W9-BUM-945

Elazar J. Pedhazur
New York University

SECOND EDITION

MULTIPLE REGRESSION IN BEHAVIORAL RESEARCH

Explanation and Prediction

HOLT, RINEHART AND WINSTON

New York • Chicago • San Francisco • Philadelphia
Montreal • Toronto • London • Sydney • Tokyo
Mexico City • Rio de Janeiro • Madrid

To Geula

Library of Congress Cataloging in Publication Data

Pedhazur, Elazar J.
Multiple regression in behavioral research.

Previous ed. published in 1973 as: Multiple regression in behavioral research / Fred N. Kerlinger, Elazar J. Pedhazur.
Includes bibliographical references and indexes.
1. Regression analysis. 2. Psychological research.
I. Kerlinger, Fred N. (Fred Nichols), 1910–
Multiple regression in behavioral research. II. Title.
HA31.3.P4 1982 519.5′36 81-20202
AACR2

ISBN 0-03-041760-0

Address correspondence to:
383 Madison Avenue, New York, N.Y. 10017

Printed in the United States of America
Published simultaneously in Canada

6789 038 987

CBS COLLEGE PUBLISHING
Holt, Rinehart and Winston
The Dryden Press
Saunders College Publishing

PREFACE TO THE SECOND EDITION

This edition constitutes a major revision and expansion of the first. While the overall objectives and the nonmathematical approach of the first edition have been retained (see Preface to the First Edition), much that is new has been incorporated in the present edition. It is not possible to enumerate here all the changes and additions. An overview of the methods presented and the perspectives from which they are viewed will be found in Chapter 1. What follows is a partial listing of major expansions and additions.

Although, as in the first edition, Part 1 is devoted to the foundations of multiple regression analysis (MR), attempts have been made to delineate more clearly the role of theory, research goals, and research design in the application of MR and the interpretation of the results. Accordingly, chapters dealing exclusively with either prediction (Chapter 6) or explanation (Chapters 7 and 8) were added.

Among new or expanded topics in Part 1 are: the analysis of residuals (Chapter 2); specification and measurement errors (Chapters 2 and 8); multicollinearity (Chapter 8); variable-selection procedures (Chapter 6); variance partitioning (Chapter 7); and the interpretation of regression coefficients as indices of the effects of variables (Chapter 8).

Computer programs from three popular packages (SPSS, BMDP, and SAS), introduced in Chapter 4, are used repeatedly throughout the book. For each run, the control cards are listed and commented upon. This is followed by excerpts of the output and commentaries, which are designed not only to acquaint the reader with the output, but also for the purpose of elaborating upon and extending the discussion of specific methods dealt with in a given chapter.

Among notable expansions and additions in Part 2 are: A more detailed treatment of multiple comparisons among means, and the use of tests of significance among regression coefficients for the purpose of carrying out such comparisons (see, in particular, Chapters 9 and 13). An expanded discussion has been provided of nonorthogonal designs, and of distinctions in the use of such designs in experimental versus nonexperimental research (Chapter 10). There is a more detailed discussion of the concept of interaction, and tests of simple main effects (Chapter 10). A longer discussion has been given of designs with continuous and categorical variables, including multiple aptitudes in aptitude-treatment-interaction designs, and multiple covariates in the analysis of covariance (Chapters 12 and 13). There is a new chapter on repeated-measures designs (Chapter 14) and a discussion of issues regarding the unit of analysis and ecological inference (Chapter 13).

Part 3 constitutes an extended treatment of causal analysis. In addition to an enlarged discussion of path analysis (Chapter 15), a chapter devoted to an introduction to LInear Structural RELations (LISREL) was added (Chapter 16). The chapter includes detailed discussions and illustrations of the application of LISREL IV to the solution of structural equation models.

Part 4 is an expanded treatment of discriminant analysis, multivariate analysis of variance, and a canonical analysis. Among other things, the relations among these methods, on the one hand, and their relations to MR, on the other hand, are discussed and illustrated.

In the interest of space, it was decided to delete the separate chapters dealing with research applications. It will be noted, however, that research applications are discussed in various chapters in the context of discussions of specific analytic techniques.

I am grateful to Professors Ellis B. Page, Jum C. Nunnally, Charles W. McNichols, and Douglas E. Stone for reviewing various parts of the manuscript and for their constructive suggestions for its improvement.

Ellen Koenigsberg, Professor Liora Pedhazur Schmelkin, and Dr. Elizabeth Taleporos have not only read the entire manuscript and offered valuable suggestions, but have also been always ready to listen, willing to respond, eager to discuss, question, and challenge. For all this, my deepest appreciation.

My thanks to the administration of the School of Education, Health, Nursing, and Arts Professions of New York University for enabling me to work consistently on the book by granting me a sabbatical leave, and for the generous allocation of computer time for the analyses reported in the book.

To Bert Holland, of the Academic Computing Center, my thanks for expert assistance in matters concerning the use of the computing facilities at New York University.

My thanks to Brian Heald and Sara Boyajian of Holt, Rinehart and Winston for their painstaking work in preparing the manuscript for publication.

I am grateful to my friends Sheldon Kastner and Marvin Sontag for their wise counsel.

It has been my good fortune to be a student of Fred N. Kerlinger, who has stimulated and nourished my interest in scientific inquiry, research design and methodology. I was even more fortunate when as a colleague and friend he generously shared with me his knowledge, insights, and wit. For all this, and more, thank you, Fred, and may She. . .

My wife, Geula, has typed and retyped the entire manuscript—a difficult job for which I cannot thank her enough. And how can I thank her for her steadfast encouragement, for being a source of joy and happiness, for sharing? Dedicating this book to her is but a small token of my love and appreciation.

Elazar J. Pedhazur
Brooklyn, New York

PREFACE TO THE FIRST EDITION

Like many ventures, this book started in a small way: we wanted to write a brief manual for our students. And we started to do this. We soon realized, however, that it did not seem possible to write a brief exposition of multiple regression analysis that students would understand. The brevity we sought is possible only with a mathematical presentation relatively unadorned with numerical examples and verbal explanations. Moreover, the more we tried to work out a reasonably brief manual the clearer it became that it was not possible to do so. We then decided to write a book.

Why write a whole book on multiple regression analysis? There are three main reasons. One, multiple regression is a general data analytic system (Cohen, 1968) that is close to the theoretical and inferential preoccupations and methods of scientific behavioral research. If, as we believe, science's main job is to "explain" natural phenomena by discovering and studying the relations among variables, then multiple regression is a general and efficient method to help do this.

Two, multiple regression and its rationale underlie most other multivariate methods. Once multiple regression is well understood, other multivariate methods are easier to comprehend. More important, their use in actual research becomes clearer. Most behavioral research attempts to explain one dependent variable, one natural phenomenon, at a time. There is of course research in which there are two or more dependent variables. But such research can be more profitably viewed, we think, as an extension of the one dependent variable case. Although we have not entirely neglected other multivariate methods, we have concentrated on multiple regression. In the next decade and beyond, we think it will be seen as the cornerstone of modern data analysis in the behavioral sciences.

Our strongest motivation for devoting a whole book to multiple regression is that the behavioral sciences are at present in the midst of a conceptual and technical revolution. It must be remembered that the empirical behavioral sciences are young, not much more than fifty to seventy years old. Moreover, it is only recently that the empirical aspects of inquiry have been emphasized. Even after psychology, a relatively advanced behavioral science, became strongly empirical, its research operated in the univariate tradition. Now, however, the availability of multivariate methods and the modern computer makes possible theory and empirical research that better reflect the multivariate nature of psychological reality.

The effects of the revolution are becoming apparent, as we will show in the latter part of the book when we describe studies such as Frederiksen et al.'s (1968) study of organizational climate and administrative performance and the now well-known *Equality of Educational Opportunity* (Coleman et al., 1966). Within the decade we will probably see the virtual demise of one-variable thinking and the use of analysis of variance with data unsuited to the method. Instead, multivariate methods will be well-accepted tools in the behavioral scientist's and educator's armamentarium.

The structure of the book is fairly simple. There are five parts. Part 1 provides the theoretical foundations of correlation and simple and multiple regression. Basic calculations are illustrated and explained and the results of such calculations tied to rather simple research problems. The major purpose of Part 2 is to explore the relations between multiple regression analysis and analysis of variance and to show the student how to do analysis of variance and covariance with multiple regression. In achieving this purpose, certain technical problems are examined in detail: coding of categorical and experimental variables, interaction of variables, the relative contributions of independent variables to the dependent variable, the analysis of trends, commonality analysis, and path analysis. In addition, the general problems of explanation and prediction are attacked.

Part 3 extends the discussion, although not in depth, to other multivariate methods: discriminant analysis, canonical correlation, multivariate analysis of variance, and factor analysis. The basic emphasis on multiple regression as the core method, however, is maintained. The use of multiple regression analysis—and, to a lesser extent, other multivariate methods—in behavioral and educational research is the substance of Part 4. We think that the student will profit greatly by careful study of actual research uses of the method. One of our purposes, indeed, has been to expose the student to cogent uses of multiple regression. We believe strongly in the basic unity of methodology and research substance.

In Part 5, the emphasis on theory and substantive research reaches its climax with a direct attack on the relation between multiple regression and scientific research. To maximize the probability of success, we examine in some detail the logic of scientific inquiry, experimental and nonexperimental research, and, finally, theory and multivariate thinking in behavioral research. All these problems are linked to multiple regression analysis.

In addition to the five parts briefly characterized above, four appendices are included. The first three address themselves to matrix algebra and the computer. After explaining and illustrating elementary matrix algebra—an indispensable and, happily, not too complex a subject—we discuss the use of the computer in data analysis generally and we give one of our own computer programs in its entirety with instructions for its use. The fourth appendix is a table of the *F* distribution, 5 percent and 1 percent levels of significance.

Achieving an appropriate level of communication in a technical book is always a difficult problem. If one writes at too low a level, one cannot really explain many important points. Moreover, one may insult the background and intelligence of some readers, as well as bore them. If one writes at too advanced a level, then one loses most of one's audience. We have tried to write at a fairly elementary level, but have not hesitated to use certain advanced ideas. And we have gone rather deeply into a number of important, even indispensable, concepts and methods. To do this and still keep the discussion within the reach of students whose mathematical and statistical backgrounds are bounded, say, by correlation and analysis of variance, we have sometimes had to be what can be called excessively wordy, although we hope not verbose. To compensate, the assumptions behind multiple regression and related methods have not been emphasized. Indeed, critics may find the book wanting in its lack of discussion of mathematical and statistical assumptions and derivations. This is a price we had to pay, however, for what we hope is comprehensible exposition. In other words, understanding and intelligent practical use of multiple regression are more important in our estimation than rigid adherence to statistical assumptions. On the other hand, we have discussed in detail the weaknesses as well as the strengths of multiple regression.

The student who has had a basic course in statistics, including some work in inferential statistics, correlation, and, say, simple one-way analysis of variance should have little difficulty. The book should be useful as a text in an intermediate analysis or statistics course or in courses in research design and methodology. Or it can be useful as a supplementary text in such courses. Some instructors may wish to use only parts of the book to supplement their work in design and analysis. Such use is feasible because some parts of the books are almost self-sufficient. With instructor help, for example, Part 2 can be used alone. We suggest, however, sequential study since the force of certain points made in later chapters, particularly on theory and research, depends to some extent at least on earlier discussions.

We have an important suggestion to make. Our students in research design courses seem to have benefited greatly from exposure to computer analysis. We have found that students with little or no background in data processing, as well as those with background, develop facility in the use of packaged computer programs rather quickly. Moreover, most of them gain confidence and skill in handling data, and they become fascinated by the immense potential of analysis by computer. Not only has computer analysis helped to illustrate and enhance the subject matter of our courses; it has also relieved students of laborious calculations, thereby enabling them to concentrate on the interpretation and meaning of data. We therefore suggest that instructors with access to computing facilities have their students use the computer to analyze the examples given in the text as well as to do exercises and term projects that require computer analysis.

We wish to acknowledge the help of several individuals. Professors Richard Darlington and Ingram Olkin read the entire manuscript of the book and made many helpful suggestions, most of which we have followed. We are grateful for their help in improving the book. To Professor Ernest Nagel we express our thanks for giving us his time to discuss philosophical aspects of causality. We are indebted to Professor Jacob Cohen for first arousing our curiosity about multiple regression and its relation to analysis of variance and its application to data analysis.

The staff of the Computing Center of the Courant Institute of Mathematical Sciences, New York University, has been consistently cooperative and helpful. We acknowledge, particularly, the capable and kind help of Edward Friedman, Neil Smith, and Robert Malchie of the Center. We wish to thank Elizabeth Taleporos for valuable assistance in proofreading and in checking numerical examples. Geula Pedhazur has given fine typing service with ungrateful material. She knows how much we appreciate her help.

New York University's generous sabbatical leave policy enabled one of us to work consistently on the book. The Courant Institute Computing Center permitted us to use the Center's CDC-6600 computer to solve some of our analytic and computing problems. We are grateful to the university and to the computing center, and, in the latter case, especially to Professor Max Goldstein, associate director of the center.

Finally, but not too apologetically, we appreciate the understanding and tolerance of our wives who often had to undergo the hardships of talking and drinking while we discussed our plans, and who had to put up with, usually cheerfully, our obsession with the subject and the book.

This book has been a completely cooperative venture of its authors. It is not possible, therefore, to speak of a ''senior'' author. Yet our names must appear in some order on the cover and title page. We have solved the problem by listing the names alphabetically, but would like it understood that the order could just as well have been the other way around.

FRED N. KERLINGER
ELAZAR J. PEDHAZUR

Amsterdam, The Netherlands
Brooklyn, New York
March 1973

CONTENTS

PART 1

FOUNDATIONS OF MULTIPLE REGRESSION ANALYSIS

1

OVERVIEW

Remarkable advances in the analysis of educational, psychological, and sociological data have been made in recent decades. Much of this increased understanding and mastery of data analysis has come about through the wide propagation and study of statistics and statistical inference, and especially from the analysis of variance. The expression "analysis of variance" is well chosen. It epitomizes the basic nature of most data analysis: the partitioning, isolation, and identification of variation in a dependent variable due to different independent variables.

Other analytic statistical techniques, such as multiple regression analysis and multivariate analysis, have been applied less frequently until very recently, not only because they are less well understood by behavioral researchers but also because they generally involve numerous and complex computations that in most instances require the aid of a computer for their execution. The recent widespread availability of computer facilities and "package" programs not only has liberated researchers from the drudgery of computations but also has put the most sophisticated and complex analytic techniques within the easy reach of anyone who has the rudimentary skills required to process data by computer. This development has not been free of drawbacks, as it has increased the frequency of blind or mindless application of methods without regard to their suitability for the solution of the problem at hand, or even in the complete absence of a clearly formulated problem. It is a truism that methods per se mean little unless they are integrated within a theoretical context and are applied to data obtained in an appropriately designed study. In short: "The important question about methods is not 'how' but 'why' " (Tukey, 1954, p. 36).

Nevertheless, much of this book is about the "how" of methods because it is indispensable for an appreciation of their potentials, for an awareness of their limitations, and for an understanding of their role in the overall research endeavor. Data do *not* speak for themselves but through the medium of the analytic techniques applied to them. It is important to realize that analytic techniques not only set limits to the scope and nature of the answers one may obtain from data, but also affect the type of questions a researcher asks and the manner in which the questions are formulated. "It comes as no particular surprise to discover that a scientist formulates problems in a way which requires for their solution just those techniques in which he himself is especially skilled" (Kaplan, 1964, p. 28).

Analytic techniques may be viewed from a variety of perspectives, among which are an analytic perspective and a research perspective. The term "analytic perspective" is used here to refer to such aspects as the mechanics of the calculations of a given technique, the meaning of its elements and the interrelations among them, and the statistical assumptions that underlie its valid application. Knowledge of these aspects is, needless to say, essential for the use of any analytic technique. But the analytic perspective is a narrow one, and the sole preoccupation with it poses the threat of losing sight of the role of analysis in scientific inquiry. It is one thing to know how to calculate a correlation coefficient or a t ratio, for example, and quite another to know when such techniques are applicable and what bearing the results they yield have on the question(s) addressed in a research study. Regrettably, while students are able to recite chapter and verse of a method, say a t ratio for the difference between means, they are often unable to determine when it is appropriate to apply it and how to interpret the results obtained through its application.

To fully appreciate the role and meaning of an analytic technique it is necessary to view it from the broader research perspective, which includes such aspects as the purpose of the study, its theoretical framework, and the type of research. In a book such as this one it is not possible to deal with the research perspective in the detail that it deserves, because this would require, among other things, detailed discussions of the philosophy of scientific inquiry, of theories in specific disciplines (psychology, sociology, and political science, for example), and of research design. Efforts are, however, made throughout the book to discuss the analytic techniques from a research perspective; to return to the question of why a given method is used and to comment on its role in the overall research setting. Thus it is shown, for example, how certain elements of an analytic technique are applicable in one research setting but not in another, or that the interpretation of elements of a method depends on the research setting in which it is applied.

The aforementioned perspectives are used in this chapter as a means of organizing the overview of the contents and major themes of this book. It is important to recognize that no appreciable depth of understanding can be accomplished at this stage; nor is it intended. The purpose is rather to set the stage, to provide an orientation, for things to come. Therefore, do not be concerned if you do not understand some of the concepts and techniques mentioned or briefly commented upon. A certain degree of ambiguity is inevitable at this stage. It is hoped that this will be diminished when topics outlined or mentioned here are discussed in detail in subsequent chapters.

THE ANALYTIC PERSPECTIVE

The fundamental task of science is to explain phenomena. As Braithwaite (1953) says, its basic aim is to discover or invent general explanations of natural events. Natural phenomena are complex. The phenomena and constructs of the behavioral sciences—learning, achievement, anxiety, conservatism, social class, aggression, reinforcement, authoritarianism, and so on—are especially complex. "Complex" in this context means that the phenomenon has many facets and many causes. In a research-analytic context, "complex" means that a phenomenon has several sources of variation. To study a construct or a variable scientifically we must be able to identify the sources of the variable's variation. Broadly speaking, a variable is any attribute on which objects or individuals vary. This means that when we apply an instrument that measures the variable to a sample of individuals we obtain more or less different scores for each of them. We talk about the variance of college grade-point average (as a measure of achievement), or the variability among individuals on a scale designed to measure locus of control, ego strength, learned helplessness, and so on.

It can be asserted that the scientist is essentially interested in explaining variance. In the behavioral sciences, variability is itself a phenomenon of great scientific curiosity and interest. The large differences in the intelligence and achievement of children, for instance, and the considerable differences between schools and socioeconomic groups in critical educational variables are phenomena of deep interest and concern to behavioral scientists.

In their attempts to explain the variability of a phenomenon of interest (often referred to as the dependent variable), scientists study its relations or covariations with other variables (referred to as the independent variables). In essence, information from the independent variables is brought to bear on the dependent variables. Educational researchers seek to explain the variance of school achievement by studying its relations with intelligence, aptitude, social class, race, home background, school atmosphere, teacher characteristics, and so on. Political scientists seek to explain voting behavior by studying variables presumed to influence such behavior: sex, age, income, education, party affiliation, motivation, place of residence, and the like. Psychologists seek to explain aggressive behavior by searching for variables that may elicit it: frustration, noise, heat, crowding, exposure to acts of violence on TV.

Various analytic techniques have been developed for the purpose of studying relations between independent variables and dependent variables, or the effects of the former on the latter. Following is a synopsis of techniques presented in this book. This section concludes with a statement about the use of computer programs for statistical analysis.

Simple and Multiple Regression Analysis

Broadly speaking, regression analysis is a method of analyzing the variability of a dependent variable by resorting to information available on one or more independent variables. Among other things, an answer is sought to the question: What are the expected changes in the dependent variable as a result of changes (observed or induced) in the independent variables?

When only one independent variable is used, the analysis is referred to as *simple regression*—a topic to which Chapter 2 is devoted. When more than one independent variable is used, it is of course possible to apply simple regression analysis to each of the independent variables and the dependent variable. But doing this overlooks the possibility that the independent variables may be intercorrelated, or that they may interact in their effects on the dependent variable. *Multiple regression analysis* (MR) is eminently suited for analyzing the collective and separate effects of two or more independent variables on a dependent variable.

The bulk of this book deals with various aspects of applications and interpretations of MR in scientific research. In Chapter 3, the foundations of MR are introduced for the case of two independent variables. The generalization of MR to any number of independent variables is then presented (Chapter 4), via the use of matrix algebra. It should be noted that most of the subject matter of this book can be mastered without resorting to matrix algebra. But because some topics (such as multivariate analysis of variance) require the use of matrix algebra, and because matrix algebra is extremely useful and general for the conceptualization and analysis of diverse designs, it is strongly suggested that you develop a working knowledge of it. To this end, Appendix A presents an introduction to matrix algebra. In addition, in order to facilitate your acquisition of logic and skills in this very important subject, some topics in this book are presented twice: first in ordinary algebra and then in matrix algebra (see, for example, Chapters 3 and 4).

Methods of statistical control useful in their own right (e.g., partial correlation) or that are important elements of MR (e.g., semipartial correlation) constitute the subject matter of Chapter 5. Chapters 6 through 8 address different approaches to the use and interpretation of MR with a particular emphasis on its use for explanation or prediction (see below).

MR and the Analysis of Variance (ANOVA)

Part 1 of the book deals exclusively with designs in which the independent variables are *continuous* or quantitative—that is, variables on which individuals or objects differ in degree. Examples of such variables are height, weight, age, drug dosage, intelligence, motivation, study time. There is another class of variables—*categorical* or qualitative—on which individuals differ in kind. Broadly speaking, on such variables individuals are identified according to the category or group to which they belong. Race, sex, political party affiliation, different experimental treatments are but some examples of categorical variables.

Conventionally, designs with categorical independent variables have been analyzed by ANOVA. Until recent years ANOVA and MR have been treated by many as two distinct analytic approaches. It is not uncommon to encounter students or researchers who have been trained exclusively in the use of ANOVA, and who therefore cast their research questions in this mold even when it is inappropriate or undesirable to do so. As is shown in Part 2 of this book, ANOVA can be treated as a special case of MR. The advantages of doing this are discussed in Part 2. For now, two points will be made. (1) Conceptually, continuous and categorical variables are treated alike in MR—that is, both types of variables are viewed as providing information about the status of individuals, be it their measured aptitude, their income, or the group to which they belong, the type of treatment they have been administered. (2) MR is applicable to designs in which the variables are continuous, categorical, or combinations of both, thereby eschewing the inappropriate or undesirable practice of categorizing continuous variables (such as designating individuals above the mean as high and those below the mean as low) in order to fit them in what is considered, often erroneously, an ANOVA design.

Analytically, it is necessary to code categorical variables so that they may be used in MR. Chapter 9 details different methods of coding categorical variables and demonstrates how they are used to analyze designs with a single categorical independent variable, or what is often referred to as simple ANOVA. Designs consisting of more than one categorical independent variable (factorial designs) are discussed in detail in Chapter 10.

Combinations of continuous and categorical variables may be used in various designs for different purposes. For example, in an experiment with several treatments (a categorical variable), aptitudes of subjects (a continuous variable) may be used in order to study the interaction between these variables in their effect on a dependent variable. This is an example of aptitude-treatments-interaction (ATI) designs. Instead of using aptitudes in order to study their possible interactions with treatments, they may be used to control for individual differences, as in the analysis of covariance (ANCOVA). In Chapters 12 and 13 it is shown how MR is used to analyze ATI, ANCOVA, and related designs (e.g., comparing regression equations obtained from two or more groups). In addition to the above-noted designs, it is shown how MR is applied for the analysis of trends or curvilinear relations (Chapters 11 and 13), and in repeated-measures designs (Chapter 14).

In sum, MR is versatile and useful for the analysis of diverse designs. To repeat: the overriding conception is that information from independent variables (continuous, categorical, or combinations of both types of variables) is brought to bear in attempts to explain variability of a dependent variable.

Causal Analysis

In recent years, social and behavioral scientists have been showing a steadily growing interest in studying patterns of causation among variables. Various approaches to the analysis of causation have been proposed. Part 3 of this book serves as an introduction to some of them. In Chapter 15 it is shown how the analysis of certain types of causal models is accomplished by repeated applications of multiple regression analysis. A recently developed powerful approach (LISREL) that accommodates, among other things, models with reciprocal causation, multiple indicators of unobserved variables, and measurement errors is introduced in Chapter 16.

Multivariate Analysis

Multiple regression analysis is applicable in designs consisting of a single dependent variable and two or more independent variables. Because there is only one dependent variable, the analysis of such designs is often referred to as univariate analysis. In many instances, the interest is in studying the effects of independent variables on more than one dependent variable simultaneously, or in studying relations between sets of independent and dependent variables. Under such circumstances, multivariate analysis has to be applied.

It will be noted in passing that some authors view multiple regression analysis as a multivariate analytic technique whereas others reserve the term "multivariate analysis" for approaches in which multiple dependent variables are analyzed simultaneously. The specific nomenclature is not all-important. One may view multivariate analytic techniques as extensions of multiple regression analysis or, alternatively, the latter may be viewed as a special case subsumed under the former.

Part 4 of this book is designed to serve as a introduction to different methods of multivariate analysis. While Chapter 16 presents discriminant analysis and multivariate analysis of variance for any number of groups, it is also shown that for two groups such analyses may be carried out through multiple regression analysis. Canonical analysis that is used to study relations between sets of variables is presented in Chapter 18, where it is shown, among other things, that discriminant analysis and multivariate analysis of variance can be viewed as special cases of this most general analytic approach.

Computer Programs

The widespread availability of computer programs for statistical analysis has been noted earlier. Such programs are invaluable in facilitating applications of the analytic techniques presented in this book. Three "packages" of computer programs are introduced in Chapter 4 and are then used repeatedly in various other chapters. In addition, special programs, notably LISREL (Chapter 16), are introduced when the need for them arises. In all instances, all the control cards are given and commented upon. The results are then presented, along with commentaries. The emphasis is on the interpretation, the meaning of specific terms reported in the output, and on the overall meaning of the results. Consequently, computer output is not reproduced in its entirety. Instead, the most pertinent information for the discussion of a given topic is presented.

It was decided to use more than one "package" so that you may become familiar with the unique features of each, with its strengths and weaknesses, and with the specific format of input and output used in each. It is hoped that you will thereby develop flexibility in using any program that may be available to you, or the one you deem most suitable when seeking specific pieces of information in the results.

It is suggested that you begin to use computer programs at the early stages of learning the subject matter presented in this book. The time and effort saved in the calculations will free you to pay greater attention to the meaning of the methods presented, thereby developing a better understanding and appreciation of them. Yet there is no substitute for hand calculations in order to gain understanding of a method and a "feel" for what is going on when the data are analyzed by computer. It is therefore strongly recommended that at the initial stages of learning a new topic you solve the numerical examples by hand as well as with the aid of a computer. Comparisons between the two solutions and the identification of specific aspects of the computer output can be a valuable part of the learning process. With this in mind, the numerical examples are purposely small so that they can be solved by hand with little effort.

THE RESEARCH PERSPECTIVE

It was said earlier that role and meaning of an analytic technique can be fully understood and appreciated only when viewed from the broad research perspective. The purpose of this section is to elaborate on the preceding statement by commenting on some aspects of the research perspective. The discussion is neither exhaustive nor detailed, yet it is hoped that it will serve to underscore from the beginning the paramount role of the research perspective in determining how a specific method is applied and how the results it yields are interpreted. The presentation is limited to the following aspects: (1) the purpose of the study; (2) the type of research; and (3) the theoretical framework of the study. The section concludes with some comments about the use of illustrative research applications in this book.

Purpose of Study

In the broadest sense, a study may be designed for the purpose of predicting or explaining a given phenomenon. These purposes are not mutually exclusive. Yet it is fairly easy to identify studies, and even broad research areas, in which the main concern is with either prediction or explanation. For example, a college admissions officer may be interested in determining whether, and to what extent, a set of variables (mental ability, aptitudes, achievement in high school, socioeconomic status, interests, motivation) is useful in *predicting* academic achievement in college. Being interested solely in prediction, the admissions officer has a great deal of latitude in the selection of predictors. Among other things, he or she may examine potentially useful predictors individually or in sets in order to determine which of them are to be retained and which are to be discarded. To this end, various approaches designed to identify the minimum number of variables to be retained so that little, or nothing, of the predictive power of the entire set of variables under consideration is sacrificed have been developed. These are described in Chapter 6, where it is shown, among other things, that different variable-selection procedures applied to the same data result in the retention of different variables. Nevertheless, this does not pose any problems in a predictive study. Any procedure that meets the specific needs and inclinations of the researcher (economy, ready availability of some variables, ease of obtaining specific measurements) will do.

The great liberty in the selection of variables in predictive research is countervailed by the constraint that no statement may be made about their meaningfulness and effectiveness from a theoretical frame of reference. Thus, for example, it is argued in Chapter 6 that when variable-selection procedures are used for the purpose of optimizing the prediction of a criterion, regression coefficients should not be interpreted as indices of the effects of the predictors on the criterion. Furthermore, it is shown (see, in particular Chapters 6, 7, and 8) that a major source of confusion and misinterpretation of results obtained in some landmark studies in education is their reliance on variable-selection procedures despite the fact that they were aimed at explanation of phenomena. In sum, when variables are selected for the purpose of optimizing prediction, all one can say is, given a specific procedure and specific constraints placed by the researcher, which combination of variables best predicts the criterion.

Contrast the preceding example with a study whose purpose is to *explain* academic achievement in college. Under such circumstances, the choice of variables and the analytic approach are largely determined by the theoretical framework (see below). Chapters 7 and 8 are devoted to detailed discussions of different approaches in the use of multiple regression analysis in explanatory research. For example, in Chapter 7 it is argued that the popular approaches of incremental partitioning of variance and commonality analysis cannot yield answers to questions about the relative importance of independent variables or their relative effects on the dependent variable. As is noted in Chapter 7, these approaches are discussed in detail because they are often misapplied in various areas of social and behavioral research. Chapter 8 is devoted to a discussion of issues related to the interpretation of regression coefficients as indices of the effects of the variables with which they are associated. Differences in the use of standardized and unstandardized coefficients are discussed, and advantages and disadvantages of each are examined. Adverse effects on regression coefficients of high intercorrelations among independent variables, measurement errors, and errors in specifying the model that presumably reflects the process by which the independent variables affect the dependent variables are some of the major issues addressed in Chapter 8.

Types of Research

Of the various classifications of types of research one of the most useful is their division into experimental, quasi-experimental, and nonexperimental. Much has been written about these types of research with a special emphasis on issues regarding their internal and external validity (see, for example, Campbell & Stanley, 1963; Cook & Campbell, 1979; Kerlinger, 1973). While, as was noted earlier, it is not possible to discuss these issues in this book, attention is drawn in various chapters to the fact that the interpretation of results yielded by a given analytic technique depends, in part, on the type of research in which it is applied.

Contrasts between the different types of research recur in different contexts, among which are: (1) the interpretation of regression coefficients (Chapter 8); (2) the potential for specification errors (Chapter 8); (3) designs with unequal sample sizes or unequal cell frequencies (Chapters 9 and 10); (4) the meaning of interactions among independent variables (Chapters 10 through 13); and (5) applications and interpretations of the analysis of covariance (Chapter 13).

Theoretical Framework

Explanation implies, among other things, a theoretical formulation about the nature of the relations among the variable under study. The theoretical framework determines, to a large extent, the choice of the analytic technique, the manner in which it is to be applied, and the interpretation of the results. This is demonstrated in various parts of the book. In Chapter 5, for example, it is shown that the calculation of a partial correlation coefficient is predicated on a specific theoretical statement regarding the patterns of relations among the variables. Similarly, it is shown (Chapter 7) that within certain theoretical frameworks it may be meaningful to calculate semipartial correlations, whereas in others such statistics are not meaningful. In Chapters 7, 8, and 15 the same data are analyzed several times in accordance with the degree of elaboration of the theoretical framework, and it is shown how elements obtained in each of the analyses are interpreted.

In sum, in explanatory research data analysis is designed to shed light on theory. The potential of accomplishing this goal is predicated, among other things, on the use of analytic techniques that are commensurate with the theoretical framework.

Research Applications

Examples of research applications of specific methods are summarized and commented upon in various chapters. The choice of the examples was guided by two aims: (1) illustration of the application of a specific method or approach discussed in a given chapter, and (2) sharpening your critical thinking in evaluating published research in which methods presented in this book have been used.

Generally, the presentations are brief, and the focus is on the application and interpretation of specific analytic techniques. Hence, other aspects of the research are briefly commented upon only when necessary. Some studies are, however, dealt with in greater detail (see Chapters 7 and 8) because of their scope and their great impact on educational and social policies. It was felt that their very importance required that they be more carefully scrutinized. Moreover, it was believed that this will enhance your understanding of the analytic techniques and approaches used in these studies.

2

SIMPLE LINEAR REGRESSION AND CORRELATION

This chapter is devoted to the fundamentals of regression analysis. Following a brief review of variance and covariance, linear regression analysis with one independent variable is presented and discussed in detail. This is followed by a presentation of tests of statistical significance. The assumptions underlying regression analysis, and some consequences of their violations, are then detailed. The study of residuals is presented next, as an aid in the detection of possible violations of the assumptions of regression analysis. The chapter concludes with a brief presentation of the correlation model.

VARIANCE AND COVARIANCE

Much of behavioral research is concerned with the study of variability, be it among individuals, groups, cultures, or within individuals across time and settings. It is the phenomenon of variability that arouses the curiosity of people and motivates some to search for its origins, to attempt to explain it. When scientists attempt to explain the variability of a variable, they resort, among other things, to the study of its covariations with other variables. Among indices used in the study of variation and covariation are the variance and the covariance, which are briefly reviewed now.

Variance

Recall that the variance of a sample when it is used as an estimator of the population variance is defined as:

$$s_x^2 = \frac{\Sigma(X - \bar{X})^2}{N - 1} = \frac{\Sigma x^2}{N - 1} \tag{2.1}$$

where s_x^2 = sample variance of X; Σx^2 = sum of the squared deviations of X from the mean of X; N = sample size.

When the calculations are done by hand, or with the aid of a calculator, it is more convenient to obtain the deviation sum of squares by applying a formula in which only raw scores are used:

$$\Sigma x^2 = \Sigma X^2 - \frac{(\Sigma X)^2}{N} \tag{2.2}$$

where ΣX^2 = sum of the squared raw scores; $(\Sigma X)^2$ = square of the sum of raw scores. Henceforth, "sum of squares" is used to refer to deviation sum of squares unless there is ambiguity, in which case "deviation sum of squares" will be used.

The calculations of the sums of squares and the variances for X and Y are now illustrated for sample data reported in Table 2.1.

Table 2.1 Illustrative Data for *X* and *Y*

	X	X^2	Y	Y^2	XY
	1	1	3	9	3
	1	1	5	25	5
	1	1	6	36	6
	1	1	9	81	9
	2	4	4	16	8
	2	4	6	36	12
	2	4	7	49	14
	2	4	10	100	20
	3	9	4	16	12
	3	9	6	36	18
	3	9	8	64	24
	3	9	10	100	30
	4	16	5	25	20
	4	16	7	49	28
	4	16	9	81	36
	4	16	12	144	48
	5	25	6	36	30
	5	25	7	49	35
	5	25	10	100	50
	5	25	12	144	60
Σ:	60	220	146	1196	468
M:	3.00		7.30		

$$\Sigma x^2 = 220 - \frac{60^2}{20} = 40 \qquad \Sigma y^2 = 1196 - \frac{146^2}{20} = 130.2$$

$$s_x^2 = \frac{40}{19} = 2.11 \qquad s_y^2 = \frac{130.2}{19} = 6.85$$

The standard deviation (s) is, of course, the square root of the variance:

$$s_x = \sqrt{2.11} = 1.45 \qquad\qquad s_y = \sqrt{6.85} = 2.62$$

Covariance

The sample covariance is defined as:

$$s_{xy} = \frac{\Sigma(X - \bar{X})(Y - \bar{Y})}{N - 1} = \frac{\Sigma xy}{N - 1} \tag{2.3}$$

where s_{xy} = covariance of X and Y; Σxy = sum of the cross products deviations of pairs of X and Y scores from their respective means. Note the analogy between the variance and the covariance. The variance of a variable can be conceived of as its covariance with itself. For example:

$$s_x^2 = \frac{\Sigma(X - \bar{X})(X - \bar{X})}{N - 1}$$

In short, the variance indicates the variation of a set of scores from their mean, whereas the covariance indicates the covariation of two sets of scores from their respective means.

As in the case of sums of squares, it is convenient to calculate the sum of the cross products deviations (henceforth referred to as "sum of cross products") by using the following algebraic identity:

$$\Sigma xy = \Sigma XY - \frac{(\Sigma X)(\Sigma Y)}{N} \tag{2.4}$$

where ΣXY is the sum of the products of pairs of raw X and Y scores; ΣX and ΣY are the sums of raw scores of X and Y, respectively.

For the data of Table 2.1:

$$\Sigma xy = 468 - \frac{(60)(146)}{20} = 30$$

$$s_{xy} = \frac{30}{19} = 1.58$$

Sums of squares, sums of cross products, variances, and covariances are the staples of regression analysis; hence it is essential to understand them thoroughly and to be able to calculate them routinely. If necessary, refer to statistics texts (e.g., Hays, 1981) for further study of these concepts.

SIMPLE LINEAR REGRESSION

It was said above that among approaches used to explain the variability of a variable is the study of its covariations with other variables. The most powerful method of doing this is the experiment, whose simplest form is one in which the effect of an independent variable, X, on a dependent variable, Y, is being studied. In such a setting, the researcher wishes to determine how induced variations in the independent variable lead to variations in the dependent variable. Stated differently, the goal is to determine how, and to what extent, does variability in the dependent variable depend upon manipulations of the independent variable. For example, it may be desired to determine the effects of hours of study, X, on achievement in vocabulary, Y (see numerical example, below), or the effects of different dosages of a drug, X, on anxiety, Y. Because performance on Y may be affected by factors other than X, or by random errors, it is very unlikely that all individuals who are administered a given level of X will exhibit identical performance on Y. But if X does affect Y, the means of the Y's at different levels of X would be expected to differ from each other. When the Y means for the different levels of X differ from each other and lie on a straight line, it is said that there is a simple linear regression of Y on X. By "simple" is meant that only one independent variable, X, is used. The preceding ideas can be expressed succinctly by the following linear model:

$$Y_i = \alpha + \beta X + \epsilon_i \tag{2.5}$$

where Y_i = score of individual i; α (alpha) = mean of the population when the value of X is zero, or the Y intercept; β (beta) = regression coefficient in the population, or the slope of the regression line; ϵ_i (epsilon) = random disturbance, or error, for individual i.[1] The regression coefficient (β) indicates the effect of the independent variable on the dependent variable. Specifically, for each unit change of the independent variable, X, there is an expected change equal to the size of β in the dependent variable, Y.

From the foregoing it can be seen that each person's score, Y_i, is conceived of being composed of two parts: (1) A fixed part indicated by $\alpha + \beta X$, that is, part of the Y score of an individual administered a given level of X is equal to $\alpha + \beta X$. Thus, all individuals administered the same level of X are said to have the same part of the Y score. (2) A random part, ϵ_i, unique to each individual, i.

Linear regression analysis is by no means limited to experimental research. As is amply demonstrated in subsequent chapters, it is often applied in nonexperimental research for the purpose of explaining or predicting phenomena. While the calculations of regression statistics are the same regardless of the type of research in which they are applied, the interpretation of the results depends on the specific research design. These issues are discussed in detail in subsequent chapters (see, for example, Chapters 6 through 8). For now, however, the concern is with the general analytic approach.

Equation (2.5) was expressed in parameters. The equation for a sample is:

$$Y = a + bX + e \tag{2.6}$$

where a is an estimator of α, b is an estimator of β, and e is an estimator of ϵ.

[1]The term "linear" refers also to the fact that parameters in equations such as (2.5) are expressed in linear form even though the regression of Y on X is nonlinear. For example, $Y = \alpha + \beta X + \beta X^2 + \beta X^3 + \epsilon$ describes the cubic regression of Y on X. Note, however, that it is X, not the β's, that is raised to second and third powers. Such equations, which are subsumed under the general linear model, are dealt with in Chapter 11.

Note that for convenience no subscripts have been used in (2.6). This practice of omitting subscripts will be followed throughout the book, unless there is danger of ambiguity. Subscripts for individuals will be used when it is desired to identify given individuals. In equations with more than one independent variable (see subsequent chapters) subscripts will be used to identify each of the variables.

The meaning of the statistics in (2.6) and the mechanics of their calculations are discussed and illustrated in the context of a numerical example to which we now turn.

A Numerical Example

Assume that in an experiment on the effects of hours of study, X, on task performance, Y (e.g., mathematics, vocabulary), 20 subjects were randomly assigned to different levels of X. Specifically, there are five levels of X, ranging from one to five hours of study. Four subjects were randomly assigned to one hour of study, four other subjects were assigned to two hours of study, and so on to five hours of study for the fifth group of subjects. The dependent variable measure is the number of items answered correctly on a subsequent test. Other examples may be: the effect of the number of exposures to a list of words on the retention of the words; the effects of different dosages of a drug on reaction time or on blood pressure. Alternatively, X may be a nonmanipulated variable (e.g., age, grade in school), and Y may be height or verbal achievement. For illustrative purposes, the data reported in Table 2.1 will be treated as if they were obtained in a learning experiment, as described above.

The goal of scientific inquiry is the explanation or prediction of phenomena. The ideal is, of course, perfect explanation—that is, without error. Being unable to achieve this state, however, the scientist attempts to minimize the errors. In the present example, the purpose is to explain Y, task performance, on the basis of X, hours of study. It is, however, very unlikely that students studying the same number of hours will achieve the same level of performance. Obviously, many other variables (e.g., mental ability, motivation), as well as errors of measurement, will lead to variability in students' performance. All sources of variability of Y, other than X, are subsumed under e in Equation (2.6). In other words, e represents the part of the Y score that is not explained by, or predicted from, X.

The purpose, then, is to find a solution for the constants, a and b of (2.6), so that explanation, or prediction, of Y will be maximized. Stated differently, a solution is sought for a and b so that e, the errors committed in using X to explain Y, will be at a minimum. The intuitive solution of minimizing the sum of the errors turns out to be unsatisfactory because positive errors will cancel negative ones, thereby leading to the possibly false impression that small errors have been committed when their sum is small, or that no errors have been committed when their sum turns out to be zero. Instead, it is the sum of the squared errors (Σe^2) that is minimized, hence the name *least squares* given to this solution.

Given certain assumptions (discussed below), the least-squares solution leads to estimators that have the desirable properties of being Best Linear Unbiased Estimators (BLUE). An estimator is said to be unbiased if its average (i.e., expected value) obtained from repeated samples of size N is equal to the parameter. Thus b, for example, is an unbiased estimator of β if the average of the former in repeated samples is equal to the latter. Unbiasedness is only one desirable property of an estimator. In addition, it is desirable that the variance of the distribution of such an estimator (i.e., its sampling distribution) be as small as possible. The smaller the variance of the sampling distribution, the smaller the error in estimating the parameter. Least-squares estimators are said to be "best" in the sense that the variance of their sampling distributions is the smallest from among linear unbiased estimators (for a thorough discussion of BLUE see Hanushek & Jackson, 1977, pp. 46–56. For discussions of sampling distributions and unbiasedness see, for example, Hays, 1981, Chapter 5). Later in the chapter it is shown how the variance of the sampling distribution of b is used in statistical tests of significance and for establishing confidence intervals. We turn now to the calculation of least-squares estimators and to a discussion of their meaning.

The two constants are calculated as follows:

$$b = \frac{\Sigma xy}{\Sigma x^2} \tag{2.7}$$

$$a = \bar{Y} - b\bar{X} \tag{2.8}$$

Using these constants, the equation for predicting Y from X, or the *regression equation*, is:

$$Y' = a + bX \tag{2.9}$$

where Y' = predicted score on the dependent variable, Y. Note that (2.9) does not include e, which is the error that results from using the prediction equation. In other words, $e = Y - Y'$, where Y = observed score and Y' = predicted score. It is the $\Sigma(Y - Y')^2$, referred to as the sum of squared residuals (see below), that is minimized in the least-squares solution for a and b of (2.9).

For the data of Table 2.1, $\Sigma xy = 30$ and $\Sigma x^2 = 40$ (see calculations above). $\bar{Y} = 7.3$ and $\bar{X} = 3.0$ (see Table 2.1).

$$b = \frac{30}{40} = .75$$

$$a = 7.3 - (.75)(3.0) = 5.05$$

Therefore,

$$Y' = 5.05 + .75X$$

In order, then, to predict Y for a given X, multiply the X by b (.75) and add the constant a (5.05). From the above it can be seen that b indicates the expected change in Y associated with a unit change in X. In other words, for each increment of one unit in X one predicts a .75 increment in Y. In our example this means that for every additional hour of study, X, there is an expected gain of .75 unit in Y, task performance. Knowledge of a and b is necessary and sufficient to predict Y from X so that squared errors of prediction are minimized.

Let us take a closer look at the regression equation. Substituting (2.8) in (2.9):

$$\begin{aligned} Y' &= a + bX \\ &= (\bar{Y} - b\bar{X}) + bX \\ &= \bar{Y} + b(X - \bar{X}) \\ &= \bar{Y} + bx \end{aligned} \tag{2.10}$$

Note that Y' can be expressed as being composed of two components: the mean of Y and the product of the deviation of X from the mean of X (x) by the regression coefficient (b). Therefore, when the regression of Y on X is zero (i.e., $b = 0$), or when X does not affect Y, the regression equation would lead to a predicted Y being equal to the mean of Y for each value of X. This makes intuitive sense. When attempting to guess at, or predict, scores of people on a variable Y in the absence of information, except for the knowledge that they are members of the group being studied, the best prediction, in a statistical sense, is the mean of Y for each individual.

Such a prediction policy will minimize squared errors, because the sum of the squared deviations is minimized when the errors are taken from the mean as opposed to any other constant (see, for example, Edwards, 1964, pp. 5–6). Further, when more information about the people is available in the form of their status on another variable, X, but when variations in X are not associated with variations in Y, the best prediction for each individual is still the mean of Y, and the regression equation will lead to the same prediction. Note from (2.7) that when X and Y do not covary, Σxy is zero, resulting in $b = 0$. Applying (2.10) when $b = 0$ leads to $Y' = \bar{Y}$ regardless of the specific values of X.

When, however, b is not zero (that is, when X and Y covary), the application of the regression equation will lead to a reduction in errors of prediction as compared with the errors resulting from predicting $\bar{Y}$ for each individual. The degree of reduction in errors of prediction is closely linked to the concept of the partitioning of the sum of squares of the dependent variable (Σy^2), to which we now turn.

Partitioning the Sum of Squares

The data of Table 2.1 are repeated in Table 2.2. Since the values of X and Y for each individual are known, it is possible to note how accurately each Y is predicted by using the regression equation. Applying the regression equation calculated above, $Y' = 5.05 + .75X$, to each person's X score yields the predicted Y's listed in Table 2.2 in the column labeled Y'. In addition, the following are reported for each person: $Y' - \bar{Y}$, the deviation of the predicted Y from the mean of Y, referred to as deviation due to regression, and its square

Table 2.2 Regression Analysis of a Learning Experiment

	X	Y	Y'	$Y' - \bar{Y}$	$(Y' - \bar{Y})^2$	$Y - Y'$	$(Y - Y')^2$
	1	3	5.80	−1.5	2.25	−2.80	7.84
	1	5	5.80	−1.5	2.25	−.80	.64
	1	6	5.80	−1.5	2.25	.20	.04
	1	9	5.80	−1.5	2.25	3.20	10.24
	2	4	6.55	−.75	.5625	−2.55	6.5025
	2	6	6.55	−.75	.5625	−.55	.3025
	2	7	6.55	−.75	.5625	.45	.2025
	2	10	6.55	−.75	.5625	3.45	11.9025
	3	4	7.30	.00	.00	−3.30	10.89
	3	6	7.30	.00	.00	−1.30	1.69
	3	8	7.30	.00	.00	.70	.49
	3	10	7.30	.00	.00	2.70	7.29
	4	5	8.05	.75	.5625	−3.05	9.3025
	4	7	8.05	.75	.5625	−1.05	1.1025
	4	9	8.05	.75	.5625	.95	.9025
	4	12	8.05	.75	.5625	3.95	15.6025
	5	6	8.80	1.5	2.25	−2.80	7.84
	5	7	8.80	1.5	2.25	−1.80	3.24
	5	10	8.80	1.5	2.25	1.20	1.44
	5	12	8.80	1.5	2.25	3.20	10.24
Σ:	60	146	146	.00	22.50	.00	107.7

$(Y' - \bar{Y})^2$; $Y - Y'$, the deviation of the observed Y from the predicted Y, which is referred to as the residual, or error of prediction; and the squared residual $(Y - Y')^2$.

Careful study of Table 2.2 will reveal important elements of regression analysis, some of which are noted at this stage. The sum of predicted scores $(\Sigma Y')$ is equal to ΣY. Consequently, the mean of predicted scores is always equal to the mean of the dependent variable. The sum of the residuals $[\Sigma(Y - Y')]$ is always zero. These are consequences of the least-squares solution. Each Y score is broken down into three components: $\bar{Y}$, $Y' - \bar{Y}$, and $Y - Y'$. Note the identity:

$$Y = \bar{Y} + (Y' - \bar{Y}) + (Y - Y') \tag{2.11}$$

Each Y is expressed as being composed of the mean of Y; the deviation of the predicted Y from the mean of Y, or the deviation due to regression; and the deviation of the observed Y from the predicted Y, the residual. For the data of Table 2.2, $\bar{Y} = 7.30$. The first subject's score on Y (3) can therefore be expressed as

$$\begin{aligned} 3 &= 7.30 + (5.80 - 7.30) + (3 - 5.80) \\ &= 7.30 + (-1.5) + (-2.80) \end{aligned}$$

Similar statements can be made for each of the subjects of Table 2.2.

It was noted earlier that when no information about an independent variable is available, or when the available information is irrelevant, the best prediction for each individual is $\bar{Y}$, and the sum of squared errors of prediction is Σy^2. When doing a regression analysis, one wishes to determine by how much these errors of prediction can be reduced. In other words, one is interested in knowing how much of the Σy^2 can be explained on the basis of knowledge about the regression of Y on X.

The solution to this problem is approached by using the above-noted identity (2.11):

$$Y = \bar{Y} + (Y' - \bar{Y}) + (Y - Y')$$

Subtracting $\bar{Y}$ from each side:

$$Y - \bar{Y} = (Y' - \bar{Y}) + (Y - Y')$$

Squaring and summing:

$$\begin{aligned}\Sigma(Y - \bar{Y})^2 &= \Sigma[(Y' - \bar{Y}) + (Y - Y')]^2 \\ &= \Sigma(Y' - \bar{Y})^2 + \Sigma(Y - Y')^2 + 2\Sigma(Y' - \bar{Y})(Y - Y')\end{aligned}$$

It can be shown that the *last* term on the right equals zero. Therefore,

$$\Sigma y^2 = \Sigma(Y' - \bar{Y})^2 + \Sigma(Y - Y')^2 \tag{2.12}$$

or

$$\Sigma y^2 = ss_{\text{reg}} + ss_{\text{res}}$$

where ss_{reg} = regression sum of squares and ss_{res} = residual sum of squares.

This central principle in regression analysis states that the deviation sum of squares of the dependent variable, Σy^2, is partitioned into two parts: $\Sigma(Y' - \bar{Y})^2$ is the sum of squares due to regression, or the regression sum of squares; and $\Sigma(Y - Y')^2$ is the sum of squares due to residuals, or the residual sum of squares. When $\Sigma(Y' - \bar{Y})^2 = 0$ it means that Σy^2 is equal to the residual sum of squares, or the errors, indicating that nothing has been gained by resorting to information from X. When, on the other hand, $\Sigma(Y - Y')^2 = 0$, all the variability in Y is explained by regression, or by the information X provides.

Dividing each of the elements in the above equation by the total sum of squres; Σy^2,

$$\begin{aligned}\frac{\Sigma y^2}{\Sigma y^2} &= \frac{ss_{\text{reg}}}{\Sigma y^2} + \frac{ss_{\text{res}}}{\Sigma y^2} \\ 1 &= \frac{ss_{\text{reg}}}{\Sigma y^2} + \frac{ss_{\text{res}}}{\Sigma y^2}\end{aligned} \tag{2.13}$$

The first term on the right-hand side of the equal sign indicates the proportion of the sum of squares of the dependent variable that is due to regression. The second term indicates the proportion of the sum of squares due to error, or residual. For the present example:

$$\frac{22.5}{130.2} + \frac{107.7}{130.2} = .1728 + .8272 = 1$$

About 17% of the sum of squares of Y is due to regression, and about 83% of Σy^2 is left unexplained (i.e., attributed to error).

The calculations in Table 2.2 are rather lengthy even with a small number of cases. They were presented in this form in order to illustrate what each element of the regression analysis means. Following are three equivalent formulas for the calculation of the regression sum of squares. The terms in the formulas are not defined, since they should be clear by now. Each of the formulas is applied to the data of Table 2.2.

$$ss_{\text{reg}} = \frac{(\Sigma xy)^2}{\Sigma x^2} = \frac{(30)^2}{40} = \mathit{22.5} \tag{2.14}$$

$$ss_{\text{reg}} = b\Sigma xy = (.75)(30) = \mathit{22.5} \tag{2.15}$$

$$ss_{\text{reg}} = b^2 \Sigma x^2 = (.75)^2(40) = \mathit{22.5} \tag{2.16}$$

It was shown above that

$$\Sigma y^2 = ss_{\text{reg}} + ss_{\text{res}}$$

Therefore,

$$ss_{\text{res}} = \Sigma y^2 - ss_{\text{reg}} = 130.2 - 22.5 = \mathit{107.7} \tag{2.17}$$

Above, the regression sum of squares was divided by the total sum of squares, thus obtaining the proportion of the latter that is due to regression. Using the right-hand term of (2.14) as an expression of the regression sum of squares, and dividing by the total sum of squares:

$$r^2_{xy} = \frac{(\Sigma xy)^2}{\Sigma x^2 \Sigma y^2} \tag{2.18}$$

where r^2_{xy} is the squared Pearson product moment coefficient of correlation between X and Y. This important formulation, which is used repeatedly in the book, states that the squared correlation between X and Y indicates the proportion of the sum of squares of $Y(\Sigma y^2)$ that is due to regression. It follows that the proportion of Σy^2 that is due to errors, or residuals, is $1 - r^2_{xy}$.

Using these formulations, it is possible to arrive at the following expressions of the regression and residual sum of squares:

$$ss_{\text{reg}} = r_{xy}^2 \Sigma y^2 \qquad (2.19)$$

For the data of Table 2.2, $r_{xy}^2 = .1728$, and $\Sigma y^2 = 130.2$.

$$ss_{\text{reg}} = (.1728)(130.2) = 22.5$$

and

$$\begin{aligned} ss_{\text{res}} &= (1 - r_{xy}^2)\Sigma y^2 \\ &= (1 - .1728)(130.2) = 107.7 \end{aligned} \qquad (2.20)$$

Finally, it will be noted that instead of partitioning the sum of squares of the dependent variable, one may partition its *variance:*

$$s_y^2 = r_{xy}^2 s_y^2 + (1 - r_{xy}^2)s_y^2 \qquad (2.21)$$

where $r_{xy}^2 s_y^2$ = the portion of the variance of Y that is due to its regression on X; $(1 - r_{xy}^2)s_y^2$ = portion of the variance of Y that is due to residuals, or errors. r^2, then, is also interpreted as the proportion of the variance of the dependent variable that is accounted for by the independent variable, and $1 - r^2$ is the proportion of variance of the dependent variable that is not accounted for. In subsequent presentations, sums of squares or variances are partitioned, depending on the topic under discussion. Frequently, both approaches are used in order to underscore their equivalence.

Graphic Depiction of Regression Analysis

The data of Table 2.2 are plotted in Figure 2.1. Although the points are fairly scattered, they do depict a linear trend in which increments in X are associated with increments in Y. The line that best fits the regression of Y on X, in the sense of minimizing the sum of the squared deviations of the observed Y's from it, is referred to as the regression line. This line depicts pictorially the regression equation, where a represents the point on the ordinate, Y, intercepted by the regression line, and b represents the slope of the line. Of various methods for graphing the regression line, the following is probably the easiest. Two points are necessary to draw a line. One of the points that may be used is the value of a (the intercept) calculated by (2.8). Equation (2.10) is repeated with a new number:

$$Y' = \bar{Y} + bx \qquad (2.22)$$

from which it can be seen that, regardless of what the regression coefficient (b) is, $Y' = \bar{Y}$ when $x = 0$—that is, when $X = \bar{X}$. In other words, the means of X and Y are always on the regression line. Consequently, the intersection of lines

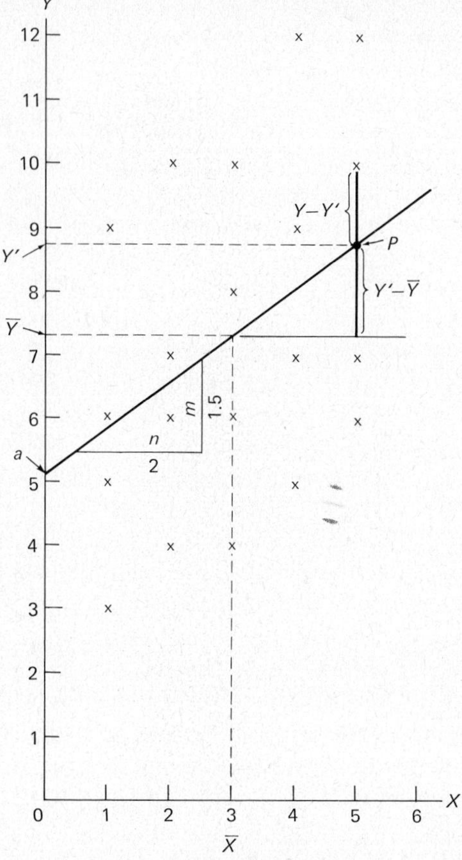

Figure 2.1

drawn from the horizontal (abscissa) and the vertical (ordinate) axes at the means of X and Y provides the second point for graphing the regression line. See the intersection of the broken lines in Figure 2.1.

In Figure 2.1 two lines, m and n, were drawn, paralleling the Y and X axes, respectively, thus constructing a right triangle whose hypotenuse is a segment of the regression line. The slope of the regression line, b, can now be expressed trigonometrically: it is the length of the vertical line, m, divided by the horizontal line, n. In Figure 2.1, $m = 1.5$ and $n = 2.0$. Therefore, $1.5/2.0 = .75$, which is equal to the value of b calculated earlier. It can be seen now that b indicates the rate of change of Y associated with the rate of change of X. Because we are dealing with a straight line, the above holds true no matter where along the regression line the triangle is constructed.

Since $b = m/n$, $m = bn$. This provides another approach to the graphing of the regression line. Draw a horizontal line of length n originating from the intercept (a). At the end of n draw a line m perpendicular to n. The endpoint of line m serves as one point and the intercept as the other point for graphing the regression line.

Two other concepts are illustrated graphically in Figure 2.1: the deviation due to residual ($Y - Y'$) and the deviation due to regression ($Y' - \bar{Y}$). For illustrative purposes the individual whose scores are 5 and 10 on X and Y, respectively, is being used. This individual's predicted score (8.8) is found by drawing a line perpendicular to the ordinate (Y) from the point P on the regression line (see Figure 2.1, and also Table 2.2 where the same Y' was obtained by using the regression equation). Now, this individual's Y score deviates 2.7 points from the mean of Y (10 − 7.3 = 2.7). It is the sum of the squares of all such deviations (Σy^2) that we wish to partition into two parts: regression sum of squares, and residual sum of squares. For the individual under consideration, the residual: $Y - Y' = 10 - 8.8 = 1.2$. This is indicated by the vertical line drawn from the point for this individual to the regression line. The deviation due to regression, $Y' - \bar{Y} = 8.8 - 7.3 = 1.5$, is indicated by the extension of the same line until it meets the horizontal line originating from $\bar{Y}$ (see Figure 2.1, and also Table 2.2). Note that $Y' = 8.8$ for all the individuals whose $X = 5$. It is their residuals that differ. Some points are closer to the regression line and thus their residuals are small (e.g., the individual whose $Y = 10$), and some are farther from the regression line, indicating larger residuals (e.g., the individual whose $Y = 12$).

Finally, note that the residual sum of squares is relatively large when the scatter of the points about the regression line is relatively large. Conversely, the closer the points are to the regression line the smaller the residual sum of squares. When all the points are on the regression line, the residual sum of squares is zero, and explanation, or prediction, of Y using X is perfect. If, on the other hand, the regression of Y on X is zero, the regression line has no slope and will be drawn horizontally originating from $\bar{Y}$. Under such circumstances, $\Sigma y^2 = \Sigma(Y - Y')^2$, and all the deviations are due to error. Knowledge of X does not enhance the prediction of Y.

TESTS OF SIGNIFICANCE

Sample statistics are most often used for the purpose of making inferences about unknown parameters of a defined population. It will be recalled that tests of statistical significance are resorted to in order to determine whether the probability of obtaining a given estimate is small, say .05, so as to lead to the rejection of the null hypothesis that the population parameter is of a given value, say zero. Thus, for example, a small probability associated with an obtained b (the statistic) would lead to the rejection of the hypothesis that β (the parameter) is zero.

It is assumed that you are familiar with the logic and principles of statistical hypothesis testing (if necessary, review this topic in a statistics book, e.g., Hays, 1981, Chapter 7). But because such tests are used repeatedly in this book it is important to place them in a proper perspective of the overall research endeavor. Statistical tests of significance are a major source of controversy among social scientists (for a compilation of articles on this topic, see Morrison & Henkel, 1970). The controversy is due, in part, to various misconceptions of the role and meaning of such tests in the context of scientific inquiry (a good discussion of misconceptions and "fantasies" about tests of significance is provided by Carver, 1978).

It is necessary to remember that all that is meant by a statistically significant finding is that the probability of its occurrence is small, assuming that the null hypothesis is true. But it is the substantive meaning of the finding that is paramount. Of what use is a statistically significant finding if it is deemed to be substantively not meaningful? Bemoaning the practice of exclusive reliance on tests of significance, Nunnally (1960) stated: "We should not feel proud when we see the psychologist smile and say 'the correlation is significant beyond the .01 level.' Perhaps that is the most he can say, but he has no reason to smile" (p. 649).

It is well known that given a sufficiently large sample, the probability of rejecting the null hypothesis is high. "If rejection of the null hypothesis were the real intention in psychological experiments, there usually would be no need to gather data" (Nunnally, 1960, p. 643. See also Rozeboom, 1960). Sound principles of research design dictate that the researcher first decide upon the magnitude of the effect, or relation, that is to be considered substantively meaningful in a specific area of research. Having done this, the level of significance (Type I error) and the desired power of the statistical test (1 − Type II error) are selected. Based on the preceding decisions, the requisite sample size is calculated. Using this approach, the researcher can avoid arriving at findings that are substantively meaningful but statistically not significant, or to be fooled by findings that are statistically significant but substantively not meaningful (for extensive discussions of this topic, see Cohen, 1977; Cohen & Cohen, 1975).

In sum, the major emphasis should be on substantive meaningfulness of findings, that is, on magnitudes of relations among variables, magnitudes of differences among means, magnitudes of treatment effects, and the like. In view of the foregoing, you probably wonder why criteria for meaningfulness of findings are not discussed in this book. The reason is that meaningfulness is specific to a given research area. For example, a mean difference between two groups that is considered meaningful in one area may be viewed as trivial in another area. Moreover, even within the same research area researchers may disagree about the meaningfulness of a finding when they consider, for example, the costs involved in obtaining it. In short, criteria for substantive meaningfulness cannot be arrived at in a research vacuum. Admittedly, some authors (notably Cohen, 1977) provide guidelines for criteria of meaningfulness. But being guidelines in the abstract, they are, inevitably, bound to be viewed as unsatisfactory by some researchers when they examine their specific findings. For example, Cohen suggests that accounting for 1% of the variance of the dependent variable be viewed as a small meaningful effect. It is not difficult to envision various researchers dismissing such a finding as trivial in their own research.

In a book such as the present one it is easy to show how to conduct tests of significance. But because the data used are illustrative, and because it is not possible to elaborate on the substantive meaning of findings without thorough discussions of the theories underlying the research as well as the specific aspects of the research design, comments about meaningfulness will be made occasionally only as reminders of the preceding discussion. It is hoped that these will suffice to serve as warnings against exclusive reliance on tests of significance.

Instead of presenting here special formulas for tests of significance for the case of simple linear regression, it was decided to present general formulas that are used throughout the book, because simple linear regression is subsumed under them.

Testing the Regression of *Y* on *X*

It was shown earlier that the sum of squares of the dependent variable (Σy^2) can be partitioned into two components: regression sum of squares (ss_{reg}), and residual sum of squares (ss_{res}). Each of these sums of squares has associated with it a number of degrees of freedom *(df)*. Dividing each sum of squares by its *df* yields a mean square. The ratio of the mean square regression to the mean square residual follows an *F* distribution with df_1 for the numerator and df_2 for the denominator (see below). When the obtained *F* exceeds the tabled value of *F* at a preselected level of significance, the conclusion is to reject the null hypothesis (for thorough discussions of the *F* distribution and the concept of *df*, see, for example, Hays, 1981; Kirk, 1968; Winer, 1971). The formula for *F*, then, is:

$$F = \frac{ss_{\text{reg}}/df_1}{ss_{\text{res}}/df_2} = \frac{ss_{\text{reg}}/k}{ss_{\text{res}}/(N - k - 1)} \tag{2.23}$$

where df_1 associated with ss_{reg} are equal to the number of independent variables, *k*; df_2 associated with ss_{res} are equal to *N* (sample size) minus *k* (number of independent variables) minus 1. In the case of simple linear regression, $k = 1$. Therefore, 1 *df* is associated with the numerator of the *F* ratio. The *df* for the denominator are: $N - 1 - 1 = N - 2$.

For the numerical example of Table 2.2: $ss_{\text{reg}} = 22.5$; $ss_{\text{res}} = 107.7$; $N = 20$.

$$F = \frac{22.5/1}{107.7/18} = 3.76$$

with 1 and 18 *df*.

Assuming that the researcher set α (level of significance) = .05, it is found that the tabled *F* with 1 and 18 *df* is 4.41 (see Appendix B for a table of the *F* distribution). As the obtained *F* is smaller than the tabled value, it is concluded that the regression of *Y* on *X* is not significantly different from zero. Referring to the variables dealt with in the present example (recall that the data are illustrative), one would conclude that the regression of task performance on study time is not significant at the .05 level, or that study time does not significantly affect task performance (at the .05 level). But recall the important distinction between statistical significance and substantive meaningfulness discussed above.

Testing the Proportion of Variance Accounted for by Regression

Earlier, it was said that r^2 indicates the proportion of variance of the dependent variable accounted for by the independent variable. Also, $1 - r^2$ is the proportion of variance of the dependent variable not accounted for by the independent variable, or the proportion of error variance. The significance of r^2 is tested as follows:

$$F = \frac{r^2/k}{(1 - r^2)/(N - k - 1)} \tag{2.24}$$

where k is the number of independent variables.

For the data of Table 2.2, $r^2 = .1728$; hence

$$F = \frac{.1728/1}{(1 - .1728)/(20 - 1 - 1)} = 3.76$$

with 1 and 18 *df*. Note that the same F ratio is obtained whether one uses sums of squares or r^2. The identity of the two formulas for the F ratio may be noted by substituting (2.19) and (2.20) in (2.23):

$$F = \frac{r^2 \Sigma y^2/k}{(1 - r^2)\Sigma y^2/(N - k - 1)} \tag{2.25}$$

where $r^2\Sigma y^2 = ss_{\text{reg}}$ and $(1 - r^2)\Sigma y^2 = ss_{\text{res}}$. Canceling Σy^2 from the numerator and the denominator of (2.25) results in formula (2.24).

From the foregoing it is evident that it makes no difference whether sums of squares or proportions of variance are used for testing the significance of the regression of Y on X. In subsequent presentations one or both of the above interchangeable approaches will be used so that you may develop a flexibility in using whichever you may prefer.

Testing the Regression Coefficient

Like other statistics, the regression coefficient, b, has a standard error associated with it. But before presenting the standard error of b and its use in testing the significance of b, it is necessary to introduce the concepts of the variance of estimate and the standard error of estimate.

Variance of Estimate. The variance of scores about the regression line is referred to as the variance of estimate. The parameter is written as $\sigma^2_{y.x}$, which means the variance of Y given X. The sample unbiased estimator of $\sigma^2_{y.x}$ is $s^2_{y.x}$, and is calculated as follows:

$$s^2_{y.x} = \frac{\Sigma(Y - Y')^2}{N - k - 1} = \frac{ss_{\text{res}}}{N - k - 1} \tag{2.26}$$

where Y = observed Y; Y' = predicted Y; N = sample size; k = number of independent variables. The variance of estimate, then, is the variance of the residuals. It indicates the degree of variability of the points about the regression line. Note that the rightmost expression of $s^2_{y.x}$ is the same as the denominator of the F ratio presented earlier [see Equation (2.23)]. The variance of estimate, then, is the Mean Square Residual *(MSR)*.

For the data of Table 2.2,

$$s^2_{y.x} = MSR = \frac{107.7}{18} = 5.983$$

The *standard error of estimate* is the square root of the variance of estimate. That is, it is the standard deviation of the residuals.

$$s_{y.x} = \sqrt{\frac{\Sigma(Y - Y')^2}{N - k - 1}} = \sqrt{\frac{ss_{\text{res}}}{N - k - 1}} \tag{2.27}$$

For our data: $s_{y.x} = \sqrt{5.983} = 2.446$

The *standard error of b,* the regression coefficient, is:

$$s_b = \sqrt{\frac{s^2_{y.x}}{\Sigma x^2}} = \frac{s_{y.x}}{\sqrt{\Sigma x^2}} \tag{2.28}$$

where s_b = standard error of b; $s^2_{y.x}$ = variance of estimate; $s_{y.x}$ = standard error of estimate; Σx^2 = sum of squares of the independent variable, X. s_b is the standard deviation of the sampling distribution of b, and can therefore be used for testing the significance of b:

$$t = \frac{b}{s_b} \tag{2.29}$$

where t is the t ratio with *df* associated with $s^2_{y.x}$: $N - k - 1$ (N = sample size; k = number of independent variables).

For the data of Table 2.2: $b = .75$; $s^2_{y.x} = 5.983$; $\Sigma x^2 = 40$ (see calculations above). Hence

$$t = \frac{.75}{\sqrt{\frac{5.983}{40}}} = \frac{.75}{\sqrt{.1496}} = 1.94$$

with 18 *df* (20 − 1 − 1), $p > .05$. Recall that $t^2 = F$ when the numerator *df* for F is 1, which is the case in the present example. Therefore, $1.94^2 = 3.76$, the F ratio obtained above. In simple linear regression, testing the significance of b is the same as testing the regression of Y on X by using sums of squares or proportions of variance, as was done earlier. The conclusions are, of course, the same. On the basis of the above test it is concluded that the regression coefficient *(b)* is not significantly different from zero (at the .05 level).

There are, however, situations when the use of a t ratio is preferable to the use of F. First, while (2.29) was used to test whether b differs significantly from zero, it may be used to test whether b differs significantly from any hypothesized value. The formula takes the following form:

$$t = \frac{b - \beta}{s_b} \tag{2.30}$$

where β is the hypothesized regression coefficient.

Assume that in the numerical example under consideration there was reason to hypothesize that the regression coefficient in the population is .50. To test whether the obtained b differs significantly from the population β, one would calculate

$$t = \frac{.75 - .50}{.3868} = .65$$

with 18 *df*. This is obviously not significant at the .05 level. In other words, the obtained b is not significantly different from the hypothesized regression coefficient.

Second, using a t ratio one can set confidence intervals around the regression coefficient. The use of confidence intervals in preference to tests of statistical significance has been strongly advocated by various authors (see, for example, Hays, 1981; Nunnally, 1960; Rozeboom, 1960). Because of space considerations this topic is not discussed here, except to list some of the arguments advanced in favor of the use of confidence intervals. Probably the most important argument is that a confidence interval provides more information than the information provided by a statement about the rejection of (or the failure to reject) a null hypothesis, which is almost always false anyway. Moreover, a confidence interval enables one to test simultaneously all possible null hypotheses. The narrower the confidence interval, the smaller the range of possible null hypotheses, and hence the greater the confidence in one's findings. It is therefore suggested that confidence intervals become an integral part of research reports, or that standard errors of the statistics be reported so that a reader may use them to better assess the findings.

The confidence interval for a b is:

$$b \pm t(\alpha/2, df)s_b$$

where t is the tabled t ratio at $\alpha/2$ with *df* associated with standard error of estimate and s_b is the standard error of b. Assuming one wishes to obtain the 95% confidence interval in the present example: the tabled t at .05/2 (0.25) with 18 *df* is 2.101 (see table of t distribution in statistics books, or take $\sqrt{F}$ with 1 and 18 *df* from Appendix B), $b = .75$, and $s_b = .3868$. The 95% confidence interval is:

$$.75 \pm (2.101)(.3868) = -.0627 \text{ and } 1.5627.$$

It can therefore be stated with 95% confidence that the parameter lies within this range; that is,

$$-.0627 \leq \beta \leq 1.5627$$

Note that the interval includes zero, thereby indicating that b is not significantly different from zero at the .05 level.

Third, using a t ratio instead of F, one may apply one-tailed tests of significance. Assume that the researcher had reason to test the b at .05 using a one-tailed test, then the t obtained above (1.94 with 18 df) would have been declared statistically significant (a t of 1.73 is required for a one-tailed test at .05 with 18 df). For discussions of one-tailed versus two-tailed tests of significance, see Edwards (1972) and Guilford and Fruchter (1978).

FACTORS AFFECTING THE PRECISION OF THE REGRESSION EQUATION

Careful study of the formulas for tests of significance in regression analysis will reveal that three factors affect them: (1) sample size N; (2) the scatter of points about the regression line, indicated by $\Sigma(Y - Y')^2$; and (3) the range of values selected for the X variable, reflected by Σx^2.

Some of the formulas used earlier are repeated with new numbers in order to demonstrate these points.

$$F = \frac{ss_{\text{reg}}/k}{ss_{\text{res}}/(N - k - 1)} \tag{2.31}$$

Other things equal, the larger N the smaller the denominator, the larger the F ratio. Holding N constant, the smaller the scatter about the regression line (i.e., the smaller the ss_{res}) the larger ss_{reg}, and consequently the larger the F ratio. Hence

$$t = \frac{b}{\sqrt{\dfrac{s^2_{y.x}}{\Sigma x^2}}} \tag{2.32}$$

Other things equal, the larger Σx^2, the smaller the s_b, and consequently the larger the t ratio. Holding X constant, $s^2_{y.x}$ is a function of the scatter of points about the regression line. Therefore, the smaller $s^2_{y.x}$, the smaller the s_b, and the larger the t ratio. Similar reasoning applies also to formulas in which the proportion of variance accounted for is tested for significance.

The effects of the above-noted factors are illustrated by selecting, in turn, different parts of the data of Table 2.2. These are reported in Table 2.3 and are plotted in Figure 2.2. Also given in Table 2.3, for easy reference, are some of the formulas used in this chapter. It is suggested that you repeat some of the calculations of Table 2.3 as an exercise. Obtaining the same results by using one or more algebraic identities will assist in making the concepts of regression analysis part of your vocabulary.

Several things will be noted about Table 2.3 and Figure 2.2. The regression

Table 2.3 Four Sets of Illustrative Data

	(a)		(b)		(c)		(d)	
	X	Y	X	Y	X	Y	X	Y
	1	5	1	3	1	3	2	4
	1	6	1	9	1	5	2	6
	2	6	2	4	1	6	2	7
	2	7	2	10	1	9	2	10
	3	6	3	4	5	6	3	4
	3	8	3	10	5	7	3	6
	4	7	4	5	5	10	3	8
	4	9	4	12	5	12	3	10
	5	7	5	6			4	5
	5	10	5	12			4	7
							4	9
							4	12
N:	10		10		8		12	
ss:	20	20.9	20	108.5	32	59.5	8	70.67
a:	4.85		5.25		5.00		5.08	
b:	.75		.75		.75		.75	
r^2:	.54		.10		.30		.06	
ss_{reg}:	11.25		11.25		18.00		4.50	
ss_{res}:	9.65		97.25		41.50		66.17	
$s_{y.x}$:	1.10		3.49		2.63		2.57	
F:	9.33 (1, 8)		.93 (1, 8)		2.60 (1, 6)		.68 (1,10)	
t:	3.05 (8)		.96 (8)		1.61 (6)		.82 (10)	

$$b = \frac{\Sigma xy}{\Sigma x^2} \qquad a = \bar{Y} - b\bar{X} \qquad ss_{\text{reg}} = b\Sigma xy = b^2\Sigma x^2 = r^2\Sigma y^2$$

$$ss_{\text{res}} = \Sigma y^2 - ss_{\text{reg}} = (1 - r^2)\Sigma y^2 \qquad F = \frac{ss_{\text{reg}}/k}{ss_{\text{res}}/(N - k - 1)} \qquad t = \frac{b}{s_b}$$

coefficient in the four sets of data is the same ($b = .75$). The F ratio associated with the b, however, is significant only in set (a). Compare and contrast set (a) with set (b): having an identical b and identical Σx^2 (20), the regression sum of squares ($b^2\Sigma x^2$) is the same in both (11.25). N is also the same in both. They differ in the residual sum of squares—that is, 9.65 for (a) and 97.25 for (b)—which reflects the scatter of points about the regression line. Consequently, the standard error of estimate, which is the standard deviation of the residuals, of (a) is about one-third of what it is for (b), and similarly for the standard errors of the two b's. Note also that the proportion of variance (r^2) accounted for in (a) is .54, and in (b) it is .10.

Compare and contrast sets (c) and (d). The former is composed of the extreme values of X (1 and 5), whereas the latter is composed of the intermediate values of X (2, 3, and 4). Σx^2 in (c) is four times that of (d): 32 and 8 respectively. Since the b's are the same in both sets, ss_{reg} in (c) is four times that of (d). Note also that the standard errors of estimate are very similar in both sets. Although the $s_{y.x}$ is slightly larger in (c), the standard error of b for set (c) is .4649, as compared with .9086, which is the standard error of b in set (d). This

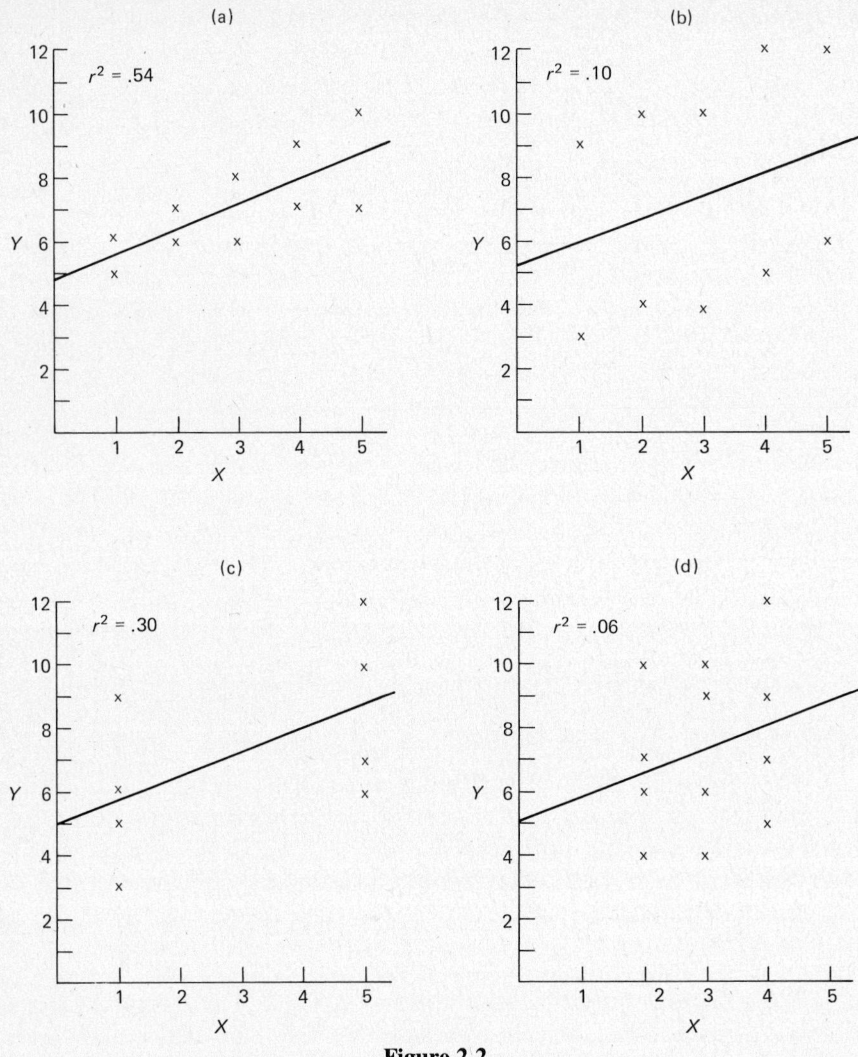

Figure 2.2

is directly a function of the different Σx^2's in the two sets, leading to a t of 1.61 in (c) and a t of .82 in (d). Also, the proportion of variance (r^2) accounted for in (c) is .30, whereas in (d) it is .06.

It is suggested that you study this example carefully to note the relations and principles that were discussed as well as others that were not detailed.

ASSUMPTIONS

Nothing has been said about assumptions until now. Unfortunately, preoccupation with assumptions seems to frighten students, or bore them. Intelligent use of analytic methods, however, requires knowledge of the rationale and thus the assumptions behind the methods. It requires knowledge and understanding when departures from, or violations of, assumptions lead to serious biases, and when they have little impact on estimators and test statistics. With the preceding remarks in mind, the assumptions underlying simple linear regression are discussed, and some consequences of violations of the assumptions are noted.

It is assumed the X, the independent variable, is a fixed variable. What this means is that if the experiment were to be replicated, the same values of X would have to be used. Referring to the numerical example used earlier, this means that the same values of hours of study would have to be used if the experiment were to be replicated. When the study is nonexperimental, as in the regression of verbal ability on age, the requirement of fixed X means that in repeated samples the same values of X, age in the present example, would be used.[2]

From the foregoing, it is clear that the researcher is at liberty to fix the values of X in an experimental study, or to select the values of X in a nonexperimental study. A question that comes to mind is: What are the considerations in selecting values of X? It was shown earlier that the larger Σx^2, the smaller the standard error of the regression coefficient. Therefore, selecting extreme values of X will optimize tests of statistical significance. In the limiting case, selecting only two extreme values of X will maximize the Σx^2. But it is important to note that this will force the regression to be linear even when it is curvilinear along the X continuum. Using only two X values thus precludes the possibility of determining whether the regression departs from linearity (see Chapter 11). In general, it is recommended that X values be fixed at evenly spaced intervals along the continuum of interest. There are, however, situations when other approaches to the selection of X values are preferable (for a detailed discussion, see Draper & Smith, 1981, pp. 51–55).

It is further assumed that X is measured without error.

The population means of the Y's at each level of X are assumed to be on a straight line. In other words, the regression of Y on X is assumed to be linear.

Unlike X, Y is a random variable, which means that Y has a range of possible values, each having an associated probability (for detailed discussions of random variables, see Edwards, 1964, Chapter 4; Hays, 1981, pp. 83–85; Winer, 1971, Appendix A). But recall that each observation of Y (Y_i) is assumed to be composed of two components: a fixed component, $\alpha + \beta X$, and a random error, ϵ_i. Therefore, the remaining assumptions are concerned with the errors.

The assumptions regarding the errors are: (1) The mean of errors for each observation, Y_i, over many replications is zero. (2) Errors associated with one observation, Y_i, are not correlated with errors associated with any other observation, Y_j. (3) The variance of errors at all values of X is constant. That is, the variance of errors is the same at all levels of X. This property is referred to as *homoscedasticity*. When the variance of errors differs at different values of X, *heteroscedasticity* is indicated. (4) The errors are assumed to be not correlated with the independent variable, X.

The preceding assumptions are necessary in order to obtain best linear unbiased estimators (see discussion earlier in the chapter). For the purpose of

[2]Linear regression analysis when X is a random variable is discussed later in this chapter.

conducting tests of significance, an additional assumption is required, namely that the errors are normally distributed.

Violation of Assumptions

It has been demonstrated that regression analysis is generally robust in the presence of departures from assumptions, except for measurement errors and specification errors (for detailed discussions see Bohrnstedt & Carter, 1971; Fox, 1968; Ezekiel & Fox, 1959; Hanushek & Jackson, 1977; Johnston, 1972; Kmenta, 1971; Snedecor & Cochran, 1967). Therefore, it is to the aforementioned issues that this section is devoted.

Measurement Errors. Measurement errors in the dependent variable do not lead to bias in the estimation of the regression coefficient, but they do lead to an increase in the standard error of estimate, thereby weakening the test of statistical significance. Errors of measurement in the independent variable, however, lead to underestimation of the regression coefficient. It can be shown that the underestimation is related to the reliability of the measure of the independent variable. Reliability is a complex concept that cannot be discussed here (for different models of reliability and approaches to its estimation, see Nunnally, 1978, Chapters 6 and 7). For the present purposes it will only be noted that, broadly speaking, reliability refers to the accuracy of measurement. The reliability of a measure, symbolized as r_{tt}, can range from .00 to 1.00. The higher the r_{tt}, the more accurate the measure. Now,

$$b = \beta r_{tt} \tag{2.33}$$

where b = the statistic and β = the parameter. From (2.33) it can be seen that with perfect reliability of X ($r_{tt} = 1.00$) $b = \beta$. When the reliability is less than 1.00, as it almost always is, b underestimates β. When $r_{tt} = .70$, for example, there will be a 30% underestimation of β. In experimental research, the independent variable is under the direct control of the experimenter. Consequently, it is reasonable to expect that, with proper care, the reliability of X is high. In nonexperimental research, on the other hand, the reliability of the measure of the independent variable tends to be low to moderate (i.e., ranging from about .5 to about .8). This is particularly so with some of the attributes used in such research (e.g., cognitive styles, self-concept, ego strength, attitudes). Therefore, the bias in estimating the regression coefficient in nonexperimental research may be considerable. Researchers have generally been complacent about the biasing effects of measurement errors, even when they were aware of them, because they believed that they were being conservative since the bias leads to underestimation rather than overestimation of the regression coefficient. But two things have to be borne in mind. First, when one wishes to test whether the regression of Y on X is the same in two groups, say, as in Aptitude-Treatment-Interaction (ATI) designs (see Chapter 12), one's conclusions may be seriously in error if the reliabilities of X in each group differ greatly from each other. Similarly, in Analysis of Covariance designs, or in some designs dealing with test bias (see Chapter 13). Second, the effects of measurement errors when more than one independent variable is used (i.e., in multiple regression) are much more complex, and their bias may be in overestimation as well as in underestimation (see Chapter 8). The above remarks apply to the effects of random errors of measurement. Effects of nonrandom errors are more complex and difficult to trace.

Specification Errors. In a broad sense, specification errors refer to any errors committed in specifying the model to be tested or to the violation of any of the assumptions that underlie the model. The term is generally used in a narrower sense to refer to errors in model specification (see Hanushek & Jackson, 1977, pp. 79–86; Johnston, 1972, pp. 168–169; Kmenta, 1971, pp. 391–405). The model used (i.e., the regression equation) is actually a representation of the theory that generated it. When the model is not tenable from a theoretical frame of reference, specification errors have been committed. Among such errors are: (1) omission of relevant variables from the equation; (2) inclusion of irrelevant variables in the equation; (3) specifying that the regression is linear when it is curvilinear.

Specification errors are discussed in detail in Chapter 8. At this stage, the purpose is only to draw attention to the serious biasing effects such errors may have. Earlier, it was said that under the errors, e, are subsumed all variables, other than X, that affect the dependent variable, Y. It was also said that e is assumed to be not correlated with X. This situation is depicted in Figure 2.3. Now, suppose that a relevant variable (or variables) not included in the equation is correlated with X. Since such a variable is subsumed under e, it follows that e and X will be correlated, thus violating a crucial assumption and leading to bias in the estimation of the regression coefficient associated with X. The nature of the bias is shown in Chapter 8. For now, suffice it to say that it may be very serious and lead to erroneous conclusions about the effect of X on Y.

It should also be noted that the type of research in which regression analysis is used may lead to a greater or lesser potential for specification errors of the kind described above. Specifically, it is important to distinguish between experimental and nonexperimental research. In experimental research, subjects are randomly assigned to different levels of X, and it is therefore reasonable to assume that the effects of all variables, other than X, are equally distributed in the various groups. In other words, the assumption about the absence of a relation between X and e is tenable, though not a certainty. The assumption

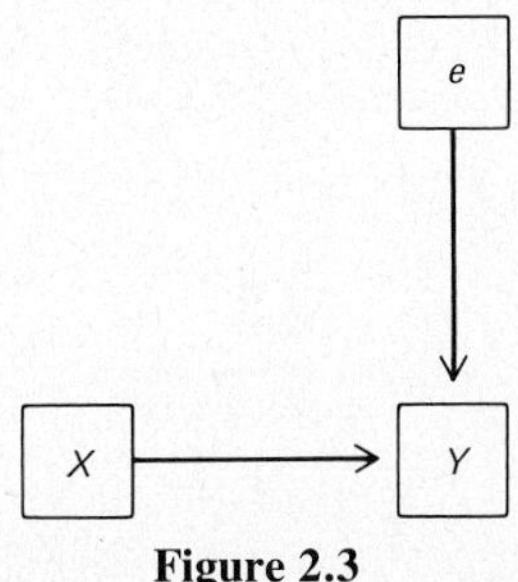

Figure 2.3

may be highly questionable when the research is nonexperimental, particularly when X "explains" a relatively small proportion of the variance in Y. Assume, for example, that the proportion of variance due to regression is .10, that is, that 10 percent of the variance is accounted for. Such a finding would be considered by most researchers in the social sciences as meaningful and being of medium magnitude (see Cohen, 1977). But since 90% of the variance is unaccounted for, it is very questionable that of all the variables "responsible" for this percentage of the variance none is related to X.

In a very good discussion of the biasing effects of measurement and specification errors, Bohrnstedt and Carter (1971) point out that researchers often ignore such errors. The authors then state: "We can only come to the sobering conclusion, then, that many of the published results based on regression analysis . . . are possible distortions of whatever reality may exist" (p. 143). This is, admittedly, a strong indictment. It should serve to alert researchers to possible distortions in their analyses and to the need to take steps to avoid them or to cope with them.

Plotting Data and Residuals

An indispensable approach to a better understanding of one's results and to discerning whether some of the assumptions (e.g., linearity, homoscedasticity) are tenable is to study carefully plots of the data. For a very good discussion and instructive illustrations, see Anscombe (1973).

Another very useful approach is the plotting and study of residuals. This is too broad a topic to discuss here in detail. Only a brief sketch is therefore given. Of the various plotting approaches, probably the simplest and most useful is the one in which standardized residuals are plotted against the standardized predicted Y's.

You have, assuredly, encountered standard scores in introductory courses in statistics and measurement. Recall that:

$$z = \frac{X - \bar{X}}{s} \tag{2.34}$$

where z = standard score; X = raw score; $\bar{X}$ = mean; s = standard deviation. As was noted earlier, the mean of residuals is always zero. The standard deviation of residuals is the standard error of estimate ($s_{y.x}$). Therefore, to standardize residuals, divide each residual by $s_{y.x}$. The predicted scores (Y') are, of course, obtained by the application of the regression equation.

The data of Table 2.2 are used to illustrate the plotting of residuals as well as to discuss some approaches to studying them. In Table 2.2 the predicted Y's are reported under the column labeled Y', and the residuals are reported under a column labeled $Y - Y'$. Dividing each residual by 2.446 ($s_{y.x}$) yields a standardized residual. The standardized residuals of Table 2.2 are plotted against the predicted Y's in Figure 2.4.

Several things are being sought when studying plots like those of Figure 2.4. First, do the points appear to scatter randomly about the line originating from

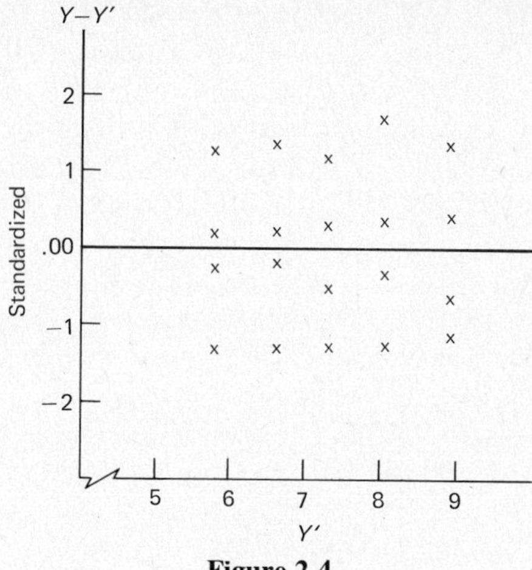

Figure 2.4

the mean of the residuals, describing what appears to be a rectangle? If, for example, the points describe a curve as in Figure 2.5, it serves as a signal that the regression is nonlinear.

Second, are the points scattered evenly about the line originating from the mean of the residuals? If they are not, as, for example, in Figure 2.6, heteroscedasticity is indicated.

Third, are there extreme residuals, or outliers? Extreme residuals may seriously distort the results. While there are statistical tests of significance to determine which residuals are extreme (see, for example, Snedecor & Cochran, 1967, pp. 157–158), a good rule of thumb is to consider standardized residuals greater than 2 (i.e., $z > 2.00$) as extreme. Extreme residuals deserve special attention and study, inasmuch as various factors may give rise to them. The most obvious cause of an extreme residual is a recording or keypunching error. Assume, for example, that instead of recording, or keypunching, the last value of Y in Table 2.2 as 12, one recorded 22. This single error will lead to a regression equation of $Y' = 4.05 + 1.25X$ instead of $Y' = 5.05 + .75X$ obtained when this error was not made. Note that the b has increased by .50, leading to a

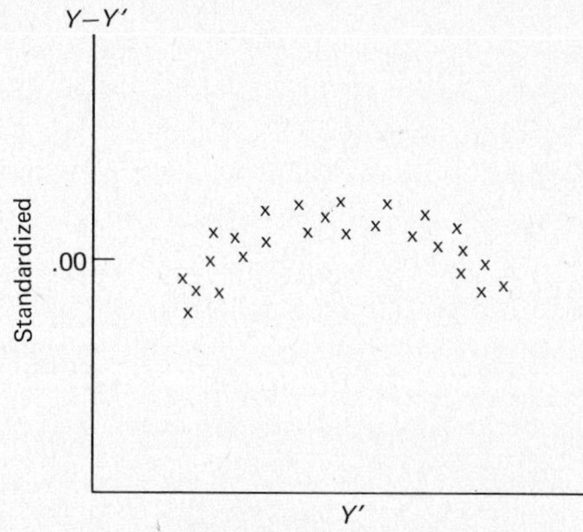

Figure 2.5

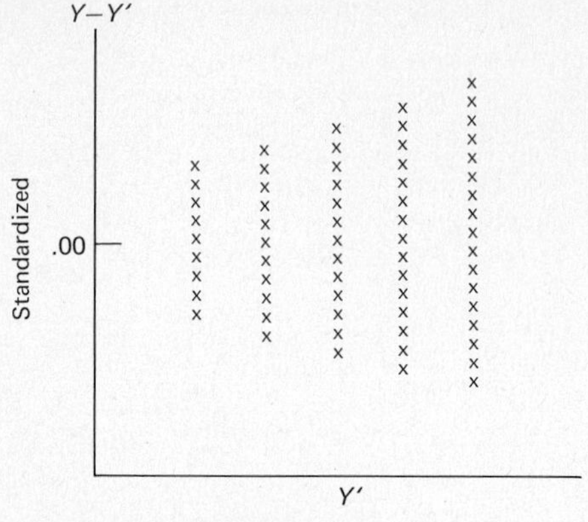

Figure 2.6

statement that the effect of study time (our fictitious example) is much stronger. The residual for the erroneous value is 11.7, and $s_{y.x} = 3.776$. The standardized residual (3.10) will lead one to suspect this value, and perhaps be able to track the recording or keypunching error. If, instead, the error in the same score were in the opposite direction, say, a 2 instead of 12, the regression equation would be $Y' = 6.05 + .25X$. In this case, $s_{y.x} = 2.67$, the residual is -5.30. Incidentally, the r^2 obtained in analyses with extreme residuals may differ considerably from those in which such values are corrected or removed. For example, $r^2 = .17$ for the data of Table 2.2 (see calculations earlier in this chapter). For the case in which $Y = 12$ was erroneously recorded as $Y = 2$, $r^2 = .02$. It is suggested that you calculate and plot the above examples as an exercise.

Other kinds of errors may lead to extreme residuals—for example, errors of measurement, the malfunctioning of an instrument, or the inappropriate use of instructions when administering a treatment to a given subject. Detecting the errors and correcting them, or deleting those that cannot be corrected, is the recommended procedure in such cases.

Although the above-noted factors may be subsumed under a broad category of errors, extreme residuals may occur in the absence of any errors. In fact, these are the most interesting and intriguing. Individuals with a unique attribute, or a unique combination of attributes, may react so uniquely to a treatment as to make them stand out and deviate extremely from the rest of the group. Discovery of such occurrences may lead to greater insights into the phenomenon under study and to the designing of research to further explore and extend such insights.

Although computer programs are discussed in subsequent chapters, it will be noted here that most computer packages (e.g., BMDP, SAS, SPSS) have subroutines for data plotting. The multiple regression programs in such packages have options for the calculation and the plotting of residuals. BMDP1R, in particular, has a variety of choices for residual plots. Some programs (e.g., BMDP1R, SPSS) also use special symbols to alert the user to the existence of extreme residuals.

It is hoped that the foregoing discussion will serve to indicate both the importance of studying residuals and the complexity in dealing with extreme residuals, or outliers. Detailed treatments of these topics may be found in the following sources: Anscombe (1960); Anscombe and Tukey (1963); Chatterjee and Price (1977); Draper and Smith (1981); Hoaglin and Welsch (1978); Larsen and McCleary (1972).

REGRESSION ANALYSIS WHEN *X* IS A RANDOM VARIABLE

Thus far, the discussion was limited to designs in which X is fixed. But, as is well known, in much of social science research the researcher does not, or cannot, fix X. Instead, a sample is drawn from a defined population, and measures of X and Y are obtained. Thus, both X and Y are random variables. It has been demonstrated (see, for example, Kmenta, 1971, pp. 297–304; Snedecor & Cochran, 1967, pp. 149–150; Wonnacott & Wonnacott, 1970, pp. 38–39) that when the other assumptions are reasonably met, particularly the assumption that X and e are not correlated, the least-squares estimators and the tests of significance presented earlier apply equally to the situation when both X and Y are random variables.

When both variables are random, the researcher may choose to study the regression of Y on X, or the regression of X on Y. The equation for the regression of X on Y is:

$$X' = a + bY \tag{2.35}$$

where X' is the predicted X. It is very important to note that the values of a and b are not those obtained when one studies the regression of Y on X, as is indicated by the formulas used to calculate them:

$$b = \frac{\Sigma xy}{\Sigma y^2} \tag{2.36}$$

$$a = \bar{X} - b\bar{Y} \tag{2.37}$$

[Compare (2.36) and (2.37) with (2.7) and (2.8).] Generally, subscripts are used to distinguish between the constants of the two equations. Thus, for example, b_{yx} is used to designate the regression coefficient for the regression of Y on X, whereas b_{xy} is used to designate the regression coefficient for the regression of X on Y. When there is no ambiguity about the designations of the independent variable and the dependent variable, one may dispose of the use of subscripts. This is why subscripts were not used in preceding sections of this chapter.

Finally, using the respective regression equations, one can draw the regression line for Y on X, and that for X on Y. The two lines will coincide only when all the observed scores lie on a straight line, that is, when the errors of predicting Y from X, or X from Y, are all equal to zero.

THE CORRELATION MODEL

Unlike the regression model with which we have been concerned up to this point, the correlation model does not distinguish between an independent and a dependent variable. Instead, the model seeks to study the degree of relation, or association, between two variables. Recall that in the regression model Y is a random variable assumed to be normally distributed, whereas X is fixed, its values being determined by the researcher. In the correlation model both X and Y are random variables and are assumed to follow a bivariate normal distribution. That is, the joint distribution of the two variables is assumed to be normal. The assumptions about homoscetasticity and about the residuals are the same in both models, and will not be gone into here. The population correlation coefficient is:

$$\rho = \frac{\Sigma xy}{N\sigma_x \sigma_y} = \frac{\sigma_{xy}}{\sigma_x \sigma_y} \tag{2.38}$$

where ρ (rho) = population correlation coefficient; Σxy = sum of the cross products; σ_{xy} = covariance of X and Y; σ_x, σ_y = standard deviation of X and Y, respectively. The concept of covariance was discussed earlier in the chapter. Although it is a useful concept, it is difficult to interpret because its magnitude is affected by the specific scales that are being used. For example, in studying the covariance between height and weight one might express height in inches, say, and weight in ounces. If, instead, one were to express height in feet and weight in pounds, the underlying relation between the two variables will, of course, not change but the value of the covariance will change. In order to overcome this problem, one may use the correlation coefficient, which is essentially a standardized covariance. It was noted earlier that dividing a deviation score by the standard deviation yields a standard score, z, as in Equation (2.34). Inspection of (2.38), particularly the first term on the right, will indicate that the scores on X and Y are being standardized. To make this statement more explicit, ρ is expressed in standard score form:

$$\rho = \frac{\Sigma z_x z_y}{N} \tag{2.39}$$

from which it can be seen clearly that the correlation coefficient is a covariance of standard scores. It is not dependent on the specific units used to measure X and Y. It can be shown that the maximum value of ρ is $|1.00|$. $\rho = +1.00$ indicates a perfect positive correlation, whereas $\rho = -1.00$ indicates a perfect negative correlation. $\rho = .00$ indicates no linear relation between X and Y. The closer ρ is to one the stronger the relation between X and Y. Also, the correlation coefficient is a symmetric index: $\rho_{xy} = \rho_{yx}$.

The sample correlation, r, is

$$r_{xy} = \frac{s_{xy}}{s_x s_y} \tag{2.40}$$

where s_{xy} = sample covariance; s_x, s_y = sample standard deviations of X and

Y, respectively. Of various other formulas available to calculate r, two that are particularly easy to use are

$$r_{xy} = \frac{\Sigma xy}{\sqrt{\Sigma x^2 \Sigma y^2}} \tag{2.41}$$

where Σxy = sum of the products; Σx^2, Σy^2 = sums of squares of X and Y, respectively, and

$$r_{xy} = \frac{N\Sigma XY - (\Sigma X)(\Sigma Y)}{\sqrt{N\Sigma X^2 - (\Sigma X)^2}\sqrt{N\Sigma Y^2 - (\Sigma Y)^2}} \tag{2.42}$$

where all the terms are expressed in raw scores. Formula (2.42) is particularly useful for calculations by hand, or with the aid of a calculator.

Although r and r^2 enter into regression calculations, it is very important to distinguish between the regression model and the correlation model. In the regression model, r is irrelevant, and its interpretation as the linear relation between X and Y is inappropriate. Look back at Figure 2.2 and note that the b's are the same in the four sets of data, but the r's range from a low of .24 to a high of .73. Careful study of the figure and the calculations associated with it will reveal that r changes as a function of scatter of points about the regression line and the variability of X. The greater the scatter, other things equal, the lower the r value. The smaller the variability of X, other things equal, the lower the r value. As was discussed earlier, in regression analysis the researcher may increase the variability of X at will, thereby increasing r. There is nothing wrong in doing so as long as one does not interpret r as the sample estimate of the linear correlation between two random variables.

It was noted earlier that r^2 is a meaningful term in regression analysis, indicating the proportion of variance of Y accounted for by X. Moreover, $1 - r^2$ is closely related to the variance of estimate and the standard error of estimate. Earlier, the residual sum of squares was expressed as

$$ss_{\text{res}} = (1 - r^2)\Sigma y^2 \tag{2.43}$$

and the variance of estimate as

$$s^2_{y.x} = \frac{(1 - r^2)\Sigma y^2}{N - 2} \tag{2.44}$$

From (2.43) and (2.44) it can be seen that when $1 - r^2$ is zero, the ss_{res}, and $s^2_{y.x}$ are zero. In other words, no error is committed. This, of course, happens when $r^2 = 1.00$, indicating that all the variance is due to regression. The larger the r^2, the smaller the $1 - r^2$ (the proportion of variance due to error). It is this use of r^2 that is legitimate and meaningful in regression analysis, and not the use of its square root (i.e., r) as an indicator of the linear correlation between two random variables.

When the focus of the research is on the explanation of, or the prediction of, a dependent variable, the regression model is appropriate. The regression model is most directly and intimately related to the primary goals of scientific inquiry: explanation and prediction of phenomena. When a scientist wishes to state, for example, what changes in Y are expected as a consequence of manipulations of, or changes in, X it is the regression coefficient, b, that provides this information. Because of the greater potency of the regression model, some writers (e.g., Blalock, 1968; Tukey, 1954) argue that it be used whenever possible and that the correlation model be used only when the former cannot be applied. Tukey (1954), who refers to himself as a member of the "informal society for the suppression of the correlation coefficient" (p. 38), advances strong arguments against its use. He maintains that: "It is an enemy of generalization, a focuser on the 'here and now' to the exclusion of the 'there and then' " (Tukey, 1969, p. 89). Only bad reasons come to Tukey's mind when he considers the question why the correlation coefficient is so attractive to many researchers. He argues:

> Given two perfectly meaningless variables, one is reminded of their meaninglessness when a regression coefficient is given, since one wonders how to interpret its value. A correlation coefficient is less likely to bring up the unpleasant truth—we *think* we know what $r = -.7$ means. *Do we?* How often? Sweeping things under the rug is the enemy of good data analysis. Often, using the correlation coefficient is "sweeping under the rug" with a vengeance.

Expressing the same point of view, though in a less impassioned tone, Fisher (1958) says: "The regression coefficients are of interest and scientific importance in many classes of data where the correlation coefficient, if used at all, is an artificial concept of no real utility" (p. 129).

These are, admittedly, postures with which some writers may disagree. The important point, however, is that the researcher be aware of the differences between the regression and the correlation models, and apply the one most suited for the given research problem.

For further discussions of the distinction between the two models, see Binder (1959); Ezekiel and Fox (1959, pp. 279–280); Fox (1968, pp. 167–190, 211–223); Kendall (1951); Warren (1971). Although the correlation model is occasionally dealt with, the primary concern in this book is with the regression model.

SUMMARY

In this chapter the basic elements of simple linear regression analysis were presented. The mechanics of the calculations, as well as basic issues regarding the interpretation of the results were dealt with. The assumptions underlying the valid applications of tests of significance were presented and discussed. It was pointed out that measurement errors in the independent variable and specification errors require special attention because they may lead to serious distortions of the results of regression analysis. The importance of plotting the data and the residuals and the careful study of such plots were discussed and illustrated. Finally, the distinction between the regression and the correlation models was discussed.

A single independent variable is probably in most instances not sufficient to provide thorough explanation of the complex phenomena that are the subject matter of the social sciences. Multiple independent variables may affect a given dependent variable, and it is to the study of their simultaneous effects that we now turn. Chapter 3 is devoted to the analysis and interpretation with two independent variables. Chapter 4 presents the generalization to any number of independent variables.

STUDY SUGGESTIONS

1. You will do well to study simple regression from a standard text. The following two sources are excellent—and quite different: Hays (1981, Chapter 13), and Snedecor and Cochran (1967, Chapter 6). Although these two chapters are somewhat more difficult than certain other treatments, they are both worth the effort.
2. Here are a set of X and a set of Y scores (the second, third, and fourth pairs of columns are simple continuations of the first pair of columns):

X	Y	X	Y	X	Y	X	Y
2	2	4	4	4	3	9	9
2	1	5	7	3	3	10	6
1	1	5	6	6	6	9	6
1	1	7	7	6	6	4	9
3	5	6	8	8	10	4	10

Calculate:
(a) The means, sums of squares and cross products, standard deviations, and the correlation between X and Y.
(b) The regression equation of Y on X.
(c) Regression and residual sums of squares.
(d) The F ratio for the test of significance of the regression of Y on X, using sums of squares (i.e., ss_{reg} and ss_{res}) and using r^2_{xy}.
(e) The variance of estimate, and the standard error of estimate.
(f) The standard error of the regression coefficient.
(g) The t ratio for the test of the regression coefficient. What should the square of the t equal? (That is, what statistic calculated above should it equal?)
(h) Using the regression equation, calculate each person's predicted score, Y', on the basis of the X's.
(i) The sum of the predicted scores and their mean.
(j) The residuals, $Y - Y'$; their sum, $\Sigma(Y - Y')$; and the sum of the squared residuals, $\Sigma(Y - Y')^2$.
(k) Plot the data, the regression line, and the residuals against the predicted scores.

3. Following are summary data from a study: $N = 200$; $\overline{X} = 60$; $\overline{Y} = 100$; $s_x = 6$; $s_y = 9$; $r_{xy} = .7$. Calculate:
(a) The sums of squares for X and Y, and the sum of the cross products.
(b) The proportion of variance of Y accounted for by X.
(c) The regression equation of Y on X.
(d) The regression sum of squares.
(e) The residual sum of squares.
(f) The F ratio for the significance of the regression of Y on X.

ANSWERS

2. (a) $\overline{X} = 4.95$; $\overline{Y} = 5.50$; $\Sigma x^2 = 134.95$; $\Sigma y^2 = 165.00$; $\Sigma xy = 100.50$; $s_x = 2.6651$; $s_y = 2.9469$; $r_{xy} = .6735$
(b) $Y' = 1.81363 + .74472X$

(c) $ss_{\text{reg}} = 74.84439$; $ss_{\text{res}} = 90.15561$
(d) $F = 14.94$, with 1 and 18 *df*
(e) $s^2_{y.x} = 5.00865$; $s_{y.x} = 2.23800$
(f) $s_b = .19265$
(g) $t = 3.87$, with 18 *df*; $t^2 = F$ obtained in (d), above.
(h) $Y'_1 = 3.30307 \ldots$; $Y'_{20} = 4.79251$
(i) $\Sigma Y' = 110.00 = \Sigma Y$; $\bar{Y}' = 5.50 = \bar{Y}$
(j) $Y_1 - Y'_1 = -1.30307 \ldots$; $Y_{20} - Y'_{20} = 5.20749$; $\Sigma(Y - Y') = 0$; $\Sigma(Y - Y')^2 = 90.15561 = ss_{\text{res}}$

3. (a) $\Sigma x^2 = (N - 1)s^2_x = (199)(36) = 7164$;
$\Sigma y^2 = (N - 1)s^2_y = 16{,}119$;
$\Sigma xy = (r_{xy}s_x s_y)(N - 1) = 7522.2$;
(b) $.49 = r^2_{xy}$
(c) $Y' = 37 + 1.05X$
(d) $ss_{\text{reg}} = 7898.31$
(e) $ss_{\text{res}} = 8220.69$
(f) $F = 190.24$, with 1 and 198 *df*

ELEMENTS OF MULTIPLE REGRESSION ANALYSIS: TWO INDEPENDENT VARIABLES

In this chapter, regression theory and analysis are extended to the case of two independent variables. Although the concepts introduced here apply equally to multiple regression analysis with any number of independent variables, the decided advantage of limiting this introduction to two independent variables is in the relative simplicity of the calculations that it necessitates. It is hoped that by not having to engage in, or follow, complex calculations you will be able to concentrate on the meaning of the concepts being presented, thereby grasping the basic elements of multiple regression analysis. Generalization to more than two independent variables is straightforward, although it involves complex calculations that are best handled by matrix algebra—a topic introduced in Chapter 4.

THE BASIC IDEAS

In Chapter 2 the equation for simple linear regression was given as (2.6). The equation is repeated with a new number. (For your convenience, this procedure of repeating equations, but attaching new numbers to them, is resorted to frequently.)

$$Y = a + bX + e \tag{3.1}$$

where Y = raw score on the dependent variable; a = intercept; b = regression coefficient; X = raw score on the independent variable; e = error, or residual.

Equation (3.1) can be extended to any number of independent variables or X's:

$$Y = a + b_1X_1 + b_2X_2 + \cdots + b_kX_k + e \qquad (3.2)$$

where $b_1, b_2, \ldots, b_k$ are regression coefficients associated with the independent variables $X_1, X_2, \ldots, X_k$; e is the error, or residual. The assumptions discussed in relation to simple linear regression (see Chapter 2) apply equally to the case of multiple regression, except that instead of one X used in the former, more than one X is used in the latter. As was the case in simple linear regression, a solution is sought for the constants (a and the b's) such that the sum of the squared errors of prediction (Σe^2) is minimized. This, it will be recalled, was referred to as the *principle of least squares*. In other words, a solution in which the independent variables are differentially weighted is sought so that the sum of the squared errors of prediction is minimized, or that prediction is optimized.

The prediction equation in multiple regression analysis is

$$Y' = a + b_1X_1 + b_2X_2 + \cdots + b_kX_k \qquad (3.3)$$

where Y' = predicted Y score. All other terms are as defined under (3.2). One of the main calculation problems of multiple regression is to solve for the b's in Equation (3.3). With only two independent variables, the problem is not difficult, as is shown later in this chapter. With more than two X's, however, it is considerably more difficult, and reliance on matrix operations becomes essential. To repeat, the principles and interpretations discussed with two independent variables apply equally to problems with any number of independent variables.

In Chapter 2, data from an experiment in which one independent variable was used were analyzed. Among other things, it was pointed out that r^2 (the square of the correlation between the independent and the dependent variable) indicates the proportion of variance accounted for by the independent variable. And, of course, $1 - r^2$ is the proportion of variance not accounted for, or the error. Since the aim of scientific research is to minimize the errors, or optimize explanation, the researcher could use more than one independent variable. Assuming two independent variables, X_1 and X_2, are used, one would calculate $R^2_{y.x_1x_2}$, where R^2 = squared multiple correlation of Y (the dependent variable) with X_1 and X_2 (the independent variables). In order to avoid cumbersome notation of subscripts, the dependent variable will be frequently referred to as Y, and the independent variables will be identified by numbers. Thus, $R^2_{y.x_1x_2} = R^2_{y.12}$; $r^2_{yx_1} = r^2_{y1}$; $r^2_{x_1x_2} = r^2_{12}$.

$R^2_{y.12}$ indicates the proportion of variance of Y accounted for by X_1 and X_2. In experimental research, the experimenter designs the study so that there is no correlation between the independent variables (i.e., $r_{12} = .00$). Under such circumstances, the calculation of R^2 is simple and straightforward.

$$R^2_{y.12} = r^2_{y1} + r^2_{y2} \qquad (\text{when } r_{12} = .00)$$

Each r^2 indicates the proportion of variance accounted for by a given independent variable.[1] Calculations of other regression statistics (e.g., the regression equation) are similarly simple.

[1]It is also possible, as shown in Chapter 10, to study the interaction between X_1 and X_2.

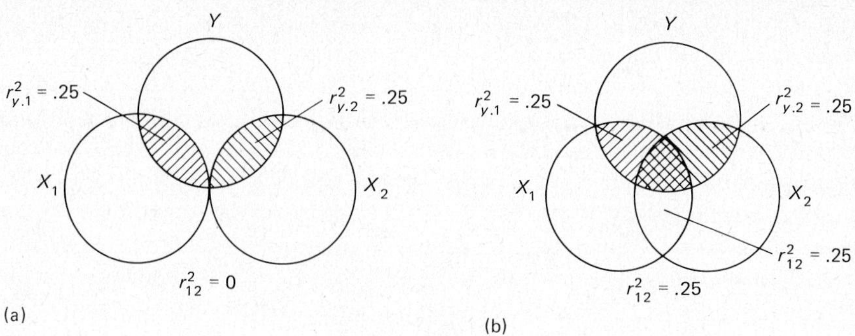

Figure 3.1

When $r_{12} \neq .00$, that is, when there is a correlation between the two independent variables, or two predictors, it is necessary to take the correlation into account when calculating multiple regression statistics because the nonzero correlation indicates that the two independent variables, or predictors, provide a certain amount of redundant information.

These ideas can perhaps be clarified by Figure 3.1, where each set of circles represents the variance of a Y variable and two X variables, X_1 and X_2. The set on the left labeled (a), is a simple situation where $r_{y1} = .50$, $r_{y2} = .50$, and $r_{12} = 0$. If we square the correlation coefficients of X_1 and X_2 with Y and add them—that is, $(.50)^2 + (.50)^2 = .25 + .25 = .50$—we obtain the proportion of variance of Y accounted for by both X_1 and X_2, or $R^2_{y.12} = .50$.

But now study the situation in (b). The sum of r^2_{y1} and r^2_{y2} is not equal to $R^2_{y.12}$ because r_{12} is not equal to 0. (The degree of correlation between two variables is expressed by the amount of overlap of the circles.[2]) The hatched areas of overlap represent the variances common to pairs of depicted variables. The one doubly hatched area represents that part of the variance of Y that is common to the X_1 and X_2 variables. Or, it is part of r^2_{y1}; it is part of r^2_{y2}; and it is part of r^2_{12}. Therefore, to calculate that part of Y that is determined by X_1 *and* X_2, it is necessary to subtract this doubly hatched overlapping part so that it will not be counted twice.

Careful study of Figure 3.1 and the relations it depicts should help you to grasp the principle stated earlier. Look at the right-hand side of the figure. In order to explain or predict more of Y, so to speak, it is necessary to find other variables whose variance circles will intersect the Y circle and, at the same time not intersect each other, or at least minimally intersect each other. As was noted above, this can be accomplished fairly easily in experimental research. In nonexperimental research, however, the independent variables are almost always intercorrelated. It seems that much of the world is correlated—especially the world of the kind of variables that are being studied in nonexperimental research. Once a variable or two have been found to correlate substantially with school achievement, say, then it becomes difficult to find additional variables that correlate substantially with school achievement and *not* with the other variables. For instance, one might think that verbal ability would correlate substantially with school achievement. It does. Then one would think

[2]The above figure is used only for pedagogical purposes. It is not always possible to express all the complexities of possible relations among variables with such figures.

that the need to achieve, or *n* achievement, as McClelland calls it, would correlate substantially with school achievement. Evidently it does (McClelland et al., 1953). One might also reason that *n* achievement should have close to zero correlation with verbal ability, since verbal ability, while acquired to some extent, is in part a function of genetic endowment. It turns out, however, that *n* achievement is significantly related to verbal ability (McClelland et al., 1953, pp. 234–238, especially Table 8.8, p. 235). This means that, while it may increase the R^2 when added to the regression equation, its predictive power in the regression is decreased by the presence of verbal ability because part of its predictive power is already provided by verbal ability. The same reasoning applies to the situation in which one adds verbal ability to an equation in which *n* achievement has already been taken into account.

AN EXAMPLE WITH TWO INDEPENDENT VARIABLES

An example in which the two independent variables are correlated is purposely used, as it is the more general case under which is subsumed the special case of $r_{12} = 0$. It is the case of correlated independent variables that poses so many of the interpretational problems that will occupy us not only in this chapter but also in subsequent ones.

Suppose we have reading achievement, verbal aptitude, and achievement motivation scores on 20 eighth-grade pupils. (There will, of course, usually be many more than 20 subjects.) We want to calculate the regression of Y, reading achievement, on *both* verbal aptitude *and* achievement motivation. But since verbal aptitude and achievement motivation are correlated, it is necessary to take the correlation into account when studying the regression of reading achievement on both variables.

Calculation of Basic Statistics

Assume that the measures obtained for the 20 pupils are those given in Table 3.1. In order to do a regression analysis, a number of statistics have to be calculated. The sums, means, and the sums of squares of raw scores on the three sets of scores are given in the three lines directly below the table. In addition, the following statistics will be needed: the deviation sums of squares of the three variables, their deviation cross products, and their standard deviations. They are calculated as follows:

$$\Sigma y^2 = \Sigma Y^2 - \frac{(\Sigma Y)^2}{N} = 770 - \frac{(110)^2}{20} = 770 - 605 = \mathit{165.00}$$

$$\Sigma x_1^2 = \Sigma X_1^2 - \frac{(\Sigma X_1)^2}{N} = 625 - \frac{(99)^2}{20} = 625 - 490.05 = \mathit{134.95}$$

$$\Sigma x_2^2 = \Sigma X_2^2 - \frac{(\Sigma X_2)^2}{N} = 600 - \frac{(104)^2}{20} = 600 - 540.80 = \mathit{59.20}$$

$$\Sigma x_1 y = \Sigma X_1 Y - \frac{(\Sigma X_1)(\Sigma Y)}{N} = 645 - \frac{(99)(110)}{20} = 645 - 544.50 = \mathit{100.50}$$

$$\Sigma x_2 y = \Sigma X_2 Y - \frac{(\Sigma X_2)(\Sigma Y)}{N} = 611 - \frac{(104)(110)}{20} = 611 - 572 = \mathit{39.00}$$

$$\Sigma x_1 x_2 = \Sigma X_1 X_2 - \frac{(\Sigma X_1)(\Sigma X_2)}{N} = 538 - \frac{(99)(104)}{20} = 538 - 514.80 = \mathit{23.20}$$

$$s_y = \sqrt{\frac{\Sigma y^2}{N - 1}} = \sqrt{\frac{165}{20 - 1}} = \sqrt{8.6842} = \mathit{2.9469}$$

$$s_{x_1} = \sqrt{\frac{\Sigma x_1^2}{N - 1}} = \sqrt{\frac{134.95}{20 - 1}} = \sqrt{7.1026} = \mathit{2.6651}$$

$$s_{x_2} = \sqrt{\frac{\Sigma x_2^2}{N - 1}} = \sqrt{\frac{59.20}{20 - 1}} = \sqrt{3.1158} = \mathit{1.7652}$$

The results of the calculations are pulled together for visual convenience in Table 3.2. Since the correlations between the variables will be needed later, they are included below the principal diagonal of the matrix. (.6735, .3946, and .2596).

Table 3.1 Illustrative Data: Reading Achievement (Y), Verbal Aptitude (X_1), and Achievement Motivation (X_2)

	Y	X_1	X_2	Y'	$Y - Y' = e$
	2	2	4	3.0305	−1.0305
	1	2	4	3.0305	−2.0305
	1	1	4	2.3534	−1.3534
	1	1	3	1.9600	−.9600
	5	3	6	4.4944	.5056
	4	4	6	5.1715	−1.1715
	7	5	3	4.6684	2.3316
	6	5	4	5.0618	.9382
	7	7	3	6.0226	.9774
	8	6	3	5.3455	2.6545
	3	4	5	4.7781	−1.7781
	3	3	5	4.1010	−1.1010
	6	6	9	7.7059	−1.7059
	6	6	8	7.3125	−1.3125
	10	8	6	7.8799	2.1201
	9	9	7	8.9504	.0496
	6	10	5	8.8407	−2.8407
	6	9	5	8.1636	−2.1636
	9	4	7	5.5649	3.4351
	10	4	7	5.5649	4.4351
Σ:	110	99	104	110	0
M:	5.50	4.95	5.20		
SS:	770.	625.	600.	$\Sigma e^2 = 81.6091$	

Note: *SS* = sum of the squared raw scores.

Table 3.2 Deviation Sums of Squares and Cross Products, Correlation Coefficients, and Standard Deviations of Data of Table 3.1[a]

	y	x_1	x_2
y	165.00	100.50	39.00
x_1	*.6735*	134.95	23.20
x_2	*.3946*	*.2596*	59.20
s	2.9469	2.6651	1.7652

[a]The tabled entries are as follows: the first line gives, successively, Σy^2, the deviation sum of squares of Y, the cross product of the deviations of X_1 and Y, or $\Sigma x_1 y$, and finally $\Sigma x_2 y$. The entries in the second and third lines, on the diagonal or above, are Σx_1^2, $\Sigma x_1 x_2$, and (in the lower right corner) Σx_2^2. The italicized entries *below* the diagonal are the correlation coefficients. The standard deviations are given in the last line.

There is more than one way to calculate the essential statistics of multiple regression analysis. Ultimately, all of them will be covered. Now, however, we concentrate on calculations that use sums of squares, because they have the virtue of being additive and intuitively comprehensible.

Reasons for the Calculations

Before we proceed with the calculations it will be useful to review why we are doing all this. First, we want to calculate the constants (a, b_1, and b_2) in the regression equation, $Y' = a + b_1X_1 + b_2X_2$, so that we can, if we wish, use the X's of individuals and predict the Y' values. This means, in the present example, that if we have scores of individuals on verbal aptitude and achievement motivation, we can insert them into the equation and obtain Y' values, or predicted reading achievement scores.

Second, we want to know the proportion of variance "accounted for," that is $R^2_{y.12}$. In other words, we want to know how much of the total variance of Y, reading achievement, is due to its regression on the X's, on verbal aptitude and achievement motivation.

Third, we wish to test the results for statistical significance in order to be able to state, for example, whether the regression of Y on the X's is statistically significant, or whether each regression coefficient, b, in the regression equation is statistically different from zero.

Finally, we wish to determine the relative importance of the different X's in explaining Y. We wish to know, in this case, the relative importance of X_1 and X_2, verbal aptitude and achievement motivation, in explaining verbal achievement. As we will see, this is the most difficult question to answer. In this chapter the complexities attendant on such questions, and some alternative approaches to answering them, are dealt with briefly. A deeper knowledge of multiple regression analysis is necessary for fully comprehending the various approaches and the complexities of each of them. In succeeding chapters the scope of the different uses and interpretations of multiple regression analysis is broadened and deepened.

Calculation of Regression Statistics

The calculation of the b's of the regression equation is done rather mechanically with formulas for two X variables. They are

$$b_1 = \frac{(\Sigma x_2^2)(\Sigma x_1 y) - (\Sigma x_1 x_2)(\Sigma x_2 y)}{(\Sigma x_1^2)(\Sigma x_2^2) - (\Sigma x_1 x_2)^2}$$

$$b_2 = \frac{(\Sigma x_1^2)(\Sigma x_2 y) - (\Sigma x_1 x_2)(\Sigma x_1 y)}{(\Sigma x_1^2)(\Sigma x_2^2) - (\Sigma x_1 x_2)^2} \tag{3.4}$$

Taking the appropriate values from Table 3.2 and substituting them in the formulas, we calculate the b's:

$$b_1 = \frac{(59.20)(100.50) - (23.20)(39.00)}{(134.95)(59.20) - (23.20)^2} = \frac{5949.60 - 904.80}{7989.04 - 538.24} = \frac{5044.80}{7450.80} = .6771$$

$$b_2 = \frac{(134.95)(39.) - (23.20)(100.50)}{(134.95)(59.20) - (23.20)^2} = \frac{5263.05 - 2331.60}{7989.04 - 538.24} = \frac{2931.45}{7450.80} = .3934$$

The formula for a is given by

$$a = \bar{Y} - b_1\bar{X}_1 - b_2\bar{X}_2 \tag{3.5}$$

Substituting the appropriate values yields

$$a = 5.50 - (.6771)(4.95) - (.3934)(5.20) = .1027$$

The regression equation can now be written with the calculated values of a and the b's:

$$Y' = .1027 + .6771X_1 + .3934X_2$$

As examples of the use of the equation in prediction, calculate the predicted Y's for the fifth and the twentieth subjects of Table 3.1:

$$Y'_5 = .1027 + (.6771)(3) + (.3934)(6) = 4.4944$$

$$Y'_{20} = .1027 + (.6771)(4) + (.3934)(7) = 5.5649$$

The *obtained* Y's are: $Y_5 = 5$ and $Y_{20} = 10$. The residuals or $e = Y - Y'$, are

$$e_5 = 5 - 4.4944 = .5056$$

$$e_{20} = 10 - 5.5649 = 4.4351$$

One residual is quite small and the other quite large. The predicted Y's and the residuals, e, are given in the last two columns of Table 3.1. About half the e's are positive and about half negative, and most of them are relatively small. The a and the b's of the regression equation, recall, were calculated to satisfy the least-squares principle, that is, to minimize the squares of the errors of prediction. If we square each of the residuals or e's and add them, as we did in Chapter 2, we obtain $\Sigma e^2 = 81.6091$. (Note that $\Sigma e = 0$.) This can be symbolized Σy^2_{res} or ss_{res}, as was also shown earlier. In short, the residual sum of squares expresses that portion of the total Y sum of squares, Σy^2, that is *not* due to the regression. Actually, as is shown below, there is no need to go through these involved calculations. The residual sum of squares can be calculated much more readily. We went through the lengthy calculations to show clearly what this sum of squares is.

The regression sum of squares is calculated with the following general formula:

$$ss_{reg} = b_1 \Sigma x_1 y + \cdots + b_k \Sigma x_k y \tag{3.6}$$

where k = the number of X or independent variables. In the case of two X variables, $k = 2$, the formula reduces to

$$ss_{reg} = b_1 \Sigma x_1 y + b_2 \Sigma x_2 y \tag{3.7}$$

Taking the b values calculated earlier and the deviation sums of cross products from Table 3.2, and substituting in (3.7),

$$ss_{reg} = (.6771)(100.50) + (.3934)(39.00) = \mathit{83.3912}$$

This is that portion of the total sum of squares of Y, or Σy^2, that is due to the regression of Y on the two X's. Note that the total sum of squares of Y is 165.00 (from Table 3.2). In Equation (2.12) it was shown that

$$\Sigma y^2 = ss_{reg} + ss_{res} \tag{3.8}$$

Therefore,

$$ss_{res} = 165.00 - 83.3912 = \mathit{81.6088}$$

which is, within rounding errors, the same as the value obtained through the lengthy calculations of Table 3.1.

Alternative Calculations

In order to reinforce and broaden your understanding of multiple regression analysis, the regression statistics are calculated by other methods, in which correlation coefficients are used. Before presenting the alternative calculations, it is necessary to digress briefly to discuss the distinction between standardized and unstandardized regression coefficients, and how they are related to each other.

Regression Weights: *b* and β

Earlier, *b* was used as a symbol for the statistic and β as a symbol for the parameter. There is, however, another way in which these symbols are frequently used: *b* is the unstandardized regression coefficient, and β is the standardized regression coefficient (these are discussed below). Unfortunately, there is no consistency in the use of symbols. For example, some authors use b^* as the symbol for the standardized regression coefficient, others use $\hat{\beta}$ as the symbol for the estimator of β (the unstandardized coefficient) and $\hat{\beta}^*$ as the symbol for the standardized coefficient. To add to the confusion, it will be recalled that β is also used as a symbol for Type II error (see Hays, 1981, p. 245). While the use of the different symbols, as exemplified above, is meant to avoid confusion, it is believed that they are unnecessarily cumbersome and may therefore result in even greater confusion. Consequently, *in subsequent presentations b is used as the symbol for the sample unstandardized regression coefficient and* β *as the symbol for the sample standardized coefficient*. Occasionally, it will be necessary to refer to the earlier usage of β, namely as a parameter. But since such usage will be explicitly stated, it is hoped that no ambiguity will arise.

When raw scores are used, as was done until now, *b*'s are calculated and applied to the *X*'s (raw scores) in the regression equation. If, however, one were first to standardize the scores for the *Y* and the *X*'s (i.e., convert them to *z* scores), β's would be calculated and applied to *z*'s in the regression equation. For simple regression, the equation in which standard scores are used is:

$$z'_y = \beta z_x \tag{3.9}$$

where z'_y = predicted standard score of *Y*; β = standardized regression coefficient; and z_x = standard score of *X*. As in the case of *b*, β is interpreted as the expected change in *Y* associated with a unit change in *X*. But because the standard deviation of *z* scores is equal to 1.00, a unit change in *X*, when it has been standardized, refers to a change of one standard deviation in *X*. Distinctions in the use and interpretation of *b*'s and β's are discussed later in this chapter.

With one independent variable, the formula for the calculation of β is:

$$\beta = \frac{\Sigma z_x z_y}{\Sigma z_x^2} \tag{3.10}$$

In Chapter 2 it was shown that *b* is calculated as follows:

$$b = \frac{\Sigma xy}{\Sigma x^2} \tag{3.11}$$

Note the similarity between (3.10) and (3.11). Whereas sum of cross products and sum of squares of standard scores are used in the former, the latter requires the deviation sum of cross products and sum of squares. It is, however, not necessary to carry out the calculations indicated in (3.10) because b and β are related as follows:

$$\beta = b\frac{s_x}{s_y}$$

and (3.12)

$$b = \beta\frac{s_y}{s_x}$$

where β = standardized regression coefficient; b = unstandardized regression coefficient; and s_x, s_y = standard deviations of X and Y, respectively. Substituting (3.11) and the formulas for the standard deviations of X and Y in (3.12), we obtain

$$\beta = b\frac{s_x}{s_y} = \frac{\Sigma xy\sqrt{\Sigma x^2}\sqrt{N-1}}{\Sigma x^2\sqrt{N-1}\sqrt{\Sigma y^2}} = \frac{\Sigma xy}{\sqrt{\Sigma x_2}\sqrt{\Sigma y^2}} = r_{xy} \quad (3.13)$$

Note that with one independent variable $\beta = r_{xy}$. Note also that when using standard scores, the intercept, a, is zero. The reason for this is readily seen when it is recalled that the mean of z scores is zero. Therefore, $a = \bar{Y} - \beta\bar{X} = 0 - \beta 0 = 0$.

For two independent variables, X_1 and X_2, the regression equation with standard scores is

$$z'_y = \beta_1 z_1 + \beta_2 z_2 \quad (3.14)$$

where β_1 and β_2 are the standardized regression coefficients; z_1 and z_2 are standard scores on X_1 and X_2, respectively. The formulas for calculating the β's when two independent variables are used are

$$\beta_1 = \frac{r_{y1} - r_{y2}r_{12}}{1 - r^2_{12}} \qquad \beta_2 = \frac{r_{y2} - r_{y1}r_{12}}{1 - r^2_{12}} \quad (3.15)$$

Note that when the independent variables are not correlated (i.e., $r_{12} = 0$), $\beta_1 = r_{y1}$ and $\beta_2 = r_{y2}$, as is the case in simple linear regression. This holds true for any number of independent variables: When there is no correlation among the independent variables, β for a given independent variable is equal to the product-moment correlation coefficient *(r)* of that variable with the dependent variable.

The correlations for the data of Table 3.1 (see Table 3.2) are $r_{y1} = .6735$; $r_{y2} = .3946$; $r_{12} = .2596$.

$$\beta_1 = \frac{.6735 - (.3946)(.2596)}{1 - .2596^2} = .6123$$

$$\beta_2 = \frac{.3946 - (.6735)(.2596)}{1 - .2596^2} = .2356$$

The regression equation, in standard scores, for the data of Table 3.1 is

$$z'_y = .6123z_1 + .2356z_2$$

Having calculated the β's, one can obtain the corresponding b's, the unstandardized regression coefficients, by the following equation:

$$b_j = \beta_j \frac{s_y}{s_j} \tag{3.16}$$

where b = unstandardized regression coefficient; $j = 1, 2$; β = standardized regression coefficient; s_y and s_j = standard deviations of Y and X_j respectively. For the data of Table 3.1,

$$s_y = 2.9469 \qquad s_1 = 2.6651 \qquad s_2 = 1.7652$$

$$b_1 = .6123 \frac{2.9469}{2.6651} = .6770 \qquad b_2 = .2356 \frac{2.9469}{1.7652} = .3933$$

which are, within rounding errors, the same values obtained earlier. Once the b's are calculated, one can obtain a by applying (3.5).

THE SQUARED MULTIPLE CORRELATION COEFFICIENT

In Chapter 2 it was shown that the ratio of ss_{reg} to the total sum of squares, Σy^2, equals the square of the correlation coefficient between the independent and the dependent variable. The same principle applies to the case of multiple independent variables, except that the ratio indicates the squared multiple correlation:

$$R^2 = \frac{ss_{\text{reg}}}{\Sigma y^2} \tag{3.17}$$

R^2, then, indicates the proportion of variance of the dependent variable accounted for by the independent variables. Substituting the sums of squares calculated earlier, we obtain:

$$R^2 = \frac{83.3912}{165.0000} = .5054$$

About 50% of the variance in reading achievement is accounted for by verbal aptitude and n achievement.

Another way of viewing R^2 is to note that it is the squared product-moment correlation of the Y's (observed Y's) and the predicted Y's, Y'_i, which are of course a linear combination of the X's.

$$R^2_{y.12} = r^2_{yy'} = \frac{(\Sigma yy')^2}{\Sigma y^2 \Sigma y'^2} \tag{3.18}$$

The values of Equation (3.18) can be calculated from the Y and Y' columns of Table 3.1. We already have $\Sigma y^2 = 165$. The comparable value of $\Sigma y'^2$ is calculated as follows:

$$\Sigma y'^2 = \Sigma Y'^2 - \frac{(\Sigma Y')^2}{N} = 688.3969 - \frac{(110)^2}{20} = 83.3969$$

The sum of the deviation cross products is:

$$\Sigma yy' = \Sigma YY' - \frac{(\Sigma Y)(\Sigma Y')}{N} = 688.3939 - \frac{(110)(110)}{20} = 83.3939$$

(The difference of .003 in the two sums of squares is due to errors of rounding. Actually, $\Sigma y'^2$ must equal $\Sigma yy'$. The calculated values are used as they are, however, since it makes no difference in R^2 calculation.) Substituting in Equation (3.18), R^2 is obtained:

$$R^2 = \frac{(83.3939)^2}{(83.3969)(165)} = \frac{6954.5426}{13{,}760.4885} = .5054$$

The positive square root of R^2 gives R. Unlike r, which can take positive as well as negative values, R may vary from .00 to 1.00. For the data of Table 3.1.

$$R_{y.12} = \sqrt{.5054} = .7109$$

or

$$R_{y.12} = r_{yy'} = \frac{\Sigma yy'}{\sqrt{\Sigma y^2}\sqrt{\Sigma y'^2}} = \frac{83.3939}{\sqrt{(83.3969)(165)}} = .7109$$

For completeness of presentation, R was calculated even though it may be irrelevant in regression analysis. As was discussed in the case of simple linear regression (see Chapter 2), r^2, not r, is the meaningful term in regression analysis; so is R^2, not R, the meaningful term in multiple regression analysis.

Calculation of the Squared Multiple Correlation Coefficient

There are various formulas for the calculation of R^2. Following is one in which β's and r's are used:

$$R^2_{y.12} = \beta_1 r_{y1} + \beta_2 r_{y2} \tag{3.19}$$

For the present data:

$$R^2_{y.12} = (.6123)(.6735) + (.2356)(.3946) = .5054$$

which is the same value obtained in the lengthier calculations.

Yet another formula for the calculation of R^2 can be obtained by substituting (3.15) in (3.19)

$$R^2_{y.12} = \frac{r^2_{y1} + r^2_{y2} - 2r_{y1}r_{y2}r_{12}}{1 - r^2_{12}} \tag{3.20}$$

Formula (3.20) is very simple and very useful for the calculation of R^2 with two independent variables. All one needs are the three r's. When the correlation between the independent variables is zero (i.e., $r_{12} = 0$) then (3.20) reduces to $R^2_{y.12} = r^2_{y1} + r^2_{y2}$, as was noted earlier.

For the data of Table 3.1,

$$R^2_{y.12} = \frac{.6735^2 + .3946^2 - 2(.6735)(.3946)(.2596)}{1 - .2596^2} = .5054$$

Again, this is the same value as was obtained earlier.

TESTS OF SIGNIFICANCE AND INTERPRETATIONS

The role of tests of significance and the assumptions underlying them were discussed in Chapter 2. Therefore, these issues are not dealt with here.

There are several tests of significance that one may apply to results of multiple regression analysis. Three of them are presented here: (1) test of R^2; (2) tests of regression coefficients; and (3) tests of increments in the proportion of variance accounted for by a given variable.

Test of R^2

The test of R^2 proceeds in the same manner that r^2 was tested in Chapter 2.

$$F = \frac{R^2/k}{(1 - R^2)/(N - k - 1)} \tag{3.21}$$

with k and $N - k - 1$ *df*, where k = number of independent variables; N = sample size. For the data of Table 3.1, $R^2_{y.12} = .5054$, $N = 20$.

$$F = \frac{.5054/2}{(1 - .5054)/(20 - 2 - 1)} = \frac{.2527}{.0291} = 8.684$$

with 2 and 17 *df*, $p < .01$. One can, of course, calculate F using the appropriate sums of squares. The formula is

$$F = \frac{ss_{\text{reg}}/df_{\text{reg}}}{ss_{\text{res}}/df_{\text{res}}} \tag{3.22}$$

The degrees of freedom associated with ss_{reg} are $k = 2$, the number of independent variables. The degrees of freedom associated with ss_{res} are $N - k - 1 = 17$. Earlier we calculated $ss_{reg} = 83.3912$ and $ss_{res} = 81.6088$. Therefore,

$$F = \frac{83.3912/2}{81.6088/17} = \frac{41.6956}{4.8005} = 8.686$$

This agrees with the F calculated using R^2 (within rounding error).

Whether one uses (3.21) or (3.22) is a matter of taste, as the same test is being performed. The identity of the two tests can be seen when it is noted that $ss_{reg} = R^2\Sigma y^2$ and $ss_{res} = (1 - R^2)\Sigma y^2$. Substituting these equivalencies in (3.22) will enable one to cancel Σy^2 from the numerator and the denominator, thus obtaining (3.21).

On the basis of R^2 one would conclude that verbal aptitude and achievement motivation account for about 50% of the variance in reading achievement, and that this finding is statistically significant at the .01 level.

The test of R^2 indicates whether the regression of Y on the independent variables taken together is statistically significant. Stated differently, testing R^2 is tantamount to testing whether one or more than one regression coefficient differs from zero. It is very important to note that failure to reject the null hypothesis leads to the conclusion that all the regression coefficients do not differ significantly from zero (this point is discussed below).

When, however, one wishes to determine whether the effect of a given variable is significantly different from zero, it is the regression coefficient, b, associated with it that needs to be tested.

Tests of Regression Coefficients

Each b in a multiple regression equation indicates the expected change in Y associated with a unit change in the variable under consideration while controlling for, or holding constant, the effects of the other independent variables. Therefore the b's in multiple regression are actually referred to as partial regression coefficients or partial slopes. In order to avoid cumbersome notation, certain subscripts were omitted from the multiple regression equations presented thus far. It is now shown how the regression equation with two independent variables, for example, is written

$$Y' = a + b_{y1.2}X_1 + b_{y2.1}X_2 \tag{3.23}$$

where $b_{y1.2}$ and $b_{y2.1}$ are partial regression coefficients. Each of the b's is referred to as a first-order partial regression coefficient, the order pertaining to the number of variables that are held constant, or partialed. With two independent variables, each b is of a first order because one variable is partialed in each case. With three independent variables, there are three second-order partial coefficients since two variables are partialed in the calculation of each b. With k independent variables, the order of each b is $k - 1$. The notation of (3.23) will not be used as there is no ambiguity as to which variables are being partialed.

In Chapter 2 it was stated that dividing a b by its standard error yields a t ratio. The same holds true in multiple regression analysis, where each b has a standard error associated with it. The standard error of b_1, for example, when there are k independent variables is

$$s_{b_{y1.2...k}} = \sqrt{\frac{s^2_{y.12...k}}{\Sigma x_1^2 (1 - R^2_{1.2...k})}} \tag{3.24}$$

where $s_{b_{y1.2...k}}$ = standard error of b_1; $s^2_{y.12...k}$ = variance of estimate; Σx_1^2 = sum of squares of X_1; $R^2_{1.2...k}$ = the squared multiple correlation between X_1, used as a dependent variable, and X_2 to X_k as the independent variables. Similarly, for all other b's. For the case of two independent variables,

$$s_{b_{y1.2}} = \sqrt{\frac{s^2_{y.12}}{\Sigma x_1^2 (1 - r^2_{12})}} \qquad s_{b_{y2.1}} = \sqrt{\frac{s^2_{y.12}}{\Sigma x_2^2 (1 - r^2_{12})}} \tag{3.25}$$

The denominator of (3.24), or (3.25), reveals very important aspects of tests of significance of b's, namely the effects of the correlations among the independent variables on the standard errors of the b's. The topic of high intercorrelations among independent variables is discussed in detail in Chapter 8 (see the section on Multicollinearity). For now, it will only be pointed out that the higher the intercorrelation among the independent variables, the larger the standard errors of the b's. It therefore follows that when the independent variables are highly intercorrelated, it may turn out that none of the b's is statistically significant when each is tested separately. Note, on the other hand, that when, for example, $r_{12} = 0$ the denominator of (3.25) reduces to Σx^2, as was the case when a single independent variable was used [see (2.28) and the discussion related to it]. These properties of the s_b underscore the virtue of designing studies in which the independent variables are not correlated among themselves, as one is able to do in experimental research.

Before illustrating the calculations of standard errors of b's and their use in tests of significance, it is very important to distinguish between the test of R^2 and the test of a given b in a multiple regression equation. It was said above that the test of R^2 is tantamount to testing all the b's simultaneously. But when a given b is tested for significance, the question being addressed is whether it differs from zero *while controlling for the effects of the other independent variables*. It is clear, then, that the two tests are addressed to different questions.

Failure to distinguish between the purposes of the two tests has led some researchers to maintain that they might lead to contradictory or puzzling results. For example, it is possible to find that R^2 is statistically significant, leading to the conclusion that one or more of the regression coefficients are different from zero. And yet, when each regression coefficient is tested separately it may turn out that *none* of them is statistically significant. A possible reason for such an occurrence was mentioned above, namely that the standard errors of the b's become relatively large when the independent variables are highly intercorrelated. As long as the different questions addressed by the test of R^2 and by the test of a single b are borne in mind there should be no reason for puzzlement about seemingly contradictory results that they may yield.[3]

The tests of statistical significance are now applied to the b's of the present example. It will be recalled that

$$s^2_{y.12} = \frac{ss_{\text{res}}}{N - k - 1} \tag{3.26}$$

where $s^2_{y.12}$ = variance of estimate; ss_{res} = residual sum of squares; N = sample size; k = number of independent variables. Earlier we calculated ss_{res} = 81.6088.

$$s^2_{y.12} = \frac{81.6088}{20 - 2 - 1} = 4.8005$$

$$\Sigma x_1^2 = 134.95 \qquad \Sigma x_2^2 = 59.20$$

$$b_1 = .6671 \qquad b_2 = .3934 \qquad r_{12} = .2596$$

(See calculations earlier in the chapter.)

$$s_{b_1} = \sqrt{\frac{4.8005}{134.95(1 - .2596^2)}} = \sqrt{\frac{4.8005}{125.8554}} = \sqrt{.03814} = .1953$$

$$t_{b_1} = \frac{b_1}{s_{b_1}} = \frac{.6771}{.1953} = 3.47$$

with 17 *df* (*df* associated with the variance of estimate: $N - k - 1$), $p < .01$.

$$s_{b_2} = \sqrt{\frac{4.8005}{59.20(1 - .2596^2)}} = \sqrt{\frac{4.8005}{55.2104}} = \sqrt{.08695} = .2949$$

$$t_{b_2} = \frac{b_2}{s_{b_2}} = \frac{.3934}{.2949} = 1.33$$

with 17 *df*, $p > .05$. It is concluded that the effect of X_2, achievement motivation, is not statistically significant (at the .05 level). You are reminded not to overlook the important distinction between statistically significant and substantively meaningful findings (see Chapter 2).

As was discussed in Chapter 2, it is desirable to set confidence intervals around the regression coefficient. The procedure for doing this in multiple regression analysis is the same as in simple regression analysis, namely:

$$b \pm t(\alpha/2, df)s_b$$

where t is the tabled t ratio at $\alpha/2$ with *df* associated with the variance of estimate, or the mean square residual; s_b is the standard error of the b. For the

[3]For a good discussion of the logic of tests of significance in multiple regression analysis, see Cramer (1972).

present example, $df = 17$. Assuming it is desired to set the 95% confidence interval for the present example: the tabled t at .05/2 (.025) with 17 df is 2.11 (see table of t in statistics books, or take $\sqrt{F}$ with 1 and 17 df from Appendix B).

Using the results obtained above, the 95% confidence intervals for the first and second regression coefficients, respectively, are

$$.6771 \pm (2.11)(.1953) = \quad .2650 \text{ and } 1.0892$$

$$.3934 \pm (2.11)(.2949) = -.2288 \text{ and } 1.0156$$

Note that the second confidence interval includes zero, as would be expected on the basis of the tests of significance of the two b's (see above).

In Chapter 2, several factors that affect the precision of regression statistics were discussed. One of these factors is the variability of X as reflected by Σx^2. The effect of the variability of X in the present example may be noted from the two standard errors of the b's. Except for Σx^2, all other terms are identical in both standard errors. Since $\Sigma x_1^2 = 134.95$ and $\Sigma x_2^2 = 59.20$, the standard error of b_1 is much smaller than the standard error of b_2 (.1953 and .2949, respectively). Other things equal, division by a smaller standard error will, of course, yield a larger t ratio.

It was found above that b_1 is significantly different from zero, whereas b_2 is not. Without dealing at this stage with complex aspects of interpretation, it is noted that the researcher may decide to delete X_2 as being not useful. When $r_{12} = 0$, such a decision is unambiguous and proper. When, however, $r_{12} \neq 0$, the decision is not that simple, and is discussed in detail in subsequent chapters.

When the independent variables are correlated, it is necessary to recalculate the regression statistics following the deletion of one or more than one variable from the regression equation. Assuming that in the present example a decision is made to delete X_2, this would necessitate the calculation of regression statistics with X_1 only. This is done without elaborating on each step, since what is being done should be clear by now. (If you encounter difficulties, it is suggested that you review the material covered in Chapter 2.)

$$b_1 = \frac{\Sigma x_1 y}{\Sigma x_1^2} = \frac{100.5}{134.95} = \mathit{.7447}$$

$$ss_{\text{reg}} = b\Sigma xy = (.7447)(100.5) = \mathit{74.8424}$$

$$ss_{\text{res}} = \Sigma y^2 - ss_{\text{reg}} = 165. - 74.8424 = \mathit{90.1576}$$

$$a = \bar{Y} - b\bar{X}_1 = 5.50 - (.7447)(4.95) = \mathit{1.8137}$$

$$Y' = 1.8137 + .7447X_1$$

$$R^2_{y1} = \frac{ss_{\text{reg}}}{\Sigma y^2} = \frac{74.8424}{165.0000} = \mathit{.4536}$$

$$F = \frac{R^2/k}{(1 - R^2)/(N - k - 1)} = \frac{.4536/1}{(1 - .4536)/(20 - 1 - 1)} = \frac{.4536}{.0304} = \mathit{14.92}$$

with 1 and 18 df, $p < .01$. Or, using Formula (3.22),

$$F = \frac{ss_{\text{reg}}/df_{\text{reg}}}{ss_{\text{res}}/df_{\text{res}}} = \frac{74.8424/1}{90.1576/18} = \frac{74.8424}{5.0088} = 14.94$$

Earlier in the chapter a distinction was made between b, the unstandardized regression coefficient, and β, the standardized regression coefficient. It was noted that b is applied in an equation in which raw scores are being used, and that β is applied to standard scores. It can be shown how one tests β's for statistical significance, but this is not done here because the t (or F) obtained for a given b is the same as the one that would be obtained for its corresponding β (see, earlier in the chapter, the formulas for obtaining β from b, and vice versa). In other words, testing a b is the same as testing the β that corresponds to it.

Testing Increments in Proportion of Variance Accounted For

In multiple regression analysis, it is possible to test whether an increment in the proportion of variance accounted for by a given variable, or a set of variables, is statistically significant. This approach is discussed in detail in subsequent chapters. At this stage, only the basic ideas are introduced. The test for an increment in the proportion of variance accounted for is given by

$$F = \frac{(R^2_{y.12\ldots k_1} - R^2_{y.12\ldots k_2})/(k_1 - k_2)}{(1 - R^2_{y.12\ldots k_1})/(N - k_1 - 1)} \tag{3.27}$$

where $R^2_{y.12\ldots k_1}$ = the squared multiple correlation coefficient for the regression of Y on k_1 variables (the larger coefficient, referred to as the full model); $R^2_{y.12\ldots k_2}$ = the squared multiple correlation for the regression of Y on k_2 variables, where k_2 = the smaller set of variables selected from among those of k_1 (referred to as the restricted model); N = sample size. The F ratio has $k_1 - k_2$ *df* for the numerator and $N - k_1 - 1$ *df* for the denominator. Formula (3.27) could also be used to test increments in regression sum of squares. The test is, of course, identical, inasmuch as a regression sum of squares is a product of a proportion of variance multiplied by the total sum of squares; for example,

$$ss_{\text{reg}.12\ldots k_1} = (R^2_{y.12\ldots k_1})\Sigma y^2$$

For the example under consideration, one may use (3.27) to test the increment due to X_2 (i.e., over and above what X_1 accounts for), and the increment due to X_1 (i.e., over and above X_2), respectively.

$$F = \frac{(R^2_{y.12} - R^2_{y.1})/(2 - 1)}{(1 - R^2_{y.12})/(N - 2 - 1)}$$

and

$$F = \frac{(R^2_{y.12} - R^2_{y.2})/(2 - 1)}{(1 - R^2_{y.12})/(N - 2 - 1)}$$

As we calculated earlier, $r^2_{y1} = R^2_{y.1} = .4536$ and $r^2_{y2} = R^2_{y.2} = .1557$. X_1 by itself accounts for about 45% of Y, and X_2 by itself accounts for about 16% of the variance of Y. Together, the two variables account for about 50% of the variance ($R^2_{y.12} = .5054$).

Testing the increment due to X_2:

$$F = \frac{(.5054 - .4536)/(2-1)}{(1 - .5054)/(20-2-1)} = \frac{.0518}{.02909} = 1.78$$

with 1 and 17 *df*, $p > .05$. Although, as noted above, X_2 by itself accounts for 16% of the variance, its increment to the accounting of variance over X_1 is about 5% (.0518). This is, of course, because X_1 and X_2 are correlated. The increment due to X_2 is not statistically significant.

Testing the increment due to X_1:

$$F = \frac{(.5054 - .1557)/(2-1)}{(1 - .5054)/(20-2-1)} = \frac{.3497}{.02909} = 12.02$$

with 1 and 17 *df*, $p < .01$. The increment in variance due to X_1 is about 35% (.3497) and statistically significant at the .01 level. Recall that by itself, X_1 accounted for about 45% of the variance of Y. Again, the reduction from 45% to 35% reflects the correlation between X_1 and X_2.

Two things will be noted about this procedure at this stage. First, testing the increment in proportion of variance accounted for by a single variable is equivalent to the test of the b associated with the variable. Earlier we found $b_1 = .6771$ with $t = 3.47$ (17 *df*); $b_2 = .3934$ with $t = 1.33$ (17 *df*). Recall that $t = \sqrt{F}$, when F has one degree of freedom for the numerator. Therefore, $\sqrt{1.78} = 1.33$, and $\sqrt{12.02} = 3.47$. To repeat, the same value is obtained whether one tests the b or the increment due to the variable with which it is associated. Second, the increment in the proportion of variance accounted for by a given variable (or by a set of variables) may be considerably different from the proportion of variance it accounts by itself, the difference being directly a function of the correlations of the variable with the other variables in the equation.

RELATIVE IMPORTANCE OF VARIABLES

In their attempts to explain the dependent variable, researchers often resort to different approaches for the purpose of determining the relative importance of the independent variables under study. This is an extremely complex topic to which much of the remainder of the book is devoted (see, in particular, Chapters 7 and 8). For now, therefore, only several brief comments will be made about the use of regression coefficients and increments in proportion of variance accounted for as indices of the relative importance of variables.

b's and β's

The magnitude of the b is affected, in part, by the scale of measurement that is being used to measure the variable with which the b is associated. Assume, for example, a simple linear regression in which X is length of objects measured in feet. Suppose that, instead of using feet, one were to express X in inches. The nature of the regression of Y on X will, of course, not change, nor will the test of significance of the b. The magnitude of the b, however, will change drastically. In the present case the b associated with X when measured in inches will be one-twelfth of the b obtained when X is measured in feet. This should alert you to two things: (1) A relatively large b may be neither substantively meaningful nor statistically significant, whereas a relatively small b may be both meaningful and statistically significant. (2) In multiple regression analysis one should not compare the magnitude of the b's associated with different X's when attempting to determine the relative importance of variables (see Chapter 8).

Let us assume that in the numerical example analyzed above both b's were found to be statistically significant. It would not be appropriate to compare the magnitude of the b's because they are based on different scales of measurement. Incidentally, because the b is affected by the scale being used, it is necessary to calculate b's to several decimal places. For a given scale, the b may, for example, be .0003 and yet be substantively meaningful and statistically significant. Had one solved only to two decimal places, the b would have been declared to be zero. In general, it is recommended that you carry out the calculations of regression analysis to as many decimal places as is feasible. Further rounding may be done at the end of the calculations.

Because of the incomparability of b's, researchers who wish to speak of relative importance of variables resort to comparisons among β's, as they are based on standard scores. In the numerical example analyzed above we found $\beta_1 = .6123$ and $\beta_2 = .2356$. Assuming, again, that both β's are statistically significant, one may wish to conclude that the effect of X_1 is more than 2.5 times as great as the effect of X_2. Although such an interpretation is legitimate, it is not free of problems because the β's are affected, among other things, by the variability of the variable with which they are associated. It was shown above that in simple linear regression $\beta = r$. In Chapter 2 it was shown how r varied as a function of the variability of X, while the b remained constant. The same principle operates in multiple regression analysis (for a discussion of this point, and numerical examples, see Chapter 8). The present discussion was meant to indicate that one needs to be cautious when comparing magnitudes of β's for the purpose of arriving at conclusions about the relative importance of variables. Other issues regarding the interpretation of regression coefficients are, as noted above, postponed until after a more thorough presentation of multiple regression analysis has been given.

Increment in Proportion of Variance Accounted For

Issues regarding the use of the increment in the proportion of variance accounted for by an independent variable as an indication of its relative importance cannot be discussed without dealing with the broader problem of variance partitioning—a topic to which Chapter 7 is devoted in its entirety. All that can be said here is that when the independent variables are intercorrelated, the proportion of variance incremented by a variable depends, among other things, on its point of entry into the regression analysis. Assuming that all the variables are positively intercorrelated, the later the point of entry of a variable, the smaller is the proportion of variance it is shown to account for in the dependent variable. Questions that undoubtedly come to your mind are: How, then, does one determine the order of entry of the variables? Is there a "correct" order? As is shown in Chapters 6 and 7, attempts to answer such questions are closely related to considerations of the theory that has generated the research and its focus—that is, explanation or prediction.

In sum, your sense of frustration at the lack of definitive answers to questions about the relative importance of variables is not difficult to imagine. Yet, attempts to come to grips with such questions must be postponed until after multiple regression analysis has been explored in greater detail and depth. Only then will it become evident that there is more than one answer to such questions, and that the ambiguity of some situations is not entirely resolvable.

CONCLUDING REMARKS

It is hoped that by now you understand, to a limited extent at least, the basic principles of multiple regression analysis. Although only two independent variables were used, enough of the subject has been presented to lay the foundations for the use of multiple regression analysis in scientific research. A severe danger in studying a subject like multiple regression, however, is that we become so preoccupied with formulas, numbers, and number manipulations that we lose sight of the larger purposes. We become so enwrapped in techniques and manipulations that we become the servants of methods rather than the masters. While it has been necessary to go through a good deal of number and symbol manipulations, this poses the real threat of losing one's way. It is therefore important to pause and take stock of why we are doing what we are doing.

In Chapter 1 it was said that multiple regression analysis may be used for two major purposes: explanation and prediction. Enough has been said thus far to gain somewhat more insight into this statement. To draw the lines clearly but oversimply, if we were interested only in prediction, we might be satisfied with selecting a set of predictors that optimizes R^2, and with using the regression equation for the predictors thus selected to predict individuals' performance on the criterion of interest. Success in high school or college as predicted by certain tests is a classic case. In much of the research on school success, the interest has been on prediction of the criterion. One need not probe too deeply into the whys of success in college; one wants mainly to be able to predict successfully. And this is of course no mean achievement to be lightly derogated. As is detailed in Chapter 6, which is devoted solely to the use of multiple regression analysis for prediction, various approaches are available to achieve this goal.

In much of behavioral research, however, prediction, successful or not, is not enough. We want to know why; we want to explain phenomena. This is the main goal of science. We want to explain, for example, phenomena such as problem solving, achievement, creativity, aggression, prejudice, job satisfaction. When the goal is explanation, the focus shifts to the interpretation of the regression equation. We want to know the magnitudes of the effects of independent variables on the dependent variable as they are reflected by the regression coefficients. But which ones should be used: unstandardized (b) or standardized (β) regression coefficients? In this chapter, it was possible to offer only a glimpse at the answer to this question. A detailed treatment of the study of effects of variables in nonexperimental research is given in Chapter 8. Much of Part 2 of this book is devoted to study of effects of variables in experimental research. Another approach to the use of elements of multiple regression analysis for the purpose of explanation—increments in the proportion of variance accounted for by independent variables—was alluded to in this chapter. This complex, often abused, approach is discussed in detail in Chapter 7.

In sum, then, Chapters 2 and 3 were designed to set the stage for the study of analytic and technical problems encountered in the use of elements of multiple regression analysis in predictive and explanatory scientific research. It is believed that mastery of the technical aspects of an analytic approach is a prerequisite for its valid application and an important antidote against misapplications. Needless to say, the study and mastery of the technical aspects of research are necessary but not sufficient conditions for the solution of research problems.

Finally, it will be recalled that in the beginning of this chapter it was said that the presentation was limited to two independent variables because of the ease this affords in discussing elements of multiple regression analysis. Although the meaning of elements of multiple regression analysis with more than two independent variables is the same as for the case of two independent variables, their calculations are best accomplished by the use of matrix algebra—a topic to which the first part of Chapter 4 is devoted.

STUDY SUGGESTIONS

1. Use the following illustrative data for calculations indicated below.

X_1	X_2	Y	X_1	X_2	Y
2	5	2	4	3	3
2	4	1	3	6	3
1	5	1	6	9	6
1	3	1	6	8	6
3	6	5	8	9	10
4	4	4	9	6	9
5	6	7	10	4	6
5	4	6	9	5	6
7	3	7	4	8	9
6	3	8	4	9	10

The second set of three columns is merely a continuation of the first set. The X_1 and Y scores are the same as those of Table 3.1; the X_2 scores, however, are different. Even though the calculations with X_1 and Y were given earlier in the chapter, it is suggested that you do all the calculations and then check the text. Set up a table like Table 3.2 to keep things orderly. Calculate:

(a) Sums, means, standard deviations, sums of squares and cross products, and the three r's.

(b) The regression equation of Y on X_1 and X_2.

(c) ss_{reg}, ss_{res}, $R^2_{y.12}$, F, $s^2_{y.12}$.
(d) The t ratios for the two regression coefficients.
(e) The increment in the proportion of variance accounted for by X_2, over and above X_1, and the F ratio for the test of this increment. What should this F be equal to?
(f) The increment in the proportion of variance accounted for by X_1, over and above X_2, and the F ratio for the test of this increment. What should this F be equal to?
(g) Using the regression equation, calculate the predicted Y's, the residuals, $Y - Y'$, $\Sigma(Y - Y')$, $\Sigma(Y - Y')^2$.
(h) The squared correlation between Y' and Y. What should this equal: that is, what statistic calculated earlier should be the same?

2. Consider the following two correlation matrices.

	X_1	X_2	Y
X_1	1.0	0	.7
X_2	0	1.0	.6
Y	.7	.6	1.0

A

	X_1	X_2	Y
X_1	1.0	.4	.7
X_2	.4	1.0	.6
Y	.7	.6	1.0

B

(a) For which matrix will $R^2_{y.12}$ be higher? Why?
(b) Calculate $R^2_{y.12}$ for each matrix.
(c) Calculate the regression equation for each matrix.
(d) Assume that each matrix is based on a sample of 100 people. Calculate the F ratio for each of the R^2 values obtained in (b) above.

ANSWERS

1. (a) $\bar{X}_1 = 4.95$; $\bar{X}_2 = 5.50$; $\bar{Y} = 5.50$; $s_1 = 2.6651$; $s_2 = 2.1151$; $s_y = 2.9469$; $\Sigma x_1^2 = 134.95$; $\Sigma x_2^2 = 85.00$; $\Sigma y^2 = 165.00$; $\Sigma x_1 x_2 = 15.50$; $\Sigma x_1 y = 100.50$; $\Sigma x_2 y = 63.00$; $r_{12} = .14472$; $r_{y1} = .67350$; $r_{y2} = .53197$
   (b) $Y' = -1.23561 + .67370X_1 + .61833X_2$
   (c) $ss_{\text{reg}} = 106.66144$; $ss_{\text{res}} = 58.33856$; $R^2_{y.12} = .64643$; $F = 15.54$, with 2 and 17 *df*; $s^2_{y.12} = 3.43168$
   (d) For b_1: $t = 4.18$, with 17 *df*; for b_2: $t = 3.04$, with 17 *df*.
   (e) .1928; $F = 9.27$, with 1 and 17 *df*. F is equal to t^2 for b_2
   (f) .3634; $F = 17.47$, with 1 and 17 *df*. F is equal to t^2 for b_1
   (g) $\Sigma(Y - Y') = 0$; $\Sigma(Y - Y')^2 = 58.3386$
   (h) $r^2_{yy'} = R^2_{y.12} = .64643$
2. (a) Matrix **A**
   (b) For matrix **A:** $R^2_{y.12} = .85$; for matrix **B:** $R^2_{y.12} = .61$
   (c) For matrix **A:** $z'_y = .7z_1 + .6z_2$; for matrix **B:** $z'_y = .55z_1 + .38z_2$
   (d) For matrix **A:** $F = 274.83$, with 2 and 97 *df*; for matrix **B:** $F = 75.86$, with 2 and 97 *df*

4

GENERAL METHOD OF MULTIPLE REGRESSION ANALYSIS: MATRIX OPERATIONS AND COMPUTER PROGRAMS

The main purpose of Chapter 3 was to introduce the basic elements of multiple regression theory and analysis. Although only two independent variables were used, it was pointed out that the same approach applies to any number of independent variables. The presentation in Chapter 3 was limited to two independent variables because algebraic formulas for analyses with more than two independent variables become unwieldy and intractable. The powerful and elegant techniques of matrix algebra are eminently suited for the solution of multivariable problems, of which multiple regression analysis is an important case.

In this chapter, the use of matrix algebra in multiple regression analysis is discussed and illustrated. Despite its generality, the application of matrix algebra is limited here to the case of one and two independent variables. The reason for doing so is to enable you to concentrate on the meaning of the method instead of getting bogged down in numerous calculations. While matrix equations are elegant and succinct, some operations on matrices (particularly the calculation of inverses) are extremely laborious. This is why matrix solutions with more than two independent variables are almost always done by computer. The virtue of working through the matrix algebra with two independent variables is that it will provide you with an understanding of the matrix equations that are applicable to regression analysis with any number of independent variables.

To enhance your learning and understanding of the method further, it is purposely applied to numerical examples analyzed in Chapters 2 and 3. It is suggested that you refer frequently to the analyses in Chapters 2 and 3 when you are working through the matrix operations presented in this chapter. Compare results obtained earlier with those obtained in this chapter. Study specific elements of the various matrices and see whether you can identify them in the analyses presented in Chapters 2 and 3. Above all, be patient and study the material presented systematically. It will pay off in better understanding.

Since the analyses in subsequent chapters are done almost exclusively by computer, three "package" programs that will be used repeatedly (i.e., SPSS, BMD, SAS) are introduced in this chapter. Relevant aspects of control cards used in each program are discussed. This is followed by a presentation of excerpts of output and commentaries. The programs are applied to a problem that is solved by hand calculations in the beginning of the chapter. Comparisons of the computer output with the results obtained by hand calculations should serve to acquaint you with specific features of each of the programs.

If you have no knowledge of matrix algebra, you are urged to study first Appendix A, which is a systematic elementary treatment of certain fundamental aspects of matrix algebra. The treatment of the subject is specifically geared to the multiple regression needs of this book and should be sufficient to enable you to grasp the material presented in this chapter and in subsequent ones.

You are particularly urged to study to the point of being familiar with the following aspects of matrix algebra: matrix manipulations analogous to simple algebraic manipulations, particularly matrix multiplication; the notion of a determinant and an inverse of a matrix; and the ability to calculate them for a 2 × 2 matrix. These topics are covered in Appendix A.

REGRESSION ANALYSIS: MATRIX OPERATIONS

In Chapter 2 and 3 equations were presented that expressed a score on a dependent variable, Y, as a linear combination of independent variables, X's, plus a constant, a, and an error term, e.

For k independent variables the equation is

$$Y = a + b_1X_1 + b_2X_2 + \cdots + b_kX_k + e \tag{4.1}$$

where a = intercept; b's = regression coefficients applied to the X's; e = residual, or error. Recall that a solution was sought for the constants (a and the b's) so that the sum of the squared residuals (Σe^2) will be at a minimum. Using matrix notation, Equation (4.1) is expressed as follows:

$$\underset{N \times 1}{\mathbf{Y}} = \underset{N \times (1+k)}{\mathbf{X}} \quad \underset{(1+k) \times 1}{\mathbf{b}} + \underset{N \times 1}{\mathbf{e}} \tag{4.2}$$

where **Y** is a column vector of raw scores on the dependent variable for N individuals (i.e., an N by 1 vector); **X** is an N by $1 + k$ matrix of raw scores for N individuals on k independent variables and a unit vector (a vector of 1's) for the intercept; **b** is a $1 + k$ column vector consisting of a, the intercept, and b_k regression coefficients;[1] **e** is an N by 1 column vector of errors, or residuals. To

[1]In matrix presentations of multiple regression analysis it is customary to use b_0, instead of a, as a symbol for the intercept. Because comparisons among intercepts from two or more regression equations are studied extensively in subsequent chapters, it was felt that using a as a symbol for the intercept will better serve to distinguish it from the regression coefficients.

make sure that you understand Equation (4.2), it is spelled out in the form of matrices.

$$\begin{bmatrix} Y_1 \\ Y_2 \\ Y_3 \\ \cdot \\ \cdot \\ \cdot \\ Y_N \end{bmatrix} = \begin{bmatrix} 1 & X_{11} & X_{12} & X_{13} & \cdots & X_{1k} \\ 1 & X_{21} & X_{22} & X_{23} & \cdots & X_{2k} \\ 1 & X_{31} & X_{32} & X_{33} & \cdots & X_{3k} \\ \cdot & \cdot & \cdot & \cdot & & \cdot \\ \cdot & \cdot & \cdot & \cdot & & \cdot \\ \cdot & \cdot & \cdot & \cdot & & \cdot \\ 1_N & X_{N1} & X_{N2} & X_{N3} & \cdots & X_{Nk} \end{bmatrix} \begin{bmatrix} a \\ b_1 \\ b_2 \\ \cdot \\ \cdot \\ \cdot \\ b_k \end{bmatrix} + \begin{bmatrix} e_1 \\ e_2 \\ e_3 \\ \cdot \\ \cdot \\ \cdot \\ e_N \end{bmatrix}$$

where Y_1, for example, is the first person's score on the dependent variable, Y; X_{11} is the first person's score on X_1; X_{12} is the first person's score on X_2; and so on up to X_{1k}, the first person's score on X_k. In other words, each row of **X** represents the scores of a given individual on the independent variables, X's, plus a constant (1) for the intercept *(a)*. e_1 is the residual associated with the first person, and so on for all the others in the group. Multiplying **X** by **b** and adding **e** yields N equations like (4.1), one for each person in the group. Using the principle of least squares, we seek a solution for **b** so that **e'e** will be minimized. (**e'** is the transpose of **e**, or **e** expressed as a row vector. Multiplying **e'** by **e** is the same as squaring each e and summing them, i.e., Σe^2.)

The solution for **b** that minimizes **e'e** is:

$$\mathbf{b} = (\mathbf{X'X})^{-1}\mathbf{X'Y} \tag{4.3}$$

where **b** is column vector of a (intercept) plus b_k regression coefficients. **X'** is the transpose of **X**, the latter being an N by $1 + k$ matrix composed of a unit vector and k column vectors of scores on the independent variables. $(\mathbf{X'X})^{-1}$ is the inverse of $(\mathbf{X'X})$. **Y** is an N by 1 column of dependent variable scores.

A Numerical Example with One Independent Variable

We turn now to the solution of a numerical example with one independent variable using matrix operations. For purposes of comparisons, the example introduced and analyzed in Chapter 2 (see Table 2.1) is being used. In order to make sure that you follow what is being done the matrices are written in their entirety. For the data of Table 2.1, see facing page.

$$\mathbf{b} = \left\{ \underset{\mathbf{X}'}{\begin{bmatrix} 11111111111111111111 \\ 11112222333344445555 \end{bmatrix}} \underset{\mathbf{X}}{\begin{bmatrix} 1 & 1 \\ 1 & 1 \\ 1 & 1 \\ 1 & 1 \\ 1 & 2 \\ 1 & 2 \\ 1 & 2 \\ 1 & 2 \\ 1 & 3 \\ 1 & 3 \\ 1 & 3 \\ 1 & 3 \\ 1 & 4 \\ 1 & 4 \\ 1 & 4 \\ 1 & 4 \\ 1 & 5 \\ 1 & 5 \\ 1 & 5 \\ 1 & 5 \end{bmatrix}} \right\}^{-1} \underset{\mathbf{X}'}{\begin{bmatrix} 11111111111111111111 \\ 11112222333344445555 \end{bmatrix}} \underset{\mathbf{Y}}{\begin{bmatrix} 3 \\ 5 \\ 6 \\ 9 \\ 4 \\ 6 \\ 7 \\ 10 \\ 4 \\ 6 \\ 8 \\ 10 \\ 5 \\ 7 \\ 9 \\ 12 \\ 6 \\ 7 \\ 10 \\ 12 \end{bmatrix}}$$

multiplying **X′** by **X**:

$$\mathbf{X'X} = \begin{bmatrix} \underset{N}{20} & \underset{\Sigma X}{60} \\ \underset{\Sigma X}{60} & \underset{\Sigma X^2}{220} \end{bmatrix}$$

Under each number, the term that it represents is indicated. Thus, $N = 20$, $\Sigma X = 60$, $\Sigma X^2 = 220$. Compare with the calculations in Chapter 2.

$$\mathbf{X'Y} = \begin{bmatrix} \underset{\Sigma Y}{146} \\ \underset{\Sigma XY}{468} \end{bmatrix}$$

Again, the same values were obtained in Chapter 2.

Calculating the Inverse of a 2 × 2 Matrix

To calculate the inverse of the 2 × 2 **X**, where

$$\mathbf{X} = \begin{bmatrix} a & b \\ c & d \end{bmatrix}$$

$$\mathbf{X}^{-1} = \begin{bmatrix} \dfrac{d}{ad - bc} & \dfrac{-b}{ad - bc} \\ \dfrac{-c}{ad - bc} & \dfrac{a}{ad - bc} \end{bmatrix}$$

Note that the denominator is the determinant of **X**—that is, $|\mathbf{X}|$. Note also that the elements of the principal diagonal (a and d) are interchanged and that the signs of the other two elements (b and c) are changed.

For our data, calculate first the determinant of $(\mathbf{X}'\mathbf{X})$:

$$|\mathbf{X}'\mathbf{X}| = \begin{vmatrix} 20 & 60 \\ 60 & 220 \end{vmatrix} = (220)(20) - (60)(60) = 800$$

Now calculate the inverse of $(\mathbf{X}'\mathbf{X})$:

$$(\mathbf{X}'\mathbf{X})^{-1} = \begin{bmatrix} \dfrac{220}{800} & \dfrac{-60}{800} \\ \dfrac{-60}{800} & \dfrac{20}{800} \end{bmatrix} = \begin{bmatrix} .275 & -.075 \\ -.075 & .025 \end{bmatrix}$$

We are now ready to calculate:

$$\mathbf{b} = (\mathbf{X}'\mathbf{X})^{-1}\mathbf{X}'\mathbf{Y} = \begin{bmatrix} .275 & -.075 \\ -.075 & .025 \end{bmatrix} \begin{bmatrix} 146 \\ 468 \end{bmatrix} = \begin{bmatrix} 5.05 \\ .75 \end{bmatrix}$$

$$a = 5.05 \quad \text{and} \quad b_1 = .75$$

or

$$Y' = 5.05 + .75X$$

which is the regression equation obtained in Chapter 2.

Regression and Residual Sum of Squares

The regression sum of squares in matrix form is:

$$ss_{\text{reg}} = \mathbf{b}'\mathbf{X}'\mathbf{Y} - \frac{(\Sigma Y)^2}{N} \tag{4.4}$$

where **b**′ is the row vector of *b*'s; **X**′ is the transpose of **X** matrix of scores on independent variables plus a unit vector; **Y** is a column vector of dependent variable scores; $(\Sigma Y)^2/N$ is a correction term used to arrive at deviation scores (see Formula (2.2) in Chapter 2).

As we calculated above,

$$\mathbf{X'Y} = \begin{bmatrix} 146 \\ \\ 468 \end{bmatrix} \qquad \mathbf{b'} = [5.05 \quad .75] \qquad \Sigma Y = 146$$

$$ss_{\text{reg}} = [5.05 \quad .75] \begin{bmatrix} 146 \\ 468 \end{bmatrix} - \frac{(146)^2}{20} = 1088.3 - 1065.8 = \mathit{22.5}$$

The same value was obtained in Chapter 2.

The residual sum of squares is

$$\mathbf{e'e} = \mathbf{Y'Y} - \mathbf{b'X'Y} \tag{4.5}$$

where **e**′ and **e** are row and column vectors of the residuals, respectively. As was noted above, premultiplying a column by its transpose is the same as squaring and summing the elements of the column. In other words, $\mathbf{e'e} = \Sigma e^2$. Similarly $\mathbf{Y'Y} = \Sigma Y^2$, the sum of raw scores squared.

$$\mathbf{Y'Y} = 1196 \qquad \mathbf{b'X'Y} = 1088.3$$

$$ss_{\text{res}} = \mathbf{e'e} = 1196 - 1088.3 = \mathit{107.7}$$

Squared Multiple Correlation Coefficient

Recall that the squared multiple correlation coefficient (R^2, or r^2 with a single independent variable) indicates the proportion of variance, or sum of squares, of the dependent variable accounted for by the independent variable. In matrix form,

$$R^2 = \frac{\mathbf{b'X'Y} - (\Sigma Y)^2/N}{\mathbf{Y'Y} - (\Sigma Y)^2/N} = \frac{ss_{\text{reg}}}{\Sigma y^2} \tag{4.6}$$

where $(\Sigma Y)^2/N$ in the numerator and the denominator is the correction term.

$$R^2 = \frac{1088.3 - (146)^2/20}{1196 - (146)^2/20} = \frac{22.5}{130.2} = \mathit{.1728}$$

Also,

$$R^2 = 1 - \frac{\mathbf{e'e}}{\mathbf{Y'Y} - (\Sigma Y)^2/N} = 1 - \frac{ss_{\text{res}}}{\Sigma y^2}$$

We could, of course, test the regression sum of squares, or the proportion of variance accounted for (R^2), for significance. Because the tests are the same as those used frequently in Chapters 2 and 3, they are not repeated here.

In the above analysis matrix algebra was applied to simple linear regression analysis. One can well sympathize with the puzzled reader who wonders why all these matrix operations were necessary when one could have used the methods presented in Chapter 2, which certainly looked simpler, particularly to one who is not accustomed to the use of matrix algebra. Had regression analyses in the social sciences been limited to one or two independent variables, there would have been no need to resort to matrix algebra. The methods presented in Chapters 2 and 3 would have sufficed. Needless to say, more than two independent variables are used in much, if not all, of behavioral research. For such analyses, matrix algebra is essential. As was said earlier, it is easy to demonstrate the application of matrix algebra with one and two independent variables. Study the analyses in this chapter until you understand them well and feel comfortable with them. After that, you can let the computer do the matrix operations for you. But you will know what is being done and will therefore better understand how to use and interpret the results of your analyses.

AN EXAMPLE WITH TWO INDEPENDENT VARIABLES: DEVIATION SCORES

The data of Table 3.1 will now be analyzed by matrix operations. This time, however, we work with matrices of deviation scores rather than raw scores, and subsequently we do the same analysis with a matrix of correlation coefficients. You will thus become familiar with three variations on the same theme. The equation for the b's using deviation scores is

$$\mathbf{b} = (\mathbf{x}'\mathbf{x})^{-1}\mathbf{x}'\mathbf{y} \tag{4.7}$$

where **b** is a column of regression coefficients, **x** is an $N \times k$ matrix of deviation scores on k independent variables, and $\mathbf{x}'$ is the transpose of **x**. Unlike the solution with raw scores, **x** does not include a unit vector because multiplication of a column vector by a unit row vector is the same as adding the elements of the column vector (see Appendix A). Now, each column of **x** consists of deviation scores from their mean, and therefore the sum of each column is zero. When (4.7) is applied, a solution is obtained for the b's only. The intercept, a, is calculated separately (see below).

$(\mathbf{x}'\mathbf{x})$ is a $k \times k$ matrix of deviation sums of squares and cross products. For k independent variables:

$$(\mathbf{x}'\mathbf{x}) = \begin{bmatrix} \Sigma x_1^2 & \Sigma x_1x_2 & \cdots & \Sigma x_1x_k \\ \Sigma x_2x_1 & \Sigma x_2^2 & \cdots & \Sigma x_2x_k \\ \cdot & \cdot & & \cdot \\ \cdot & \cdot & & \cdot \\ \cdot & \cdot & & \cdot \\ \Sigma x_kx_1 & \Sigma x_kx_2 & & \Sigma x_k^2 \end{bmatrix}$$

Note that the diagonal is composed of sums of squares, and that the off-diagonals are sums of cross products. $\mathbf{x}'\mathbf{y}$ is a $k \times 1$ column of cross products of x_k variables with y, the dependent variable.

$$\mathbf{x'y} = \begin{bmatrix} \Sigma x_1 y \\ \Sigma x_2 y \\ \cdot \\ \cdot \\ \cdot \\ \Sigma x_k y \end{bmatrix}$$

Before applying (4.7) to the data of Table 3.1, it will be instructive to spell out the equation for the case of two independent variables using symbols.

$$\mathbf{b} = \underset{\mathbf{x'x}}{\begin{bmatrix} \Sigma x_1^2 & \Sigma x_1 x_2 \\ \Sigma x_2 x_1 & \Sigma x_2^2 \end{bmatrix}^{-1}} \underset{\mathbf{x'y}}{\begin{bmatrix} \Sigma x_1 y \\ \Sigma x_2 y \end{bmatrix}}$$

First, calculate the determinant of $(\mathbf{x'x})$:

$$|\mathbf{x'x}| = \begin{vmatrix} \Sigma x_1^2 & \Sigma x_1 x_2 \\ \Sigma x_2 x_1 & \Sigma x_2^2 \end{vmatrix} = (\Sigma x_1^2)(\Sigma x_2^2) - (\Sigma x_1 x_2)^2$$

Second, calculate the inverse of $(\mathbf{x'x})$:

$$(\mathbf{x'x})^{-1} = \begin{bmatrix} \dfrac{\Sigma x_2^2}{(\Sigma x_1^2)(\Sigma x_2^2) - (\Sigma x_1 x_2)^2} & \dfrac{-\Sigma x_1 x_2}{(\Sigma x_1^2)(\Sigma x_2^2) - (\Sigma x_1 x_2)^2} \\ \dfrac{-\Sigma x_2 x_1}{(\Sigma x_1^2)(\Sigma x_2^2) - (\Sigma x_1 x_2)^2} & \dfrac{\Sigma x_1^2}{(\Sigma x_1^2)(\Sigma x_2^2) - (\Sigma x_1 x_2)^2} \end{bmatrix}$$

Note that: (1) the denominator for each term in the inverse is the determinant of $(\mathbf{x'x})$, $|\mathbf{x'x}|$; (2) the sums of squares $(\Sigma x_1^2, \Sigma x_2^2)$ were interchanged; (3) the signs for the sum of the cross products were reversed. Now solve for **b:**

$$\mathbf{b} = \underset{(\mathbf{x'x})^{-1}}{\begin{bmatrix} \dfrac{\Sigma x_2^2}{(\Sigma x_1^2)(\Sigma x_2^2) - (\Sigma x_1 x_2)^2} & \dfrac{-\Sigma x_1 x_2}{(\Sigma x_1^2)(\Sigma x_2^2) - (\Sigma x_1 x_2)^2} \\ \dfrac{-\Sigma x_2 x_1}{(\Sigma x_1^2)(\Sigma x_2^2) - (\Sigma x_1 x_2)^2} & \dfrac{\Sigma x_1^2}{(\Sigma x_1^2)(\Sigma x_2^2) - (\Sigma x_1 x_2)^2} \end{bmatrix}} \underset{\mathbf{x'y}}{\begin{bmatrix} \Sigma x_1 y \\ \Sigma x_2 y \end{bmatrix}}$$

$$= \begin{bmatrix} \dfrac{(\Sigma x_2^2)(\Sigma x_1 y) - (\Sigma x_1 x_2)(\Sigma x_2 y)}{(\Sigma x_1^2)(\Sigma x_2^2) - (\Sigma x_1 x_2)^2} \\ \dfrac{(\Sigma x_1^2)(\Sigma x_2 y) - (\Sigma x_1 x_2)(\Sigma x_1 y)}{(\Sigma x_1^2)(\Sigma x_2^2) - (\Sigma x_1 x_2)^2} \end{bmatrix}$$

Note that the solution is identical with the algebraic formula for the b's given in Chapter 3 (see 3.4). These matrix operations were presented not only to show the identity of the two approaches, but also to give you an idea how unwieldy algebraic formulas would become had one attempted to develop them for the case of more than two independent variables. Again, this is why one resorts to matrix algebra.

Let us now apply the matrix algebra to the data of Table 3.1. In Chapter 3 we have calculated:

$$\Sigma x_1^2 = 134.95 \qquad \Sigma x_2^2 = 59.20 \qquad \Sigma x_1 x_2 = 23.20$$

$$\Sigma x_1 y = 100.50 \qquad \Sigma x_2 y = 39.00$$

Therefore,

$$\mathbf{b} = \underset{\mathbf{x'x}}{\begin{bmatrix} 134.95 & 23.20 \\ 23.20 & 59.20 \end{bmatrix}^{-1}} \underset{\mathbf{x'y}}{\begin{bmatrix} 100.50 \\ 39.00 \end{bmatrix}}$$

First find the determinant of $\mathbf{x'x}$:

$$|\mathbf{x'x}| = \begin{vmatrix} 134.95 & 23.20 \\ 23.20 & 59.20 \end{vmatrix} = (134.95)(59.20) - (23.20)^2 = 7450.8$$

Now invert $(\mathbf{x'x})$:

$$(\mathbf{x'x})^{-1} = \begin{bmatrix} \dfrac{59.20}{7450.8} & \dfrac{-23.20}{7450.8} \\ \dfrac{-23.20}{7450.8} & \dfrac{134.95}{7450.8} \end{bmatrix} = \begin{bmatrix} .0079455 & -.0031138 \\ -.0031138 & .0181121 \end{bmatrix}$$

$$\mathbf{b} = \begin{bmatrix} .0079455 & -.0031138 \\ -.0031138 & .0181121 \end{bmatrix} \begin{bmatrix} 100.50 \\ 39.00 \end{bmatrix} = \begin{bmatrix} .6771 \\ .3934 \end{bmatrix}$$

Note that the b's are identical with those obtained in Chapter 3. The intercept can now be calculated using the following formula:

$$a = \bar{Y} - b_1\bar{X}_1 - b_2\bar{X}_2 \tag{4.8}$$

$$a = 5.50 - (.6771)(4.95) - (.3934)(5.20) = .1027$$

The regression equation is

$$Y' = .1027 + .6771X_1 + .3934X_2$$

Regression and Residual Sums of Squares

The regression sum of squares when using matrices of deviation scores is:

$$ss_{\text{reg}} = \mathbf{b'x'y} \tag{4.9}$$

$$= \underset{\mathbf{b'}}{[.6771 \quad .3934]} \underset{\mathbf{x'y}}{\begin{bmatrix} 100.50 \\ 39.00 \end{bmatrix}} = 83.3912$$

and the residual sum of squares is:

$$ss_{\text{res}} = \mathbf{e'e} = \mathbf{y'y} - \mathbf{b'x'y}$$
$$= 165 - 83.3912 = \mathit{81.6088} \tag{4.10}$$

which agree with the values obtained in Chapter 3.

One could, of course, proceed now to calculate R^2, as well as to do tests of significance. But since these calculations will be identical with those presented in Chapter 3, they are not presented here. Instead, the variance/covariance matrix of the b's is introduced.

Variance/Covariance Matrix of the b's

As discussed in Chapters 2 and 3, each b has a variance associated with it (i.e., the variance of its sampling distribution. The square root of the variance of a b is the standard error of the b). It is also possible to calculate the covariance of two b's. The variance/covariance matrix of the b's is:

$$\mathbf{C} = \frac{\mathbf{e'e}}{N - k - 1}(\mathbf{x'x})^{-1} = s^2_{y.12\ldots k}(\mathbf{x'x})^{-1} \tag{4.11}$$

where $\mathbf{C}$ = the variance/covariance matrix of the b's; $\mathbf{e'e}$ = residual sum of squares; N = sample size; k = number of independent variables; $(\mathbf{x'x})^{-1}$ = inverse of the matrix of deviation scores on the independent variables, $\mathbf{x}$, premultiplied by its transpose, $\mathbf{x}'$, that is, the inverse of the matrix of the sums of squares and cross products. As indicated in the right-hand term of (4.11), $\frac{\mathbf{e'e}}{N - k - 1} = s^2_{y.12\ldots k}$ is the variance of estimate, or the mean square residual, which was used repeatedly in Chapters 2 and 3. The matrix $\mathbf{C}$ plays a very important role in significance testing, and is used extensively in subsequent chapters (see, in particular, Chapters 9 and 13). At this point the meaning of its elements is indicated, and it is shown how they are used in tests of statistical significance.

Each diagonal element of $\mathbf{C}$ is the variance of the b with which it is associated. Thus c_{11}—that is, the first element of the principal diagonal—is the variance of b_1, c_{22} is the variance of b_2, and so on. The $\sqrt{c_{11}}$ is the standard error of b_1, $\sqrt{c_{22}}$ is the standard error of b_2. The off diagonal elements are the covariances of the b's with which they are associated. Thus, $c_{12} = c_{21}$ is the covariance of b_1 and b_2, and similarly for the other off diagonal elements. Since there is no danger of confusion—diagonal elements are variances, off diagonal elements are covariances—it will be more convenient to refer to $\mathbf{C}$ as the covariance matrix of the b's.

$\mathbf{C}$ for the present example is now calculated, and its elements are used in statistical tests in order to illustrate and clarify what was said above. We calculated above $\mathbf{e'e} = ss_{\text{res}} = 81.6088$; $N = 20$; $k = 2$. Using these values and $(\mathbf{x'x})^{-1}$, which was calculated earlier, we obtain:

$$\mathbf{C} = \frac{81.6088}{20 - 2 - 1}\begin{bmatrix} .0079455 & -.0031138 \\ -.0031138 & .0181121 \end{bmatrix} = \begin{bmatrix} .03814 & -.01495 \\ -.01495 & .08695 \end{bmatrix}$$

As noted above, the first term on the right is the variance of estimate ($s^2_{y.12}$ = 4.8005) which is, of course, the same value as was obtained in Chapter 3 [see calculations following Equation (3.26)]. The diagonals of **C** are the variances of the b's. Therefore, the standard errors of b_1 and b_2 are $\sqrt{.03814} = .1953$ and $\sqrt{.08695} = .2949$, respectively. These agree with the values obtained in Chapter 3. Now test the two b's as follows:

$$t = \frac{b_1}{s_{b_1}} = \frac{.6771}{.1953} = 3.47$$

$$t = \frac{b_2}{s_{b_2}} = \frac{.3934}{.2949} = 1.33$$

Again, the values agree with those obtained in Chapter 3. Each t has 17 df associated with it (i.e., $N - k - 1$).

It was said above that the off-diagonal elements of **C** are the covariances of their respective b's. The standard error of the difference between b_1 and b_2 is

$$s_{b_1 - b_2} = \sqrt{c_{11} + c_{22} - 2c_{12}} \tag{4.12}$$

where c_{11} and c_{22} are the diagonal elements of **C** and $c_{12} = c_{21}$ is the off-diagonal element of **C**. It is worth noting that extensions of (4.12) to designs with more than two independent variables would become unwieldy. But, as is shown in subsequent chapters, such designs can be handled with relative ease by matrix algebra.

Applying (4.12) to the present numerical example,

$$s_{b_1 - b_2} = \sqrt{.03814 + .08695 - 2(-.01495)} = \sqrt{.15499} = .3937$$

$$t = \frac{b_1 - b_2}{s_{b_1 - b_2}} = \frac{.6771 - .3934}{.3937} = \frac{.2837}{.3937} = .72$$

with 17 df ($N - k - 1$).

Such a test is meaningful and useful only when the two b's are associated with variables that are of the same kind and that are measured by the same type of scale. In the present example this test is not meaningful. It was introduced here in order to acquaint you with the method used frequently in some subsequent chapters, in which not only are tests of the difference between two b's performed, but also tests of linear combinations of more than two b's.

Increments in Regression Sum of Squares

The notion of increments in regression sum of squares, or proportion of variance, due to a given variable was discussed and illustrated in Chapter 3.

That is, we studied what portion of the sum of squares is due to a given variable, over and above the other variables already in the equation. Such increments can be easily calculated when using matrix operations. An increment in the regression sum of squares due to variable j is:

$$ss_{\text{reg}(j)} = \frac{b_j^2}{x^{jj}} \tag{4.13}$$

where $ss_{\text{reg}(j)}$ = increment in regression sum of squares due to variable j; b_j = regression coefficient for variable j; x^{jj} = diagonal element of the inverse of $(\mathbf{x}'\mathbf{x})$ associated with variable j. As calculated above, $b_1 = .6771$, $b_2 = .3934$, and

$$(\mathbf{x}'\mathbf{x})^{-1} = \begin{bmatrix} .0079455 & -.0031138 \\ -.0031138 & .0181121 \end{bmatrix}$$

The increment in the regression sum of squares due to X_1 is:

$$ss_{\text{reg}(1)} = \frac{.6771^2}{.0079455} = \frac{.458464}{.0079455} = 57.70114$$

And due to X_2:

$$ss_{\text{reg}(2)} = \frac{.3934^2}{.0181121} = \frac{.1547644}{.0181121} = 8.54478$$

If, instead, one wished to express the increments in proportion of variance, all one would have to do is to divide each increment by the sum of squares of the dependent variable (Σy^2). For the present example, $\Sigma y^2 = 165$. Therefore, the increment in proportion of variance accounted for due to X_1 is:

$$\frac{57.70114}{165.} = .3497$$

And due to X_2:

$$\frac{8.54478}{165.} = .0518$$

Compare these results with those obtained in Chapter 3, where it was also shown how one tests such increments for significance. The approach presented in this section is discussed in detail in Chapter 7. At this stage, it was only designed to show how easily the terms can be obtained when one uses matrix algebra.

AN EXAMPLE WITH TWO INDEPENDENT VARIABLES: CORRELATION COEFFICIENTS

As was discussed in Chapter 3, when all the variables are expressed in standard scores *(z)*, one can calculate the regression statistics using correlation coefficients. For two variables, the regression equation is:

$$z'_y = \beta_1 z_1 + \beta_2 z_2 \tag{4.14}$$

where z'_y is the predicted Y in standard scores; β_1 and β_2 are standardized regression coefficients; z_1 and z_2 are standard scores on X_1 and X_2, respectively.

The matrix equation for the solution of the standardized coefficients is:

$$\boldsymbol{\beta} = \mathbf{R}^{-1}\mathbf{r} \tag{4.15}$$

where $\boldsymbol{\beta}$ is a column vector of standardized coefficients; **R** is the correlation matrix of the independent variables; **r** is a column vector of correlations between each independent variable and the dependent variable. Equation (4.15) is applied now to the data of Table 3.1. In Chapter 3 (see Table 3.2) we calculated:

$$r_{12} = .2596 \qquad r_{1y} = .6735 \qquad r_{2y} = .3946$$

Therefore,

$$\mathbf{R} = \begin{bmatrix} 1.0000 & .2596 \\ .2596 & 1.0000 \end{bmatrix}$$

r_{11} and r_{22} are, of course, equal to 1.00.

The determinant of **R** is:

$$|\mathbf{R}| = \begin{vmatrix} 1.0000 & .2596 \\ .2596 & 1.0000 \end{vmatrix} = (1.0000)^2 - (.2596)^2 = .93261$$

The inverse of **R** is:

$$\mathbf{R}^{-1} = \begin{bmatrix} \dfrac{1.0000}{.93261} & \dfrac{-.2596}{.93261} \\[2ex] \dfrac{-.2596}{.93261} & \dfrac{1.0000}{.93261} \end{bmatrix} = \begin{bmatrix} 1.07226 & -.27836 \\ -.27836 & 1.07226 \end{bmatrix}$$

Applying (4.15),

$$\boldsymbol{\beta} = \begin{bmatrix} 1.07226 & -.27836 \\ -.27836 & 1.07226 \end{bmatrix} \begin{bmatrix} .6735 \\ .3946 \end{bmatrix} = \begin{bmatrix} .6123 \\ .2356 \end{bmatrix}$$

The regression equation is: $z'_y = .6123z_1 + .2356z_2$. Compare with the β's obtained in Chapter 3. One can now use the following formula to calculate the b's.

$$b_j = \beta_j \frac{s_y}{s_j} \tag{4.16}$$

where b_j = unstandardized coefficient for variable j; β_j = standardized coefficient for variable j; s_y = standard deviation of the dependent variable, Y; s_j = standard deviation of variable j. Equation (4.16) is not applied here as this was done in detail in Chapter 3.

Squared Multiple Correlation

The squared multiple correlation can be calculated as follows:

$$R^2 = \boldsymbol{\beta}'\mathbf{r} \tag{4.17}$$

where $\boldsymbol{\beta}'$ is a row vector of β's (the transpose of $\boldsymbol{\beta}$), and $\mathbf{r}$ is a column of correlations of each independent variable with the dependent variable. For our data,

$$R^2 = [.6123 \quad .2356] \begin{bmatrix} .6735 \\ \\ .3946 \end{bmatrix} = .5054$$

This is the same value as the one obtained in Chapter 3.

One can, of course, test the significance of R^2, as was shown in Chapter 3.

Increment in Proportion of Variance

It was shown above how one may determine the increment in regression sum of squares due to a given variable. Using matrices based on standard scores, one can calculate the proportion of variance incremented by a given variable, as follows:

$$prop_{(j)} = \frac{\beta_j^2}{r^{jj}} \tag{4.18}$$

where $prop_{(j)}$ = increment in proportion of variance due to variable j; r^{jj} = the diagonal element of the inverse of $\mathbf{R}$ ($\mathbf{R}^{-1}$) associated with variable j. As calculated above,

$$\beta_1 = .6123 \qquad \beta_2 = .2356$$

and

$$\mathbf{R}^{-1} = \begin{bmatrix} 1.07226 & -.27836 \\ \\ -.27836 & 1.07226 \end{bmatrix}$$

The increment in proportion of variance due to X_1 is

$$prop_{(1)} = \frac{.6123^2}{1.07226} = \frac{.37491}{1.07226} = .3496$$

The increment due to X_2 is

$$prop_{(2)} = \frac{.2356^2}{1.07226} = \frac{.05551}{1.07226} = .0518$$

These values are, of course, the same as those obtained above and in Chapter 3.

Finally, just as one may obtain increments in proportion of variance from increments in regression sums of squares (see calculations above), so can one do the reverse operation. That is, having increments in proportions of variance one can calculate increments in regression sum of squares. All one need do is multiply each increment by the sum of squares of the dependent variable (Σy^2). For the present example, $\Sigma y^2 = 165$. Therefore,

$$ss_{\text{reg}(1)} = (.3496)(165) = 57.684$$

$$ss_{\text{reg}(2)} = (.0518)(165) = 8.547$$

These values agree (within errors of rounding) with those obtained above.

COMPUTER PROGRAMS

Rarely does one encounter in the behavioral sciences regression analysis problems in which the number of variables and the number of subjects are small so that all the necessary calculations may be done efficiently by hand, or with the aid of a calculator. Therefore, reliance on computer programs has become the rule in much, if not most, of behavioral research. In this book, computer programs are introduced for two purposes: (1) to provide guidance in the use of some popular programs; (2) to use programs for the analysis of specific numerical examples, so as to not be sidetracked by laborious calculations. Of the two, the second purpose is the more important one. Even if no attempt were made to provide guidance in the use of computer programs, their output would have been used to report and discuss results of analyses of specific problems.

If you are well versed in the use of a specific program being presented, or if you have no access to the program, or if you prefer to use another program, feel free to skip the listings of the control cards and the comments about them. *But you are strongly urged not to skip the output and the commentaries about it.* In subsequent chapters, certain problems are analyzed by computer only, and substantive comments are made about the output in connection with the specific analytic method being discussed or the specific problem at hand. *Therefore, you are urged to study the output and the substantive comments about it, even when the specific program that generated the output is of no interest, or irrelevant, to you.*

With the above remarks in mind, we turn to a description of the format that will be used in the presentation of computer programs and their output. This is followed by some remarks about the use of package programs.

Package Programs and Their Use

In this section, three computer programs for multiple regression analysis are introduced and applied. There is a large number of such programs, and many more will probably be available by the time this book is published. It is therefore appropriate to offer some explanation for the choices made here. Programs were selected because they: (1) are readily available in computing centers in many countries; (2) are relatively easy to use; (3) provide great flexibility for data editing and data manipulations; (4) have a variety of options in the analyses, as well as the types of output one may obtain; (5) are part of package programs, which are updated periodically and for which published comprehensive manuals are available.

The presentation is not designed to be exhaustive, nor is it intended to supplant the manuals for the programs. On the contrary, it is hoped that the presentation will help you use the manuals and the programs more efficiently. Specific features and requirements of the programs are not dealt with, unless they are directly related to the topic being discussed or to the numerical example that is being analyzed. For example, each program has several options for the format of reading in the data. Although it is shown how the data were read in, the format is generally not commented upon. Moreover, the examples are not meant to imply that the "best" or the most efficient approach was used. "Best" and "efficient" are situation-specific, and depend, among other things, on the amount of data, the type of facilities and support services available, and the overall analytic plan for a given data set.

In short, the aim is to acquaint you with the programs and to help you identify and understand the meaning of different parts of the output. For each program, the control cards that have been used to analyze the numerical example under consideration are shown. The choices of certain options for the analyses and output may not be the ones that you will find most suited for your specific problem. Because of the small data sets used here it was not necessary to worry about costs in central and peripheral processes. Consequently, certain options are sometimes called for even though no reference is made to results that are generated by them. With large data sets one would, of course, have to be more careful and more cost conscious. For example, in the SPSS program STATISTICS ALL is specified even when there is no interest in some of the options and therefore the output generated by them is not reported.

Following the listing of the control cards, parts of the output are reported, along with comments and explanations that, it is hoped, will help you understand the special features of each program and enable you to use them to the best advantage. Several considerations guided the decision to use the present format instead of reproducing the output of a program in its entirety. First, and most important, it was felt that reporting excerpts interspersed by commentaries is the most flexible and efficient format for concentrating on specific pieces of information, and providing more or less elaboration as seems to be called for by a given topic. Thus, whereas a given piece of information may require a brief comment, another piece of information may require a more detailed discussion. Second, the format used permits the exclusion of output relevant to topics that have not yet been introduced, thereby avoiding confusion and frustration. For example, the programs used in this chapter report, among other things, the adjusted R^2. But because this concept has not yet been introduced, it is not reported here as part of the output. When the adjusted R^2 is discussed in a subsequent chapter, a reference is made to computer programs that report it. Third, the present format enables one to conserve space by reporting, when desired, only output that is unique to a given program, thereby avoiding duplication of information that has already been included in the reporting of the output of another program.

It is suggested that you run the examples being discussed on programs available to you, and that you study their output along with the ones reported in the book. Doing this will facilitate identification and understanding of information provided by the programs to which you have access or ones you prefer to use. Discussions of the output include references to formulas or calculations presented in the chapter in order to enhance your understanding of the analytic methods as well as the computer output. When necessary, it is shown how some parts of the output may be used in order to obtain results that are not reported.

Before the programs are presented, some general remarks about the use of package programs seem advisable. Package programs have to be approached with care and circumspection. You must know what the program can and cannot do and be alert to possible mishaps. Computer programs can, and sometimes do, have incorrect procedures. Hence in order to avoid, or minimize, errors you must know what you are doing, and you must test each program before you use it for the analysis of "real" data. Knowledge of what you are doing will enable you to detect results that do not make sense, thereby indicating the need to investigate what went wrong. More often than not, the fault is not with the computer program but with the person using it. It is possible, for example, that the data were read in with the wrong format, or that some of the variables read in were not those relevant to the analysis, or that inappropriate options were called for in the analysis. Be always alert to the GIGO principle: Garbage In, Garbage Out.

Yet, as was noted above, there may be something wrong with the program you are using. The simplest way to test a program is to use it with a "model" problem for which the complete solution is available. You will probably find an appropriate "model" problem in various textbooks. When necessary, calculate a small example by hand and by the computer program so that you may determine whether you are getting what you are supposed to be getting, or to discern what it is that you are getting. Another useful approach to the testing of programs, as well as to becoming familiar with their output and unique features, is to run the "model" problem with several programs and compare the results. Doing this may enable you, for example, to determine that two programs provide the same piece of information but that each labels it somewhat differently.

Computer programs are frequently revised and updated. The specific version of each program being used in this book is indicated when the program is first introduced. It is almost certain that by the time this book is published a new version will be available for one or more of them. Fortunately, the basic approach used in each of the packages does not change from one revision to another. Usually, revisions involve additional options or additional programs. Consequently, the general guides given here will probably be applicable for subsequent revisions of the packages used. It is, however, suggested that you check the documentation of the specific version you are using in order to make sure that you are using it correctly and to the best advantage.

We turn now to the separate programs. Inasmuch as the job control cards may vary from one institution to another, they are not given here. The concern is only with the control cards internal to the program, not with the procedures to access a specific program at a specific computing center.

SPSS

SPSS (Hull & Nie, 1979; Nie, Hull, Jenkins, Steinbrenner, & Bent, 1975) is a versatile set of interrelated programs that affords great flexibility in data manipulation, data editing, and data analysis. The programs are very easy to use because the control cards and the general layout for reading in the data—calling for the different procedures, options, and so on—are uniform. The manual presents detailed explanations and examples. In addition, clear introductions to each procedure are also given.

There are different versions of SPSS for different computers. Although most of the options and the output are identical in all the versions, there are some differences from one version to another both in type of output given and in the specific layout and labeling of the output. The following two versions are used here: IBM OS/360, VERSION H, RELEASE 8.0, 1979; and CDC VERSION 8.0, 1979. When necessary, it is indicated, usually by enclosing IBM or CDC in parentheses, from which of these two versions the output was obtained.

Following is a listing of the control cards used to analyze the data of Table 3.1, which were also used earlier in this chapter to illustrate the application of matrix algebra in multiple regression analysis.

Control Cards

```
1                   1
                    6
RUN NAME            ANALYSIS OF DATA FROM TABLE 3.1
VARIABLE LIST       Y, X1, X2
N OF CASES          20
INPUT FORMAT        FIXED (3F2.0)
LIST CASES          CASES = 20/ VARIABLES = Y TO X2/
REGRESSION          VARIABLES = Y TO X2/
                    REGRESSION = Y WITH X1(4) X2(2)/
                    REGRESSION = Y WITH X1(2) X2(4)/
STATISTICS          ALL
```

```
READ INPUT DATA
 2 2 4
 1 2 4
 . . .
 . . .
 . . .
10 4 7
```

Commentary

LIST CASES. This procedure card enables you to list your input. When working with a small data set it is always advisable to list the data. This will enable you to detect whether you have made some punching error, or whether you have made an error in your variable format statement. Listing the data is particularly useful when one does data manipulations prior to the analysis. In later chapters, for example, columns are multiplied or variables are raised to powers. Listing the data after such operations affords one the opportunity to note whether the appropriate manipulations were executed. With large data sets, you may wish to call for a listing of, say, the first 10 or 20 subjects.

REGRESSION = Y WITH X1(4) X2(2)/ Note that a regression analysis in two stages is called for. This is done in order to acquaint you with some of the features of this command, which is used frequently in subsequent chapters. In the present case, X1 will be entered first (it has the higher inclusion level), followed by X2. A second REGRESSION statement, in which the order of entry of the variables is reversed, is also included. Therefore, two regression analyses will be done for the same data.

Following is a partial listing of the output with accompanying commentaries. Even though some of the output is reported to a relatively large numer of decimal places, results are rounded to five places, or even less, whenever feasible.

Output

```
VARIABLES(S) ENTERED ON STEP 1 . . X1
R SQUARE  .45360          STANDARD ERROR  2.2380
                     ANALYSIS OF VARIANCE
REGRESSION    DF   SUM OF SQUARES   MEAN SQUARE      F
               1      74.84439        74.84439    14.94
RESIDUAL      18      90.15561         5.00865

- - - - - - - - - - - -VARIABLES IN EQUATION- - - - - - - - - - - -
VARIABLE          B      BETA   STD ERROR B     F
X1            .74472   .67350      .19265     14.94
(CONSTANT)   1.81364
```

Commentary

The first step in this analysis is, of course, the simple linear regression of Y on X_1. Therefore, $R = r$, and $R^2 = r^2$.

STANDARD ERROR (IBM), STD DEVIATION (CDC) is what was labeled earlier the standard error of estimate, $s_{y.x}$; see Formula (2.27).

MEAN SQUARE RESIDUAL is what was also called earlier the variance of estimate, $s^2_{y.x}$; see Formula (2.26). It is obtained by dividing the ss_{res} by its degrees of freedom. Of course, $\sqrt{5.00865} = 2.23800$, the standard error of estimate.

The F ratio is a test of the R^2, or the regression sum of squares. As this is a simple linear regression, it is also the test of the b (note that the same F ratio is reported in both places). When you want the t ratio for a given b, take $\sqrt{F}$ that corresponds to it. In the present case: $\sqrt{14.94} = 3.87 = t$.

CONSTANT is the intercept a, B is the unstandardized coefficient, and BETA is the standardized coefficient. STANDARD ERROR B is for the unstandardized regression coefficient. $F = b^2/s_b^2$. For this example, $74472^2/.19265^2 = 14.94$.

The total sum of squares (Σy^2) may be obtained by adding ss_{reg} and ss_{res}. In the present example, $74.84439 + 90.15561 = 165$.

Output

VARIABLE(S) ENTERED ON STEP 2 . . X2

R SQUARE .50540 STANDARD ERROR 2.19101

ANALYSIS OF VARIANCE

REGRESSION	DF	SUM OF SQUARES	MEAN SQUARE	F
	2	83.39090	41.69545	8.69
RESIDUAL	17	81.60910	4.80054	

- - - - - - - - - - - - - -VARIABLES IN EQUATION- - - - - - - - - - - - - -

VARIABLE	B	BETA	STANDARD ERROR B	F
X1	.67708	.61233	.19530	12.02
X2	.39344	.23567	.29487	1.78
(CONSTANT)	.10255			

Commentary

At this step variable X_2 is added to the equation. $R^2 = .50540$ is the squared multiple correlation of Y with X_1 and X_2. Consequently, if you wish to determine the increment in the proportion of variance due to X_2, subtract R^2 obtained in the preceding step (step 1) from R^2 obtained at this step: $.50540 - .45360 = .0518$ (compare with the analysis done earlier in the chapter).

Similarly, the regression sum of squares, 83.39090, is due to X_1 and X_2. Therefore, the regression sum of squares incremented by X_2: $83.39090 - 74.84439 = 8.54651$ (compare with the analysis done earlier in the chapter).

MEAN SQUARE RESIDUAL is 4.80054 with 17 *df*. Therefore, the F for the increment due to X_2 is:

$$F = \frac{8.54651}{4.80054} = \mathit{1.78}\ (1, 17)$$

which is, of course, the same value obtained when testing the b for X_2. Recall that the test of a b is the same as testing the proportion of variance, or sum of squares, incremented by the variable with which it is associated (see discussion of this point in (Chapter 3).

Output

SUMMARY TABLE

VARIABLE	MULTIPLE R	R SQUARE	RSQ CHANGE	SIMPLE R
X1	.67350	.45360	.45360	.67350
X2	.71091	.50540	.05180	.39460

Commentary

The SUMMARY TABLE is very useful. It is discussed in greater detail in subsequent chapters (see, for example, Chapter 6). At this stage, only some of the terms are commented upon. MULTIPLE R and R SQUARE are the multiple correlation coefficient and its square, respectively, at each step. SIMPLE R is the simple correlation coefficient of each variable with the dependent variable. Since on the first line only X_1 was entered, the SIMPLE R is equal to the MULTIPLE R, and R SQUARE is the square of this R, or r^2 ($.67350^2 = .45360$). On the second line the MULTIPLE R and the R SQUARE are for *both* X_1 and X_2. The RSQ CHANGE is what was referred to earlier as the increment in the proportion of variance accounted for by a given variable. When X_1 is entered into the equation, no other variable has yet been entered. Consequently, RSQ CHANGE is the same as R SQUARE on the same line (the line for X_1). But when X_2 is entered, RSQ CHANGE indicates the proportion of variance it increments: .05180. It is the difference between the two R SQUARES in the preceding column: $.50540 - .45360 = .0518$. The SIMPLE R for X_2 is .39460. While the increment in the proportion of variance accounted for by X_2 is .0518, it could, by itself, account for .1557 proportion of the variance ($.39460^2$).

Note that when one wishes to determine the proportion of variance incremented by X_1, it is necessary to run a regression analysis in which X_2 is entered first (i.e., assigned a higher inclusion level). Such an analysis was called for in the second REGRESSION card (see above). In order to conserve space, the output of the second analysis is not reported here. It is suggested, however, that you run both regressions, study the results, and compare them with the results and the discussion given earlier in this chapter.

Finally, it will be pointed out that when the interest is only in the overall regression analysis, and not in an incremental analysis, all the variables may be assigned the same level of entry. Alternatively, no level of entry need be assigned when the overall regression analysis is being sought. By default, the program assigns the same level of entry to all the variables.

Output (CDC only)

COEFFICIENTS AND CONFIDENCE INTERVALS

VARIABLE	B	STD ERROR B	T	95.0 PCT CONFIDENCE INTERVAL
X1	.67708	.19530	3.47	.26503 , 1.08913
X2	.39344	.29487	1.33	−.22868 , 1.01556

Commentary

In Chapter 2 the advantages of using t ratios, instead of F's, for tests of the b's were discussed. Among other things, it was pointed out that the t ratio may be used to set confidence intervals for each of the b's. The above output reports just that. The B's and the STD ERROR B's are, of course, the same as those reported earlier. T is the t ratio, each of which is equal to the square root of the F reported above for each of the b's. Thus the F for b_1 was reported above as 12.02. ($\sqrt{12.02} = 3.47$.) Note that the confidence interval for b_2 includes zero, since it ranges from $-.22868$ to 1.01556. Consequently, b_2 is not significantly different from zero (at the .05 level). This, of course, can also be discerned from the $t = 1.33$ (17), $p > .05$. But a confidence interval provides important information that is not available from the t ratio only. Assume, for example, that the confidence interval for b_1, which is statistically significant, was .57708–.77708, or .07708–1.27708, and the value of calculating confidence intervals for b's becomes obvious.

Output (CDC Only)

VARIANCE/COVARIANCE OF THE
UNNORMALIZED REGRESSION COEFFICIENTS

X1	.03814	
X2	−.01495	.08695
	X1	X2

Commentary

This is what was called earlier the covariance matrix of the b's, **C**. The diagonal elements of this matrix are the variances of the b's, or the squares of the standard errors of the b's reported above. The off-diagonal element is the covariance of b_1 and b_2. See the discussion of **C** and its use earlier in this chapter. As was pointed out in that discussion, this matrix is used extensively in some of the subsequent chapters.

BMDP1R

BMDP (Dixon & Brown, 1979) is a package of computer programs for a great variety of analytic techniques. The manual describes each program in detail, along with sample analyses and comments. In addition, the formulas for the analytic techniques used in each program are given. The 1979 version is used here. The specific program used for the analysis of the present example is BMDP1R. Following is a listing of the control cards for the problem analyzed above by SPSS.

Control Cards

```
/PROBLEM TITLE IS 'TABLE 3.1'.
/INPUT VARIABLES ARE 3 FORMAT IS '(3F2.0)'.
```

```
/VARIABLE NAMES ARE Y, X1, X2.
/REGRESS DEPENDENT IS Y. INDEPENDENT ARE X1, X2.
/PRINT CORRELATION. COVARIANCE. RREG.
/END
 2 2 4
 1 2 4
 . . .
 . . .
 . . .
10 4 7
```

Output and Comments

Following is a partial listing of the output with accompanying comments.

Output

R-SQUARE .5054 STD. ERROR OF EST. 2.1910

ANALYSIS OF VARIANCE

	SUM OF SQUARES	DF	MEAN SQUARE	F RATIO
REGRESSION	83.391	2	41.696	8.686
RESIDUAL	81.609	17	4.801	

VARIABLE	COEFFICIENT	ST. ERROR	STD. REG COEFF	T	P (2 TAIL)
INTERCEPT	.10255				
X1	.67708	.195	.612	3.467	.003
X2	.39344	.295	.236	1.334	.200

Commentary

You should encounter no difficulties in interpreting the above output, particularly if you compare it with the output from SPSS (STEP 2), as well as with the calculations presented earlier in this chapter. Consequently, only some brief comments are made.

$\Sigma y^2 = ss_{\text{reg}} + ss_{\text{res}} = 83.391 + 81.609 = 165$
COEFFICIENT = unstandardized regression coefficient, b.
ST. REG COEFF = standardized regression coefficient.

The program reports t ratios for each of the b's. Squaring the t's yields F ratios, which are the same as the F's reported in the SPSS output. The program also reports the two-tail probabilities for each of the t ratios.

Output

CORRELATION MATRIX OF REGRESSION COEFFICIENTS

	X1	X2
X1	1.0000	
X2	−.2596	1.0000

Commentary

The above matrix is obtained by calling for RREG in the PRINT card (see above). From this matrix one can easily obtain the covariance matrix of the b's, **C**. To obtain **C**, replace each diagonal element in the above matrix by the square of the standard error of the b associated with it. The standard errors are reported in the output above: .195 for b_1, and .295 for b_2. For each of the off-diagonal elements, multiply the correlation reported in the above matrix by the standard errors of the b's corresponding to it. In other words, for the element 21 multiply the reported correlation by the standard errors of b_1 and b_2. Following is the **C** matrix obtained by carrying out the operations indicated above.

$$\mathbf{C} = \begin{bmatrix} .195^2 & \\ (-.2596)(.195)(.295) & .295^2 \end{bmatrix} = \begin{bmatrix} .0380 & \\ -.0149 & .0870 \end{bmatrix}$$

Compare with the SPSS output and with the calculations reported earlier in this chapter.

SAS

SAS (Helwig & Council, 1979) is a computer package with a variety of programs, as well as procedures for matrix manipulations. A useful feature of SAS is that while using it one may call for the execution of programs from SPSS and BMD. The *User's Guide* and the *Supplemental Library User's Guide* describe the programs and provide some sample runs. RELEASE 79 is used here. The procedure used is GLM (General Linear Model). Following is a listing of the control cards for the problem analyzed above by SPSS and BMDP1R.

Control Cards

```
DATA; INPUT Y 1-2 X1 3-4 X2 5-6; CARDS;
 2 2 4
 1 2 4
 . . .
 . . .
 . . .
10 4 7
PROC PRINT;
PROC GLM; MODEL Y = X1 X2/XPX I;
TITLE TABLE 3.1
```

Commentary

PROC PRINT is the procedure card used to list the data or parts of the data. PROC GLM calls for the execution of the General Linear Model procedure. MODEL Y = X1 X2 designates Y as the dependent variable, and X_1, X_2 as the independent variables.

XPX calls for the reporting of **X′X.**
I calls for the inverse of **X′X, (X′X)**$^{-1}$ (see Commentaries below).

Following is a partial listing of output generated by the GLM procedure, along with commentaries.

Output

THE X′X MATRIX

	INTERCEPT	X1	X2
INTERCEPT	20.00	99.00	104.00
X1	99.00	625.00	538.00
X2	104.00	538.00	600.00

Commentary

The above matrix is obtained by calling for XPX in the PROC GLM card (see above). **X** is the matrix of raw scores for N subjects on k independent variables plus a unit vector. **X′** is the transpose of **X.** The first element of the principal diagonal is equal to N (i.e., 20). The other diagonal elements are raw score sums of squares for independent variables, the X's. Thus $\Sigma X_1^2 = 625$; $\Sigma X_2^2 = 600$ (see Table 3.1 for the calculations of these values). The off-diagonal elements of the first row and first column (i.e., those labeled INTERCEPT) are the sums of the raw scores for the X's. Thus $\Sigma X_1 = 99$; $\Sigma X_2 = 104$ (see Table 3.1). The other off-diagonal elements are raw scores sums of products of the X's. In the present example, there is only one sum of cross products: $\Sigma X_1 X_2 = 538$ (see calculations related to Table 3.1).

Output

X′X INVERSE MATRIX

	INTERCEPT	X1	X2
INTERCEPT	.574140	−.023138	−.078770
X1	−.023138	.007945	−.003114
X2	−.078770	−.003114	.018112

Commentary

The above matrix **(X′X)**$^{-1}$, introduced in Formula (4.3), is obtained by calling for **I** in the PROC GLM card (see above). Recall that **(X′X)**$^{-1}$ is used for the calculation of the intercept and the b's. It was used earlier in this chapter in the analysis of data with only one independent variable. In the analysis of the example with two independent variables, **(x′x)**$^{-1}$, the inverse of the deviation sum of squares and cross products, was used instead. Note, however, that the part of **(X′X)**$^{-1}$ that corresponds to the X's (i.e., excluding the elements in the raw and column labeled INTERCEPT) is the same as the inverse of **(x′x)** that was obtained by hand calculations. This is always the case. Therefore, when you wish to obtain **(x′x)**$^{-1}$, all you have to do is take the elements of **(X′X)**$^{-1}$ excluding the row and column labeled INTERCEPT.

Earlier in this chapter, some applications using elements of **(x′x)**$^{-1}$ were shown. For example, it was shown that one can calculate the regression sum of squares incremented by a variable by squaring the b associated with it and dividing by the diagonal element of $(\mathbf{x}'\mathbf{x})^{-1}$ for that variable (i.e., b^2/x^{jj}; see Formula (4.13)). To calculate the regression sum of squares incremented by X_1, divide $b_1^2 = .67708^2$ (reported later in the output) by $x^{11} = .007945$. Hence,

$$ss_{\text{reg}(1)} = \frac{.67708^2}{.007945} = 57.701$$

and

$$ss_{\text{reg}(2)} = \frac{.39344^2}{.018112} = 8.547$$

Compare with the calculations done when Formula (4.13) was introduced, as well as with calculations done earlier in this chapter. SAS does not report the covariance matrix of the b's, **C**. But it is very simple to obtain it from the output that SAS does report. Earlier in this chapter, **C** was defined as follows (see Formula 4.11):

$$\mathbf{C} = \frac{\mathbf{e}'\mathbf{e}}{N - k - 1}(\mathbf{x}'\mathbf{x})^{-1} = s^2_{y.12...k}\,(\mathbf{x}'\mathbf{x})^{-1}$$

where $s^2_{y.12...k}$ is the variance of estimate, or the square of the standard error of estimate. To obtain **C** from SAS output, multiply $s^2_{y.12...k}$ by that part of $(\mathbf{X}'\mathbf{X})^{-1}$ that is associated with the X's. In other words, exclude the row and column labeled INTERCEPT. The $s^2_{y.12...k}$ is the MEAN SQUARE ERROR reported later in the output. For our example, $s^2_{y.12...k} = 4.8005$. Multiplying this value by the appropriate elements from $(\mathbf{X}'\mathbf{X})^{-1}$ reported above, we obtain

$$\mathbf{C} = 4.8005\begin{bmatrix} .007945 & -.003114 \\ -.003114 & .018112 \end{bmatrix} = \begin{bmatrix} .03814 & -.01495 \\ -.01495 & .08695 \end{bmatrix}$$

Compare with the output we have obtained from SPSS, as well as with the calculations of **C** done earlier in this chapter.

The rest of the SAS output is the same as that of SPSS and BMD, although the layout and some of the labels used are different. You should encounter no difficulty in reading it. When necessary, compare with the SPSS and BMD outputs, or with the calculations done earlier in this chapter.

Finally, it will be noted that another SAS program, SYSREG, includes an option (COVB) for the printing of the covariance matrix of the b's, **C**.

SUMMARY

Matrix algebra for the calculation of multiple regression statistics was introduced and illustrated in the first part of this chapter. This was done with data expressed in raw scores, sums of squares, and correlation coefficients. Small numerical examples were used despite the fact that such examples cannot begin to convey the generality, power, and elegance of the matrix approach. The reason for using small numerical examples was to enable you to concentrate on the understanding of the properties of the matrices used and on the matrix operations. Since the matrix equations are the same regardless of the number of variables used, what is important is to grasp the meaning of the equations and the matrix operations indicated in them. For example, Equation (4.3) for the solution of the b's, $\mathbf{b} = (\mathbf{X}'\mathbf{X})^{-1}\mathbf{X}'\mathbf{Y}$, could refer to one, two, three, or any number of independent variables. Therefore, to repeat, what is important is to understand the meaning of this equation, the properties of its elements, and the matrix operations that are called for. In any case, with large data sets the calculations are best done by computers.

It would not be surprising if at this stage you do not appreciate, or are unimpressed by, some of the ideas presented regarding the properties of the matrices used in multiple regression analysis. Rest assured, however, that these are elaborated upon and used extensively in subsequent chapters. For example, at this stage you cannot see the virtue of using the variance/covariance of the b's (**C**) for the purpose of testing differences among b's. But in Chapter 9 it is shown how this approach can be used efficiently for testing multiple comparisons among means, and in Chapter 13 it is shown how this approach is used to test multiple comparisons among adjusted means in the analysis of covariance. Similarly, important properties of the inverse of the correlation matrix of the independent variables, $\mathbf{R}^{-1}$, introduced in this chapter, are used extensively in subsequent chapters (see, for example, Chapters 7 and 8) to enhance the understanding of elements of multiple regression analysis or to facilitate the calculation of such elements. In short, appreciation of the full force of the matrix approach will have to await until additional topics in multiple regression analysis are introduced. When this is done, you are urged to go back to this chapter whenever you experience difficulties in understanding the matrix operations used.

In the second part of this chapter, three computer programs from three popular packages—SPSS, BMD, and SAS—were introduced. These programs are used extensively in subsequent chapters. It is suggested that you refer to the presentation in this chapter whenever you encounter difficulties in using these programs.

STUDY SUGGESTIONS

1. The following correlation matrices, **A** and **B**, were used in Study Suggestion 2 of Chapter 3. This time do the calculations indicated below using matrix algebra. Compare the results with those obtained in Chapter 3.

A

	X_1	X_2	Y
X_1	1.0	0	.7
X_2	0	1.0	.6
Y	.7	.6	1.0

B

	X_1	X_2	Y
X_1	1.0	.4	.7
X_2	.4	1.0	.6
Y	.7	.6	1.0

(a) Calculate the inverse of the correlation matrix of the independent variables, X_1 and X_2, for **A** and for **B**.

(b) Multiply each of the inverses obtained in (a) by the column of the zero-order correlations of the X's with Y. What is the meaning of the resulting values?

(c) Multiply each row of β's obtained in (b) by the column of the zero-order correlations of the X's with Y. What is the meaning of the resulting values?

2. The following summary statistics were taken from Study Suggestion 1 of Chapter 3. They are presented in the format used in Table 3.2. That is, the diagonal elements are sums of squares; the off-diagonal elements, above the diagonal, are sums of cross products; the off-diagonal elements, below the diagonal, are zero-order correlations. The last line contains the standard deviations.

	y	x_1	x_2
y	165.00	100.50	63.00
x_1	.6735	134.95	15.50
x_2	.5320	.1447	85.00
s	2.9469	2.6651	2.1151

Use matrix algebra to do the calculations indicated below, and compare the results with those obtained in Chapter 3.

(a) Calculate the inverse of the matrix of the sums of squares and cross products of the X's: $(\mathbf{x'x})^{-1}$.

(b) Calculate $(\mathbf{x'x})^{-1}\,\mathbf{x'y}$, where $\mathbf{x'y}$ is a column of the cross products of the X's with Y. What is the meaning of the resulting values?

(c) Using the b's obtained above, and the standard deviations of the variables, calculate the standardized regression coefficients (β's).

(d) Calculate $\mathbf{b'x'y}$, where $\mathbf{b'}$ is a row vector of the b's obtained above. What is the meaning of the obtained result?

(e) Calculate the residual sum of squares, and $s^2_{y.12}$.

(f) Calculate $s^2_{y.12}\,(\mathbf{x'x})^{-1}$. What is the resulting matrix?

(g) Using relevant values from the matrix obtained in (f), calculate the t ratios for the b's.

(h) Using the b's and relevant values from $(\mathbf{x'x})^{-1}$ calculate: (1) the increment in the regression sum of squares due to X_1, over and above X_2; and (2) the increment in the regression sum of squares due to X_2, over and above X_1.

(i) Calculate $R^2_{y.12}$ and the F ratio for the test of this R^2. ($N = 20$.)

3. Following are summary data from a study based on a sample of 200 people.

	R		
	X_1	X_2	Y
X_1	1.0	.4	.5
X_2	.4	1.0	.6
Y	.5	.6	1.0
M:	50.0	80.0	100.0
s:	8.50	10.25	12.75

R = correlation matrix; M = means; s = standard deviations.

Use a computer program that enables you to read in means, standard deviation, and a correlation matrix (e.g., SPSS). Read in the summary data given above, and do a multiple regression analysis of Y on X_1 and X_2.

In addition, determine: (a) the proportion of variance and regression sum of squares incremented by X_2, over and above X_1; (b) the F ratio for the test of this increment; (c) the proportion of variance and regression sum of squares incremented by X_1, over and above X_2; (d) the F ratio for the test of this increment. What tests of significance in the overall analysis are equivalent to the tests in (b) and (d)?

ANSWERS

1. (a) $\underset{\mathbf{A}}{\begin{bmatrix} 1.0 & 0 \\ 0 & 1.0 \end{bmatrix}}$ $\underset{\mathbf{B}}{\begin{bmatrix} 1.19048 & -.47619 \\ -.47619 & 1.19048 \end{bmatrix}}$

   (b) **A:** [.7 .6]; **B:** [.54762 .38096]. These are the standardized regression coefficients, β's, for each of the matrices. Note that the β's for **A** are equal to the zero-order correlations of the X's with Y. Why?

   (c) **A:** .85; **B:** 61. These are the R^2's of Y with X_1 and X_2 in **A** and **B**, respectively.

2. (a) $(\mathbf{x}'\mathbf{x})^{-1} = \begin{bmatrix} .00757 & -.00138 \\ -.00138 & .01202 \end{bmatrix}$

   (b) [.67384 .61857]. These are the unstandardized regression coefficients: b's.

   (c) $\beta_1 = .60940$; $\beta_2 = .44397$

   (d) $106.69083 = ss_{\text{reg}}$

   (e) $ss_{\text{res}} = 58.30917$; $s^2_{y.12} = 3.42995$

   (f) $\begin{bmatrix} .02596 & -.00473 \\ -.00473 & .04123 \end{bmatrix}$

   This is the variance/covariance matrix of the b's: **C.**

   (g) t for $b_1 = 4.18$, with 17 *df*; t for $b_2 = 3.05$, with 17 *df*

   (h) (1) 59.98156; (2) 31.83268

   (i) $R^2_{y.12} = .6466$; $F = 15.55$, with 2 and 17 *df*

3. Excerpts of output from SPSS (REGRESSION):

DEPENDENT VARIABLE Y   R SQUARE .44048

ANALYSIS OF VARIANCE

	DF	SUM OF SQUARES	MEAN SQUARE	F
REGRESSION	2	14249.37723	7124.68862	77.54
RESIDUAL	197	18100.56027	91.88102	

- - - - - - - - - - - - - - - - - -VARIABLES IN THE EQUATION- - - - - - - - - - - - - - - - - -

VARIABLE	B	BETA	STD ERROR B	F
X1	.46429	.30952	.08722	28.33
X2	.59233	.47619	.07233	67.06
(CONSTANT)	29.39895			

(a) .19048 and 6161.89285; (b) 67.06, with 1 and 197 *df;* (c) .08048 and 2603.39973; (d) 28.33, with 1 and 197 *df*. The tests in (b) and (d) are equivalent to the tests of significance of b_2 and b_1, respectively.

5

STATISTICAL CONTROL: PARTIAL AND SEMIPARTIAL CORRELATION

Preceding chapters have been aimed at helping you understand the basic principles of multiple regression analysis. Some complex issues of analyses, applications, and interpretations were not discussed in order to avoid overwhelming you. Before turning to these issues, however, it will be instructive to discuss partial and semipartial correlations, both because these are meaningful techniques in their own right and because they are integral parts of multiple regression analysis. Understanding these techniques is therefore bound to lead to a better understanding of multiple regression analysis.

STATISTICAL CONTROL OF VARIABLES

Studying the relations among variables is not easy. The most severe problem is expressed in the question: Is this relation I am studying really the relation I think it is? This can be called the problem of the validity of relations. Science is basically preoccupied with formulating and verifying statements of the form, if *p*, then *q*—if dogmatism, then ethnocentrism, for example. The problem of validity of relations boils down essentially to the question of whether it is *this p* that is related to *q*, or, in other words, whether the discovered relation between *this* independent variable and the dependent variable is truly the relation we think it is. In order to have some confidence in the validity of any particular if *p*, then *q* statement, we have to have some confidence that it is really *p* that is related to *q* and not *r* or *s* or *t*. To attain such confidence scientists invoke techniques of control.

Reflecting the complexity and difficulty of studying relations, control is itself a complex subject. Although fundamentally important, it cannot be discussed in detail.[1] Nevertheless, the technical analytic notions to be discussed in this chapter are best understood if they are approached as part of the subject of control. Therefore it is necessary to discuss control, to some extent at least.

In scientific research, control means control of variance. There are a number of ways to control variance. The best known is to set up an experiment, whose most elementary form is an experimental group and a so-called control group. The scientist tries to increase the difference, the variance, between the two groups by experimental manipulation. To set up a research design is itself a form of control. One designs a study, in part, to maximize systematic variance, minimize error variance, and control extraneous variance. Another well-known form of variance control is matching subjects. One also controls variance by subject selection. If one wants to control the variable sex, for example, one can select as subjects only males or only females. This of course reduces sex variability to zero.

Potentially the most powerful form of control in research is to assign subjects randomly to experimental groups. Other things being equal, if random assignment has been used, one can assume that one's groups are equal in all possible characteristics. In a word, all variables except the one that forms the basis for the groups—different methods of changing attitudes, say—are controlled. Control here means that the variations among the subjects due to anything that makes them different are scattered, by definition at random, throughout the several groups. Unfortunately, in much behavioral research random assignment is not possible because such research is nonexperimental in nature. Nonexperimental research is that research in which the independent variable or variables have already "occurred," so to speak, and the investigator cannot control them directly by manipulation. The independent variables are beyond the manipulative control of the researcher.

Testing alternative hypotheses to the hypothesis under study is a form of control, although different in kind from those discussed above and below. The point of this whole discussion is that different forms of control are similar in function. They are different expressions of the one principle: control is control of variance. And so it is with the statistical form of control to be discussed in this chapter. Statistical control means that one uses statistical methods to identify, isolate, or nullify variance in a dependent variable that is presumably "caused" by one or more independent variables that are extraneous to the particular relation or relations under study. Statistical control is particularly important when one is interested in the joint or mutual effects of more than one independent variable on a dependent variable because one has to be able to sort out and control the effects of some variables while studying the effects of other variables. Multiple regression and related forms of analysis provide ways to achieve such control.

Some Examples

In his preface to *The Doctor's Dilemma,* Shaw (1963) offers some interesting examples of the pitfalls in interpreting relations among variables as being "real" because other relevant variables were not controlled.

[1]For detailed discussions, see Kerlinger (1969; 1973, pp. 306–311, 380–381). See also Kish (1975).

> . . . comparisons which are really comparisons between two social classes with different standards of nutrition and education are palmed off as comparisons between the results of a certain medical treatment and its neglect. Thus it is easy to prove that the wearing of tall hats and the carrying of umbrellas enlarges the chest, prolongs life and confers comparative immunity from disease; for the statistics shew that the classes which use these articles are bigger, healthier, and live longer than the class which never dreams of possessing such things. It does not take much perspicacity to see that what really makes this difference is not the tall hat and the umbrella, but the wealth and nourishment of which they are evidence, and that a gold watch or membership of a club in Pall Mall might be proved in the same way to have the like sovereign virtues. A university degree, a daily bath, the owning of thirty pairs of trousers, a knowledge of Wagner's music, a pew in the church, anything, in short, that implies more means and better nurture than the mass of laborers enjoy, can be statistically palmed off as a magic-spell conferring all sort of privileges. (pp. 53–54)

The examples provided by Shaw illustrate what are referred to as spurious correlations. When two variables are correlated solely because they are both affected by the same cause, the correlation is referred to as being spurious. Once the effects of the common cause are controlled, or removed from the two variables, the correlation between them vanishes. A spurious correlation between variables Z and Y is depicted in Figure 5.1. Removing the effects of the common cause, X, from both Z and Y will result in a zero correlation between them. As is shown below, this can be accomplished by the calculation of the partial correlation between Z and Y, when X is partialed out.

Here is another example of what is probably a spurious correlation. On July 19, 1971, the *New York Post* reported a story under the heading: "Prof Fired after Finding Sex Great for Scholars." According to the report: "Active sex contributes to academic success, says a sociologist who conducted a survey of undergraduates at the University of Puerto Rico." Basically, Dr. Martin Sagrera found a positive correlation between reported frequency of sexual intercourse and Grade-Point Average (GPA). The finding was taken seriously not only by the university's administration, who fired Sagrera, but also by Sagrera himself, who is quoted as saying: "These findings appear to contradict the Freudian view that sublimation of sex is a powerful factor in intellectual achievement." Problems of research based on self-reports notwithstanding, it requires little imagination to formulate hypotheses about the factor, or factors, that might be responsible for the observed correlation between the frequency of sexual intercourse and GPA.

An example of what some medical researchers believe is a spurious correla-

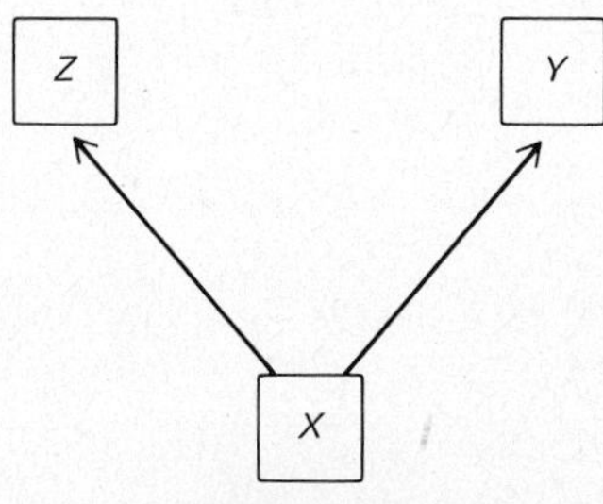

Figure 5.1

tion was reported in the *New York Times,* October 29, 1973, under the heading: "New Heart Study Absolves Coffee." The researchers are reported to challenge the view held by other medical researchers that there is a causal relation between the consumption of coffee and heart attacks. While they do not deny that the two variables are correlated, they claim that the correlation is spurious. "Rather than coffee drinking itself, other traits associated with coffee drinking habits—such as personality, national origin, occupation and climate of residence—may be the real heart-disease risk factors, the California researchers suggested."

A variable which, when left uncontrolled in behavioral research, often leads to spurious correlations is chronological age. Taking a group of children varying in age, say from 4 to 15, it is possible to show, for example, that there is a very high correlation between the size of the right-hand palm and mental ability, or between shoe size and intelligence. In short, there is bound to be a high correlation between any two variables that are affected by age, when the latter is not controlled for. Age may be controlled for by using a sample of children of the same age. Alternatively, age may be controlled statistically by calculating the partial correlation coefficient between two variables, with age being partialed out. Terman (1926, p. 168), for example, reports correlations of .835 and .876 between mental age and standing height for groups of heterogeneous boys and girls, respectively. After partialing out age, these correlations dropped to .219 and .211 for boys and girls, respectively. It is conceivable that controlling for an additional variable, or variables, will result in reducing the correlation between intelligence and height to zero. The assumptions that need to be met when one exercises such statistical controls are discussed below. At this stage, the aim is only to introduce the meaning of statistical control.

The examples presented thus far illustrated the potential use of partial correlations for the purpose of detecting spurious correlations. Another use of partial correlations is in the study of the effects of a variable as it is mediated by another variable. Assume, for example, that it is hypothesized that Socioeconomic Status (SES) does not affect Achievement (ACH) directly but only indirectly through the mediation of Achievement Motivation (AM). In other words, it is hypothesized that SES affects AM, which in turn affects ACH. This hypothesis, which is depicted in Figure 5.2, may be tested by calculating the correlation between SES and ACH while controlling for, or partialing out, AM. A zero, or close to zero partial correlation between SES and ACH would lend support to this hypothesis. Carroll (1975), for example, reports that: "Student socioeconomic background tended *not* to be associated with performance when other variables, such as student interest, etc., were controlled" (p. 29). Such a statement should, of course, not be construed that socioeconomic background is not an important variable, but that its effects on performances may be mediated by other variables, such as student interest.

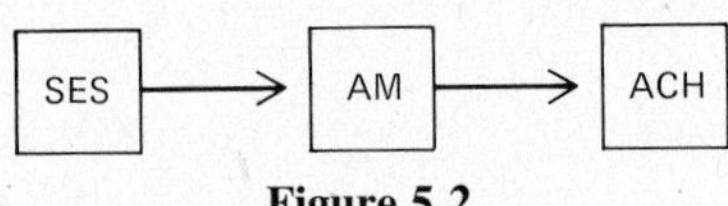

Figure 5.2

THE NATURE OF CONTROL BY PARTIALING

The formulas for calculating partial correlation coefficients are comparatively simple. What they accomplish, however, is not so simple. To help achieve the understanding of what is being accomplished, a detailed analysis of what is behind the statistical operations is presented. You are encouraged to work through the calculations and the reasoning presented.

The symbol for expressing the correlation between two variables with a third variable partialed out is $r_{12.3}$, which means the correlation between variables 1 and 2, partialing out variable 3. Similarly, $r_{xy.z}$ is the partial correlation between X and Y when Z is controlled or partialed out. Basically, the idea of a partial correlation is that it is a correlation between two variables after removing from them the effects, or the linear relations, of another variable (or variables). Stated differently, a partial correlation is an estimate of the correlation between two variables in a population that is homogeneous on the variable (or variables) that is being controlled for, or whose effect is being removed. Assume, for example, that we are interested in the correlation between height and intelligence and that the sample consists of a heterogeneous group of children ranging in age from 4 to 10. In order to control for age, we can calculate the correlation between height and intelligence within each age group. That is, we can calculate the correlation among children of age 4, 5, 6, and so on. Or we could, instead, accomplish the same thing by calculating the partial correlation between height and intelligence, when age is partialed out. The partial correlation thus calculated will be equal to a weighted average of the correlations between the two variables when calculated within each age group in the range of ages under consideration. In order to see how this is accomplished we turn to a discussion of some elements of regression analysis.

Partial Correlation and Regression Analysis

Suppose that we have data on three variables, X_1, X_2, and X_3 as reported in Table 5.1. Using the methods presented in Chapter 2 we calculate the regression equation for predicting X_1 from X_3, which is:[2]

$$X'_1 = 1.2 + .6X_3$$

Similarly, we calculate the regression equation for predicting X_2 from X_3:

$$X'_2 = .3 + .9X_3$$

Having calculated the two regression equations, we calculate for each subject predicted values for X_1 and X_2 as well as the residuals for each variable; that is, $e_1 = X_1 - X'_1$ and $e_2 = X_2 - X'_2$. The residuals for X_1 and X_2 are reported in Table 5.1 in columns e_1 and e_2, respectively.

[2]It is suggested that you perform these and other calculations presented in this chapter. Also, do not be misled by the simplicity and the uniformity of the numbers and variables in this example. These very simple numbers were chosen so that the discussion could be followed easily.

Table 5.1 Illustrative Data for Three Variables, and Residuals for Two

	X_1	X_2	X_3	e_1	e_2
	1	3	3	−2.0	0
	2	1	2	−.4	−1.1
	3	2	1	1.2	.8
	4	4	4	.4	.1
	5	5	5	.8	.2
Σ:	15	15	15	0	0

NOTE: e_1 are the residuals when X_1 is predicted from X_3; e_2 are the residuals when X_2 is predicted from X_3.

It is useful to pursue some of the relations among the variables reported in Table 5.1. In order to facilitate the calculations and to provide a succinct summary of them, summary statistics for Table 5.1 are reported in Table 5.2. The diagonal of Table 5.2 is composed of deviation sums of squares, while the values above the diagonal are sums of cross product deviations. Correlations are reported below the diagonal.

One of the formulas for the correlation coefficient introduced in Chapter 2, Equation (2.41), is repeated here:

$$r_{x_1x_2} = \frac{\Sigma x_1 x_2}{\sqrt{\Sigma x_1^2 \ \Sigma x_2^2}} \tag{5.1}$$

Using the appropriate sum of cross products and sums of squares from Table 5.2, calculate

$$r_{x_3e_1} = \frac{0}{\sqrt{(10)(6.4)}} = .00 \quad \text{and} \quad r_{x_3e_2} = \frac{0}{\sqrt{(10)(1.9)}} = .00$$

Note that since the sum of cross products in each case is zero, the correlation is necessarily zero. This illustrates an important principle: The correlation between a predictor and the residuals of another variable, calculated on the basis of the predictor, is always zero. This makes sense because the residual is that part of the criterion variable that is not predictable on the basis of the predictor—that is, the error. When we generate a set of residuals for X_1 by

Table 5.2 Deviation Sums of Squares and Cross Products and Correlations, Based on Data of Table 5.1

	X_1	X_2	X_3	e_1	e_2
X_1	10.	7.	6.	6.4	1.6
X_2	*.70*	10.	9.	1.6	1.9
X_3	*.60*	*.90*	10.	0	0
e_1			*.00*	6.4	1.6
e_2			*.00*	*.46*	1.9

NOTE: The sums of squares are in the diagonal, the cross products above the diagonal. Correlations, shown italicized, are below the diagonal.

regressing it on X_3 we say that we residualize X_1 with respect to X_3. In Table 5.1, e_1 and e_2 were obtained by residualizing X_1 and X_2 with respect to X_3. Consequently, e_1 and e_2 represent those parts of X_1 and X_2 that are not shared with X_3, or those parts that are left over after the effects of X_3 are taken out from X_1 and X_2. Therefore, calculating the correlation between e_1 and e_2 is tantamount to determining the relation between two residualized variables. Stated differently, it is the correlation between X_1 and X_2 after the effects of X_3 were taken out, or partialed, from both of them. This, then, is the meaning of a partial correlation coefficient. For the data of Table 5.1,

$$r_{12.3} = r_{e_1e_2} = \frac{1.6}{\sqrt{(6.4)(1.9)}} = .46$$

We have gone through these rather lengthy calculations in order to convey the meaning of the partial correlation. It is, however, not necessary to calculate the residuals in order to obtain the partial correlation coefficient. It may be obtained through the application of a simple formula in which the correlations among the three variables are used:

$$r_{12.3} = \frac{r_{12} - r_{13}r_{23}}{\sqrt{1 - r_{13}^2}\sqrt{1 - r_{23}^2}} \tag{5.2}$$

Using the appropriate sums of products and sums of squares from Table 5.2, calculate

$$r_{12} = \frac{7}{\sqrt{(10)(10)}} = .7 \qquad r_{13} = \frac{6}{\sqrt{(10)(10)}} = .6 \qquad r_{23} = \frac{9}{\sqrt{(10)(10)}} = .9$$

and

$$r_{12.3} = \frac{(.7) - (.6)(.9)}{\sqrt{1 - .6^2}\sqrt{1 - .9^2}} = \frac{.7 - .54}{\sqrt{.64}\sqrt{.19}} = \frac{.16}{.3487} = .46$$

The same value was obtained when the correlation between the residuals, e_1 and e_2, was calculated. From the foregoing discussion and illustrations it should be evident that the partial correlation is symmetrical: $r_{12.3} = r_{21.3}$.

The partial correlation between two variables when one variable is partialed out is referred to as a first-order partial correlation. As is shown below, it is possible to partial out, or hold constant, more than one variable. For example, $r_{12.34}$ is the second-order partial correlation between variables 1 and 2 from which 3 and 4 were partialed out. And $r_{12.345}$ is a third-order partial correlation. The order of the partial correlation coefficient is indicated by the number of variables that are being controlled—that is, the number of variables that appear after the point. Consistent with this terminology, the correlation between two variables from which no other variables are partialed out is referred to as a zero-order correlation. Thus, r_{12}, r_{13}, and r_{23}, which are used in Formula (5.2), are zero-order correlations.

In the above example, the zero-order correlation between variables 1 and 2 (r_{12}) is .7, whereas the first-order partial correlation between 1 and 2 when 3 is partialed out ($r_{12.3}$) is .46. Careful study of Formula (5.2) will indicate that the sign and the magnitude of the partial correlation coefficient are determined by the signs and the magnitudes of the zero-order correlations among the variables. It is possible, for example, for the sign of the partial correlation to be different from the sign of the zero-order correlation coefficient between the same variables. Also, the partial correlation coefficient may be larger or smaller than the zero-order correlation coefficient between the variables.

Suppressor Variable. A special case when a partial correlation is larger than its respective zero-order correlation involves what has been termed a *suppressor variable*. A suppressor variable is a variable that has a zero, or close to zero, correlation with the criterion but is correlated with one or more than one of the predictor variables. The inclusion of a suppressor variable in the analysis increases the partial correlation because it serves to suppress, or control for, irrelevant variance, that is, variance that is shared with the predictor and not with the criterion, thereby ridding the analysis of irrelevant variation, or noise. For example, assume the following zero-order correlations:

$$r_{12} = .3 \qquad r_{13} = .0 \qquad r_{23} = .5$$

If variable 1 is the criterion, it is evident that variable 3 shares nothing with it. Variable 3 is, however, related to variable 2, and whatever it is that these two variables share is evidently different from what 1 and 2 share. Calculate now:

$$r_{12.3} = \frac{.3 - (.0)(.5)}{\sqrt{1 - .0^2}\sqrt{1 - .5^2}} = \frac{.3}{\sqrt{.75}} = \frac{.3}{.866} = .35$$

Repeating what was said above: The partial correlation is larger than its respective zero-order correlation because a certain amount of irrelevant variance was suppressed, thereby purifying, so to speak, the relation between variables 1 and 2.

It is instructive to note the effect of a suppressor variable on the squared multiple correlation. Using Formula (3.20), calculate $R^2_{1.23}$ for the above numerical example:

$$R^2_{1.23} = \frac{r^2_{12} + r^2_{13} - 2r_{12}r_{13}r_{23}}{1 - r^2_{23}} = \frac{.3^2 + .0^2 - 2(.3)(.0)(.5)}{1 - .5^2} = \frac{.09}{.75} = .12$$

While variable 2 accounts for 9% of the variance of variable 1 ($r^2_{12} = .3^2 = .09$), adding variable 3, whose correlation with variable 1 is zero, results in an increase of 3% in the variance accounted for in variable 1. The above should serve as a reminder that inspection of the zero-order correlations is not sufficient to reveal the potential usefulness of variables when they are used simultaneously to predict or explain a dependent variable. Using Formula (3.15), calculate the β's for variables 2 and 3:

$$\beta_2 = \frac{r_{12} - r_{13}r_{23}}{1 - r_{23}^2} = \frac{.3 - (.0)(.5)}{1 - .5^2} = \frac{.3}{.75} = .4$$

$$\beta_3 = \frac{r_{13} - r_{12}r_{23}}{1 - r_{23}^2} = \frac{.0 - (.3)(.5)}{1 - .5^2} = \frac{-.15}{.75} = -.2$$

Note that the suppressor variable gets a negative regression coefficient. As we are dealing here with standard scores, the manner in which the suppressor variable operates in the regression equation can be clearly seen. People whose scores are above the mean on the suppressor variable (3) have positive z scores, and those whose scores are below the mean have negative z scores. Consequently, when the regression equation is applied, predicted scores for people who score above the mean on the suppressor variable will be lowered as a result of multiplying a negative regression coefficient by a positive z score. And, conversely, predicted scores of those below the mean on the suppressor variable will be raised as a result of multiplying a negative regression coefficient by a negative z score. In other words, people who are high on the suppressor variable are penalized, so to speak, for being high, whereas those who are low on the suppressor variable are compensated for being low.

Horst (1966) gives a good research example of the above phenomenon. In a study of prediction of success in pilot training during World War II it was found that tests of mechanical, numerical, and spatial abilities had positive correlations with the criterion, but that verbal ability had a very low positive correlation with the criterion. Verbal ability did, however, have relatively high correlations with the three predictors. This was not surprising as all the abilities were measured by paper-and-pencil tests, and therefore: "Some verbal ability was necessary in order to understand the instructions and the items used to measure the other three abilities" (Horst, 1966, p. 355). Verbal ability, therefore, served as a suppressor variable. "To include the verbal score with a negative weight served to suppress or subtract irrelevant ability, and to discount the scores of those who did well on the test simply because of their verbal ability rather than because of abilities required for success in pilot training."

Discussions of suppressor variables, and extensions of the ideas presented here, may be found in: Cohen & Cohen (1975, pp. 87–91); Conger (1974); Conger and Jackson (1972); Darlington (1968); Lord and Novick (1968, pp. 271–272); Tzelgov and Stern (1978); Velicer (1978); Wiggins (1973, pp. 30–38).

Higher-Order Partials

It was noted above that one may partial, or control for, more than one variable. The basic idea and analytic approach are the same as those presented in relation to first-order partial correlations. For example, $r_{12.34}$ is the second-order partial correlation between X_1 and X_2, partialing X_3 and X_4. One could calculate $r_{12.34}$ by residualizing X_1 and X_2, with respect to X_3 and X_4, thereby creating two sets of residuals, e_1 (the residuals of X_1) and e_2 (the residuals of X_2). The correlation between e_1 and e_2 is $r_{12.34}$. Note, however, that the process is quite laborious. To obtain e_1, for example, it is necessary to: (1) regress X_1 on X_3 and X_4 (i.e., do a multiple regression analysis); (2) obtain the regression equation: $X'_1 = a + b_3X_3 + b_4X_4$; (3) obtain X'_1 on the basis of this regression equation; and (4) calculate the residuals (i.e., $e_1 = X_1 - X'_1$). A similar set of operations would have to be done in order to residualize X_2 with respect to X_3 and X_4 and to obtain e_2.

As in the case of a first-order partial correlation, however, it is not necessary to go through the calculations outlined above. They were outlined in order to indicate what in effect is being accomplished when a second-order partial correlation is calculated. The formula for calculating $r_{12.34}$ is:

$$r_{12.34} = \frac{r_{12.3} - r_{14.3}r_{24.3}}{\sqrt{1 - r^2_{14.3}}\sqrt{1 - r^2_{24.3}}} \tag{5.3}$$

Note that the format of (5.3) is the same as (5.2), except that the terms in the former are all first-order partials, whereas those in the latter are zero-order correlations.

The calculation of $r_{12.34}$ is demonstrated by using the zero-order correlations reported in Table 5.3. First, it is necessary to calculate three first-order partial correlations:

$$r_{12.3} = \frac{r_{12} - r_{13}r_{23}}{\sqrt{1 - r^2_{13}}\sqrt{1 - r^2_{23}}} = \frac{.6735 - (.5320)(.1447)}{\sqrt{1 - .5320^2}\sqrt{1 - .1447^2}} = .7120$$

$$r_{14.3} = \frac{r_{14} - r_{13}r_{34}}{\sqrt{1 - r^2_{13}}\sqrt{1 - r^2_{34}}} = \frac{.3475 - (.5320)(.0225)}{\sqrt{1 - .5320^2}\sqrt{1 - .0225^2}} = .3964$$

$$r_{24.3} = \frac{r_{24} - r_{23}r_{34}}{\sqrt{1 - r^2_{23}}\sqrt{1 - r^2_{34}}} = \frac{.3521 - (.1447)(.0225)}{\sqrt{1 - .1447^2}\sqrt{1 - .0225^2}} = .3526$$

Now applying Formula (5.3):

$$r_{12.34} = \frac{r_{12.3} - r_{14.3}r_{24.3}}{\sqrt{1 - r^2_{14.3}}\sqrt{1 - r^2_{24.3}}} = \frac{.7120 - (.3964)(.3526)}{\sqrt{1 - .3964^2}\sqrt{1 - .3526^2}} = \frac{.5722}{.8591} = .6660$$

In this particular example, the zero-order correlation does not differ much from the second-order partial correlation: .6735 and .6660, respectively.

Formula (5.3) can be extended to calculate partial correlations of any order. The higher the order of the partial correlation, however, the larger the number of lower-order partials one would have to calculate. For a systematic approach to successive partialing, see Nunnally (1978, pp. 168–175). Various computer

Table 5.3 Correlation Matrix for Four Variables

	X_1	X_2	X_3	X_4
X_1	1.0000	.6735	.5320	.3475
X_2	.6735	1.0000	.1447	.3521
X_3	.5320	.1447	1.0000	.0225
X_4	.3475	.3521	.0225	1.0000

program packages include programs for the calculation of partials of any order, starting with either raw data or a correlation matrix (see, for example, SPSS and BMDP6R). Instead of presenting formulas for partials of higher orders, we turn to an alternative approach in which partials of any order are calculated through the use of multiple correlations. This approach not only is more straightforward and does not require special computer programs for the calculation of partial correlations, but it also demonstrates the relations among partial and multiple correlations.

Partial Correlations Via Multiple Correlations

Partial correlation can be viewed as a relation between residual variances in a somewhat different way than described above. $R^2_{1.23}$ expresses the variance in X_1 accounted for by X_2 and X_3. It was noted earlier that $1 - R^2_{1.23}$ expresses the variance in X_1 *not* accounted for by the regression of X_1 on X_2 and X_3. Similarly, $1 - R^2_{1.3}$ expresses the variance *not* accounted for by the regression of X_1 on X_3. The square of the partial correlation of X_1 with X_2, partialing X_3 is expressed as follows:

$$r^2_{12.3} = \frac{R^2_{1.23} - R^2_{1.3}}{1 - R^2_{1.3}} \tag{5.4}$$

The numerator of (5.4) indicates the proportion of variance incremented by variable 2, that is, the proportion of variance accounted for by X_2 after the effects of X_3 have already been taken into account. The denominator of (5.4) indicates the residual variance, that is, the variance left after what X_3 is able to account for. Therefore, the square of the partial correlation coefficient is a ratio of variance incremented to residual variance.

In order to apply Formula (5.4) to the data of Table 5.1, it is necessary to calculate first $R^2_{1.23}$. From Table 5.2, $r_{12} = .7$, $r_{13} = .6$, and $r_{23} = .9$. Using Formula (3.20),

$$R^2_{1.23} = \frac{r^2_{12} + r^2_{13} - 2r_{12}r_{13}r_{23}}{1 - r^2_{23}} = \frac{.7^2 + .6^2 - 2(.7)(.6)(.9)}{1 - .9^2} = \frac{.094}{.19} = .4947$$

Apply now Formula (5.4):

$$r^2_{12.3} = \frac{.4947 - .6^2}{1 - .6^2} = \frac{.1347}{.64} = .2105$$

$r_{12.3} = \sqrt{r^2_{12.3}} = \sqrt{.2105} = .46$, which is the same as the value obtained when Formula (5.3) was used.

An alternative formula for the calculation of the squared partial correlation via the multiple correlation is

$$r^2_{12.3} = \frac{R^2_{2.13} - R^2_{2.3}}{1 - R^2_{2.3}} \tag{5.5}$$

Note the pattern in the numerators of (5.4) and (5.5): The first term is the squared multiple correlation of one of the primary variables (X_1 or X_2) with the remaining variables; the second term is the squared zero-order correlation of the same primary variable with the control variable—that is, variable 3. For more than one control variable, see Equations (5.6) and (5.7) below. In (5.4) and (5.5), the denominator is one minus the right-hand term of the numerator. Formula (5.5) is applied to the numerical example analyzed above.

$$R^2_{2.13} = \frac{r^2_{21} + r^2_{23} - 2r_{21}r_{23}r_{13}}{1 - r^2_{13}} = \frac{.7^2 + .9^2 - 2(.7)(.9)(.6)}{1 - .6^2} = \frac{.544}{.64} = .85$$

$$r^2_{12.3} = \frac{.85 - .81}{1 - .81} = \frac{.04}{.19} = .2105$$

which is the same value as the one obtained when Formula (5.4) was used. It was noted above that the partial correlation is symmetrical; that is, $r_{12.3} = r_{21.3}$.

Because Formula (5.4) or (5.5) yields the squared partial correlation coefficient it is not possible to tell whether the sign of the partial correlation coefficient is positive or negative. The sign of the partial correlation coefficient is the same as the sign of the regression coefficient (b or β) in which any control variables are partialed out. Thus, if Formula (5.4) is used to calculate $r^2_{12.3}$, the sign of $r_{12.3}$ is the same as the sign of $\beta_{12.3}$ (or $b_{12.3}$) in the equation in which X_1 is regressed on X_2 and X_3. Similarly, if (5.5) is used, the sign of $r_{12.3}$ is the same as that of $\beta_{21.3}$ (or $b_{21.3}$) in the equation in which X_2 is regressed on X_1 and X_3.

Generalization of (5.4) or (5.5) to higher-order partial correlations is straightforward. Thus the formula for the squared second-order partial correlation via multiple correlations is

$$r^2_{12.34} = \frac{R^2_{1.234} - R^2_{1.34}}{1 - R^2_{1.34}} \tag{5.6}$$

or

$$r^2_{12.34} = \frac{R^2_{2.134} - R^2_{2.34}}{1 - R^2_{2.34}} \tag{5.7}$$

The formula for a squared third-order partial correlation is

$$r^2_{12.345} = \frac{R^2_{1.2345} - R^2_{1.345}}{1 - R^2_{1.345}} = \frac{R^2_{2.1345} - R^2_{2.345}}{1 - R^2_{2.345}} \tag{5.8}$$

Formula (5.6) is used now for the calculation of squared second-order partial correlations for the data of Table 5.3. Using a computer program for multiple regression analysis, calculate $R^2_{1.234} = .66375$ and $R^2_{1.34} = .39566$.

$$r^2_{12.34} = \frac{R^2_{1.234} - R^2_{1.34}}{1 - R^2_{1.34}} = \frac{.66375 - .39566}{1 - .39566} = \frac{.26809}{.60434} = .44361$$

Hence

$$r_{12.34} = \sqrt{r^2_{12.34}} = \sqrt{.44361} = .6660$$

which is the same value as the one obtained above when Formula (5.3) was applied.

Alternatively,

$$R^2_{2.134} = .52300 \qquad R^2_{2.34} = .14269$$

$$r^2_{12.34} = \frac{R^2_{2.134} - R^2_{2.34}}{1 - R^2_{2.34}} = \frac{.52300 - .14269}{1 - .14269} = \frac{.38031}{.85731} = .44361$$

Again, the same value of $r^2_{12.34}$ is obtained.

Using the correlations from Table 5.3, calculate $r^2_{14.23}$. First calculate

$$R^2_{1.234} = .66375 \qquad R^2_{1.23} = .64647$$

$$r^2_{14.23} = \frac{R^2_{1.234} - R^2_{1.23}}{1 - R^2_{1.23}} = \frac{.66375 - .64647}{1 - .64647} = \frac{.01728}{.35353} = .0489$$

$$r_{14.23} = \sqrt{r^2_{14.23}} = \sqrt{.0489} = .2211$$

Whereas $r_{14} = .3475$, $r_{14.23} = .2211$.

The meaning of the above calculations can perhaps be further clarified by study of Figure 5.3. The figure has been drawn to represent the situation in calculating $r^2_{14.23}$. The area of the whole square represents the total variance of X_1: it equals 1. The horizontally hatched area represents $1 - R^2_{1.23} = 1 - .64647 = .35353$. The vertically hatched area (it is doubly hatched due to the overlap with the horizontally hatched area) represents $R^2_{1.234} - R^2_{1.23} = .66375 - .64647 =$

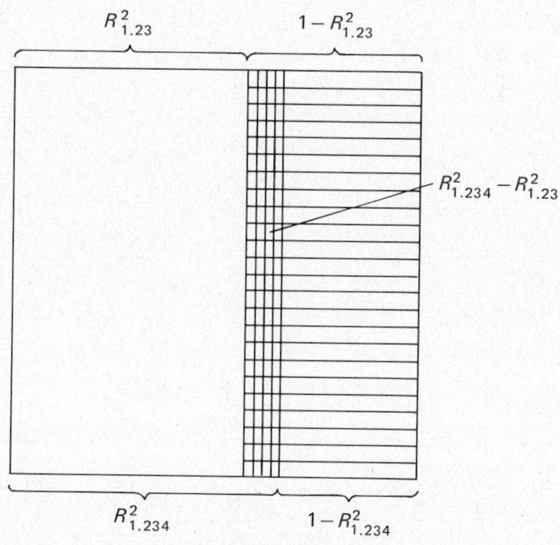

Figure 5.3

.01728. (The areas $R^2_{1.23}$ and $R^2_{1.234}$ are labeled in the figure.) The squared partial correlation coefficient is the ratio of the doubly hatched area to the horizontally hatched area, or

$$\frac{.66375 - .64647}{.35353} = \frac{.01728}{.35353} = .0489$$

CAUSAL ASSUMPTIONS

Partial correlation is not an all-purpose method of control. Its valid application is predicated on a sound theoretical model. Controlling variables without regard to the theoretical considerations about the pattern of relations among them may amount to a distortion of reality and result in misleading or meaningless results. Emphasizing the need for a causal model when calculating partial correlations, Fisher (1958) contends:

> If . . . we choose a group of social phenomena with no antecedent knowledge of the causation or the absence of causation among them, then the calculation of correlation coefficients, total or partial, will not advance us a step towards evaluating the importance of the causes at work. . . . In no case, however, can we judge whether or not it is profitable to eliminate a certain variate unless we know, or are willing to assume, a qualitative scheme of causation. (pp. 190–191)

In an excellent discussion of what he labels the partialing fallacy, Gordon (1968) maintains that the routine presentation of all higher-order partial correlations in a set of data is a sure sign that the researcher has not formulated a theory that attempts to explain the relations among the variables under consideration. Even with three variables only, there is a relatively large number of possible causal models, two of which are depicted in Figure 5.4. Note that $r_{xz.y} = .00$ is consistent with both models depicted in Figure 5.4. The two models are, however, radically different from each other. In (a), Y is conceived of as mediating the effects of X on Z, whereas in (b), Y is conceived of as the common cause that leads to a spurious correlation between X and Z. On the basis of $r_{xz.y} = .00$ it is not possible to determine whether model (a) or model (b) is tenable. It is theory that dictates the appropriate analytic method to be used, not the other way around.

Two additional patterns of possible causation among three variables are depicted in Figure 5.5, where (a) describes a situation in which X affects Z directly as well as through Y, whereas in (b) it is assumed that X and Y are correlated causes of Z. In either of these situations, partial correlation is inap-

Figure 5.4

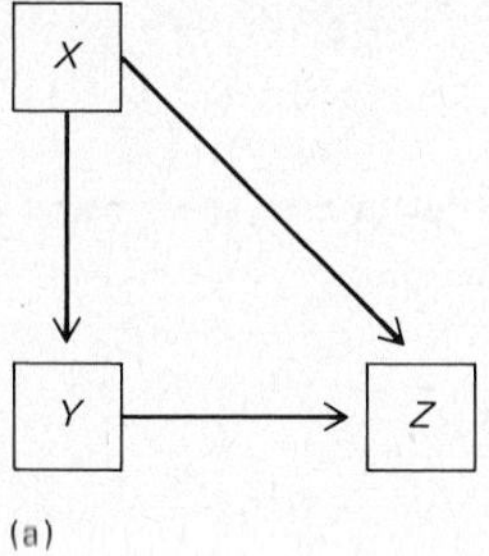

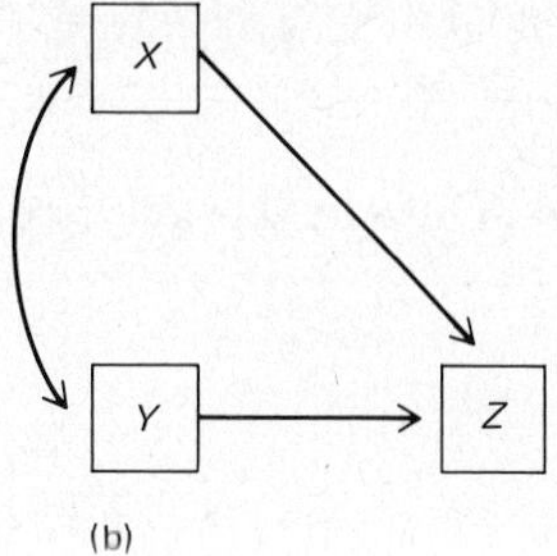

Figure 5.5

propriate, as it may result in partialing too much of the relation. Burks (1928) offers a good example of partialing too much. Assume that X = parent's intelligence, Y = child's intelligence, Z = child's academic achievement, and that one is interested in assessing the effect of the child's intelligence on achievement when parent's intelligence is controlled for.

> If we follow the obvious procedure of partialling out parental intelligence, we indeed succeed in eliminating all effect of parental intelligence. But . . . we have partialled out more than we should, for the *whole* of the child's intelligence, including that part which can be predicted from parents' intelligence as well as the parts that are due to all other conditioning factors, properly belongs to our problem. We are interested in the contribution made to school achievement by intelligence of a normal range of variability rather than by the narrow band of intelligence that would be represented by children whose parents' intelligence was a constant. The partial-correlation technique has made a clean sweep of parental intelligence. But the influence of parental intelligence that affects achievement indirectly *via* heredity (i.e., *via* the child's intelligence) should stay; only the direct influence should go. Thus, the partial-correlation technique is inadequate to this situation. Obviously, it is inadequate to any other situation of this type. (p. 14)

In sum, the calculation of partial correlations is inappropriate when one assumes causal models as those depicted in Figure 5.5. Later in this book (see Chapter 15) analytic methods appropriate for such models are presented.

Another potential pitfall in the application of partial correlation coefficients without regard to theory is what Gordon (1968) has referred to as partialing the relation out of itself. This will happen when, for example, two measures of a given variable are available and one partials out one of the measures in order to study the relation of the second measure with a given criterion. It will make no sense to control, for example, for one measure of mental ability while correlating another measure of mental ability with academic achievement when the purpose of the study is to determine the relation between mental ability and academic achievement. As noted above, this will be tantamount to partialing a relation out of itself and may lead one to the fallacious conclusion that mental ability and academic achievement are not correlated.

Good discussions of causal assumptions and the conditions necessary for appropriate applications of partial correlation technique will be found in Blalock (1964); Burks (1926a, 1926b); Duncan (1970); Linn & Werts (1969).

MEASUREMENT ERRORS

The effects of errors of measurement on regression statistics were discussed in Chapter 2. Measurement errors also lead to biased estimates of zero-order and partial correlation coefficients. While the concern here is with the effects of measurement errors on partial correlation coefficients, it will be instructive to discuss briefly the effects of such errors on zero-order correlations.

When errors are present in the measurement of either X_1 or X_2, or both, the correlation between the two variables is attenuated; that is, it is lower than it would have been had true scores on X_1 and X_2 been used. In other words, when the measures of either or both variables have less than perfect reliabilities, the correlation between the variables is attenuated. In the behavioral sciences the presence of measurement errors is the rule rather than the exception. In fact, many of the measures used in the behavioral sciences have only moderate reliabilities (i.e., .7–.8).

In order to estimate what the correlation between two variables would have been had they been measured without error, one may use the so-called correction for attenuation formula:

$$r^*_{12} = \frac{r_{12}}{\sqrt{r_{11}}\sqrt{r_{22}}} \tag{5.9}$$

where r^*_{12} = the correlation between X_1 and X_2 corrected for attenuation; r_{12} = the observed correlation; r_{11} and r_{22} = reliability coefficients of X_1 and X_2, respectively (see Nunnally, 1978, pp. 219–220). From the denominator of (5.9) it is evident that $r^*_{12} = r_{12}$ only when $r_{11} = r_{22} = 1.00$, that is when the reliabilities of both measures are perfect. With less than perfect reliabilities, r_{12} will always underestimate r^*_{12}. Assume, for the purpose of illustration, that $r_{12} = .7$, and and $r_{11} = r_{22} = .8$. Applying Formula (5.9),

$$r^*_{12} = \frac{r_{12}}{\sqrt{r_{11}}\sqrt{r_{22}}} = \frac{.7}{\sqrt{.8}\sqrt{.8}} = \frac{.7}{.8} = .875$$

The estimated correlation between X_1 and X_2, had both variables been measured without error, is .875. One may choose to correct for the unreliability of either X_1 only or X_2 only. For a discussion of this and related issues, see Nunnally (1978, pp. 237–239).

Using the above conceptions one may derive formulas for the estimation of partial correlation coefficients corrected for one or all the measures involved. Probably most important is the correction for unreliability of the measure of the variable that is controlled, or partialed out, in the calculation of the partial-correlation coefficient. The formula is:

$$r_{12.3^*} = \frac{r_{33}r_{12} - r_{13}r_{23}}{\sqrt{r_{33} - r^2_{13}}\sqrt{r_{33} - r^2_{23}}} \tag{5.10}$$

where $r_{12.3^*}$ is the estimated partial correlation coefficient when X_3 is corrected for unreliability; r_{33} is the reliability coefficient of X_3. Note that when X_3 is measured without error (i.e., $r_{33} = 1.00$), Formula (5.10) reduces to (5.2), the formula for the first-order partial correlation introduced earlier in this chapter. Unlike the zero-order correlation, which as was shown above underestimates the correlation in the presence of measurement errors, the partial correlation coefficient uncorrected for measurement errors may result in either overestimation or underestimation.

For the purpose of illustration, assume that

$$r_{12} = .7 \qquad r_{13} = .5 \qquad r_{23} = .6$$

Applying first Formula (5.2),

$$r_{12.3} = \frac{r_{12} - r_{13}r_{23}}{\sqrt{1 - r_{13}^2}\sqrt{1 - r_{23}^2}} = \frac{.7 - (.5)(.6)}{\sqrt{1 - .5^2}\sqrt{1 - .6^2}} = \frac{.4}{.6928} = .58$$

Assuming now that the reliability of the variable being controlled for, X_3, is .8 (i.e., $r_{33} = .8$), and applying Formula (5.10):

$$r_{12.3^*} = \frac{r_{33}r_{12} - r_{13}r_{23}}{\sqrt{r_{33} - r_{13}^2}\sqrt{r_{33} - r_{23}^2}} = \frac{(.8)(.7) - (.5)(.6)}{\sqrt{.8 - .5^2}\sqrt{.8 - .6^2}} = \frac{.26}{.4919} = .53$$

In the present case, $r_{12.3}$ overestimated $r_{12.3^*}$.

Here is another example:

$$r_{12} = .7 \qquad r_{13} = .8 \qquad r_{23} = .7 \qquad r_{33} = .8$$

Applying Formula (5.2),

$$r_{12.3} = \frac{r_{12} - r_{13}r_{23}}{\sqrt{1 - r_{13}^2}\sqrt{1 - r_{23}^2}} = \frac{.7 - (.8)(.7)}{\sqrt{1 - .8^2}\sqrt{1 - .7^2}} = \frac{.14}{.4285} = .33$$

Applying now Formula (5.10),

$$r_{12.3^*} = \frac{r_{33}r_{12} - r_{13}r_{23}}{\sqrt{r_{33} - r_{13}^2}\sqrt{r_{33} - r_{23}^2}} = \frac{(.8)(.7) - (.8)(.7)}{\sqrt{.8 - .8^2}\sqrt{.8 - .7^2}} = .00$$

When X_3 is corrected for unreliability the correlation between X_1 and X_2 appears to be spurious; or it may be that X_3 mediates the effect of X_1 on X_2. (For a discussion of this point, see earlier sections of this chapter.) A quite different conclusion is reached when X_3 is not corrected for unreliability.

Assume now that the correlations among the three variables are the same as above but that $r_{33} = .75$ instead of .8. $r_{12.3}$ is the same as obtained above (i.e., .33). Applying (5.10):

$$r_{12.3^*} = \frac{r_{33}r_{12} - r_{13}r_{23}}{\sqrt{r_{33} - r_{13}^2}\sqrt{r_{33} - r_{23}^2}} = \frac{(.75)(.7) - (.8)(.7)}{\sqrt{.75 - .8^2}\sqrt{.75 - .7^2}} = \frac{-.035}{.1691} = -.21$$

This time, the two estimates differ not only in magnitude but also in sign (i.e., $r_{12.3} = .33$ and $r_{12.3^*} = -.21$). The above illustrations suffice to indicate the importance of correcting for the unreliability of the partialled variable. For further discussions, see Blalock (1964, pp. 146–150); Kahenman (1965); Linn and Werts (1973); Lord (1963, 1974).

As was noted above, it is possible to correct for the unreliability of all the measures used in the calculation of a partial correlation coefficient. The formula is

$$r_{12.3}^* = \frac{r_{33}r_{12} - r_{13}r_{23}}{\sqrt{r_{11}r_{33} - r_{13}^2}\sqrt{r_{22}r_{33} - r_{23}^2}} \tag{5.11}$$

where $r_{12.3}^*$ is the corrected partial correlation coefficient; r_{11}, r_{22}, and r_{33} are the reliability coefficients for X_1, X_2, and X_3 respectively (see Bohrnstedt & Carter, 1971, pp. 136–137). Two things will be noted about Formula (5.11): (1) When the three variables are measured with perfect reliability (i.e., $r_{11} = r_{22} = r_{33} = 1.00$), Formula (5.11) reduces to (5.2); and (2) the numerators of (5.11) and (5.10) are identical. Only the denominator changes when one introduces corrections for the unreliability of the measures of the primary variables, in addition to the correction for the unreliability of the measure of the control variable.

For illustrative purposes, Formula (5.2) is applied to the following data:

$$r_{12} = .7 \qquad r_{13} = .5 \qquad r_{23} = .6$$

$$r_{12.3} = \frac{r_{12} - r_{13}r_{23}}{\sqrt{1 - r_{13}^2}\sqrt{1 - r_{23}^2}} = \frac{.7 - (.5)(.6)}{\sqrt{1 - .5^2}\sqrt{1 - .6^2}} = \frac{.4}{.6928} = .58$$

Assume now, for the sake of simplicity, that $r_{11} = r_{22} = r_{33} = .8$. Applying Formula (5.11),

$$r_{12.3}^* = \frac{r_{33}r_{12} - r_{13}r_{23}}{\sqrt{r_{11}r_{33} - r_{13}^2}\sqrt{r_{22}r_{33} - r_{23}^2}} = \frac{(.8)(.7) - (.5)(.6)}{\sqrt{(.8)(.8) - .5^2}\sqrt{(.8)(.8) - .6^2}} = \frac{.26}{.3305} = .79$$

In the present example, $r_{12.3}$ underestimated $r_{12.3}^*$. Depending on the pattern of intercorrelations among the variables, and the reliabilities of the measures used, the uncorrected $r_{12.3}$ may either underestimate or overestimate $r_{12.3}^*$.

In conclusion, it will be noted again that the most important correction is the one applied to the variable that is being controlled, or partialed out. Stated differently, the application of Formula (5.10) may serve as a minimum safeguard against erroneous interpretations of partial correlation coefficients. For a good discussion and illustrations of the adverse effects of measurement error on the use of partial correlations in hypothesis testing, see Brewer, Crano, and Campbell (1970).

SEMIPARTIAL CORRELATION

Until now we were concerned with the situation in which a variable (or several variables) was partialed out from *both* variables whose correlation was being sought. There are, however, situations in which it is desired to partial out a variable from only one of the variables that are being correlated. For example, suppose that a college admissions officer is dealing with the following three variables: X_1 = grade-point average; X_2 = entrance examination; and X_3 = intelligence. One would expect intelligence and the entrance examination to be positively correlated. Assuming that the admissions officer is interested in the relation between the entrance examination and grade-point average, while controlling for intelligence, the $r_{12.3}$ will provide this information. Similarly, $r_{13.2}$ will indicate the correlation between intelligence and grade-point average, while controlling for performance on the entrance examination. It is possible, however, that of greater interest to the admission officer is the predictive power of the entrance examination after that of intelligence has already been taken into account. Stated differently, the interest is in the increment in the proportion of variance in grade-point average accounted for by the entrance examination that is over and above the proportion of variance accounted for by intelligence. In such a situation intelligence should be partialed out from the entrance examination, but not from grade-point average where it belongs. This can be accomplished by calculating the squared *semipartial* correlation. Some authors (e.g., DuBois, 1957, pp. 60–62; McNemar, 1962, pp. 167–168) refer to such correlations as *part correlations*.

It will be recalled that a partial correlation is a correlation between two variables that were residualized on a third variable. The semipartial correlation is the correlation between a variable that is unmodified and a variable that was residualized. The symbol for a first-order semipartial correlation is $r_{1(2.3)}$, which means the correlation between X_1 (unmodified) and X_2, after it has been residualized on X_3, or after X_3 was partialed out from X_2. Referring to the variables noted above, $r_{1(2.3)}$ is the semipartial correlation between grade-point average and an entrance examination, after intelligence was partialed out from the latter. Similarly, $r_{1(3.2)}$ is the semipartial correlation of grade-point average and intelligence, after an entrance examination was partialed out from the latter.

To demonstrate concretely the meaning of a semipartial correlation, we return to the numerical example introduced earlier in Table 5.1. Recall that e_1 and e_2 of Table 5.1 are the residuals of X_1 and X_2, respectively, when X_3 was used to predict each of these variables. It was demonstrated earlier that $r_{x_3e_1} = r_{x_3e_2} = .00$, and that therefore the correlation between e_1 and e_2 is the relation between those two parts of X_1 and X_2 which are not shared with X_3, that is, the partial correlation between X_1 and X_2, after X_3 was partialed out from both variables. To calculate, instead, the semipartial correlation between X_1 (unmodified) and X_2, after X_3 is partialed out from it, correlate X_1 with e_2. From Table 5.2 we obtain the following:

$$\Sigma x_1^2 = 10 \qquad \Sigma e_2^2 = 1.9 \qquad \Sigma x_1 e_2 = 1.6$$

Therefore,

$$r_{x_1e_2} = r_{1(2.3)} = \frac{\Sigma x_1 e_2}{\sqrt{\Sigma x_1^2 \, \Sigma e_2^2}} = \frac{1.6}{\sqrt{(10)(1.9)}} = \frac{1.6}{4.359} = .37$$

We can, similarly, calculate $r_{2(1.3)}$—that is, the semipartial correlation between X_2 (unmodified) and X_1, after X_3 was partialed out from it. This is tantamount to correlating X_2 with e_1. Again, taking the appropriate values from Table 5.2,

$$\Sigma x_2^2 = 10 \qquad \Sigma e_1^2 = 6.4 \qquad \Sigma x_2 e_1 = 1.6$$

and

$$r_{x_2e_1} = r_{2(1.3)} = \frac{\Sigma x_2 e_1}{\sqrt{\Sigma x_2^2 \, \Sigma e_1^2}} = \frac{1.6}{\sqrt{(10)(6.4)}} = \frac{1.6}{8} = .2$$

The foregoing calculations were presented in order to show the meaning of the semipartial correlation. But, as in the case of partial correlations, there are simple formulas for the calculation of semipartial correlations. For the purpose of comparison, the formula for a first-order partial correlation (5.2) is repeated:

$$r_{12.3} = \frac{r_{12} - r_{13}r_{23}}{\sqrt{1 - r_{13}^2}\sqrt{1 - r_{23}^2}} \tag{5.12}$$

The formula for $r_{1(2.3)}$ is

$$r_{1(2.3)} = \frac{r_{12} - r_{13}r_{23}}{\sqrt{1 - r_{23}^2}} \tag{5.13}$$

and

$$r_{2(1.3)} = \frac{r_{12} - r_{13}r_{23}}{\sqrt{1 - r_{13}^2}} \tag{5.14}$$

Note that the numerators for the semipartial correlations are the same as the numerator for the partial correlation that corresponds to them. The denominator in the formula for the partial correlation (5.12) is composed of two standard errors, whereas the denominators in the formulas for the semipartial correlation, (5.13) and (5.14), have only one standard error. In each case it is the standard error for the variable from which the control variable is partialed out.

From the denominators of the formulas for the partial and semipartial correlations it can be seen that $r_{12.3}$ will be larger than either $r_{1(2.3)}$ or $r_{2(1.3)}$, except when r_{13} or r_{23} equal zero, in which case the partial correlation will be equal to the semipartial correlation.

To demonstrate the application of (5.13) and (5.14) we return again to the data of Table 5.1. The correlations among the variables of Table 5.1 (see calculations accompanying the table, and a summary of the calculations in Table 5.2) are as follows:

$$r_{12} = .7 \qquad r_{13} = .6 \qquad r_{23} = .9$$

Applying Formula (5.13),

$$r_{1(2.3)} = \frac{r_{12} - r_{13}r_{23}}{\sqrt{1 - r_{23}^2}} = \frac{(.7) - (.6)(.9)}{\sqrt{1 - .9^2}} = \frac{.16}{.4359} = .37$$

The same value was obtained above when X_1 was correlated with e_2. In addition,

$$r_{2(1.3)} = \frac{r_{12} - r_{13}r_{23}}{\sqrt{1 - r_{13}^2}} = \frac{(.7) - (.6)(.9)}{\sqrt{1 - .6^2}} = \frac{.16}{.8} = .20$$

Again, this is the same as the value obtained when X_2 was correlated with e_1.

Earlier we calculated $r_{12.3} = .46$, which, as was noted above, is larger than either of the semipartial correlations.

Having gone through the mechanics of the calculations, it is necessary to address the question of when to use a partial correlation and when a semipartial correlation would be more appropriate. Moreover, assuming that a semipartial correlation is called for, it is still necessary to decide which of two semipartial correlations should be calculated. Answers to such questions depend on the theory and causal assumptions that underlie the research (see Werts & Linn, 1969). As is discussed in greater detail below, and in Chapter 7, squared semipartial correlations are used by some researchers in their attempts to partition the variance of the dependent variable. It was noted several times earlier that the validity of any analytic approach is predicated on the purpose of the study and on the soundness of the theoretical model that underlies it. For the present, though, an example of the meaning and implications of a choice between two semipartial correlations may help demonstrate some of the complexities as well as serve to underscore the paramount role played by theory in the choice and valid interpretation of an analytic method.[3]

Suppose, for the sake of illustration, that in research on the effects of schooling one is dealing with three variables only: I = a student input variable (e.g., aptitude, home background); S = a school quality variable (e.g., teachers' verbal ability, or attitudes); and C = a criterion variable (e.g., achievement, or graduation). Most researchers who study the effects of schooling, in the context of the above noted variables, are inclined to calculate the following squared semipartial correlation:

$$r_{C(S.I)}^2 = \frac{(r_{CS} - r_{CI}r_{SI})^2}{1 - r_{SI}^2} \tag{5.15}$$

[3]The remainder of this section is adapted from Pedhazur (1975), by permission from the American Educational Research Association.

In (5.15) the student variable is partialed out from the school variable. In essence, what one obtains by calculating (5.15) is the proportion of variance of the criterion variable that the school variable accounts for over and above the variance accounted for by the student input variable.

Some researchers, notably Astin and his associates (see, for example, Astin, 1968, 1970; Astin & Panos, 1969) take a different analytic approach to the same problem. In an attempt to control for the student input variable, they residualize the criterion variable on it. They then correlate the residualized criterion with the school variable in order to determine the effect of the latter on the former. For the example under consideration, this approach amounts to calculating the following squared semipartial correlation:

$$r^2_{\text{S(C.I)}} = \frac{(r_{\text{CS}} - r_{\text{CI}}r_{\text{SI}})^2}{1 - r^2_{\text{CI}}} \tag{5.16}$$

Since Equations (5.15) and (5.16) have the same numerators, it follows that the magnitude of the proportion of variance attributed to the school variable under each of the approaches depends on the relative magnitudes of r_{SI} and r_{CI}. When $r_{\text{SI}} = r_{\text{CI}}$, the two methods yield the same results. When $|r_{\text{SI}}| > |r_{\text{CI}}|$, then $r^2_{\text{C(S.I)}} > r^2_{\text{S(C.I)}}$. The reverse is, of course, true when $|r_{\text{CI}}| > |r_{\text{SI}}|$. Which approach should be followed? Werts and Linn (1969) answer facetiously that it depends on the kind of hypothesis one wishes to support. After presenting four approaches (two of which are the ones discussed here), Werts and Linn provide the reader with a flow diagram for selecting the approach that holds the greatest promise for supporting one's hypothesis. Barring inspection of the intercorrelations among the variables prior to a commitment to an approach, the choice between the two discussed here depends on whether one wishes to show a greater or a lesser effect of the school variable. A hereditarian, for example, would choose the approach in which the school variable is residualized on the student input (5.15). The reason is that in educational research correlations of student input variables with the criterion tend to be greater than correlations of student input variables with school variables. Consequently, the application of the approach exemplified by (5.15) will result in a smaller proportion of variance attributed to the school variable than will the approach exemplified by (5.16). An environmentalist, on the other hand, may be able to squeeze a little more variance for the school by applying (5.16). Needless to say, this advice is not meant to be taken seriously. It does, however, underscore the complex nature of the choice between the different approaches.

The important point to bear in mind is that the complexities arise, among other things, because the student input variable is correlated with the school quality variable. As long as the researcher is unwilling, or unable, to explain how this correlation comes about, it is not possible to determine whether (5.15) or (5.16) is more appropriate. As discussed later on (see Chapter 7), in certain instances neither of them leads to a valid answer about the effects of schooling.

Until now, only first-order semipartial correlations have been presented. Instead of presenting special formulas for the calculation of higher-order semipartial correlations, it is shown how semipartial correlations of any order may be obtained via multiple correlations.

Semipartial Correlations Via Multiple Correlations

It was said above that a squared semipartial correlation indicates the proportion of variance in the dependent variable accounted for by a given independent variable after another independent variable(s) was partialed out from it. The same idea may be stated somewhat differently: a squared semipartial correlation indicates the proportion of variance of the dependent variable accounted for by a given independent variable after another variable(s) has already been taken into account. Stated thus, a squared semipartial correlation is indicated by the difference between two squared multiple correlations. It is this approach that affords the straightforward calculation of squared semipartial correlations of any order. For example,

$$r^2_{1(2.3)} = R^2_{1.23} - R^2_{1.3} \tag{5.17}$$

where $r^2_{1(2.3)}$ = squared semipartial correlation of X_1 with X_2 after X_3 has been partialed out from X_2. Note that the first term to the right of the equal sign of (5.17) indicates the proportion of variance in X_1 accounted for by X_2 and X_3, whereas the second term indicates the proportion of variance in X_1 accounted for by X_3 alone. The difference between the two terms therefore indicates the proportion of variance due to X_2 after X_3 has already been taken into account. Note also that the right-hand side of (5.17) is the same as the numerator in the formula for the square of the partial correlation of the same order (see Formula (5.4) and the discussion related to it). The difference between (5.17) and (5.4) is that the latter has a denominator (i.e., $1 - R^2_{1.3}$), whereas the former has no denominator. Since $1 - R^2_{1.3}$ is a fraction (except when $R^2_{1.3}$ is zero) and both formulas have the same numerator, it follows, as was noted earlier, that the partial correlation is larger than its corresponding semipartial correlations.

Analogous to (5.17), the $r^2_{1(3.2)}$ is calculated as follows:

$$r^2_{1(3.2)} = R^2_{1.23} - R^2_{1.2} \tag{5.18}$$

This time the increment in proportion of variance accounted for by X_3, after X_2 is already in the equation, is obtained.

The present approach may be used to obtain semipartial correlations of any order. Following are some examples:

$$r^2_{1(2.34)} = R^2_{1.234} - R^2_{1.34} \tag{5.19}$$

which is the squared second-order semipartial correlation of X_1 with X_2, when X_3 and X_4 are partialed out from X_2.

Similarly,

$$r^2_{1(3.24)} = R^2_{1.234} - R^2_{1.24} \tag{5.20}$$

which is the squared second-order semipartial correlation of X_1 with X_3, after X_2 and X_4 were partialed out from X_3.

The squared third-order semipartial of X_3 with X_1, after X_2, X_4, and X_5 are partialed out from X_1 is

$$r^2_{3(1.245)} = R^2_{3.1245} - R^2_{3.245} \tag{5.21}$$

From the above examples it should be clear that to calculate a squared semipartial of any order, it is necessary to: (1) calculate the squared multiple correlation of the dependent variable with all the independent variables; (2) calculate the squared multiple correlation of the dependent variable with the variables that are being partialed out; (3) subtract the R^2 of step 2 from the R^2 of step 1, thereby obtaining the squared semipartial correlation.

The semipartial correlation is, of course, equal to the square root of the squared semipartial correlation. As was noted earlier in relation to the partial correlation, the sign of the semipartial correlation is the same as the sign of the regression coefficient (b or β) that corresponds to it.

Numerical Examples

In order to demonstrate the application of the present approach, and to provide for comparisons with the calculations of partial correlations, the correlation matrix which was introduced earlier in Table 5.3 will be used. It is repeated here for convenience as Table 5.4. Using data from Table 5.4 different squared semipartial correlations are calculated and briefly commented upon.

$$r^2_{1(2.3)} = R^2_{1.23} - R^2_{1.3}$$

$$= .64647 - .28302 = .36345$$

Note that while X_2 by itself can account for about .45 of the variance in X_1 (i.e., $r^2_{12} = .6735^2 = .4536$), or 45% of the variance in X_1, it accounts for about 36% of the variance after partialing X_3 from it, or after allowing X_3 to enter first into the regression equation.

$$r^2_{1(3.2)} = R^2_{1.23} - R^2_{1.2}$$

$$= .64647 - .45360 = .19287$$

Variable X_3 by itself can account for about 28% of the variance in X_1 (i.e., $r^2_{13} \times 100$). But it accounts for about 19% of the variance after X_2 is partialed out from it.

Table 5.4 Correlation Matrix for Four Variables

	X_1	X_2	X_3	X_4
X_1	1.0000	.6735	.5320	.3475
X_2	.6735	1.0000	.1447	.3521
X_3	.5320	.1447	1.0000	.0225
X_4	.3475	.3521	.0225	1.0000

$$r^2_{1(2.34)} = R^2_{1.234} - R^2_{1.34}$$

$$= .66375 - .39566 = .26809$$

Having partialed out X_3 and X_4 from X_2, the latter accounts for about 26% of the variance in X_1. Compare with the variance accounted for by the zero-order correlation (45%) and by the first-order semipartial correlation (36%). Compare also with the squared partial correlation of the same order: $r^2_{12.34} = .4436$ (see calculations earlier in this chapter).

$$r^2_{1(4.23)} = R^2_{1.234} - R^2_{1.23}$$

$$= .66375 - .64647 = .01728$$

Variable X_4 by itself can account for about 12% of the variance in X_1 (i.e., $r^2_{14} \times 100$). But when X_2 and X_3 are partialed out from X_4, the latter accounts for about 2% of the variance in X_1. The squared partial correlation corresponding to this squared semipartial correlation (i.e., $r^2_{14.23}$) was calculated earlier as .0489.

The successive reductions in the proportions of variance accounted for by a given variable as one goes from a zero-order correlation to a first-order semipartial, and then to a second-order semipartial, is due to the fact that all the correlations among the variables under consideration are of the same sign (in the present case they are all positive). The successive partialing takes out information that is redundant with the information provided by the variables that are being controlled. It should be noted that, similar to a partial correlation, a semipartial correlation may be larger than its corresponding zero-order correlation. The semipartial correlation may also have a different sign than the zero-order correlation to which it corresponds. The magnitude and the sign of the semipartial correlation are determined by the magnitudes and the pattern of the correlations among the variables under consideration.

To illustrate what was said above, assume that $r_{12} = .6735$, $r_{13} = .5320$ (these are the same values as in Table 5.4), but that $r_{23} = -.1447$ (this is the same correlation as the one reported in Table 5.4, but with a change in its sign). Using Formula (5.13) calculate:

$$r_{1(2.3)} = \frac{r_{12} - r_{13}r_{23}}{\sqrt{1 - r^2_{23}}} = \frac{.6735 - (.5320)(-.1447)}{\sqrt{1 - (-.1447)^2}} = \frac{.75048}{.98948} = .75846$$

Note that X_2 by itself accounts for about 45% of the variance in X_1. But when X_3 is partialed out from X_2, the latter accounts for about 58% of the variance in X_1 (i.e., $.75846^2 \times 100$).

The above demonstration could, of course, have been accomplished also through the application of Formula (5.17). Formula (5.13) was used, instead, because one can see clearly what is taking place. Inspect the numerator first. Because r_{13} and r_{23} have different signs, their product will be added to r_{12}, resulting, of course, in a value larger than r_{12}. Moreover, the denominator is a fraction. Consequently, $r_{1(2.3)}$ must be larger than r_{12} in the present case.

What was said, and demonstrated, above applies also to semipartial correlations of higher orders, although the pattern is more complex and therefore not as easily tractable as in a first-order semipartial correlation.

TESTS OF SIGNIFICANCE

A formula for testing the significance of an increment in the proportion of variance of the dependent variable accounted for by any number of independent variables was first introduced in Chapter 3 [see Formula (3.27) and the discussion related to it]. The formula is repeated here:

$$F = \frac{(R^2_{y.12\ldots k_1} - R^2_{y.12\ldots k_2})/(k_1 - k_2)}{(1 - R^2_{y.12\ldots k_1})/(N - k_1 - 1)} \tag{5.22}$$

where $R^2_{y.12\ldots k_1}$ = the squared multiple correlation coefficient for the regression of Y on k_1 variables (the larger coefficient); $R^2_{y.12\ldots k_2}$ = the squared multiple correlation for the regression of Y on k_2 variables; k_2 = the smaller set of variables selected from among those of k_1; N = sample size. The F ratio has $(k_1 - k_2)$ *df* for the numerator, and $(N - k_1 - 1)$ *df* for the denominator.

As the squared semipartial correlation indicates the increment in proportion of variance of the dependent variable accounted for by a given independent variable, after controlling for the other independent variables, it is evident that the formula for testing its statistical significance is a special case of Formula (5.22). For a squared semipartial correlation, k_1 is the total number of independent variables, whereas k_2 is the total number of independent variables minus one, that being the variable whose semipartial correlation with the dependent variable is being sought. Consequently, the numerator of the F ratio will always have one *df*.

Assuming that the correlation matrix of Table 5.4 is based on $N = 20$, it is demonstrated now how the above obtained squared semipartial correlations are tested for significance.

For $r^2_{1(2.3)}$,

$$F = \frac{R^2_{1.23} - R^2_{1.3}}{(1 - R^2_{1.23})/(N - k_1 - 1)} = \frac{.64647 - .28302}{(1 - .64647)/(20 - 2 - 1)} = \frac{.36345}{.0208} = 17.47$$

with 1 and 17 *df*.

For $r^2_{1(3.2)}$,

$$F = \frac{R^2_{1.23} - R^2_{1.2}}{(1 - R^2_{1.23})/(N - k_1 - 1)} = \frac{.64647 - .45360}{(1 - .64647)/(20 - 2 - 1)} = \frac{.19287}{.0208} = 9.27$$

with 1 and 17 *df*.

For $r^2_{1(2.34)}$,

$$F = \frac{R^2_{1.234} - R^2_{1.34}}{(1 - R^2_{1.234})/(N - k_1 - 1)} = \frac{.66375 - .39566}{(1 - .66375)/(20 - 3 - 1)} = \frac{.26809}{.02102} = 12.75$$

with 1 and 16 *df*.

For $r^2_{1(4.23)}$,

$$F = \frac{R^2_{1.234} - R^2_{1.23}}{(1 - R^2_{1.234})/(N - k_1 - 1)} = \frac{.66375 - .64647}{(1 - .66375)/(20 - 3 - 1)} = \frac{.01728}{.02102} = .82$$

with 1 and 16 *df*.

Testing the significance of a squared semipartial correlation is identical to testing the significance of the regression coefficient (b or β) associated with it. Thus, testing $r^2_{1(2.3)}$ for significance is the same as testing the significance of $b_{12.3}$ in an equation in which X_1 was regressed on X_2 and X_3. Similarly, testing $r^2_{1(2.34)}$ for significance is the same as testing $b_{12.34}$ in an equation in which X_1 was regressed on X_2, X_3, and X_4. In short, testing the significance of any regression coefficient (b or β) is tantamount to testing the increment in the proportion of variance that the independent variable associated with the b (or β) accounts for in the dependent variable when it is entered last into the regression equation (see Chapter 7 for a discussion of this point).

Finally, specialized formulas for testing the significance of partial correlations are available (see, for example, Blalock, 1972, pp. 466–467). These are not necessary, however, because testing the significance of a partial correlation coefficient is tantamount to testing the significance of the semipartial correlation, or the regression coefficient, that corresponds to it. Thus, to test $r_{12.3}$ for significance, test $r_{1(2.3)}$, or $b_{12.3}$.

MULTIPLE REGRESSION AND SEMIPARTIAL CORRELATIONS

The conceptual and computational complexity and difficulty of multiple regression analysis arise from the intercorrelations among the independent variables. When the correlations among the independent variables are all zero, the solution and interpretation are simple. The squared multiple correlation is simply the sum of the squared zero-order correlations of each independent variable with the dependent variable:

$$R^2_{y.12\ldots k} = r^2_{y1} + r^2_{y2} + \cdots + r^2_{yk} \tag{5.23}$$

Furthermore, it is possible to state unambiguously the proportion of variance in the dependent variable accounted for by each of the independent variables. For each independent variable it is the square of its correlation with the dependent variable. The simplicity of the case in which the correlations among the independent variables are zero is easily explained: each variable offers unique information not shared with any of the other independent variables.

One of the advantages of experimental research is that, when appropriately planned and executed, the independent variables are not correlated. Consequently, the researcher is able to speak unambiguously about the effects of each of the independent variables, as well as of the interactions among them.

Much, if not most, of behavioral research is, however, nonexperimental. In this type of research the independent variables are usually correlated, sometimes substantially. The ubiquity of smaller and larger intercorrelations of independent variables and the difficulty of unambiguous interpretation of data are well illustrated in the large and important study, *Equality of Educational Opportunity* (Coleman et al., 1966, Appendix). The intercorrelations of the independent variables ranged from negative to positive and from low to high. (Problems of interpretation in this and other studies are dealt with in detail in Chapter 7.)

It is possible to view multiple regression analysis as a method of adjusting a set of correlated variables so that they become uncorrelated. This may be accomplished by using, successively, semipartial correlations. Formula (5.23) can be altered to express this viewpoint. For four independent variables,

$$R^2_{y.1234} = r^2_{y1} + r^2_{y(2.1)} + r^2_{y(3.12)} + r^2_{y(4.123)} \tag{5.24}$$

(For simplicity, only four independent variables are used rather than the general formula. Once the idea is grasped, the formula can be extended to accommodate as many independent variables as is necessary.)

Formula (5.23) is a special case of (5.24) (except for the number of variables). If the correlations among the independent variables are all zero, then (5.24) reduces to (5.23). Note what the formula says. The first independent variable, 1, since it is the first to enter the formula, expresses the variance shared by variable y and 1. Subsequent expressions will have to express the variance of added variables without duplicating or overlapping this first variance contribution. The second expression, $r^2_{y(2.1)}$, is the squared semipartial correlation between variable y and 2, partialing out the variance shared by variables 1 and 2.

The third term, $r^2_{y(3.12)}$, is the second-order semipartial correlation. When variable 3 is introduced, we want to take out of it whatever it shares with variables 1 and 2 so that the variance it contributes to the prediction of the dependent variable is not redundant to that already contributed by 1 and 2. It expresses the variance common to variables y and 3, after variables 1 and 2 have been partialed out from variable 3. The last term, $r^2_{y(4.123)}$, is the variance common to variables y and 4, partialing out the influence of variables 1, 2, and 3. In short, the formula spells out a procedure that residualizes each successive independent variable on the independent variables that preceded it. It is tantamount to creating new variables (i.e., residualized variables) that are not correlated with each other.

It was shown earlier that a squared semipartial correlation can be expressed as a difference between two squared multiple correlations. It will therefore be instructive to restate (5.24) accordingly:

$$\begin{aligned} R^2_{y.1234} &= R^2_{y.1} + (R^2_{y.12} - R^2_{y.1}) + (R^2_{y.123} - R^2_{y.12}) + (R^2_{y.1234} - R^2_{y.123}) \\ &= r^2_{y1} + r^2_{y(2.1)} + r^2_{y(3.12)} + r^2_{y(4.123)} \end{aligned} \tag{5.25}$$

(For the sake of uniformity, the zero-order correlation between X_1 and Y, r_{y1}, is expressed as $R_{y.1}$.) Removing the parentheses in (5.25) and performing the indicated operations will result in the algebraic identity: $R^2_{y.1234} = R^2_{y.1234}$.

As far as the calculation of R^2 is concerned, it makes no difference in what order the independent variables enter the equation and the calculations. That is, $R^2_{y.123} = R^2_{y.213} = R^2_{y.312}$. But the order in which the independent variables are entered into the equation makes a great deal of difference in the amount of variance incremented by each variable. A variable, if entered first, almost invariably will account for a much larger proportion of the variance than if it is entered second or third. In general, when the independent variables are correlated, the more they are correlated and the later they are entered in the regression equation, the less the variance they account for.

With four independent variables there are 24 (i.e., 4!) different orders in which the variables may be entered into the equation. In other words, it is possible to develop 24 equations like (5.24) or (5.25), each of which will be equal to $R^2_{y.1234}$. But the proportion of variance of the dependent variable attributed to a given independent variable will depend upon its specific point of entry into the equation. Is the choice of the order of entry of variables, then, arbitrary, or are there criteria for its determination? Attempts to answer this question are postponed to Chapter 7, in which the present approach is dealt with in the context of methods of variance partitioning. For now, it will only be noted that the criteria for a valid choice of a given order of entry for the variables depend on whether the research is designed for purposes of prediction only or whether the goal is explanation. The choice in predictive research relates to such issues as economy and feasibility, whereas the choice in explanatory research is predicated on the theory and hypotheses that are being tested (see Chapters 6 and 7).

COMPUTER ANALYSIS

The effect of the order of entry of the variables into the equation on the proportion of variance attributed to a given variable is now demonstrated numerically using the correlation matrix reported in Table 5.4. The same data are chosen so that comparisons with earlier analyses may be made. This time the REGRESSION program of SPSS is being used. As was done in Chapter 4, the control cards are presented first, followed by excerpts from the output and commentaries.

Control Cards

```
1               1
                6
RUN NAME        DIFFERENT ORDERS OF ENTRY
VARIABLE LIST   X1, X2, X3, X4
N OF CASES      20
REGRESSION      VARIABLES = X1 TO X4/
                REGRESSION = X1 WITH X2(6) X3(4) X4(2)/
                REGRESSION = X1 WITH X2(2) X3(4) X4(6)/
                REGRESSION = X1 WITH X2(4) X3(6) X4(2)/
OPTIONS         4
```

```
STATISTICS        ALL
READ MATRIX
10000    6735    5320    3475
 6735   10000    1447    3521
 5320    1447   10000    0225
 3475    3521    0225   10000
```

Commentary

In this example a correlation matrix is read in as input, instead of raw data. In SPSS it is required that correlation matrices be read in according to an 8F10.7 format. That is, each card consists of up to 8 fields of 10 columns each, with 7 digits after the decimal place. Because of this, there is no INPUT FORMAT card. Instead, OPTIONS 4 indicates that a matrix is to be read in. It is not necessary to punch the decimal points, but the numbers must be punched in the appropriate columns. The four values of the first card are punched as follows: 10000 in columns 3–7; 6735 in columns 14–17; 5320 in columns 24–27; 3475 in columns 34–37. The other cards are similarly punched. It is, of course, not necessary to punch the three additional zeros that follow the decimal point in each of the values of the matrix.

In this analysis, X_1 is treated as the dependent variable. In SPSS one may determine the order of entry of the independent variables into the equation by assigning an inclusion level to each variable, or to sets of variables. This is accomplished by inserting even numbers, in parentheses, following each variable, or each set of variables. The analysis is performed hierarchically, entering first the variable assigned the highest inclusion level, followed by the variable assigned a lower inclusion level, and so on until the variable assigned the lowest inclusion level is entered last into the equation. As can be seen from the control cards, three different orders of entry for the variables have been specified. Accordingly, three regression analyses will be done using the following hierarchies: (1) X_2, X_3, and X_4; (2) X_4, X_3, and X_2; (3) X_3, X_2, and X_4.

In order to conserve space, the separate steps and the statistics associated with them are not reported. They should pose no problems of interpretation since they follow the same pattern of output presented and discussed in detail in Chapter 4. There is, however, one difference between the output obtained here and the one obtained in Chapter 4. This has to do with the regression equations reported in the output. In Chapter 4, raw data were read in. Consequently, regression equations for raw scores (i.e., a and b's) as well as for standard scores (β's only) were reported. In the present analysis, a correlation matrix is read as input. Consequently, the program reports the b's and the β's as being the same. Also, the constant (a) is reported as being equal to zero, as it always is with standard scores. Incidentally, SPSS enables one to read in means and standard deviations, along with a correlation matrix. This is done by using OPTIONS 4 and 5. When both options are used, the output is identical to the one reported in Chapter 4.

It is suggested that you run the example as presented, or with different orders of entry for the variables, and study each step carefully. When doing so, you will probably benefit from going back to the analyses in Chapter 4. You will note, for example, that two different orders of entry for the independent variables were used in Chapter 4. Also, it was shown there how one may obtain the increment in the proportion of variance due to a given variable (i.e., the squared semipartial correlation) by subtracting the R^2 reported for the step preceding the entry of the given variable from the R^2 reported when the variable was entered. The same approach applies, of course, in the present example, although the SUMMARY TABLE (discussed below) is used instead.

As the R^2 and the regression equation are the same regardless of the order in which the variables are entered into the equation, results from the first regression analysis only are reported.

Output

R SQUARE .66375

- - - - - - - - - - - - - -VARIABLES IN EQUATION- - - - - - - - - - - - -

VARIABLE	B	BETA	STANDARD ERROR B	F
X2	.55921	.55921	.15657	12.76
X3	.44792	.44792	.14658	9.34
X4	.14052	.14052	.15496	.82
(CONSTANT) 0.0				

Commentary

This is the final step in the first analysis. The three variables are now in the equation. As was noted above, B = BETA because only statistics associated with standard scores can be calculated from a correlation matrix. It was pointed out earlier that tests of regression coefficients are the same as tests of partial and semipartial correlations to which they correspond. Thus, for example, the test of the BETA for X_2, $\beta_{12.34}$, has an F (1, 16) = 12.76, which is the same as the F ratio obtained earlier when $r^2_{1(2.34)}$ was tested for significance. Similarly, testing $\beta_{14.23}$ is the same as testing $r^2_{1(4.23)}$.

Finally, the output for the other two regression analyses will be the same as the one reported above, even though the variables are entered in different orders. To repeat: R^2 and the regression equation are not affected by the order in which the variables are entered into the analysis, but the proportion of variance attributed to a given variable is affected by the order of its entry into the analysis.

Output

SUMMARY TABLE

1			2		
VARIABLE	R SQUARE	RSQ CHANGE	VARIABLE	R SQUARE	RSQ CHANGE
X2	.45360	.45360	X4	.12076	.12076
X3	.64647	.19287	X3	.39566	.27491
X4	.66375	.01728	X2	.66375	.26809

3

VARIABLE	R SQUARE	RSQ CHANGE
X3	.28302	.28302
X2	.64647	.36345
X4	.66375	.01728

Commentary

For each regression analysis a SUMMARY TABLE is reported. The elements of such tables are discussed in detail in Chapter 4. In the present example, only relevant parts of the summary tables are reported. They are given here in a single table so as to facilitate comparisons among them. Thus the part labeled 1 is for the first regression analysis; 2 is for the second; and 3 is for the third regression analysis.

Looking first at the part of the summary table labeled 1, it will be noted that R SQUARE for X_2 is actually the squared zero-order correlation between X_1 and X_2, r^2_{12}. The RSQ CHANGE for this variable is the same as R SQUARE, as no other variable has as yet entered into the analysis. The R SQUARE printed alongside X_3 (i.e., .64647) is the squared multiple correlation of X_1 with X_2 *and* X_3, $R^2_{1.23}$. RSQ CHANGE alongside X_3 is equal to $R^2_{1.23} - R^2_{1.2} = .64647 - .45360 = .19287$. This, then, is the increment in the proportion of variance due to X_3 after X_2 is already taken into account. It was shown earlier that this increment is equal to $r^2_{1(3.2)}$. Similarly, R SQUARE reported alongside X_4 is $R^2_{1.234}$, and the RSQ CHANGE associated with this variable is equal to $R^2_{1.234} - R^2_{1.23} = .66375 - .64647 = .01728$. Again, RSQ CHANGE for X_4 is the same as the squared semipartial correlation of X_1 with X_4, partialing all the preceding variables from X_4, $r^2_{1(4.23)}$. Using the values reported in the column labeled RSQ CHANGE one can express $R^2_{1.234}$ as was done earlier in Formula (5.24):

$$R^2_{1.234} = r^2_{12} + r^2_{1(3.2)} + r^2_{1(4.23)}$$

$$.45360 + .19287 + .01728 = .66375$$

The summary table for the second and third regression analyses are similarly used and interpreted. Thus, for the second regression analysis:

$$R^2_{1.234} = r^2_{14} + r^2_{1(3.4)} + r_{1(2.34)}$$

$$= .12076 + .27491 + .26809 = .66375$$

Note, for example, that when X_4 enters last it accounts for about 2% of the variance (see SUMMARY TABLE 1). But, when it enters first it accounts for about 12% of the variance (see SUMMARY TABLE 2). Similarly, when X_2 is entered first it accounts for about 45% of the variance (see SUMMARY TABLE 1). When X_2 is entered second, it accounts for about 36% of the variance (see SUMMARY TABLE 3). And when X_2 is entered last, it accounts for about 27% of the variance (see SUMMARY TABLE 2). Compare these, and other results, with those obtained earlier in this chapter.

Finally, Formulas (5.5) and (5.6) for squared partial correlations are repeated here in order to show how one may obtain squared partial correlations from the SUMMARY TABLE.

$$r^2_{12.3} = \frac{R^2_{1.23} - R^2_{1.3}}{1 - R^2_{1.3}}$$

The numerator is, as was discussed earlier, $r^2_{1(2.3)}$. In the present output it is equal to RSQ CHANGE reported alongside X_2 in SUMMARY TABLE 3 (i.e., .36345). The denominator is simply one minus the value of R SQUARE reported in the same table for X_3 (i.e., .28302). Therefore,

$$r^2_{12.3} = \frac{.36345}{1 - .28302} = .50692$$

And,

$$r^2_{12.34} = \frac{R^2_{1.234} - R^2_{1.34}}{1 - R^2_{1.34}}$$

The necessary values may be obtained from SUMMARY TABLE 2, where RSQ CHANGE reported for X_2, .26809, is equal to the numerator, $R^2_{1.234} - R^2_{1.34}$. The denominator is simply one minus $R^2_{1.34}$, which is the value of R SQUARE reported alongside X_3 (.39566). Therefore,

$$r^2_{12.34} = \frac{.26809}{1 - .39566} = .44361$$

Compare with the value obtained earlier in this chapter.

MULTIPLE PARTIAL AND SEMIPARTIAL CORRELATIONS

Until now we have dealt with a correlation between two variables while partialing out other variables from *both* of them (i.e., partial correlations) or from only *one* of them (i.e., semipartial correlations). Logical extensions of such correlations are the multiple partial and the multiple semipartial correlations.

Multiple Partial Correlation

A multiple partial correlation may be used to calculate the squared multiple correlation of a dependent variable with a set of independent variables, after controlling, or partialing out, the effects of another variable, or variables, from the dependent and the independent variables. The difference, then, between a partial and a multiple partial correlation is that in the former there is only one independent variable, whereas in the latter more than one independent variable is being used. For example, suppose that a researcher is interested in the squared multiple correlation of academic achievement with mental age and motivation. Since, however, his sample is heterogeneous in age, he wishes to control for this variable while studying the relations among the other variables. He can accomplish this by the calculation of a multiple partial correlation. Note that had only one independent variable been involved (i.e., either mental age or motivation) a partial correlation would be called for.

Conceptually and analytically, the multiple partial correlation and the partial correlation are designed to accomplish the same goal. In the above example this means that academic achievement, mental age, and motivation are residualized on age. The residualized variables may then be used as ordinary variables in a multiple regression analysis. As with partial correlations, one may partial out more than one variable. In the above example, one may partial out age as well as, say, socioeconomic status.

We use the following notation: $R^2_{1.23(4)}$, which means the squared multiple correlation of X_1 with X_2 and X_3, after X_4 has been partialed out from the other variables. Note that the variable that is being partialed out is placed in parentheses. Similarly, $R^2_{1.23(45)}$ is the squared multiple correlation of X_1 with X_2 and X_3, after X_4 and X_5 have been partialed out from the other three variables.

The calculation of squared multiple partial correlations is similar to the calculation of squared partial correlations:

$$R^2_{1.23(4)} = \frac{R^2_{1.234} - R^2_{1.4}}{1 - R^2_{1.4}} \tag{5.26}$$

Note the similarity between (5.26) and (5.4), the formula for the squared partial correlation. Had there been only one independent variable (i.e., X_2 or X_3), Equation (5.26) would have been reduced to (5.4). To calculate the squared multiple partial correlation, then: (1) calculate the squared multiple correlation of the dependent variable with all the other variables (i.e., the independent and the control variables); (2) calculate the squared multiple correlation of the dependent variable with the control variables only: (3) subtract the R^2 obtained in step 2 from the R^2 obtained in step 1; (4) divide the value obtained in step 3 by one minus the R^2 obtained in step 2.

The formula for the calculation of the squared multiple partial correlation with two control variables is:

$$R^2_{1.23(45)} = \frac{R^2_{1.2345} - R^2_{1.45}}{1 - R^2_{1.45}} \tag{5.27}$$

Extensions of (5.26) or (5.27) to any number of independent variables and any number of control variables are straightforward.

Numerical Examples. A correlation matrix for five variables is reported in Table 5.5. Assume that it is desired to calculate the squared multiple partial correlation of achievement (X_1) with mental ability (X_2) and motivation (X_3),

Table 5.5 Correlation Matrix for Five Variables (Illustrative Data)

	1 *Achievement*	2 *Mental Ability*	3 *Motivation*	4 *Age*	5 *SES*
1	1.00	.80	.60	.70	.30
2	.80	1.00	.40	.80	.40
3	.60	.40	1.00	.30	.35
4	.70	.80	.30	1.00	.04
5	.30	.40	.35	.04	1.00

while controlling for age (X_4). Using a computer program to calculate the relevant R^2's, and applying Formula (5.26):

$$R^2_{1.23(4)} = \frac{R^2_{1.234} - R^2_{1.4}}{1 - R^2_{1.4}} = \frac{.74570 - .49000}{1 - .49000} = \frac{.2557}{.51} = .50137$$

While $R^2_{1.23} = .73333$, the squared multiple partial correlation is .50137. Controlling for age reduced by about 23% the variance that mental ability and motivation account for in achievement.

Assume now that it is desired to control for both age (X_4) and SES (X_5); that is, it is desired to calculate $R^2_{1.23(45)}$. Calculating the relevant R^2's and applying Formula (5.27):

$$R^2_{1.23(45)} = \frac{R^2_{1.2345} - R^2_{1.45}}{1 - R^2_{1.45}} = \frac{.74747 - .56410}{1 - .56410} = \frac{.18337}{.4359} = .42067$$

Controlling for both age and SES, the squared multiple correlation of achievement with mental ability and motivation is .42067. Compare with $R^2_{1.23} = .73333$.

Multiple Semipartial Correlation

Instead of partialing out variables from both the independent and dependent variables, it is possible to partial out variables from the independent variables only. For example, one may wish to calculate the squared multiple correlation of X_1 with X_2 and X_3, after X_4 has been partialed out from X_2 and X_3. This, then is an example of a squared multiple semipartial correlation. The notation is: $R^2_{1(23.4)}$. Note the analogy between this notation and the squared semipartial correlation. The dependent variable is outside the parentheses. The control variable (or variables) is placed after the dot. Similarly, $R^2_{1(23.45)}$ is the squared multiple semipartial correlation of X_1 with X_2 and X_3, after X_4 and X_5 have been partialed out from X_2 and X_3.

Analogous to the squared semipartial correlation, the squared multiple semipartial correlation indicates the increment in the proportion of variance of the dependent variable that is accounted for by more than one independent variable. In other words, in the case of the squared semipartial correlation the increment is due to one independent variable, whereas in the case of the squared multiple semipartial correlation the increment is due to more than one independent variable. Accordingly, the squared multiple semipartial correlation is calculated as one would calculate a squared semipartial correlation, except that more than one independent variable is being used for the former, For example,

$$R^2_{1(23.4)} = R^2_{1.234} - R^2_{1.4} \tag{5.28}$$

Formula (5.28) indicates the proportion of variance in X_1 accounted for by X_2 and X_3 after the contribution of X_4 has been taken into account. Note that the expression of (5.28) is the same as the numerator of (5.26), the formula for the squared multiple partial correlation. A similar relationship was shown between the formulas for the squared semipartial and the squared partial correlations.

Using the data of Table 5.5, calculate:

$$R^2_{1(23.4)} = R^2_{1.234} - R^2_{1.4} = .74570 - .49000 = .2557$$

After partialing out X_4 from X_2 and X_3, these two variables account for about 26% of the variance in X_1. That is, the increment in the percent of variance in achievement (X_1) accounted for by mental ability (X_2) and motivation (X_3), over and above what age (X_4) accounts for, is 26%.

Calculate now:

$$R^2_{1(23.45)} = R^2_{1.2345} - R^2_{1.45} = .74747 - .56410 = .18337$$

After controlling for both age and SES, mental ability and motivation account for about 18% of the variance in achievement.

The calculation of the squared multiple partial correlation and the squared multiple semipartial correlation can be facilitated when one uses a computer program that permits the assignment of inclusion levels for variables or sets of variables. For example, using SPSS for the calculation of $R^2_{1(23.45)}$, one would specify (beginning in column 16); REGRESSION = X1 WITH X4, X5(4) X2, X3(2)/. Summing the increments due to X_2 and X_3, reported in the SUMMARY TABLE as RSQ CHANGE, yields $R^2_{1(23.45)}$.

The decision whether to calculate a squared multiple partial or a squared multiple semipartial correlation depends on one's theory and specific purposes (see Variance Partitioning in Chapter 7).

Tests of Significance

Tests of significance for squared multiple partial and squared multiple semipartial correlations yield identical results. Basically, the increment in proportion of variance of the dependent variable accounted for by a set of independent variables is tested. Consequently, Formula (5.22) is used for this purpose. To illustrate, assume that the matrix of Table 5.5 is based on $N = 300$. Testing $R^2_{1(23.4)}$:

$$F = \frac{(R^2_{1.234} - R^2_{1.4})/(k_1 - k_2)}{(1 - R^2_{1.234})/(N - k_1 - 1)} = \frac{(.74570 - .49000)/(3 - 1)}{(1 - .74570)/(300 - 3 - 1)} = \frac{.12785}{.00086} = 148.7$$

with 2 and 296 *df*. This is also a test of $R^2_{1.23(4)}$.

Testing $R^2_{1(23.45)}$:

$$F = \frac{(R^2_{1.2345} - R^2_{1.45})/(k_1 - k_2)}{(1 - R^2_{1.2345})/(N - k_1 - 1)} = \frac{(.74747 - .56410)/(4 - 2)}{(1 - .74747)/(300 - 4 - 1)} = \frac{.09168}{.00086} = 106.6$$

with 2 and 295 *df*. This is also a test of $R^2_{1.23(45)}$.

SUMMARY

The main ideas of this chapter have been the control and explication of variables through partial and semipartial correlations. It was shown that a partial correlation is a correlation between two variables that have been residualized on one or more control variables. A semipartial correlation, on the other hand, was shown to be a correlation between an unmodified variable and a variable that has been residualized on one or more control variables.

The role of theory in dictating which variables are to be controlled and what type of control is to be exercised was stressed. It was argued that the absence of a theory about the causes of the relations among the variables under consideration precludes the exercise of meaningful controls of variables. When, for example, it is desired to study the relation between two variables after the effects of their common causes have been removed, a partial correlation is called for. When, on the other hand, it is desired to study the relation between an independent variable and a dependent variable after removing the effects of other independent variables from only the former, a semipartial correlation is called for. Clearly, the preceding statements imply different theoretical formulations regarding the relations among the variables being studied.

It was shown that the squared semipartial correlation indicates the proportion of variance that a given independent variable accounts for in the dependent variable, after taking into account the effects of other independent variables. Consequently, it was said, and demonstrated, that the order in which independent variables are entered into the analysis is crucial when it is desired to determine the proportion of variance incremented by each of them. Issues regarding the determination of the order of entry of independent variables into the analysis as well as the meaning of increments in the proportion of variance accounted for were commented upon briefly. It was noted that these topics are discussed in detail in Chapter 7.

Adverse effects of measurement errors on the attempts to study the relation between two variables while controlling for other variables were discussed and illustrated. The chapter concluded with a presentation of extensions of the partial and semipartial correlations to multiple partial and multiple semipartial correlations.

STUDY SUGGESTIONS

1. Suppose that the correlation between the size of palm and verbal ability is .55; between size of palm and age, .70; and between age and verbal ability, .80. What is the correlation between size of palm and verbal ability after partialing out age? How might one label the zero-order correlation between size of palm and verbal ability?
2. Assume that the following correlations were obtained in a study: .51 between level of aspiration and school achievement; .40 between social class and school achievement; .30 between level of aspiration and social class.
   (a) Suppose it is desired to determine the correlation between level of aspiration and school achievement after controlling for social class. What is this correlation?
   (b) The reliability of the measurement of social class is .82. What is the correlation between level of aspiration and school achievement after controlling for social class and correcting for the unreliability of its measurement? Interpret the results.
3. How does a semipartial-correlation coefficient differ from a partial-correlation coefficient?
4. Express the following as differences between R^2's: (a) $r^2_{1(3.2)}$; (b) $r^2_{1(3.24)}$; (c) $r^2_{5(1.234)}$.
5. Express $R^2_{2.1435}$ as:
   (a) one squared zero-order correlation and a set of squared semipartial correlations.
   (b) one squared zero-order correlation and a set of terms composed of differences between R^2's.
6. Read in the following correlation matrix in a program for multiple regression. Call for the necessary R^2's, entering the independent variables in appropriate hierarchies, so that you may use relevant output for the calculation of the terms indicated below. ($N = 500$.)

	Variables				
	1	*2*	*3*	*4*	*5*
1	1.00	.35	.40	.52	.48
2	.35	1.00	.15	.37	.40
3	.40	.15	1.00	.31	.50
4	.52	.37	.31	1.00	.46
5	.48	.40	.50	.46	1.00

   (a) (1) $r^2_{13.2}$ and $r^2_{1(3.2)}$
   (2) $r^2_{14.23}$ and $r^2_{1(4.23)}$
   (3) $r^2_{15.234}$ and $r^2_{1(5.234)}$
   (b) (1) $r^2_{32.4}$ and $r^2_{3(2.4)}$
   (2) $r^2_{35.24}$ and $r^2_{3(5.24)}$
   (3) $r^2_{31.245}$ and $r^2_{3(1.245)}$

ANSWERS

1. −.02; spurious.
2. (a) The partial correlation between level of aspiration and school achievement is .45.
   (b) After correcting for the unreliability of measurement of social class, the partial correlation between level of aspiration and school achievement is .43.
4. (a) $R^2_{1.32} - R^2_{1.2}$; (b) $R^2_{1.324} - R^2_{1.24}$; (c) $R^2_{5.1234} - R^2_{5.234}$
5. (a) $r^2_{21} + r^2_{2(4.1)} + r^2_{2(3.14)} + r^2_{2(5.143)}$
   (b) $r^2_{21} + (R^2_{2.14} - R^2_{2.1}) + (R^2_{2.143} - R^2_{2.14}) + (R^2_{2.1435} - R^2_{2.143})$
   (a) (1) .14079 and .12354; (2) .14984 and .11297; (3) .03139 and .02012
   (b) (1) .00159 and .00144; (2) .18454 and .16654; (3) .03957 and .02912

PREDICTION

Prediction and explanation are central concepts in scientific research, as indeed they are in human action and thought. It is probably because of their preeminence that these concepts have acquired a variety of meanings and usages, resulting in ambiguities and controversies. Philosophers of science have devoted a great deal of efforts to the explication of prediction and explanation, some viewing them as structurally and logically identical, others considering them as being distinct and predicated on different logical structures.

Hempel (1965), for example, argues:

> Thus, the logical structure of a scientific prediction is the same as that of a scientific explanation. . . . The customary distinction between explanation and prediction rests mainly on a pragmatic difference between the two: While in the case of an explanation, the final event is known to have happened, and its determining conditions have to be sought, the situation is reversed in the case of a prediction: here, the initial conditions are given, and their "effect"—which, in the typical case, has not yet taken place—is to be determined (p. 234).

De Groot (1969) equates knowledge with the ability to predict: "The criterion *par excellence* of true knowledge is to be found in the ability to predict the results of a testing procedure. *If one knows something to be true, he is in a position to predict; where prediction is impossible, there is no knowledge*" (p. 20).

Scriven (1959), on the other hand, claims that there is "a gross difference" (p. 480) between prediction and explanation. Among other things, Scriven points out that in certain situations it is possible to predict phenomena without being able to explain them, and vice versa. "Roughly speaking, the prediction requires only a correlation, the explanation requires more. This difference has as one consequence the possibility of making predictions from indicators of causes—for example, predicting a storm from a sudden drop in the barometric pressure. Clearly we could not say that the drop in pressure in our house caused the storm: it merely presaged it'' (p. 480).

Kaplan (1964) maintains that from the standpoint of a philosopher of science the ideal explanation is probably one that allows prediction.

> The converse, however, is surely questionable; predictions can be and often are made even though we are not in a position to explain what is being predicted. This capacity is characteristic of well-established empirical generalizations that have not yet been transformed into theoretical laws. . . . In short, explanations provide understanding, but we can predict without being able to understand, and we can understand without necessarily being able to predict. It remains true that if we can predict successfully on the basis of certain explanations we have good reason, and perhaps the best sort of reason, for accepting the explanation (pp. 349–350).

The foregoing was meant to provide only a glimpse at the complex problems attendant with attempts to delineate the status and role of prediction and explanation in scientific research. In addition to the sources cited above, discussions of prediction and explanation may be found in Brodbeck (1968, Part Five); Doby (1967, Chapter 4); Feigl and Brodbeck (1953, Part IV); Scheffler (1957); Sjoberg and Nett (1968, Chapter 11).

Regardless of one's philosophical orientation concerning prediction and explanation, it is necessary to distinguish between research designed primarily for predictive purposes and that designed primarily for explanatory purposes. In predictive research the main emphasis is on practical applications, whereas in explanatory research the main emphasis is on the understanding of phenomena. This is not to say that the two research activities are unrelated, or that they have no bearing on each other. Predictive research may, for example, serve as a source of hunches and insights that lead to theoretical formulations. This state of affairs is probably most characteristic of the initial stages of the development of a science. Explanatory research may serve as the most powerful means for prediction. Yet the importance of distinguishing between the two types of research activities cannot be overemphasized.

The distinction between predictive and explanatory research is particularly germane to the valid use and interpretation of results from regression analysis. In predictive research, the goal is to optimize prediction of criteria such as income, social adjustment, election results, academic achievement, or delinquency. Consequently, the choice of variables in research of this kind is primarily determined by their contribution to the prediction of the criterion. ''If the correlation is high, no other standards are necessary. Thus if it were found that accuracy in horseshoe pitching correlated highly with success in college, horseshoe pitching would be a valid means of predicting success in college'' (Nunnally, 1978, p. 88). Cook and Campbell (1979) make the same point:

> For purely forecasting purposes, it does not matter whether a predictor works because it is a symptom or a cause. For example, your goal may be simply to predict who will finish high school. In that case, entering the Head Start experience into a predictive equation

as a negative predictor which reduces the likelihood of graduation may be efficient even if the Head Start experience improved the chances of high school graduation. This is because receiving Head Start training is also evidence of massive environmental disadvantages which work against completing high school and which may be only slightly offset by the training received in Head Start. In the same vein, while psychotherapy probably reduces a depressed person's likelihood of suicide, for forecasting purposes it is probably the case that the more psychotherapy one has received the greater is the likelihood of suicide. (p. 296)

In a reanalysis of data from the Coleman Report, Armor (1972) found that an index of nine household items (e.g., having a television set, telephone, refrigerator, dictionary) had the highest correlation with verbal achievement, namely .80 and .72 for black and white sixth-grade students, respectively. It is valid to treat such an index as a useful predictor of verbal achievement. But would one venture to use it as a cause of verbal achievement? Would even a naive researcher be tempted to recommend that the government scrap the very costly and controversial compensatory educational programs in favor of a less costly program, that of supplying all families who do not have them with the nine household items, thereby leading to the enhancement of verbal achievement? Yet, as will be shown in this and in the next chapter, social science researchers frequently fall into such traps when they use purely predictive studies for the purpose of explaining phenomena.

The fact that the usefulness of variables in a predictive study is empirically determined should not be taken to mean that theory plays no role, or is irrelevant, in the choice of such variables. On the contrary, theory is the best guide in the selection of criteria and predictors, as well as in the development of measures of such variables. The chances of attaining substantial predictability while minimizing costs and efforts are enhanced when the predictor variables are selected as a result of theoretical considerations. Discussions of criterion-related validity are largely devoted to issues related to the selection and measurement of criterion and predictor variables (see, for example, Cronbach, 1971; Nunnally, 1978; Thorndike, 1949).

As a safeguard against confusing the two types of research, some writers have proposed different terminologies for each of them. Thus, Wold and Jureen (1953) proposed that in predictive research the predictors be referred to as *regressors* and the criterion be referred to as the *regressand*. In explanatory research, on the other hand, they propose the label *cause* (or *explanatory*) for what is generally referred to as an independent variable, and the label *effect* for the dependent variable.[1] In this book, the terms *predictor* and *criterion* are used in the context of predictive research. The terms *independent* and *dependent* variables are used in the context of explanatory research. Responding to the necessity for distinguishing between predictive and explanatory research, Tukey (1954) has suggested that regression analysis used in the former be referred to as "predictive regression," whereas regression analysis in the latter be referred to as "structural regression."

[1]Wold and Juréen's (1953, Chapter 2) discussion of the distinction between predictive and explanatory research in the context of regression analysis is probably the best available on this topic. See also Blalock (1964) for a very good discussion of these issues.

In predictive research, the researcher is at liberty to interchange the roles of the predictor and the criterion variables. From a predictive frame of reference it is just as tenable to use, for example, mental ability to predict motivation as it is to use motivation for the purpose of predicting mental ability. Similarly, a researcher may use self-concept to predict achievement, or reverse the role of these variables and use achievement to predict self-concept. Numerous examples of the arbitrary designation of variables as predictors and criteria abound in the social sciences. There is nothing wrong with such strategies, so long as one does not accord the variables the status and role of independent and dependent variables, and so long as one does not interpret the results as if they were obtained in explanatory research.

Finally, it will be noted that, when appropriately used, regression analysis in predictive research poses little difficulties in interpretation. It is the use and interpretation of regression analysis in explanatory research that is fraught with ambiguities and potential misinterpretations, and it is within this context that controversies abound. The present chapter is devoted to the application and interpretation of regression analysis in predictive research. Explanatory research is dealt with in detail in Chapters 7 and 8. It is hoped that dealing with the two types of research in separate chapters will further stress the importance of distinguishing between them.

REGRESSION ANALYSIS IN SELECTION

One of the major uses of regression analysis in predictive research is for the selection of applicants, be it for a job, a training program, college, the armed forces, to name but a few examples. Basically, a regression equation is being sought so that on the basis of an applicant's status on a set of predictors his or her performance on a criterion may be predicted. It should be noted that while our concern here is exclusively with the development of such prediction equations, there are various other factors (e.g., the ratio of available positions to the number of applicants, cost, utility) that enter into the complex decisions related to selection. For detailed treatments of these and related topics see, for example, Cronbach and Gleser (1965); Thorndike (1949); Wiggins (1973).

In order to develop the prediction equation, it is necessary first to select a criterion (e.g., success on the job, achievement in school), define it, and have valid and reliable measures to assess it. This is a most complex topic that cannot be dealt with here (for extensive discussions, see, for example, Cronbach, 1971; Cureton, 1951; Nunnally, 1978; Wiggins, 1973). Assuming one has a valid and reliable measure of the criterion, predictor variables are selected, preferably on the basis of theoretical considerations and previous research evidence. It is necessary to have a representative sample of potential applicants for whom scores on the predictors as well as the criterion are available. The regression equation developed on the basis of the sample is then used in predicting criterion scores for future applicants.

As was done in earlier chapters, a numerical example with illustrative data is used in order to illustrate the analysis as well as various concepts related to the use of regression analysis in predictive research.

Table 6.1 Illustrative Data for a Selection Problem; $N = 30$[a]

Ss	*GPA*	*GREQ*	*GREV*	*MAT*	*AR*	*Predicted*	*Lower 95% CL Individual*	*Upper 95% CL Individual*
1	3.2	625	540	65	2.7	3.33	2.44	4.22
2	4.1	575	680	75	4.5	3.81	2.97	4.66
3	3.0	520	480	65	2.5	2.79	1.94	3.64
4	2.6	545	520	55	3.1	2.83	2.00	3.66
5	3.7	520	490	75	3.6	3.17	2.32	4.03
6	4.0	655	535	65	4.3	3.67	2.79	4.56
7	4.3	630	720	75	4.6	4.11	3.25	4.97
8	2.7	500	500	75	3.0	3.02	2.15	3.89
9	3.6	605	575	65	4.7	3.59	2.74	4.45
10	4.1	555	690	75	3.4	3.59	2.73	4.45
11	2.7	505	545	55	3.7	2.79	1.91	3.67
12	2.9	540	515	55	2.6	2.73	1.89	3.57
13	2.5	520	520	55	3.1	2.73	1.89	3.57
14	3.0	585	710	65	2.7	3.43	2.54	4.32
15	3.3	600	610	85	5.0	4.09	3.21	4.96
16	3.2	625	540	65	2.7	3.33	2.44	4.22
17	4.1	575	680	75	4.5	3.81	2.97	4.66
18	3.0	520	480	65	2.5	2.79	1.94	3.64
19	2.6	545	520	55	3.1	2.83	2.00	3.66
20	3.7	520	490	75	3.6	3.17	2.32	4.03
21	4.0	655	535	65	4.3	3.67	2.79	4.56
22	4.3	630	720	75	4.6	4.11	3.25	4.97
23	2.7	500	500	75	3.0	3.02	2.15	3.89
24	3.6	605	575	65	4.7	3.59	2.74	4.45
25	4.1	555	690	75	3.4	3.59	2.73	4.45
26	2.7	505	545	55	3.7	2.79	1.91	3.67
27	2.9	540	515	55	2.6	2.73	1.89	3.57
28	2.5	520	520	55	3.1	2.73	1.89	3.57
29	3.0	585	710	65	2.7	3.43	2.54	4.32
30	3.3	600	610	85	5.0	4.09	3.21	4.96
M:	3.31	565.33	575.33	67.00	3.57			
s:	.60	48.62	83.03	9.25	.84			

[a]GPA = Grade-Point Average; GREQ = Graduate Record Examination—Quantitative; GREV = Graduate Record Examination—Verbal; MAT = Miller Analogies Test; AR = Average Rating.

A Numerical Example

Assume that for the purpose of selecting applicants for graduate study, a psychology department has decided to use grade-point average (GPA) as a criterion. Four predictors are used. Of these, three are measures administered to each student at the time of application. They are: (1) Graduate Record Examination—Quantitative (GREQ); (2) Graduate Record Examination—Verbal (GREV); and (3) Miller Analogies Test (MAT). In addition, each applicant is interviewed by three professors, each of whom rate the applicant on a five-point scale, five indicating a very promising candidate. The average rating (AR) given by the three professors is the fourth predictor. A set of illustrative data for 30 subjects on the five variables is reported in Table 6.1. Also included in the table is a column consisting of predicted scores and two columns labeled Lower 95% CL Individual and Upper 95% CL Individual (these are discussed below).

For reasons discussed below, the GLM program from SAS was used to analyze the data. Except for some parts of the MODEL statement, which are discussed later, the control cards are identical to the ones presented in Chapter 4, and will therefore not be commented upon.

Control Cards

```
DATA;
INPUT GPA 1-2 1 GREQ 3-6 GREV 7-10 MAT 11-13 AR 14-16 1;
CARDS;
32  625  540  65  27
41  575  680  75  45
...
...
...
33  600  610  85  50
PROC PRINT;
PROC GLM; MODEL GPA = GREQ GREV MAT AR/P CLI I;
TITLE DATA OF TABLE 6.1;
```

Output

Following are excerpts of the computer output (some of the values were rounded to five decimal places).

DEPENDENT VARIABLE: GPA

SOURCE	DF	SUM OF SQUARES	MEAN SQUARE	F VALUE	R-SQUARE
MODEL	4	6.68313	1.67078	11.13	.64047
ERROR	25	3.75153	.15006		
TOTAL	29	10.43466			

PARAMETER	ESTIMATE	T FOR HO: PARAMETER = 0	STD ERROR OF ESTIMATE
INTERCEPT	−1.73811	−1.83	.95074
GREQ	.00400	2.18	.00183
GREV	.00152	1.45	.00105
MAT	.02090	2.19	.00955
AR	.14423	1.28	.11300

Commentary

The four predictors account for about 64% of the variance of GPA (R^2 = .64047). The F ratio for the total regression is obtained by dividing the MEAN SQUARE MODEL (in SPSS and BMD programs this value is labeled RE-

GRESSION) by the MEAN SQUARE ERROR (1.67078/.15006 = 11.13), with 4 and 25 *df*, $p < .001$. The reported F ratio is, of course, also a test of R^2. To see this, use Formula (3.21) to calculate:

$$F = \frac{R^2/k}{(1 - R^2)/(N - k - 1)} = \frac{.64047/4}{(1 - .64047)/(30 - 4 - 1)} = \frac{.16012}{.01438} = 11.13$$

with 4 and 25 *df*.

The regression equation, reported above under the column labeled ESTIMATE, is:

$$\text{GPA}' = -1.73811 + .00400\ \text{GREQ} + .00152\ \text{GREV} + .02090\ \text{MAT} + .14423\ \text{AR}$$

The t ratio for each regression coefficient is obtained by dividing the regression coefficient by its standard error. Each t has 25 *df* (the degrees of freedom associated with the error term).

Using $\alpha = .05$, it is evident from the output reported above that the regression coefficients for GREV and AR are not statistically different from zero. It should be noted that this is due, in part, to the small sample size used here for illustrative purposes only. Normally, a much larger sample size is called for (see discussion below). Assume, for the sake of illustration, that the sample size is adequate. Note that the largest regression coefficient (.14423 for AR) has the smallest t ratio (1.28). It was pointed out earlier (see Chapter 3, Relative Importance of Variables) that the magnitude of the b is affected, among other things, by the units of the scale being used to measure the variable with which the b is associated. AR is measured with a scale that may range from 1 to 5, whereas GREV and GREQ are based on scales with much larger ranges; hence the larger coefficient for AR. Also, because the range of scores for the criterion is relatively small, all the b's are relatively small. It was suggested earlier that calculations be carried out to as many decimal places as is possible. When the calculations are done by hand it is suggested that they be carried to at least five decimal places. Note that had one calculated the b's for the present example to two decimal places only, the b for GREQ, which is significant, would have been incorrectly reported as equal to .00.

Deleting Variables from the Equation

On the basis of the tests of significance, it appears that GREV and AR may be deleted from the equation without a substantial loss in predictability. Recall that the test of a b is tantamount to testing the proportion of variance incremented by the variable with which the b is associated when the variable is entered last in the equation (see discussions of this point in Chapter 3, Testing Increments in Proportion of Variance Accounted for, and in Chapter 4, Increments in Regression Sum of Squares and Proportion of Variance). Depending on the pattern of the intercorrelations among the variables, it is possible that a variable that has been shown to have a nonsignificant b will turn out to have a significant b when another variable (or variables) is deleted from the equation. In the present example, it is possible for the b associated with GREV to be statistically significant when AR is deleted, or for the b associated with AR to be significant when GREV is deleted. Deleting both variables simultaneously will, of course, not provide this type of information. It is therefore recommended that variables be deleted one at a time so that the effect of the deletion on the magnitudes and the tests of significance of the b's for the remaining variables may be noted. For the present example, it is necessary to calculate two regression analyses: one in which AR is deleted, and one in which GREV is deleted. Following are the two regression equations that were obtained from such analyses for the data of Table 6.1. The t ratios (each with 26 df) are given in parentheses underneath the regression coefficients.

$$\text{GPA}' = -2.14877 + \underset{(2.90)}{.00493}\ \text{GREQ} + \underset{(2.99)}{.02612}\ \text{MAT} + \underset{(1.52)}{.00161}\ \text{GREV}$$

$$\text{GPA}' = -1.68902 + \underset{(2.80)}{.00492}\ \text{GREQ} + \underset{(2.67)}{.02492}\ \text{MAT} + \underset{(1.35)}{.15506}\ \text{AR}$$

In the present case, neither GREV nor AR has a significant b when the other variable is deleted from the equation. It is therefore decided to delete both variables from the equation. The final regression equation is:

$$\text{GPA}' = -2.12938 + \underset{(3.76)}{.00598}\ \text{GREQ} + \underset{(3.68)}{.03081}\ \text{MAT}$$

Using only GREQ and MAT, $R^2 = .58300$, as compared with $R^2 = .64047$ when the four predictors are used. In other words, using GREV and AR one could account for an additional 6% of the variance ($.64047 - .58300 = .05747$). Such an increment would not be viewed as trivial in most social science research. It is, however, not statistically significant, largely because of the small sample size. (This example is further analyzed later in the chapter.)

Although the discussion thus far, and the numerical example, dealt with a selection problem, it should be clear that the same approach is applicable whenever one's aim is to predict to a criterion. Thus, the analysis will proceed in the same way as above if, for example, one were interested in predicting delinquency, using family size, socioeconomic status, health, sex, race, and school achievement as predictors. In short, the analytic approach is the same, regardless of the specific criterion and predictors, and regardless of the specific predictive use to which the analysis is being put.

Finally, note carefully that *no* interpretation of the b's as indices of the effects of the variables on the criterion has been made. This is because such an interpretation of b's is inappropriate in predictive research. This topic is discussed in detail in Chapter 8.

CONFIDENCE INTERVALS FOR PREDICTED SCORES

When a regression equation is used to predict a new value of Y on the basis of given X's, errors that are associated with the regression equation as well as random errors of Y affect the accuracy of the prediction. As with other statistics, it is possible to calculate the standard error of a predicted score and to use it in setting up confidence intervals around the predicted score.

The following presentation is based on the assumption that the conditions under which the regression equation was developed remain unchanged. Changes in the situation may diminish the usefulness of the regression equation, or even render it useless. If, for example, the criterion is grade-point average in college, and there have been important changes in grading policies, a regression equation derived in a situation prior to such changes may not apply any longer. A similar problem would occur if there has been a radical change in the type of applicants.

Standard Error of a Predicted Score: One Predictor

The standard error of a predicted score is presented first for the case of one predictor. Extensions to multiple predictors are presented subsequently. The formula for the standard error of a predicted score is

$$s_{y'} = s_{y.x}\sqrt{1 + \frac{1}{N} + \frac{(X - \bar{X})^2}{\Sigma x^2}} \tag{6.1}$$

where $s_{y'}$ = standard error of predicted $Y(Y')$; $s_{y.x}$ = standard error of estimate (see Formula (2.27) and related discussion); N = sample size; X = score on the predictor; $\bar{X}$ = mean of the predictor; Σx^2 = deviation sum of squares of the predictor. Note that the standard error of a predicted score has the smallest possible value when the score on the predictor is equal to the mean of the predictor. When $X = \bar{X}$, the last term of (6.1) is equal to zero. The more X deviates from $\bar{X}$, the larger the standard error of the predicted score. This is a consequence of $(X - \bar{X})^2$ in (6.1). It makes sense intuitively that the more deviant, or extreme, a score, the more prone it is to error. Other things equal, the smaller the standard error of estimate ($s_{y.x}$), the smaller the standard error of a predicted score. Also, the larger the variability of the predictor (X), the smaller the standard error of a predicted score.

The numerical example presented in Chapter 2 (Tables 2.1 and 2.2) is used to illustrate the calculations of standard errors of predicted scores. The following were calculated in Chapter 2:

$$s_{y.x} = 2.446 \qquad \bar{X} = 3.00 \qquad \Sigma x^2 = 40$$

$$Y' = 5.05 + .75X$$

For $X = 1$,

$$Y' = 5.05 + .75(1) = 5.8$$

Calculate now the $s_{y'}$, recalling that $N = 20$.

$$s_{y'_1} = 2.446\sqrt{1 + \frac{1}{20} + \frac{(1-3)^2}{40}} = 2.446\sqrt{1.15} = 2.623$$

For $X = 2$,

$$Y' = 5.05 + .75(2) = 6.55$$

$$s_{y'_2} = 2.446\sqrt{1 + \frac{1}{20} + \frac{(2-3)^2}{40}} = 2.446\sqrt{1.075} = 2.536$$

For $X = 3$,

$$Y' = 5.05 + .75(3) = 7.3$$

$$s_{y'_3} = 2.446\sqrt{1 + \frac{1}{20} + \frac{(3-3)^2}{40}} = 2.446\sqrt{1.05} = 2.506$$

Confidence Intervals

The confidence interval for Y' is

$$Y' \pm t(\alpha/2, df)s_{y'} \tag{6.2}$$

where α = level of significance; df = degrees of freedom associated with the standard error of estimate, $s_{y.x}$, or with the residual sum of squares. In the present example, $N = 20$ and k (number of predictors) = 1. Therefore, df for (6.2) are $N - k - 1 = 20 - 1 - 1 = 18$. Assume, for example, that the 95% confidence interval is desired. The t (.025, 18) = 2.101 (see a t table in statistics books, or take $\sqrt{F}$ with 1 and 18 df from Appendix B).

For $X = 1$, it was found above that $Y' = 5.8$ and $s_{y'} = 2.623$. The 95% confidence interval for $Y' = 5.8$ is therefore

$$5.8 \pm (2.101)(2.623) = .29 \text{ and } 11.31$$

For $X = 2$: $Y' = 6.55$ and $s_{y'} = 2.536$ (see calculations above). The 95% confidence interval is

$$6.55 \pm (2.101)(2.536) = 1.22 \text{ and } 11.88$$

For $X = 3$: $Y' = 7.3$ and $s_{y'} = 2.506$. The 95% confidence interval is

$$7.3 \pm (2.101)(2.506) = 2.03 \text{ and } 12.57$$

These confidence intervals are fairly large, partly because of the small sample size. This demonstrates, again, the importance of working with large samples.

Standard Error of a Predicted Score: Multiple Predictors

With multiple predictors, the algebraic formulas for $s_{y'}$ become unwieldy. Matrix notation is simpler, and will therefore be used. The formula for the variance of a predicted score, $s^2_{y'}$, is:

$$s^2_{y'} = s^2_{y.12\ldots k}\,[1 + \mathbf{p}'(\mathbf{X}'\mathbf{X})^{-1}\mathbf{p}] \tag{6.3}$$

where $s^2_{y'}$ = variance of a predicted score; $s^2_{y.12\ldots k}$ = variance of estimate, or mean square residuals (MSR); $\mathbf{p}'$ = a vector of raw scores on the predictors and a 1 for the intercept. $\mathbf{X}'$ is the transpose of $\mathbf{X}$, the latter being an N by $1 + k$ matrix composed of a unit vector and k column vectors of scores on the predictor variables. $(\mathbf{X}'\mathbf{X})^{-1}$ is the inverse of $(\mathbf{X}'\mathbf{X})$. (See Chapter 4 for detailed discussions and numerical examples of $(\mathbf{X}'\mathbf{X})$ and $(\mathbf{X}'\mathbf{X})^{-1}$.) $\mathbf{p}$ is a column vector of scores on the predictor variables and a 1 for the intercept. Note that $\mathbf{p}'$ is the transpose of $\mathbf{p}$. Also, $\mathbf{p}'$ is any one row of $\mathbf{X}$, the raw score matrix.

With several predictors, the matrix calculations, particularly those of the inverse, are lengthy, laborious, and prone to error when done by hand. It is therefore suggested that they be done with the aid of a computer. Any computer package that includes matrix operations will do. As discussed below, however, one may obtain the confidence intervals for predicted scores directly from one of the SAS programs.

In order to save on computational labor, and to conserve space, the application of Formula (6.3) will be demonstrated for the case of a single predictor. Moreover, it will be applied to the same numerical example that was used above with Formula (6.1). It is hoped that this will suffice to show how Formula (6.3) is applied. Recall that the numerical example used above for the calculation of standard errors of predicted scores and confidence intervals was taken from Chapter 2 (Table 2.1). In Chapter 4, this example was used to demonstrate matrix algebra applications in regression analysis. (If you are encountering difficulties with the following demonstration, it is suggested that you review related materials in Chapter 4 and in Appendix A.)

Using the data of Table 2.1, it was shown in Chapter 4 that

$$(\mathbf{X}'\mathbf{X})^{-1} = \begin{bmatrix} .275 & -.075 \\ -.075 & .025 \end{bmatrix}$$

The variance of estimate, $s^2_{y.x}$, is 5.9833 (see calculations in Chapter 2, and also in Chapter 4).

Applying now (6.3) to the case when $X = 1$:

$$s^2_{y'_1} = 5.9833\left(1 + [1 \quad 1]\begin{bmatrix} .275 & -.075 \\ -.075 & .025 \end{bmatrix}\begin{bmatrix} 1 \\ 1 \end{bmatrix}\right)$$

Note that in the present case $\mathbf{p}' = [1 \quad 1]$. The first 1 is for the intercept, and will appear always, regardless of the scores on the predictor variables. The second 1 is the score on X.

Calculating first:

$$[1 \quad 1]\begin{bmatrix} .275 & -.075 \\ -.075 & .025 \end{bmatrix} = [.2 \; -.05]$$

and

$$[.2 \; -.05]\begin{bmatrix} 1 \\ 1 \end{bmatrix} = .15$$

$$s^2_{y'_1} = 5.9833(1 + .15) = (5.9833)(1.15) = 6.8808$$

$$s_{y'_1} = \sqrt{6.8808} = 2.623$$

The same value was obtained when (6.1) was used.

As another example, (6.3) is applied to the case when $X = 2$:

$$s^2_{y'_2} = 5.9833\left(1 + [1 \quad 2]\begin{bmatrix} .275 & -.075 \\ -.075 & .025 \end{bmatrix}\begin{bmatrix} 1 \\ 2 \end{bmatrix}\right)$$

Calculating,

$$[1 \quad 2]\begin{bmatrix} .275 & -.075 \\ -.075 & .025 \end{bmatrix} = [.125 \quad -.025]$$

and

$$[.125 \quad -.025]\begin{bmatrix} 1 \\ 2 \end{bmatrix} = .075$$

$$s^2_{y'_2} = 5.9833(1 + .075) + 6.4320$$

$$s_{y'_2} = \sqrt{6.4320} = 2.536$$

Again, the same value was obtained when (6.1) was used.

The calculation of confidence intervals is, of course, the same as above and is therefore not repeated here.

Confidence Intervals by Computer Program

Using the GLM procedure of SAS one may obtain confidence intervals for predicted scores as part of the output. This is how the confidence intervals reported in Table 6.1 were obtained. The PROC GLM card listed earlier is repeated here:

```
PROC GLM; MODEL GPA = GREQ GREV MAT AR/P CLI I;
```

In this card, PROC GLM calls for the General Linear Model program. In the model statement GPA is indicated as the criterion and the remaining variables as the predictors. P calls for the printing of observed, predicted, and residual values for each individual. CLI calls for confidence limits for individual predicted scores. Note that when CLI is used, P must also be used. One may also specify the ALPHA level for the confidence interval. When ALPHA is not specified, .05 is used.

Using P and CLI, the GLM program will, of course, provide confidence intervals only for X values that were used in the original study. Using the regression equation, one may obtain predicted values for new predictor values (X's) that are within the range of the X's used in the original study. Note that extrapolation (i.e., using predictor values that are outside the range of the original X's) is questionable and should be used with caution (see Chapter 11). To obtain confidence intervals for predicted scores based on new X's, Formula (6.3) has to be applied. The main difficulty is in obtaining $(\mathbf{X}'\mathbf{X})^{-1}$, which is part of Formula (6.3). Using GLM, $(\mathbf{X}'\mathbf{X})^{-1}$ may be obtained by including the option I in the MODEL statement, as was done above. (For a discussion of $(\mathbf{X}'\mathbf{X})$ and $(\mathbf{X}'\mathbf{X})^{-1}$ see Chapter 4.)

Finally, note that the predicted scores and the confidence intervals reported in Table 6.1 are based on the regression equation in which all the predictors were used. When predictors are deleted because they do not contribute meaningfully, or significantly, to the prediction, the predicted scores and the confidence intervals are, of course, calculated on the basis of the regression equation for the predictors that were retained. Using the GLM program, this would necessitate a MODEL statement in which only the retained predictors appear.

SHRINKAGE

The choice of a set of weights in a regression analysis is designed to yield the highest possible correlation between the independent variables and the dependent variable. Recall that the multiple correlation can be expressed as the correlation between the predicted scores based on the regression equation and the observed criterion scores. If one were to apply a set of weights derived in one sample to the predictor scores of another sample and then correlate these predicted scores with the observed criterion scores, the resulting R would almost always be smaller than the R obtained in the sample for which the weights were originally calculated. This phenomenon is referred to as the shrinkage of the multiple correlation. The reason for shrinkage is that in calculating the weights to obtain a maximum R, the zero-order correlations are treated as if they were error-free. This is of course never the case. Consequently, there is a certain amount of capitalization on chance, and the resulting R is biased upwards.

The degree of the overestimation of R is affected, among things, by the ratio of the number of independent variables to the size of the sample. Other things being equal, the larger this ratio, the greater the overestimation of R. Some authors recommend that the ratio of independent variables to sample size be at least 30 subjects per independent variable. This is a rule of thumb that does not satisfy certain researchers who say that samples should have at least 400 subjects. Needless to say, the larger the sample the more stable the results. It is therefore advisable to work with fairly large samples.

The importance of having a small ratio of number of variables to number of subjects may be noted when one considers the expectation of R^2. Even when R^2 in the population is zero, the expectation of the sample R^2 is $k/(N - 1)$, where k is the number of predictors, and N is the sample size (see, for example, Finn, 1974, p. 184; Harris, 1975, p. 19). What this means is that when the number of predictors is equal to the number of subjects minus one, a perfect correlation will be obtained even when in the population the predictors have zero correlations with the criterion. Take, for example, the case of one predictor and two subjects. Since the scores of the two subjects are represented by two points, a straight line may be drawn between them, regardless of what variables are being used—hence a perfect correlation. (In the foregoing statement it was assumed that the two subjects have different scores on the two variables. When their scores on one of the variables are equal to each other, the correlation coefficient is undefinable.) Although the above example is admittedly extreme, it should serve to alert the user of regression analysis to the hazards of overfitting, which will occur whenever the number of predictors approaches the sample size.

Even though it is not possible to determine exactly the shrinkage of R^2, several formulas for the estimation of the shrinkage have been proposed (see, for example, Carter, 1979; Darlington, 1968). It will be noted, however, that with samples of moderate size (about 50) the various formulas lead to virtually identical estimates. Following is one of the formulas used to estimate the shrinkage of R^2:

$$\hat{R}^2 = 1 - (1 - R^2)\frac{N - 1}{N - k - 1} \tag{6.4}$$

where $\hat{R}^2$ = adjusted squared multiple correlation; R^2 = obtained squared multiple correlation; N = size of sample; k = number of predictors.

The application of Formula (6.4) is demonstrated for three different sample sizes. Assume that the squared multiple correlation between three independent variables and a dependent variable is. .36. What will $\hat{R}^2$ be if the ratios of the independent variable to the sample size were 1:5, 1:30, 1:50? In other words, what will $\hat{R}^2$ be if the sample sizes for which the R^2 was obtained were 15, 90, and 150?

For a sample of 15 (1:5 ratio),

$$\hat{R}^2 = 1 - (1 - .36)\left(\frac{15 - 1}{15 - 3 - 1}\right) = 1 - (.64)\left(\frac{14}{11}\right) = 1 - .81 = .19$$

For a sample of 90 (1:30 ratio),

$$\hat{R}^2 = 1 - (1 - .36)\left(\frac{90 - 1}{90 - 3 - 1}\right) = 1 - (.64)\left(\frac{89}{86}\right) = 1 - .66 = .34$$

For a sample of 150 (1:50 ratio),

$$\hat{R}^2 = 1 - (1 - .36)\left(\frac{150 - 1}{150 - 3 - 1}\right) = 1 - (.64)\left(\frac{149}{146}\right) = 1 - .65 = .35$$

Note that with a ratio of 1:5, $\hat{R}^2$ is about half the size of R^2 (.19 and .36 respectively); when the ratio is 1:30, the estimated shrinkage of R^2 is about .02 (from .36 to .34); and with a ratio of 1:50, it is about .01 (from .36 to .35).

From Formula (6.4) it may also be noted that, other things equal, the higher the R^2 the less the estimated shrinkage. Assume that $R^2 = .60$. Using the same number of predictors and the same sample sizes as in the above demonstration, the application of (6.4) leads to the following:

$$\hat{R}^2 = .491 \qquad \text{for } N = 30$$

$$\hat{R}^2 = .586 \qquad \text{for } N = 90$$

$$\hat{R}^2 = .592 \qquad \text{for } N = 150$$

The above discussion and Formula (6.4) apply to the case when all the variables are retained in the equation. When a selection procedure is used to retain only some of the variables (see below), capitalization on chance is even greater, resulting in greater shrinkage. The use of large samples (about 500) is therefore particularly crucial when a number of variables is to be selected from a larger pool of variables.

Finally, it will be noted that various computer programs for multiple regression analysis report routinely the $\hat{R}^2$. SPSS and BMDP, for example, use Formula (6.4) and label the result ADJUSTED R SQUARE.

CROSS-VALIDATION

Probably the best method for estimating the degree of shrinkage is to perform a cross-validation (Herzberg, 1969; Lord & Novick, 1968, pp. 285 ff.; Mosier, 1951). This is done by using two samples. For the first sample a regular regression analysis is performed, and R^2 and the regression equation are calculated. The regression equation is then applied to the predictor variables of the second sample, thus yielding a Y' for each subject. The first sample is referred to as the *screening sample,* and the second as the *calibration sample* (Lord & Novick, 1968, p. 285). (If a selection of variables is used in the screening sample, the regression equation is applied to the same variables in the calibration sample.) A Pearson r is then calculated between the observed criterion scores (Y) in the calibration sample and the predicted criterion scores (Y'). This $r_{yy'}$ is analogous to a multiple correlation in which the equation used is the one obtained in the screening sample.

The difference between R^2 of the screening sample and R^2 of the calibration sample is an estimate of the amount of shrinkage. If the shrinkage is small and the R^2 is considered meaningful, the regression equation obtained in the screening sample may be applied to future predictions. As pointed out by Mosier (1951), however, a regression equation based on the combined samples (the screening and calibration samples) has greater stability due to the larger number of subjects on which it is based. It is therefore recommended that after deciding that the shrinkage is small, the two samples be combined and the regression equation for the combined samples be used in future predictions.

Cross-validation, then, needs two samples. Long delays in assessing the findings in a study sometimes may occur due to difficulties in obtaining a second sample. In such circumstances an alternative approach is recommended. A large sample (say 500) is randomly split into two subsamples. One subsample is used as the screening sample, and the other is used for calibration.

Double Cross-Validation

Some researchers are not satisfied with cross-validation and insist on double cross-validation (Mosier, 1951). The procedure outlined above is applied twice. For each sample (or random subsample of a given sample), R^2 and the regression equation are calculated. Each regression equation obtained in one sample is then applied to the predictor variables of the other sample, and R^2 is calculated by using $r_{yy'}$. One thus has two R^2's calculated directly in each sample, and two R^2's calculated on the basis of regression equations obtained from alternate samples. It is then possible to study the differences between the R^2's as well as the differences in the two regression equations. If the results are close, one may combine the samples and calculate the regression equation to be used in prediction. Double cross-validation is strongly recommended as the most rigorous approach to the validation of results from regression analysis in a predictive framework.

SELECTING VARIABLES FOR PREDICTION

Because many of the variables used in the behavioral sciences are intercorrelated, it is often possible and useful to select from a pool of variables, a smaller set which will be as efficient, or almost as efficient, as the entire set for the purpose of prediction. When variables are selected from an available pool, the aim is usually the selection of the minimum number of variables necessary to account for almost as much of the variance as is accounted for by the total set.

But practical considerations, such as relative costs in obtaining measures of the variables, ease of administration, and the like, often enter into the selection process. Under such circumstances, one may end up with a larger number of variables than the minimum that would be selected when the sole criterion is to account for almost as much of the variance as does the total set of variables. A researcher may, for example, select five variables in preference to three others that would yield about the same R^2 but at much greater cost.

Because practical considerations vary with given sets of circumstances, it is not possible to formulate a systematic selection method that takes such considerations into account. The researcher must select the variables on the basis of the specific means, needs, and circumstances. When, however, the sole aim is to select variables so that the "best" regression equation is obtained, various selection procedures may be used. The term "best" is placed in quotation marks to indicate that there is more than one criterion for what best means. The use of different criteria may result in the selection of different sets of variables (see Draper & Smith, 1981, Chapter 6). In the present discussion, "best" will be defined as the equation that maximizes the R^2. Of the various selection methods, the following are presented: All Possible Regressions, Forward Selection, Backward Elimination, Stepwise Selection, and Blockwise Selection. For a thorough review of selection methods, see Hocking (1976); see also Daniel and Wood (1980); Darlington (1968); Draper & Smith (1981, Chapter 6).

All Possible Regressions

The search for the "best" subset of predictors may proceed by calculating all possible regression equations, beginning with an equation in which only the intercept is used, followed by all the one-predictor equations, two-predictor equations, and so on, until all the predictors are used in a single equation. A serious shortcoming of this approach is that a very large number of equations must be examined even when the number of predictors is relatively small. The number of all possible regressions with k predictors is 2^k. Thus, with three predictors, for example, eight equations are calculated: one equation in which none of the predictors is used, three one-predictor equations, three two-predictor equations, and one three-predictor equation. This can, of course, be accomplished with relative ease. Suppose, however, that the number of predictors is 12. In this case, 4096 (or 2^{12}) regression equations are calculated. With 20 predictors, 1048576 (or 2^{20}) regression equations are called for. In view of the foregoing, it is unwise to use the method of all possible regressions when the number of predictors is relatively large. Not only is computer time wasted under such circumstances, but also the output consists of numerous equations that a researcher has to plod through in an effort to decide which of them is the "best." It will be noted in passing that an alternative approach, namely all possible subset regressions (referred to as regression by leaps and bounds) is available for use when the number of predictors is large (for a discussion of this approach, see Daniel & Wood, 1980, Chapter 6; Draper & Smith, 1981, Chapter 6; Hocking, 1976).

Criteria for the Selection of a Subset. No single criterion is available for determining how many, and which, predictors are to comprise the "best" subset. One may use a criterion of meaningfulness, statistical significance, or a combination of both. For example, it may be decided to select an equation from all the possible four-predictor equations because in the next stage (i.e., all possible five-predictor equations) no equation leads to a meaningful increment in R^2. Meaningfulness is, in part, situation-specific. What is considered a meaningful increment in R^2 in one situation may be considered not meaningful in another situation. Moreover, different researchers may use different criteria of meaningfulness even in the same situation.

A seemingly less problematic criterion is whether the increment in R^2 is statistically significant. With large samples, however, even a minute increment in R^2 may be declared statistically significant. Since the use of large samples is mandatory in regression analysis, particularly when a subset of predictors is to be selected, it is obvious that it is imprudent to rely solely on tests of statistical significance. What good is a statistically significant increment in R^2 if it is not substantively meaningful? It is therefore recommended that meaningfulness be the primary consideration in deciding what is the "best" equation and that tests of statistical significance be used as adjuncts in such decisions.

Even after the number of predictors to be selected has been decided upon, further complications may arise. It is possible, for example, that several equations with the same number of predictors yield virtually the same R^2. If so, which one of them is to be chosen? One factor in the choice among the competing equations may be economy. Assuming that some of the predictors are costlier to obtain than others, the choice would then appear obvious. Yet, other factors (e.g., stability of regression coefficients) need to be considered. For further discussions of criteria for selecting the "best" from among all possible regressions, see Daniel and Wood (1980, Chapter 6) and Draper & Smith (1981, Chapter 6).

A Numerical Example. The example introduced earlier in this chapter (see Table 6.1)—and analyzed in detail subsequently—is used for the purpose of illustrating the method of all possible regressions as well as the other methods of variable selection presented in this chapter. It is hoped that comparisons of results from the different methods applied to the same data will contribute to a better understanding of the unique features of each of them.

For the purpose of this demonstration the RSQUARE program from SAS package is used. Although there is no limitation on the number of predictors one may use, the authors recommend no more than 14. The general layout of the control cards is the same as given above, and is therefore not repeated here. The program is executed by the statement: PROC RSQUARE. This is followed by:

```
MODEL GPA = GREQ GREV MAT AR;
```

Note that the model statement is identical to the one given earlier for GLM. Like GLM, RSQUARE has its own options (e.g., the stage at which the analysis should be terminated, printing only the "best" models of any given size). In the present example no options were specified.

Output

Following is the output obtained from RSQUARE of SAS, using data of Table 6.1, and designating GPA as the criterion. The results were rounded to five decimal places.

N = 30 REGRESSION MODELS FOR DEPENDENT VARIABLE GPA

NUMBER IN MODEL	R-SQUARE	VARIABLES IN MODEL
1	.33809	GREV
1	.36509	MAT
1	.37350	GREQ
1	.38530	AR
2	.48524	GREQ GREV
2	.49232	MAT AR
2	.49348	GREV MAT
2	.50330	GREQ AR
2	.51549	GREV AR
2	.58300	GREQ MAT
3	.57161	GREQ GREV AR
3	.57187	GREV MAT AR
3	.61020	GREQ MAT AR
3	.61704	GREQ GREV MAT
4	.64047	GREQ GREV MAT AR

Commentary

The results are printed in ascending order, beginning with one-predictor equations and concluding with a four-predictor equation. At each stage, R^2's are presented in ascending order. Thus, at the first stage, GREV has the lowest R^2 with GPA, whereas AR has the highest. As single predictors are used at this stage, the R^2's are, of course, the squared zero-order correlations of each predictor with the criterion.

Note that AR alone accounts for about 38% of the variance in GPA. Had one desired a single predictor, AR would appear to be the best choice. Recall, however, that various factors may affect the final choice. AR is the average rating of an applicant by three professors who interview him or her. This is a time-consuming process. Assuming that the sole purpose of the interview is to obtain the AR for predictive purposes (an unrealistic assumption), it is conceivable that one would choose GREQ instead of AR because it is less costly and it yields about the same level of predictability. For that matter, MAT is an equally likely candidate for selection instead of AR. The foregoing brief discussion serves to reiterate what was said earlier about decisions regarding what is the "best" equation.

Moving on to the results with two predictors, the combination of GREQ and MAT appears to be the best. The next best (i.e., GREV and AR) accounts for about 7% less of the variance as compared to GREQ and MAT. Note that the "best" variable at the first stage (i.e., AR) is not included in the "best" equation at the second stage. This is due to the pattern of intercorrelations among the variables. Note also that the same two variables were retained when tests of significance of *b*'s were used for deletion of variables (see Deleting Variables from the Equation, earlier in this chapter). This, however, would not always happen. Of the three-variable equations the best combination is GREQ, GREV, and MAT, together accounting for about 62% of the variance. The increment from the best subset of two predictors to the best subset of three is about 4%. This increment may be tested for significance in the manner shown several times earlier:

$$F = \frac{(R^2_{k_1} - R^2_{k_2})/(k_1 - k_2)}{(1 - R^2_{k_1})/(N - k_1 - 1)} = \frac{(.61704 - .58300)/(3 - 2)}{(1 - .61704)/(30 - 3 - 1)} = 2.31$$

with 1 and 26 *df*, $p > .05$. The result is not significant because of the small sample size, which is used for illustrative purposes only.

Before turning to the next method of variable selection, it will be noted that with no more than ten predictors BMDP9R may be used to obtain all possible regressions in a manner similar to that obtained from RSQUARE of SAS. Unlike the latter program, however, BMDP9R can also be used to obtain all possible subset regressions (see above) for any number of predictors. BMDP9R is also superior to RSQUARE of SAS in that it prints the regression equations at each stage and provides for different definitions of "best," as well as extensive analyses of residuals.

Forward Selection

This solution proceeds in the following manner. The correlations of all the independent variables with the dependent variable are calculated. The independent variable that has the highest zero-order correlation with the dependent variable is entered first into the analysis. The next variable to enter is the one that produces the greatest increment to R^2, after having taken into account the variable already in the equation. In other words, it is the variable that has the highest squared semipartial correlation with the dependent variable, after partialing the variable already in the equation. The squared semipartial correlation indicates the increment in the R^2, or the incremental variance, attributed to the second variable. The third variable to enter is the one that has the highest squared semipartial correlation with the dependent variable after having partialed out the first two variables already in the equation. Some authors work with partial rather than with semipartial correlations. The results are, of course, the same since, as was shown in Chapter 5, semipartial correlations are proportional to partial correlations. Criteria for determining the "best" equation were discussed earlier in connection with All Possible Regressions, and are therefore not elaborated upon here.

A Numerical Example. The method of Forward Selection is now illustrated with the data of Table 6.1. The computer program used for this purpose is the subprogram REGRESSION of SPSS. Incidentally, only the Forward Selection Method is available on SPSS. Following is a listing of the layout used.

Control Cards

```
1                     1
                      6
RUN NAME              FORWARD SELECTION. DATA OF TABLE 6.1
VARIABLE LIST         GPA GREQ GREV MAT AR
N OF CASES            30
INPUT FORMAT          FIXED (F2.1, 2F4.0, F3.0, F3.1)
PRINT FORMATS         GPA AR(1)/
LIST CASES            CASES = 30/VARIABLES = GPA TO AR/
REGRESSION            VARIABLES = GPA TO AR/
                      REGRESSION = GPA(4, 4.0) WITH GREQ
                      TO AR(1)/
STATISTICS            ALL
READ INPUT DATA
32 625 540 65 27
41 575 680 75 45
 .   .   .  .  .
 .   .   .  .  .
 .   .   .  .  .
33 600 610 85 50
```

Commentary

Inasmuch as the REGRESSION control cards were discussed in some detail in Chapter 4, comments here will be made only about two statements. In Chapter 4 it was suggested that when the data set is small it may be advisable to list all the cases. When LIST CASES is specified, SPSS prints only whole numbers with no digits to the right of the decimal point. In order to print data with digits to the right of the decimal point, it is necessary to include the statement: PRINT FORMATS. In the present example it is indicated that for variables GPA and AR one digit be printed to the right of the decimal point (see *SPSS Manual*, pp. 61–62).

Following the designation of the criterion variable (i.e., GPA) on the REGRESSION statement, two numbers appear in the parentheses. The first number, 4, refers to the maximum number of variables to be entered. In the present case it was set to be equal to the number of predictors. When working with many variables, it is frequently useful to set a limit to the number of variables to be entered. The second number in the parentheses, 4.00, is the F ratio to enter. This governs the entry of variables into the equation. A variable whose increment in the proportion of variance accounted for at a given step is associated with an $F \geq 4.00$ will be entered. Variables with F ratios smaller than 4.00 will not enter at all. Note, that although in the REGRESSION statement a maximum of four predictors was specified to enter, less than four may be entered, depending on whether the specified F level is met. An $F = 4.00$ was chosen to demonstrate such an occurrence with the present example (see below).

Since the option of F-to-enter (and F-to-remove) is a feature of virtually all programs designed for the selection of predictors from a larger pool of variables, it will be noted here that there are no simple rules for deciding what value of F to specify. The probabilities of F-to-enter (and F-to-remove) when a set of predictors is selected from a larger pool do not correspond to those of the tabled F. "However, F-to-enter and F-to-remove are still useful values for guiding the regression program's variable selection, but probability statements are tough" (*BMDP Manual,* 1979, p. 855; see also Draper & Smith, 1981, Chapter 6). It is advisable to select F-to-enter on the "lenient" side, say 2.00, so that the analysis would not be terminated too soon. Using a small F-to-enter will generally result in entering several more variables than one would wish to finally use. But this has the advantage of providing the option of backing up from the last step in the output to a step in which the set of variables included is deemed most useful.

Output

Following are excerpts of the output from SPSS subprogram REGRESSION for the data of Table 6.1. Only these parts of the output directly pertinent to the present topic are presented. Some of the results were rounded to a smaller number of decimal places than that reported in the output.

CORRELATION COEFFICIENTS

	GPA	GREQ	GREV	MAT	AR
GPA	1.00000	.61115	.58145	.60423	.62072
GREQ	.61115	1.00000	.46806	.26691	.50784
GREV	.58145	.46806	1.00000	.42572	.40532
MAT	.60423	.26691	.42572	1.00000	.52479
AR	.62072	.50784	.40532	.52479	1.00000

DEPENDENT VARIABLE . . GPA
VARIABLE(S) ENTERED ON STEP NUMBER 1 . . AR
R SQUARE .38529

- -VARIABLES IN EQUATION- -			VARIABLES NOT IN EQUATION		
VARIABLE	B	F	VARIABLE	PARTIAL	F
AR	.44408	17.550	GREQ	.43814	6.414
(CONSTANT)	1.72944		GREV	.46022	7.255
			MAT	.41727	5.692

- -

VARIABLE(S) ENTERED ON STEP NUMBER 2 . . GREV
R SQUARE .51549

- -VARIABLES IN EQUATION- -			VARIABLES NOT IN EQUATION		
VARIABLE	B	F	VARIABLE	PARTIAL	F
AR	.32962	9.886	GREQ	.34032	3.406

GREV	.00285	7.255	MAT	.34113	3.424
(CONSTANT)	.49718				

- -

F-LEVEL OR TOLERANCE-LEVEL INSUFFICIENT FOR FURTHER COMPUTATION

Commentary

Because AR has the highest zero-order correlation with GPA, it is selected to enter first into the regression equation. Note, however, that the correlation of AR with GPA is only slightly higher than the correlations of the other predictors with GPA (see correlation matrix). Even though the slight differences in the correlations of the predictors with the criterion may be due to random fluctuations, or measurement errors, AR is preferred over the other predictors.

Look now at the section labeled VARIABLES NOT IN EQUATION (STEP 1). For each variable a partial correlation is reported. This is the partial correlation of the variable with the criterion, after partialing out the variable that is already in the equation (i.e., AR). For example, the partial correlation of GPA with GREQ, controlling for AR, is .43814. The F ratios are tests of significance of the partials or, equivalently, the test of the regression coefficient associated with a given variable if it were to enter in the subsequent step. Note that the F ratio for the partial correlation associated with GREV in STEP 1 (i.e., 7.255) is the same as the F ratio for the b associated with GREV in STEP 2, where it is in the equation (see earlier chapters, particularly Chapter 5, for a discussion of equivalence of tests of b's, β's, and partial and semipartial correlations). Of the VARIABLES NOT IN EQUATION, STEP 1, GREV has the highest partial correlation with GPA. Equivalently, it has the largest F ratio. Consequently, it is the one selected to enter in STEP 2.

Since the F ratios associated with the two variables not in the equation (GREQ and MAT) are smaller than the F-to-enter (see REGRESSION statement above, where the F-to-enter is 4.00) neither is entered, and the analysis is terminated. Had, for example, F-to-enter of 3.00 been specified, or had the default level (F = .01) been chosen, MAT would have been entered in STEP 3, and GREQ in STEP 4 (see section on Stepwise Selection below).

Returning now to the "best" equation obtained above, it will be noted that neither AR nor GREV was included in the "best" set when all possible regressions were calculated (see preceding section). In the previous analysis the "best" set of two predictors was the one that included GREQ and MAT (R^2 = .58300). In the present solution, R^2 = .51549. Incidentally, even if MAT were also brought into the equation (i.e., in STEP 3), the R^2 for the three variables would have been .57187; still smaller than R^2 based on GREQ and MAT only. This demonstrates what was said earlier—namely, that what emerges as the "best" equation depends on the particular method that is being used.

A serious shortcoming of the Forward Selection procedure is that no allowance is made for studying the effect the introduction of new predictors may have on the usefulness of the predictors that are already in the equation. It is possible, due to the combined contribution of predictors introduced at a later stage of the analysis, and the relations of those predictors with those already in the equation, that a predictor introduced at an earlier stage may be disposed of with very little loss in R^2 (see Backward Elimination, below). In Forward Selection the predictors are "locked in" in the order in which they were introduced into the equation. It should be noted, however, that at each step the regression equation and tests of significance of the regression coefficients are reported. Consequently, when it is decided to terminate the analysis at a given step the tests of significance of the regression coefficients should be examined in order to note whether a variable entered at an earlier step has been rendered not statistically significant or useful in the presence of variables that were entered at later steps. (Recall that the test of a regression coefficient is tantamount to testing the proportion of variance that the variable with which it is associated will account for if it were entered last into the analysis.)

Backward Elimination

The backward solution starts out with the squared multiple correlation of all independent variables with the dependent variable. The independent variables are deleted from the regression equation one at a time, and the loss to R^2 due to the deletion of the variable is studied. In other words, each variable is treated as if it were entered last in the equation. It is thus possible to observe which variable adds the least when entered last. The loss in R^2 that occurs as a result of the deletion of a variable may be assessed against a criterion of meaningfulness as well as significance. A variable considered not to add meaningfully or significantly to prediction is deleted.

If no variable is deleted, the analysis is terminated. Evidently all the variables contribute meaningfully to the prediction of the criterion. If, on the other hand, a variable is deleted, then the process described above is repeated for the remaining variables. That is, each of the remaining variables is deleted, in turn, and the one with the smallest contribution to R^2 is studied. Again, it may be either deleted or retained on the basis of the criteria used by the researcher. If the variable is deleted, one repeats the process described above to determine whether an additional variable may be deleted. The analysis continues as long as one deletes variables that produce no meaningful or significant loss to R^2. When the deletion of any one variable produces a meaningful or significant loss to R^2, the analysis is terminated.

A Numerical Example. The data of Table 6.1 are now used to illustrate the Backward Elimination procedure. The STEPWISE procedure of SAS is used for this purpose. This procedure enables one to apply five different variable-selection methods, one of which is Backward Elimination. As the general layout is the same as given above for All Possible Regressions, only the Procedure and Model statements are given here.

```
PROC STEPWISE;
MODEL GPA = GREQ GREV MAT AR/BACKWARD SLS = .05;
```

Commentary

The stepwise procedure is executed by the statement: PROC STEPWISE. In the MODEL statement GPA is designated as the criterion and the remaining variables as the predictors. Following the slash the method of variable selection is indicated. While it is possible to execute all five selection methods simultaneously, only BACKWARD is called for in the present example. SLS refers to the significance level for retaining a variable in the equation. In the present example, .05 was selected for illustrative purposes.

Output

Following are excerpts of the SAS STEPWISE output for Backward Elimination as applied to the data of Table 6.1. Only output that is pertinent to the present discussion is presented. Some of the results were rounded to five decimal places.

STEP 0	ALL VARIABLES ENTERED		R SQUARE = .64047	
	B VALUE	STD ERROR	F	PROB F
INTERCEPT	−1.73811			
GREQ	.00400	.00183	4.77	.0385
GREV	.00152	.00105	2.11	.1593
MAT	.02090	.00955	4.79	.0382
AR	.14423	.11300	1.63	.2135

STEP 1	VARIABLE AR REMOVED		R SQUARE = .61704	
	B VALUE	STD ERROR	F	PROB F
INTERCEPT	−2.14877			
GREQ	.00493	.00170	8.39	.0076
GREV	.00161	.00106	2.31	.1405
MAT	.02612	.00873	8.95	.0060

STEP 2 VARIABLE GREV REMOVED			R SQUARE = .58300	
	B VALUE	STD ERROR	F	PROB F
INTERCEPT	−2.12938			
GREQ	.00598	.00159	14.11	.0008
MAT	.03081	.00836	13.56	.0010

ALL VARIABLES IN THE MODEL ARE SIGNIFICANT AT THE .05 LEVEL.

Commentary

The analysis begins with all the variables in the equation (STEP 0). Variables with F ratios whose probabilities exceed the .05 level specified in the MODEL statement (see above, SLS = .05) are candidates for removal. As AR has an F ratio with the largest such probability (.2135), it is removed first (STEP 1). It was noted several times earlier that each F ratio is a test of a regression coefficient, and equivalently a test of the proportion of variance accounted for by a variable if it were to be entered last in the equation. In the present context the F test can be viewed as a test of the reduction in R^2 that will result from the removal of a predictor from the equation. Removing AR will result in the smallest reduction in R^2, as compared to the removal of any one of the other predictors. Note that in Forward Selection AR was entered first and was shown to account for about 38% of the variance (see above, Forward Selection), but when the other predictors are in the equation it loses almost all of its usefulness (incrementing R^2 by only about 2%) and may therefore be disposed of.

GREV is removed next as the probability associated with its F ratio is .1405. The two remaining predictors in STEP 2 have F ratios with probabilities $< .05$. Therefore neither is removed, and the analysis is terminated.

Selecting two predictors only, Forward Selection led to the selection of AR and GREV ($R^2 = .5155$), whereas the Backward Elimination led to the selection of GREQ and MAT ($R^2 = .58300$). To repeat: what is the "best" regression equation depends, in part, on the selection method that is being used.

Finally, it will be recalled that the probability statements are problematic when variable-selection procedures are implemented. Therefore, as with the F-to-enter, they should be used as rough guidelines (see comments under Forward Selection; see also Draper & Smith, 1981, pp. 310–312).

Stepwise Selection

Stepwise Selection is a variation on Forward Selection. It was noted earlier that a serious shortcoming of the latter is that predictors entered into the equation are retained despite the fact that they have lost their usefulness in view of contributions made by variables entered at later stages. In Stepwise Selection, tests are performed at each step to determine the contribution of each predictor already in the equation if it were to enter last. It is thus possible to identify predictors that were considered to be "good" at an earlier stage but have lost their usefulness when additional predictors were brought into the equation and may therefore be removed from it. As before, criteria for the removal of predictors that are not useful may be meaningfulness, statistical significance, or a combination of both.

A Numerical Example. The data of Table 6.1 are used to illustrate Stepwise Selection. While SAS STEPWISE procedure may be used for this purpose also, BMDP2R is used instead in order to provide an example of another program for variable-selection methods. BMDP2R is probably the most versatile program for variable selection, as it not only provides for different selection methods, but it also has a variety of options not available in other programs of this kind.

Control Cards

```
/PROBLEM TITLE IS 'STEPWISE SELECTION. DATA OF TABLE 6.1'.
/INPUT VARIABLES ARE 5 FORMAT IS '(F2.1, 2F4.0, F3.0, F3.1)'.
/VARIABLE NAMES ARE GPA, GREQ, GREV, MAT, AR.
```

```
/REGRESS DEPENDENT IS GPA. ENTER = 3.0. REMOVE = 2.0.
/END
32 625 540 65 27
41 575 680 75 45
 .   .   .   .   .
 .   .   .   .   .
 .   .   .   .   .
33 600 610 85 50
```

Commentary

Since the general layout for BMDP2R is the same as that for BMDP1R (see Chapter 4), it is not commented upon. The following comments are limited to the REGRESS paragraph.

When all the predictors are to be considered, only the criterion has to be specified; hence, DEPENDENT IS GPA. The values for ENTER and REMOVE refer to F ratios to enter and remove variables from the equation. The decision about the magnitudes of the F-to-enter and F-to-remove is largely "a matter of personal preference" (Draper & Smith, 1981, p. 309). Specifying an F-to-remove that is smaller than an F-to-enter may sometimes lead to a cycle of entering and removing variables. On the other hand, specifying an F-to-remove that is larger than the F-to-enter may result in retaining variables that turn out to be not useful in the presence of other variables that have been entered at a later step (see Draper & Smith, 1981, Chapter 6, for detailed discussions and suggestions).

For illustrative purposes, the following have been specified in the present analysis:

ENTER = 3.00.   REMOVE = 2.00.

This means that at any given step, variables not in the equation whose F ratios are equal to or larger than 3.00 are candidates for entry in the subsequent step. The predictor that is entered is the one that has the largest F from among those having F ratios larger or equal to 3.00. At each step, predictors already in the equation, and whose F ratios are equal or less than 2.00 (F-to-remove) are candidates for removal. The predictor with the smallest F ratio from among those having $F \leq 2.00$ is removed. (By assigning appropriate values for F-to-enter and F-to-remove it is possible to obtain Forward Selection and Backward Elimination. See *BMDP Manual*, 1979, pp. 406–407.) Following are excerpts from the output of BMDP2R as applied to the data of Table 6.1.

Output

```
STEP NO. 1 VARIABLE ENTERED AR
R-SQUARE      .3853
                 VARIABLES IN EQUATION
VARIABLE         COEFFICIENT   STD ERROR     F TO
                                OF COEFF    REMOVE
(Y-INTERCEPT          1.729)
AR                     .444          .106     17.55
```

VARIABLES NOT IN EQUATION

VARIABLE	PARTIAL CORR.	F TO ENTER
GREQ	.43813	6.41
GREV	.46022	7.26
MAT	.41727	5.69

- -

STEP NO. 2 VARIABLE ENTERED GREV
R-SQUARE .5155

VARIABLES IN EQUATION

VARIABLE	COEFFICIENT	STD ERROR OF COEFF	F TO REMOVE
(Y-INTERCEPT	.497)		
GREV	.003	.001	7.26
AR	.330	.105	9.89

VARIABLES NOT IN EQUATION

VARIABLE	PARTIAL CORR.	F TO ENTER
GREQ	.34031	3.41
MAT	.34113	3.42

- -

STEP NO. 3 VARIABLE ENTERED MAT
R-SQUARE .5719

VARIABLES IN EQUATION

VARIABLE	COEFFICIENT	STD ERROR OF COEFF	F TO REMOVE
(Y-INTERCEPT	−.144)		
GREV	.002	.001	4.83
MAT	.019	.010	3.42
AR	.242	.111	4.76

VARIABLES NOT IN EQUATION

VARIABLE	PARTIAL CORR.	F TO ENTER
GREQ	.40028	4.77

- -

STEP NO. 4 VARIABLE ENTERED GREQ
R-SQUARE .6405

VARIABLES IN EQUATION

VARIABLE	COEFFICIENT	STD ERROR OF COEFF	F TO REMOVE
(Y-INTERCEPT	−1.738)		
GREQ	.004	.002	4.77
GREV	.002	.001	2.10
MAT	.021	.010	4.79
AR	.144	.113	1.63

VARIABLES NOT IN EQUATION		
VARIABLE	PARTIAL CORR.	F TO ENTER

- -

STEP NO. 5 VARIABLE REMOVED AR
R-SQUARE .6170

VARIABLES IN EQUATION

VARIABLE	COEFFICIENT	STD ERROR OF COEFF	F TO REMOVE
(Y-INTERCEPT	−2.149)		
GREQ	.005	.002	8.39
GREV	.002	.001	2.31
MAT	.026	.009	8.95

VARIABLES NOT IN EQUATION

VARIABLE	PARTIAL CORR.	F TO ENTER
AR	.24735	1.63

- -

F-LEVELS(3.00, 2.00) INSUFFICIENT FOR FURTHER STEPPING

Commentary

The first two steps are the same as those obtained above by the Forward Selection method, and are therefore not commented upon. Look now at STEP 2, VARIABLES NOT IN EQUATION. Both predictors (GREQ and MAT) have F TO ENTER larger than 3.00, and are therefore both candidates for entry in STEP 3. A point deserving special attention, however, is that the *F* ratios for these predictors are almost identical (3.41 and 3.42). This is because both predictors have almost identical partial correlations with GPA, after GREV and AR are controlled for (.34031 and .34113). A difference this small is almost certainly due to random fluctuations. Yet the predictor with the slightest edge (MAT) is the one that is given preference and is entered next into the equation. Had the correlation between GREQ and MAT been higher than what it is in the present fictitious example (.2669) it is conceivable that, after entering MAT, GREQ may have not met the criterion of F TO ENTER and would have therefore not been entered at all. Thus it is possible that of two equally good predictors, one may be selected and the other not, just because of a slight difference between their correlations with the criterion. We return to this point later on (see also Multicollinearity in Chapter 8). In the present example, GREQ qualifies for entry in STEP 4.

Thus far a Forward Selection was obtained because at no step has the F TO REMOVE for any predictor fallen below 2.00. At STEP 4, however, AR has an F TO REMOVE of 1.63, and it is therefore removed from the equation (see

STEP 5). Here, again, is a point worth special attention: a predictor that has been shown as the "best" when no other predictors are in the equation turns out to be the "worst" when the other predictors are in the equation. Recall that AR is the average rating given an applicant by three professors who interview him or her. In view of the above results, is one to conclude that AR is not a "good" variable; that interviewing applicants for graduate study is worthless? Not at all! At least, not on the basis of the above evidence. All one may conclude is that if the sole purpose of interviewing candidates is to obtain AR in order to use it as one of the predictors of GPA, the effort and the time expanded may not be warranted, as after taking GREQ, GREV, and MAT into account AR adds about 2% to the accounting of the variance in the criterion.

As can be seen in STEP 5, the regression coefficient associated with GREV is not statistically significant at the .05 level ($F = 2.31, 1, 26$). Recall, however, that a small sample size was used for illustrative purposes only. When entered last, GREV accounts for about 3% of the variance in GPA. Assuming that the F ratio associated with GREV were significant, one would still have to decide whether it is worthwhile to retain it in the equation. Unlike AR, GREV is relatively inexpensive to obtain. It is therefore conceivable that, had the results obtained above all been statistically significant, a decision would have been made to remove AR but to retain GREV. In short, the final decision rests with the researcher's judgment about the usefulness of a predictor in relation to the cost and effort required to obtain it.

Blockwise Selection

Blockwise Selection is a method of predictor selection in which Forward Selection is applied to *blocks,* or sets, of predictors, while using any of the predictor-selection methods, or combination of such methods, to select predictors from each block. As there are various variations on this theme, it will be useful to describe first in detail one such variation and then comment on other possibilities.

Basically, the predictors are grouped in blocks on the basis of theoretical and psychometric considerations (e.g., different measures of socioeconomic status may comprise a block). Beginning with the first block, a Stepwise Selection is applied. At this stage, predictors in other blocks are ignored, while those of the first block compete for entry into the equation on the basis of specified criteria for entry (e.g., F-to-enter, increment in R^2). Since the method used is Stepwise Selection, predictors that entered at an earlier step are deleted on the basis of criteria for removal (e.g., F-to-remove). When the first stage is completed, the analysis proceeds to the stage in which a Stepwise Selection is applied to the predictors of the second block with the restriction that the predictors that survived the first stage of selection remain in the equation. In other words, although the predictors of the second block compete for entry into the equation, their usefulness is assessed in view of the presence of first-block predictors in the equation. Thus, for example, a predictor in the second block, which in relation to the other variables in the block may be considered useful, will not be selected if it is correlated highly with one, or more than one, of the predictors from the first block that are already in the equation.

The second stage having been completed, a Stepwise Selection is applied to the predictors of the third block. The usefulness of predictors from the third block is assessed in view of the presence of predictors from the first two blocks in the equation. The procedure is repeated sequentially until predictors from the last block are selected.

A substantive example may further clarify the meaning of Blockwise Selection. Assume that for the purpose of predicting academic achievement one has many predictors that can be grouped in the following four blocks: (1) home background variables; (2) student aptitudes; (3) student interests and attitudes; and (4) school variables. Using Blockwise Selection, the researcher may specify, for example, that the order of entry of the blocks be the one indicated above. This means that home background variables will be considered first, and that those that meet the criteria for entry and survive the criteria for removal will be retained in the equation. Next, a Stepwise Selection will be applied to the student aptitude measures, while locking in the predictors that survived during the first stage of the analysis (i.e., home background predictors). Having completed the second stage, student interests and attitudes will be considered as candidates for entry into the equation that already includes the predictors that survived during the first two stages of the analysis. Finally, school variables that meet the criteria for entry, in the presence of predictors selected at preceding stages, compete among themselves for entry into the equation.

Because the predictors in the various blocks tend to be intercorrelated, it is clear that whether or not a predictor is entered into the equation depends, in part, on the order of entry assigned to the block to which it belongs. Generally speaking, variables belonging to blocks assigned an earlier order of entry stand a better chance to be selected than those belonging to blocks assigned a later order of entry. Depending on the pattern of the intercorrelations among all the variables, it is conceivable that an entire block of predictors may not meet the entry criterion because it was assigned a late order of entry. The obvious question, therefore, is: What is the correct order? In predictive research the "correct" order is the one that meets the specific needs of the researcher. There is nothing wrong in any ordering of blocks so long as the researcher does not use the results for explanatory purposes. Referring to the above example, a researcher may validly state, for example, that after considering the first two blocks (home background and student aptitudes) the remaining blocks add little or nothing to the prediction of achievement. It would, however, be entirely incorrect to conclude on the basis of such results that student interests and attitudes, and school variables are not important determiners of achievement. It is conceivable that a change in the order of the blocks would lead to the opposite conclusion.

Anticipating the detailed discussion of the cross-national studies conducted under the auspices of the International Association for the Evaluation of Educational Achievement (IEA) in Chapter 7, it will be noted here that, despite the fact that results of these studies were used for explanatory purposes, their analyses were almost exclusively based on Blockwise Selection. Moreover, an extremely lenient criterion for the entry of variables into the equation was used, namely, a predictor qualified for entry if the increment in the proportion of variance due to its inclusion was .00025 or more (see, for example, Peaker, 1975, p. 79). "It was clear that the probable result of taking anything but a lenient value for the cut-off would be to fill [the tables] mainly with blanks"(!) (Peaker, 1975, p. 82). This and other issues relating to the analyses and interpretation of results in the IEA studies are discussed in detail in Chapter 7.

It was said earlier that there is a large number of variations on the theme of Blockwise Selection. For example, instead of doing Stepwise Selection for each block, other selection methods (e.g., Forward, Backward) may be used. Furthermore, one may choose to do what is essentially a Forward Selection of blocks. In other words, one may do a hierarchical regression analysis in which blocks of predictors are forced into the equation, regardless of whether individual predictors within a block meet the criterion for entry, for the sole purpose of noting whether blocks entered at later stages add meaningfully to the prediction of the criterion. Note that in this case no selection is applied to the predictors within a block.

A combination of forcing some blocks into the equation and doing Blockwise Selection on others is particularly useful in applied settings. For example, a personnel selection officer may have demographic information about the applicants, their performance on several inexpensive paper-and-pencil tests, and their scores on a test battery that is individually administered to each of them by a psychologist. Being interested in predicting a specific criterion, the selection officer may decide to do the following hierarchical analysis: (1) force into the equation the demographic information; (2) force into the equation the results of the paper-and-pencil test; (3) do a Stepwise Selection on the results of the individually administered test battery. Such a scheme is entirely reasonable from a predictive frame of reference since it enables one to determine whether it is necessary to obtain more expensive information after having taken into account the information that is less expensive to obtain.

The importance of forcing certain predictors into the equation and then noting whether additional predictors increase predictability is brought out forcefully in discussions of incremental validity (see, for example, Sechrest, 1963). Discussing test validity, Conrad (1950) states: ". . . we ought to know what is the contribution of this test over and beyond what is available from other, easier sources. For example, it is very easy to find out the person's chronological age; will our measure of aptitude tell us something that chronological age does not already tell us?" (p. 65). Similarly, Cronbach and Gleser (1965) maintain: "Tests should be judged on the basis of their contribution over and above the best strategy available that makes use of prior information" (p. 34).

In their attempts to predict criteria of achievement and creativity, Cattell and Butcher (1968) used measures of abilities and personality. In one set of analyses they first forced into the equation the ability measures, and then noted whether the personality measures increased the predictive power. The increments in proportions of variance due to the personality measures were not statistically significant in about half of these analyses. Cattell and Butcher (1968) correctly note: "In this instance, each test of significance involved the addition of fourteen new variables. . . . If for each criterion one compared not abilities alone and abilities plus fourteen personality factors, but abilities alone and abilities plus three or four factors most predictive of that particular criterion, there is little doubt that one could obtain statistically significant improvement in almost every case" (p. 192). Here, then, is an example in which one would force the ability measures into the equation and then apply a Stepwise Selection, say, to the 14 personality measures.

The main thing to bear in mind when applying any of the predictor-selection procedures outlined above is that they are designed to provide information for predictive, not explanatory, purposes. Finding, for example, that intelligence does not enhance the prediction of achievement over and above age, say, does not mean that intelligence is not an important determiner of achievement. The point has, perhaps, been made most forcefully by Meehl (1956), who is one of the central figures in the debate about clinical versus statistical prediction. Commenting on studies in which statistical prediction has been shown superior to clinical prediction, Meehl said:

> After reading these studies, it almost looks as if the first rule to follow in trying to predict the subsequent course of a student's or a patient's behavior is carefully to avoid talking to him, and that the second rule is to avoid thinking about him! (p. 263)

RECAPITULATION AND CAVEATS

This chapter began with an examination of the important distinction between predictive and explanatory research. From the discussion and illustrations of the different methods for the selection of predictors from a larger pool, it should be evident that such methods are valid and useful only in predictive research. It was amply demonstrated that different selection methods may lead to different results. Moreover, it was shown that, because the criteria used in the selection of predictors are purely statistical, a predictor with a slight edge (even when this may be due to random fluctuations or measurement errors) is selected in preference to another equally useful predictor. This crucial point warrants some further elaboration and examples.

Consider a situation in which one of several intercorrelated predictors has a slightly higher correlation with the criterion than do the rest of them. Not only will this predictor be selected first, but also there is a high probability that none of the remaining predictors will meet the criterion for entry into the equation. Recall that an increment in the proportion of variance accounted for is actually a squared semipartial correlation (see Chapter 5). Partialing out from one predictor another predictor with which it is highly correlated will generally result in a small, even meaningless, semipartial correlation. Situations of this kind are particularly prone to occur when several indicators of the same variable are being used, either by intent or because the researcher erroneously treats them as distinct variables. For example, one may use income, education, size of family, occupation, and the like as indicators of socioeconomic status, or they may be treated (erroneously) as distinct variables. Be that as it may, such indicators tend to be moderately to highly intercorrelated. If income, say, has a slightly higher correlation with a given criterion, it is possible that it alone will survive when a given variable-selection procedure is used. Assuming that this does happen, it is one thing to conclude that income is the best predictor for the given criterion and that the other indicators do not enhance predictability over and above that which income provides. It is an entirely different (and erroneous) thing to conclude on the basis of such results that income has an important effect on the criterion, whereas the other indicators have no noticeable effect on the criterion. Unfortunately, social science research is replete with misinterpretations of this kind (for examples of misinterpretations of Forward Selection procedures in political science research, see Lewis-Beck, 1978).

To highlight the point that has been made above, an example taken from one of the IEA studies (Carroll, 1975), which concerned the study of French as a foreign language in eight countries, will be analyzed. The correlation matrix reported in Table 6.2 was taken from Carroll (1975, p. 268). The criteria are: French Reading Test (Reading), and French Listening Test (Listening). The predictors "have been selected to represent the major types of factors that have been identified as being important *influences* on a student's proficiency in French" (Carroll, 1975, p. 267; italics added). The concern at this stage is exclusively with two predictors: student's aspiration to understand spoken French, and student's aspiration to be able to read French. Issues of validity and reliability notwithstanding, it is not surprising that the correlation between the two is .762 (see Table 6.2) since they are indicators of the same underlying variable—namely, self-reported aspirations to acquire skills in French.

For illustrative purposes, a Forward Selection procedure was applied twice. Reading was used as the criterion in the first analysis; Listening was the criterion in the second analysis. The seven remaining measures, listed in Table 6.2, were used as predictors in both analyses. A summary of the results of the Forward Selection applied to the data of Table 6.2 is reported in Table 6.3, where one may note the step at which a given predictor was entered into the equation, and the increment in the proportion of criterion variance attributed to it (see column labeled R SQUARE CHANGE).

Turning first to the results relating to the prediction of Reading, it will be noted that student's aspiration to understand spoken French and student's aspiration to be able to read French have almost identical correlations with the predictor that enters first into the equation, the amount of instruction (.180 and .188, respectively). Because aspiration to be able to read French has a slightly higher correlation with Reading than does aspiration to understand spoken French (.385 and .344, respectively), it is selected to enter at STEP 2 and is shown to account for about 7.34% of the variance in Reading, after the contribution of amount of instruction has been taken into account. It will be recalled that the two indicators provide a good deal of redundant information (the correlation between them is .762). Consequently, after aspiration to be able to read French enters into the equation, aspiration to understand spoken French cannot add much to the prediction of Reading. In fact, it enters at STEP 6, and is shown to account for an increment of only .04% of the variance in Reading.

The situation is even more dramatic when one considers the results of the analysis in which the criterion is Listening. In this case, the correlation of aspiration to understand spoken French with Listening is ever so slightly higher than the correlation of aspiration to be able to read French with Listening (.337

Table 6.2 Correlation Matrix of Seven Predictors and Two Criteria

		1	*2*	*3*	*4*	*5*	*6*	*7*	*8*	*9*
1	Teacher's Competence in French	1.000	.076	.269	−.004	−.017	.077	.050	.207	.299
2	Teaching Procedures	.076	1.000	.014	.095	.107	.205	.174	.092	.179
3	Amount of Instruction	.269	.014	1.000	.181	.107	.180	.188	.633	.632
4	Student Effort	−.004	.095	.181	1.000	.108	.185	.198	.281	.210
5	Student Aptitude for Foreign Language	−.017	.107	.107	.108	1.000	.376	.383	.277	.235
6	Aspiration to Understand Spoken French	.077	.205	.180	.185	.376	1.000	.762	.344	.337
7	Aspiration to Be Able to Read French	.050	.174	.188	.198	.383	.762	1.000	.385	.322
8	Reading Test	.207	.092	.633	.281	.277	.344	.385	1.000	
9	Listening Test	.299	.179	.632	.210	.235	.337	.322		1.000

NOTE: Data taken from J. B. Carroll, *The Teaching of French as a Foreign Language in Eight Countries*, p. 268. Copyright 1975 by John Wiley & Sons. Reprinted by permission.

Table 6.3 Summary of Forward Selection for French Reading and Listening Tests[a]

READING				LISTENING			
STEP	*VARIABLE*	*R SQUARE*	*R SQUARE CHANGE*	*STEP*	*VARIABLE*	*R SQUARE*	*R SQUARE CHANGE*
1	Amount of Instruction	.40069	.40069	1	Amount of Instruction	.39942	.39942
2	Aspiration to Be Able to Read French	.47404	.07335	2	Aspiration to Understand Spoken French	.45093	.05150
3	Student Effort	.48968	.01564	3	Teacher's Competence in French	.46709	.01616
4	Student Aptitude for Foreign Language	.50281	.01313	4	Teaching Procedures	.48090	.01381
5	Teacher's Competence in French	.50543	.00262	5	Student Aptitude for Foreign Language	.49005	.00915
6	Aspiration to Understand Spoken French	.50588	.00045	6	Student Effort	.49358	.00353
7	Teaching Procedures	.50616	.00029	7	Aspiration to Be Able to Read French	.49494	.00135

[a]Data from Table 6.2.

and .322, respectively; see Table 6.2). This time, therefore, aspiration to understand spoken French is the preferred indicator, entering at STEP 2 and accounting for 5.15% of the variance in Listening. Aspiration to be able to read French, on the other hand, enters last and is shown to account for an increment of about .14% of the variance in Listening.

The foregoing analyses were designed to demonstrate that variable-selection procedures are blind to the substantive aspects of the measures being used. Each vector is treated as if it were a distinct variable.[2] The moral is that, as in any other research activity, it is the researcher, not the method, that should be preeminent. It is the researcher's theory, specific goals, and knowledge about the measures being used that should serve as guides in the selection of analytic methods and the interpretation of the results. Had one (erroneously) used the above results for the purpose of explanation, instead of prediction, the inescapable conclusions would have been that, of the two aspiration "variables," only the aspiration to be able to read French is an important determiner of Reading, and that only aspiration to understand spoken French is an important determiner of Listening. The temptation to accept such conclusions as meaningful and valid would have been particularly great in the present case because they appear to be consistent with "commonsense" expectations.[3]

Speaking of the availability of "stepwise" computer programs, Maxwell (1975) maintains that: "The routine procedure today is to feed into a computer all the independent variates that are available and to hope for the best" (p. 53). Needless to say, any meaningful analysis applied to complex problems is never routine. It is the unwary researcher who applies routinely all sorts of analytic methods and then compounds the problem by selecting the results that are consistent with his or her expectations and preconceptions. Not until this type of approach is abandoned, or at least drastically reduced, is there hope of resolving some of the controversies in social science research by arriving at a greater consistency of findings that may be accepted and acted upon with greater confidence.

Study Suggestions

1. Distinguish between explanation and prediction. Give examples of studies in which the emphasis is on one or the other.
2. In Study Suggestion 2 of Chapter 2 a set of 20 observations on X and Y was used. Following are some of the results obtained with those data (see Answers to Chapter 2): $\bar{X} = 4.95$; $\Sigma x^2 = 134.95$; $s_{y.x} = 2.23800$; Y'_1 (predicted score for the first person whose $X = 2$) $= 3.30307$; Y'_{20} (predicted score for the last person whose $X = 4$) $= 4.79251$.

   Use the preceding information to calculate:

   (a) The standard error for Y'_1.
   (b) The 95% confidence interval for Y'_1.
   (c) The standard error for Y'_{20}.

[2]A particularly troublesome situation is when variable-selection methods are used when some or all the predictors are categorical variables. For a discussion of this topic, see Chapter 10.

[3]Carroll (1975) did not use a variable-selection procedure for this particular example. Instead, he interpreted the standardized regression coefficients as "the relative degree to which each of the seven variables contribute independently to the prediction of the criterion" (p. 289). This approach to the interpretation of the results is dealt with in Chapter 8.

(d) The 95% confidence interval for Y'_{20}.

3. In Study Suggestion 1 of Chapter 3 a set of 20 observations on X_1, X_2, and Y was used. Following are some of the results obtained with those data (see Answers to Chapter 3): $Y' = -1.23561 + .67370X_1 + .61833X_2$; $s^2_{y.12} = 3.43168$. The inverse of $(\mathbf{X'X})$, see Equation (6.3), is:

$$(\mathbf{X'X})^{-1} = \begin{matrix} .52380 & -.02987 & -.05926 \\ -.02987 & .00757 & -.00138 \\ -.05926 & -.00138 & .01202 \end{matrix}$$

Use the preceding information to calculate:

(a) Y'_1 (predicted score for the first person, whose scores are $X_1 = 2$; $X_2 = 5$).
(b) The standard error for Y'_1, applying Equation (6.3).
(c) The 95% confidence interval for Y'_1.
(d) Y'_{20} (predicted score for the last person, whose scores are $X_1 = 4$; $X_2 = 9$).
(e) The standard error for Y'_{20}.
(f) The 95% confidence interval for Y'_{20}.

4. If you have access to SAS package, use the GLM program with the data of Study Suggestion 2 of Chapter 2, and those of Study Suggestion 1 of Chapter 3. Call for the inverse of $(\mathbf{X'X})$ and for the 95% confidence interval for the predicted scores. Compare with the results given in 2 and 3, above.
5. What is meant by "shrinkage" of the multiple correlation? What is the relation between shrinkage and the size of the sample?
6. What is cross-validation? How is it used?
7. Calculate the "shrunken" R^2's for the following:
   (a) $R^2_{y.12} = .40$; $N = 30$
   (b) $R^2_{y.123} = .55$; $N = 100$
   (c) $R^2_{y.1234} = .30$; $N = 200$
8. Here is an illustrative correlation matrix ($N = 300$). The dependent variable is verbal achievement. The independent variables are race, IQ, school quality, self-concept, and level of aspiration.

	1 *Race*	*2* *IQ*	*3* *School Quality*	*4* *Self-Concept*	*5* *Level of Aspiration*	*6* *Verbal Achievement*
1	1.00	.30	.25	.30	.30	.25
2	.30	1.00	.20	.20	.30	.60
3	.25	.20	1.00	.20	.30	.30
4	.30	.20	.20	1.00	.40	.30
5	.30	.30	.30	.40	1.00	.40
6	.25	.60	.30	.30	.40	1.00

1. Using a computer program (e.g., SPSS, REGRESSION) do a forward selection for the above data. Specify $F = 4.00$ as a criterion for the entry of a variable into the analysis.

ANSWERS

2. (a) 2.36264; (b) −1.66084 and 8.26698; (c) 2.30056; (d) −.04097 and 9.62599
3. (a) $Y'_1 = 3.20344$; (b) 1.95601; (c) −.92374 and 7.33062; (d) $Y'_{20} = 7.02416$; (e) 2.04071; (f) 2.71826 and 11.33006
7. (a) .36; (b) .54; (c) .29
8. Excerpts from SPSS output:

SUMMARY TABLE

STEP	VARIABLE ENTERED	R SQUARE	R SQUARE CHANGE
1	X2	.36000	.36000
2	X5	.41319	.05319
3	X3	.42978	.01659
4	X4	.43919	.00941

Note that X1 (Race) did not meet the criterion for entry into the analysis. Also, after taking X2 (IQ) and X5 (Level of Aspiration) into account, the remaining two variables (X3 and X4) add little to the proportion of variance accounted for (see R SQUARE CHANGE).

7

EXPLANATION: VARIANCE PARTITIONING

Chapter 6 was devoted to the application of multiple regression analysis in predictive research. We turn our attention now to the use and interpretation of multiple regression analysis in explanatory research. Unlike prediction, which is relatively straightforward and may be accomplished even in the absence of a theoretical frame of reference, explanation is inconceivable without theory. Some authors equate scientific explanation with theory, whereas others maintain that it is theory that enables one to arrive at explanation.[1] Explanation is probably the ultimate goal of scientific inquiry, not only because it satisfies the need to understand phenomena, but also because it is the key for creating the requisite conditions for the achievement of specific objectives. Only by identifying the variables and understanding the processes by which they lead to learning, mental health, social mobility, personality development, intergroup conflicts, international conflicts, drug addiction, inflation, recession, unemployment, to name but a few, is there promise of creating the conditions most conducive to the eradication of social and individual ills and the achievement of goals deemed desirable and beneficial.

In their search for explanation of phenomena, behavioral scientists have attempted not only to identify the major variables causing them but also to determine the relative importance of such variables. Various theories, research strategies, and analytic techniques have been resorted to in the pursuit of such explanations. This chapter and Chapter 8 are limited to a discussion of methods subsumed under multiple regression analysis used for the purpose of identifying and determining the relative importance of variables assumed to be affecting a

[1]For discussions of scientific explanation, see Brodbeck (1968, Part Five); Feigl & Brodbeck (1953, Part IV); Kaplan (1964, Chapter IX); Sjoberg & Nett (1968, Chapter 11).

phenomenon under study. These methods are not mutually exclusive, but they differ in the way in which they use multiple regression analysis and in their emphases on different statistics obtained from regression analysis. In the broadest terms, it is possible to distinguish two approaches under which the methods presented herein can be subsumed: (1) variance partitioning, to which this chapter is devoted, and (2) the analysis of effects, presented in Chapter 8.

It is important to recognize at the outset that while multiple regression analysis may be used in both experimental and nonexperimental research, the interpretation of the results is by far simpler and more straightforward in experimental research. In experimental research, independent variables are manipulated, and the effects of such manipulations on dependent variables may be observed. Moreover, in balanced experimental designs the independent variables are not correlated. Consequently, it is possible to study the distinct effects of each independent variable as well as their joint effects (i.e., their interactions). In nonexperimental research, on the other hand, the independent variables tend to be correlated, sometimes substantially. This makes it difficult, if not impossible, to untangle the effects of each variable. In addition, some of the variables may serve as proxies for the "true" variables—a situation that when overlooked may lead to useless or nonsensical conclusions.

Since the complexities in the interpretation of results from multiple regression analysis are primarily related to nonexperimental research, it is with this type of research that this chapter and the next one are concerned. Issues and procedures pertaining to the application of multiple regression analysis in experimental research are discussed in subsequent chapters (see, for example, Chapters 9 and 10). Extra care and caution are called for when applying multiple regression analysis in nonexperimental settings. Sound thinking within a theoretical frame of reference, and a clear understanding of the analytic method being used are probably the best safeguards against drawing unwarranted, illogical, or nonsensical conclusions.

THE NOTION OF VARIANCE PARTITIONING

Variance partitioning refers to attempts at the partitioning of R^2 into portions attributable to different independent variables, or to different sets of independent variables. This idea has already been introduced in Chapter 5 in connection with the discussion of semipartial correlations, where it was shown that R^2 can be expressed as the sum of the squared zero-order correlation of the dependent variable with the first independent variable entered into the analysis, and squared semipartial correlations, of successive orders, for additional variables being entered (see, for example, (5.24) and the discussion related to it). It was pointed out, and illustrated numerically, in Chapter 5 that although R^2 is invariant regardless of the order of entry of the independent variables into the analysis, the proportion of variance incremented by a given variable depends upon its specific point of entry, except when the independent variables are not intercorrelated.

The partitioning of R^2 indicated above is but one of various approaches, all of which have been apparently inspired and sustained by different but algebraically equivalent formulas for R^2. Various researchers seem to have been intrigued by the different formulas for R^2, and have attempted to invest the individual elements of such formulas with substantive meaning. That such attempts may lead to questionable, even ludicrous, interpretations has been brought out in a witty statement by Ward (1969), who characterized them by formulating two Ward laws:

> If a *meaningful number* can be computed as the sum of several numbers, then each term of the sum must be as *meaningful as* or more *meaningful than the sum.*
> If results of a meaningful analysis do not agree with expectations, than a more meaningful analysis must be performed. (pp. 473–474)

Various other authors have argued against attempts at partitioning R^2 when the independent variables are intercorrelated. Thus, Darlington (1968) states: "It would be better to simply concede that the notion of 'independent contribution to variance' has no meaning when predictor variables are intercorrelated" (p. 169). And according to Duncan:

> Indeed the "problem" of partitioning R^2 bears no essential relationship to estimating or testing a model, and it really does not add anything to our understanding of how the model works. The simplest recommendation—one which saves both work and worry—is to eschew altogether the task of dividing up R^2 into unique causal components. In a strict sense, it just cannot be done, even though many sociologists, psychologists, and other quixotic persons cannot be persuaded to forego the attempt. (1975, p. 65)

As may have been gathered from the preceding remarks, and as will become evident from the discussions that follow, variance partitioning is *not* a valid approach for the purpose of determining the relative importance of the effects of independent variables on a dependent variable.

A question that undoubtedly comes to mind is: *If the preceding statement is correct, why devote an entire chapter to variance partitioning?* The answer is that variance partitioning is widely used in the social sciences, often for the purpose of determining the relative importance of independent variables. Prime examples of major studies that relied almost exclusively on variance partitioning are *Equality of Educational Opportunity* (Coleman et al., 1966) and studies conducted under the auspices of the International Association for the Evaluation of Educational Achievement (IEA). While these and other studies are discussed in detail later in this chapter, it will be pointed out here that the controversy surrounding the Coleman Report (as *Equality of Educational Opportunity* is often called) is largely one concerning the validity of using variance partitioning for the purpose of assessing the relative importance of variables affecting academic achievement.

Because of the widespread use, often abuse, of variance partitioning in the social sciences, it was felt that it deserves a thorough examination. In particular, it was felt essential to discuss the conditions under which it may be validly applied; the questions that it may be used to answer; and the nature of the answers obtained. In short, it was felt that, as with any analytic approach, a thorough understanding of its properties is an important requisite for its valid application, or for the evaluation of research studies in which it has been applied.

Before turning to specific approaches of variance partitioning dealt with in this chapter it is very important to note that R^2—the portion that is being partitioned—is sample-specific. That is, R^2 may vary from sample to sample even when the effects of the independent variables on the dependent variable are identical in all the samples. In Chapter 2 (see Table 2.3 and the discussion related to it) it was shown that while the regression coefficient *(b)* was identical for four sets of data, r^2 for these sets of data ranged from a low of .06 to a high of .54. The same phenomenon may occur in multiple regression analysis. Thus, it is possible for the regression equations to be identical in several samples while the R^2's in the samples may vary widely. The reason is that R^2 is affected, among other things, by the variability of a given sample on: (1) the variables being studied; (2) the variables *not* included in the study; (3) the errors of measurement of the dependent variable. Recall that (2) and (3) are subsumed under the error term, or the residual. Therefore, other things equal, the larger the variability of a given sample on variables not included in the study, or on measurement errors, the smaller the R^2. Also, other things equal, the larger the variability of a given sample on the independent variables, the larger the R^2. To repeat: R^2's may differ in different samples even when the regression equations are identical (for further discussions, see Blalock, 1964; Ezekiel & Fox, 1959; Fox, 1968; Hanushek & Jackson, 1977).

The above noted properties of R^2 limits its generalizability, thereby casting further doubts about the usefulness of methods designed to partition it. It is therefore not surprising that Tukey (1954), who addresses the question of variance partitioning, concludes: "Since we know that the question arises in connection with specific populations, and that in general determination is a complex thing, we see that we do not lose much by failing to answer the question" (p. 45).

With the above remarks in mind, we turn to an examination of what are currently the two most popular approaches to variance partitioning: Incremental Partitioning of Variance, and Commonality Analysis.

INCREMENTAL PARTITIONING OF VARIANCE

In this approach, the proportion of variance accounted by all the independent variables (i.e., R^2) is partitioned incrementally by noting the increment in the proportion of variance accounted for by each independent variable (or by a set of independent variables) at the point at which it is entered into a regression analysis. As was noted above, this type of partitioning of variance, which is accomplished by a process of successive partialing, was introduced in Chapter 5 (see, in particular, the section entitled Multiple Regression and Semipartial Correlations).

Since the order of entry of variables into the analysis is crucial to the incremental partitioning approach, the question is: How is the order determined? In answer to this question it is necessary to distinguish between two major purposes for which incremental partitioning of variance is used: (1) to study the effect of an independent variable(s) on the dependent variable after having controlled for another variable(s), and (2) to study the relative effects of a set of independent variables on the dependent variable. The first purpose, that of control, is valid and useful in various designs. For example, the analysis of covariance (see Chapter 13) can be viewed as an incremental partitioning of variance in which the covariate(s) is entered first into the analysis, thereby controlling for it while studying the effects of treatments on the dependent variable. The important thing to bear in mind is that such an analysis is not intended to provide information about the relative importance of variables, but rather about the effect of a variable(s) after having controlled for another variable(s).

It is the aim of the sections that follow to show why incremental partitioning of variance is not a valid approach when the purpose is to determine the relative importance of variables. Before turning to this topic, however, some additional remarks need to be made about the use of incremental partitioning of variance for the purpose of controlling for a variable(s) while studying the effect(s) of another variable(s).

The decision to control for a variable(s) is by no means an arbitrary one. Unless one has formulated a theory about the pattern of the relations among the variables under study there is no logical way to decide which variables should be controlled.[2] Unfortunately, variables are often controlled without theoretical justifications or with what appear to be questionable justifications. Probably the justification advanced most often of the need to control for a variable is that its effect has occured earlier in a time sequence. Thus, for example, Coleman et al. (1966) argued that because student background characteristics are "prior to school influence, and shape the child before he reaches school, they will . . . be controlled when examining the effects of school factors" (p. 198).

Merely because one independent variable precedes another independent variable in a time sequence is not sufficient justification to control the one while studying the effect of the other. As was said above, the problem of controlling certain variables while studying the effects of others depends upon the theoretical formulations about the entire pattern of relations among the variables under study. Suppose, for the sake of illustration, that one is dealing with three variables only: B = student background characteristics; S = school quality; A = achievement. Figure 7.1 illustrates possible models relevant to variance partitioning.

To understand the difference between the models of Figure 7.1 and others presented subsequently, it is necessary to digress briefly and discuss the distinction made in causal models between exogenous and endogenous variables.[3] An *exogenous* variable is a variable whose variability is assumed to be determined by causes outside the causal model under consideration. Stated differently, no attempt is made to explain the variability of an exogenous variable or its relations with other exogenous variables. An *endogenous* variable, on the other hand, is one whose variation is to be explained by exogenous and other endogenous variables in the causal model.

[2]See discussion of the logic of control in Chapter 5.

[3]Some of the terminology and methods used in this chapter are closely related to those of path analysis. Study of introductory presentations of path analysis (e.g., Chapter 15) will enhance the understanding of the present discussion.

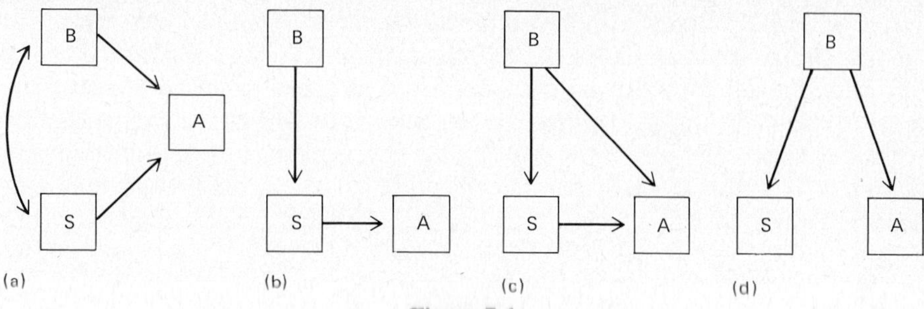

Figure 7.1

Examples of exogenous and endogenous variables will be given by reference to some of the models depicted in Figure 7.1. In model (a), B and S are treated as exogenous variables, whereas A is treated as an endogenous variable. In model (b), on the other hand, only B is treated as an exogenous variable, whereas S and A are treated as endogenous variables.

Whether or not a variable can be meaningfully controlled while studying the effects of another variable depends, among other things, on the causal model postulated by the researcher and upon the specific questions that are being addressed. This is illustrated in connection with the models of Figure 7.1. Turning first to model (a), it will be noted that the two exogenous variables (B and S) are correlated. This is indicated by the curved line, with arrowheads at both ends, connecting these variables. What this means is that the correlation between B and S is treated as "given." In other words, the model does not address the question why the variables are correlated. (This is always the case when correlated exogenous variables are used in a causal model.) Attempts to explain the correlation between B and S would require the introduction of one or more additional variables into the model, or a revised model in which one of these variables is treated as an endogenous variable (e.g., model (c)).

The choice of a model is, of course, not arbitrary, nor is it determined by considerations regarding the analytic approach one wishes to use. A model reflects one's theory about the interrelations among the variables being studied, and the process by which the independent variables affect the dependent variable.

It is important to note that when the exogenous variables are correlated, as in model (a), there is no justification to do an incremental partitioning of variance in an effort to control for one variable while studying the effect of the other, even if the former precedes the latter in time. The reason is that the researcher is unable, or unwilling, to state why the two variables are correlated. It is possible, for example, that the variables are correlated because one of them affects the other, or because they are affected by a common cause(s). Whatever the reason for the correlation between B and S, if B is entered first into the analysis because it precedes S in time, the variance in A attributed to it will include also the explanatory power that it has by virtue of its correlation with S. In other words, the shared explanatory power of B and S is allocated exclusively to B when it is entered first into the regression analysis.

Suppose, however, that the theoretical considerations indicate that the pattern of the relations among the three variables is due to a process as depicted in model (b), Figure 7.1, according to which the school (S) mediates the effects of the background characteristics (B) on achievement (A). Note that according to this model B does not affect A directly (there is no arrow from the former to the latter). Direct and indirect effects are discussed below. In such a model it is valid to control for B, that is to enter it first into the analysis, in order to study the effect of S after B has been controlled. This can be accomplished by calculating

$$R^2_{\text{A.BS}} - R^2_{\text{A.B}}$$

where $R^2_{\text{A.BS}}$ indicates the proportion of variance of A accounted for by *both* B and S, and $R^2_{\text{A.B}}$ indicates the proportion of variance of A accounted for by B alone. The difference between these two terms, then, indicates the proportion of variance accounted for by S over and above what B accounts for.

It is important to recognize what it is that the proportion of variance incremented by S represents. As can be seen from model (b), S transmits the effect of B on A. In addition, S by itself may affect A, that is apart from the effect of B that it transmits. Now, the increment in the proportion of variance accounted for that is attributed to S reflects the part of the effect of this variable on A that is independent of B. In other words, the increment in the proportion of variance attributed to S *does not* include the effect of B on A that S transmits. Clearly, then, one may choose to control for B in model (b) if it is desired to address the question about the effect of S on A that is independent of B. As is discussed below, however, this should not be construed as an answer to the question which of the two variables (B or S) has a greater effect on A, or which of the two variables is more important.

What was said above about model (b) applies also to model (c). The difference between the two models is that in the former B is hypothesized to affect A only indirectly, via S, whereas in the latter it is hypothesized that B affects A directly as well as indirectly (analyses of such alternative models are presented in Chapter 15).

Turning to model (d) of Figure 7.1, it will be noted that according to this model it is hypothesized that the correlation between school quality (S) and achievement (A) is due to a common cause, student background characteristics (B). This, then, is an instance in which B would be controlled by partialing it out from *both* S and A in order to determine whether the correlation between S and A is spurious (see Chapter 5).

The brief discussion about the four alternative models of Figure 7.1 was designed to underscore the point that it is not possible to decide whether and how to control for a variable without first formulating a causal model about the process by which the independent variables affect the dependent variable. To repeat, however, even when variables are controlled in accordance with a causal model it is *not* valid to compare the proportions of variance accounted for by the different variables for the purpose of determining their relative effects on the dependent variable, or their relative importance. It is to this issue that we now turn by examining the properties of elements obtained in an incremental partitioning of variance.

The Meaning of Incremental Partitioning of Variance

The meaning of elements obtained in an incremental partitioning of variance will be examined first in a three-variable model, and then in several four-variable models. In the course of the discussion it will be necessary to resort to some concepts used in the analysis of causal models. These concepts, which are discussed in detail in Chapter 15, are introduced here on an intuitive level only. It is hoped that this will suffice for the present purpose. (To gain a deeper understanding of topics discussed here, it is suggested that you refer to relevant sections of Chapter 15.)

In the analysis of causal models, a distinction is made between direct and indirect effects of independent variables on dependent variables. A *direct effect* of an independent variable on a dependent variable is defined as the part of its effect that is not mediated, or transmitted, by other variables. An *indirect effect*, on the other hand, is the part of the effect of the independent variable that is mediated, or transmitted, by another variable or other variables.

These concepts are illustrated by reference to the three-variable models presented earlier in Figure 7.1. In model (a), B and S are said to have direct effects on A, as indicated by the arrows that emanate from B and S to A. In this model, there are no indirect effects because there are no variables that mediate the effects of B and S on A. As was noted earlier, the curved line with arrowheads at both ends indicates that the two exogenous variables are correlated.

Turning to model (b) of Figure 7.1, it will be noted that B has a direct effect on S, as indicated by the arrow from the former to the latter. B has no direct effect on A (there is no arrow connecting the two variables). B does, however, affect A indirectly, via S. The indirect effect of B on A is indicated by B → S → A. Finally, because there are no variables intervening between S and A, the former has only a direct effect on the latter.

Contrast model (b) with model (c) of Figure 7.1. The difference between the two models is that in the former it is hypothesized that B has only an indirect effect on A, whereas in the latter B is hypothesized to have both a direct and an indirect effect on A.

One additional term to be introduced here is that of a total effect. A *total effect* of an independent variable on a dependent variable is defined as the sum of its direct and indirect effect(s). Depending on the causal model, a variable may or may not have a direct effect on another variable. Moreover, a variable may have more than one indirect effect on another variable (see four-variable models, below). In Chapter 15 it is shown how the direct and indirect effects are calculated. For the present purposes it is only necessary to bear in mind that a total effect of a variable is the sum of its direct and indirect effect(s). When a variable has only a direct effect on another variable, this is its total effect. Similarly, the total effect of a variable that has no direct effect on another variable is equal to its indirect effect, or the sum of its indirect effects. We are ready now to study the meaning of elements obtained in incremental partitioning of variance. This is done first in a three-variable model and then in several four-variable models.

A Three-Variable Model

Assume that the model of Figure 7.2 is hypothesized to reflect the process of school achievement.[4] That is, it is hypothesized that Student Background (B) affects Achievement (A) directly as well as indirectly, via School Quality (S). Note also that in this model B has a direct effect on S, and that S has a direct effect on A. For illustrative purposes, assume that the correlations among the three variables are

$$r_{BS} = .5 \qquad r_{AB} = .4 \qquad r_{AS} = .65$$

$R^2_{A.BS}$ is calculated, applying Formula (3.20)

$$R^2_{A.BS} = \frac{r^2_{AB} + r^2_{AS} - 2r_{AB}r_{AS}r_{BS}}{1 - r^2_{BS}} = \frac{.4^2 + .65^2 - 2(.4)(.65)(.5)}{1 - .5^2} = .43$$

B and S account for 43% of the variance of A. To do an incremental partitioning of variance according to the model depicted in Figure 7.2, it is necessary to calculate the proportion of variance in A accounted for by B, and the proportion of variance in A accounted for by S after B has been taken into account, or the increment in the proportion of variance accounted for that is due to S. Symbolically this may be stated as

$$R^2_{A.BS} = r^2_{AB} + r^2_{A(S.B)} = R^2_{A.B} + (R^2_{A.BS} - R^2_{A.B})$$

where the first term is the squared zero-order correlation of A with B, and the second term is the squared semipartial correlation of A with S, after B has been partialed out from the latter.

For the present data, the proportion of variance accounted for by B is .16 (r^2_{AB}), and the increment in the proportion of variance accounted for due to S is

$$R^2_{A.BS} - R^2_{A.B} = .43 - .16 = .27$$

It is concluded that Student Background accounts for 16% of the variance in Achievement, and that School Quality accounts for an additional 27% of the variance in Achievement, that is, over and above what Student Background accounts for.

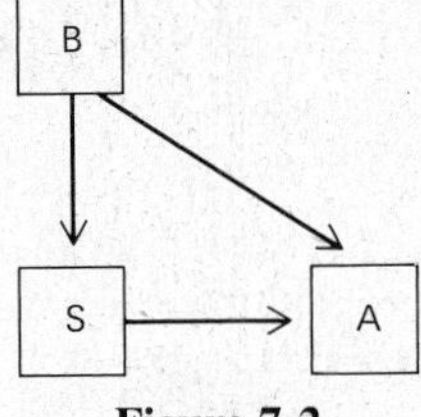

Figure 7.2

[4]This oversimplified model is, of course, inadequate to explain school achievement. It is used for illustrative purposes only.

The main question for the present purposes is: *What do these two elements represent?* It can be shown[5] that the proportion of variance accounted for by B (.16) is equal to the square of its total effect on A. In other words, it is equal to the square of the sum of the direct effect of B on A and its indirect effect on A, via S. The increment in the proportion of variance due to S, on the other hand, is *not* equal to the square of its total effect. It can be shown that the square of the total effect of S on A is .36. But the increment in the proportion of variance due to S (.27) represents only that part of the effect of S on A that is independent of B. That is, the effect of B on A that is transmitted by S is *not* included in this quantity.

The preceding discussion could have been avoided by simply noting that the increment in the proportion of variance accounted for by S is equal to the squared semipartial correlation, $r^2_{A(S.B)}$, thereby indicating that it is the proportion of variance S accounts for after B was partialed out from it. The reason for going through the above presentation was to show that the two elements represent different types of effects, and that it is therefore inappropriate to compare them for the purpose of determining the relative importance of the variables with which they are associated.

Finally, it will be noted that it is appropriate, and sometimes useful, to compare total effects of different variables in an effort to determine their relative effects on the dependent variable. In the present example this would mean a comparison between the total effect of B on A, which may be shown to be .4, and the total effect of S on A, which may be shown to be .6. This approach is discussed in detail in Chapter 15, where the total effect is also referred to as the effect coefficient.

Four-Variable Models

Assume that one wishes to explain grade-point average (GPA) of college students by resorting to the following independent variables: socioeconomic status (SES), intelligence (IQ), and need achievement (*n* Ach).[6] An illustrative correlation matrix for these variables is reported in Table 7.1. It is obvious that different theoretical formulations may be advanced regarding the relations

Table 7.1 Correlation Matrix for Three Independent Variables and a Dependent Variable; $N = 300$

	1 *SES*	*2* *IQ*	*3* *n Ach*	*Y* *GPA*
1	1.00	.30	.41	.33
2	.30	1.00	.16	.57
3	.41	.16	1.00	.50
Y	.33	.57	.50	1.00

[5]See Chapter 15, where some of the models presented in this chapter are reanalyzed.

[6]No attempt will be made to justify the choice of these variables or the omission of other important variables. It is felt that the use of substantive variables, instead of labeling them X_1, X_2, and so on, will enhance the understanding of the illustrations.

among the variables under considerations. Without attempting to justify them on theoretical grounds, three possible models will be examined for the sole purpose of noting what type of variance partitioning, if any, is appropriate for each, and what effects the partitioned elements represent.

Model A. We begin with the model depicted in Figure 7.3, according to which SES affects IQ; SES and IQ affect *n* Ach; and SES, IQ, and *n* Ach affect GPA. To avoid cumbersome subscript notation, GPA is designated as *Y*, and the independent variables are referred to by the numbers attached to them in Table 7.1 and in Figure 7.3. Accordingly, 1 = SES, 2 = IQ, and 3 = *n* Ach.

Doing an incremental partitioning of variance, beginning with SES, it is determined that it accounts for about 11% of the variance in GPA:

$$r^2_{y1} = .33^2 = .1089$$

Without presenting the calculations, it will be noted that $R^2_{y.12} = .35268$, and $R^2_{y.123} = .49647$. To obtain the increment in the proportion of variance of GPA accounted for by IQ, calculate

$$R^2_{y.12} - R^2_{y.1} = .35268 - .1089 = .24378$$

IQ adds about 24% to the variance accounted for in GPA.

The proportion of variance of GPA that *n* Ach accounts for, over and above SES and IQ, is:

$$R^2_{y.123} - R^2_{y.12} = .49647 - .35268 = .14379$$

In sum, the three variables combined account for about 50% of the variance of GPA ($R^2_{y.123} = .49647$), of which SES accounts for about 11%, IQ adds 24%, and *n* Ach adds another 14%.

According to the model depicted in Figure 7.3 SES has a direct effect on GPA as well as three indirect effects. The latter are: (1) SES → *n* Ach → GPA; (2)

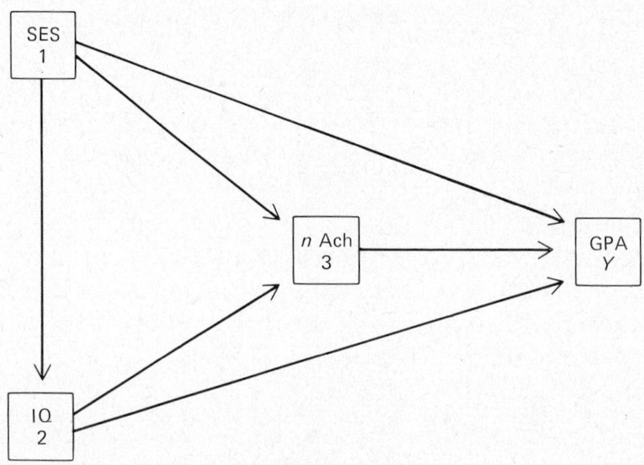

Figure 7.3

SES → IQ → GPA; and (3) SES → IQ → *n* Ach → GPA. The total effect of SES on GPA, then, is equal to the sum of its direct effect and the three indirect effects. Now, it can be shown that the proportion of variance of GPA accounted for by SES (.1089) is equal to the square of its total effect.

Turning now to IQ, it will be noted that according to the model depicted in Figure 7.3 it has a direct effect on GPA as well as an indirect effect: IQ → *n* Ach → GPA. It can be shown that the total effect (the direct plus the indirect effect) of IQ on GPA is .52. But the proportion of variance incremented by IQ (.24) is *not* equal to the square of its total effect on GPA. The proportion of variance incremented by IQ reflects the part of the effect of this variable on GPA that is independent of SES.

Finally, the total effect of *n* Ach on GPA is equal to its direct effect because there are no variables mediating the effect of the former on the latter. It can be shown that the total effect of *n* Ach on GPA is .42. The proportion of variance of GPA accounted for by *n* Ach, over and above SES and IQ, (.14) is *not* equal to the square of its total effect, but rather to the square of its effect that is independent of SES and IQ.

On the basis of the preceding discussion it is clear that the proportions of variance attributed to the three variables reflect different types of effects: for SES it is the square of its total effect; for IQ it is the square of its effect that is independent of SES; and for *n* Ach it is the square of its effect that is independent of SES and IQ. On the basis of the preceding analysis it is valid to make statements about the proportion of variance accounted for by IQ after controlling for SES, and about the proportion of variance accounted for by *n* Ach after controlling for SES and IQ (assuming, of course, that the model that led to this partitioning of the variance is valid and sound from a theoretical frame of reference. Alternative models for the four variables are presented below.). But because the different elements obtained in the preceding analysis reflect different types of effects it is *not* valid to compare them for the purpose of determining the relative effects of the variables with which they are associated on GPA, or the relative importance of the three independent variables.

Model B. Assume now that the model related to the data of Table 7.1 is as depicted in Figure 7.4. The difference between Model A (Figure 7.3) and Model B (Figure 7.4) is that in the former only SES is treated as an exogenous variable, whereas in the latter SES and IQ are treated as exogenous variables. In Model A the correlation between SES and IQ is conceived of as a consequence of the former affecting the latter. In Model B, on the other hand, the correlation between SES and IQ is left unexplained. The two variables are treated as correlated causes of *n* Ach and GPA.

As is discussed in Chapter 15, the concept of a total effect of either SES or IQ on either *n* Ach or on GPA is, to say the least, ambiguous because the correlation between SES and IQ remains unanalyzed. In other words, as long as the correlation between SES and IQ is left unexplained, it is not possible to tell whether, for example, the former affects the latter or vice versa. Some authors (e.g., Duncan, 1975, p. 41; MacDonald, 1979, p. 295) maintain that when exogenous variables are correlated, the concept of a total effect is inapplicable to any of them. Other authors (e.g., Alwin & Hauser, 1975, pp. 38–39) use the

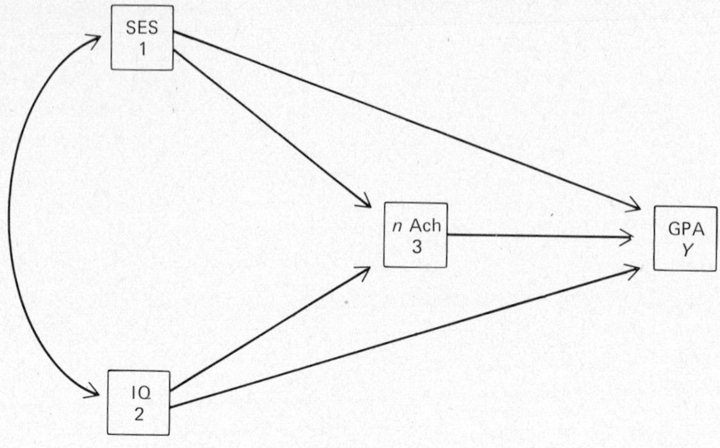

Figure 7.4

term *total effect* to indicate the direct and indirect effect(s) of an exogenous variable even when it is correlated with other exogenous variables. Thus, following Alwin and Hauser, and referring to Model B, one would consider the total effect of SES, for example, on GPA to be equal to its direct effect plus its indirect effect: SES → *n* Ach → GPA.

Whether or not one decides to apply the concept of total effects to correlated exogenous variables, the important thing to note is that under such circumstances it is not possible to detect parts of their (probable) effects on a given endogenous variable. For example, from Model B, Figure 7.4, it can be discerned that part of the correlation between SES and GPA is due to the correlation of SES with another cause of GPA, IQ. As is shown in Chapter 15 (see section entitled The Decomposition of Correlations) this part of the correlation between SES and GPA remains unanalyzed (as is the part of the correlation between IQ and GPA that is due to the correlation between IQ and SES).

The implication of the preceding discussion for the topic under consideration is that when exogenous variables are intercorrelated it is not possible to untangle some of their relations with a given endogenous variable, hence to partition the variance of the latter into distinct portions attributable to each of the former. As MacDonald (1979) states: "Since then we cannot (while retaining our model as specified) assign 'total effects' to our exogenous variables, we equally cannot produce any decomposition of variance amongst them" (p. 295). MacDonald refers to attempts to partition variance among exogenous variables as "nonsense" (p. 295).

All one can do when variance is partitioned in the presence of correlated exogenous variables is to determine the proportion of variance they account for simultaneously. Referring to Model B, this means that one may calculate the proportion of variance of GPA accounted for by SES and IQ taken together, and the proportion of variance incremented by *n* Ach over and above what SES and IQ account for. Using the correlations reported in Table 7.1, such a partitioning of variance is:

1) Due to SES and IQ: $R^2_{y.12}$ $= .35268$
2) Increment due to *n* Ach: $R^2_{y.123} - R^2_{y.12} = .14379$
$R^2_{y.123} = .49647$

SES and IQ together account for about 35% of the variance of GPA. *n* Ach accounts for an additional 14% of the variance of GPA.

Two things will be noted about the preceding analysis. First, had a researcher erroneously applied an incremental partitioning of variance beginning with SES only, the implication would have been that Model A, *not* B, reflects the pattern of causal relations among the variables under study. Second, as in the analysis of Model A, the increment in the proportion of variance accounted for by *n* Ach reflects that part of its effect that is independent of SES and IQ.

Model C. This time it is assumed that the model related to the data of Table 7.1 is as in Figure 7.5. The three independent variables are treated as exogenous. In this model it is still possible to determine the direct effects of each of the exogenous variables on GPA (this is done in Chapters 8 and 15). But there is no meaningful way to partition the variance of GPA and to attribute distinct portions to each of the independent variables. All one can do is determine the proportion of variance accounted for by the three variables, simultaneously, that is, that $R^2_{y.123} = .49647$.

The three models presented above differ in the degree of their theoretical elaboration; Model A being the most elaborate, and Model C the least elaborate. Note that the more elaborate the model, the more explicit are the statements about the causal relations among the variables, the greater the freedom in partitioning the variance. When no causal statement is made about the relations among the independent variables (i.e., they are treated as exogenous variables, as in Model C) the researcher is in effect professing ignorance, or unwillingness to make a statement, about the reasons for the correlations among the independent variables. Be that as it may, the absence of a statement that ex-

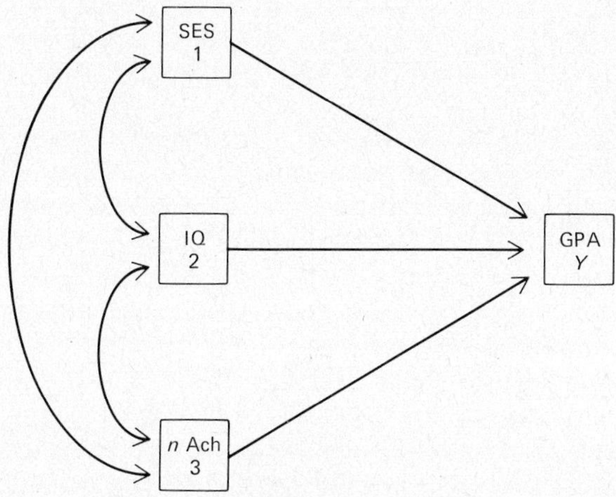

Figure 7.5

plains the correlations among the independent variables precludes the possibility of partitioning the variance of the dependent variable.

RECAPITULATION

It is worthwhile to recapitulate the major points discussed in the preceding sections. First, it was pointed out that one may use incremental partitioning of variance for the purpose of controlling for a variable(s) while studying the effect(s) of another variable(s) on a given dependent variable. Second, it was stressed that, to be meaningful, controls should be applied in accordance with a specific causal model. Third, it was stated that the increment in the proportion of variance accounted for by a given variable reflects that part of its effect that is independent of the variables that have been controlled. Finally, it was argued that because the elements obtained in incremental partitioning of variance reflect different types of effects, it is *not* valid to compare them for the purpose of determining their relative effects on a dependent variable (for further discussions of the points made in the preceding sections, see Coleman, 1975a, 1976; MacDonald, 1979).

In conclusion, it will be recalled that in the beginning of this chapter reservations were expressed regarding the use of variance partitioning for the purpose of determining the relative importance of independent variables. It was said that because of their popularity such approaches deserve a thorough examination in order to better understand what can and cannot be accomplished by their application. It will be noted that there exist more appropriate and more powerful methods for the analysis of models, such as the ones presented in the preceding sections. In fact, in Chapter 15 the models presented in this chapter are reanalyzed through Path Analysis, and comparisons between the two approaches are drawn. In light of the discussion of incremental partitioning of variance, we turn to an examination of some large-scale studies that relied almost exclusively on this approach.

RESEARCH APPLICATIONS

Incremental partitioning of variance is used frequently in social science research, often inappropriately. Instead of briefly reviewing a large number of studies in which this method was used, it was felt that it would be more beneficial to concentrate on a couple of important and influential studies. It should be noted, however, that the presentation is not designed to serve as a summary of the studies, nor is it intended to provide statements about their substantive findings. The sole purpose of this section is to illustrate the application of incremental partitioning of variance, to scrutinize the rationale (if any) in support of the analysis, and to examine the validity of some of the conclusions in the light of the unique properties of the analytic method being used. Issues concerning the overall research design that are not directly related to the variance partitioning (e.g., sampling, measurement, unit of analysis) are not commented upon, although it is, of course, crucial to appraise them whenever substantive findings of a study are being assessed.

Equality of Educational Opportunity

Equality of Educational Opportunity (Coleman et al., 1966)—or the Coleman Report, as it is popularly referred to—is perhaps the most important single study of American education in recent decades. It is certainly the most controversial. Opposing factions (e.g., supporters and opponents of school integration, advocates and detractors of the schools) have used the report's "findings," or what they believed the findings to be, as evidence in support of their political ideologies or educational philosophies. This may have been an inevitable reaction to an influential statement about strongly held beliefs in American society. Reactions of social scientists to the report varied greatly, ranging from commendations to condemnations, from acceptance without questioning to total rejection.

Despite its shortcomings, some of which were acknowledged by its authors, the Coleman Report has made important contributions to educational and social scientific research. It has demonstrated the feasibility of collecting and analyzing huge amounts of data in the form of responses to several hundred items by about 600,000 children in grades 1, 3, 6, 9, and 12, and about 60,000 teachers in about 4000 schools across the country. More important, the study provided valuable information about various aspects of American education with special emphasis on equality of educational opportunity. In this area, "the findings constitute the most powerful empirical critique of the myths (the unquestioned assumptions, the socially received beliefs) of American education ever produced" (Mosteller & Moynihan, 1972b, p. 5).

The major source of the controversy surrounding the report, at least among social scientists, stems from the attempts of its authors to explain student achievement, particularly verbal ability (see Coleman et al., 1966, Chapter 3). One of their main goals was to assess the effects of schools relative to other factors. The analytic method used for this purpose was almost exclusively incremental partitioning of variance. As argued below, this method was applied inappropriately. Moreover, its use has led to serious misconceptions among social scientists, policymakers, and the general public. Yet the publication of the report had the unintended salutary effect of stimulating numerous exchanges among social scientists, resulting in a sharper focus on the problems at hand, as well as in a better understanding of the potential uses and abuses, scope and limitations, of multiple regression analysis in nonexperimental research (for some examples of reanalyses and discussions of the Coleman Report, see Bowles & Levin, 1968a, 1968b; Cain & Watts, 1968, 1970; Coleman, 1970; Mosteller & Moynihan, 1972a; Smith, 1968).

The most telling criticism of the incremental partitioning of variance used by Coleman and his colleagues in their attempt to explain verbal achievement is the absence of a theory to guide the analysis. In response to criticism on this point (e.g., Cain & Watts, 1970, pp. 238–241), Coleman (1970, p. 243) concedes the absence of theory in the report, but argues that his critics, too, were unable to specify a theoretical model of achievement. Although this is true, it does not alter the fact that doing an incremental partitioning of variance without reference to a theory that such a partitioning presumably reflects not only may be meaningless but also may lead to serious misconceptions about the process of achievement. That it did, at the very least, lead to ambiguous results in the Coleman Report is demonstrated below. Following an outline of the analysis, a critique of the analytic approach and conclusions based on it is given.

Outline of the Analysis. First, the large number of items was reduced to 60 by combining some into composite indices, and deleting others on the basis of initial analyses or a priori judgments. Second, variables were grouped in blocks—for example, objective student background characteristics; subjective student characteristics including the student's interests in school, self-concept, and sense of control of the environment; student body characteristics; school resources; and teacher variables. Third, incremental partitioning of variance was done, in which verbal achievement was used as the dependent variable and the various blocks as the independent variables. In all the analyses the student background variables were entered first into the equation. The treatment of the remaining blocks varied; in some analyses they were entered in a fixed order, whereas in other analyses the order of entry of the blocks was varied so as to note the proportion of variance incremented by a given block depending upon its specific point of entry into the equation.

Coleman and his associates justify their decision to enter student background characteristics first, saying:

> Because the background differences are prior to school influence, and shape the child before he reaches school, they will, to the extent we have succeeded in measuring them, be controlled when examining the effect of school factors. This means that the achievement differences among schools which are due only to differences in student input can be in part controlled, to allow for more accurate examination of the apparent effects of differences in school or teacher factors themselves. (p. 298)

After going through a variety of analyses in which it was shown that the school variables add little to the proportion of variance accounted for, the authors assert: "Taking all these results together, one implication stands out above all: That schools bring little influence to bear on a child's achievement that is independent of his background and general social context" (p. 325). Though not intended by the authors of the report, it is this conclusion that has led to the greatest misconceptions, particularly among laymen, leading many to conclude that schooling is a waste of children's time and taxpayers' money or, at the very least, that schools are inefficient and therefore do not deserve the continued support they have been getting, let alone increased support. The validity of the report's conclusion notwithstanding, it *does not* refer to a comparison between schooling and no schooling, but rather to differential effects of different types of schools, or different degrees of school resources.

As implied above, neither the report's conclusion about the differential effects of schools nor other conclusions regarding the process of verbal achievement are warranted in view of the analytic procedures that were used to arrive at them. The remainder of this section constitutes an elaboration of this statement.

Critique. Earlier in this chapter, it was pointed out that incremental partitioning of variance for the purpose of controlling a variable while studying the effect of another variable is meaningful only when it is done in accordance with a causal model. The rationale given in the report for entering student background characteristics first is commented upon below. It should be noted that no theoretical rationale was given in the report for the order of entry of the remaining blocks of variables. In fact, as was noted above, in some instances several analyses were done, using different orders of entry for these blocks of variables. Moreover, it will be recalled that even when variance partitioning is done in accordance with a causal model, comparisons among proportions of variance accounted for by given variables, or blocks of variables, for the purpose of determining their relative importance are not valid. Although the foregoing arguments suffice to cast serious doubts about the report's analysis of achievement, it will be instructive to pursue some of the complexities a little further.

Consider, for example, the status of student background characteristics and school resources. It is well known that one of the important determiners of the choice of a place of residence, particularly among middle-class parents, is the quality of its school system. There is therefore a relatively high correlation between student background characteristics and school quality. When, as was done in the Coleman Report, student characteristics are entered first into the equation, or are "controlled" for, one may actually be partialing out school effects. At the very least, the proportion of variance attributed to student background characteristics includes also the variance that they share with school resources (for further discussions of this point, see Bowles & Levin, 1968, pp. 14–16; Smith, 1972, p. 239). Even if one were to assume that the causal flow is unidirectional from student background characteristics to school resources, it is necessary to bear in mind that when school resources are entered into the analysis after student background characteristics the proportion of variance attributed to them does not include that part of the student characteristics effect that they transmit. Because the correlation between student background characteristics and school resources was left unexplained in the report, the only course of action open to its authors was to treat the two blocks as exogenous, and hence to eschew attempts to determine the variance that each accounts for separately in achievement.

What was said about the status of student background characteristics and school quality applies equally to the other variables dealt with in the analysis of achievement. It is known that they are intercorrelated, to a greater or lesser extent, with student background characteristics, as well as among themselves, but the process responsible for the observed relations is not known; at least it is not stated in the report. Consequently, all one could do is treat all of them as exogenous variables. When, however, student background characteristics are entered first, the proportion of variance accounted for that is attributed to them reflects their total effect, thereby implying that they affect achievement directly as well as indirectly, via the intermediate variables in the system.

Another example of the ambiguous status of the variables used to explain achievement is student body characteristics, about which the report states: "*Attributes of other students account for far more variation in achievement of minority group children than do any attributes of school facilities and slightly more than do attributes of staff.* In general, as the educational aspirations and backgrounds of fellow students increase, the achievement of minority group children increases" (Coleman et al., 1966, p. 302). Even the authors of the report concede that this result may be confounded by the minority group children's own aspirations and background. Other factors (e.g., mental abilities of minority group children) also may confound the results. Yet, the above-cited "finding" had a great impact on the views and decisions of social scientists, policymakers, and the courts regarding the "optimal" composition of the student body, leading some to expect that implementation of programs to achieve "optimal" racial composition in the school (e.g., through busing) will result in greater achievement for minority group children (see Grant, 1973; Young & Bress, 1975, for detailed discussions of this issue).

The discussion to this point focused on problems concerning the interrelations among the "independent" variables. The situation becomes even more complex and ambiguous when one considers possible patterns of causal relations between the "independent" variables and the "dependent" variable (i.e., achievement). Jencks (1972), for example, states:

> It is almost never clear whether a school characteristic affects student achievement or vice versa. If schools with accelerated curriculums and language laboratories enroll overachievers, are we to assume that the curriculum and the laboratory boosted their achievement? Or are we to assume that the school developed the curriculum and got the laboratory because it already enrolled overachievers . . .? Similar ambiguities recur everywhere. (p. 83)

Or, consider the block of variables labeled in the report as attitudes of students. This block is composed of: (1) students' interests in school and outside reading, (2) self-concept, specifically as it relates to learning and success in school, (3) sense of control of one's environment. Referring to this block, Coleman and his colleagues (1966) say: "Of all the variables measured in the survey, including all measures of family background and school variables, these attitudes showed the strongest relation to achievement" (p. 319). But the authors themselves concede that the causal relation "may very well be two-directional, with both the attitude and the achievement affecting each other" (p. 320). Consequently, attributing an effect to attitudes in an incremental partitioning of variance is, to say the least, questionable. The Coleman Report errs also in its attempt to note whether the school affects these attitudes, saying: "If family background characteristics are controlled, almost none of the remaining variance in self-concept and control of environment is accounted for by the school factors measured in this survey" (p. 323). Other issues notwithstanding, if, as was noted earlier, all that can be said about the student background and school variables is that they are correlated, it is not appropriate to partition the variance in student attitudes among these variables.

Finally, it will be noted that achievement was appropriately analyzed separately for social and ethnic groups. The report then compared increments in the proportion of variance accounted for by a given variable in different groups in order to arrive at statements about its relative effectiveness in those groups. For example, seven selected teacher variables accounted for a greater proportion of achievement variance among minority children, particularly among black children in the South.

Two things will be noted regarding such comparisons. First, the authors report that the selection of the seven teacher variables was done "after eliminating a number of characteristics that appeared, in early regressions, to have little effect. Other variables were eliminated because they were highly correlated with one or more of the remaining, and thus their effects could not easily be distinguished" (p. 316). The authors concede that the seven remaining variables may be surrogates of other variables with which they are correlated, and therefore recommend caution in the interpretation. Yet, soon afterwards they say: "This result is an extremely important one, for it suggests that good teachers matter more for children from minority groups which have educationally deficient backgrounds" (p. 317).

Second, it was said earlier that R^2 is sample-specific, and that it is therefore possible for it to vary across samples even when the effects of the variables under study are the same in all the samples. Consequently, conclusions about the relative importance of variables in different samples, arrived at on the basis of comparisons of proportions of variance incremented by the variables, are highly questionable. (Methods of cross-sample comparisons are discussed in Chapters 8, 12, and 13.)

In sum, the questions posed explicitly or implicitly by Coleman and his associates regarding the process of achievement cannot be answered in the absence of a theoretical model about the relations among the variables under study. Moreover, even when such a model is specified, incremental partitioning of variance provides answers that have no bearing on the question of the relative importance of the variables.

The International Evaluation of Educational Achievement (IEA)

A set of cross-national studies of achievement in various topics (e.g., reading, science, literature, civic education) has been conducted under the auspices of the International Association for Evaluation of Educational Achievement. In the past several years nine volumes reporting on various aspects of these studies have been published (for summaries and reviews, see Härnqvist, 1975; Inkeles, 1977; Purves & Levine, 1975). Although the studies differ in the application of some specific analyses, they share a major theme and a major analytic approach (for a technical report and some summaries, see Peaker, 1975). The major theme is the explanation of achievement by resorting to blocks of independent variables. The major analytic technique used for this purpose is incremental partitioning of variance. The present discussion is limited to this aspect of the analysis in the IEA studies.[7] Because the concern here is exclusively

[7]Other analytic methods used in some of the IEA studies are discussed later in this chapter and in Chapter 8.

with the validity of the analyses and the conclusions drawn from them, no attempt will be made to summarize the findings or to distinguish between specific studies. Illustrations and statements from the various studies will be used eclectically for the sole purpose of shedding light on the analytic approach. Consequently, some of the comments may be more or less applicable to some of the studies.

The Variables. The large number of variables was reduced to a smaller and more manageable one by combining some into composite indices and by deleting others. The variables were then grouped in the following blocks.

1. Home and Student Background, including father's education, mother's education, number of books in the home, and size of family. In some of the studies this block included also the age and sex of the student.
2. Type of School and Type of Program in which the student was enrolled.
3. Learning Conditions, including variables that reflect school practices and teachers' characteristics and training. In some of the studies this block also included the amount of prior instruction.
4. Kindred Variables, including students' attitudes toward school life and learning, current reading habits, leisure activities, expected occupation, parental expectations, and parental involvement in students' work.
5. School Achievement, including one or more dependent measures of achievement in the specific area under study (e.g., science, French, literature).

Outline of the Analysis. The dependent variable, School Achievement, was regressed on the blocks of the independent variables in the order in which they were presented above. That is, Home Background was entered first into the equation, followed by School Type, Learning Conditions, and Kindred Variables. When each block was entered, a stepwise regression analysis was done on the variables included in it. Variables that met a prespecified criterion were retained, whereas those that did not meet the criterion were discarded. At the conclusion of the stepwise regression analysis within a given block, the proportion of variance incremented by it was noted. In short, the analysis was based on blockwise incremental partitioning of variance, with the added restriction that variables that did not meet a prespecified criterion at the stepwise regression stage of the analysis were deleted (see section entitled Blockwise Selection in Chapter 6).

Rationale for the Analysis. The authors of the various studies use almost identical language in support of the incremental partitioning of variance. Basically, it is maintained that the analysis reflects a causal model in which variables entered at an earlier stage of the analysis are assumed to affect those that are entered at later stages. Thus, for example, in the study of Science Education (Comber & Keeves, 1973) the authors state: "The basic proposition underlying the development of this causal model was that earlier events in the life of an individual student have influenced later events in the student's life and schooling. It seemed reasonable to use this proposition rather than any other to guide the order in which the variables were entered into the regression equation'' (p. 191). (See also Purves, 1973, pp. 117–119; Torney, Oppenheim, & Farnen, 1975, pp. 127–129.)

Critique. The most important criticism that may be leveled against the causal model advanced in the IEA studies is that its sole justification appears to be a presumed time sequence, or temporal priority, in the occurrence of the variables under study. ''Time provided the rationale for the ordering of the blocks to be entered into the regression equation'' (Purves, 1973, p. 118). This is a fallacious approach because it treats temporal priority as a sufficient rather than a necessary condition for a causal relation between two variables. In other words, on logical grounds we are not willing to accept the notion that an event that occurred later in time caused one that preceded it. But a temporal sequence of events is not in and of itself evidence that a causal process is taking place.[8] It should also be noted that the temporal sequence of variables in the IEA studies is itself questionable. For example, are Learning Conditions temporally prior to Kindred Variables, or is it the other way around? The most plausible assumption is that the sequence of their occurrence is cyclical.

The situation is even more problematic when one considers the presumed causal status of the variables, including the dependent variable. That such problems exist is conceded to by the authors of the IEA studies in their discussions of the status of the Kindred Variables in relation to School Achievement. Thus Purves (1973), for example, says:

> The fourth set of variables is not perhaps part of a model of causation, since it consists of concomitants of achievement. . . . In addition there are some variables related to the home and the attitude of the parents toward learning and school. *All these variables influence achievement or are influenced by it . . ., but they can hardly be termed causative.* (p. 118; italics added)

Or as Schwille (1975) says: ''Kindred variables, that is, variables which, though expected to correlate with test scores, did not fit in other blocks, usually because they might be considered *either cause or effect of achievement*'' (p. 127; italics added). Similar doubts, though not expressed by the authors of the IEA studies, may be raised about the causal relations among the other blocks of variables. Do, for example, Learning Conditions affect School Achievement, or does the latter affect the former? There is probably a reciprocal causation between them.

Attempts to depict graphically the causal model of the IEA studies further highlight its dubious nature. Setting aside the questions raised about the validity of the temporal sequence and about the causal status of the blocks of variables, it is still not possible to tell from the IEA reports whether a given block is assumed to affect subsequent ones directly or indirectly, or both. To clarify this point, two of various possible models are depicted in Figure 7.6. It will be noted that in model (a) *all* the possible direct and indirect effects are posited, whereas model (b) describes a strict chain of causation. No claims are being made here

[8]For further discussions of the concept of causation, see Chapter 15.

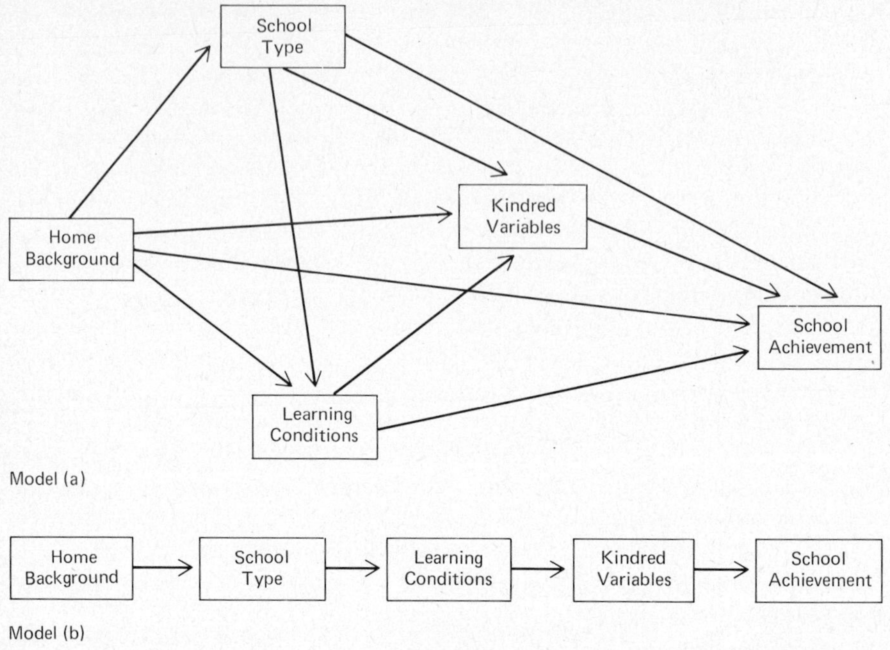

Figure 7.6

for the plausibility of either of the models depicted in Figure 7.6, but it should be noted that both of them, and others that could have been depicted, reflect the temporal sequence assumed by the authors of the IEA studies. While there are methods for testing whether a causal model is consistent with a given set of data,[9] incremental partitioning of variance (the method used in the IEA studies) is not one of them. In other words, knowledge about the proportion of variance incremented by blocks of variables entered in a given sequence sheds no light on the specific causal model one may be working with. Consider, for example, the squared correlation between Home Background and School Achievement. From earlier discussions in this chapter we know that it reflects the total effect of the former on the latter. The total effect may, however, at one extreme, reflect the direct effect and all possible indirect effects, as depicted in model (a) of Figure 7.6. At the other extreme, the total effect of Home Background on School Achievement may be only due to indirect effects, as depicted in model (b) of Figure 7.6. Intermediate statements between these extremes are also possible. For example, Home Background may affect School Achievement directly, and in addition indirectly through the mediation of some, but not all of the remaining blocks. In other words, it may be hypothesized that some of the indirect effects are zero, or close to zero. The main point is that merely knowing the proportion of achievement variance accounted for by Home Background is insufficient for one even to attempt to conjecture which of several possible models of causation is more tenable. Incidentally, the inclusion of age and sex as part of the Home Background block in some of the IEA studies

[9]See Chapters 15 and 16.

is an additional hindrance to attempts to unravel the process of School Achievement.

The main purpose of doing incremental partitioning of variance in the IEA studies was to determine the relative importance of the various blocks of variables. Peaker (1975), for example, states: "Our concern is to assess *the differential effects* of those recent conditions that we have measured, and in doing this we must do our best to make a due discount for the effects of earlier conditions, whether at home or at school" (p. 53; italics added). It was reasoned earlier in this chapter that it is not valid to use incremental partitioning of variance for the purpose of arriving at statements about the relative importance of the variables with which they are associated.[10]

That the authors of the IEA studies were somewhat ambivalent about their use of incremental partitioning of variance for the purpose of explaining the process of School Achievement is evident, among other things, from their attempts to note the changes in the proportion of variance attributed to given blocks as a result of changes in the order of their entry into the regression equation. Schwille (1975), in particular, reports the percentage of variance accounted for by each block at different points of entry into the equation. Thus, for example, the median percentage of variance accounted for by Home Background when it was entered first (the usual position for this block) is 18. When entered in the third or fourth position, Home Background accounted for 2% of the variance. The median percentage of variance accounted for by Learning Conditions when it was entered in its usual third position is 12. But when it was entered first it accounted for 32% of the variance. When Learning Conditions was entered fourth it accounted for 9% of the variance (see Schwille, 1975, p. 138).

Had the percent of variance accounted for in an incremental partitioning of variance been a valid indicator of the relative importance of a variable, the inevitable conclusion from the above results would have been that Learning Conditions are more important than Home Background because in the three entry positions they accounted for a greater proportion of variance than did the latter. Such a conclusion would run counter to the one drawn by the authors of the IEA studies, namely that Home Background is the most important block of variables. To repeat, however, neither of the above conclusions is supportable on the basis of incremental partitioning of variance.[11] Furthermore, the attempts to note the effects of changes in the order of entry of the blocks on the manner in which the variance is partitioned evidence the absence of a clearly stated theoretical model about the relations among the variables under study.

Another interesting example of the ambiguity of the theoretical frame of reference in the IEA studies comes from the manner in which measures that may be construed as indices of verbal ability were treated in some of them. For example, in the study of *Literature Education in Ten Countries* (Purves, 1973) two such measures were: Word Knowledge and Reading Comprehension. Dis-

[10]For further discussions of this point, with special reference to the IEA studies, see Coleman (1975a, 1976).

[11]Other examples of the effects of changes in the order of entry of the blocks into the regression equation abound. See, for example, Peaker (1975, pp. 90–91).

cussing these measures, and the decision at what point to enter them into the equation, Purves (1975) says:

> The critical reading of Literature is certainly a specialized aspect of reading, and reading ability is a form of a general verbal strength. . . . One might expect therefore, that reading ability as measured by the Reading test would be the most powerful predictor of cognitive ability in Literature. For that reason it must be considered in the analysis, *but to consider it first would deny any of the other predictors a chance to show their contribution to achievement in Literature.* Word knowledge and Reading ability are therefore considered last. (p. 156; italics added)

The considerable differences in the proportion of variance attributed to the measures of verbal ability when they are entered first or last into the equation are evident in the various tables reported by Purves (1973). For example, in Table 6.1 (p. 160) the mean correlation of Word Knowledge with Literature Achievement Score is .51, and that for Reading Comprehension with Literature Achievement is .67. Consequently, when Word Knowledge is entered first it accounts for about 26% of the variance ($.51^2 \times 100$). When Reading Comprehension is entered first it accounts for about 45% of the variance ($.67^2 \times 100$). From Table 6.4 (p. 163) it may be noted that Word Knowledge was entered as the fifth block, accounting for an average of about 7% of the variance. Reading Comprehension, which was entered last, accounted for an average of about 11% of the variance (see Table 6.4, p. 163). Together, then, the verbal ability measures account for about 18% of the variance when they are entered last into the equation.

It is more important, however, to note what would have happened to the proportion of variance attributed to the other blocks had the verbal ability measures been entered first. From Table 6.4 (p. 163) it may be noted that the mean percentage of variance accounted for by the six blocks together is about 55. It was noted above that, on the average, Reading Comprehension alone can account for 45%, leaving 10% of the variance to the remaining blocks. If Word Knowledge is used together with Reading Comprehension as the first block, virtually nothing of the variance in Literature Achievement Scores is left to the remaining blocks.

Another example of the same problem comes from the study of *Teaching of French as a Foreign Language in Eight Countries* (Carroll, 1975). Speaking of a measure of Word Knowledge, Carroll says:

> Probably because this block occurred at the end of the blockwise regression analysis, its variances are relatively small. The Word Knowledge test presumably measures a general verbal ability dimension that is highly associated with school performance. *The reason for extracting its variance late in the analysis was that it was desired to allow all other types of variables to "show their colors" independently even if they happened also to be correlated with verbal ability.* (p. 207; italics added)

To say that one wishes to allow the other types of variables to show what they contribute independently of verbal ability even if they happen(!) to be correlated with it, is questionable reasoning particularly when one considers the nature of the variables and the analytic method that is being used. Be that as it may, the determination of the order of entry of verbal ability into the regression equation should not be made on the basis of how this might affect the proportion of variance attributed to the other variables, but on the basis of theoretical considerations. In the absence of a theoretical model about the relations among the variables, no meaningful decision about the order of entry of variables into the regression equation can be made. And even when variables are entered according to a theoretical model, the major objections to the use of incremental partitioning of variance for the determination of the relative importance of variables prevail.

One final point about the use of incremental partitioning of variance in the IEA studies will be made here. In the various studies, incremental partitioning of variance was done separately for each of the participating countries. The authors then proceeded to compare the proportions of variance accounted for by a given block across countries in order to determine in which of them the block is more or less important. As was noted several times earlier, variance partitioning is sample-specific, and depends largely on the degree of variability of the variables within a given sample. Therefore, conclusions about the relative importance of a variable on the basis of comparisons of the proportion of variance it accounts for in different samples are questionable.[12]

COMMONALITY ANALYSIS

Commonality analysis is a method of variance partitioning designed to identify proportions of variance in the dependent variable that may be attributed uniquely to each of the independent variables, and proportions of variance that are attributed to various combinations of independent variables. Mood (1969, 1971) and Mayeske et al. (1969), who developed the method, have applied it to data of the Coleman Report. It will be noted that two researchers in England, Newton and Spurrell (1967a, 1967b), independently developed the same system and applied it to industrial problems. They referred to the method as elements analysis. For comments on some earlier and related attempts, see Creager (1971).

The unique contribution of an independent variable is defined as the variance attributed to it when it is entered last in the regression equation. Thus defined, the unique contribution is actually a squared semipartial correlation between the dependent variable and the variable of interest, after partialing all the other independent variables from it. With two independent variables, the unique contribution of variable 1 is defined as follows:

$$\mathrm{U}(1) = R^2_{y.12} - R^2_{y.2} \tag{7.1}$$

where $\mathrm{U}(1)$ = unique contribution of variable 1; $R^2_{y.12}$ = squared multiple correlation of Y with variables 1 and 2; $R^2_{y.2}$ = squared correlation of Y with variable 2. Similarly, the unique contribution of variable 2 is defined as follows:

$$\mathrm{U}(2) = R^2_{y.12} - R^2_{y.1} \tag{7.2}$$

[12]For methods of cross-sample comparisons, see Chapters 8, 12, and 13.

where U(2) = unique contribution of variable 2. The definition of the commonality of variables 1 and 2 is

$$C(12) = R^2_{y.12} - U(1) - U(2) \tag{7.3}$$

where C(12) = commonality of variables 1 and 2. Substituting the right-hand sides of Formulas (7.1) and (7.2) for U(1) and U(2) in Formula (7.3), we obtain

$$\begin{aligned} C(12) &= R^2_{y.12} - (R^2_{y.12} - R^2_{y.2}) - (R^2_{y.12} - R^2_{y.1}) \\ &= R^2_{y.12} - R^2_{y.12} + R^2_{y.2} - R^2_{y.12} + R^2_{y.1} \\ &= R^2_{y.2} + R^2_{y.1} - R^2_{y.12} \end{aligned} \tag{7.4}$$

As a result of determining unique and common contribution of variables, it is possible to express the correlation between any independent variable and the dependent variable as a composite of the unique contribution of the variable of interest plus its commonalities with other independent variables. Thus $R^2_{y.1}$ in the above example can be expressed as follows:

$$R^2_{y.1} = U(1) + C(12) \tag{7.5}$$

That this is so can be demonstrated by restating Formula (7.5) using the right-hand sides of Formulas (7.1) and (7.4):

$$R^2_{y.1} = (R^2_{y.12} - R^2_{y.2}) + (R^2_{y.2} + R^2_{y.1} - R^2_{y.12})$$

Similarly,

$$R^2_{y.2} = U(2) + C(12) \tag{7.6}$$

The commonality of variables 1 and 2 is referred to as a second-order commonality. With more than two independent variables second-order commonalities are determined for all the possible pairs of variables. In addition, third-order commonalities are determined for all possible sets of three variables, fourth-order commonalities for all sets of four variables, and so forth up to one commonality whose order is equal to the total number of independent variables. Thus, for example, with three variables, *A*, *B*, and *C*, there are three unique components, namely U(*A*), U(*B*), and U(*C*); three second-order commonalities, namely C(*AB*), C(*AC*), and C(*BC*), and one third-order commonality, namely C(*ABC*). Altogether, there are seven components in a three-variable problem. In general, the number of components is equal to $2^k - 1$, where k is the number of independent variables. Thus, with four independent variables there are $2^4 - 1 = 15$ components, four of which are unique, six are second-order, four are third-order, and one is a fourth-order commonality. With five independent variables there are $2^5 - 1 = 31$ components. Note that with each addition of an independent variable there is a considerable increase in the number of components, a point discussed below.

Rules for Writing Commonality Formulas

Mood (1969) and Wisler (1969) offer a rule for writing formulas for the unique and commonality components in a commonality analysis. This rule can be explained by an example. Suppose we have three independent variables, X_1, X_2, and X_3, and a dependent variable, Y. To write the formula for the unique contribution of variable X_2, for example, we first construct the following product:

$$-(1 - X_2)X_1X_3$$

The variable of interest, X_2, is subtracted from one and this term is multiplied by the remaining independent variables, which in the present example are X_1 and X_3. The above product is now expanded:

$$-(1 - X_2)X_1X_3 = -(X_1X_3 - X_1X_2X_3) = -X_1X_3 + X_1X_2X_3$$

After expanding the product, each term is replaced by R^2 of the dependent variable with the variables indicated in the given term. Thus, using the above expansion, the unique contribution of variable X_2 is

$$\mathrm{U}(X_2) = -R^2_{y.x_1x_3} + R^2_{y.x_1x_2x_3}$$

or, written more succinctly,

$$\mathrm{U}(2) = -R^2_{y.13} + R^2_{y.123}$$

How the rule applies to the writing of the formula for the commonality of two variables—namely, X_2 and X_3—will now be illustrated. First, construct the product. This time, however, there are two terms in which each of the variables of interest is subtracted from one. The product of these terms is multiplied by the remaining independent variable(s), which in the present example is X_1. The product to be expanded for the commonality of X_2 and X_3 is therefore

$$-(1 - X_2)(1 - X_3)X_1$$

After expansion,

$$-(1 - X_2)(1 - X_3)X_1 = -X_1 + X_1X_2 + X_1X_3 - X_1X_2X_3$$

Replacing each term in the right-hand side of this equation by R^2, we obtain

$$\mathrm{C}(23) = -R^2_{y.1} + R^2_{y.12} + R^2_{y.13} - R^2_{y.123}$$

To write the formula for the commonality of X_1 and X_3 one expands the product $-(1 - X_1)(1 - X_3)X_2$ and then replaces each term by the appropriate R^2.

For the commonality of all the independent variables in the above example, it is necessary to expand the following product:

$$-(1 - X_1)(1 - X_2)(1 - X_3)$$

After expansion, the above product is equal to

$$-1 + X_1 + X_2 - X_1X_2 + X_3 - X_1X_3 - X_2X_3 + X_1X_2X_3$$

When the rule is applied to the writing of the formula for the commonality of all the independent variables, the expansion of the product has one term equal to -1. This term is deleted and the remaining terms are replaced by R^2's in the manner illustrated above. Accordingly, using the expansion for the product terms of X_1, X_2, and X_3, the formula for the commonality of these variables is

$$C(123) = R^2_{y.1} + R^2_{y.2} - R^2_{y.12} + R^2_{y.3} - R^2_{y.13} - R^2_{y.23} + R^2_{y.123}$$

The rule illustrated above applies to any number of independent variables. This is illustrated for some components in a problem with k independent variables. To obtain, for example, the unique contribution of variable X_1, the following product is constructed:

$$-(1 - X_1)X_2X_3 \ldots X_k$$

After expanding this product, each term is replaced by R^2 of the dependent variable with the independent variables indicated in the given term. To write the formula for the commonality of variables X_1, X_2, X_3, and X_4, for example, the following product is expanded:

$$-(1 - X_1)(1 - X_2)(1 - X_3)(1 - X_4)X_5X_6 \ldots X_k$$

Again, each term after the expansion is replaced by the appropriate R^2. The formula for the commonality of all k independent variables is obtained by expanding the following product:

$$-(1 - X_1)(1 - X_2) \ldots (1 - X_k)$$

As noted above, after expansion with all the independent variables there is one term equal to -1. This term is deleted, and all other terms are replaced by R^2's in the manner shown above.

A Numerical Example

Before discussing some aspects and problems in interpreting results from commonality analysis, the method is applied to an illustrative numerical example. The same example was used earlier in this chapter in connection with incremental partitioning of variance. Three independent variables were used:

socioeconomic status (SES), intelligence (IQ), and need achievement (n Ach). The dependent variable was the grade-point average (GPA) of college students. The intercorrelations among these variables are repeated in part I of Table 7.2. In part II of the table the various R^2's necessary for a commonality analysis are reported.

The rule for writing the formulas for the various components is now applied to the present example. In order to avoid cumbersome symbolism, however, the following symbols are used: X_1 = SES; X_2 = IQ; X_3 = n Ach; Y = GPA. For the unique contribution of X_1 expand the following product:

$$-(1 - X_1)X_2X_3 = -X_2X_3 + X_1X_2X_3$$

Replacing each of the terms in the expansion by the appropriate R^2's from Table 7.2, we obtain

$$\text{U}(1) = -R^2_{y.23} + R^2_{y.123} = -.49641 + .49647 = .00006$$

The unique contributions of X_2 and X_3 are similarly obtained. They are

$$\text{U}(2) = -R^2_{y.13} + R^2_{y.123} = -.26878 + .49647 = .22769$$

$$\text{U}(3) = -R^2_{y.12} + R^2_{y.123} = -.35268 + .49647 = .14379$$

For the commonality of X_1 and X_2 we expand the following product:

$$-(1 - X_1)(1 - X_2)X_3 = -X_3 + X_1X_3 + X_2X_3 - X_1X_2X_3$$

Replacing each term in the expansion by the appropriate R^2's from Table 7.2,

$$\text{C}(12) = -R^2_{y.3} + R^2_{y.13} + R^2_{y.23} - R^2_{y.123}$$

$$= -.2500 + .26878 + .49641 - .49647 = .01872$$

Table 7.2 Illustrative Data for a Commonality Analysis[a]

I:	*Correlation Matrix*			
	1 *SES*	*2* *IQ*	*3* *n Ach*	*Y* *GPA*
1	1.0000	.3000	.4100	.3300
2	.0900	1.0000	.1600	.5700
3	.1681	.0256	1.0000	.5000
Y	.1089	.3249	.2500	1.0000

II: Squared Multiple Correlations

$R^2_{y.123} = .49647$ $\quad R^2_{y.12} = .35268$

$R^2_{y.13} = .26878$ $\quad R^2_{y.23} = .49641$

[a]The entries above the principal diagonal of the correlation matrix are zero-order correlations, whereas those below the diagonal are squared zero-order correlations. For example $r_{12} = .3000$, $r^2_{12} = .0900$.

The commonality of X_1 and X_3, and that of X_2 and X_3 are similarly obtained. They are

$$C(13) = -R^2_{y.2} + R^2_{y.12} + R^2_{y.23} - R^2_{y.123}$$
$$= -.3249 + .35268 + .49641 - .49647 = .02772$$
$$C(23) = -R^2_{y.1} + R^2_{y.12} + R^2_{y.13} - R^2_{y.123}$$
$$= -.1089 + .35268 + .26878 - .49647 = .01609$$

The commonality of variables X_1, X_2, and X_3 is obtained by the following expansion:

$$-(1 - X_1)(1 - X_2)(1 - X_3) = -1 + X_1 + X_2 - X_1X_2 + X_3 - X_1X_3 - X_2X_3 + X_1X_2X_3$$

Deleting the -1 and replacing the remaining terms by the R^2's from Table 7.2,

$$C(123) = R^2_{y.1} + R^2_{y.2} - R^2_{y.12} + R^2_{y.3} - R^2_{y.13} - R^2_{y.23} + R^2_{y.123}$$
$$= .1089 + .3249 - .35268 + .2500 - .26878 - .49641 + .49647 = .0624$$

The analysis is summarized in Table 7.3 in the manner suggested by Mayeske et al. (1969). Several observations may be made about this table. Note that each term in the last line, the line labeled Σ, is equal to the squared zero-order correlation of the variable with which it is associated and the dependent variable. Thus, for example, in the last line under SES we have .1089, which is equal to the squared zero-order correlation between SES and GPA ($.3300^2$; see Table 7.2).

Reading down each column in Table 7.3 it is possible to note how the proportion of variance accounted for by a given variable is partitioned into various components. The proportion of variance accounted for by SES, for example, is partitioned as follows: .00006 unique to SES, .01872 common to SES and IQ, .02772 common to SES and *n* Ach, and .06240 common to SES, IQ, and *n* Ach. From this analysis it is evident that SES makes practically no unique contribu-

Table 7.3 Summary of Commonality Analysis of Data of Table 7.2

	Variables		
	1 *SES*	*2* *IQ*	*3* *n Ach*
Unique to 1, SES	.00006		
Unique to 2, IQ		.22769	
Unique to 3, *n* Ach			.14379
Common to 1 and 2	.01872	.01872	
Common to 1 and 3	.02772		.02772
Common to 2 and 3		.01609	.01609
Common to 1, 2, and 3	.06240	.06240	.06240
Σ:	.1089	.3249	.2500

tion. Most of the variance accounted for by SES (.1089) is due to its commonalities with the other independent variables. In contrast, intelligence and need achievement show relatively large unique contributions, about 23% and 14%, respectively.

The squared multiple correlation can be written as a composite of all the unique and common components. Thus, for the present problem,

$$R^2_{y.123} = \text{U}(1) + \text{U}(2) + \text{U}(3) + \text{C}(12) + \text{C}(13) + \text{C}(23) + \text{C}(123)$$

$$.49647 = .00006 + .22769 + .14379 + .01872 + .02772 + .01609 + .06240$$

From this form of partitioning of the variance it appears that the unique contributions of IQ and *n* Ach comprise about 37% of the variance accounted for, and all the commonalities account for the remaining 13%.

A Closer Look at Uniqueness

The unique contribution of a variable was defined above as the increment in the proportion of variance it accounts for when it is entered last into the regression equation. When the independent variables are not correlated, the uniqueness of each variable is equal to the squared zero-order correlation between it and the dependent variable. Under such circumstances, the commonalities of the independent variables are zero. Consequently, there is no ambiguity about the partitioned variance. When the independent variables are correlated, as indeed they almost always are in nonexperimental research, the uniqueness and the commonality elements are affected by the magnitudes and the signs of the intercorrelations among the variables. Assuming, for example, that all the variables are positively intercorrelated, the higher the correlations among the independent variables, the smaller the uniqueness and the larger the relative proportions of variance attributed to the commonality of variables.

It was noted earlier that the uniqueness of a variable is equal to its squared semipartial correlation with the dependent variable, when all the other independent variables are partialed out from the one under consideration. An equivalent way of expressing the uniqueness of a variable, say X_1, is $\beta^2_{y1.23\ldots k}(1 - R^2_{1.23\ldots k})$, where $\beta^2_{y1.23\ldots k}$ is the squared standardized coefficient of X_1 in the regression equation of Y on all the X's, and $R^2_{1.23\ldots k}$ is the squared multiple correlation of X_1 with the remaining independent variables. Consequently, $1 - R^2_{1.23\ldots k}$ is what X_1 *does not* share with the other X's, or the residual variance. Now, the β's are partial regression coefficients, and their magnitude is affected, among other things, by the intercorrelations among the independent variables. In addition, other things equal, the smaller the residual variance of a given variable (i.e., the higher the squared multiple correlation between it and the other independent variables), the smaller the uniqueness associated with it. This formulation of uniqueness is now illustrated with the numerical example of Table 7.2. Regressing Y on the three X's, the following regression equation is obtained:

$$z'_y = .00919z_1 + .50066z_2 + .41613z_3$$

Calculate:

$$R^2_{1.23} = .22449 \qquad R^2_{2.13} = .09165 \qquad R^2_{3.12} = .16960$$

Using the above results, the unique contributions of the three variables are

$$\text{U}(1) = (.00919^2)(1 - .22449) = .00006$$

$$\text{U}(2) = (.50066^2)(1 - .09165) = .22769$$

$$\text{U}(3) = (.41613^2)(1 - .16960) = .14379$$

The same values are reported in Table 7.3.

Before turning to a simpler method of calculating the uniqueness, it will be noted that some authors (e.g., Purves, 1973, p. 134) use the above terminology in their discussions of the uniqueness of variables. Similarly, Coleman (1968, pp. 241–242; 1972, p. 156) expresses the same ideas using the notation $b^2(1 - C^2)$, where b^2 is the squared standardized regression coefficient, β^2, associated with the variable whose uniqueness is being calculated, and $1 - C^2$ is the residual variance of this variable, as defined above.

Darlington (1968, pp. 168–169) uses the term *usefulness* for what has been labeled here *uniqueness* (see discussion in the next section) and shows how it may be calculated from the overall regression of the dependent variable on all the independent variables. In Chapter 5 it was said that testing the significance of a partial correlation, a semipartial, a b, and a β, are all equivalent. Computer programs for multiple regression analysis routinely report the F ratios for the tests of the significance of the regression coefficients (some computer programs report t ratios instead. But in the present case $t^2 = F$, since each F ratio has one degree of freedom for the numerator.). The uniqueness of a variable, say X_1, can be calculated as follows:

$$\text{U}(1) = \frac{F_1(1 - R^2_{y.12\ldots k})}{N - k - 1} \tag{7.7}$$

where F_1 is the F ratio for testing the significance of the regression coefficient associated with X_1; $R^2_{y.12\ldots k}$ is the squared multiple correlation of Y with all the independent variables; N is the sample size; k is the number of independent variables.

In order to demonstrate the application of Formula (7.7) to the data of Table 7.2, it was assumed that $N = 300$. The three F ratios associated with the β's reported above are: F_1 (for SES) $= .038$; F_2 (for IQ) $= 133.849$; F_3 (for *n* Ach) $= 84.529$. Each of these F's and 1 and 296 *df*. $R^2_{y.123} = .49647$. Applying Formula (7.7),

$$\text{U}(1) = \frac{(.038)(1 - .49647)}{300 - 3 - 1} = \frac{.019134}{296} = .00006$$

$$\text{U}(2) = \frac{(133.849)(1 - .49647)}{296} = \frac{67.39699}{296} = .22769$$

$$\text{U}(3) = \frac{(84.529)(1 - .49647)}{296} = \frac{42.56289}{296} = .14379$$

The same values were obtained earlier.

Yet another way of observing the effect of the intercorrelations among independent variables on the uniqueness of each is to note the manner in which the uniqueness of a variable is related to the inverse of the correlation matrix of the independent variables. In Chapter 4 (see Formula (4.18) and the discussion related to it) the following formula was introduced for the calculation of the increment in the proportion of variance accounted for by a given variable:

$$prop_{(j)} = \frac{\beta_j^2}{r^{jj}} \tag{7.8}$$

where $prop_{(j)}$ = increment in the proportion of variance accounted for by variable j; r^{jj} = the diagonal element of the inverse of $\mathbf{R}$($\mathbf{R}^{-1}$) associated with variable j. When the correlations among all the independent variables are zero, the inverse of the correlation matrix ($\mathbf{R}^{-1}$) is an identity matrix—that is, a matrix whose diagonal elements are 1's and the off-diagonal elements are 0's (see Appendix A). Under such circumstances, then, the application of Formula (7.8) for the calculation of uniqueness will lead to the conclusion that the uniqueness of each variable is equal to the squared β associated with it. But when variables are not intercorrelated, each β is equal to the zero-order correlation of the variable with which it is associated and the dependent variable. Therefore, squaring the β to obtain the uniqueness is the same as squaring the zero-order correlation.

When the independent variables are intercorrelated, the diagonal elements of $\mathbf{R}^{-1}$ are larger than unity. They become relatively large when the intercorrelations among the independent variables are relatively large (see discussion of Multicollinearity in Chapter 8). Consequently, when the independent variables are intercorrelated, the uniqueness of a variable will always be smaller than its squared β, approaching the vanishing point as the diagonal elements of $\mathbf{R}^{-1}$ become increasingly larger.

The inverse of the correlation matrix of the independent variables for the data of Table 7.2 is:

$$\mathbf{R}^{-1} = \begin{bmatrix} 1.28947 & -.310192 & -.479051 \\ -.310192 & 1.10089 & -.0489638 \\ -.479051 & -.0489638 & 1.20425 \end{bmatrix}$$

Note that all the diagonal elements of $\mathbf{R}^{-1}$ exceed unity, but not by very much. The reason is that the correlations among the independent variables are relatively low (see Table 7.2). Having the $\mathbf{R}^{-1}$ it is now possible to apply Formula (7.8) to obtain the unique contributions of each of the variables. Recall that the regression equation for the data of Table 7.2 is

$$z_y' = .00919z_1 + .50066z_2 + .41613z_3$$

Using, in turn, each of the diagonal elements of $\mathbf{R}^{-1}$ reported above and applying Formula (7.8),

$$U(1) = \frac{.00919^2}{1.28947} = .00006$$

$$U(2) = \frac{.50066^2}{1.10089} = .22769$$

$$U(3) = \frac{.41613^2}{1.20425} = .14379$$

These values were obtained several times earlier.

The discussion in this section was limited to an examination of the effects of the intercorrelations among the independent variables on the uniqueness of each of them. It is possible also to show the parts that make up the commonality of variables. These, however, become unweildy when the commonalities are of higher orders (i.e., beyond the second and the third). More important, they elude straightforward interpretations. They are therefore not presented here.[13]

Problems in the Interpretation of Commonality Analysis

As with any analytic method, it is imperative to determine the meaning of results obtained from commonality analysis. Referring to the commonality analysis of the illustrative data of Table 7.2, several questions come immediately to mind. Do the results enable one to answer the question about the relative importance of independent variables? May one conclude that SES is not an important variable, since it makes almost no unique contribution to GPA (.00006; see Table 7.3)? Or does the larger proportion of variance attributed uniquely to IQ, as compared with *n* Ach, indicate that it is the more important variable of the two? And what do the commonality elements mean?

The key to answering these and other questions is in the realization that commonality analysis is useful and meaningful in predictive but not in explanatory research. By its very nature, commonality analysis evades the problem of explanation, or, at the very least, fails to come to grips with it. This becomes particularly evident when it is realized that, given a set of independent variables and a dependent variable, commonality analysis is applied in exactly the same way, and of course yields identical results, regardless of one's causal model concerning the variables under study or in the absence of any such model.

Advocates of commonality analysis extol its virtues as being safe. Cooley and Lohnes (1976), for example, say: "The commonality method of partitioning of variance in multivariate regression is an informative, conservatively safe method for most situations likely to arise in evaluations, and it is therefore strongly recommended as the usual style of analysis for evaluative researches" (p. 219). There is no denying that the method is conservative and safe, but its safety stems from the fact that it does not address questions relating to attempts at explaining phenomena. It is informative only for predictive research, where it can be used for decisions about which variables may be elimi-

[13]See Wisler (1969) for a mathematical development in which commonality analysis is expressed as squared semipartial correlations. See also Beaton (1973).

nated while sacrificing little in overall predictability. In short, commonality analysis can be used as an alternative to other variable-selection procedures (e.g., stepwise selection; see Chapter 6). In fact, Newton and Spurrell (1967a, 1967b) maintain that commonality analysis is superior to other selection methods currently used, and give empirical evidence in support of this claim. Among several rules they formulate for the selection of variables from a larger pool is that variables with small commonalities and large unique components are to be preferred. This rule makes good sense in a predictive framework. Its application in an explanatory framework, however, may be highly misleading.

Beaton, who played a major role in developing methodological approaches for the extensive reanalyses of data from the Coleman Report (Mayeske et al., 1972, 1973a, 1973b, 1975), distinguishes between the use of regression analysis for predictive purposes and for the estimation of parameters in a causal model. He proceeds to state: "Commonality analysis is an attempt to understand the relative *predictive* power of the regressor variables, both individually and in combination. [It] may be used as a procedure to guide a stepwise regression" (Beaton, 1973, p. 2; italics added).

In their response to criticism of commonality analysis, Lohnes and Cooley (1978) urge researchers to revert to Darlington's term *usefulness* instead of *uniqueness*. This is probably a good idea as it may serve as a safeguard against misinterpretations of such elements, provided that one is mindful of what Darlington (1968) says about usefulness: "When the focus is on the *prediction* of X_0, *rather than causal analysis,* usefulness is clearly the measure of greatest interest" (p. 168; italics added). Even Lohnes and Cooley (1978) end up saying: "In this context 'useful' refers to the *utility of the predictor in estimating* the dependent variable after all the predictors have been introduced" (p. 7; italics added).

Uniqueness, then, is useful in a predictive framework, but not in an explanatory one. This, however, is not how the measure is interpreted by leading exponents of commonality analysis. Mayeske and his associates (1972), for example, say: "It does not seem unreasonable to assume that some degree of proportionality exists between the percent of variance of a dependent variable that can be uniquely associated with a set of variables and its *causal influence*" (p. 52; italics added). One fails to see the justification for this statement. Or, when he discusses the difficulties that arise when commonalities are large and the unique components are small, Mood (1971, p. 197) does not attribute it to the analytic method being used, but to "our state of ignorance about educational variables." He further maintains that commonality analysis helps us "identify indicators which are failing badly with respect to specificity" (p. 197).

While it is true that large commonalities are a consequence of high correlations among variables, it does not necessarily follow that a high correlation reflects lack of specificity of variables. Creager (1971) comments on this point, saying: "Correlations between sets may be of substantive importance and not solely artifacts of the inadequacy of the proxy variables" (p. 675). It is possible, for example, that two variables are highly correlated because one of them is a cause of the other. Commonality analysis, however, does not differentiate between situations in which variables lack specificity and those in which causal relations exist. Applying commonality analysis in the latter situation may lead to the erroneous conclusion that a presumed cause lacks specificity or is unimportant because it has little or no uniqueness, on the one hand, and large commonalities with other variables on the other hand. For example, in the reanalysis of the Coleman Report data, Mayeske and his colleagues (1972) used student's racial-ethnic group membership as a student variable and teacher's racial-ethnic group membership as a school variable. Not surprisingly, these variables were found to be correlated highly, thus contributing to high commonalities for school and student variables when attempting to explain dependent variables such as achievement. It is obvious, however, that the high correlation between student and teacher racial composition does not reflect a lack of specificity of these variables but is primarily a consequence of a policy of segregation.

Finally, it is important to note that there is nothing absolute about the uniqueness of a variable, inasmuch as it depends on the relations among the specific variables under study. Addition or deletion of variables may change drastically the uniqueness attributed to some or all of the variables. Peaker (1975), who played a major role in determining the analytic methods used in the IEA studies, has this to say about the use and interpretation of uniqueness: "At first sight this analytic position appears safe, if unenterprising, but the safety is only apparent, since the 'unique' variances are unique only for a particular choice of variables. There is nothing absolute about their uniqueness" (p. 148).

The problems of interpreting unique elements in an explanatory framework pale in comparison with the difficulties encountered in the interpretation of commonality elements in such a framework. Witness, for example, the statement about the commonality between two sets of variables by one of the leading exponents of commonality analysis. "In the strictest sense this common portion represents an intermediate situation. That is to say, we cannot tell to which of the two sets . . . all or some part of this common portion should be attributed" (Mayeske, 1970, p. 105). This statement refers to a second-order commonality, that is, between two variables or two sets of variables. With more than two independent variables the difficulty increases: one obtains higher-order commonalities that will amost always elude explanation. Yet one encounters interpretations of commonalities even as indications of interactions between variables (e.g., Hanushek & Kain, 1972; Purves, 1973). Such interpretations are incorrect, since commonality is a result of a correlation among predictors and does not reflect an interaction in the sense in which the term is used in experimental research. An interaction between two independent variables, for example, means that there is a dependent-variable variance that neither variable alone accounts for; both variables operate jointly to produce it. Commonality, on the other hand, reflects variation in the dependent variable that would be accounted for by either variable alone.

Another problem with commonality elements is that they may have negative signs.[14] Negative commonalities may be obtained in situations where some of the variables act as suppressors, or when some of the correlations among the independent variables are positive and others are negative. There seems to be no need to elaborate on the logical problem of dealing with a negative propor-

[14]Unique elements are always positive. They may, however, be equal to zero.

tion of variance attributed to the commonality of a set of variables. And the problem is not solved by saying, as Mayeske et al. (1972) did: "Negative commonalities will be regarded as equivalent to zero" (p. 49).

Still another problem with commonality analysis, alluded to earlier, is the proliferation of higher-order commonalities that results from the addition of independent variables. Even with five independent variables only, there are 31 components, 26 of which are commonalities. Although it may be possible, but by no means always easy, to explain a second- or a third-order commonality, it is extremely difficult, and even impossible, to explain commonalities of higher orders. Mood and Mayeske recognize this difficulty and suggest as a remedy that independent variables be grouped and that commonality analysis be done on the grouped variables. Wisler (1969), for example, maintains that "It is by grouping variables and performing commonality analyses that one can begin to discern the structure in nonexperimental, multivariate data" (p. 359). While admittedly simpler, commonality analysis with grouped variables may still lead to results that are difficult to interpret. One can find examples of such difficulties in the reanalysis of data from the Coleman Report by Mayeske and associates (1969). For example, Mood (1971) reproduces one such analysis from Mayeske, in which two grouped independent variables, peer quality and school quality, were used. Each of these variables was obtained as a result of grouping about 30 indicators. In an analysis of achievement in grades 3, 6, 9, and 12 it was found that the unique contributions of each of the grouped variables ranged from .04 to .11, while their commonalities ranged from .45 to .75. Mood (1971) concludes: "The overlap between peer quality and school quality is so large that there seems hardly any point in referring to them as different factors; or perhaps the problem is that we are so ignorant about specificity of indicators that ours have almost no specificity at all" (p. 198).

In view of the above-noted difficulties with the interpretation of commonality elements it is not surprising that some researchers (e.g., Cooley & Lohnes, 1976; Purves, 1973) report the uniqueness of each variable, or set of variables, and lump together all the commonalities. It is interesting to note that although Cooley and Lohnes (1976, pp. 224–227) label the combined commonalities as the "Jointly Explained" proportion of variance, their characterization, in parentheses, of this quantity as "confounded" more appropriately reflects its ambiguous status. Authors who do report separate commonalities either confess their inability to explain them, or make some general comments about them (e.g., that they tend to be large compared with the unique elements).

RESEARCH APPLICATIONS

"Currently, enthusiasm for commonality partitioning of variance is running high" (Cooley & Lohnes, 1976, p. 220), especially among researchers engaged in evaluation studies in general, and studies on the effect of schooling in particular. Most of the studies in which commonality analysis has been used were aimed at explaining phenomena (e.g., school achievement). Assuming that one accepts the views expressed above that commonality analysis is not an appropriate method for explanatory research, one would have to question seriously, if not reject, the conclusions of the explanatory studies in which the method was used. On these grounds it would have been justified to refrain from reviewing, or commenting upon, specific studies. It was felt, however, that such an omission would be unwise because some of the studies have had, and will probably continue to have, a strong impact not only on educational researchers but also on educational policymakers, educators, and the general public. It was therefore decided to comment briefly on some major studies in the hope of drawing attention to them as serious, though flawed, attempts to explain very complex phenomena under very severe constraints. Additionally, it is hoped that the comments will illustrate and highlight some of the problems in the application of commonality analysis in explanatory research. Needless to say, the brief statements that follow cannot begin to do justice to the broad scope and extensive efforts that have gone into the studies being considered. Furthermore, attention is being directed here only to commonality analysis, which is one of several methods used in some of these studies. In short, the following presentations are neither summaries nor reviews of the studies. The interested reader is encouraged to read the original reports and judge whether, and to what degree, they help explain the phenomena under consideration.

Reanalyses of the Coleman Report Data

Probably the most extensive use of commonality analysis is to be found in a set of studies conducted by personnel of the United States Office of Education under the leadership of Mayeske (e.g., Mayeske et al., 1972, 1973a, 1973b, 1975). One of the major goals of these studies was to determine the relative effects of student background characteristics and schooling on student cognitive and noncognitive functioning. For example, in the preface to *A Study of Our Nation's Schools* (Mayeske et al., 1972), Mayeske states that one of its major purposes was: "to show the extent to which the structural properties of the data will permit answers to be obtained about possible influences that schools may have on their students" (p. vii).

In this study, approximately 400 questionnaire items of the Coleman Report were initially reduced to about 70 variables. These were subsequently grouped in blocks, the two major ones being Background (B) and School (S) variables. The most pervasive finding that emerged from repeated applications of commonality analysis is that nearly all of the achievement variance is attributable to commonality elements. For example, for the twelfth grade: U(B) = .08, U(S) = .04, and C(BS) = .75. While C(BS) is considerably larger than U(S) and U(B) at all grade levels, there are some differences in the relative magnitudes of these elements across the grade levels. The authors comment on these differences, saying, for example: "A reversal in the unique portion of B and S occurs at the third grade, and this persists at the higher grades. The second-order commonality coefficient shows a progressive increase from the first to the 12th grades" (Mayeske et al., 1972, p. 46). Such comparisons are unwarranted because the unique and commonality elements are sample-specific.

The precarious nature of such cross-sample comparisons is even more striking when the authors attempt to study the effects of different aspects of schooling by partitioning S into three subsets: School Personnel and Personnel Expenditure variables (T), Pupil Programs and Policies variables (P), and Facilities variables (F). At all grade levels the unique elements are small, though they differ from each other. For example, U(T) is .06 at the first-grade level; .03 at the third- and sixth-grade levels; and .02 at the ninth- and twelfth-grade levels. Of all the commonalities, C(BT) is the largest, ranging from .28 in the first grade to .55 in the sixth (see Table 5.4.2.5 in Mayeske et al., 1972, p. 51). The authors comment:

> A diminishing role is played by T at the higher grade levels. The fact that the unique portion is so high at the lower grade levels is somewhat puzzling until one observes that the second-order commonality coefficient, C(BT), increases for higher grade levels. This suggests that T comes to share more of the predictable variance in Achievement at the higher grade levels instead of making an independent contribution. . . . The variables we have called F, with P and B, share an increasing amount of variance at the ninth and 12th grades. . . . The relative ordering, however, is for B to be slightly to appreciably larger than T, and for T to be larger than F—until the 12th grade. These results suggest that B and T may play an important role in the development of achievement. If P and F play a role, it would be by virtue of their shared variances with B and T. (Mayeske et al., 1972, p. 51)

All of the above amounts to nothing more than a statement that the patterns and magnitudes of the correlations among the variables differ in the different grades. This may, in part, be due to differences in the variabilities of the variables at the different grade levels. Be that as it may, the use of uniqueness of variables as indicators of their effects on Achievement is, to say the least, questionable. To compare such indices across samples is even more questionable. The foregoing comments apply also to comparisons of unique and common elements across different dependent variables (e.g., Achievement, Motivation, Attitudes).

Reservations about specific aspects of the analyses, and specific conclusions notwithstanding, the overall findings reflect a situation in which commonality analysis cannot help untangle the highly correlated variables, nor does it help determine whether, how, and to what extent each of them produces an effect. This inevitable conclusion is reached also by the authors of the report, who say: "The principal findings are as follows. On the whole, the influence of the school cannot be separated from that of the student's social background—and vice versa. Moreover, the common influence of the school and the student's social background exceeds either of their distinguishable influences" (Mayeske et al., 1972, p. ix).

Because the purpose of the above presentation was to illustrate some of the difficulties in the application of commonality analysis to the Coleman Report data, it was more convenient to use illustrations from only one of the studies. It should be noted, however, that the comments made above apply equally to those sections of the other studies in which commonality analysis was used. Although other analytic approaches were also used (see, in particular, Mayeske et al., 1975), all the studies relied primarily on commonality analysis.

In response to criticisms of their reliance on commonality analysis, Mayeske et al. (1975) tried alternative approaches to variance partitioning and concluded: "We tested several of these alternative models, and found them unproductive. The most promising approach, it seems to us, lay in further refinements of the commonality model" (p. 130). The crucial issue is that none of the variance-partitioning approaches can provide answers to the questions raised by Mayeske and his associates. Moreover, in the absence of a theory of the process of achievement it is not possible to tell which analytic method is potentially useful. Mood, who has written forewords to the various Mayeske studies, defends their use of commonality analysis on the grounds that no theory of education exists. Mood says: "When it comes to quantitative models, education . . . is still in the Stone Age: true theoretical models are still lacking, as are reproducible conceptual connections that might give us a few clues on constructing even a simple model. . . . We shall eventually develop some believable theory. As we proceed along that path *we shall abandon partitions of variance as soon as possible*" (Mood, 1973, p. iv; italics added).

There is no denying the validity of Mood's contention of the lack of a theory of education. But to use an analytic technique in a theoretical vacuum is not only the least promising route for arriving at one, but may inhibit the development of theory by deflecting one's attention from this paramount goal. Furthermore, the seemingly valid answers obtained by relying solely on analytic methods may result in deleterious consequences for educational practices and policies (see Chapter 8, section entitled Social Sciences and Social Policy).

The International Evaluation of Educational Achievement (IEA)

The IEA studies are described earlier in this chapter, along with a detailed discussion of the major type of analysis used in them—namely, incremental partitioning of variance. Commonality analysis was also used in some of the studies. Illustrative findings are drawn from the study of *Literature Education in Ten Countries* (Purves, 1973) because commonality analysis was used extensively in it. Additional examples may be found in other IEA studies and also in a technical report (Peaker, 1975) that provides a general discussion of the methodology of the IEA studies, as well as some summaries of their findings.

In the Literature study, the following six blocks of variables were used: (1) Home Background, (2) Type of School, (3) Learning Conditions, (4) Kindred Variables, (5) Word Knowledge, and (6) Reading Comprehension.[15] In a commonality analysis with six blocks, 63 elements (i.e., $2^6 - 1$) may be obtained (see discussion of commonality analysis earlier in this chapter). Of the 63 elements, 6 are unique and 57 are commonalities (15 second-order, 20 third-order, 15 fourth-order, 6 fifth-order, and 1 sixth-order). Purves (1973) does not report the proportion of variance attributed to the separate elements. Instead, he reports the sum of the unique elements, and the sum of all the commonalities, which he labels "joint contribution of the variables."

Overall, the finding in the different populations is that most of the variance of

[15]For a description of these blocks, see section on Incremental Partitioning of Variance earlier in this chapter.

Achievement in Literature is due to commonalities. For example, in Population II, the total percent of variance accounted for in the ten countries ranges from 66.6 to 93.2. The sum of the unique contributions ranges from 7% to 44.3%, whereas the sum of the commonalities ranges from 40.7% to 82.2% (see Purves, 1973, Table 5.3, p. 133).

The higher the intercorrelations among the blocks within a given country, the smaller the sum of the unique elements and the larger the sum of the commonalities. This is demonstrated dramatically for Population II in England and in Finland. In England the variance accounted for by the six blocks is 89.5%, of which 7.3% is the sum of the unique contributions and 82.2% is the sum of the commonalities. In Finland the six blocks account for 92.8% percent of the variance, of which 7.0% is the sum of the unique contributions and 85.9% is the sum of the commonalities. It is clear, then, that results like these afford little insight into the process of achievement in Literature, except for the obvious conclusion that the blocks are highly intercorrelated. Purves was prudent in not reporting the separate commonalities, since they would have certainly eluded any meaningful interpretation. It will be noted, however, that Purves' occasional reference to commonalities as interactions is potentially misleading. Thus, he says: "That so much of the variance is accounted for not only by the unique contribution of the variables but by their *interactions* also reflects the tight relationship between them" (Purves, 1973, pp. 133–134; italics added).[16]

An additional point regarding the above-cited results is worth noting. As discussed earlier in this chapter, the major analytic approach in the IEA studies was incremental partitioning of variance in which the six blocks were entered in a fixed order, beginning with Home Background. For Population II, Home Background accounts for 68.4% of the variance in England and 79.1% in Finland (see Purves, 1973, Table 5.3, p. 133). But, as reported above, the sum of the unique contributions, *including Home Background,* is 7.3 and 7.0 in England and Finland, respectively. Is, then, Home Background an important block? It is obvious that the answer depends on which of the two analyses one proceeds to interpret. In the incremental partitioning of variance, Home Background appears to have the overwhelming effect, as it accounts for about 80% of the variance accounted for by the six blocks together. In the commonality analysis, on the other hand, it accounts for a fraction of 7% of the total variance. The crucial point is that, as discussed earlier, neither incremental partitioning of variance nor commonality analysis is a valid approach for ascertaining the relative importance of variables.

Purves reports a large number of analyses that not only are of dubious explanatory value but also are potentially misleading. These are analyses in which the unique contribution of each variable is assessed when only the variables of the block in which it appears are used in a commonality analysis. Thus, for example, using only the variables that comprise Block I, in Population II, Age of the student in school is reported to have a uniqueness of 1.0% in the United States, 1.5% in Finland, none in Sweden and England (see Purves, 1973, Table 5.5, p. 136). Or, using only the block of Student Attitudes and

[16]See discussion of this point earlier in this chapter.

Interests (Table 5.6), Reading books about art makes a unique contribution in Sweden only (3.6%), and Reading travel and mystery makes a unique contribution only in Chile (2.1%). And so it goes in table after table which, except for sprinklings of small unique elements, are mostly blank (see, for example, Purves, 1973, pp. 138, 146–149, 166–167, 176–178). There is, of course, nothing absolute about the uniqueness of these values that would certainly change in the presence of other blocks in the analysis. Furthermore, to the extent that the logic and the method of grouping variables were valid in the first place, one would expect the variables within a block to be intercorrelated. Consequently, the sum of the unique elements within a block would be expected to be small relative to the sum of their commonalities. Most important, however, is that one fails to see the validity of such analyses in explanatory research.

Measures of School Effectiveness

In a recent study, Madaus, Kellaghan, Rakow, and King (1979) argue that the failure to detect differential effects of schooling is due primarily to the exclusive reliance on standardized achievement tests as measures of the dependent variable. These authors maintain that curriculum-based tests are more sensitive and therefore more appropriate as measures of the dependent variable in studies of the effect of schooling. In support of their premise, Madaus and associates offer results of a study conducted in secondary schools in the Republic of Ireland. This study is reviewed here because it is a recent example of the application of commonality analysis and because it affords an opportunity for illustrating some serious conceptual and methodological problems in the use of commonality analysis in explanatory research.

Beginning with 82 predictor variables, Madaus et al. grouped them in five blocks. It will be noted in passing that little or no justification is given in support of the clustering of rather disparate variables into a block. Thus, for example, the authors say: "Variables describing the student, such as sex, age, attitude to education, and academic self-concept, were assigned to an *individual* block" (Madaus et al., p. 212). The situation is further confounded by the fact that the unit of analysis is the classroom and not the individual. That is, class means, or class indices, presumably describe the individual.

After grouping the predictors in blocks, a two-stage process was undertaken in order to reduce their number. In the first stage, "eight 'key' dependent variables [of a total of 18] were selected. . . . Each selected dependent variable was regressed separately in a step-wise fashion on the variables in each block. To be retained within a block, a regressor variable had to be a significant predictor (.05 level) of any four or more of the 'key' variables" (Madaus et al., p. 213). Of the original 82 variables, 42 survived this stage of the analysis.

> In the second stage of the screening of variables, a single set of predictor variables was selected for each dependent variable by a step-wise regression on all the predictor variables, regardless of block, that were retained from the first stage of analysis. Variables were eliminated *as predictors of a specific variable* if they did not contribute significantly to the prediction of that dependent variable. At this stage a *unique set of*

predictor variables was associated with each dependent variable. These were the variables used in subsequent analyses to estimate the shares of variance attributable to each block. (p. 213; italics added)

Several points will be noted. Earlier in this book (see Chapter 6) it was argued that stepwise regression analysis is useful in predictive research only. In the present chapter it was shown that the uniqueness of a variable is directly related to the test of significance of the regression coefficient associated with the variable. Therefore, the stepwise regression analysis, coupled with the criterion of significant *b*'s, favored predictors whose unique contributions were relatively large. Since the uniqueness of a variable is larger the less it is correlated with the other predictors, the predictor-selection process at the first stage of the analysis necessarily resulted in blocks composed of relatively heterogeneous predictors (i.e., predictors whose intercorrelations are relatively small). This may be useful in predictive but not in explanatory research, where the substantive meaning of each block is paramount. In short, beginning with a grouping of variables that was questionable in the first place, Madaus and coworkers ended up with an even more questionable grouping.

In the second stage of the analysis, each of 18 measures was regressed on the 42 predictors that survived the first-stage selection process. Again, a stepwise regression analysis was used, and predictors whose *b*'s were statistically significant were retained. Thus, at this stage, too, the analysis favored predictors with relatively large unique contributions. This time, however, different combinations of predictors were selected for each dependent variable. It is not known how many variables from each block were retained in each of the 18 analyses, nor is one told of the degree of redundancy with which each of the predictors was selected. For example, 13 predictors of the first block survived the first stage of the variable-selection process. How many of these predictors survived in each of the 18 analyses of the second stage? How many times was a given predictor selected? In principle, it is possible that two different subsets of the 13 predictors that comprised the first block were retained in two separate analyses in the second stage of the variable-selection process. And yet both subsets would be treated as representing an *individual* block.

Treating each of 18 measures of achievement as a separate dependent variable is, to say the least, questionable. Moreover, in the second stage of the variable-selection process, stepwise analyses were done with 42 predictors for classes whose numbers ranged from a low of 51 to a high of 101. Dangers of capitalization on chance and the resulting shrinkage (see Chapter 6) loom large indeed. They are magnified by the two-stage process in the selection of predictors.

At the conclusion of the second stage of the variable selection, the specific variables that were retained in each of the 18 analyses were grouped into their original blocks. These were then used in commonality analyses for each of the 18 measures of achievement. Earlier, it was argued at length that commonality analysis is not useful for the purpose of determining the relative importance of variables. It was also stated that comparisons of proportions of variance accounted for in different measures are not valid indicators of the relative importance of independent variables. On these grounds alone, one would have to question the analyses done by Madaus et al., not to mention their interpretations of the results. The two-stage process of variable selection that preceded the commonality analysis aggravated the problems that arise when one attempts to use it in explanatory research.

VARIANCE PARTITIONING: RETROSPECT

Variance partitioning was discussed in detail in this chapter because it is frequently used *inappropriately* for the purpose of studying the relative importance of the effects of independent variables on a dependent variable. Several major studies that relied heavily on some form of variance partitioning were scrutinized in order to illustrate some of the problems and difficulties attendant with the application of such methods.

In the beginning of this chapter it was stated that incremental partitioning of variance may be used when it is desired to control for a variable(s) while studying the effect of another variable(s), provided that this is done in accordance with a causal model. It was, however, stressed that results from such an analysis should not be construed as shedding light on the question of the relative importance of the effects of independent variables on the dependent variable. It is worth noting that, following Cohen and Cohen (1975), some researchers use the term hierarchical regression analysis, or hierarchical model, for what was labeled in this chapter as incremental partitioning of variance. It goes without saying that, regardless of one's preference for one label or the other, the discussion of incremental partitioning of variance applies equally to hierarchical regression analysis.

Finally, it is important to recognize that, even when appropriately applied, results obtained from an incremental partitioning of variance are of dubious value, if not useless, as guides for policy and decision making (for a discussion, see Cain & Watts, 1968, p. 170). What are the policy implications of a finding that a given variable accounts for, say, 10% of the variance of the dependent variable? What should be done in order to increase, or decrease, its effect on the dependent variable? Assuming that the variable can be manipulated by the researcher, by how much should it be changed? What will be the costs of a specific change? What will be its measurable consequences? Such questions are unanswerable in the context of variance partitioning. They are greatly aggravated when, as is done in virtually all major studies, the partitioned variance is attributed to blocks of variables instead of to single ones. Assume, for example, that a researcher finds that a block of variables describing the teacher (e.g., years of experience, salary, level of education, attitudes toward education) accounts for a certain proportion of the variance in student achievement. How can such a finding be translated into policy? Even if all the variables were under the control of the decision maker (an admittedly unrealistic assumption), by how much should each of them be changed in order to achieve a desired effect? What is a desired effect when the proportion of variance accounted for is used as the index? As complex as these problems are, they pale compared with those arising in the more realistic stituation in which most or all of the variables comprising the block are nonmanipulable; that some may be multiple indicators of a variable; that others may be proxies of variables. If the situation appears hopeless, it is because it is indeed so in the context of variance partitioning. Other approaches, presented in subsequent chapters, are more appropriate and hold more promise for attempts to explain complex phenomena with which behavioral scientists are concerned.[17]

STUDY SUGGESTIONS

1. The following illustrative correlation matrix ($N = 300$) was used in Study Suggestion 8 of Chapter 6.

	1 Race	*2* IQ	*3* School Quality	*4* Self-Concept	*5* Level of Aspiration	*6* Verbal Achievement
1	1.00	.30	.25	.30	.30	.25
2	.30	1.00	.20	.20	.30	.60
3	.25	.20	1.00	.20	.30	.30
4	.30	.20	.20	1.00	.40	.30
5	.30	.30	.30	.40	1.00	.40
6	.25	.60	.30	.30	.40	1.00

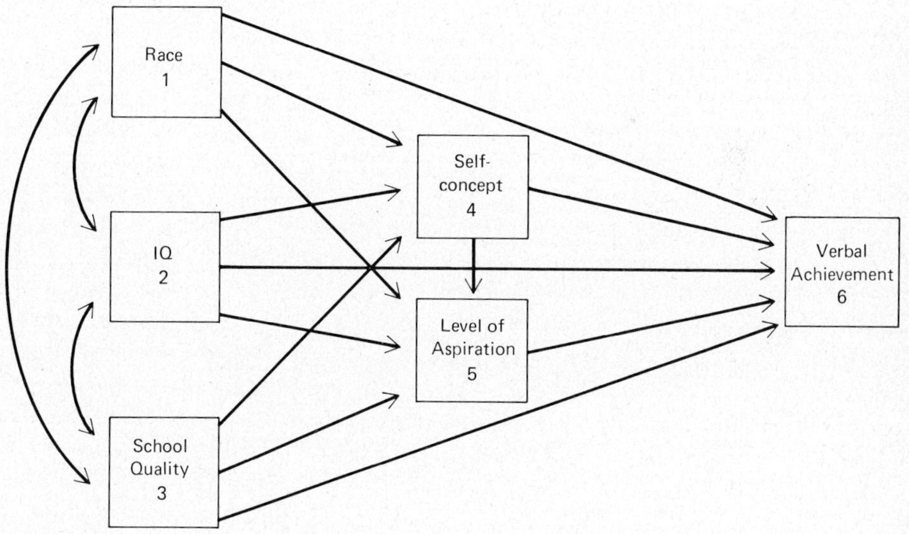

[17]For some general observations about the use of variance partitioning in explanatory research, and about possible effects of results of such research on policymakers and the general public, see the concluding section of Chapter 8.

Assume that the causal model that is depicted in the figure above reflects the theoretical framework about the relations among the variables under consideration.

(a) Which variables are treated as exogenous?

(b) Which variables are treated as endogenous?

(c) What is the proportion of variance of Verbal Achievement that is accounted for by the five independent variables?

(d) Assuming that it is desired to partition the variance obtained in (c) in a manner that is consistent with the causal model depicted in the figure, outline the necessary steps to accomplish this.

(e) Do the variance partitioning as indicated in (d). Determine the different components, and explain what each of them means.

(f) Can the results obtained in (e) be used for the purpose of assessing the relative importance of the variables under consideration? Explain.

2. Assume that one wishes to do a commonality analysis, using the variables of Study Suggestion 1 and treating Verbal Achievement as the dependent variable.

(a) How many components will be obtained in such an analysis?

(b) Indicate the number of components of each type (e.g., how many unique, second-order, etc.) that would be obtained.

(c) Using the correlation matrix of Study Suggestion 1, apply Formula (7.7) to calculate the uniqueness of the five independent variables.

(d) Use R^2's to indicate how you would go about calculating the following: C(12), C(235).

3. In what way does the causal model depicted in the figure under Study Suggestion 1 affect the manner in which commonality analysis would be applied to the variables under consideration?

ANSWERS

1. (a) Race, IQ, and School Quality.
   (b) Self-Concept, Level of Aspiration, and Verbal Achievement.
   (c) $.43947 = R^2_{6.12345}$
   (d) (1) Proportion of variance accounted for by 1, 2, and 3: $R^2_{6.123}$.
   (2) Proportion of variance incremented by 4: $R^2_{6.1234} - R^2_{6.123}$.
   (3) Proportion of variance incremented by 5: $R^2_{6.12345} - R^2_{6.1234}$.
   (e) (1) Proportion of variance accounted for by 1, 2, and 3: .39510.
   (2) Proportion of variance incremented by 4: .02275.
   (3) Proportion of variance incremented by 5: .02161.
   (f) No. For an explanation, see beginning of this chapter.
2. (a) $31 = 2^5 - 1$
   (b) 5 unique, 10 second-order, 10 third-order, 5 fourth-order, 1 fifth-order.
   (c) U(1) = .0003, U(2) = .2190, U(3) = .0148, U(4) = .0097, U(5) = .0216
   (d) $C(12) = -R^2_{6.345} + R^2_{6.1345} + R^2_{6.2345} - R^2_{6.12345}$
   $C(235) = -R^2_{6.14} + R^2_{6.124} + R^2_{6.134} - R^2_{6.1234} + R^2_{6.145} - R^2_{6.1245} - R^2_{6.1345} + R^2_{6.12345}$
3. The causal model does not affect the manner in which commonality analysis is carried out. Given a set of independent variables and a dependent variable, commonality analysis is carried out in exactly the same manner, regardless of the specific causal model advanced by the researcher, or in the absence of any causal model.

EXPLANATION: THE ANALYSIS OF EFFECTS

Chapter 7 was devoted to methods of variance partitioning, with particular attention to difficulties that arise when such methods are used for the purpose of explaining phenomena. The dubious value of variance partitioning as a guide for policymaking was also discussed. In the present chapter we turn our attention to the use of the regression equation for the purpose of explaining phenomena, particularly to the use of regression coefficients as indices of the effects of independent variables on the dependent variable. In earlier chapters it was said that the partial regression coefficient (i.e., a regression coefficient obtained in the regression of a dependent variable on a set of interrelated independent variables) indicates the expected change in the dependent variable associated with a unit change in a given independent variable while controlling for the other independent variables. This interpretation of the regression coefficient has great appeal for many theoreticians and research workers because it holds the promise for unraveling complex phenomena and for effecting desired changes in it. It is necessary, however, to take a closer look at the properties of regression coefficients, paying particular attention to factors that may lead to their biased estimation or instability, as well as to the restrictive conditions under which they can be validly interpreted as indices of the effects of the variables with which they are associated.

A sober examination of the properties of the regression equation is particularly pressing because its apparent simplicity is deceptive and can easily lead its unwary user to serious misconceptions, misinterpretations, and misapplications. Rather than being exhaustive, the present chapter concentrates on the major sources of error, on the most serious pitfalls to be avoided. Some of these topics have been introduced in earlier chapters. The present chapter expounds on the earlier discussions and focuses on the interpretation of regression coefficients as indices of effects.

The chapter begins with a discussion of the distinction between experimental and nonexperimental research as it relates to the interpretation of regression coefficients. This is followed by a discussion of the following major topics: (1) specification errors; (2) measurement errors; (3) multicollinearity; (4) standardized versus unstandardized regression coefficients; and (5) the role of theory. Research applications that illustrate some of the interpretive problems discussed earlier are then presented. The chapter concludes with some observations about social sciences and social policy.

EFFECTS IN EXPERIMENTAL AND NONEXPERIMENTAL RESEARCH

The important distinction between experimental and nonexperimental research was discussed several times earlier (see, in particular, Chapters 5, 6, and 7). It was noted, among other things, that in experimental research the researcher is not only manipulating the independent variables but is also better able to control extraneous variables directly or by randomization. Under such circumstances the researcher may feel reasonably confident in concluding, on the basis of regression coefficients, that certain actions need be taken in order to produce a desired effect on the dependent variable. The policymaker can note the investment necessary in changing a unit of an independent variable and the returns that are expected to accrue from the change. Accordingly, one is in a position to decide how the efforts and investments should be allocated.

The situation is considerably more complex and more ambiguous when the regression equation is obtained in nonexperimental research. Cook and Campbell (1979, Chapter 7); Michelson (1970); Mood (1970); Smith (1972), and Snedecor and Cochran (1967; pp. 393–397), among other authors, address themselves to the problems involved in the interpretation of regression equations calculated from data collected in nonexperimental research. The most important thing to note is that such equations reflect average relations between a dependent and a set of independent variables, and not necessarily the process by which the latter produce the former. For example, in their discussion of the findings of the Coleman Report, Mosteller and Moynihan (1972b) note that "we can estimate the difference in achievement between schools not having and those having a language laboratory, say. But we cannot tell whether actually adding or removing a language laboratory would produce nearly the same difference. Through the years, regression forecasts made in this manner in other fields have often failed in their predictions" (p. 35).

Following his excellent discussion of uses and abuses of regression analysis, Box (1966) concludes: "To find out what happens to a system when you interfere with it you have to interfere with it (not just passively observe it)" (p. 629). Although one cannot take issue with Box's dictum, it is necessary to recognize that following it to the letter will result in the exclusion of much, if not most, of human behavior from the realm of scientific inquiry. Because of ethical considerations, or because manipulations of variables are infeasible, or because it is desired to study behavior in complex field settings, nonexperimental research is frequently the only mode of research available to the behavioral researcher. Such research can and does lead to meaningful findings, provided that it is designed with forethought and executed with care and that its results are interpreted with circumspection.

Used wisely, regression analysis can play an important role in nonexperimental research. Unfortunately, all too frequently one encounters almost mindless interpretations of regression analysis in nonexperimental research. Several examples of erroneous, or potentially erroneous, conclusions based on interpretations of results obtained in nonexperimental research have been given in earlier chapters (see, in particular, Chapters 5, 6, and 7). The literature of studies of effects of schooling abounds with such examples. A striking example of misinterpretation of regression coefficients comes from Burt's work in the area of mental ability. Burt (1921) collected data on the following four variables: (1) mental age as measured by a modification of the Binet-Simon Scale (Binet); (2) school attainment expressed in terms of educational age (School Work); (3) Burt's reasoning test, which he considered as a measure of intelligence (Intelligence); and (4) chronological age (Age).

Using the Binet score as a criterion, and the remaining variables as predictors, Burt (1921, p. 183) obtained the following regression equation:

$$\text{Binet}' = .54\ \text{School Work} + .33\ \text{Intelligence} + .11\ \text{Age}$$

As the regression coefficients happen to sum to about one (actually, their sum is .98), Burt interprets each coefficient as a percent of the variance of the Binet attributable to the *effect* of the variable with which the given coefficient is associated. Thus, Burt (1921) argues:

> Of the gross result, then, one-ninth is attributable to age, one-third to intellectual development, and over one-half to school attainment. School attainment is thus the preponderant contributor to the Binet-Simon tests. To school the weight assigned is nearly double that of intelligence alone, and distinctly more than that of intelligence and age combined. *In determining the child's performance in the Binet-Simon Scale, intelligence can bestow but little more than half the share of the school, and age but one-third of intelligence.* (p. 183)

To bolster his argument, Burt uses as evidence results that he has obtained from the calculation of all the possible first- and second-order partial correlations for the four variables (see Chapter 5 for a warning against doing this). Burt says:

> With both age and intelligence constant, the partial correlation between school attainments and Binet results remains at .61. Of all the partial coefficients of the second order this is the largest. There can therefore be little doubt that *with the Binet-Simon Scale a child's mental age is a measure not only of the amount of intelligence with which he is congenitally endowed, not only of the plane of intelligence at which in the course of life and growth he has eventually arrived; it is also an index, largely if not mainly, of the mass of scholastic information and skill which in virtue of attendance more or less*

regular, by dint of instruction more or less effective, he has progressively accumulated in school. (p. 182)

Holzinger and Freeman (1925), who have criticized Burt's interpretation of the regression equation, used his results to calculate three additional regression equations, treating in turn each of the variables as the criterion. Following is their equation in which age was used as the criterion:

$$\text{Age}' = .15 \text{ Binet} + .51 \text{ School Work} + .03 \text{ Intelligence}$$

In order to highlight the fallacies in Burt's interpretation, Holzinger and Freeman (1925) interpret this equation in a manner done by Burt, using some of the very same expressions he has used.

It appears at once that over half of a child's age is "attributable" to school attainment. This is truly alarming. We had always supposed that age was a comparatively simple thing, when it could be discovered, but now we find that there can be little doubt that age is a measure not only of the amount of age with which a child is congenitally endowed—but it is also an index, largely, if not mainly, of the mass of scholastic information and skill which in virtue of attendance more or less regular, by dint of instruction more or less effective, he has accumulated in school. Isolated from scholastic progress and from development in mental age, intelligence subscribes but a paltry portion. Indeed, if the child were removed from school and his mental age taken away from him, he would probably not get old at all. The secret of eternal youth has at last been discovered! (pp. 581–582)

While one might be tempted to attribute Burt's erroneous interpretations to the fact that they were committed at a time when regression theory was clearly understood by relatively few researchers, two things should be noted: (1) In a fourth edition of Burt's book (1962) the same interpretation is repeated without as much as changing a single word (Burt comments on Hozinger & Freeman's critique in Appendix VI). (2) More important, as is shown in this chapter, similar errors were committed in some of the most recently published influential research studies.

The major sources of errors of interpretation of regression analysis in nonexperimental research constitute the body of this chapter and will therefore not be enumerated here. As a broad frame of reference, however, two points will be made. First, variables used in nonexperimental research may be, and often are, proxies for causal variables that are not included in the regression equation (e.g., number of books in the house as a proxy for home background). Needless to say, manipulating a proxy variable will not bring about a desired effect regardless of the magnitude of the regression coefficient associated with it. Yet, one encounters frequently not only the interpretation of proxies as if they were causal variables but also recommendations for policy decisions on the basis of such interpretations. Thus, for example, in a nonexperimental study of reading achievement, Heim and Perl (1974) speak of cost effectiveness of different "inputs" and conclude, among other things:

Using the additional $100 per pupil available to upgrade the degree status of principals seemed most cost effective, suggesting an astounding 14 percentile gain. Use of these resources to upgrade teacher-degree-status levels is associated with a 9 percentile point gain, making this strategy the second most cost effective. (p. 26)

It requires but little imagination to come up with a variety of variables for which the above indices may serve as proxies.

Second, variables in nonexperimental research tend to be intercorrelated. Since more often than not researchers neither understand the causes of the interrelations nor attempt to study them, implications of regression coefficients for policy decisions are questionable. Specifically, statements about achieving a desired effect by changing a given independent variable while holding all others constant tend to have an air of fantasy about them. Consider the following example. A researcher wishes to study the effects of a set of independent variables on academic achievement. Assume that among these are: self-concept, locus of control, and motivation. It is known that these variables are intercorrelated, though the causes of the correlations are not clear, or are debatable, depending upon one's theoretical formulations, assuming that such have been attempted in the first place. Be that as it may, the notion of varying one of the variables while holding the others constant may be tenable from a statistical frame of reference (i.e., effecting a partialing process), but it is much more problematic from a theoretical or a practical frame of reference. Assuming that one can arrive at a clear explication of the relations among the variables, it is conceivable that varying one while holding the others constant is neither theoretically meaningful nor practically feasible. Hence, the air of fantasy. (See Smith, 1972, on this and related issues.)

With these remarks in mind we turn now to detailed discussions of major sources of errors in the interpretation of regression coefficients as indices of effects.

SPECIFICATION ERRORS

The concept of specification errors was introduced in Chapter 2, where it was indicated that such errors refer to the use of a wrong or inappropriate model in the regression analysis—for example, when relevant variables are omitted from the regression equation, when irrelevant variables are included, when a linear model is postulated though a nonlinear model is more appropriate, or when an additive model is postulated even though a nonadditive model is more appropriate.

The most important thing to note about the foregoing statement is that it refers to a situation in which the researcher enunciated a theoretical model that describes the manner in which the independent variables affect the dependent variable. The regression equation, whose coefficients are to be estimated, is meant to reflect this model. Consequently, the absence of a model precludes a meaningful interpretation of the estimated coefficients. In short, specification errors refer to a misspecified model, not to its absence. Following are some of the major aspects and consequences of specification errors.[1]

[1]For further discussions, see Bohrnstedt and Carter (1971); Deegan (1974); Duncan (1975, Chapter 8); Hanushek and Jackson (1977, pp. 79–86); Hocking (1974); Kmenta (1971, pp. 391–405).

Omission of Relevant Variables

When relevant variables are omitted from the regression equation and they are correlated with the variables remaining in the equation, estimation of the coefficients for the latter is biased. The nature of the bias is demonstrated for the case of two independent variables. Assume that the true model is

$$Y = a + b_1X_1 + b_2X_2 + e \tag{8.1}$$

but instead the researcher postulates the following:

$$Y = a + b_1X_1 + e' \tag{8.2}$$

In Chapter 2 it was pointed out that one of the assumptions underlying regression analysis is that the variables not included in the model, and subsumed under the error term, are not correlated with the variables in the model (i.e., in (8.1) it is assumed the e is not correlated with X_1 or X_2). Under such circumstances the estimation of regression coefficients for the variables in the model is not biased. If, however, in the above noted example, the researcher uses Equation (8.2) instead, and if X_1 is correlated with X_2, it is obvious that the e', under which X_2 is subsumed, is correlated with X_1, thereby leading to bias in the estimation of the regression coefficient for X_1. It can be shown that[2]

$$b_{y1} = b_{y1.2} + b_{y2.1}b_{21} \tag{8.3}$$

where b_{y1} is the regression coefficient obtained from regressing Y on X_1 only; $b_{y1.2}$ and $b_{y2.1}$ are partial regression coefficients obtained from the regression of Y on X_1 and X_2; b_{21} is the regression coefficient obtained from regressing X_2 (the omitted variable) on X_1. b_{21} may be calculated as follows:

$$b_{21} = r_{21}\left(\frac{s_2}{s_1}\right) \tag{8.4}$$

where r_{21} is the correlation coefficient between X_2 and X_1; and s_2 and s_1 are standard deviations of X_2 and X_1, respectively. Substituting (8.4) in (8.3),

$$b_{y1} = b_{y1.2} + b_{y2.1}r_{21}\left(\frac{s_2}{s_1}\right) \tag{8.5}$$

It is now clear that the source of bias in estimating b_{y1} is due to r_{21}. When $r_{21} = .00$, the second term on the right of (8.5) vanishes, and the estimation of b_{y1} is not biased. The magnitude and the direction of the bias, when X_2 is omitted, are a function of the magnitudes and the signs of r_{21} and $b_{y2.1}$.

Equation (8.3) is applied now to two sets of data, one in which the two independent variables are correlated and one in which there is no correlation between the independent variables. The illustrative data of Table 8.1 are used for

[2]For proofs, see references cited in Footnote 1. Note that the estimation of a is also biased, although this is not dealt with here.

Table 8.1 Illustrative Correlation Matrix, Means, and Standard Deviations; $N = 100$

	Y	X_1	X_2	X_3
Y	1.0	.7	.5	.5
X_1	.7	1.0	.6	.0
X_2	.5	.6	1.0	.4
X_3	.5	.0	.4	1.0
M:	50	30	40	40
s:	6	4	5	5

this purpose. Assume, first, that the researcher regresses Y on X_1 only, and that the omitted variable is X_2. Using (8.4), calculate:

$$b_{y1} = r_{y1}\left(\frac{s_y}{s_1}\right) = .7\left(\frac{6}{4}\right) = 1.05$$

$$b_{21} = r_{21}\left(\frac{s_2}{s_1}\right) = .6\left(\frac{5}{4}\right) = .75$$

Using Formulas (3.15) and (3.16) from Chapter 3, calculate:

$$b_{y1.2} = \frac{r_{y1} - r_{y2}r_{12}}{1 - r_{12}^2}\left(\frac{s_y}{s_1}\right) = \frac{.7 - (.5)(.6)}{1 - .6^2}\left(\frac{6}{4}\right) = .9375$$

$$b_{y2.1} = \frac{r_{y2} - r_{y1}r_{12}}{1 - r_{12}^2}\left(\frac{s_y}{s_2}\right) = \frac{.5 - (.7)(.6)}{1 - .6^2}\left(\frac{6}{5}\right) = .15$$

Because the wrong model was used—that is, (8.2) instead of (8.1)—the estimation of the regression coefficient for X_1, with the present data, is biased upwards (from .9375 to 1.05).

Using the above results in Equation (8.3):

$$b_{y1} = .9375 + (.15)(.75) = 1.05$$

Assume now that the researcher regresses Y on X_1, but that the omitted variable this time is X_3. Using the data of Table 8.1, calculate:

$$b_{y1} = 1.05 \text{ (as above)}$$

$$b_{31} = r_{31}\frac{s_3}{s_1} = .00\left(\frac{5}{4}\right) = .00$$

$$b_{y1.3} = \frac{r_{y1} - r_{y3}r_{13}}{1 - r_{13}^2}\left(\frac{s_y}{s_1}\right) = \frac{.7 - (.5)(.0)}{1 - .0^2}\left(\frac{6}{4}\right) = 1.05$$

$$b_{y3.1} = \frac{r_{y3} - r_{y1}r_{13}}{1 - r_{13}^2}\left(\frac{s_y}{s_3}\right) = \frac{.5 - (.7)(.0)}{1 - .0^2}\left(\frac{6}{5}\right) = .6$$

It is obvious that the estimation of b_{y1} is not biased (i.e., $b_{y1} = b_{y1.3}$). Applying (8.3),

$$b_{y1} = 1.05 + (.6)(.0) = 1.05$$

This is, of course, because $r_{31} = .00$; hence $b_{31} = .00$.

Extensions of the above formulation to more than two independent variables are straightforward, although they are not presented here (see the references cited in Footnote 1).

In view of the fact that no estimation bias occurs when the omitted variables are not correlated with those of the model, one may be tempted to conclude that no harm is done by omitting such variables. It should be noted, however, that when relevant variables not correlated with those in the equation are omitted, the standard errors of the latter are biased upwards, thereby reducing the sensitivity of their statistical tests of significance and increasing the magnitudes of their confidence intervals. This is because the omitted variables are treated as error, resulting in a larger standard error of estimate, hence in larger standard errors for the b's.

What was said above may be illustrated by using the data for variables Y, X_1, and X_3 of Table 8.1. The results will be stated without showing the calculations (you may wish to do the calculations as an exercise either by using formulas presented in Chapter 3 or 4, or by using a computer program). It was shown above that because the correlation between X_1 and X_3 is zero, the regression coefficient for X_1 is the same regardless of whether Y is regressed on X_1 only or on X_1 and X_3:

$$b_{y1} = b_{y1.3} = 1.05$$

When Y is regressed on X_1 only, the standard error of estimate ($s_{y.1}$) is 4.30667, and the standard error of $b_{y1} = .10821$. Consequently, the t ratio for this b is 9.70, with 98 df. But when Y is regressed on X_1 and X_3, the standard error of estimate ($s_{y.12}$) is 3.09079, and the standard error of $b_{y1.3}$ is .07766. Therefore, the t ratio for the regression coefficient is 13.52, with 97 df. In sum, the reduction in the standard error of the b for X_1 in the second analysis is a direct function of the reduction in the standard error of estimate which is due to the inclusion in the analysis of a variable, X_3, that is not correlated with X_1.

Inclusion of Irrelevant Variables

In an attempt to offset the deleterious consequences of omitting relevant variables, researchers are tempted to "play it safe" by including variables regarding whose effects they have no theoretical expectations. Sometimes, a researcher will include irrelevant variables in order to "see what will happen." Such approaches have been referred to as "kitchen sink models" (Kmenta, 1971, p. 397).

When irrelevant variables are included in the equation, the estimation of the regression coefficients is not biased. The inclusion of irrelevant variables has, however, two consequences. One, there is a loss in degrees of freedom, resulting in a larger standard error of estimate. This is not a serious problem when the sample size is relatively large, as it should always be. Two, to the extent that the irrelevant variables are correlated with relevant ones, the standard errors of the regression coefficients for the latter will be larger than when the irrelevant variables are not included in the equation.

In sum, then, although the inclusion of irrelevant variables is not nearly as serious as the omission of relevant ones, it should not be resorted to routinely and thoughtlessly. While the estimates of the regression coefficients are not biased in the presence of irrelevant variables, the efficiency of the tests of significance of the coefficients of the relevant variables may be decreased.

Nonlinearity and Nonadditivity

The application of a linear additive model when a nonlinear or nonadditive one is called for is another instance of specification errors. Some forms of nonlinear relations may be handled in the context of multiple regression analysis by using powered vectors of variables, as is indicated in Equation (8.6) for the case of a single independent variable:

$$Y' = a + b_1X + b_2X^2 + \cdots + b_kX^k \tag{8.6}$$

Such models are discussed in Chapter 11.

Nonadditivity is generally treated under the heading of interaction, or joint, effects of independent variables on the dependent variable. In a two-variable model, for example, this approach takes the following form:

$$Y' = a + b_1X_1 + b_2X_2 + b_3X_1X_2 \tag{8.7}$$

where the product of X_1 and X_2 is meant to reflect the interaction between these variables. The topic of interaction is discussed in detail in subsequent chapters (see, for example, Chapter 10).

Detecting and Minimizing Specification Errors

Some of the consequences of specification errors were demonstrated by contrasting parameter estimation in true and in misspecified models. The rub, however, is that the true model is seldom, if ever, known. "Indeed it would require no elaborate sophistry to show that we will never have the 'right' model in any absolute sense. Hence, we shall never be able to compare one of our many wrong models with a definitely right one" (Duncan, 1975, p. 101). The researcher is therefore faced with the most difficult task of detecting specification errors and minimizing them while not knowing what the true model is. Obviously there is neither a simple nor an entirely satisfactory solution to this problem.

Some specification errors are easier to detect and, consequently, to eliminate or minimize than others. The simplest error to detect is probably the inclusion of irrelevant variables (see Kmenta, 1971, pp. 402–404, for testing procedures). The detection of some forms of nonlinearities can be accomplished by, for example, comparing models with and without powered vectors of the variables (see Chapter 11). The need for fitting a nonlinear model can also be ascertained from the study of plots of residuals. (See Chapter 2 for a general discussion, and the references cited therein for more advanced treatments of the topic. Figure 2.5 illustrates a residual plot that indicates the need for curvilinear analysis.)

The most pernicious specification errors are also the most difficult to detect. These are errors of omitting relevant variables. One possible approach is to plot residuals against a variable suspected to have been erroneously omitted. A nonrandom pattern in such a plot would suggest the need for the inclusion of the variable in the model. The absence of a specific pattern in the residual plot, however, does not provide assurance that a specification error was not committed by not including the variable in the model (see Rao & Miller, 1971, p. 115).

The most important safeguard against the commission of specification errors is theory. The role of theory is aptly captured in the following anecdote related by Ulam (1976): "Once someone asked, 'Professor Whitehead, which is more important: ideas or things?' 'Why, I would say ideas about things,' was his instant reply" (pp. 118–119). It is the ideas about the data that count, it is they that provide the cement, the integration. Nothing can substitute for a theoretical model, which, as noted earlier, the regression equation is meant to reflect. No amount of fancy statistical acrobatics will undo the harm that may result by using an ill-conceived theory, or a caricature of a theory.[3]

MEASUREMENT ERRORS

In Chapter 2 it was stated that one of the assumptions of regression analysis is that the independent variables are measured without error. Various types of errors are subsumed under the generic term *measurement errors*. Jencks and co-workers (1979, pp. 34–36) classify such errors into three broad categories: conceptual, consistent, and random (see also Cochran, 1968, pp. 637–639).

Conceptual errors are committed when a proxy is used instead of the variable of interest either because of lack of knowledge of how to measure the latter or because the measurement of the former is more convenient and/or less expensive. For example, sometimes a measure of vocabulary is used as a proxy for mental ability. It is evident that an inference about the effect of mental ability on the basis of a regression coefficient associated with a measure of vocabulary will be biased. The nature and magnitude of the bias is generally not discernible because it depends, among other things, on the relation between the proxy and the variable of interest, which is rarely known.

Consistent, or systematic, errors occur for a variety of reasons. Respondents may, for example, provide systematically erroneous information (e.g., about income, age, years of education). Reporting errors may be conscious or unconscious. Respondents are not the only source of systematic errors. Such errors may emanate from measuring instruments, research settings, interviewers, raters, and researchers, to name but a few. The presence of systematic errors introduces bias in the estimation of regression coefficients. The direction and magnitude of the bias cannot be determined without knowledge of the direction and magnitude of the errors—an elusive task in most instances.

[3]See the section entitled The Role of Theory, below.

Random, or nonsystematic, errors occur, among other things, as a result of temporary fluctuations in respondents, raters, interviewers, settings, and the like. Much of psychometric theory is concerned with the effects of such errors on the reliability of measurement instruments (see Guilford, 1954; Nunnally, 1978).

Most of the work on the effects of measurement errors on regression statistics was done with reference to random errors. Even in this area the work is limited to rudimentary, hence largely unrealistic, models. Yet what is known about the effects of measurement errors should be a serious cause of concern to researchers using multiple regression analysis. Unfortunately, most researchers do not seem to be bothered about measurement errors—either because they are unaware of their effects or because they do not know what to do about them. Jencks et al. (1972) characterized this general attitude, saying: "The most frequent approach to measurement error is indifference" (p. 330). It is to this indifference that much of the inconsistencies and untrustworthiness of findings in social science research may be attributed.

Following is a summary of what is known about the effects of measurement errors on regression statistics and some of the suggested remedies. You are encouraged to study the references cited below in order to gain a better understanding of this topic.

The effects of measurement errors in simple regression analysis were discussed in Chapter 2. Briefly, it was pointed out that measurement errors in the dependent variable are absorbed in the residual term and do not lead to bias in the estimation of the unstandardized regression coefficient (b). The standardized regression coefficient is attenuated by measurement errors in the dependent variable. It was also pointed out that measurement errors in the independent variable lead to a downward bias in the estimation of both the b and the β.

Turning now to multiple regression analysis, it will be noted that measurement errors in the dependent and/or the independent variables lead to a downward bias in the estimation of R^2. Cochran (1970), who discusses this point in detail, maintains that errors of measurement are largely responsible for the disappointingly low R^2 values that are obtained in much of the research in the social sciences. Commenting on studies in which complex human behavior was measured, Cochran (1970) says: "The data were obtained by questionnaires filled out in a hurry by apparently disinterested graduate students. The proposal to consign this material at once to the circular file (except that my current wastebasket is rectangular) has some appeal" (p. 33).

As is the case in simple regression analysis, errors in the dependent variable do not lead to bias in the estimation of the b's, but do lead to a downward bias in the estimation of the β's.

Unlike simple regression analysis, errors of measurement in the independent variables in a multiple regression analysis may lead to either an upward or a downward bias in the estimation of the regression coefficients. The effects of the errors are "complicated" (Cochran, 1968, p. 655).

In general, the lower the reliabilities of the measures or the higher the intercorrelation among the variables (see Multicollinearity below) the greater the distortions in the estimation of the regression coefficients that result from measurement errors. It should also be noted that even if some of the independent variables are measured without error, the estimation of their regression coefficients may not be bias free because of the relations of such variables with others that are measured with errors.

Because of the complicated effects of measurement errors it is possible, for example, that while $\beta_1 > \beta_2$, $\beta_1' < \beta_2'$, where β_1 and β_2 are the standardized regression coefficients that would be obtained if X_1 and X_2 are measured without error; β_1' and β_2' are the standardized coefficients obtained when errors are present in the measurement of X_1 and/or X_2. "Thus, interpretation of the relative sizes of different regression coefficients may be severely distorted by errors of measurement" (Cochran, 1968, p. 656). (See discussion below: Standardized or Unstandardized Coefficients?)

Measurement errors will also bias results of commonality analysis. For example, since the uniqueness of a variable is related, among other things, to the size of the β associated with it (see Chapter 7), it follows that a biased β will lead to a biased estimation of uniqueness. Estimation of commonality elements, too, will be biased as a result of measurement errors (see Cochran, 1970, p. 33, for some examples).

It is evident that the presence of measurement errors may be very damaging to results of multiple regression analysis, and that being indifferent to problems arising from the use of imperfect measures will certainly not make them go away. What, then, can be done about them? Various remedies and approaches have been suggested. When the reliabilities of the measures are relatively high and one is willing to make the rather restrictive assumption that the errors are random, it is possible to introduce conventional corrections for attenuation prior to the calculation of regression statistics (Lord & Novick, 1968; Nunnally, 1978). The use of corrections for attenuation, however, precludes tests of significance of regression coefficients in the usual way (Kenny, 1979, p. 83). Corrections for attenuation create other problems, particularly when there are high intercorrelations among the variables or when there is a fair amount of variability in the reliabilities of the measures being used (see Jencks et al., 1972, pp. 332–336; 1979, pp. 34–37).

Other approaches designed to detect and offset biasing effects of measurement errors are discussed and illustrated in the following references: Bibby (1977); Blalock, Wells, & Carter (1970); Duncan (1975, Chapter 9); Johnston (1972, pp. 278–281); Kenny (1979, Chapter 5); and Zeller & Carmines (1980). A structural equation model that can handle, among other things, measurement errors is presented later in this book (Chapter 16).

In conclusion, although various proposals to deal with measurement errors are important and useful, the goal of bridging the gap between theory and observed behavior by constructing highly valid and reliable measures deserves greater attention, sophistication, and expertise on the part of behavioral scientists.

MULTICOLLINEARITY

In preceding chapters it was shown several times that correlations among independent variables may lead to difficulties in the estimation of regression statistics. Problems emanating from intercorrelations among independent variables are generally discussed under the heading of multicollinearity. There is, however, no consensus about the meaning of this term. Some use it to refer to the existence of any correlations among the independent variables, whereas others reserve the term to describe a situation in which the independent variables are highly correlated, although there is, understandably, no agreement what "high" means. Still others speak of different degrees of multicollinearity.

One of the reasons for the different uses of the term *multicollinearity* is the failure to distinguish between its definition and its effects on the estimation of regression statistics. The least ambiguous definition of multicollinearity is that it refers to the absence of orthogonality in a set of independent variables (Farrar & Glauber, 1967, p. 100). Orthogonal means at right angles (90°). When two variables are orthogonal, they are independent of each other, and the correlation between them is zero. Multicollinearity is absent when a matrix of variables is orthogonal. Note that multicollinearity refers to the interrelations among the independent variables only.

Even though the presence and degree of multicollinearity is immediately apparent in the case of two independent variables (it is the correlation between them), the general approach to the detection of multicollinearity and some of its effects will be pursued first for this special case because of the ease with which it can be demonstrated and grasped. Examples with more than two independent variables are presented subsequently.

In Chapter 4 the use of matrix algebra for the calculation of regression statistics was presented and demonstrated. For the case of standardized variables (i.e., when correlations are used) the following formula (see (4.15) and the discussion associated with it) was presented:

$$\boldsymbol{\beta} = \mathbf{R}^{-1}\mathbf{r} \tag{8.8}$$

where $\boldsymbol{\beta}$ is a column vector of standardized coefficients; $\mathbf{R}$ is the correlation matrix of the independent variables; $\mathbf{r}$ is a column vector of correlations between each independent variable and the dependent variable. The key to the detection of multicollinearity and its effects of the estimation of regression statistics is in the inverse of the correlation matrix. In Chapter 4 the inversion of a 2×2 matrix was demonstrated several times (see also Appendix A). Briefly, given

$$\mathbf{A} = \begin{bmatrix} a & b \\ c & d \end{bmatrix}$$

then to invert **A,** find its determinant: $|\mathbf{A}| = ad - bc$; interchange the elements of the main diagonal (i.e., a with d); change the signs of b and c; and divide each of the elements by $|\mathbf{A}|$. The resulting matrix is the inverse of **A.** When the matrix is one of correlations, its main diagonal consists of 1's and its off-diagonal elements are correlation coefficients. For two independent variables,

$$\mathbf{R} = \begin{bmatrix} 1.00 & r_{12} \\ r_{21} & 1.00 \end{bmatrix}$$

$$|\mathbf{R}| = (1)(1) - (r_{12})(r_{21}) = 1 - r_{12}^2$$

and

$$\mathbf{R}^{-1} = \begin{bmatrix} \dfrac{1}{1 - r_{12}^2} & \dfrac{-r_{12}}{1 - r_{12}^2} \\ \\ \dfrac{-r_{21}}{1 - r_{12}^2} & \dfrac{1}{1 - r_{12}^2} \end{bmatrix}$$

Note that when $r_{12} = .00$, **R** is an identity matrix:

$$\mathbf{R} = \begin{bmatrix} 1.00 & 0 \\ 0 & 1.00 \end{bmatrix}$$

$|\mathbf{R}| = 1.00$, and $\mathbf{R}^{-1} = \mathbf{R}$. Applying (8.8) under such circumstances,

$$\boldsymbol{\beta} = \begin{bmatrix} 1.00 & 0 \\ 0 & 1.00 \end{bmatrix} \begin{bmatrix} r_{y1} \\ r_{y2} \end{bmatrix} = \begin{bmatrix} r_{y1} \\ r_{y1} \end{bmatrix}$$

When the matrix is orthogonal, each β is equal to the zero-order correlation of the variable with which it is associated and the dependent variable ($\beta_1 = r_{y1}$; $\beta_2 = r_{y2}$). When the determinant of a correlation matrix (of any size) is 1 it indicates that the matrix is orthogonal.

Consider what happens when $|r_{12}| > 0$. The determinant of **R** is a fraction that becomes increasingly smaller as the correlation between X_1 and X_2 increases. When r_{12} reaches its maximum (i.e., 1.00), $|\mathbf{R}| = .00$. Because it is necessary to divide each of the elements of **R** by its determinant in order to obtain the inverse of **R,** it is obvious that when the determinant is zero, **R** cannot be inverted. A matrix that cannot be inverted is said to be *singular*. Perfect collinearity results in a singular matrix. Under such circumstances, the regression coefficients are indeterminate.

In sum, then, when the matrix is orthogonal, its determinant, $|\mathbf{R}|$, is 1. When, on the other hand, there is perfect multicollinearity in **R,** $|\mathbf{R}| = 0$. The determinant of **R** may vary between 0 and 1. The closer it is to zero, the greater the degree of multicollinearity, though the gradient between the two limits is not well defined. Consequently, it is not possible to tell when the determinant is too small, except in extreme cases (see discussion of tests of significance, below).

A matrix is singular when it contains at least one linear dependency. A *linear dependency* means that one vector in the matrix may be derived on the basis of another vector, or on the basis of a linear combination of more than one of the other vectors in the matrix. Some examples of linear dependencies are: $X_2 = 3X_1$, that is, when each element in vector X_2 is three times its corresponding element in X_1; $X_1 = X_2 + X_3$; $X_3 = .5X_1 + 1.7X_2 - .3X_4$. Although linear dependencies do not generally occur in social science research, they may be introduced by an unwary researcher. For example, assume that one is using a test battery that consists of four subtests as part of the matrix of the independent variables. If, in addition to the scores on the subtests, their sum is used as a total score, a linear dependency is introduced, causing the matrix to be singular. Other examples of linear dependencies that may be introduced inadvertently by a researcher are: (1) when a categorical variable is coded for use in multiple regression analysis, and the number of coded vectors is equal to the number of categories (see Chapter 9); (2) when an ipsative measure (e.g., a rank-order scale) is used in multiple regression analysis (see Clemans, 1965).

When a matrix contains linear dependencies, information provided by some of the variables is completely redundant with the information available from other variables and hence useless for the purpose of regression analysis. In the case of two independent variables, the existence of a linear dependency is immediately evident when the correlation between them is perfect. Under such circumstances, either one of the variables, but not both, may be used in a regression analysis. When more than two independent variables are used, it is not possible to tell on the basis of the inspection of the zero-order correlations among them whether linear dependencies exist in the matrix. When the determinant of the matrix is zero, at least one linear dependency is indicated.

It was noted above that the closer the determinant is to zero, the higher the multicollinearity in the matrix—and the greater the redundancy of the information available. High multicollinearity leads to imprecise estimation of regression coefficients. Slight fluctuations in the correlations (e.g., due to sampling or random errors) in the presence of multicollinearity may lead to very large fluctuations in the estimation of regression coefficients (see demonstrations below).

High multicollinearity has extremely adverse effects on the standard errors of the regression coefficients, hence on tests of their statistical significance and their confidence intervals. This can be easily seen by inspecting the formula for the standard error of the regression coefficient. With two independent variables the standard error for b_1, for example, is (see Formula (3.25) and the discussion related to it):

$$s_{b_{y1.2}} = \sqrt{\frac{s^2_{y.12}}{\Sigma x_1^2 (1 - r_{12}^2)}} \tag{8.9}$$

Note that the denominator includes the correlation between the two independent variables (r_{12}). The larger r_{12}, other things equal, the larger the standard error of the b. When $r_{12} = 1.00$, the denominator is zero, and the standard error of b is indeterminate. As the t ratio for a given b is obtained by dividing the latter by its standard error (see Chapter 3), it follows that the t ratio will become increasingly smaller, and the confidence interval for the b increasingly wider, as the standard error of the b becomes increasingly larger.

The same consequences prevail for the case of k independent, where the standard error of b_1, for example, is:

$$s_{b_{y1.23\ldots k}} = \sqrt{\frac{s^2_{y.12\ldots k}}{\Sigma x_1^2 (1 - R^2_{1.23\ldots k})}} \tag{8.10}$$

Note that (8.9) is a special case of (8.10). In (8.10), $R^2_{1.23\ldots k}$ indicates the squared multiple correlation of X_1 when it is regressed on the remaining independent variables. The larger this R^2 the larger the standard error of the b, and hence the smaller its t ratio and the wider the confidence interval for the b. $R^2_{1.23...k} = 1.00$ indicates that X_1 is a linear dependency of some or all the X's. Under such circumstances the denominator of (8.10) is zero and the standard error indeterminate.

The ideas regarding the effect of multicollinearity on the standard errors of the regression coefficients are now demonstrated via matrix algebra. In Chapter 4 it was shown that when the square root of a diagonal element of the inverse of the matrix of the independent variables is multiplied by the standard error of estimate ($s_{y.12...k}$) one obtains the standard error of the b for the variable with which the given diagonal element is associated. This approach is now used with a 2×2 correlation matrix in order to relate it to the concept of multicollinearity. The inverse of a 2×2 **R** matrix was shown above as:

$$\mathbf{R}^{-1} = \begin{bmatrix} \dfrac{1}{1 - r^2_{12}} & \dfrac{-r_{12}}{1 - r^2_{12}} \\ \\ \dfrac{-r_{21}}{1 - r^2_{12}} & \dfrac{1}{1 - r^2_{12}} \end{bmatrix}$$

As noted above, the higher the correlation between r_{12}, the larger the diagonal elements of $\mathbf{R}^{-1}$, hence the larger the standard errors of the β's. It is instructive to note the relation between the diagonal elements of $\mathbf{R}^{-1}$ and the squared multiple correlation of each of the independent variables with the remaining ones.

$$R^2_i = 1 - \frac{1}{r^{ii}} \tag{8.11}$$

where R^2_i is the squared multiple correlation of X_i with the remaining independent variables; r^{ii} is the diagonal element of the inverse of the correlation matrix for variable i. From (8.11) it is evident that the larger r^{ii} the higher the squared multiple correlation of X_i with the remaining X's. When $r_{12} = .00$, $r^{ii} = 1.00$, $R^2_i = .00$. (Recall that in an orthogonal correlation matrix all the diagonal elements of $\mathbf{R}^{-1}$ are 1's.) Applying (8.11) to the 2×2 matrix given above,

$$R^2_1 = 1 - \frac{1}{\left(\dfrac{1}{1 - r^2_{12}}\right)} = 1 - (1 - r^2_{12}) = r^2_{12}$$

and similarly for R^2_2, because only two independent variables are being used.

An overall indication of the multicollinearity in **R**, as reflected by its determinant, is useful but it does not enable one to pinpoint the specific variables contributing to it. A zero, or very small, determinant may reflect widely different patterns of multicollinearity. Unless one can identify the specific variables that are highly multicollinear, one would not be in a position to attempt to explain the phenomena, or to take remedial steps when possible (see below). It is the diagonal elements of $\mathbf{R}^{-1}$ that provide the information about specific sources of high multicollinearity. When a diagonal element of $\mathbf{R}^{-1}$ is 1.00, it means that the independent variable associated with this element is not correlated with the remaining independent variables. A relatively large diagonal element of $\mathbf{R}^{-1}$ indicates that the variable associated with it is highly correlated with the remaining independent variables. Using (8.11) one can, of course, calculate the R^2 values of each independent variable with all the others.

Popular package computer programs for multiple regression analysis do not report $\mathbf{R}^{-1}$, thus precluding the application of (8.11) in order to pinpoint sources of high multicollinearity. Output reported routinely by such programs can, however, be used to calculate the R^2 values of each independent variable with all the others. A simple formula for doing this (see Lemieux, 1978, for its derivation) is:

$$R_i^2 = 1 - \frac{(1 - R^2)F_i}{(N - k - 1)\beta_i^2} \tag{8.12}$$

where R_i^2 is the squared multiple correlation of X_i with the other independent variables; R^2 is the squared multiple correlation of the dependent variable with the independent variables; F_i is the F ratio for testing the significance of the regression coefficient for X_i; β_i is the standardized regression coefficient for X_i; N is the sample size; k is the number of independent variables. When using a computer program that reports only the unstandardized regression coefficients (b's), one can easily convert them to β's by multiplying each b by the ratio of the standard deviation for the variable with which it is associated to the standard deviation of the dependent variable, as given in Formula (3.12). If the computer program reports t ratios, instead of F's, one can obtain the latter by squaring the former, since each of the F's has one degree of freedom for the numerator.

Numerical Examples[4]

The ideas presented in the preceding section, and some extensions of them, are now illustrated by several numerical illustrative examples. In Table 8.2, two correlation matrices, (a) and (b), are presented. In both matrices there are three independent variables whose correlations with the dependent vari-

Table 8.2 Two Correlation Matrices for Three Independent Variables and a Dependent Variable; $N = 100$

	1	*2*	*3*	*Y*		*1*	*2*	*3*	*Y*
1	1.00	.20	.20	.50	1	1.00	.20	.20	.50
2	.20	1.00	.10	.50	2	.20	1.00	.85	.50
3	.20	.10	1.00	.50	3	.20	.85	1.00	.50
Y	.50	.50	.50	1.00	*Y*	.50	.50	.50	1.00
		(a)					(b)		

[4]The numerical examples in this section are patterned after those in Gordon's (1968) excellent paper, which deserves careful study.

ables are identical (.50). The correlations between X_1 and X_2 and X_1 and X_3 are also identical in both matrices (.20). The only difference, then, between (a) and (b) is that in the former the correlation between X_2 and X_3 is low (.10) whereas in the latter it is high (.85).

The data were analyzed twice, once using the MATRIX procedure of SAS, and once using the REGRESSION program of SPSS. Excerpts from the output of either one or both programs will be presented as the topic discussed warrants. As control cards for the use of SPSS with a correlation matrix were given before (see Chapter 5), none are given here. For the first analysis with SAS the control cards are given along with commentaries. For subsequent analyses, only the pertinent results are reported.

SAS Control Cards

MATRIX is a very versatile and comprehensive procedure for the manipulation of matrices and the solution of complex problems with matrices. Although the example used here demonstrates the application of MATRIX to a multiple regression analysis, it should be noted that other types of analyses (e.g., multivariate analysis of variance, canonical correlation analysis) can be easily done with this procedure. Following is a listing of the control cards for matrix (a) of Table 8.2.

```
PROC MATRIX PRINT;
A = 1.0   .2   .2   .5/
     .2  1.0   .1   .5/
     .2   .1  1.0   .5/
     .5   .5   .5  1.0;
B = A (1 2 3, 1 2 3);
C = DET (B);
D = INV (B);
E = D * A (1 2 3, 4);
F = E' * A (1 2 3, 4);
TITLE TABLE 8.2 MATRIX (A)
```

Commentary

PROC MATRIX is the statement that is used to call for the MATRIX procedure of SAS. When PRINT is specified, the results of each matrix statement are printed (for other options, see SAS manual).

A = is used to set up the matrix input **A.** The end of each line of **A** is indicated by a slash (/) and the last line of **A** is indicated by a semicolon (;).

B = A (1 2 3, 1 2 3); defines a matrix **B** which is composed of the first three rows and the first three columns of **A.** For the present example, **B** is the correlation matrix of the independent variables.

C = DET (B); instructs the program to calculate the determinant of **B** ($|\mathbf{R}|$).

D = INV (B); instructs the program to calculate the inverse of **B** ($\mathbf{R}^{-1}$).

E = D * A (1 2 3, 4); In this statement, a column vector composed of the first three rows and the fourth column of **A** is defined. This, then, is a column vector of the correlations of the dependent variable with the independent variables. Multiplying **D,** which is $\mathbf{R}^{-1}$, by this column yields the standardized regression coefficients. In other words, this statement is equivalent to: $\boldsymbol{\beta} = \mathbf{R}^{-1}\,\mathbf{r}$ (see Formulas (4.15) and (8.8)).

F = E′ * A (1 2 3, 4); **E′** is the transpose of **E.** That is, **E′** is a row vector consisting of the standardized regression coefficients. When this row is multiplied by the column of the correlations of the dependent variable with the independent variables, A (1 2 3, 4), $R^2_{y.123}$ is obtained. In other words, $R^2 = \boldsymbol{\beta}'\mathbf{r}$ (see Formula (4.17)).

Output

DET = .918

Commentary

The determinant of the correlation matrix among the independent variables is close to 1, indicating that there is little multicollinearity among the variables. This is, of course, evident from the inspection of the matrix of the correlations. But with larger matrices, and with a more complex pattern of interrelations among the variables, inspection will not suffice.

Output

INV			
	1.07843	−.196078	−.196078
	−.196078	1.04575	−.0653595
	−.196078	−.0653595	1.04575

Commentary

This is the inverse of the correlation matrix of the independent variables ($\mathbf{R}^{-1}$). Note that the diagonal elements are close to 1. This is because of the low multicollinearity in the matrix. Recall that in an orthogonal matrix the diagonal elements are 1's. As was discussed earlier, see (8.11), the diagonal elements of the inverse can be used to calculate the squared multiple correlation of each independent variable with the other independent variables. For example,

$$R^2_{1.23} = 1 - \frac{1}{1.07843} = .07273$$

Similarly, for the other R^2 values.

Output

E′ = .343137 .392157 .392157

Commentary

E′ is the transpose of **E,** which is a column vector of β's. Recall that **E** was obtained by multiplying $\mathbf{R}^{-1}$ by **r** ($\mathbf{R}^{-1}\mathbf{r}$; see commentary under Control Cards, above).

Output

F = .563725

Commentary

F yields $R^2_{y.123} = .563725$. It was obtained by multiplying $\boldsymbol{\beta}'$ by $\mathbf{r}$ ($\boldsymbol{\beta}'\mathbf{r}$; see commentary under Control Cards, above). The three independent variables account for about 56% of the variance in Y.

It is possible, of course, to use the MATRIX procedure of SAS to calculate additional statistics (e.g., standard errors of β's, F ratios). Instead of doing this, results of analysis of the same data by SPSS are reported.

SPSS Analysis

Matrix (a) from Table 8.2 was analyzed by the REGRESSION program of SPSS. Following are excerpts of the output, along with commentaries.

Output

R SQUARE .56373

- - - - - - - - - - - - - -VARIABLES IN EQUATION- - - - - - - - - - - - -

VARIABLE	BETA	STD ERROR B	F
V1	.34314	.07001	24.025
V2	.39216	.06894	32.360
V3	.39216	.06894	32.360

Commentary

The results are, of course, the same as obtained above with SAS. They are reported here in order to demonstrate the application of Formula (8.12) for the calculation of the squared multiple correlation of each independent variable with the remaining ones, as a means of pinpointing sources of high multicollinearity. For example,

$$R^2_{1.23} = 1 - \frac{(1 - R^2_{y.123})F_1}{(N - k - 1)\beta_1^2} = 1 - \frac{(1 - .56373)(24.025)}{(100 - 3 - 1)(.34314)^2} = .07273$$

which is the same as the value obtained from the application of (8.11) to the output from SAS (see above).

Analysis of Matrix (b)

Matrix (b), Table 8.2, is identical to Matrix (a), except for the correlation between X_2 and X_3, which is .1 in (a) and .85 in (b). The purpose of changing this correlation is to note its effects on the regression statistics. Matrix (b) was analyzed by the MATRIX procedure of SAS in the same manner as was done above for Matrix (a). Following are the results, along with commentaries.

Output

DET = .2655

Commentary

Note that while the determinant for Matrix (a) was close to 1 (.918), the determinant for Matrix (b) is low, indicating a relatively high degree of multicollinearity. In the present case, the source of high multicollinearity is obvious. With larger and more complex matrices it will not necessarily be obvious.

Output

INV	1.0452	−.112994	−.112994
	−.112994	3.61582	−3.05085
	−.112994	−3.05085	3.61582

Commentary

Inspection of the diagonal elements of the inverse indicates the sources of the high multicollinearity. The diagonal element for X_1 is close to 1, indicating that there is a very low correlation between it and the remaining two independent variables. This, however, is not the case for the diagonal elements associated with X_2 and X_3. Applying (8.11),

$$R^2_{1.23} = 1 - \frac{1}{1.0452} = .04325$$

$$R^2_{2.13} = 1 - \frac{1}{3.61582} = .72344$$

Since the diagonal element for X_3 is the same as the one for X_2, then $R^2_{3.12} =$ .72344.

It is clear, then, that whereas X_1 provides information that is relatively unique to it, the information provided by X_2 and X_3 is highly redundant.

Output

$E' = \boldsymbol{\beta}' =$ .409605 .225989 .225989

Commentary

These are the standardized regression coefficients for X_1, X_2, and X_3, respectively. It is instructive to compare the β's obtained above for Matrix (a) with those obtained in the present analysis. The β's for X_2 and X_3 in the present analysis are about half the size of the β's for the same variables in Matrix (a). Since the two matrices are identical in all respects, except for r_{23}, the effect of the high intercorrelation between these two variables is clearly evident. Because a β is a partial regression coefficient, its magnitude is drastically reduced when a variable (or variables) highly correlated with it is partialed out.

In connection with the present discussion, it is very useful to introduce a distinction made by Gordon (1968) between *redundancy* (or *high correlation* between independent variables, no matter what the number of variables), and *repetitiveness* (or the *number* of redundant variables, regardless of the degree of redundancy among them). An example of repetitiveness would be the use of more than one measure of a variable (e.g., using two or more measures of intelligence). Gordon provides dramatic examples of the effect of repetitiveness, which leads to a reduction in the magnitude of the β's associated with the variables that comprise the repeated set. To clarify the point, consider an analysis in which intelligence is one of the independent variables, and that a single measure of this variable is being used. The β associated with intelligence will presumably reflect its effect on the dependent variable, while partialing out all the other independent variables. Assume now that the researcher considers intelligence as being the more important variable and therefore decides to obtain two measures of it, while obtaining single measures of the other independent variables. In a regression analysis with the two measures of intelligence, the β that was originally obtained for the single measure will split among the two measures, leading to a conclusion that intelligence is less effective than it appeared to have been when it was represented by a single measure. Using three measures for the same variable will split the β among the three of them. In sum, then, increasing repetitiveness leads to increasingly smaller β's. For the sake of illustration, assume that X_2 and X_3 of Matrix (b), Table 8.2, are measures of the same variable. Had Y been regressed on X_1 and X_2 only (or on X_1 and X_3 only), that is, had only one measure of the variable been used, $\beta_{y2.1}$ (or $\beta_{y3.1}$) would have been .41667. But when both measures are used, the β splits, resulting in $\beta = .22599$ for each of the measures (see above). Note also that, with the present sample size (100), $\beta_{y2.1}$ (or $\beta_{y3.1}$) would be declared statistically significant ($F = 27.714$; 1, 97), whereas the F ratio for $\beta_{y2.13}$ (or $\beta_{y3.12}$) is not statistically significant at the .05 level ($F = 2.382$; 1, 96. See SPSS output below.). Using one measure for the variable, then, it would have been concluded that it has a statistically significant effect on the dependent variable. But using two measures of the same variable would have led to the conclusion that neither has a statistically significant effect on the dependent variable (see discussion below).

Researchers frequently introduce multicollinearity by using multiple indicators for variables in which they have greater interest or which they consider more important from a theoretical point of view. This is not to say that multiple indicators are not useful or that they should be avoided. On the contrary, they are of utmost importance (see Chapter 16). When, however, multiple indicators are used in a regression analysis, they can play havoc with regression statistics. As noted above, the β that would have been obtained for an indicator of a variable had it been the only one used in the equation will split when several indicators of the variable are used, resulting in relatively small β's for each of them. Under such circumstances, a researcher using β's as indices of effects may have to conclude that what was initially considered a tangential variable, and therefore represented in the regression equation by a single indicator, is more important, or has a stronger effect, than a variable that was considered important and was therefore represented by several indicators.

SPSS Analysis

Following are some of the results obtained from the analysis of Matrix (b), Table 8.2, by SPSS.

Output

R SQUARE .43079

- - - - - - - - - - - - - -VARIABLES IN EQUATION- - - - - - - - - - - - -

VARIABLE	BETA	STD ERROR B	F
V1	.40960	.07872	27.073
V2	.22599	.14642	2.382
V3	.22599	.14642	2.382

Commentary

R^2 in this analysis is considerably smaller than R^2 obtained in the analysis of Matrix (a) (i.e., .56373) because of the redundancy between X_2 and X_3 in Matrix (b).

The comments made above about the magnitudes of the β's and the fact that those of X_2 and X_3 are not statistically significant (at the .05 level) are now elaborated upon. It was noted several times before that the square root of the diagonal element of $\mathbf{R}^{-1}$ multiplied by the standard error of estimate equals the standard error of the regression coefficient for the variable associated with the diagonal element. It was also noted that the higher the multicollinearity the larger the diagonal elements of $\mathbf{R}^{-1}$ for the variables that are highly multicollinear. The diagonal element of $\mathbf{R}^{-1}$ for X_1 was found above to be equal to 1.0452, whereas those for X_2 and X_3 are 3.61582. This discrepancy between the diagonal elements results in the standard error for β_1 (.07872) to be about half the size of the standard error for β_2, or that of β_3 (i.e., .14642).

In sum, the high correlation between X_2 and X_3 leads not only to a reduction in the magnitudes of their β's, but also to an increase in their standard errors. Because of such effects, the presence of high multicollinearity may lead to seemingly puzzling results, as when the squared multiple correlation of the dependent variable with a set of independent variables is statistically significant but *none* of the regression coefficients is statistically significant. While some people view such results as contradictory, there is nothing contradictory about them. Each of the tests is addressed to a different model, and is designed to answer a different question. The test of R^2 refers to the question of whether one or more of the regression coefficients are significantly different from zero against the hypothesis that all of them are equal to zero. The test of a single regression coefficient, on the other hand, refers to the question of whether it differs from zero, while partialing out all the other variables.[5]

Finally, the output from SPSS is used to demonstrate again the application of Formula (8.12) for the purpose of detecting sources of high multicollinearity in Matrix (b). For example,

[5]See the discussion of this point in Chapter 3.

$$R^2_{2.13} = 1 - \frac{(1 - R^2_{y.123})F_2}{(N - k - 1)\beta_2^2} = 1 - \frac{(1 - .43079)(2.382)}{(100 - 3 - 1)(.22599)^2} = .72346$$

The same value (within rounding errors) was obtained above when Formula (8.11) was applied to the diagonal element of $\mathbf{R}^{-1}$.

We turn now to two other numerical examples that demonstrate another aspect of the deleterious effects of multicollinearity.

Examples in Which Correlations with the Dependent Variable Differ

In the preceding two examples the three independent variables had identical correlations with the dependent variable (.50). The examples in this section are designed to demonstrate the effects of multicollinearity when there are slight differences in the correlations between the independent and dependent variables. The data reported in Table 8.3 will be used for this purpose. Note that the correlations among the independent variables in Matrices (a) and (b) of Table 8.3 are identical with those of Matrices (a) and (b), respectively, of Table 8.2. Therefore, no attention will be directed here to their determinants and inverses, inasmuch as this was done in great detail in the preceding section. The focus here is on the correlations of the independent variables with the dependent variable, specifically on the difference between r_{y2} (.50) and r_{y3} (.52) in both matrices. Following are the results of the analyses of the two matrices of Table 8.3 as obtained from SPSS.

Output

Matrix (a)

R SQUARE .57983

VARIABLES IN EQUATION

VARIABLE	BETA	STD ERROR	F
V1	.33922	.06870	24.378
V2	.39085	.06765	33.376
V3	.41307	.06765	37.279

Matrix (b)

R SQUARE .44128

VARIABLES IN EQUATION

VARIABLE	BETA	STD ERROR	F
V1	.40734	.07799	27.277
V2	.16497	.14507	1.293
V3	.29831	.14507	4.229

Commentary

Because of the high correlation between X_2 and X_3 in Matrix (b), $R^2_{y.123}$ is considerably smaller for this matrix than $R^2_{y.123}$ for Matrix (a), although the correlations of the independent variables with Y are identical in both matrices. This is not surprising since there is a greater redundancy of information in Matrix (b) than in Matrix (a).

Table 8.3 Two Correlation Matrices for Three Independent Variables and a Dependent Variable; $N = 100$

	1	*2*	*3*	*Y*		*1*	*2*	*3*	*Y*
1	1.00	.20	.20	.50	1	1.00	.20	.20	.50
2	.20	1.00	.10	.50	2	.20	1.00	.85	.50
3	.20	.10	1.00	.52	3	.20	.85	1.00	.52
Y	.50	.50	.52	1.00	*Y*	.50	.50	.52	1.00
		(a)					(b)		

The results relating to the regression coefficients of X_2 and X_3 in the two matrices are not consistent with commonsense expectations. After all, the difference between r_{y2} and r_{y3} is slight (.02) and could certainly be obtained as a result of sampling or measurement errors. In Matrix (a), where the multicollinearity is low, β_3 is slightly greater than β_2. But in Matrix (b) the high multicollinearity tips the scales in favor of the variable that has the slight edge, and as a result of this β_3 is about twice the size of β_2. Moreover, β_3 is statistically significant (at the .05 level), whereas β_2 is not. One would therefore have to arrive at the paradoxical conclusion that although X_2 and X_3 are highly correlated (.85), and may even be measures of the same variable, X_3 has a significant effect on Y but X_2 does not. Even if β_2 were statistically significant, the difference in the magnitudes of β_2 and β_3 would have to be interpreted as the latter having about twice the effect that the former has (see below for an example from the IEA studies).

Inspection of the standard errors of the β's in the two matrices (see Output, above) indicates clearly the effect of high multicollinearity on the precision with which they are estimated. In Matrix (a) the standard errors of the three β's are almost identical. But in Matrix (b) the standard errors for β_2 and β_3 (the variables that are highly correlated) are about twice the size of the standard error of β_1.

In sum, high multicollinearity leads to imprecise, and sometimes surprising, estimates of regression statistics. For example, high multicollinearity may lead to counterintuitive results: a regression coefficient may have a negative sign when the variable with which it is associated is expected to have a positive effect (see Philadelphia School District Studies, below).

Further Considerations and Remedies

Earlier, it was noted that there is no agreement about what constitutes high multicollinearity. Some authors (Farrar & Glauber, 1967; Rockwell, 1975) propose the testing of the departure of a correlation matrix from singularity as a means of determining whether or not multicollinearity exists in the matrix. Basically, a chi-squared test is used to determine whether the determinant of the correlation matrix differs significantly from zero. Failure to reject the null hypothesis is taken as an indication that the matrix is singular. This approach has serious drawbacks, the most important being the validity of the test itself. Since multicollinearity is a characteristic of the sample, not of the population, the application of tests of significance under such circumstances is not appropriate (Kmenta, 1971, p. 380; Kumer, 1975; Schmidt & Muller, 1978, pp. 272–274). Even when used "heuristically" (Haitovsky, 1969), it is necessary to bear in mind that the χ^2 test is affected, among other things, by the sample size. Therefore, given a sufficiently large sample, the null hypothesis may be rejected even in the presence of high multicollinearity. In sum, judgment about the severity of multicollinearity in a correlation matrix remains just that: a judgment.

Methods other than those presented in this chapter have been proposed for the purpose of determining the degree of multicollinearity and the detection of its sources. Probably the most useful approach is via the study of the eigenvalues and eigenvectors of the correlation matrix (see Chatterjee & Price, 1977, Chapter 7; Gunst & Mason, 1977).

Regardless of what method is being used, the crucial question is: Having detected high multicollinearity, what can be done about it? In other words: Are there remedies? Before answering this question, it will be pointed out that high multicollinearity does not pose difficulties when the researcher's sole purpose is the determination and interpretation of R^2. This, however, is a very modest research goal in that it does not shed any light on the process by which the independent variables affect the dependent variable.

It should be clear by now that high multicollinearity may lead not only to serious distortions in the estimations of the magnitudes of regression coefficients but also to reversals in their signs. Therefore, the presence of high multicollinearity poses serious threats to the interpretation of regression coefficients as indices of effects. What, then, can be done? A solution that probably comes first to mind is to delete variables that have been identified as causes of high multicollinearity. It is, however, necessary to recognize that when attempts are being made to detect multicollinearity it is assumed that the model is correctly specified. Consequently, deletion of variables to reduce the degree of multicollinearity may lead to specification errors (Chatterjee & Price, 1977).

One of the proposed remedies is the collection of additional data in the hope that this may ameliorate the condition of high multicollinearity. Another set of remedies relates to the grouping of variables either in blocks on the basis of a priori judgments or by the use of such methods as principal components analysis and factor analysis (Chatterjee & Price, 1977, Chapter 7; Gorsuch, 1974; Harman, 1976; Mulaik, 1972). These approaches are not free of problems. When blocks of variables are used in a regression analysis (e.g., in the Coleman Report and the IEA studies), it is not possible to obtain a regression coefficient for a block unless one has first arrived at combinations of variables so that each block is represented by a single vector. Coleman (1975a, 1976) has proposed a method of arriving at a summary coefficient for each block of variables used in the regression analysis (see also Igra, 1979). Referring as they do to blocks of variables, such summary statistics are of dubious value when one wishes to make statements about the effects of a variable, not to mention policy implications. What was said above applies also to situations in which the correlation matrix is orthogonalized by subjecting it, for example, to a principal components analysis. The regression coefficients based on the orthogonalized matrix may not lend themselves to meaningful interpretations as indices of effects because the components with which they are associated may lack substantive meaning.

Another set of proposals for dealing with high multicollinearity is to abandon Ordinary Least-Squares analysis, and use instead other methods of estimation. One such method that has been gaining in popularity is Ridge Regression (see Chatterjee & Price, 1977, Chapter 8; Horel & Kennard, 1970a, 1970b; Marquardt & Snee, 1975; Mason & Brown, 1975; Price, 1977; Schmidt & Muller, 1978. For a recent critique of ridge regression, see Rozeboom, 1979).

In conclusion, it is important to note that none of the proposed methods of dealing with high multicollinearity constitutes a cure. High multicollinearity is symptomatic of insufficient, or deficient, information, which no amount of data manipulation can rectify. As thorough an understanding as is possible of the causes of multicollinearity in a given set of data is the best guide for the action to be taken. Farrar and Glauber (1967) conclude their discussion of multicollinearity saying: "It would be pleasant to conclude on a note of triumph that the problem has been solved. . . . Such a feeling, clearly would be misleading. Diagnosis, although a necessary first step, does not insure cure. No miraculous 'instant orthogonalization' can be offered" (p. 107). These sentiments are probably as apt today as they were at the time when they were uttered.

STANDARDIZED OR UNSTANDARDIZED COEFFICIENTS?

The distinction between standardized (β) and unstandardized (b) regression coefficients was introduced and discussed briefly in Chapter 3. The interpretation of β is analogous to the interpretation of b, except that β is interpreted as indicating the expected change in the dependent variable, expressed in standard scores, associated with a one standard deviation change in an independent variable, while holding the remaining variables constant. Unlike the b's, β's are scale-free indices and therefore can be compared across different variables. It is this property of the β's that appeals to a great many researchers, who use their relative magnitudes as an indication of the relative importance of the variables with which they are associated.

It is important, however, to bear in mind that the magnitude of a β reflects not only the presumed effect of the variable with which it is associated but also the variances and the covariances of the variables included in the model, as well as the variance of the variables not included in the model and subsumed under the error term. Because some, or all, of these factors may vary from one population to another, it is possible for a given variable to have a relatively large β in one sample and be declared important and a relatively small β in another sample and be declared unimportant or less important. In short, β is sample-specific and can therefore not be used for the purpose of generalizations across settings and populations.

The unstandardized coefficient, on the other hand, remains fairly stable despite differences in the variances and the covariances of the variables in different settings or populations. Examples of this property of the b were shown early in the book in connection with the discussion of simple linear regression.

In Chapter 2, Table 2.3, it was shown that $b_{yx} = .75$ for four sets of fictitious data, but that because of differences in the variances of X, Y, or both, in these data sets, r_{yx} varied from a low of .24 to a high of .73. It was also shown (see Chapter 3, Equation (3.13)) that $\beta = r$ when one independent variable is being used. Interpreting β as an index of the effect of X on Y, one would reach the conclusion that it varies greatly in the four data sets of Table 2.3. Interpreting b as an index of the effect of X on Y, on the other hand, the conclusion would be that the effect is identical in these four data sets.

The same phenomenon, which may occur in situations when more than one independent variable is used, is demonstrated now for two sets of illustrative data reported in Table 8.4. Using methods presented in Chapter 3 or 4, or using a computer program, regress Y on X_1 and X_2 for both sets of data of Table 8.4. The regression equation for raw scores in both data sets is

$$Y' = 10 + 1.0X_1 + .8X_2$$

The regression equations in standard score form are

$$z'_y = .6z_1 + .4z_2 \qquad \text{for set (a)}$$

$$z'_y = .5z_1 + .25z_2 \qquad \text{for set (b)}$$

The relation between β and b was shown earlier (see Chapter 3, Equation (3.16)) as being

$$\beta_j = b_j\left(\frac{s_j}{s_y}\right) \tag{8.13}$$

where β_j = standardized regression coefficient associated with variable j; b_j = unstandardized regression coefficient associated with variable j; s_j and s_y = the standard deviations of j and the dependent variable, Y, respectively. From (8.13) it is evident that the magnitude of β is affected by the ratio of the standard deviation with which it is associated to the standard deviation of the dependent variable. For data set (a) in Table 8.4,

$$\beta_1 = 1.0\left(\frac{12}{20}\right) = .6$$

Table 8.4 Two Sets of Illustrative Data with Two Independent Variables in Each

	1	2	Y		*1*	2	Y
1	1.00	.50	.80	1	1.00	.40	.60
2	.50	1.00	.70	2	.40	1.00	.45
Y	.80	.70	1.00	Y	.60	.45	1.00
s:	12	10	20	*s:*	8	5	16
M:	50	50	100	*M:*	50	50	100
	(a)				(b)		

$$\beta_2 = .8\left(\frac{10}{20}\right) = .4$$

and for data set (b),

$$\beta_1 = 1.0\left(\frac{8}{16}\right) = .5$$

$$\beta_2 = .8\left(\frac{5}{16}\right) = .25$$

Assume that the two data sets of Table 8.4 were obtained in the same experimental setup, except that in (a) the researcher has used values of X_1 and X_2 which were more variable than those used in (b). Interpreting the unstandardized regression coefficients as indices of the effects of the X's on Y, the conclusion would be that they are identical in both data sets. The conclusion that the X's have stronger effects in (a) than in (b) would be reached if one were to interpret the β's as indices of their effects.

The same reasoning applies also when it is assumed that the data of Table 8.4 were obtained in nonexperimental research.[6] For example, data set (a) may have been obtained from a sample of males, or a sample of whites, and data set (b) may have been obtained from a sample of females, or blacks. If the variances in one group differ from those of the other group, the corresponding b's in the two groups may be identical, or very similar to each other, whereas the differences between the β's across groups may be considerable. To repeat: assuming that the model is valid, one would reach different conclusions about the effects of X_1 and X_2, depending on whether the b's or the β's are interpreted as the indices of their effects. Smith (1972), who reanalyzed the Coleman Report data, offers numerous examples in which comparisons based on β's or b's for different groups (e.g., blacks and whites, different grade levels, different regions of the country) led to contradictory conclusions about the relative importance of the same variables.

Because of the relative stability of the b's in different populations, most authors prefer them over the β's as indices of the effects of the variables with which they are associated (e.g., Blalock, 1964, 1968; Kim & Mueller, 1976; Schoenberg, 1972; Tukey, 1954; Turner & Stevens, 1959; Wright, 1976). For discussions of this issue in the context of research on educational effects, see Bowles and Levin (1968a), Cain and Watts (1968, 1970), Hanushek and Kain (1972), Linn, Werts, and Tucker (1971), Smith (1972), and Werts and Watley (1968). The common theme in these papers is that the unstandardized coefficients come closest to statements of scientific laws. For a dissenting view, see Hargens (1976), who argues that the choice between b and β should be made on the basis of theoretical considerations that relate to the scale representation of the variable. Thus, Hargens maintains that when the theoretical model refers to one's standing on a variable not in an absolute sense but relative to others in the group to which one belongs, standardized coefficients are the appropriate indices of the effects of the variables in the model.

[6]A more tenable assumption as $r_{12} \neq .00$—a situation that is less likely to occur in an experiment that has been appropriately designed and executed.

Most authors, however, recommend that β's be used when it is desired to compare the effects of different variables within *a single population,* but that b's be used when it is desired to compare the effects of given variables *across populations.*[7] Whatever one's choice for the purpose of interpretation, it is strongly recommended that both b's and β's be reported or that the standard deviations of all the variables be reported so that a reader may be in a position to derive one set of coefficients from the other. Needless to say, the information provided by the standard deviations is important in and of itself and should therefore always be part of the report of a research study. It is unfortunate that current practices are frequently limited to the reporting of correlation matrices, thereby not only precluding the possibility of calculating the unstandardized coefficients but also omitting important information about the sample, or samples, under study.

In addition to their relative stability, unstandardized coefficients are recommended on the grounds that, unlike the β's, they are directly translatable into guides for policy decisions. It should be noted, however, that the interpretation of b's is not free of problems. In the first place, their magnitudes depend on the units used in the measurement of the given variables. Changing units from dollars to cents, say, will result in a change in the coefficient associated with the variable. Consequently, b's in a given equation cannot be compared for the purpose of assessing the relative importance of the variables with which they are associated. Second, many of the measures used in social research are not on an interval level. Statements about a unit change at different points of such scales are, to say the least, questionable. A corollary of the preceding is that the meaning of a unit change in many of the scales used in the social sciences is substantively unknown or ambiguous. What, for example, is the substantive meaning of a unit change on a specific measure of teacher attitudes or warmth? Or what is the substantive meaning of a unit change on a specific scale measuring student locus of control or educational aspirations? Third, when the reliabilities of the measures of independent variables differ across samples, comparisons of the b's associated with such variables may lead to erroneous conclusions.

The foregoing discussion and those of the preceding sections have emphasized problems and potential pitfalls related to the interpretation of regression coefficients as indices of the effects of the variables with which they are

[7]The method for comparing b's across different samples is presented in detail in Chapters 12 and 13. In the present context it will only be noted that one frequently encounters analyses in which data from two or more than two groups were pooled without determining first whether the pooling was warranted. For example, data from males and females are analyzed together without determining first whether the regression equations in the two groups are similar to each other. Sometimes the analysis of pooled data includes one or more than one coded vectors to represent group membership. As is demonstrated in Chapters 12 and 13, when data from two, or more than two, groups are used in a single regression analysis in which no coded vectors are included to represent group membership, it is assumed that the regression equations (intercepts as well as regression coefficients) are not different from each other in the groups under study. When coded vectors representing group membership are included in such analyses it is assumed that the intercepts of the regression equations for the different groups differ from each other but that the regression coefficients do not differ across groups. Obviously, neither the question about the equality of intercepts nor that about the equality of regression coefficients should be relegated to assumptions. Both require to be tested before one may decide whether or not the data from different groups may be pooled.

associated. It is hoped that these discussions will serve to alert the researcher to the need for constant vigilance, for being ever mindful of the theory that generated the research, of the research design, of the psychometric properties of the measures being used, and of the principles and properties of multiple regression analysis.

It was said several times earlier that the regression equation reflects the researcher's theoretical model of the process by which the independent variables affect the dependent variable. It will be instructive to demonstrate the pivotal role of theory in the context of attempts to determine the effects of independent variables on the basis of the β's associated with them. This will be done by using a miniature example, to which we now turn.

THE ROLE OF THEORY

In Chapter 7 a simple example was presented in which attempts were made to explain Grade-Point Average (GPA) by resorting to the following variables: Socioeconomic Status (SES), Intelligence (IQ), and the need for Achievement (n Ach). For the sake of illustration, the two alternative models depicted in Figure 8.1 will be considered here. In model (a) the three independent variables are treated as exogenous variables (see Chapters 7 and 15 for definitions of exogenous and endogenous variables). This means that no theory exists, or that none is advanced, about the relations among the independent variables. The equation (in standard scores) that reflects this model is:

$$z_y = \beta_{y1}z_1 + \beta_{y2}z_2 + \beta_{y3}z_3 + e_y$$

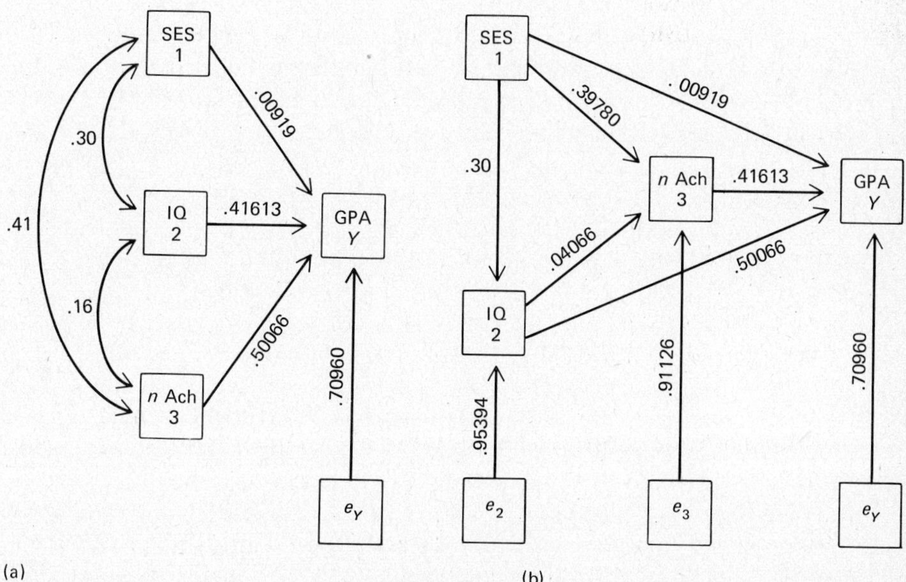

Figure 8.1

where the subscripts refer to the variable numbers given in Figure 8.1. This type of model is the most prevalent in the application of multiple regression analysis in the social sciences either because a theory of the causal relations among the independent variables is not formulated or because it is not recognized that the regression equation reflects a specific theoretical model. Be that as it may, when a single regression equation is used to study the effects of a set of independent variables on a dependent variable, a model such as (a) of Figure 8.1 is used either by design or by default.

Turning now to model (b) of Figure 8.1 it will be noted that only SES (variable No. 1) is treated as an exogenous variable, whereas the remaining variables are treated as endogenous variables. The equations that reflect this model are:

$$z_1 = e_1$$

$$z_2 = \beta_{21}z_1 + e_2$$

$$z_3 = \beta_{31}z_1 + \beta_{32}z_2 + e_3$$

$$z_y = \beta_{y1}z_1 + \beta_{y2}z_2 + \beta_{y2}z_3 + e_y$$

Note that the last equation is the same as the single equation given above for model (a). The difference, then, between the two models is that in model (a) the relations among SES, IQ, and *n* Ach (variables 1, 2, and 3) are left unanalyzed, whereas model (b) specifies the causes for the relations among these variables. For example, in model (a) it is noted that SES is correlated with *n* Ach, but no attempt is made to determine the cause of this relation. In model (b), on the other hand, it is hypothesized that the correlation between SES and *n* Ach is due to: (1) the direct effect of the former on the latter, as indicated by SES → *n* Ach; and (2) the indirect effect of the former on the latter, as indicated by SES → IQ → *n* Ach.

The implications of the two models for the study of effects of independent variables on a dependent variable will be shown by using the correlation matrix reported in Table 8.5 (this matrix was introduced in Chapter 7 as Table 7.1). For illustrative purposes, the effect of SES on GPA in the two models will be scrutinized.

The effects of SES, IQ, and *n* Ach on GPA for model (a) can be calculated by regressing the latter on the former variables. Without showing the calculations (you may wish to do them as an exercise) it will be noted that the regression equation is:

$$z'_y = .00919z_1 + .50066z_2 + .41613z_3$$

Because the effects are expressed as standardized coefficients (β's), one would have to conclude that the effect of SES on GPA (i.e., .00919) is virtually zero. In other words, it would be concluded that SES has no meaningful effect on GPA.

Turning to model (b), however, it will be noted that according to this model SES affects GPA indirectly via the following paths:(1) SES → *n* Ach → GPA; (2) SES → IQ → GPA; and (3) SES → IQ → *n* Ach → GPA. It can be shown

Table 8.5 Correlation Matrix for Three Independent Variables and a Dependent Variable

	1 *SES*	*2* *IQ*	*3* *n Ach*	*Y* *GPA*
1	1.00	.30	.41	.33
2	.30	1.00	.16	.57
3	.41	.16	1.00	.50
Y	.33	.57	.50	1.00

that, given certain assumptions, the effects for model (b) can be calculated by regressing: (1) IQ on SES; (2) *n* Ach on SES and IQ; and (3) GPA on SES, IQ, and *n* Ach.[8] The three equations that are thus obtained for the data of Table 8.5 are:

$$z_2' = .30z_1$$

$$z_3' = .39780z_1 + .04066z_2$$

$$z_y = .00919z_1 + .50066z_2 + .41613z_3$$

In Chapter 7 the concepts of direct, indirect, and total effects of a variable were introduced (see also Chapter 15). In connection with the results obtained above for model (b) it will be noted that the direct effect of SES on GPA is .00919, which is the same as the effect of SES on GPA obtained in model (a). But, as was noted above, in model (b) SES is said to have indirect effects on GPA. It can be shown (this is done in Chapter 15) that the sum of the indirect effects of SES on GPA is equal to .32081. Since the total effect of a variable is equal to the sum of its direct effect and its indirect effects (see Chapters 7 and 15), it follows that the total effect of SES on GPA in model (b) is .33 (i.e., .00919 + .32081).

In view of the foregoing analyses it is clear that radically different conclusions would be reached about the effect of SES on GPA, depending on whether model (a) or model (b) is used. Specifically, if model (a) is used, the conclusion is that SES has practically no effect on GPA. If, on the other hand, model (b) is used, the conclusion is that whereas SES has practically no direct effect on GPA, it has meaningful indirect effects whose sum is equal to .32081.

The choice between models (a) and (b) is, needless to say, not an arbitrary one. On the contrary, it is predicated on one's theoretical formulations. As was noted earlier, in model (a) the researcher is unwilling, or unable, to make statements about the causes of the relations among SES, IQ, and *n* Ach (they are treated as exogenous variables). In model (b), on the other hand, a pattern of causation among these variables is specified, thereby enabling one to study indirect effects in addition to direct effects.

In conclusion, the sole purpose of the above demonstration was to show that different theoretical models dictate different approaches to the analysis, and

[8]Methods for the analysis of causal models are presented in Chapter 15, where the models discussed here are reanalyzed.

may lead to different conclusions about the effects of the independent variables. The analysis of causal models is treated in detail in Chapters 15 and 16.

RESEARCH APPLICATIONS

In this section, selected examples from research applications are presented. As in earlier chapters, the purpose is not to provide summaries of the studies but rather to use segments of their analyses in order to illustrate or highlight some of the major issues discussed throughout this chapter. You are therefore cautioned, again, not to pass judgment about any of the studies solely on the basis of the present discussions. There is no substitute for reading the original reports, which you are strongly urged to do.

International Evaluation of Educational Achievement (IEA)

This set of cross-national studies was described in some detail in Chapter 7, where it was noted that the primary analytic approach used in them was variance partitioning. In some of the studies, regression equations were also used for explanatory purposes. Before dealing with a specific example, several general comments about the use and interpretation of regression equations in the IEA studies are in order. Overall, these comments apply to all the studies in which regression coefficients were interpreted as indices of effects. But because the studies vary in their reliance on such interpretations, the relevance of the general comments varies depending upon the specific study to which one may wish to apply them.

The most important point, from which several others follow, is that in order to interpret the regression coefficients validly as indices of effects, one must have reasonable assurances that the regression equation validly reflects the process by which the independent variables affect the dependent variable. In other words, it is necessary to assume that there are no specification errors, or at least that they are minimal (see discussion earlier in this chapter). Peaker (1975), who was largely responsible for the methodology used in the IEA studies, aptly states: "Underlying any interpretation is the general proviso—'*If* this is how the thing works *these* equations are the most relevant. But if not, not' " (p. 29). Do, then, the regression equations used in the IEA studies reflect "how the thing works"? Regrettably, the answer is no! Even the authors of the IEA studies acknowledge that their models are deficient not only regarding omitted variables, possible nonlinearities, and the like, but also because of the questionable status of variables included in the models (see, for example, the discussion of the status of Kindred Variables in Chapter 7). The editors of a symposium on the IEA studies (Purves & Levine, 1975) state that there was agreement among the participants, some of whom were authors of IEA studies, that multiple regression analysis "would not suffice" (p. ix) to deal with the complexity of the relations among the variables under study.

Even if one were to overlook the above reservations, it must be noted that the routine use of stepwise regression analysis in the IEA studies renders their results useless, or at least questionable, for the purpose of explanation (see Chapter 6 for a discussion of this point). This may explain, in part, some of the puzzling, inconsistent, and contradictory results obtained in the various studies, of which the following are but a few examples.

> In four countries the time spent in hours per week on Science homework was positively related to the level of achievement in Science. . . . However, in three other countries . . . a negative relationship was noted. The nature of this relationship is indicated by the signs of the regression coefficients. (Comber & Keeves, 1973, p. 231)

> *Teacher's University Training in French.* Seven of the *t*-values reach the critical level of significance, some favoring larger amounts of training and other lesser amounts.
> *Teacher's Time in Marking Student Papers.* The results for this variable are highly inconsistent, with 5 strong positive values, and 7 strong negative values, the remaining 10 being nonsignificant. (Carroll, 1975, pp. 217–218)

> Students in schools where the civics teachers were specialized generally did better in three countries, but worse in one. Students who reported stress on facts in Civic Education classes were generally less successful in Italy, New Zealand and Ireland, but in Finland they did better than other students. (Torney, Oppenheim, & Farnen, 1975, p. 147)

In their discussions of the blocks of variables the authors of the IEA studies have put forward a multistage causal model, which they have used as the rationale for incremental partitioning of variance (see Chapter 7). Assuming that the multistage model is valid (see, however, Chapter 7 for a critique), one would have to question the usefulness of regression coefficients as indices of effects when these were arrived at on the basis of an analysis in which the dependent variable was regressed on all the independent variables simultaneously. It was shown in the preceding section that in such an analysis the regression coefficients indicate the direct effects only. Consequently, conclusions about the importance of variables on the basis of direct effects only overlook the possibility that their effects may be mostly, or solely, indirect.

Two final general comments will be made regarding the use of regression equations in the IEA studies. First, standardized regression coefficients were compared across samples and countries for the purpose of determining the relative importance of the variables associated with them (for a discussion of potential problems with such an approach, see earlier sections of this chapter). Second, while the authors of some of the studies (e.g., Carroll, 1975, p. 213; Comber & Keeves, 1973, pp. 291–292) report of considerable differences between boys and girls on various variables, they have used only a coded vector to represent sex, thereby assuming that the difference between boys and girls is limited to the intercepts of the regression equations (see Footnote 7).

It will be instructive now to turn to a more detailed analysis of a specific example because it serves to illustrate dramatically some important issues discussed earlier in this chapter. This example, which is taken from the *Teaching of French as a Foreign Language in Eight Countries* (Carroll, 1975), was introduced and discussed in Chapter 6 in connection with stepwise regression analysis (see Tables 6.2 and 6.3 and the discussion related to them). For convenience, Table 6.2 is repeated here as Table 8.6. Briefly, a Reading test and a Listening test in French (variables 8 and 9 of Table 8.6) were regressed in turn on the first seven variables listed in Table 8.6. The sole purpose here is to illustrate the effects of high multicollinearity and small discrepancies between zero-order correlations of independent variables with the dependent variables on the standardized coefficients. Consequently, the focus is on what happens to the β's associated with variables 6 and 7. Although inspection of the zero-order correlation between these two variables (.762) is sufficient to alert one to a source of trouble, it is instructive to calculate the determinant and the inverse of the correlation matrix of the independent variables in order to illustrate some of the points discussed earlier in the chapter. The results reported here were obtained from the MATRIX procedure of SAS (examples of control cards for this program are given earlier in this chapter).

The determinant of the correlation matrix of the independent variables is .274691. Recall that the higher the multicollinearity, the closer the determinant is to zero. It was shown earlier that it is possible to pinpoint sources of high multicollinearity by studying the diagonal elements of the inverse of the correlation matrix of the independent variables. Instead of reporting the inverse for the data of Table 8.6, it will be pointed out that the diagonal elements associated with the first five variables are close to 1.00, indicating that each of them is not highly correlated with the remaining variables. The diagonal elements for variables 6 and 7, on the other hand, are 2.47818 and 2.47723, respectively.

It was shown earlier in Formula (8.11) how one can use a diagonal element of the inverse in order to calculate the squared multiple correlation between the variable with which the element is associated and the remaining variables. Apply (8.11) to the diagonal elements associated with variables 6 and 7:

$$R^2_{6.123457} = 1 - \frac{1}{2.47818} = .596$$

$$R^2_{7.123456} = 1 - \frac{1}{2.47723} = .596$$

In the present case both R^2 values are the same because variables 6 and 7 have similar correlations with the remaining variables. Moreover, except for the high correlation between themselves, variables 6 and 7 have low correlations with the other independent variables. Hence, the relatively high values of R^2 reported above are primarily a function of the correlation between variables 6 and 7 (compare $r^2_{67} = .762^2 = .581$ with .596 obtained above).

Regressing variables 8 and 9 of Table 8.6 on the remaining seven variables, the following equations are obtained:

$$z'_8 = .0506z_1 + .0175z_2 + .5434z_3 + .1262z_4 + .1231z_5 + .0304z_6 + .1819z_7$$

$$z'_9 = .1349z_1 + .1116z_2 + .5416z_3 + .0588z_4 + .0955z_5 + .1153z_6 + .0579z_7$$

Only the coefficients associated with variables 6 and 7 are commented upon, since the purpose of this demonstration is to show how they are affected by the

Table 8.6 Correlation Matrix of Seven Predictors and Two Criteria

		1	*2*	*3*	*4*	*5*	*6*	*7*	*8*	*9*
1	Teacher's Competence in French	1.000	.076	.269	−.004	−.017	.077	.050	.207	.299
2	Teaching Procedures	.076	1.000	.014	.095	.107	.205	.174	.092	.179
3	Amount of Instruction	.269	.014	1.000	.181	.107	.180	.188	.633	.632
4	Student Effort	−.004	.095	.181	1.000	.108	.185	.198	.281	.210
5	Student Aptitude for Foreign Language	−.017	.107	.107	.108	1.000	.376	.383	.277	.235
6	Aspiration to Understand Spoken French	.077	.205	.180	.185	.376	1.000	.762	.344	.337
7	Aspiration to Be Able to Read French	.050	.174	.188	.198	.383	.762	1.000	.385	.322
8	Reading Test	.207	.092	.633	.281	.277	.344	.385	1.000	
9	Listening Test	.299	.179	.632	.210	.235	.337	.322		1.000

NOTE: Data taken from J. B. Carroll, *The Teaching of French as a Foreign Language in Eight Countries*, p. 268. Copyright 1975 by John Wiley & Sons. Reprinted by permission.

high multicollinearity. It was shown earlier that when independent variables are highly intercorrelated and when one of them has a slightly higher correlation with the dependent variable than do the remaining ones, the magnitudes of the β's are seriously affected. Specifically, the variable whose correlation with the dependent variable is slightly higher gets a highly disproportionate β as compared to the β's associated with the other variables in the set. This phenomenon is illustrated in the present example for variables 6 and 7. Note that these two variables have similar correlations with dependent variable 8 ($r_{86} = .344$ and $r_{87} = .385$), but that because they are highly intercorrelated ($r_{67} = .762$) the magnitude of β_7 (.1819) is about six times that of β_6 (.0304). The situation is reversed when variable 9 is treated as the dependent variable. This time the discrepancy between the correlations of 6 and 7 with the dependent variable is even smaller ($r_{96} = .337$ and $r_{97} = .322$). But because variable 6 has the slightly higher correlation with dependent variable its β (.1153) is about twice as large as the β for variable 7 (.0579).

The discrepancies between the correlations of 6 and 7 with 8, and of 6 and 7 with 9, can plausibly be attributed to measurement errors and/or sampling fluctuations. Therefore, an interpretation of the highly discrepant β's as indicating important differences in the effects of the two variables is highly questionable. More important, 6 and 7 are not distinct variables but appear to be two indicators of the same variable. The former presumably indicates aspirations to understand spoken French, and the latter presumably indicates aspirations to be able to read French.

Carroll (1975) does not interpret the β's as indices of effects but does use them as indices of "the relative degree to which each of the seven variables contribute independently to the prediction of the criterion" (p. 269). Moreover, he proceeds and compares the β's across the two equations, saying:

> *Student Aspirations:* Of interest is the fact that aspirations to learn to understand spoken French makes *much more contribution* to Listening scores than to Reading, and conversely, aspirations to learn to read French makes *much more contribution* to Reading scores than to Listening scores. (p. 274; italics added)

Such statements may lead to misconceptions among researchers and the general public who do not distinguish between explanatory and predictive research. Furthermore, in view of what was said about the behavior of the β's in the presence of high multicollinearity and small discrepancies between the correlations of predictors with the criterion, one would have to question Carroll's interpretations even in a predictive framework. Finally, the validity of treating Reading and Listening as two distinct variables is also subject to doubt.

Philadelphia School District Studies

Two related studies are scrutinized in this section. The first, which was conducted under the auspices of the Federal Reserve Bank of Philadelphia (FRB), was designed to identify factors that affect student achievement. Its "findings" and recommendations have probably received wide publicity in the form of a booklet provided free of charge to the general public by the FRB

(Summers & Wolfe, 1975). A notice about the availability of this booklet was included in a report of the study's "findings" and recommendations in the *New York Times* (February 2, 1975). A more technical report was also published (Summers & Wolfe, 1977). Henceforth, this study will be referred to as Study I.

When "it became evident that the School District had no intention of utilizing this study for policy development or decision making purposes" (Kean, Summers, Raivetz, & Farber, 1979, p. 14), a second study was designed as a result of cooperation and agreement between FRB and the School District of Philadelphia. While the concern of the second study (henceforth referred to as Study II) was with the identification of factors affecting Reading, it not only utilized the same analytic techniques as in Study I but also included among the people who have planned and executed it the authors of Study I. A report of Study II (Kean et al., 1979) is available, free of charge, from the Office of Research and Evaluation, the School District of Philadelphia.

As was done earlier with other studies, comments about these studies are limited to analytic approaches and interpretations purported to indicate the effects of the independent variables on the dependent variable. Unless otherwise stated, the comments apply equally to both studies.

To begin with, it will be pointed out that the dependent variable was a measure of growth obtained by subtracting a premeasure from a postmeasure. Problems in the use and interpretation of difference scores have been dealt with extensively and are therefore not commented upon here (see, for example, Bohrnstedt, 1969; Cronbach & Furby, 1970; Harris, 1963). It will be noted, however, that the problems were compounded by the use of the differences between grade equivalents as measure of growth in Study I. Among the major shortcomings of grade equivalents is that they are not expressed on an equal-intervals scale (Coleman & Karweit, 1972, Chapter Five; Thorndike & Hagen, 1977, pp. 118–120). This in itself renders them of dubious value as a measure of the dependent variable, not to mention the further complication of using the differences between such measures. The authors of Study I have evidently had second thoughts about the use of grade equivalents, as is evidenced by their use of other types of measures in Study II, "thereby *avoiding the problems of subtracting grade equivalents* or percentile ranks" (Kean et al., 1979, pp. 31–32; italics added).

The most important criticism of the Philadelphia studies is that they are devoid of theory, as is evidenced by the following statements. About Study I the authors say:

> In winnowing down the original list of variables to get the equation of "best fit," *many regressions have been run*. The data have been mined, of course. One starts with so few hypotheses convincingly turned up by theory that classical hypothesis testing is in this application sterile. The data are there to be looked at for what they can reveal. (Summers & Wolfe, 1977, p. 642; italics added)

In describing the model and estimation procedures of Study II, the authors say:

> In this study, which examined the determinants of reading achievement growth, there is no one agreed-upon body of theory to test. What has been done, then, in its absence, is

to substitute an alternative way of arriving at a theoretical model and a procedure for testing it. More specifically, the following steps were taken:
1. The data were . . . looked at to see what they said—i.e., through a series of multiple regression equations they were mined extensively . . .
2. *The final equation was regarded as The Theory*—the hypothesized relationship between growth in reading achievement . . . and many inputs. (Kean et al., 1979, p. 37; italics added)

Whereas in Study I the reader is left to guess how many is "many" regression analyses, in Study II one is told: "Over 500 [!] multiple regression equations were run" (Kean et al., 1979, p. 7).

In view of the route by which the final regression equation was reached, it is necessary to examine, albeit briefly, some of the decisions and choices made by the researchers in order to determine what, if anything, is the meaning of the equation. The authors of the studies stress that an important aspect of their analytic approach is the study of interactions between variables by means of cross-product vectors. Problems in the use and interpretation of cross-product vectors in regression analysis of data obtained in nonexperimental research are discussed in Chapter 10. In the present context it will only be noted that even the staunchest advocates of such an approach have warned that the simultaneous analysis of vectors and their cross products "results in general in the distortion of the partial regression coefficients" (Cohen, 1978, p. 861) associated with the vectors from which the cross products were generated. This occurs because there is generally a high correlation between the original vectors and their cross products, thereby resulting in the latter appropriating some (often much) of the variance of the former. Cohen (1978) points out that when the original vectors and their cross products are included in a simultaneous analysis, the coefficients associated with the former are, "in general, arbitrary nonsense" (p. 861). The solution, according to Cohen (1978), "is the use of a hierarchical model in which IVs [independent variables] are entered in a predetermined sequence so that earlier entering variables are partialed from later ones and *not* vice versa" (p. 861).

The merits of Cohen's solution aside, it appears that the equations reported in the Philadelphia studies have been obtained by using the variables and their cross products in simultaneous analyses. Some examples of the deleterious consequences of this approach are noted from Study I, in which the regression equations with and without the cross-product vectors are reported (Summers & Wolfe, 1977, Table 1, p. 643). Thus, for example, the b for Race when cross-product vectors are not included in the regression equation is -3.34 ($t = -2.58$), as compared to a b of $-.23$ ($t = -.10$) when the cross-product vectors are included in the regression equation. For Income, $b = .17$ ($t = 1.08$) without cross-product vectors, and $.06$ ($t = .34$) with cross-product vectors. The most glaring consequence occurs in connection with Third-Grade Score, which appears four times in the equation in the form of cross products with other variables (i.e., presumably reflecting interactions), but it *does not* appear by itself in the regression equation (i.e., presumably implying that it has no main effect). In the absence of additional information, it is not possible to tell why this has occurred, except to point out that the authors say that they have used tests of statistical significance only as a crude guide. "But, to the final formulations and interpretations of coefficients, more informal standards were applied" (Summers & Wolfe, 1977, p. 642).

Finally, it will be noted that in Study I the adjusted R^2 for the regression equation in which nine cross-product vectors were included is .27, whereas the R^2 for the equation in which the cross-product vectors were omitted is .24. Taken together, then, the "interactions" add 3% to the proportion of variance accounted for by the "main effects." It is doubtful whether this is a meaningful increment, even if one were to assume that the analyses are valid. Moreover, in either case (i.e., with or without "interactions") about 75% of the variance in the dependent variable is left unexplained, leading one to the strong suspicion of the existence of specification errors, particularly because the research is nonexperimental. It, therefore, comes as no surprise that not only are some of the results puzzling but also the results for specific variables in Study I are at odds with those obtained for the same variables in Study II. Following are but a few examples.

Class Size. In Study I the authors claim to have found that "Low-achieving students . . . did worse in classes with more than 28 students: high-achieving students . . . did better . . . ; those around the grade level appeared unaffected" (Summers & Wolfe, 1977, p. 645). It is interesting to note that in a booklet designed for the general public, the results are reported as follows: "Elementary students in our sample who are below grade level *gain* in classes with less than 28 students, but *the rest of the students* can, without any negative effects on achievement, be in classes up to 33. *For all elementary students,* in the sample, *being in classes of 34 or more has a negative effect, and increasingly so as the size of the class increases*" (Summers & Wolfe, 1975, p. 12; italics added). Incidentally, the latter version was used also in a paper presented to the Econometric Society (Summers & Wolfe, 1974, pp. 10–11). Whatever the version, and other issues notwithstanding, it should be noted that the conclusions about the differential effects of class size are based on the regression coefficient associated with the cross product of one of the dummy vectors representing class size and Third-Grade Score, a variable whose questionable status in the regression equation was noted earlier.

The findings of Study II are purported to indicate that "students do better in larger classes" (Kean et al., 1979, p. 46). The authors attempt to explain the contradictory findings about the effect of class size. Thus, when they have presumably found that classes of 34 or more have a negative effect, the following explanation is given: "It is possible that the negative relationship may arise from a teacher's hostile reaction to a class size larger than mandated by the union contract, rather than from largeness itself" (Summers & Wolfe, 1975, p. 12). But when class size seems to have a positive effect, the authors say: "In interpreting the finding, however, it is important to emphasize that it is a finding which emerges when many other variables are controlled—that is, what the positive coefficients are saying is that larger classes are better, *after* controlling for such instructional characteristics as the degree of individualization in teaching reading" (Kean et al., 1979, pp. 46–47). One of the authors is reported to have come up with another explanation of the positive effect of class size. In a publication of Division H (School Evaluation and Program Development) of the American Educational Research Association it is reported that:

> A Federal Reserve Bank economist, Anita Summers, . . . one of the authors of the study, had a possible explanation for this interesting finding. She felt that the reason why the larger classes seem to show greater growth could be tied to the fact that teachers with larger classes may be forced to instill more discipline and prescribe more silent reading (which appears to positively affect reading achievement) (*Pre Post Press,* September 1979, *1,* p. 1).

There are, of course, many other alternative explanations, the simplest and most plausible being that the model reflected by the regression equation has little or nothing to do with a theory of the process of achievement in reading. It is understandable that authors are reluctant to question their own work, let alone to find fault with it. But it is unfortunate that a publication of a division of the American Education Research Association prints a front-page feature on the study, entitled: "Philadelphia Study Pinpoints Factors in Improving Reading Achievement," listing all kinds of presumed findings without the slightest hint that the study may be deficient.

Disruptive Incidents. When they find that "for students who are at or below grade level, more Disruptive Incidents are associated with greater achievement growth" (Summers & Wolfe, 1977, p. 647), the authors attempt to explain this result. They then conclude: "In any case, it would seem a bit premature to engage in a policy of encouraging disruptive incidents to increase learning!" (Summers & Wolfe, 1977, p. 647).

Ratings of Teachers Colleges. The colleges from which the teachers have graduated were rated on the Gourman Scale, which the authors describe as follows:

> The areas rated include (1) individual departments, (2) administrations, (3) faculty (including student/staff ratio and research), (4) student services (including financial and honor programs), and (5) general areas such as facilities and alumni support. The Gourman rating is a *simple average* of all of these. (Summers & Wolfe, 1975, p. 14).

One cannot help but question whether a score derived as described above has any meaning. In any case, the authors dichotomized the ratings so that colleges with ratings of 525 or higher were considered high, whereas those with ratings below 525 were considered low. Their finding: "Teachers who received B.A.'s from higher rated colleges . . . were associated with students whose learning rate was greater . . ." (Summers & Wolfe, 1977, p. 644). Even if one were to give credence to this finding, it would at least be necessary to entertain the notion that the Gourman Scale may serve as a proxy for a variety of variables (teachers' ability or motivation to name but two). It is noteworthy that when the Ratings of Teachers Colleges were found not to contribute significantly to the results of Study II, this fact is mentioned, almost in passing (see Kean et al., 1979, p. 45), without the slightest hint that it is at odds with what was considered a major finding in Study I.

Lest the reader feel that these points are unduly belabored, it is to be noted that not only did the authors reject any questioning of their findings, but also advocated that they be used as guides for policy changes in the educational system. The following are but two instances in support of this contention.

In response to criticisms of their work, the authors of Study I are reported to have "*implied that it's time educators stopped using technicalities as excuses for not seeking change*" (*Education U.S.A.*, 1975, *17*, p. 179). Further, they are quoted as having said that: "The broad findings . . . are firm enough in this study and supported enough by other studies to warrant confidence. We think that this study provides useful information for policy decisions."

The same tone of confidence by the authors of Study I about the implications of their findings is evidenced in the following excerpts from a *New York Times* (February 2, 1975) report about their study.

> On the basis of their findings, the authors advocated not only a reordering of priorities to support those factors that make the most difference in achievement, but also "making teacher salary scales more reflective of productivity."
>
> "For example," they wrote, "Graduating from a higher-rated college seems to be a 'productive' characteristic of teachers in terms of achievement growth, though currently this is not rewarded or even used as a basis for hiring."

SOCIAL SCIENCES AND SOCIAL POLICY

In the course of reading this and the preceding chapter you have most likely experienced uneasiness about the state of social science research in general, and educational research in particular. You have undoubtedly been nagged by questions concerning the researchers whose studies were discussed in these chapters, and perhaps about others with whose work you are familiar. The authors of the studies reviewed in these chapters are prominent researchers. Some of them have even broken new ground in social science research. Is it possible, then, that they are not aware of the shortcomings and the limitations of the methods they have used? Of course they are aware of them, as is attested to by their own writings and caveats. Why, then, do they seem to ignore the limitations of the methods they are using? The answer is not a simple one. In fact, more than one answer may be conjectured.

Some researchers (e.g., Coleman, 1970) justify the use of rather crude analytic approaches on the grounds that our state of theory is, at best, rudimentary and does not warrant the use of more sophisticated analytic approaches. In response to his critics, Coleman (1970) argues that neither he nor anyone else has been able to formulate a theoretical model of achievement, and maintains that: "As with any problem, one must start where he is, not where he would like to be" (p. 243).

Similarly, Lohnes and Cooley (1978) defend the use of commonality analysis, saying: "We favor weak over strong interpretations of regressions. This stems from our sense that Congress and other policy agents can better wait for converging evidence of the effects of schooling initiatives than they can recover from confident advisements on what to do which turn out to be wrong" (p. 4).

And the authors of the IEA studies, each in his own way, insert statements of reservation and caution about the analytic methods they have been using. Some, for example, even show how incremental partitioning of variance yields dramatically different results when the order of the entry of the blocks into the regression equation is altered.

Yet the reservations, the cautions, and the caveats seem to have a way of fading into the woodwork, of being swept under the carpet. Despite the desire to make weak and qualified statements, strong and absolute pronouncements and prescriptions seem to emerge and develop a life of their own. Perhaps this is "because the indices produced by this method [commonality analysis], being pure numbers (proportions or percentages), are especially prone to float clear of their data bases and achieve transcendental quotability and memorableness" (Cooley & Lohnes, 1976, p. 220). Perhaps it is because of a desperate need to make a conclusive statement after having expended large amounts of money and a great deal of energy in designing, executing, and analyzing large-scale research studies. One may sense the feeling of frustration that accompanies inconclusive findings in the following statement by one of the authors of the IEA studies: "As one views the results on school factors related to reading achievement *it is hard not to feel somewhat disappointed and let down.* There is so little that provides a basis for any positive or constructive action on the part of teachers or administrators" (Thorndike, 1973, p. 122; italics added).

Perhaps it is the sincere desire to reform society and its institutions that leads to a blurring of the important distinction between the role of the social scientist qua scientist and his or her role as an advocate of social policies to which he or she is committed. It is perhaps this process that leads researchers to overlook, or to mute, their own reservations about their research findings, and to forget their own exhortations about the necessary caution in interpreting them and in translating them into policy decisions (see Young & Bress, 1975, for a critique of Coleman's role as an advocate of social policy, and Coleman's 1975b reply).

One can surely come up with other explanations of the schism between researchers' knowledge about their research design and methods, and their findings, or what they say they have found. Whatever the explanations, whatever the motives, which are best left to the psychology and the sociology of scientific research, the unintended damage of conclusions and actions based on questionable research designs and the inappropriate use of analytic methods is incalculable.

Few policymakers and judges are sufficiently versed in methodology as to be in a position to assess the validity of the conclusions based on voluminous research reports chock-full of tables, bristling with formulas and tests of statistical significance. Fewer still probably even attempt to read the reports. Probably most obtain their information from summaries or reports of such summaries by the news media. Very often the summaries do not reflect faithfully the findings of the study, not to mention the caveats with which they were presented in the report itself. In case of government-sponsored research, summaries of studies may be prepared under the direction of, or even exclusively by, government officials who are not only poorly versed in methodology but are more concerned with the political repercussions that the summary may have than with its veracity. A case in point is the summary of the Coleman Report.

Grant (1973) provides a penetrating and detailed description of the tortuous route of the summary of the Coleman Report to its publication. No less than three different versions were being written by different people, while the policymakers at the U.S. Office of Education were bickering about what the public should and should not be told in the summary. When it was finally published, there was general agreement among those who have studied the Report that its summary was misleading. Yet, it is the summary, or news reports about it, that has had the greatest impact on the courts, Congress, and other policymakers.

The gap between what the findings of the Coleman Report were and what policymakers knew about them is perhaps best demonstrated by the candid statement of Howard Howe, then U.S. commissioner of education, whom Grant (1973) quotes as saying:

> I think the reason I was nervous was because I was dealing with something I didn't fully understand. I was not on top of it. You couldn't read the summary and get on top of it. You couldn't read the whole damn thing so you were stuck with trying to explain publicly something that maybe had all sorts of implications, but you didn't want to say the wrong thing, yet you didn't know what the hell to say so it was a very difficult situation for me. (p. 29)

This from a person who was supposed to draw policy implications from the report (see Howe, 1976, for general observations regarding the promise and problem of educational research). Is there any wonder that other, perhaps less candid, policymakers have drawn from the report whatever conclusions they found compatible with their own views?

Often, policymakers and the general public learn about findings of a major study from reports of news conferences held by one or more of the researchers who have participated in the study or on the basis of news releases prepared by the researchers and/or the sponsoring agency. It is, admittedly, not possible or useful to provide reporters with intricate information about analyses and other research issues because, lacking the necessary training, they could not be expected to follow them, or even to be interested in them. It is time, however, that social scientists rethink their role in the dissemination of results of their studies to the general public. It is time they realize that the present practices are bound to lead to oversimplification, misunderstandings, selectivity, and even outright distortions consistent with one's preconceived notions, beliefs, or prejudices.

In connection with the critique of the Philadelphia School District studies, earlier in this chapter, it was shown, through excerpts from a report in the *New York Times,* what the public was told about the "findings" of these studies, and the recommendations that were presumably based on them. Following are a couple of examples of what the public was told about the IEA studies. Reporting on a news conference regarding the IEA studies, the *New York Times* (May 25, 1973) ran the story under the heading: "Education Study Cites Home." The major conclusions presented are that "family background, and the presence of classmates from affluent homes had more bearing on achievement in school than school itself." The findings are said to support earlier findings of the Coleman Report. On November 18, 1973, the *New York Times* reported on another news conference regarding the IEA studies. This time the headline, which ran across the entire page, proclaimed: "Study Questions Belief That Home Is More Vital to Pupil Achievement than the School." Among other things, it reported that: "Perhaps the most intriguing result of the study was that while home background did seem to play an important role in reading, literature and civics, school conditions were generally more important when it came to science and foreign languages. Home background was found to account for 11.5 per cent of the variation on the average for all subjects in all countries, and learning conditions amounted to 10 per cent on the average."

Is there any wonder that readers are bewildered about what it is that the IEA studies have found? Moreover, faced with conflicting reports, are policymakers to be blamed for selecting the "findings" that appear to them more reasonable, or more socially just?

Commenting on the technical complexities of the Coleman Report, Mosteller and Moynihan say:

> We have noted that the material is difficult to master, even for those who had the time, facilities, and technical equipment to try. As a result, in these technical areas society must depend upon the judgment of experts. (Thus does science re-create an age of faith!) Increasingly the most relevant findings concerning the state of society are the work of elites, and must simply be taken—or rejected—by the public at large, at times even by the professional public involved, on such faith. Since specialists often disagree, however, the public is frequently at liberty to choose which side it will, or, for that matter, to choose neither and continue comfortable in the old myths. (1972b, p. 32)

Fred H. Hechinger, who has been education editor of the *New York Times*, has recently reacted to the contradictory "findings" about the effects of schooling. In an article titled "Frail Sociology" (*New York Times*, November 5, 1979) Hechinger says: "The surgeon general should consider labeling all sociological studies: 'Keep out of reach of politicians and judges.' Indiscriminate use of these suggestive works can be dangerous to the nation's health." He proceeds to point out that the same researchers offer contradictory findings.

> For example, take the pronouncement in 1966 by James S. Coleman that school integration helps black children learn more. The Coleman report became a manual for political and court actions involving busing and other desegregation strategies. But in 1975 Mr. Coleman proclaimed that busing was a failure. "What once appeared to be fact is now known to be fiction," Coleman II said, reversing Coleman I.

Hechinger points out, however, that Coleman does not deserve condemnation because the original caveats were lost sight of in the rush toward busing. Contradictions are also pointed out in Jencks' work and in the work of others. Not surprisingly, Hechinger concludes that in matters of social policy we should do what we believe is right and eschew seeking support for such policies in results obtained from frail studies.

In sum, then, disseminating "findings" based on questionable research designs and analyses may lead to either selectivity of results on the part of policymakers and the public to suit specific goals or to the heeding of suggestions such as Hechinger's to ignore social scientific research altogether. Either course of action is, of course, undesirable and may further erode the support for social science research as a means of studying social phenomena and destroy what little credibility it has as a guide for social policy.[9]

STUDY SUGGESTIONS

1. The illustrative correlation matrix (N = 300) used in the Study Suggestions of Chapters 6 and 7 is repeated here. Using a computer program, regress Verbal Achievement on the five independent variables.

	1 Race	*2* IQ	*3* School Quality	*4* Self-Concept	*5* Level of Aspiration	*6* Verbal Achievement
1	1.00	.30	.25	.30	.30	.25
2	.30	1.00	.20	.20	.30	.60
3	.25	.20	1.00	.20	.30	.30
4	.30	.20	.20	1.00	.40	.30
5	.30	.30	.30	.40	1.00	.40
6	.25	.60	.30	.30	.40	1.00

   (a) What is R^2?
   (b) What is the regression equation?
   (c) What information would you need in order to convert the β's obtained in (b) into b's?
   (d) Assuming you were to use the magnitude of the β's as indices of the effects of the variables with which they are associated, interpret the results.
   (e) The validity of the preceding interpretation is predicated, among other things, on the assumptions that the model is correctly specified, and that the measures of the independent variables are perfectly reliable. Discuss the implications of this statement.
   (f) Using relevant information from the computer output and applying a formula given in this chapter, calculate R^2's for each of the independent variables with the remaining independent variables. Of what use is such information?

2. Use a computer program that enables you to do matrix operations (e.g., SAS).
   (a) Calculate the determinant of the correlation matrix of the five independent variables in 1 above.
   (b) What would the determinant be if the matrix were orthogonal?
   (c) What would the determinant be if there were perfect multicollinearity in the matrix?
   (d) Assuming that the determinant were equal to 1.00, what would the regression equation be?

[9]When this book was in press, Coleman and associates released a report in which they claim to have found that private high schools provide a better education than public high schools. The report has sparked anew controversies regarding methodological issues as well as the role of social scientists as advocates of social policy. For some reports and exchanges, see the *New York Times*, April, 7, 8, 10, 12, 19, and 20, 1981; May 11, 1981; June 9 and 20, 1981.

(e) Calculate the inverse of the correlation matrix of the five independent variables.

(f) Using relevant values from the inverse and a formula given in this chapter, calculate R^2's for each of the independent variables with the remaining ones. Compare the results with those obtained under 1(f), above. If you do not have access to a computer program for matrix operations, use the inverse given in the Answers to this chapter to solve for the R^2's.

(g) What would the inverse of the correlation matrix among the independent variables be if all the correlations among them were equal to zero?

ANSWERS

1. (a) .43947
   (b) $z'_6 = -.01865z_1 + .50637z_2 + .13020z_3 + .11004z_4 + .17061z_5$
   (c) The standard deviations.
   (d) IQ has the largest effect on Verbal Achievement. The effect of Race on Verbal Achievement is neither meaningful nor statistically significant. The effects of the remaining three variables are about the same.
   (f) $R^2_{1.2345} = .18327$; $R^2_{2.1345} = .14601$; $R^2_{3.1245} = .12691$
   $R^2_{4.1235} = .19967$; $R^2_{5.1234} = .25749$ [by Formula (8.12)]. To pinpoint sources of high multicollinearity.
2. (a) .54947
   (b) 1.00
   (c) .00
   (d) $z'_6 = .25z_1 + .60z_2 + .30z_3 + .30z_4 + .40z_5$. That is, each β is equal to a zero-order correlation of a given independent variable with the dependent variable.
   (e)

1.22883	−.24369	−.16689	−.22422	−.15579
−.24369	1.17096	−.09427	−.05032	−.22977
−.16689	−.09427	1.14530	−.06433	−.23951
−.22422	−.05032	−.06433	1.24944	−.39811
−.15579	−.22977	−.23951	−.39811	1.34676

   (f) $R^2_{1.2345} = .18622$; $R^2_{2.1345} = .14600$; $R^2_{3.1245} = .12687$; $R^2_{4.1235} = .19964$; $R^2_{5.1234} = .25748$. By Formula (8.11).
   (g) An identity matrix.

PART 2

REGRESSION ANALYSIS WITH CATEGORICAL AND CONTINUOUS VARIABLES

DUMMY, EFFECT, AND ORTHOGONAL CODING OF CATEGORICAL VARIABLES

The treatment of regression analysis in preceding chapters was limited to situations in which the independent variables or the predictors are continuous. A *continuous variable* is one on which subjects differ in amount or degree. Weight, height, study time, dosages of a drug, frequency of reinforcement, motivation, and mental ability are but some examples of continuous variables. Note that a continuous variable expresses gradations; that is, a person is more or less motivated, say, or has studied more or less.[1]

Another type of variable frequently encountered is a *categorical variable,* on which subjects differ in type or kind. For example, when in experimental research subjects are randomly assigned to different treatments (e.g., different teaching methods, different modes of communication, different kinds of rewards), the treatments constitute a set of mutually exclusive categories that differ from each other in kind, not in degree. Or, when people are classified into groups or categories on the basis of attributes such as race, occupation, political party affiliation, marital status, religious affiliation, the classification is comprised of a set of mutually exclusive categories. Unlike a continuous variable, which reflects a condition of "more or less," a categorical variable reflects a condition of "either/or." On a categorical variable, a person either belongs to a given category or does not belong to it.

In principle, one should be able to use information provided by a categorical

[1]Strictly speaking, a continuous variable has infinite gradations. When measuring height, for example, one may resort to ever finer gradations. Any choice of gradations on such a scale depends on the degree of accuracy called for in the given situation. When, on the other hand, one is measuring the number of children in a set of families, one is dealing with a variable that has only discrete values. This type of variable, too, is referred to as a continuous variable in this book. Some writers use the terms *qualitative* and *quantitative* for *categorical* and *continuous,* respectively.

variable to explain or predict phenomena in much the same manner as continuous variables are used for such purposes. Indeed, one of the major reasons for creating classifications is to study how they relate to, or help explain, other variables (for discussions of the role of classification in scientific inquiry, see Hempel, 1952, pp. 50–54; 1965, pp. 137–145). Actually, it is possible to use categorical variables in regression analysis, but in order to do that it is necessary first to code such variables. The present chapter details procedures for coding a categorical variable and the manner in which it is then used in regression analysis. In Chapter 10 these ideas are extended to multiple categorical variables. In Chapters 12 and 13 it is shown how regression analysis is applied to designs consisting of both continuous and categorical independent variables or predictors.

The present chapter begins with a brief discussion of the concept of coding a categorical variable. It is then shown how simple regression analysis of a dependent variable on a coded variable can be used to analyze data from two groups, and that the results thus obtained are identical to results obtained from the application of the t test for the difference between two means.

Multiple regression analysis in which a dependent variable is regressed on coded vectors that represent a categorical variable with more than two categories is then presented. It is shown that such an analysis yields results identical to those obtained from the application of the analysis of variance. The properties of three coding methods are discussed and it is shown that while they yield overall identical results, intermediate results obtained from the application of each are useful for specific purposes, particularly for doing specific types of multiple comparisons among means.

The first part of the chapter deals with designs in which the sample sizes are equal. This is followed by a presentation of the analysis of designs with unequal sample sizes. The chapter concludes with some general observations about multiple regression analysis versus the analysis of variance.

Before turning to the substance of this chapter it is important to note that, as with continuous variables, categorical variables may be used in research that is experimental as well as nonexperimental, explanatory as well as predictive. Consequently, what was said about these topics in connection with continuous variables (see, in particular, Chapters 6, 7, and 8) applies equally to categorical variables. For example, one may wish to use a categorical variable such as occupation in order to predict or explain a given phenomenon—say, attitudes toward the use of nuclear power plants, or voting behavior.

When the goal is explanation, it is essential to formulate a theoretical model and to be alert to potential threats to a valid interpretation of the results, particularly to specification and measurement errors. It is necessary, for example, to be cognizant of the fact that occupation is correlated with a variety of variables or that it may serve as a proxy for a variable not included in the model. Depending on the specific occupations being used, there may be a strong relation between occupation and education. Is it, then, occupation or education that determines attitudes or voting behavior, or do both of them affect such phenomena? Some occupations are held primarily by women and others are held primarily by men. Assuming that such occupations are used in explanatory research, is sex or occupation (or are both) the "cause" (or "causes") of the phenomenon being studied? Moreover, it is possible that neither sex nor occupation affects the phenomenon under study, but that they appear to affect it because they are related with variables that do affect it.

It was said in earlier chapters that experimental research has the potential of providing less ambiguous answers to research questions than does nonexperimental research. This holds true whether the independent variables are continuous or categorical. It should be recognized, however, that experimental research does not always lead to less ambiguous answers than nonexperimental research (see the discussion of definition of variables in the next section). The method of coding categorical variables and the manner in which they are used in regression analysis is the same whether the research is experimental or nonexperimental, explanatory or predictive. Consequently, although brief comments and reminders about the importance of distinguishing between these types of research will be made occasionally, no detailed discussions of such distinctions will be given, since these are treated in detail in books on research design (e.g., Kerlinger, 1973). You are urged to pay particular attention to discussions regarding the internal and external validity of experimental, quasi-experimental, and nonexperimental designs (Campbell & Stanley, 1963; and Cook & Campbell, 1979). With these remarks in mind, we turn now to the topic of coding a categorical independent variable or a predictor.

CODING AND METHODS OF CODING

A *code* is a set of symbols to which meanings can be assigned. For example, a set of symbols {A, B, C} can be assigned to three different treatments or to three groups of people, such as Protestants, Catholics, and Jews. Or the set {0, 1} can be assigned to a control and an experimental group, or to males and females. Whatever the symbols, they are assigned to objects of mutually exclusive subsets of a defined universe to indicate subset or group membership.

The assignment of symbols follows a rule or a set of rules determined by the definition of the variable under consideration. For some variables the rule may be obvious and need little or no explanation, as in the assignment of 1's and 0's to males and females, respectively. There are, however, variables that require elaborate explication of rules, or definitions, about which there may not be agreement among all or most observers. For example, the definition of a variable such as occupation may involve a complex set of rules about which there may not be universal agreement. An example of even greater complexity is the explication of rules for the classification of mentally ill patients according to their diseases, as what is called for is a complex process of diagnosis about which psychiatrists may not agree or may strongly disagree. The validity of findings of research in which categorical nonmanipulated variables are used depends, among other things, on the validity and reliability of their definitions (i.e., the classification rules). Indeed, "the establishment of a suitable system of classification in a given domain of investigation may be considered as a special kind of scientific concept formation" (Hempel, 1965, p. 139).

What was said about the definition of nonmanipulated categorical variables applies equally to manipulated categorical variables, that is, to variables used in experimental research. Some manipulated variables are relatively easy to define theoretically and operationally, whereas the definition of others may be very difficult, as is evidenced by attempts to define, through manipulations, variables such as anxiety, motivation, prejudice, and the like. For example, do different instructions to subjects or exposure to different films lead to different levels of anxiety? Assuming they do, are exposures to different instructions the same as exposures to different films, so far as anxiety arousal is concerned? And what other variables might have been affected by the above noted treatments? The preceding are but some questions the answers to which have important implications for the valid interpretation of results. In short, as in nonexperimental research, the validity of conclusions drawn from experimental research is predicated, among other things, on the validity and reliability of the definitions of the variables.

Whatever the definition of a categorical variable and whatever the coding, subjects given the same symbol are treated as equal to each other on the variable. If one defines rules of membership in political parties and assigns 1's, say, to Democrats and 0's to Republicans, it is necessary to recognize that all subjects assigned 1's are considered equally as Democrats, no matter how different they may be on other variables and no matter how they may differ in their devotion, activity, and commitment to the Democratic party.

Note that the numbers are used as symbols and therefore do not reflect quantities or a rank ordering of the categories to which they are assigned. Any set of numbers may be used: $\{1, 0\}$, $\{-99, 123\}$, $\{1, 0, -1\}$, $\{24, 5, -7\}$, and so on. Some coding methods, however, have properties that make them more useful than others. This is especially so when the symbols are used in statistical analysis. Three coding methods: *dummy, effect,* and *orthogonal* are used in this book. It should be noted that the overall analysis and results are identical regardless of which of the three methods is used in multiple regression analysis. As is shown below, however, some intermediate results and the statistical tests of significance associated with the three methods are different. Therefore, a given coding method may be more useful in one situation than in another. We turn now to a detailed treatment of each of the methods of coding categorical variables.

DUMMY CODING

The simplest method of coding categorial variables is dummy coding. In this method one generates a number of vectors such that, in any given vector, membership in a given group or category is assigned 1, while nonmembership in the category is assigned 0. Let us begin with the simplest case, in which the categorical variable is composed of two categories only, as when one has an experimental group and a control group, or males and females.

A Numerical Example

Assume that the data reported in Table 9.1 were obtained in an experiment in which E represents the Experimental group and C represents the Control

Table 9.1 Illustrative Data for an Experimental *(E)* and a Control *(C)* Group

	E	C
	20	10
	18	12
	17	11
	17	15
	13	17
Σ:	85	65
$\bar{Y}$:	17	13
Σy^2:	26	34

group. Alternatively, the data under E may have been obtained from males and those under C from females, or those under E from people who own homes and those under C from people who rent (recall, however, the comments made above about the need to distinguish between experimental and nonexperimental research).

As is well known, a t test may be used in order to determine whether the mean of the Experimental group is significantly different from the mean of the Control group. This is done here for the purpose of comparison with the analysis of the same data via regression methods. The formula for a t test for the difference between two means is:

$$t = \frac{\bar{Y}_1 - \bar{Y}_2}{\sqrt{\dfrac{\Sigma y_1^2 + \Sigma y_2^2}{N_1 + N_2 - 2}\left(\dfrac{1}{N_1} + \dfrac{1}{N_2}\right)}} \tag{9.1}$$

where $\bar{Y}_1$ and $\bar{Y}_2$ are the means of groups 1 and 2, respectively (for the data of Table 9.1, consider $\bar{Y}_1 = \bar{Y}_E$, and $\bar{Y}_2 = \bar{Y}_C$); Σy_1^2 and Σy_2^2 are the sums of squares for E and C, respectively; N_1 is the number of people in E; and N_2 is the number of people in C. The t ratio has $N_1 + N_2 - 2$ degrees of freedom. (For detailed discussions of the t test, see Edwards, 1972, Chapter 5, and Hays, 1981, Chapter 8). The means and sums of squares for the two groups are reported in Table 9.1, where:

	E	C
$\bar{Y}$:	17	13
Σy^2:	26	34
N:	5	5

Using these figures, calculate:

$$t = \frac{17 - 13}{\sqrt{\dfrac{26 + 34}{5 + 5 - 2}\left(\dfrac{1}{5} + \dfrac{1}{5}\right)}} = \frac{4}{\sqrt{3}} = \frac{4}{1.732} = 2.31$$

with 8 *df*, $p < .05$. Using the .05 level of significance it is concluded that the mean of the Experimental group is significantly different from the mean of the Control group.

The data of Table 9.1 are now used to illustrate the application of dummy coding and regression analysis. They are displayed in Table 9.2, where the measures of the dependent variable for both groups are combined in a single vector, Y. In addition, three vectors are displayed in Table 9.2. X_1 is a unit vector (i.e., all subjects are assigned 1's in this vector). In X_2, subjects in E are assigned 1's, whereas those in C are assigned 0's. Conversely, in X_3 subjects in C are assigned 1's and those in E are assigned 0's. X_2 and X_3, then, are dummy vectors in which a categorical variable with two categories (e.g., E and C; male and female) was coded.

One could now proceed and regress Y on the X's in order to note whether the latter help explain, or predict, some of the variance of Y. In other words, one seeks to determine whether information about membership in different groups, be they naturally existing ones or created for the purpose of an experiment, helps explain some of the variability of the subjects on the dependent variable, Y.

In Chapter 4, it was shown how one may use matrix algebra to solve the equation:

$$\mathbf{b} = (\mathbf{X}'\mathbf{X})^{-1}\mathbf{X}'\mathbf{Y} \tag{9.2}$$

where $\mathbf{b}$ is a vector of b's plus the intercept (a); $\mathbf{X}$ is a matrix of scores on the independent variables plus a unit vector; $\mathbf{Y}$ is a vector of scores on the dependent variable. Equation (9.2) applies equally when $\mathbf{X}$ is a matrix of scores on continuous variables or, as in the present example, when it is composed of coded vectors. In Table 9.2, $\mathbf{X}$ is composed of a unit vector and two dummy vectors. Inspection of this matrix will reveal that it contains a linear depen-

Table 9.2 Dummy Coding for Experimental and Control Groups, Based on Data from Table 9.1

	Y	X_1	X_2	X_3
	20	1	1	0
	18	1	1	0
	17	1	1	0
	17	1	1	0
	13	1	1	0
	10	1	0	1
	12	1	0	1
	11	1	0	1
	15	1	0	1
	17	1	0	1
M:	15	1	.5	.5
ss:	100	0	2.5	2.5
		$\Sigma yx_2 = 10$	$\Sigma yx_3 = -10$	

NOTE: M = mean; ss = deviation sum of squares.

dency: $X_2 + X_3 = X_1$. Therefore $(\mathbf{X'X})$ is singular and cannot be inverted, thus precluding a solution for Equation (9.2). To see clearly that $(\mathbf{X'X})$ is singular, carry out the matrix operations with the three X vectors of Table 9.2 to obtain:

$$\mathbf{X'X} = \begin{bmatrix} 10 & 5 & 5 \\ 5 & 5 & 0 \\ 5 & 0 & 5 \end{bmatrix}$$

Note that the first row, or column, of the matrix is equal to the sum of the two other rows, or columns. The determinant of $(\mathbf{X'X})$ is zero. (If you are encountering difficulties with this presentation, it is strongly suggested that you review Chapter 4, where these topics are dealt with in detail.)

The problem of the linear dependency in $\mathbf{X}$ may be easily resolved when one notes that either X_2 or X_3 of Table 9.2 is necessary and sufficient to represent membership in two categories of a variable. In other words, using both vectors provides completely redundant information. To repeat: X_2, or X_3, alone contains all the information about group membership. Therefore, it is sufficient to use X_1 and X_2, or X_1 and X_3, as $\mathbf{X}$ in Equation (9.2). The overall results are the same regardless of which set is used; however, as shown below, the regression equations obtained for the two sets differ.

Because the calculations of regression statistics with a single independent variable (in the present case a single coded vector, i.e., X_2 or X_3) were presented in detail in Chapter 2 using algebraic formulas and in Chapter 4 using matrix operations,there appears to be no need to repeat them here. Instead, the calculations of statistics for the regression of Y on X_2 and Y on X_3 of Table 9.2 are summarized in Table 9.3. For your convenience, the algebraic formulas used in the calculations are also included in Table 9.3. If necessary, refer to Chapter 2 for detailed discussions of each of them. We turn now to a discussion of relevant results obtained in Table 9.3.

The Regression Equation. Consider first the regression Y on X_2:

$$Y' = a + bX_2 = 13 + 4X_2$$

Since X_2 is a dummy vector, the predicted Y for each person assigned 1 (i.e., members of the Experimental group) is:

$$Y' = a + bX_2 = 13 + 4(1) = 17$$

And the predicted Y for each person assigned 0 (members of the Control group) is:

$$Y' = a + bX_2 = 13 + 4(0) = 13$$

Thus, the regression equation leads to a predicted score that is equal to the mean of the group to which an individual belongs (see Table 9.1, where $\bar{Y}_E = 17$ and $\bar{Y}_C = 13$).

Table 9.3 Calculation of Statistics for the Regression of Y on X_2 and Y on X_3, Based on Data from Table 9.2

	(a) Y on X_2	(b) Y on X_3
$b = \frac{\Sigma xy}{\Sigma x^2}$	$\frac{10}{2.5} = 4$	$\frac{-10}{2.5} = -4$
$a = \bar{Y} - b\bar{X}$	$15 - (4)(.5) = 13$	$15 - (-4)(.5) = 17$
$Y' = a + bX$	$13 + 4X$	$17 - 4X$
$ss_{\text{reg}} = b\Sigma xy$	$(4)(10) = 40$	$(-4)(-10) = 40$
$ss_{\text{res}} = \Sigma y^2 - ss_{\text{reg}}$	$100 - 40 = 60$	$100 - 40 = 60$
$s^2_{y.x} = \frac{ss_{\text{res}}}{N - k - 1}$	$\frac{60}{10 - 1 - 1} = 7.5$	$\frac{60}{10 - 1 - 1} = 7.5$
$s_b = \sqrt{\frac{s^2_{y.x}}{\Sigma x^2}}$	$\sqrt{\frac{7.5}{2.5}} = 1.732$	$\sqrt{\frac{7.5}{2.5}} = 1.732$
$t = \frac{b}{s_b}$	$\frac{4}{1.732} = 2.31$	$\frac{-4}{1.732} = -2.31$
$r^2 = \frac{ss_{\text{reg}}}{\Sigma y^2}$	$\frac{40}{100} = .4$	$\frac{40}{100} = .4$
$F = \frac{r^2/k}{(1 - r^2)/(N - k - 1)}$	$\frac{.4/1}{(1 - .4)/8} = 5.33$	$\frac{.4/1}{(1 - .4)/8} = 5.33$

Note that the intercept *(a)* is equal to the mean of the group assigned 0 in X_2 (i.e., the Control group):

$$Y'_C = \bar{Y}_C = a + b(0) = a = 13$$

Also, the regression coefficient *(b)* is equal to the deviation of the mean of the group assigned 1 in X_2 from the mean of the group assigned 0 in the same vector:

$$Y'_E = \bar{Y}_E = a + b(1) = a + b = 17$$

$$\bar{Y}_E - \bar{Y}_C = (a + b) - a = b = 17 - 13 = 4$$

Turning now to the regression Y on X_3, as in Table 9.3:

$$Y' = a + bX_3 = 17 - 4X_3$$

and applying it to the scores on X_3:

$$Y'_E = 17 - 4(0) = 17$$

$$Y'_C = 17 - 4(1) = 13$$

In X_3, members of the Control group were assigned 1's, whereas those in the Experimental group were assigned 0's. Although the regression equation on X_3—that is, in part (b) of Table 9.3—differs from the one in (a), both lead to the same predicted Y, the mean of the group to which the individual belongs.

Note that, as in (a), the intercept for the regression equation in (b) is equal to the mean of the group assigned 0 in X_3 (i.e., the mean of the Experimental group). And, again, as in (a), the regression coefficient in (b) is equal to the deviation of the mean of the group assigned 1 in X_3 (i.e., Control group) from the mean of the group assigned 0 (i.e., Experimental; $\bar{Y}_C - \bar{Y}_E = 13 - 17 = -4 = b$).

In sum, the properties of the regression equations in (a) and (b) of Table 9.3 are the same, although the specific values of the intercept and the regression coefficient differ depending on which group is assigned 1 and which is assigned 0. The predicted scores are the same, regardless of which of the two regression equations is used.

Test of the Regression Coefficient. It was noted above that the regression coefficient *(b)* is equal to the deviation of the mean of the group assigned 1 from the mean of the group assigned 0. In other words, b is equal to the difference between the two means. The same value is, of course, obtained in (a) and (b), except that in the former it is positive (i.e., $\bar{Y}_E - \bar{Y}_C$) whereas in the latter it is negative (i.e., $\bar{Y}_C - \bar{Y}_E$). Therefore testing the b for significance is tantamount to testing the difference between the two means. Not surprisingly, then, the t ratio of 2.31 with 8 *df* ($N - k - 1$) is the same as the one obtained earlier when Formula (9.1) was applied to the test of the difference between the means of the Experimental and Control groups.

Regression and Residual Sums of Squares. Note that these two sums of squares are identical in (a) and (b), inasmuch as they reflect the same information about group membership regardless of the specific symbols assigned to members of a given group.

Squared Correlation. The squared correlation, r^2, between the independent variable (i.e., the coded vector) and the dependent variable, Y, is also the same in (a) and (b), .4, indicating that 40% of the Σy^2 is due to regression or that 40% of the variance of Y is due to its regression on X_2 or on X_3. Testing r^2 for significance, $F = 5.33$ with 1 and 8 *df*. Since the numerator for the F ratio has one degree of freedom, $t^2 = F$ ($2.31^2 = 5.33$; see Table 9.3). One, would, of course, obtain the same F ratio if the ss_{reg} were tested for significance (see Chapter 2).

A NUMERICAL EXAMPLE OF A VARIABLE WITH MULTIPLE CATEGORIES

We turn now to an example in which the categorical independent variable, or predictor, is composed of more than two categories. Even though a variable with three categories is used, extensions to variables with any number of categories are straightforward. As was done in the numerical example analyzed above, the present example is first analyzed using the more conventional approach of the Analysis of Variance (ANOVA). As is well known, when it is desired to test the significance of the difference among more than two means a one-way, or simple, ANOVA is the appropriate analytic method. As is shown below, using multiple regression analysis one may accomplish the same purpose. In fact, the reason ANOVA is presented here is to show the equivalence of the two approaches. If you are not familiar with ANOVA you may skip the next section without loss of continuity, or you may choose to study an introductory treatment of one-way ANOVA (e.g., Edwards, 1972, Chapter 7; Kirk, 1968, Chapter 4).

One-Way Analysis of Variance

In Table 9.4 illustrative data for three groups are presented. You may think of these data as having been obtained in an experiment in which, for example, A_1 and A_2 are different kinds of drugs for the treatment of obesity and A_3 is a placebo. Or, A_1, A_2, and A_3 may represent three different methods of teaching reading. Alternatively, the data may be viewed as having been obtained in nonexperimental research. For example, one might be interested in studying the relation between marital status of adult males and their attitudes to the awarding of child custody to the father after a divorce. A_1 may be married males, A_2 may be single males, and A_3 may be divorced males. Scores on Y would indicate their attitudes. The three groups can, of course, represent three

Table 9.4 Illustrative Data for Three Groups and Analysis of Variance Calculations

	A_1	A_2	A_3	
	4	7	1	
	5	8	2	
	6	9	3	
	7	10	4	
	8	11	5	
ΣY:	30	45	15	$\Sigma Y_t = 90$
$\bar{Y}$:	6	9	3	$(\Sigma Y_t)^2 = 8100$
				$\Sigma Y^2 = 660$

$$C = \frac{8100}{15} = 540$$

$$\text{Total} = 660 - 540 = 120$$

$$\text{Between} = \frac{30^2 + 45^2 + 15^2}{5} - 540 = 90$$

Source	*df*	*ss*	*ms*	*F*
Between	2	90	45.00	18.00
Within	12	30	2.50	
Total	14	120		

other kinds of categories, for example, religious groups, countries of origin, professions, political parties, and so on.

Data such as those reported in Table 9.4 may be analyzed by what is called a one-way analysis of variance, "one-way" referring to the fact that only one independent variable is being used. The ANOVA calculations are presented in Table 9.4, and are not commented upon except to note that the F ratio [18 (2, 12), $p < .01$] indicates that there are significant differences among the three means. Specific elements of Table 9.4 will be commented upon after the analysis of the same data by multiple regression methods to which we now turn.

Multiple Regression Analysis

The data of Table 9.4 are used now to illustrate the application of dummy coding to a variable with multiple categories. The measures of the dependent variable are combined in a single vector, Y, in Table 9.5. This procedure of combining all the measures of the dependent variable in a single vector is always followed, regardless of the number of categories of the independent variable and regardless of the number of independent variables (see Chapter 10). The reason for doing this is to cast the data in the form appropriate for a multiple regression analysis in which a dependent variable is regressed on two or more independent variables. That in the present case there is only one categorical independent variable composed of three categories does not alter the basic conception of bringing information from a set of independent variables to bear on a dependent variable. The information may be obtained from continuous independent variables (as in Part 1 of the book) or it may be obtained from multiple categorical variables (as in Chapter 10) or from a combination of con-

Table 9.5 Dummy Coding for Illustrative Data from Three Groups[a]

Group	Y	X_1	X_2
	4	1	0
	5	1	0
A_1	6	1	0
	7	1	0
	8	1	0
	7	0	1
	8	0	1
A_2	9	0	1
	10	0	1
	11	0	1
	1	0	0
	2	0	0
A_3	3	0	0
	4	0	0
	5	0	0

[a] The same data were analyzed by ANOVA in Table 9.4.

tinuous and categorical variables (as in Chapters 12 and 13). The overall approach and conception are the same, although the interpretation of specific aspects of the results depends on the type of variables used. Furthermore, as is shown in this chapter, specific methods of coding categorical variables yield results that lend themselves to specific interpretations.

For the example under consideration, we know that the measures of the dependent variable, Y, of Table 9.5 were obtained from three groups. It is this information about group membership that is coded to represent the independent variable in the regression analysis. Using dummy coding, two vectors, X_1 and X_2, are created in Table 9.5. In X_1, subjects in group A_1 are assigned 1's, while the subjects not belonging to A_1 are assigned 0's. In X_2, subjects in group A_2 are assigned 1's, while those not belonging to A_2 are assigned 0's. We can also create another vector in which subjects of group A_3 will be assigned 1's, and those not belonging to this group will be assigned 0's. Note, however, that such a vector is not necessary since the information about group membership is exhausted by the two vectors that were created. A third vector will not add any information to that contained in the first two vectors (see discussion above about the linear dependency in **X** when the number of coded vectors is equal to the number of groups, and about $(\mathbf{X}'\mathbf{X})$ therefore being singular).

Stated another way, knowing an individual's status in reference to the first two coded vectors is sufficient information about his or her group membership. Thus, an individual who has a 1 in X_1 and a 0 in X_2 belongs to group A_1; one who has a 0 in X_1 and a 1 in X_2 is a member of group A_2; and an individual who has 0's on both vectors is a member of group A_3. In general, to code a categorical variable with g categories or groups it is necessary to create $g - 1$ vectors, each of which will have 1's for the members of a given group and 0's for subjects not belonging to the group. Because only $g - 1$ vectors are created, it follows that members of one of the groups will have 0's in all the vectors. In the present example there are three categories and therefore two vectors were created. The members of group A_3 are assigned 0's in both vectors. Instead of assigning 1's to groups A_1 and A_2, two different vectors could have been created. For example, in the first vector 1's could be assigned to members of group A_2, and in the second vector 1's could be assigned to members of group A_3. In this case, members of group A_1 will be assigned 0's in both vectors. The specific choice of the group to be assigned 0's is discussed below. Note, however, that regardless of which groups are assigned 1's, the number of vectors necessary and sufficient for information about group membership in the present example is two.

Since the data of Table 9.5 consist of two coded vectors, the regression statistics can be easily done by hand using formulas presented in Chapter 3, or matrix operations presented in Chapter 4. The calculations are particularly easy as the correlations between dummy vectors are easily obtained by a simplified formula (see Cohen, 1968):

$$r_{ij} = -\sqrt{\frac{n_i n_j}{(n - n_i)(n - n_j)}} \tag{9.3}$$

where n_i = sample size in group i; n_j = sample size in group j; and n = total sample in the g groups. When the groups are of equal size (in our case, $n_1 = n_2 = n_3 = 5$), Formula (9.3) reduces to

$$r_{ij} = -\frac{1}{g-1} \tag{9.4}$$

where g is the number of groups. In the present example $g = 3$. Therefore the correlation between X_1 and X_2 of Table 9.5 is

$$r_{12} = -\frac{1}{3-1} = -.5$$

Formulas (9.3) and (9.4) are applicable to any number of dummy vectors. Thus, for example, for five groups or categories four dummy vectors have to be created. Assuming that the groups are of equal size, then the correlation between any two of the dummy vectors is

$$r_{ij} = -\frac{1}{5-1} = -.25$$

The calculation of the correlation between any dummy vector and the dependent variable can also be simplified. Using, for example, Formula (2.42) for the correlation between dummy vector X_2 and Y:

$$r_{y2} = \frac{N\Sigma YX_2 - (\Sigma Y)(\Sigma X_2)}{\sqrt{N\Sigma Y^2 - (\Sigma Y)^2}\sqrt{N\Sigma X_2^2 - (\Sigma X_2)^2}}$$

it may be noted that ΣYX_2 is equal to ΣY for the group assigned 1 in vector X_2; $\Sigma X_2 = \Sigma X_2^2$ is the number of people in the group assigned 1 in vector X_2; and similarly for the correlation of any dummy vector with the dependent variable.

Despite the ease of the calculations for the present example, they are not presented here (you may wish to do them as an exercise). Instead, computer output is presented and discussed. As was done in earlier chapters, excerpts of the output are given, interspersed by comments. Obviously, any computer program for multiple regression analysis may be used. The output presented here was obtained from the REGRESSION program of SPSS.

SPSS Control Cards

Because the control cards for the REGRESSION program of SPSS have been given several times before (see, for example, Chapter 4) they are not given here. A general comment about the number of "variables" read in when coded vectors are used seems advisable, however. Note that "variables" was placed in quotation marks. Computer programs do not distinguish between a variable and a coded vector that may be one of several vectors representing a variable. As far as the program is concerned each vector is a "variable." Thus, if you are using a computer program that requires a statement about the number of variables read in, you would have to count each coded vector as a variable. For the data of Table 9.5 this would mean that three "variables" are read in, although only two are involved (i.e., the dependent variable and two dummy vectors that represent the independent variable). Or, assuming that a single independent variable with six categories is used, then five dummy vectors will be required. The number of "variables" read in (including the dependent variable) will therefore be six. To repeat: the computer program does not distinguish between a coded vector and a variable. It is the user who should bear the distinction in mind when interpreting the results. Consequently, some parts of the output may be irrelevant for a given solution, or parts of the output may have to be combined in order to obtain the relevant information (as shown below and in Chapter 10).

SPSS does not require a statement about the number of variables read in, but it does require a variable list. Such a list must include the dependent variable and all the coded vectors, using any of the SPSS conventions for indicating a variable list. For the data of Table 9.5 the variable list may take, for example, the following form:

```
                                          1
1                                         6
VARIABLE LIST                             Y, X1, X2
```

(Note that in programs like SPSS, BMDP, and SAS a unit vector is automatically inserted for the intercept and therefore should not be read in by the user.)

Output

DEPENDENT VARIABLE Y   R SQUARE .75

		ANALYSIS OF VARIANCE		
	DF	SUM OF SQUARES	MEAN SQUARE	F
REGRESSION	2	90.00	45.00	18.00
RESIDUAL	12	30.00	2.50	

Commentary

$R^2_{y.12} = .75$; that is, 75% of the variance of Y is explained by (or predicted from) the independent variable. The F ratio of 18.00 with 2 and 12 *df* is a test of this R^2:

$$F = \frac{R^2/k}{(1 - R^2)/(N - k - 1)} = \frac{.75/2}{(1 - .75)/(15 - 2 - 1)} = 18.00$$

Note that when the above formula was first introduced, as Formula (3.21), k was defined as the number of independent variables. When, however, coded vectors are used to represent a categorical variable, k is the number of coded vectors, which is equal to the number of groups minus one ($g - 1$). In other words, k is the number of degrees of freedom associated with treatments, groups, or categories (see discussion above under SPSS Control Cards).

Alternatively, the F ratio is a ratio of the mean square regression to the mean square residuals: 45.00/2.50 = 18.00. Compare the results given above with those obtained when the same data were subjected to a one-way analysis of variance (Table 9.4). Note that the Regression Sum of Squares (90.00) is the same as the Between-Groups Sum of Squares obtained in Table 9.4, and that the Residual Sum of Squares (30.00) is the same as the Within-Groups Sum of Squares. The degrees of freedom are, of course, also the same in both tables. Consequently, the mean squares and the *F* ratio are identical in both analyses. The total sum of squares (120) is the sum of the Regression and Residual Sums of Squares, or the sum of the Between-Groups and the Within-Groups Sums of Squares.

When ANOVA is calculated one may obtain the proportion of the total sum of squares accounted for by the independent variable by calculating η^2 (eta squared; see Hays, 1981, p. 349, and Kerlinger, 1973, pp. 230–231):

$$\eta^2 = \frac{ss \text{ between groups}}{ss \text{ total}} \tag{9.5}$$

Using the results from ANOVA of Table 9.4:

$$\eta^2 = \frac{90}{120} = .75$$

Note that $\eta^2 = R^2$.

The equivalence of ANOVA and multiple regression analysis with coded vectors should now be evident. In view of their equivalence, and assuming that you are more familiar and more comfortable with ANOVA, you are probably wondering what, if any, the advantages are in using multiple regression analysis in preference to ANOVA. You are probably questioning whether there is anything to be gained by learning what may seem to be a more complicated analysis. In subsequent sections, some of the advantages of using multiple regression analysis instead of ANOVA are shown. A summary statement contrasting both approaches is given at the end of the chapter.

Output

- - - - - - - - - - - - -VARIABLES IN THE EQUATION- - - - - - - - - - - - -

VARIABLE	B	STD ERROR B	F
X1	3.00	1.00	9.00
X2	6.00	1.00	36.00
(CONSTANT)	3.00		

Commentary

The *regression equation* is

$$Y' = 3.00 + 3.00X_1 + 6.00X_2$$

The means of the three groups (see Table 9.4) are

$$\bar{Y}_{A_1} = 6.00 \qquad \bar{Y}_{A_2} = 9.00 \qquad \bar{Y}_{A_3} = 3.00$$

It is now possible to see the properties of the regression equation obtained when dummy coding is applied to the categorical independent variable. The intercept a (CONSTANT in the above output) is equal to the mean of group A_3, the group whose members were assigned 0's throughout. This will always be the case when dummy coding is used. Furthermore, each b is equal to the deviation of the mean of the group assigned 1 in the vector with which the b is associated from the mean of the group that was assigned 0 in all the vectors. Thus, in X_1 members of group A_1 were assigned 1's (see Table 9.5). The mean of this group is 6.00. Therefore

$$\bar{Y}_{A_1} - \bar{Y}_{A_3} = 6.00 - 3.00 = 3.00 = b_1$$

Similarly, in X_2 members of A_2 were assigned 1's. Since $\bar{Y}_{A_2} = 9.00$,

$$\bar{Y}_{A_2} - \bar{Y}_{A_3} = 9.00 - 3.00 = 6.00 = b_2$$

If the dummy coding were to be assigned differently to the data of the present example, the overall results (i.e., R^2 and F) would be identical to those obtained above. The regression equation, however, will not be the same as the one obtained above. Instead, it will reflect the specific pattern of dummy coding being used. For example, assume that for the data of Table 9.5 members of group A_2 are assigned 1's in X_1 and members of group A_3 are assigned 1's in X_2. Consequently, members of group A_1 will be assigned 0's in both vectors. Regressing Y on X_1 and X_2, the regression equation will be

$$Y' = 6.00 + 3.00X_1 - 3.00X_2$$

The intercept this time (6.00) is equal to the mean of A_1, the group assigned 0's in both vectors.

$$b_1 = \bar{Y}_{A_2} - \bar{Y}_{A_1} = 9.00 - 6.00 = \mathit{3.00}$$

$$b_2 = \bar{Y}_{A_3} - \bar{Y}_{A_1} = 3.00 - 6.00 = \mathit{-3.00}$$

(You may wish to run the example of Table 9.5 by changing the dummy coding, each time assigning the 0's in both vectors to another group and noting the changes in the regression equations. Using SPSS this can be done easily in one run by including an additional vector X_3 in which 1's are assigned to members of group A_3. Using three REGRESSION statements you may select each time two different coded vectors as the independent "variables.")

As was said above, the overall results will be the same regardless of which of the groups was assigned 0's throughout. Hence is there any pattern of codes that is preferable? This is discussed below under tests of regression coefficients. But first we return to the regression equation obtained above. From what was said about the properties of the regression equation it should be evident that when it is applied to the scores of a given individual, it will yield a predicted score that is equal to the mean of the group to which the individual belongs. The scores on the coded vectors are 1's and 0's. Individuals whose group was assigned a 1 in a given vector will have a score of 1 in that vector and

0's in all the others. The scores for individuals who belong to a group that was assigned 0 in all the vectors will, of course, be 0's in all the vectors. For the present example, $Y' = 3.00 + 3.00X_1 + 6.00X_2$. The scores for members of group A_1 are 1 on X_1 and 0 on X_2 (see Table 9.5). Therefore for individuals in this group:

$$Y' = 3.00 + 3.00(1) + 6.00(0) = \mathit{6.00}$$

which is the mean of group A_1.

Similarly, for members of group A_2,

$$Y' = 3.00 + 3.00(0) + 6.00(1) = \mathit{9.00}$$

which is the mean of group A_2.

And for members of group A_3,

$$Y' = 3.00 + 3.00(0) + 6.00(0) = \mathit{3.00}$$

the mean of group A_3.

In other words, the mean of any group is equal to a (the intercept) plus the regression coefficient associated with the vector in which members of the group were assigned 1's. Obviously, the mean of the group assigned 0's throughout is, as was noted above, equal to the intercept (a).

Tests of Regression Coefficients. In earlier chapters (see, in particular, Chapters 3 and 4) it was shown that dividing the b by its standard error yields a t ratio with df equal to those associated with the residual sum of squares. SPSS reports F ratios instead of t's. But since each of the F ratios has one degree of freedom for the numerator, the t ratio for each regression coefficient is equal to the $\sqrt{F}$ associated with it. For the present example, $t = 3.00$ for b_1, and $t = 6.00$ for b_2. Each of the t ratios has 12 df (see output above).

From what was said above about the b's in a regression equation with dummy coding it should be evident that the test of a b is tantamount to testing the difference between the mean of the group assigned 1 in the vector with which the b is associated and the mean of the group assigned 0's in all the vectors. The tests of the b's are therefore relevant when one wishes to test, in turn, the differences between the means of each group assigned 1 in a given vector and that of the group assigned 0's in all the vectors. An example of such a design is when there are several treatments and a control group, and it is desired to compare each of the treatments with the control (see, for example, Edwards, 1972, pp. 147–150; Winer, 1971, pp. 201–204).

The t ratios associated with the b's are identical to the t ratios obtained when following Dunnett (1955): one calculates multiple t ratios between each treatment mean and the control group mean. Such tests are done subsequent to a one-way analysis of variance in the following manner:

$$t = \frac{\bar{X}_1 - \bar{X}_C}{\sqrt{MS_W\left(\frac{1}{n_1} + \frac{1}{n_C}\right)}} \tag{9.6}$$

where $\bar{X}_1$ = mean of treatment 1; $\bar{X}_C$ = mean of control group; MS_W = mean square within groups from the analysis of variance; n_1, n_C = number of subjects in treatment 1 and the control group, respectively. Incidentally, Formula (9.6) is a special case of a t test between any two means subsequent to an analysis of variance. For the general case, the numerator of (9.6) is $\bar{X}_i - \bar{X}_j$ (i.e., the difference between $\bar{X}_i$ and $\bar{X}_j$). The denominator is similarly altered only with respect to the subscripts. When $n_1 = n_C$, Formula (9.6) can be stated as follows:

$$t = \frac{\bar{X}_1 - \bar{X}_C}{\sqrt{\dfrac{2MS_W}{n}}} \tag{9.7}$$

where n = number of subjects in one of the groups. All other terms are as defined for (9.6).

For the sake of illustration, assume that group A_3 of Table 9.4 is a control group, while A_1 and A_2 are two treatment groups. From Table 9.4,

$$\bar{Y}_{A1} = 6.00 \qquad \bar{Y}_{A2} = 9.00 \qquad \bar{Y}_{A3} = 3.00$$

$$n_1 = n_2 = n_3 = 5$$

$$MS_W = 2.50$$

Comparing the mean of A_1 with A_3 (the control):

$$t = \frac{6.00 - 3.00}{\sqrt{\dfrac{2(2.50)}{5}}} = \frac{3.00}{\sqrt{1}} = \frac{3}{1} = 3.00$$

Comparing A_2 with A_3:

$$t = \frac{9.00 - 3.00}{\sqrt{\dfrac{2(2.50)}{5}}} = \frac{6.00}{1} = 6.00$$

The two t ratios are identical to the ones obtained for the two b's associated with the dummy vectors of Table 9.5, where A_3 was assigned 0 in both vectors and therefore each mean of the other groups was compared with the mean of A_3.

In order to determine whether a given t ratio for the comparison of a treatment mean with the control mean is significant at a prespecified level, one may check a special table prepared by Dunnett. This table is reproduced in various statistics books, including Edwards (1972) and Winer (1971). For the present case, where the analysis was performed as if there were two treatments and a control group, the tabled values of a one-tailed t with 12 df are 2.11 (.05 level), 3.01 (.01 level), and for a two-tailed test: 2.50 (.05 level), 3.39 (.01 level).

To recapitulate, the F ratio associated with the R^2 of the dependent variable with the dummy vectors indicates whether there are significant differences among some or all the means of the groups. This is, of course, equivalent to the overall F ratio of the analysis of variance. The t ratio for each b is equivalent to the t ratio for the difference between the mean of the group assigned 1 in the vector with which the b is associated and the mean of the group assigned 0 throughout. In other words, the t ratios for the b's in effect treat the group assigned 0 in all the vectors as a control group.

Dummy coding is not restricted to situations in which there are several treatment groups and a control group. They can be used to code any categorical variable. When there is no control group in the design, the designation of the group to be assigned 0 in all the vectors is arbitrary. Under such circumstances, the t ratios for the b's are irrelevant. Instead, the overall F ratio for the R^2 is interpreted. In order to determine specifically which group means are significantly different from each other, it is necessary to apply one of the methods for multiple comparisons between means. This topic is taken up in a subsequent section.

If, on the other hand, one has a design in which several treatment means are to be compared with a control mean, the control group is the one assigned 0 in all vectors. Doing this, all one needs in order to determine which treatment means differ significantly from the control group mean is to note which of the t ratios associated with the b's exceed the critical value in Dunnett's table.

EFFECT CODING

Effect coding is so named because, as shown below, the regression coefficients yielded by its use reflect the effects of the treatments of the analysis. The code numbers used are 1's, 0's, and -1's. Effect coding is thus similar to dummy coding. The difference is that in dummy coding one group or category is assigned 0's in all the vectors, whereas in effect coding the same group is assigned -1's in all the vectors. (See -1's assigned to A_3 in Table 9.6.) Although it makes no difference which group is assigned -1's, it is convenient to assign them to members of the last group. One generates k vectors (k = number of groups minus one). In each vector, members of one group are assigned 1's; all other subjects are assigned 0's except for members of the last group, who are assigned -1's.

The application of effect coding to the data earlier analyzed by dummy coding is illustrated in Table 9.6. Note that in vector X_1 of Table 9.6 members of group A_1 are assigned 1's, members of group A_2 are assigned 0's, and members of group A_3 are assigned -1's. In vector X_2, members of A_1 are assigned 0's, those of A_2 are assigned 1's and those of A_3 are assigned -1's.

The data of Table 9.6 were analyzed by the REGRESSION program of SPSS. Following are excerpts of the output and commentaries.

Output

DEPENDENT VARIABLE Y R SQUARE .75

		ANALYSIS OF VARIANCE		
	DF	SUM OF SQUARES	MEAN SQUARE	F
REGRESSION	2	90.00	45.00	18.00
RESIDUAL	12	30.00	2.50	

Table 9.6 Effect Coding for Illustrative Data from Three Groups[a]

Group	*Ss*	*Y*	X_1	X_2
	1	4	1	0
	2	5	1	0
A_1	3	6	1	0
	4	7	1	0
	5	8	1	0
	6	7	0	1
	7	8	0	1
A_2	8	9	0	1
	9	10	0	1
	10	11	0	1
	11	1	−1	−1
	12	2	−1	−1
A_3	13	3	−1	−1
	14	4	−1	−1
	15	5	−1	−1
M:		6	0	0

[a]Vector *Y* is repeated from Table 9.5.

Commentary

The above output is identical to the one obtained earlier with dummy coding and is therefore not commented upon, except to note that the overall results are the same regardless of what method one uses to code the categorical variable. The difference between the two methods is in the properties of the regression equations that result from their application. The properties of the regression equation obtained when dummy coding is used were discussed above. We turn now to an examination of the regression equation when effect coding is used.

Output

```
- - - - - - - - - - - -VARIABLES IN THE EQUATION- - - - - - - - - - - -
VARIABLE              B              STD ERROR B              F
      X1              0                .57735                 0
      X2              3.00             .57735             27.00
(CONSTANT)            6.00
```

Commentary

The *regression equation* is

$$Y' = 6 + 0X_1 + 3X_2$$

Note that *a* (the intercept) is equal to the grand mean of the dependent variable, $\bar{Y}$, while each *b* is equal to the deviation of the mean of the group assigned 1's in the vector with which it is associated from the grand mean. Thus, b_1 is equal to the deviation of mean A_1 from the grand mean ($\bar{Y}$); that is, $6.00 - 6.00 = 0$. b_2 is equal to $\bar{Y}_{A_2} - \bar{Y} = 9.00 - 6.00 = 3.00$. It is evident, then, that *each b reflects a treatment effect;* b_1 reflects the effect of treatment A_1, while b_2 reflects the effect of treatment A_2. This method of coding thus generates a regression equation whose b coefficients reflect the effects of the treatments. In order to appreciate the properties of the regression equation that results from the use of effect coding, it is necessary to digress for a brief presentation of the linear model. After this presentation the discussion of the regression equation is resumed.

The Fixed Effects Linear Model

The fixed effects one-way analysis of variance is presented by some authors (for example, Graybill, 1961; Scheffé, 1959; Searle, 1971) in the form of the linear model:

$$Y_{ij} = \mu + \beta_j + \epsilon_{ij} \tag{9.8}$$

where Y_{ij} = the score of individual i in group or treatment j; μ = the population mean; β_j = the effect of treatment j; ϵ_{ij} = error associated with the score of individual i in group or treatment j. "Linear model" means that an individual's score is conceived as a linear composite of several components. In (9.8) it is a composite of three parts: the grand mean, a treatment effect, and an error term. The error is the part of Y_{ij} not explained by the grand mean and the treatment effect. This can be seen from a restatement of (9.8) as follows:

$$\epsilon_{ij} = Y_{ij} - \mu - \beta_j \tag{9.9}$$

The method of least squares is used to minimize the sum of squared errors ($\Sigma\epsilon_{ij}^2$). In other words, an attempt is being made to explain as much of Y_{ij} as possible by the grand mean and a treatment effect. In order to obtain a unique solution to the problem, the restraint that $\Sigma\beta_g = 0$ is used (g = number of groups). The meaning of this condition is simply that the sum of the treatment effects is zero. It is shown below that such a restraint results in expressing each treatment effect as the deviation of the mean of the treatment whose effect is studied from the grand mean.

Although Equation (9.8) is expressed in parameters, or population values, in actual analyses statistics are used as estimates of these parameters:

$$Y_{ij} = \bar{Y} + b_j + e_{ij} \tag{9.10}$$

where $\bar{Y}$ = the grand mean; b_j = effect of treatment j; e_{ij} = error associated with individual i under treatment j.

The sum of squares, $\Sigma(Y - \bar{Y})^2$, can be expressed in the context of the regression equation. It will be recalled from Equation (2.10) that $Y' = \bar{Y} + bx$. Therefore,[2]

[2]See Chapter 2 for a presentation that parallels the one given here.

$$Y = \bar{Y} + bx + e$$

A deviation of a score from the mean of the dependent variable can be expressed thus:

$$Y - \bar{Y} = \bar{Y} + bx + e - \bar{Y}$$

Substituting $Y - \bar{Y} - bx$ for e in the above formula, we obtain

$$Y - \bar{Y} = \bar{Y} + bx + Y - \bar{Y} - bx - \bar{Y}$$

Now, $\bar{Y} + bx = Y'$ and $Y - \bar{Y} - bx = Y - Y'$. By substitution,

$$Y - \bar{Y} = Y' + Y - Y' - \bar{Y}$$

Rearranging the terms on the right,

$$Y - \bar{Y} = (Y' - \bar{Y}) + (Y - Y') \tag{9.11}$$

Since we are interesting in explaining the sum of squares,

$$\begin{aligned}\Sigma y^2 &= \Sigma[(Y' - \bar{Y}) + (Y - Y')]^2 \\ &= \Sigma(Y' - \bar{Y})^2 + \Sigma(Y - Y')^2 + 2\Sigma(Y' - \bar{Y})(Y - Y')\end{aligned}$$

It can be demonstrated that the last term on the right equals zero. Therefore

$$\Sigma y^2 = \Sigma(Y' - \bar{Y})^2 + \Sigma(Y - Y')^2 \tag{9.12}$$

The first term on the right, $\Sigma(Y' - \bar{Y})^2$, is the sum of squares due to regression. It is analogous to the between-groups sum of squares of the analysis of variance. $\Sigma(Y - Y')^2$ is the residual sum of squares, or what is termed the within-groups sum of squares in the analysis of variance. $\Sigma(Y' - \bar{Y})^2 = 0$ means that Σy^2 is all due to residuals, and we thus have explained nothing by knowledge of X. If, on the other hand, $\Sigma(Y - Y')^2 = 0$, all the variability is explained by regression, or by the information X provides. We return now to the regression equation that resulted from the analysis with effect coding.

The Meaning of the Regression Equation

From the foregoing discussion it can be seen that the use of effect coding results in a regression equation that reflects the linear model. This is illustrated by applying the regression equation obtained above ($Y' = 6 + 0X_1 + 3X_2$) to some of the subjects of Table 9.6. For subject number 1 we obtain

$$Y'_1 = 6 + 0(1) + 3(0) = 6$$

This is, of course, the mean of the group to which this subject belongs, namely the mean of A_1. The residual for subject 1 is

$$e_1 = Y_1 - Y'_1 = 4 - 6 = -2$$

Expressing the score of subject 1 in components of the linear model:

$$Y_1 = a + b_1 + e_1$$

$$4 = 6 + 0 + (-2)$$

Since a is equal to the grand mean ($\bar{Y}$), and for each group (except for the one assigned -1's) there is only one vector in which it is assigned 1's, the predicted score for each subject is a composite of a and the b for the vector in which the subject is assigned 1. In other words, *a predicted score is a composite of the grand mean and the treatment effect of the group to which the subject belongs.* Thus, for subjects in group A_1 the application of the regression equation results in $Y' = 6 + 0(1)$, because subjects in this group are assigned 1's in the first vector only, and 0's in all others, regardless of the number of groups involved in the analysis.

For subjects of group A_2 the regression equation is, in effect, $Y' = 6 + 3(1)$, 6 being the a (intercept), and 3 the b associated with the vector in which subjects of group A_2 are assigned 1's. Since the predicted score for any subject is the mean of his group expressed as a composite of $a + b$, and since a is the grand mean, it follows that b is the deviation of the group mean from the grand mean. As stated earlier, b is equal to the treatment effect for the group with which it is associated. For group A_1 the treatment effect is $b_1 = 0$, and for group A_2 the treatment effect is $b_2 = 3$.

Applying now the regression equation to subject number 6 (the first subject of group A_2) we obtain

$$Y'_6 = 6 + (0)(0) + (3)(1) = 9$$

$$e_6 = Y_6 - Y'_6 = 7 - 9 = -2$$

Expressing the score of subject 6 in components of the linear model:

$$Y_6 = a + b_2 + e_6$$

$$7 = 6 + 3 + (-2)$$

The treatment effect for the group assigned -1 is easily obtained when considering the constraint $\Sigma b_g = 0$. In the present problem this means

$$b_1 + b_2 + b_3 = 0$$

Substituting the values for b_1 and b_2 obtained above,

$$0 + 3 + b_3 = 0$$

$$b_3 = -3$$

In general, the treatment effect for the group assigned -1's is $-\Sigma b_k$ (k = number of coded vectors, or $g - 1$, number of groups minus one). For the present problem,[3]

$$b_3 = -\Sigma(b_k) = -\Sigma(0 + 3) = -3$$

The mean of A_3 is 3, and its deviation from the grand mean ($\bar{Y} = 6.00$) is -3, which is the value of b_3, the treatment effect for A_3.

Applying the regression equation to subject 11 (the first subject in group A_3),

$$\begin{aligned} Y'_{11} &= 6 + 0(-1) + 3(-1) \\ &= 6 - 3 = 3 \end{aligned}$$

This is the mean of A_3. All other subjects in A_3 will have the same predicted Y.

$$\begin{aligned} e_{11} &= Y_{11} - Y'_{11} = 1 - 3 = -2 \\ Y_{11} &= a + b_3 + e_{11} \\ 1 &= 6 + (-3) + (-2) \end{aligned}$$

The foregoing discussion can perhaps be best summarized and illustrated by examining Table 9.7. Several points will be noted in reference to this table.

Each person's score is expressed as being composed of three components: (1) $\bar{Y}$—the grand mean of the dependent variable. In the regression equation with effect coding this is equal to the intercept (a). (2) b_j—the effect of the treatment administered to the group to which a person belongs, defined as the deviation of the treatment mean from the grand mean. In the regression equation with effect coding this is equal to the b for the vector in which a given treatment was assigned 1. For the treatment assigned -1's in all the vectors, it is equal to $-\Sigma b_j$. (3) e_{ij}—the residual for person i in treatment j.

Squaring and summing the treatment effects (column b_j of Table 9.7) one obtains the regression sum of squares, or 90 (see the last line of Table 9.7). Clearly, then, the regression sum of squares reflects the differential effects of the treatments.

Squaring and summing the residuals (column e_{ij} of Table 9.7) one obtains the residual sum of squares, or 30 (see the last line of Table 9.7). Clearly, this is the sum of the squared errors of prediction.

In Equation (2.2) it was shown that a deviation sum of squares may be obtained as follows:

$$\Sigma y^2 = \Sigma Y^2 - \frac{(\Sigma Y)^2}{N}$$

[3]Note that b_3 is not part of the regression equation, which consists of two b's only because there are only two coded vectors. For convenience, b_{k+1} will be used to represent the effect of the treatment for the group assigned -1's in all the vectors. Thus, if there are, for example, five groups, there will be four b's for the four coded vectors. b_5 will be used to refer to the effect of the treatment for the group assigned -1's in all the vectors.

Table 9.7 Data for Three Groups Expressed as Components of the Linear Model

Group	*Ss*	Y	$\bar{Y}$	b_j	Y'	$e_{ij} = Y - Y'$
	1	4	6	0	6	−2
	2	5	6	0	6	−1
A_1	3	6	6	0	6	0
	4	7	6	0	6	1
	5	8	6	0	6	2
	6	7	6	3	9	−2
	7	8	6	3	9	−1
A_2	8	9	6	3	9	0
	9	10	6	3	9	1
	10	11	6	3	9	2
	11	1	6	−3	3	−2
	12	2	6	−3	3	−1
A_3	13	3	6	−3	3	0
	14	4	6	−3	3	1
	15	5	6	−3	3	2
Σ:		90	90	0	90	0
SS:		660	540	90	630	30

NOTE: Vector Y is repeated from Table 9.6. SS = sum of the squared elements in each of the columns. Thus, $SS_Y = \Sigma Y^2$, $SS_{\bar{Y}} = \Sigma \bar{Y}^2$, and so forth.

From Table 9.7,

$$\Sigma y^2 = 660 - \frac{(90)^2}{15} = 120$$

It is this sum of squares that is partitioned into ss_{reg} (90) and ss_{res} (30).

An alternative formula for the calculation of Σy^2 is:

$$\Sigma y^2 = \Sigma(Y - \bar{Y})^2 = \Sigma Y^2 - \Sigma \bar{Y}^2$$

$$= 660 - 540 = 120 \qquad \text{(from last line of Table 9.7)}$$

Similarly,

$$ss_{reg} = \Sigma(Y' - \bar{Y})^2 = \Sigma Y'^2 - \Sigma \bar{Y}^2$$

$$= 630 - 540 = 90 \qquad \text{(from last line of Table 9.7)}$$

$$ss_{res} = \Sigma(Y - Y')^2 = \Sigma Y^2 - \Sigma Y'^2$$

$$= 660 - 630 = 30 \qquad \text{(from last line of Table 9.7)}$$

Pooling the above together:

$$\Sigma y^2 = ss_{reg} + ss_{res}$$

$$\Sigma Y^2 - \Sigma \bar{Y}^2 = (\Sigma Y'^2 - \Sigma \bar{Y}^2) + (\Sigma Y^2 - \Sigma Y'^2)$$

$$660 - 540 = (630 - 540) + (660 - 630)$$

$$120 = 90 + 30$$

The second line is an algebraic equivalent of Equation (9.12). The third and fourth lines are numeric expressions of this equation for the data of Table 9.7.

One final comment will be made about the regression equation obtained with effect coding. Although each of the b's can be tested for significance (computer programs report such tests routinely; see above output), they are generally not used in the present context because the interest is not in whether a mean for a given group differs significantly from the grand mean (which is what the b reflects) but rather whether there are significant differences among the means, or treatments.

MULTIPLE COMPARISONS BETWEEN MEANS

A significant F ratio for R^2 leads to the rejection of the null hypothesis that there is no relation between group membership, or treatments, and performance on the dependent variable. With a categorical independent variable the significant R^2 in effect means that the null hypothesis $\mu_1 = \mu_2 = \cdots = \mu_g$ (g = number of groups, or categories) is rejected. Rejection of the null hypothesis, however, does not necessarily mean that all the means are significantly different from each other. In order to determine which of the means differ significantly from each other, one of the methods of multiple comparisons of means must be used.

There are two types of comparisons of means: planned comparisons and post hoc comparisons. *Planned comparisons* are hypothesized by the researcher prior to the overall analysis. Consequently, they are also referred to as a priori comparisons. *Post hoc,* or a posteriori, comparisons are performed following the rejection of the overall null hypothesis. Only when the F ratio associated with R^2 is significant may one proceed with post hoc comparisons between means in order to detect where significant differences exist.

The topic of post hoc comparisons is complex.[4] Various methods are available, but there is no universal agreement about their appropriateness. For a presentation and a discussion of the various methods the reader is referred to Games (1971), Kirk (1968), Miller (1966), and Winer (1971). The presentation here is limited to a method developed by Scheffé (1959). The Scheffé, or the S, method is the most general method of multiple comparisons. It enables one to make all possible comparisons between individual means as well as between combinations of means. In addition, it is applicable to equal as well as unequal frequencies in the groups or the categories of the variable. It is also the most conservative test. That is, it is less likely than other tests to show differences as significant. A *comparison,* a *contrast,* or a *difference* is a linear combination of the form

[4]Planned comparisons are discussed later in this chapter.

$$D = C_1\overline{Y}_1 + C_2\overline{Y}_2 + \cdots + C_j\overline{Y}_j \tag{9.13}$$

where D = difference or contrast; C = coefficient by which a given mean, $\overline{Y}$, is multiplied; j = number of means involved in the comparison. It is required that $\Sigma C_j = 0$. That is, the sum of the coefficients in a given contrast must equal zero. Thus, contrasting $\overline{Y}_1$ with $\overline{Y}_2$ one can set $C_1 = 1$ and $C_2 = -1$. Accordingly,

$$D = (1)(\overline{Y}_1) + (-1)(\overline{Y}_2) = \overline{Y}_1 - \overline{Y}_2$$

A contrast is not limited to individual means. One may, for example, contrast the average of $\overline{Y}_1$ and $\overline{Y}_2$ with that of $\overline{Y}_3$. This can be accomplished by setting $C_1 = 1/2$; $C_2 = 1/2$; $C_3 = -1$. Accordingly,

$$D = \left(\frac{1}{2}\right)(\overline{Y}_1) + \left(\frac{1}{2}\right)(\overline{Y}_2) + (-1)(\overline{Y}_3)$$
$$= \frac{\overline{Y}_1 + \overline{Y}_2}{2} - \overline{Y}_3$$

A comparison is considered statistically significant if $|D|$ (the absolute value of D) exceeds a value S, which is defined as follows:

$$S = \sqrt{kF_{\alpha};\, k,\, N - k - 1}\ \sqrt{MSR\left[\Sigma\frac{(C_j)^2}{n_j}\right]} \tag{9.14}$$

where k = number of coded vectors, or number of groups minus one; $F_{\alpha}; k, N - k - 1$ = tabled value of F with k and $N - k - 1$ degrees of freedom at a prespecified α level; MSR = mean square residuals or, equivalently, the mean square error from the analysis of variance; C_j = coefficient by which the mean of group j is multiplied; n_j = number of subjects in group j.

The method is now illustrated for some comparisons between the means of the example of Table 9.7. For this example $\overline{Y}_{A_1} = 6.00$; $\overline{Y}_{A_2} = 9.00$; $\overline{Y}_{A_3} = 3.00$; $MSR = 2.50$; $k = 2$; $N - k - 1 = 12$ (see Table 9.4 or SPSS output above). The tabled F ratio for 2 and 12*df* for the .05 level is 3.88. Contrasting $\overline{Y}_{A_1}$ with $\overline{Y}_{A_2}$,

$$D = (1)(\overline{Y}_{A_1}) + (-1)(\overline{Y}_{A_2}) = 6.00 - 9.00 = -3.00$$

$$S = \sqrt{(2)(3.88)}\ \sqrt{2.50\left[\frac{(1)^2}{5} + \frac{(-1)^2}{5}\right]} = \sqrt{7.76}\ \sqrt{2.50\left(\frac{2}{5}\right)}$$
$$= \sqrt{7.76}\ \sqrt{\frac{5}{5}} = (2.79)(1.00) = 2.79$$

Since $|D|$ exceeds S it is concluded that $\overline{Y}_{A_1}$ is significantly different from $\overline{Y}_{A_2}$ at the .05 level. Because $n_1 = n_2 = n_3$, S is the same for any comparison between two means. It can therefore be concluded that the difference between $\overline{Y}_{A_1}$ and $\overline{Y}_{A_3}$ (6.00 − 3.00) and that between $\overline{Y}_{A_2}$ and $\overline{Y}_{A_3}$ (9.00 − 3.00) are also significant. In the present example all the possible comparisons between individual means are significant.

Suppose that one also wished to compare the average of the means for groups A_1 and A_3 with the mean of group A_2. This can be done in the following manner:

$$D = \left(\frac{1}{2}\right)(\bar{Y}_{A_1}) + \left(\frac{1}{2}\right)(\bar{Y}_{A_3}) + (-1)(\bar{Y}_{A_2})$$

$$D = \left(\frac{1}{2}\right)(6.00) + \left(\frac{1}{2}\right)(3.00) + (-1)(9.00) = -4.50$$

$$S = \sqrt{(2)(3.88)}\sqrt{(2.50)\left[\frac{(.5)^2}{5} + \frac{(.5)^2}{5} + \frac{(-1)^2}{5}\right]}$$

$$= \sqrt{7.76}\sqrt{(2.50)\frac{(1.50)}{5}} = \sqrt{7.76}\sqrt{\frac{3.75}{5}} = \sqrt{7.76}\sqrt{.75}$$

$$= (2.79)(.87) = 2.43$$

$|D|$ (4.50) is larger than S (2.43) and it is concluded that there is a significant difference between $\bar{Y}_{A_2}$ and $(\bar{Y}_{A_1} + \bar{Y}_{A_3})/2$.

In order to avoid working with fractions one may multiply the coefficients by a constant. For the above comparison, for example, the coefficients may be multiplied by 2, thereby setting $C_1 = 1$, $C_2 = 1$, $C_3 = -2$. This will result in testing $(\bar{Y}_{A_1} + \bar{Y}_{A_3}) - 2\bar{Y}_{A_2}$, which is equivalent to the above test.

$$D = (1)(6.00) + (1)(3.00) + (-2)(9.00) = -9.00$$

$$S = \sqrt{(2)(3.88)}\sqrt{(2.50)\left[\frac{(1)^2}{5} + \frac{(1)^2}{5} + \frac{(-2)^2}{5}\right]}$$

$$= 2.79\sqrt{(2.50)\left(\frac{6}{5}\right)} = 2.79\sqrt{3.00} = (2.79)(1.73) = 4.83$$

The ratios of D to S in both instances are the same, within rounding errors. The second D is twice as large as the first D, and the second S is twice as large as the first S. The conclusion from either the first or the second calculation is therefore the same.

Any number of means and any combination of means can be compared similarly. The only constraint is that the sum of the coefficients of each comparison must be zero.

An alternative approach for performing the Scheffé test is as follows:

$$F = \frac{[C_1(\bar{Y}_1) + C_2(\bar{Y}_2) + \cdots + C_j(\bar{Y}_j)]^2}{MSR\left[\Sigma\frac{(C_j)^2}{n_j}\right]} \tag{9.15}$$

where the numerator is the square of a comparison as defined in (9.13). In the denominator: MSR = mean square residuals; C_j = coefficient by which the mean of group j is multiplied; n_j = number of subjects in group j. The F ratio has 1 and $N - k - 1$ df. In order for a comparison to be declared statistically significant, the F associated with it has to exceed $kF_\alpha; k, N - k - 1$, where k the number of coded vectors, or the number of groups minus one; $F_\alpha; k, N - k - 1$ = tabled value of F with k and $N - k - 1$ degrees of freedom at a prespecified α level.

For the data of Table 9.7, $\bar{Y}_{A_1} = 6.00$; $\bar{Y}_{A_2} = 9.00$; $\bar{Y}_{A_3} = 3.00$; $MSR = 2.50$; $k = 2$; $N - k - 1 = 12$.

Equation (9.15) is applied now to the same comparisons performed above where (9.14) was used. Testing the difference between $\bar{Y}_{A_1}$ and $\bar{Y}_{A_2}$,

$$F = \frac{[(1)(6.00) + (-1)(9.00)]^2}{2.5\left[\frac{(1)^2}{5} + \frac{(-1)^2}{5}\right]} = \frac{9}{1} = 9$$

The tabled F ratio for 2 and 12 df for the .05 level is 3.88. The obtained F above exceeds $(2)(3.88) = 7.76$ (kF_α; k, $N - k - 1$ as described above), and it is therefore concluded that the comparison is significant at the .05 level.

Contrasting the means of A_1 and A_3 with that of A_2:

$$F = \frac{[(1)(6.00) + (-2)(9.00) + (1)(3.00)]^2}{2.5\left[\frac{(1)^2}{5} + \frac{(-2)^2}{5} + \frac{(1)^2}{5}\right]} = \frac{81}{3} = 27.00$$

This F ratio exceeds 7.76 (kF_α; k, $N - k - 1$), and it is therefore concluded that the contrast is significant at the .05 level.

The conclusions based on the use of (9.15) are, of course, identical to those arrived at when (9.14) was applied. It is now shown how multiple comparisons among means can be accomplished by testing differences among regression coefficients (b's) associated with coded vectors.

Multiple Comparisons Via *b*'s

It was shown above that the mean of a given group is a composite of the grand mean and the treatment effect for the group. For effect coding this was expressed earlier as $\bar{Y}_j = a + b_j$, where $\bar{Y}_j$ = mean of group j; a = intercept, or grand mean, $\bar{Y}$; and b_j = the effect of treatment j, or $\bar{Y}_j - \bar{Y}$. Accordingly, when contrasting, for example, $\bar{Y}_{A_1}$ with $\bar{Y}_{A_2}$,

$$\begin{aligned} D = (1)(\bar{Y}_{A_1}) + (-1)(\bar{Y}_{A_2}) &= (1)(a + b_1) + (-1)(a + b_2) \\ &= a + b_1 - a - b_2 \\ &= b_1 - b_2 \end{aligned}$$

Similarly,

$$\begin{aligned} D = (1)(\bar{Y}_{A_1}) + (-2)(\bar{Y}_{A_2}) + (1)(\bar{Y}_{A_3}) &= (1)(a + b_1) + (-2)(a + b_2) + (1)(a + b_3) \\ &= a + b_1 - 2a - 2b_2 + a + b_3 \\ &= b_1 + b_3 - 2b_2 \end{aligned}$$

Therefore, testing differences between b's is tantamount to testing differences between means. The notion of testing the difference between two b's was introduced in Chapter 4 in connection with the covariance matrix of the b's

(C).[5] But before it is shown how elements of **C** are used for testing of differences between b's, it is necessary to augment **C**. The meaning and purpose of this operation are explained in the next section.

Augmented C: C*

In Chapter 4 it was noted that one may obtain **C** from the CDC version of SPSS. Alternatively, it was shown how one may use BMDP or SAS output to obtain **C**. For the numerical example of Table 9.6, **C**, as obtained from SPSS, is:

$$\mathbf{C} \begin{bmatrix} .33333 & -.16667 \\ -.16667 & .33333 \end{bmatrix}$$

Note that **C** is a 2×2 matrix corresponding to the two b's associated with the two coded vectors of Table 9.6 (b_1 and b_2 reported above in the output). That is, it provides the variances and the covariance for b_1 and b_2 only. Consequently, information is available for contrasts between treatments A_1 and A_2 (recall that b_1 indicates the effect of treatment A_1 and b_2 indicates the effect of treatment A_2). In order to test differences that involve treatment A_3 it is necessary to obtain the variance for b_3 as well as the covariances of b_3 with the remaining b's. This can be easily accomplished in a manner analogous to that done above for the calculation of b_3 (i.e., the effect of the treatment assigned -1's in all the coded vectors). Recall that $b_3 = -\Sigma b_j$. The same approach is taken to augment **C** so that it includes the missing elements for b_3. A missing element in a row (or column) of **C** is equal to $-\Sigma c_i$ (or $-\Sigma c_j$), where i is row i of **C** and j is column j of **C**. Note that what this means is that the sum of each row (and column) of the augmented matrix (**C***) is equal to zero. For the present example,

$$\mathbf{C}^* = \begin{array}{cc:c} .33333 & -.16667 & -.16667 \\ -.16667 & .33333 & -.16667 \\ \hdashline -.16667 & -.16667 & .33333 \end{array}$$

where the dashes have been inserted to indicate the elements that were added to **C**.

Note that the diagonal elements are equal to each other. Also the off-diagonal elements are equal to each other. This will always be the case when the n's (n = number of people in a group or treatment) are equal. Therefore, it is not necessary to go through the above outlined procedure in order to obtain the missing elements. All that is necessary to obtain **C*** from **C** when n's are equal is to add a diagonal element equal to those of the diagonal of **C**, and similarly for the off-diagonal elements.

The reason the procedure for obtaining **C*** was outlined above is that when the n's are unequal, or when both categorical and continuous independent vari-

[5]If you are encountering difficulties with the presentation in this section, it is suggested that you review relevant discussions of **C** and its properties in Chapter 4.

ables are used, the diagonal elements of **C** will generally not be equal to each other, nor will the off-diagonal elements be equal to each other. But the method of augmenting **C** applies equally to such situations, as does the method of using elements of **C*** for doing multiple comparisons. Although the method is illustrated below for the case of a categorical variable with equal n's, it is for situations in which a categorical as well as continuous independent variables are used that the method is particularly useful (see Chapter 13). We are ready now to test differences between b's.

Tests of Differences Between *b*'s

The variance of estimate of the difference between two b's is

$$s^2_{b_i - b_j} = c_{ii} + c_{jj} - 2c_{ij} \tag{9.16}$$

where $s^2_{b_i - b_j}$ = variance of estimate of the difference between b_i and b_j; c_{ii} = diagonal element of **C*** for i, and similarly for c_{jj}; $c_{ij} = c_{ji}$ are the off-diagonal elements of **C*** corresponding to ij (see also Equation (4.12)).

$$F = \frac{[(1)(b_i) + (-1)(b_j)]^2}{s^2_{b_i - b_j}} \tag{9.17}$$

with 1 df for the numerator and $N - k - 1$ df for the denominator (i.e., df associated with the mean square residual).

The regression equation obtained above for the data of Table 9.6 is:

$$Y' = 6.00 + 0X_1 + 3X_2$$

(see output above) and

$$b_3 = -\Sigma b_j = -\Sigma(0 + 3) = -3$$

Obtaining the appropriate elements from **C*** (reported above), calculate F for the difference between b_1 and b_2:

$$F = \frac{[(1)(0) + (-1)(3)]^2}{.33333 + .33333 - 2(-.16667)} = \frac{9}{1} = 9$$

The same value was obtained when Equation (9.15) was applied to test the difference between $\bar{Y}_{A_1}$ and $\bar{Y}_{A_2}$ (see above). It was noted earlier that when the Scheffé procedure is applied the obtained F has to exceed kF_α; $k, N - k - 1$ (see discussion above). The sole purpose here has been to demonstrate that identical results are obtained when (9.15) and (9.17) are applied.

As was the case with (9.15), Equation (9.17) can be expanded to accommodate comparisons between combinations of b's. For this purpose, the numerator of the F ratio consists of the squared linear combination of b's and the denominator consists of the variance of estimate of this linear combination.

Although it is possible to express the variance of estimate of a linear combination of b's in a form analogous to (9.16), this becomes unwieldy when several b's are involved. It is therefore more convenient and more efficient to use matrix notation. Thus, for a linear combination of b's,

$$F = \frac{[a_1(b_1) + a_2(b_2) + \cdot \cdot \cdot + a_j(b_j)]^2}{\mathbf{a}'\mathbf{C}^*\mathbf{a}} \tag{9.18}$$

where $a_1, a_2, \ldots, a_j$ are coefficients by which b's are multiplied (a's are used here instead of c's so as not to confuse them with elements of $\mathbf{C}^*$, the augmented matrix); $\mathbf{a}'$ and $\mathbf{a}$ are the row and column vectors, respectively, of the coefficients of the linear combination; $\mathbf{C}^*$ is the augmented covariance matrix of the b's. Since some of the a's of a given linear combination may be 0's, thus excluding the b's associated with them from consideration, it is convenient to exclude such a's from the numerator and the denominator of (9.18). Accordingly, only that part of $\mathbf{C}^*$ whose elements correspond to nonzero a's will be used in the denominator of (9.18). This is now illustrated by the application of (9.18) to the b's of the numerical example under consideration. First, calculate the F for the contrast between b_1 and b_2 (the same contrast that was used when (9.17) was applied). Recall that $b_1 = 0$ and $b_2 = 3$. From $\mathbf{C}^*$ obtain the values that correspond to the variances and covariances of these b's.

$$F = \frac{[(1)(0) + (-1)(3)]^2}{[1 \quad -1]\begin{bmatrix} .33333 & -.16667 \\ -.16667 & .33333 \end{bmatrix}\begin{bmatrix} 1 \\ -1 \end{bmatrix}} = \frac{9}{1} = 9$$

The same value was obtained when (9.17) was applied above.

Earlier, $\bar{Y}_{A_1}$ and $\bar{Y}_{A_3}$ were contrasted with $\bar{Y}_{A_2}$, using (9.15). It is now shown that the same F ratio (27.00) is obtained when contrasting b_1 and b_3 with b_2 applying (9.18). Recall that $b_1 = 0$, $b_2 = 3$, $b_3 = -3$.

$$F = \frac{[(1)(0) + (-2)(3) + (1)(-3)]^2}{[1 \quad -2 \quad 1]\begin{bmatrix} .33333 & -.16667 & -.16667 \\ -.16667 & .33333 & -.16667 \\ -.16667 & -.16667 & .33333 \end{bmatrix}\begin{bmatrix} 1 \\ -2 \\ 1 \end{bmatrix}} = \frac{81}{3} = 27.00$$

One can, similarly, test any other linear combination of b's. For example, contrasting b_2 with b_3:

$$F = \frac{[(1)(3) + (-1)(-3)]^2}{[1 \quad -1]\begin{bmatrix} .33333 & -.16667 \\ -.16667 & .33333 \end{bmatrix}\begin{bmatrix} 1 \\ -1 \end{bmatrix}} = \frac{36}{1} = 36.00$$

The same F ratio will be obtained if one were to use (9.15) for testing the difference between $\bar{Y}_{A_2}$ and $\bar{Y}_{A_3}$.

In view of the special features of $\mathbf{C}^*$ when sample sizes are equal (equal n's) the calculation of $\mathbf{a}'\mathbf{C}^*\mathbf{a}$—that is, the denominator of (9.18)—can be greatly simplified. Recall that each element of $\mathbf{C}^*$ is equal to the variance of the b with which it is associated (s_b^2). But with equal n's the variances of the b's are equal to each other. Each off-diagonal element of $\mathbf{C}^*$ (when n's are equal) is equal to $-c_{ii}/k$, where c_{ii} is a diagonal element of $\mathbf{C}^*$, and k is the number of coded vectors.

Now,

$$\mathbf{a'C^*a} = \left(c_{ii} + \frac{c_{ii}}{k}\right)\Sigma a^2 = \left(s_b^2 + \frac{s_b^2}{k}\right)\Sigma a^2$$

where Σa^2 is the sum of the squared coefficients used in a given contrast. The application of this procedure is now illustrated for the comparisons calculated above. The standard error of b (s_b) in the example under consideration is .57735 (recall that all the standard errors of b's are the same when n's are equal in all groups). Therefore $c_{ii} = .57735^2 = .33333$. The number of coded vectors in the present example is two. In the first comparison above, $\bar{Y}_{A_1}$ was contrasted with $\bar{Y}_{A_2}$, with the coefficients (a's): 1 and -1. Using the procedure outlined above,

$$\mathbf{a'C^*a} = \left(.57735^2 + \frac{.57735^2}{2}\right)[(1)^2 + (-1)^2] = \mathit{1.00}$$

which is the same as the value obtained above using the matrix operations. Note that because n's are equal $\mathbf{a'C^*a}$ will be the same (in the present case 1.00) no matter which two means are compared.

In the second comparison above $\bar{Y}_{A_1}$ and $\bar{Y}_{A_3}$ were contrasted with $\bar{Y}_{A_2}$. The coefficients (a's) used were: 1, -2, and 1. Therefore,

$$\mathbf{a'C^*a} = \left(.57735^2 + \frac{.57735^2}{2}\right)[(1)^2 + (-2)^2 + (1)^2] = \mathit{3.00}$$

again, the same value as was obtained via the matrix operations. $\mathbf{a'C^*a} = 3.00$ will be the same for any comparison between two means and a third one, when the above coefficients are used.

The shortcut procedure for the calculation of $\mathbf{a'C^*a}$ applies to any linear combination of b's, regardless of the specific coefficients used and the number of groups, provided that the sample sizes in all the groups are equal. With unequal sample sizes the matrix operations will have to be carried out. The important thing, however, is that the procedures outlined earlier for augmenting $\mathbf{C}$ and for the testing of linear combinations of b's apply equally to situations when n's are equal or unequal (see below). The great advantage of doing the tests of linear combinations of b's in lieu of the conventional calculations of multiple comparisons among means will become evident when categorical and continuous variables are used together, as in the analysis of covariance (see Chapter 13).

Before turning to the next topic, several points will be made about the procedure for testing linear combinations of b's. The approach was used here to apply it in the Scheffé procedure; however, it is applicable whenever the testing of a linear combination of b's is appropriate. Note that the procedure yields an F ratio with 1 and $N - k - 1$ *df*, regardless of the specific purpose for which one wishes to use this F. If one wishes to apply the F in a Scheffé procedure, then it has to exceed kF_{α}; k, $N - k - 1$ (see discussion above). But several other multiple comparison procedures involve an F ratio of the type obtained above, sometimes only requiring to compare it with specially prepared tables for the given procedure (see references cited above in connection with multiple comparisons). Also, some multiple comparison procedures require a t ratio instead. But since the F obtained with the present procedure has one degree of freedom for the numerator, all that is necessary is to take $\sqrt{F}$ (see below, Planned Nonorthogonal Comparisons).

It is worthwhile to amplify and numerically illustrate some of the foregoing comments. Recall that when dummy coding was presented it was shown that it is particularly suited for a design in which several treatments are compared with a control group. Suppose, however, that effect coding was used instead. Using the approach outlined above one can accomplish the same purpose. Assume that in the data of Table 9.6 it is desired to treat A_3 as a control group (i.e., the group that was treated as a control when dummy coding was used; see Table 9.5 and the calculations related to it). The procedure will be applied as follows: (1) Calculate two F ratios, one for the difference between b_1 and b_3, and one for the difference between b_2 and b_3. (2) Take the square root of each F to obtain t's. (3) Refer to a Dunnett table. In fact, one such comparison was done above. When b_2 was compared with b_3 the F ratio was 36.00. The t is therefore 6.00, which is the same value obtained for this comparison when dummy coding was used earlier.

Note that if, instead, A_2 were to be treated as a control group and effect coding was used, then applying the above procedure one would test the difference between b_1 and b_2, and that of b_3 and b_2, obtain t's from the F's and refer to a Dunnett table. (The decision as to which group is assigned -1's in all the vectors is, of course, immaterial.)

Suppose now that effect coding was used but one wished to do orthogonal comparisons or planned nonorthogonal comparison. The above approach still applies. Provided, for example, one constructed an appropriate set of orthogonal comparisons of b's obtained from effect coding, the results would be the same as those obtained from orthogonal coding (see below).

To repeat: tests of linear combinations of b's obtained from effect coding may be used for various purposes, although their application above was illustrated in connection with the Scheffé procedure of multiple comparisons among means.

ORTHOGONAL CODING

In the preceding section post hoc comparisons between means were illustrated using the Scheffé method. It was pointed out that such comparisons are performed subsequent to a significant R^2 in order to determine which means, or treatment effects, differ significantly from each other. Instead of a post hoc approach, however, it is possible to take an a priori approach in which differences between means, or treatment effects, are hypothesized prior to the analysis of the data. The tests of significance for a priori, or planned, comparisons are more powerful than those for post hoc comparisons. In other words, it is possible for a specific comparison to be not significant when tested by post hoc methods but significant when tested by a priori methods. This advantage of the planned comparisons stems from the demands on the researcher, who must hypothesize the differences prior to the analysis, and who is limited to those comparisons about which hypotheses were formulated.

Post hoc comparisons, on the other hand, enable the researcher to engage in so-called data snooping by performing any or all of the conceivable comparisons between means. Tests of significance using this approach are thus more conservative than those for the planned comparisons approach, as they should be. The choice between the two approaches depends on the state of the knowledge in the area under study and the goals of the researcher. The greater the knowledge, the less one has to rely on omnibus tests and data snooping, and the more one is in a position to formulate planned comparisons.

There are two types of planned comparisons: orthogonal and nonorthogonal. This section is devoted principally to the former. A brief comment is made about the latter at the conclusion of this section. Before it is shown how one can use orthogonal coding for the purpose of testing orthogonal comparisons, it is necessary to discuss briefly the meaning of such comparisons.

Orthogonal Comparisons

Two comparisons are orthogonal when the sum of the products of the coefficients for their respective elements is zero. Consider the following two comparisons:

$$D_1 = (1)(\bar{Y}_1) + (-1)(\bar{Y}_2) + (0)(\bar{Y}_3)$$

$$D_2 = \left(-\frac{1}{2}\right)(\bar{Y}_1) + \left(-\frac{1}{2}\right)(\bar{Y}_2) + (1)(\bar{Y}_3)$$

In the first comparison, D_1, $\bar{Y}_1$ is contrasted with $\bar{Y}_2$. In comparison D_2, the average of $\bar{Y}_1 + \bar{Y}_2$, is contrasted with $\bar{Y}_3$. To determine whether these two comparison are orthogonal we multiply the coefficients for each element in the two comparisons and sum. Accordingly:

$$1: \quad (1) + (-1) + (0)$$

$$2: \quad \left(-\frac{1}{2}\right) + \left(-\frac{1}{2}\right) + (1)$$

$$1 \times 2: \quad (1)\left(-\frac{1}{2}\right) + (-1)\left(-\frac{1}{2}\right) + (0)(1) = 0$$

D_1 and D_2 are obviously orthogonal.

Consider now the following two comparisons:

$$D_3 = (1)(\bar{Y}_1) + (-1)(\bar{Y}_2) + (0)(\bar{Y}_3)$$

$$D_4 = (-1)(\bar{Y}_1) + (0)(\bar{Y}_2) + (1)(\bar{Y}_3)$$

The sum of the products of the coefficients of these comparisons is

$$(1)(-1) + (-1)(0) + (0)(1) = -1$$

Table 9.8 Some Possible Comparisons between Means of Three Groups

	Groups		
Comparison	A_1	A_2	A_3
1	1	-1	0
2	$-\frac{1}{2}$	$-\frac{1}{2}$	1
3	1	$-\frac{1}{2}$	$-\frac{1}{2}$
4	0	1	-1
5	1	0	-1
6	$-\frac{1}{2}$	1	$-\frac{1}{2}$

Comparisons D_3 and D_4 are not orthogonal.

The number of orthogonal comparisons one can perform within a given analysis is equal to the number of groups minus one, or the number of coded vectors necessary to describe group membership. For three groups, for example, one can perform two orthogonal comparisons. Several possible comparisons for three groups are listed in Table 9.8. Comparison 1, for example, contrasts the mean of A_1 with the mean of A_2, while comparison 2 contrasts the mean of A_3 with the average of the means A_1 and A_2. It was shown above that comparisons 1 and 2 are orthogonal. Comparisons 1 and 3, on the other hand, are not orthogonal.

Table 9.8 contains three alternative sets of two orthogonal comparisons, namely 1 and 2, 3 and 4, 5 and 6. The specific set of orthogonal comparisons one chooses is dictated by the theory from which the hypotheses are derived. If, for example, A_1 and A_2 are two experimental treatments while A_3 is a control group, one may wish, on the one hand, to contrast means A_1 and A_2, and, on the other hand, to contrast the average of means A_1 and A_2 with the mean of A_3. (Comparisons 1 and 2 of Table 9.8 will accomplish this.) Or, referring to nonexperimental research, one might have samples from three populations (e.g., married, single, and divorced males; blacks, whites, and Hispanics) and formulate two hypotheses about the difference among their means. Thus, for example, one hypothesis may refer to the difference between married and single males in their attitudes toward the awarding of child custody to the father after a divorce. The second hypothesis will be about the difference between these two groups and divorced males. Comparison 1 will contrast the mean of married males with that of single males. Comparison 2 will contrast the mean of married and single males with the mean of divorced males.

Regression Analysis with Orthogonal Coding

When hypothesizing orthogonal comparisons it is possible to use coefficients of the hypothesized contrasts as the numbers in the coded vectors in regression analysis. The application of this method, referred to here as orthogonal coding, yields results that are directly interpretable. In addition, it is shown below that the use of orthogonal coding simplifies the calculations of the regression analysis.

Orthogonal coding is now applied to an analysis of the data earlier analyzed with dummy coding and effect coding. Using the three methods of coding with the same illustrative data enables one to compare the overall results as well as to study the unique properties of each method.

In Table 9.9 the Y vector of Tables 9.5 and 9.6 is repeated. It will be recalled that this vector consists of scores on a dependent variable for three groups: A_1, A_2, and A_3. Vectors X_1 and X_2 of Table 9.9 represent two orthogonal comparisons, the first being a contrast between mean A_1 and mean A_2, whereas the second contrasts the average of mean A_1 and A_2 with the mean of A_3. It was shown earlier that these two comparisons are orthogonal (see Table 9.8, comparisons 1 and 2). Note, however, that in comparison 2 of Table 9.8 two of the coefficients are fractions. As was done above in the case of effect coding, all the coefficients were transformed into integers as a result of multiplying each of them by a constant (2), yielding the coefficients of -1, -1, and 2, which are used as the codes of X_2 of Table 9.9. Such a transformation, for convenience of calculation by hand or for punching data on cards for computer analysis, may be done for any comparison. Thus, if one had for example four groups, A_1, A_2, A_3, and A_4 and wished to compare the average of groups A_1, A_2, and A_3 with that of A_4, the comparison called for is:

$$\frac{\bar{Y}_{A_1} + \bar{Y}_{A_2} + \bar{Y}_{A_3}}{3} - \bar{Y}_{A_4}$$

or

$$\frac{1}{3}(\bar{Y}_{A_1}) + \frac{1}{3}(\bar{Y}_{A_2}) + \frac{1}{3}(\bar{Y}_{A_3}) + (-1)(\bar{Y}_{A_4})$$

To convert the coefficients to integers multiply each by 3, obtaining

$$(1)(\bar{Y}_{A_1}) + (1)(\bar{Y}_{A_2}) + (1)(\bar{Y}_{A_3}) + (-3)(\bar{Y}_{A_4})$$

As another example, assume that five groups are involved and that one wished to make the following comparison:

$$\frac{\bar{Y}_{A_1} + \bar{Y}_{A_2} + \bar{Y}_{A_3}}{3} - \frac{\bar{Y}_{A_4} + \bar{Y}_{A_5}}{2}$$

or

$$\frac{1}{3}(\bar{Y}_{A_1}) + \frac{1}{3}(\bar{Y}_{A_2}) + \frac{1}{3}(\bar{Y}_{A_3}) + \left(-\frac{1}{2}\right)(\bar{Y}_{A_4}) + \left(-\frac{1}{2}\right)(\bar{Y}_{A_5})$$

To convert the coefficients to integers, multiply by 6 (the common denominator), obtaining

$$(2)(\bar{Y}_{A_1}) + (2)(\bar{Y}_{A_2}) + (2)(\bar{Y}_{A_3}) + (-3)(\bar{Y}_{A_4}) + (-3)(\bar{Y}_{A_5})$$

Table 9.9 Orthogonal Coding for Illustrative Data from Three Groups

Group	Y	X_1	X_2
	4	1	−1
	5	1	−1
A_1	6	1	−1
	7	1	−1
	8	1	−1
	7	−1	−1
	8	−1	−1
A_2	9	−1	−1
	10	−1	−1
	11	−1	−1
	1	0	2
	2	0	2
A_3	3	0	2
	4	0	2
	5	0	2
Σ:	90	0	0
M:	6	0	0
ss:	120	10	30
$\Sigma x_1 y = -15$	$\Sigma x_2 y = -45$	$\Sigma x_1 x_2 = 0$	
$r^2_{y1} = .1875$	$r^2_{y2} = .5625$	$r^2_{12} = 0$	

The results of the regression analysis and the tests of significance will be the same regardless of whether one uses the fractional coefficients or the integers to which they have been converted (see, however, below for comments about the effects of such transformations on the magnitudes of the regression coefficients).

We turn now to the analysis of the data of Table 9.9. Instead of reporting computer output, as was done for the analysis of the same data with dummy and effect coding, it will be instructive to do the analysis of Table 9.9 by hand, using algebraic formulas presented in Chapter 3.[6] The main reason for doing this is that it affords an opportunity to review and illustrate numerically some of the ideas discussed in earlier chapters, particularly those regarding the absence of ambiguity in the interpretation of results when the independent variables are not correlated. Note carefully that in the present example there is only *one* independent variable (i.e., group membership in A, whatever the groupings in A represent); however, because the two coded vectors representing this variable are not correlated, the example still affords an illustration of ideas relevant to situations in which the independent variables are not correlated.

[6]The simplest and most efficient method is the use of matrix operations. Recall that a solution is sought to $\mathbf{b} = (\mathbf{X'X})^{-1}\mathbf{X'Y}$ (see Chapter 4). When orthogonal coding is used, $(\mathbf{X'X})$ is a diagonal matrix; that is, all the off-diagonal elements are 0. The inverse of a diagonal matrix is a diagonal matrix whose elements are the reciprocals of the diagonal elements of $(\mathbf{X'X})$. You may wish to analyze the present example by matrix operations in order to appreciate the ease with which this can be done when orthogonal coding is used. For guidance in doing this, see Chapter 4.

A secondary purpose of doing the calculations by hand is to demonstrate the ease with which this can be accomplished when the independent variables are not correlated (again, in the present example there is only one independent variable, but it is represented by two vectors that are not correlated).

Since the formulas to be used in this demonstration have been used frequently in earlier chapters, they are generally not commented upon. You should encounter no difficulties in following the presentation. If you do, it is suggested that you review earlier chapters, particularly Chapter 3.

Before calculating the regression statistics some observations about the calculations reported at the bottom of Table 9.9 will be useful. Note that the sums, and consequently the means, of X_1 and X_2 are 0, as they will always be with this type of coding. Because of that the *ss* (deviation sum of squares) for a coded vector is simply equal to the sum of its squared elements (i.e., 10 for X_1 and 30 for X_2). Also, because $\Sigma X = 0$, Σxy (deviation sum of products) is simply the sum of the products of the two vectors. Thus, $\Sigma x_1 y = \Sigma X_1 Y$. Similarly, $\Sigma x_2 y = \Sigma X_2 Y$. Note the properties of these sums of products. To obtain $\Sigma x_1 y$ values of X_1 are multiplied by values of Y and added. But look at these two columns in Table 9.9 and note that each Y of A_1 is multiplied by 1, and that each Y of A_2 is multiplied by -1. Consequently, $\Sigma x_1 y = \Sigma Y_{A_1} - \Sigma Y_{A_2}$. This shows clearly that X_1 which was designed to contrast $\bar{Y}_{A_1}$ with $\bar{Y}_{A_2}$ does that, except that total scores are used instead of means.

Examine now $\Sigma x_2 y$. Each of the scores of Y_{A_1} and Y_{A_2} is multiplied by -1, whereas each score of Y_{A_3} is multiplied by 2. Consequently, $\Sigma x_2 y = 2\Sigma Y_{A_3} - (\Sigma Y_{A_1} + \Sigma Y_{A_2})$, which the second comparison is designed to accomplish, except that the contrast is made in terms of sums instead of means.

Finally, $\Sigma x_1 x_2 = 0$ indicates that X_1 and X_2 are orthogonal. Of course, $r_{12} = 0$.

With these observation in mind, we turn first to the calculation and interpretation of the regression equation.

The Regression Equation. Because $r_{12} = 0$, the calculation of each of the regression coefficients is simply $\Sigma xy/\Sigma x^2$, as in the case of simple linear regression. Taking the appropriate values from the bottom of Table 9.9,

$$b_1 = \frac{\Sigma x_1 y}{\Sigma x_1^2} = \frac{-15}{10} = -1.5$$

$$b_2 = \frac{\Sigma x_2 y}{\Sigma x_2^2} = \frac{-45}{30} = -1.5$$

It will be recalled that

$$a = \bar{Y} - b_1\bar{X}_1 - b_2\bar{X}_2$$

But since the means of the coded vectors are equal to zero, $a = \bar{Y} = 6.00$. With orthogonal coding, as with effect coding, a is always equal to $\bar{Y}$, the grand mean of the dependent variable. The regression equation for the data of Table 9.9 is therefore

$$Y' = 6.00 - 1.5X_1 - 1.5X_2$$

Applying this equation to the scores (i.e., codes) of a subject on X_1 and X_2 will, of course, yield a predicted score equal to the mean of the group to which the subject belongs. For example, for the first subject of Table 9.9,

$$Y' = 6.0 - 1.5(1) - 1.5(-1) = 6$$

which is equal to $\bar{Y}_{A_1}$, the mean of the group to which this subject belongs. Similarly, for the last subject of Table 9.9:

$$Y' = 6.0 - 1.5(0) - 1.5(2) = 3$$

which is equal to $\bar{Y}_{A_3}$.

We turn now to an examination of the b's. From what was said above about the sums of cross products (i.e., $\Sigma x_1 y$ and $\Sigma x_2 y$) it can be seen that each b reflects the contrast described by the vector with which it is associated. Thus b_1 reflects the comparison $\bar{Y}_{A_1} - \bar{Y}_{A_2}$. Look at X_1 of Table 9.9 and note that the scores in group A_1 are +1's, while those in A_2 are −1's. Since $b_1 = -1.50$, then $(-1.50)(1) - (-1.50)(-1) = -3.00$, which is equal to the difference between $\bar{Y}_{A_1}$ and $\bar{Y}_{A_2}$ (that is, $6.00 - 9.00 = -3.00$). Similarly, b_2 reflects the second comparison; that is,

$$\bar{Y}_{A_3} - \frac{\bar{Y}_{A_1} + \bar{Y}_{A_2}}{2} = 3.00 - \frac{6.00 + 9.00}{2} = 3.00 - 7.5 = -4.5$$

Applying b_2, −1.50, to the codes of X_2: $(-1.5)(2) - (-1.5)(-1) = -4.5$.

While each b reflects the contrast described in the vector with which it is associated, the numerical value of a b is dependent upon the specific values that are used as the codes in a given comparison. Thus, for example, if instead of the 1's and −1's of X_1 one were to use $\frac{1}{2}$ and $-\frac{1}{2}$ (that is, coefficients that are half the size of those that were used), the results would have been: $\Sigma x^2 = 2.5$, and $\Sigma x_1 y = -7.5$, leading to $b_1 = -7.5/2.5 = -3.00$. Note that this b is twice the size of the one obtained above. But now apply this b to the second set of coefficients: $(-3)(\frac{1}{2}) - (-3)(-\frac{1}{2}) = -3.00$. Again, the difference between the two means $(\bar{Y}_{A_1} - \bar{Y}_{A_2})$ is obtained.

Differences in the b's obtained for the same comparison when different codes are used reflect the scaling factor by which the codes differ. This can be further clarified when one considers another method of calculating b's; that is, $b_j = \beta_j s_y/s_j$. Recall that when the independent variables are not correlated, each β (standardized regression coefficient) is equal to the zero-order correlation between the variable with which it is associated and the dependent variable. Thus $\beta_{y1} = r_{y1}$, $\beta_{y2} = r_{y2}$, and so on. Now, multiplying or dividing X_1 by a constant does not change its correlation with Y. Consequently, the β will also not change. What will change is the standard deviation of X_1, which will be equal to the constant times the original standard deviation. Concretely, then, when X_1 is multiplied by 2, for example, $b_1 = \beta_1 s_y/(2)s_1$, resulting in a b that is half the size of the one originally obtained. The main point, however, is that the

b reflects the contrast regardless of the factor by which the codes were scaled, and that the test of significance of the b is the test of the significance of the comparison that it reflects. Before this is demonstrated we turn to the partitioning of the sum of squares of the dependent variable (Σy^2).

Partitioning the Sum of Squares

One of the methods of obtaining the regression sum of squares is:

$$ss_{\text{reg}} = b_1\Sigma x_1 y + b_2\Sigma x_2 y$$

Using the b's obtained above, and the sums of products from Table 9.9:

$$ss_{\text{reg}} = (-1.5)(-15) + (-1.5)(-45)$$
$$= 22.5 + 67.5 = \mathit{90.00}$$

This regression sum of squares is of course the same as that obtained in the earlier analyses of the same data with dummy and effect coding. But unlike the earlier analyses, the present analysis affords a partitioning of ss_{reg} into two independent components, each of which is associated with one degree of freedom. Thus ss_{reg} due to X_1 (the first comparison) is 22.5 and ss_{reg} due to X_2 (the second comparison) is 67.5. That this is so can perhaps best be seen when one recalls that

$$R^2_{y.12} = r^2_{y1} + r^2_{y2} \qquad (\text{when } r_{12} = 0)$$

The proportion of variance of Y accounted for by X_1 is independent of that accounted for by X_2, and similarly for any number of independent variables, or coded vectors, as long as they are orthogonal. From Table 9.9,

$$R^2_{y.12} = .1875 + .5625 = .75$$

Together, the two comparisons account for 75% of the variance of Y (the same R^2 was, of course, obtained in the earlier analyses of these data). The first comparison accounts for about 19% of the variance of Y, and the second comparison accounts for about 56% of the variance of Y. Now, multiplying a proportion by Σy^2 yields a sum of squares. For the data of Table 9.9, $\Sigma y^2 = 120$. Therefore,

$$ss_{\text{reg}(1)} = (.1875)(120) = \mathit{22.5}$$

$$ss_{\text{reg}(2)} = (.5625)(120) = \mathit{67.5}$$

which are the same as the values obtained above. It was noted above that each of these sums of squares has one degree of freedom. Therefore the mean square for each is equal to its ss_{reg}. Each of the mean squares can be tested separately for significance. In order to do that it is necessary to calculate the mean square residuals (*MSR*).

$$ss_{\text{res}} = \Sigma y^2 - ss_{\text{reg}}$$
$$= 120 - 90 = 30$$

Equivalently,

$$ss_{\text{res}} = (1 - R^2_{y\ 12})(\Sigma y^2) = (1 - .75)(120) = 30$$

and

$$MSR = \frac{ss_{\text{res}}}{N - k - 1} = \frac{30.00}{15 - 2 - 1} = \frac{30}{12} = 2.50$$

Testing each ss_{reg}:

$$F_1 = \frac{ss_{\text{reg}(1)}}{MSR} = \frac{22.50}{2.50} = 9.00$$

with 1 and 12 degrees of freedom, $p < .05$. This F ratio indicates that the difference between the means of groups A_1 and A_2 (that is, $6.00 - 9.00 = -3.00$) is significant at the .05 level.

For the second comparison,

$$F_2 = \frac{ss_{\text{reg}(2)}}{MSR} = \frac{67.50}{2.50} = 27.00$$

with 1 and 12 *df*, $p < .005$. The average of the means of groups A_1 and A_2, 7.50, is significantly different from the mean of group A_3, 3.00, at the .005 level of significance.[7]

The same F ratios could have, of course, been obtained by testing the proportions of variance accounted for. For example, for comparison 1, $r^2_{y1} = .1875$. Recall that $R^2_{y.12} = .75$. Therefore,

$$F = \frac{r^2_{y1}/1}{(1 - R^2_{y.12})/(15 - 2 - 1)} = \frac{.1875}{(1 - .75)/12} = 9.00$$

and similarly for the second F.

Note the interesting relation between the F ratios for the individual degrees of freedom and the overall F ratio. The latter is an average of all the F ratios obtained from the orthogonal comparisons. In the present case, $(9.00 + 27.00)/2 = 18.00$, which is the value of the overall F ratio. This demonstrates the advantage of orthogonal comparisons. Unless the treatment effects are equal, some orthogonal comparisons will have F ratios larger than the overall F ratio. Even when the overall F ratio is not significant, some of the orthogonal comparisons

[7]Although the sums of squares of each comparison are independent, the F ratios associated with them are not, because the same mean square error is used for all the comparisons. When the number of degrees of freedom for the mean square error is large, the comparisons can be viewed as independent. For a discussion of this point the reader is referred to Hays (1981) and Kirk (1968).

may have significant F ratios. Furthermore, while a significant overall F ratio is a necessary condition for the application of post hoc comparisons between means, the calculation of the overall F ratio is not necessary for orthogonal comparison analysis. The interest in such analysis is in the F ratios for the individual degrees of freedom corresponding to the specific differences hypothesized prior to the analysis.

The foregoing analysis is summarized in Table 9.10, where it is possible to see clearly how the total sum of squares is broken into the various components.

Since each F ratio obtained in the analysis with orthogonal coding has one degree of freedom for the numerator it is, of course, possible to take $\sqrt{F}$ in order to obtain t for a given comparison. It will now be shown that tests of significance of the b's yield the same t's that would be obtained from taking $\sqrt{F}$ calculated above.

Testing the Regression Coefficients. Recall that a standard error of a b is:

$$s_{b_1} = \sqrt{\frac{s^2_{y.12...k}}{\Sigma x_1^2(1 - R^2_{1.2...k})}}$$

where $s^2_{y.12...k}$ is the variance of estimate or the MSR and $R^2_{1.2...k}$ is the squared multiple correlation of independent variable 1 with the remaining independent variables. But because with orthogonal coding the vectors representing the independent variable(s) are not correlated, the formula for the standard error of a b reduces to:

$$s_{b_1} = \sqrt{\frac{s^2_{y.12...k}}{\Sigma x_1^2}}$$

Note carefully that this formula *applies only when the independent variables are orthogonal*. $s^2_{y.12} = MSR$ was found above to be equal to 2.50; from Table 9.9, $\Sigma x_1^2 = 10$, $\Sigma x_2^2 = 30$.

$$s_{b_1} = \sqrt{\frac{2.50}{10}} = \sqrt{.25} = .50$$

Table 9.10 Summary of the Analysis with Orthogonal Coding, Based on Data of Table 9.9

Source	*df*		*ss*		*ms*		*F*
Total regression	2		90.00		45.00		18.00
Regression due to X_1		1		22.50		22.50	9.00
Regression due to X_2		1		67.50		67.50	27.00
Residual	12		30.00		2.50		
Total	14		120.00				

Since $b_1 = -1.50$, then

$$t_{b_1} = \frac{b_1}{s_{b_1}} = \frac{-1.50}{.50} = -3.00$$

Note that $t_{b_1}^2 = 9.00$, which is equal to the F ratio obtained above for $ss_{\text{reg}(1)}$. An examination of the test of the b will now demonstrate what was said above—namely, that multiplying (or dividing) a coded vector by a constant affects the magnitude of the b associated with it but does not affect its test of significance. Assume, for the sake of illustration, that a coded vector is multiplied by a constant of 2. It was shown above that this will result in a b that is half the size of the b that would be obtained for the same vector prior to the multiplication by 2. But note that when each value of the coded vector is multiplied by 2, the sum of squares of the vector, Σx^2, will be multiplied by 2^2. Since $s_{y.12\ldots k}^2$ will not change, and since Σx^2 is quadrupled, the square root of the ratio of the former to the latter will be half its original size. In other words, the standard error of b will be half its original size. It is clear, then, that when the coded vector is multiplied by 2 the b as well as its standard error are half their original size, thus leaving the t ratio invariant.

Calculate now the standard error of b_2:

$$s_{b_2} = \sqrt{\frac{2.50}{30}} = \sqrt{.08333} = .28867$$

Since $b_2 = -1.50$,

$$t_{b_2} = \frac{-1.50}{.28867} = -5.19624$$

$t_{b_2}^2 = -5.19624^2 = 27.00$, which is the same as the F ratio obtained above for $ss_{\text{reg}(2)}$.

In sum, then, the test of a b when orthogonal coding is used is the test of the comparison reflected in the vector with which the b is associated. The degrees of freedom for each b are equal to the degrees of freedom associated with the residual sum of squares: $(N - k - 1)$. For the present example, $N = 15$, $k = 2$ (coded vectors). Each t ratio has 12 *df*.

In order not to lose sight of the main purpose of orthogonal coding, it is advisable to provide a brief summary. When one has hypothesized a priori orthogonal comparisons among a set of means, it is necessary to generate orthogonally coded vectors, each of which reflects one of the hypotheses. Regressing Y on the coded vectors, proportions of variance (or ss) due to each comparison may be obtained. These may be tested separately for significance. But the tests of the b's provide the same information; that is, each t ratio is a test of the comparison reflected in the vector with which the b is associated. Thus, when a computer program is used for multiple regression analysis, all that is necessary is to inspect the t ratios that are reported for the b's in order to note which hypotheses were supported.

It will be recalled that the number of orthogonal comparisons possible among g groups is $g - 1$. Assume that a researcher is working with five groups. Four orthogonal comparisons are therefore possible. Suppose, however, that the researcher has only two a priori hypotheses that are orthogonal. These can still be tested in the manner outlined above provided that, in addition to the two orthogonally coded vectors representing these hypotheses, two more orthogonally coded vectors are included in the analysis. This is necessary in order to exhaust all the information about group membership (recall that for g groups $g - 1 = k$ coded vectors are necessary; this holds true regardless of the method of coding). Having done this, the researcher will inspect only those t ratios that are associated with the b's that reflect the a priori hypotheses. As to the remaining means, comparisons among them may still be pursued by one of the methods for post hoc comparisons (e.g., Scheffé).

Finally, in the beginning of this section it was said that one may have planned comparisons that are nonorthogonal. We turn now to a brief treatment of this topic.

Planned Nonorthogonal Comparisons

Some authors, notably Ryan (1959a, 1959b), have argued that there are neither logical nor statistical reasons for the distinction between planned and post hoc comparisons, and that all comparisons may be treated by a uniform approach and from a common frame of reference. The topic is too complex to be discussed here. Instead, it will be pointed out that the approach that has been recommended has been variously referred to as *Bonferroni t statistics* (Miller, 1966) or the Dunn (1961) procedure. Basically, this procedure involves the calculation of F or t ratios for the hypothesized comparisons (the number of comparisons may be relatively large and any given comparison may refer to differences between pairs of means or combinations of means) and adjusting the overall α level for the number of comparisons being performed. An example will be used to illustrate these ideas. Suppose that, in research with seven groups, five planned nonorthogonal comparisons are hypothesized and that the overall α is .05. One would proceed and calculate F or t ratios for each of the comparisons. But the obtained t's or F's will have to exceed the critical value for .01 ($\alpha/5 = .05/5$) and not those of the .05 level. Suppose that for the same number of groups (7) one wanted to perform all pairwise comparisons among the means. This means that $(7)(6)/2 = 21$ comparisons are to be performed. Assuming that the overall $\alpha = .05$, then the critical value to be exceeded is one with $\alpha/21 = .05/21 = .002$.

In general, then, given c (number of comparisons), and α (the overall level of significance), a t or F for a comparison will have to exceed the critical value at α/c. The degrees of freedom for t are those associated with the mean square residual *(MSR)*, $N - k - 1$, while those for F are 1 and $N - k - 1$.

The procedure outlined above will frequently require critical values at α levels not found in conventional tables of t or F. Tabled values for what are either referred to as Bonferroni test statistics or the Dunn Multiple Comparison Test may be found in statistics books (e.g., Kirk, 1968; Myers, 1979). Such tables are entered with the number of comparisons (c) and $N - k - 1$ (df for MSR). For example, suppose that for the data of Table 9.9 one hypothesized pairwise comparisons between the means (i.e., $\bar{Y}_{A_1} - \bar{Y}_{A_2}; \bar{Y}_{A_1} - \bar{Y}_{A_3}; \bar{Y}_{A_2} - \bar{Y}_{A_3}$), and that the overall $\alpha = .05$. There are three comparisons, and df for MSR are 12 (see analysis above). Entering the Dunn table with these values it is found that the critical t ratio is 2.78. Thus, an obtained t ratio for a given comparison must exceed 2.78 to be declared significant.

The Bonferroni, or Dunn, procedure is very versatile. For further discussions and applications, as well as comparisons between this procedure and other multiple comparisons procedures, see Bielby and Kluegel (1977), Davis (1969), Kirk (1968), Myers (1979), Perlmuter and Myers (1973).

In concluding the discussion of multiple comparisons it will be noted that the method of testing differences among b's using elements of $\mathbf{C}^*$ (the augmented covariance matrix of the b's) presented earlier may be applied whether one does post hoc, planned orthogonal, or planned nonorthogonal comparisons. Basically, a t or F ratio is obtained for a contrast among b's. How it is used depends on the specific procedure for multiple comparisons one is applying. If the Scheffé procedure is used the F is checked against $kF_{\alpha}, k, N - k - 1$ (see discussion of the Scheffé procedure earlier in this chapter). If, on the other hand, the Bonferroni approach is applied then the obtained t is checked against t with α/c, where c is the number of comparisons. Using orthogonal coefficients for tests among b's obtained from effect coding, one will obtain the same F's or t's that would be obtained from a regression analysis in which orthogonal coding is used. In fact, of the two orthogonal comparisons used in Table 9.9 the first was obtained earlier in the section on Multiple Comparisons via b's, though there it was used to illustrate the calculation of post hoc comparisons. Note that the F ratio associated with this comparison (9.00) is the same as the one obtained in this section.

In sum, when effect coding is used one may still obtain planned orthogonal or nonorthogonal comparisons by testing linear combinations of b's. When, however, the planned comparisons are orthogonal, it is more efficient to use orthogonal coding, since doing this obviates the need for further testing subsequent to the overall analysis. All the necessary information is provided by the tests of the b's in the overall analysis.

UNEQUAL SAMPLE SIZES IN GROUPS

It is desirable that sample sizes of groups be equal. There are two major reasons: the statistical tests presented in this chapter are more sensitive when they are based on equal n's, and equal n's minimize distortions that may occur when there are departures from certain assumptions underlying these statistical tests.[8] But statistical issues notwithstanding, it is necessary to examine briefly other issues relevant to the use of unequal n's because they may have serious implications for the valid interpretation of the results. Unequal n's may occur

[8]For further discussion of the advantages of equal sample sizes, see Li (1964, I, pp. 147–148, 197–198).

by design or because of the loss of subjects in the course of an investigation, frequently referred to as subject mortality or subject attrition. These two types of occurrences are examined, in turn, in the context of experimental and nonexperimental research.

In experimental research, a researcher may find it necessary or desirable to randomly assign subjects in varying numbers to different treatments that vary, for example, in costs. Other reasons for designing experimental research with unequal *n*'s come readily to mind, though they will not be enumerated here. The use of unequal *n*'s by design does not pose threats to the internal validity of the experiment, that is, to the valid conclusions about the effects of the treatments.[9] Subject mortality, however, may pose very serious threats to internal validity. The degree of bias introduced as a result of subject mortality is often not easy to assess, because it requires a thorough knowledge of the reasons for the loss of subjects. Assume that an experiment was begun with equal *n*'s but that in the course of its implementation subjects were lost. Losses may occur for myriad reasons, from such simple and traceable ones as errors in the recording of scores for some subjects, or the malfunctioning of equipment, necessitating the elimination of the affected subjects, to very complex and intractable reasons that may relate to subjects' motivations or reactions to specific treatments leading them to drop out. Subject mortality may of course result in equal *n*'s when equal numbers of subjects are lost from each of the treatments. The threats to internal validity are not diminished just because the loss of subjects resulted in groups with equal *n*'s, although such an occurrence may generally be more reasonably attributed to a random process, thus posing less serious threats to the internal validity of the experiment. Be that as it may, it is obvious that subject mortality may reflect a process of self-selection resulting in groups composed of different kinds of people, thereby raising serious doubts as to whether the results are due to the effects of the treatments, or largely, perhaps solely, due to differences among subjects in the different treatment conditions. The less one is able to discern the reasons for subject mortality, the greater is its potential threat to the internal validity of the experiment.

In nonexperimental research, too, unequal *n*'s may be used by design or they may be a consequence of subject mortality. The use of equal or unequal *n*'s by design is directly related to the sampling plan, and to the questions the study is designed to answer. Thus, when the aim is to study the relation between a categorical and a continuous variable in a defined population, it is essential that the categories or subgroups that comprise the categorical variable be represented in accordance with their proportions in the population. For example, if the purpose is to study the relation between race and income in the United States, it is necessary that the sample include whites, blacks, and so on in the same proportions that such groups are in the population, thereby resulting in a categorical variable with unequal *n*'s.

Probably more often, researchers are interested in making comparisons among subgroups, or what are referred to as strata in sampling terminology. Thus, the main interest may be in comparisons of income among different rac-

[9]For discussions of internal validity of experiments, see Campbell and Stanley (1963), and Cook and Campbell (1979).

ial groups. For such purposes it is desirable to have equal n's in the subgroups. This is accomplished by what is referred to as disproportionate or unequal probabilities sampling. In studies on the effects of schooling disproportionate sampling is often done so that the sample include equal numbers of students from the different racial or ethnic groups. It should be evident that the sampling plans discussed above are not interchangeable, and that each is directed toward attempts to answer different questions (for discussions of these and related issues, see Kish, 1953, 1965; Sudman, 1976).

Regardless of the sampling plan, subject mortality may occur for a variety of reasons and affect the validity of the results to a greater or lesser extent. Probably one of the most serious threats to the validity of the results stems from what could broadly be characterized as nonresponse and undercoverage. Sampling experts have developed various techniques designed to adjust the results for such occurrences (see, for example, Namboodiri, 1978, Part IV). The main thing to bear in mind is that nonresponse reflects a process of self-selection, thus casting doubts about the representativeness of the subgroups that are being compared.

The foregoing brief review of situations that may give rise to unequal n's and the potential threats some of them pose to the validity of the results should suffice to alert one to the dangers of not being attentive to these issues. We turn now to the regression analysis of a continuous variable on a categorical variable whose categories are composed of unequal n's. Dummy and effect coding are presented first together. This is followed by a treatment of orthogonal coding.

Dummy and Effect Coding for Unequal *N*'s

Dummy or effect coding of a categorical variable with unequal n's proceeds in the same manner as that for equal n's. This is illustrated with part of the illustrative data used earlier in this chapter. The example analyzed with the

Table 9.11 Dummy and Effect Coding for Unequal *n*'s

		Dummy Coding		*Effect Coding*	
Group	Y	X_1	X_2	X_3	X_4
	4	1	0	1	0
A_1	5	1	0	1	0
	6	1	0	1	0
	7	0	1	0	1
	8	0	1	0	1
A_2	9	0	1	0	1
	10	0	1	0	1
	1	0	0	−1	−1
	2	0	0	−1	−1
A_3	3	0	0	−1	−1
	4	0	0	−1	−1
	5	0	0	−1	−1

three coding methods consisted of three groups, each composed of 5 subjects. For the present analysis, the scores of the fourth and the fifth subjects from group A_1 and the score of the fifth subject from group A_2 are deleted. Group A_3 remains intact. Accordingly, there are 3, 4, and 5 subjects in groups A_1, A_2 and A_3, respectively. The scores for these groups, along with dummy and effect coding are reported in Table 9.11. Note that the methods used are identical to those used with equal n's (see Tables 9.5 and 9.6). X_1 and X_2 of Table 9.11 are dummy coding, while X_3 and X_4 are effect coding. The calculations of multiple regression analysis are done in the same way as with equal n's. Instead of doing them here by hand, therefore, excerpts of SPSS output are reported and commented upon.

Output

DEPENDENT VARIABLE Y — R SQUARE .79921

ANALYSIS OF VARIANCE

	DF	SUM OF SQUARES	MEAN SQUARE	F
REGRESSION	2	67.66667	33.83333	17.91
RESIDUAL	9	17.00000	1.88889	

Commentary

This output is identical for dummy and effect coding. The categorical variable accounts for about 80% of the variance of Y (R^2). The F ratio with 2 ($k = 2$ coded vectors) and 9 ($N - k - 1 = 12 - 2 - 1$) is 17.91, $p < .01$. Regression sum of squares is equal to $R^2 \Sigma y^2 = (.79921)(84.66667)$, and residual sum of squares is equal to $(1 - R^2) \Sigma y^2 = (1 - .79921)(84.66667)$.

Output (for Dummy Coding)

DEPENDENT VARIABLE Y

VARIABLES IN THE EQUATION

VARIABLE	B	STD ERROR B	F
X1	2.00	1.00370	3.97
X2	5.50	.92195	35.59
(CONSTANT)	3.00		

Commentary

The *regression equation for dummy coding* is

$$Y' = 3.00 + 2.00X_1 + 5.50X_2$$

Applying this equation to the codes of a subject will lead to a predicted score that is equal to the mean of the group to which the subject belongs.

For subjects in Group A_1,

$$Y' = 3.00 + 2.00(1) + 5.50(0) = 5.00 = \bar{Y}_{A_1}$$

for those in Group A_2,

$$Y' = 3.00 + 2.00(0) + 5.50(1) = 8.50 = \bar{Y}_{A_2}$$

and for those in Group A_3,

$$Y' = 3.00 + 2.00(0) + 5.50(0) = 3.00 = \bar{Y}_{A_3}$$

Note that the properties of this equation are the same as those of the regression equation with equal n's; that is, a (CONSTANT) is equal to the mean of the group assigned 0's throughout ($\bar{Y}_{A_3}$), b_1 is equal to the deviation of $\bar{Y}_{A_1}$ from $\bar{Y}_{A_3}$ (5.00 − 3.00 = 2.00), and b_2 is equal to the deviation of $\bar{Y}_{A_2}$ from $\bar{Y}_{A_3}$ (8.50 − 3.00 = 5.50).

It was stated earlier that with dummy coding the group assigned 0's throughout acts as a control group, and testing each b for significance amounts to testing the difference between the mean of the group with which the given b is associated and the mean of the control group. The same holds true for unequal n's. Assuming that A_3 is indeed a control group, then

$$t_{b_1} = \sqrt{F_1} = \sqrt{3.97} = 1.99$$
$$t_{b_2} = \sqrt{F_2} = \sqrt{35.59} = 5.97$$

Assuming that a two-tailed test at the .05 level is desired, the critical t value reported in the Dunnett table for two treatment groups and a control, with 9 df is 2.61. One would therefore conclude that $\bar{Y}_{A_1}$ is not significantly different from $\bar{Y}_{A_3}$, but that $\bar{Y}_{A_2}$ is significantly different from $\bar{Y}_{A_3}$.

If the dummy coding were used for convenience and $\bar{Y}_{A_3}$ is not a control group, the tests of the b's are ignored. One proceeds instead with multiple comparisons among means—a topic discussed below under effect coding.

Output (for Effect Coding)

DEPENDENT VARIABLE Y

VARIABLES IN THE EQUATION

VARIABLE	B
X3	−.50
X4	3.00
(CONSTANT)	5.50

Commentary

Note that while the output includes standard errors of b's and an F ratio for each b, they are not reported here as they are not used in the present context. Instead multiple comparisons among means will be done (see below).

The *regression equation for effect coding* is

$$Y' = 5.50 - .50X_3 + 3.00X_4$$

Although this regression equation has the same properties as the one obtained for effect coding with equal *n*'s, there are some differences between the two situations. When the categorical variable is composed of unequal *n*'s, *a* (CONSTANT) is *not* equal to the grand mean of the dependent variable $(\bar{Y})$, but rather to the unweighted mean of Y, that is, the average of the group means. In the present example $\bar{Y} = 5.33$, which is a weighted mean:

$$\bar{Y} = \frac{(3)(5.00) + (4)(8.50) + (5)(3.00)}{3 + 4 + 5} = 5.33$$

But a is equal to the unweighted mean:

$$a = \frac{5.00 + 8.50 + 3.00}{3} = 5.50$$

When the sample sizes are equal, the average of the means is the same as the grand mean, since all the means are weighted by a constant (the sample size).

As shown previously, each b indicates the effect of the treatment with which it is associated or the deviation of the group mean with which the b is associated from the overall mean. In the case of unequal *n*'s, the overall mean from which deviations of group means are calculated is the *unweighted* mean; $b_3 = -.50$ is equal to the deviation of $\bar{Y}_{A_1}$ from the *unweighted* mean (5.00 – 5.50); $b_4 = 3.00$ is the deviation of $\bar{Y}_{A_2}$ from the *unweighted* mean (8.50 – 5.50). The effect of A_3 is $-\Sigma b_j = -\Sigma(-.50 + 3.00) = -2.50$, which is the deviation of $\bar{Y}_{A_3}$ from the *unweighted* mean (3.00 – 5.50).

The application of the regression equation to the codes of a subject on X_3 and X_4 will, of course, yield the mean of the group to which the subject belongs. Thus, for subjects in A_1,

$$Y' = 5.50 + (-.50)(1) + 3.00(0) = 5.00 = \bar{Y}_{A_1}$$

For those in group A_2,

$$Y' = 5.50 + (-.50)(0) + 3.00(1) = 8.50 = \bar{Y}_{A_2}$$

And for those in group A_3,

$$Y' = 5.50 + (-.50)(-1) + 3.00(-1) = 3.00 = \bar{Y}_{A_3}$$

Multiple Comparisons among Means

As in the case of equal *n*'s, one performs multiple comparisons among means when *n*'s are unequal. These may take the form of post hoc, planned nonorthogonal, and planned orthogonal. Assume that in the present example no planned comparisons were hypothesized. Because the overall F ratio is significant, one may proceed with post hoc comparisons—say, the Scheffé procedure.

For illustrative purposes two comparisons will be calculated:

$$\bar{Y}_{A_1} - \bar{Y}_{A_2} \quad \text{and} \quad \frac{\bar{Y}_{A_1} + \bar{Y}_{A_2}}{2} - \bar{Y}_{A_3}$$

Formula (9.15) will be applied first to both comparisons. This will be followed by tests among the b's for the same comparisons.

For the comparison between $\bar{Y}_{A_1}$ and $\bar{Y}_{A_2}$,

$$F = \frac{[C_1(\bar{Y}_{A_1}) + C_2(\bar{Y}_{A_2})]^2}{MSR\left[\Sigma\frac{(C_j)^2}{n_j}\right]} = \frac{[(1)(5.00) + (-1)(8.50)]^2}{1.88889\left[\frac{(1)^2}{3} + \frac{(-1)^2}{4}\right]} = \frac{(-3.50)^2}{1.10185} = 11.12$$

For the comparison between $(\bar{Y}_{A_1} + \bar{Y}_{A_2})/2$ and $\bar{Y}_{A_3}$:

$$F = \frac{[C_1(\bar{Y}_{A_1}) + C_2(\bar{Y}_{A_2}) + C_3(\bar{Y}_{A_3})]^2}{MSR\left[\Sigma\frac{(C_j)^2}{n_j}\right]} = \frac{[(1)(5.00) + (1)(8.50) + (-2)(3.00)]^2}{1.88889\left[\frac{(1)^2}{3} + \frac{(1)^2}{4} + \frac{(-2)^2}{5}\right]}$$

$$= \frac{(7.5)^2}{2.61296} = 21.53$$

Using the Scheffé procedure, each of the obtained F's has exceeded $kF_{\alpha};\, k,\, N - k - 1$, which for the present example is (2)(4.26) = *8.52*, where 4.26 is the tabled F ratio with 2 and 9 *df* at the .05 level. Both comparisons are significant at the .05 level.

It is now demonstrated how one can perform the same tests by using the b's and elements of $\mathbf{C}^*$ (the augmented covariance matrix of the b's). From SPSS output,

$$\mathbf{C}^* = \left[\begin{array}{cc|c} .37428 & -.20288 & -.17140 \\ -.20288 & .32181 & -.11893 \\ \hline -.17140 & -.11893 & .29033 \end{array}\right]$$

The values enclosed in the dashed lines are the ones reported in the output. The remaining values were obtained in the manner described earlier (i.e., a missing element in a row i is equal to $-\Sigma c_i$, and similarly for a missing element in a column). When $\mathbf{C}^*$ was discussed in connection with equal n's it was said that when unequal n's are used the diagonal elements will not be equal to each other, nor will the off-diagonal elements be equal to each other. The $\mathbf{C}^*$ obtained above illustrates that point. Yet, the manner of obtaining the missing elements is the same as in the case of equal n's.

We turn now to multiple comparisons among means via tests of differences among b's. Recall that the regression equation is

$$Y' = 5.50 - .50X_3 + 3.00X_4$$

and that the b for the group assigned -1's, say b_5, is -2.50.

In order to test $\bar{Y}_{A_1} - \bar{Y}_{A_2}$ test the difference between b_3 and b_4 using the appropriate elements from **C***:

$$F = \frac{[(1)(-.50) + (-1)(3.00)]^2}{[1 \quad -1]\begin{bmatrix} .37428 & -.20288 \\ -.20288 & .32181 \end{bmatrix}\begin{bmatrix} 1 \\ -1 \end{bmatrix}} = \frac{(-3.50)^2}{1.10185} = \mathit{11.12}$$

which is the same as the F ratio obtained above.

To test $(\bar{Y}_{A_1} + \bar{Y}_{A_2})/2 - \bar{Y}_{A_3}$, test $(b_3 + b_4)/2 - b_5$:

$$F = \frac{[(1)(-.50) + (1)(3.00) + (-2)(-2.50)]^2}{[1 \quad 1 \quad -2]\begin{bmatrix} .37428 & -.20288 & -.17140 \\ -.20288 & .32181 & -.11893 \\ -.17140 & -.11893 & .29033 \end{bmatrix}\begin{bmatrix} 1 \\ 1 \\ -2 \end{bmatrix}} = \frac{(7.5)^2}{2.61297} = \mathit{21.53}$$

It is very important to note that when n's are unequal, tests of linear combinations of means (or b's) are done on *unweighted* means. In the second comparison above it was the *average* of the means for groups A_1 and A_2 that was contrasted with the mean of group A_3. In other words, the fact that $\bar{Y}_{A_1}$ and $\bar{Y}_{A_2}$ are obtained from different numbers of people is not taken into account. Each group is given equal weight. Let us examine the meaning of this by using a concrete example. Suppose that A_1 represents a group of blacks, A_2 a group of Hispanics, and A_3 a group of whites. When the average of the means of the blacks and Hispanics is contrasted with the mean of the whites (as in the second comparison above), the fact that blacks may outnumber Hispanics, or vice versa, is ignored.[10]

Whether or not comparisons among unweighted means are meaningful depends on the specific questions one wishes to answer. Assume that A_1, A_2, and A_3 were three treatments in an experiment and that the researcher has used unequal n's by design (i.e., the unequal n's are not a consequence of subject mortality). It makes sense that the researcher may wish to compare unweighted means, thus ignoring the unequal n's. Or, in the example used above the researcher may wish to contrast minority group members with those of the majority, ignoring the fact that one minority group is larger than the other. It is conceivable, however, that one would be interested instead to contrast weighted means—in other words, weighting each mean by the number of people in the group. For the numerical example under consideration this would mean

$$\frac{\bar{Y}_{A_1} + \bar{Y}_{A_2}}{2} - \bar{Y}_{A_3} = \frac{(3)(5.00) + (4)(8.50)}{3 + 4} - 3.00 = 7.00 - 3.00 = \mathit{4.00}$$

as compared with the contrast between unweighted means: $(5.00 + 8.50)/2 - 3.00 = \mathit{3.75}$. Comparisons among weighted means are dealt with in the section on Orthogonal Coding.

[10]For a discussion of this topic, and some examples, see Cohen and Cohen (1975, pp. 199–200).

ORTHOGONAL CODING WITH UNEQUAL *n*'S

For samples with unequal n's, a comparison is defined as

$$D = n_1C_1 + n_2C_2 + \cdots + n_jC_j = 0 \tag{9.19}$$

where D = difference, or comparison; $n_1, n_2 \ldots n_j$ = number of subjects in groups 1, 2, . . . , j, respectively; C = coefficient. Note that with equal n's formula (9.19) reduces to the requirement stated earlier in this chapter—namely, that $\Sigma C_j = 0$. For the example with unequal n's, analyzed above with dummy and effect coding, the number of subjects is 3, 4, and 5 in groups A_1, A_2, and A_3, respectively. Suppose we want to compare $\bar{Y}_{A_1}$ with $\bar{Y}_{A_2}$ and assign 1's to members of group A_1, -1's to members of group A_2, and 0's to members of group A_3. By Equation (9.19),

$$D = (3)(1) + (4)(-1) + (5)(0) = -1$$

It will be noted that these coefficients are not appropriate, since $D \neq 0$. It is necessary to find a set of coefficients that will satisfy the requirement that D equal zero. The simplest way to satisfy Equation (9.19) is to use n_2 (4) as the coefficient for group A_1, and $-n_1$ (-3) as the coefficient for group A_2. Accordingly the comparison between groups A_1 and A_2 is

$$D = (3)(4) + (4)(-3) + (5)(0) = 0$$

Suppose we now wish to contrast groups A_1 and A_2 with group A_3. For this comparison we use $-n_3$ (-5) as the coefficients for groups A_1 and A_2, and $n_1 + n_2 = 7$ as the coefficient for group A_3. This comparison, too, satisfies the requirement of Equation (9.19):

$$D = (3)(-5) + (4)(-5) + (5)(7) = 0$$

Are these two comparisons orthogonal? With unequal n's two comparisons are orthogonal if

$$n_1C_{11}C_{21} + n_2C_{12}C_{22} + n_3C_{13}C_{23} = 0 \tag{9.20}$$

where the first subscript for each C refers to the number of the comparison, and the second subscript refers to the number of the group. For example, C_{11} means the coefficient of the first comparison for group 1, and C_{21} is the coefficient of the second comparison for group 1, and similarly for the other coefficients. For the two comparisons under consideration:

$$D_1 = (3)(4) + (4)(-3) + (5)(0)$$

$$D_2 = (3)(-5) + (4)(-5) + (5)(7)$$

$$(3)(4)(-5) + (4)(-3)(-5) + (5)(0)(7) = (3)(-20) + (4)(15) + 0 = 0$$

The two comparisons are orthogonal. Using the coefficients of the two comparisons, two coded vectors are generated, each reflecting one of the orthogonal comparisons. It is now possible to do a multiple regression analysis where Y is the dependent variable and the two coded vectors are treated as independent variables. The data for the three groups, along with the orthogonal vectors, are reported in Table 9.12, where X_1 reflects the comparison between $\bar{Y}_{A_1}$ and $\bar{Y}_{A_2}$, and X_2 reflects the comparison between the weighted average of $\bar{Y}_{A_1}$ and $\bar{Y}_{A_2}$ and the mean of group A_3, $\bar{Y}_{A_3}$. This will be discussed in greater detail later.

The data of Table 9.12 were analyzed by the SPSS REGRESSION program. Following are excerpts of the output and commentaries.

Output

DEPENDENT VARIABLE Y R SQUARE .79921

ANALYSIS OF VARIANCE

	DF	SUM OF SQUARES	MEAN SQUARE	F
REGRESSION	2	67.66667	33.83333	17.91
RESIDUAL	9	17.00000	1.88889	

Commentary

The above output is identical to that obtained for the same data when dummy or effect coding was used. It is therefore not commented upon, as this was done earlier. It was said several times earlier that the overall results of the analysis are the same regardless of the method of coding the categorical variables.

Table 9.12 Orthogonal Coding for Unequal *n*'s

Group	Y	X_1	X_2
	4	4	−5
A_1	5	4	−5
	6	4	−5
	7	−3	−5
A_2	8	−3	−5
	9	−3	−5
	10	−3	−5
	1	0	7
	2	0	7
A_3	3	0	7
	4	0	7
	5	0	7
Σ:	64	0	0
M:	5.33333	0	0
ss:	84.66667	84.00000	420.00000
	$\Sigma x_1 y = -42$	$\Sigma x_2 y = -140$	$\Sigma x_1 x_2 = 0$
	$r_{y1} = -.49803$	$r_{y2} = -.74242$	$r_{12} = .00000$

NOTE: X_1 reflects the comparison between $\bar{Y}_{A_1}$ and $\bar{Y}_{A_2}$. X_2 reflects the comparison between the weighted average of $\bar{Y}_{A_1}$ and $\bar{Y}_{A_2}$ with $\bar{Y}_{A_3}$.

Note from Table 9.12 that $r_{12} = 0$, as it should be when orthogonal coding is used. Moreover, $R^2_{y.12} = r^2_{y1} + r^2_{y2} = (-.49803)^2 + (-.74242)^2 = .79922$, which is, within rounding errors, the same as R^2 reported in the output above. The first comparison accounts for about 25% of the variance of Y, $(-.49803)^2 \times 100$, and the second comparison accounts for about 55% of the variance of Y, $(-.74242)^2 \times 100$.

Recall that when planned comparisons are hypothesized the primary interest is in tests of such comparisons. It is to this aspect of the analysis that we now turn.

Output

VARIABLES IN THE EQUATION

VARIABLE	B	STD ERROR B	F
X1	−.50000	.14996	11.12
X2	−.33333	.06706	24.71
(CONSTANT)	5.33333		

Commentary

The *regression equation* is

$$Y' = 5.33 - .50X_1 - .33X_2$$

Applying the regression equation to the codes of a subject on X_1 and X_2 will yield a predicted score that is equal to the mean of the group to which the subject belongs.

Note that, as in the analysis with orthogonal coding when n's are equal, a (CONSTANT) is equal to the grand mean of the dependent variable ($\bar{Y}$; see Table 9.12). In other words, a is equal to the *weighted* mean of Y when orthogonal coding is used with unequal n's.

Although the magnitude of the b's is affected by the specific codes being used (see discussion of this point in the section on Orthogonal Coding with Equal n's) each b reflects the specific planned comparison with which it is associated. Thus b_1 reflects the contrast between the means of groups A_1 and A_2, and b_2 reflects the contrast between the *weighted* means of groups A_1 and A_2 with the mean of A_3. Consequently, the test of a b amounts to a test of the comparison it reflects. Thus, the first comparison has an F ratio of 11.12 with 1 and 9 *df*, or a $t = 3.33$ ($\sqrt{F}$) with 9 *df*. The second comparison has an F ratio of 24.71 with 1 and 9 *df*, or $t = 4.97$.

Partitioning the Regression Sum of Squares

Recall that:

$$ss_{\text{reg}} = b_1\Sigma x_1y + b_2\Sigma x_2y$$

From Table 9.12, $\Sigma x_1y = -42$ and $\Sigma x_2y = -140$. Hence

$$ss_{reg} = (-.50)(-42) + (-.33333)(-140)$$
$$= 21.0000 + 46.6662 = 67.6662$$

The regression sum of squares was partitioned into two independent components, which together are equal to the regression sum of squares (see output above). Each ss_{reg} can be tested for significance, where ss_{reg} is the numerator of an F ratio and the denominator is the mean square residual *(MSR)*. From the output, $MSR = 1.88889$. Hence

$$F_1 = \frac{21}{1.88889} = 11.12$$

$$F_2 = \frac{46.6662}{1.88889} = 24.71$$

The F ratios, each with 1 and 9 *df*, are the same as those obtained for the b's.

Alternatively, because $r_{12} = 0$,

$$ss_{reg} = r^2_{y1}\Sigma y^2 + r^2_{y2}\Sigma y^2$$

From Table 9.12, $r_{y1} = -.49803$, $r_{y2} = -.74242$, and $\Sigma y^2 = 84.66667$. Therefore

$$ss_{reg} = (-.49803)^2(84.66667) + (-.74242)^2(84.66667)$$
$$= 21.00020 + 46.66721$$
$$= 67.66741$$

which are (within rounding errors) the same as the values obtained above. One could, of course, test each r^2 for significance. The F ratios will be the same as above.

The foregoing analysis is summarized in Table 9.13, where one can see clearly how the total sum of squares is broken into the various components. (The slight difference between some of the figures of Table 9.13 and those reported above from the computer output are due to rounding errors.)

Earlier, the question of whether to do multiple comparisons among weighted or unweighted means was discussed. It was shown that when one uses effect coding and proceeds with tests of linear combinations of means (or b's) it is unweighted means that are being contrasted. In this section it was shown that by using orthogonal coding, linear combinations of weighted means are tested. It is also possible to test linear combination of weighted means when applying

Table 9.13 Summary of Analysis with Orthogonal Coding for Unequal n's

Source	*df*		*ss*		*ms*	*F*
Total regression	2		67.6662		33.8331	17.91
Regression due to X_1		1		21.0000	21.0000	11.12
Regression due to X_2		1		46.6662	46.6662	24.71
Residual	9		17.00047		1.8889	
Total	11		84.66667			

post hoc or planned nonorthogonal procedures. Basically, what is required is to select coefficients for each desired contrast such that Equation (9.19) will be satisfied; that is, the sum of the products of the coefficients by their respective n's will be equal to zero in each comparison. When a set of such comparisons is not orthogonal, one may apply procedures outlined earlier for planned nonorthogonal or post hoc comparisons.

MULTIPLE REGRESSION VS. ANALYSIS OF VARIANCE

Early in this chapter, the equivalence between multiple regression analysis (MR) and the analysis of variance (ANOVA) when the independent variable is categorical was shown. At that juncture, the question was raised as to whether there are any advantages to using MR in preference to ANOVA. A partial answer to this question may be discerned from contents of this chapter. Thus, it was shown that using the appropriate method of coding the categorical independent variable in MR obviates the need for doing additional calculations that are required subsequent to ANOVA (e.g., using dummy coding when one wishes to contrast each of several treatments with a control, using orthogonal coding for the purpose of testing orthogonal comparisons). Had, however, a reduction in some of the calculations been the only advantage, it would understandably not have sufficed to convince one to abandon ANOVA in favor of MR, particularly when one is more familiar and comfortable with the former.

Although the superiority of MR will become progressively clearer as additional topics are presented in subsequent chapters, some general comments about it are in order here. The most important reason for preferring MR to ANOVA is that it is a more comprehensive and general approach on the conceptual as well as the analytic level. On the conceptual level, all variables, be they categorical or continuous, are viewed from the same frame of reference: information available when attempting to explain or predict a dependent variable. On the analytic level, too, different types of variables (i.e., categorical and continuous) can be dealt with in MR. On the other hand, ANOVA is limited to categorical independent variables (except for manipulated continuous variables).

Following is a partial listing of situations in which MR is the superior or the only appropriate method of analysis: (1) when the independent variables are continuous; (2) when some of the independent variables are continuous and some are categorical, as in analysis of covariance, aptitude–treatment interactions, or treatments by levels designs; (3) when cell frequencies in a factorial design are unequal and disproportionate; (4) when studying trends in the data—linear, quadratic, and so on. These and other related topics are presented in subsequent chapters.

SUMMARY

Three methods of coding categorical variables were presented in this chapter. They were called dummy coding, effect coding, and orthogonal coding. Regardless of the coding method used, the results of the overall analysis are the same. When a regression analysis is done with Y as the dependent variable and k coded vectors (k = number of groups minus one) reflecting group membership as the independent variables, the overall R^2, regression sum of squares, residual sum of squares, and the F ratio are the same with any coding method. The predictions based on the regression equations resulting from the different coding methods are also identical. In each case the predicted score is equal to the mean of the group to which the subject belongs. The coding methods do differ in the properties of their regression equations. A brief summary of the major properties of each method follows.

With *dummy coding*, k coded vectors consisting of 1's and 0's are generated. In each vector, in turn, subjects of one of the groups are assigned 1's and all others are assigned 0's. Since k is equal to the number of groups minus one, it follows that members of one of the groups are assigned 0's in all the vectors. This group is treated as a control group in the analysis. In the regression equation, the intercept, a, is equal to the mean of the control group. Each b coefficient is equal to the deviation the mean of the group assigned 1's in the vector associated with the b from the mean of the control group. The test of significance of a given b is a test of significance between the mean of the group associated with the b and the mean of the control group. Although dummy coding is particularly useful when one does in fact have several experimental groups and one control group, it may also be used in situations in which no particular group serves as a control for all others. The properties of dummy coding are the same for equal or unequal sample sizes.

Effect coding is similar to dummy coding. The difference is that in dummy coding one of the groups is assigned 0's in all the coded vectors, whereas in effect coding one of the groups is assigned -1's in all the vectors. As a result, the regression equation reflects the linear model. In other words, the intercept, a, is equal to the grand mean of the dependent variable, $\bar{Y}$, and each b is equal to the treatment effect for the group with which it is associated, or the deviation of the mean of the group from the grand mean, $\bar{Y}$. When effect coding is used with unequal sample sizes, the intercept of the regression equation is equal to the unweighted mean of the group means. Each b is equal to the deviation of the mean of the group with which it is associated from the unweighted mean.

Orthogonal coding consists of k coded vectors of orthogonal coefficients. The selection of orthogonal coefficients for equal and unequal sample sizes was discussed and illustrated. In the regression equation, a is equal to the grand mean, $\bar{Y}$, for equal as well as unequal sample sizes. Each b reflects the specific comparison with which it is related. Testing a given b for significance amounts to testing the specific hypothesis that the comparison reflects.

Which method of coding one chooses depends on one's purpose and interest. When one wishes to compare several treatment groups with a control group, dummy coding is the preferred method. Orthogonal coding is most efficient when one's sole interest is in orthogonal comparisons among means. It was shown, however, that the different types of multiple comparisons—orthogonal, planned nonorthogonal, and post hoc—can be easily performed by testing differences among regression coefficients obtained from effect coding. Consequently, effect coding is generally the preferred method of coding categorical variables.

STUDY SUGGESTIONS

1. Distinguish between categorical and continuous variables. Give examples of each.
2. The regression of moral judgment on religious affiliation (e.g., Catholic, Jewish, Protestant) was studied.
   (a) What is the independent variable?
   (b) What is the dependent variable?
   (c) What kind of a variable is religious affiliation?
3. In a study with six different groups, how many coded vectors are necessary to exhaust the information of group membership? Explain.
4. Under what conditions is dummy coding particularly useful?
5. In a research study with three treatments, A_1, A_2, A_3, and a control group, C, dummy vectors were constructed as follows: vector X_1 consisted of 1's for subjects in treatment A_1, 0's for all others; vector X_2 consisted of 1's for subjects in treatment A_2, 0's for all others; vector X_3 consisted of 1's for subjects in treatment A_3, 0's for all others. A multiple regression analysis was done in which the dependent variable measure was regressed on the three dummy vectors. The regression equation obtained in the analysis was

$$Y' = 8.00 + 6.00X_1 + 5.00X_2 - 2.00X_3$$

   (a) What are the means of the four groups on the dependent variable measure?
   (b) What is the zero-order correlation between each pair of coded vectors, assuming equal n's in the groups?
6. In a study of problem solving, subjects were randomly assigned to two different treatments, A_1 and A_2, and a control group, C. At the conclusion of the experiment, the subjects were given a set of problems to solve. The problem-solving scores for the three groups were:

A_1	A_2	C
7	2	3
6	3	3
4	2	4
7	5	4
8	3	2
4	5	2

   Using dummy coding, do a multiple regression analysis in which the problem-solving scores are regressed on the coded vectors. It is suggested that you do the calculations by hand as well as with a computer program. Calculate:
   (a) R^2.
   (b) Regression sum of squares.
   (c) Residual sum of squares.
   (d) The regression equation.
   (e) The overall F ratio.
   (f) t ratios for the test of the difference of each treatment mean from the control mean.
   (g) What table would you use to check whether the t's obtained in (f), above, are statistically significant?
   (h) Interpret the results.
7. The following regression equation was obtained from an analysis with effect coding for four groups with equal n's:
   $Y' = 102.5 + 2.5X_1 - 2.5X_2 - 4.5X_3$
   (a) What is the grand mean, $\bar{Y}$?
   (b) What are the means of the four groups, assuming that the fourth group was assigned -1's?
   (c) What is the effect of each treatment?
8. In a study consisting of four groups, each with ten subjects, the following results were obtained:
   $\bar{Y}_1 = 16.5$ $\quad \bar{Y}_2 = 12.0$ $\quad \bar{Y}_3 = 16.0$
   $\bar{Y}_4 = 11.5$ $\quad MSR = 7.15$
   (a) Write the regression equation that will be obtained if effect coding is used. Assume that subjects in the fourth group are assigned -1's.
   (b) What are the effects of the four treatments?

(c) What is the residual sum of squares?
(d) What is the regression sum of squares? [*Hint:* use the treatment effects obtained in (b), above.]
(e) What is R^2?
(f) What is the overall F ratio?
(g) Do Scheffé tests for the following comparisons, using the .05 level of significance: (1) between $\bar{Y}_1$ and $\bar{Y}_2$; (2) between the mean of $\bar{Y}_1$ and $\bar{Y}_2$, and $\bar{Y}_3$; (3) between the mean of $\bar{Y}_1$ $\bar{Y}_2$, $\bar{Y}_4$, and $\bar{Y}_3$.

9. A researcher studied the regression of attitudes toward school busing on political party affiliation. She administered an attitude scale to samples of Conservatives, Republicans, Liberals, and Democrats, and obtained the following scores. The higher the score, the more favorable the attitude. (The scores are illustrative.)

Conservatives	*Republicans*	*Liberals*	*Democrats*
2	3	5	4
3	3	6	5
4	4	6	5
4	4	7	7
6	5	7	7
6	6	9	7
7	8	10	9
7	8	10	9
8	9	11	10
8	10	12	10

(a) Using dummy coding, do a regression analysis of these data. Calculate: (1) R^2; (2) ss_{reg}; (3) ss_{res}; (4) the regression equation; (5) the overall F ratio.
(b) Using effect coding, do a regression analysis of the data. Calculate the same statistics as in (a), above. In addition, calculate **C*** (the augmented variance/covariance matrix of the b's).
(c) Using the regression equations obtained under (a) and (b), above, calculate the means of the four groups.
(d) Calculate F ratios for the following comparisons: (1) between Conservatives and Republicans; (2) between Liberals and Democrats; (3) between the mean of Conservatives and Republicans, and that of Liberals and Democrats; (4) between the mean of Conservatives, Republicans, and Democrats, and the mean of Liberals.
(e) Taken together, what type of comparisons are 1, 2, 3 in (d), above?
(f) Assuming it is desired to use the Scheffé test at the .05 level of significance for the comparisons under (d), above, what is the F ratio that is to be exceeded so that a comparison would be declared statistically significant?
(g) Using the regression coefficients obtained from the analysis with effect coding and **C*** [under (b), above] calculate F ratios for the same comparisons as those done under (d), above. In addition, calculate F ratios for the following comparisons: (1) between Republicans and Democrats; (2) between Liberals and Democrats, against the Conservatives.
(h) Assume that the researcher had the following a priori hypotheses: that Republicans have more favorable attitudes toward school busing than do Conservatives; that Liberals are more favorable than Democrats; that Liberals and Democrats are more favorable toward school busing than are Conservatives and Republicans.

Use orthogonal coding to express these hypotheses and do a regression analysis. Calculate the following: (1) R^2; (2) the regression equation; (3) the overall F ratio; (4) t ratios for each of the b coefficients; (5) regression sum of squares due to each hypothesis; (6) residual sum of squares; (7) F ratios for each hypothesis. (8) What should each of these F ratios be equal to? (9) What should the average of these F ratios be equal to?

Interpret the results obtained under (a)–(h) above.

Note: Using a computer program, you can do the three regression analyses required above in a single run. For example, using SPSS you will read in Y and three sets of coded vectors (dummy, effect, and orthogonal). Use three REGRESSION statements, each specifying Y as the dependent variable and a given set of coded vectors as the independent "variables."

You may also wish to try and read in only Y and four dummy vectors, one for each of the groups. Manipulating these vectors by, for example, COMPUTE statements in SPSS you can generate the effect and the orthogonal coding vectors, instead of punching them. Alternatively, you may wish to experiment with IF statements in order to generate coded vectors, instead of having to punch them.

ANSWERS

2. (a) Religious affiliation.
   (b) Moral judgment.
   (c) Categorical.
3. 5
4. When it is desired to test the difference between the mean of each experimental group and a control group.
5. (a) $\bar{Y}_{A_1} = 14.00$, $\bar{Y}_{A_2} = 13.00$, $\bar{Y}_{A_3} = 6.00$, $\bar{Y}_C = 8.00$.
   (b) $-.33$.
6. (a) .54275.
   (b) 32.44444.
   (c) 27.33333.
   (d) $Y' = 3.00 + 3.00X_1 + .33X_2$.
   (e) $F = 8.90$, with 2 and 15 *df*.
   (f) t for b_1 (i.e., the difference between $\bar{Y}_{A_1}$ and $\bar{Y}_C$) is 3.85, with 15 *df*, $p < .01$. t for b_2 (i.e., the difference between $\bar{Y}_{A_2}$ and $\bar{Y}_C$) is .43, with 15 *df*, $p > .05$.
   (g) Dunnett.
7. (a) 102.5.
   (b) $\bar{Y}_1 = 105$, $\bar{Y}_2 = 100$, $\bar{Y}_3 = 98$, $\bar{Y}_4 = 107$.
   (c) $T_1 = 2.5$, $T_2 = -2.5$, $T_3 = -4.5$, $T_4 = 4.5$.
8. (a) $Y' = 14.0 + 2.5X_1 - 2.0X_2 + 2.0X_3$.
   (b) $T_1 = 2.5$, $T_2 = -2.0$, $T_3 = 2.0$, $T_4 = -2.5$.
   (c) 257.4 ($MSR \times df$).
   (d) $205.0 = [(2.5)^2 + (-2.0)^2 + (2.0)^2 + (-2.5)^2]\,(10)$.
   (e) $.44334 = ss_{reg}/\Sigma y^2$, where $\Sigma y^2 = 257.4 + 205.0 = 462.4$.
   (f) 9.56, with 3 and 36 *df*.
   (g) (1) $|D| = 4.5$; $S = 3.5$; significant;
   (2) $|D| = 3.5$; $S = 6.1$; not significant;
   (3) $|D| = 8.0$; $S = 8.6$; not significant.
9. (a) (1) $R^2 = .19868$.
   (2) $ss_{reg} = 48.275$.
   (3) $ss_{res} = 194.700$.

(4) $Y' = 7.3 - 1.8X_1 - 1.3X_2 + 1.0X_3$.
(5) $F = 2.98$, with 3 and 36 *df*.

(b) All the results are the same as under (a), above, except for the regression equation:

$$Y' = 6.775 - 1.275X_1 - .775X_2 + 1.525X_3.$$

$$\mathbf{C}^* = \begin{bmatrix} .40563 & -.13521 & -.13521 & -.13521 \\ -.13521 & .40563 & -.13521 & -.13521 \\ -.13521 & -.13521 & .40563 & -.13521 \\ -.13521 & -.13521 & -.13521 & .40563 \end{bmatrix}$$

(c) Conservatives = 5.5; Republicans = 6.0; Liberals = 8.3; Democrats = 7.3.

(d) (1) .23; (2) .92; (3) 7.77; (4) 5.73. Each of these F ratios has 1 and 36 *df*.

(e) Orthogonal.

(f) 8.58 ($kF_\alpha; k, N - k - 1$).

(g) The F ratios for the comparisons under (d) are the same as those obtained above. For the two additional comparisons, the F ratios are: (1) 1.56; (2) 6.52.

(h) (1) $R^2 = .19868$.
(2) $Y' = 6.775 + .250X_1 + .500X_2 + 1.025X_3$.
(3) $F = 2.98$ with 3 and 36 *df*.
(4) t for $b_1 = .48$; t for $b_2 = .96$; t for $b_3 = 2.79$. Each t has 36 *df*.
(5) $ss_{\text{reg}(1)} = 1.24889$; $ss_{\text{reg}(2)} = 5.00043$; $ss_{\text{reg}(3)} = 42.02496$.
(6) $ss_{\text{res}} = 194.70000$.
(7) $F_1 = .23$; $F_2 = .92$; $F_3 = 7.77$. Each F has 1 and 36 *df*. Note that the same results were obtained when the regression equation from effect coding and $\mathbf{C}^*$ were used. See (d) above.
(8) Each F in (7) is equal to the square of its corresponding t in (4).
(9) The average of the three F's in (7) should equal the overall F (i.e., 2.97).

10

MULTIPLE CATEGORICAL VARIABLES AND FACTORIAL DESIGNS

As in the case of continuous variables, the use of regression analysis is not limited to a single categorical independent variable or predictor. Complex phenomena almost always require the use of more than one variable if substantial explanation or prediction is to be achieved. Multiple categorical variables may be used in predictive or explanatory, experimental or nonexperimental research. The context of the research in which the variables are used should always be borne in mind so that risks of arriving at erroneous interpretations and conclusions may be reduced.

As is shown below, the major advantage of designs with multiple independent variables is in the opportunities they afford for studying, in addition to the effects of each of the independent variables, their joint effects or interactions. In earlier chapters it was argued that results obtained in experimental research are generally easier to interpret than those obtained in nonexperimental research (see Chapter 9). In the present chapter the major concern with the distinction between the two types of research settings is with the status of the concept of interaction within each of them. The first part of the chapter is devoted exclusively to experimental research with equal cell frequencies or orthogonal designs. This is followed by a discussion of nonorthogonal designs in experimental and nonexperimental research. It is within the context of the latter section that issues regarding the use of the concept of interaction in nonexperimental research are addressed.

Methods of coding categorical variables, introduced in Chapter 9 for designs with a single independent variable, are extended in this chapter to designs with multiple categorical independent variables. In addition, another approach—Criterion Scaling—that may be useful for certain purposes is introduced at the end of the chapter.

FACTORIAL DESIGNS

In the context of the analysis of variance, independent variables are also referred to as *factors*. A factor is a variable; for example, methods of teaching, sex, levels of motivation. The two or more subdivisions or categories of a factor are, in set theory language, *partitions* (Kemeny, Snell, & Thompson, 1966, Chapter 3). The subdivisions in a partition are subsets and are called cells. If a sample is divided into male and female, there are two cells, A_1 and A_2, with males in one cell and females in the other. In a factorial design, two or more partitions are combined to form a *cross partition*, which consists of all subsets formed by the intersections of the original partitions. For instance, the intersection of two partitions or sets, $A_i \cap B_j$, is a cross partition. (The cells must be disjoint and they must exhaust all the cases.) It is possible to have $2 \times 2, 2 \times 3, 3 \times 3, 4 \times 5$, and in fact, $p \times q$ factorial designs. Three or more factors with two or more subsets per factor are also possible: $2 \times 2 \times 2, 2 \times 3 \times 3, 3 \times 3 \times 5, 2 \times 2 \times 3 \times 3, 2 \times 3 \times 3 \times 4$, and so on.

A factorial design is customarily displayed as in Figure 10.1. There are two

	B_1	B_2	B_3
A_1	A_1B_1	A_1B_2	A_1B_3
A_2	A_2B_1	A_2B_2	A_2B_3

Figure 10.1

independent variables, A and B, with two subsets of A: A_1 and A_2, and three subsets of B: B_1, B_2, and B_3. The cells obtained by the cross partitioning are indicated by A_1B_1, A_1B_2, and so on.

Advantages of Factorial Designs

There are several advantages to studying the effects on a dependent variable of several independent variables. The first and perhaps most important advantage is that it is possible to determine whether the independent variables interact in their effect on the dependent variable. An independent variable can "explain" a relatively small proportion of variance of a dependent variable, whereas its interaction with other independent variables may explain a relatively large proportion of the variance. Studying the effects of independent variables in isolation cannot reveal the interaction between them.

Second, factorial designs afford the researcher greater control, and, consequently, more sensitive statistical tests than the statistical tests used in analyses with single variables. When a single independent variable is used, the variance not explained by it is relegated to the error term. Needless to say, the larger the error term the less sensitive the statistical test in which it is used. One method of reducing the magnitude of the error term is to identify as many sources of systematic variance of the dependent variable as is possible, feasible, and meaningful under a given set of circumstances. For example, suppose one is studying the effect of different styles of leadership on group productivity. If no other variable is included in the design, all the variance not explained by leadership styles becomes part of the error term. Suppose, however, that each group has an equal number of males and females, and that there is a correlation between sex and the type of productivity under study. In other words, some of the variance of productivity is due to sex. Under such circumstances, the introduction of sex as another independent variable will result in a reduction in the error estimate by reclaiming that part of the dependent variable variance due to sex. Note that the proportion of variance due to leadership styles will remain unchanged. But since the error term will be decreased, the test of significance for the effect of leadership styles will be more sensitive. The same reasoning of course applies to testing the effect of sex. In addition, as noted above, an interaction between the two factors may be detected. For example, one style of leadership may lead to greater productivity among males, whereas another style may lead to greater productivity among females.

Third, factorial designs are efficient. One can test the separate and combined effects of several variables using the same number of subjects one would have to use for separate experiments.

Fourth, in factorial experiments the effect of a treatment is studied across different conditions of other treatments. Consequently, generalizations from factorial experiments are broader than generalizations from single-variable experiments. Factorial designs are examples of efficiency, power, and elegance. They also expeditiously accomplish scientific experimental purposes.

Manipulated and Classificatory Variables

A factorial design may consist of either manipulated variables only or of manipulated and classificatory variables. A classificatory, or grouping, variable is one in which subjects either come from naturally existing classes or are classified by the researcher into two or more classes for research purposes. Examples of the former are sex and marital status. Examples of the latter are extravert, introvert; and psychotic, neurotic, and normal (see Chapter 9 for a discussion of classification rules). The distinction between the types of designs is not in the data analysis but in the interpretation of the results.

In an experiment with manipulated variables only, subjects are randomly assigned to different treatment combinations in order to study the separate effects of each manipulated variable as well as their joint effects (i.e., interactions). For example, one may wish to study the effects of three methods of teaching and three types of reinforcements. This, then, would be a 3×3 design in which both variables are manipulated. Subjects would be randomly assigned to the nine cells (treatment combinations) and the researcher would then study the effects of teaching methods, reinforcement, and their interaction on the dependent variable—say, reading achievement. Assuming the research is well designed and executed, the interpretation of the results is relatively straightforward, depending, among other things, upon the soundness and elaborateness of the theory from which the hypotheses have been derived and upon the knowledge, abilities, and sophistication of the researcher.

Suppose now that classificatory variables are used in combination with manipulated variables. One of the purposes of such designs is control of extraneous variables, as when in studying the effects of certain treatments one might introduce sex as a factor in the design for the purpose of isolating variance due to sex, thereby increasing the sensitivity of the analysis. Another purpose for introducing classificatory variables in experimental research is explanation; that is, it is desired to test hypotheses about the effects of such variables and/or interactions among themselves and with manipulated variables. It is this usage of classificatory variables that may give rise to serious problems in the interpretation of the results.

An example with one manipulated and one classificatory variable will help clarify this point. Assume, again, that one wishes to study the effects of three methods of teaching, but that it is hypothesized that the methods interact with the regions in which the schools are located. That is, it is hypothesized that given methods have differential effects depending on whether they are used in urban, suburban, or rural schools. This, then, is also a 3×3 design, except that this time it consists of a manipulated and a classificatory variable.

To validly execute such a study, subjects from each region (urban, suburban, and rural) have to be randomly assigned to the teaching methods. The analysis then proceeds in the same manner as in a study in which all the variables are manipulated. But what about the interpretation of the results? Suppose that in the example under consideration it is found that region has a significant effect on the dependent variable or that there is a significant interaction between region and teaching methods. Such results would not be easily interpretable because region is correlated with many other variables whose effects it may be reflecting. For example, it is well known that in some parts of the country urban schools are attended mostly by minority group children, whereas all or most of the students in the suburban and the rural schools are white. Should the findings regarding the classificatory variable be attributed to region, to race, to both? To complicate matters further, it is known that race is correlated with many variables. Is it race, then, or variables correlated with it that interact with teaching methods? There is no easy answer to such questions. All one can say is that when using classificatory variables in experimental research it is necessary to consider variables associated with them as possible alternative explanations regarding findings about their effects or interactions with the manipulated variables. The greater one's knowledge of the area being studied, the greater the probability of arriving at a valid interpretation of the results, although the inherent ambiguity of the situation cannot be resolved entirely. As the sole purpose of the presentation that follows is to show how data from factorial designs are analyzed by multiple regression methods, no further comments will be made about the distinction between designs in which only manipulated variables are used and those that include also classificatory variables.

ANALYSIS OF A THREE-BY-THREE DESIGN

Regression analysis with multiple categorical independent variables is illustrated for the case of two independent variables, each having three categories. The same procedure, however, applies to any number of independent variables consisting of any number of categories. A set of illustrative data for two factors (*A* and *B*), each with three categories, is given in Table 10.1. It is assumed that the researcher is interested in making inferences only about the categories included in the design. In other words, the concern is with a fixed effects model (see, Hays, 1981; Kirk, 1968; Winer, 1971, for discussions of fixed and random effects models). The data are analyzed first using effect coding. Orthogonal and dummy coding are discussed subsequently.

Effect Coding

The scores on the dependent variable are placed in a single vector, *Y*, representing the dependent variable. This is always done, regardless of the type of design and of the number of factors of which it is composed. Coded vectors are then generated to represent the independent variables or factors of the design. When this is done, each factor is coded separately as if it were the only one in the design. In other words, when one factor or variable is being coded, all other independent variables are ignored. As was the case when a single categorical variable was used (Chapter 9), for each variable in a factorial design one generates a number of coded vectors equal to the number of categories of the variable minus one, or the number of degrees of freedom associated with a given variable. Thus, each set of coded vectors identifies one independent variable, be it manipulated or classificatory. In the present example it is necessary to generate two coded vectors for each of the categorical variables.

The procedure outlined in the preceding paragraph is followed regardless of the method of coding (effect, orthogonal, dummy). In this section it is illustrated with effect coding. Effect coding was introduced in Chapter 9, where it was noted that the coding is 1, 0, −1. In each coded vector, members of a category being identified are assigned 1's, all others are assigned 0's, except that the members of one category (for convenience the last category of the variable is used) are assigned −1's. In Table 10.2 the scores of Table 10.1 are repeated, this time in the form of a single vector, *Y*. The coded vectors (1

Table 10.1 Illustrative Data for a Three-by-Three Design

	B_1	B_2	B_3	$\bar{Y}_A$
A_1	16 14	20 16	10 14	15
A_2	12 10	17 13	7 7	11
A_3	7 7	10 8	6 4	7
$\bar{Y}_B$	11	14	8	$\bar{Y} = 11$

NOTE: $\bar{Y}_A$ = means for the three categories of *A*; $\bar{Y}_B$ = means for the three categories of *B*; $\bar{Y}$ = grand mean.

Table 10.2 Effect Coding for a 3 × 3 Design, Based on Data of Table 10.1

Cell	*Y*	*1*	*2*	*3*	*4*	*5* (1 × 3)	*6* (1 × 4)	*7* (2 × 3)	*8* (2 × 4)
A_1B_1	16	1	0	1	0	1	0	0	0
	14	1	0	1	0	1	0	0	0
A_2B_1	12	0	1	1	0	0	0	1	0
	10	0	1	1	0	0	0	1	0
A_3B_1	7	−1	−1	1	0	−1	0	−1	0
	7	−1	−1	1	0	−1	0	−1	0
A_1B_2	20	1	0	0	1	0	1	0	0
	16	1	0	0	1	0	1	0	0
A_2B_2	17	0	1	0	1	0	0	0	1
	13	0	1	0	1	0	0	0	1
A_3B_2	10	−1	−1	0	1	0	−1	0	−1
	8	−1	−1	0	1	0	−1	0	−1
A_1B_3	10	1	0	−1	−1	−1	−1	0	0
	14	1	0	−1	−1	−1	−1	0	0
A_2B_3	7	0	1	−1	−1	0	0	−1	−1
	7	0	1	−1	−1	0	0	−1	−1
A_3B_3	4	−1	−1	−1	−1	1	1	1	1
	6	−1	−1	−1	−1	1	1	1	1
ss:	340	12	12	12	12	8	8	8	8
M:	11	0	0	0	0	0	0	0	0

NOTE: Y = dependent variable; vectors 1 and 2 represent factor A; vectors 3 and 4 represent factor B; vectors 5 through 8 represent the interaction of A and B.

through 8) necessary for the analysis of this 3 × 3 design are given beside the Y vector. Vectors 1 and 2 represent the codes for factor A. Note that in vector 1, subjects belonging to category A_1 are assigned 1's, subjects in category A_2 are assigned 0's, while subjects in category A_3 are assigned −1's. In vector 2, subjects in category A_3 are still assigned −1's, but now subjects in category A_1 are assigned 0's, while subjects in A_2 are assigned 1's. As was said above, when one factor or independent variable is coded, the other factors are ignored. Thus, when in vector 1, subjects in category A_1 are assigned 1's; the fact that they belong to different categories of B is not taken into account—and similarly, for all other vectors representing a given factor. One could now regress Y on vectors 1 and 2 of Table 10.2. Such an analysis is legitimate, and its results may be interpreted exactly as was done in Chapter 9 because the data are treated as if they were obtained in a design with a single categorical independent variable. But doing such an analysis would defeat the very purpose for which factorial designs are being used, since the effects of B and the interaction between A and B would be ignored. In fact, they would be relegated to the error term, or the residual.

As was done when factor A was coded, factor B is coded as if A does not exist. This was done in vectors 3 and 4 of Table 10.2. In these two vectors category B_3 is assigned −1's, whereas B_1 is assigned 1's in vector 3 and category B_2 is assigned 1's in vector 4.

To repeat, vectors 1 and 2 of Table 10.2 represent factor *A* and vectors 3 and 4 represent factor *B*. These four vectors represent what are referred to as the main effects of factors *A* and *B*. Before proceeding with the analysis it is necessary to generate coded vectors that represent the interaction between *A* and *B*. This is done by cross-multiplying, in succession, each of the vectors of one factor with each of the vectors of the other factor. Vectors 5 through 8 of Table 10.2 are obtained in this manner. That is, the product of vectors 1 and 3 yields vector 5, 1 × 4 yields vector 6, 2 × 3 yields vector 7, and 2 × 4 yields vector 8. The number of vectors thus generated is equal to the number of degrees of freedom associated with the interaction. The degrees of freedom for an interaction equals the product of the degrees of freedom associated with each of the variables whose interaction is being considered. In the present example, *A* has 2 *df* and *B* has 2 *df*, and the interaction (*A* × *B*) has 4 *df*. Had one worked, for example, with a design in which *A* was composed of 4 categories and *B* of 5 categories (i.e., a 4 × 5 design), it would have been necessary to generate three coded vectors to represent factor *A* and four coded vectors to represent *B*. This would have been accomplished in exactly the same manner as above. Cross-multiplying each vector of *A* by each vector of *B*, 12 vectors representing the interaction would have been obtained. *A* would have had 3 *df*, *B* would have 4 *df*, and *A* × *B* would have 12 *df*. (For analyses with more than two categorical independent variables, see below.)

When one uses a computer program that allows for manipulation of vectors (most do) it is not necessary to punch the cross-product vectors since this can be done by using the appropriate command. Thus, using SPSS, for example, one can obtain cross-product vectors by using the command COMPUTE with the appropriate expression. For example, to obtain vector 5 of Table 10.2, the following expression will be used:

```
COMPUTE V5 = V1*V3
```

(It is assumed that the coded vectors were read in as V1, V2, and so on. One could, of course, use other variable names, as long as they conform to the requirements of the given computer program.)

We are ready now to do the analysis by regressing *Y* on vectors 1 through 8 of Table 10.2. Before this is done an additional comment will be made about the coded vectors of Table 10.2. Note that the sum of the codes in each vector is equal to zero, and therefore the mean of each vector is zero. This will always be the case when effect coding is used, regardless of the number of factors and the number of categories within a factor, as long as the design consists of equal *n*'s in the cells (designs with unequal *n*'s are treated below). Therefore, when a computer program is used for the analysis it is advisable to check the means of the coded vectors. A nonzero mean for a vector indicates that an error was made either in the punching of the data or in the variable format used for reading in the data.

The data of Table 10.2 were analyzed by the REGRESSION program of SPSS. Excerpts of the output are presented and commented upon as each aspect of the analysis is being discussed.

Control Cards

Since control cards for SPSS REGRESSION have been shown several times before (see in particular Chapter 4) they are not shown here. Only the REGRESSION statement used is shown.
Beginning in column 16:

```
REGRESSION = Y WITH V1, V2(6), V3, V4(4), V5 TO V8(2)/
```

The regression will be done in three steps. In the first step, V1 and V2 will be entered because they were given the highest inclusion level(6). V3 and V4 will be entered in the second step, and V5 TO V8 will be entered in the third step. The reason for doing this is explained below.

The Overall Analysis

Output

DEPENDENT VARIABLE Y R SQUARE .90588

ANALYSIS OF VARIANCE

	DF	SUM OF SQUARES	MEAN SQUARE	F
REGRESSION	8	308.00	38.50	10.83
RESIDUAL	9	32.00	3.55556	

Commentary

Altogether, about 91% of the variance of Y ($R^2 \times 100$) is accounted for by A, B, and $A \times B$. It is instructive to examine the meaning of R^2 in the present context. With two independent variables, each having three categories, there are nine distinct combinations that can be treated as nine separate groups. There is, for example, a group under conditions A_1B_1, another group under conditions A_1B_2, and so forth for the rest of the combinations. If one were to perform a multiple regression analysis of Y with nine distinct groups (or a one-way analysis of variance for nine groups) one would obtain the same R^2 as that above. The F ratio associated with $R^2_{y.12345678}$ is the overall F ratio that would be obtained if one were to perform a regression analysis in which each cell was treated as a separate group. In other words, the overall R^2 indicates the proportion of the variance of Y that is explained by all the available information.

In what way, then, is the above output useful when it is obtained from an analysis of a factorial design? It is useful only for the purpose of ascertaining whether overall one is explaining a meaningful proportion of variance. Meaningfulness depends on what a given researcher deems meaningful in a specific research area and considering, among other things, the investment of time, money, and energy on the part of the experimenter and the subjects in obtaining the results. (Do not be misled by the very high R^2 obtained in the illustrative example above. This was done so that even with small *n*'s the results will be statistically significant. R^2's as large as the one obtained here are rarely, if ever, obtained in social science research.) When a researcher deems the overall R^2 to be not meaningful there is no point in interpreting the remainder of the analysis. Assuming that the experiment was appropriately executed, one has to conclude that the desired effects (whatever they were) were not obtained. The next step (e.g., abandoning research in the area, designing a new study) will depend on a reconsideration and reexamination of every aspect of the study that has failed to yield the expected results (e.g., theory, operational definitions of the variables, types of subjects).

It is possible for an overall R^2 that is considered meaningful to be associated with a nonsignificant F ratio. This should not lead one to conclude that none of the results is statistically significant. The reason is that when the overall R^2 is tested for significance it is done by using all the degrees of freedom for the main effects and the interaction. Assume, for example, that only one factor accounts for a meaningful proportion of the variance of Y, while the remaining ones and the interactions have negligible effects. When the overall R^2 is tested for significance, all the variance accounted for is lumped together, as are all the degrees of freedom for the main effects and the interactions. This may lead to a relatively small numerator for the overall F ratio, possibly resulting in a nonsignificant one.

It is worthwhile to illustrate this phenomenon with a numerical example. For this purpose, the results of the analysis of the data of Table 10.2 are altered. It is shown below that factor A accounts for .56 of the variance. Assume now that B and $A \times B$ together account for only .04 of the variance (in our example they actually account for about .35). The overall R^2 would therefore be .60. Using the formula for testing this overall R^2 with $N = 18$ (number of people in the sample) and $k = 8$ (number of coded vectors for the main effects and the interaction):

$$F = \frac{R^2/k}{(1 - R^2)/(N - k - 1)} = \frac{.60/8}{(1 - .60)/(18 - 8 - 1)} = \frac{.075}{.044} = 1.70$$

Clearly, the F ratio is not significant. This is because the numerator has appropriated 8 *df*, leading to a relatively small mean square regression (.075). But, test now the proportion of variance accounted for by A alone:

$$F = \frac{.56/2}{(1 - .6)/(18 - 8 - 1)} = \frac{.28}{.044} = 6.36$$

with 2 and 9 *df*, $p < .05$. Note that the denominator is the same for both F ratios, as it should be because it reflects the error, that portion of Y that is not accounted for by A, B, and $A \times B$. But because in the numerator of the second F ratio two degrees of freedom are used (those associated with A), the mean square regression is considerably larger than the one for the first F ratio (.28 as compared with .075). What happened when everything was taken together (i.e., overall R^2) is that a proportion of .04 brought with it, so to speak, 6 *df* leading to an overall relatively small mean square regression. In sum, the overall R^2, not its test of significance, is a useful piece of information when a factorial design is analyzed.

All that was said about the overall R^2 applies equally to the overall partitioning of the sum of squares of Y. In the present example, $\Sigma y^2 = 340$ (see Table 10.2). In the above output, $ss_{reg} = 308.00$ and $ss_{res} = 32.00$. Of course, $ss_{reg}/\Sigma y^2 = R^2$; that is, $308/340 = .90588$. Therefore, it makes no difference whether one examines the overall ss_{reg} or the overall R^2, except that the latter is more readily interpretable because it is a pure number independent of the particular scale values used in the measurement of Y. When analyzing a factorial design, the objective is to partition the regression sum of squares or the proportion of variance accounted for by each factor and by the interaction. We turn first to the partitioning of the regression sum of squares. The partitioning of the proportion of variance accounted for is presented subsequently.

Partitioning the Regression Sum of Squares

In effect coding, the vectors representing the main effects and the interactions are mutually orthogonal. This means that although the coded vectors representing a given factor or an interaction are intercorrelated, there is no correlation between coded vectors across factors or interactions. Stated differently, the coded vectors of one factor are not correlated with the coded vectors of the other factors, nor are they correlated with the coded vectors representing interactions. In the present analysis, for example, vectors 1 and 2 of Table 10.2 represent factor A, and vectors 3 and 4 represent factor B. Consequently, $r_{13} = r_{14} = r_{23} = r_{24} = .00$.

Because of these properties of effect coding, each set of coded vectors representing a main effect or an interaction contains information that is independent of the information of the other sets of coded vectors. Consequently, the regression of Y on a given set of coded vectors will yield an independent component of the overall regression sum of squares, and equivalently an independent component of the proportion of variance accounted for (see below). The vectors within each set should, of course, not be treated as separate variables because it is as a set that they represent a given variable (see Chapter 9 for a discussion of this point) or an interaction term. In fact, depending on how the codes are assigned, a given vector may be shown to appropriate a smaller or a larger amount of the overall regression sum of squares. But, taken together, the set of coded vectors representing a given factor or an interaction term will always appropriate the same amount of regression sum of squares, regardless of the specific codes assigned to a given category.

In view of the foregoing, when a factorial design with effect coding is analyzed it is necessary to group the contribution made by a set of vectors that represent a given factor. This can be done regardless of the order in which the individual vectors are entered into the analysis (i.e., even when vectors are entered in a mixed order). It is, however, more convenient and more efficient to group each set of vectors representing a factor or an interaction term and force each set into the analysis in a sequence. The sequence itself is immaterial because, as was noted above, the sets of coded vectors are mutually orthogonal. It is this procedure of entering sequentially sets of vectors that was followed in the present analysis. This was accomplished by assigning different inclusion levels for variables on the REGRESSION card (see Control Cards above). In this specific analysis the vectors for *A* were to be entered first, followed by those of *B*, and then by the vectors representing the interaction. To repeat: the order of the entry of the sets makes no difference.

Following are relevant excerpts of output from the regression analysis of the data of Table 10.2, together with commentaries.

Output

STEP NO	VARIABLES ENTERED	ANALYSIS OF VARIANCE	DF	SUM OF SQUARES	MEAN SQUARE	F
1	V1 V2	REGRESSION	2	192.00	96.00	
2	V3 V4	REGRESSION	4	300.00		
3	V5 V6 V7 V8	REGRESSION	8	308.00	38.50	10.83
		RESIDUAL	9	32.00	3.55556	

Commentary

The output is organized in a format that differs somewhat from the one used by SPSS in order to make the relevant information easily accessible. Also, irrelevant information is not presented. Looking first at STEP NO 1, it is noted that the REGRESSION SUM OF SQUARES associated with V1 and V2 is 192.00. As each vector appropriates 1 *df,* the MEAN SQUARE is 96.00. The program reports also a residual sum of squares, mean square, and an *F* ratio for STEP 1. This information is, however, irrelevant for the present purposes because it is based on a treatment of the data as if only one factor is being used, namely factor *A* (represented by V1 and V2).

At STEP 2, V3 and V4 are added to the analysis. These vectors represent factor *B*. Note that the DF and the SUM OF SQUARES for step 2 refer to all the vectors that have been entered up to this point. This is why the MEAN SQUARE that is given in the output was not reported above. It is irrelevant for the present purposes. What we want is a sum of squares regression and *df* for V3 and V4 by themselves. These are easily obtained from the output. The *df* for V3 and V4 are, of course, 2 as two vectors are involved. This is the same as subtracting the DF of STEP 1 (2) from those of STEP 2 (4). The SUM OF SQUARES is similarly obtained: 300.00 − 192.00 (i.e., SUM OF SQUARES of STEP 2 minus SUM OF SQUARES of STEP 1) = 108.00. Dividing this sum of squares by 2 *(df)* one obtains the mean square for *B:* 108.00/2 = 54.

At STEP 3, the vectors for the interaction are entered. Again, the DF and SUM OF SQUARES refer to all the vectors that have been entered up to and including this step. Therefore, *df* for $A \times B$ are 4, and the regression sum of squares is 8.00 (i.e., 308.00 − 300.00: the SUM OF SQUARES at STEP 3 minus the SUM OF SQUARES of the preceding step). The mean square for $A \times B$ is therefore 8.00/4 = 2.00.

STEP 3 is the last one in the analysis. Therefore the REGRESSION SUM

OF SQUARES reported at this step refers to the overall regression sum of squares, as does the F ratio. In fact, it is from this step that the information reported earlier about the overall F ratio, R^2, and so on, was taken. Because this is the last step the RESIDUAL SUM OF SQUARES and MEAN SQUARE are relevant and are therefore reported here. To obtain F ratios for each factor and for the interaction the mean square for each is divided by the MEAN SQUARE RESIDUAL (3.55556). This is done in Table 10.3, where the analysis is summarized. The F ratio for A is 27.00 (2, 9), $p < .01$. The F ratio for B is 15.19 (2, 9), $p < .01$. The two variables have significant main effects. The interaction between them is not significant ($F < 1$).

Table 10.3 Summary of Multiple Regression Analysis, Based on Data of Table 10.2

Source	*ss*	*df*	*ms*	*F*
A (V1, V2)	192.00	2	96.00	27.00
B (V3, V4)	108.00	2	54.00	15.19
$A \times B$ (V5, V6, V7, V8)	8.00	4	2.00	< 1
Residual	32.00	9	3.55556	
Total	340.00	17		

NOTE: V1 through V8 are coded vectors using effect coding. See Table 10.2.

Partitioning the Variance

Although it is possible to obtain the proportion of variance accounted for by each factor and the interaction by subtracting from the R^2 at each step the R^2 of the preceding step, the SUMMARY TABLE of SPSS will be used for this purpose in order to explain some of its properties. Following are excerpts of the summary table for the analysis of the data of Table 10.2.

Output

SUMMARY TABLE

VARIABLE ENTERED	R SQUARE	R SQUARE CHANGE	SIMPLE R
V1	.56471	.56471	.75147
V2	.56471	.00000	.37573
V3	.64412	.07941	.28180
V4	.88235	.23824	.56360
V5	.88382	.00147	.03835
V8	.90588	.02206	.15339
V7	.90588	.00000	.07670
V6	.90588	.00000	.07670

Commentary

Summary tables like the one reported here have been discussed several times earlier (see Chapters 4 and 5). Therefore, only some brief comments relevant to the topic of partitioning of the variance will be made. Examine first the rows for V1 and V2. Recall that these represent the effect coding for factor *A* in Table 10.2. Note that the correlation of V1 with *Y* is .75147 (SIMPLE R in the output) and its square is .56471. Look now at the row for V2 and note that although V2 correlates .37573 with *Y*, the increment in R^2 due to it (R SQUARE CHANGE) is .00000. This is because R SQUARE CHANGE is a squared semipartial correlation. For each row, it is the squared semipartial correlation of the dependent variable with the variable of the given row while partialing out from it all the variables in preceding rows (see Chapter 5, Computer Analysis, for a discussion and illustrations of the interpretation of R SQUARE CHANGE). Thus R SQUARE CHANGE for V2 is equal to $r^2_{y(2.1)}$. To show this, $r_{y(2.1)}$ is calculated using the following: $r_{y1} = .75147$, $r_{y2} = .37573$, $r_{12} = .50$. (Incidentally, the correlation between any two vectors in which effect coding was used for a single categorical variable, or for the main effects of multiple categorical variables, is .50 when *n*'s are equal.)

$$r_{y(2.1)} = \frac{.37573 - (.75147)(.50)}{\sqrt{1 - .50^2}} = .00$$

This demonstrates that after V1 is entered, V2 is shown to add nothing to the proportion of variance accounted for in *Y*. This, however, does not mean that V2 may be deleted from the analysis, because it is V1 and V2 together that provide the information about the categories of factor A. That is, together they account for .56471 of the variance of *Y*. The manner in which this proportion is sliced up between the two vectors is irrelevant and would change with a change in the order of entry of the vectors or with a change in the choice as to which category of *A* is assigned −1 and which is assigned 1 in a given vector. For the present case, had V2 been entered first it would have accounted for .14117 (the square of its correlation with *Y*). Consequently V1 would have accounted for an increment (R SQUARE CHANGE) equal to .42354 [$r^2_{y(1.2)}$]. To repeat: all of this makes no difference because it is the proportion of variance due to V1 and V2 that we want (i.e., $R^2_{y.12}$), and that will always be the same.

Look now at V3. It is reported to have an R SQUARE CHANGE of .07941. This, too, is a squared semipartial correlation, $r^2_{y(3.12)}$. But since V3 is not correlated with V1 and V2 because the vectors associated with different factors are not correlated (see discussion above), $r^2_{y3} = r^2_{y(3.12)}$. V3, then, accounts for a proportion of variance equal to its squared zero-order correlation with *Y* ($.28180^2$). V4 is the second vector reflecting factor *B*, and it is correlated with V3. Therefore the R SQUARE CHANGE for V4 is equal to $r^2_{y(4.3)}$. Together V3 and V4 account for .31765 of the variance of *Y* (i.e., the sum of the two elements of the R SQUARE CHANGE, .07941 + .23824). In other words, $R^2_{y.34} = .31765$.

The principles discussed above apply also to vectors 5 through 8 that are associated with the interaction. Since V5 is not correlated with the vectors preceding it, the R SQUARE CHANGE for this vector (.00147) is equal to the square of its zero-order correlation with Y. But the R SQUARE CHANGE for V8 is equal to $r^2_{y(8.5)}$, because V8 and V5 are correlated. For reasons that need not concern us here the vectors for the interaction are not entered in the order in which they were generated. But since V5 through V8 are to be treated as a set, their internal ordering is of no consequence. To obtain the proportion of variance accounted for by the interaction the elements of R SQUARE CHANGE corresponding to V5 through V8 are added, regardless of the order in which they were entered into the analysis. Therefore, the proportion of variance accounted for by the interaction for the data of Table 10.2 is .02353. This is equivalent to $R^2_{y.5678} = .02353$.

In sum, when in using SPSS for the analysis of a factorial design it is desired to partition the variance accounted for, it is probably simplest to do so by using the SUMMARY TABLE. All one needs do to obtain a proportion accounted for by a given component is to sum the elements of R SQUARE CHANGE that correspond to the coded vectors representing the component. Such a sum is actually the R^2 of the dependent variable with the vectors representing the component being considered.

The partitioning of the proportion of variance accounted for in the data of Table 10.2 may be summarized as follows:

$$
\begin{array}{lll}
\text{For factor } A\text{:} & R^2_{y.12} = .56471 + .00000 & = .56471 \\
\text{For factor } B\text{:} & R^2_{y.34} = .07941 + .23824 & = .31765 \\
\text{For } A \times B\text{:} & R^2_{y.5678} = .00147 + .02206 + .0000 + .0000 & = \underline{.02353} \\
 & & \Sigma : .90589
\end{array}
$$

Each of these R^2's may be tested for significance in the usual manner, as long as in the denominator for each of the F ratios $1 - R^2_{y.12345678}$ is used because it is the overall error term. Thus to test the proportion of variance due to A:

$$F = \frac{R^2_{y.12}/2}{(1 - R^2_{y.12\ldots8})/(N - 8 - 1)} = \frac{.56471/2}{(1 - .90589)/(18 - 8 - 1)} = 27.00$$

with 2 and 9 *df*. This is the same value as the one obtained when the regression sum of squares due to A was tested for significance, and similarly for the tests of the other proportions.

Having proportions due to separate components one may obtain the regression sum of squares for each, and vice versa. Thus

$$
\begin{aligned}
ss_{\text{reg}} &= ss_{\text{reg}(A)} + ss_{\text{reg}(B)} + ss_{\text{reg}(A \times B)} \\
&= R^2_{y.12}\Sigma y^2 + R^2_{y.34}\Sigma y^2 + R^2_{y.5678}\Sigma y^2 \\
&= (.56471)(340) + (.31765)(340) + (.02353)(340) \\
308.00 &= 192.00 + 108.00 + 8.00
\end{aligned}
$$

Compare with the results obtained earlier and summarized in Table 10.3.

Conversely, dividing a regression sum of squares due to a given component by the total sum of squares (Σy^2) yields a proportion. For example,

$$ss_{\text{reg}(A)}/\Sigma y^2 = 192.00/340.00 = .56471 = R^2_{y.12}$$

and similarly for the other components.

The Regression Equation

In Chapter 9 it was shown that the regression equation for effect coding with one categorical independent variable reflects the linear model. The same is true for the regression equation for effect coding in factorial designs. For two categorical independent variables, the linear model is

$$Y_{ijk} = \mu + \alpha_i + \beta_j + (\alpha\beta)_{ij} + \epsilon_{ijk} \tag{10.1}$$

where Y_{ijk} = the score of subject k in row i and column j, or the treatment combination α_i and β_j; μ = the population mean; α_i = the effect of treatment i; β_j = the effect of treatment j; $(\alpha\beta)_{ij}$ = the effect of the interaction between treatments α_i and β_j; ϵ_{ijk} = the error associated with the score of individual k under treatment combination α_i and β_j.

Equation (10.1) is expressed in parameters. In statistics the linear model for two categorical independent variables is

$$Y_{ijk} = \bar{Y} + a_i + b_j + (ab)_{ij} + e_{ijk} \tag{10.2}$$

where the terms on the right are estimates of the respective parameters of Equation (10.1). Thus, for example, $\bar{Y}$ = the grand mean of the dependent variable and is an estimate of μ in Equation (10.1)—and similarly for the remaining terms. The score of a subject is conceived as composed of five components: the grand mean, the effect of treatment a_i, the effect of treatment b_j, the interaction between treatment a_i and b_j, and error.

In the light of the above, we turn our attention to the regression equation for the 3 × 3 design analyzed with effect coding (the original data are given in Table 10.2). From the computer output we obtain

$$Y' = 11 + 4X_1 + 0X_2 + 0X_3 + 3X_4 + 0X_5 + 0X_6 + 0X_7 + 1X_8$$

Note that a is equal to the grand mean of the dependent variable, $\bar{Y}$. Of the eight b's, the first four are associated with the vectors representing the main effects. Specifically, b_1 and b_2 are associated with vectors 1 and 2 of Table 10.2, the vectors representing factor A. Similarly, b_3 and b_4 are associated with the main effects of factor B, and b_5 through b_8 are associated with the interaction ($A \times B$). We deal separately with the regression coefficients for the main effects and those for the interaction.

Regression Coefficients for the Main Effects

In order to facilitate the understanding of the regression coefficients for the main effects, the means of the treatment combinations (cells), as well as the treatment means and the treatment effects, are given in Table 10.4. From the table it can be noted that each b is equal to the treatment effect with which it is associated.[1] Thus, in vector 1 of Table 10.2, subjects belonging to category A_1 were assigned 1's. Accordingly, the coefficient for vector 1, b_1, is equal to the effect of category, or treatment, A_1. That is, $b_1 = \bar{Y}_{A_1} - \bar{Y} = 15 - 11 = 4$. Vector 2 identifies category A_2, and the coefficient associated with this vector, b_2, indicates the effect of category A_2: $b_2 = \bar{Y}_{A_2} - \bar{Y} = 11 - 11 = 0$. Similarly, the coefficients of vectors 3 and 4, b_3 and b_4, indicate the treatment effects of B_1 and B_2 respectively (see Table 10.4 and note that $\bar{Y}_{B_1} - \bar{Y} = 11 - 11 = 0 = b_3$, and that $\bar{Y}_{B_2} - \bar{Y} = 14 - 11 = 3 = b_4$).

The remaining treatment effects—that is, those associated with the categories that are assigned -1's (in the present example these are A_3 and B_3)—can be easily obtained in view of the constraint that $\Sigma a_i = \Sigma b_j = 0$. That is, the sum of the effects of any factor equals zero. Therefore, the effect for $A_3 = -\Sigma a_i = -(4 + 0) = -4$. The effect for $B_3 = -\Sigma b_j = -(0 + 3) = -3$. Compare these values with those of Table 10.4.

Before dealing with the regression coefficients for the interaction, we digress for a discussion of the meaning of the interaction.

Table 10.4 Cell and Treatment Means and Treatment Effects for Data of Table 10.2

	B_1	B_2	B_3	$\bar{Y}_A$	$\bar{Y}_A - \bar{Y}$
A_1	15	18	12	15	4
A_2	11	15	7	11	0
A_3	7	9	5	7	-4
$\bar{Y}_B$	11	14	8	$\bar{Y} = 11$	
$\bar{Y}_B - \bar{Y}$	0	3	-3		

NOTE: $\bar{Y}_A$ = means for the three categories of factor A; $\bar{Y}_B$ = means for the three categories of factor B; $\bar{Y}$ = grand mean; $\bar{Y}_A - \bar{Y}$ and $\bar{Y}_B - \bar{Y}$ = treatment effects for a category of factor A and a category of factor B, respectively.

THE MEANING OF INTERACTION

In the preceding section it was shown how one may determine the effects of each independent variable, which are referred to as main effects because they reflect the effects of a variable that are independent of the effects of the other variables. For example, it was shown that the effects of factor A for the data of

[1]The example was contrived so that the means of the cells, the main effects, and the grand mean are integers. Although results of this kind are rarely obtained in actual data analysis, it was felt that avoiding fractions would facilitate the presentation and the discussion. It was also noted earlier that the proportion of variance accounted for in this example is very large compared to that generally obtained in behavioral research. Again this was contrived so that the results would be significant despite the small number of subjects involved.

Table 10.2 are $A_1 = 4$, $A_2 = 0$, and $A_3 = -4$ (see Table 10.4). This means that when considering the scores of subjects administered treatment A_1, one part of their scores (i.e., 4) is attributed to the fact that they have received this treatment. Note that in the preceding statement no reference has been made to the fact that subjects under A_1 received different B treatments, hence the term *main effect*. The effects of the other categories of A, and those of B, are similarly interpreted.

In short, when main effects are studied, each factor's independent effects are being considered separately. It is, however, possible for factors to have joint effects. That is, a given combination of treatments (one from each factor) may be particularly effective because they enhance the effects of each other, or particularly ineffective because they operate at cross purposes, so to speak. Referring to examples discussed earlier, it is possible that a combination of a given teaching method (A) with a certain type of reinforcement (B) is particularly advantageous in producing achievement that is higher than what would be expected on the basis of their separate effects. Conversely, a combination of a teaching method and a type of reinforcement may be particularly disadvantageous in leading to achievement that is lower than would be expected on the basis of their separate effects. Or, to take another example, a specific teaching method may be particularly effective in a given region—say, urban—whereas another teaching method may be particularly effective in another region—say, suburban.

When no effects are observed over and above the separate effects of the various factors, it is said that the variables do not interact, or that they do not have joint effects. When, on the other hand, in addition to the separate effects of the factors they have joint effects as a consequence of specific treatment combination, it is said that the factors interact with each other. Formally, for two factors an interaction is defined as follows:

$$(AB)_{ij} = (\bar{Y}_{ij} - \bar{Y}) - (\bar{Y}_{A_i} - \bar{Y}) - (\bar{Y}_{B_j} - \bar{Y}) \tag{10.3}$$

where $(AB)_{ij}$ = interaction of treatments A_i and B_j; $\bar{Y}_{ij}$ = mean of treatment combination A_i and B_j, or the mean of cell ij; $\bar{Y}_{A_i}$ = mean of category, or treatment, i of factor A; $\bar{Y}_{B_j}$ = mean of category, or treatment, j of factor B; $\bar{Y}$ = grand mean. Note that $\bar{Y}_{A_i} - \bar{Y}$ in Equation (10.3) is the effect of treatment A_i, and that $\bar{Y}_{B_j} - \bar{Y}$ is the effect of treatment B_j. From Equation (10.3) it follows that when the deviation of a cell mean from the grand mean is equal to the sum of the treatment effects related to the given cell, then the interaction term for the cell is zero. Stated differently, in order to predict the mean of such a cell it is sufficient to know the grand mean and the treatment effects.

Using (10.3) we calculate the interaction term for each of the treatment combinations. These are reported in Table 10.5. For example, the term for the cell A_1B_1 is obtained as follows:

$$\begin{aligned} A_1 \times B_1 &= (\bar{Y}_{A_1B_1} - \bar{Y}) - (\bar{Y}_{A_1} - \bar{Y}) - (\bar{Y}_{B_1} - \bar{Y}) \\ &= (15 - 11) - (15 - 11) - (11 - 11) \\ &= 4 - 4 - 0 = 0 \end{aligned}$$

The other terms of Table 10.5 are similarly obtained. In five of the cells of Table 10.5 the interaction terms are zero, which means that for these cells it is possible to express each individual's score as a composite of the grand mean, main effects, and error. The four remaining cells of Table 10.5 have nonzero interaction terms, indicating that part of each individual's score in these cells is due to an interaction between factors *A* and *B*.

Table 10.5 Interaction Effects for the Data of Table 10.2

	B_1	B_2	B_3	Σ
A_1	0	0	0	0
A_2	0	1	−1	0
A_3	0	−1	1	0
Σ:	0	0	0	

Another way of ascertaining whether an interaction exists is to examine, in turn, differences between cell means of two treatment levels of one factor across all the levels of the other factor. This can perhaps be best understood by referring to the example under consideration. Look back at Table 10.4 and consider first rows A_1 and A_2. In row A_1 are the means of groups that were administered treatment A_1, and in row A_2 are the means of groups that were administered treatment A_2. If the effects of these two treatments are independent of the effects of factor *B* (i.e., if there is no interaction), it follows that the difference between any two means under a given level of *B* should be equal to a constant, that being the difference between the effect of treatment A_1 and that of A_2. In Table 10.4 the effect of A_1 is 4 and that of A_2 is zero. Therefore, if there is no interaction, the difference between any two cell means under the separate *B*'s should be equal to 4 (i.e., 4 − 0). Stated another way, if there is no interaction, $A_1 - A_2$ under B_1, $A_1 - A_2$ under B_2, and $A_1 - A_2$ under B_3 should be equal to each other because for each difference between the *A*'s *B* is constant. This can be further clarified by noting that when *A* and *B* do not interact each cell mean can be expressed as a composite of three elements: the grand mean ($\bar{Y}$), the effect of treatment *A* administered to the given group (a_i), and the effect of treatment *B* (b_j) administered to the group. For cell means in rows A_1 and A_2 of Table 10.4 this translates into

$$A_1B_1 = \bar{Y} + a_1 + b_1$$

$$A_2B_1 = \bar{Y} + a_2 + b_1$$

Subtracting the second row from the first $a_1 - a_2$ is obtained: the difference between the effects of treatments A_1 and A_2.

Similarly,

$$A_1B_2 = \bar{Y} + a_1 + b_2$$

$$A_2B_2 = \bar{Y} + a_2 + b_2$$

Again, the difference between these two cell means is equal to $a_1 - a_2$, and

$$A_1B_3 = \bar{Y} + a_1 + b_3$$

$$A_2B_3 = \bar{Y} + a_2 + b_3$$

Once again, the difference between the two cells is equal to $a_1 - a_2$.

Consider now the numerical example of Table 10.4:

$$A_1B_1 - A_2B_1 = 15 - 11 = 4$$

$$A_1B_2 - A_2B_2 = 18 - 15 = 3$$

$$A_1B_3 - A_2B_3 = 12 - \ \ 7 = 5$$

The differences between the cell means are not equal, thereby indicating that there is an interaction between A and B. Stated differently, to express the mean of a given cell it is not sufficient to resort to the grand mean and the main effects; it is also necessary to include a term for the interaction. The interaction terms for each cell for the example under consideration were given in Table 10.5. Consider, for example, the difference between cell means of A_1B_2 and A_2B_2 when each is expressed as a composite of the grand mean, main effects, and an interaction term:

$$A_1B_2 = 11(\bar{Y}) + 4(a_1) + 3(b_2) + 0(a_1b_2) = 18$$

$$A_2B_2 = 11(\bar{Y}) + 0(a_2) + 3(b_2) + 1(a_2b_2) = 15$$

Subtracting the second row from the first, the difference between the two-cell mean (3) is obtained. Had the interaction terms been ignored in the above calculations, the mean for cell A_1B_2 would still have been predicted as being 18. But the mean for cell A_2B_2 would have erroneously been predicted as being 14, leading to a difference of 4 between the means. That is, a difference equal to that between treatments A_1 and A_2 (4 – 0). It should therefore be clear that only when there is no interaction will all the elements in tables such as Table 10.5 be equal to zero.

In the above presentation, cell means in rows A_1 and A_2 were compared across the levels of B. Even if all the differences were equal to each other, this would have not sufficed to warrant a conclusion that there is no interaction between A and B. The reason is that differences between cell means may not be equal when two other rows, say A_1 and A_3, are compared. In order to conclude that there is no interaction in the present example it is necessary and sufficient for two comparisons of the kind described above to satisfy the condition that differences between cell means are equal. Any two comparisons will do—that is, between rows A_1 and A_2 and between A_1 and A_3, or between A_1 and A_2 and between A_2 and A_3. This is because when any two out of three possible comparisons satisfy the condition that the differences between cell means of one factor across the levels of the other factor are equal, then the third comparison also satisfies this condition. This is indicated by the fact that factor A has 2 *df*.

Instead of doing the comparisons by rows, one may do them by columns.

That is, for example, differences between cell means of columns B_1 and B_2 across the levels of A, and those between cells means of columns B_1 and B_3 may be compared. The same condition holds: an interaction is indicated if the mean differences for any one of the two comparisons are not equal. Note, however, that it is *not* necessary to carry out the comparisons for both columns and rows, because the same information is contained in either set of comparisons.

Graphing the Interaction

The ideas expressed above can be clearly depicted in a graphic presentation. Assigning one of the factors (it does not matter which one) to the abscissa, its cell means are plotted across the levels of the other factor. The points representing a set of cell means at a given level of a factor are then connected by straight lines. This was done for the data of Table 10.4 in part (a) of Figure 10.2. When there is no interaction between the factors, the line segments connecting respective cell means at the levels of one of the factors would all be parallel. Note that this condition is not met in (a) of Figure 10.2. The line segments connecting cell means of A_1 and A_2 at levels of B_1, B_2, and B_3 are not parallel, nor are those connecting A_2 and A_3. This is to be expected since an interaction was found in the present data.

Look now at part (b) of Figure 10.2 and note that the line segments are parallel, indicating that A and B do not interact. From the figure it may be noted, for example, that cell means associated with treatment B_1 are equally larger than those associated with treatment B_2, regardless of the levels of A. Similarly, for the comparisons between any two other lines: the respective cell means are equidistant from each other, when two lines are contrasted. Without presenting a substantive research example it is difficult to fully convey the meaning of graphs like the ones depicted in Figure 10.2. In order to impart at least some of their meaning it will be assumed in the following discussions that the higher the mean of the dependent variable, whatever it is, the more desirable the result. Returning to part (b) of Figure 10.2 it may be concluded that the most potent treatment from among the B's is B_1, and that its potency does not depend upon the type of A treatments with which it is combined. The least potent treatment is B_3. The effect of B_2 is intermediate between these two. Similar interpretations may be advanced regarding the independent effects of the A treatments. Thus, the meaning of the main effects in the absence of interactions is clearly evident in part (b) of Figure 10.2.

Disordinal and Ordinal Interactions

Two different examples of an interaction between A and B are depicted in parts (c) and (d) of Figure 10.2. Turning first to (c) it is clear that references to main effects of A or B are not meaningful because the effect of a given treatment of one factor depends largely on the type of treatment of the other factor with which it is paired. Consider, for example, B_3. In combination with A_3 it leads to the best results, this cell mean being the highest. But when B_3 is combined with A_1, the lowest mean is obtained. Or, A_1 with B_1 is the second best

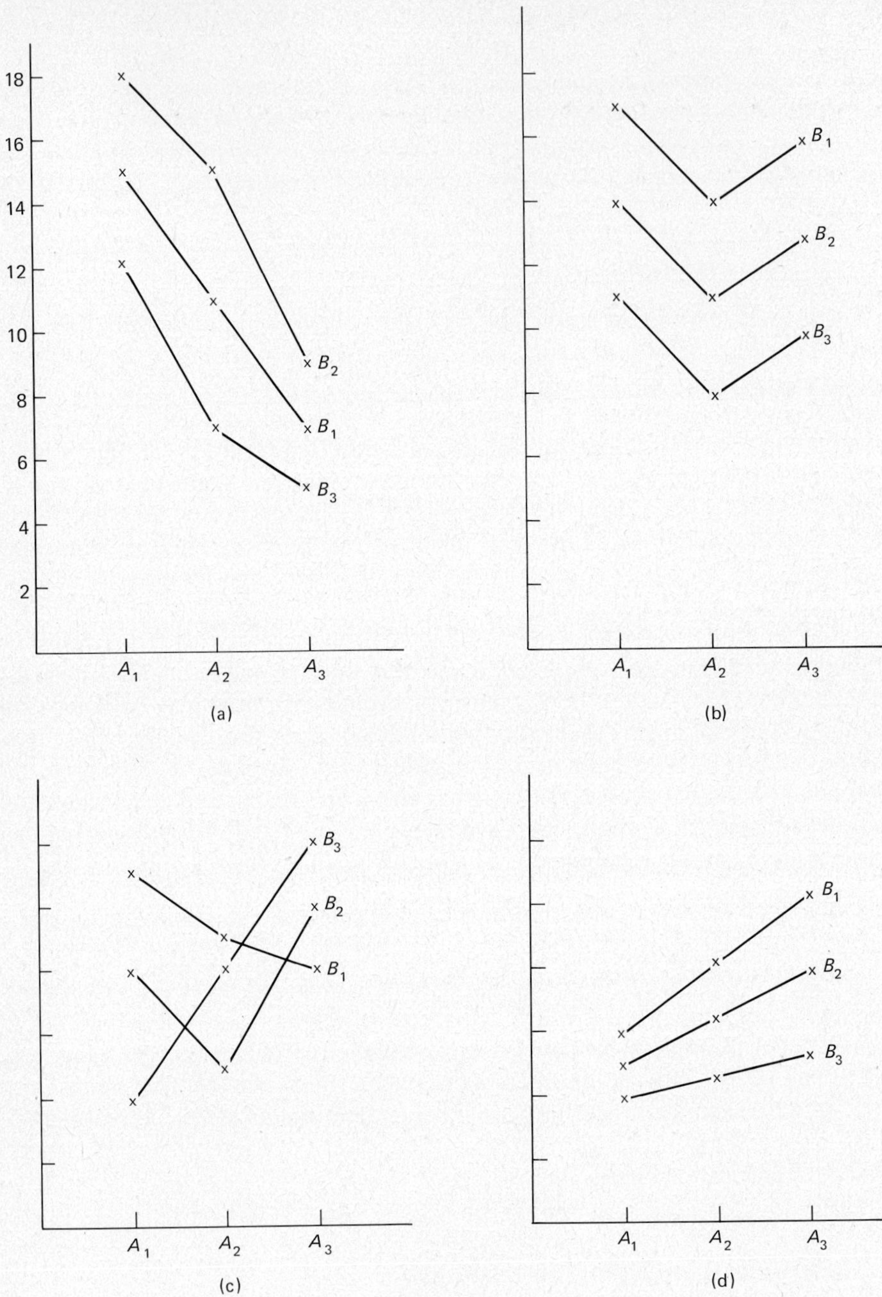

Figure 10.2

combination, leading to the second highest mean, whereas, as noted above, the combination of A_1 and B_3 results in the weakest effect. To repeat: it is not possible to speak of main effects in (c) as no treatment leads consistently to higher means than do the other treatments, but rather the rank order of effects of the treatment changes depending on their specific pairings. For example, under A_3 the rank order of the effectiveness of the B treatments is B_3, B_2, and B_1. But under A_1 the rank order of the B's is B_1, B_2, B_3. An interaction in which the rank order of the treatment effects changes is referred to as a *disordinal interaction* (Lubin, 1961).

Look now at part (d) of Figure 10.2. Here, too, an interaction between A and B is depicted. But this time it is an *ordinal interaction*. That is, the rank order of the treatment effects remains constant. B_1 is consistently superior to B_2, and B_2 is consistently superior to B_3. But the differences among the three treatments are not constant. They vary depending upon their specific combinations with the A treatments, hence the ordinal interaction. When combined with A_1, the differences among the three B's are much smaller than those under the combination of the B's with A_3. Similar interpretations may be advanced regarding the effects of the B's when combined with A_2 or the effects of the A's when combined with the different B's. For example, combined with B_3, the A treatments have relatively small differential effects. When, however, the A's are combined with B_1, their differential effects are appreciably larger. But the rank order of the effects of A treatments does not change. A_3 has the strongest effect, followed by A_2, with A_1 having the weakest effect.

When the interaction is ordinal, one may make statements about the main effects of the treatments, although such statements are generally of dubious value because they ignore the fact that treatments of a factor differ in their effectiveness depending on their combination with the treatments of another factor. For example, B_1 is clearly the most effective treatment regardless of the levels of A. But what is important to consider is its differential effectiveness. Assume that B_1 is a very expensive treatment to administer. On the basis of results like those in (d) of Figure 10.2, a researcher may decide that the investment involved in using B_1 is worthwhile only when it can be administered in combination with A_3. If A_1 is to be used, for whatever reasons, the researcher may decide to select a less expensive B treatment, say B_2 or B_3. In fact, when tests of statistical significance are done pursuant to an interaction (see below) it may be found, for example, that the differences among the B's at A_3 are significant but those at A_1 are not.

Finally, it will be pointed out that what may appear as interactions in a given set of data may be due to random fluctuations or errors of measurement. Whether nonzero interactions are to be considered sufficiently large to be attributed to other than random fluctuations is determined by statistical tests of significance. In the absence of a significant interaction it is sufficient to speak of main effects only. When an interaction is significant, it is necessary to pursue it with tests of simple main effects (see below).

We return now to the regression equation in order to examine the properties of the regression coefficients for the interaction terms.

Regression Coefficients for the Interaction

The regression equation for the 3 × 3 design of the data given in Table 10.2 is repeated:

$$Y' = 11 + 4X_1 + 0X_2 + 0X_3 + 3X_4 + 0X_5 + 0X_6 + 0X_7 + 1X_8$$

The first four b weights in this equation were discussed earlier. It was shown that b_1 and b_2 refer to effects of factor A and that b_3 and b_4 refer to effects of factor B. The remaining four b's refer to interaction effects. Specifically, each b refers to the cell with which it is associated. Look back at Table 10.2 and note that vector 5 is obtained as a product of vectors 1 and 3, that is, the vectors identifying A_1 and B_1. Therefore, the regression coefficient associated with vector 5, b_5, is associated with cell A_1B_1. Note that $b_5 = 0$, as is the cell for A_1B_1 in Table 10.5.

Similarly, b_6, b_7, and b_8 refer to cells A_1B_2, A_2B_1, and A_2B_2, respectively. As with the main effects, the remaining terms for the interaction can be obtained in view of the constraint that $\Sigma(ab)_{ij} = 0$. That is, the sum of the interaction terms for each row or column equals zero (see Table 10.5). Thus, for example, the b for $A_2B_3 = -\Sigma(0 + 1) = -1$.

Applying the Regression Equation

The discussion of the properties of the regression equation for effect coding, as well as the overall analysis of the data of Table 10.2, can best be summarized by using the regression equation to predict the scores of the subjects. Applying the regression equation obtained above to the coding of the first row of Table 10.2—that is, the coding for the first subject—we obtain

$$Y' = 11 + 4(1) + 0(0) + 0(1) + 3(0) + 0(1) + 0(0) + 0(0) + 1(0)$$

$$= 11 + 4 + 0 + 0 = 15$$

Note that 15 is the mean of the cell to which the first subject belongs, A_1B_1. The regression equation will always yield the mean of the cell to which a subject belongs. Note, too, that in arriving at a statement about the predicted score of the subject, terms that belong to a given factor or to the interaction were collected. For example, the second and third terms refer to factor A, and they were therefore collected; that is, $4(1) + 0(0) = 4$. Similarly, the fourth and the fifth terms were collected to express factor B, and the last four terms were collected to express the interaction.

The residual, or error, for the first subject is $Y - Y' = 16 - 15 = 1$. It is now possible to express the score of the first subject as a composite of the five components of the linear model. To demonstrate this, Equation (10.2) is repeated with a new number:

$$Y_{ijk} = \bar{Y} + a_i + b_j + (ab)_{ij} + e_{ijk} \tag{10.4}$$

where Y_{ijk} = the score of subject k in row i and column j, or in treatment combination a_i and b_j; $\bar{Y}$ = grand mean; a_i = the effect of treatment i of factor A; b_j = the effect of treatment j of factor B; $(ab)_{ij}$ = the effect of the interaction between a_i and b_j; e_{ijk} = the error associated with the score of individual k under treatments a_i and b_j. For the first subject in cell A_1B_1 the expression of Equation (10.4) takes the following form:

$$16 = 11 + 4 + 0 + 0 + 1$$

where 11 = the grand mean; 4 = the effect of treatment A_1; 0 = the effect of treatment B_1; 0 = the effect of the interaction for cell A_1B_1; 1 = the residual, $Y - Y'$.

As another example, the regression equation is applied to the last subject of Table 10.2:

$$
\begin{aligned}
Y' &= 11 + 4(-1) + 0(-1) + 0(-1) + 3(-1) + 0(1) + 0(1) + 0(1) + 1(1) \\
&= 11 - 4 - 3 + 1 = 5
\end{aligned}
$$

Again, the predicted score, Y', is equal to the mean of the cell to which the subject belongs, A_3B_3. The residual for this subject is $Y - Y' = 6 - 5 = 1$. Expressing the scores of the last subject of Table 10.2 in the components of the linear model,

$$6 = 11 - 4 - 3 + 1 + 1$$

In this way the scores for all the subjects of Table 10.2 are reported in Table 10.6 as components of the linear model. A close study of Table 10.6 will enhance understanding of the analysis of these data. Note that squaring and summing the elements in the column for the main effects of factor A (a_i) yield a sum of squares of 192. This is the same sum of squares obtained earlier for factor A (see, for example, Table 10.3). Similarly, the sum of the squared elements for

Table 10.6 Data for a 3 × 3 Design Expressed as Components of the Linear Model

Cell	Y	$\bar{Y}$	a_i	b_j	ab_{ij}	Y'	$Y - Y'$
A_1B_1	16	11	4	0	0	15	1
	14	11	4	0	0	15	−1
A_2B_1	12	11	0	0	0	11	1
	10	11	0	0	0	11	−1
A_3B_1	7	11	−4	0	0	7	0
	7	11	−4	0	0	7	0
A_1B_2	20	11	4	3	0	18	2
	16	11	4	3	0	18	−2
A_2B_2	17	11	0	3	1	15	2
	13	11	0	3	1	15	−2
A_3B_2	10	11	−4	3	−1	9	1
	8	11	−4	3	−1	9	−1
A_1B_3	10	11	4	−3	0	12	−2
	14	11	4	−3	0	12	2
A_2B_3	7	11	0	−3	−1	7	0
	7	11	0	−3	−1	7	0
A_3B_3	4	11	−4	−3	1	5	−1
	6	11	−4	−3	1	5	1
ss:			192	108	8		32

NOTE: Y = observed score; $\bar{Y}$ = grand mean; a_i = effect of treatment i of factor A; b_j = effect of treatment j of factor B; ab_{ij} = interaction between a_i and b_j; Y' = predicted score, where in each case it is equal to the sum of the elements in the four columns preceding it; $Y - Y'$ = residual, or error; ss = sum of squares.

the effects of factor B (b_j), the interaction between $A \times B$ $(ab)_{ij}$, and the residuals, $Y - Y'$, are 108, 8, and 32. The same values were obtained earlier. Adding the four sums of squares obtained in Table 10.6, the total sum of squares of Y is obtained:

$$\Sigma y^2 = 192 + 108 + 8 + 32 = 340$$

MULTIPLE COMPARISONS

As in the case of a single categorical variable (see Chapter 9) multiple comparisons among means may be conducted in a factorial design. The kinds of comparisons that are called for are predicated on whether or not the interaction is significant. When the interaction is not significant, multiple comparisons among main effects are appropriate. When, however, the interaction is significant, tests of simple main effects are more meaningful. The two kinds of comparisons are treated separately, beginning with comparisons among main effects.

Comparisons Among Main Effects

When the interaction is not significant, multiple comparisons among main effects are carried out in the same manner as was shown earlier for comparisons among means when a single categorical variable was used (see Chapter 9). When doing comparisons among the main effects of one factor the other factor is ignored. One proceeds exactly as if a single categorical variable is used, except that the value of mean square residuals *(MSR)* involved in the comparisons is the one obtained from the overall analysis of the factorial design. Because all that was said in Chapter 9 about multiple comparisons among means for a single categorical variable (i.e., post hoc, planned orthogonal, and nonorthogonal) applies equally to the case of multiple comparisons among main effects, this discussion is not repeated. Instead, using the data of Table 10.2, comparisons among the main effects of B will be illustrated.

In Equation (9.15) an F test for a comparison was presented. Such a test when applied to a comparison among the main effects of a given factor, say B, takes the following form:

$$F = \frac{[(C_1)(\bar{Y}_{B_1}) + (C_2)(\bar{Y}_{B_2}) + \cdots + (C_j)(\bar{Y}_{B_j})]^2}{MSR\left[\Sigma\frac{(C_j)^2}{n_j}\right]} \qquad (10.5)$$

where C is a coefficient applied to the mean of a given treatment (recall from Chapter 9 that the sum of the coefficients for a given comparison is zero); MSR is the mean square residual from the overall analysis of the factorial design; n_j is the number of subjects in treatment j—that is, all the subjects administered treatment B_j regardless of what treatments of A they were administered. The F ratio has 1 and $N - k - 1$ df, where k is the number of coded vectors in the factorial design (i.e., for the main effects and the interaction). In other words, the denominator degrees of freedom are equal to those of the *MSR*. An expression similar to (10.5) is used for a comparison among main effects of *A*, except that $\bar{Y}_{B_j}$ and n_j are replaced by $\bar{Y}_{A_i}$ and n_i.

Equation (10.5) is now applied to a comparison between the average of main effects B_1 and B_2, and the effect of B_3. From Table 10.4, $\bar{Y}_{B_1} = 11$, $\bar{Y}_{B_2} = 14$, $\bar{Y}_{B_3} = 8$. And from Table 10.3, $MSR = 3.55556$. $n_j = 6$, that is, there are 6 subjects under each *B* treatment. Using these numbers.

$$F = \frac{[(1)(11) + (1)(14) + (-2)(8)]^2}{3.55556\left[\frac{1^2}{6} + \frac{1^2}{6} + \frac{(-2)^2}{6}\right]} = \frac{9^2}{3.55556} = \frac{81}{3.55556} = 22.78$$

with 1 and 9 *df*.

As was discussed in Chapter 9, this *F* ratio is used differently depending on whether post hoc, planned orthogonal, or planned nonorthogonal comparisons among the main effects of *B* are used. Assuming that the above comparison was one of the two possible orthogonal comparisons hypothesized prior to the data collection, then the obtained *F* is compared with the tabled value of *F* for 1 and 9 *df* in order to determine whether the given comparison is statistically significant. Using, for example, the .01 level of significance, the tabled value for 1 and 9 *df* is 10.56. It would therefore be concluded that the average of main effects B_1 and B_2 is significantly different from the main effect of B_3.

If, on the other hand, the comparison obtained above is one of several post hoc comparisons using the Scheffé procedure, the obtained *F* will have to exceed $k_B F_\alpha; k_B, N - k - 1$, where k_B is the number of coded vectors used to represent factor *B* or the number of *df* associated with factor *B*. $F_\alpha; k_B, N - k - 1$ is the tabled value of *F* at α with k_B *df* for the numerator and $N - k - 1$ *df* for the denominator, where *k* is the total number of coded vectors for the factorial design. In other words $N - k - 1$ are the *df* associated with the *MSR*. For the present example, $k_B = 2$ and $N - k - 1 = 9$. Assuming $\alpha = .01$, then the tabled *F* with 2 and 9 *df* is 8.02. The value that *F* for a given comparison has to exceed is therefore, $(2)(8.02) = 16.04$. As the *F* obtained for the comparison calculated above is 22.78, it would be concluded that it is significant when using the Scheffé procedure.

Finally, assuming that the above comparison is one of several planned nonorthogonal comparisons, then one may apply the Bonferroni or Dunn procedure by splitting the α among the comparisons (see Chapter 9).

In Chapter 9 it was shown that instead of using an equation like (10.5) for tests of multiple comparisons among means, the same purpose can be accomplished by doing multiple comparisons among regression coefficients. The same procedure is applicable to tests of multiple comparisons among main effects, and is now illustrated for comparisons among main effects of *B*.[2]

The *F* ratio for testing a linear combination of *b*'s was presented and discus-

[2]If you are encountering difficulties with the presentation that follows it is suggested that you review the extensive discussion of **C*** and its use in Chapter 9.

sed in connection with Equation (9.18). To test a linear combination of b's associated with the main effects—say, of B:

$$F = \frac{[a_1(b_1) + a_2(b_2) + \cdots + a_j(b_j)]^2}{\mathbf{a}'\mathbf{C}^*\mathbf{a}} \tag{10.6}$$

where $a, a_2, \ldots, a_j$ are coefficients by which the b's are multiplied (a's are used here instead of c's so as not to confuse them with elements of $\mathbf{C}^*$, the augmented matrix of variances and covariances of the b's); b_j is the regression coefficient associated with the effect of treatment B_j; $\mathbf{a}'$ and $\mathbf{a}$ are the row and column vectors, respectively, of the coefficients of the linear combination; $\mathbf{C}^*$ is the augmented matrix of the variances and covariances of the b's. In Chapter 9, very simple methods were shown for generating $\mathbf{C}^*$ when $\mathbf{C}$ (note this is not the augmented matrix, hence the absence of an asterisk) is not reported in the computer output. Therefore they are not repeated here. Moreover, an even simpler method for calculating $\mathbf{a}'\mathbf{C}^*\mathbf{a}$ was shown in Chapter 9. It is this method, which is repeated here without elaboration, that will be used for testing multiple comparisons among the main effects of B. In Chapter 9 it was shown that

$$\mathbf{a}'\mathbf{C}^*\mathbf{a} = \left(s_b^2 + \frac{s_b^2}{k_j}\right)\Sigma a^2$$

where s_b is the standard error of a b associated with one of the coded vectors for factor B (recall that with equal n's, as in the present example, the standard errors of the b's associated with a given factor will be equal to each other); k_j is the number of coded vectors used to represent the factor under consideration; Σa^2 is the sum of the squared coefficients used in a given linear combination. From the computer output, s_b for either of the b's associated with factor B is .62854; $k_j = 2$ (two coded vectors, V3 and V4, were used to represent factor B; see Table 10.2); $b_3 = 0$ is the effect of treatment B_1; and $b_4 = 3.00$ is the effect of B_2 (see Table 10.4 and the regression equation reported above). It is necessary also to obtain the effect for treatment B_3, the one assigned -1's. Recall that the effect of the category assigned -1's in effect coding is equal to $-\Sigma b_j$. In accordance with the practice introduced in Chapter 9, the subscript for the b representing the category assigned -1 will be $k + 1$, where k is the number of coded vectors in the design. In the present case there are 8 coded vectors. Therefore, the b for treatment B_3 is designated b_9. This procedure is followed so as not to confuse this coefficient with any of the ones that are part of the regression equation. For the present data, $b_9 = -(3.00 + 0) = -3.00$.

Using this information, tests of multiple comparisons among main effects of B are now illustrated. Let us begin with the same comparison that was tested above by the application of Equation (10.5). That is, it is desired to test the average of the effects of B_1 and B_2 against the effect of B_3.

$$F = \frac{[(1)(b_3) + (1)(b_4) + (-2)(b_9)]^2}{\mathbf{a}'\mathbf{C}^*\mathbf{a}} = \frac{[(1)(0) + (1)(3) + (-2)(-3)]^2}{\mathbf{a}'\mathbf{C}^*\mathbf{a}} = \frac{81}{\mathbf{a}'\mathbf{C}^*\mathbf{a}}$$

Using the method outlined above, and recalling that s_b = .62854 and k = 2 (coded vectors):

$$\mathbf{a'C^*a} = \left(.62854^2 + \frac{.62854^2}{2}\right)[(1)^2 + (-1)^2 + (-2)^2]$$

$$= (.59259)(6) = 3.55554$$

Therefore,

$$F = \frac{81}{3.55554} = 22.78$$

which is the same F ratio that was obtained above when (10.5) was applied.

Assume now that it is desired to compare the effect of treatment B_1 with that of B_2.

$$F = \frac{[(1)(b_3) + (-1)(b_4)]^2}{\mathbf{a'C^*a}} = \frac{[(1)(0) + (-1)(3)]^2}{\mathbf{a'C^*a}} = \frac{9}{\mathbf{a'C^*a}}$$

$$\mathbf{a'C^*a} = \left(.62854^2 + \frac{.62854^2}{2}\right)[(1)^2 + (-1)^2]$$

$$= (.59259)(2) = 1.18518$$

Therefore,

$$F = \frac{9}{1.18518} = 7.59$$

How one interprets these F ratios depends, as discussed above, on the type of comparisons that are being performed. Assume that the two comparisons calculated above are to be treated as planned comparisons. Since the sum of the products of their coefficients is zero, they are orthogonal. Therefore, the two obtained F ratios, each with 1 and 9 *df*, are relevant tests for the two planned orthogonal comparisons. The same F ratios would be obtained if one were to do a factorial analysis of variance and follow it by tests of orthogonal comparisons. Also, the same F ratios would be obtained if one were to use orthogonal coding for the regression analysis instead of the effect coding used here (see below).

If the above comparisons are to be treated as post hoc, say Scheffé, then the obtained F's will have to exceed tabled F values multiplied by the appropriate constant, as shown above. And if the above comparisons are to be treated as part of a set of planned nonorthogonal comparisons, then the α level will have to be split among the comparisons in a manner shown in Chapter 9.

The important thing is that having done a regression analysis with effect coding one can test linear combinations of regression coefficients to accomplish any type of comparison desired among main effects: post hoc, planned nonorthogonal, and planned orthogonal. Comparisons among main effects are meaningful when the interaction is not significant. When the interaction is significant, one proceeds with tests of simple main effects, to which we now turn.

Simple Main Effects

When the interaction is significant it is generally not meaningful to interpret the main effects. This is because the presence of an interaction indicates that the treatments of a given factor do not have constant effects, but rather that their effects vary depending on the treatments of the other factors with which they are combined. When the idea of a disordinal interaction was presented earlier, it was shown that a given treatment may be the best in combination with one level of another factor, and the worst when it is combined with another level of that factor (see Figure 10.2(c) and the discussion related to it). Consequently, with certain patterns of interactions it is possible even to obtain main effects that are all zero or negligible.

The idea behind simple main effects is that differential effects of treatments of one factor are studied, in turn, for each treatment of the other factor. Referring to the 3×3 design we have been working with, this means that one would study separately the differences among treatments B_1, B_2, and B_3 at level A_1, at A_2, and at A_3. In effect it is as if one had been dealing with three separate designs each consisting of the same categorical variable B. But each of these studies, so to speak, is conducted within the context of a different treatment of A. If this fact does not matter, then the differences among the B's across the three "studies" should be equal, or relatively small because of random fluctuations. This, of course, would occur when A and B do not interact. If, on the other hand, A and B interact, it will be found that the pattern of the differences among the B's in the three separate levels of A differ. Thus, for example, it may be found that under A_1 the effects of B_1, B_2, and B_3 are equal to each other. At A_2, on the other hand, it may be found that the effect of B_1 is the strongest, that of B_2 the weakest, and that of B_3 somewhere in between these two effects. At A_3 the effects of the three B's may be reversed.

From the foregoing it should be clear that the 3×3 design is sliced into three slabs, each consisting of an A level and the three B levels. Each such slab is analyzed separately. But the 3×3 design could also be sliced by columns. Thus one would have one slab for the three levels of A under condition B_1, another slab under condition of B_2, and a third under B_3. Slicing the table this way, one could study separately the differential effects of the A treatments under each level of B. This, then, is the idea of studying simple main effects.

In order to test the simple main effect for B, for example, one could regress the dependent variable, Y, on coded vectors representing the B's separately for each level of A. Referring to the example under consideration, there would be only two coded vectors for the B's, and each separate regression analysis would consist of six subjects. This is because there are two subjects in each cell and three cells of B are used in each separate analysis. The regression sum of squares obtained from each such analysis is divided, as usual, by its degrees of freedom to obtain a mean square regression. But instead of using the mean square residual from each separate analysis as the denominator of the F ratio, it is the MSR from the overall analysis of the factorial design that is used.

What was said about the testing of simple main effects for B applies equally to such tests for A. Doing both for the 3×3 design would therefore require six separate analyses. It will now be shown, however, that having done an overall regression analysis with effect coding one may easily obtain the regression sum of squares for each simple main effect. Even though the interaction was found to be not significant in the analysis of the numerical example of the 3×3 design, it will be used to illustrate the method of obtaining the regression sums of squares for simple main effects.

In order to facilitate the presentation, the effects that were obtained via the regression equation are displayed in a 3×3 format in Table 10.7. Note that the main effects of A and B were placed in the marginals of the table, each identified by a b with a subscript corresponding to coded vector associated with the given effect (see Table 10.2). Thus, b_1 is associated with vector 1 in which A_1 was assigned 1's, and therefore b_1 represents the treatment effect of A_1. All this was described in detail earlier. It was repeated here to make sure that you understand the layout of Table 10.7. Note that two of the marginals, one for A and one for B, have no b's attached to them. This is done in order to show that they were not obtained directly from the regression equation, but rather on the basis of the constraint that the sum of the effects of a given factor is zero. This, too, was discussed in detail earlier.

Table 10.7 Main Effects and Interactions for Data of Table 10.2

	B_1	B_2	B_3	
A_1	$0 = b_5$	$0 = b_6$	0	$4 = b_1$
A_2	$0 = b_7$	$1 = b_8$	-1	$0 = b_2$
A_3	0	-1	1	-4
	$0 = b_3$	$3 = b_4$	-3	

The entries in the body of Table 10.7 are the interaction terms for each cell. These were given earlier in Table 10.5, except that here their respective b's from the regression equation are indicated. Again, entries that have no b's attached to them were not obtained directly from the regression equation but on the basis of the constraint that the sum of interaction terms in rows or columns equals zero.

In order to provide a feel for what it is that we are after in Table 10.7, look at the marginals for factor A. The first marginal (4) is, of course the treatment effect of A_1. Six subjects received this treatment (there are two subjects in each cell). In other words, part of the score on Y for each of these subjects is 4, and similarly for the other marginals of A, each of which belongs to six other subjects. Now each of the marginals represents a deviation of the mean of the treatment from the grand mean (this is how an effect is defined). Therefore, to obtain the regression sum of squares due to A, square each effect of A and multiply by the number of subjects to whom the effect refers. But since the number of subjects is the same for each effect, this reduces to

$$ss_{\text{reg}}(A) = 6\,[(4)^2 + (0)^2 + (-4)^2] = 192$$

which is, of course, the same value that was obtained earlier. Actually what was done here with the information of Table 10.7 was done earlier in Table 10.6, except that in the latter the effects for each person in the design were spelled out.

To obtain the regression sum of squares due to B, use the marginals of B in Table 10.7 thus:

$$ss_{\text{reg}}(B) = 6\,[(0)^2 + (3)^2 + (-3)^2] = 108$$

which, again, is the same value as obtained earlier.

Now, for the interaction. Each cell is based on 2 subjects. Therefore,

$$ss_{\text{reg}}(A \times B) = 2\,[(0)^2 + (0)^2 + (0)^2 + (0)^2 + (1)^2 + (-1)^2 + (-0)^2 + (-1)^2 + (1)^2] = 8$$

which is, again, the same as the value obtained earlier.

All the foregoing values were obtained from the overall regression analysis. They were recalculated here in order to provide a better understanding of how one would obtain sum of squares for simple main effects by following the same approach. This is now illustrated, beginning with simple main effects for A. Look at Table 10.7 and consider only the first column (B_1). As the effect of B_1 is a constant, the differences between A_1, A_2, and A_3 under B_1 may be expressed as a composite of effects of A and the interaction. Thus for cell A_1B_1 this translates into $4 + 0$, for A_2B_1 it is $0 + 0$, and for cell A_3B_1 it is $-4 + 0$. Each of these elements is related to two subjects. Following the approach outlined above, the regression sum of squares for simple main effects for A is:

$$\begin{aligned}
&\text{For } A \text{ at } B_1\text{:} \quad 2\,[(4 + 0)^2 + (0 + 0)^2 + (-4 + 0)^2] &&= 64\\
&\text{For } A \text{ at } B_2\text{:} \quad 2\,[(4 + 0)^2 + (0 + 1)^2 + (-4 + -1)^2] &&= 84\\
&\text{For } A \text{ at } B_3\text{:} \quad 2\,[(4 + 0)^2 + (0 + -1)^2 + (-4 + 1)^2] &&= \underline{52}\\
& &&\Sigma : 200
\end{aligned}$$

Note that the sum of the regression sum of squares for simple main effects for A is equal to $ss_A + ss_{A \times B} = 192 + 8 = 200$. This is not surprising inasmuch as the effects of A and the interaction between A and B were used in the calculation of the simple main effects.

The simple main effects for B are obtained in a similar manner:

$$\begin{aligned}
&\text{For } B \text{ at } A_1\text{:} \quad 2\,[(0 + 0)^2 + (3 + 0)^2 + (-3 + 0)]^2 &&= 36\\
&\text{For } B \text{ at } A_2\text{:} \quad 2\,[(0 + 0)^2 + (3 + 1)^2 + (-3 + -1)]^2 &&= 64\\
&\text{For } B \text{ at } A_3\text{:} \quad 2\,[(0 + 0)^2 + (3 + -1)^2 + (-3 + 1)]^2 &&= \underline{16}\\
& &&\Sigma : 116
\end{aligned}$$

Again, the sum of the regression sum of squares for the simple main effects of B is equal to $ss_B + ss_{A \times B} = 108 + 8 = 116$.

Each of the regression sum of squares for the simple main effects has 2 *df* in the present example since in each case three treatments are being compared. Dividing each sum of squares by the *df* yields a mean square for the numerator of the F ratio. The denominator of all the F ratios is, as was said above, the *MSR* of the overall analysis of the factorial design. From the overall analysis it was found earlier that $ss_{res} = 32.00$ with 9 *df*, and $MSR = 32.00/9 = 3.55556$. Calculating mean squares for each simple main effect and dividing by *MSR*, the *F* ratios for each test are obtained. This is done for the present example in a summary form in Table 10.8.

Table 10.8 Summary of Tests of Simple Main Effects for Data of Table 10.2

Source	*ss*	*df*	*ms*	*F*
A at B_1	64	2	32	9.00
A at B_2	84	2	42	11.81
A at B_3	52	2	26	7.31
B at A_1	36	2	18	5.06
B at A_2	64	2	32	9.00
B at A_3	16	2	8	2.25
Residual	32	9	3.55556	

Each of the *F* ratios of Table 10.8 has 2 and 9 *df*. It is recommended that the α level be divided by the number of simple main effects tested for a given factor and that the obtained *F* ratios then be checked against tabled *F*'s with α thus obtained. In the present example three tests for simple main effects were done for each factor. Assume the initial $\alpha = .01$. Then the critical value for the *F*'s of Table 10.8 is a tabled *F* at $\alpha/3 = .01/3 \approx .003$, with 2 and 9 *df*. Had factor *A* in the present example consisted of four treatments, then the tabled *F* for tests of simple main effects for factor *B*, assuming overall $\alpha = .01$, would be $\alpha/4 = .01/4 = .0025$ with 2 *df* for the numerator and whatever *df* associated with *MSR* for the denominator.

When an *F* ratio for a simple main effect is significant, it is followed up by multiple comparisons in the same manner as was outlined earlier. Depending on the hypotheses that were advanced, post hoc or planned comparisons are performed. It is thus possible to pinpoint which treatments differ significantly from each other at a given level of the other factor.

It will be recalled that in the numerical example under consideration the interaction was not significant. Therefore tests of simple main effects are not called for. They were carried out in order to illustrate the method of obtaining the regression sum of squares for each simple main effect. The generalization of this method to higher-order designs (i.e., designs with more than two factors) is straightforward, except that in such designs one obtains additional terms depending on which of the interaction terms are significant. For example, if in a three-factor design the second-order interaction is significant (i.e., the interaction between the three factors), then one would test simple first-order (i.e., two-factor) interactions and simple main effects (see, for example, Kirk, 1968, pp. 222–224; Winer, 1971, pp. 456–457).

ORTHOGONAL CODING

As in the case of a single categorical variable, when one has hypothesized orthogonal comparisons in a factorial design, the coefficients of such comparisons

Table 10.9 Orthogonal Coding for a 3 × 3 Design for Data of Table 10.1

Cell	*Y*	*1*	*2*	*3*	*4*	*5* (*1* × *3*)	*6* (*1* × *4*)	*7* (*2* × *3*)	*8* (*2* × *4*)
A_1B_1	16	1	1	1	1	1	1	1	1
	14	1	1	1	1	1	1	1	1
A_2B_1	12	−1	1	1	1	−1	−1	1	1
	10	−1	1	1	1	−1	−1	1	1
A_3B_1	7	0	−2	1	1	0	0	−2	−2
	7	0	−2	1	1	0	0	−2	−2
A_1B_2	20	1	1	−1	1	−1	1	−1	1
	16	1	1	−1	1	−1	1	−1	1
A_2B_2	17	−1	1	−1	1	1	−1	−1	1
	13	−1	1	−1	1	1	−1	−1	1
A_3B_2	10	0	−2	−1	1	0	0	2	−2
	8	0	−2	−1	1	0	0	2	−2
A_1B_3	10	1	1	0	−2	0	−2	0	−2
	14	1	1	0	−2	0	−2	0	−2
A_2B_3	7	−1	1	0	−2	0	2	0	−2
	7	−1	1	0	−2	0	2	0	−2
A_3B_3	4	0	−2	0	−2	0	0	0	4
	6	0	−2	0	−2	0	0	0	4
ss:	340	12	36	12	36	8	24	24	72
M:	11	0	0	0	0	0	0	0	0
r:		.37573	.65079	−.28180	.48809	.03835	−.06642	−.06642	.11504

NOTE: *r* is the correlation between the coded vector under which the value appears and the dependent variable *Y*. Thus, for example, the correlation between vector 1 and *Y* is .37573, the value listed under vector 1. Similarly for all other vectors. The correlation between any two coded vectors is, of course, zero.

may be used to code the factors. The dependent variable Y is then regressed on the coded vectors. As in effect coding, each factor is coded separately, and interaction vectors are obtained by generating cross-product vectors of each of the vectors of one factor by each of the vectors of the other factor. In view of the similarity of this approach to that presented in Chapter 9 for a single categorical variable, there does not appear to be a need for describing it in detail here. Instead, its application to the 3×3 design analyzed above with effect coding is illustrated.

In Table 10.9 the factors of the 3×3 design of Table 10.1 were coded to reflect orthogonal comparisons. Note that vectors 1 and 2 represent orthogonal coding for factor A. In vector 1 subjects in category A_1 are assigned 1's, those in category A_2 are assigned -1's, and those in category A_3 are assigned 0's. Accordingly, vector 1 contrasts category A_1 with category A_2. Remember that when coding one factor, ignore the other factor. Thus, for example, subjects assigned 1's in vector 1 all belong to category A_1 but to different categories of B.

In vector 2 of Table 10.9 subjects in categories A_1 and A_2 are assigned 1's, whereas subjects in category A_3 are assigned -2's. Accordingly, vector 2 contrasts categories A_1 and A_2 with category A_3. It can be easily verified that vectors 1 and 2 are orthogonal (the sum of their cross products is equal to zero). As there are three categories in Factor A, only two orthogonal comparisons are possible. The specific set chosen is, of course, the one that reflects the hypotheses.

Vectors 3 and 4 of Table 10.9 reflect two orthogonal comparisons for Factor B. Thus, in vector 3, B_1 is contrasted with B_2. In vector 4, B_1 and B_2 are contrasted with B_3. Vectors 5 through 8 are obtained by cross multiplying each of the vectors of factor A by each of the vectors of Factor B (see Table 10.9).

At the bottom of Table 10.9 the zero-order correlations between each coded vector and the dependent variable, Y, are given. Because all the coded vectors in the table are orthogonal, the square of the zero-order correlation of a coded vector with Y indicates the proportion of variance accounted for by the comparison that the vector reflects. And, of course, the sum of the squared zero-order correlations of the coded vectors with Y is equal to the overall R^2. These properties of the coded vectors render regression statistics and tests of significance easily obtainable by hand calculations, although these are not shown here (you may wish to do them as an exercise). Instead excerpts of computer output obtained from SPSS are given and commented upon.

Output

- - - -VARIABLES IN THE EQUATION- - - -

VARIABLE	B	STD ERROR B	F	BETA
V1 (A_1 vs. A_2)	2.00	.54433	13.50	.37573
V2 ($A_1 + A_2$ vs. A_3)	2.00	.31427	40.50	.65079
V3 (B_1 vs. B_2)	−1.50	.54433	7.59	−.28180

V4 ($B_1 + B_2$ vs. B_3)	1.50	.31427	22.78	.48809
V5	.25	.66667	.14	.03835
V6	−.25	.38490	.42	−.06642
V7	−.25	.38490	.42	−.06642
V8	.25	.22222	1.27	.11504
(CONSTANT)	11.00			

Commentary

The overall analysis is the same as the one obtained earlier with effect coding and is therefore not reported here. The BETAs (standardized regression coefficients) were reported above to demonstrate what was said in earlier chapters, namely, that when the independent variables are not correlated, $\beta_{yi} = r_{yi}$. That is, each β is equal to the zero-order correlation of the coded vector with which it is associated and the dependent variable (compare the BETAs with the last line of Table 10.9 where the zero-order correlations are given). In the present example there are two independent variables (factors A and B) whose main effects and interaction are represented by 8 coded vectors. But since the coded vectors are orthogonal, what was said above still holds. The sum of the squared BETAs is .90588 = $R^2_{y.12\ldots 8}$.

As was the case with effect coding, a (CONSTANT) is equal to the grand mean of the dependent variable ($\bar{Y}$ = 11.00). Each regression coefficient (B) reflects a specific contrast. The contrasts for the orthogonal comparisons for the main effects are indicated in parentheses in the output reported above. It will be recalled that the magnitude of each B is affected by the specific codes that are used (see Chapter 9), but that as long as orthogonal coding was used the test of each B is a test of the comparison that it reflects. Each of the B's has an F ratio with 1 and 9 df ($N - k - 1$). Thus the test of B for vector 1 is a test of the difference between the means of categories A_1 and A_2 of factor A. Similarly, for the other B's. Since each F ratio has 1 df for the numerator, t's can be obtained by taking the square roots of the F's.

In conclusion, it will be noted that the comparisons reflected by vectors 3 and 4 above (i.e., B_1 vs. B_2, and $B_1 + B_2$ vs. B_3) were also tested in the preceding section where linear combinations of b's were tested subsequent to the analysis of the same data. Not surprisingly, the same F ratios were obtained by the two approaches. It was said in the preceding section that subsequent to an analysis with effect coding one may test linear combinations of b's to accomplish any type of comparison (e.g., orthogonal, post hoc). What, then, is the advantage of using orthogonal instead of effect coding? The only advantage of orthogonal coding is that the tests of the orthogonal comparisons are obtained directly from the output (i.e., the tests of the B's). On the other hand, effect coding is simpler and leads to a regression equation that is directly interpretable in the context of the linear model. Moreover, multiple comparisons subsequent to an analysis with effect coding involve very simple calculations (see illustration in the section on Effect Coding). In view of the foregoing, it appears that Effect Coding is the preferred method even when orthogonal comparison are hypothesized, except when the calculations are to be done by hand.

DUMMY CODING

The presentation thus far has been devoted to factorial design with orthogonal and effect coding. It is of course possible to do the analysis of the 3×3 design with dummy coding. Some general comments about the method will suffice.

First, the method of coding the main effects with dummy coding is the same as with effect coding, except that instead of assigning -1's to the last category of each factor, 0's are assigned. As in the previous analyses, the vectors for the interaction are obtained by cross multiplying the vectors for the main effects.

Second, the overall results obtained with dummy coding are the same as those obtained with orthogonal and effect coding. The regression equation, however, is different. The a (intercept) equals the mean of the cell that as a result of the dummy coding has 0's in all the vectors. Using as an example the 3×3 design analyzed with the other methods of coding, the cell that will have 0's in all the vectors is A_3B_3. Without going into a lengthy explanation about the b's, it is pointed out that their determination, too, is related to the cell that is assigned 0's in all the vectors.

Third, while the vectors of the main effects for one factor are not correlated with the vectors of the main effects for the other factors, there is a correlation between the vectors for the interaction and those for the main effects. With orthogonal and effect coding there is no correlation between the vectors for the interaction and the vectors for the main effects. Using the 3×3 design as an example, it should be noted that, unlike orthogonal and effect coding, with dummy coding,

$$R^2_{y.12345678} \neq R^2_{y.12} + R^2_{y.34} + R^2_{y.5678}$$

where $R^2_{y.12\ldots8}$ = squared multiple correlation of Y with eight dummy vectors for a 3×3 design; $R^2_{y.12}$ = squared multiple correlation of Y with the dummy vectors for factor A; $R^2_{y.34}$ = squared multiple correlation of Y with the dummy vectors for factor B; $R^2_{y.5678}$ = squared multiple correlation of Y with the vectors for the interaction.

When doing the calculations, it is important to make the adjustment for the intercorrelations between the coded vectors. In the 3×3 example, the calculation of all the necessary terms can be done as follows:

For factor A, calculate:	$R^2_{y.12}$
For factor B, calculate:	$R^2_{y.34}$
For A, B, $A \times B$, calculate:	$R^2_{y.12345678}$
For $A \times B$, calculate:	$R^2_{y.12345678} - (R^2_{y.12} + R^2_{y.34})$
For residuals, calculate:	$1 - R^2_{y.12345678}$

Using a computer program that enables one to force in sets of variables or vectors in a sequence (e.g., SPSS) one may obtain the correct partitioning of variance by assigning the lowest inclusion level to the interaction vectors. Doing this in SPSS, for example, one may then use the R SQUARE CHANGE from the SUMMARY TABLE to obtain R^2 for each component in the same manner as was shown earlier for the analysis with effect coding.

The properties of dummy coding in factorial designs were described for completeness of presentation, though it is recommended that this method not be used in such designs. The use of effect coding (or orthogonal coding when desired) is preferable in factorial designs.

ANALYSES WITH MORE THAN TWO CATEGORICAL VARIABLES

Procedures for coding categorical independent variables and using them in regression analysis were demonstrated for the case of two categorical variables, each consisting of three categories. The same approach may be extended to any number of independent variables with any number of categories. All that is necessary is to code each categorical variable as if it were the only one in the design. Cross-product vectors are then generated to represent the interactions.

In designs with more than two categorical variables, higher-order interactions are of course calculated. The vectors for such interactions are also obtained by cross multiplying the vectors of the pertinent variables. Suppose, for example, that one has a design with three variables as follows: A with two categories, B with three categories, and C with four categories; then A will have one coded vector (say vector number 1), variable B will have two vectors (2 and 3), and variable C will have three vectors (4, 5, and 6). The first-order interactions, $A \times B$, $A \times C$, and $B \times C$, are obtained in the manner described earlier: by cross multiplying vectors 1 and 2, 1 and 3, and so on. The second-order interaction, that is, $A \times B \times C$, is obtained by cross multiplying the vectors associated with these variables as follows: $1 \times 2 \times 4$; $1 \times 3 \times 4$; $1 \times 2 \times 5$; $1 \times 3 \times 5$; $1 \times 2 \times 6$; $1 \times 3 \times 6$. Altogether, six vectors are generated to represent 6 degrees of freedom associated with this interaction (the degrees of freedom for A, B, and C, respectively, are 1, 2, and 3; the degrees of freedom for the interaction $A \times B \times C$ are therefore $1 \times 2 \times 3 = 6$). Having generated the necessary vectors, one does a multiple regression analysis using the coded vectors as the independent variables and the scores on the dependent measure as the dependent variable. The procedure of obtaining the results from computer output is the same as for the case of a two-factor design, except that higher-order interactions are also obtained. For interpretation of results from factorial designs with more than two factors, see Edwards (1972, Chapter 10), Kirk (1968, Chapter 7), and Winer (1971, Chapters 5 and 6).

Note the flexibility of the coding approach. Researchers frequently encounter difficulties in obtaining computer programs that meet their specific needs. A researcher may, for example, have a four-variable design and discover to his or her chagrin that the computer center to which he or she has access has only a three-variable program. With coding, any multiple regression program can be used for the analysis with ease.

From what was said about coding categorical variables in Chapter 9 and in this chapter it should be evident that, used judiciously, this approach can be extended to designs other than those considered here. For example, sometimes it is desired to use one or more control groups even though they do not fit into the factorial design that is being contemplated. Under such circumstances, the control groups are attached to the factorial design (see Himmelfarb, 1975; Hornbeck, 1973; Winer, 1971, pp. 468–473). Such designs can be easily accommodated by the coding methods presented here and subjected to a multiple regression analysis, and similarly for other designs (e.g., Hierarchical, Latin Squares). Multiple regression analysis of repeated-measures designs with coded vectors are presented in Chapter 14. The use of coded vectors in multivariate analysis is presented in Chapters 17 and 18.

NONORTHOGONAL DESIGNS

The topic of unequal *n*'s in designs with one independent variable was discussed in Chapter 9, where special issues regarding their use in experimental and nonexperimental research were noted. In addition, an important distinction was made between situations in which unequal *n*'s are used by design and those in which they are a consequence of subject mortality. Note that for the sake of convenience the term *subject mortality* is used to cover all contingencies that lead to a loss of subjects, though some (e.g., errors in the recording of some scores) do not pose nearly as great a threat to the internal validity of the study as others (e.g., subjects unwilling to continue to participate because of what appear to be reasons related to specific aspects of certain treatments). While it was shown that the analysis with unequal *n*'s for one categorical variable is straightforward, it was noted that the researcher is faced with choices (e.g., whether to compare unweighted or weighted means) and with ambiguities in the interpretation of the results, depending upon the specific design and the specific causes that have given rise to the unequal *n*'s.

In factorial designs, too, unequal *n*'s may occur in experimental or nonexperimental research, either by design or because of subject mortality. The analysis and interpretation of the results in factorial designs with unequal *n*'s are, however, considerably more complex and more ambiguous than in the case of a single independent variable. The reason is that when the frequencies in the cells of a factorial design are unequal, the treatment effects and their interactions are correlated, thereby rendering the attribution of a portion of the sum of squares to each main effect and to the interaction ambiguous. In other words, the design is not orthogonal and it is therefore not possible to partition the regression sum of squares to separate and independent components in the manner shown earlier in this chapter for orthogonal designs (i.e., designs with equal cell frequencies).

Factorial designs with unequal *n*'s are variously referred to in the literature as nonorthogonal, unbalanced, or designs with unequal cell frequencies. It should be noted that there is no single agreed-upon method for the analysis of nonorthogonal designs. In fact, this topic has generated lively debate and controversy among social scientists, as is evidenced by published arguments and counterarguments, comments, replies to comments, and comments on the replies to comments. Most of these are purposely not referenced here because instead of clarifying the problems they further obfuscate them, bearing witness to Appelbaum and Cramer's (1974) apt observation that: "The nonorthogonal multifactor analysis of variance is perhaps the most misunderstood analytic technique available to the behavioral scientists, save factor analysis'' (p. 335).

Because issues regarding the analysis and interpretation of nonorthogonal designs in experimental research are largely distinct from those relevant to nonexperimental research, the two research setting are treated separately, beginning with experimental research.

Nonorthogonal Designs in Experimental Research

Unequal cell frequencies in experimental research may occur either by design or because of subject mortality. A researcher may, for example, decide to use different numbers of subjects with different treatments because some are costlier than others. Under such circumstances, the probability is very high that the researcher will design a study in which the cell frequencies, though unequal, are proportional. A factorial design is said to have proportional cell frequencies when the ratio of cell frequencies in the rows is constant across columns, or equivalently, when the ratio of cell frequencies in columns is constant across rows. Consider the following 2 × 3 design in which the numbers refer to frequencies:

	B_1	B_2	B_3	
A_1	10	20	30	60
A_2	20	40	60	120
	30	60	90	180

By inspection, it may be noted that the ratio of row frequencies is 1:2:3, and that of column frequencies is 1:2. In general, proportionality of cell frequencies is indicated when

$$n_{ij} = \frac{n_{i.}n_{.j}}{n_{..}}$$

where n_{ij} = frequency in cell of row i and column j; $n_{i.}$ = frequency in row i; $n_{.j}$ = frequency in column j; $n_{..}$ = total frequency in the table. Basically, then, when each cell frequency is equal to the product of its marginal frequencies divided by the total frequency, the design is proportional. For the 2 × 3 given above, (30)(60)/180 = 10, (30)(120)/180 = 20, and so forth.

A design with proportional cell frequencies is analyzed and interpreted in the same manner as one with equal cell frequencies. In other words, in such designs it is still possible to partition the regression sum of squares to orthogonal components due to main effects and interaction. Consequently, all that was said about designs with equal cell frequencies applies also to designs with proportional cell frequencies.

The absence of orthogonality and the resultant ambiguity occur in designs in which the cell frequencies are disproportionate. In experimental research this will most often happen because of subject mortality. A researcher may start with equal or proportional cell frequencies but may lose subjects for some reason or another. Under such circumstances, the validity of the analysis and the interpretation of the results are predicated on the assumption that the loss of subjects is due to a random process. In other words, it is assumed that subject mortality is not related in a systematic manner to the treatment combinations. When this assumption is not tenable, "there would seem to be no remedy short of pretending that the missing observations are random" (Appelbaum & Cramer, 1974, p. 336).

The presentation that follows is closely patterned after those by Appelbaum and Cramer (1974), and Cramer and Appelbaum (1980). Theirs is probably the most lucid and logical treatment of the topic of nonorthogonal designs, and it deserves careful study. Basically, they argue that on logical and conceptual grounds there is no difference between orthogonal and nonorthogonal designs. In both cases the method of least squares is applied, and tests of significance are used to compare different linear models in an attempt to determine which of them appears to be most consistent with the data at hand.

Parenthetically, it will be noted that prior to the widespread availability of computer facilities analytic approaches that are generally less satisfactory than the least-squares solutions have been used (e.g., unweighted-means analysis; see Kirk, 1968, Chapter 7; Snedecor & Cochran, 1967, Chapter 16; Winer, 1971, Chapter 6). It is interesting that although Snedecor and Cochran present the least-squares solution, they do so after presenting the other methods, saying: "*Unfortunately,* with unequal cell numbers the exact test of the null hypothesis that interactions are absent requires the solution of a set of linear equations like those in a multiple regression" (1967, pp. 473–474; italics added). Fortunately, conditions have changed drastically since the time the preceding statement was made. The ready availability of computer facilities and programs for multiple regression analysis renders the use of the other methods unnecessary. Here, then, is yet another example of the superiority of multiple regression over the analysis of variance approach.

The least-squares solution for the case of nonorthogonal designs will be presented in the context of a numerical example. For convenience, a 2×2 design is used. The same approach may be extended to designs with more than two factors, each consisting of any number of categories.

A Numerical Example

Assume an experiment on attitude change toward the use of marijuana. The experiment consists of two factors, each with two treatments, as follows. Factor A refers to source of information, where A_1 = a former addict, and A_2 = a nonaddict. Factor B refers to fear arousal, where B_1 = mild fear arousal, and B_2 = intense fear arousal. Without going into the details of the design, assume further, for the sake of illustration, that five subjects are randomly assigned to each treatment combination.

In short, the experiment consists of four treatment combinations—namely, A_1B_1, A_1B_2, A_2B_1, and A_2B_2. This is, of course, a 2×2 factorial design. Assume that the experiment has been in progress for several sessions and that subject attrition has occurred. During the final session, measures of attitude change were available for only 14 of the 20 original subjects. The scores for these subjects, the cell means, and the unweighted treatment means are given in Table 10.10.

The methods of coding categorical independent variables in a design with unequal cell frequencies are the same as in designs with equal cell frequencies. For the present example, effect coding is used. In Table 10.11 the data originally given in Table 10.10 are repeated, together with the effect coding. Note

Table 10.10 Illustrative Data from an Experiment on Attitude Change

	Fear Arousal		
Source of Information	B_1	B_2	*Unweighted Means*
A_1	4 3 2 $\bar{Y} = 3.00$	8 10 $\bar{Y} = 9.00$	6.00
A_2	3 2 5 6 4 $\bar{Y} = 4.00$	5 4 5 6 $\bar{Y} = 5.00$	4.50
Unweighted Means	3.50	7.00	5.25

Table 10.11 Effect Coding for Data from an Experiment on Attitude Change

	Y	*1*	*2*	*3* (*1* × *2*)
A_1B_1	4	1	1	1
	3	1	1	1
	2	1	1	1
A_2B_1	3	−1	1	−1
	2	−1	1	−1
	5	−1	1	−1
	6	−1	1	−1
	4	−1	1	−1
A_1B_2	8	1	−1	−1
	10	1	−1	−1
A_2B_2	5	−1	−1	1
	4	−1	−1	1
	5	−1	−1	1
	6	−1	−1	1
Σy^2:	64.35714			

NOTE: Y = data originally given in Table 10.10; 1 = coded vector for factor A; 2 = coded vector for factor B; 3 = coded vector for the interaction between A and B.

that vector 1 of Table 10.11 identifies factor A (since there are two categories in factor A, one coded vector is necessary). Similarly, vector 2 of Table 10.11 identifies factor B. Vector 3, obtained by the multiplication of vectors 1 and 2, represents the interaction.

Thus far, the procedure is the same as the one used earlier in the chapter for the case of orthogonal designs. Recall that in orthogonal designs the coded vectors representing separate main effects and interactions are mutually orthogonal. Consequently, it is possible in such designs to partition the variance or the regression sum of squares into a set of orthogonal components. It was shown earlier that in orthogonal designs the R^2 of Y with a set of coded vectors representing a given factor, or an interaction, indicates the proportion of variance accounted for by the factor being considered. This is not true for the case of nonorthogonal designs because the coded vectors are correlated across factors and the interactions. (Referring to the coded vectors of Table 10.11, $r_{12} = .04303$, $r_{13} = .14907$, and $r_{23} = -.28868$.) Therefore, when doing an analysis for a nonorthogonal design it is necessary to take into account, or adjust for, the intercorrelations among main effects and interactions, depending upon the specific hypothesis that is being tested.

Appelbaum and Cramer (1974) point out that for a two-factor design one of the following five models may be the most consistent with the data:

1. $Y_{ijk} = \mu + \alpha_i + \beta_j + (\alpha\beta)_{ij} + \epsilon_{ijk}$
2. $Y_{ijk} = \mu + \alpha_i + \beta_j + \epsilon_{ijk}$
3. $Y_{ijk} = \mu + \alpha_i + \epsilon_{ijk}$
4. $Y_{ijk} = \mu + \beta_j + \epsilon_{ijk}$
5. $Y_{ijk} = \mu + \epsilon_{ijk}$

Note that Model 1 was introduced earlier as Equation (10.1). It is the most comprehensive model, since it conceives of an individual k's score under treatment combination ij as being composed of the grand mean, μ; two main effects, α_i and β_j; an interaction effect, $(\alpha\beta)_{ij}$; and a residual, ϵ_{ijk}. Model 1 is appropriate and sufficient to test separately the estimates of the effects in the case of an orthogonal design. On the basis of such tests it is possible to determine whether it is necessary to retain Model 1 or whether some of its elements may be deleted, thereby leading to a more parsimonious model. For example, if the interaction term in an orthogonal design is not significant, but the two main effects are significant, it will be concluded that Model 2 is to be retained.

In nonorthogonal designs, on the other hand, the validity of estimates of effects depends on the tenability of the model being used. To clarify this point, consider, for example, Models 2 and 3. Model 2 requires estimates of α and β, whereas Model 3 requires an estimate of α only. When the effects are nonorthogonal, the estimate of α will differ depending on whether it is done within the context of Model 2 or Model 3. How, then, does one determine which of the models is to be retained? The answer is sought by doing a sequence of tests, beginning with the most comprehensive model.

Test of the Interaction

The first test is addressed to the question of whether Model 1 or Model 2 is to be retained. In other words, the contrast between these two models is designed to answer the question of whether an interaction term is necessary or whether it is sufficient to retain the model in which only main effects are included. Testing whether the interaction is significant is accomplished in the usual manner by testing the difference between two R^2's—one in which the interaction is included (usually referred to as the full model) and one in which it is excluded (the restricted model). This may be expressed as follows:

$$R^2_{y.A,B,AB} - R^2_{y.A,B}$$

where A stands for one or more than one coded vectors representing factor A; B stands for one or more than one coded vectors representing factor B; and AB stands for the interaction.

It is instructive to note that, in an orthogonal design,

$$R^2_{y.A,B,AB} - R^2_{y.A,B} = R^2_{y.AB}$$

In a nonorthogonal design, however, the difference between the two R^2's is actually a squared multiple semipartial correlation: $R^2_{y(AB.A,B)}$ (see Chapter 5). In other words, it is the squared multiple correlation of Y with the interaction vectors after partialing out from the latter what they share with A and B. For the numerical example under consideration the proportion of variance due to the interaction is:

$$R^2_{y.123} - R^2_{y.12}$$

where the subscripts refer to the numbers of the coded vectors in Table 10.11. Using a computer program that enables one to enter variables sequentially (e.g., SPSS), the simplest way to obtain the information necessary for the test of the interaction is to enter vector 3 of Table 10.11 last and note in the SUMMARY TABLE the proportion of variance increment by it (i.e., R SQUARE CHANGE). For the data of the Table 10.11, $R^2_{y.12} = .44869$ and $R^2_{y.123} = .75139$. The increment in the proportion of variance accounted for due to the interaction (R SQUARE CHANGE for vector 3) is .3027, and it is this proportion that is tested for significance:

$$F = \frac{(R^2_{y.123} - R^2_{y.12})/1}{(1 - R^2_{y.123})/(N - 3 - 1)} = \frac{.75139 - .44869}{(1 - .75139)/(14 - 3 - 1)} = \frac{.30270}{.02486} = 12.18$$

with 1 and 10 *df*, $p < .01$. It is therefore concluded that the interaction is significant and Model 1 is to be retained.

Before discussing what the next step is, it will be noted that because in the present example the interaction is represented by a single vector one could obtain the test for the interaction without going through the process outlined above. Recall that a test of a regression coefficient (b) is the same as a test of the proportion of variance accounted for by the variable with which it is associated when the variable is entered last in the analysis. Therefore, for the case of a 2×2 design all that is necessary is to note the F (or t) ratio associated with the b for the interaction vector. With designs larger than a 2×2 the procedure outlined above has to be followed.

We return now to a consideration of what is to be done if, as in the present example, the interaction is significant. The decision is exactly the same as in the case of an orthogonal design. Recall that earlier in the chapter it was argued that when the interaction is significant it is not meaningful to test main effects, although such tests are not wrong from a statistical point of view. Instead, one proceeds with tests of simple main effects in order to gain insight into the differential effects of treatments of one factor depending upon their combinations with treatments of the other factor. The same holds true for the case of a nonorthogonal design. Because the interaction for the present example is significant one would test the differences between the two fear arousal conditions (B_1 and B_2) at each category of source of information (A_1 and A_2). In other words, one would test the difference between the mean of cell A_1B_1 and that of A_1B_2, and the difference between the mean of cell A_2B_1 and that of A_2B_2. Similarly, one may test the simple main effects of sources of information (A_1 and A_2) at each level of fear arousal (B_1 and B_2). These tests, which are done in the same manner as presented earlier for the case of orthogonal designs, are not carried out here because the only concern is with the problem of unequal cell frequencies. It is instructive, however, to note by inspection that the difference between B_1 and B_2 at level A_1 (9.00 − 3.00) is considerably larger than that between the same treatments at level A_2 (5.00 − 4.00). Note also the difference between A_1 and A_2 at B_1 (4.00 − 3.00) and that of A_1 and A_2 at B_2 (9.00 − 5.00). All this, of course, is what the interaction is all about.

Tests of the Main Effects

When the interaction is not significant, one proceeds with tests of main effects as in the case of orthogonal designs, except that each main effect is tested after it has been adjusted for its correlation with the other main effect. Appelbaum and Cramer (1974) prefer to refer to this test as a test of a main effect after eliminating the other main effect. Searle (1971) prefers to speak of a test of a main effect after another main effect. The specific terminology notwithstanding, they all refer to the same thing—namely, a test of a squared multiple semipartial correlation or a test of the increment in the proportion of variance due to one main effect after the contribution of the other main effect has been taken into account. Referring to the five models listed above, the testing of the main effect of B is accomplished by contrasting Model 2 (in which B is included) with Model 3 (in which B is not included). Expressed as a test of the difference between two R^2's, the test of B after it has been adjusted for A is

$$R^2_{y.A,B} - R^2_{y.A}$$

A significant F ratio would indicate that B has to be retained in Model 2.

Similarly, one tests the main effect of A after it has been adjusted for B; that is,

$$R^2_{y.A,B} - R^2_{y.B}$$

If this test, too, is significant, the decision is to retain Model 2.

If only one of the main effects is significant, the model containing it is retained. If neither of the main effects is significant, Appelbaum and Cramer (1974) suggest two additional tests: one in which A is tested while ignoring B and one in which B is tested while ignoring A. Note carefully that these tests do not take into account the correlation between A and B. When A is tested, Model 3, which includes A, is compared to Model 5, which includes only the grand mean. Similarly, when B is tested, Model 4 is compared with Model 5. Several patterns of results may emerge from such tests: (1) Both A and B are significant. This is, of course, an indication of serious confounding between the two variables. Recall that these tests are done when both A and B are not significant after each is adjusted for the other. Appelbaum and Cramer say that if both A and B are significant one should retain one factor only in the final model—"the choice is indeterminate" (p. 341). (2) Only one of the factors is significant. The one that is significant is retained in the final model. (3) Neither of the tests is significant. Then a model in which only the grand mean appears is retained. In other words, there are no main and interaction effects.

It is important to note that Appelbaum and Cramer (1974) urge caution in interpreting results of tests of main effects when the other factors are ignored. Since the significance of such tests basically serves to underscore the fact that the factors are seriously confounded due to relatively extreme disproportionality, one is inclined to suggest that they not be carried out at all. The potential danger of misinterpreting the results based on such tests outweighs whatever benefits may be gained in using them. More important, extreme disproportionality of cell frequencies should be a cause of grave concern because it raises serious doubts about the assumption that subject mortality is due to a random process, thereby casting doubts on the internal validity of the experiment. Retaining, under such circumstances, a factor that has been shown to be significant only when the other factor was ignored is, to say the least, hazardous. If, despite the foregoing, one chooses to follow Appelbaum and Cramer's suggestion to carry out tests of each main effect while ignoring the other factor (after it has been established that neither is significant when one is adjusted for the other), one would also be well advised to heed their call for caution in interpreting results of such tests.

Finally, note that only in the case of nonorthogonal designs may one encounter patterns of results in which main effects are not significant when adjusted for one another, but one or both are significant when each is tested without taking the other into account. In orthogonal designs, the regression sum of squares due to a given main effect will not change when it is adjusted for other main effects because the main effects (and interactions) are not correlated. This, of course, is the meaning of orthogonality.

Summary of Testing Sequence

It will be useful now to summarize the sequence of the testing in nonorthogonal designs:

1. Begin with a test of the interaction. If the interaction is significant, do tests of simple main effects. If the interaction is not significant, go to step 2.

2. Test each factor while adjusting it for the other factor. That is, test *A* after *B*, and *B* after *A*. Retain one or both, depending on whether they are statistically significant. If neither is significant, you may choose to conclude that Model 5 is tenable, that is, that there are no main effects and interactions. Or, you may choose to go to step 3.
3. Test each factor while ignoring the other. Treat the results of such tests with great caution.

Numerical Example (Continued)

In the numerical example analyzed above it was found that the interaction is significant, and it was noted that tests of simple main effects are called for. Nevertheless, in order to illustrate the procedure of testing adjusted main effects it will be assumed that the interaction is not significant. When a computer program is used, it is necessary to perform two analyses: (1) entering *A* first, and noting the increment in the proportion of variance, or regression sum of squares, due to *B;* (2) entering *B* first and noting the increment due to *A*. Each of the increments is then divided by its degrees of freedom to obtain a mean square, which is tested for significance by using the overall error term. For the data of Table 10.11 the increment in the proportion of variance due to either of the factors has one degree of freedom.

The analysis of the data of Table 10.11 is summarized in Table 10.12. The increments are expressed as sums of squares by multiplying each proportion by the total sum of squares (Σy^2). One could, of course, carry out the tests on the proportions of variance accounted for. The choice between the two is a matter of taste.

The first thing to note about Table 10.12 is that the sum of the separate components (65.15003) is not equal to Σy^2 (64.35714). This is a consequence of the correlations among the main effects and the interaction. The discrepancy between the two sums will be greater or smaller depending on the correlations among the vectors representing the main effects and the interaction, which are

Table 10.12 Analysis of Variance Summary Table for Data of Table 10.11

Source	*ss*	*df*	*ms*	*F*	*p*
A	$\Sigma y^2 (R^2_{y.12} - R^2_{y.2})$ 64.35714(.44869 − .39077) = 3.72757	1	3.72757	2.33	n.s.
B	$\Sigma y^2 (R^2_{y.12} - R^2_{y.1})$ 64.35714(.44869 − .04560) = 25.94172	1	25.94172	16.21	.01
A × *B*	$\Sigma y^2 (R^2_{y.123} - R^2_{y.12})$ 64.35714(.75139 − .44869) = 19.48091	1	19.48091	12.18	.01
Residual	$\Sigma y^2 (1 - R^2_{y.123})$ 64.35714(1 − .75139) = 15.99983	10	1.59998		
	Σy^2 = 64.35714 Σ: 65.15003	13			

NOTE: *A* = Source of Information; *B* = Fear Arousal; Σy^2 = total sum of squares of the dependent variable, *Y;* 1 = coded vector for factor *A;* 2 = coded vector for factor *B;* 3 = coded vector for *A* × *B*.

affected by the degree and the pattern of disproportionality of the cell frequencies.

Assuming, for the sake of illustration, that the interaction is not significant, it will be noted that factor A is not significant, whereas factor B is significant. It would therefore be concluded that Model 4 in which the grand mean, factor B, and a residual term appear is to be retained (see above for a listing of the five models). To repeat, the interaction in the present case is significant. Consequently, one would not carry out the tests of adjusted main effects, which were done here for illustrative purposes only.

The procedure outlined above may be extended to higher-order designs. For a discussion, see Appelbaum and Cramer (1974). We turn now to an examination of the properties of the regression equation with effect coding when the design is nonorthogonal.

The Regression Equation

Following is an excerpt of the output of the analysis of the data of Table 10.11 as obtained from SPSS.

Output

	- - - -VARIABLES IN THE EQUATION- - - -		
VARIABLE	B	STD ERROR B	F
V1 *(A)*	.75	.35824	4.38
V2 *(B)*	−1.75	.35824	23.86
V3 *(AB)*	−1.25	.35824	12.18
(CONSTANT)	5.25		

Commentary

Since effect coding was used (see Table 10.11), the regression equation has the same properties as the regression equation obtained from effect coding in orthogonal designs. In the case of nonorthogonal designs, however, the terms in the equation refer to unweighted means (this is similar to the case of unequal n's with one independent variable; see Chapter 9). Thus, the intercept, 5.25, is equal to the unweighted grand mean, or the mean of the cell means (see Table 10.10). The weighted grand mean $(\bar{Y})$ for the present data is 4.7857. b_1 (.75) is equal to the difference between the unweighted mean of A_1 (6.00; see Table 10.10) and the unweighted grand mean. In other words, b_1 is equal to the effect of treatment A_1 (see Table 10.11, where subjects in A_1 were assigned 1's), in which each cell mean is given equal weight regardless of the number of subjects in the cell. If the assumption about the missing data being due to a random process is reasonable, it makes sense to arrive at statements of treatment effects in this manner. If, on the other hand, subject mortality is not due to a random process, the entire analysis is questionable.

As usual, the effect of the treatment assigned -1 is equal to $-\Sigma b_i$. In the present example, the effect of treatment A_2 is $-.75$, which is the deviation of the unweighted mean of A_2 (4.50; see Table 10.10) from the unweighted grand mean.

b_2 (−1.75) is equal to the effect of B_1 (subjects in B_1 were assigned 1's in vector 2 of Table 10.11). Again, it is the deviation of the unweighted mean of B_1 from the unweighted grand mean. The effect of B_2 is 1.75.

b_3 (−1.25) is the interaction effect for cell A_1B_1. This is the same as in an orthogonal design (see the discussion in earlier parts of this chapter). But, as is the case for the main effects in a nonorthogonal design, it is an unweighted interaction effect. To show this, values from Table 10.10 are repeated:

$$\bar{Y}_{A_1B_1} = 3.00 \qquad \bar{Y}_{A_1} = 6.00 \qquad \bar{Y}_{B_1} = 3.50 \qquad \bar{Y} = 5.25$$

(Note that the last three are unweighted means.) Applying Equation (10.3) to obtain the interaction term for cell A_1B_1:

$$A_1B_1 = (3.00 - 5.25) - (6.00 - 5.25) - (3.50 - 5.25) = -1.25$$

In view of the constraint that the sum of interaction effects for each row and each column is zero, the other terms for the cell may be easily obtained. Thus, for A_1B_2, the interaction effect is 1.25, and so forth.

Applying the regression equation to the codes of a subject on the three vectors will yield a predicted score that is equal to the mean of the cell to which the subject belongs. This will always be the case, as long as all the coded vectors (i.e., for main effects and interaction) are included in the analysis.

F ratios for tests of the regression coefficients were reported earlier. Because in the present example each vector represents a different component (V1 represents factor *A;* V2 represents factor *B,* and V3 represents the interaction), it will be useful to examine the meaning of the tests of the *b*'s. Beginning with the test of V3 it will be noted that the *F* ratio associated with it (12.18) is the same as the one obtained earlier for the interaction. This illustrates what was said earlier—namely, that in a 2 × 2 design the test of the *b* associated with the vector representing the interaction is the same as the test of the proportion of variance incremented by the interaction term when it is entered last (i.e., after the main effects). Note that in designs with more than two categories per factor one has to test the interaction in the manner shown earlier (i.e., by testing the difference between two R^2's).

Turning now to the tests of the *b*'s associated with the main effects, it should be evident that the test of each *b* is one in which the factor with which it is associated is adjusted for the other factor *and* for the interaction. This, of course, is the meaning of a test of a partial regression coefficient. But this is not what we wish to do in a nonorthogonal design. Recall that if the interaction is not significant, we adjust each main effect for the other main effect. If, on the other hand, the interaction is significant, no adjustments are made. Instead, tests of simple main effects are performed.

In sum, the tests of the *b*'s for the main effects reported above are irrelevant, even though we are dealing with a 2 × 2 design and therefore each *b* is associated with one of the main effects. Compare the *F* ratios for *A* (V1) and *B* (V2) reported from the computer output with those given in Table 10.12, where it was assumed that the interaction was not significant, and note that they are not the same. The latter are based on adjustments for main effects only, whereas the former are based on adjustments for main effects *and* the interaction. To repeat, it is the adjustment for main effects only that we are interested in when the interaction is found to be not significant in nonorthogonal designs.

It will be noted now that some authors, notably Overall, Spiegel, and Cohen (1975), argue that the main effects should be adjusted also for the interaction (see also Carlson & Timm, 1974; Edwards, 1979, Chapter 13). In the context of the numerical example under consideration, Overall and associates would maintain that the tests of the *b*'s, reported in the computer output above, are the appropriate tests of the main effects—not those reported in Table 10.12. From what was said about the strategy of testing in orthogonal and nonorthogonal designs, depending on whether the interaction is or is not significant, it should be evident why the adjustment of main effects for interactions is not recommended here. For a critique of the approach used by Overall and his colleagues, see Cramer and Appelbaum (1980).

When the topic of nonorthogonal designs was introduced, it was said that there was no agreement about the partitioning of the regression sum of squares to main effects and interactions. The contrast between the approach advocated by Appelbaum and Cramer and that advocated by Overall and his colleagues is but one illustration of the disagreement about the appropriate analysis of nonorthogonal designs in experimental research. It is therefore useful to conclude the presentation by noting what Cochran and Cox (1950) have to say about the problem of missing data: "The only complete solution of the 'missing data' problem is not to have them" (p. 74).

Nonorthogonal Designs in Nonexperimental Research

Unequal cell frequencies in experimental research result in correlations among the coded vectors that represent the independent variables. The reverse is true in nonexperimental research, where unequal cell frequencies are generally obtained *because* of correlations among independent variables or predictors. Consider, for example, a 2 × 2 design in which one variable *(A)* is race (A_1 = black; A_2 = white), and the other variable *(B)* is education (B_1 = high school; B_2 = college). Assume that the dependent variable is income. As this appears to be similar to a 2 × 2 experimental design, researchers are often inclined to treat it as such. That is, they seek answers to questions about main effects and interactions. In the present example this would mean that one may be tempted to determine the effects of race and education as well as their interaction on income. It is necessary, however, to recognize that race and education are correlated. Consequently, when drawing representative samples of blacks and whites from defined populations one is bound to obtain more college-educated whites than blacks. Assuming that one finds that whites earn significantly more than blacks (i.e., a main effect for race), it is necessary to realize that the difference may be partly, or entirely, due to differences in education, not to mention a host of other variables that are related to race and education.

A statement about the effect of education is equally questionable. Furthermore, the notion of an interaction between race and education is, as discussed below, inherently ambiguous.

Before turning to issues of analysis and interpretation of such designs another example may be useful. This time, assume that one is interested in studying the educational attitudes of elementary school personnel and that one variable (A) is status (A_1 = administrator; A_2 = teacher), and the other variable (B) is sex (B_1 = male; B_2 = female). It is well known that these variables are correlated: most school administrators are males, whereas the majority of teachers are females. Is, then, an observed difference in educational attitudes between administrators and teachers due to status or due to sex? Conversely, does a difference between males and females reflect a difference due to sex or due to status? And what, if any, is the meaning of an interaction between status and sex? Again, the situation is further complicated because status and sex are correlated with many other variables that are not included in the design.[3]

In view of the foregoing, it should be evident that what was said earlier about the analysis of nonorthogonal designs in experimental research is not applicable to such designs in nonexperimental research. When the topic of unequal n's in nonexperimental research was introduced for the case of one categorical variable (Chapter 9), it was noted that for certain purposes one may sample disproportionately from the different strata in order to arrive at a design with equal n's. The temptation to use a similar approach in designs with multiple categorical variables should be resisted because the use of equal cell frequencies when the variables are correlated is tantamount to pretending that they are not correlated. Such artificial orthogonalizations of nonorthogonal designs is (borrowing a phrase from Hoffman, 1960) a *dismemberment of reality*. Humphreys and Fleishman (1974) aptly label designs that have been artificially orthogonalized as being "pseudo-orthogonal" designs.

How, then, are nonorthogonal designs in nonexperimental research to be treated? Except for the fact that the variables are categorical, such designs are conceptually and analytically not different from designs in which continuous variables are used in nonexperimental research. Therefore, all that was said in earlier chapters about analytic approaches in nonexperimental research with continuous variables applies equally to designs with categorical variables. But because categorical variables that consist of more than two categories are represented by more than one coded vector, analyses with such variables must take this into account. For example, assume that multiple categorical variables are used in a predictive study and that it is desired to apply a variable-selection procedure (e.g., stepwise regression analysis; see Chapter 6). Unless each of the variables consists of two categories only it is inappropriate to apply the variable-selection method to the coded vectors because each of them will be treated as a distinct variable. Instead, the selection needs to be applied to sets of coded vectors, each representing a given variable.[4]

The analysis with categorical variables in explanatory research is, as in the

[3]For other examples and a very good discussion of problems relevant to factorial designs in nonexperimental research, see McNemar (1969, pp. 444–449).

[4]This point is discussed in detail below under Criterion Scaling.

case of continuous variables, predicated on the theoretical model advanced by the researcher and on the questions he or she wishes to answer. Thus, if it is desired to partition the variance of the dependent variable, it is necessary that a causal model about the correlations among the independent variables be formulated. It will be recalled that if all the independent variables are treated as being exogenous (i.e., no explanation is advanced about the correlations among them), then there is no meaningful way of partitioning the variance of the dependent variable (see Chapter 7 for a detailed discussion of this and related issues). If, on the other hand, some of the independent variables are treated as endogenous (i.e., as being affected by other independent variables), then the analysis proceeds in the same manner as was done for the case of continuous variables (Chapter 7), except the coded vectors are used to represent the categorical variables.

Consider the first hypothetical example introduced above. It may be argued that race *(A)* affects to some extent one's level of education *(B)*. The converse is obviously not the case. Consequently, one may decide to determine first the proportion of the variance in income *(Y)* that is due to race, and then the proportion of variance that is incremented by education. This is done in the usual manner: $R^2_{y.A}$ is the proportion of variance due to race, and $R^2_{y.AB} - R^2_{y.A}$ is the proportion of variance incremented by education. Each of the proportions of variance is tested for significance in the usual manner. Note that *A* and *B* above represent a factor, or a categorical variable, regardless of the number of categories of which it is composed. Thus while in the example under consideration each factor consisted of only two categories, the same approach will be taken if each factor consisted of more than two categories, except that more than one coded vector will be necessary to represent a factor. In other words, each factor is coded in the usual manner and then an incremental, or hierarchical, partitioning of variance is done to reflect the pattern of causality among the independent variables. When testing the significance of each proportion, the degrees of freedom for the numerator of a given F ratio are, of course, the number of coded vectors used to represent the factor under consideration. The error term is, as always, 1 minus the overall R^2 (i.e., R^2 for all the factors) divided by the degrees of freedom associated with the residual (i.e., $N - k - 1$, where k is the total number of coded vectors in the design).

Finally, it should be recalled that an incremental, or hierarchical, partitioning of variance does not provide answers to questions about the relative importance of the independent variables and that the proportion of variance incremented by a variable is of dubious value for policy decisions (see Chapter 7 for a detailed discussion of these topics).

Assume now that instead of partitioning the variance of the dependent variable one wishes to study the effects of independent categorical variables in a manner analogous to the study of regression coefficients for continuous variables (see Chapter 8). It is obvious that when each of the categorical variables consists of two categories only, the b's would be tested in the same manner as is done for the case of continuous variables. Thus, in the above hypothetical example the test of the b associated with the vector representing race is a test of this factor after adjusting for its correlation with education. Similarly, for the test of the b that is associated with the vector that represents education.

When the categorical variables consist of more than two categories, it is necessary to test, in turn, the proportion of variance accounted for by a given categorical variable after it has been adjusted for the other categorical variables. Stated differently, one would test, in turn, the proportion of variance due to a given categorical variable when it is entered last into the equation. For the purpose of illustration, assume a design with three categorical variables as follows: A with 3 categories; B with 4 categories, and C with 5 categories. A would therefore require 2 coded vectors; B, 3 coded vectors; and C, 4 coded vectors. The proportion of variance due to A, for example, is: $R^2_{y.ABC} - R^2_{y.BC}$. And similarly for the other factors. The test of the proportion of variance due to A is:

$$F = \frac{(R^2_{y.ABC} - R^2_{y.BC})/(k_1 - k_2)}{(1 - R^2_{y.ABC})/(N - k_1 - 1)}$$

where k_1 is the *df* associated with the overall R^2 (i.e., the one in which A, B, and C are included). In the present example, $k_1 = 9$. k_2 is the *df* associated with the R^2 for B and C, which in the present example are 7. Therefore the degrees of freedom for the numerator of the above F ratio are 2 (i.e., 9 − 7), or the number of coded vectors that represent the factor under consideration—namely, factor A. Tests for the other factors are carried out in a similar manner.

Multiplicative or Joint Relations

In the above presentation no mention was made of interactions among the categorical variables. This omission was intentional because the aim was to present first procedures in which the analyses with categorical variables in nonexperimental research follow along the same lines as analyses with continuous variables in similar settings. It will be recalled that in factorial designs in experimental research the interaction terms were obtained by cross multiplying the coded vectors for the main effects. The same procedure can be followed in designs with multiple categorical variables in nonexperimental research. It is suggested, however, that in such settings the term *multiplicative,* or *joint, relations* be used to refer to the relations of combinations of categorical variables with the dependent variable. It is hoped that the use of different labels will not be viewed as an exercise in semantics, but rather as a constant reminder of the important differences between experimental and nonexperimental research.

In experimental research, the administration of combinations of treatments is totally under the control of the researcher. Moreover, random assignment of subjects to treatment combinations minimizes specification errors. In other words, one may assume that variables not included in the design are not correlated with variables whose effects are being studied. Under such circumstances, statements about main effects and interactions are straightforward and unambiguous. This is not to say that the substantive meaning of specific findings, particularly of higher-order interactions, is always clear-cut. Whether or not the interpretation of results is simple or complex, clear-cut or ambiguous, depends not on the analysis per se but, among other things, on the substantive meaning of the variables being used and their operational definitions (see Chapter 9), on the theory, and the overall validity of the research design.

In nonexperimental research, on the other hand, the variables are almost always correlated with each other. Frequently, it is not possible to unravel the reasons for the correlations among the variables. In addition, the probability of specification errors in such designs is generally high since it is very likely that variables being studied are correlated with variables that are not considered in the design. Often, variables included in the design serve as proxies for variables that affect the dependent variable but are not included in the study. Under such circumstances, references to the main effects of variables, not to mention references to interactions, may be misleading. References to interactions are equally misleading when one postulates a pattern of causal relations among the variables that are treated as the independent variables.

Yet cross-product vectors in nonexperimental research may be associated with a meaningful increment in the proportion of variance accounted for, although the interpretation of such increments will generally pose serious difficulties. Some of the difficulties may, perhaps, be best understood in the context of a concrete example. Let us return to the hypothetical study in which race and education are used to explain income. It is known that race and education are correlated. As discussed earlier, it is plausible to assume that race affects education to some extent. It is a fact that when, in addition to the coded vectors that represent race and education, cross products of these vectors are used, the cell means of the combinations of the two variables will be predictable from the regression equation. In other words, errors of prediction will be minimized when cross-product vectors are used in addition to the vectors that represent the variables. Assuming that in the example under consideration the multiplicative term accounts for a meaningful increment in the proportion of variance accounted for, how is one to interpret such a finding? Using the terminology of experimental research one may be tempted to conclude that race and education interact in their effects on income. Stated differently, one may be tempted to conclude, for example, that the effect of race on income depends on the level of education. But such a conclusion would not be tenable if the assumption that race affects education is tenable. Even if one were to exclude the possibility of a causal relation between race and education, it is necessary to recognize that other variables may be operating. Consider, for example, the combinations of blacks with a college education, and that of whites with a high school education only. Both of these may be, in part, a consequence of mental ability, motivation, and socioeconomic status, to name but three variables. These variables, too, tend to be intercorrelated, and the causes of the correlations are, to say the least, not clear. In view of the foregoing, it is evident that although it is valid to state that predicted income varies depending on specific combinations of categories of race and education, the conclusion that there is an interaction between race and education is clearly questionable.

Whether or not one accepts the proposed distinction between interactions and multiplicative relations, it will be noted that there appears to be general agreement that the analysis should be carried out hierarchically.[5] That is, the

[5]This point is discussed in detail in Chapter 11 in connection with attempts to interpret products of continuous variables as interactions.

cross-product vectors are adjusted for their correlations with the vectors representing the variables, but not the other way around. In other words, the purpose is to note whether the multiplicative, or joint, relations add meaningfully and significantly to the proportion of variance accounted for by the variables themselves. In the context of the example under consideration this means that one tests whether the product of race *(A)* and education *(B)* increments significantly the proportion of variance in income *(Y)* accounted for by race and education alone. That is, one tests $R^2_{y.A,B,AB} - R^2_{y\,A,B}$, where *AB* stands for the cross product of the *A* and *B* vectors. If this increment is not significant, the multiplicative term is deleted and the analysis proceeds as outlined in the preceding section: each variable's contribution is studied after it has been adjusted for its correlations with the other variables. Thus, for the proportion of variance incremented by *A*, test $R^2_{y.A,B} - R^2_{y.B}$. Similarly, for the proportion of variance incremented by *B*.

When the multiplicative term is significant, it is necessary to study the joint relations and attempt to unravel their causes. Although the analytic procedure is not unlike the study of simple main effects in experimental research, the interpretation is much more complex in view of the correlation among the variables and the high risk of specification errors.

It is not difficult to envision the sense of frustration that you may have experienced while reading this section. It is, however, not possible to relieve the frustration by providing simple solutions because there are none. It is very simple to construct coded vectors to represent categorical variables. It is also very simple to generate cross-product vectors and label them interactions. But having done this, the interpretational problems do not disappear. Consider, for example, a study in which race, religion, political party affiliation, and sex are used to explain attitudes toward the Equal Rights Amendment. Sounds simple! And it is simple so far as the mechanics of coding the variables and generating cross-product vectors is concerned. But what about interpretations of results? What does an interaction between, say, race, religion, and political party affiliation mean, particularly when these variables not only are intercorrelated but also are correlated with variables not included in the design, and may even serve as proxies for some? This does not just sound complicated; it is complicated.

The best antidote against erroneous interpretations of results from complex studies is clear thinking and sound theory. It is first and foremost important not to be trapped by the mechanics of the analysis. Second, the more one knows about the causes for the patterns of relations among the variables under study, the sounder the theoretical formulation, the better will one be able not only to select the most appropriate analytic approach but also to interpret the results thus obtained.

CRITERION SCALING

Although the method of coding categorical independent variables or predictors is straightforward and is generalizable to any number of variables with any number of categories, it becomes unwieldy when the number of variables is large, or even with a small number of variables when each consists of many categories. For example, it has been estimated (Beaton, 1969a) that about 600 vectors would be required to code the variables for the ninth-grade students in the Coleman Report. Even the large computers now in use cannot economically handle hundreds of vectors, not to mention cross-product vectors that may run into the millions. Beaton (1969a) has estimated that 10^{75} vectors would be required to represent the cross-product vectors for the variables noted above.

To handle the problem, Beaton (1969a, 1969b) has proposed a coding method that he has labeled *criterion scaling*. The idea of criterion scaling is very simple. It will be recalled that the regression equation obtained from the regression of the dependent variable on a set of coded vectors yields predicted scores that are equal to the means of the group or categories on the dependent variable. In other words, errors of prediction are minimized when the predicted score for each individual is equal to the mean on the criterion for the group to which he or she belongs. A categorical variable is said to be criterion scaled when it is transformed to a single vector in which each individual's score is equal to the criterion mean of the group to which he or she belongs. Stated differently, a criterion-scaled variable is one that is composed of the predicted scores of the individuals under consideration.

Recall that $R^2_{y.12\ldots k} = r^2_{yy'}$, where $R^2_{y.12\ldots k}$ is the squared multiple correlation of Y with k independent variables or coded vectors, and $r^2_{yy'}$ is the squared correlation of Y with the predicted Y's (see Chapter 3, Equation (3.18) and the discussion related to it). Therefore, by criterion scaling the categorical variable a multiple regression analysis can be replaced by a bivariate regression analysis in which the dependent variable is regressed on the criterion-scaled variable. This holds true regardless of the number of categories of the categorical variable and for equal as well as unequal n's.

A Numerical Example

The scaling of a categorical variable with three categories and the regression calculations are illustrated for a numerical example in Table 9.11 and the analysis related to it, thereby demonstrating the identity of the results obtained when coded vectors and criterion scaling are used to represent the categorical variable. In Table 10.13, vector Y, the criterion, is the same as Y of Table 9.11. Instead of using two coded vectors (as in Table 9.11), the categorical variable has been criterion scaled and is represented by Y' in Table 10.13. Note that Y' is composed of the means of the three groups on the dependent variable, or the criterion. Thus, for the first three subjects $Y' = 5$, which is the mean of the group ($\bar{Y}_{A_1}$) to which they belong. Similarly, for the other groups.

The calculations of the regression of Y on Y' are now done without commenting on the mechanics, as these should be clear by now.[6] Using values reported at the bottom of Table 10.13, calculate:

$$\Sigma y^2 = \Sigma Y^2 - \frac{(\Sigma Y)^2}{N} = 426 - \frac{(64)^2}{12} = 84.66667$$

[6]For an analysis identical to the one done here, except that the independent variables were continuous, see Chapter 3.

$$\Sigma y'^2 = \Sigma Y'^2 - \frac{(\Sigma Y'^2)}{N} = 409 - \frac{(64)^2}{12} = 67.66667$$

$$\Sigma yy' = \Sigma YY' - \frac{(\Sigma Y)(\Sigma Y')}{N} = 409 - \frac{(64)(64)}{12} = 67.66667$$

$$r^2_{yy'} = \frac{(\Sigma yy')}{(\Sigma y^2)(\Sigma y'^2)} = \frac{67.66667^2}{(84.66667)(67.66667)} = .79921$$

Compare $r^2_{yy'}$ with $R^2_{y.12}$ obtained in the analysis of the same data with coded vectors (Chapter 9) and note that they are identical. That is, the proportion of variance accounted for by the categorical variable is the same, regardless of whether it is represented by coded vectors or by criterion scaling. It will be noted, however, that it would be incorrect to test $r^2_{yy'}$ as if it were a squared zero-order correlation. Instead, the proportion of variance represented by $r^2_{yy'}$ has to be tested, using the appropriate degrees of freedom for the numerator and the denominator of the F ratio. For the present example, the numerator degrees of freedom are 2 (there are three categories). Therefore,

$$F = \frac{.79921/2}{(1 - .79921)/(12 - 2 - 1)} = \frac{.39660}{.02231} = 17.91$$

with 2 and 9 *df*. Not surprisingly, the same F ratio was obtained when these data were analyzed with coded vectors representing the categorical variable (see Chapter 9). Note that had the data of Table 10.13 been run on a computer program, the proportion of variance accounted for, the regression and residual sums of squares would have been correct. But the F ratio reported in the output would have been *incorrect* because it would have been calculated as if the proportion of variance accounted for (or the regression sum of squares) is as-

Table 10.13 Criterion Scaling of a Variable Consisting of Three Categories

	Y	Y^2	Y'	Y'^2	YY'
A_1	4	16	5	25	20
	5	25	5	25	25
	6	36	5	25	30
A_2	7	49	8.5	72.25	59.5
	8	64	8.5	72.25	68
	9	81	8.5	72.25	76.5
	10	100	8.5	72.25	85
A_3	1	1	3	9	3
	2	4	3	9	6
	3	9	3	9	9
	4	16	3	9	12
	5	25	3	9	15
Σ:	64	426	64	409	409
M:	5.33		5.33		

sociated with one degree of freedom. This will always be the case because when a categorical variable is criterion scaled only one vector is used to represent the independent variable.

In sum, when a categorical variable is criterion scaled, the squared zero-order correlation of the dependent variable with the criterion-scaled variable is equal to the squared multiple correlation of the dependent variable with a set of coded vectors that represent the categorical variable. The proportion of variance accounted for thus obtained is tested in the usual manner.

Turning now to the regression equation with a criterion-scaled variable:

$$b = \frac{\Sigma yy'}{\Sigma y'^2} = \frac{67.66667}{67.66667} = 1.00$$

$$a = \bar{Y} - b\bar{Y}' = 5.33 - (1.00)(5.33) = 0$$

Note the properties of the regression equation with criterion scaling: (1) The regression coefficient is always one, because $\Sigma yy' = \Sigma y'^2$. That $b = 1.00$ makes sense intuitively because the values on the predictor variable (i.e., the criterion-scaled variable) are actually the predicted scores. (2) The intercept is equal to zero. This will always be so, because $\bar{Y} = \bar{Y}'$ (see Chapter 2), and b is always one.

The regression sum of squares was obtained above: $\Sigma y'^2 = 67.66667$—or, using one of the formulas introduced in Chapter 2,

$$ss_{\text{reg}} = b\Sigma yy' = (1.00)(67.66667) = 67.66667$$

Compare with the results of the analysis of the same data in Chapter 9.

Finally, it will be noted that when n's are equal, total scores for each group on the dependent variable may be used instead of the means for the purpose of criterion scaling. This is so because all it means is that the criterion-scaled variable was multiplied by a constant (n), and therefore $r^2_{yy'}$ will not be affected. Using totals whenever possible is advisable because possible rounding errors due to the use of means that may have been rounded is thus avoided.[7] Note carefully that with unequal n's *means* must be used for criterion scaling.

For convenience, criterion scaling was demonstrated for the case of a categorical variable with three categories only. Of course, the main advantage of criterion scaling is when the variable consists of many categories that would necessitate many coded vectors. There are two additional advantages to the use of criterion scaling. One, when data are missing for subjects on the categorical variable, these subjects are treated as another category. That is, their mean on the dependent variable is used as the score on the criterion-scaled variable. This amounts to using "the information that we have no information on X to assist us in the estimation of Y" (Beaton, 1969b, p. 342). Two, criterion scaling can be used to scale variables that are expressed on an ordinal level. Doing this will accomplish the same results as using a set of coded vectors to represent the ordinal variable. Because researchers try to avoid the proliferation of coded

[7]For an example of the use of totals see Chapter 14.

vectors when they use ordinal variables, they resort to scaling schemes (mostly judgmental) for the assignment of scale values to the different levels of the variable. The authors of the Coleman Report, for example, have resorted to such schemes. In a reanalysis of some of the data of the Coleman Report, Beaton (1969a) has demonstrated that using criterion scaling for the ordinal variables resulted in accounting for larger proportions of variance as compared with the variance accounted for when such variables were assigned scale values on the basis of the researchers' judgments.

Multiple Categorical Variables

Thus far, the discussion of criterion scaling was limited to a single categorical variable. The same approach can be extended to multiple categorical variables. Each variable is criterion scaled separately, thereby leading to a number of criterion-scaled variables equal to the number of categorical variables. The dependent variable is then regressed on the criterion-scaled variables instead of on coded vectors. It should be noted that only when the categorical variables are not correlated (i.e., when the cell frequencies are equal) will this approach yield the same results as the ones in which coded vectors are used to represent the categorical variables. When, on the other hand, the categorical variables are correlated the results from using criterion-scaled variables will be discrepant from those in which coded vectors are used. The degree of the discrepancy cannot be exactly determined, although it generally appears to be small (Beaton, 1969a, 1969b; Gocka, 1973).

Even though the solution with criterion-scaled variables is not exact when the categorical variables are correlated, it may still be a useful or even the only feasible approach when the number of coded vectors required is prohibitively large. It will also be noted that terms representing interactions may also be criterion scaled by using cell means as a criterion-scaled variable, in addition to the criterion-scaled vectors that represent the main effects (see Beaton, 1969a, 1969b).

A situation in which criterion scaling is particularly useful occurs when one wishes to apply a variable-selection procedure (e.g., stepwise regression; see Chapter 6) to a set of categorical variables. Using such a procedure when the variables are represented by coded vectors treats each vector as a separate variable. Consequently, one is almost always bound to obtain results in which parts of variables (i.e., some of the coded vectors representing a variable) in a mixed order are retained. Such results are not only difficult to interpret but may in fact have little or no bearing on the questions posed by the researcher. If, for example, one wishes to make a statement about increments in proportions of variance accounted for by predictors as they are entered successively into the analysis, one is not in a position to do so when vectors representing different variables are entered in a mixed order and only parts of variables are retained in the final analysis.

Examples of stepwise regression analysis applied to independent variables represented by coded vectors occur in the research on college effects of Astin and his associates. Astin and Panos (1969), for example, report a large number of such analyses in which they treated coded vectors as if each represented an independent variable or a distinct predictor. Thus, when predicting persistence in college, 19 out of 90 coded vectors were retained as a result of the application of a stepwise regression analysis. Of the 19 vectors, 5 represent high school grade average (out of 9 categories), 3 are career choices (out of 30 categories), 2 are father's education (out of 6 categories), and so on. Moreover, the vectors that represent fragments of variables were entered in a mixed order. Yet Astin and Panos proceed to report, and test for significance, the increment in the proportion of variance due to each vector as it is entered into the analysis. Needless to say such results are not meaningful.

It should be evident that criterion scaling can be used to avoid the difficulties encountered by the use of coded vectors when variable-selection procedures are used. In fact, one may apply such analyses to what Gocka (1973) refers to as mixed-mode variables—namely, interval as well as categorical or ordinal variables that have been criterion scaled. While the analysis proceeds in the usual manner, it is necessary to adjust the degrees of freedom for the categorical variables, since each is represented in the analysis by one vector, regardless of the number of degrees of freedom associated with it. It is probably preferable to follow Gocka's (1973) suggestion to do the analysis in two stages. First, the variable selection procedure is applied to the criterion-scaled variables (and the interval variables if there are such in the design). Second, having decided which variables are to be retained, on the basis of the results of the first analysis, the categorical variables that have been retained are entered in the form of coded vectors (along with any interval variables that were retained) and the analysis proceeds in the usual manner. The virtue of this two-stage process is that chances are that a relatively small number of variables will be retained as a result of the application of the first stage of the analysis. Consequently, the use of coded vectors to represent the categorical variables in the second stage of the analysis will be feasible.

In conclusion, Beaton's words should be borne in mind: "Criterion scaling does not attempt to produce an absolute scale for a factor but instead to scale the factor with reference to an external criterion" (Beaton, 1969b, p. 343). Therefore, the categories of a variable may be assigned different scale values, and even change in their rank order, when different criterion variables are used in the process of criterion scaling. Examples of criterion scaling applied to data from the Coleman Report may be found in Beaton (1969a) and Mayeske et al. (1969).

SUMMARY

In this chapter the notion of coding categorical independent variables was extended to factorial designs. It was shown that regardless of the coding method used, the basic approach and the overall results are the same. As in the case of one categorical independent variable, the scores on the dependent variable measure are regressed on a set of coded vectors. In factorial designs, however, there are subsets of coded vectors, each subset representing the main effects of a factor, or the interaction between factors.

For the main effects, each independent variable is coded separately as if it were the only variable in the design. For each variable one generates a number of coded vectors equal to the number of categories of the variable minus one. The vectors for the interaction between any two variables, or factors, are obtained by cross multiplying each of the vectors of one factor by each of the vectors of the other factor. Vectors for higher-order interactions are similarly obtained. That is, each of the vectors of one factor is multiplied by each of the vectors of the factors whose higher-order interaction is being considered.

Tests for main effects and interaction can be made either by using the proportions of variance accounted for by each subset of coded vectors, or by using the regression sums of squares attributable to each subset of coded vectors. Multiple comparisons among main effects may take the form of orthogonal, planned nonorthogonal, and post hoc, depending upon the specific hypotheses formulated by the researcher. It was noted, however, that when the interaction is statistically significant, it is more meaningful to perform tests of simple main effects.

Although the three coding methods—effect, orthogonal, and dummy—may be used in factorial designs, effect coding is the most useful and straightforward, and has therefore received the most detailed treatment in the chapter. It was shown how tests of significance among regression coefficients obtained from effect coding may be used to perform any kind of comparison among main effects. In addition, it was shown how these coefficients may be used to obtain the appropriate sums of squares necessary for tests of simple main effects.

Nonorthogonal designs were then discussed in the context of experimental and nonexperimental research. It was argued, among other things, that the concept of interaction be used in the former only. For the latter, it was suggested that the cross-product vectors be referred to as multiplicative, or joint, relations.

The chapter concluded with a presentation of the method of criterion scaling. It was pointed out that this method is particularly useful when it is desired to apply a variable-selection procedure when the independent variables are categorical variables or when they are a mixture of categorical and continuous variables.

STUDY SUGGESTIONS

1. Discuss the advantages of a factorial experiment as compared to single-variable experiments.
2. In a factorial experiment, factors A, B, and C have 3, 3, and 5 categories respectively. Indicate the number of coded vectors necessary to represent each of the main effects, and each of the interaction terms.
3. In an experiment with two factors, A with 3 categories and B with 6 categories, there are 10 subjects per cell or treatment combination. What are the degrees of freedom associated with the F ratios for each of the main effects, and for the interaction?
4. In a factorial design with orthogonal coding, there are three coded vectors, 1, 2, and 3, for factor A. the zero-order correlations between each of these vectors and the dependent variable, Y, are: $r_{y1} = .36$; $r_{y2} = .41$; $r_{y3} = .09$. The total sum of squares, Σy^2, is 436.00.
   (a) What are the β's associated with each of the coded vectors for factor A?
   (b) What is the proportion of variance accounted for by factor A?

(c) What is the regression sum of squares for factor A?
(d) What is the mean square regression for factor A?
(e) What additional information do you need in order to test the main effect of A?

5. In a factorial analysis effect coding was used. Factor B consists of four categories. In the regression equation obtained from the analysis, a (intercept) = 8.5. The three b coefficients associated with the coded vectors for B are: $b_1 = .5$, $b_2 = -1.5$, $b_3 = 2.5$. What are the means of the four levels of factor B?
6. In a factorial analysis with three factors, the following coded vectors were used: 1 and 2 for factor A; 3, 4, and 5 for factor B; 6, 7, and 8 for factor C. There are five subjects per cell. The proportion of variance accounted for by all the factors and their interactions is .37541. The proportion of variance accounted for by factor B is .23452. What is the F ratio for factor B?
7. Using effect coding, analyze the following data obtained from a 2 × 3 factorial experiment:

	B_1	B_2	B_3
	5	4	9
A_1	6	5	10
	7	6	11
	3	7	5
A_2	4	8	6
	5	9	7

(a) What is the proportion of variance accounted for by each of the factors, and by their interaction?
(b) What is the regression sum of squares due to each factor, and their interaction?
(c) What is the mean square residuals?
(d) What is the regression equation?
(e) What are the F ratios for each factor, and for the interaction?
(f) Draw a 2 × 3 table. In the marginals of the table indicate the main effects of A and B. In each cell indicate the interaction term (an example of such a table was given in this chapter, Table 10.7).
(g) Using relevant values from the table under (f), above, and relevant n's, show how the regression sums of squares for A, B, and $A \times B$ may be obtained.
(h) Since the F ratio for the interaction is statistically significant [see (e), above], what type of tests are indicated?
(i) Using relevant values from the table under (f), above, and relevant n's, calculate sums of squares for simple main effects for A and for B. Calculate the F ratios for the simple main effects and display the results in a table, using a format as in Table 10.8.
(j) What should the sum of the sums of squares for the simple main effects for A be equal to?
(k) What should the sum of the sums of squares for the simple main effects for B be equal to?
(l) Show how by using relevant values from the table under (f), above, and the intercept (a) from the regression equation obtained under (d) above, one can calculate the mean of each cell.

8. Discuss the importance of distinguishing between nonorthogonal designs in experimental and nonexperimental research.

ANSWERS

2. $A = 2$; $B = 2$; $C = 4$; $A \times B = 4$; $A \times C = 8$; $B \times C = 8$; $A \times B \times C = 16$
3. F for A: 2 and 162 df; F for B: 5 and 162 df; F for $A \times B$: 10 and 162 df.

4. (a) $\beta_1 = .36$; $\beta_2 = .41$; $\beta_3 = .09$
   (b) .3058
   (c) 133.3288
   (d) 44.44293
   (e) The mean square residual.
5. $\bar{Y}_{B_1} = 9$, $\bar{Y}_{B_2} = 7$, $\bar{Y}_{B_3} = 11$, $\bar{Y}_{B_4} = 7$
6. $F = 24.03$, with 3 and 192 *df*. (*df* for total = 239. *df* for: $A = 2$, $B = 3$, $C = 3$, $AB = 6$, $AC = 6$, $BC = 9$, $ABC = 18$. Therefore, *df* for main effects and interaction are 47. *df* for error: 239 − 47 = 192.)
7. (a) $A = .05455$; $B = .32727$; $A \times B = .47272$
   (b) $A = 4.50$; $B = 27.00$; $A \times B = 39.00$
   (c) $MSR = 1.00$
   (d) $Y' = 6.5 + .5X_1 - 1.5X_2 + 0X_3 + .5X_4 - 2.0X_5$. The following coded vectors were used in obtaining this equation: in X_1, A_1 was assigned 1 and A_2 −1; in X_2, B_1 was assigned 1, B_2 0, and B_3 −1; in X_3, B_1 was assigned 0, B_2 was assigned 1, and B_3 −1. X_4 and X_5 are the products of X_1 and X_2, and X_1 and X_3, respectively.
   (e) $F(1, 12) = 4.50$ for A
   $F(2, 12) = 13.50$ for B
   $F(2, 12) = 19.50$ for $A \times B$

   (f)

	B_1	B_2	B_3	
A_1	$.5 = b_4$	$-2.0 = b_5$	1.5	$.5 = b_1$
A_2	$-.5$	2.0	-1.5	$-.5$
	$-1.5 = b_2$	$0 = b_3$	1.5	

   (g) $ss_A = [(.5)^2 + (-.5)^2]\,(9) = 4.5$
   $ss_B = [(-1.5)^2 + (0)^2 + (1.5)^2]\,(6) = 27.0$
   $ss_{AB} = [(.5)^2 + (-2.0)^2 + (1.5)^2 + (-.5)^2 + (2.0)^2 + (-1.5)^2]\,(3) = 39.0$
   (h) Simple main effects.
   (i) For example, A at $B_1 = (3)[(.5 + .5)^2 + (-.5 + -.5)^2] = 6.0$ Similarly, for the remaining terms. If you encounter difficulties, see text.

Source	*ss*	*df*	*ms*	*F*
A at B_1	6.0	1	6.0	6.0
A at B_2	13.5	1	13.5	13.5
A at B_3	24.0	1	24.0	24.0
B at A_1	42.0	2	21.0	21.0
B at A_2	24.0	2	12.0	12.0
Residual	12.0	12	1.00	

   (j) $ss_A + ss_{AB} = 4.5 + 39.0 = 43.5 = 6.0 + 13.5 + 24.0$
   (k) $ss_B + ss_{AB} = 27.0 + 39.0 = 66.0 = 42.0 + 24.0$
   (l) For example, the mean for cell A_1B_1 is:

$$\underset{a}{6.5} + \underset{A_1}{.5} + \underset{B_1}{(-1.5)} + \underset{A_1B_1}{(.5)} = 6.0$$

   Similarly, for the other cells.

11

TREND ANALYSIS: LINEAR AND CURVILINEAR REGRESSION

In Chapters 9 and 10 it was demonstrated that multiple regression and the analysis of variance yield identical results. We have dealt, however, with categorical independent variables. For different teaching methods, for example, the choice between regression analysis and analysis of variance is quite arbitrary and will probably depend on one's familiarity with the two methods as well as the availability of computer programs and other computing facilities.[1]

As pointed out in Chapter 9, one cannot order objects on a categorical variable. The only operation possible is the assignment of each object to one of a set of mutually exclusive categories. Even though one may assign numbers to the different categories, as is done when creating dummy variables, the numbers are used solely for identification of group or category membership. Needless to say, however, experiments in the behavioral sciences are not limited to categorical variables. In learning experiments, for example, one encounters continuous independent variables such as hours of practice, schedules of reinforcement, hours of deprivation, intensity of electric shock, and the like. In studies over time or practice, one may observe so-called growth trends, which are often referred to as growth curves. For discussions and examples of growth curves in the development of intelligence, see Bayley (1955) and Guilford (1967).

When the independent variable is continuous, the choice between analysis of

[1]The multiple regression approach is preferable since it is more flexible and allows more direct interpretation. What is more important, however, is that under certain circumstances the multiple regression approach is called for even when the independent variables are categorical. This was demonstrated in Chapter 10 for the case of unequal cell frequencies. When one analyzes both categorical and continuous variables, as in analysis of covariance, the multiple regression approach must be used.

variance and regression analysis is not arbitrary. Although either approach may be used, each of them is addressed to a different question. Applying simple analysis of variance, or multiple regression analysis with coded vectors, when the independent variable is continuous amounts to treating it as if it were a categorical variable. In other words, the answer that is being sought is whether or not one may infer that the population means for the different treatment levels are different from each other. Applying regression analysis when the independent variable is continuous, one seeks to answer the question about the nature of the relation between the independent and the dependent variable. For example, one may determine whether the regression of the dependent variable on the independent variable is linear or curvilinear. Moreover, assuming that the regression is curvilinear, it is possible to determine its specific form.

The first section of the chapter is devoted to the study of linear regression and departures therefrom. This is followed by a treatment of curvilinear regression analysis. As in preceding chapters, analyses in experimental research are presented first. These are followed with a presentation of curvilinear analysis in nonexperimental research.

Analysis of Variance with a Continuous Independent Variable

Let us assume that 15 subjects have been randomly assigned to five treatments in a learning experiment with paired associates. The treatments vary so that one group is given one exposure to the list, a second group is given two exposures, and so on to five exposures for the fifth group. The dependent variable measure is the number of correct responses on a subsequent test. In this example the independent variable is continuous: different numbers of exposures to the list.

The data for the five groups, as well as the calculations of the analysis of variance, are presented in Table 11.1. The F ratio of 2.10 with 4 and 10 degrees of freedom is not significant at the .05 level. Consequently, it is concluded that the hypothesis $\mu_1 = \mu_2 = \mu_3 = \mu_4 = \mu_5$ cannot be rejected.[2] In this analysis the continuous independent variable was treated as if it were categorical; that is, as if there were five distinct treatments. We now analyze the data treating the independent variable as continuous.

Linear Regression Analysis of the Learning Experiment

When doing a linear regression analysis, one should first establish that the data follow a linear trend. For linear regression to be applicable, the means of the arrays (or the five treatments in the present case) should fall on the regression line. It is possible, however, that even though the means of the population fall on the regression line, the means of the samples do not fall exactly on it, but

[2]We are not concerned here with the important distinction between statistical significance and meaningfulness, but with the two statistical analyses applied to the same data. It is possible that on the basis of meaningfulness one would conclude that the experiment should be replicated with larger n's in order to increase the power of the test.

Table 11.1 Illustrative Data for a Learning Experiment and Analysis of Variance Calculations

	Number of Exposures					
	1	*2*	*3*	*4*	*5*	
	2	3	3	4	4	
	3	4	4	5	5	
	4	5	5	6	6	
ΣY:	9	12	12	15	15	$\Sigma Y_t = 63$
$\bar{Y}$:	3	4	4	5	5	$(\Sigma Y_t)^2 = 3969$
						$\Sigma Y_t^2 = 283$

$$C = \frac{3969}{15} = 264.60$$

$$\text{Total} = 283 - 264.60 = 18.40$$

$$\text{Between} = \frac{9^2 + 12^2 + 12^2 + 15^2 + 15^2}{3} - 264.60 = 8.40$$

Source	*df*	*ss*	*ms*	*F*
Between	4	8.40	2.10	2.10 (n.s.)
Within	10	10.00	1.00	
Total	14	18.40		

are sufficiently close to describe a linear trend. The question is therefore whether there is a linear trend in the data, or, in other words, whether the deviation from linearity is statistically significant. If it is not statistically significant, linear regression analysis is appropriate. If, on the other hand, the deviation from linearity is statistically significant, one can still do an analysis in which the continuous variable is treated as a categorical variable—that is, an analysis of variance.[3] In what follows, the methods of regression and analysis of variance are applied to the data.

The data presented in Table 11.1 can be displayed for the purpose of regression analysis as in Table 11.2. Following the procedures outlined in Chapter 2 we obtain

$$\Sigma y^2 = \Sigma Y^2 - \frac{(\Sigma Y)^2}{N} = 283 - \frac{(63)^2}{15} = 18.40$$

$$\Sigma x^2 = \Sigma X^2 - \frac{(\Sigma X)^2}{N} = 165 - \frac{(45)^2}{15} = 30.00$$

$$\Sigma xy = \Sigma XY - \frac{(\Sigma X)(\Sigma Y)}{N} = 204 - \frac{(63)(45)}{15} = 15.00$$

$$ss_{\text{reg}} = \frac{(\Sigma xy)^2}{\Sigma x^2} = \frac{(15.00)^2}{30.00} = 7.50$$

[3]The alternative of applying curvilinear regression analysis is dealt with later in the chapter.

Table 11.2 Data from the Learning Experiment, Laid Out for Regression Analysis

X	Y	XY
1	2	2
1	3	3
1	4	4
2	3	6
2	4	8
2	5	10
3	3	9
3	4	12
3	5	15
4	4	16
4	5	20
4	6	24
5	4	20
5	5	25
5	6	30
Σ: 45	63	204
SS: 165	283	

$$b = \frac{\Sigma\, xy}{\Sigma\, x^2} = \frac{15.00}{30.00} = .50$$

$$a = \bar{Y} - b\bar{X} = 4.20 - (.50)(3.00) = 2.70$$

Look back at Table 11.1, in which the between-treatments sum of squares was found to be 8.40. The sum of squares due to deviation from linearity is calculated by subtracting the regression sum of squares from the between-treatments sum of squares.

$$SS_{\text{dev}} = SS_{\text{treat}} - SS_{\text{reg}}$$

$$SS_{\text{dev}} = 8.40 - 7.50 = .90$$

The Meaning of the Deviation Sum of Squares

Before interpreting the results, the meaning of the sum of squares due to deviation from linearity should be explained. This is done with the aid of a figure as well as by direct calculation. In Figure 11.1 the 15 scores of Table 11.2 are plotted. The regression line is drawn following the procedures discussed in Chapter 2 and using the regression equation calculated above. The mean of each of the five arrays is symbolized by a circle. Note that while the circles are close to the regression line, none of them is actually on the line. The vertical distance between the mean of an array and the regression line is the deviation of that mean from linear regression. Since the regression line is expressed by the formula $Y' = 2.7 + .5X$, this equation can be used to calculate the predicted Y's for each of the X's:

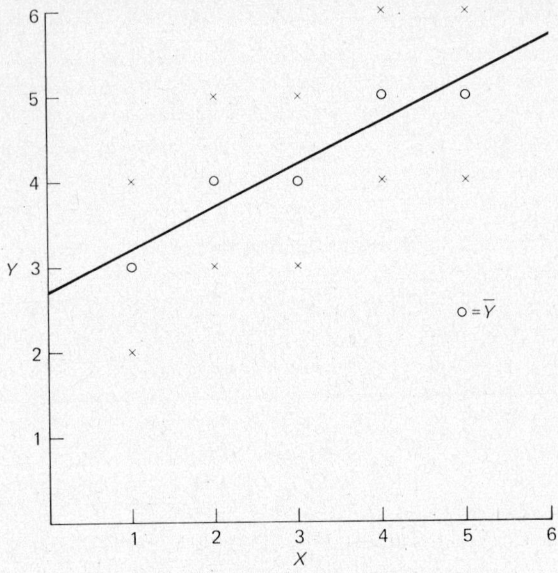

Figure 11.1

$$Y'_1 = 2.7 + .5X_1 = (2.7) + (.5)(1) = 3.2$$

$$Y'_2 = 2.7 + .5X_2 = (2.7) + (.5)(2) = 3.7$$

$$Y'_3 = 2.7 + .5X_3 = (2.7) + (.5)(3) = 4.2$$

$$Y'_4 = 2.7 + .5X_4 = (2.7) + (.5)(4) = 4.7$$

$$Y'_5 = 2.7 + .5X_5 = (2.7) + (.5)(5) = 5.2$$

The five predicted Y's fall on the regression line and it is the deviation of the mean of each from its Y' that describes the deviation from linearity. They are

$$3.00 - 3.2 = -.2$$

$$4.00 - 3.7 = +.3$$

$$4.00 - 4.2 = -.2$$

$$5.00 - 4.7 = +.3$$

$$5.00 - 5.2 = -.2$$

In each case the predicted Y of a given array is subtracted from the mean of the Y's of that array. For example, the predicted Y for the array of X's with the value of 1 is 3.2, while the mean of the Y's of that array is 3.00 [(2 + 3 + 4)/3]. Squaring each deviation listed above, weighting the result by the number of scores in its array, and summing all the values yields the sum of squares due to deviation from regression:

$$(3)(-.2^2) + (3)(+.3^2) + (3)(-.2^2) + (3)(+.3^2) + (3)(-.2^2)$$
$$= .12 + .27 + .12 + .27 + .12 = .90$$

The same value (.90) was obtained by subtracting the regression sum of squares from the treatment sum of squares. When calculating the sum of squares due to deviation from linearity one is asking the question: What is the difference between putting a restriction on the data so that they conform to a linear trend and putting no such restriction on the data? When the between-treatments sum of squares is calculated there is no restriction on the trend of the treatment means. If the means are in fact on a straight line, the between-treatments sum of squares will be equal to the regression sum of squares. With departures from linearity the between-treatments sum of squares will always be larger than the regression sum of squares. What is necessary is a method that enables one to decide when the difference between the two sums of squares is sufficiently small to warrant the use of linear regression analysis.

Test of the Deviation Sum of Squares

The method of testing the significance of deviation from linearity is straightforward. Instead of the one F ratio obtained for the between-treatments sum of squares, two F ratios are obtained—one for the sum of squares due to linear regression and one for the sum of squares due to deviation from linearity. These two sums of squares are components of the between-treatments sum of squares, as shown above. The sum of squares due to linear regression has 1 degree of freedom, while the deviation sum of squares has $g - 2$ degrees of freedom (g = number of treatments). Dividing each sum of squares by its degrees of freedom yields a mean square. Each mean square is divided by the mean square error from the analysis of variance, thus yielding two F ratios. If the F ratio associated with the sum of squares due to deviation from linearity is not significant, one may conclude that the data describe a linear trend, and that the application of linear regression analysis is appropriate. If, on the other hand, the F ratio associated with the sum of squares due to deviation from linearity is significant, a nonlinear trend is indicated. This procedure, as applied to the data from the learning experiments, is summarized in Table 11.3.

Note how the treatments sum of squares is broken down into two components, as are the degrees of freedom associated with the treatments sum of squares. The mean square for deviation from linearity (.30) is divided by the mean square error (1.00) to yield an F ratio of .30, which is not significant. One therefore concludes that the deviation from linearity is not significant, and that linear regression analysis is appropriate. The F ratio associated with the linear

Table 11.3 Analysis of Variance Table: Test for Linearity of Learning Experiment Data

Source	*df*		*ss*		*ms*	*F*
Between Treatments	4		8.40			
Linearity		1		7.50	7.50	7.50
Deviation from Linearity		3		.90	.30	<1
Within Treatments	10		10.00		1.00	
Total	14		18.40			

trend is 7.50. Since it is significant at the .01 level the researcher may conclude that the linear trend is significant. In effect, this means that the regression coefficient (b_{yx}) is significantly different from zero. For each unit increment in the independent variable (number of exposures) there is an expected .50 (b) unit increment in the dependent variable (number of correct responses).

MULTIPLE REGRESSION ANALYSIS OF THE LEARNING EXPERIMENT

The analysis of variance and the regression analysis of the same data were presented in detail in order to show clearly the process and meaning of testing deviation from linearity. It is now demonstrated how the same results may be obtained in the context of multiple regression analysis. The necessary calculations have already been done. The basic approach is displayed in Table 11.4. Look first at the vectors Y and X. These are the same as the Y and X vectors in Table 11.2. Consequently we know (see calculations following Table 11.2) that $\Sigma xy = 15.00; \Sigma x^2 = 30.00; \Sigma y^2 = 18.40$. It is therefore possible to calculate

$$r^2_{xy} = \frac{(15.00)^2}{(30.00)(18.40)} = \frac{225}{552} = .40761$$

The linear regression of Y and X accounts for about 41% of the variance in the Y scores.

Table 11.4 Data from Learning Experiment, Laid Out for Multiple Regression Analysis

Treatment	Y	X	1	2	3	4
	2	1	1	0	0	0
1	3	1	1	0	0	0
	4	1	1	0	0	0
	3	2	0	1	0	0
2	4	2	0	1	0	0
	5	2	0	1	0	0
	3	3	0	0	1	0
3	4	3	0	0	1	0
	5	3	0	0	1	0
	4	4	0	0	0	1
4	5	4	0	0	0	1
	6	4	0	0	0	1
	4	5	0	0	0	0
5	5	5	0	0	0	0
	6	5	0	0	0	0

Suppose, now, it is decided not to restrict the data to a linear regression. In other words, suppose a multiple regression analysis is calculated in which Y is the dependent variable, and group membership in the various treatments levels is the independent variable. It will be recalled from Chapter 9 that any method of coding group membership will yield the same results. Look now at Table 11.4 in which vectors 1 through 4 describe group membership using dummy coding. When these vectors are used, the independent variable is treated as if it were a categorical variable. It is now possible to calculate $R^2_{y.1234}$. It will be recalled that this is equivalent to a one-way analysis of variance, and that $R^2_{y.1234}$ is equal to η^2_{yx}, or the ratio of the between-treatments sum of squares to the total sum of squares (see Chapter 9). The numerical value of $R^2_{y.1234}$ is .45652. When a restriction of linearity was placed on the data, it was found that the proportion of variance accounted for was .40761 (r^2_{yx}). When, on the other hand, no trend restriction was placed on the data, the proportion of variance accounted for by X was .45652 ($R^2_{y.1234}$). It is now possible to test whether the increment in the proportion of variance accounted for is significant when no restriction is placed on the data. In other words, is the deviation from linearity significant? For this purpose, a formula used frequently in earlier chapters is adapted:

$$F = \frac{(R^2_{y.1234} - R^2_{y.x})/(k_1 - k_2)}{(1 - R^2_{y.1234})/(N - k_1 - 1)} \tag{11.1}$$

where $R^2_{y.1234}$ = squared multiple correlation of the dependent variable, Y, and vectors 1 through 4 of Table 11.4; $R^2_{y.x} = r^2_{yx}$ = squared correlation of Y with the X vector of Table 11.4, in which the independent variable is treated as continuous; k_1 = number of vectors associated with the first R^2; k_2 = number of vectors associated with the second R^2; N = number of subjects. The degrees of freedom for the F ratio are $k_1 - k_2$ and $N - k_1 - 1$ for the numerator and the denominator respectively.

Note that $R^2_{y.1234} \geq R^2_{y.x}$. That is, $R^2_{y.1234}$ must be larger than or equal to $R^2_{y.x}$. When the regression of Y on X is exactly linear, that is, when the Y means for all X values are on a straight line, $R^2_{y.1234} = R^2_{y.x}$. When, on the other hand, there is a deviation from linearity $R^2_{y.1234} > R^2_{y.x}$. It is this deviation from linearity that is tested by Formula (11.1). For the data of Table 11.4,

$$F = \frac{(.45652 - .40761)/(4 - 1)}{(1 - .45652)/(15 - 4 - 1)} = \frac{(.04891)/3}{(.54348)/10} = \frac{.01630}{.05435} = .30$$

The F ratio of .30 with 3 and 10 degrees of freedom is the same as that obtained before (see Table 11.3). We conclude, of course, that the deviation from linearity is not significant.

Using Formula (11.1) we test for the significance of the linear trend: F = .40761/.05435 = *7.50*, with 1 and 10 degrees of freedom. The numerator is r^2_{yx} and the denominator is the same as the error term used in calculating the F ratio for the deviation from linearity. The F ratio of 7.50 is the same as the F ratio obtained in Table 11.3 with the same degrees of freedom.

The procedure and calculation of the various sums of squares are illustrated below:

$$\text{Overall regression} = (R^2_{y.1234})(\Sigma y^2) = (.45652)(18.40) = 8.40$$

$R^2_{y.1234}$ indicates the proportion of variance accounted for by the overall regression when no restriction for trend is placed on the data. Σy^2 = total sum of squares of the dependent variable, Y. The sum of squares due to overall regression, 8.40, is equal to the between-treatments sum of squares obtained in the analysis of variance (see Table 11.1).

$$\text{Linear regression} = (r^2_{yx})(\Sigma y^2) = (.40761)(18.40) = 7.50$$

The sum of squares due to deviation from linearity can, of course, be obtained by subtracting the regression sum of squares due to linearity from the overall regression sum of squares. Symbolically the sum of squares due to deviation from linearity is

$$(R^2_{y.1234})(\Sigma y^2) - (r^2_{yx})(\Sigma y^2) = (R^2_{y.1234} - r^2_{yx})(\Sigma y^2)$$

For the present data,

$$\text{Deviation from linearity} = (.45642 - .40761)(18.40) = .90$$

The sum of squares due to error is, as always, $(1 - R^2)(\Sigma y^2)$; that is, the proportion of variance not accounted for multiplied by the total sum of squares. For the present data,

$$\text{Error} = (1 - R^2_{y.1234})(\Sigma y^2) = (1 - .45652)(18.40) = 10.00$$

All the sums of squares obtained above are identical to those obtained in Table 11.3.

CURVILINEAR REGRESSION ANALYSIS

The presentation has been, until now, restricted to linear regression analysis. If the data depart significantly from linearity, one can do a multiple regression analysis in which the continuous variable is treated as a categorical variable. All that such an analysis can tell, however, is whether there is some trend in the data. When it is desired to study the nature of the trend, it is necessary to resort to nonlinear models. Such models may be classified into two categories: (1) intrinsically linear models and (2) intrinsically nonlinear models. An intrinsically linear model is one that is linear in its parameters but nonlinear in the variables. By an appropriate transformation, a model that is nonlinear in the variables may be reduced to a linear model, hence the name intrinsically linear model. Examples of transformations are raising variables to powers (see below), expressing variables as logarithms, or taking square roots of variables. Intrinsically linear models may be analyzed by the method of ordinary least squares. In effect, the nonlinear variables are replaced by their transformations, and the latter are used in a multiple regression analysis.

Intrinsically nonlinear models, on the other hand, are nonlinear in the parameters. The use of ordinary least squares is generally not appropriate for such models. The presentation here is limited to intrinsically linear models. Specifically, only polynomial regression is discussed and illustrated. For other transformations in intrinsically linear models, see Cohen and Cohen (1975, Chapter 6), Draper and Smith (1981, Chapter 5), and Kmenta (1971, pp. 451–460). For good introductions to analyses of intrinsically nonlinear models, see Draper and Smith (1981, Chapter 10), Kmenta (1971, pp. 461–472), and Williams (1959, Chapter 4).

The Polynomial Equation

The method of curvilinear regression analysis is similar to linear regression analysis. The difference between the two approaches is in the regression equation used. Curvilinear regression analysis uses a polynomial regression equation. This means that the independent variable is raised to a certain power. The highest power to which the independent variable is raised indicates the degree of the polynomial. The equation

$$Y' = a + b_1X + b_2X^2$$

is a second-degree polynomial, since X is raised to the second power.

$$Y' = a + b_1X + b_2X^2 + b_3X^3$$

is a third-degree polynomial equation.

The order of the equation indicates the number of bends in the regression curve. A first-degree polynomial, like $Y = a + bX$, describes a straight line. A second-degree polynomial describes a single bend in the regression curve, and is referred to as a quadratic equation. A third-degree polynomial has two bends and is referred to as a cubic equation. The highest order that any given equation may take is equal to $g - 1$, where g is the number of distinct values in the independent variable. If, for example, a continuous independent variable consists of seven distinct values, these values may be raised to the sixth power. When this is done, the regression equation will yield predicted Y's that are equal to the means of the different Y arrays, thus resulting in the smallest possible value for the residual sum of squares. In fact, when the highest-degree polynomial is used with any set of data the resulting R^2 is equal to η^2, since both analyses permit as many bends in the curve as there are degrees of freedom minus one for the between-treatments sum of squares.

One of the goals of scientific research, however, is parsimony. Our interest is not in the predictive power of the highest-degree polynomial equation possible, but rather in the highest-degree polynomial equation necessary to describe a set of data.[4]

Polynomial regression analysis is carried out as an ordinary multiple regression analysis, except that powered vectors are included and the analysis is done *hierarchically*. That is, the analysis is carried out in a series of steps, beginning with the first-degree polynomial and followed by successively higher-degree polynomials. At each step, the proportion of variance of the dependent variable incremented by a higher-degree polynomial is tested for statistical significance.

Suppose, for example, that one has a continuous variable with five distinct values. The increments in the proportion of variance accounted for at each stage are obtained as follows:

Linear: $R^2_{y.x}$

Quadratic: $R^2_{y.x,x^2} - R^2_{y.x}$

Cubic: $R^2_{y.x,x^2,x^3} - R^2_{y.x,x^2}$

Quartic: $R^2_{y.x,x^2,x^3,x^4} - R^2_{y.x,x^2,x^3}$

At each state, the significance of an increment in the proportion of variance accounted is tested with an F ratio. For the quartic element in above example the F ratio is

$$F = \frac{(R^2_{y.x,x^2,x^3,x^4} - R^2_{y.x,x^2,x^3})/(k_1 - k_2)}{(1 - R^2_{y.x,x^2,x^3,x^4})/(N - k_1 - 1)} \tag{11.2}$$

where N = number of subjects; k_1 = degrees of freedom for the larger R^2 (in the present case 4); k_2 = degrees of freedom for the smaller R^2 (in the present case 3). This type of F ratio has been used extensively in this book. Note, however, that the R^2 in the present example is based on one independent variable raised to a certain power, while in the earlier uses of the formula R^2 was based on several independent variables.

Curvilinear Regression: A Numerical Example

Suppose we are interested in the effect of time spent in practice on the performance of a visual discrimination task. Suppose, further, that subjects have been randomly assigned to different levels of practice. After practice, a test of visual discrimination is administered, and the number of correct responses recorded for each subject. We focus attention on the regression of visual discrimination performance on practice time. In the illustrative data of Table 11.5 there are three subjects for each of six levels of practice. Since there are six levels, the highest-degree polynomial possible for these data is the fifth. The aim, however, is to determine the lowest-degree polynomial that best fits the data.

[4]It was demonstrated in the first part of this chapter that a linear equation was sufficient to describe a set of data. Using higher-degree polynomials on such data will not appreciably and significantly enhance the description of the data and the predictions based on regression equations derived from the data.

Table 11.5 Illustrative Data from a Study of Visual Discrimination[a]

	Practice Time (in Minutes)					
	2	4	6	8	10	12
	4	7	13	16	18	19
	6	10	14	17	19	20
	5	10	15	21	20	21
Σ:	15	27	42	54	57	60
$\bar{Y}$:	5	9	14	18	19	20

[a]The dependent variable measure is the number of correct responses.

In Table 11.6 the data are displayed in the form in which they were used for computer analysis with the REGRESSION program of SPSS. The first and last values of X raised successively to higher powers are listed for illustrative purposes only. Only the vectors for Y and X were read as input. The remaining vectors were generated by COMPUTE statements. Thus, X^2 was generated as follows:

```
COMPUTE        X2 = X**2
```

X^3 was generated by

```
COMPUTE        X3 = X**3
```

and similarly for the other vectors.

Table 11.6 Illustrative Data from Visual Discrimination Study Laid Out for Curvilinear Regression

Y	X	X^2	X^3	X^4	X^5
4	2	4	8	16	32
6	2	.	.	.	.
5	2	.	.	.	.
7	4	.	.	.	.
10	4	.	.	.	.
10	4	.	.	.	.
13	6	.	.	.	.
14	6	.	.	.	.
15	6	.	.	.	.
16	8	.	.	.	.
17	8	.	.	.	.
21	8	.	.	.	.
18	10	.	.	.	.
19	10	.	.	.	.
20	10	.	.	.	.
19	12	.	.	.	.
20	12	.	.	.	.
21	12	144	1728	20736	248832

NOTE: Y = visual discrimination, X = practice time in minutes.

The control cards are not given here because they have been shown several times earlier (see, in particular, Chapter 4). Instead, only the regression card used in the analysis is given. Beginning in column 16:

```
REGRESSION = Y WITH X(10)X2(8)X3(6)X4(4)X5(2)/
```

Note that by using the inclusion numbers in the parentheses a hierarchical regression analysis is called for, beginning with the first-order polynomial and entering at each step a higher-order polynomial.

Following are excerpts from the computer output, along with commentaries.

Output

STEP	VARIABLE ENTERED	R SQUARE	R SQUARE CHANGE	SUM OF SQUARES
1	X (Linear)	.88324	.88324	509.18571
2	X2 (Quadratic)	.94277	.05953	543.50714
3	X3 (Cubic)	.94627	.00350	545.52381
4	X4 (Quartic)	.95091	.00464	548.20238
5	X5 (Quintic)	.95143	.00052	548.50000
	RESIDUAL			28.00000

STEP	VARIABLE ENTERED	SUM OF SQUARES CHANGE	DF	MEAN SQUARE	F
1	X (Linear)	509.18571	1	509.18571	218.22
2	X2 (Quadratic)	34.32143	1	34.32143	14.71
3	X3 (Cubic)	2.01667	1	2.01667	<1
4	X4 (Quartic)	2.67857	1	2.67857	1.15
5	X5 (Quintic)	.29762	1	.29762	<1
	RESIDUAL		12	2.33333	

Commentary

Before discussing the results, some comments will be made about the organization of the output reported above. To conserve space, and for convenience of reference, the information was organized in a format that differs from the one reported in the computer output. Some of the information reported above is not given in the computer output but has been calculated (see below).

The first four columns were obtained from the SUMMARY TABLE reported in the computer output. The SUMS OF SQUARES were obtained from the successive steps of the analysis. Thus, 509.18571 is the REGRESSION sum of squares reported at the first step (i.e., for the linear component), 543.50714 is the REGRESSION sum of squares reported at the second step (i.e., for the linear and the quadratic components), and similarly for the remaining terms. The elements in the column labeled SUM OF SQUARES therefore parallel those reported under R SQUARE, except that the latter indicate the proportions of variance accounted for, whereas the former provide the same information but expressed in terms of sums of squares. One is, of course, obtainable from the other. For example, for STEP 1: (R SQUARE)(Σy^2) = (.88324)(576.50) = 509.18786, which is (within rounding) the same as the SUM OF SQUARES reported at STEP 1.

SUM OF SQUARES CHANGE is *not* reported in the output but was obtained by subtracting successively each element in the column labeled SUM OF SQUARES from the element that succeeds it in the same column. For example, 543.50714 − 509.18571 = 34.32143. The elements in the column labeled SUM OF SQUARES CHANGE thus parallel those in the column labeled R SQUARE CHANGE.

As is indicated in the column labeled DF, each degree of the polynomial has 1 *df*. Consequently, the MEAN SQUARE for each term is equal to the SUM OF SQUARES associated with it. The information contained in the last line (RESIDUAL) was obtained from STEP 5 of the computer output.

We are ready now to discuss the results. Turning first to R SQUARE it will be noted that $R^2_{y.x,x^2,x^3,x^4,x^5} = .95143$. This means, of course, that 95% of the variance in the dependent variable is accounted for by the fifth-degree polynomial of the independent variable. This R^2 is tested in the usual manner:

$$F = \frac{.95143/5}{(1 - .95143)/(18 - 5 - 1)} = 47.01$$

with 5 and 12 *df*, $p < .01$.

Or, using the SUM OF SQUARES reported at STEP 5 and the MEAN SQUARE RESIDUAL, reported in the last line:

$$F = \frac{548.50/5}{2.33333} = 47.01$$

This is the overall F ratio that is reported in the computer output for the last step (in the present case STEP 5) of the analysis. The same F ratio will be obtained if the data are subjected to a one-way analysis of variance. Testing the highest-degree polynomial possible in a set of data is tantamount to a test of whether the means of the arrays are equal, which is equivalent to testing whether the means of the treatments differ from each other when a one-way analysis of variance is applied.[5] In fact, η^2 is equal to R^2 of the highest-degree polynomial possible—that is, .95143.

At this stage, all we know is that there is a significant trend in the data. In order to see what degree polynomial best fits these data it is necessary to turn attention to the hierarchical analysis in which the increments due to each degree of the polynomial are tested successively. The F ratios for these tests are reported above in the last column under Output. Note that with output like the one obtained from SPSS the simplest approach to the testing of the increment due to each degree of the polynomial is to calculate the SUM OF SQUARES CHANGE as described above. Since each such increment is associated with 1

[5]For further discussion of this point, see Li (1964, Vol. II, pp. 171–174).

df, it is also the mean square of the numerator of F ratio. The denominator for the F ratios is the MEAN SQUARE RESIDUAL reported at the last step of the analysis. In the present case, it is 2.33333 with 12 *df*.

Looking now at the F ratios reported above it is noted that only the ones for the linear and the quadratic terms are statistically significant. It is therefore concluded that the regression of Y on X is quadratic. The same F ratios could, of course, be obtained by testing the increments in R^2 in the usual manner. In the present case, the linear component accounts for about 88% of the variance of Y. The increment due to the quadratic component is about 6%. Note that the remaining terms add very little to the accounting of the variance of Y (see R SQUARE CHANGE under Output, above).

The Regression Equation

We turn now to a discussion of the regression equation obtained in polynomial regression analysis. For this purpose, two regression equations will be reported and commented upon: one for the fifth-degree and one for the second-degree polynomial.

Output

VARIABLE	B	STD ERROR B	F
X	5.12500	27.88806	.033
X2	−1.71875	10.17245	.028
X3	.40104	1.67769	.057
X4	−.03906	.12775	.093
X5	.00130	.00365	.128
(CONSTANT)	−1.00000		

VARIABLE	B	STD ERROR B	F
X	3.49464	.50105	48.646
X2	−.13839	.03503	15.604
(CONSTANT)	−1.90000		

Commentary

Look first at the equation for the fifth-degree polynomial and note that none of the b's is statistically significant (all the F ratios are < 1). Recall that these are partial regression coefficients, also that a test of a partial regression coefficient is equivalent to a test of the proportion of variance incremented by the variable with which it is associated, when the variable is entered last into the analysis. In other words, it is equivalent to a test of the squared semipartial correlation of the dependent variable with a given vector when all the other vectors are partialed out from it (see Chapters 5 and 8 for discussions of these points). For example, the test of the b associated with the linear component (X of Table 11.6) is equivalent to a test of:

$$r^2_{y(x.x^2,x^3,x^4,x^5)} = R^2_{y.x,x^2,x^3,x^4,x^5} - R^2_{y.x^2,x^3,x^4,x^5}$$

Now, powered vectors tend to be highly intercorrelated. For the present data, correlations between vectors range from .85744 (between X and X^5) to .99606 (between X^4 and X^5). In view of the high multicollinearity in these data one would not expect any of the vectors to have a meaningful squared semipartial correlation with the dependent variable. Note also the relatively large standard errors of the b's (see Output, above), which are due to the high multicollinearity in the present data (see Chapter 8). It is therefore not surprising that none of the b's is statistically significant.

An analysis in which the b's are tested as above is referred to as a simultaneous analysis. But in the preceding section it was said that tests of significance in polynomial regression analysis should proceed hierarchically, beginning with the linear component. It therefore follows that only the test of the b for the highest-degree polynomial is relevant in polynomial regression analysis. In the present example, the test of the b associated with the fifth-degree term is the same as the test of the increment in the proportion of variance due to the quintic term, over and above the lower-order terms (compare with the output reported earlier). The tests of the remaining b's are irrelevant because they go counter to the requirement of the hierarchical testing.

What is necessary is to determine the degree of the polynomial that fits the data following the procedures outlined in the preceding section (i.e., doing the tests hierarchically) and then to recalculate the regression equation with the terms that have been retained. In the present example it was found that none of the terms beyond the quadratic added significantly to the proportion of variance of Y accounted for. Therefore, it is necessary to calculate the regression equation of Y on X and X^2 only. Using a computer program that enables one to enter vectors hierarchically (e.g., SPSS; see REGRESSION statement above), what is necessary is to take the regression equation reported at the step that corresponds to the degree of the polynomial to be retained. In the present example, it is the equation reported at STEP 2 (see Output above).

When the regression is calculated only with the terms that are to be retained (linear and quadratic, in the present example), higher-order polynomials are relegated to the error term. In fact, whenever higher-order polynomials are not statistically significant, their sums of squares may be pooled with the residual sum of squares. This generally results in a smaller mean square error term for testing the components retained in the equation, because the relatively small increase in the residual sum of squares is offset by the increase in the degrees of freedom for the residual sum of squares. For the present data, the pooled residual sum of squares is 32.99286 (28.000 + 2.01667 + 2.67857 + .29762; see Output in the preceding section), with 15 degrees of freedom. The residual mean square is therefore 2.19952, compared with 2.33333 in the analysis with the fifth-degree polynomial (see Output in preceding section). The SUM OF

SQUARES CHANGE for the Quadratic component was shown earlier to be 34.32143. Therefore the F ratio for this component is 34.32143/2.19952 = 15.604, with 1 and 15 *df*. Compare with the F ratio for the same component obtained in the analysis with the fifth-degree polynomial (14.71 with 1 and 12 *df;* see Output in the preceding section).[6] Note that the F ratio for the b associated with X^2 in the quadratic equation is the same as the one obtained here (15.604). This demonstrates what was said above—namely, that of the F ratios for the b's the only meaningful one is the F ratio associated with the b for the highest-degree polynomial in the equation, which in the present case is X^2. To reiterate, the F ratio for the b associated with X in the quadratic equation is not meaningful because it tests the increment of the linear component over and above the quadratic component. This is not the test we want. To test the linear component divide the sum of squares due to the linear component by the mean square residual. For the present data the sum of squares due to the linear component is 509.18571 (see Output in the preceding section). The mean square residual in the quadratic equation was calculated above to be 2.19952. Therefore the F ratio for the linear trend in the quadratic equation is 509.18571/2.19952 = 231.50, with 1 and 15 *df*. Compare this F ratio with the one obtained for the b associated with the X vector in the quadratic equation (48.646 with 1 and 15 *df;* see Output above).

In sum, when a polynomial regression analysis is performed, the tests of the trend components are done hierarchically. Once the highest-degree polynomial that fits the data has been determined, the regression equation is calculated with the terms that are to be retained. Only the test of the b associated with the highest-degree polynomial in the equation is meaningful. Therefore, even when F ratios for b's of lower-order polynomials are not significant, the vectors associated with such b's should *not* be deleted. In other words, all the vectors up to and including the highest-degree polynomial that has been determined to best fit the data are retained.

Having the regression equation one can, of course, calculate predicted scores. For the present data,

$$Y' = -1.90000 + 3.49464X - .13839X^2$$

For subjects practicing for 2 minutes,

$$Y' = -1.90000 + (3.49464)(2) + (-.13839)(4) = \mathit{4.54}$$

That is, for subjects practicing for 2 minutes, the prediction is 4.54 correct responses on the visual discrimination test. For subjects practicing 8 minutes,

$$Y' = -1.90000 + (3.49464)(8) + (-.13839)(64) = \mathit{17.20}$$

It is also possible to use the regression equation to predict performance on the dependent variable for values not used originally in the study, as long as

[6]For a detailed discussion of different models for the error term in polynomial regression, see Cohen and Cohen (1975, pp. 234–236).

such values are within the range of those originally used. In other words, interpolation is generally acceptable. If one wanted, for example, to make a prediction for 5 minutes of practice (a condition not used in the experiment):

$$Y' = -1.90000 + (3.49464)(5) + (-.13839)(25) = \mathit{12.11}$$

For 5 minutes of practice, the prediction is a score of 12.11 on the visual discrimination test. The same procedure may be applied to other intermediate values.

Extrapolation, on the other hand, is dangerous, and should be avoided. In other words, one should *not* engage in predictions for values of the independent variable that are outside the range used in the study. To indicate the potential danger of extrapolation, the scores of the present example are plotted in Figure 11.2. The circles indicate the means of the arrays. Note that for the values 2, 4, 6, and 8 of the independent variable the trend is virtually linear. Had only these value been used in the study, one might have been led to believe that the trend is generally linear. As can be seen from Figure 11.2, and as has been concluded on the basis of the analysis of these data, the curve is quadratic. There is no way of telling what the shape of the curve would be if one were to increase practice time beyond 12 minutes (the maximum time in the present experiment). If one is interested in the effects of values outside the range of those under consideration, they should be included in the study or in a subsequent study.

Some comments about the interpretation of the b's are now in order. Generally, the b's do not lend themselves to easy interpretation. Following are some of the reasons. First, in polynomial regression a variable is represented by more than one vector. Therefore the usual interpretation of a b as the expected change in Y associated with a unit change in the variable under consideration while holding the other variables constant does not make sense in polynomial regression. In the present example, it makes little sense to interpret the b associated with X^2 as the effect of this "variable" while holding X constant, because when the latter does not vary the former cannot vary either. Stated differently, visual discrimination (the dependent variable in the present exam-

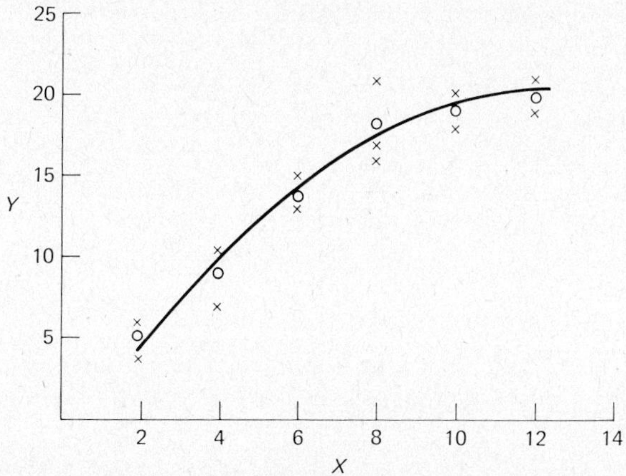

Figure 11.2

ple) does not depend on practice time and on practice time squared as if these were distinct variables. Instead, what the analysis indicates is that the regression of visual discrimination on practice time is quadratic.

Second, the relative magnitudes of the b's in polynomial regression cannot be compared because the variances of higher-order terms generally become increasingly larger, thereby leading to increasingly smaller b's. In the present example, $s_x^2 = 12.35$; $s_{x^2}^2 = 2526.59$; $s_{x^3}^2 = 392555.25$, and increasingly larger variances for higher-order terms.

Third, when X is subjected to a linear transformation not only do the variances of the vectors representing the different components of the polynomial change, but the correlations among these vectors also change. For example, the correlation between X and X^2 may be changed at will by an appropriate transformation of X. For the present data, $r_{x,x^2} = .97892$. Suppose, that instead of using X, one were to use deviations from the mean of X (i.e., $(X - \bar{X})$ and $(X - \bar{X})^2$). In other words, a constant (in the present case, $\bar{X}$) is subtracted from X prior to the squaring operation. The variance of X will, of course, not change as a result of the above transformation, but the variance of $(X - \bar{X})^2$ will change (105.41, as compared with 2526.59, which is the variance of X^2). Moreover, the correlation between $(X - \bar{X})$ and $(X - \bar{X})^2$ will be zero, as compared with .97892 (the correlation between X and X^2). Incidentally, whenever the X's are distributed symmetrically around the mean of X (as is the case in the present example), the correlation between $(X - \bar{X})$ and $(X - \bar{X})^2$ is zero.

As a result of the above changes due the transformation of X, the regression equation for the transformed X differs from the one obtained prior to the transformation. It was shown above that

$$Y' = -1.90000 + 3.49464X - .13839X^2$$

When $(X - \bar{X})$ is used,

$$Y' = 15.78125 + 1.55714(X - \bar{X}) - .13839(X - \bar{X})^2$$

Note that the b for the linear component in the second equation is less than half the size of the b for the linear component in the first equation. The b for the quadratic term, on the other hand, is identical in both equations.[7]

The foregoing should suffice to illustrate the problems that arise when one attempts to interpret b's in a polynomial regression as if they were associated with distinct variables. For an approach to the interpretation of the b's in polynomial regression in terms of partial derivatives, see Stimson, Carmines, and Zeller (1978) and Stolzenberg (1979).

Finally, it is important to note that despite the transformation of X and despite the effect it has on the correlations among the powered vectors, the hierarchical regression analysis is invariant. That is, the proportions of variance accounted for by successive introduction of higher-order polynomials are not affected by the linear transformation of X. Therefore, the conclusion about

[7]For further details of the effects of linear transformations of X on the regression equation and other regression statistics see Allison (1977) and Cohen (1978).

the nature of the regression of Y on X will be identical regardless of the linear transformation of X (see Cohen, 1978, for further details).

Yet it may be useful to transform X in order to reduce the high multicollinearity that generally exists among powered vectors. It was shown earlier that in the present data the correlations run as high as .99606. With high multicollinearity, inaccuracies due to rounding may be introduced even when the analysis is done by a computer (see Longley, 1967, for a detailed discussion and examples). The most common linear transformations of X are subtraction of the mean, or standardization (i.e., conversion to z scores). For detailed discussions of transformations for the purpose of reducing multicollinearity see Bradley and Srivastava (1979) and Smith and Sasaki (1979). A special kind of transformation of X is the use of orthogonal polynomials, to which we now turn.

CURVILINEAR REGRESSION ANALYSIS AND ORTHOGONAL POLYNOMIALS

Curvilinear regression analysis may be done by using a set of orthogonal vectors coded to reflect the various degrees of the polynomials. The coefficients in such vectors are called *orthogonal polynomials*. The calculations involved in curvilinear regression analysis are considerably reduced when orthogonal polynomials are used instead of the original values of the continuous independent variable. The underlying principle of orthogonal polynominals is basically the same as that discussed with the orthogonal coefficients coding method (see Chapter 9). Orthogonal coefficients were constructed to contrast groups, whereas now the orthogonal coefficients are constructed to describe the different degrees of the polynomials.

When the levels of the continuous independent variable are equally spaced, and there is an equal number of subjects at each level, the construction of orthogonal polynomials is simple (see, for example, Myers, 1979, pp. 441–443). Rather than constructing them, however, the necessary coefficients may be found in tables of orthogonal polynomials, such as the one given in Appendix B. More extensive tables can be found in Fisher and Yates (1963). The magnitude of the difference between the levels is immaterial as long as it is equal between all levels. In other words, it makes no difference whether one is dealing with levels such as 2, 4, 6, and 8, or 5, 10, 15, and 20, or 7, 14, 21, and 28, or any other set of levels. The orthogonal polynomial coefficients obtained from the tables apply equally to any set, provided they are equally spaced and there is an equal number of subjects at each level. Since the experimenter is interested in studying a trend, the levels of the continuous independent variable can be equally spaced, and an equal number of subjects can be assigned randomly to each level.

It is possible, though somewhat complicated, to construct orthogonal polynomial coefficients for continuous variables that are not equally spaced, or when the number of subjects at each level are not equal. For a treatment of this subject see Myers (1979) and Kirk (1968). Tabled coefficients of orthogonal polynomials may be used when n's are unequal. Under such circumstances, the coded vectors will not be orthogonal, but the hierarchical regression analysis with such vectors will yield the same results as the ones obtained from an analysis with powered vectors. Coefficients of orthogonal polynomials may also be adapted for the case of an unequally spaced variable. For details, see Cohen and Cohen (1975, p. 238).

Analysis of Visual Discrimination Data

To illustrate the method, the illustrative data of the visual discrimination experiment are now reanalyzed using orthogonal polynomials. These data and a set of orthogonal vectors, whose coefficients were obtained from Appendix B are given in Table 11.7. Note that the sum of the coefficients in each vector is zero, as is the sum of the cross products of any two vectors. These conditions, recall, are necessary to satisfy orthogonality. Look now at the pattern of the signs of the coefficients in each column. In column 1, Table 11.7, the signs change once from −5 to +5. In column 2, the signs change twice from +5 to +5. In column 3 they change three times from −5 to +5. These changes in signs correspond to the degree of the polynomial. Vector 1 has one sign change; it describes the linear trend. Vector 2 has two sign changes; it describes the quadratic trend. The other vectors are handled similarly.

Following are excerpts of computer output for the analysis of the data of Table 11.7, as obtained from SPSS.

Table 11.7 Illustrative Data from Visual Discrimination Study, Laid Out for Analysis with Orthogonal Polynomials

	Y	1	2	3	4	5
	4	−5	5	−5	1	−1
	6	−5	5	−5	1	−1
	5	−5	5	−5	1	−1
	7	−3	−1	7	−3	5
	10	−3	−1	7	−3	5
	10	−3	−1	7	−3	5
	13	−1	−4	4	2	−10
	14	−1	−4	4	2	−10
	15	−1	−4	4	2	−10
	16	1	−4	−4	2	10
	17	1	−4	−4	2	10
	21	1	−4	−4	2	10
	18	3	−1	−7	−3	−5
	19	3	−1	−7	−3	−5
	20	3	−1	−7	−3	−5
	19	5	5	5	1	1
	20	5	5	5	1	1
	21	5	5	5	1	1
M:	14.16667	0	0	0	0	0
s:	5.82338	3.51468	3.85013	5.63602	2.22288	6.66863

Output

VARIABLE	R SQUARE	R SQUARE CHANGE	SIMPLE R	B	F
LINEAR	.88324	.88324	.93981	1.55714	218.22
QUAD	.94277	.05953	−.24400	−.36905	14.71
CUBIC	.94627	.00350	−.05914	−.06111	.86
QUART	.95091	.00465	.06816	.17857	1.15
QUINT	.95143	.00052	.02272	.01984	.13
			(CONSTANT)	14.16667	

Commentary

As was done in preceding sections, the output was organized in a format that differs from the one used by SPSS. The columns labeled R SQUARE, R SQUARE CHANGE, and SIMPLE R were obtained from the SUMMARY TABLE of SPSS. The columns labeled B and F were obtained from the last step of the analysis—that is, the step in which all the coded vectors of Table 11.7 were included.

The first thing to be noted is that $R^2_{y.12345} = .95143$, which is the same as the value obtained earlier when powered vectors of X were used. Note also that the column R SQUARE CHANGE is identical to the one obtained in the earlier analysis. In the present analysis, however, since the coded vectors are orthogonal, the proportion of variance accounted for by each vector is equal to the squared zero-order correlation of a given vector with the dependent variable. Look at the output and note that the squared SIMPLE R for a given row is equal to R SQUARE CHANGE for the same row. For example, $.93981^2 = .88324$ (for Linear); $-.24400^2 = .05953$ (for Quadratic). Similarly, for the remaining terms. R^2 is, of course, equal to the sum of the squared zero-order correlations of the coded vectors with the dependent variable.

Recall that when the coded vectors are orthogonal to each other each F (or t) ratio associated with a given b weight is independently interpretable (see Chapter 9). Look at the output and note that the F ratios associated with the b's are the same as those obtained earlier in the hierarchical analysis of the same data. Recall that in the analysis with powered vectors of X the tests of the b's were irrelevant. In the present analysis, however, the tests of the b's amount to tests of the separate trend components and are obtainable directly from the output, whereas in the previous analysis additional calculations were necessary to obtain the F ratios. As always, each F ratio has 1 *df* for the numerator and $N - k - 1$ *df* for the denominator (i.e., the *df* associated with the residual sum of squares). In the present example: $N - k - 1 = 18 - 5 - 1 = 12$.

The results of the analysis are not interpreted further here because the interpretation is identical to the one given earlier when the same data were analyzed with powered vectors of X. Instead, we turn to a discussion of the regression equation with orthogonal polynomials.

The Regression Equation

In the previous analysis it was noted that in order to obtain a regression equation that includes only the significant components of the trend, one has to reanalyze the data with the number of terms to be included in the regression equation. This was necessary because b weights change when the variables that are deleted are correlated with those remaining in the equation. In the case of orthogonal vectors, however, the b weights do not change when vectors are deleted. Furthermore, the intercept, a, is also not affected by deletion of vectors—when the vectors are orthogonal. Now,

$$a = \bar{Y} - b_i \bar{X}_i \qquad (11.3)$$

Since each orthogonal vector has, by definition, a mean of zero, a will always be equal to the mean of the dependent variable. In the present case the mean of Y is 14.66667 (see Table 11.7), and this is the value of the intercept, a. It is clear, therefore, that each dependent variable score is expressed as a composite of the mean of the dependent variable and the contribution of those components of the trend that are included in the regression equation.

To obtain the regression equation for any degree of the polynomial it is sufficient to read from the output the appropriate b weights. The quadratic equation for the present data is therefore

$$Y' = 14.16667 + 1.55714X_1 - .36905X_2$$

Note that in the equation X_1 and X_2 are used to represent vectors 1 and 2 of Table 11.7. When using the regression equation for the purpose of prediction, the values inserted in it are the coded values that correspond to a given level and a given degree of the polynomial. For example, subjects who practiced for 2 minutes were assigned a -5 in the first vector (linear), and a $+5$ in the second vector (quadratic). For such subjects one would therefore predict

$$Y' = 14.16667 + 1.55714(-5) + (-.36905)(5) = 4.54$$

For subjects practicing for 8 minutes,

$$Y' = 14.16667 + 1.55714(1) + (-.36905)(-4) = 17.20$$

The same predicted values were obtained in the earlier calculations, when the original values of the independent values were inserted in the regression equation.

In sum, then, when coding is not used, the regression equation needs to be recalculated with the degree of polynomial desired. The values inserted in such an equation are those of the original variable. When orthogonal polynomials are used, on the other hand, one can obtain the regression equation at any degree desired without further calculation. The values inserted in the regression equation thus obtained are the coefficients that correspond to a given level and a given degree of the polynomial.

Calculation without a Computer

It should be evident that when using orthogonal polynomials it is fairly easy to do a curvilinear regression analysis even when a computer is not available. Simply calculate the zero-order correlation of the coded vectors with the dependent variable, the mean of the dependent variable, and the standard deviations of the dependent variable and the coded vectors. Each squared zero-order correlation indicates the proportion of variance accounted for by a given component. R^2 is, as indicated earlier, the sum of the squared zero-order correlations. The b weights can be easily obtained by using the formula

$$b = r_{xy} \frac{s_y}{s_x} \tag{11.4}$$

For example, the b weight for the linear trend

$$b_{\text{lin}} = .93981 \frac{5.82338}{3.51468} = 1.55714$$

is the same value that was obtained above and reported in the Output above. The intercept is, as indicated in the previous section, equal to the mean of the dependent variable.

Factorial Designs

The use of orthogonal polynomials can be extended to designs with more than one continuous independent variable or to designs in which continuous and categorial independent variables are used. When the independent variables are continuous, code each variable with orthogonal polynomial coefficients as if it is the only one in the design. Generate cross-product vectors by multiplying, in turn, the vectors of one variable by those of the other. The cross-product vectors represent the interaction. The approach is similar when the design includes continuous and categorical independent variables. The latter are coded in the usual manner (see Chapters 9 and 10), and the former are coded by orthogonal polynomial coefficients. Again, cross products of the vectors of variables represent the interactions. An example of such an analysis is given in Chapter 12.

Examples of trend analysis in factorial designs are given in Kirk (1968, pp. 189–198), Myers (1979, pp. 445–456), and Winer (1971, pp. 388–391 and 478–484), as well as in other texts. It is suggested that you use a multiple regression program to analyze some of the numerical examples given in these, or other, texts. A comparison of the results you obtain with those reported in the text, and a careful study of the discussion of the results, will enhance your understanding of such designs.

CURVILINEAR REGRESSION IN NONEXPERIMENTAL RESEARCH

The discussion and numerical examples presented thus far dealt with data obtained in experimental research. The method of studying trends, however, is equally applicable to data obtained in nonexperimental research. When, for example, a researcher studies the regression of one attribute variable on another, it is imperative that the trend of the regression be determined. Using linear regression analysis only can lead to erroneous conclusions. A researcher may, for example, conclude on the basis of linear regression analysis that the regression of variable Y on X is weak, or even nonexistent, when in fact it is strong but curvilinear.

In what he refers to as a "light-hearted" example, Eysenck (1965) reasons that the study of curvilinear relations may help resolve the contradiction between "two hypotheses which are held equally strong by popular imagination. One says that 'absence makes the heart grow fonder'. . . . Exactly the opposite is postulated by those who believe 'out of sight out of mind' " (p. 11). Eysenck maintains that both may be right, and that the regression of fondness on length of absence may be curvilinear. According to this conception, fondness increases with increments in length of absence up to an optimal point beyond which fondness decreases with increments in length of absence.

It should also be recognized that a relatively high r^2 does not constitute evidence that the regression is linear. In a very instructive paper, Anscombe (1973) demonstrates how several sets of fictitious data which differ widely with respect to the type of relation between X and Y yield identical r^2's and identical regression equations when Y is regressed on X. Although Anscombe does not calculate curvilinear regression for his data (the purpose of his paper was to demonstrate the importance of graphing data) it will be noted that for one set of his data (y_2 and x_1, Table, p. 19) $r^2_{yx} = .67$, but $R^2_{y.x,x^2} = 1.00$![8]

A Numerical Example

A researcher was interested in studying the regression of satisfaction with a given job on mental ability. An intelligence test was administered to a random sample of 40 employees. In addition, each employee was asked to rate his or her satisfaction with the job, using a 10-point scale, 1 indicating very little satisfaction, 10 indicating a great deal of satisfaction. The data (illustrative) are presented in Table 11.8, where Y is job satisfaction and X is intelligence.

In the examples presented earlier in the chapter, there were several distinct values of the independent variable. Moreover, the researcher was able to select values that were equally spaced with an equal number of subjects at each level.

[8]Other aspects of Anscombe's (1973) paper are also very important and merit careful study.

Table 11.8 Illustrative Data for Intelligence and Job Satisfaction, $N = 40$

Y	X	X^2	X^3	Y	X	X^2	X^3
2	90	8100	729000	9	104	10816	1124864
2	90	•	•	10	105	•	•
3	91	•	•	10	105	•	•
4	92	•	•	9	107	•	•
4	93	•	•	9	107	•	•
5	94	•	•	10	110	•	•
5	94	•	•	9	110	•	•
6	95	•	•	8	112	•	•
5	96	•	•	9	112	•	•
6	96	•	•	10	115	•	•
5	97	•	•	8	117	•	•
5	98	•	•	8	118	•	•
6	98	•	•	7	120	•	•
7	100	•	•	7	120	•	•
6	100	•	•	7	121	•	•
7	102	•	•	6	124	•	•
8	102	•	•	6	124	•	•
9	103	•	•	6	125	•	•
9	103	•	•	5	127	•	•
10	104	10816	1124864	5	127	16129	2048383

NOTE: Y = job satisfaction; X = intelligence.

Consequently, the study of trends was simplified by the use of orthogonal polynomials. The researcher could fit the highest-degree polynomial possible or go to any desired level. In nonexperimental research, however, attribute variables may have many distinct values, unequally spaced,[9] with unequal numbers of subjects at each level. The procedure, therefore, is to raise the independent variable successively to higher powers, to calculate at each stage the squared multiple correlation of Y with the independent variable raised to a given power, and to test at each stage whether a higher-degree polynomial adds significantly to the proportion of variance accounted for in Y. This procedure is now applied to the illustrative data of Table 11.8. Note that the first and last values of X^2 and X^3 in each column are given for illustrative purposes. Only vectors Y and X are necessary. The remaining vectors are generated by the computer program.

Following are excerpts of SPSS output for the analysis of the data of Table 11.8. A hierarchical regression was called for, entering X, X^2, X^3, and X^4 in this order.

[9]"Unequally spaced" does not mean that the measure used is not an interval scale, but rather that not all values within a given range are observed in a given sample. Consequently, the observed values are not equally spaced. Trend analysis relies heavily on the assumption that the independent variable measures form an interval scale. When one knows, or even suspects, serious departures from this assumption, it is advisable not to do a trend analysis. At the least, extra caution must be used with the interpretation of the data.

Output

DEPENDENT VARIABLE Y R SQUARE .13350

ANALYSIS OF VARIANCE

	DF	SUM OF SQUARES	MEAN SQUARE	F
REGRESSION	1	25.95249	25.95249	5.85
RESIDUAL	38	168.44751	4.43283	

Commentary

These are the results of the linear regression of Y on X: $r^2_{yx} = R^2_{y.x} = .13350$. The F ratio of 5.85 with 1 and 38 *df* is significant at .05 level. Had the analysis been terminated at this point, it would have been concluded that the regression of job satisfaction on intelligence is linear, and that approximately 13% of the variance in satisfaction is accounted for by intelligence. Furthermore, since the sign of r_{yx} is positive, it would have been concluded that the higher the intelligence of an employee the more he or she tends to be satisfied with the job. But let us see the results of the quadratic regression analysis.

Output

DEPENDENT VARIABLE Y R SQUARE .89141

ANALYSIS OF VARIANCE

	DF	SUM OF SQUARES	MEAN SQUARE	F
REGRESSION	2	173.29029	86.64514	151.87
RESIDUAL	37	21.10971	.57053	

- - - - - - - - - - - - -VARIABLES IN THE EQUATION- - - - - - - - - - - -

VARIABLE	B	F
X	3.77115	267.82
X2	−.01707	258.25
(CONSTANT)	−199.03392	

Commentary

$R^2_{y.x,x^2} = .89141$. This is, of course, the proportion of variance of Y accounted for by both the linear and the quadratic term. The F ratio of 151.88 with 2 and 37 *df* is a test of this R^2, which is significant at the .001 level. But we wish to note the proportion of variance incremented by the quadratic term:

$$R^2_{y.x,x^2} - R^2_{y.x} = .89141 - .13350 = .75791$$

It is evident that the quadratic term increases dramatically the proportion of variance accounted for. This increment can be tested for significance in the usual manner. It will be recalled, however, that the test of the b for the highest-degree polynomial in the equation is equivalent to a test of the proportion of variance accounted for that is incremented by the highest-degree polynomial. Look at the output above and note that the *b* for X2 has an *F* ratio of 258.25 with 1 and 37 *df* (i.e., *df* for the residual). This, then, is the same as the test of increment in the proportion of variance accounted for by the quadratic term. The equivalence of the two tests can be shown easily by using the regression sums of squares reported in the first and second steps of the analysis. The regression sum of squares for the linear term is reported above as 25.95249. For the linear and the quadratic terms, the regression sum of squares is 173.29029. Therefore

$$F = \frac{(173.29029 - 25.95249)/(2 - 1)}{.57053} = 258.25$$

The denominator of this *F* ratio is the MEAN SQUARE RESIDUAL reported at the second step of the analysis. The same *F* ratio would, of course, be obtained if one were to test the difference between the two R^2's. To repeat, however, no additional calculations are necessary as the *F* ratio associated with the *b* for the quadratic term provides the required information. Before turning to the cubic term, it will be noted that no comments were made about the test of the *b* for the linear component. While the *F* ratio associated with this *b* was reported for completeness of presentation, it will be recalled that it is irrelevant in this context (see discussion earlier in this chapter).

Output

DEPENDENT VARIABLE Y R SQUARE .89194

ANALYSIS OF VARIANCE

	DF	SUM OF SQUARES	MEAN SQUARE	F
REGRESSION	3	173.39400	57.59800	99.05
RESIDUAL	36	21.00600	.58350	

- - - - - - - - - - - - -VARIABLES IN THE EQUATION- - - - - - - - - - - -

VARIABLE	B	F
X	5.41789	1.92
X2	−.03242	.79
X3	.00005	.18

Commentary

It is evident that the proportion of variance incremented by the cubic term is very small:

$$R^2_{y.x,x^2,x^3} - R^2_{y.x,x^2} = .89194 - .89141 = .00053$$

Using a criterion of meaningfulness such an increment would be dismissed, regardless of whether or not it is statistically significant. But for completeness of presentation it will be pointed out the *F* ratio for the *b* associated with X3 (.18 with 1 and 36 *df*) is the test of the increment due to the cubic term. Again, the tests of the other two *b*'s are irrelevant. Note that had the tests of all of the

b's been used it would have been concluded that none is statistically significant. As was discussed earlier in this chapter, we are interested in a hierarchical, not a simultaneous, analysis when doing polynomial regression, and therefore the tests of b's are ignored, except the one for the highest-degree polynomial in a given equation.

For reasons indicated below, it is advisable to test one more polynomial beyond the first nonsignificant one. The results of the analysis with the quartic term are not reported here, although it will be noted that the increment in proportion of variance due to this term is neither meaningful nor statistically significant.

In behavioral research, particularly with attribute variables, it is rare to find significant trends beyond the quadratic. Moreover, the higher the degree of the polynomial the more it is affected by the reliability of the measure involved, and the more difficult it is to interpret. When the reliability is not very high, trends may seem to appear when in fact they do not exist, or trends that do exist may be overlooked. Unlike manipulated variables, attribute variables used in the behavioral sciences tend to have only moderate reliabilities. It is therefore recommended that analyses with such variables not be carried out beyond the quadratic term. Furthermore, results from analyses with variables whose measures are not highly reliable should be interpreted with caution. (For discussions of reliability see, for example, Nunnally, 1978; Thorndike & Hagen, 1977.)

Revised *F* Ratios

The F ratios obtained in the preceding analysis were based on different error terms, because with the successive appropriations of variance by higher-order polynomials the error term is decreased successively. Proceeding with the analysis in the manner outlined above may result in declaring a component to be nonsignificant because the error term used at the given stage includes variance that may be due to higher-order polynomials yet to be identified. The error term for the linear component, for example, includes variance that may be appropriated by higher-order polynomials. It is for this reason that it was suggested above that an additional degree of polynomial be tested beyond the first nonsignificant one.

When the analysis outlined above is terminated and a decision is made about the degree of polynomial that best fits the data, it is possible to recalculate the F ratios for the components retained in the equation, using a common error term for each component. This procedure is illustrated for the example under consideration.

Recall that the trends beyond the quadratic were not statistically significant. The common error term for the linear and the quadratic components is .57053 (i.e., the mean square residual reported above for the analysis in which X and X^2 were included). All that is necessary to obtain the F ratio for the linear component is to divide the regression sum of squares associated with the linear component by the common error term. For the present example,

$$F = \frac{25.95249}{.57053} = 45.49$$

with 1 and 37 *df*. Compare this *F* ratio with the *F* ratio obtained when only the linear component was used in the analysis (5.85, with 1 and 38 *df*). The difference, of course, results from the great reduction in the error term due to the identification of a quadratic trend. As noted above, a given component that may be found nonsignificant in the initial analysis may be shown to be significant when the revised *F* ratio is based on the error term associated with the highest-degree polynomial that best fits the data. It is not necessary to recalculate the *F* ratio for the quadratic term. As was noted above, it is the *F* ratio associated with the *b* for X^2 (258.25, with 1 and 37 *df*). This always applies to the last component retained in the analysis. The *F* ratios for all the components but the highest retained will change.

Finally, it will be recalled that even if some of the *F* ratios for intermediate terms are not statistically significant, such terms should not be deleted from the regression equation. All terms up to and including the highest that best fit the data have to be included when doing a polynomial regression analysis (see discussion of this point earlier in the chapter).

The Regression Equation

The quadratic equation for the present data was reported above in the output. It is:

$$Y' = -199.03392 + 3.77115X - .01707X^2$$

Using this equation one may calculate predicted Y's for X's along the continuum of X. Such predicted values may be used to plot a smoothed curve. This was done in Figure 11.3, along with the regression line for the linear trend (i.e., using the linear regression equation). Note how the curve for the quadratic

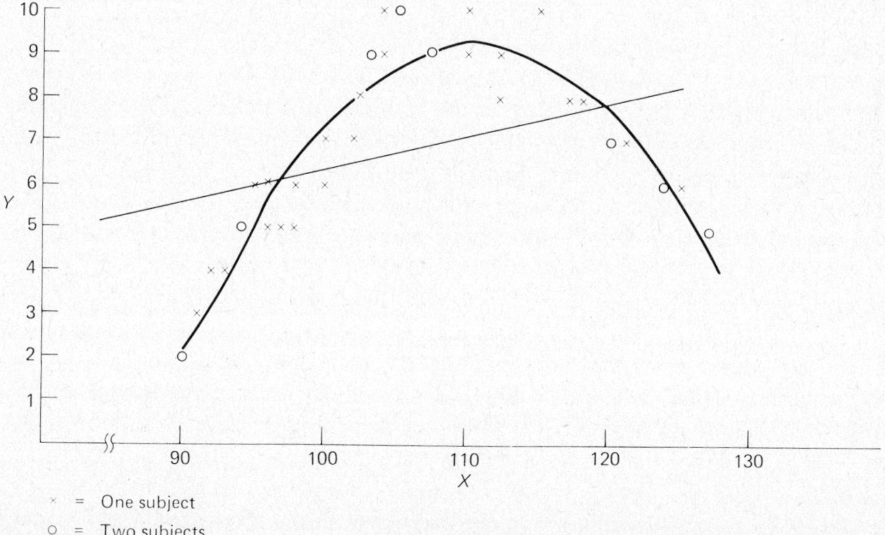

Figure 11.3

trend fits the data much better than does the one for the linear regression analysis. On the basis of the present analysis it can be concluded that subjects of relatively low or relatively high intelligence tend to be less satisfied with the job, as compared with subjects of average intelligence. One may speculate that the type of job under study is moderately demanding intellectually and therefore people of average intelligence seem to be most satisfied with it.

MULTIPLE CURVILINEAR REGRESSION

As in experimental research, polynomial regression analysis with multiple independent variables may be applied also in nonexperimental research. The mechanics of the analysis are fairly simple, but the interpretation of the results is far from simple. For the purpose of the present discussion, a second-degree polynomial equation with two independent variables will be used. This takes the following form:

$$Y' = a + b_1X + b_2Z + b_3XZ + b_4X^2 + b_5Z^2$$

where XZ is the cross product of X and Z. The analysis proceeds hierarchically. The first thing that is generally determined is whether the regression of Y on X and Z is linear or curvilinear. In effect, one tests whether $\beta_3 = \beta_4 = \beta_5 = 0$ (note that these are parameters; *not* standardized regression coefficients). This can be easily accomplished by testing whether the last three terms in the above equation add significantly to the proportion of variance accounted for. That is,

$$F = \frac{(R^2_{y.x,z,xz,x^2,z^2} - R^2_{y.x,z})/(5-2)}{(1 - R^2_{y.x,z,xz,x^2,z^2})/(N-5-1)}$$

with 3 and $N - 5 - 1$ *df*. If the increment is not statistically significant, it is concluded that the regression equation that best fits the data is

$$Y' = a + b_1X + b_2Z$$

In other words, it is concluded that the regression is linear. (The analysis and interpretation of multiple linear regression were discussed in great detail in earlier chapters; see, in particular, Chapters 3, 4, and 8.)

When the increment in the proportion of variance due to XZ, X^2, and Z^2 is statistically significant, it is concluded that the regression is curvilinear. But because the above test involved three terms, it is useful to test each of them singly, or to test first whether $\beta_4 = \beta_5 = 0$; that is, if X^2 and Z^2 add significantly to the proportion of variance accounted for by X, Z, and XZ. Assuming that this null hypothesis cannot be rejected, one can then test whether $\beta_3 = 0$—that is, whether XZ adds significantly to proportion of variance accounted for by X and Z. Other tests are also possible, though they will not be detailed here, except to note that they proceed in the manner indicated above (i.e., hierarchically).

So far so good. But what about the interpretation of the results? Consider the cross-product term (i.e., XZ). Some authors, notably Cohen (1978), emphatically refer to the *increment* in the proportion of variance accounted for by XZ, over and above X and Z as indicating an interaction between X and Z (see also Ahlgren & Walberg, 1975; Allison, 1977). XZ is also referred to as the linear interaction, or nonadditivity. Allison (1977) and Cohen (1978) discuss in detail models that include product terms. Among other things, they demonstrate that the regression coefficient associated with the product term, the proportion of variance incremented by the product term, and the t ratio associated with it are invariant under linear transformations of either or both of the original variables (i.e., X and Z). Both these authors also demonstrate that the regression coefficients for X and Z are affected by such transformation, and note that it is generally not meaningful to interpret such coefficients when the product term is included in the equation in which they have been estimated. Thus, Allison (1977) states: "When one or more of the variables in the product term are measured on interval scales, it is useless to attempt to substantively interpret or test hypotheses about the coefficients for the other variables entered singly" (p. 148). Furthermore: "It is an exercise in futility to attempt to determine the relative importance of main effects and interaction by examining the standardized coefficients. Even when variables are measured on ratio scales, this will probably not be an informative comparison" (p. 149).

And Cohen (1978) states: "The simultaneous analysis of X, Z, and XZ results in general in the distortion of the partial coefficients for X and Z, since they are generally (usually substantially) correlated with XZ" (p. 861). It is worthwhile noting that the very same point was made earlier in this chapter in connection with the interpretation and the testing of partial regression coefficients in simple curvilinear regression (i.e., with one independent variable). It was also demonstrated that because of high multicollinearity none of the regression coefficients was statistically significant, when each was tested in a simultaneous analysis. The similarity between the two situations becomes evident when it is realized that the squaring of a variable, for example, may be conceived of as the creation of a cross-product vector by multiplying the variable by itself (i.e., $X^2 = XX$).

In view of the foregoing, Cohen (1978) concludes:

> Thus, even aside from the lack of invariance over linear transformation, such simultaneous analysis is, in general, inappropriate for analytic purposes when product variables are involved. The partialed XZ,X,Z *is the interaction,* but X or Z from which XZ is partialed is, in general, *arbitrary nonsense*. (p. 861; italics added)

Where, then, does all this lead to? Allison (1977) says: "Perhaps the best measure of importance of the interaction [?] is simply the increment to R^2 with the inclusion of the product term" (p. 149). The reference to the product term as an interaction notwithstanding, it will be recalled that the proportion of variance accounted for by a variable is not a useful index of its effect, not only because it is sample-specific but also because of the special properties of the process of variance partitioning (see Chapter 7, which is entirely devoted to this topic). A corollary of the latter point is that because there are, in general, high correlations between product vectors and the variables from which they were generated, increments in proportions of variance due to product terms will frequently be very small—in many instances, substantively meaningless. A case in point is Cronbach's (1968) reanalysis of the Wallach-Kogan data. This paper is noteworthy not only because of the care with which Cronbach approaches the analyses and the interpretation of the results, but particularly because it is one of the two singled out by Cohen (1978) to buttress his strong advocacy for treating product vectors as interactions. Cohen argues that if the "indictment" of the product vectors were to be taken seriously "the methodological clock would be turned back at least a decade, and we would consign to limbo, *inter alia,* the Coleman Report . . . and the Cronbach . . . reanalysis of the Wallach-Kogan data" (Cohen, 1978, pp. 858–859).[10]

For the present purpose, it is not necessary to scrutinize and summarize Cronbach's paper. It is not even necessary to mention the substantive issues with which it deals. As the sole interest here is in Cronbach's use of product terms, it will be noted that in 33 regression analyses in which such terms were used the increments in the proportion of variance they accounted for ranged from .000 to .081, with a median of .003 (see Cronbach, 1968, Table 2). These are, to say the least, not impressive results. In discussing one of these findings, Cronbach himself notes: "But the interaction effect is weak . . . [It] accounts for no more than three percent of the variance . . ." (1968, p. 497). Note carefully that this is said about an increment of .03 in the proportion of variance accounted for. What, then, is one to say about the large number of zero, or close to zero, increments? Be that as it may, the validity of an analytic method is not predicated on whether or not its application leads to impressive or meaningful results. Cronbach's results were noted because it appears that Cohen considers them as exemplifying the usefulness of product terms. To repeat: because of high multicollinearity, increments in the proportion of variance accounted for by product terms are generally very meager.[11]

The test of the increment in the proportion of variance accounted for by a product term is the same as the test of the b associated with it. Would it, therefore, be preferable to focus on the b, instead of on the proportion of variance incremented, when interpreting the effect of a product term? The interpretation of a regression coefficient for a product term as an index of effect poses logical problems in that one attempts to make a statement about the expected change in Y as a result of a unit change in XZ while holding X and Z constant.

The foregoing arguments aside, should the product term be interpreted as an interaction? The situation dealt with here is not unlike the one discussed in

[10]As can be seen from the discussion that follows, no objections are raised here to the use of product terms per se but rather to Cohen's emphatic claim that they *are* interactions. Incidentally, Cohen's demonstration of the invariance of the product term, and his discussion of polynomial regression analysis are very clear and deserve careful study.

[11]The other study mentioned by Cohen (the Coleman Report) is not discussed here because it was discussed extensively in Chapter 7 and 8. In view of the present concern with the effect of high multicollinearity on the contribution of product terms, however, it will be noted that one of the recurring criticisms of the Coleman Report is that its data suffer from severe multicollinearity. For example, Bowles and Levin (1968b) point out that when all the school facilities, teacher characteristics and student variables were included in a regression analysis, $|\mathbf{R}|$ (the determinant of the correlation matrix; see Chapter 8 for a discussion of $|\mathbf{R}|$ in relation to multicollinearity) was .0005 for twelfth-grade blacks and .0032 for twelfth-grade whites.

detail in Chapter 10, when cross-product vectors of categorical variables were used in the analysis of data obtained in nonexperimental research. It was argued there that the increment in the proportion of variance accounted for by product vectors should be interpreted as indicating multiplicative or joint relations, and that the term "interaction" be used only in experimental research. Except for the fact that the cross-product vectors in the present chapter are obtained by the multiplication of continuous variables, it is believed that the arguments advanced about the interpretation of product terms in Chapter 10 apply equally in the present situation. Therefore, they are not repeated here, except to recall that a distinction between interactions and multiplicative relations was suggested as a safeguard against the routine, frequently mindless, use of product terms in nonexperimental research. Unfortunately, one encounters all too often inappropriate use and misinterpretation of product terms in nonexperimental research in the behavioral sciences. Some researchers even test and interpret regression coefficients for variables and their products, when these are obtained in a simultaneous analysis.[12] Worse yet, applications of such methods of stepwise regression analysis in designs that include product terms are not uncommon (see Research Applications, below).

The discussion thus far has been limited to product vectors. What about the powered vectors? It has already been noted that such vectors can be conceived of as product terms. Furthermore, issues and problems regarding the analysis and interpretation of designs with powered vectors were discussed earlier in this chapter for the case of simple curvilinear regression. The same problems not only prevail in multiple curvilinear regression analysis but are aggravated because of the presence in the equation of correlated variables and their products.

In conclusion, several additional points will be made. First, the preceding discussion was limited to a second-degree polynomial equation with two variables. Needless to say, analyses and interpretations when higher-degree polynomials and/or more than two variables are used are considerably more complex. The danger of getting lost in a forest of terms for product and powered vectors is indeed a very real one.

Second, there is a fairly extensive literature in which curvilinear regression analysis is couched in terminology of response surface methodology (e.g., Box, 1954, 1968; Cox, 1958, pp. 120–125; Li, 1964, Chapter 31; Meyer, 1963). It will be well to remember that response surface methodology was designed to be applied in the analysis of data obtained in experimental research. In such settings, the concepts of main effects and interactions may be meaningfully interpreted. This is not to say that the interpretation of such terms is always simple and straightforward. Meaningful interpretation depends, among other things, on the complexity of the design, the theory from which the hypotheses were derived, and the competence and insights of the researcher. Now, admittedly, it is possible to depict results from nonexperimental research as response surfaces (for examples, see Ezekiel & Fox, 1959, Chapter 21). There is nothing wrong in doing this for descriptive purposes. In fact, it may enhance the under-

[12]For an example and a discussion of such research, see Chapter 8 under Philadelphia School District Studies.

standing of what is going on in the data. But the interpretation of response surfaces in nonexperimental research as depicting main effects and interactions is subject to the same criticisms as those advanced when regression equations in nonexperimental research are thus interpreted.

Third, attempts have been made to interpret effects of interactions and nonlinearities by extending the approaches presented in this chapter, as well as by resorting to other models. For examples, see Southwood (1978) and Stolzenberg (1974, 1979).

RESEARCH APPLICATIONS

In order to illustrate the application of curvilinear regression analysis, several research examples will be briefly summarized. You are urged to search the literature in your field of interest for additional examples. When reviewing the literature you will probably encounter instances in which data lent themselves to curvilinear regression analysis but were subjected instead to cruder analyses.

It was felt that an example of the misuse of product terms will enhance your understanding of the discussion of this topic. One such example is therefore discussed briefly at the conclusion of this section.

The Effect of Induced Muscular Tension on Heart Rate and Performance on a Learning Task

Wood and Hokanson (1965) tested an aspect of the theory of physiological activation, which states that subjects under moderate levels of tension will perform better than subjects under no tension. Under high levels of tension, however, the theory predicts a decrement in performance. Wood and Hokanson hypothesized that there is a linear relation between muscular tension and heart rate: increased muscular tension leads to increased heart rate. The researchers hypothesized further that there is a quadratic relation between muscular tension and performance on a simple learning task (a digit symbol task). In other words, increased muscular tension will lead to higher performance on a learning task up to an optimal point, after which further increase in such tension will lead to a decline in performance on the task.

Subjects were assigned to five different levels of induced muscular tension. Changes in heart rate and the learning of digit symbols were subjected to trend analyses. Both hypotheses were supported. Specifically, for the heart rate only the linear trend was significant, while for the digit symbols only the quadratic trend was significant.

Compare these results with those that would have been obtained had Wood and Hokanson done only an analysis of variance treating muscular tensions as a categorical variable with five categories. For digit symbols, for example, the authors report an F ratio of 4.5417, with 4 and 76 degrees of freedom, for the differences among the five levels of induced tension. When the analysis for trend is done, however, the F ratio for the linear trend is less than one. The F

ratio for the quadratic trend is 16.0907, with 1 and 76 degrees of freedom. The F ratio for the cubic trend is 0.00, and the F ratio for the quartic trend is slightly larger than one. It is thus seen clearly that the trend for the digit symbol data is, as predicted by the authors, quadratic.

Group Size and Imitative Behavior

Milgram, Bickman, and Berkowitz (1969) studied the effect of the size of the group on the imitative behavior of passersby on a busy New York City sidewalk. Using groups ranging in size from 1 to 15, the researchers had them stop on a signal and look up for 60 seconds at a sixth-floor window across the street. Five randomly ordered trials were conducted for each of the group sizes. Motion pictures taken of the observation area were analyzed to determine the percentage of passersby who looked up but continued walking, and the percentage who stopped and looked up.

The independent variable, then, is group size. Two dependent variables were used: looking up only, and stopping and looking up. Milgram et al. first report the results of two one-way analyses of variance. For the percentage stopping: F $(5, 24) = 20.63$, $p < .001$. For the percentage looking up: $F\ (5, 24) = 16.28$, $p <$ .001. In these two analyses, group size was treated as if it were a categorical variable. The authors then report the results of a trend analysis:

> There is a significant linear trend ($F = 101.7$, $p < .01$) and a nonsignificant quadratic trend ($F = .42$) for the passersby who stopped. However, for the passersby who looked up, there are both significant linear ($F = 57.2$, $p < .01$) and quadratic ($F = 11.6$, $p < .01$) components. (p. 198)

The two trends are clearly evident from the authors' plots of the data. For the stopping behavior, there is a fairly constant increase from 4% of passersby who stopped alongside a single individual who was looking up, to 40% who stopped alongside a group of 15 people who were looking up. For the looking behavior, on the other hand, the percent of passersby increases steeply from 42 when a single individual was looking up, to 80 when five individuals were looking up. The curve then flattens, indicating very small increases for groups larger than five.

In sum, the analyses in this study (identical to those with illustrative data in the beginning of this chapter) demonstrate that when the independent variable is continuous, trend analysis is more informative than a one-way analysis of variance.

Political and Social Indicators

The preceding examples were taken from experimental research—the first in a laboratory setting and the second in a field setting. Interesting examples of second- and third-order polynomial regression analysis in nonexperimental research may be found in Russett, Alker, Deutsch, and Lasswell (1964, pp. 304–310). For example, they report first a negative linear regression for Population

Growth on Adult Literacy, using countries as the unit of analysis. The authors then demonstrate how a quadratic curve provides a better fit for the data: increases in population growth are associated with increases in the percentage of literacy up to 30%, beyond which the regression is negative.

Cognitive Style and School Achievement

A study by Robinson and Gray (1974) provides an example of the misuse of product terms. The authors used 11 measures of achievement (e.g., Vocabulary, Reading Comprehension) for fifth-grade boys and girls as dependent variables. Of the five independent variables, two were measures of mental ability (Verbal and Nonverbal IQ), and three were measures of cognitive style (Categorical, Descriptive, and Relational). Before describing the analysis, it will be noted that the correlations among the five independent variables are high, ranging from .58 to .78 (see Robinson & Gray, 1974, Table 2). It is therefore doubtful whether they should be treated as distinct variables, particularly when one considers the reliabilities of the cognitive style measures (.78, .80, and .84; the reliabilities of the IQ measures are not reported).

The foregoing reservation notwithstanding, the method of analysis is now described. Using the five independent variables, the authors generated 10 product terms by using all the possible pairings among them (e.g., Categorial by Verbal IQ; Verbal IQ by Nonverbal IQ; Categorical by Relational). Twenty-two multiple regression analyses were done by regressing, in turn, each of the 11 measures of achievement on the 15 vectors (five variables and ten product terms) for boys and girls separately. "For each analysis, verbal and nonverbal IQ were forced into the equation, then the remaining 13 independent variables [sic] entered freely into the regression equation" (p. 797). In other words, after entering the two IQ measures, the remaining 13 vectors were subjected to a stepwise regression analysis (see Chapter 6 for a detailed discussion of the properties of this method of analysis). This goes counter to all that was said earlier in this chapter about analyses in which product vectors are also included.

It is instructive to summarize briefly the results regarding the entry of vectors after verbal and nonverbal IQ were forced into the analysis. Of 22 regression analyses: (1) no additional vectors were entered in six; (2) one vector entered in each of seven analyses (in all instances, it was a *product term*); (3) two vectors entered in each of the remaining nine analyses. In all instances, a product term entered *first,* followed by a "variable" in its original form.

It is hoped that in view of what you have learned about the method of analysis used in this study, and considering the high multicollinearity among the variables (not to mention their products), these results come as no surprise to you. Therefore, no further comments will be made about them or about the meaningfulness of the "findings." If you have some doubts, or questions, it is suggested that you read relevant sections of Chapter 6 about the use of stepwise regression analysis, and the discussion of analysis with product terms in the present chapter.

SUMMARY

It is a sign of relatively sophisticated theory when predictions derived from it are not limited to statements about differences between conditions or treatments, but also address themselves to the pattern of the differences. At the initial stages of formulating a theory one can probably state only that the phenomena under study differ under different conditions. A relatively sophisticated theory generally provides more specific predictions about relations among variables.

The methods presented in this chapter provide the means for testing predicted trends in the data. When cruder analyses are applied to data for which a trend analysis is appropriate, the consequences may be failure to support the hypothesis being tested or, at the very least, a loss of information.

The studies summarized in the previous section make it clear that the relation between theory and analytic method is close. It was the use of trend analysis that enabled the researchers to detect relations predicted by theory. Trend analysis is, of course, also useful when a researcher has no hypothesis about the specific pattern of relations among the variables under study, but wishes to learn what the pattern is. The discovery of trends may lead the researcher to reformulate theory and conduct subsequent studies to test such reformulations.

It was pointed out that for trend analysis the independent variable has to be continuous. In addition, the measurement of the variable should have relatively high reliability, or trends may seem to appear when in fact they do not exist, or trends that do exist may be overlooked.

Problems in the interpretation of products of variables were discussed. It was argued that product terms should not be accorded the status of interaction.

In sum, trend analysis is a powerful technique that, when appropriately applied, can enhance the predictive and explanatory power of scientific inquiry.

STUDY SUGGESTIONS

1. Why is it not advisable to transform a continuous variable into a categorical variable?
2. Discuss the hazards of extrapolation from the regression line.
3. Under what condition is $\eta^2_{yx} = r^2_{yx}$?
4. In a study with a continuous independent variable consisting of eight distinct values, the following results were obtained: proportion of variance due to overall regression = .36426; proportion of variance due to linear regression = .33267. The total number of subjects was 100. Calculate the F ratios for the following:
   (a) overall regression;
   (b) linear regression;
   (c) deviation from linearity.
5. When a continuous independent variable has six distinct values, what is the highest-degree polynomial that can be fitted to the data?
6. In a study with a continuous independent variable, a third-degree polynomial was fitted. Some of the results are: $R^2_{y.x} = .15726$; $R^2_{y.x,x^2} = .28723$; $R^2_{y.x,x^2,x^3} = .31626$. The total number of subjects was 150. Calculate the F ratios for the following components:
   (a) linear;
   (b) quadratic;
   (c) cubic.

7. Why should curvilinear regression analysis be carried out hierarchically (i.e., first X, then X^2, etc.)?
8. In a regression equation with polynomial terms, are the tests of the b's meaningful? Explain.
9. A continuous independent variable consists of seven distinct values equally spaced. There is an equal number of subjects for each value of the independent variable. Using an appropriate table, indicate the orthogonal polynomials for the following components:
   (a) linear;
   (b) quadratic;
   (c) cubic.
10. A researcher studied the regression of risk-taking on ego-strength. To a sample of 25 subjects she administered a measure of risk-taking and one of ego-strength. The data (illustrative) are as follows:

Risk-Taking	*Ego-Strength*
2	1
3	1
4	2
4	2
5	2
5	3
5	3
6	3
8	4
8	4
9	5
10	5
10	5
10	6
11	6
11	7
12	7
12	7
12	8
12	8
11	8
12	9
12	9
12	10
12	10

(a) What are the proportions of variance accounted for by the following components: (1) linear; (2) quadratic; (3) cubic?
(b) What are the initial F ratios associated with the following components: (1) linear; (2) quadratic; (3) cubic?
(c) What is the degree of polynomial that best fits the data?
(d) What are the revised F ratios for the components retained in (c), above?
(e) Plot the data, and interpret the results.

ANSWERS

3. When the regression is linear.
4. (a) $F = 7.53$, with 7 and 92 *df*.
   (b) $F = 48.14$, with 1 and 92 *df*.
   (c) $F = .76$, with 6 and 92 *df*.
5. 5
6. (a) $F = 33.58$, with 1 and 146 *df*.
   (b) $F = 27.75$, with 1 and 146 *df*.
   (c) $F = 6.20$, with 1 and 146 *df*.
8. Only the test of the b for the highest-degree polynomial in the equation is meaningful.
9. (a) linear: -3 -2 -1 0 1 2 3
   (b) quadratic: 5 0 -3 -4 -3 0 5
   (c) cubic: -1 1 1 0 -1 -1 1

10. (a) (1) linear = .88542; (2) quadratic = .08520; (3) cubic = .00342
    (b) (1) $F = 177.73$, with 1 and 23 *df*.
        (2) $F = 63.79$, with 1 and 22 *df*.
        (3) $F = 2.77$, with 1 and 21 *df*.
    (c) quadratic.
    (d) linear: $F = 662.91$, with 1 and 22 *df*;
        quadratic: $F = 63.79$, with 1 and 22 *df*.

12

CONTINUOUS AND CATEGORICAL INDEPENDENT VARIABLES; APTITUDE-TREATMENT INTERACTION; COMPARISONS OF REGRESSION EQUATIONS

In the preceding chapters analysis of data obtained in designs with continuous and categorical independent variables was discussed and illustrated, but the two kinds of variables were treated separately. In the present chapter and in Chapter 13 they are treated together: multiple regression analysis is applied to designs in which both continuous and categorical variables are used. The two chapters thus serve as an integration of methods that have been treated by some researchers as distinct and by others as even incompatible.

The present chapter begins with a discussion and an analysis of an experimental design in which one of the independent variables is continuous and another is categorical. Next, the inadvisability of categorizing continuous variables is discussed and illustrated. This is followed by a presentation of experimental designs consisting of a categorical variable that is manipulated and a continuous variable that is not manipulated. Designs in which neither the categorical nor the continuous variables are manipulated (i.e., nonexperimental designs) are then discussed. This is followed by a discussion and illustration of curvilinear regression analysis when one of the independent variables is continuous and another is categorical. The chapter concludes with some examples of research applications.

ANALYSIS OF DATA FROM AN EXPERIMENT IN RETENTION

A researcher is studying the effect of an incentive on the retention of subject matter and is also interested in the effect on retention of time devoted to study. Another question to be pursued is whether there is an interaction between the two variables in their effect on retention. Subjects are randomly assigned to two groups, one receiving and the other not receiving an incentive. Within these groups, subjects are randomly assigned to 5, 10, 15, or 20 minutes of study of a passage specifically prepared for the experiment. At the end of the study period, a test of retention is administered. An illustrative set of data from such an experiment is reported in Table 12.1. Note that one of the variables, Incentive–No Incentive, is categorical, while the other variable, Study Time, is continuous.

Table 12.1 Illustrative Data from a Retention Experiment with One Continuous and One Categorical Variable

	Study Time (in Minutes)				
Treatments	*5*	*10*	*15*	*20*	
	3	4	5	7	
No Incentive	4	5	6	8	
	5	6	8	9	$\bar{Y}_{\text{No Inc.}} = 5.83$
	7	9	8	10	
Incentive	8	10	11	11	
	9	11	12	13	$\bar{Y}_{\text{Inc.}} = 9.92$
$\bar{Y}$:	6.00	7.50	8.33	9.67	$\bar{Y}_t = 7.875$

In order to lay the groundwork for discussion of the analysis, the data have been plotted in Figure 12.1. Circles identify subjects who received an incentive (I), while crosses identify subjects who received no incentive (NI). The regression lines of retention on study time for the two groups are also drawn in the figure. Two questions may be asked about these regression lines. The first is whether the slopes of the two lines (indicated by the b coefficients) are equal.

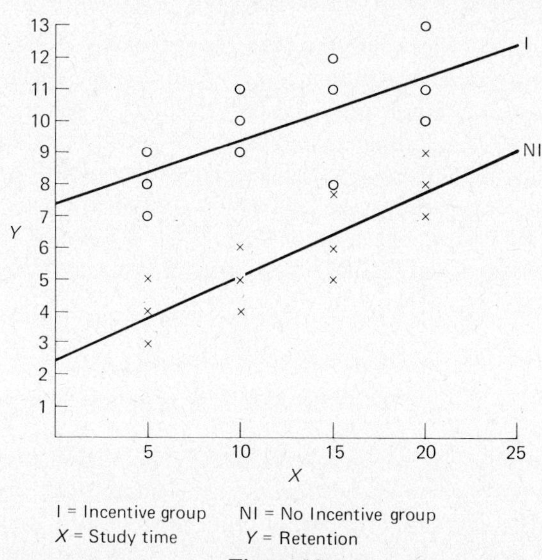

Figure 12.1

Stated differently, are the two lines parallel? Equality of slopes means that the effect of the continuous variable (Study Time) is the same in both groups. Assuming the b's to be equal, one can ask the second question: Are the intercepts (a's) of the two regression lines equal? The second question is addressed to the elevation of the regression lines. Equality of intercepts means that a single regression line fits the data for both groups, so that there is really no difference between them. If, on the other hand, the b's are equal while the a's are not, this indicates that one group is superior to the other group along the continuum of the continuous variable.

From Figure 12.1 it is evident that the regression lines are not parallel. It is possible, however, that the departure from parallelism is due to chance. This hypothesis can be tested by testing the significance of the difference between the b's. If the b's are not significantly different, one can then test the significance of the difference between the a's.

The calculations of the regression equations for the Incentive and No Incentive group are summarized in Table 12.2. The regression equation for the Incentive group is

$$Y' = 7.33330 + .20667X$$

and for the No Incentive group

$$Y' = 2.49996 + .26667X$$

While the b's are quite alike, there is a marked difference between the a's. The procedures for testing differences between regression coefficients and differences between intercepts are outlined below and applied to the data.

Tests of Differences between Regression Coefficients

As discussed in earlier chapters (see, in particular, Chapter 9), a test of significance can be conceived as an attempt to answer the question: Does additional information add significantly to the explanation of the dependent variable? Applied to the topic under discussion, the question is: Does using separate regression coefficients for each group add significantly to the regression sum of squares, as compared to the regression sum of squares obtained when a common regression coefficient is used?

A common regression coefficient for several groups may be calculated by the following formula:

$$b_c = \frac{\Sigma xy_1 + \Sigma xy_2 + \cdots + \Sigma xy_k}{\Sigma x_1^2 + \Sigma x_2^2 + \cdots + \Sigma x_k^2} \tag{12.1}$$

where b_c = common regression coefficient; Σxy_1 = sum of the products in group 1, and similarly for all other terms in the numerator; Σx_1^2 = sum of the squares in group 1, and similarly for all other terms in the denominator. Note that the numerator in (12.1) is the pooled sum of products within groups, while

Table 12.2 Calculation of Regression Equations from the Retention Experiment

	No Incentive			Incentive		
	Y	X	XY	Y	X	XY
	3	5	15	7	5	35
	4	5	20	8	5	40
	5	5	25	9	5	45
	4	10	40	9	10	90
	5	10	50	10	10	100
	6	10	60	11	10	110
	5	15	75	8	15	120
	6	15	90	11	15	165
	8	15	120	12	15	180
	7	20	140	10	20	200
	8	20	160	11	20	220
	9	20	180	13	20	260
Σ:	70	150	975	119	150	1565
M:	5.83333	12.500		9.91667	12.500	
SS:	446	2250		1215	2250	

No Incentive:

$$\Sigma xy = 975 - \frac{(70)(150)}{12} = 100$$

$$\Sigma x^2 = 2250 - \frac{(150)^2}{12} = 375$$

$$b = \frac{\Sigma xy}{\Sigma x^2} = \frac{100}{375} = .26667$$

$$a = \bar{Y} - b\bar{X} = 5.83333 - (.26667)(12.5) = 2.49996$$

$$Y' = 2.49996 + .26667X$$

$$ss_{\text{reg}} = \frac{(\Sigma xy)^2}{\Sigma x^2} = \frac{(100)^2}{375} = 26.66667$$

Incentive:

$$\Sigma xy = 1565 - \frac{(119)(150)}{12} = 77.5$$

$$\Sigma x^2 = 2250 - \frac{(150)^2}{12} = 375$$

$$b = \frac{\Sigma xy}{\Sigma x^2} = \frac{77.5}{375} = .20667$$

$$a = \bar{Y} - b\bar{X} = 9.91667 - (.20667)(12.5) = 7.33330$$

$$Y' = 7.33330 + .20667X$$

$$ss_{\text{reg}} = \frac{(\Sigma xy)^2}{\Sigma x_2} = \frac{(77.5)^2}{375} = 16.01667$$

the denominator is the pooled sum of squares within groups. For the present example (see Table 12.2)

No Incentive group: $\Sigma xy = 100.00$; $\Sigma x^2 = 375.00$

Incentive group: $\Sigma xy = 77.50$; $\Sigma x^2 = 375.00$

$$b_c = \frac{77.50 + 100.00}{375.00 + 375.00} = .23667$$

Recall that the calculation of a regression coefficient is based on the principle of least squares: b is calculated so that the sum of the squared residuals is minimized. This, of course, results in maximizing the regression sum of squares. Now, when regression lines are parallel the b's are obviously identical. Consequently, the sum of the regression sums of squares obtained from using each b for its own group is the same as the regression sum of squares obtained from using a common b for all groups.

When, however, regression lines are not parallel, the common b is not equal to the separate b's. Since the b for each group provides the best fit for the group data, the sum of the regression sums of squares obtained from using the separate b's is larger than the regression sum of the squares obtained from using a common b. The discrepancy between the sum of the regression sums of squares obtained from separate b's and the regression sum of squares obtained from a common b is due to the departure from parallelism of the regression lines of the separate groups. When the increment in the regression sum of squares due to the use of separate b's is not significant, it is concluded that there are no significant differences between the b's. In other words, the common b is tenable for all the groups.

Note that such a conclusion is predicated on the failure to reject the null hypothesis and is therefore tantamount to accepting the null hypothesis of no differences among the b's. In order to minimize type II error (i.e., failure to reject the null hypothesis when it should have been rejected; see Edwards, 1972, pp. 21–22; Hays, 1981, p. 245) it is suggested that a relatively large level of significance (e.g., $\alpha = .10$ or even .25) be used for tests of significance of the differences among the b's.

In the calculations of Table 12.2 separate b's were used for each group. The regression sum of squares for the No Incentive group is 26.66667 and for the Incentive group is 16.01667. The sum of these regression sums of squares is 42.68334. The regression sum of squares due to a common b may be obtained as follows:

$$ss_{\text{reg}} \text{ for common } b = \frac{(\text{pooled } \Sigma xy)^2}{\text{pooled } \Sigma x^2} \tag{12.2}$$

For the present data we obtain

$$\frac{(77.50 + 100.00)^2}{375.00 + 375.00} = \frac{177.50^2}{750.00} = \mathit{42.00833}$$

The discrepancy between the sum of the regression sums of squares for the separate b's and the regression sum of squares for the common b is 42.68334 – 42.00833 = *.67501*. It is this value that is tested for significance.

The foregoing presentation was meant as an explanation of the approach to testing the difference between the b's. Although the procedure presented can, of course, be used to do the calculations, it is demonstrated now how the analysis is done in the context of the procedures of preceding chapters.

In Table 12.3 the data from the retention experiment are displayed for such an analysis. Vector 1 in the table identifies group membership: No Incentive (NI) and Incentive (I). The continuous variable, Study Time (ST), is given as vector 2. As in the case of categorical variables (see Chapter 10), vectors for the interaction are obtained by cross multiplying the vectors representing the variables. In the present case, vector 3 is the product of vectors 1 and 2.

The data of Table 10.3 were analyzed by the REGRESSION program of SPSS. Following are excerpts of the output and commentaries.

Table 12.3 Data from the Retention Experiment, Laid Out for Regression Analysis

Treatment	*Y*	*1*	*2*	*3 (1 × 2)*
	3	1	5	5
	4	1	5	5
	5	1	5	5
	4	1	10	10
	5	1	10	10
No Incentive	6	1	10	10
	5	1	15	15
	6	1	15	15
	8	1	15	15
	7	1	20	20
	8	1	20	20
	9	1	20	20
	7	−1	5	−5
	8	−1	5	−5
	9	−1	5	−5
	9	−1	10	−10
	10	−1	10	−10
Incentive	11	−1	10	−10
	8	−1	15	−15
	11	−1	15	−15
	12	−1	15	−15
	10	−1	20	−20
	11	−1	20	−20
	13	−1	20	−20
	Σy^2: 172.625			

NOTE: *Y* = measures of retention originally presented in Table 12.1; 1 = coded vector for Incentive–No Incentive; 2 = Study Time; 3 = product vector of 1 and 2.

Output

```
- - - - - - - - - - - - -VARIABLES IN THE EQUATION- - - - - - - - - - - -
               VARIABLE           B        F
               X1 (NI-I)     -2.41667
               X2 (ST)         .23667
               X3 (X1*X2)      .03000    .45
               CONSTANT       4.91667
```

Commentary

The first test to be performed is whether there is a significant difference between the *b*'s for the two groups. This is accomplished by testing whether the product vector adds significantly to the regression sum of squares (or the proportion of variance accounted for) over and above what is accounted for by the variables themselves. But this is the same as testing the b associated with the product vector (see earlier chapters, particularly Chapter 8). The F ratio for X3 (.45) is clearly not significant. It is concluded that the coefficients for the regression of Retention on Study Time in the two groups (NI and I) are not significantly different from each other.

Note that F ratios for X1 and X2 were not given above, although they are reported in the computer output. The reason is that tests associated with these vectors depend on whether or not the b's for the separate groups are significantly different from each other. Before dealing with these tests we turn our attention to the properties of the regression equation in which product vectors are included. Henceforth, a regression equation that includes product terms will be referred to as an overall regression equation.

The Overall Regression Equation

Regression equations in which product terms have been included were discussed in earlier chapters. In Chapter 10, where the product vectors were obtained by multiplying vectors representing categorical variables, it was shown that the coefficients of the overall regression equation have specific meanings. Problems and difficulties in the interpretation of the overall regression equation when the product vectors were obtained by multiplying continuous variables were discussed in Chapter 11. In the present chapter the product vectors are obtained by multiplying coded vectors of a categorical variable by a continuous variable. In such cases the interpretation of the overall regression equation depends on the method of coding that was used to represent the categorical variable. In the numerical example under consideration, effect coding was used (see Table 12.3). The properties of the overall regression equation when effect coding is used to represent the categorical variable are now discussed. The properties of such equations with dummy coding are discussed later in this chapter.

The overall regression equation obtained above is repeated:

$$Y' = 4.91667 - 2.41667X_1 + .23667X_2 + .03000X_3$$

where X_1 = vector 1 of Table 12.3 (NI-I): X_2 = vector 2 of Table 12.3 (ST); X_3 = the product of X_1 and X_2. Earlier, the separate regression equations for the No Incentive and Incentive groups were calculated:

$$Y'_{\text{NI}} = 2.49996 + .26667X$$

$$Y'_{\text{I}} = 7.33330 + .20667X$$

where Y is Retention and X is Study Time.

Now, the intercept, a, of the overall equation is equal to the average of the intercepts of the separate regression equations:

$$\frac{2.49996 + 7.33330}{2} = 4.91663$$

The b associated with a coded vector in the overall regression equation is equal to the deviation of the intercept for the group identified in the vector (i.e., the group assigned 1) from the average of the intercepts. Consequently, the a for the group assigned 1 in a given vector is equal to the average of the intercepts, or the a of the overall regression equation, plus the b associated with this vector. In the present example, the No Incentive group was assigned 1 in vector 1 (see Table 12.3). The b for this vector (the b for X_1) is -2.41667. Accordingly, the intercept for the No Incentive group is:

$$4.91667 + (-2.41667) = \mathit{2.5}$$

which is (within rounding error) the same value that was obtained earlier in the separate analyses.

The intercept for the group assigned -1 in all the coded vectors is equal to the intercept obtained from the overall regression equation minus the sum of the b's associated with all the coded vectors in the overall regression equation. In the present example there is only one coded vector (X_1), whose coefficient is -2.41667. The Incentive group was assigned -1 in this vector. Therefore the intercept for this group is:

$$4.91667 - (-2.41667) = \mathit{7.33334}$$

which is (within rounding error) the same as the value obtained earlier in the separate analyses.

We turn now to the regression coefficients associated with the continuous variable and the product vectors. The b for the continuous variable in the overall regression equation is equal to the average of the b's of the separate regression equations:

$$\frac{.26667 + .20667}{2} = \mathit{.23667}$$

This is the b coefficient associated with X_2 (ST) in the overall regression equation reported above.

The b associated with each product vector in the overall regression equation is equal to the deviation of the b for the group assigned 1 in the vector that was used to generate the product vector from the average of the b's. In the present example the product vector, X_3, was generated by multiplying X_1, in which the No Incentive group was assigned 1, by the vector of the continuous variable, X_2. The b for X_3 was shown above to be .03000. Therefore the b for the No Incentive group is

$$.23667 + .03000 = \mathit{.26667}$$

Compare with the b obtained in the separate analysis of this group (Table 12.2).

The b for the group assigned -1 in all the coded vectors is equal to the average of the regression coefficients (i.e., the b for the continuous variable in the overall regression equation) minus the sum of the b's for all the product vectors in the overall regression equation. In the present example there is only one product vector, X_3, whose coefficient is .03000. The b for the group assigned -1 (that is, the Incentive group) is therefore:

$$.23667 - (.03000) = .20667$$

This is the b obtained earlier when a separate analysis was done for the data of the Incentive group (see Table 12.2).

Several things will be noted. First, in the present example the categorical variable consisted of two categories only. The same approach is taken, and the overall regression equation is similarly interpreted, when the categorical variable consists of more than two categories. When this is the case, it is obviously necessary to generate a number of coded vectors equal to the number of categories minus one, or the number of degrees of freedom associated with the categorical variable. Each of the coded vectors is multiplied by the continuous variable.

Second, in the present example only one continuous variable was used. The properties of the overall regression equation generalize to any number of continuous variables. When multiple continuous variables are used, product vectors are obtained by multiplying the coded vectors of the categorical variable by each of the continuous variables. Examples of analyses with categorical variables consisting of more than two categories, and with multiple continuous variables, are given in Chapter 13.

Third, because there is only one product vector in the present example it was possible to perform the test of the difference between the two separate b's (for NI and I) by testing the b for the product vector. In fact, in view of the foregoing discussion of the properties of this b it can be clearly seen what is being tested when only two groups are used. Recall that the b for the continuous variable in the overall regression equation is equal to the average of the b's for the two groups in their separate equations, and that the b for the product term is a deviation of the b for one of the groups from the average of the two b's. It is obvious therefore that when the two b's in the separate equations are equal to each other, the b for the product term in the overall equation must be zero. When, on the other hand, the separate b's are not equal to each other, the test of the b for the product term is a test of the deviation of one of the b's from their average. But the deviation of the other b is the same, except for a reversal of its sign.

When more than two groups are involved, more than one product vector has to be formed. Under such circumstances, the test of the differences among the separate b's is done by testing the increment in the proportion of variance accounted for (or regression sum of squares) by all the product vectors, over and above what the original variables account for. Numerical examples with categorical variables consisting of more than two categories are given in Chapter 13. We return now to the analysis of the data of Table 12.3.

The Common Regression Coefficient

It will be recalled that the regression coefficients for the two groups were found to be statistically not significantly different from each other. Consequently, a common regression coefficient may be used. Earlier, Formula

(12.1) was used to calculate the common coefficient for the data of Table 12.3. b_c was found to be equal to .23667. Instead of applying Formula (12.1), the common regression coefficient may be calculated by regressing the dependent variable on the original variables only—that is, by doing a multiple regression analysis without product vectors. The regression coefficient associated with the continuous variable in such an analysis *is the common regression coefficient.* In the present example, it is necessary to regress Y (Retention) on X_1 (NI-I) and X_2 (ST). The regression coefficient for X_2 is b_c. As is shown below, using the coded vector and the continuous vector without the product vector is tantamount to placing a restriction on the data of the two groups so that their regression equations will have two separate intercepts but the same regression coefficient. In other words, the regression lines are constrained to be parallel to each other. Following is an excerpt of the output for such an analysis for the data of Table 12.3.

Output

------------VARIABLES IN THE EQUATION-----------

VARIABLE	B	F
X1 (NI-I)	−2.04167	68.71
X2 (ST)	.23667	28.85
CONSTANT	4.91667	

Commentary

The common regression coefficient is .23667, which is the same as the value obtained earlier in the chapter. Note carefully that in the present example b_c is equal to the average of the two b's discussed earlier in connection with the overall regression equation (i.e., the b associated with the continuous variable in the overall regression equation). This will happen only when the Σx^2's (sums of squares for the continuous independent variable) for all groups are equal to each other. In the present example:

$$\Sigma x^2_{\text{NI}} = \Sigma x^2_{\text{I}} = 375.00$$

(see calculations following Table 12.2). To see why this is so, an algebraic equivalent of Formula (12.1) is stated:

$$b_c = \frac{\Sigma x_1^2 b_1 + \Sigma x_2^2 b_2 + \cdots + \Sigma x_k^2 b_k}{\Sigma x_1^2 + \Sigma x_2^2 + \cdots + \Sigma x_k^2}$$

From this equation it can be seen that b_c is a weighted average of the b's, in which each b is weighted by Σx^2 for its group. When all Σx^2's are equal to each other, the weighted average of the b's (i.e., b_c) is the same as the average of the b's.

To repeat: *the b associated with the continuous variable in the overall regression equation is equal to the average of the separate b's. The b associated with the continuous variable in the regression equation in which the product vectors are not included is the common b.*

Test of the Common Regression Coefficient

Having obtained b_c, it is necessary to determine whether it is significantly different from zero. In the context of the present example this test is addressed to the question of whether the continuous variable, Study Time, has a significant effect on the dependent variable, Retention. The test of b_c is done in the usual manner. That is, dividing b_c by its standard error, a t ratio is obtained. In SPSS an F ratio (t^2) is reported instead. The F ratio for b_c in the present example is 28.85 (see Output above). The *df* for this F ratio are, as always, 1 for the numerator and $N - k - 1$ for the denominator. In the present example: $N = 24$ (number of subjects in both groups); $k = 2$ (one vector for NI-I and one for ST). Therefore the *df* for the denominator of the F ratio are 21. These are, of course, the *df* associated with the mean square residual reported in the computer output (not given here) for the regression of Y on X_1 and X_2.

In view of the obtained F ratio it is concluded that Study Time has a significant effect on Retention. The expected change in the latter associated with a unit change in the former is .23667 (b_c) units.

Test of the Difference between Intercepts

A test of the difference between intercepts is performed only after it has been established that the b's do not differ significantly from each other.[1] Only then does it make sense to ask whether one of the treatments is more effective than the other along the continuum of the continuous variable. Testing the difference between intercepts amounts to testing the difference between the treatment effects of the categorical variable. This test is accomplished by testing the increment in the proportion of variance accounted for (or the regression sum of squares) by the coded vectors, over and above the proportion of variance accounted for by the continuous variable. This is a test between two R^2's encountered so frequently in the book.

Because in the present example there is only one coded vector, the same results may be obtained by testing the b associated with this coded vector. In the Output reported above, the F ratio for the b associated with the coded vector (X_1) is 68.71, with 1 and 21 *df*. This, then, is a test of the difference between the two intercepts. It is concluded that the effect of No Incentive is significantly different from the effect of Incentive on Retention. Or, that there is a constant difference between No Incentive and Incentive along the continuum of Study Time. In X_1, No Incentive was assigned 1 (see Table 12.3). The b for X_1 is -2.04167 (see Output above). Therefore, the effect of No Incentive is -2.04167. The effect of Incentive is 2.04167. The difference between the two treatments is therefore:

$$2.04167 - (-2.04167) = \mathit{4.08334}$$

Had there been more than two treatments in the categorical variable it would have been necessary to use more than one coded vector. Under such cir-

[1]When the b's are significantly different from each other an interaction between the categorical and the continuous variable is indicated. This topic is treated later in the chapter.

cumstances the test among the intercepts is done by testing the increment in the proportion of variance accounted for by the coded vectors (i.e., a test of the difference between two R^2's). If on the basis of this test it is concluded that there are significant differences among the intercepts, it is necessary to do multiple comparisons in order to determine which of the treatments, or categories, differ significantly from each other along the continuum of the continuous variable. Such tests are discussed and illustrated in Chapter 13. To reiterate: because the categorical variable in the present example consists of two categories only, it is sufficient to test the b associated with the coded vector representing this variable in order to determine whether the two treatments, or the two intercepts, differ significantly from each other.

Separate Regression Equations

Let us assume that the test of the difference between the intercepts in the present example is not statistically significant, but that the common regression coefficient (b_c) is statistically different from zero. If this were the case, it would have been concluded that a single regression line would provide a good fit for the data of both groups. The regression equation for such an occurrence is calculated by regressing Y on the continuous variable only (X_2). Note that by omitting the coded vector no distinction is made between scores obtained under the No Incentive and those obtained under the Incentive condition. In other words, it is decided to calculate a regression equation in which both groups are treated as if they come from the same population. For the present data, such a regression equation would be:

$$Y' = 4.91667 + .23667X_2$$

where X_2 is the continuous variable, Study Time.

Recall, however, that in the present example the difference between the intercepts is statistically significant. Also, the difference between the b's is not significant, and the common b is significantly different from zero. Accordingly, two separate regression equations in which the intercepts differ but the b's are the same are indicated. These can be easily derived following the same procedures outlined above, except that instead of using the overall regression equation, the equation in which product vectors are *not* included is used. For the present example, this equation is:

$$Y' = 4.91667 - 2.04167X_1 + .23667X_2$$

where X_1 is the coded vector for No Incentive–Incentive, and X_2 is Study Time. In X_1 the No Incentive group was assigned 1 (see Table 12.3). Therefore the intercept for this group is:

$$4.91667 + (-2.04167) = \mathit{2.87500}$$

The Incentive group was assigned -1 in X_1. Therefore its intercept is:

$$4.91667 - (-2.04167) = \mathit{6.95834}$$

Using the common coefficient reported above (.23667), the two regression equations are:

$$Y'_{\text{NI}} = 2.87500 + .23667X$$

$$Y'_{\text{I}} = 6.95834 + .23667X$$

where X is Study Time. Note that the difference between the two intercepts, $6.95834 - 2.87500 = 4.08334$, is (as was noted above) the difference between the effects of the two treatments of the categorical variable along the continuum of the continuous variable. In the context of the present example this means that along the continuum of Study Time, subjects who were given an incentive are expected to have 4.08334 higher scores than subjects who were not given an incentive. This, of course, is the same as saying that there is no interaction between the categorical and the continuous variable.

Proportions of Variance Accounted For

Since the design under consideration is orthogonal (see Table 12.1, where the cell frequencies are equal), it is possible to state unambiguously the proportion of variance accounted for by each variable.[2] From the output,

$$R^2_{y.12} = .82288$$

About 82% of the variance in Retention is accounted for by Study Time and No Incentive–Incentive. The proportion of variance due to Study Time is:

$$R^2_{y.12} - R^2_{y.1} = R^2_{y.2} \qquad \text{(because } r_{12} = 0\text{)}$$

$$.82288 - .57953 = .24335$$

And the proportion of variance due to No Incentive–Incentive is:

$$R^2_{y.12} - R^2_{y.2} = R^2_{y.1}$$

$$.82288 - .24335 = .57953$$

These proportions of variance accounted for can be tested in the usual manner. This is done here to show the equivalence between these tests and the tests of the b's corresponding to them.

$$F_{\text{ST}} = \frac{.24335/1}{(1 - .82288)/(24 - 2 - 1)} = 28.85$$

with 1 and 21 *df*, and

$$F_{\text{NI-I}} = \frac{.57953/1}{(1 - .82288)/(24 - 2 - 1)} = 68.71$$

[2]For an extensive discussion of orthogonal and nonorthogonal designs, see Chapter 10.

with 1 and 21 *df*. Compare these F ratios with those reported in the Output for the tests of the b's in the equation in which product vectors were *not* included.

Recapitulation

Quite a bit of ground has been covered up to this point. It would therefore be useful to recapitulate what has been said in order to clarify the analytic sequence. The steps to be followed are presented in the form of a set of questions. Depending on the nature of the answer to a given question, one may either have to go to another step or terminate the analysis and summarize the results.

Create a vector Y that will include the measures of the dependent variable for all subjects. Create coded vectors to indicate group membership in the categories of the categorical variable. This is done in the usual manner, as described extensively in Chapter 9. Create a vector, or vectors, that will include the values of the continuous variable, or variables, for all subjects. Generate new vectors by multiplying the vectors representing the categorical variable by the vector for the continuous variable. When more than one continuous variable is used, the vectors representing the categorical variable are multiplied, in turn, by each of the vectors for the continuous variables. The product vectors represent the interaction terms.

To make the following presentation concise, an example of one categorical and one continuous variable will be used. The categorical variable is symbolized by the letter A. Note that A may refer to more than one coded vector, the number being equal to the number of categories of the categorical variable minus one (see Chapter 9). The letter B is used to represent the continuous variable. The product vectors are symbolized by the letter C.

1. *Is the proportion of variance accounted for meaningful?* Calculate $R^2_{y.abc}$. This indicates the proportion of variance accounted for by the main effects and the interaction. If $R^2_{y.abc}$ is too small to be meaningful within the context of your theoretical formulation and your knowledge of the findings in the field of study, terminate the analysis. Whether R^2 is significant or not, if in your judgment its magnitude has little substantive meaning, there is no point in going further. If $R^2_{y.abc}$ is meaningful, go to step 2.

2. *Is there a significant interaction?* Calculate $R^2_{y.ab}$. Test

$$F = \frac{(R^2_{y.abc} - R^2_{y.ab})/(k_1 - k_2)}{(1 - R^2_{y.abc})/(N - k_1 - 1)}$$

where k_1 is the number of vectors (the coded vectors, the continuous variable, and the product vectors) associated with $R^2_{y.abc}$; k_2 is the number of vectors (the coded vectors and the continuous variable) associated with $R^2_{y.ab}$. A nonsignificant F ratio with $k_1 - k_2$ and $N - k_1 - 1$ *df* indicates that the interaction is not significant. If the interaction is not significant, go to step 3. If it is significant, go to step 7.

3. *Is the common regression coefficient (b_c) significant?* Calculate $R^2_{y.a}$. Test

$$F = \frac{(R^2_{y.ab} - R^2_{y.a})/(k_1 - k_2)}{(1 - R^2_{y.ab})/(N - k_1 - 1)}$$

where k_1 is the number of vectors (the coded vectors and the continuous variable) associated with $R^2_{y.ab}$; k_2 is the number of coded vectors associated with $R^2_{y.a}$. This test was presented for uniformity of format. It can be accomplished in a simpler manner. Remember that the b associated with the continuous variable in a regression equation in which product vectors are *not* included is b_c. Therefore, testing this b in the usual manner is equivalent to the above test. If this test is not significant go to step 4. If it is significant, go to step 5.

4. *Do the treatments of the categorical variable differ significantly from each other?* Calculate $R^2_{y.a}$. Test

$$F = \frac{R^2_{y.a}/k}{(1 - R^2_{y.a})/(N - k - 1)}$$

where k is the number of coded vector used to represent the categorical variable. Note that because it was concluded (step 3) that b_c is not significant, the design here is reduced to one in which only a categorical independent variable is used. Therefore, it is analyzed and interpreted in the same way as was done in Chapter 9.

5. *Are the intercepts significantly different?* Calculate $R^2_{y.b}$. Test

$$F = \frac{(R^2_{y.ab} - R^2_{y.b})/(k_1 - k_2)}{(1 - R^2_{y.ab})/(N - k_1 - 1)}$$

where k_1 is the number of vectors (the coded vectors and the continuous variable) associated with $R^2_{y.ab}$; $k_2 = 1$ (one continuous variable is used in the present context). If this test is not significant, go to step 6. If this test is significant, calculate separate regression equations in which the intercepts differ, but all have the same b (i.e., b_c). This is done by using the regression equation in which product vectors are *not* included. When the categorical variable consists of more than two categories, it is possible to do multiple comparisons among the intercepts. This topic is discussed in Chapter 13.

6. Having determined (step 5) that the intercepts are not significantly different from each other, calculate a single regression equation for all subjects by regressing the dependent variable on the continuous variable. The analysis is terminated, and the results are interpreted.

7. Having determined that the interaction is significant (step 2), *calculate separate regression equations*. This is done by using the overall regression equation. *Establish regions of significance*. This topic is discussed later in the chapter.

CATEGORIZING CONTINUOUS VARIABLES

Behavioral scientists frequently partition continuous independent variables into dichotomies, trichotomies, and so on, and then analyze the data as if they came from discrete categories of an independent variable. Several broad classes of research in which there is a tendency to partition continuous variables can be identified. The first class may be found in experiments in which a manipulated variable is continuous and is treated in the analysis as categorical. The retention experiment discussed in this chapter is an illustration. One variable was categorical (Incentive–No Incentive), while the other was continuous (Study Time) with four levels. Instead of doing an analysis of the kind discussed earlier, some researchers will treat the continuous variable as composed of four distinct categories and analyze the data with a 2×4 factorial analysis of variance.[3]

The second class of research studies in which one frequently encounters categorization of a continuous variable is what is referred to as the treatments-by-levels design. In such designs the continuous variable is primarily a control variable. For example, a researcher may be interested in the difference between two methods of instruction. Since the subjects differ in intelligence, he or she may wish to control this variable. One way of doing this is to block or create groups with different levels of intelligence and to randomly assign an equal number of subjects from each level to each of the treatments. The levels are then treated as distinct categories and a factorial analysis of variance is done. The purpose of introducing the levels into the design is to decrease the error term. This is done by identifying the sum of squares due to intelligence, thereby reducing the error sum of squares. A more sensitive F test for the main effect, methods of instruction, is thereby obtained. The reduction in the error term depends on the correlation between the continuous variable and the dependent variable. The larger the correlation the greater the reduction will be in the error term.

The third class of studies in which researchers tend to categorize continuous variables is similar to the second class just discussed. While the categorization in the second class was primarily motivated by the need for control, the categorization in this class of studies is motivated by an interest in the possible interaction between the independent variables. This approach is referred to as Aptitude-Treatment Interaction (ATI) or Trait-Treatment Interaction (TTI). It is important in the behavioral sciences, since it may help identify relations that will otherwise go unnoticed. Behavioral scientists and educators have frequently voiced concern that while lip service is paid to the fact that people differ and that what may be appropriate for some may not be appropriate for others, little has been done to search for and identify the optimal conditions of performance for different groups of people.

If, for example, in a study of the effectiveness of different teaching methods the variable of intelligence is included not only for the purposes of control but also for the purpose of seeking possible interactions between teaching methods and intelligence the research is in the ATI framework. Note that the point of departure of the researcher is a search for optimal methods of teaching subjects with different levels of intelligence. The analysis is the same as in the treatments-by-levels design, that is, a factorial analysis of variance. In both cases the researcher studies the main effects and the interaction. The difference between the two approaches is in the conceptualization of the research. Does the

[3]Whether one uses the conventional calculating methods or performs the calculations by the methods presented in this book (see Chapter 10), the results will, of course, be the same.

researcher include the continuous variable primarily for the purpose of control or for the purpose of studying interaction?

One may point to various areas in which categorization of variables in the framework discussed above is done. With achievement motivation, for example, researchers measure need achievement, dichotomize it into high and low need achievement, and treat it as a categorical variable. Researchers also tend to partition variables like authoritarianism, dogmatism, cognitive style, self-esteem, and ego-defense similarly.

For the most exhaustive treatment of ATI research to date see Cronbach and Snow (1977), the first four chapters of which consist of an excellent discussion of introductory and advanced topics in the design and analysis of ATI studies. The remainder of the book is devoted to a critical review of ATI research in various substantive areas (e.g., Learning, Personality). See also Berliner and Cahen (1973) and Bracht (1970).

A fourth class of studies in which continuous variables are categorized is in nonexperimental research with attribute variables. This is potentially the most misleading and harmful use of categorization because it casts the design in what appears to be a factorial analysis of variance. Researchers resort to this approach either because they are unfamiliar with other methods (e.g., multiple regression analysis) or because they *erroneously* believe that by categorizing the attributes and doing an analysis of variance they may study interactions among the attributes.

Problems regarding the use of the concept of interaction in nonexperimental research have been discussed in detail in Chapters 10 and 11. In the present context it will therefore suffice to point out that the categorization of continuous variables further aggravates the problems. In a good critique of the inappropriateness of categorizing continuous variables, Humphreys (1978) states:

> The basic fact is that a measure of individual differences is not an independent variable, and it does not become one by categorizing the scores and treating the categories as if they defined a variable under experimental control in a factorially designed analysis of variance. (p. 873)

In short, categorizing attribute variables and treating them as if they define a factorial analysis of variance "not infrequently produces in both the investigator and his audience the illusion that he has experimental control over the independent variable. Nothing could be more wrong" (Humphreys & Fleishman, 1974, p. 468).

Categorization of attribute variables is all too frequently resorted to in the social sciences. An area in which this is currently being done almost with a vengeance is sex role research. Most often, median splits are being used in order to identify, for example, people who are masculine, feminine, androgynous, and undifferentiated. For a critique of such research, see Pedhazur and Tetenbaum (1979).

There are two major questions on the categorization of continuous variables: "On what basis does one categorize?" and "What effect does the categorization have on the analysis?" The first question cannot be easily answered, since categorization is an arbitrary process. One researcher may choose to split the group at the median and label those above the median as high and those below the median as low. All subjects within a given subgroup are treated as if they had identical scores on what is essentially a continuous variable. This is particularly questionable when the variability of the continuous measure is relatively large. Moreover, in a median split, a difference of one unit on the continuous variable may result in labeling a subject as high or low. In order to avoid this possibility, some researchers create a middle group and use it in the analysis or ignore it altogether. There are other variations on the theme. One can take the continuum of intelligence, for example, and create as many categories as one fancies or believes to be appropriate. There are no solid principles to guide the categorization of continuous variables. It can be said, however, that one should not categorize a continuous variable because there is nothing to be gained; indeed there is danger of loss.

It is possible that some of the conflicting evidence in the research literature of a given area may be attributed to the practice of categorization of continuous variables. For example, let us assume that two researchers are independently studying the relation between dogmatism and susceptibility to a prestigious source. Suppose, further, that the researchers follow identical procedures in their research designs. That is, they have the same type of prestigious source, the same type of suggestion, the same number of subjects, and so on. They administer the Dogmatism Scale to their subjects, split them at the median and create a high Dogmatism and a low Dogmatism group. Subjects from each of these groups are then randomly assigned to a prestigious or a nonprestigious source. The result is a 2 × 2 factorial analysis of variance—two sources and two levels of Dogmatism. Note, however, that the determination of "high" and "low" is entirely dependent on the type of subjects involved. It is true that in relation to one's group it is appropriate to say that a subject is "high" or "low." But it is possible that the "highs" of the first researcher may be more like the "lows" of the second researcher due to differences in samples. When the two studies are reported, it is likely that little specific information about the subjects is offered. Instead, reporting is generally restricted to statements about high and low dogmatists, as if this were determined in an absolute fashion rather than relative to the distribution of dogmatism of a given group. It should therefore not come as a surprise that under such circumstances the "highs" in one research study behave more like the "lows" in the other study, thus leading to conflicting results in what are presumably similar studies.

The answer to the second question—"What effects does the categorization have on the analysis?"—is clear-cut. Categorization leads to a loss of information, and consequently to a less sensitive analysis. For example, in the research illustration on dogmatism and susceptibility to a prestigious source, the researcher is interested in the relation between these two variables. Once dogmatism has been dichotomized into high and low, statements can be made about differences between the two subgroups. Attempts to estimate the relation between the variables, however, will be limited due to the reduction in the variability of dogmatism resulting from the categorization.

As mentioned above, all subjects within a category are treated alike even though they may have originally been quite different on the continuous variable. For example, if one's cutting score for the high group on intelligence is 115, then all subjects above this score are considered alike on intelligence. In the subsequent analysis no distinction is made between a subject whose score was 115, and another whose score was, say, 130. But if, in the first place, the choice of the continuous variable (intelligence) was made because of its relation to the dependent variable, then one would expect a difference in performance between the two subjects, even though they were given the same treatment. It is this loss of information about the differences between subjects, or the reduction in the variability of the continuous variable, that leads to a reduction in the sensitivity of the analysis, not to mention the meaningfulness of the results.

A Numerical Example

In order to illustrate the decrease in sensitivity of the analysis caused by the categorization process, the data of the retention experiment reported in Table 12.1 are reanalyzed. Now, however, the continuous variable, Study Time, is treated as if it were a categorical variable consisting of four categories. It may also be useful to think of the data as if they were obtained in treatments-by-levels design, or an ATI design. For example, instead of the variable Incentive–No Incentive (the categorical variable in the retention experiment reported in Table 12.1) think of two methods of teaching, or two sources of information, or two methods of attitude change. Instead of Study Time (the continuous variable in the retention experiment) think of four levels of intelligence, or four levels of authoritarianism.[4]

The data from Table 12.1 are displayed in Table 12.4 for an analysis in which both independent variables are treated as categorical variables. The procedures for such an analysis were discussed and illustrated in Chapter 10 and are therefore not repeated here. Note that vector 1 in Table 12.4 identifies the Incentive–No Incentive variable. Vectors 2, 3, and 4 express the variable Study Time (treated now as a categorical variable). Vectors 5, 6, and 7 express the interaction between the independent variables. In Chapter 10 it was demonstrated that when the frequencies in each cell are equal, the vectors identifying each variable and the interaction are mutually orthogonal, when orthogonal or effect coding is used. Note that effect coding is used in Table 12.4. Following are excerpts of output from the REGRESSION program of SPSS which was used to analyze the data of Table 12.4.

Output

VARIABLE	R SQUARE	R SQUARE CHANGE	SUM OF SQUARES CHANGE
X1 (No Incentive–Incentive)	.57953	.57953	100.04167
X2–X4 (Study Time)	.82549	.24596	42.45833
X5–X7 (Interaction)	.83780	.01231	2.12500
RESIDUAL			28.00000

[4]That the values associated with the continuous variable in this example are 5, 10, 15, and 20 should pose no problem. If you wish, add, for example, a constant of 100 to each of the values, and you may now think of the scores as IQ's. The results will not be affected by the addition of a constant.

VARIABLE	DF	MEAN SQUARE	F
X1 (No Incentive–Incentive)	1	100.04167	57.17
X2–X4 (Study Time)	3	14.15278	8.09
X5–X7 (Interaction)	3	.70833	.40
RESIDUAL	16	1.75000	

Table 12.4 Data from the Retention Experiment, Laid Out for Analysis in Which the Independent Variables Are Treated as Categorical Variables

Y	*1*	*2*	*3*	*4*	*5* (*1* × *2*)	*6* (*1* × *3*)	*7* (*1* × *4*)
3	1	1	0	0	1	0	0
4	1	1	0	0	1	0	0
5	1	1	0	0	1	0	0
4	1	0	1	0	0	1	0
5	1	0	1	0	0	1	0
6	1	0	1	0	0	1	0
5	1	0	0	1	0	0	1
6	1	0	0	1	0	0	1
8	1	0	0	1	0	0	1
7	1	−1	−1	−1	−1	−1	−1
8	1	−1	−1	−1	−1	−1	−1
9	1	−1	−1	−1	−1	−1	−1
7	−1	1	0	0	−1	0	0
8	−1	1	0	0	−1	0	0
9	−1	1	0	0	−1	0	0
9	−1	0	1	0	0	−1	0
10	−1	0	1	0	0	−1	0
11	−1	0	1	0	0	−1	0
8	−1	0	0	1	0	0	−1
11	−1	0	0	1	0	0	−1
12	−1	0	0	1	0	0	−1
10	−1	−1	−1	−1	1	1	1
11	−1	−1	−1	−1	1	1	1
13	−1	−1	−1	−1	1	1	1
Σy^2:	172.625						

NOTE: Y = measures of retention originally given in Table 12.1; 1 = coded vector for Incentive–No Incentive; 2, 3, and 4 = coded vectors for Study Time; 5, 6, and 7 = vectors expressing the interaction between Incentive–No Incentive and Study Time.

Commentary

As was done in earlier examples, the output was organized in a format that differs from the one given by SPSS. The numbers attached to the *X*'s (under VARIABLE in Output) refer to the vector numbers of Table 12.4. Note that in the output given here the vectors referring to a given component were grouped together, as was the information relevant to them (i.e., R SQUARE, R SQUARE CHANGE). The SUM OF SQUARES CHANGE, DF, MEAN SQUARE, and F are not reported in this form by SPSS but were calculated by using information that the program does report (for detailed discussions of how this is done with SPSS output, see Chapters 10 and 11). In what follows, the present analysis is contrasted with the one done earlier in this chapter, where Study Time was treated as a continuous variable.

Beginning with the categorical variable, No Incentive–Incentive, it will be noted that the proportion of variance it accounts for is identical in both analyses (.57953; see Output above, and section entitled Proportions of Variance Accounted For). The *F* ratios for the test of this proportion, however, are not the same in the two analyses. In the earlier analysis the *F* ratio for the categorical variable is 68.71 with 1 and 21 *df,* whereas in the present analysis the *F* ratio is 57.17 with 1 and 16 *df* (see Output above). This is due to the smaller mean square residual in the earlier analysis. It is interesting to note that the residual sum of squares in the present analysis is smaller than the one obtained in the earlier analysis (28.00000 and 30.57500, respectively). But this is offset by the larger number of *df* associated with the residual sum of squares in the earlier analysis as compared with the present one (21 and 16, respectively), thereby leading to a smaller mean square residual in the earlier analysis.

Turning now to the main concern of the contrast between the two analyses, it will be noted that Study Time accounts for barely a slightly larger proportion of the variance in Retention (the dependent variable) in the present analysis than what it accounted for in the earlier analysis (.24596 and .24335, respectively). But notice the dramatic difference between the two *F* ratios associated with Study Time. When this variable was treated as continuous, the *F* ratio was 28.85 with 1 and 21 *df,* whereas in the present analysis the *F* ratio is 8.09 with 3 and 16 *df.*

Since the proportion of variance accounted for by Study Time in both analyses is almost identical, and the mean square residuals are very similar in both analyses, it is clear that the difference between the two *F* ratios is due primarily to the difference in the *df* for their numerators (1 *df* in the earlier analysis, and 3 *df* in the present one). Consequently, the numerator of the *F* ratio in the present analysis is about a third of what it is in the earlier analysis. Although both *F* ratios are significant beyond the .01 level for the illustrative data being used, it should be evident that it is possible that treating a continuous variable in its original form may result in a significant *F* ratio at a prespecified level of significance, whereas the *F* ratio for the same variable may fail to reach significance when it is treated as if it were a categorical variable. A numerical example of such an occurrence was given at the beginning of Chapter 11.

But why the difference in *df*? To answer this question it is necessary to recall the discussion in Chapter 11, where it was pointed out that two different models are being used when a continuous variable is treated either in its original form or as a categorical variable. When the continuous variable is treated in its original form, the analysis is addressed to questions regarding possible trends in the regression of the dependent variable on the continuous independent variable. When, on the other hand, the continuous variable is treated as if it were categorical, the analysis is addressed to the question whether there are significant differences among the means under the different levels of the continuous variable. In the earlier analysis, only the linear component of Study Time was used. Although it was possible to use higher-degree polynomials with Study Time, this was not done in the earlier analysis. In essence, then, the analysis proceeded as if it were known that trends beyond the linear were not meaningful, hence 1 *df*.[5] When the continuous variable was treated as being categorical in the present analysis the test of the proportion of variance (or sum of squares) it accounted for was addressed to the question whether there are significant differences among the four means under the different levels of Study Time, hence 3 *df*.

It will be recalled (see Chapter 11) that the proportion of variance accounted for by a continuous variable when it is treated as if it were categorical is equal to the proportion of variance that will be accounted for by the continuous variable when it is raised to the highest-degree polynomial possible in the given set of data. As Study Time consists of four distinct levels, it may be raised to the third power. Had this been done, it would have accounted for .24596 of the variance of the dependent variable (the same as in the present analysis). That there is no meaningful trend beyond the linear can be seen by calculating the proportion of variance due to deviation from linearity: $.24596 - .24335 = .00261$.[6]

The contrast between using polynomial regression analysis or treating the continuous variable as if it were categorical is that with the former approach it is possible to determine what degree of polynomial fits the data, whereas in using the latter approach a curve is fitted to go through the means. To repeat: the proportion of variance accounted for when a continuous variable is treated as if it were categorical is equal to the proportion of variance accounted for by the highest-degree polynomial possible with a given set of values. Therefore, treating the continuous variable as if it were categorical cannot result in a loss of information so far as the proportion of variance accounted for is concerned. But there is a serious loss in the meaningfulness of the results. By ignoring the fact that the variable is continuous one forfeits the opportunity for studying trends in the data and is constrained to speak only of differences among means. It was shown above that the deviation from linearity in the present data is minuscule (.00261)—an issue that is not addressed at all when the continuous variable is treated as if it were a categorical one.

What was said above about the continuous variable applies equally to its interaction with the categorical variable. Using three vectors (one for the

[5]Although, as is shown below, the deviation from linearity is very small in the present data, one should always study the trends in the data and not assume that the regression is linear. Curvilinear regression analysis is discussed later in the chapter, where the present example is reanalyzed for illustrative purposes.

[6]See Footnote 5.

categorical variable, one for the continuous, and one for their product) as was done in the earlier analysis, the only question that could be answered regarding the interaction is whether there is a significant interaction between the categorical variable and the linear trend of the continuous variable (remember that it was not significant). But calculating the interaction, when the continuous variable is treated as a categorical variable, is tantamount to calculating the proportion of variance that is accounted for by the interaction with all the terms of the polynomials, whether or not they are meaningful. Note carefully that as in the case of the main effect, the question of trends is not addressed when the interaction is based on a treatment of the continuous variable as a categorical one. There is simply a lumping of the variance accounted for by what could be identified as interactions with different trends when curvilinear regression analysis is applied. This is demonstrated later in the chapter when the data used here are subjected to such an analysis.

Until now, the discussion and the numerical demonstration were limited to the case of a manipulated continuous variable consisting of a small number of distinct values. When the continuous variable consists of many values, as is frequently the case with attribute variables (e.g., intelligence), it would be absurd to attempt to raise it to the highest-degree polynomial possible. Therefore, when such a variable is arbitrarily categorized (it should not be!), the equivalence in proportion of variance accounted for by the two alternative analyses that was shown above does not hold anymore. Arbitrarily categorizing a continuous variable will lead to loss of information, the degree of which will depend on the number of categories used and the type of trend that exists in the data.

The obvious conclusion from the foregoing discussion is: Do not treat a continuous variable with a few distinct values as if it were a categorical variable, and do not categorize a continuous variable that consists of a relatively large number of values.

THE STUDY OF INTERACTION

The concept of interaction was introduced and discussed in detail in Chapter 10, where it was limited to situations in which the independent variables are categorical. The topic was dealt with again in Chapter 11, where the concern was with interactions between continuous variables. In this chapter, interactions between continuous and categorical variables are discussed. The type of variables notwithstanding, to ask whether independent variables interact is, in effect, to ask about the model that best fits the data. When an interaction is not significant, an additive model is sufficient to describe the data. This means that a subject's score on the dependent variable is conceived of as a composite of several additive components. In the most general case, these are an intercept, treatment effects, and an error term. For the Retention experiment analyzed in the beginning of the chapter, the additive model is:

$$Y = a + b_1X_1 + b_2X_2 + e \qquad (12.3)$$

where X_1 is group membership (NI and I), X_2 is the continuous variable (ST; see Table 12.3), and b_1 and b_2 are the regression coefficients associated with these vectors.

If, on the other hand, the interaction is significant, this means that an additive model is not adequate to describe the data. One needs to add terms that reflect the interaction. For the present example this may take the form

$$Y = a + b_1X_1 + b_2X_2 + b_3X_1X_2 + e \tag{12.4}$$

The difference between Equations (12.3) and (12.4) is that in the latter a term that is the product of the values of the independent variables has been added (that is, X_1X_2). It is, of course, possible to determine whether this new term adds significantly to the proportion of variance accounted for, thereby testing whether the additive model is adequate or not. In fact, this was done earlier in the chapter with the data of the Retention experiment. Moreover, it was shown that when one of the variables is categorical and the other is continuous, the test of the interaction addresses the question whether the regression lines of the dependent variable on the continuous variable are parallel for all the categories of the categorical variable. Stated differently, a test of the interaction addresses the question of whether the regression coefficients in a set of separate regression equations are different from each other.

Before pursuing further the study of interaction it is necessary to recognize that in experimental research the continuous variable may be a manipulated or an attribute variable. In the Retention experiment, presented in the beginning of this chapter, the continuous variable, Study Time, was manipulated. It is possible, however, to use a nonmanipulated continuous variable in conjunction with a manipulated categorical variable. A prime example of such research is the area of Aptitude-Treatment Interaction (ATI), where the aptitude is some attribute of the subjects. A test of the interaction indicates whether or not the regression coefficients in the separate regression equations are different from each other (or whether or not the regression lines are parallel) regardless of whether the continuous variable is manipulated or not. The interpretation of the interaction, however, is less ambiguous when the continuous variable is manipulated. The reason is that under such circumstances complete randomization is possible, and it is therefore plausible to assume that the continuous variable is not correlated with other variables that are subsumed under the error term—for example, e in Equation (12.4). When the continuous variable is not manipulated, subjects may be randomly assigned only to the treatments that comprise the categorical variable. The purpose of such randomization is to "equate" the groups assigned to the different treatments, but this does not preclude the possibility that the continuous variable being used in the study is correlated with other variables that are not included in the model. Consequently, when a continuous nonmanipulated variable is used, it is necessary to be cognizant of the possibility that variables other than the one under consideration may be partly, or even wholly, responsible for its interaction with a manipulated categorical variable. The best guides for the interpretation of the results are, as always, theory and knowledge about the specific problem under study. And the best safeguard for avoiding misinterpretations is clear and critical thinking.[7] Because the presentation that follows is devoted solely to analytic issues, the important distinction between interactions with manipulated and nonmanipulated variables will not be dealt with. You should not, however, overlook this distinction when you are doing research and when you are reading research reports.

Ordinal and Disordinal Interactions

The concepts of ordinal and disordinal interactions were introduced in Chapter 10 in connection with interactions between categorical variables. Although the overall conception is the same for the case of interactions between continuous and categorical variables, it will become apparent from the following presentation that the specifics of the definitions, graphic depictions, and tests of significance differ in the two situations. The differences stem from the fact that in the present situation we are dealing with regression equations, regression lines, and comparisons among them, whereas in Chapter 10 we were dealing with means, line segments connecting means, and comparisons between mean differences.

An ordinal interaction between a continuous and a categorical variable is indicated when nonparallel regression lines do not intersect within the research range of interest (see explanation below), whereas a disordinal interaction is indicated when regression lines intersect within the research range of interest. This distinction can best be illustrated graphically, as in Figure 12.2. In Figure 12.2(a), a situation in which there is no interaction is depicted. The two regression lines are parallel. There is a constant difference between Treatments I and II along the continuum of the continuous variable. In other words, the b weights for the two regression lines are identical, and the difference between the treatments is entirely accountable by the difference between the intercepts of the regression lines. In (b), while Treatment I is still superior to Treatment II along the continuum, it is relatively more effective at the lower end of the X variable than at the upper end. Note, however, that in no instance is Treatment II superior to Treatment I. Thus this is an ordinal interaction.

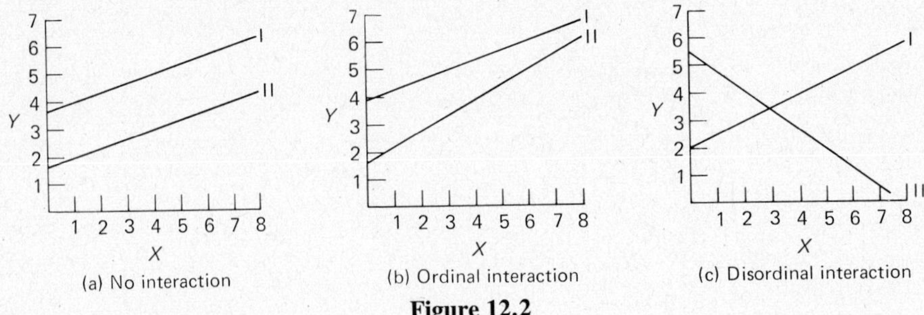

Figure 12.2

[7]For a discussion that parallels the one given above, see in Chapter 10 the section entitled Manipulated and Classificatory Variables.

In Figure 12.2(c), the regression lines cross. This is an example of a disordinal interaction. Treatment II is superior at the lower levels of X (up to 3), while Treatment I is superior at the upper regions of X (from 3 and up). At the value of $X = 3$ the two treatments seem to be equally effective.

It is obvious that if the regression lines of Figure 12.2(b) are extended, they will cross each other as in a disordinal interaction. Therefore, the question is: When is an interaction considered ordinal and under what conditions is it considered disordinal? The answer lies in the range of interest of the researcher.

The Research Range of Interest

The research range of interest is defined by the values of the continuous variable (X) of relevance to the purposes of the research. Recall that extrapolation from regression lines is hazardous (see Chapter 11). Therefore, values within the research range of interest should be included in the actual study. In the Retention experiment analyzed earlier in this chapter the research range of interest was presumably from 5 to 20 minutes of Study Time. Or, using an example with a nonmanipulated continuous variable, say IQ, the research range of interest may be from 90 to 120. In other words, it is for subjects within this range of intelligence that one wishes to make statements about the effectiveness of teaching methods or some other treatment.

The decision as to whether an interaction is ordinal or disordinal is based on the point at which the regression lines cross each other. If this point is outside the range of interest, the interaction is considered ordinal. If, on the other hand, the point at which the lines intersect is within the range of interest, then the interaction is considered disordinal. To illustrate, let us assume that for Figure 12.2 the researcher's range of interest is from 1 to 8 on the X variable. It is evident that the regression lines in (b) do not intersect within the range of interest, while those in (c) cross each other well within the range of interest (at the point where $X = 3$).

Determining the Point of Intersection

It is possible to calculate the point at which the regression lines intersect. Note that at the point of intersection the predicted Y for Treatment I is equal to the predicted Y for Treatment II. When the regression lines are parallel, a prediction of equal Y's for two treatments at a given value of X will not occur. The regression equations for two parallel lines consist of different intercepts and identical b weights. For example, assume that in a given research study consisting of two treatments (A and B) the regression lines are parallel. Assume further that the intercept for Treatment A is 7 while the intercept for Treatment B is 2, and that the b weights for each of the regression lines is .8. The two regression equations are

$$Y'_A = 7 + .8X$$

$$Y'_B = 2 + .8X$$

For any value of X the value of Y'_A will be 5 points higher than the value of Y'_B (this is the difference between the intercepts, and it is constant along the continuum of X).

Suppose, however, that the two equations are

$$Y'_A = 7 + .3X$$

$$Y'_B = 2 + .8X$$

An inspection of these two equations indicates that when the values of X are relatively small, Y'_A will be larger than Y'_B. The reason is that the intercept plays a more important role relative to the b weight in the prediction of Y. But as X increases, the b weight plays an increasingly important role, thus offsetting the difference between the intercepts, until a point is reached where a balance is struck and $Y'_A = Y'_B$. Beyond that point, Y'_B will be larger than Y'_A. The point of intersection can be calculated with the following formula:

$$\text{Point of intersection } (X) = \frac{a_1 - a_2}{b_2 - b_1} \qquad (12.5)$$

where the a's are the intercepts of the regression lines, and the b's are the regression coefficients. For the above example, $a_1 = 7$, $a_2 = 2$, $b_1 = .3$, $b_2 = .8$.

$$X = \frac{7 - 2}{.8 - .3} = \frac{5}{.5} = 10$$

The point at which the lines intersect is at the value of $X = 10$. This is illustrated in Figure 12.3. If the range of interest in the research depicted in Figure 12.3 is from 3 to 15, then the interaction is disordinal since the lines intersect within this range.

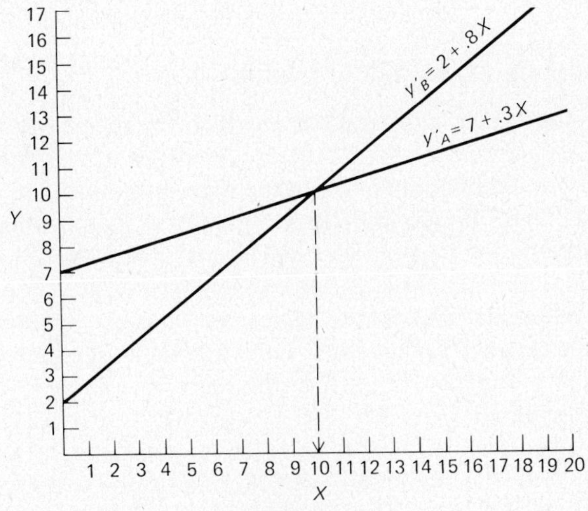

Figure 12.3

The regression equations for the two lines of Figure 12.3 are now applied to several values of X in order to illustrate the major points made in the discussion above. For $X = 10$,

$$Y'_A = 7 + (.3)(10) = 10$$

$$Y'_B = 2 + (.8)(10) = 10$$

The same value is predicted for subjects under treatments A or B. This is because the lines intersect at $X = 10$. For $X = 5$,

$$Y'_A = 7 + (.3)(5) = 8.5$$

$$Y'_B = 2 + (.8)(5) = 6$$

The value of $X = 5$ is below the point of intersection, and the regression equation for Treatment A leads to higher predicted value of Y than does the regression equation for Treatment B. The reverse is true for values of X that are above the point of intersection. For example, for $X = 12$,

$$Y'_A = 7 + (.3)(12) = 10.6$$

$$Y'_B = 2 + (.8)(12) = 11.6$$

AN EXAMPLE WITH INTERACTION

It has been maintained that students' satisfaction with the teaching styles of their teachers depends, among other variables, on the students' tolerance of ambiguity. Specifically, students whose tolerance of ambiguity is relatively low prefer teachers whose teaching style is largely directive, while students whose tolerance of ambiguity is relatively high prefer teachers whose style is largely nondirective. To test this hypothesis students were randomly assigned to "directive" and "nondirective" teachers. In the beginning of the semester the students were administered a measure of tolerance of ambiguity on which the higher the score the greater the tolerance. At the end of the semester students rated their teacher on a 7-point scale, 1 indicating very little satisfaction, 7 indicating a great deal of satisfaction. This then is an example of an ATI or TTI study.

Illustrative data for two classes, each consisting of 20 students, are reported in Table 12.5. Note that both dummy (vector 1) and effect (vector 2) coding are used to represent the categorical variable, teaching styles.[8] It is, of course, not necessary to use both coding methods. The properties of the overall regression equation with effect coding were discussed earlier in this chapter. Dummy coding is included here in order to show the properties of the overall regression equation with this method of coding. Vector 3 in Table 12.5 represents the con-

[8]When the categorical variable consists of two categories, effect coding and orthogonal coding are indistinguishable. For more than two categories, the methods presented here also apply with orthogonal coding.

Table 12.5 Tolerance of Ambiguity and Rating of Teachers, Illustrative Data

Teaching Styles	*Y*	*1*	*2*	*3*	*4* (*1* × *3*)	*5* (*2* × *3*)
	2	1	1	5	5	5
	1	1	1	7	7	7
	2	1	1	10	10	10
	2	1	1	15	15	15
	3	1	1	17	17	17
	3	1	1	20	20	20
	3	1	1	25	25	25
Nondirective	4	1	1	23	23	23
	4	1	1	27	27	27
	5	1	1	30	30	30
	6	1	1	35	35	35
	5	1	1	37	37	37
	5	1	1	40	40	40
	5	1	1	42	42	42
	6	1	1	45	45	45
	6	1	1	47	47	47
	6	1	1	50	50	50
	7	1	1	55	55	55
	7	1	1	60	60	60
	6	1	1	62	62	62
	7	0	−1	5	0	−5
	7	0	−1	7	0	−7
	7	0	−1	9	0	−9
	6	0	−1	13	0	−13
	5	0	−1	12	0	−12
	6	0	−1	16	0	−16
	5	0	−1	18	0	−18
	5	0	−1	21	0	−21
	5	0	−1	22	0	−22
	4	0	−1	27	0	−27
Directive	4	0	−1	26	0	−26
	3	0	−1	32	0	−32
	3	0	−1	35	0	−35
	2	0	−1	40	0	−40
	3	0	−1	45	0	−45
	2	0	−1	47	0	−47
	2	0	−1	49	0	−49
	1	0	−1	53	0	−53
	2	0	−1	58	0	−58
	1	0	−1	63	0	−63

NOTE: Y = ratings of teachers; vector 1 = teaching styles, where 1 is for nondirective and 0 is for directive; vector 2 = teaching styles, where 1 is for nondirective and −1 is for directive; 3 = tolerance of ambiguity.

tinuous variable, tolerance of ambiguity. Vector 4 is a product of vectors 1 and 3, and vector 5 is a product of vectors 2 and 3. Although vectors 4 and 5 are presented in Table 12.5, they need not be punched on cards since they can be generated by the computer program.

The data of Table 12.5 were analyzed by the REGRESSION program of SPSS. Two regression analyses were called for: (1) the regression of Y on X_1, X_3, and X_4: (2) the regression of Y on X_2, X_3, and X_5. Because it was desired to note the proportion of variance accounted for by the interaction, X_4 and X_5 were assigned lower-level inclusion numbers in their respective regression equations.

Beginning in column 16, the two regression statements are:
REGRESSION = Y WITH X1 X3(4) X4(2)/
REGRESSION = Y WITH X2 X3(4) X5(2)/

Following are excerpts of the output and commentaries.

Output

SUMMARY TABLE
Dummy Coding

VARIABLE ENTERED	R SQUARE	R SQUARE CHANGE
X1	.01140	.01140
X3	.01580	.00440
X4	.90693	.89113

SUMMARY TABLE
Effect Coding

VARIABLE	R SQUARE	R SQUARE CHANGE
X2	.01140	.01140
X3	.01580	.00440
X5	.90693	.89113

Commentary

The SUMMARY TABLES from the analyses with dummy and effect coding are given alongside each other to show that they lead to identical results, as would be expected. As is shown below, the regression equations for the two analyses differ. Again, this is to be expected because of the different coding methods.

Note that although $R^2_{y.134} = R^2_{y.235} = .90693$, the major part of the proportion of variance accounted for is due to the increment accounted for by the interaction: .89113 (R SQUARE CHANGE). It is this increment that is tested for significance.

$$F = \frac{.89113/1}{(1 - .90693)/(40 - 3 - 1)} = 344.69$$

with 1 and 36 *df*. It was shown earlier that with two groups this test is equivalent to the test of the *b* associated with the interaction vector. Since the test of the *b* is given in the output, the calculation of the above *F* ratio is not necessary. It was done for completeness of presentation. When the design consists of more than two groups, the above approach has to be used (for a numerical example, see Chapter 13).

Output

Dummy Coding			Effect Coding		
VARIABLES IN THE EQUATION			VARIABLES IN THE EQUATION		
VARIABLE	B	F	VARIABLE	B	F
X1	−5.99972		X2	−2.99986	
X3	−.10680		X3	−.00422	
X4	.20516	344.68	X5	.10258	344.68
CONSTANT	7.19321		CONSTANT	4.19336	

Commentary

The results from both analyses are given alongside each other for comparative purposes. Note that although the regression equations for the two coding methods differ, the *F* ratios for the *b*'s associated with the product vectors (X4 in Dummy Coding and X5 in Effect Coding) are identical. This is (within rounding) the same as the *F* ratio obtained above, when the increment in proportion of variance accounted for by the interaction vector was tested. The *F* ratios for the other vectors were not given above, though they are reported in the output, because they are irrelevant. All we want to know at this stage is whether the interaction is significant. It is clearly significant, indicating that the regressions of ratings of teachers on tolerance of ambiguity differ under the conditions of nondirective and directive teachers. Consequently, it is necessary to obtain the separate regression equations.

Separate Regression Equations

Earlier, it was shown how the separate regression equations may be obtained from the overall regression equation with effect coding. Therefore, only minimal comments will be made here about this approach. Subsequently, it is shown how the separate regression equations may be obtained from the overall regression equation with dummy coding.

Effect Coding. The overall regression equation given above is:

$$Y' = 4.19336 - 2.99986X_2 - .00422X_3 + .10258X_5$$

where X_2, X_3, and X_5 refer to vectors 2, 3, and 5 of Table 12.5. The average of the intercepts of the two separate regression equations is 4.19336 *(a)*. In vector

2, the group taught by the nondirective teacher was assigned 1. Therefore, the intercept for this group is

$$4.19336 + (-2.99986) = \mathit{1.19350}$$

The intercept for the group assigned -1 in vector 2 (group taught by directive teacher) is

$$4.19336 - (-2.99986) = \mathit{7.19322}$$

The average of the regression coefficients for the separate regression equations is $-.00422$ (b for X_3). The deviation of the regression coefficient for the group taught by the nondirective teacher is .10258 (b for X_5). The regression coefficient for this group is therefore:

$$-.00422 + .10258 = \mathit{.09836}$$

The regression coefficient for the group taught by the directive teacher is

$$-.00422 - (.10258) = -\mathit{.10680}$$

On the basis of the above calculations the regression equations for the two groups are

$$Y'_{\text{ND}} = 1.19350 + .09836X$$

$$Y'_{\text{D}} = 7.19322 - .10680X$$

where ND = nondirective; D = directive; X = tolerance of ambiguity. The same regression equations would be obtained if one calculated them separately for each group. You may wish to do this as an exercise.

Dummy Coding. The overall regression equation with dummy coding is:

$$Y' = 7.19321 - 5.99972X_1 - .10680X_3 + .20516X_4$$

where X_1, X_3, and X_4 refer to vectors 1, 3, and 4 of Table 12.5. It is now shown how the separate regression equations may be obtained from the overall regression equation.

The intercept, a, in the overall regression equation is equal to the intercept of the group that is assigned 0's in all the coded vectors.[9] In the present example the group taught by the directive teacher was assigned 0 in vector 1 (see Table 12.5). Consequently, the intercept of the regression equation for this group is 7.19321.

Each b for a coded vector in the overall regression equation is equal to the

[9]Because the procedure applies equally to situations when the categorical variable consists of more than two categories, the statements here are made in the plural form.

deviation of the intercept of the regression equation for the group identified by the vector (that is, the group assigned 1 in the vector) from the intercept of the regression equation for the group assigned 0's in all the coded vectors. Therefore, in order to obtain the intercept for a given group add the a from the overall regression equation and the b for the coded vector in which the group was assigned 1. In the present example there is only one dummy vector (vector 1 of Table 12.5) in which the group taught by the nondirective teacher was assigned 1. The b for this vector is -5.99972. The intercept for the group taught by the nondirective teacher is therefore

$$7.19321 + (-5.99972) = \mathit{1.19349}$$

The method of obtaining the regression coefficients for the separate regression equations is analogous to the method outlined above for obtaining the intercepts for the separate regression equations. Specifically, the b for the continuous variable in the overall regression equation is equal to the b for the continuous variable in the regression equation for the group assigned 0's throughout. In the present example the b for vector 3 representing tolerance of ambiguity (see Table 12.5) was reported above as $-.10680$. This, then, is the b for tolerance of ambiguity in the regression equation for the group taught by the directive teacher.

The b associated with each of the interaction vectors in the overall regression equation is equal to the deviation of the b for the group assigned 1 in the coded vector that was used to generate the product vector from the b for the group assigned 0's throughout. Recall that the latter is equal to the b associated with the continuous variable in the overall regression equation. In the present example vector 1 was multiplied by vector 3 to obtain vector 4. In vector 1 the group taught by the nondirective teacher was assigned 1. Accordingly, the b associated with vector 4 in the overall regression equation (.20516) is equal to the deviation of the b taught by the nondirective teacher from the b for the continuous variable ($-.10680$). The b for the group taught by the nondirective teacher is therefore

$$-.10680 + .20516 = \mathit{.09836}$$

The separate regression equations obtained from the overall regression equation with dummy coding are, of course, the same as those obtained from the overall regression equation with effect coding.

The Point of Intersection

Having obtained the separate regression equations one can calculate the point of intersection of the two regression lines. For convenience the two regression equations are repeated:

$$Y'_{\text{D}} = 7.19322 - .10680X$$

$$Y'_{\text{ND}} = 1.19350 + .09836X$$

where D = directive; ND = nondirective; X = tolerance of ambiguity. Applying Formula (12.5) to the values of these equations, obtain the point of intersection:

$$X = \frac{7.19322 - 1.19350}{(.09836) - (-.10680)} = \frac{5.99972}{.20516} = 29.24$$

The value of X at which the regression lines intersect is well within the range of scores of the continuous variable (the scores range from 5 to 63). The interaction is therefore disordinal.

The data of Table 12.5 are plotted in Figure 12.4, along with the two regression lines. For the group taught by a nondirective teacher the regression of teacher ratings on tolerance of ambiguity is positive. The situation is reversed for the group taught by a directive teacher. This, of course, is also evident from the regression coefficients of the separate regression equations. It appears, then, that students who are more tolerant of ambiguity prefer a nondirective teacher and students who are less tolerant of ambiguity prefer a directive teacher.

In the example analyzed above, the number of subjects in the groups was equal. The same approach applies to designs with unequal n's.

Regions of Significance and the Johnson-Neyman Technique

Inspection of Figure 12.4 indicates that students whose scores on tolerance of ambiguity are closer to the point of intersection of the regression lines (29.24)

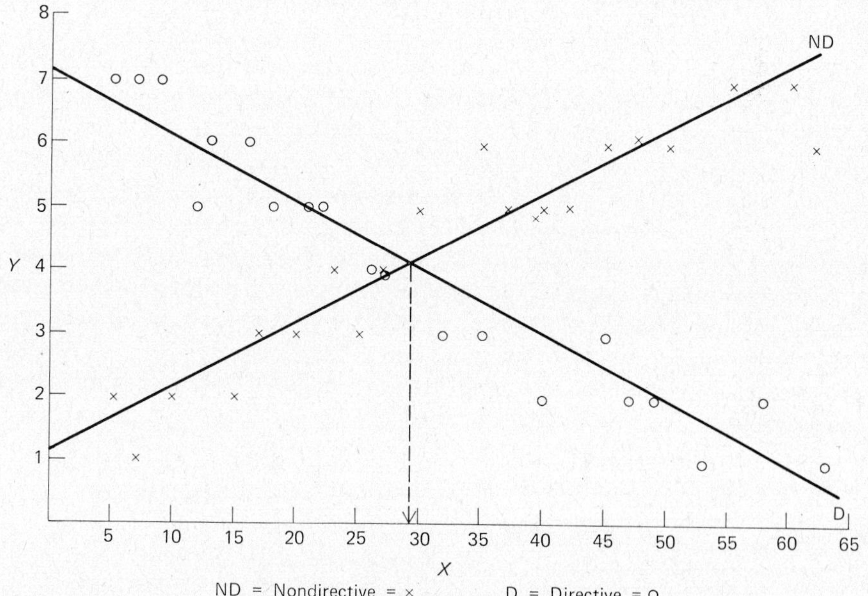

Figure 12.4

differ less in their satisfaction with the teachers, as compared with students whose scores on tolerance are farther from the point of intersection. In other words, the differential effects of teaching styles are more marked for students whose scores on tolerance of ambiguity are relatively high or low compared to students whose scores on ambiguity are in the middle of the range.

It will be recalled (see Chapter 10) that when a significant interaction is found in a factorial design, it is pursued by tests of simple main effects. Analogously, when a significant interaction is found between a continuous and a categorical variable, it is pursued by the calculation of regions of significance. An approach to the establishment of regions of significance developed by Johnson and Neyman (1936) will be presented here.[10]

The application of the Johnson-Neyman technique is demonstrated for the above example. In order to establish the regions of significance it is necessary to solve for the two values of X in the following formula[11]:

$$X = \frac{-B \pm \sqrt{B^2 - AC}}{A} \tag{12.6}$$

The terms of Equation (12.6) are defined as follows:

$$A = \frac{-F_\alpha}{N-4}(ss_{\text{res}})\left(\frac{1}{\Sigma x_1^2} + \frac{1}{\Sigma x_2^2}\right) + (b_1 - b_2)^2 \tag{12.7}$$

$$B = \frac{F_\alpha}{N-4}(ss_{\text{res}})\left(\frac{\bar{X}_1}{\Sigma x_1^2} + \frac{\bar{X}_2}{\Sigma x_2^2}\right) + (a_1 - a_2)(b_1 - b_2) \tag{12.8}$$

$$C = \frac{-F_\alpha}{N-4}(ss_{\text{res}})\left(\frac{N}{n_1 n_2} + \frac{\bar{X}_1^2}{\Sigma x_1^2} + \frac{\bar{X}_2^2}{\Sigma x_2^2}\right) + (a_1 - a_2)^2 \tag{12.9}$$

where F_α = tabled F ratio with 1 and $N - 4$ degrees of freedom at a selected level of α; N = total number of subjects, or number of subjects in both groups; n_1, n_2 = number of subjects in groups 1 and 2, respectively; ss_{res} = residual sum of squares obtained from the overall regression analysis, or, equivalently, the pooled residual sum of squares from separate regression analyses for each group; $\Sigma x_1^2, \Sigma x_2^2$ = sum of squares of the continuous independent variable (X) for groups 1 and 2, respectively; $\bar{X}_1, \bar{X}_2$ = means of groups 1 and 2, respectively, on the continuous independent variable, X; b_1, b_2 = regression coefficients of the regression equations for groups 1 and 2, respectively; a_1, a_2 = intercepts of the regression equations for groups 1 and 2, respectively.

The values necessary for the application of the above formulas to the data of Table 12.5 are[12]

[10]For detailed descriptions of the Johnson-Neyman technique see Huitema (1980, Chapter 13), and Johnson and Jackson (1959, pp. 430–444).

[11]The formulas used here were adapted from formulas given by Walker and Lev (1953, p. 401).

[12]Note that the first two terms in Formulas (12.7), (12.8), and (12.9) are the same, except that in Formulas (12.7) and (12.9) their sign is negative, whereas in Formula (12.8) the sign is positive.

$$ss_{res} = 13.06758 \qquad \Sigma x_1^2 = 5776.80 \qquad \Sigma x_2^2 = 6123.80$$

$$\bar{X}_1 = 32.60 \qquad \bar{X}_2 = 29.90$$

$$a_1 = 1.19350 \qquad a_2 = 7.19322$$

$$b_1 = .09836 \qquad b_2 = -.10680$$

The tabled F value with 1 and 36 degrees of freedom at the .05 level is 4.11.

$$A = \frac{-4.11}{36}(13.06758)\left(\frac{1}{5776.80} + \frac{1}{6123.80}\right) + (.20516)^2 = .04160$$

$$B = \frac{4.11}{36}(13.06758)\left(\frac{32.60}{5776.80} + \frac{29.90}{6123.80}\right) + (-5.99972)(.20516) = -1.21521$$

$$C = \frac{-4.11}{36}(13.06758)\left(\frac{40}{400} + \frac{32.60^2}{5776.80} + \frac{29.90^2}{6123.80}\right) + (-5.99972)^2 = 35.35519$$

$$X = \frac{1.21521 \pm \sqrt{1.21521^2 - (.04160)(35.35519)}}{.04160}$$

$$X_1 = 31.07 \qquad X_2 = 27.36$$

The two X values are now used to establish the region of nonsignificance. Values of Y for subjects whose scores lie within the range of 27.36 and 31.07 on X are not significantly different across groups. There are two regions of significance, one for X scores above 31.07 and one for X scores below 27.36. In other words, the ratings indicated by students whose scores on tolerance of ambiguity are above 31.07 or below 27.36 are significantly different in the two groups. Note that in the present example the region of nonsignificance is narrow: about 4 points on X. Practically all the X values are in the regions of significance. On the basis of the analysis it is concluded that students whose scores on tolerance of ambiguity are above 31.07 are more satisfied with a nondirective teacher, while students whose scores on tolerance of ambiguity are below 27.36 are more satisfied with a directive teacher.

Applications and Extensions of the Johnson-Neyman Technique

In the example analyzed above the interaction was disordinal. The Johnson-Neyman technique is equally applicable to ordinal interactions. The procedure is the same except that with ordinal interactions one of the regions of significance is outside the research range of interest.[13]

The technique is not limited to the case of a categorical variable with two categories, or two groups, nor is it limited to one continuous independent variable. For extensions to more than two categories, or groups, and more than one

[13]For a discussion of the research range of interest, see earlier sections of the chapter. For an example of regions of significance when the interaction is ordinal, see Study Suggestion 8 at the end of the chapter.

continuous variable, see Abelson (1953), Johnson and Fay (1950), Johnson and Jackson (1959, pp. 438–441), Potthoff (1964), and Walker and Lev (1953, pp. 404–411).

Finally, it will be pointed out that Potthoff (1964) has argued that the regions of significance described above are nonsimultaneous ones. That is, such regions are appropriate when it is desired to make a statement about the difference between two treatments or two groups at any specific point of the continuous variable, X, but that ". . . it does *not* follow that one can state with 95 per cent confidence that there is a nonzero difference between the groups simultaneously for *all* points in the region" (Potthoff, 1964, p. 241). Potthoff has proposed extensions of the Johnson-Neyman technique for the purpose of establishing simultaneous regions of significance. The calculation of such regions for the example under consideration (two groups and one continuous variable) requires a minor modification of Equations (12.7) through (12.9). Specifically, the tabled F ratio with 1 and $N - 4$ degrees of freedom in these equations is replaced by $2F(2, N-4)$—that is, two times the tabled F ratio with 2 and $N - 4$ degrees of freedom.

Simultaneous regions of significance are more conservative than nonsimultaneous ones because they refer to the entire range of nonzero differences between treatments rather than to a nonzero difference at a given point of X. Detailed discussions of the two types of regions of significance as well as other issues regarding comparisons of regression equations will be found in Rogosa (1980, 1981).

Computer Programs for ATI Designs

From the foregoing discussions and numerical examples it should be clear that a computer program for multiple regression analysis is all that one needs for the purpose of analyzing data when the independent variables are categorical and continuous. Nevertheless, because it is necessary to calculate regions of significance when the interaction is significant, it will be useful to note the availability of specialized computer programs that incorporate the calculation of regions of significance as well as plots of such regions. These programs (Borich, Godbout, & Wunderlich, 1976), are, however, limited to the following designs: (1) Two groups (or treatments), one continuous variable—linear regression. (2) Two groups, two continuous variables—linear regression. (3) Two groups, one continuous variable—curvilinear regression. The manual for these programs includes numerical examples, as well as useful methodological notes.[14]

Sample Output

To show the type of output provided by the above noted programs, one of them (ATLIN1) was used to analyze the data of Table 12.5. Because this numerical example was commented upon in detail in the preceding sections, no

[14]The programs and the manual are distributed by International Educational Services, P. O. Box A3650, Chicago, Illinois 60690.

additional comments are made here. The sole purpose is to show how the program reports the separate regression equations, tests of significance, and Johnson-Neyman regions of significance. Following are excerpts of the output.

THE REGRESSION EQUATION FOR GROUP 1 (Nondirective) IS Y = 1.1935 + 0.0984X

THE REGRESSION EQUATION FOR GROUP 2 (Directive) IS Y = 7.1932 − 0.1068X

THE REGRESSION LINES INTERSECT AT PREDICTOR VALUE OF 29.2447

THE F-VALUE FOR THE TEST OF HOMOGENEITY OF GROUP REGRESSIONS IS 344.6628 WITH 1 AND 36 DEGREES OF FREEDOM WHICH HAS A PROBABILITY OF 0.0000

THE F-VALUE FOR THE TEST OF COMMON INTERCEPTS, ASSUMING HOMOGENEITY OF GROUP REGRESSIONS IS 0.4683 WITH 1 AND 37 DEGREES OF FREEDOM WHICH HAS A PROBABILITY OF 0.5049

LEFT REGION OF SIGNIFICANCE IS BOUNDED BY: 5.0000 27.3312 WHERE 5.0000 IS THE MINIMUM OBSERVED APTITUDE VALUE

RIGHT REGION OF SIGNIFICANCE IS BOUNDED BY: 31.1101 63.0000 WHERE 63.0000 IS THE MAXIMUM OBSERVED APTITUDE VALUE

Note that the first test given above is for the difference between the regression coefficients in the separate regression equations, or the test of the interaction between the continuous and the categorical variables.

Although the program reports the results of the test between the intercepts of the separate regression equations, this test is not relevant here because a significant interaction was found. In other words, the group regressions are not homogeneous.

Compare the results reported here with those given in preceding sections.

COMPARING REGRESSION EQUATIONS IN NONEXPERIMENTAL RESEARCH

Thus far, the discussion and examples were limited to designs in which both the categorical and the continuous variables were manipulated, or to ones in which only the categorical variable was manipulated (e.g., ATI designs). We turn now to designs in which neither the categorical nor the continuous variable is manipulated—that is, to nonexperimental designs. It will be noted, at the outset, that the analytic approach in such designs is identical to the one used in experimental designs. The difference between the two is in the interpretation of the results, which is generally more ambiguous and more complex in nonexperimental designs (see discussion below).

Whenever the regression of a variable on one or more than one variable is being studied in samples from different populations it is imperative to determine whether the regression equations in the various samples differ from each other. Doing a combined regression analysis across samples is tantamount to an assumption that the separate regression equations for the different groups are identical. Stated differently, the fact that subjects belong to different groups is overlooked when they are combined in one analysis; all subjects are treated as if they come from the same population.

Often, researchers appear to be operating under the mistaken assumption that in order to take into account a classificatory, or grouping, variable (e.g., sex, race, religious affiliation) all that is necessary is to include in the analysis, in addition to the continuous variables, coded vectors that represent the classificatory variable.[15] It was shown in the preceding section that when product vectors between the categorical and the continuous variable are *not* included in the combined analysis the separate regression equations for the groups under consideration are assumed to differ only in their intercepts. In other words, separate regression equations with identical regression coefficients but with different intercepts are fitted when product terms are *not* included in the combined regression analysis.

To demonstrate the possible deleterious consequences of ignoring a classificatory variable, or of not treating it appropriately in the analysis, we return to the numerical example of Table 12.5. It will be recalled that the example was concerned with a continuous variable (tolerance of ambiguity) and a categorical manipulated variable (teaching styles). Assume now that the categorical variable is a classificatory one (e.g., male–female, black–white). If one were to do an analysis in which this variable is ignored (i.e., regressing the dependent variable on the continuous variable only), the regression coefficient for the data of Table 12.5 would be $-.00626$.[16] R^2 would be .00335—a finding that is neither meaningful nor statistically significant.

Now suppose that a coded vector were also to be included to represent the classificatory variable. This time the regression coefficient associated with the continuous variable would be $-.00721$. It will be recalled that this coefficient has been referred to as the common regression coefficient (b_c). For both the continuous and the classificatory variable, R^2 would be .01580, which is not significant ($F < 1$). Using either of the analyses outlined above, a researcher would be forced to conclude that the results are not meaningful. But it will be recalled that a strong interaction was found for the data of Table 12.5, and that its presence was detected by the inclusion of the product vector in the analysis. One group had a b of $-.10680$, whereas the b for the other group was .09836. Recall also that the inclusion of the product vector led to an R^2 of .90693, as compared to $R^2 = .01580$ in the analysis without the product vector.[17]

In short, when a categorical and a continuous variable are used in nonexperimental research, the analysis should proceed in exactly the same sequence

[15]Examples of such analyses were discussed in Chapter 8 in connection with the review of the IEA studies.

[16]The properties of such coefficients—referred to as total regression coefficients—are discussed in Chapter 13 under the heading Unit of Analysis.

[17]The topic of this section is discussed further below, in the section on The Study of Test Bias.

as in experimental research.[18] But, as was said above, the interpretation of the results differs in the two research settings. For example, a finding that regression equations differ from each other is interpreted as an interaction between the categorical and the continuous variable when the research is experimental. In nonexperimental research, on the other hand, such an interpretation may be misleading. The reasons for limiting the use of the term interaction to experimental research were discussed in detail in earlier chapters (see, in particular, Chapters 10 and 11) and will therefore not be repeated here. Instead, the unique problems in the type of design under consideration here will be scrutinized.

Categorical variables may be narrow or broad in scope. Although this obviously does not imply a dichotomy, it is necessary to indicate what is meant here by this distinction. Consider, for example, an attitude or an interest question to which the possible responses are: Yes, No; or: Yes, No, Undecided. Either of these sets of responses can be represented as a categorical variable in a regression analysis (the first set would require one coded vector; the second set would require two vectors). Contrast this categorical variable with one that represents a broad classification (e.g., sex, race, religious affiliation, marital status, professional status) and the intended distinction between categorical variables that are broad or narrow in scope will, it is hoped, become clear. The main point is that broad categorical variables are related to, or subsume, or cause a host of other variables.

When regression equations are compared in nonexperimental research, the categorical variable is almost always a broad classificatory, or grouping, variable. Under such circumstances, the interpretation of differences between regression coefficients as indicating an interaction not only may be misleading but also may appear to provide answers, when in fact it should be viewed as raising questions. This can, perhaps, be clarified by a relatively simple example. Suppose that the dependent variable is achievement and that two independent variables are used: sex and achievement motivation. Further, assume that the analysis was carried out in the proper sequence, and that it was found that the regression of achievement on achievement motivation for males differs from that for females. Should these results be interpreted as an interaction between sex and achievement motivation, one may be led to believe that an answer has been found regarding the differential effects of achievement motivation on achievement among males and females. Issues of absence of randomization and manipulation, and attendant problems of specification errors notwithstanding (see Chapter 8), the focus here is on the categorical variable. Sex is a broad classificatory variable that, as noted above, is related to, or subsumes, or causes a host of variables. Therefore, to say that sex interacts with achievement motivation either says nothing or appears to say everything. Neither is, of course, the case. Suffice it to note only the potential consequences due to different socialization practices for males and females (e.g., aspirations, motivation, self-concept) in order to realize the complexity of the situation.

In conclusion, it is important to note that so far as the general arguments advanced in this book against the use of the term interaction in nonexperimen-

[18]See preceding sections. For a summary of the analytic sequence, see section entitled Recapitulation.

tal research are concerned there is no difference between the design discussed in this chapter and those discussed in earlier chapters. The discussion here was given a special slant because it is believed that the use of broad classificatory variables in the type of designs discussed in this chapter is generally more prone to misinterpretation and therefore requires extra vigilance.

The Study of Test Bias

The literature on test bias has been growing steadily in recent years, primarily in response to civil rights legislation and to court rulings on ever-increasing challenges to the use of tests in such diverse areas as selection for employment, admissions to colleges and professional schools, promotion on the job, wages. It is not the intention to review here this literature or to discuss the various definitions of test fairness that have been advanced (see, for example, Cole, 1973; *Federal Register,* 1978; Hunter & Schmidt, 1976; *Journal of Eudcational Measurement* 13, Spring 1976; Linn, 1973). The sole purpose here is to illustrate the central role played by the analytic approach presented in this chapter in *one* of the definitions of test bias.

A definition of test bias that has probably enjoyed the widest currency has been proposed by Cleary (1968):

> A test is biased for members of a subgroup of the population if, in the prediction of the criterion for which the test was designed, consistent nonzero errors of prediction are made for members of the subgroup. In other words, the test is biased if the criterion score predicted from the common regression line is consistently too high or too low for members of the subgroup. (p. 115)

In view of this definition, it should come as no surprise that it has been labeled the Regression Model. In fact, all it amounts to is a comparison of regression equations for different subgroups. This is illustrated graphically in Figure 12.5 for the case of two groups: A and B. The situations depicted in Figure 12.5 are but three of many possible patterns, but they will suffice to illustrate the definition of bias in the Regression Model. Consider first situation (a). Note that the regression lines for groups A and B are parallel and very close to each other. In other words, the regression coefficients are identical and the intercepts are very similar to each other. It appears, then, that using a common regression line (or a common regression equation) in this situation will not result in bias toward members of either of the groups.

Let us turn now to the situation depicted in (b) of Figure 12.5. Again, the regression lines are parallel. But this time they are relatively apart. Using the common regression line under these circumstances will result in consistent overprediction for members of group B, and consistent underprediction for members of group A. This, then, would constitute positive bias for group B and negative bias for group A.

Yet another situation is depicted in (c). This time the regression lines intersect, indicating that the regression coefficients for the two groups differ from each other. Using the common regression line will result in positive bias for

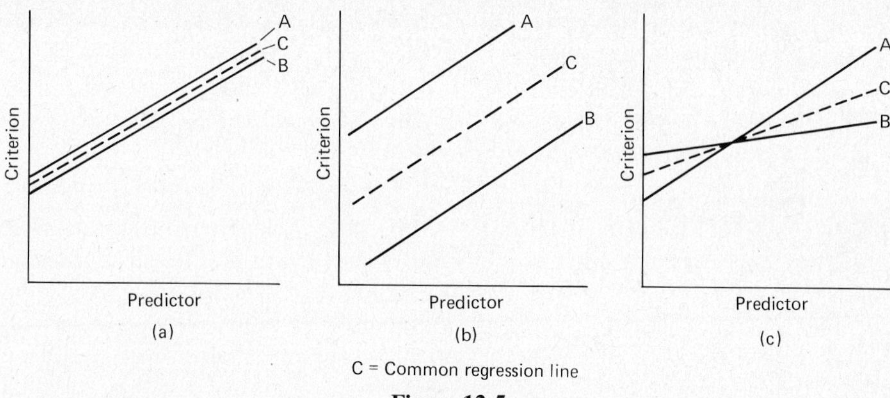

C = Common regression line

Figure 12.5

members of group A and negative bias for members of group B whose scores are below the point of intersection on the predictor. The reverse is true for subjects whose scores are above the point of intersection. As a cutting score on the predictor is used for the purpose of selection, it can be seen that if, for example, this score is above the point of intersection in (c), the use of a common regression line will consistently overpredict for members of group B and underpredict for members of group A, although the extent of over- and underprediction will vary depending on the specific score on the predictor. The further the score is from the point of intersection, the larger the over- or underprediction.

It is important to note that the comments made in the preceding section about problems regarding the interpretation of differences between regression equations in nonexperimental research apply equally to the use of this approach for the purpose of detecting test bias. For example, assume that a test of Scholastic Aptitude is used for decisions about admission to college. A conclusion that the use of a common regression equation constitutes bias implies, among other things, that other variables (e.g., mental ability, motivation, study habits) are not related to the predictor.

In conclusion, it is very important to reiterate what was said earlier: The purpose of this section was *not* to provide a discussion of the very complex topic of test bias, but only to show how multiple regression analysis is used in one of the approaches to its definition and detection.

CURVILINEAR REGRESSION ANALYSIS

In the numerical examples presented thus far it was clear from the plots of the data (see Figures 12.1 and 12.4) that the regression is linear. In many instances, however, the trend may not be that obvious. Moreover, one should not rely on visual inspection alone, although the study of plotted data is always valuable. It is the application of tests for trends that enables one to make a decision about the analysis that is most appropriate for a given set of data. In this section curvilinear regression analysis in designs with one categorical and one continuous variable is demonstrated. First, an example in which the continuous variable is manipulated is analyzed. This is followed by an example in which the continuous variable is an attribute.

Regression with Orthogonal Polynomials

Curvilinear regression analysis is applied to the data from the retention experiment presented in the beginning of this chapter. The reason for returning to this example is because it was analyzed twice earlier: first linear regression analysis was used (i.e., it was *assumed* that the regression is linear) and then the data were analyzed as if the continuous variable were categorical. Reanalyzing these data by using curvilinear regression analysis will therefore afford comparisons and contrasts with the earlier analyses. It will be recalled that the continuous variable, Study Time, had four levels. The highest-degree polynomial for these data is therefore cubic (number of levels minus one). This may be obtained by raising the values of the continuous variable to the second and the third powers. Since the experiment also involved a categorical variable (Incentive–No Incentive), we must study the interactions on the linear, quadratic, and cubic levels. To perform the entire analysis it is necessary to have the following vectors for the independent variables: (1) Incentive–No Incentive, (2) linear trend in Study Time, (3) quadratic trend (Study Time squared), (4) cubic trend (Study Time raised to the third power), (5) linear interaction (product of vectors 1 and 2), (6) quadratic interaction (product of vectors 1 and 3), and (7) cubic interaction (product of vectors 1 and 4).

Because the retention experiment consisted of equal cell frequencies and equal intervals for the continuous variable, it is possible to simplify the analysis by the use of orthogonal polynomials—a method introduced in Chapter 11. The data from the experiment are repeated in Table 12.6, along with the necessary vectors to test for trends and interactions. Vector Y, as in earlier tables, identifies the dependent variable. Vector 1 identifies Incentive–No Incentive. Vectors 2, 3, and 4 represent the linear, quadratic, and cubic components for Study Time. The coefficients for these vectors were obtained from a table of orthogonal polynomials (see Appendix B). Vectors 5, 6, and 7 are obtained by multiplying, in turn, vector 1 by vectors 2, 3, and 4. Thus vector 5 represents the linear interaction, and is a product of vectors 1 and 2. Vectors 6 and 7 represent the quadratic and cubic interactions, respectively. It will be noted that all the vectors are orthogonal to each other. The analysis is therefore straightforward, and the results directly indicate the proportion of variance accounted for by each vector.

The data of Table 12.6 were analyzed by the REGRESSION program of SPSS. Following are excerpts of the output and commentaries.

Output

VARIABLE	R SQUARE	R SQUARE CHANGE	B	F
V1 (NI-I)	.57953	.57953	−2.04167	57.17
V2 (Linear)	.82288	.24335	.59167	24.00
V3 (Quadratic)	.82312	.00024	−.04167	.02

Table 12.6 Data from the Retention Experiment, Laid Out for Trend Analysis

Y	*1*	*2*	*3*	*4*	*5* (*1* × *2*)	*6* (*1* × *3*)	*7* (*1* × *4*)
3	1	−3	1	−1	−3	1	−1
4	1	−3	1	−1	−3	1	−1
5	1	−3	1	−1	−3	1	−1
4	1	−1	−1	3	−1	−1	3
5	1	−1	−1	3	−1	−1	3
6	1	−1	−1	3	−1	−1	3
5	1	1	−1	−3	1	−1	−3
6	1	1	−1	−3	1	−1	−3
8	1	1	−1	−3	1	−1	−3
7	1	3	1	1	3	1	1
8	1	3	1	1	3	1	1
9	1	3	1	1	3	1	1
7	−1	−3	1	−1	3	−1	1
8	−1	−3	1	−1	3	−1	1
9	−1	−3	1	−1	3	−1	1
9	−1	−1	−1	3	1	1	−3
10	−1	−1	−1	3	1	1	−3
11	−1	−1	−1	3	1	1	−3
8	−1	1	−1	−3	−1	1	3
11	−1	1	−1	−3	−1	1	3
12	−1	1	−1	−3	−1	1	3
10	−1	3	1	1	−3	−1	−1
11	−1	3	1	1	−3	−1	−1
13	−1	3	1	1	−3	−1	−1
Σy^2: 172.625							

NOTE: *Y* = measures of retention originally given in Table 12.1; 1 = coded vector for Incentive–No Incentive; 2 = vector for linear component of Study Time; 3 = quadratic; 4 = cubic; 5, 6, and 7 = interaction between Incentive–No Incentive and Study Time.

V4 (Cubic)	.82549	.00237	.05833	.23
V5 (V1*V2)	.82940	.00391	.07500	.39
V6 (V1*V3)	.83543	.00603	.20833	.60
V7 (V1*V4)	.83780	.00237	−.05833	.23
		(CONSTANT)	7.87500	

Commentary

Following the practice adopted in earlier chapters, the output is organized in a format that differs from that used by SPSS. The first three columns were obtained from the SUMMARY TABLE. The fourth and fifth columns were obtained from that part of the output in which the regression equation is reported. The numbers in the first column refer to the vector numbers given in Table 12.6.

Look first at the row for V1. The variable No Incentive–Incentive accounts for .57953 of the variance, a finding identical to the ones obtained in the earlier analyses. The same applies to V2, the linear component of Study Time (.24335). As can be seen in the column labeled R SQUARE CHANGE, the proportions of variance added by the quadratic and cubic components as well as by the interaction are very small. Each of the F ratios, with 1 and 16 *df*, refers to a test of the B in its row. But because the vectors are orthogonal the F is also a test of the R SQUARE CHANGE in its row. It is obvious, then, that the only two terms that are both meaningful and statistically significant are the contribution of the categorical variable and the linear component of the continuous variable.

What, then, is the difference between the present analysis and the analyses of the same data done earlier in the chapter? Turning first to the analysis in which only the linear regression was used (see Table 12.3 and the presentation that follows it), it was noted above that the results regarding the linear component and the categorical variable are identical. Also, the proportion of variance due to the linear interaction (.00391; see V5 in the Output above) is the same as would be obtained if one were to calculate the increment in proportion of variance accounted for by the product vector of the categorical and the continuous variable in the earlier analysis. The only difference between the two analyses is that in the earlier one the regression was *assumed* to be linear whereas in the present analysis the acceptance of the linear component only of Study Time was done as a result of determining that trends beyond the linear were neither meaningful nor statistically significant.

Turning now to a comparison between the present analysis and the one in which the continuous variable was treated as if it were categorical (see Table 12.4 and the presentation that follows it), it will be noted that Study Time accounted for .24596 of the variance. In the present analysis, too, the same proportion of variance is accounted for by Study Time (i.e., the sum of R SQUARE CHANGE for vectors 2, 3, and 4: .24335 + .00024 + .00237 = .24596). But from the present analysis it is possible to tell that almost all of the variance accounted for is due to the linear component (.24335), whereas in the earlier analysis all the components were lumped together, and similarly for the interaction term. Adding the elements of R SQUARE CHANGE for vectors 5, 6, and 7 (.00391 + .00603 + .00237 = .01231) one obtains the same value of the proportion of variance accounted for as was obtained in the earlier analysis. Again, in the present analysis separate components of the interaction are identified, whereas in the earlier analysis they were lumped together. The reason it was not possible to identify separate components in the earlier analysis is, of course, a consequence of treating the continuous variable as a categorical one—an analysis that was carried out for the sole purpose of demonstrating why one should not engage in such practices.

In sum, it is neither appropriate to assume that the regression is linear nor advisable to treat the continuous variable as if it were categorical. When one of the variables is continuous, it is necessary to do a curvilinear regression analysis in order to determine the model that best fits the data. With continuous variables that consist of several distinct values the analytic approach used above is the most efficient. This approach is, of course, not feasible when the continuous variable consists of many values—a topic to which we now turn.

Curvilinear Regression with an Attribute Variable

When the continuous variable is manipulated, the researcher is in a position to select values that are equally spaced and to randomly assign equal numbers of subjects to each level. This, it will be recalled, makes the use of orthogonal polynomials simple and straightforward. When the continuous variable is an attribute (e.g., IQ, motivation, anxiety, cognitive styles) the values of the variable may not be equally spaced. Moreover, such variables tend to consist of many values with unequal numbers of subjects for the different values.[19] One must still test deviation from linearity. In certain studies a trend other than linear may be part of the hypothesis. In other words, on the basis of theoretical formulations a researcher may hypothesize a quadratic or a cubic trend. Obviously, such hypotheses need to be tested.

The procedures for testing the deviation for linearity, or given trends, with attribute variables follow a sequence of steps. At each step a decision needs to be made about the next appropriate one to be taken. These procedures are now illustrated with a numerical example.

A Numerical Example

A set of illustrative scores on Y and X for two groups (T_1 and T_2) is given in Table 12.7. You may think of these data as having been obtained in experimental research where the categorical variable, T, represents two treatments, or a treatment and a control, and X represents an attribute. This, then, would be an example of an ATI design. If, instead, you choose to view the data as having been obtained in nonexperimental research, the categorical variable would represent two groups (e.g., male–female, black–white). In this case the purpose of the research would be to compare the regression equations of Y on X for the two groups. The analysis proceeds in the same manner, regardless of whether the design is experimental or nonexperimental. It is the interpretations of the results that differ in the two research settings (see discussions earlier in this chapter). For convenience, the categorical variable will be referred to as representing treatments, T, in the following presentation.

The data were analyzed by the REGRESSION program of SPSS. Only Y, X, and T were read as input. The remaining vectors of Table 12.7 were generated by the use of COMPUTE statements. The first and last three values in each of these vectors in Table 12.7 are given for illustrative purposes only. Note that in the present example X is raised to the second power only. Using the same strategy presented below, one could carry out an analysis in which X is raised to higher-order polynomials.

[19]Detailed discussions of the distinction between the two types of variables, the meaning of equally spaced values, and of equal n's at each level are given in Chapter 11.

Table 12.7 Illustrative Data for Curvilinear Regression Analysis

	Y	X	T	XT	X^2	X^2T
	4	2	1	2	4	4
	5	2	1	2	4	4
	7	3	1	3	9	9
	6	3	1	·	·	·
	5	4	1	·	·	·
	7	5	1	·	·	·
	6	5	1	·	·	·
	9	7	1	·	·	·
	8	7	1	·	·	·
T_1	6	7	1	·	·	·
	9	10	1	·	·	·
	8	10	1	·	·	·
	11	11	1	·	·	·
	12	11	1	·	·	·
	9	13	1	·	·	·
	12	13	1	·	·	·
	11	14	1	·	·	·
	12	15	1	·	·	·
	11	16	1	·	·	·
	10	16	1	·	·	·
	3	2	−1	·	·	·
	5	3	−1	·	·	·
	4	4	−1	·	·	·
	6	4	−1	·	·	·
	8	6	−1	·	·	·
	6	6	−1	·	·	·
	8	8	−1	·	·	·
	9	8	−1	·	·	·
	9	10	−1	·	·	·
T_2	8	10	−1	·	·	·
	10	12	−1	·	·	·
	8	12	−1	·	·	·
	8	14	−1	·	·	·
	8	15	−1	·	·	·
	6	16	−1	·	·	·
	8	17	−1	·	·	·
	5	17	−1	·	·	·
	7	18	−1	−18	324	−324
	5	18	−1	−18	324	−324
	6	19	−1	−19	361	−361

NOTE: T = Treatments; $N_{T_1} = N_{T_2} = 20$.

The analysis may proceed by different routes, depending on the specific questions one wishes to answer. The route taken here is presented in the form of a set of questions and tests designed to answer them. As can be seen below, the kind of questions raised at a later stage of the analysis depend on the kind of answers that were obtained at earlier stages.

1. *Is the proportion of variance accounted for by the second-degree polynomial meaningful?* Calculate $R^2_{y.x,t,xt,x^2,x^2t} = .79873$, where the subscripts here, and in the rest of the presentation, refer to the vectors of Table 12.7. It was said several times earlier that meaningfulness depends on a researcher's judgment within a given research setting. If the overall R^2 is deemed not meaningful, there is no point in continuing with the analysis. Instead, it is necessary to scrutinize and rethink all aspects of the study in order to arrive at a decision about the steps to be taken (e.g., designing a new study, using other measures, abandoning the research in the area).

In the numerical example being analyzed no reference has been made to a substantive area. It will only be noted that the overall R^2 is high (.79873), and that it is therefore appropriate to proceed to the next question.

2. *Is there a quadratic trend in the data?* Calculate $R^2_{y.x,t,xt} = .58362$. Test

$$F = \frac{(R^2_{y.x,t,xt,x^2,x^2t} - R^2_{y.x,t,xt})/(k_1 - k_2)}{(1 - R^2_{y.x,t,xt,x^2,x^2t})/(N - k_1 - 1)}$$

$$= \frac{(.79873 - .58362)/(5 - 3)}{(1 - .79873)/(40 - 5 - 1)} = \frac{.21511/2}{.20127/34} = 18.17$$

with 2 and 34 *df*, $p < .01$. Note that in this test of the difference between two R^2's, the first R^2 includes also the quadratic terms, whereas these terms are excluded from the second R^2. The difference between the two R^2's, then, indicates the increment in the proportion of variance accounted for by the quadratic terms. In the present example this increment is .21511 and is statistically significant. Accordingly, one asks the next question (see 3 below).

Before turning to question 3, however, it will be noted that when the F ratio for the test of the quadratic terms is not significant, the next set of questions would be addressed to models in which only X, T, and XT are included. The sequence of testing different models with such terms was shown earlier in this chapter and was summarized in the section entitled Recapitulation. Briefly, test first whether there is a significant linear interaction. If the interaction is significant, use the Johnson-Neyman technique to establish regions of significance and interpret the results. If the linear interaction is not significant, test the difference between the intercepts. If the intercepts differ significantly, two parallel lines fit the data. That is, one treatment is superior to the other along the continuum of the continuous variable. If the intercepts do not differ significantly, a single regression line describes the data adequately. In other words, the treatments do not differ significantly.

In the present example it was found that there is a quadratic trend. One may therefore proceed to the next question.

3. *Is there an interaction between the categorical and the continuous variable?* Stated differently: *Are the two regression curves parallel?* Calculate $R^2_{y.x,t,x^2} = .72067$. Test

$$F = \frac{(R^2_{y.x,t,xt,x^2,x^2t} - R^2_{y.x,t,x^2})/(k_1 - k_2)}{(1 - R^2_{y.x,t,xt,x^2,x^2t})/(N - k_1 - 1)}$$

$$= \frac{(.79873 - .72067)/(5 - 3)}{(1 - .79873)/(40 - 5 - 1)} = \frac{.07806/2}{.20127/34} = 6.59$$

with 2 and 34 *df*, $p < .01$. It is concluded that the regression curves are not parallel, or that two separate regression equations, one for each treatment, or group, are required.

Before turning to the separate regression equations, it will be useful to comment on the steps to be taken when it is determined that the regression curves are parallel (i.e., when the above F ratio is not significant). Under such circumstances, the appropriate question would be whether the intercepts of the two parallel curves differ from each other. This is accomplished by testing the difference between two R^2's: $R^2_{y\ x,x^2,t} - R^2_{y\ x,x^2}$. A nonsignificant F ratio would indicate that a single quadratic equation, $Y' = a + bX + bX^2$, adequately describes the data for both treatments or both groups. In other words, there is no significant difference between the treatments or the groups. If, on the other hand, the F ratio is significant, two regression equations that differ in their intercepts only would be required. This, of course, means that there is a significant difference between the treatments, or groups, along the continuum of the continuous variable.

In the present example, a significant interaction has been found. As was noted above, this means that the regression of Y on X under one treatment, or for one group, differs from that under the other treatment, or for the other group. Because the difference may take divers forms it is necessary to derive and examine the separate regression equations.

Earlier in this chapter it was shown how the overall regression equation may be used in order to obtain separate regression equations. The same procedure is applicable to situations in which the regression is curvilinear. Consequently, the procedure is applied here without comments. If necessary, review the section entitled The Overall Regression Equation, earlier in this chapter.

The overall regression equation for the data of Table 12.7 is:

$$Y' = 1.874199 + 1.140738X + 1.120435T - .266946XT - .042344X^2 + .019838X^2T$$

$$a_{T_1} = 1.874199 + 1.120435 = \mathit{2.994634}$$

$$a_{T_2} = 1.874199 - 1.120435 = \mathit{.753764}$$

$$bX_{T_1} = 1.140738 - .266946 = \mathit{.873792}$$

$$bX_{T_2} = 1.140738 + .266946 = \mathit{1.407684}$$

$$bX^2_{T_1} = -.042344 + .019838 = \mathit{-.022506}$$

$$bX^2_{T_2} = -.042344 - .019838 = \mathit{-.062182}$$

The two separate regression equations are:

$$Y'_{T_1} = 2.994634 + .873792X - .022506X^2$$

$$Y'_{T_2} = .753764 + 1.407684X - .062182X^2$$

It is necessary to examine each of these equations in order to determine whether the quadratic terms are required in both of them. Doing a separate regression analysis of Y on X and X^2 for T_1 it is found that:

$$R^2_{y\ x} = .77415 \qquad R^2_{y\ x,x^2} = .79872$$

It is evident that the quadratic term adds very little to the proportion of variance accounted for: .79872 − .77415 = *.02457*. Testing this increment,

$$F = \frac{(R^2_{y\,x,x^2} - R^2_{y\,x})/(k_1 - k_2)}{(1 - R^2_{y\,x,x^2})/(N - k_1 - 1)} = \frac{(.79872 - .77415)/1}{(1 - .79872)/(20 - 2 - 1)} = 2.08$$

with 1 and 17 *df*, $p > .05$. It appears, then, that a linear regression equation would suffice to describe the data for T_1. Because X and X^2 are correlated, it is necessary to recalculate the regression equation with X only. This equation is

$$Y' = 4.28229 + .47330X$$

We turn now to a separate regression analysis for T_2:

$$R^2_{y\,x} = .05437 \qquad R^2_{y\,x,x^2} = .72384$$

Unlike T_1, the increment in the proportion of variance accounted for by the quadratic term in T_2 is very large: .72384 − .05437 = *.66947*. Testing this increment,

$$F = \frac{(R^2_{y\,x,x^2} - R^2_{y\,x})/(k_1 - k_2)}{(1 - R^2_{y\,x,x^2})/(N - k_1 - 1)} = \frac{(.72384 - .05437)/1}{(1 - .72384)/(20 - 2 - 1)} = 41.21$$

with 1 and 17 *df*, $p < .001$. It is clear, then, that the regression of Y on X is quadratic under T_2, whereas under T_1 it is essentially linear.[20]

Using the linear regression equation for T_1 and the quadratic equation for T_2 (see above) the two regression curves are drawn in Figure 12.6, where the fit of each to its data may be observed.

Because more often than not researchers analyze their data as if the regression were linear, it will be instructive to conclude this section with a demonstration of the consequences of such an approach when applied to the data of Table 12.7. This time the data are analyzed using X, T, and XT only. In other words, the regression of Y on X under both treatment conditions is assumed to be linear. The researcher first proceeds to test whether there is a linear interaction. Following the procedures presented earlier in the chapter, calculate

$$R^2_{y\,x,t} = .39867 \qquad R^2_{y\,x,t,xt} = .58362$$

Now test the interaction

$$F = \frac{(.58362 - .39867)/(3 - 2)}{(1 - .58362)/(40 - 3 - 1)} = \frac{.18495/1}{.41638/36} = 15.99$$

with 1 and 36 *df*, $p < .001$. Clearly, the interaction accounts for a meaningful increment in the proportion of variance (.18495), and is statistically significant. Accordingly, two separate regression equations are required.

[20]A substantive example of such a finding is given below in the section entitled Research Applications (see Involvement, Discrepancy of Information, and Attitude Change).

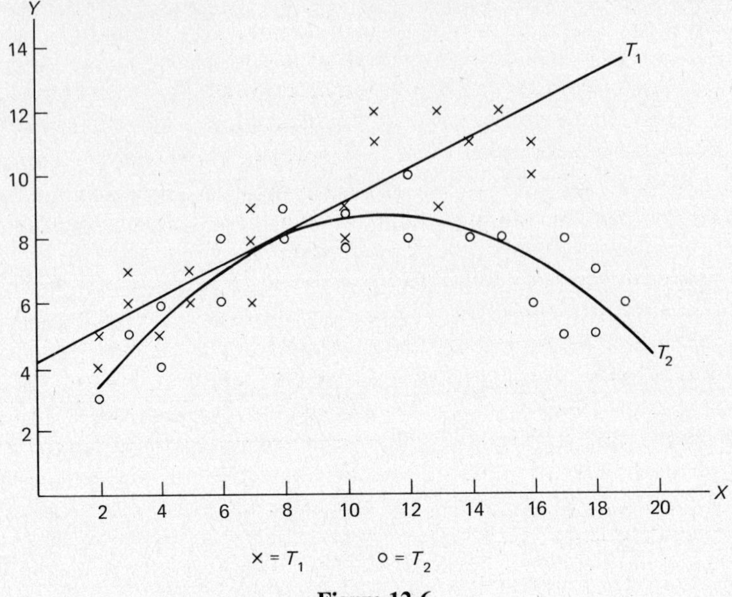

Figure 12.6

The overall regression equation is

$$Y' = 5.147031 + .274925X - .864740T + .198375XT$$

Using this equation to obtain the values for the separate regression equations:

$$a_{T_1} = 5.147031 - .864740 = 4.28229$$

$$a_{T_2} = 5.147031 + .864740 = 6.01177$$

$$bX_{T_1} = .274925 + .198375 = .47330$$

$$bX_{T_2} = .274925 - .198375 = .07655$$

The separate regression equations are:

$$Y'_{T_1} = 4.28229 + .47330X$$

$$Y'_{T_2} = 6.01177 + .07655X$$

Not surprisingly, the linear regression equation for T_1 is the same as obtained above, when it was concluded that a first-degree polynomial is sufficient to describe the data for this treatment. Note, however, what has happened to the regression equation for T_2. The test for the interaction (see above) indicated that the two b's are significantly different. Considering the magnitude of these b's one would have to conclude that the effect of X under T_1 is much larger than its effect under T_2. It will be noted that $R^2_{y.x} = .77415$ under T_1, and $R^2_{y.x} = .05437$ under T_2. Incidentally, because of the small sample size under each treatment R^2 for T_2 is not significant [$F = 1.04$ (1, 18)]. Nevertheless, the two regression lines are drawn in Figure 12.7 for the purpose of comparison with Figure 12.6.

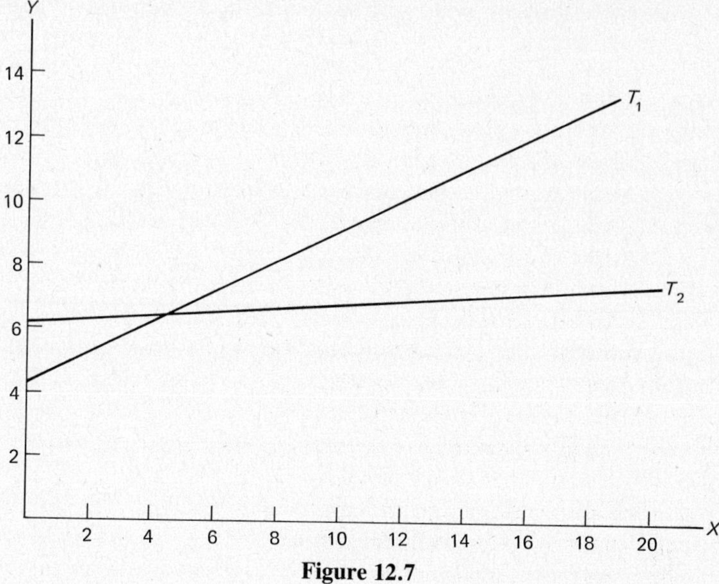

Figure 12.7

Without belaboring the point, it should be obvious that strikingly different conclusions would be reached depending on which of the two analyses was to be used with the data of Table 12.7. The moral of this demonstration is also obvious: Do not assume that the trend in your, or in anyone else's, data is linear! Also, always plot your data, and study the plot.

RESEARCH APPLICATIONS

Several studies in which the methods presented in this chapter have been used are briefly summarized. Because the sole purpose is to illustrate the applications of these methods, no comments are made about the theory or design aspects of the studies (e.g., sampling, sample size, controls, adequacy of measuring instruments). Substantive conclusions drawn by the authors are briefly stated, but their validity is not examined. You are urged to read the studies cited critically and to draw your own conclusions.

Sex, Age, and the Perception of Violence

Moore (1966) used a stereoscope to present a viewer with pairs of pictures simultaneously. One eye was presented with a "violent" picture, and the other eye was presented with a "nonviolent" picture. One of the pairs, for example, was a mailman and a man who had been knifed. Under such conditions of binocular rivalry, binocular fusion takes place: the subject sees only one picture. Various researchers have demonstrated that binocular fusion is affected by cultural and personality factors. Moore hypothesized that when presented with pairs of violent–nonviolent pictures in a binocular rivalry situation, males will see more violent pictures than will females. Moore further hypothesized that there is a positive relation between age and the perception of violent pictures, regardless of sex.

Subjects in the study were males and females from grades 3, 5, 7, 9, 11, and college freshmen. (Note that grade is a continuous independent variable with six levels.) As predicted, Moore found that males perceived significantly more violent pictures than did females, regardless of the grade level. Furthermore, within each sex there was a significant linear trend between grade (age) and the perception of violent pictures. Moore interpreted his findings within the context of differential socialization of sex roles across age.

Involvement, Discrepancy of Information, and Attitude Change

There is a good deal of evidence that relates attitude change to discrepancy of new information about the object of the attitude. That is, in some studies it has been found that the more discrepant new information about an attitude object is from the attitude held by an individual, the more change there will be in his attitude toward the object. In addition, other studies have considered the initial involvement of the individual with the object of the attitude. Freedman (1964) hypothesized that under low involvement the relation between the discrepancy of information and attitude change is monotonic. This means, essentially, that as the discrepancy between the information and the attitude held increases, there is a tendency toward an increase in attitude change. In any event, an increase in the discrepancy will not lead to a decrease in attitude change. With high involvement, however, Freedman hypothesized that the relation is nonmonotonic: with increased discrepancy between information and attitude there is an increase in attitude change up to an optimal point. Further increase in discrepancy will lead to a decrease in attitude change, or what has been called a "boomerang" effect.

Freedman induced the conditions experimentally and demonstrated that in the low involvement group only the linear trend was significant, whereas in the high involvement group only the quadratic trend was significant. In the high involvement group moderate discrepancy, as predicted, resulted in the greatest attitude change. Freedman maintains that the relation between discrepancy and attitude change is nonmonotonic also when the level of involvement is low. In other words, he claims that in the low involvement group the relation is also quadratic. That he obtained a linear relation in the low involvement group Freedman attributes to the range of discrepancy employed in his study. He claims that with greater discrepancy a quadratic trend will emerge in the low involvement group also. Be this as it may, one should not extrapolate from the linear trend. To test Freedman's notions one would have to set up the appropriate experimental conditions.

Test Bias

Cleary (1968) was interested in determining whether the use of the Scholastic Aptitude Test (SAT) for the prediction of Grade-Point Average (GPA) in college is biased toward blacks or whites.[21] Three integrated colleges were used. In each school, GPA was regressed on SAT (Verbal and Mathematical scores), and on SAT and High School Rank (HSR; for two schools only) for the following groups: (1) all black students; (2) a random sample of white students; (3) a sample of white students matched with the black students on curriculum and class (for two schools only).

Differences among regression coefficients within each school were found to be small and not statistically significant. In two of the schools, there were also no significant differences among the intercepts. In one of the schools, the intercepts for the whites were significantly larger than those for the blacks. Cleary concludes:

> In the three schools studied . . . there was little evidence that the Scholastic Aptitude Test is biased as a predictor of college grades. In the two eastern schools, there were not significant differences in the regression lines for Negro and white students. In the one college in the southwest, the regression lines for Negro and white students were significantly different: the Negro students' scores were overpredicted by the use of the white or common regression lines. When high school grades or rank-in-class are used in addition to the SAT as predictors, the degree of positive bias for the Negro students increases. (p. 123)

Teaching Styles, Manifest Anxiety, and Achievement

This study by Dowaliby and Schumer (1973) is an example of the use of an ATI design. College students were assigned to either a teacher-centered or a student-centered class in introductory psychology. Among other measures, the Taylor Manifest Anxiety scale was administered to the students. Two multiple-choice examinations served as the measures of the criterion. Regressing each of these measures on Manifest Anxiety, the authors found a disordinal interaction between the latter and the two teaching styles. Students low on Manifest Anxiety achieved more under the student-centered condition than under the teacher-centered condition. The reverse was found to be true for students high in Manifest Anxiety. The authors report also the regions of significance as established by the application of the Johnson-Neyman technique.

SUMMARY

The collection and analysis of data in scientific research are guided by hypotheses derived from theoretical formulations. Needless to say, the closer the fit between the analytic method and the hypotheses being tested, the more one is in a position to draw appropriate and valid conclusions. The overriding theme of this chapter was that certain analytic methods considered by some researchers as distinct or even incompatible are actually part of the multiple

[21]Cleary's definition of test bias is given earlier in the chapter in the section entitled The Study of Test Bias.

regression approach. To this end, methods introduced separately in preceding chapters were brought together.

Whether the independent variables are continuous, categorical, or a combination of both, the basic approach is to bring all the information to bear on the explanation of the variance of the dependent variable. Used appropriately, this approach can enhance the researcher's efforts to explain phenomena. It was shown, for example, that the practice of categorizing continuous variables leads to loss of information. More important, however, is the loss of explanatory power in that the researcher is not able to study the trend of the relation between the continuous variable that was categorized and the dependent variable.

The analytic methods presented in this chapter were shown to be particularly useful for testing hypotheses about trends and interactions between continuous and categorical variables. The application of these methods not only enables the researcher to test specific hypotheses but also to increase the general sensitivity of the analysis.

The numerical examples used in this chapter were limited to a single continuous variable and a categorical variable consisting of only two levels. As is shown in Chapter 13, extensions to designs with multiple continuous variables and categorical variables consisting of more than two levels are straightforward.

Finally, the methods presented in this chapter were discussed in the context of experimental research, ATI designs, and comparisons of regression equations. As is shown in Chapter 13, the same analytic approaches are applicable in the context of the analysis of covariance.

STUDY SUGGESTIONS

1. In a study of the regression of Y on X in three separate groups, some of the results were: $\Sigma x_1y_1 = 72.56$; $\Sigma x_2y_2 = 80.63$; $\Sigma x_3y_3 = 90.06$; $\Sigma x_1^2 = 56.71$; $\Sigma x_2^2 = 68.09$; $\Sigma x_3^2 = 75.42$. The subscripts refer to group numbers 1, 2, and 3 respectively. Using these data, calculate:
   (a) the three separate b coefficients;
   (b) the common b coefficient;
   (c) the regression sum of squares when the separate b's are used;
   (d) the regression sum of squares when the common b is used.
2. Distinguish between ordinal and disordinal interaction.
3. What is meant by "the research range of interest"?
4. In a study with two groups, A and B, the following regression equations were obtained:

$$Y'_A = 22.56 + .23X$$

$$Y'_B = 15.32 + .76X$$

   At what value of X do the two regression lines intersect?
5. What is meant by "aptitude-treatment interaction"? Give examples of research problems in which the study of ATI may be important.
6. Suppose that a researcher regresses Y on a continuous variable, X, and on a categorical variable, A, without using the product(s) of X and A. What is he or she in effect assuming?
7. In an ATI study with three treatments, A_1, A_2, and A_3, and an aptitude, X, effect coding was used to code the treatments as follows: in vector E1, subjects receiving treatment A_1 were assigned 1's, those receiving A_2 were assigned

0's, and those receiving A_3 were assigned -1's; in vector E2, subjects receiving treatment A_1 were assigned 0's, those receiving A_2 were assigned 1's, and those receiving A_3 were assigned -1's. Product vectors were generated: XE1 and XE2. The overall regression equation obtained from regressing Y on E1, E2, X, XE1, and XE2 is:

$$Y' = 20.35 + 5.72\text{E1} - 3.70\text{E2} + 2.37X + 1.12X\text{E1} + .76X\text{E2}$$

(a) What are the separate regression equations for the three groups?
(b) What vectors should be included in a regression analysis if it is desired to calculate the common regression coefficient (b_c)?

8. A researcher wished to determine whether the regression of achievement on achievement motivation is the same for males and females. For a sample of males ($N = 12$) and females ($N = 12$) she obtained measures of achievement and achievement motivation. Following are the data (illustrative):

Males

Achievement Motivation	*Achievement*
3	16
3	19
5	19
6	21
7	22
7	19
8	20
9	22
9	19
10	24
10	23
10	19

Females

Achievement Motivation	*Achievement*
1	17
1	15
3	16
3	18
4	17
5	18
7	17
7	17
8	18
8	17
9	18
9	18

(a) What is the correlation between achievement motivation and achievement in each of the groups?
(b) What is the proportion of variance accounted for by sex, achievement motivation, and their product?
(c) What is the proportion of variance accounted for by the product of sex and achievement motivation?
(d) What is the F ratio for the product vector?
(e) What is the overall regression equation for achievement motivation, sex, and the product vector (when effect coding [1 -1] is used for sex)?
(f) What are the regression equations for the two groups?
(g) What is the point of intersection of the regression lines?
(h) What is the region of significance at the .05 level? Plot the regression lines and interpret the results.

ANSWERS

1. (a) $b_1 = 1.28$; $b_2 = 1.18$; $b_3 = 1.19$
(b) $b_c = 1.21$
(c) $ss_{\text{reg}} = 295.86$
(d) $ss_{\text{reg}} = 295.53$

4. $X = 13.66$
6. That the regression coefficients for Y on X in the separate groups do not differ from each other. Or that the use of a common regression coefficient is tenable.
7. (a) $Y'_{A_1} = 26.07 + 3.49X$
   $Y'_{A_2} = 16.65 + 3.13X$
   $Y'_{A_3} = 18.33 + .49X$
   (b) E1, E2, X
8. (a) .64291 for males, and .59352 for females.
   (b) .68511
   (c) .04676
   (d) 2.97, with 1 and 20 *df*, $p < .10$.
   (e) $Y' = 16.18120 + .37227(\text{AM}) + .02987(\text{S}) + .18482(\text{INT})$
   (f) $Y'_{\text{M}} = 16.21107 + .55709(\text{AM})$
   $Y'_{\text{F}} = 16.15133 + .18745(\text{AM})$
   (g) −.16162
   (h) Males and females whose scores on achievement motivation range from 4 to 10 differ significantly in achievement. Note that this is a nonsimultaneous region of significance. For a discussion of the calculation of simultaneous regions of significance see Applications and Extensions of the Johnson-Neyman Technique in this chapter.

   Note the similarity between the two correlation coefficients in the two groups [see (a), above], as contrasted with the difference between the two b's [see (f), above]. In the present example, the correlations are equal to β's. For a discussion of properties of β's and b's, and recommendations when to use one or the other, see earlier chapters, particularly Chapter 8.

13

ANALYSIS OF COVARIANCE; THE UNIT OF ANALYSIS

This chapter consists of two major sections. In the first section, topics introduced in Chapter 12 are expanded within the context of the analysis of covariance (ANCOVA). After a general discussion of ANCOVA, analyses with one and two covariates are illustrated and discussed in detail. This is followed by a discussion of problems of interpretations related to ANCOVA designs.

The second section, which is broadly subsumed under the heading of The Unit of Analysis, deals with such topics as cross-level inferences, ecological correlations and fallacies, and group and contextual effects. It is shown that much of the analytic complexities regarding these topics may be understood within the context of ANCOVA. The chapter concludes with a brief discussion of multilevel analysis.

ANALYSIS OF COVARIANCE

In traditional statistics books the analysis of covariance (ANCOVA) is presented as a separate topic. Students who are not familiar with regression analysis are frequently baffled by ANCOVA and tend to do the calculations blindly. Needless to say, little understanding is gained. The picture becomes even more complicated when more than one covariate is used, or when one is dealing with a factorial ANCOVA.

Viewed from a regression frame of reference, ANCOVA is not different from the methods that have been presented in the preceding chapter. The concern is still with comparisons of regression equations, except that in ANCOVA one or more variables (usually continuous) are introduced for the sole purpose of control. In Chapter 10 it was shown how one may exercise direct control of extraneous variance by introducing the source of such variance as a factor in a factorial design. It was noted there that such control is designed to lead to a reduction of the error term, thereby increasing the precision of the analysis. For example, suppose one wishes to study the differential effectiveness of different instructional methods. Subjects are randomly assigned to treatments, whose effects on the dependent variable are studied by comparing the mean responses of the different groups on a measure of the dependent variable. This type of design was discussed in detail in Chapter 9 (for the case of one manipulated variable), and in Chapter 10 (for multiple manipulated variables). Assuming that the study was properly designed and executed, the conclusions based on the analysis of differences among mean responses on the dependent variable serve as a valid indication of the differential effects of the treatments.

It will be noted, however, that the precision of the analysis in such designs is affected to a greater or lesser extent, depending on the degree to which subjects differ on variables that are related to performance on the dependent variable. This is because when the variance that is due to individual differences is not isolated, it becomes part of the error term, thereby leading to a less precise analysis. Note carefully that it is the precision, not the valid estimation of treatment effects, that is affected by relegating the individual differences to the error term.

Relevant individual differences may be controlled for directly by introducing their source variables into the design. Thus, if in the above example the subjects differ in mental ability, and it is known that this variable is related to performance on the dependent variable, this source of variability may be directly controlled. One may, for example, group subjects according to different levels of mental ability, and then randomly assign subjects from each level to the different instructional methods. Mental ability is thus included as a factor, and the design is generally referred to as a treatments-by-levels design (Lindquist, 1953, Chapter 5). Or one may match subjects on mental ability and then randomly assign them to the instructional treatments, thereby using what is referred to as a randomized blocks design (Edwards, 1972, Chapter 13; see also Chapter 14 of this book). Other approaches for the direct control of extraneous variance are also possible.

Instead of controlling extraneous variance directly, it is possible to control for it indirectly by the use of statistical techniques. Basically, this is accomplished by partialing out of the dependent variable the variable, or variables, one wishes to control for. Thus, referring to the above example, instead of introducing mental ability as a factor in the design, one would study the effects of the instructional methods after partialing out from the dependent variable the effect of mental ability. This, then, is an example of an ANCOVA in which mental ability is referred to as a covariate or a concomitant variable.[1]

It is shown below that comparisons among treatments in ANCOVA are tantamount to comparisons among the intercepts of the regression equations in which the dependent variable is regressed on the covariate. Note the similarity between ANCOVA and the ATI designs discussed in Chapter 12. In the latter,

[1]See Feldt (1958) for comparisons among ANCOVA, treatments-by-levels, and randomized-blocks designs.

an aptitude (mental ability of the present example) was introduced because it was desired to study how it interacts with treatments (instructional methods of the present example). In ANCOVA, on the other hand, the aptitude is introduced for the purpose of control. In sum, it is for the purpose of controlling extraneous variables statistically, thereby increasing the precision of the analysis, that ANCOVA was developed (Fisher, 1958).[2]

Other uses, nay abuses, of ANCOVA abound in the social sciences. All of them share a common goal, namely an attempt to "equate" groups that are essentially nonequivalent, or to "adjust" for differences among preexisting groups on a covariate. Several broad areas in which ANCOVA is thus used will be identified. One, when one or more manipulated variables are used with nonequivalent groups ANCOVA is resorted to in an effort to "equate" or "adjust" for initial differences among the groups on relevant variables. Such designs, often referred to as quasi-experimental designs (Campbell & Stanley, 1963; Cook & Campbell, 1979), are frequently encountered in social intervention programs. Some examples that come immediately to mind are programs in compensatory education (e.g., Head Start), drug rehabilitation, birth control, health care, and the like. A common characteristic of such programs is that most often subjects are *not* randomly assigned to them. On the contrary, it is those who are deemed most in need or most deserving that are assigned to such programs. Sometimes, a process of self-assignment, or self-selection, takes place, as when a program is made available to people who wish to participate in it. In either case, an attempt is made to assess the effectiveness of the program by comparing the group that has received it with one that has not received it. ANCOVA is used to "equate" the groups on one or more relevant variables on which they differ.

Other examples of the use of ANCOVA in quasi-experimental designs are encountered in settings in which, because of administrative or other considerations, subjects cannot be assigned randomly to treatments. Instead, the treatments are administered to intact groups. This happens very often in educational settings. For example, suppose again that one is studying the effects of different teaching methods on achievement. The school in which the study is conducted does not permit random assignment of pupils to treatments, but insists that intact classes be used. The researcher suspects, or knows, that classes differ in mental ability. Under such conditions, it is possible that the classes higher in mental ability will perform better regardless of the teaching method to which they are assigned. This may therefore lead to the erroneous conclusion that a given method is superior, when its apparent superiority is due to the mental ability of the subjects assigned to it. To avoid such a blunder, the researcher attempts to "equalize" the groups on mental ability by the use of ANCOVA. In other words, an attempt is made to take into account, or "adjust" for initial group differences in mental ability. The same reasoning is extended to more than one variable. Thus if the researcher believes that the groups differ in motivation as well as mental ability, an "adjustment" is made for initial group differences on both variables; that is, both are used as covariates.

[2]For very good discussions of ANCOVA, its uses and assumptions, see Cochran (1957), Elashoff (1969), and Reichardt (1979).

Second, ANCOVA is often used in nonexperimental research when it is desired to compare the performance of two or more groups on a given variable while controlling for one or more relevant variables. For example, when comparing the achievement of subjects from different ethnic or religious groups, researchers use ANCOVA to control for relevant variables such as intelligence, motivation, socioeconomic status. Or, when comparing the reading achievement of males and females, ANCOVA is used to "equate" the groups on, say, motivation or study time.

Third, it is sometimes desired to compare regression equations obtained in intact groups while controlling for relevant variables. For example, one may wish to compare the regression of achievement on locus of control among males and females while controlling for motivation. In such situations, too, a variation of ANCOVA is resorted to.

The foregoing illustrates how pervasive is the use of ANCOVA in the social sciences. Unfortunately, the applications of ANCOVA in quasi-experimental and nonexperimental research are by and large not valid. It is felt, however, that a discussion of problems of using ANCOVA in these settings will be more beneficial and meaningful after the logic and the method are presented and illustrated. It should be noted that the analytic approach is the same whether ANCOVA is applied in experimental, quasi-experimental, or nonexperimental research. It is the interpretation of the results in the latter settings that is, to say the least, questionable.

The Logic of Analysis of Covariance

It will be recalled that when a variable is residualized, the correlation between the predictor variable and the residuals is zero (see Chapter 5). In other words, the residualized variable is one from which whatever it shared with the predictor variable has been purged. Suppose now that one were studying the effects of different teaching methods on achievement and wished to adjust the achievement score for differences in intelligence. The independent variable is teaching methods, the dependent variable is achievement, and the covariate is intelligence. One can first use the subjects' intelligence scores to predict their achievement on intelligence. If Y_{ij} is the actual achievement of individual i in group j, then Y'_{ij} is his predicted score. $Y_{ij} - Y'_{ij}$ is, of course, the residual. Calculating the residuals for all subjects, one arrives at a set of scores (residuals) that have zero correlations with intelligence. A test of significance between the residuals of the various groups will indicate whether the groups differ significantly *after* their scores have been adjusted for possible differences in intelligence. This is the logic behind the analysis of covariance. It can be summarized by the following formula:

$$Y_{ij} = \bar{Y} + T_j + b(X_{ij} - \bar{X}) + e_{ij} \tag{13.1}$$

where Y_{ij} = the score of subject i under treatment j; $\bar{Y}$ = the grand mean on the dependent variable; T_j = the effect of treatment j; b = a common regression coefficient for Y on X; X_{ij} = the score on the covariate for subject i under treatment j; $\bar{X}$ = the grand mean of the covariate; e_{ij} = the error associated with the score of subject i under treatment j. Formula (13.1) can be rewritten as

$$Y_{ij} - b(X_{ij} - \bar{X}) = \bar{Y} + T_j + e_{ij} \tag{13.2}$$

which clearly shows that after adjustment $[Y_{ij} - b(X_{ij} - \bar{X})]$, a score is conceived as composed of the grand mean, a treatment effect, and an error term. The right-hand side of Formula (13.2) is an expression of the linear model presented in Chapter 9. In fact, if b were zero, that is, if the covariate were not related to the dependent variable, Formula (13.2) would be identical to Formula (9.10).

Homogeneity of Regression Coefficients

The process of adjustment for the covariate (X) in Formula (13.1) involves the application of a common regression coefficient (b) to the deviation of X from the grand mean of X $(\bar{X})$. The use of a common b weight is based on the assumption that the b weights for the regression of Y on X in each group are not significantly different. This assumption is also referred to as the homogeneity of regression coefficients. The testing of the assumption proceeds in exactly the same manner as the testing of the differences between regression coefficients, which was discussed and illustrated in the preceding chapter. Essentially, one tests whether the use of separate regression coefficients adds significantly to the proportion of variance accounted for, as compared to the proportion of variance accounted for by the use of a common regression coefficient.

Having established that the use of a common regression coefficient is appropriate, one can determine whether there is a significant difference between the means of the treatment groups after adjusting the scores on the dependent variable for possible differences on the covariate. As shown below, this is equivalent to a test of differences among intercepts, which was also presented in the preceding chapter.

It will be recalled that tests among intercepts are carried out only after it has been established that the b's in the separate groups are not significantly different from each other. The same holds true for ANCOVA. When the b's are found to be heterogeneous, ANCOVA should not be used. One can instead proceed and study the pattern of regressions in the separate groups, and establish regions of significance as was shown in Chapter 12. The interpretation of the results (e.g., whether one interprets differences among the b's as an interaction between the covariate and the treatments) depends on the specific research setting. This topic, too, was discussed in detail in Chapter 12.

The logic of the ANCOVA was presented as an analysis of residuals for the purpose of clarifying what in effect is being accomplished by such an analysis. One need not, however, actually calculate the residuals. From the foregoing discussion it should be clear that the calculations of ANCOVA follow the same pattern as described in the preceding chapter. We turn now to a numerical example in order to illustrate the calculations of ANCOVA.

A Numerical Example

Illustrative data for four groups on a dependent variable, Y, and two covariates, X and Z, are given in Table 13.1. For convenience, the groups are referred to as treatments. A substantive example is intentionally not given so that you may view the data as having been obtained in any setting, that is, experimental, quasi-experimental, nonexperimental. It was said above that the analysis is the same regardless of the research setting. The concern here is solely with the analysis. Issues regarding interpretation are dealt with later.

The data of Table 13.1 will be used for two analyses: (1) with X only as a covariate; (2) with X and Z as covariates. Doing this will afford an opportunity to illustrate the analytic approach with a single covariate and with multiple covariates. Moreover, the general approach in these analyses will also serve to illustrate extensions of analyses presented in Chapter 12. That is, instead of thinking of X and Z as covariates you may view them as aptitudes in an ATI design. Or, if you wish, you may view the data of Table 13.1 as having been obtained from four groups, and that the interest is in comparing the separate regression equations, as one would do, for example, in a study of test bias (see Chapter 12). In short, the general analytic approach is the same. The interpretations differ, of course, depending on the specific research setting and the specific questions one wishes to answer.

Table 13.1 Illustrative Data for ANCOVA

	Treatments											
		I			*II*			*III*			*IV*	
	Y	*X*	*Z*	*Y*	*X*	*Z*	*Y*	*X*	*Z*	*Y*	*X*	*Z*
	6	1	6	13	4	12	20	7	8	27	7	16
	9	1	7	16	4	12	22	7	14	28	8	10
	8	2	15	15	5	17	24	9	11	25	8	13
	8	3	13	16	6	9	26	9	11	27	9	7
	12	3	18	19	6	20	24	10	16	31	9	15
	12	4	9	17	8	18	25	11	20	29	10	20
	10	4	16	19	8	16	28	11	19	32	10	16
	8	5	10	23	9	20	27	12	19	30	12	21
	12	5	16	19	10	10	29	13	12	32	12	15
	13	6	18	22	10	17	26	13	16	33	14	21
M:	9.8	3.4	12.8	17.9	7.0	15.1	25.1	10.2	14.6	29.4	9.9	15.4
s:	2.35	1.71	4.49	3.11	2.31	4.04	2.73	2.20	4.06	2.63	2.18	4.60

Analysis with a Single Covariate

The data of Table 13.1 for Y and X only are displayed in Table 13.2 in a format suitable for multiple regression analysis. As always, the scores on the dependent variable, Y, and on the covariate, X, are displayed in single vectors. Note that effect coding was used to code group membership in vectors 1, 2, and 3. Vectors XV1, XV2, and XV3 are obtained by multiplying X, in turn, by vectors 1, 2, and 3. The approach taken here is identical to the one used repeatedly in Chapter 12, except that there the categorical variable consisted of two categories whereas here it consists of four categories. The product vectors are given in the table for illustrative purposes only. Normally, they would be generated by the computer program. In SPSS, for example, this can be accomplished by the use of COMPUTE statements. The data of Table 13.2 were analyzed by the REGRESSION program of SPSS. Anticipating the sequence of the analysis, the vectors were entered in the following hierarchy: *X;* vectors 1, 2, and 3; vectors *X*V1, *X*V2, and *X*V3. This was accomplished by the use of different inclusion levels in the REGRESSION statement as follows:

REGRESSION = Y WITH X(6) V1 TO V3(4) XV1 TO XV3(2)/

Following are excerpts of the output and commentaries.

Table 13.2 Illustrative Data for ANCOVA with *X*

	Y	*X*	*V1*	*V2*	*V3*	*XV1*	*XV2*	*XV3*
	6	1	1	0	0	1	0	0
	9	1	1	0	0	1	0	0
I	.	.	.	.	.	.	.	.
	12	5	1	0	0	5	0	0
	13	6	1	0	0	6	0	0
	13	4	0	1	0	0	4	0
	16	4	0	1	0	0	4	0
II	.	.	.	.	.	.	.	.
	19	10	0	1	0	0	10	0
	22	10	0	1	0	0	10	0
	20	7	0	0	1	0	0	7
	22	7	0	0	1	0	0	7
III	.	.	.	.	.	.	.	.
	29	13	0	0	1	0	0	13
	26	13	0	0	1	0	0	13
	27	7	−1	−1	−1	−7	−7	−7
	28	8	−1	−1	−1	−8	−8	−8
IV	.	.	.	.	.	.	.	.
	32	12	−1	−1	−1	−12	−12	−12
	33	14	−1	−1	−1	−14	−14	−14

NOTE: The scores for the first and last two subjects in each group are given here. For the full data see Table 13.1. V1–V3 are effect coding vectors for treatments. *X*V1–*X*V3 are products of *X* with the coded vectors.

Output

VARIABLE	R SQUARE	R SQUARE CHANGE
X	.79189	.79189
V1–V3	.95944	.16755
XV1–XV3	.95984	.00040

VARIABLE	SUM OF SQUARES	SUM OF SQUARES CHANGE	DF	MEAN SQUARE
X	1965.38621	1965.38621	1	
V1–V3	2381.22741	415.84120	3	
XV1–XV3	2382.23359	1.00618	3	.33539
RESIDUAL	99.66641		32	3.11458

Commentary

As was done in earlier chapters, the output is organized in a format that differs from that used by SPSS. Only relevant information is included and grouped together for the purpose of the analysis. Thus, for example, the MEAN SQUARE is reported only for the product vectors (XV1–XV3) and the RESIDUAL because the other mean squares are not relevant at this stage.

The first question to be answered is whether the *b*'s are homogeneous. Recall that if the *b*'s are found to be heterogeneous ANCOVA should not be applied. The test of whether the *b*'s differ significantly from each other could be accomplished by using either the SUM OF SQUARES CHANGE or the R SQUARE CHANGE associated with the product vectors. With output like the one reported above the simplest approach is to use the MEAN SQUARE for the product vectors and that for the residual, Thus,

$$F = \frac{.33539}{3.11458} = .11$$

with 3 and 32 *df*.

Equivalently, one can test the proportion of variance incremented (R SQUARE CHANGE) by the product vectors:

$$F = \frac{.00040/3}{(1 - .95984)/(40 - 7 - 1)} = .11$$

Clearly, there is no significant difference among the *b*'s. Note that the increment in the proportion of variance accounted for by XV1–XV3 is minute. It is concluded that the use of a common *b* is appropriate for the present data.

Regression Equations with Separate *b*'s

Even though for the present data it is not necessary to derive regression equations with separate *b*'s, this is done here to show that the method described in Chapter 12 for the case of two groups applies equally to any number of groups. The overall regression equation as reported in the SPSS output is:

$$Y' = 12.84198 + .99947X - 6.10713\text{V1} - 2.67115\text{V2} + 1.54334\text{V3} - .09795X\text{V1} + .10470X\text{V2} + .05099X\text{V3}$$

where V1, V2, and V3, refer to vectors 1, 2, and 3 of Table 13.2. And similarly, for X and XV1–XV3.

Because the properties of the overall regression equation were described in detail in Chapter 12, the separate regression equations are derived here without comments. If necessary, refer to Chapter 12 for a detailed explanation. The intercepts for the separate groups are

$$a_{\text{I}} = 12.84198 + (-6.10713) = 6.73485$$

$$a_{\text{II}} = 12.84198 + (-2.67115) = 10.17083$$

$$a_{\text{III}} = 12.84198 + (1.54334) = 14.38532$$

$$a_{\text{IV}} = 12.84198 - [(-6.10713) + (-2.67115) + (1.54334)] = 20.07692$$

The b's for the separate regression equations are

$$b_{\text{I}} = .99947 + (-.09795) = .90152$$

$$b_{\text{II}} = .99947 + (.10470) = 1.10417$$

$$b_{\text{III}} = .99947 + (.05099) = 1.05046$$

$$b_{\text{IV}} = .99947 - [(-.09795) + (.10470) + (.05099)] = .94173$$

The separate regression equations are

$$Y'_{\text{I}} = 6.73485 + .90152X$$

$$Y'_{\text{II}} = 10.17083 + 1.10417X$$

$$Y'_{\text{III}} = 14.38532 + 1.05046X$$

$$Y'_{\text{IV}} = 20.07692 + .94173X$$

It was established earlier that the separate b's are not significantly different from each other. Inspection of the b's reveals that they are very similar to each other. Using the four regression equations, the regression lines are plotted in Figure 13.1, where it may be noted that they are nearly parallel.

Because one may use a common b with these data, the next step is to test the differences among the intercepts, to which we now turn.

Differences among Intercepts

As was shown in Chapter 12, a test of the difference among intercepts is accomplished by comparing two models, one in which separate intercepts are fitted to each of the groups and one in which a common intercept is fitted to all of them. If the regression sum of squares (or the proportion of variance accounted for) in the model with separate intercepts does not differ significantly from that obtained when a common intercept is used, it is concluded that the latter model is appropriate to describe the data.

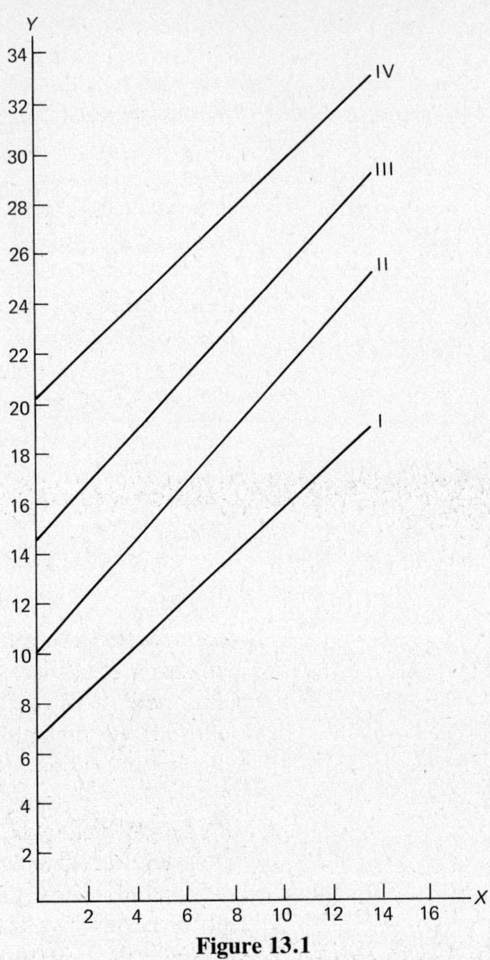

Figure 13.1

Output

VARIABLE	R SQUARE	R SQUARE CHANGE
X	.79189	.79189
V1–V3	.95944	.16755

VARIABLE	SUM OF SQUARES	SUM OF SQUARES CHANGE	DF	MEAN SQUARE
X	1965.38621	1965.38621	1	
V1–V3	2381.22741	415.84120	3	138.61373
RESIDUAL	100.67259		35	2.87636

Commentary

The output reported here is the same as the one reported earlier for the first two steps (i.e., after X and V1 to V3 have been entered into the analysis). Note that because XV1–XV3 have been shown earlier as adding very little to the proportion of variance accounted for, the values associated with these vectors have been relegated to the error term. Thus, for example, in the earlier output the *df* for the residual were 32, whereas in the present analysis they are 35 (the 3 *df* for XV1–XV3 were incorporated in the residual *df*). Similarly for the sum of squares.

From the output reported here it can be noted that using X only (i.e., using a common intercept) .79189 of the variance is accounted for. The increment in the proportion of variance accounted for by V1–V3 is .16755 (R SQUARE CHANGE), indicating that a meaningful proportion of variance is accounted for by the use of separate intercepts. This increment is tested for significance in the usual manner:

$$F = \frac{.16755/3}{(1 - .95944)/(40 - 4 - 1)} = 48.19$$

with 3 and 35 *df*, $p < .001$.

With output like the one reported above there is even a more direct way to obtain this F ratio: (a) Divide the sum of squares change due to V1–V3 by its *df* (3) to obtain a mean square; (b) divide the mean square for V1–V3 by the mean square residual reported in the computer output.

$$F = \frac{415.84120/3}{2.87636} = 48.19$$

Note the usefulness of entering the vectors in the hierarchy that was shown earlier on the REGRESSION statement. Examine first the last step of the analysis to determine whether the b's are homogeneous. Having determined that they are, go to the second step of the output to obtain the information for the test of the differences among the intercepts. Assuming that there are no significant differences among the intercepts (in the present example they are significantly different from each other), go to the first step of the output, where only X has been entered, and obtain a single regression equation for all groups.

Because in the present example significant differences have been found among the intercepts, it is necessary to arrive at four separate regression equations which consist of a common b and separate intercepts. This is accomplished by using the regression equation reported at the step at which the product vectors (XV1–XV3) are not included. From the computer output:

$$Y' = 12.82548 + 1.01305X - 6.46986\text{V1} - 2.01684\text{V2} + 1.94139\text{V3}$$

As was noted in Chapter 12, the b associated with the continuous variable (X) in the equation in which product vectors are *not* included is the common b (b_c). In the present case, then, $b_c = 1.01305$. One tests this b, as always, by dividing it by its standard error. From the computer output, the F ratio for the common b is 57.41, with 1 and 35 df, $p < .001$. It is concluded that the covariate (X) contributes significantly to the proportion of variance accounted for.

Obtain now the separate intercepts by using information in the regression equation reported above:

$$a_{\text{I}} = 12.82548 + (-6.46986) = 6.35562$$

$$a_{\text{II}} = 12.82548 + (-2.01684) = 10.80864$$

$$a_{\text{III}} = 12.82548 + (1.94139) = 14.76687$$

$$a_{\text{IV}} = 12.82548 - [(-6.46986) + (-2.01684) + (1.94139)] = 19.37079$$

It was found above that there are significant differences among these intercepts. As is the case with other statistics, one can now do pairwise comparisons between intercepts, or comparisons between combinations of intercepts. Before it is shown how this is done, it will be useful to discuss the concept of adjusted means.

Adjusted Means

The means for the four treatment groups on the dependent variable were reported in Table 13.1. They are

$$\bar{Y}_{\text{I}} = 9.8 \qquad \bar{Y}_{\text{II}} = 17.9 \qquad \bar{Y}_{\text{III}} = 25.1 \qquad \bar{Y}_{\text{IV}} = 29.4$$

These means reflect not only differences in treatment effects but also differences among the groups that are presumably due to their differences on the covariate. It is possible to adjust each of the means and observe the differences among them after the effect of the covariate has been removed. For one covariate, the formula is

$$\bar{Y}_{j(\text{adj})} = \bar{Y}_j - b(\bar{X}_j - \bar{X}) \tag{13.3}$$

where $\bar{Y}_{j(\text{adj})}$ = the adjusted mean of treatment j; $\bar{Y}_j$ = the mean of treatment j before the adjustment; b = the common regression coefficient; $\bar{X}_j$ = the mean of the covariate for treatment group j; $\bar{X}$ = the grand mean of the covariate.

To appreciate what is accomplished by Formula (13.3), let us assume that in a study in which ANCOVA is used, subjects are randomly assigned to treatments. Assume, further, that because of randomization all treatment groups end up having identical means on the covariate. This means that $\bar{X}_j = \bar{X}$ in Formula (13.3). The application of (13.3) under such circumstances will result in no adjustments of the means of $\bar{Y}_j$. This makes sense, since the groups are equal on the covariate. Note that in this case the function of the covariate is to identify a systematic source of variance and thereby reduce the error term. Although randomization of subjects will generally not result in equal group means on the covariate, the differences among such means will tend to be small when relatively large groups are being used. Consequently, the adjustments of means by Formula (13.3) will be relatively small.

When, on the other hand, intact groups are being used, they may differ to a greater or lesser extent on the covariate. The greater the differences, the larger will the adjustment be. The present numerical example was designed to illustrate the nature of the adjustment when the groups differ on the covariate. From Table 13.1,

$$\bar{X}_{\text{I}} = 3.4 \qquad \bar{X}_{\text{II}} = 7.0 \qquad \bar{X}_{\text{III}} = 10.2 \qquad \bar{X}_{\text{IV}} = 9.9$$

The grand mean on X is therefore 7.625. Using these figures, the common b, and the $\bar{Y}$'s reported above the adjusted means are calculated by the application of Formula (13.3). They are

$$\bar{Y}_{\text{I(adj)}} = 9.8 - (1.01305)(3.4 - 7.625) = 14.08014$$

$$\bar{Y}_{\text{II(adj)}} = 17.9 - (1.01305)(7.0 - 7.625) = 18.53316$$

$$\bar{Y}_{\text{III(adj)}} = 25.1 - (1.01305)(10.2 - 7.625) = 22.49139$$

$$\bar{Y}_{\text{IV(adj)}} = 29.4 - (1.01305)(9.9 - 7.625) = 27.09531$$

The adjusted means are closer to each other than are the unadjusted ones. This is because the means on the dependent variable for groups whose covariate means are low are adjusted upward, while those for groups whose covariate means are high are adjusted downward. The more the group mean on the covariate deviates from the grand mean of the covariate, the larger the adjustment. For example, the deviation of the covariate mean from the grand mean for group I is the largest (−4.225). Consequently, the adjustment for this group is the largest (from 9.8 to 14.08). The covariate mean for group II, on the other hand, does not deviate much from the grand mean, and the resulting adjustment is therefore small (from 17.9 to 18.53).

The adjustments are, of course, predicated on the covariate having a meaningful correlation with the dependent variable. This is reflected in the common b used in Formula (13.3). In the extreme case, when the covariate is not correlated with the dependent variable, $b_c = 0$, and no adjustment will take place when Formula (13.3) is applied. This makes sense because an adjustment would be made for differences among groups on a variable that is irrelevant to the phenomenon under study. It has been shown (Cochran, 1957; Feldt, 1958) that the use of a covariate whose correlation with the dependent variable is less than .3 does not lead to an appreciable increase in the precision of the analysis.

Tests among Adjusted Means

The topic of multiple comparisons among means was discussed in detail in Chapter 9. The discussion is therefore not repeated here, except to note that in ANCOVA the same type of comparisons (i.e., a priori and post hoc) are applied to the adjusted means. The F ratio for a comparison between two adjusted means, I and II, is

$$F = \frac{[\bar{Y}_{I(adj)} - \bar{Y}_{II(adj)}]^2}{MSR\left[\frac{1}{n_I} + \frac{1}{n_{II}} + \frac{(\bar{X}_I - \bar{X}_{II})^2}{ss_{res(X)}}\right]} \tag{13.4}$$

where $\bar{Y}_{I(adj)}$ and $\bar{Y}_{II(adj)}$ = adjusted means for treatments I and II respectively; MSR = mean square residual of the analysis of covariance; n_I, n_{II} = number of subjects in groups I and II respectively; $ss_{res(X)}$ = residual sum of squares of the covariate *(X)* when it is regressed on the treatments—that is, when X is used as a dependent variable and the coded vectors for the treatments are used as the independent variable. The *df* for the F ratio of (13.4) are 1 and $N - k - 2$, where k is the number of coded vectors for treatments. The reason the denominator *df* are $N - k - 2$, and not $N - k - 1$, as used in earlier chapters, is that an additional *df* is lost because of the use of a covariate. Note that $N - k - 2$ are the *df* associated with the residual sum of squares of the ANCOVA. To obtain a t ratio, take $\sqrt{F}$ in (13.4). The *df* for the t ratio are $N - k - 2$.

Several things will be noted about Formula (13.4). First, it was said above that when all the treatment groups have equal means on the covariate, no adjustment of means takes place. Therefore the numerator of Formula (13.4) will consist of unadjusted means when all the treatment groups have equal means on the covariate. Second, when the treatment means on the covariate are equal to each other, the last term in the denominator vanishes, and (13.4) reduces to the conventional formula for a test of the difference between two means, except that the *MSR* is the one obtained in ANCOVA. Given a covariate that is meaningfully correlated with the dependent variable, *MSR* from ANCOVA will be smaller than *MSR* obtained without the use of the covariate. This, of course, is the reason for using ANCOVA in the first place. Third, when subjects are randomly assigned to treatments, the numerator of the last term of the denominator (i.e., $\bar{X}_1 - \bar{X}_{II}$) will generally be small because the means for the treatment groups on the covariate will be similar, though not necessarily equal, to each other. Fourth, with intact groups that differ on the covariate, the last term of the denominator of (13.4) will lead to a larger error term. The larger the difference between $\bar{X}_I$ and $\bar{X}_{II}$, the larger the error term will be. This therefore has serious implications for testing differences between adjusted means when intact groups are used. Fifth, inspection of the denominator of (13.4) will show that the error term changes depending on the specific covariate means for the groups whose adjusted means are being compared. Finney (1946) has therefore suggested the use of a general error term, as indicated in the following formula

$$F = \frac{[\bar{Y}_{I(adj)} - \bar{Y}_{II(adj)}]^2}{MSR\left(\frac{1}{n_I} + \frac{1}{n_{II}}\right)\left[1 + \frac{ss_{reg(X)}}{k\,ss_{res(X)}}\right]} \tag{13.5}$$

where $ss_{reg(X)}$ = regression sum of squares of the covariate *(X)* when it is regressed on the treatments; k = number of coded vectors for treatments, or the degrees of freedom for treatments. All other terms are as defined for (13.4).

Formula (13.4) is now applied to a test between the adjusted means of groups I and II of the numerical example under consideration. The following values were reported above:

$\bar{Y}_{\text{I(adj)}} = 14.08$ $\bar{Y}_{\text{II(adj)}} = 18.53$ $\bar{X}_{\text{I}} = 3.4$ $\bar{X}_{\text{II}} = 7.0$

$n_{\text{I}} = 10$ $n_{\text{II}} = 10$ $MSR = 2.87636$

In order to apply (13.4) it is necessary to calculate the residual sum of squares of the covariate when it is regressed on the treatment. In the present example, this means doing a multiple regression analysis in which X is used as the dependent variable and the coded vectors (1, 2, and 3 of Table 13.2) are used as the independent variable. Doing this, one obtains $ss_{\text{res}(X)} = 160.9$. Applying now (13.4) to the test of the difference between the adjusted means of groups I and II:

$$F = \frac{(14.08 - 18.53)^2}{2.87636\left[\frac{1}{10} + \frac{1}{10} + \frac{(3.4 - 7.0)^2}{160.9}\right]} = \frac{19.8025}{.80695} = 24.54$$

with 1 and 35 df, $p < .001$.

One could, similarly, test the differences between other pairs of means. Or one may use (13.5) instead in order to avoid the calculation of different error terms for each comparison.

Until now, the concern was only with pairwise comparisons of adjusted means. But, as in the case of designs when a covariate was not used (see Chapter 9), one can test linear combinations of more than two adjusted means in ANCOVA. The formula for the F ratio is similar to the one given in Equation (9.15), except that MSR in the denominator is the one obtained from the ANCOVA, and the denominator also includes an additional term as in (13.5) above (see also Kirk, 1968, p. 472).

The reason the F ratio for the test of linear combinations of more than two adjusted means was described only briefly, and the reason for not illustrating its application to the numerical example is that a more direct approach for doing multiple comparisons in ANCOVA is presented below. But before this is done it is necessary to discuss briefly the relation between the intercepts of the separate regression equations and the adjusted means.

Intercepts and Adjusted Means

Recall that with one independent variable, X, the intercept, a, is calculated as follows:

$$a = \bar{Y} - b\bar{X} \tag{13.6}$$

compare this with the formula for the calculation of an adjusted mean in ANCOVA (13.3), which is repeated here:

$$\bar{Y}_{j\text{(adj)}} = \bar{Y}_j - b(\bar{X}_j - \bar{X}) \tag{13.7}$$

Note that the difference between (13.6) and (13.7) is a constant, $b\bar{X}$. Therefore, the intercept for each treatment group is simply equal to the adjusted mean minus this constant. In the present example, $b = 1.01305$ and $\bar{X} = 7.625$. The constant, then, is $(1.01305)(7.625) = 7.72451$. For example, the adjusted mean for group I was found above to be equal to 14.08014. The intercept of the regression equation for this group was found above to be equal to 6.35562. Now,

$$14.08014 - 6.35562 = 7.72452$$

and similarly for the differences between each of the other adjusted means and its respective intercept.

From the foregoing it follows that testing the difference between intercepts is the same as testing the difference between their respective adjusted means. For the test between the adjusted means of groups I and II given above,

$$14.08014 - 18.53316 = -4.45302 = 6.35562 - 10.80864$$

where the last two values are the intercepts for groups I and II respectively, calculated above.

Look back now at the method of obtaining separate intercepts from the overall regression equation and note that each of them is composed of two components: (1) a constant that is equal to their average, this being the a from the equation consisting of the covariate and the coded vectors for treatments, and (2) the deviation of each intercept from the average of the intercepts, this being the b associated with a coded vector in which a given group was identified. Thus, the intercepts for groups I and II are

$$a_{\text{I}} = a + b_{\text{I}}$$

$$a_{\text{II}} = a + b_{\text{II}}$$

where a = intercept of an equation consisting of the covariate and the coded vectors for treatments. In the present example it is the equation for X and vectors 1, 2, and 3 of Table 13.2. b_{I} is the regression coefficient for the coded vector in which treatment I was assigned 1, and similarly for b_{II}.

Note that subtracting a_{II} from a_{I} is equivalent to subtracting b_{II} from b_{I} (because a is a constant in both a_{I} and a_{II}). For the numerical example under consideration,

$$a_{\text{I}} - a_{\text{II}} = 6.35562 - 10.80864 = -4.45302$$

$$b_{\text{I}} - b_{\text{II}} = (-6.46986) - (-2.01684) = -4.45302$$

The same holds true for the difference between any two b's that are associated with coded vectors that represent treatments.

The above can be viewed from still another perspective. Recall that an effect is defined as the deviation of a treatment mean from the grand mean of the dependent variable. This is true whether the design does not include a covariate (as in Chapter 9) or it does. In the latter case, however, the effect is defined as the deviation of the adjusted mean from the grand mean of the dependent variable. Using the adjusted means calculated above and the grand mean of Y (20.55) calculate the effects of the four treatments:

$$T_{\text{I}} = 14.08014 - 20.55 = -6.46986$$

$$T_{\text{II}} = 18.53316 - 20.55 = -2.01684$$

$$T_{\text{III}} = 22.49139 - 20.55 = 1.94139$$

$$T_{\text{IV}} = 27.09531 - 20.55 = 6.54531$$

Not surprisingly, the first three values are the same as the b's for the respective coded vectors in the regression equation in which the product vectors are not included. For convenience, this equation is repeated:

$$Y' = 12.82548 + 1.01305X - 6.46986\text{V1} - 2.01684\text{V2} + 1.94139\text{V3}$$

where V1, V2, and V3 are the coded vectors for the treatments in Table 13.2. Clearly, then, the b's represent the treatment effects after adjustment for the covariate. As always, the effect of the treatment assigned -1's in all the vectors is equal to $-\Sigma b_j$.

This somewhat lengthy detour was designed to demonstrate the equivalence of testing differences among b's, among intercepts, or among adjusted means. Consequently, the approach of testing differences among effects via differences among b's is applicable also in ANCOVA designs. It is to such an approach that we now turn.

Multiple Comparisons among Adjusted Means via *b*'s

In Chapter 4 the variance/covariance matrix of the b's (**C**) was introduced and discussed in detail. It was shown there how elements of **C** may be used to test differences between b's. The **C** was then introduced again in Chapter 9, where it was shown how one augments this matrix to obtain **C***, and how elements of **C*** are used for the purpose of testing multiple comparisons among b's. It was shown in Chapter 9 that doing this is equivalent to testing multiple comparisons among means. One of the reasons that this approach was introduced in earlier chapters was in anticipation of its use in ANCOVA designs, with which we are now concerned. As will become evident from the presentation given below, this approach is more direct and involves a minimal amount of calculations. This is particularly true when the design includes multiple covariates (see later in this chapter).

The variance/covariance matrix of the b's (**C**) for the numerical example of Table 13.2 as obtained from SPSS is[3]

	V1	V2	V3
V1	.53484	−.02470	−.26640
V2	−.02470	.22271	−.10068
V3	−.26640	−.10068	.33426

[3]If the SPSS version you are using does not report **C**, this matrix may be obtained from other programs. In Chapter 4 it was shown how **C** may be obtained from output reported by BMDP1R and the GLM program of SAS.

where V1, V2, and V3 refer to coded vectors 1, 2, and 3 of Table 13.2—that is, the vectors that represent treatments I, II, and III, respectively. Thus, for example, .53484 is the square of the standard error of b_1, the coefficient associated with vector 1 in which treatment I was assigned 1 (see Table 13.2). The covariance of b_1 and b_2 is −.02470, and similarly for other elements of **C**.[4]

It will be noted that in the output **C** includes also the variance of the b associated with the covariate (X) and the covariances of this b with the b's of the coded vectors. But since the interest here is only in the b's for the coded vectors, only the segment of **C** that refers to them was reproduced above.

Also, **C** reported above does not include the variance of the b for the treatment that was assigned −1's in the three vectors (i.e., treatment IV) as well as the covariance of this b with the remaining three b's. Recall that this information is obtained by augmenting **C** to obtain **C*** (see Chapter 9 for a detailed discussion). The missing elements can be easily obtained by recalling that the sum of each row and column of **C*** is equal to zero. **C*** for the numerical example of Table 13.2 is therefore

	V1	V2	V3	(V4)
V1	.53484	−.02470	−.26640	−.24374
V2	−.02470	.22271	−.10068	−.09733
V3	−.26640	−.10068	.33426	.03282
(V4)	−.24374	−.09733	.03282	.30825

where V4 was placed in parentheses and the values corresponding to it separated by dashed lines to indicate that these are *not* obtained from the output.

The relevant b's for vectors 1, 2, and 3 in the equation that includes also the covariate were reported earlier. They are repeated here:

$$b_1 = -6.46986 \qquad b_2 = -2.01684 \qquad b_3 = 1.94139$$

It is necessary now to obtain a b for the treatment that was assigned −1 in the three coded vectors (i.e., treatment IV). This b, which will be labeled b_4, is obtained in the usual manner; that is, $b_4 = -\Sigma b_j$. Using the values reported above:

$$b_4 = -[(-6.46986) + (-2.01684) + (1.94139)] = 6.54531$$

We are ready now to test multiple comparisons among the four b's. To this end, the formula for the F ratio used extensively in earlier chapters (see, in particular, Formula (9.18) and the discussion that follows it) is repeated:

$$F = \frac{[a_1(b_1) + a_2(b_2) + \cdots + a_j(b_j)]^2}{\mathbf{a'C^*a}} \qquad (13.8)$$

[4]If you are encountering difficulties with the presentation in this section, it is strongly suggested that you review discussions of **C** in earlier chapters, particularly those in Chapter 9.

where $a_1, a_2, \ldots, a_j$ are coefficients by which b's are multiplied (a's are used here instead of c's so as not to confuse them with elements of $\mathbf{C}^*$, the augmented $\mathbf{C}$); $\mathbf{a}'$ and $\mathbf{a}$ are the row and column vectors, respectively, of the coefficients of the linear combination; $\mathbf{C}^*$ is the augmented matrix of variance covariance of the b's. Since some of the a's of a given linear combination may be 0's, thus excluding the b's associated with them from consideration, it is convenient to exclude such a's from the numerator and the denominator of (13.8). Accordingly, only that part of $\mathbf{C}^*$ whose elements correspond to nonzero a's will be used in the denominator of (13.8).

The application of (13.8) is now illustrated for the numerical example under consideration. Assume, first, that it is desired to test the significance of the difference between b_1 (−6.46986) and b_2 (−2.01684):

$$F = \frac{[(1)(-6.46986) + (-1)(-2.01684)]^2}{[1 \quad -1]\begin{bmatrix} .53484 & -.02470 \\ -.02470 & .22271 \end{bmatrix}\begin{bmatrix} 1 \\ -1 \end{bmatrix}} = \frac{19.82939}{.80695} = 24.57$$

with 1 and 35 df. Note that the same F ratio (within rounding) was obtained earlier when Formula (13.4) was applied to a test of the difference between the adjusted means of treatments I and II. This, then, demonstrates the equivalence of testing differences between adjusted means and testing differences between b's associated with coded vectors that identify the groups whose adjusted means are being used.

Following are several examples of tests of linear combinations of b's. For each test, the relevant values for the denominator are obtained from $\mathbf{C}^*$ reported above. Test the average of b_1 (−6.46986) and b_2 (−2.01684) against b_3 (1.94139):

$$F = \frac{[(1)(-6.46986) + (1)(-2.01684) + (-2)(1.94139)]^2}{[1 \quad 1 \quad -2]\begin{bmatrix} .53484 & -.02470 & -.26640 \\ -.02470 & .22271 & -.10068 \\ -.26640 & -.10068 & .33426 \end{bmatrix}\begin{bmatrix} 1 \\ 1 \\ -2 \end{bmatrix}} = \frac{153.00404}{3.51351} = 43.55$$

with 1 and 35 df. This is the same as testing the average of the adjusted means for treatments I and II against the adjusted mean of treatment III.

Test the difference between the average of b_1 (−6.46986) and b_3 (1.94139) with that of the average of b_2 (−2.01684) and b_4 (6.54531):

$$F = \frac{[(1)(-6.46986) + (-1)(-2.01684) + (1)(1.94139) + (-1)(6.54531)]^2}{[1 \quad -1 \quad 1 \quad -1]\begin{bmatrix} .53484 & -.02470 & -.26640 & -.24374 \\ -.02470 & .22271 & -.10068 & -.09733 \\ -.26640 & -.10068 & .33426 & .03282 \\ -.24374 & -.09733 & .03282 & .30825 \end{bmatrix}\begin{bmatrix} 1 \\ -1 \\ 1 \\ -1 \end{bmatrix}}$$

$$= \frac{82.02816}{1.3452} = 60.98$$

with 1 and 35 df. This is the same as testing the difference between the average of the adjusted means of treatments I and III with that of the average of the adjusted means of treatments II and IV.

Finally, test the difference between the average of b_1, b_2, and b_3 against b_4:

$$F = \frac{[(1)(-6.46986) + (1)(-2.01684) + (1)(1.94139) + (-3)(6.54531)]^2}{[1 \quad 1 \quad 1 \quad -3]\begin{bmatrix} .53484 & -.02470 & -.26640 & -.24374 \\ -.02470 & .22271 & -.10068 & -.09733 \\ -.26640 & -.10068 & .33426 & .03282 \\ -.24374 & -.09733 & .03282 & .30825 \end{bmatrix}\begin{bmatrix} 1 \\ 1 \\ 1 \\ -3 \end{bmatrix}}$$

$$= \frac{685.45733}{4.932} = 138.98$$

with 1 and 35 *df*. This is the same as testing the average of the adjusted means of treatments I, II, and III against the adjusted mean of treatment IV.

As was described in detail in Chapter 9, the above tests may be used for any type of comparison (planned orthogonal, planned nonorthogonal, or post hoc). For example, if it is assumed that the above comparisons were part of a set of Scheffé comparisons, then an obtained F ratio would have to exceed $kF_\alpha; k, N - k - 2$ in order to be declared significant. In the preceding expression k is the number of coded vectors for treatments. $F_\alpha; k, N - k - 2$ is the tabled F value at a prespecified α with k and $N - k - 2$ *df* (the denominator *df* are equal to those associated with the residual sum of squares of the ANCOVA). For further details of tests among b's, see Chapter 9.

Tabular Summary of ANCOVA

The major results of the ANCOVA are reported in Table 13.3, thus providing a succinct summary of the procedures followed in the analysis. Part I of Table 13.3 reports the results of the ANCOVA. Part II reports the original and adjusted means of the dependent variable.

Table 13.3 Summary of ANCOVA for Data of Table 13.1

I: Source	Proportion of Variance	*ss*	*df*	*ms*	*F*
$R^2_{y.x}$	.79189	1965.38621	1	1965.38621	
Treatments (after adjustment) $R^2_{y.x123} - R^2_{y.x}$	.16755	415.84120	3	138.61373	48.19
Error $(1 - R^2_{y.x123})$	.04056	100.67259	35	2.87636	
Total	1.00000	2481.90000			

II:	Treatments *I*	*II*	*III*	*IV*
Original means:	9.8	17.9	25.1	29.4
Adjusted means:	14.08	18.53	22.49	27.10

NOTE: Y = dependent variable; X = covariate; 1, 2, 3 = coded vectors for treatments. See Table 13.2.

Recapitulation

In order not to lose sight of what has been presented thus far, the major points are briefly summarized.

ANCOVA was initially developed in the context of experimental research for the purpose of increasing the precision of statistical analyses by controlling for sources of systematic variations.

Subsequently, ANCOVA also came into frequent use in attempts to "equate" intact groups in quasi-experimental and nonexperimental research.

ANCOVA is a special case of the general analytic approach in designs with categorical and continuous variables. Following is an outline of the sequence of steps in ANCOVA with one covariate.

1. Create a vector, Y, that includes the scores on the dependent variable for all subjects.
2. Create a vector, X, that includes the scores on the covariate for all subjects.
3. Create coded vectors to represent group membership.
4. Multiply X by each of the coded vectors.
5. Test whether the product vectors add significantly to the proportion of variance accounted for. If yes, it means that the b's are not homogeneous. Proceed with the analysis as in Chapter 12. If no, proceed to 6.
6. Test whether the coded vectors add significantly to the proportion of variance accounted for, over and above the covariate. If no, calculate a single regression equation in which only the covariate is used. If yes, it means that the intercepts are significantly different from each other. Equivalently, this means that the adjusted means differ from each other. Go to 7.
7. When the categorical variable consists of more than two categories, multiple comparisons among adjusted means are necessary. Probably the simplest approach for doing this is via tests of differences among the b's associated with the coded vectors. To this end, the augmented variance/covariance matrix of the b's, $\mathbf{C}^*$, is used.

ANCOVA WITH MULTIPLE COVARIATES

In this section, ANCOVA with multiple covariates is discussed and illustrated. Although for convenience only two covariates are used, it should be clear that the same approach may be extended to more than two covariates. Also, even though the present discussion is couched in ANCOVA terminology, the same overall analytic approach is applicable when the continuous variables are not viewed as covariates. For example, with two or more aptitudes in an ATI design the analysis will proceed in the same manner as in the present section, although the focus will change. Thus, whereas in ANCOVA the continuous variables are used for control purposes, in ATI designs they are used for the purpose of studying their possible interactions with treatments. Therefore, the test of the differences among regression coefficients, for example, serves different purposes in the two designs. In ANCOVA it is used to test the assumption about homogeneity of regression coefficients, whereas in ATI the test is used for the purpose of detecting an interaction between the aptitudes and the treatments. Recall, however, that when in ANCOVA the *b*'s are not homogeneous the interpretation is the same as in an ATI design—that is, that the covariates interact with the treatments.

A Numerical Example

For a numerical example with two covariates (or two aptitudes) we return to the data of Table 13.1. Note that for the four treatments, three variables (*Y*, *X*, and *Z*) are listed. In the preceding sections ANCOVA was applied with one covariate, *X*. This time, *Z* is also used as an additional covariate. In view of the fact that the present analysis is an extension of the one presented in preceding sections, comments will generally be briefer here, except when a point is particularly relevant to the case of ANCOVA with more than one covariate. Moreover, when it appears that no comments are necessary, because the analysis parallels the one given earlier with one covariate, none will be made. Instead, the results will be stated, and conclusions drawn.

In Table 13.4 the data of Table 13.1 are displayed for the purpose of doing a multiple regression analysis. This table is similar to Table 13.2, except that it contains two covariates and two sets of product vectors: one for the products of the coded vectors with *X*, and one for the products of the coded vectors with *Z*. The data of Table 13.4 were analyzed by the REGRESSION program of SPSS, with the variables entered in the hierarchy indicated by the inclusion levels in the following Regression statement:

```
REGRESSION = Y WITH X Z(6) V1 TO V3(4) XV1 TO ZV3(2)/
```

Following are excerpts of the output and commentaries.

Output

VARIABLE	R SQUARE	R SQUARE CHANGE
X Z	.79311	.79311
V1–V3	.96241	.16930
XV1–ZV3	.96555	.00314

VARIABLE	SUM OF SQUARES	SUM OF SQUARES CHANGE	DF	MEAN SQUARE
X Z	1968.40817	1968.40817	2	
V1–V3	2388.59757	420.18940	3	
XV1–ZV3	2396.40189	7.80432	6	1.30072
RESIDUAL	85.49811		28	3.05350

Table 13.4 Illustrative Data for ANCOVA with *X* and *Z*

	Y	*X*	*Z*	*V1*	*V2*	*V3*	*XV1*	*XV2*	*XV3*	*ZV1*	*ZV2*	*ZV3*
	6	1	6	1	0	0	1	0	0	6	0	0
	9	1	7	1	0	0	1	0	0	7	0	0
I	•	•	•	•	•	•	•	•	•	•	•	•
	12	5	16	1	0	0	5	0	0	16	0	0
	13	6	18	1	0	0	6	0	0	18	0	0
	13	4	12	0	1	0	0	4	0	0	12	0
	16	4	12	0	1	0	0	4	0	0	12	0
II	•	•	•	•	•	•	•	•	•	•	•	•
	19	10	10	0	1	0	0	10	0	0	10	0
	22	10	17	0	1	0	0	10	0	0	17	0
	20	7	8	0	0	1	0	0	7	0	0	8
	22	7	14	0	0	1	0	0	7	0	0	14
III	•	•	•	•	•	•	•	•	•	•	•	•
	29	13	12	0	0	1	0	0	13	0	0	12
	26	13	16	0	0	1	0	0	13	0	0	16
	27	7	16	−1	−1	−1	−7	−7	−7	−16	−16	−16
	28	8	10	−1	−1	−1	−8	−8	−8	−10	−10	−10
IV	•	•	•	•	•	•	•	•	•	•	•	•
	32	12	15	−1	−1	−1	−12	−12	−12	−15	−15	−15
	33	14	21	−1	−1	−1	−14	−14	−14	−21	−21	−21

NOTE: The scores for the first and last two subjects in each group are given here. For full data, see Table 13.1. V1–V3 are effect coding vectors for treatments. *X*V1–*Z*V3 are products of *X* and *Z* with the coded vectors.

Commentary

It is evident that the increment in the proportion of variance due to the six product vectors is very small (.00314). One could test this increment for significance in the usual way. Instead, the two mean squares reported above will be used:

$$F = \frac{1.30072}{3.05350} < 1$$

It is concluded that the regression coefficients are homogeneous. Stated differently, it is appropriate to use common *b*'s for the four treatments.

The next step is to note whether there are significant differences among the intercepts. Instead of reporting more output, in which the results may be obtained more directly, the output given above will be used for this purpose.

$$F = \frac{.16930/3}{(1 - .96241)/(40 - 5 - 1)} = 51.04$$

with 3 and 34 *df*, $p < .001$. Clearly, there are significant differences among the intercepts or, equivalently, among the adjusted means.

Before illustrating the application of multiple comparisons among adjusted means, the regression equation is reported.

Output

VARIABLES IN EQUATION

VARIABLE	B	F
X	.89525	36.07
Z	.11996	2.69
V1	−6.76662	
V2	−2.16544	
V3	2.22973	
(CONSTANT)	11.98726	

Commentary

The common coefficients for X and Z, respectively, are .89525 and .11996. Note that the common b for Z is not significant at the .05 level [$F = 2.69(1,34)$]. Assuming that the .05 level of significance was selected for the study, Z would be removed from the equation. Doing this would bring us back to the analysis done earlier in the chapter, where only X was used as a covariate. It is interesting to note that $R^2_{y.x123} = .95944$, whereas $R^2_{y.xz123} = .96241$, indicating that Z adds very little to the proportion of variance accounted for by X and the three coded vectors. Because the sole purpose of this section is to illustrate the analysis with two covariates, the issue of significance of the b associated with Z will be ignored.

In the output reported above, F ratios were not given for the coded vectors (although they are given in the SPSS output) because they are irrelevant. The relevant test regarding the differences among the intercepts was done above, and found to be statistically significant.

The regression equation given above will now be used to calculate: (1) separate regression equations for the four treatments; (2) adjusted means for the four treatments.

Separate Regression Equations

$$a_{\text{I}} = 11.98726 + (-6.76662) = 5.22064$$

$$a_{\text{II}} = 11.98726 + (-2.16544) = 9.82182$$

$$a_{\text{III}} = 11.98726 + (2.22973) = 14.21699$$

$$a_{\text{IV}} = 11.98726 - [(-6.76662) + (-2.16544) + (2.22973)] = 18.68959$$

$$Y'_{\text{I}} = 5.22064 + .89525X + .11996Z$$

$$Y'_{\text{II}} = 9.82182 + .89525X + .11996Z$$

$$Y'_{\text{III}} = 14.21699 + .89525X + .11996Z$$

$$Y'_{\text{IV}} = 18.68959 + .89525X + .11996Z$$

Note that because it was established earlier that the regression coefficients do not differ significantly from each other, the regression equations have common *b*'s but separate *a*'s.

Adjusted Means

In order to calculate adjusted means, it is necessary to have the treatment as well as the grand means on the variables. These are reported in Table 13.5. Using relevant values from this table and the common *b*'s the adjusted means are calculated:

$$\bar{Y}'_{\text{I(adj)}} = 9.8 - .89525(3.4 - 7.625) - .11996(12.8 - 14.475) = 13.78336$$

$$\bar{Y}'_{\text{II(adj)}} = 17.9 - .89525(7.0 - 7.625) - .11996(15.1 - 14.475) = 18.38456$$

$$\bar{Y}'_{\text{III(adj)}} = 25.1 - .89525(10.2 - 7.625) - .11996(14.6 - 14.475) = 22.77974$$

$$\bar{Y}'_{\text{IV(adj)}} = 29.4 - .89525(9.9 - 7.625) - .11996(15.4 - 14.475) = 27.25234$$

As was explained in detail earlier in the chapter, the differences between any two adjusted means is equal to the difference between the two intercepts that correspond to them. Therefore, testing differences between intercepts is the same as testing differences between adjusted means to which they correspond. But it was also shown earlier that the *b*'s associated with coded vectors for treatments indicate the treatment effects after having adjusted for the covariates. Therefore, tests among such *b*'s are the same as tests among adjusted means to which they correspond. As was done earlier, tests among adjusted means will be done via tests of differences among *b*'s.

Table 13.5 Treatment and Grand Means for Data of Table 13.1

	Treatments				
	I	*II*	*III*	*IV*	*M*
$\bar{Y}$:	9.8	17.9	25.1	29.4	20.550
$\bar{X}$:	3.4	7.0	10.2	9.9	7.625
$\bar{Z}$:	12.8	15.1	14.6	15.4	14.475

NOTE: M = grand mean.

Multiple Comparisons via *b*'s

The *b*'s for the three coded vectors of Table 13.4 were reported above:

$$b_1 = -6.76662 \qquad b_2 = -2.16544 \qquad b_3 = 2.22973$$

As always, the b for the treatment assigned -1's is:

$$b_4 = -[(-6.76662) + (-2.16544) + (2.22973)] = 6.70233$$

Recall that in order to test linear combinations of b's we need the augmented $\mathbf{C}^*$. The relevant segment of $\mathbf{C}^*$ for the coded vectors of Table 13.4 is:

	V1	V2	V3	(V4)
V1	.54305	−.00715	−.28602	−.24988
V2	−.00715	.22070	−.11201	−.10154
V3	−.28602	−.11201	.34986	.04817
(V4)	−.24988	−.10154	.04817	.30325

The matrix enclosed by the dashed lines was obtained from SPSS. The values for V4 were obtained in the manner shown several times earlier (recall that the sum of each row and each column is equal to zero).

Assume that it is desired to test the difference between the adjusted means for treatments I and II. First the following equivalences will be shown:

$$\bar{Y}_{\text{I(adj)}} - \bar{Y}_{\text{II(adj)}} = 13.78336 - 18.38456 = -4.6012$$

$$a_{\text{I}} - a_{\text{II}} = 5.22064 - 9.82182 = -4.60118$$

$$b_1 - b_2 = -6.76662 - (-2.16544) = -4.60118$$

Using relevant values from $\mathbf{C}^*$ test the difference between b_1 and b_2:

$$F = \frac{[(1)(-6.76662) + (-1)(-2.16544)]^2}{[1 \quad -1]\begin{bmatrix} .54305 & -.00715 \\ -.00715 & .22070 \end{bmatrix}\begin{bmatrix} 1 \\ -1 \end{bmatrix}} = \frac{21.17086}{.77805} = 27.21$$

with 1 and 34 df, $p < .001$.

It is instructive to show now how the same test is done when the conventional approach to the calculations of ANCOVA is used (see, for example, Kirk, 1968, p. 475). The F ratio for the comparison between adjusted means I and II is:

$$F = \frac{[(1)\,\bar{Y}_{\text{I(adj)}} + (-1)\,\bar{Y}_{\text{II(adj)}}]^2}{MSR\left[\frac{2}{n} + \frac{\Sigma z^2(\bar{X}_{\text{I}} - \bar{X}_{\text{II}})^2 - 2\Sigma xz\,(\bar{X}_{\text{I}} - \bar{X}_{\text{II}})(\bar{Z}_{\text{I}} - \bar{Z}_{\text{II}}) + \Sigma x^2(\bar{Z}_{\text{I}} - \bar{Z}_{\text{II}})}{\Sigma x^2\Sigma z^2 - (\Sigma xz)^2}\right]} \tag{13.9}$$

where MSR = mean square residual from ANCOVA; Σz^2 = sum of squares of Z *within* treatments or, equivalently, it is the residual sum of squares when Z is regressed on the three coded vectors of Table 13.4; Σx^2 = sum of squares of X *within* treatments; Σxz = sum of the products of X and Z *within* treatments; n = number of subjects in either of the treatments. The remaining terms in (13.9) should be clear.

Following are the values necessary for the calculation of F in (13.9):

$$\bar{Y}_{\text{I(adj)}} = 13.78336 \qquad \bar{Y}_{\text{II(adj)}} = 18.38456$$

$$\bar{X}_{\text{I}} = 3.4 \qquad \bar{X}_{\text{II}} = 7.0$$

$$\bar{Z}_{\text{I}} = 12.8 \qquad \bar{Z}_{\text{II}} = 15.1$$

$$MSR = 2.74419 \qquad n = 10$$

$$\Sigma z^2 = 667.3 \qquad \Sigma xz = 158 \qquad \Sigma x^2 = 160.9$$

$$F = \frac{[(1)(13.78336) + (-1)(18.38456)]^2}{2.74419\left[\dfrac{2}{10} + \dfrac{667.3(3.4-7.0)^2 - 2(158)(3.4-7)(12.8-15.1) + 160.9(12.8-15.1)^2}{(160.9)(667.3) - (158)^2}\right]}$$

$$= \frac{21.17104}{.77805} = 27.21$$

This is the same F ratio as obtained above for the difference between b_1 and b_2. But notice the much greater computational labor involved in the conventional approach. Consider, further, that much of what was done above will have to be recalculated for each comparison. Also, the calculations will become even more tedious when linear combinations of adjusted means are tested. Finally, imagine what an extension of (13.9) would look like had there been three covariates, and the advantage of doing multiple comparisons via the b's should become evident.

Here is another example. This time, it is desired to contrast the average of adjusted means for treatments I and II with that of III. Using the b's and the relevant values of **C*** reported above:

$$F = \frac{[(1)(-6.76662) + (1)(-2.16544) + (-2)(2.22973)]^2}{[1 \quad 1 \quad -2]\begin{bmatrix} .54305 & -.00715 & -.28602 \\ -.00715 & .22070 & -.11201 \\ -.28602 & -.11201 & .34986 \end{bmatrix}\begin{bmatrix} 1 \\ 1 \\ -2 \end{bmatrix}} = \frac{179.33281}{3.74101} = 47.94$$

with 1 and 34 df, $p < .001$.

You may wish to apply Formula (13.9) to the same comparison in order to convince yourself that the same F value is obtained through more complex calculations. If you do this, and assuming you use the coefficients 1, 1, and -2 for the comparison, the value of $2/n$ in the denominator of (13.9) will be 6/10 instead—that is, $[(1)^2 + (1)^2 + (-2)^2]/10$.

In sum, to test any linear combination of adjusted means, test the linear combination of the b's for the coded vectors that correspond to the adjusted means that are being considered. Tests of linear combinations of b's may be used for any type of multiple comparisons: planned orthogonal, planned nonorthogonal, or post hoc. Because what was said about this topic in Chapter 9 applies equally to the present situation, no further comment will be made about it here.

Factorial ANCOVA

The examples presented thus far concerned a single-factor ANCOVA with one or two covariates. ANCOVA is not limited to such designs. For example,

ANCOVA with one or more than one covariate may be part of a factorial design. The analytic procedure of factorial ANCOVA is a direct extension of the procedures presented in Chapter 10 and those presented in the present chapter. Thus, the categorical variables of the factorial design are coded in the same manner as was done in Chapter 10, that is, as if there were no covariates. The dependent variable is then regressed on the coded vectors (for main effects and interaction) and on the covariate(s).

As in the case of a single-factor ANCOVA, it is necessary to test whether the regression coefficients are homogeneous. In a factorial design, homogeneity of regression coefficients refers to the regression of the dependent variable on the covariate(s) within the cells of the design. This test is accomplished in a manner similar to the one done in a single-factor design. Specifically, multiply the coded vectors (for main effects and the interaction) by the covariate(s). Test whether these product vectors add significantly to the proportion of variance accounted for, over and above that accounted for by the covariate(s), the main effects, and the interaction. A nonsignificant F ratio indicates that the use of a common b is tenable.

For a discussion of factorial ANCOVA and numerical examples, see Winer (1971, pp. 781–792). Winer does the analysis in the conventional ANCOVA approach. You will benefit from analyzing Winer's numerical example in the manner outlined above and comparing your results with those given by him.

INTERPRETATIONAL PROBLEMS IN ANCOVA

Earlier, a distinction was made between the use of ANCOVA in experimental versus quasi-experimental and nonexperimental research. It will be recalled that the use of ANCOVA in experimental research is designed to identify and remove extraneous variance, thereby increasing the precision of the analysis. In addition to the usual assumptions of ANCOVA (see Cochran, 1957; Elashoff, 1969; Reichardt, 1979) it is necessary to ascertain that the treatments do not affect the covariate; otherwise, the adjustment for the covariate will result in removing not only extraneous variance but also variance due to the treatments. The simplest way to ensure that this will not occur is to measure the covariate prior to the inception of the experiment. Following sound principles of research design, ANCOVA may serve a very useful purpose of control in experimental research.

The situation is radically different (some say hopeless) when ANCOVA is used in quasi-experimental or nonexperimental research for the purpose of "equating" intact groups. The logical and statistical problems that arise in such situations are so serious that some authors have argued that ANCOVA should not be used in them at all. Anderson (1963) has, perhaps, best expressed the logical problem, saying: "One may well wonder what exactly it means to ask what the data would look like if they were not what they are" (p. 170). Lord (1969), who argues cogently against the use of ANCOVA for adjustment when comparing intact groups, offered the following illuminating example. Suppose that a researcher is studying the yields of "black" and "white" varieties of corn. Suppose, further, that the two are treated equally for several months, after which it is found that the white variety has yielded much more grain than the black variety. But, as Lord points out, the average height of black plants at flowering time is 6 feet, whereas that of white plants is 7 feet. In this hypothetical situation, a researcher who uses ANCOVA to adjust for differences in the height of the plants is in effect asking the question: "Would the black variety produce as much salable grain if conditions were adjusted so that it averaged 7 feet at flowering time?" (Lord, 1969, p. 336) Lord says:

> I think it is quite clear that analysis of covariance is not going to provide us with a good answer to this question. In practice, the answer depends on what we do to secure black-variety plants averaging 7 feet in height. This could be done by destroying the shorter plants, by applying more fertilizer, or by stretching the plants at night while they are young, or by other means. *The answer depends on the means used.* (pp. 336–337)

The foregoing will suffice to serve as a broad frame of reference for viewing the problems of using ANCOVA with intact groups. What follows is a relatively brief, and by no means exhaustive, discussion of some specific problems regarding the use of ANCOVA in such situations.[5]

Specification Errors

Much of the problems attendant with attempts to "equate" nonequivalent groups by the use of ANCOVA may be subsumed under the heading of specification errors. It will be recalled that such errors refer to misspecified models.[6] In Chapter 8 it was shown how specification errors lead to biased estimation of parameters. In the present context this means that specification errors will result in, among other things, a biased estimation of the common regression coefficient for the covariate, and consequently in an over- or underadjustment of treatment means. In either case, the conclusion about the differential effects of treatments, or the difference between the treatment and the "control" group, will be erroneous.

The potential for specification errors in the application of ANCOVA with intact groups is so great that it is a virtual certainty in most instances. As one example, consider the errors due to the omission of relevant variables. Recall that specification errors are committed whenever a variable in the equation (a covariate, in the present case) is correlated with variables that are not included in the equation and that are related to the dependent variable. It is not necessary to engage in great feats of imagination to realize that when intact groups are "equated" on a given variable, they may differ on many other relevant variables. Indeed, as Meehl (1970) argues convincingly, the very act of equating groups on a variable may result in accentuating their differences on other variables. Attributing, under such circumstances, the "adjusted" differences to treatments or to group membership (e.g., male–female) is erroneous and may often lead to rather strange conclusions.

[5]Excellent discussions of ANCOVA will be found in Cochran (1957), Cronbach, Rogosa, Floden, and Price (1977), and Weisberg (1979).

[6]Weisberg's (1979) discussion of ANCOVA is presented from this frame of reference.

Reichardt (1979) provides a very good example of the potential of arriving at erroneous conclusions because some of the variables on which groups differ were left uncontrolled in an ANCOVA design. He describes a situation in which a researcher is interested in assessing the effectiveness of driver education classes in promoting safe driving. In the absence of an experimental design, which would include random assignment to driver education and a control group, the researcher is faced with a myriad of variables that would have to be "controlled" for. "Perhaps those who take a course in driver education are more motivated to be safe drivers, or are more fearful of accidents, or are more law-abiding and so feel more compelled to learn all the proper procedures, or are more interested in lowering their insurance costs (if completing the course provides a discount), than those who do not attend such classes" (Reichardt, 1979, p. 174). Failure to control such variables may result in attributing observed differences in traffic violations between the groups to the fact that one of them was exposed to driver education, even when, in reality, the course may be useless.

Even if it were possible to control for all the variables noted above (not an easy task, to say the least), it is necessary to recognize that others may have been overlooked. As Reichardt points out: "Perhaps those who attend the course do so because they are unskilled at such tasks and realize that they need help. Or perhaps those who attend will end up driving more frequently than those who do not attend" (p. 175). In either case, it may turn out that the frequency of traffic violations or accidents is greater among those who have attended driver education courses. Failure to control for the initial differences among the groups would, under such circumstances, lead to the conclusion that driver education courses are harmful!

Although the above was a fictitious, but very realistic, example, it should be noted that similar situations in which social intervention programs have been shown to be harmful have been noted. For extensive discussions of conditions that may lead to the conclusion that compensatory education is harmful, see Campbell and Boruch (1975), Campbell and Erlebacher (1970); see also the section on Measurement Errors (below).

Extrapolation Errors

When there are considerable differences on the covariate between, for example, two groups so that there is little, or no, overlap between their distributions, the process of arriving at adjusted means involves two extrapolations. The regression line for the group that is lower on the covariate is extrapolated upward, whereas the regression line for the group higher on the covariate is extrapolated downward.[7] Smith's (1957) suggestion that it would be more appropriate to speak of "fictitious means" (p. 291) instead of corrected means in ANCOVA is particularly pertinent in situations of the kind described here.

[7]For a discussion of hazards of extrapolation, see Chapter 11.

Differential Growth

Social scientists are frequently interested in assessing the effectiveness of a treatment in accelerating the growth of individuals on some dependent variable. In the absence of randomization, attempts are made to adjust for pretreatment differences among nonequivalent groups. Although several methods of adjustment have been proposed, the one most commonly used is ANCOVA in which posttest measures of the dependent variable are adjusted for initial group differences on a pretest measure of the same variable. It is necessary to recognize that used thus it is assumed that the rate of growth of individuals in the nonequivalent groups is the same. When this assumption is not tenable, it is possible that observed differences among groups after adjusting for a pretest are due, in part or wholly, to the differential growth of the groups rather than to the treatments. Bryk and Weisberg (1976, 1977) discuss this topic in detail and show the type of growth patterns for which ANCOVA is appropriate, and those for which it leads to over- or underadjustment. In addition, they examine other proposed methods of adjustment for initial differences on a pretest, and offer an alternative approach for growth models. For additional discussions of this topic, see Campbell and Boruch (1975), Campbell and Erlebacher (1970), Kenny (1975; 1979, Chapter 11).

Nonlinearity

Most often, ANCOVA is applied on the basis of the assumption that the regression of the dependent variable on the covariate is linear. In fact, this assumption was made implicitly in this chapter because it was desired to concentrate on the rationale of ANCOVA in the context of a relatively simple model. ANCOVA is, however, not limited to linear regression. Linearity should not be assumed. Methods of curvilinear regression analysis presented in Chapters 11 and 12 are applicable also in ANCOVA designs. To repeat: do not assume that the regression is linear; study its shape, thereby avoiding erroneous assumptions and inappropriate analyses.

Measurement Errors

The effects of errors of measurement in the independent variables on regression statistics were discussed several times in earlier chapters. In Chapter 2 it was shown that random errors of measurement in the independent variable lead to an underestimation of the regression coefficient. It follows, therefore, that the consequence of using a fallible covariate in ANCOVA is an underadjustment for initial differences among groups. This may have far-reaching implications for conclusions about treatment effects. If, for example, the group given the treatment is lower on the covariate (this often happens in social intervention programs) than the "control" group, the underadjustment may even lead to the conclusion that not only was the treatment not beneficial but that it was actually harmful![8]

[8]For very good discussions of this point, and numerical illustrations, see Campbell and Boruch (1975) and Campbell and Erlebacher (1970).

In Chapter 5 it was shown that when the control variable is not perfectly reliable, the partial correlation is biased and may even differ in sign as compared with a partial correlation when the control variable is measured without error. In ANCOVA, the control variable is the covariate, and a partial regression coefficient is calculated instead. But the effects of measurement errors in the covariate are similar to those indicated for the partial correlation.

Problems of measurement errors with multiple independent variables were discussed in Chapter 8, where it was noted that, unlike the designs with one independent variable, measurement errors may lead to either the overestimation or the underestimation of regression coefficients. The same bias would, of course, occur when the fallible variables are covariates.

As was noted in earlier chapters, all the foregoing considerations referred to random errors of measurement. The effects of other types of errors are even more complicated, and little is known about them. But even if one were to consider the effects of random errors only, it is clear that they may lead to serious misinterpretations in ANCOVA. What, then, is the remedy? Unfortunately, there is no consensus among social scientists about the appropriate corrective measures in ANCOVA with fallible covariates. Cohen and Cohen (1975) have perhaps best characterized the prevailing state of affairs, saying: "Although the nature of the problem of fallible covariates is widely understood among methodologists, the solution to the problem is still in the realm of debate" (pp. 372–373). In this connection, it is interesting to note that Cohen and Cohen propose a method of correcting for the unreliability of the covariate but warn the reader that it "has not been proved mathematically nor even tested by extensive computer trials on data of known characteristics ('Monte Carlo' methods). It rests on no more than the judgment of the present authors and some of our colleagues" (p. 373).

It is not possible to discuss here the different proposed solutions to deal with fallible covariates without having to go into complex issues regarding measurement models. The purpose of the discussion here was only to alert you to the problem in the hope that you will reach two obvious conclusions: (1) that efforts should be directed to construct measures of the covariates that have very high reliabilities, and (2) that ignoring the problem, as is unfortunately done in most applications of ANCOVA, will not make it disappear. Detailed discussions of the effects of fallible covariates, and proposals for corrective measures, will be found in the following sources and in references cited therein: Campbell and Boruch (1975), Campbell and Erlebacher (1970), Huitema (1980), Porter and Chibucos (1974), Reichardt (1979), and Weisberg (1979).

In concluding this section it will be noted that the crux of the problems in the use and interpretation of ANCOVA with intact groups is that the researcher has no systematic control over the assignment of subjects to groups. Even when the assignment is not random but under the systematic control of the researcher, ANCOVA will lead to unbiased estimation of parameters. A case in point is a design in which the researcher assigns subjects to groups on the basis of the covariate. In certain studies it may be useful, for example, to assign subjects below a cutoff score on the covariate to a treatment and those above the cutoff score to another treatment or to a control group. Under such circumstances, the use of ANCOVA will lead to unbiased estimation of parameters. Incidentally, in such a design one should not correct for unreliability of the covariate. For further discussion of this topic, see Cain (1975), Overall and Woodward (1977a, 1977b), and Rubin (1977). See also discussions of Regression-Discontinuity Designs in Campbell and Stanley (1963) and Cook and Campbell (1979).

To repeat, then, the problems arise because one has to work with preexisting groups about whose formation one has had no control. It is the inherent inequality of preexisting groups, and the inherent impossibility of enumerating all the pertinent variables on which they differ, not to mention the task of controlling for them, that has led some methodologists to conclude that attempts to "equate" such groups are doomed to fail. Lord (1967), for example, states unequivocally: "With the data usually available for such studies, there simply is no logical or statistical procedure that can be counted on to make the proper allowances for uncontrolled preexisting differences between groups" (p. 305). Similarly, Cochran and Rubin say: "If randomization is absent, it is virtually impossible in many practical circumstances to be convinced that the estimates of the effects of treatments are in fact unbiased" (1973, p. 417).

Even though other methodologists may take a somewhat less pessimistic view of the use of ANCOVA with nonequivalent groups, all seem to agree that it is indeed a "delicate instrument" (Elashoff, 1969), and "no miracle worker that can produce interpretable results from . . . quasi-experimental designs" (Games, 1976, p. 54). And when Cronbach and Furby (1970) observe that the use of ANCOVA in studies in which assignment to groups is nonrandom "is now in bad repute" (p. 78), it is of methodologists that they seem to speak. Unfortunately, applied researchers seem to apply ANCOVA routinely, atheoretically, almost blindly. "Such blind applications of ANCOVA can result in substantial model misspecification and in considerably worse inferences than no adjustment whatsoever" (Bryk & Weisberg, 1977, p. 959).

One final note. The foregoing discussion dealt exclusively with the use of ANCOVA in quasi-experimental and nonexperimental research not because it is the only method that is being used, or recommended for use, in such settings, but because it appears to be the one most commonly used.[9] Moreover, the discussion was not intended to convey the idea that research other than experimental holds no promise for the social sciences, and should therefore be avoided. On the contrary, there are many good reasons for choosing to study certain phenomena in quasi-experimental or nonexperimental settings. And because of ethical considerations, economic or societal constraints, this type of research may be the only feasible one in various areas. But the conduct of such research, indeed all scientific research, requires sound theoretical thinking, constant vigilance, and a thorough understanding of the potential and limitations of the methods being used.

Given the state of current methodology in the social sciences, the full potential of such studies will not be realized until more appropriate methods, suited to deal with the unique problems they pose, are developed. Attempting to develop such designs ought to be

[9]For other approaches, see Cook and Campbell (1979), Kenny (1974, 1979, Chapter 11), and Rubin (1974).

a top priority of evaluation methodologists. Until we have tried to develop alternatives based not on "approximations" to randomization, we should be cautious in discounting the value of uncontrolled studies. While statistical adjustments are certainly problematic, the potential contribution of uncontrolled studies has not really been tested. (Weisberg, 1979, p. 1163)

THE UNIT OF ANALYSIS

What is the appropriate unit of analysis in social and behavioral research? In educational research, for example, should the unit of analysis be the individual student, the class, the school, the school district, the state? Similarly, in studies of voting behavior, for example, should the unit of analysis be the individual voter, electoral districts, cities, states? Social scientists have dealt with the problem of the unit of analysis from a wide spectrum of theoretical orientations and disciplines. In fact, one of the distinguishing characteristics among the social sciences is the unit of analysis on which they focus (Sherif, 1963). Even within a given discipline, researchers use different units of analysis depending, among other things, on the theoretical orientation and the type of variables and measures they use.

At this point, it is not difficult to envision your puzzlement as to why a topic that is apparently unrelated to the subject matter discussed thus far has been sprung on you, so to speak. Admittedly, this topic could have been presented as a separate chapter. But because much of the analytic complexities regarding the unit of analysis can best be clarified within the context of ANCOVA, it was decided to address them in this chapter. It is necessary, however, to recognize that issues regarding the unit of analysis are very complex, partly because they are not limited to statistical analysis but are also related, among other things, to theory and measurement. Suffice it to point out that, in addition to numerous papers, entire books have been devoted to one aspect or another of the unit of analysis in various disciplines such as econometrics (e.g., Green, 1964; Gupta, 1969; Theil, 1954, 1972), sociology and political science (e.g., Borgatta & Jackson, 1980; Dogan & Rokkan, 1969; Hannan, 1971; Merritt & Rokkan, 1966; Taylor, 1968); and education (e.g., Roberts & Burstein, 1980).

Within the confines of a brief presentation it is therefore not possible to do justice to this complex topic. It is hoped that the discussion that follows will provide you with some insights into the topic, and that it will stimulate you to study it further and in greater depth.

Writing over a decade ago, Alker (1969) commented that some of the findings regarding the unit of analysis "have now become methodologically commonplace or even passé" (p. 69). This may have been true among methodologists. It certainly was not, by and large, true among applied researchers then, nor does it appear to be the case today. Hannan and Young (1976) are probably correct when they say: "Despite the long history of concern and the recent upsurge of interest in the problem, a great deal of current research practice appears virtually unaffected" (p. 1). In the preface to an important paper dealing with analytic issues concerning research on classrooms and schools, Cronbach (1976) says:

> If any fraction of the argument herein is correct, educational research—and a great deal of social science—is in serious trouble. The implications of my analysis can be put bluntly:
>
> 1. The majority of studies of educational effects—whether classroom experiments, or evaluations of programs, or surveys—have collected and analyzed data in ways that conceal more than they reveal. The established methods have generated false conclusions in many studies. (p. 1)

Broadly speaking, it is possible to identify two major perspectives within which the issue of the unit of analysis is addressed. One concerns problems inherent in cross-level or cross-unit inferences, whereas the other addresses the questions of what are the appropriate units and what is the appropriate analysis when a given phenomenon is being studied. The two perspectives are not unrelated. Historically, social scientists have been more concerned with problems of cross-level inferences. It is only in very recent years that a shift to the other perspective seems to have taken place. Because the major issues about the unit of analysis have arisen within the context of cross-level inferences, and because much of the analytic complexity can be illustrated within this context, it is dealt with here first.

CROSS-LEVEL INFERENCES

When findings obtained from data collected using one type of unit of analysis are used to make inferences about another type of unit of analysis, a cross-level inference is being made. For example, one might study the relation between mental ability and achievement using the school as the unit of analysis. That is, school means on mental ability and achievement are used to calculate, say, a correlation coefficient between these two variables. When on the basis of the correlation coefficient thus obtained an inference is made about the relation between these variables on the level of another unit, say individual students, a cross-level inference is being made. Similarly, when the relation between race and voting behavior is calculated using data obtained from individual voters, and an inference is made about the relation between these variables on the level of counties, or states. Note that in the first example the cross-level inference is made from aggregates to individuals, whereas in the second example the inference is made from individuals to aggregates.

Cross-level inferences may also be made from one type of aggregate to another, as when the school is the unit of analysis and inferences are made to classrooms, or vice versa. Most of the discussions of cross-level inferences in the social sciences have, however, been concerned with inferences from the aggregate to the individual level. While in the following presentation it will be convenient to refer to inferences from aggregates to individuals, and vice versa, it should be borne in mind that conceptually and analytically the discussion applies also to other kinds of cross-level inferences.

A question that probably comes first to mind is: Why not study the relation between the variables using the unit that is of interest? The answer is that most often researchers use aggregate data because, for one reason or another, it is not feasible to collect data on individuals or to match data for individuals across variables. Sociology and political science are replete with examples of studies in which data on census tracts, election districts, counties, states, countries, and the like, were used because these were the only data available or obtainable in view of constraints regarding costs or confidentiality of information, to name but two. Studies of educational effects serve as other prime examples where aggregates of some kind or another are used. Numerous examples may be found in the Coleman Report (Coleman et al., 1966). Thus, because of problems of matching measures obtained from individual teachers and students they taught, teacher variables in the Coleman Report were aggregated measures of teachers on a schoolwide basis. Because of problems of feasibility (Coleman, 1968), per-pupil expenditure was arrived at on the basis of school district aggregation. In some reanalyses of the Coleman Report data (e.g., Armor, 1972; Mayeske et al., 1972), aggregate measures of schools were used for all the variables, including the dependent variable. Numerous other examples of the use of aggregate data may be found in the various IEA studies.[10]

Warnings about the dangers of engaging in cross-level inferences have been sounded relatively early in the social sciences. An interesting example of such warnings may be found in a comment made by E. L. Thorndike (1939) in connection with research reported by Burt (1925). In a study of juvenile delinquency, Burt reported correlations between rates of juvenile delinquency and a variety of indices of social conditions using aggregate data from 29 metropolitan boroughs of London. Among other correlations, Burt reported a .67 correlation between poverty and juvenile delinquency, and a .77 correlation between overcrowding and juvenile delinquency. On the basis of these correlations, and others like them, Burt concluded:

> They indicate plainly that it is in the poor, overcrowded, insanitary households, where families are huge, where the children are dependent on charity and relief for their own maintenance, that juvenile delinquency is most rife. (p. 75)

It does not seem necessary to elaborate on the far-reaching implications of accepting such correlations as reflecting the magnitude of the relations between the variables when the unit of analysis is the family. Nor is it necessary to discuss in detail the manner in which such cross-level inferences may serve to legitimize prejudices toward the poor. The important thing is that cross-level references may be, and most often are, fallacious and grossly misleading.

In order to demonstrate the potential fallacies in making cross-level inferences, E. L. Thorndike (1939) has constructed data on intelligence and number of persons per room for what were supposed to be 12 districts. When the correlation between the two variables was calculated within each of the 12 districts it was found to be equal to zero. When, instead, the data from all the districts were combined into one group and the correlation was calculated, it was found to be .45. When the averages of intelligence and persons per room for each district were used, the correlation between the variables was found to be .90.

In his demonstration, Thorndike has drawn attention to the fact that when

[10]For descriptions of the Coleman Report and the IEA studies, see earlier chapters, particularly Chapter 7.

data are available for more than one group it is possible to calculate three different correlation coefficients: (1) within groups; (2) between groups; and (3) a total correlation. These types of correlations are discussed in detail below, where it is shown that not only can they differ in magnitude, but that their signs, too, may differ. Regrettably, Thorndike's statement, that had only incompetent scientists engaged in cross-level inferences there would be no need to publish his note in a professional journal, is as timely today as it was over 30 years ago. Two recent examples of the apparent need to revisit the topic in professional journals are Knapp (1977) and Sockloff (1975).

Another early warning of the hazards of cross-level inferences was sounded by Lindquist (1940, pp. 219–224). But it was not until the publication of a paper by Robinson (1950) that social scientists, particularly sociologists and political scientists, were jolted into the awareness that cross-level inferences may be highly misleading. Using data on race (black, white) and on illiteracy (illiterate, literate), Robinson has demonstrated that the correlation between these two variables was .203, when individuals were used as the unit of analysis. When, however, the correlation for the same data was calculated with states as the unit of analysis it was .773. And when the unit of analysis was changed to census tracts (nine tracts) the correlation between race and illiteracy was .946!

To further dramatize the problem, Robinson used data on national origin (native born, foreign born) and illiteracy. Robinson reasoned that because of the lower educational background of foreign-born individuals (a plausible assumption, considering that the data were collected in 1930), the correlation between national origin and illiteracy is expected to be positive (i.e., when foreign born and illiterate are scored as 1's, whereas native born and literate are scored as 0's). Indeed, when individuals were used as the unit of analysis a small positive correlation (.118) was found between the variables. But when the same data were aggregated by census tracts the correlation was −.619! Note that in this example the correlations differ not only in magnitude but also in sign.

Robinson used the above examples to illustrate the fallacy of making inferences from correlations based on aggregate data—which he labeled ecological correlations—to individuals. This type of inference has come to be known as the ecological fallacy. Robinson's important contribution in alerting social scientists to the dangers of ecological fallacies is attested to, among other things, by the fact that almost every subsequent treatment of this topic in the social science literature views it as a point of departure in the discussion of cross-level inferences. Yet Robinson's classic paper suffers from what might be considered overstatements, as well as omissions. These are perhaps due to his zeal in conveying his very important message. Be that as it may, while Robinson's discussion of the ecological fallacy is sound and very well stated, his claim that the interest is always in individual correlations is not supportable. It is *not* true that "Ecological correlations are used simply because correlations between the properties of individuals are not available" (Robinson, 1950, p. 352). Frequently, one may be interested in ecological correlations for their own sake. Moreover, there are circumstances in which ecological correlations are either the only meaningful or the only ones that can be calculated. Thus, Menzel (1950) argued:

It can hardly be said that a researcher correlating women's court cases with boys' court cases does so in order to imply that the very individuals who land in women's court are especially likely to land in boys' court also! (p. 674)

Among other examples, Menzel points out that one may be interested in the ecological correlation between the number of physicians per capita and infant mortality rate. "This correlation may be expected to be high and negative, and loses none of its significance for the fact that a corresponding individual correlation would be patently impossible" (p. 674). (See also Converse, 1969, and Valkonen, 1969, for very good discussions of these issues.)

As is shown below, the total correlation (i.e., the correlation based on individuals) is a hybrid, so to speak, of the between and within correlations. Accordingly, contrary to Robinson's claim, this type of correlation is probably of least interest when the research involves more than one group.

It has been shown that fallacies other than ecological ones may be committed. Thus, for example, when inferences are made to the group level on the basis of correlations calculated on the individual level, individualistic fallacies may be committed (for a typology of fallacies, see Alker, 1969; see also Scheuch, 1966).

Two final points will be made in reference to Robinson's paper. First, he has failed to distinguish between problems of data aggregation, model specification, and bias in parameter estimation (see, for example, Firebaugh, 1978; Hanushek, Jackson, & Kain, 1974; Scheuch, 1966; and Smith, 1977). Second, Robinson's presentation is limited to correlations. Under certain circumstances, an ecological fallacy may be committed when correlations are used, but *not* when regression coefficients are used instead (see below).

We turn now to take a closer look at the three kinds of correlation coefficients, and the corresponding regression coefficients, that may be calculated when data are available for more than one group. The logic of the calculations is presented first. This is followed by a numerical example and a discussion of the relations among the three statistics.

Within, Between, and Total Statistics

When regression analysis was introduced for the very first time in Chapter 2, it was shown how the sum of squares of the dependent variable (Σy^2) may be partitioned into two components: regression and residual sums of squares. When the concept of regression of a continuous variable on a categorical variable was introduced in Chapter 9, it was shown that the regression sum of squares is equivalent to the between-treatments, or between-groups, sum of squares, and that the residual sum of squares is equivalent to the within-treatments, or within-groups, sum of squares.[11] That is,

$$\Sigma(Y_{ij} - \bar{Y})^2 = \sum_j \sum_i (Y_{ij} - \bar{Y}_j)^2 + \sum_j n_j (\bar{Y}_j - \bar{Y})^2 \qquad (13.10)$$

[11]See Chapter 9, particularly the discussion related to the analysis of the data of Table 9.4 and 9.7.

where Y_{ij} = score of individual i in group j; $\bar{Y}$ = grand mean of Y; $\bar{Y}_j$ = mean of group j; n_j = number of people in group j. The term on the left of the equal sign is the total sum of squares and will be designated as Σy_t^2 in the following presentation. The first term on the right of the equal sign is the pooled within-groups sums of squares, or the residual sum of squares when Y is regressed on coded vectors representing group membership. Note that for each group, the deviation scores from the group mean are squared and added. These are then pooled to comprise the within-groups sum of squares, Σy_w^2. The second term on the right of the equal sign is the between-groups sum of squares, or the regression sum of squares when Y is regressed on coded vectors representing group membership. Note that the deviation of each group mean from the grand mean is squared and weighted by the number of people in the group (n_j). These values for the j groups are added to yield the between-groups sum of squares, Σy_b^2.

When, in addition to scores on Y, there are scores on X for individuals in different groups, the total sum of squares of X, Σx_t^2, may be partitioned in the same manner as the partitioning of Σy_t^2. That is,

$$\Sigma(X_{ij} - \bar{X})^2 = \sum_j \sum_i (X_{ij} - \bar{X}_j)^2 + \sum_j n_j (\bar{X}_j - \bar{X})^2 \qquad (13.11)$$
$$\Sigma x_t^2 = \Sigma x_w^2 + \Sigma x_b^2$$

Similarly, the total sum of products, Σxy_t, is partitioned to within and between-groups sums of products:

$$\Sigma(X_{ij} - \bar{X})(Y_{ij} - \bar{Y}) = \sum_j \sum_i (X_{ij} - \bar{X}_j)(Y_{ij} - \bar{Y}_j) + \sum_j n_j (\bar{X}_j - \bar{X})(\bar{Y}_j - \bar{Y}) \qquad (13.12)$$
$$\Sigma xy_t = \Sigma xy_w + \Sigma xy_b$$

Using the different sums of squares and sums of products, three correlation coefficients may be calculated:

$$r_t = \frac{\Sigma xy_t}{\sqrt{\Sigma x_t^2 \Sigma y_t^2}} \qquad (13.13)$$

where r_t is the total correlation between X and Y. (Because it is clear that the correlations are between X and Y, subscripts identifying the variables will not be used.) Note that group membership is ignored when r_t is calculated. That is, all subjects are treated as if they belong to one group.

Using the between-groups values, a between-groups correlation of X and Y can be calculated:

$$r_b = \frac{\Sigma xy_b}{\sqrt{\Sigma x_b^2 \Sigma y_b^2}} \qquad (13.14)$$

This is in effect a correlation between the means of the groups, except that the values are weighted by the number of people in the group. With equal numbers of subjects in all groups, r_b can be obtained by simply correlating the means of X and Y for the different groups.

Finally, a within-groups correlation coefficient can be calculated:

$$r_w = \frac{\Sigma xy_w}{\sqrt{\Sigma x_w^2 \Sigma y_w^2}} \tag{13.15}$$

Note that this is a pooled within-groups correlation. It is, obviously, possible to calculate the correlation of X and Y within each group separately by using the sum of products and the sums of squares within the groups. r_w, however, is calculated on the basis of the pooled sums of products and sums of squares. To see the difference between the two types of the within correlations consider, for example, the case of two groups only. Assume that Σxy in one of the groups is equal to that of the other group but that it is positive in one group and negative in the other. Accordingly, the correlation will be positive in one of the groups and negative in the other. When these sums of products are pooled to calculate r_w, their sum will be equal to zero, and r_w will necessarily be equal to zero. From the foregoing it follows that r_w is meaningful only when the correlations within each of the groups do not differ significantly from each other.

Analogous to the three correlation coefficients, regression coefficients may be calculated. Recall, however, that whereas the correlation coefficient is symmetrical, the regression coefficient is not. That is, although $r_{xy} = r_{yx}$, b_{yx} indicates the regression of Y on X and b_{xy} indicates the regression of X on Y. In the following presentation it is assumed that Y is the dependent variable, and that therefore the interest is in b_{yx}. For convenience, the subscripts will be omitted. The three regression coefficients are calculated as follows:

$$b_t = \frac{\Sigma xy_t}{\Sigma x_t^2} \tag{13.16}$$

$$b_b = \frac{\Sigma xy_b}{\Sigma x_b^2} \tag{13.17}$$

$$b_w = \frac{\Sigma xy_w}{\Sigma x_w^2} \tag{13.18}$$

It will be noted that what has been labeled here the pooled within-groups regression coefficient (b_w) was labeled the common regression coefficient (b_c) in Chapter 12 and in earlier sections of the present chapter.

In order to clarify the calculations of the above statistics a simple numerical example for two groups will be used. Subsequently, the relations among the three statistics will be discussed.

A Numerical Example

In Table 13.6, scores for subjects in two groups, I and II, are given. In addition, the scores for the two groups were combined under T (Total). The values necessary for the calculation of the different statistics are given at the bottom of Table 13.6. The procedures for calculating these values should require no explanation since they were introduced in Chapter 2 and have been

Table 13.6 Illustrative Data for Two Groups

	I		*II*		*T*	
	X	*Y*	*X*	*Y*	*X*	*Y*
	5	1	8	6	5	1
	2	2	5	7	2	2
	4	3	7	8	4	3
	6	4	9	9	6	4
	3	5	6	10	3	5
					8	6
					5	7
					7	8
					9	9
					6	10
Σ:	20	15	35	40	55	55
M:	4	3	7	8	5.5	5.5
SS:	90	55	255	330	345	385
ss:	10	10	10	10	42.5	82.5
Σ*XY:*	60		280		340	
Σ*xy:*	0		0		37.5	

NOTE: M = mean; SS = raw scores sum of squares (for example, $\Sigma X_{\text{I}}^2 = 90$); ss = deviation sum of squares (for example, $\Sigma y_t^2 = 82.5$); ΣXY = raw scores sum of products; Σxy = deviations sum of products.

used repeatedly in subsequent chapters. In any event, here are a couple of examples:

$$\Sigma x_{\text{I}}^2 = \Sigma X_{\text{I}}^2 - \frac{(\Sigma X_{\text{I}})^2}{n} = 90 - \frac{(20)^2}{5} = 10$$

$$\Sigma xy_t = \Sigma XY_t - \frac{(\Sigma X_t)(\Sigma Y_t)}{N} = 340 - \frac{(55)(55)}{10} = 37.5$$

Using the appropriate values from the bottom of Table 13.6, and applying Formulas (13.13) through (13.18), the different correlation and regression coefficients may be calculated. Thus,

$$r_t = \frac{\Sigma xy_t}{\sqrt{\Sigma x_t^2 \Sigma y_t^2}} = \frac{37.5}{\sqrt{(42.5)(82.5)}} = .63330$$

$$b_t = \frac{\Sigma xy_t}{\Sigma x_t^2} = \frac{37.5}{42.5} = .88235$$

Instead of continuing in this manner with the calculation of the other statistics, it will be more convenient to present them in a tabular format, as given in Table 13.7. Note that values in the first three columns for the first four rows of Table 13.7 were obtained from the bottom of Table 13.6. The values for the last row (Between) may be calculated directly, as indicated in the rightmost terms of

Table 13.7 Total, Within, and Between Statistics Based on Data from Table 13.6

Source	Σy^2	Σx^2	Σxy	r	b
Total	82.5	42.5	37.5	.63330	.88235
I	10.0	10.0	0	.00000	.00000
II	10.0	10.0	0	.00000	.00000
Within	20.0	20.0	0	.00000	.00000
Between	62.5	22.5	37.5	1.00000	1.66667

Formulas (13.10) through (13.12), or by subtraction. That is, Between equals Total minus Within. Thus, for example:

$$\Sigma y_b^2 = \Sigma y_t^2 - \Sigma y_w^2 = 82.5 - 20.0 = 62.5$$

The values for the r's and the b's of Table 13.7 are obtained by using the values of the sums of squares and sum of products in their respective rows. Thus, for example,

$$r_b = \frac{37.5}{\sqrt{(62.5)(22.5)}} = 1.0000$$

Before describing the relations among the statistics reported in Table 13.7, each of these statistics will be discussed separately. Turning first to the statistics within groups, it will be noted that the correlation and the regression coefficient within each of the groups is zero. That is, within each group there is no relation between X and Y. Further, because $\Sigma xy = 0$ in both groups, $\Sigma xy_w = 0$, and r_w and b_w are necessarily zero.

While r_w and b_w are equal to zero, $r_t = .63330$ and $b_t = .88235$. Here, then, is an example of a difference between within and total statistics. It is instructive to note briefly how this has come about. Look back at the data of Table 13.6 and note that subjects in group II tend to have higher scores on X and Y than do subjects in group I. When the scores for the two groups are combined, relatively high scores on X are paired with relatively high scores on Y, and relatively low scores on X are paired with relatively low scores on Y, resulting in a positive correlation and a positive regression coefficient. This demonstration should serve as a warning against indiscriminate calculation of total statistics when data are available for more than one group.

When total statistics are calculated for the present example, a specification error is committed. A variable, group membership, which is related to, or affects, X and Y is omitted in the calculation of the total statistics. Think, for example, of group I as being composed of females, and group II as being composed of males. It is evident that the correlation between X and Y is zero among males and females. But because males tend to have higher scores than females on both X and Y, the variables are correlated when the scores for the groups are combined. In other words, when the total statistics are calculated, a specification error is committed by the omission of the sex variable. It is worthwhile to note that regressing Y on X and a vector representing group membership (e.g., effect coding) will indicate that b_c (i.e., the common, or the within, coefficient for X) is equal to zero, the intercept is 5.5, and the regression coefficient associated with the vector representing group membership is −2.5. Look back at the data of Table 13.5 and note that $\bar{Y}_{\text{I}} = 3.0$, $\bar{Y}_{\text{II}} = 8.0$, $\bar{Y} = 5.5$. Consequently, the effect of group I is −2.5 (3.0 − 5.5) and that of group II is 2.5 (8.0 − 5.5), which is what the regression coefficient associated with the coded vector for group membership indicates. Note that in the preceding an ANCOVA, in which X is used as the covariate, was described. But because $b_c = 0$, the adjusted means for the two groups are, of course, equal to their original means. From the foregoing it also follows that the partial correlation between X and Y (partialing out group membership) is equal to zero. When group membership affects both X and Y, r_t is a spurious correlation.

Turning now to the between-group statistics it is noted that $r_b = 1.00$. This is not surprising, because when the correlation between the means is considered in the present example there are only two pairs of scores—$\bar{X}$ and $\bar{Y}$ for group I, and $\bar{X}$ and $\bar{Y}$ for group II—and therefore the correlation must be perfect except when the means of the groups on one, or both, of the variables do not differ from each other. When the group means are equal on one of the variables, r_b is indeterminate because one of the vectors is a constant. A correlation coefficient is an index of a relation between two variables, not between a variable and a constant. Try to apply the formula for the correlation coefficient to a case in which one of the vectors is a variable and the other is a constant and you will find that you have to divide by zero—an unacceptable operation in mathematics.

Even though the present example is artificial and small (involving two groups only) it illustrates the ecological fallacy that Robinson and others have warned against. Using the correlation between group means to make inferences to the individual level, one would erroneously conclude that X and Y are perfectly correlated when the correlation between them, using the individual as the unit of analysis (i.e., r_t) is .63330. But, as was noted above and as is discussed in greater detail below, r_t is generally not useful when more than one group is used. In the present example, the correlation between X and Y within each of the groups is zero.

The foregoing comments about the between-groups statistics were limited to the correlation coefficient. Concerning the regression coefficient (b_b), it is necessary to recall that it is a function of the correlation between X and Y as well as the ratio of the standard deviation of Y to that of X (i.e., $b = r_{xy}s_y/s_x$). Therefore, while for the case of two groups $r_b = |1.00|$,[12] b_b may take any value, depending on s_y/s_x. Similarly, for situations when more than two groups are involved. In such situations r_b is, obviously, not necessarily 1.00. But the

[12]The absolute value of r is one. The sign of r will be positive or negative, depending on the pattern of the means in the two groups. Suppose that in the numerical example under consideration $\bar{X}$ for group II was smaller than $\bar{X}$ for group I, but that the reverse was true for the Y means, then r_b would be −1.00.

difference between r_b and b_b will depend on the ratio of the two standard deviations.

Relations among the Different Statistics

In order to show the relations among the different statistics (i.e., total, between, and within) it is necessary first to recall the meaning of η^2. In Chapter 9, it was shown that η^2 is the ratio of the between-groups sum of squares to the total sum of squares. It was also shown that η^2 is equal to R^2 that is obtained when the dependent variable is regressed on coded vectors that represent group membership. In other words, η^2, or R^2, is the proportion of variance of the dependent variable that is accounted for by group membership. In the context of the present discussion, two η^2's, or two R^2's, may be calculated: η_y^2 is the ratio of Σy_b^2 to Σy_t^2, and η_x^2 is the ratio of Σx_b^2 to Σx_t^2. In other words, it is possible to determine the proportion of variance of Y as well as that of X that is accounted for by group membership. With this in mind, the three correlation coefficients may be expressed as follows:

$$r_t = r_w\sqrt{1-\eta_x^2}\,\sqrt{1-\eta_y^2} + r_b\eta_x\eta_y \tag{13.19}$$

$$r_w = \frac{r_t - r_b\eta_x\eta_y}{\sqrt{1-\eta_x^2}\,\sqrt{1-\eta_y^2}} \tag{13.20}$$

$$r_b = \frac{r_t - r_w\sqrt{1-\eta_x^2}\,\sqrt{1-\eta_y^2}}{\eta_x\eta_y} \tag{13.21}$$

Before discussing these formulas, they will be applied to the numerical example of Table 13.6 in the hope of thereby clarifying their meaning. The terms necessary for the application of (13.19) through (13.21) are given in Table 13.7, except for the two η^2's. Regressing Y of Table 13.6 for the combined scores (i.e., under T) on a coded vector representing group membership it will be found that $R^2 = .75758$. Equivalently, using the between and total sums of squares for Y from Table 13.7 η_y^2 can be calculated

$$\eta_y^2 = \frac{\Sigma y_b^2}{\Sigma y_t^2} = \frac{62.5}{82.5} = .75758$$

and similarly,

$$\eta_x^2 = \frac{\Sigma x_b^2}{\Sigma x_t^2} = \frac{22.5}{42.5} = .52941$$

Using these η^2's and appropriate values from Table 13.7, calculate the three correlation coefficients by applying Formulas (13.19) through (13.21):

$$r_t = .00000\sqrt{1 - .52941}\ \sqrt{1 - .75758} + (1.00000)(.72761)(.87039) = .63330$$

$$r_w = \frac{.63330 - (1.00000)(.72761)(.87039)}{\sqrt{1 - .52941}\ \sqrt{1 - .75758}} = .00000$$

$$r_b = \frac{.63330 - .00000\sqrt{1 - .52941}\ \sqrt{1 - .75758}}{(.72761)(.87039)} = 1.00000$$

It will be noted that the interrelations among the three correlation coefficients are a function of the coefficients themselves as well as the two η's. Consider, for example, the case of $\eta_x^2 = \eta_y^2 = .00$. This, of course, means that there are no differences among the means of X, nor are there differences among the means of Y. In other words, $\Sigma x_b^2 = \Sigma y_b^2 = .00$. All the variability is within groups. Consequently, $r_t = r_w$, and r_b is indeterminate.

Suppose now that $\eta_x^2 = \eta_y^2 = 1.00$. In this case, all the variability is between groups. Therefore, r_w is indeterminate and $r_t = r_b$.

The two extreme situations depicted above are rarely, if ever, encountered in actual research. What usually takes place is something between these extremes, depending on the composition of the groups being studied. When, for example, the groups are relatively homogeneous, r_w will tend to be relatively small and r_b will tend to be relatively large. The total correlation, r_t, will take a value somewhere in between r_w and r_b as a compromise, so to speak, between them. Because of these properties of r_t it is generally a less useful index than r_w and r_b. A case can be made for using the pooled within-groups correlation, r_w, as an index of the relation between two variables within groups, assuming that it has been established that the correlations within the groups do not differ significantly from each other. Similarly, it is conceivable that one might wish to study the relation between two variables on an aggregate level (e.g., using group measures) and will therefore calculate r_b. Note that in the situations described here each of the correlations will be calculated for its own sake, not because it is desired to use one of them in order to make inferences about the other (i.e., cross-level inferences). A similar case cannot generally be made for r_t because it is a weighted combination of r_b and r_w and can therefore not be interpreted unambiguously, except when it is equal to r_b or r_w, or when $r_t = r_b = r_w$. Note that when r_t or b_t is calculated, Y is regressed only on X—that is, coded vectors identifying groups are not included in the analysis. It was demonstrated earlier in this chapter that such an analysis is valid only after it has been established that: (1) the b's are not significantly different from each other (the b's are homogeneous), and (2) there are no significant differences among the intercepts of the separate groups. In short, when r_t or b_t is calculated it is assumed that a single regression equation fits the data of all the groups.

In view of the foregoing, it is interesting to note that in many of the studies designed to draw attention to, and illustrate, the ecological fallacy the comparisons were made between r_b and r_t. Perhaps this was motivated by the belief that the individual is the natural unit of the analysis (see, for example, Robinson, 1950). But this is based on the questionable assumption that individuals are not affected by the groups to which they belong (see Group and Contextual Effects, below), or that groups are composed by a random process.

As in the case of the correlation coefficients, the three types of regression coefficients are also interrelated:

$$b_t = b_w + \eta_x^2(b_b - b_w) \tag{13.22}$$

Note that b_t is a function of b_w, b_b, and η_x^2. When, for example, $b_b = b_w$, then $b_t = b_b = b_w$. When $b_w = .00$, b_t is a function of b_b and η_x^2. This may be illustrated with the data of Table 13.7, where $b_b = 1.66667$, $b_w = .00000$, $b_t = .88235$, and $\eta_x^2 = .52941$. Applying Formula (13.22),

$$b_t = .00000 + .52941(1.66667 - .00000) = .88235$$

As in the case of the correlation coefficients, b_w and b_b may be meaningfully used and interpreted for different purposes. The same does not generally hold true for b_t. "Insofar as relevant experiences are associated with groups there are two matters to consider: between-groups relations and within-groups relations. *The overall analysis combines these, to everyone's confusion*" (Cronbach, 1976, p. 1.10; italics added).

There is an extensive literature devoted to the exposition of the relations among the indices introduced in this section, and the conditions under which cross-level inferences are biased and those under which such inferences are not biased (see, for example, Alker, 1969; Blalock, 1964; Duncan, Cuzzort, & Duncan, 1961; Firebaugh, 1978; Hammond, 1973; Hannan, 1971; Hannan & Burstein, 1974; Irwin & Lichtman, 1976; Langbein & Lichtman, 1978; Przeworski, 1974; Smith, 1977). It is not possible, nor is it necessary, to review here these and other treatments of the topic. Instead, it will be pointed out that although they may differ in the perspective from which they view the topic, they all focus on the process by which the groups under study have been formed. A couple of examples will, it is hoped, clarify this point. When, for example, the groups are formed by a random process, the within, between, and total statistics are expected, within random fluctuations, to be equal to each other. Consequently, cross-level inferences are expected to be not biased. When the groups are formed on the basis of individuals' scores on the independent variable (i.e., individuals who have similar scores on the independent variable are placed in the same group) r_b will be larger than r_t, but b_b will, within random fluctuations, be equal to b_t. Therefore, under such circumstances, using a between-groups correlation to make inferences about individuals will be biased. But using the between-groups *unstandardized* regression coefficient to make inferences about the *unstandardized* regression coefficient on the individual level will not be biased. Finally, when the groups are formed on the basis of individuals' scores on the dependent variable, or on the basis of a variable that is correlated both with the independent and the dependent variable, the correlations will differ from each other, as will the regression coefficients.[13]

[13]For a very good discussion of these points, and interesting numerical examples, see Blalock (1964, Chapter 11); see also Langbein and Lichtman (1978).

The main problem is that when intact groups are studied it is very difficult, often impossible, to unravel the processes by which the groups were formed. When, under such circumstances, data are available on the group level only it is generally not possible to tell the direction and the magnitude of the bias that results from inferences made about individuals.

There is a fairly extensive literature in which analyses using the individual as the unit of analysis are contrasted with ones in which aggregates are used as the unit of analysis. This literature deserves careful study not only because it illustrates the striking differences in the results one may obtain from the two analyses, but also because much of it contains discussions of methodological issues concerning the unit of analysis. For some examples, see Alexander and Griffin (1976), Bidwell and Kasarda (1975, 1976), Burstein (1976), Hannan, Freeman, and Meyer (1976), Langbein (1977), and Smith (1972).

An important point to note when studying this literature is the distinction between R^2 obtained in an analysis in which individuals are used as the unit of analysis and R^2 obtained when aggregates are used as the unit of analysis. When individuals are used as the unit of analysis, R^2 indicates the proportion of the *total* variance accounted for by the independent variables. When, on the other hand, aggregates (e.g., classes, schools) are used as the unit of analysis, R^2 indicates the proportion of variance of the *between* aggregates that is accounted for by the independent variables. Consequently, when the variance between groups is relatively small, one should be careful not to be overly impressed even when a high R^2 is obtained. For example, suppose that the variance between groups is .10. Then, an $R^2 = .8$ obtained in analysis with group data refers to an explanation of 80% of the variance between groups (i.e., of the 10%), not of the total variance. It is possible, then, to obtain high R^2's in analyses with aggregate data and yet explain only a minute proportion of the total variance. Typical are many of the studies of educational effects. Because most of the variance is within schools (in the Coleman Report, for example, it was found that about 80% of the variance was within schools), an analysis that uses the school as the unit addresses itself to a small portion of the total variance, and the R^2 obtained in such an analysis indicates the fraction of this small portion that is being explained. The potential dangers of wandering into a world of fantasy when doing analyses with aggregated data are very real indeed.

It is hoped that the preceding discussion has served its main purpose of alerting you to the potential hazards of cross-level inferences. Recall that the need to make such inferences usually arises when data on the unit of analysis that is of interest are not available, or because the researcher is constrained (by administrative, economic, or other considerations) from using them. In many research settings, however, the researcher has access to data on more than one level (e.g., individuals as well as groups to which they belong), and therefore the issue of cross-level inferences does not, or should not, arise. Engaging in cross-level inferences when the data on the unit of interest are available is "obviously either poor research strategy or a regrettable adjustment to one's limited resources" (Scheuch, 1969, p. 136). Issues that come to the fore when data are available on more than one level concern the methods of analysis and the interpretation of the results. This, then, is the second perspective that was referred to when the topic of the unit of analysis was introduced, and to which we now turn.

GROUP AND CONTEXTUAL EFFECTS

Social scientists, notably sociologists and political scientists, have long been interested in the effects of group contexts and group properties on the behavior of individuals. Based on the premise that individuals do not operate in a social vacuum, and that their behaviors vary, to a greater or lesser degree, as a function of their social environments, researchers have attempted to identify what have come to be known as group, contextual, structural, or compositional effects. There is no consensus about the definitions of these terms. Some researchers treat them as indicating distinct types of social effects, whereas others use them interchangeably. Since the treatment of the topic here is limited to some analytic aspects, no attempt will be made to define the aforementioned concepts.[14] The distinction between group and contextual effects, which is the focus of the present discussion, is discussed below. For now, however, it will be useful to offer a couple of research examples of contextual effects. Because these are given for illustrative purposes only, the question of their validity is not addressed.

The first example is taken from the Coleman Report, which devoted a good deal of attention to the effects of student body composition and properties on the achievement of individual students. Among other conclusions, the authors of the report state:

> Finally, it appears that a pupil's achievement is strongly related to the educational backgrounds and aspirations of other students in the school. . . . Analysis indicates . . . that children from a given family background, when put in schools of different social composition, will achieve at quite different levels. . . . If a minority pupil from a home without much educational strength is put with schoolmates with strong educational backgrounds, his achievement is likely to increase. (Coleman et al., 1966, p. 22)[15]

The second example is taken from an analysis of voting behavior during the 1968 presidential election. Among other findings, Schoenberger and Segal (1971) report a positive correlation of .55 between percent black and a vote for Wallace for southern congressional districts. The authors say:

> It would be a fallacy—ecological, logical, sociological and political—to infer from these data that blacks in the South provided a major source of Wallace support. Rather we suggest that our data demonstrate a contextual effect, viz., the greater the concentration of blacks in a congressional district, the greater the propensity of whites in the district to vote for Wallace. (p. 585)

[14]For some attempts at defining these concepts, see Burstein (1980a), and Karweit, Fennessey, and Daiger (1978).

[15]The pervasive impact of such statements is evident, among other things, from their use by Congress and the Courts in legislation and rulings regarding school desegregation. For extensive documentation and discussion of these issues, see Grant (1973) and Young and Bress (1975).

There is a sizable literature devoted to the presentation of substantive findings regarding contextual, compositional, or structural effects (see, for example, Alexander & Campbell, 1964; Alexander & Eckland, 1975; Alwin & Otto, 1977; Blau, 1960; Bowers, 1968; Davis, 1966; McDill, Rigsby, & Meyers, 1969; Meyer, 1970; Nelson, 1972; Sewell & Armer, 1966). While this literature contains some discussions of methodological approaches to the detection of such effects, more pertinent for the concerns of the present chapter are papers that are primarily devoted to analytic issues. Among these are Alwin (1976), Burstein (1978), Farkas (1974), Firebaugh (1979), Hauser (1970, 1971, 1974), Prysby (1976), Przeworski (1974), Sprague (1976), Tannenbaum and Bachman (1964), Valkonen (1969), and Werts and Linn (1971).

The remainder of this section is devoted to analytic issues concerning the study of group and contextual effects. Beginning with group effects, it will be noted that the method of analysis is identical to that of ANCOVA presented earlier in this chapter. Conceptually, the covariate (or covariates) is viewed as an attribute of individuals who belong to two or more groups. Assuming that the within-groups regression coefficients are homogeneous (see discussion earlier in this chapter under ANCOVA) one may test differences among groups after adjusting for, or partialing out, the effect of the attribute. It was shown earlier that this may be accomplished by using any one of three equivalent approaches. That is, testing differences among (1) adjusted means, (2) intercepts, or (3) regression coefficients associated with coded vectors that represent group membership.

It is clear, then, that so far as the analysis is concerned, the detection of group effects poses no problems. This, however, does not mean that the interpretation of the results is free of problems and ambiguity. The problems are the same as those discussed earlier in connection with the use of ANCOVA in nonexperimental research, and those discussed in connection with comparisons among regression equations (see Chapter 12), and will therefore not be repeated here. These problems notwithstanding, when a group effect is detected it is not possible to tell what it is about the group (i.e., what are the specific variables) that is responsible for the effect. It is for this reason that advocates of contextual effects call for the use of specific group variables in the analysis instead of an identification of overall group effects as is done, for example, when coded vectors are used to represent group membership.

It is useful to distinguish among different types of variables or properties that are used to describe groups. Lazarsfeld and Menzel (1961), for example, distinguish three types: analytic properties based on aggregation of data collected on members of the groups (e.g., mean intelligence, motivation, anxiety); structural properties based on data of relations among group members (e.g., patterns of sociometric choices, group cliquishness); global properties, that is, properties that are not based on information on individual members (e.g., forms of government of nations, educational policies of school districts). (See also Kendall & Lazarsfeld, 1955; Rosenberg, 1968.)

Most definitions, and most of the empirical studies, associate the effects of group analytic variables with contextual effects. That is, a contextual effect is defined as the net effect of a group analytic variable after having controlled for the effect of the same variable on the individual level. For example, when it is desired to study the contextual effect of Socioeconomic Status (SES) of region of residence on voting behavior, each individual has two scores: one's own SES score, and the mean SES of the region in which one resides. Voting behavior is regressed on both the individuals' SES scores and the SES means for the regions. The partial regression coefficient for the vector of means on SES is taken as the contextual effect of the regions' SES. Similarly, in a study of achievement one may use individuals' mental ability scores as well as the mean mental ability of their class (school, school district). Again, the partial regression coefficient associated with the vector of means on mental ability is taken as the contextual effect of the groups' mental abilities on achievement. We turn now to a numerical example to illustrate the manner in which the analysis is carried out, as well as to examine some of its properties.

A Numerical Example

For comparative purposes, a numerical example analyzed earlier through ANCOVA will now be analyzed by the approach outlined above. Specifically, data from Table 13.1 will be used. Although the analytic approach outlined above is applicable to any number of variables, the scores on Y and X only will be used for illustrative purposes. In Table 13.8 the scores on Y and X for the four groups of Table 13.1 are repeated. In addition, the vector labeled $\bar{X}$ contains the means of the four groups on X.

It will be helpful to cast the illustrative data of Table 13.8 in some substantive contexts. For example, Y may be achievement, X may be some measure of aspiration, and $\bar{X}$ is the mean aspiration of the group (e.g., class, region) to which a given individual belongs; or Y may be productivity, X some measure of anxiety, and $\bar{X}$ the mean anxiety of the group to which a given individual belongs. Other examples come readily to mind, but these will suffice to provide some substantive meaning to the analysis that follows.

As indicated above, the dependent variable, Y, is regressed on X and $\bar{X}$. In what follows, the results of such an analysis for the data of Table 13.8 are reported and discussed first in reference to R^2 and then to the regression equation. Some general observations about group and contextual effects conclude the presentation.

Squared Multiple Correlation (R^2)

Using the REGRESSION program of SPSS the Y scores of Table 13.8 were regressed on X and $\bar{X}$. $R^2_{y.x\bar{x}} = .90182$. It will be noted that when the same data were analyzed earlier through ANCOVA (i.e., using X as the covariate and three coded vectors to represent group membership), R^2 was .95944. The source of the discrepancy between these two R^2's is now examined. Look back at Table 13.8 and note that the score under $\bar{X}$ for each group is necessarily the same because it is the mean of the given group that is assigned to all its members. Suppose now that instead of placing the four X means in a single vector, as was done in Table 13.8, the means were used in separate vectors. Specifically, assume that instead of the single $\bar{X}$ vector, three vectors were gener-

Table 13.8 Illustrative Data for Contextual Analysis

Group	*Y*	*X*	$\bar{X}$
	6	1	3.4
	9	1	3.4
	8	2	3.4
	8	3	3.4
I	12	3	3.4
	12	4	3.4
	10	4	3.4
	8	5	3.4
	12	5	3.4
	13	6	3.4
	13	4	7.0
	16	4	7.0
	15	5	7.0
	16	6	7.0
II	19	6	7.0
	17	8	7.0
	19	8	7.0
	23	9	7.0
	19	10	7.0
	22	10	7.0
	20	7	10.2
	22	7	10.2
	24	9	10.2
	26	9	10.2
III	24	10	10.2
	25	11	10.2
	28	11	10.2
	27	12	10.2
	29	13	10.2
	26	13	10.2
	27	7	9.9
	28	8	9.9
	25	8	9.9
	27	9	9.9
IV	31	9	9.9
	29	10	9.9
	32	10	9.9
	30	12	9.9
	32	12	9.9
	33	14	9.9

NOTE: Data for *Y* and *X* are taken from Table 13.1.

ated as follows: vector 1, consisting of $\bar{X}$ for group I and 0's for all other groups; vector 2, consisting of $\bar{X}$ for group II and 0's for all other groups; and vector 3, consisting of $\bar{X}$ for group III and 0's for all other groups. As a result of doing this, group IV will be assigned 0's in all the vectors. What was described above is in essence a method of coding group membership, but instead of using codes like 1's and 0's, for example, the codes are the means of the groups. In Chapter 9 it was said that R^2 is the same regardless of the specific codes that are used to represent group membership. Consequently, if one were to regress Y of Table 13.8 on X and on three coded vectors in which the means of X are used as the codes, R^2 would be .95944 (i.e., the same as obtained when ANCOVA was used).

It is now possible to state the condition under which R^2 obtained when the means are placed in a single vector (i.e., in contextual analysis) will be equal to R^2 obtained when the means are placed in separate vectors (i.e., when the data are analyzed as in ANCOVA). The two R^2's will be equal only when the means of the groups on X lie exactly on the regression plane. This is the same as saying that the squared correlation of the means of Y with the means of X is equal to 1.00. Whenever this is not the case, R^2 obtained in contextual analysis will be smaller than that obtained in ANCOVA for the same data.

In the numerical example under consideration $r^2_{\bar{y}\bar{x}} = .93548$, resulting in a small discrepancy between the two R^2's. Consider, however, the data for Y and Z of Table 13.1. That is, assume that instead of using X, as was done above, Z is used as the independent variable. When Y is regressed on Z and a vector consisting of the means of Z (as in contextual analysis), $R^2_{y.z\bar{z}} = .65395$. But when the same data are analyzed as in ANCOVA, R^2 is .92253. This time the discrepancy between the two R^2's is rather large. It will be noted that $r^2_{\bar{y}\bar{z}} =$ .69920. In sum, R^2 obtained in a contextual analysis will be equal to or smaller than the R^2 obtained when the same data are subjected to ANCOVA.

The Regression Equation

The regression equation for the data of Table 13.8 is:

$$Y' = .52161 + 1.01305X + 1.61362\bar{X}$$

The first thing that will be noted is that the b associated with X (i.e., the measures of individuals) is the pooled within-groups regression coefficient (b_w or b_c). It is suggested that you review the ANCOVA for the same data earlier in this chapter and note that b_c obtained there is 1.01305. Recall that it is this b that is used to calculate the adjusted means, and that when these are not significantly different from each other it is concluded that there are no group effects.

An important difference between ANCOVA and contextual analysis can now be noted. When ANCOVA is used, it is possible to test whether the b's for the separate groups are homogeneous in order to conclude whether or not the use of a common b is tenable. Recall that it is necessary to perform this test before calculating the adjusted means for the purpose of determining whether there are any group effects. In contextual analysis, on the other hand, it is not possible to test whether the separate regression coefficients are homogeneous. A common regression coefficient is all that one obtains and ends up using even when the separate regression coefficients are heterogeneous.

The foregoing shortcoming of contextual analysis aside, the focus in such an analysis is on the b associated with the vector of the means. When this b is statistically significant it is concluded that the group variable has an effect after the individual variable has been partialed out. That is, it is concluded that a contextual effect has been detected. It can be shown that the b associated with the vector of the means is equal to the difference between the between-groups regression coefficient (b_b) and the within-groups regression coefficients (b_w). (See Alwin, 1976; Firebaugh, 1978, 1979.) Using Formula (13.17) to calculate b_b for the data of Table 13.8 it is found that $b_b = 2.62667$. Therefore, for these data,

$$b_b - b_w = 2.62667 - 1.01305 = \mathit{1.61362}$$

From the foregoing it is evident that when $b_b = b_w$, the regression coefficient for $\bar{X}$ is zero and no contextual effect is indicated. Also, the test of the b associated with $\bar{X}$ is in essence a test of the difference between b_b and b_w. It is also possible to perform such a test within the context of ANCOVA (see, for example, Myers, 1979, pp. 410–412; Schuessler, 1971, pp. 210–213). But, as is pointed out by these and other authors, such a test is valid only when the within-groups regression coefficients are homogeneous, and the regression of the means of Y on the means of X is linear. Here, then, is another weakness of contextual analysis; not only is it carried out as if the within-groups regression coefficients are homogeneous (see above), but it also assumes that the regression of the means of Y on the means of X is linear.[16] Because violations of either or both of these assumptions go undetected in contextual analysis, one cannot but deduce that such an analysis may lead to erroneous conclusions.

MULTILEVEL ANALYSIS

When the topic of the unit of analysis was introduced earlier in this chapter it was noted that there is no consensus among social scientists about what the appropriate unit is. In recent years, some authors (notable among them are Burstein, 1980a, 1980b; Burstein, Linn, & Capell, 1978; Cronbach, 1976; Cronbach & Snow, 1977; Cronbach & Webb, 1975; Keesling, 1978; Keesling & Wiley, 1974; Snow, 1977) have been calling for a change in perspective regarding the unit of analysis. These authors reason that the issue is not one of choice of the appropriate unit of analysis but rather the conceptualization and development of analytic approaches that will make full use of the different types of information contained in the different levels or units one has frequently to deal with in social science research.

[16]For the method of testing this assumption, see Schuessler (1971, pp. 212–213). For a detailed discussion of the meaning of the test of the difference between b_b and b_w, see Smith (1957).

The proposed methodologies are understandably not fully developed as yet. Nevertheless, they do serve to demonstrate the potential benefits of doing multilevel analysis and point to the need for their further refinement as well as for the development of new approaches commensurate with the complex designs that are becoming increasingly prevalent in social science research.

It is not the intention here to discuss these methods but rather to describe briefly some of their concerns and proposed solutions. This can perhaps best be accomplished by way of an example of an ATI design. Assume that classes are randomly assigned to one of two instructional methods and that it is desired to study whether there is an interaction between the methods and some aptitude of the students. This, then, is the simplest example of a study in which the researcher is faced with the dilemma of whether to use the student or the class as the unit of analysis. Traditionally, most researchers have focused on the student, although some have chosen to focus on the class instead.

The above cited authors argue, however, that the choice of one level to the exclusion of the other may result in either masking certain effects or in indicating effects when none exist. This is because certain processes operate on the group level and others operate on the individual within a specific group. Thus, for example, Cronbach and Webb (1975) reason that a high mean aptitude of a class may lead a teacher to crowd more material into the course, thereby leading to either greater or lesser achievement for the class as a whole. Treatments may also have "comparative effects within a group" (Cronbach & Webb, 1975, p. 717). If, for example, "one method provides special opportunities or rewards for whoever is ablest within a class, the experience of a student with an IQ of 110 depends on whether the mean of his class is 100 or 120" (Cronbach & Webb, 1975, p. 717). Accordingly, Cronbach (1976) proposes, among other things, that between-classes regression coefficients be studied for the purpose of detecting processes that operate on classes as units, and that within-classes regression coefficients be studied for the purpose of detecting processes that operate on individuals as units within classes.

Cronbach and Webb (1975) illustrate the benefits of such an approach by applying it to a reanalysis of data from an ATI study by Anderson (1941). Briefly, Anderson used 18 fourth-grade classes in a study of the effects of drill versus meaningful instruction on achievement in arithmetic. Using the individual as the unit of analysis, Anderson reported to have found an interaction between the methods of instruction and student ability. Cronbach and Webb (1975) reanalyzed Anderson's data separately within and between classes. Without going into the details of their analyses, which merit careful study, it will be noted that they have concluded that Anderson's data *do not* support the hypothesis of an interaction between the teaching methods and student ability.

The important role of multilevel analyses when individuals are nested within groups, and groups are nested within larger units (e.g., instructional methods) cannot be overemphasized. Witness, for example, Cronbach and Snow's (1977, p. ix) apology for having misled investigators in using a perspective that they have since found to be wanting. More important, they say that, as a result of their rethinking and reconceptualization, "We have now had to dismiss some published findings we once trusted, and have occasionally unearthed positive evidence buried beneath an author's original negative conclusion'' (Cronbach & Snow, 1977, p. ix).

Although the preceding dealt with examples of studies of the differential effects of instructional methods, it should be evident that multilevel analysis can be useful whenever groups are nested within larger units. It was said earlier that the methods of analyzing multilevel data are only at the initial stages of development. Also, it was noted that the foregoing discussion was not meant to serve as a presentation of these methods. It is hoped that the brief discussion did serve to stimulate you to study methods of multilevel analysis in the depth they deserve. The papers cited above should be very helpful in your efforts toward accomplishing this goal.

SUMMARY

This chapter began with a discussion of the logic and use of the analysis of covariance (ANCOVA). It was pointed out that in experimental research ANCOVA is used for controlling extraneous variance, thereby increasing the sensitivity of the analysis. In quasi-experimental and nonexperimental research, on the other hand, researchers use ANCOVA for the purpose of ''equating'' nonequivalent groups. Problems in the use of ANCOVA for such purposes were discussed.

Applications of ANCOVA in designs with one and two covariates were illustrated, and it was noted that the same analytic approach may be extended to designs with any number of covariates and to factorial ANCOVA. Moreover, it was noted that the same analytic approach applies to any design with continuous and categorical variables (e.g., ATI designs).

The equivalence of testing differences among adjusted means, intercepts, and regression coefficients (b's) for coded vectors was demonstrated. It was shown that tests among b's are the most direct and computationally the simplest of the three.

The second part of the chapter dealt with issues regarding the unit of analysis. Calculations of within-groups, between-groups, and total statistics were discussed and illustrated, and relations among these statistics were shown. In the context of this presentation, issues of cross-level inferences (e.g., from groups to individuals) were addressed. This was followed by a discussion of the study of group and contextual effects. It was shown that the study of group effects is the same as ANCOVA. The properties of R^2 and the regression equation obtained in contextual analysis were discussed and contrasted with those obtained in the study of group effects. The chapter concluded with general remarks about recent developments in multilevel analysis.

STUDY SUGGESTIONS

1. Distinguish between the uses of ANCOVA in experimental and nonexperimental research.
2. Why is it important to determine whether the b's are homogeneous before applying ANCOVA?

3. Discuss the similarities and the differences between ATI and ANCOVA designs.
4. An educational researcher studied the effects of three different methods of teaching on achievement in algebra. He randomly assigned 25 students to each method. At the end of the semester he obtained achievement scores on a standardized algebra test. In order to increase the sensitivity of his analysis, the researcher decided to use the students' IQ as a covariate. The data (illustrative) for the three groups are as follows:

Method A		*Method B*		*Method C*	
IQ	*Algebra*	*IQ*	*Algebra*	*IQ*	*Algebra*
90	42	90	48	90	58
92	40	91	48	92	58
93	42	93	50	93	58
94	42	94	50	94	60
95	42	95	50	95	60
96	44	96	52	96	62
97	44	97	52	97	62
98	46	98	52	99	62
99	44	99	52	100	63
100	46	100	54	102	64
102	46	101	54	103	66
103	46	102	52	104	64
104	48	103	54	105	66
106	48	104	56	107	64
107	48	105	54	108	65
108	50	106	55	110	66
109	50	108	56	111	64
111	50	109	56	112	66
113	50	111	56	113	68
114	52	112	58	115	68
116	53	114	60	116	70
118	54	115	60	118	70
119	54	116	60	118	68
120	56	118	60	120	72
121	56	120	62	121	74

Analyze the data, using effect coding for the methods, and assigning the −1's to Method C:

(a) What are the separate regression equations for the three methods?
(b) What is the common *b*?
(c) What is the *F* ratio for the test of homogeneity of regression coefficients?
(d) What is the *F* ratio for the test of the common *b?*
(e) What is the proportion of variance accounted for by the teaching methods, over and above the covariate?
(f) What is the *F* ratio for the differences among the teaching methods without covarying IQ?
(g) What is the *F* ratio for the differences among the teaching methods after covarying IQ?
(h) What is the regression equation in which the product vectors are *not* included?
(i) What are the adjusted means for the three methods?
(j) What is a test of the differences

among the b's associated with the coded vectors in the equation obtained under (h), above, equivalent to?

(k) What is the variance/covariance matrix of the b's for the coded vectors in the equation obtained under (h), above?

(l) What is the augmented variance/-covariance matrix of the b's ($\mathbf{C}^*$)?

(m) Using relevant elements of $\mathbf{C}^*$ test the differences between: (1) the b for Method A with that of Method B; (2) the b for Method B and that of Method C; (3) the b's for Methods A and C against the b for Method B.

5. Here are illustrative data on X and Y for three groups:

I		*II*		*III*	
X	*Y*	*X*	*Y*	*X*	*Y*
1	5	4	9	6	10
2	5	5	8	7	10
3	6	6	8	8	13
4	6	7	10	9	11
5	9	8	11	10	12
6	8	9	11	11	13

(a) Calculate: Σx^2, Σy^2, Σxy for (1) total (i.e., treating all groups as a single group); (2) within each group; (3) pooled within groups; (4) between groups.

(b) Use information obtained in (a) to calculate r_{yx} and b_{yx} for: (1) total; (2) within each group; (3) pooled within groups; (4) between groups. Display the results in a table, such as Table 13.6.

(c) Using information obtained in (a), calculate $\eta_{\bar{x}}^2$ and $\eta_{\bar{y}}^2$.

(d) Using information from (b) and (c), apply Equations (3.19)–(3.22).

6. Using the data given 5, above, do a contextual analysis in which Y is the dependent variable.
   (a) What is $R^2_{y.x\bar{x}}$?
   (b) What is the regression equation?
   (c) What does $b_{yx.\bar{x}}$ represent?
   (d) What does $b_{y\bar{x}.x}$ represent?
   (e) What is the F ratio for $b_{y\bar{x}.x}$?
   (f) What conclusion would a researcher doing contextual analysis reach on the basis of the result obtained in (e)?

ANSWERS

4. In the following, Y = Algebra; X = IQ; A, B and C refer to the three methods:
   (a) $Y'_A = -2.78091 + .48096X$
   $Y'_B = 8.57538 + .44152X$
   $Y'_C = 19.77527 + .42577X$
   (b) .44990
   (c) $F = 1.62$, with 2 and 69 *df.*
   (d) $F = 1136.95$, with 1 and 71 *df.*
   (e) .70365
   (f) $F = 98.16$, with 2 and 72 *df.*
   (g) $F = 1583.78$, with 2 and 71 *df.*
   (h) $Y' = 8.47106 + .44990X - 7.99065\text{V1} - .76676\text{V2}$ (subjects in Method A were assigned 1's in V1; subjects in Method B were assigned 1's in V2).
   (i) $\bar{Y}_{A\,(\text{adj})} = 47.64$ $\quad\bar{Y}_{B\,(\text{adj})} = 54.86$ $\quad\bar{Y}_{C\,(\text{adj})} = 64.38$
   (j) It is equivalent to a test of significance among adjusted means.

(k)
$$\mathbf{C} = \begin{bmatrix} .02968 & -.01487 \\ -.01487 & .02983 \end{bmatrix}$$

(l)
$$\mathbf{C}^* = \left[\begin{array}{cc:c} .02968 & -.01487 & -.01481 \\ -.01487 & .02983 & -.01496 \\ \hdashline -.01481 & -.01496 & .02977 \end{array}\right]$$

(m) (1) $F = 584.70$, with 1 and 71 *df;*
(2) $F = 1013.29$, with 1 and 71 *df;*
(3) $F = 19.70$, with 1 and 71 *df.*

5. *Source*	Σx^2	Σy^2	Σxy	r_{yx}	b_{yx}
Total	128.5	108.5	109.5	.92736	.85214
I	17.5	13.5	13.5	.87831	.77143
II	17.5	9.5	10.5	.81435	.60000
III	17.5	9.5	9.5	.73679	.54286
Within	52.5	32.5	33.5	.81100	.63810
Between	76.0	76.0	76.0	1.00000	1.00000

(c) $\eta_{\bar{x}}^2 = .59144 \quad \eta_{\bar{y}}^2 = .70046$

6. (a) $R^2_{y.x\bar{x}} = .89748$

(b) $Y' = 3.00000 + .63810X + .36190\bar{X}$

(c) $b_{yx.\bar{x}}$ is the common b or b_w. Compare with results under 5, above.

(d) $b_{y\bar{x}.x}$ is the deviation of b_b from b_w. $b_b = 1.0000$ (see under 5, above). $b_w = .63810$. $b_{y\bar{x}.x} = b_b - b_w = 1.00000 - .63810 = .36190$.

(e) $F = 5.48$, with 1 and 15 *df*, $p < .05$.

(f) That there is a contextual effect.

14

REPEATED-MEASURES DESIGNS

Preceding chapters dealt with designs in which a single measure of the dependent variable was obtained from each subject. The present chapter is devoted to designs in which subjects are measured repeatedly on the dependent variable.[1] The *sole* purpose here is to show how the analysis of data obtained in such designs can be efficiently accomplished within the context of multiple regression analysis. Consequently, issues regarding the design of such studies, problems related to their internal and external validity, and the statistical assumptions that underlie them will not be discussed. This should not be construed as implying that these issues, problems, and assumptions are not important. On the contrary, they are of utmost importance. But since excellent discussions of these topics are available in the literature, and since the concern here is only with the analytic approach, it was decided to draw attention to some of the issues and to provide references in which they are discussed in the detail that they deserve. *It is strongly suggested that you consult these references in order to gain a full understanding of the scope, advantages, and disadvantages of repeated-measures designs.*

The chapter begins with a brief discussion of the nature of repeated-measures designs. This is followed by brief comments on the advantages, potential problems, and disadvantages of such designs. The remainder of the chapter is then devoted to illustrations of the application of multiple regression analysis to different types of repeated-measures designs. All but one of the numerical examples were taken from Edwards (1972) in order to thus afford you with the opportunity of comparing the analytic approaches to repeated-measures designs that

[1]Parts of this chapter have been taken from Pedhazur (1977). Copyright 1977 by the American Psychological Association. Reprinted by permission.

are employed in most statistics books that deal with this topic with the approach that is being presented here.

The Nature of Designs with Repeated Measures

In the experimental designs that were presented in preceding chapters, subjects were randomly assigned to a single treatment (or to a combination of treatments) and the effects of the different treatments were then compared by analyzing the responses of subjects on a measure of the dependent variable. In repeated-measures designs, on the other hand, each subject is administered all the treatments, and performance on the dependent variable is measured after the administration of each of them.

A simple example may help clarify the distinction between the two types of designs. Assume that in medical research it is desired to study the differential effects of three kinds of drugs on the level of blood pressure. Using a design described in detail in Chapter 9, one can randomly assign subjects to the three drugs and then regress the measures of the dependent variable on two coded vectors that represent the treatment or, equivalently, subject the data to a one-way analysis of variance. As an alternative to the preceding design, one might choose to administer the three drugs to each subject, allowing each time for the effects of a given drug to wear off before another one is administered. This, then, is an example of a repeated-measures design with one factor.

In principle, repeated measures may be obtained in any type of design. For example, one may use a factorial design (see Chapter 10) in which each subject is administered all the treatment combinations. Very often, designs are used in which repeated measures are obtained only on some of the factors. For example, suppose that a researcher is interested in the effects of two methods of teaching and practice time on the learning of some task. Under such circumstances, it is not feasible to administer both teaching methods to the same subjects. It is, however, feasible, and in many instances of particular interest, to note the effects of practice time by measuring the subjects repeatedly instead of using different subjects for different levels of practice. In such a design, subjects are randomly assigned to one of the teaching methods, and their performance on the dependent variable is measured at the conclusion of each of the practice periods. This, then, is an example of a design in which repeated measures are obtained for one factor (practice time) but not for the other (teaching methods). Such designs have been variously referred to as mixed designs (Lindquist, 1953, Chapter 14; Myers, 1979, Chapter 8), split-plot designs (Edwards, 1972, Chapter 14; 1979, Chapter 11; Kirk, 1968, Chapter 8); factorial designs with repeated measures (Winer, 1971, Chapter 7).

The preceding example consisted of two factors. Repeated-measures designs with more than two factors are common in various areas of social science research. Again, all or some of the factors may involve repeated measures. Consider a factorial design with three factors: A, B, and C. One may, for example, randomly assign subjects to the different levels of A and administer the treatment combinations of B and C to all subjects. This, then, is an example of a mixed design in which repeated measures are obtained for factors B and C, but not for A. Finally, it will be noted that repeated measures may be used in conjunction with analysis of covariance designs (see, for example, Winer, 1971, pp. 796–809). Extensive discussions and examples of the above noted designs, and others, may be found in the references cited above.

Advantages of Repeated-Measures Designs

Probably the most important advantage of repeated-measures designs is that they afford the researcher control for individual differences among the subjects. Individual differences are probably the largest source of variation in most research studies. When left uncontrolled, as in a completely randomized design, they comprise part of the error term. In repeated-measures designs each subject serves as his own control. Consequently, it is possible to identify the variance due to individual differences and separate it from the error term (see below). This therefore leads to a more precise analysis.

Repeated-measures designs are also more economical than completely randomized designs in that they afford considerable savings in the number of subjects required for a given study. For a discussion and comparison of the statistical power of completely randomized and repeated-measures designs, see Cohen and Cohen (1975, pp. 410–412).

Finally, repeated-measures designs enable one to study phenomena across time. This is particularly useful in experiments dealing with learning (e.g., the effects of practice time in the example discussed earlier) or in developmental studies (e.g., when measures of a given phenomenon are taken at different ages).

Potential Problems and Disadvantages of Repeated-Measures Designs

Several potential problems that may affect adversely the internal and/or external validity of repeated-measures designs have been noted. Notable among them are carry-over effects, practice effects, fatigue, and sensitization. Carry-over effects refer to situations in which treatments administered earlier in the sequence continue to affect the behavior of the subjects while they are being administered a subsequent treatment. It should be noted that in certain areas of study (e.g., learning) carry-over effects are of major interest in and of themselves. The other problems noted above are self-evident and will therefore not be discussed. Various proposals have been advanced for the purpose of counteracting these and other potential threats to the validity of repeated-measures designs. For discussions, see Gaito (1961), Greenwald, (1976), Namboodiri (1972).

From a statistical frame of reference, the repeated-measures design suffers from a serious disadvantage in that the validity of the F ratio is predicated on stringent assumptions that are often not met. The problems stem from the fact that, unlike the completely randomized designs, the residuals in repeated-measures designs tend to be intercorrelated because the same subjects are measured repeatedly. Nevertheless, it has been shown that when certain conditions are met, the *F* ratio is still valid. A sufficient condition for the validity of the *F* ratio is that the covariance matrices possess the property of compound symmetry. This means that the variances of all the variables within a group are equal, as are the correlations among all the variables. In addition, the covariance matrices of all groups are equal. Other conditions under which the *F* ratio is valid have also been identified. For detailed discussions of this topic, see the references cited earlier. See also Huynh and Feldt (1970), Lana and Lubin (1963), and Rouanet and Lépine (1970).

The absence of the conditions for a valid *F* test results in increases in Type I error. That is, while the researcher may think that the α level is, say, .05 it may in fact be larger. Some authors (e.g., Greenhouse & Geisser, 1959) have therefore proposed the use of conservative *F* tests when the conditions for the validity of the *F* test are not met. Others (e.g., Bock, 1975; Davidson, 1972; Finn, 1969; McCall & Appelbaum, 1973; Poor, 1973) have advocated that multivariate analysis be used in repeated-measures designs. It should be noted, however, that when the assumptions are met, some of the univariate tests are more powerful than the multivariate ones (Davidson, 1972; Poor, 1973). Moreover, when the number of subjects is relatively small, only univariate analysis can be used.

In sum, when the number of subjects is relatively large, the use of multivariate analysis with repeated measures is generally preferable. When methods presented in this chapter are used, it is important to be alert to the potential problems outlined above. Again, you are urged to study the references cited above when you contemplate using repeated-measures designs.

A Note on Randomized-Blocks Designs

Before turning to the numerical examples it will be noted that there is another type of design that affords greater control than the completely randomized design, even though each subject is *not* measured repeatedly. In this type of design, subjects are placed in blocks on the basis of a concomitant variable that is related to the dependent variable. For example, suppose that it is desired to study the effects of four treatments while controlling for a concomitant variable such as mental ability. This can, of course, be accomplished by the use of ANCOVA (see Chapter 13). Alternatively, one may match subjects on mental ability and place them in blocks of four. Each block consists of four subjects who have the same score on mental ability. Subjects from each block are then randomly assigned to the treatments, hence the name randomized-blocks design. Such designs are discussed extensively in the references cited earlier (e.g., Edwards, 1972, Chapter 13; Kirk, 1968, pp. 131–150; see also Feldt, 1958, for a comparison between randomized-blocks designs and ANCOVA). The reason they are mentioned here is because their analyses proceed in the same manner as those of repeated-measures designs. Therefore the procedures illustrated below for using multiple regression analysis in repeated-measures designs apply equally to the analyses of randomized-blocks designs.

ONE-FACTOR REPEATED-MEASURES DESIGN

The data reported in Table 14.1 will be used to illustrate the analysis of a design in which five subjects were administered five treatments. Similarly, these data may be thought of as representing a randomized-blocks design. In this case the number of subjects is 25, but they were grouped in five blocks on the basis of a concomitant variable and then randomly assigned to one of the five treatments. Actually, this is the context in which Edwards (1972, p. 234) presents these data. As was noted above, the analytic procedure applies equally to both types of designs.

Table 14.1 Repeated-Measures Design with Five Subjects and Five Treatments

	Treatments					
Subjects	*1*	*2*	*3*	*4*	*5*	Σ
1	18	20	20	21	21	100
2	17	19	19	20	20	95
3	16	17	18	19	20	90
4	16	16	17	18	18	85
5	16	16	15	17	16	80

NOTE: Data taken from A. L. Edwards, *Experimental Design in Psychological Research* (4th ed.), p. 234. Copyright 1972 by Holt, Rinehart and Winston. Reprinted by permission.

In order to demonstrate what is being accomplished by the use of repeated measures, the data of Table 14.1 will be analyzed first as if they were obtained in a completely randomized design. That is, assume that 25 subjects were randomly assigned to five treatments. This type of design was introduced and discussed extensively in Chapter 9. Therefore, only minimal comments will be made here on the analytic procedure.

The data of Table 14.1 are presented in Table 14.2 in a format suitable for multiple regression analysis. Note that the scores on the dependent variable are strung out in a single vector Y. In vectors 1 through 4 effect coding is used to represent the treatments (see Chapter 9). Following are excerpts of the output as obtained from the SPSS REGRESSION program.

Output

```
DEPENDENT VARIABLE Y                    R SQUARE .26667
                     ANALYSIS OF VARIANCE
                  DF   SUM OF    MEAN       F
                       SQUARES   SQUARE
REGRESSION         4    20.80      5.20    1.82
RESIDUAL          20    57.20      2.86
```

Table 14.2 Data of Table 14.1 Displayed for a Randomized-Design Analysis

Y	*1*	*2*	*3*	*4*
18	1	0	0	0
17	1	0	0	0
16	1	0	0	0
16	1	0	0	0
16	1	0	0	0
20	0	1	0	0
19	0	1	0	0
17	0	1	0	0
16	0	1	0	0
16	0	1	0	0
20	0	0	1	0
19	0	0	1	0
18	0	0	1	0
17	0	0	1	0
15	0	0	1	0
21	0	0	0	1
20	0	0	0	1
19	0	0	0	1
18	0	0	0	1
17	0	0	0	1
21	−1	−1	−1	−1
20	−1	−1	−1	−1
20	−1	−1	−1	−1
18	−1	−1	−1	−1
16	−1	−1	−1	−1

Commentary

Assuming that the .05 level of significance was selected prior to the experiment, it is concluded that there are no significant differences among the five treatments. $F(4, 20) = 1.82$, $p > .05$.

Repeated-Measures Analysis

The data of Table 14.1 will now be analyzed as a repeated-measures design. In order to do so within the context of multiple regression analysis it is necessary to identify the subjects by a set of coded vectors. The coding proceeds in the same manner as one codes treatments; that is, a given subject is assigned 1's in a given vector, whereas all others are assigned 0's in that vector (dummy coding), or all others are assigned 0's, whereas one subject is assigned −1's (effect coding). Since there are five subjects in the present example, four coded vectors are required. The data of Table 14.1 and coded vectors for treatments and subjects are displayed in Table 14.3. Note that the coded vectors for treatments are the same as those used in Table 14.2. The difference, then, between Tables 14.2 and 14.3 is that in the latter four coded vectors for subjects (labeled 5 through 8) were added. Following are excerpts of output as obtained from the SPSS REGRESSION program.

Table 14.3 Data of Table 14.1 Displayed for a Repeated-Measure Analysis

Y	*1*	*2*	*3*	*4*	*5*	*6*	*7*	*8*
18	1	0	0	0	1	0	0	0
17	1	0	0	0	0	1	0	0
16	1	0	0	0	0	0	1	0
16	1	0	0	0	0	0	0	1
16	1	0	0	0	−1	−1	−1	−1
20	0	1	0	0	1	0	0	0
19	0	1	0	0	0	1	0	0
17	0	1	0	0	0	0	1	0
16	0	1	0	0	0	0	0	1
16	0	1	0	0	−1	−1	−1	−1
20	0	0	1	0	1	0	0	0
19	0	0	1	0	0	1	0	0
18	0	0	1	0	0	0	1	0
17	0	0	1	0	0	0	0	1
15	0	0	1	0	−1	−1	−1	−1
21	0	0	0	1	1	0	0	0
20	0	0	0	1	0	1	0	0
19	0	0	0	1	0	0	1	0
18	0	0	0	1	0	0	0	1
17	0	0	0	1	−1	−1	−1	−1
21	−1	−1	−1	−1	1	0	0	0
20	−1	−1	−1	−1	0	1	0	0
20	−1	−1	−1	−1	0	0	1	0
18	−1	−1	−1	−1	0	0	0	1
16	−1	−1	−1	−1	−1	−1	−1	−1

NOTE: Vectors 1 through 4 are coded vectors for treatments, and 5 through 8 are coded vectors for subjects.

Output

DEPENDENT VARIABLE Y R SQUARE .90769

VECTORS	DF	SUM OF SQUARES	MEAN SQUARE	F
V1–V4	4	20.80	5.20	11.56
V5–V8	4	50.00	12.50	
RESIDUAL	16	7.20	.45	

Commentary

In earlier chapters (see, for example, Chapter 10) it was shown that the assignment of different inclusion levels to coded vectors that represent different factors facilitates the identification of the sum of squares (or the proportion of variance) accounted for by each of the factors. The same procedure was followed in the present analysis. Specifically, vectors 1 through 4 of Table 14.3 were assigned a higher inclusion level than vectors 5 through 8. Accordingly, the sum of squares due to V1 through V4 was obtained from the first step of the analysis. The sum of squares for V5 through V8 was then obtained by subtracting the regression sum of squares reported in the first step of the analysis from the regression sum of squares reported in the second step (i.e., the one in which the eight coded vectors were included). Similarly for the degrees of freedom, which in the first step are four and in the second step are eight. Subtracting the *df* in the first step from those of the seconds yields the *df* for subjects, which are, of course, equal to the number of coded vectors used to represent the subjects. Because the vectors for treatments and those for subjects are mutually orthogonal, the same results would be obtained when the inclusion levels are reversed—that is, when vectors 5 through 8 are entered first, and vectors 1 through 4 are entered second.

Note that the mean square residual reported above (.45) is obtained directly from the output. The *F* ratio (11.56) is *not* reported in the output but has to be calculated by first calculating a mean square regression due to the treatments ($V1-V4$) and then dividing this mean square by the mean square residual.

Thus far, we were concerned with the mechanics of obtaining the values necessary for the test of significance for the differences among the treatments. We turn now to a discussion of the contrast between the present analysis and the earlier one in which the data were treated as if they were obtained in a randomized design (i.e., Table 14.2). Note that the *F* ratio in the present analysis (11.56 with 4 and 16 *df*) is significant at the .001 level, whereas the *F* ratio obtained in the earlier analysis (1.82 with 4 and 20 *df*) is not significant at the .05 level. Clearly, then, the conclusions about the significance of the differences among the treatments are dramatically different in the two analyses.

The source of the difference is in the difference between the two error terms in the two analyses. Not surprisingly, the regression sum of squares due to treatments (vectors $V1-V4$) is the same in both analyses. What is different in the two analyses is that in the earlier one the variance due to individual differences was part of the error term, whereas in the present analysis this component is identified and separated from the error term, resulting in considerably smaller mean square residuals. Specifically, the residual sum of squares of the earlier analysis (57.20 with 20 *df*) was partitioned into two parts: sum of squares due to subjects (also referred to as within-subjects sum of squares) of 50 with 4 *df*, and a residual sum of squares of 7.20 with 16 *df*. Consequently, the mean square residual in the present analysis is .45 as compared with 2.86 in the earlier analysis. Note that the loss of 4 *df* for the residual sum of squares in the present analysis, as compared with the one in the earlier analysis, was more than offset by the considerable reduction in the residual sum of squares in the present analysis.

When the topic of repeated-measures designs was introduced it was said that in much of social science research the largest source of variability is due to individual differences. The data of Table 14.3 illustrate this point. While the treatments account for about 27% of the variance of Y ($R^2_{y.1234} = .26667$), the variance accounted for by subjects is 64% ($R^2_{y.5678} = .64102$).

In sum, when subjects are randomly assigned to treatments, the variance due to individual differences is part of the error term. In repeated-measures designs this source of variability is controlled for and separated from the error term, thereby leading to greater precision in the analysis.

The method of coding subjects described above can be generalized to more complex repeated-measures and randomized-blocks designs. It suffers, however, from a serious shortcoming in that it can become unwieldy and may result in a relatively large number of vectors, exceeding the capacity of many available computer programs for multiple regression analysis. Thus, for example, a repeated measures design with 60 subjects requires 59 coded vectors for subjects, which for the purpose of the analysis are treated as 59 variables. Even when the number of subjects is relatively small, the capacity of certain computer programs may be exceeded if in addition to the vectors required to code subjects, it is necessary to generate a relatively large number of vectors to represent the categorical variables and their interactions. These difficulties can be easily overcome by using a different scheme to code subjects—to which we now turn.

Coding Subjects by Criterion Scaling

The topic of criterion scaling was introduced in Chapter 10, where it was shown that instead of using coded vectors to represent a categorical variable one may use the mean (or the total when n's are equal) of each group on the criterion (or the dependent variable) as codes for group membership, thereby requiring a single vector regardless of the number of groups. It is this property of criterion scaling that makes it particularly useful to represent subjects in repeated-measures designs, or blocks in randomized-blocks designs.

The method is now illustrated for the data of Table 14.1. In Table 14.4, vectors Y and 1 through 4 are repeated from Tables 14.2 and 14.3. Note that the treatments are coded in the same manner, regardless of the method that is used to code subjects. Vector 5 of Table 14.4 consists of the criterion scaling for subjects. Specifically, this vector consists of total scores for each subject (i.e., the sum of a subject's score on all the treatments), inserted in the rows associated with the scores of a given subject. For example, 100, the sum of the scores for subject 1 appears five times in vector 5, in the rows in which the separate scores for subject 1 appear under Y, namely, rows 1, 6, 11, 16, and 21. The same procedure is applied to the sums of the scores for the other subjects.

The analysis now proceeds in the usual manner. That is, Y is regressed on vectors 1 through 5. Following are excerpts of the output from the SPSS REGRESSION program used to analyze the data of Table 14.4.

Table 14.4 Repeated-Measures Design with Criterion Scaling for Subjects

Y	*1*	*2*	*3*	*4*	*5*
18	1	0	0	0	100
17	1	0	0	0	95
16	1	0	0	0	90
16	1	0	0	0	85
16	1	0	0	0	80
20	0	1	0	0	100
19	0	1	0	0	95
17	0	1	0	0	90
16	0	1	0	0	85
16	0	1	0	0	80
20	0	0	1	0	100
19	0	0	1	0	95
18	0	0	1	0	90
17	0	0	1	0	85
15	0	0	1	0	80
21	0	0	0	1	100
20	0	0	0	1	95
19	0	0	0	1	90
18	0	0	0	1	85
17	0	0	0	1	80
21	−1	−1	−1	−1	100
20	−1	−1	−1	−1	95
20	−1	−1	−1	−1	90
18	−1	−1	−1	−1	85
16	−1	−1	−1	−1	80

NOTE: Data are from Table 14.1. Vectors 1 through 4 represent the treatments. Vector 5 represents the criterion scaling for subjects.

Output

DEPENDENT VARIABLE Y

VECTORS	DF	SUM OF SQUARES	R SQUARE
V1–V4	4	20.80	.26667
V5	1	50.00	.64102
RESIDUAL	19	7.20	

Commentary

The information reported above was obtained by assigning different inclusion levels to vectors V1 through V4, and to V5 (see discussion of this point in the preceding section). Because the vectors representing the treatments and the one representing the subjects are orthogonal, $R^2_{y.1234}$ indicates the proportion of variance accounted for by treatments, and $R^2_{y.5}$ indicates the proportion of variance due to subjects. Note that the sums of squares and the proportions of variance accounted for (R SQUARE) are the same as those obtained earlier, when four coded vectors were used to represent the subjects (see Table 14.3 and the output related to that table). There is, however, an important difference between the two analyses regarding the degrees of freedom reported in each. This is because in the earlier analysis four vectors were used to represent the subjects, whereas in the present analysis a single vector is used to represent the same information. Consequently, the *df* for subjects in the earlier analysis are 4 (the correct number), whereas the *df* for subjects in the present analysis is 1 (an *incorrect* number). Because the computer program treats the proportion of variance, or the sum of squares, due to subjects as being associated with a single *df*, the *df* reported for the residual sum of squares are also *incorrect*. They are reported above as being 19, when in fact they should be 16. This is why the mean square residuals given in the output was not reported above.

In short, then, when criterion scaling is used to represent the subjects, the sums of squares, and the proportions of variances, due to treatments, subjects, and residual are reported correctly in the computer output. But the *df* for subjects and for the residual sums of squares, or proportion of variance, are incorrect. *Consequently, the df associated with the sum of squares for subjects, as well as those associated with the residual sum of squares, have to be adjusted when calculating their respective mean squares*. The degrees of freedom for treatments are not affected because the number of vectors representing treatments is always equal to the number of degrees of freedom associated with them.

Since the interest in repeated-measures designs is in the F ratio for treatment, all that is necessary is to adjust the *df* for the residual sum of squares in order to obtain the correct mean square residual. From the output above: $ss_{\text{res}} = 7.20$. The *df* for the residual are 16 (i.e., $25 - 4 - 4 - 1$, $25 = N$, $4 = df$ for treatments, and $4 = df$ for subjects). Or, *df* for residual: $19 - 3$ (i.e., *df* reported in the output minus an additional 3 *df* for the subjects which were absorbed in the residual term because a single vector was used to represent the subjects). The mean square residual is therefore $7.20/16 = .45$, which is the same as the one obtained in the earlier analysis when four coded vectors were used to represent subjects.

The mean square for treatments is $20.8/4 = 5.2$. The F ratio for treatments is, of course, the same as the one obtained in the earlier analysis ($5.2/.45 = 11.56$ with 4 and 16 *df*).

As always, the test of the differences among treatments could be accomplished by using proportions of variance instead of sums of squares. From the above output, $R^2_{y.12345} = .90769$. The residual proportion of variance is therefore equal to $1 - R^2_{y.12345} = 1 - .90769 = .09231$. The proportion of variance due to treatments is .26667 ($R^2_{y\,1234}$). Therefore

$$F = \frac{.26667/4}{.09231/16} = 11.56$$

The Regression Equation

It is of interest to note the properties of the regression equation that is obtained when the subjects are represented by a vector that is criterion scaled. For the data of Table 14.4 the regression equation is

$$Y' = .00 - 1.40X_1 - .40X_2 - .20X_3 + 1.00X_4 + .20X_5$$

Using the coding system displayed in Table 14.4 will always result in a Y intercept equal to zero. The regression coefficients associated with the treatment vectors have the same properties as those of effect coding in designs without repeated measures (see Chapter 9). That is, they reflect the treatment effects. Thus, -1.40 is the effect of treatment 1 (i.e., $\bar{X}_1 - \bar{X} = 16.60 - 18.00$). Similarly, for the other coefficients associated with the treatment vectors.

The coefficient associated with the vector for subjects is equal to the reciprocal of the number of repeated measures in the design. In the present case there are 5 repeated measures; hence the coefficient for the subjects' vector is .20.

MIXED DESIGNS

It was noted earlier that mixed designs are those in which repeated measures are obtained only on some of the factors. The terminology used to describe such designs varies. Some authors refer to them as split-plot designs. Others refer to them as factorial with within-subjects and between-subjects variables. The term within-subjects variables refers to variables on which repeated measures are obtained, whereas the term between-subjects variables is used to refer to variables on which no repeated measures are obtained. Still others follow Lindquist (1953, Chapter 13) in identifying different mixed designs by Roman numerals. For example, a factorial design with one within-subjects variable and one between-subjects variable is referred to as a Lindquist Type I design.

Two numerical examples of mixed designs are given below: (1) factorial with one within-subjects and one between-subjects variable; (2) factorial with two within-subjects variables and one between-subjects variable. It is hoped that these will suffice to show how criterion scaling for subjects may be used in such designs.

Factorial with One Within-Subjects and One Between-Subjects Variable

The data reported in Table 14.5 have been taken from Edwards (1972, p. 335) who describes factor A as representing three different drugs (A_1, A_2, A_3) and factor B as representing three trials (B_1, B_2, B_3). Fifteen subjects were randomly assigned to the different drugs (five subjects per treatment). In this design, A (drugs) is a between-subjects factor, and B (trials) is a within-subjects factor. The data are displayed in Table 14.6 in a format suitable for multiple regression analysis.

Table 14.5 Observations for Three Groups with Each Group Tested under a Different Drug and with Three Trials for Each Subject

Drugs	*Subjects*	Trials B_1	B_2	B_3	Σ
	1	2	4	7	13
	2	2	6	10	18
A_1	3	3	7	10	20
	4	7	9	11	27
	5	6	9	12	27
	1	5	6	10	21
	2	4	5	10	19
A_2	3	7	8	11	26
	4	8	9	11	28
	5	11	12	13	36
	1	3	4	7	14
	2	3	6	9	18
A_3	3	4	7	9	20
	4	8	8	10	26
	5	7	10	10	27

NOTE: Data are taken from A. L. Edwards, *Experimental Design in Psychological Research* (4th ed.), p. 335. Copyright 1972 by Holt, Rinehart and Winston. Reprinted by permission.

In order to demonstrate the generality of the approach, orthogonal coding is used for the drugs *(A)*. Vector 1 contrasts A_1 with A_2, and vector 2 contrasts $A_1 + A_2$ with A_3. Since Edwards (1972, pp. 340–345) also analyzes the trials for trends, *B* is represented, for comparative purposes, by orthogonal polynomials. Vector 3 represents the linear component, and vector 4 represents the quadratic components. The coding has thus far proceeded in the usual manner (see Chapter 9 for orthogonal coding, and Chapter 11 for orthogonal polynomials). Vector 5 is used to identify the source of variance due to subjects. As was done above, the total score for each subject is used in vector 5 in the same rows in which the given subject's scores on the dependent variable, *Y*, appear. For example, the scores for subject 1 under drug A_1, for trials B_1, B_2, and B_3 are 2, 4, and 7, respectively. These scores appear in rows 1, 16, and 31 of Table 14.6. Since the total score for this subject is 13 (i.e., 2 + 4 + 7), this total is inserted in vector 5 in rows 1, 16, and 31. The total score for each subject is thus repeated as many times as there are trials (3 in the present example) in the appropriate rows of vector 5.

Parenthetically, it will be noted that one could use coded vectors to represent single subjects, as was done earlier in the chapter (see Table 14.3). For the present example, such a method of coding would require 12 vectors for subjects. This is because each set of subjects within a given treatment is coded separately, using $n - 1$ coded vectors (n = number of subjects within a given treatment). Since there are five subjects within each of the *A* treatments, four coded vectors are required for each group of subjects. Note that the number of coded vectors for subjects (12) would be equal to the number of degrees of

Table 14.6 Data of Table 14.5 Displayed for Multiple Regression Analysis

			Vectors				
Cells	*Subjects*	*Y*	*1*	*2*	*3*	*4*	*5*
A_1B_1	1	2	1	1	−1	1	13
	2	2	1	1	−1	1	18
	3	3	1	1	−1	1	20
	4	7	1	1	−1	1	27
	5	6	1	1	−1	1	27
A_2B_1	1	5	−1	1	−1	1	21
	2	4	−1	1	−1	1	19
	3	7	−1	1	−1	1	26
	4	8	−1	1	−1	1	28
	5	11	−1	1	−1	1	36
A_3B_1	1	3	0	−2	−1	1	14
	2	3	0	−2	−1	1	18
	3	4	0	−2	−1	1	20
	4	8	0	−2	−1	1	26
	5	7	0	−2	−1	1	27
A_1B_2	1	4	1	1	0	−2	13
	2	6	1	1	0	−2	18
	3	7	1	1	0	−2	20
	4	9	1	1	0	−2	27
	5	9	1	1	0	−2	27
A_2B_2	1	6	−1	1	0	−2	21
	2	5	−1	1	0	−2	19
	3	8	−1	1	0	−2	26
	4	9	−1	1	0	−2	28
	5	12	−1	1	0	−2	36
A_3B_2	1	4	0	−2	0	−2	14
	2	6	0	−2	0	−2	18
	3	7	0	−2	0	−2	20
	4	8	0	−2	0	−2	26
	5	10	0	−2	0	−2	27
A_1B_3	1	7	1	1	1	1	13
	2	10	1	1	1	1	18
	3	10	1	1	1	1	20
	4	11	1	1	1	1	27
	5	12	1	1	1	1	27
A_2B_3	1	10	−1	1	1	1	21
	2	10	−1	1	1	1	19
	3	11	−1	1	1	1	26
	4	11	−1	1	1	1	28
	5	13	−1	1	1	1	36

Table 14.6 Data of Table 14.5 Displayed for Multiple Regression Analysis *(cont.)*

Cells	*Subjects*	*Y*	Vectors *1*	*2*	*3*	*4*	*5*
	1	7	0	−2	1	1	14
	2	9	0	−2	1	1	18
A_3B_3	3	9	0	−2	1	1	20
	4	10	0	−2	1	1	26
	5	10	0	−2	1	1	27

NOTE: Y = dependent variable scores; vectors 1 and 2 = orthogonal coding for *A;* vectors 3 and 4 = orthogonal polynomials for *B;* and vector 5 = criterion scaling for subjects.

freedom for subjects: $a\ (n - 1)$, where a is the number of levels of a (see below).

We return now to the analysis of the data of Table 14.6. Before doing a multiple regression analysis for these data, it is necessary to have vectors that represent the interaction between A and B. These are obtained, as usual, by cross multiplying the vectors representing one factor by those representing the other factor (see Chapter 10). For the present analysis the following vectors were generated by using COMPUTE statements in SPSS: vector 6 = 1 × 3, vector 7 = 2 × 3, vector 8 = 1 × 4, and vector 9 = 2 × 4. Note that vectors 6 through 9 represent the interaction between A and B. If, however, one wishes to test separately the $A \times B$ linear interaction, and the $A \times B$ quadratic interaction, then the proportion of variance, or the sum of squares, accounted for by vectors 6 and 7 provides the information for the former; vectors 8 and 9 provide the information for the latter.

One may now regress Y on vectors 1 through 9 in order to identify the proportion of variance, or sum of squares, associated with each component. Recall that the vectors representing the different factors and the interaction are mutually orthogonal (except, as noted below, for the correlations of the vectors for factor A and the vector for subjects, vector 5). Consequently, the proportion of variance due to a factor is simply the squared multiple correlation of Y with the vectors representing that factor. Thus, the proportion of variance due to factor A is $R^2_{y.12}$. (Incidentally, since orthogonal coding was used in the present example, each R^2 is equal to the sum of the squared zero-order correlations between each of the coded vectors and Y; for example, $R^2_{y.34} = r^2_{y3} + r^2_{y4}$.)

Note that since vector 5 of Table 14.6 exhausts all the information due to differences among subjects, it also includes the proportion of variance due to the differences among drugs (i.e., A_1, A_2, and A_3). Consequently, in order to identify the proportion of variance due to the error term for factor A (Subjects within Groups; see discussion below, and Table 14.7) it is necessary to calculate the squared semipartial correlation of Y with the subjects' vector, partialing factor A from the latter. In the present example, this translates into $r^2_{y(5.12)} = R^2_{y.125} - R^2_{y.12}$.

The data of Table 14.6 were analyzed by the REGRESSION program of SPSS. In order to facilitate the identification of the sum of squares, and the proportion of variance, due to each component the vectors representing different components were assigned different inclusion levels. For the output that follows, the coded vectors were entered in the following order: 1, 2 (*A*); 5 (Subjects); 3, 4 (*B*); 6, 7, 8, 9 ($A \times B$).

Output

DEPENDENT VARIABLE Y

VECTORS	SUM OF SQUARES CHANGE	DF CHANGE	R SQUARE CHANGE
V1–V2 (*A*)	27.77778	2	.07525
V5 (SUBJECTS)	148.00000	1	.40096
V3–V4 (*B*)	164.44444	2	.44552
V6–V9 ($A \times B$)	8.88889	4	.02409
RESIDUAL	20.00000	35	

Commentary

As was done in earlier examples, the output was organized in a format that differs from the one used in SPSS. In fact, the information about the sums of squares is not given directly by SPSS but has been obtained from the hierarchical analysis, as has been described several times earlier (see, for example, Chapter 10 and earlier in this chapter). Specifically, to obtain the SUM OF SQUARES CHANGE at a given step the REGRESSION SUM OF SQUARES reported in the step preceding it was subtracted from the REGRESSION SUM OF SQUARES reported at the step that is being considered. For example, at step 2, vectors 1, 2, and 5 have been entered. The REGRESSION SUM OF SQUARES reported at this step is 175.77778. To obtain the SUM OF SQUARES CHANGE (i.e., sum of squares for vector 5) subtract the REGRESSION SUM OF SQUARES of step 1 (27.77778) from the REGRESSION SUM OF SQUARES of step 2 (175.77778): $175.77778 - 27.77778 = 148.00$. Similarly, for the other terms in the column labeled SUM OF SQUARES CHANGE, and for the DF. The column R SQUARE CHANGE was obtained by adding the values associated with a given component as reported in the SUMMARY TABLE of SPSS.

Tests of Significance

When doing tests of significance in mixed designs, different error terms are used depending upon which component is being tested. In the design under consideration there are two error terms: one for testing the significance of the differences among the means of the between-subjects variable (*A*), and one for testing the significance of the differences among the means of the within-subjects variable (*B*) as well as the interaction ($A \times B$). For detailed discussions of tests of significance in mixed designs, see the references cited earlier.

The test of significance for factor *A* is considered first. From the output reported above, the sum of squares for *A* is 27.77778, with 2 *df*. Therefore the Mean Square for *A* is: $27.77778/2 = 13.88889$. It is necessary now to obtain the

Mean Square Error for this factor, which is labeled Subjects within Groups, or Error *(a)* (see, for example, Edwards, 1972, p. 338). In effect, the test for factor A (i.e., the between-subjects factor) is conducted as if this were a randomized design. The sum of squares for the error term for factor A is the one associated with the subjects' vector (i.e., vector 5). From the output reported above, this sum of squares is 148.00. But, as was discussed earlier in this chapter, it is necessary to adjust the *df* for this term because a single vector was used to represent the subjects. Now, as in a one-way design, each group of subjects contributes $n - 1$ *df* to the within-subjects sum of squares (n = number of subjects within a given level of A). Since there are 5 subjects under each of the three levels of A, the *df* for Subjects within Groups are: $3(5 - 1) = 12$. Therefore, dividing the SUM OF SQUARES CHANGE for vector 5 (148.00) by the appropriate *df* (12) yields the Mean Square Error for A: $148.00/12 = 12.33333$. The F ratio for A is therefore:

$$F_A = \frac{27.77778/2}{148.00000/12} = \frac{13.88889}{12.33333} = \mathit{1.13}$$

with 2 and 12 *df*. This is the same as the F ratio reported by Edwards (1972, p. 338).

We turn now to the tests of significance of B and $A \times B$. The Mean Square Error for these terms is labeled $B \times$ Subjects within Groups, or Error *(b)*. The sum of squares for this error term is the RESIDUAL SUM OF SQUARES reported in SPSS output (20.00, see above). But the *df* reported for this term (35) are *incorrect*. This is because the subjects were represented by a single vector, thereby appropriating 1 *df* instead of the 12 that are associated with this term. There is therefore a discrepancy of 11 *df*. Subtracting 11 from 35 (the *df* reported in the output for the RESIDUAL SUM OF SQUARES) yields the correct number of *df* for $B \times$ Subjects within Groups: $35 - 11 = \mathit{24}$. In general, the *df* associated with $B \times$ Subjects within Groups are: $a(n - 1)(b - 1)$, where a = number of levels of A; b = number of levels of B; and n = number of subjects within each level of A. For the present example: $3(5 - 1)(3 - 1) = \mathit{24}$.

To obtain the Mean Square Error $B \times$ Subjects within Groups divide the RESIDUAL SUM OF SQUARES reported in the output (20.00) by the adjusted *df* (24): $20.00/24 = \mathit{.83333}$. Using this Mean Square Error, and obtaining mean squares for B and $A \times B$, each of these terms is tested for significance.

$$F_B = \frac{164.44444/2}{20.00000/24} = \mathit{98.67}$$

with 2 and 24 *df*. There is a slight discrepancy between this F ratio and the one reported by Edwards (1972, p. 338). This is because Edwards has rounded to two decimal places.

$$F_{A \times B} = \frac{8.88889/4}{20.00000/24} = 2.67$$

with 4 and 24 *df*.

Table 14.7 summarizes the analysis and tests of significance for the present example. It is strongly suggested that you study the present analysis in conjunction with Edwards' (1972, pp. 334–340) presentation and discussion of this example.

As in other designs, instead of testing the significance of a factor it is possible to test components with single degrees of freedom. In the present example, one might test A_1 against A_2, separately and orthogonally from the test of $A_1 + A_2$ against A_3, or the linear component of B separately from the quadratic component. Such tests proceed in the usual manner by dividing the proportion of variance, or sum of squares, due to a given comparison by the appropriate error term. For a discussion of the error terms for the separate trend components, see Edwards (1972, pp. 340–345). (See also the other references on mixed designs, cited earlier.)

Finally, it will be noted that, as in other designs, when necessary it is possible to do multiple comparisons among main effects in mixed designs. Also, in the presence of a significant interaction, it is possible to test for simple effect in such designs. For detailed discussions, and numerical examples, of such tests in mixed designs, see Kirk (1968, Chapter 8).

Table 14.7 Summary of the Analysis of Data of Table 14.6

Source	*ss*	*df*	*ms*	*F*
$A = \Sigma y^2 R^2_{y.12}$	27.77778	2	13.88889	1.13
Subjects within Groups $= \Sigma y^2(R^2_{y.125} - R^2_{y.12})$	148.00000	12	12.33333	
$B = \Sigma y^2 R^2_{y.34}$	164.44444	2	82.22222	98.67
$A \times B = \Sigma y^2 R^2_{y.6789}$	8.88889	4	2.22222	2.67
$B \times$ Subjects within Groups $= \Sigma y^2(1 - R^2_{y.12...9})$	20.00000	24	.83333	
Total	369.11111	44		

Factorial with Two Within-Subjects Variables and One Between-Subjects Variable

In Table 14.8 data are presented for a design in which A is a between-subjects factor, and B and C are within-subject factors. In other words, repeated measures are obtained for each subject under all combinations of B and C. In Table 14.9 the same data are displayed together with the coded vectors for the purpose of a multiple regression analysis. Note that the vectors representing the main effects of A, B, and C (vectors 1, 2, and 3 of Table 14.9) are generated as one would do for a factorial design in which there are no repeated measures (see Chapter 10). This applies to any design with any number of levels for each factor. Also, one may use any coding scheme that best suits one's purposes (e.g., effect coding, orthogonal coding, orthogonal polynomials).

Vector 4 of Table 14.9 is a subjects' vector. It is composed of each subject's total score on all trials, in the same manner as was done for the design in the preceding section. For example, the total score for subject 1 under A_1 is 14. This score appears four times in vector 4, in the rows in which this subject's scores on the dependent variable appear. Vector 5 of Table 14.9 is composed of each subject's total scores on the separate levels of factor B. Thus, subject 1 under A_1 has a total score of 5 for B_1. This value appears twice in vector 5, in the first rows of cells $A_1B_1C_1$ and $A_1B_1C_2$. The same subject's total score on B_2 is 9, and it appears twice in vector 5, in the first rows of cells $A_1B_2C_1$ and $A_1B_2C_2$. In vector 6 of Table 14.9 the subjects' total scores on the levels of factor C are coded in the same manner as was done for B. For example, the total score for subject 1 for C_1 under A_1 is 8. This score appears twice, in the first rows of cells $A_1B_1C_1$ and $A_1B_2C_1$. The same subject's total score on C_2, 6, appears in the first rows of cells $A_1B_1C_2$ and $A_1B_2C_2$. In the present example, there are two levels for each within-subjects factor. The procedure outlined here is applied similarly to designs with more than two levels.

As in an ordinary factorial design, it is necessary to generate product vectors to represent interaction terms. In the present analysis the following vectors were generated by the SPSS program: vector 7 = 1 × 2 *(AB)*, vector 8 = 1 × 3 *(AC)*, vector 9 = 2 × 3 *(BC)*, and vector 10 = 1 × 2 × 3 *(ABC)*.

Having generated the interaction vectors, the scores on the dependent variable, Y, are regressed on all the coded vectors for factors, interactions among factors, and subjects. All the results can be obtained from a single run, provided the vectors are read in the proper order so as to lead to the correct partialing process. A logical ordering is to introduce sets of vectors that reflect the organization of the final analysis of variance table. That is, each set is composed of a vector or vectors that represent the main effects and interactions, followed by a subject vector that is designed to appropriate the proportion of variance, or the sum of squares for the error term for that set. Referring to the vector numbers of Table 14.9 and to those used above to identify the product vectors for the interaction terms, the ordering for the present example is as follows: 1 *(A)*, 4 (Total), 2 *(B)*, 7 *(AB)*, 5 (*B* Total), 3 *(C)*, 8 *(AC)*, 6 (*C* Total), 9 *(BC)*, and 10 *(ABC)*.

Table 14.8 Data for a Factorial with Two Within-Subjects Factors and One Between-Subjects Factor

Between-Subjects Factors	*Subjects*	*Within-Subjects Factors* B_1 C_1	B_1 C_2	B_2 C_1	B_2 C_2
A_1	1	3	2	5	4
	2	3	4	5	6
A_2	1	5	5	7	6
	2	8	6	5	6

Having entered the vectors in this sequence, one can obtain the proportions of variance, or the sums of squares, for each term from the computer output that lists the cumulated proportions of variance accounted for. In SPSS, for example, the proportions of variance can best be obtained from the column labeled R SQUARE CHANGE in the SUMMARY TABLE. The sums of squares, on the other hand, can best be obtained by following the procedures indicated in the preceding section. That is, to obtain the sum of squares for a

Table 14.9 Data of Table 14.8 Coded for Multiple Regression Analysis

			1	*2*	*3*	*4*	*5*	*6*
Cells	*Subjects*	*Y*	*A*	*B*	*C*	*Total*	*B Total*	*C Total*
$A_1B_1C_1$	1	3	1	1	1	14	5	8
	2	3	1	1	1	18	7	8
$A_2B_1C_1$	1	5	−1	1	1	23	10	12
	2	8	−1	1	1	25	14	13
$A_1B_1C_2$	1	2	1	1	−1	14	5	6
	2	4	1	1	−1	18	7	10
$A_2B_1C_2$	1	5	−1	1	−1	23	10	11
	2	6	−1	1	−1	25	14	12
$A_1B_2C_1$	1	5	1	−1	1	14	9	8
	2	5	1	−1	1	18	11	8
$A_2B_2C_1$	1	7	−1	−1	1	23	13	12
	2	5	−1	−1	1	25	11	13
$A_1B_2C_2$	1	4	1	−1	−1	14	9	6
	2	6	1	−1	−1	18	11	10
$A_2B_2C_2$	1	6	−1	−1	−1	23	13	11
	2	6	−1	−1	−1	25	11	12

NOTE: Vectors 1, 2, and 3 represent factors *A*, *B*, and *C*, respectively. Vectors 4, 5, and 6 represent overall total scores for subjects, subjects' total scores for levels of *B*, and subjects' total scores for levels of *C*, respectively.

given component subtract the REGRESSION SUM OF SQUARES reported in the step preceding the one in which the component has been entered into the analysis from the REGRESSION SUM OF SQUARES reported at the step in which the component under consideration has been included.

Following are excerpts of output obtained from the REGRESSION program of SPSS for the analysis of the data of Table 14.9.

Output

DEPENDENT VARIABLE Y

VECTOR	SUM OF SQUARES CHANGE	DF CHANGE	R SQUARE CHANGE
V1 *(A)*	16.00	1	.44444
V4 (Total)	2.50	1	.06944
V2 *(B)*	4.00	1	.11111
V7 *(AB)*	4.00	1	.11111
V5 (*B* Total)	4.50	1	.12500
V3 *(C)*	.25	1	.00694
V8 *(AC)*	.25	1	.00694
V6 (*C* Total)	2.00	1	.05556

V9 *(BC)*	.25	1	.00694
V10 *(ABC)*	.25	1	.00694
RESIDUAL	2.00	5	

Commentary

The values under R SQUARE CHANGE were obtained from the SUMMARY TABLE. The values for SUM OF SQUARES CHANGE were obtained by following the procedure outlined in the preceding section. The RESIDUAL SUM OF SQUARES reported in the output is the sum of squares for the error $BC \times$ Subjects within Groups.

Tests of Significance

As discussed earlier, it is necessary to adjust the degrees of freedom associated with each of the error terms, since each subject vector, which reflects a different error term, appropriates a single degree of freedom, regardless of the number of degrees of freedom associated with the error term that it reflects. The calculation of the F ratios then proceeds in the usual manner—by dividing the mean square for a given factor or interaction by its mean square error.

The analysis of the present example is summarized in Table 14.10. Note that the R^2 change and the *ss* were obtained from the output reported above. The *df* for the error terms, however, are *not* the ones reported in the output but rather the adjusted ones.

Finally, it will be noted that it is possible to use other approaches to the ordering of the vectors and still obtain the same results. For example, bearing in mind that the vectors representing the main effects and the interactions are mutually orthogonal, one may enter them first in any order and then enter the vector composed of subjects' overall total scores, followed by vectors com-

Table 14.10 Summary of Analysis of Data of Table 14.8

Source	*Vector*	R^2 *Change*	*ss*	*df*	*ms*	*F*
A	1	.44444	16.00	1	16.00	12.80
Subjects within Groups	4	.06944	2.50	2	1.25	
B	2	.11111	4.00	1	4.00	1.78
AB	7	.11111	4.00	1	4.00	1.78
$B \times$ Subjects within Groups	5	.12500	4.50	2	2.25	
C	3	.00694	.25	1	.25	.25
AC	8	.00694	.25	1	.25	.25
$C \times$ Subjects within Groups	6	.05556	2.00	2	1.00	
BC	9	.00694	.25	1	.25	.25
ABC	10	.00694	.25	1	.25	.25
$BC \times$ Subjects within Groups $(1 - R^2_{y\ 12\ldots10})$		.05556	2.00	2	1.00	
Total			36.00	15		

NOTE: For vector identification, see Table 14.9 and text.

posed of subjects' totals for the levels of the separate factors. Note that in order to effect the correct partialing, the vector of the overall total scores must precede the vectors composed of subjects' scores on separate factors. In the present example this alternative ordering will be as follows: vectors 1, 2, 3, 7, 8, 9, and 10, followed by vectors 4, 5, and 6.

SUMMARY

The present chapter dealt mainly with the mechanics of analyzing repeated-measures designs via multiple regression analysis. It was shown that the variables or factors in such designs are coded in the usual manner. In addition, depending on the design, one or more subject vectors are generated. These vectors are created by the procedure of criterion scaling. The dependent variable is regressed on the coded vectors, the products of such vectors representing different factors, and the subject vector(s). Entering the vectors in the analysis in an appropriate sequence enables one to identify the proportion of variance and sum of squares due to each component. After appropriate adjustments of the degrees of freedom for subjects and for the overall residual term, mean squares and F ratios are calculated.

Advantages and disadvantages of repeated-measures designs were briefly discussed, and it was pointed out that the latter are primarily due to stringent assumptions whose violation may lead to erroneous conclusions. Attention was also drawn to the alternative of analyzing repeated-measures designs via multivariate analysis of variance.

STUDY SUGGESTIONS

1. Discuss advantages and disadvantages of repeated-measures designs. Study references cited in the chapter regarding assumptions underlying such designs, and proposed alternative analytic approaches (i.e., MANOVA), particularly when the assumptions for univariate analysis are violated.
2. Following are illustrative data for six subjects, each of whom was measured under three trials, T_1, T_2, T_3.

	T_1	T_2	T_3
S_1	1	3	5
S_2	2	4	6
S_3	2	3	5
S_4	3	6	8
S_5	2	5	7
S_6	1	2	4

Code the trials and the subjects as described in the chapter. Do a multiple regression analysis of the dependent variable on the vectors for trials and the vector for subjects. Test the significance of the differences among the trials (remember to adjust the *df* for the subjects and the residual sums of squares). Display the results in a summary table.

3. Following are illustrative data for a factorial design with one between-subjects variable (A), and one within-subjects variable (B).

		B_1	B_2	B_3	B_4
	S_1	3	5	8	11
	S_2	2	3	5	8
	S_3	3	4	7	9
A_1	S_4	4	5	6	10

	S_5	3	6	8	12
	S_6	4	7	9	13
	S_1	4	7	9	13
	S_2	5	8	10	12
	S_3	6	8	10	14
A_2	S_4	6	9	11	13
	S_5	5	8	13	15
	S_6	7	10	12	14

Following the procedures shown in the chapter, code the variables and the subjects, generate product vectors for the interaction, and analyze the data. Display the results in a summary table (see, for example, Table 14.7). Remember to make the appropriate adjustments for the *df* in the output from the multiple regression analysis.

ANSWERS

2.

Source	*Prop. of Variance*	*ss*	*df*	*ms*	*F*
Trials	.66207	48.00000	2	24.00000	90.00*
Subjects	.30115	21.83333	5	4.36667	
Residual	.03678	2.66667	10	.26667	
Total	1.00000	72.50000	17		

$^*p < .001$.

3.

Source	*Prop. of Variance*	*ss*	*df*	*ms*	*F*
A	.19945	114.08333	1	114.08333	22.63*
Subjects within Groups	.08814	50.41667	10	5.04167	
B	.67599	386.66667	3	128.88889	215.81*
AB	.00510	2.91666	3	.97222	1.63
$B \times$ Subjects within Groups	.03132	17.91667	30	.59722	
Total	1.00000	572.00000	47		

$^*p < .001$.

PART 3

CAUSAL ANALYSIS

15

PATH ANALYSIS

In the present chapter path analysis—a method for studying patterns of causation among a set of variables—is presented. Because causal thinking plays a crucial role in the application of path analysis, the chapter begins with a brief discussion of causation. This is followed by a presentation of elements of path analysis and illustrations of its application to the analysis of correlations among a set of variables. The topic of testing causal models is then presented. The chapter concludes with a discussion of the analysis of covariances among a set of variables.

CAUSATION

The concept of causation has stirred a great deal of controversy among philosophers and scientists alike. The purpose of the present discussion is neither to take sides in this controversy nor to review it.[1] Instead, it is designed to draw attention to the fact that causal thinking plays an important role in scientific research. In the work of scientists, even in the work of those who are strongly opposed to the use of the term *causation,* one encounters the frequent use of terms that indicate or imply causal thinking. When behavioral scientists, for example, speak about the effects of child-rearing practices on the development of certain personality patterns, or the effect of reinforcement on subsequent behavior, or the reasons for delinquent behavior, or the influence of

[1]For discussions see, for example, Blalock (1964, 1971), Braithwaite (1953), Cook and Campbell (1979), Feigl and Brodbeck (1953), Hanson (1958, 1971), Lerner (1965), Scriven (1971, 1975), Simon (1957, 1968). For a discussion of causality in the context of multiple regression analysis, see Wold (1956) and Wold and Juréen (1953).

attitudes on perception, there is an implication of causation. Similarly, it has been noted (Alker, 1966) that while political scientists are reluctant to use causal language, they employ concepts (influence, power, decision making) that imply causal processes.

The tendency to imply causation, even when refraining from using the term, is reflected also in some of the methods employed by behavioral scientists. For example, proportions of variance are attributed to certain independent variables; or a presumed cause is partialed from two variables in order to observe whether the relation between them is spurious. "Thus, the difference between true and spurious correlations resolves into a difference between causal and noncausal connections (Brodbeck, 1963, p. 73)."[2]

Nagel (1965) summed up the status of the concept of causation, saying: "Though the *term* may be absent the *idea* for which it stands continues to have wide currency" (p. 11). Drawing attention to the fact that causal statements are frequent in the behavioral as well as the physical sciences, Nagel concludes: "In short, the idea of cause is not as outmoded in modern science as is sometimes alleged" (p. 11). That this is so is not surprising since the scientist's question of why a certain event has occurred carries with it an implication of causality. Moreover, a behavioral scientist who wishes to bring about desired changes in human behavior must be able to identify the factors affecting the behavior or, more plainly, the causes of the behavior.

In sum, scientists, qua scientists, seem to have a need to resort to causal frameworks, even though on philosophical grounds they may have reservations about the concept of causation.

Causation in Experimental and Nonexperimental Research

In experimental research the experimenter manipulates variables of interest and observes the manner in which the manipulation affects the variation of the dependent variable. In order to be reasonably sure that the observed variation in the dependent variable is indeed due to the manipulated variables, the experimenter must control other relevant variables. One of the most powerful methods of control is randomization.[3] Being in a position to manipulate and randomize, the experimenter may feel reasonably confident in making statements about the kinds of actions that need be taken in order to produce desired changes in the dependent variable.

The preceding is predicated, among other things, on the validity of the operational definition of the manipulated variable (see Chapter 9) and on the internal validity of the experiment (see Campbell & Stanley, 1963; Cook & Campbell, 1979). Although the validity of operational definitions and the internal validity of experiments are by no means always easily established, the situation is considerably more complex and more ambiguous in nonexperimental research because the researcher can neither manipulate nor randomize. While it is possible

[2]For a discussion of spurious correlations see Chapter 5. See also Blalock (1968), Brodbeck (1963), and Simon (1957, particularly Chapters 1–3).

[3]See Kerlinger (1973) for a discussion of the role of randomization in experiments.

to resort to statistical controls in lieu of randomization, the researcher must be constantly alert to the pitfalls inherent in the interpretation of analyses of data from nonexperimental research. This need for caution is probably best expressed in the oft-repeated admonition: "Correlation is no proof of causation." Nor does any other index prove causation, regardless of whether the index was derived from data collected in experimental or in nonexperimental research. Covariations or correlations among variables may be suggestive of causal linkages. Nevertheless, an explanatory scheme is not arrived at on the basis of the data, but rather on the basis of knowledge, theoretical formulations and assumptions, and logical analysis. It is the explanatory scheme of the researcher that determines the type of analysis to be applied to data, and not the other way around.

THE ROLE OF THEORY

The role of theory in the formulation of causal models has been most forcefully expressed by Hanson:

> Causes are connected with effects; but this is because our theories connect them, not because the world is held together by cosmic glue. The world *may* be glued together by imponderables, but that is irrelevant for understanding causal explanation. The notions behind "the cause x" and "the effect y" are intelligible only against a pattern of theory, namely one which puts guarantees on inferences from x to y. Such guarantees distinguish truly causal sequences from mere coincidence. (1958, p. 64)

In short, it is one's causal model about the pattern of causation among the variables under study that determines, among other things, the type of data to be collected and the method by which they are to be analyzed. Broadly speaking, the analysis of the data is designed to shed light on the question of whether or not the causal model is consistent with the data. If the model is inconsistent with the data, doubt is cast about the theory that has generated it. This is, of course, predicated on the assumption that the study was validly designed and executed. Consistency of the model with the data, however, does not constitute proof of a theory; at best it only lends support to it. Or, following Popper's (1959) contention that all one can accomplish through research is the falsification of theory, one would have to conclude that the theory has survived the test in that it has not been disconfirmed.

It is possible for competing causal models to be consistent with the same data. For example, consider the following competing models: (1) $X \rightarrow Y \rightarrow Z$; (2) $X \leftarrow Y \rightarrow Z$. The first model indicates that X affects Y, which in turn affects Z. The second model, on the other hand, indicates that Y affects X and Z. As is shown below, both models may be consistent with correlations among the three variables. The decision as to which of them is more tenable rests not on the data but rather on the theory that generated the causal model in the first place. *Therefore, although in the sequel statements will be made about a theory or a causal model being consistent with data, such statements should be under-*

stood to mean that the theory withstood the test; that it has not been disconfirmed.

What is needed, then, is a method of analysis designed to shed light on the tenability of a causal model formulated by the researcher. One such method is path analysis. In fact, one of its virtues is that in order for it to be validly applied, the researcher must make explicit his or her theoretical formulations, as well as the assumptions associated with them. Unfortunately, the popularity of path analysis has reached fad proportions, so it is frequently viewed as a panacea and is used without regard to theory and assumptions underlying its use (Bohrnstedt & Carter, 1971). Speaking of uses and abuses of path analysis in sociological research, Miller and Stokes (1975) point out: "One even hears the wail that the widespread acceptance of the technique has worked to limit what will be published. They charge that to publish in certain journals one must submit data to path analysis whether appropriate or not" (p. 193). Corroboration of this complaint is given by Coser (1975), who relates that "the editor of a major sociological journal, explained with some pride, no matter what the substantive merits of the paper might be, he would refuse to accept contributions using old-fashioned tabular methods rather than techniques of regression and path analysis" (p. 692).

It is important always to bear in mind that path analysis is a method, and as such its valid application is predicated on the competency of the person using it and the soundness of the theory that is being tested. As MacDonald (1977) so aptly put it: "If the model is not the correct model . . . parameter estimates will be returned [by the method], *no* red lights will flash, *no* alarm bells ring" (p. 84).

The following presentation is not intended to be exhaustive but rather to acquaint you with some of the basic principles and applications of path analysis. For more detailed treatments, see Blalock (1971), Duncan (1975), Heise (1975), Li (1975), and Wright (1934, 1954, 1960a, 1968).

PATH ANALYSIS

Path analysis was developed by Sewall Wright as a method for studying the direct and indirect effects of variables hypothesized as causes of variables treated as effects. As was noted above, path analysis is not a method for discovering causes, but a method applied to a causal model formulated by the researcher on the basis of knowledge and theoretical considerations. In Wright's words:

> . . . the method of path coefficients is not intended to accomplish the impossible task of deducing causal relations from the values of the correlation coefficients. It is intended to combine the quantitative information given by the correlations with such qualitative information as may be at hand on causal relations to give a quantitative interpretation. (Wright, 1934, p. 193)

> In cases in which the causal relations are uncertain, the method can be used to find the logical consequences of any particular hypothesis in regard to them. (Wright, 1921, p. 557)

Path Diagrams

The path diagram, although not essential for numerical analysis, is a useful device for displaying graphically the pattern of causal relations among a set of variables. In the causal model, a distinction is made between exogenous and endogenous variables. An *exogenous variable* is a variable whose variability is assumed to be determined by causes outside the causal model. Consequently, the determination of an exogenous variable is not under consideration in the model. Stated differently, no attempt is made to explain the variability of an exogenous variable or its relations with other exogenous variables. An *endogenous variable,* on the other hand, is one whose variation is explained by exogenous or endogenous variables in the system. The distinction between the two kinds of variables is illustrated in Figure 15.1, which depicts a path diagram consisting of four variables.

Variables 1 and 2 in Figure 15.1 are exogenous. The correlation between exogenous variables is depicted by a curved line with arrowheads at both ends, thus indicating that the researcher does not conceive of one variable being the cause of the other. Consequently, a relation between exogenous variables (in the present case r_{12}) remains unanalyzed in the system.

Variables 3 and 4 in Figure 15.1 are endogenous. Paths, in the form of unidirectional arrows, are drawn from the variables taken as causes (independent) to the variables taken as effects (dependent). The two paths leading from variables 1 and 2 to variable 3 indicate that variable 3 is dependent on variables 1 and 2.

The presentation in this chapter is limited to recursive models. This means that the causal flow in the model is unidirectional. Stated differently, it means that at a given point in time a variable cannot be both a cause and an effect of another variable. For example, if variable 2 in Figure 15.1 is taken as a cause of variable 3, then the possibility of variable 3 being a cause of variable 2 is ruled out (nonrecursive models are discussed in Chapter 16).

An endogenous variable treated as dependent in one set of variables may also be conceived as an independent variable in relation to other variables. Variable 3, for example, is taken as dependent on variables 1 and 2 and as one of the

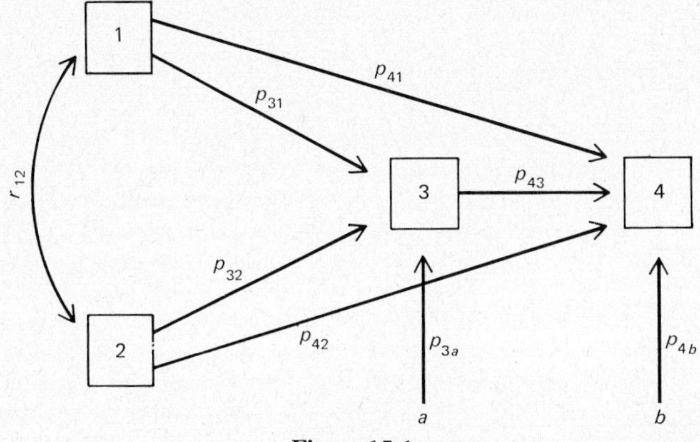

Figure 15.1

independent variables in relation to variable 4. It will be noted that in this example the causal flow is still unidirectional. Since it is almost never possible to account for the total variance of a variable, residual variables are introduced to indicate the effect of variables not included in the model. In Figure 15.1, *a* and *b* are residual variables. Note that *a* and *b* are analogous to the residual, *e*, discussed frequently in earlier chapters in the context of regression analysis (see, for example, Chapters 2 and 3).

Assumptions

Among the assumptions that underlie the application of path analysis as presented in this chapter are:

1. The relations among the variables in the model are linear, additive, and causal. Consequently, curvilinear, multiplicative, or interaction relations are excluded.

2. Each residual is not correlated with the variables that precede it in the model. Thus, for example, in Figure 15.1 it is assumed that *a* is not correlated with variables 1 and 2, and that *b* is not correlated with 1, 2, and 3. It can be shown that this implies that the residuals are not correlated among themselves. For the model depicted in Figure 15.1 this means that *a* is not correlated with *b*. The implication of the preceding statements is that all relevant variables are included in the model that is being tested. In other words, variables not included and subsumed under residuals are assumed to be not correlated with the relevant variables. Each endogenous variable is conceived of as linear combinations of exogenous and/or endogenous variables in the model and a residual. Exogenous variables are treated as "givens." Moreover, when exogenous variables are correlated among themselves, these correlations are treated as "givens" and remain unanalyzed.

3. There is a one-way causal flow in the system. That is, reciprocal causation between variables is ruled out.

4. The variables are measured on an interval scale.

5. The variables are measured without error.

It is shown below that, given the above assumptions, the method of path analysis reduces to the solution of one or more multiple linear regression analyses. Therefore, what was said earlier in this book about the consequences of violating the assumptions in multiple regression analysis (e.g., specification errors and measurement errors; see, in particular, Chapter 8) applies also to path analysis of recursive models. For additional discussions of the implications of weakening the above assumptions, see Bohrnstedt and Carter (1971), Duncan (1975), Heise (1969, 1975), and Kenny (1979).

Path Coefficients

Wright (1934) defines a path coefficient as:

> The fraction of the standard deviation of the dependent variable (with the appropriate sign) for which the designated factor is directly responsible, in the sense of the fraction which would be found if this factor varies to the same extent as in the observed data while all others (including the residual factors . . .) are constant. (p. 162)

In other words, a path coefficient indicates the direct effect of a variable hypothesized as a cause of a variable taken as an effect.

The symbol for a path coefficient is a p with two subscripts, the first indicating the effect (or the dependent variable), and the second subscript indicating the cause (the independent variable). Accordingly, p_{32} in Figure 15.1 indicates the direct effect of variable 2 on variable 3.

The Calculation of Path Coefficients

Each endogenous (dependent) variable in a causal model may be represented by an equation consisting of the variables upon which it is assumed to be dependent, and a term representing residuals, or variables not under consideration in the given model. For each independent variable in the equation there is a path coefficient indicating the amount of expected change in the dependent variable as a result of a unit change in the independent variable. Exogenous variables, it will be recalled, are assumed to be dependent on variables not included in the model, and are therefore represented by a residual term only. The letter e or u with an appropriate subscript is used to represent residuals. As an illustration, the equations for a four-variable causal model depicted in Figure 15.2 are given. Expressing all variables in standard score form (z score), the equations are

$$z_1 = e_1 \tag{15.1a}$$

$$z_2 = p_{21}z_1 + e_2 \tag{15.1b}$$

$$z_3 = p_{31}z_1 + p_{32}z_2 + e_3 \tag{15.1c}$$

$$z_4 = p_{41}z_1 + p_{42}z_2 + p_{43}z_3 + e_4 \tag{15.1d}$$

where the e's (i.e., variables not included in the model) are also expressed in standard scores. Variable 1 is exogenous and is therefore represented by a residual (e_1) only. Variable 2 is shown to be dependent on variable 1 and on e_2, which stands for variables outside the system affecting variable 2. Similar interpretations apply to the other equations. A set of equations such as (15.1) is referred to as a recursive system. It is a system of equations in which at least half of the path coefficients have been set equal to zero. Consequently, a recursive system can be organized in a triangular form, because the upper half of the matrix is assumed to consist of path coefficients which are equal to zero. For example, (15.1a) implies the following equation:

$$z_1 = e_1 + 0_{12}z_2 + 0_{13}z_3 + 0_{14}z_4$$

Similarly, for the other equations in (15.1).

As was discussed above, it is assumed that each of the residuals in (15.1) is not correlated with the variables in the equation in which it appears, nor with any of the variables preceding it in the model. It can be shown that these assumptions imply that the residuals are not correlated among themselves. Under such conditions, the solution for the path coefficients takes the form of ordinary least squares solutions for the β's (standardized regression coefficients) presented in earlier chapters of the book.

The process of calculating the path coefficients for the model depicted in Figure 15.2 is now demonstrated. Let us start with p_{21}, that is, the path coefficient indicating the effect of variable 1 on variable 2.

$$r_{12} = \frac{1}{N} \Sigma z_1 z_2$$

Substituting (15.1b) for z_2,

$$r_{12} = \frac{1}{N} \Sigma z_1(p_{21}z_1 + e_2)$$

$$= p_{21} \frac{\Sigma z_1 z_1}{N} + \frac{\Sigma z_1 e_2}{N}$$

$$r_{12} = p_{21} \tag{15.2}$$

The term $\Sigma z_1 z_1/N = \Sigma z_1^2/N = 1$ (the variance of standard scores equals one), and the covariance between variable 1 and e_2 is assumed to be zero. Thus $r_{12} = p_{21}$. It will be recalled that when dealing with a zero-order correlation β is equal to the correlation coefficient. Accordingly, $r_{12} = \beta_{21} = p_{21}$. It was thus demonstrated that the path coefficient from variable 1 to variable 2 is equal to β_{21}, which can be obtained from the data by calculating r_{12}. A path coefficient is equal to a zero-order correlation whenever a variable is conceived to be dependent on a single cause and a residual. (Note that this is the case for variable 2 in

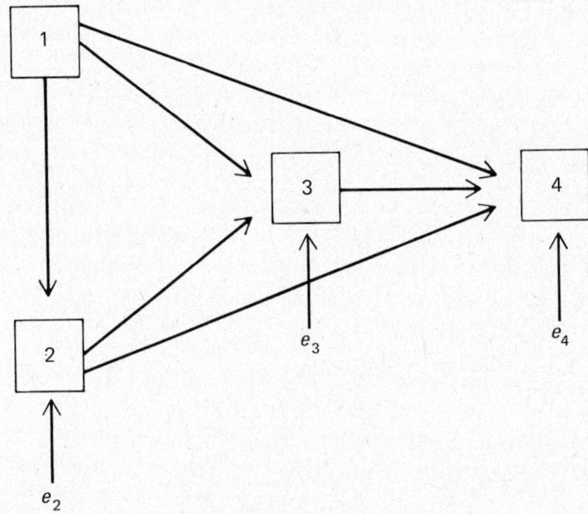

Figure 15.2

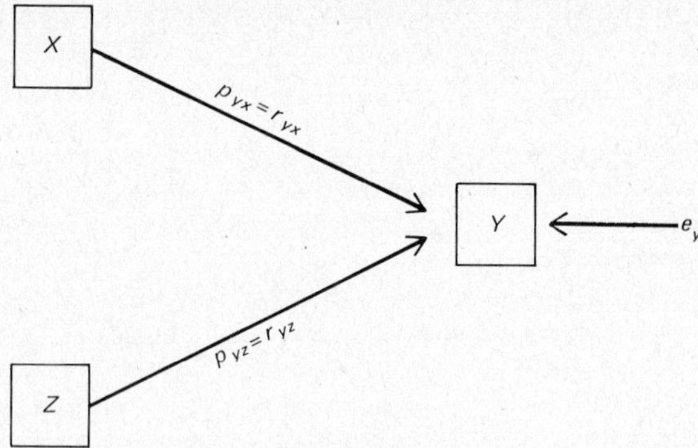

Figure 15.3

Figure 15.2.) The same principle still applies when a variable is conceived to be dependent on more than one cause, provided the causes are independent. For example, in Figure 15.3 variables X and Z are conceived as independent causes of Y. Therefore $p_{yx} = r_{yx}$ and $p_{yz} = r_{yz}$.

Returning now to Figure 15.2, it will be noted that the path coefficient from e_2 to variable 2 cannot be calculated directly because e_2 represents unmeasured variables, or variables not included in the system. In view of the assumption that e_2 is not correlated with variable 1, and recalling that all the variables are expressed in standard score form, the solution for the residual path coefficient (from e_2) is straightforward. It was said above that when causes are independent of each other, the effect of each cause (or its path coefficient) is equal to its zero-order correlation with the endogenous variables. Now, e_2 represents causes of variable 2 that are independent of variable 1. Therefore, the path coefficient from e_2 to variable 2 is equal to the correlation between e_2 and variable 2. But e_2 represents the residual term. It can be shown (see, for example, Nunnally, 1978, p. 129) that the correlation of variable 2 with its residuals (e_2) is equal to $\sqrt{1 - r^2_{12}}$. Consequently, the path coefficient from e_2 to variable 2 is equal to $\sqrt{1 - r^2_{12}}$. Note also that the variance of variable 2 accounted for by variable 1 is equal to r^2_{12}, and that accounted for by e_2 is equal to $1 - r^2_{12}$, which are the squares of the path coefficients (or the β's) for variable 1 and e_2, respectively.

Following the reasoning presented above, it may be shown that in a recursive system the path coefficient from unmeasured variables (or a residual path coefficient) to an endogenous variable, j, is equal to $\sqrt{1 - R^2_{j.12\ldots i}}$, where $R^2_{j.12\ldots i}$ is the squared multiple correlation of endogenous variable j with variables 1, 2, . . . , i that affect it. In the case of variable 2, of Figure 15.2, the preceding expression reduces to $\sqrt{1 - R^2_{2.1}} = \sqrt{1 - r^2_{21}}$.

We turn now to variable 3 of Figure 15.2. Note that this variable is affected by variables 1 and 2, which are not independent of each other. In fact, variable 2 is conceived to be dependent on variable 1 (in addition, it is dependent on e_2). It is now demonstrated how the coefficients for the two paths leading to variable 3—namely, p_{31} and p_{32}—are calculated.

$$r_{13} = \frac{1}{N} \Sigma z_1 z_3$$

Substituting (15.1c) for z_3:[4]

$$r_{13} = \frac{1}{N}\Sigma z_1(p_{31}z_1 + p_{32}z_2)$$

$$= p_{31}\frac{\Sigma z_1^2}{N} + p_{32}\frac{\Sigma z_1 z_2}{N}$$

$$r_{13} = p_{31} + p_{32}r_{12} \tag{15.3a}$$

Equation (15.3a) consists of two unknowns (p_{31} and p_{32}) and therefore cannot be solved (r_{12} and r_{13} are, of course, obtainable from the data). It is possible, however, to construct another equation with the same unknowns thereby making a solution possible. To obtain the second equation,

$$r_{23} = \frac{1}{N}\Sigma z_2 z_3$$

Again substituting (15.1c) for z_3,

$$r_{23} = \frac{1}{N}\Sigma z_2(p_{31}z_1 + p_{32}z_2)$$

$$= p_{31}\frac{\Sigma z_2 z_1}{N} + p_{32}\frac{\Sigma z_2^2}{N}$$

$$r_{23} = p_{31}r_{12} + p_{32} \tag{15.3b}$$

We thus have two equations involving the path coefficients leading to variable 3:

$$p_{31} + p_{32}r_{12} = r_{13} \tag{15.3a}$$

$$p_{31}r_{12} + p_{32} = r_{23} \tag{15.3b}$$

Equations (15.3) are similar to the normal equations used in earlier chapters for the solution of β's.[5] In fact, the above equations can be rewritten as follows:

$$\beta_{31.2} + \beta_{32.1}r_{12} = r_{13} \tag{15.4a}$$

$$\beta_{31.2}r_{12} + \beta_{32.1} = r_{23} \tag{15.4b}$$

Except for the fact that path coefficients are written without the dot notation, it is obvious that Equations (15.3) and (15.4) are identical. It is therefore possible to solve for the path coefficients in the same manner that one would solve for the β's; that is, by applying a least-squares solution to the regression of variable 3 on variables 1 and 2. Each path coefficient is equal to the β associated with the same variable. Thus, $p_{31} = \beta_{31.2}$ and $p_{32} = \beta_{32.1}$. Note that $p_{31} \neq p_{13}$. As

[4]Because of the assumptions about the residuals, or e's (see above), it is possible to drop these terms from the equations that follow, thereby simplifying the presentation.

[5]See Chapter 3, particularly the discussion in connection with Equations (3.15). Also, Chapter 4, the discussion in connection with Equation (4.15).

discussed earlier, p_{31} indicates the effect of variable 1 on variable 3, while p_{13} indicates the effect of variable 3 on variable 1. In the type of causal models under consideration in this chapter—models with one-way causation—it is not possible to have both p_{31} and p_{13}. The path coefficients that are calculated are those that reflect the causal model formulated by the researcher. If, as in the present example, the model indicates that variable 1 affects variable 3, then p_{31} is calculated.

In line with what was said earlier, the path coefficient from e_3 to variable 3 is equal to $\sqrt{1 - R^2_{3.12}}$.

Turning now to variable 4 in Figure 15.2, we note that it is necessary to calculate three path coefficients to indicate the effects of variables 1, 2, and 3 on variable 4. For this purpose three equations are constructed. This is accomplished in the same manner illustrated above. For example, the first equation is obtained as follows:

$$r_{14} = \frac{1}{N}\Sigma z_1 z_4$$

Substituting (15.1d) for z_4,

$$r_{14} = \frac{1}{N}\Sigma z_1(p_{41}z_1 + p_{42}z_2 + p_{43}z_3)$$

$$= p_{41}\frac{\Sigma z_1^2}{N} + p_{42}\frac{\Sigma z_1 z_2}{N} + p_{43}\frac{\Sigma z_1 z_3}{N}$$

$$r_{14} = p_{41} + p_{42}r_{12} + p_{43}r_{13}. \qquad (15.5a)$$

The two other equations are similarly obtained. They are

$$r_{24} = p_{41}r_{12} + p_{42} + p_{43}r_{23} \qquad (15.5b)$$

$$r_{34} = p_{41}r_{13} + p_{42}r_{23} + p_{43} \qquad (15.5c)$$

Again we have a set of normal equations (15.5), which are solved in the manner illustrated in earlier chapters.

In sum, then, when variables in a causal model are expressed in standardized form (z scores), and the assumptions discussed above are reasonably met, the path coefficients turn out to be standardized regression coefficients (β's) obtained in the ordinary regression analysis. But there is an important difference between the two analytic approaches. In ordinary regression analysis a dependent variable is regressed in a single analysis on all the independent variables under consideration. In path analysis, on the other hand, more than one regression analysis may be called for. At each stage, a variable taken as dependent is regressed on the variables upon which it is assumed to depend. The calculated β's are the path coefficients for the paths leading from the particular set of independent variables to the dependent variable under consideration. The model in Figure 15.2 requires three regression analyses for the calculation of all the path coefficients. The path from 1 to 2 (p_{21}) is calculated by regressing 2 on

1, as indicated by Equation (15.2). p_{31} and p_{32} are obtained by regressing variable 3 on variables 1 and 2, as indicated by Equations (15.3). p_{41}, p_{42}, and p_{43} are obtained by regressing variable 4 on variables 1, 2, and 3, as indicated by Equations (15.5). The path coefficient from e_4 to variable 4 is equal to $\sqrt{1 - R^2_{4.123}}$.

One of the advantages of path analysis is that it affords the decomposition of correlations among variables, thereby enhancing the interpretation of relations as well as the pattern of the effects of one variable on another. It is to these topics that we now turn.

The Decomposition of Correlations

Within a given causal model it is possible to decompose the correlation between an exogenous and an endogenous variable, or between two endogenous variables, into different components. For example, in Figure 15.4(a) variables 1 and 2 are exogenous, whereas variable 3 is endogenous. As was noted earlier, correlations among exogenous variables are treated as "givens" and can therefore not be decomposed. But what about the correlation between 1 and 3? From Figure 15.4(a) it may be noted that r_{13} consists of two parts: (1) the direct affect of 1 on 3, indicated by the path coefficient from 1 to 3 (p_{31}), and (2) that part of r_{13} that is due to the correlation of 1 with another cause of 3, namely 2, which is indicated by $r_{12}p_{32}$. Equivalently, the part of r_{13} that is due to correlated causes may be expressed as $r_{13} - p_{31}$ (because $r_{13} = p_{31} + r_{12}p_{32}$). From the viewpoint of causal explanation, the part of r_{13} that is due to correlated causes is left unanalyzed. Unless the researcher is able to state the cause, or causes, for the correlation between 1 and 2, which implies a revised causal model, there is no meaningful method of interpreting in causal terms the component of r_{13} that is due to correlated causes. This is why it is treated as unanalyzed.

The decomposition of r_{23}, of Figure 15.4(a), is similar to that of r_{13}. That is, p_{32} indicates the direct effect of 2 on 3, and $r_{12}p_{31} = r_{23} - p_{32}$ is the unanalyzed component because it is due to correlated causes (i.e., 1 and 2).

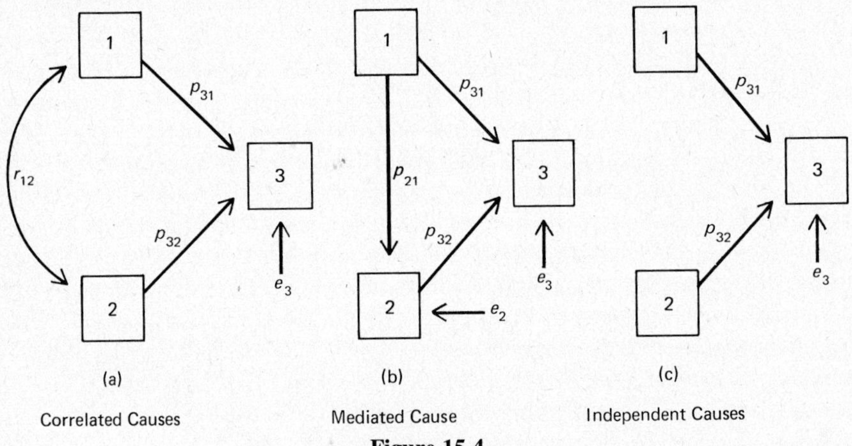

Figure 15.4

Consider now model (b) of Figure 15.4, where variable 1 is exogenous and variables 2 and 3 are endogenous. Note that variable 1 has a direct effect on variable 3 (indicated by p_{31}). In addition, variable 1 affects variable 2, which in turn affects variable 3. This latter route indicates the indirect effect of variable 1 on variable 3 as mediated by variable 2 (i.e., $p_{21}p_{32}$). r_{13} can therefore be decomposed into two parts: (1) the direct effect of 1 on 3, and (2) the indirect effect of 1 on 3 via 2. The sum of the direct and indirect effects has been labeled the total effect of one variable on another (e.g., Alwin & Hauser, 1975; Duncan, 1975; Finney, 1972). Some authors (e.g., Fox, 1980; Lewis-Beck & Mohr, 1976) have suggested that the sum of the direct and indirect effects be referred to as the effect coefficient of the variable taken as the cause on the effect variable.

In Figure 15.4(b) the total effect, or the effect coefficient, of variable 1 on variable 3 is equal to r_{13}. Contrast this with Figure 15.4(a), where variable 1 has no indirect effect on 3. While one may refer to the direct effect of 1 on 3 as the total effect (e.g., Alwin & Hauser, 1975, p. 46), some authors (e.g., Duncan, 1975, p. 41; MacDonald, 1979, p. 295) argue against such usage when referring to correlated exogenous variables. The reason is that so long as a set of variables is treated as exogenous, it is not possible to determine whether that part of the correlation between a given exogenous and an endogenous variable that is attributed to the correlation of the exogenous variable with other exogenous variables is due partly, or wholly, to some unspecified indirect effect. This point may be clarified by contrasting models (a) and (b) of Figure 15.4. In (a), variables 1 and 2 are treated as exogenous, and it is therefore not possible to tell whether either of them has an indirect effect on variable 3. In (b), on the other hand, only variable 1 is treated as exogenous, and it is possible to determine its indirect effect on variable 3, via variable 2.

Turning now to the decomposition of r_{23} of Figure 15.4(b), it will be noted that the direct effect of 2 on 3 is equal to p_{32}. The remainder of the correlation between 2 and 3 is spurious, due to the fact that they share a common cause—namely, variable 1. The spurious part of r_{23} is indicated by $p_{31}p_{21}$, or $r_{23} - p_{32}$.

In contrast to the path diagrams of Figure 15.4(a) and 15.4(b), the diagram of Figure 15.4(c) depicts a model with independent causes. In such a case the correlation between a cause and an effect is due solely to the direct effect of the former on the latter. Thus r_{13}, in Figure 15.4(c), is due to the direct effect of 1 on 3, or p_{31}, and r_{23} is due to the direct effect of 2 on 3, or p_{32}.

In sum, a correlation coefficient may be decomposed into the following components: (1) Direct Effect (DE); (2) Indirect Effects (IE); (3) Unanalyzed (U) due to correlated causes; and (4) Spurious (S) due to common causes. The sum of DI and IE is the total effect, or the effect coefficient. Some authors (e.g., Fox, 1980) refer to the sum of U and S as the noncausal part of the correlation coefficient. From the preceding discussion it should be evident that not all correlations consist of the four components indicated above. Thus, for example, spurious components may be identified only for correlations among endogenous variables. Unanalyzed components, on the other hand, may be identified only when the model consists of correlated exogenous variables. Furthermore, depending on the causal model, a variable may have only an indirect effect on another variable (see numerical examples, below).

With the above considerations in mind, we turn now to more detailed treatments of the decomposition of correlations. This is illustrated first for the four-variable model depicted in Figure 15.2. For convenience, the necessary equations that were developed in the previous section in connection with this model are repeated.

$$r_{12} = p_{21} \tag{15.2}$$

$$r_{13} = p_{31} + p_{32}r_{12} \tag{15.3a}$$

$$r_{23} = p_{31}r_{12} + p_{32} \tag{15.3b}$$

$$r_{14} = p_{41} + p_{42}r_{12} + p_{43}r_{13} \tag{15.5a}$$

$$r_{24} = p_{41}r_{12} + p_{42} + p_{43}r_{23} \tag{15.5b}$$

$$r_{34} = p_{41}r_{13} + p_{42}r_{23} + p_{43} \tag{15.5c}$$

Look back at Figure 15.2 and note that, except for the residual (e_2) which is assumed to be not correlated with variable 1, variable 2 is affected by variable 1 only. Therefore r_{12} is due solely to the direct effect of variable 1 and variable 2 as is indicated in Equation (15.2).

Consider now the correlation between variables 1 and 3. Since $r_{12} = p_{21}$, see Equation (15.2), it is possible to substitute p_{21} for r_{12} in Equation (15.3a), obtaining

$$r_{13} = \underset{\text{DE}}{p_{31}} + \underset{\text{IE}}{p_{32}p_{21}} \tag{15.3a$'$}$$

It can now be seen that r_{13} is composed of two components. The direct effect of variable 1 on 3 is indicated by p_{31}, whereas the term $p_{32}p_{21}$ indicates the indirect effect of variable 1 on variable 3 via variable 2 (see Figure 15.2 for these direct and indirect paths).

Substituting p_{21} for r_{12} in Equation (15.3b),

$$r_{23} = \underset{\text{S}}{p_{31}p_{21}} + \underset{\text{DE}}{p_{32}} \tag{15.3b$'$}$$

The decomposition of the correlation between variables 2 and 3 indicates that it is composed of two components: the direct effect of 2 on 3 (p_{32}), and a spurious component ($p_{31}p_{21}$), which is due to a common cause affecting the two variables (variable 1).

Decompose now the correlation between variables 1 and 4. In Equation (15.5a) substitute p_{21} for r_{12}. In addition, substitute for r_{13} in Equation (15.5a) the right-hand term of Equation (15.3a′). Making these substitutions:

$$\begin{aligned} r_{14} &= p_{41} + p_{42}p_{21} + p_{43}(p_{31} + p_{32}p_{21}) \\ &= \underset{\text{DE}}{p_{41}} + \underbrace{p_{42}p_{21} + p_{43}p_{31} + p_{43}p_{32}p_{21}}_{\text{IE}} \end{aligned} \tag{15.5a$'$}$$

It is evident that the correlation between variable 1 and 4 is composed of a direct effect (p_{41}) and several indirect effects as follows: $1 \rightarrow 2 \rightarrow 4$; $1 \rightarrow 3 \rightarrow 4$; $1 \rightarrow 2 \rightarrow 3 \rightarrow 4$.

Now, decompose the correlation between variable 2 and 4. In Equation (15.5b) substitute p_{21} for r_{12}, and Equation (15.3b′) for r_{23}:

$$r_{24} = p_{41}p_{21} + p_{42} + p_{43}(p_{31}p_{21} + p_{32})$$

$$= p_{41}p_{21} + p_{42} + p_{43}p_{31}p_{21} + p_{43}p_{32}$$

Rearrange the terms:

$$r_{24} = \underset{\text{DE}}{p_{42}} + \underset{\text{IE}}{p_{43}p_{32}} + \underbrace{p_{41}p_{21} + p_{43}p_{31}p_{21}}_{\text{S}} \qquad (15.5\text{b}')$$

Clearly, variable 2 affects 4 directly, as well as indirectly via variable 3. In addition, part of r_{24} is spurious, as indicated above.

Finally, in Equation (15.5c) substitute (15.3a′) for r_{13} and (15.3b′) for r_{23}, and rearrange the terms to obtain the decomposition of r_{34}.

$$r_{34} = \underset{\text{DE}}{p_{43}} + \underbrace{p_{41}p_{31} + p_{41}p_{21}p_{32} + p_{42}p_{21}p_{31} + p_{42}p_{32}}_{\text{S}} \qquad (15.5\text{c}')$$

Variable 3 has only a direct effect on variable 4. The remainder of the correlation between 3 and 4 is spurious, due to common causes (i.e., variables 1 and 2) as indicated above.

Using the four variables under consideration, it will be instructive to note how the decomposition of the correlation coefficients will be affected if causal models that differ from the one depicted in Figure 15.2 were posited. Assume, first, that the model is as depicted in Figure 15.5. Note that this time variables 1 and 2 are treated as exogenous. Consequently, unlike the model of Figure 15.2, the correlation between 1 and 2 is unanalyzed.

Following the procedures outlined above, the decomposition of the correlations among the variables in Figure 15.5 is as follows.

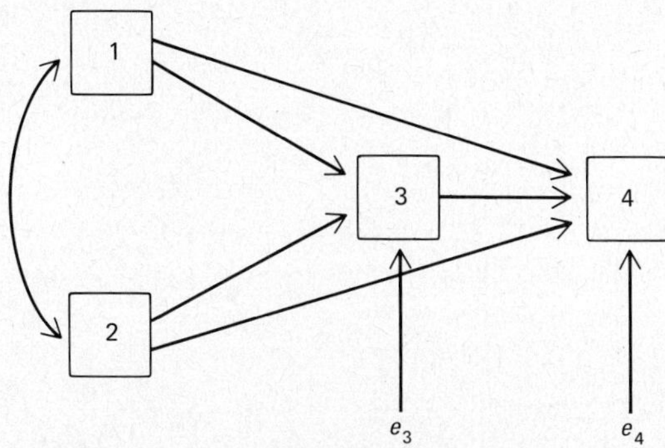

Figure 15.5

$$r_{13} = \underset{\text{DE}}{p_{31}} + \underset{\text{U}}{p_{32}r_{12}} \tag{15.6}$$

$$r_{23} = \underset{\text{DE}}{p_{32}} + \underset{\text{U}}{p_{31}r_{12}} \tag{15.7}$$

$$r_{14} = \underset{\text{DE}}{p_{41}} + \underset{\text{IE}}{p_{43}p_{31}} + \underbrace{p_{42}r_{12} + p_{43}p_{32}r_{12}}_{\text{U}} \tag{15.8}$$

$$r_{24} = \underset{\text{DE}}{p_{42}} + \underset{\text{IE}}{p_{43}p_{32}} + \underbrace{p_{41}r_{12} + p_{43}p_{31}r_{12}}_{\text{U}} \tag{15.9}$$

$$r_{34} = \underset{\text{DE}}{p_{43}} + \underbrace{p_{41}p_{31} + p_{41}p_{32}r_{12} + p_{42}p_{32} + p_{42}p_{31}r_{12}}_{\text{S}} \tag{15.10}$$

Note that although some of the elements of r_{34} involve r_{12}, they still comprise part of the spurious component because variables 1 and 2 are common, though correlated, causes of 3 and 4.

Careful study of the equations for the two causal models (Figures 15.2 and 15.5) will reveal that for a given endogenous variable the direct effects are the same. Thus, for example, the direct effects of variables 1, 2, and 3 on 4 are the same in both models. The two models differ in the degree to which remaining terms are elaborated. Contrast, for example, Equations (15.5a′) and (15.8). Both refer to the correlation between variable 1 and 4. But (15.5a′) decomposes the r_{14} into direct and indirect effects of 1 on 4, whereas (15.8) leaves the part of the correlation that involves r_{12} (the correlated causes) as unanalyzed. Similarly, r_{13} of Figure 15.2 is decomposed into a direct and indirect effect, (15.3a′), whereas r_{13} of Figure 15.5 is decomposed into a direct effect and a component that remains unanalyzed (see Equation (15.6)).

In short, the more elaborate the causal model, the better is one in a position to decompose the correlations among the variables into unambiguous components. This important point will perhaps become clearer if we turn to yet another causal model for the four variables under consideration. Consider the model depicted in Figure 15.6. This time variables 1, 2, and 3 are treated as exogenous. Consequently, the equations for this model are:

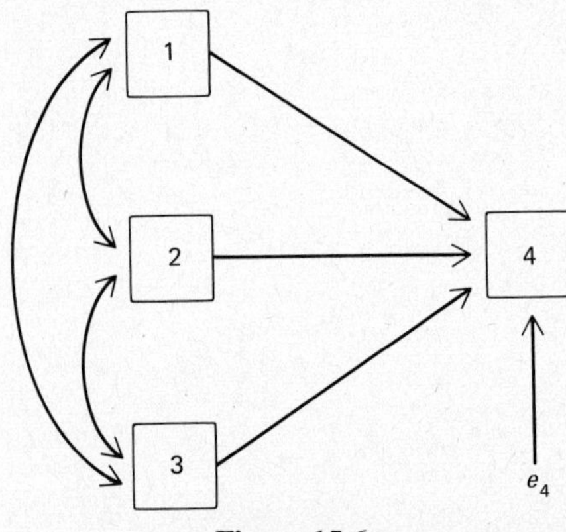

Figure 15.6

$$r_{14} = p_{41} + p_{42}r_{12} + p_{43}r_{13} \tag{15.11a}$$

$$r_{24} = p_{42} + p_{41}r_{12} + p_{43}r_{23} \tag{15.11b}$$

$$r_{34} = p_{43} + p_{41}r_{13} + p_{42}r_{23} \tag{15.11c}$$

Note that the first term in the right-hand side of Equations (15.11) indicates the direct effect of each of the exogenous variables on the endogenous variable (4). In this respect, the three models are alike. But, unlike the preceding models, all the remaining terms in Equations (15.11) are unanalyzed because they involve correlated exogenous variables. Because the model of Figure 15.6 is the least elaborate of the three, it affords the least decomposition of the correlations into unambiguous components. To further note what is taking place in the decomposition of the correlations for different models, compare Equations (15.5) with (15.11). Note that, except for the rearrangement of the terms, the two sets of equations are identical. But because (15.5) refer to a more elaborate model (Figure 15.2) it was possible to further decompose the elements (see Equations (15.5a′), (15.5b′) and (15.c′)). A similar decomposition was not possible for the model of Figure 15.6.

It is very important to note that the analyses of the three models discussed above are based on the same data. That is, the correlations among the four variables are used to calculate the different components. It should therefore be clear that the choice among these and other possible models cannot and should not be made on the basis of the data. As was said earlier, the causal model reflects the theoretical formulation regarding the relations among the variables under consideration. The absence of such a model precludes any decomposition of the correlations. Stated differently, it is not possible to speak of direct and indirect effects, or about spurious and unanalyzed components when a causal model is not posited.

Finally, it will be noted that when a dependent variable is regressed on a set of independent variables, and the β's are interpreted as indices of the effects of each of the independent variables on the dependent variable, a path analytic model is in effect being used. In other words, all the independent variables are treated as exogenous (as in Figure 15.6). Such a model is the most rudimentary possible causal model, indicating that the researcher is either unwilling or unable to explicate the causes of the relations among the exogenous variables. Consequently, all that was said earlier in this book about the interpretation of a regression equation (see, in particular, Chapter 8) applies equally to models such as the one depicted in Figure 15.6. For example, when multicollinearity is relatively high, the researcher is forced to conclude that most or all the variables have little direct effects on the dependent variable, and that the correlation of each independent variable with the dependent variable is largely due to the operation of correlated causes. But what this, in effect, means is that the researcher knows very little about the phenomenon under study, thereby precluding more elaborate analyses of the data.

NUMERICAL EXAMPLES

In the present section, several numerical examples are presented. The sole purpose here is to illustrate the calculations of path coefficients, the decomposition of correlation coefficients, and the use of path coefficients to reproduce the correlation matrix. Tests of causal models are taken up in a subsequent section.

Three-Variable Models

Suppose that a researcher has postulated a three-variable causal model as depicted in Figure 15.7. That is, variable 1 affects variables 2 and 3, and variable 2 affects variable 3. Suppose that the correlations are $r_{12} = .50$; $r_{23} = .50$; and $r_{13} = .25$. The equations of the model of Figure 15.7 are

$$z_1 = e_1$$

$$z_2 = p_{21}z_1 + e_2$$

$$z_3 = p_{31}z_1 + p_{32}z_2 + e_3$$

Following the procedures outlined in the preceding section, calculate the path coefficients:

$$p_{21} = \beta_{21} = r_{21} = .50$$

To obtain the path coefficients from variables 1 and 2 to 3 it is necessary to regress the latter on the two former variables in order to calculate $\beta_{31.2} = p_{31}$ and $\beta_{32.1} = p_{32}$. Formulas for the calculation of β's when the model consists of two independent variables have been presented earlier in the book; see, for example Formula (3.15). For the present example,

$$\beta_{31.2} = \frac{r_{31} - r_{32}r_{12}}{1 - r_{12}^2} = \frac{(.25) - (.50)(.50)}{1 - .50^2} = \frac{.25 - .25}{1 - .25} = \frac{0}{.75} = .00$$

$$\beta_{32.1} = \frac{r_{32} - r_{31}r_{12}}{1 - r_{12}^2} = \frac{(.50) - (.25)(.50)}{1 - .50^2} = \frac{.50 - .125}{1 - .25} = \frac{.375}{.75} = .50$$

Therefore $p_{31} = .00$ and $p_{32} = .50$.

The path coefficient from e_2 to variable 2 is equal to $\sqrt{1 - r_{12}^2} = \sqrt{1 - .50^2} = .866$. As was discussed in the preceding section, the path coefficient from e_3 to variable 3 is equal to $\sqrt{1 - R_{3.12}^2}$. Using Formula (3.20),

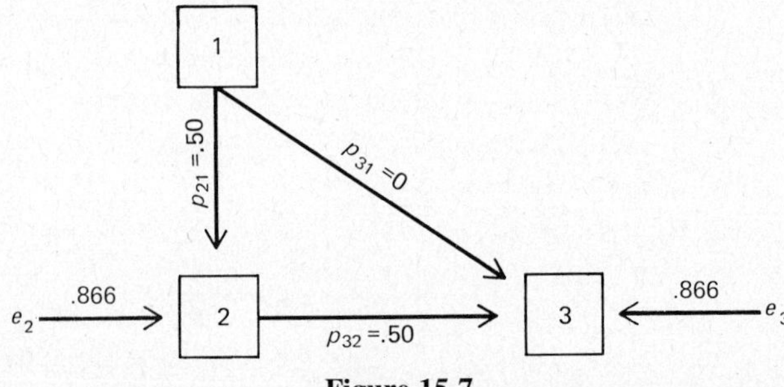

Figure 15.7

$$R^2_{3.12} = \frac{r^2_{31} + r^2_{32} - 2r_{31}r_{32}r_{12}}{1 - r^2_{12}} = \frac{(.25)^2 + (.50)^2 - 2(.25)(.50)(.50)}{1 - .50^2} = .25$$

The path coefficient from e_3 is therefore $\sqrt{1 - .25} = .866$.

We turn now to a demonstration of how the path coefficients calculated above may be used for the reproduction of the correlation coefficients among the variables. This demonstration is also an illustration of the decomposition of each of the correlation coefficients. For convenience, the following abbreviations will be used to identify the different components of the correlation coefficient: DE = Direct Effect; IE = Indirect Effect; U = Unanalyzed; S = Spurious.

The equations of the model of Figure 15.7 (see above) will be used without comment as the procedures and the assumptions that they are based upon were discussed in detail in the preceding section. Reproduce:

$$r_{12} = \frac{1}{N}\Sigma z_1 z_2 = \frac{1}{N}\Sigma z_1(p_{21}z_1) = p_{21} = \underset{\text{DE}}{.50}$$

Since there are no intervening variables between variables 1 and 2, variable 1 can have only a direct effect on variable 2. Accordingly, this is also the total effect of 1 on 2.

Turning now to r_{13}, and using the relevant equations of the model of Figure 15.7 (see above),

$$r_{13} = \frac{1}{N}\Sigma z_1 z_3 = \frac{1}{N}\Sigma z_1(p_{31}z_1 + p_{32}z_2) = p_{31} + p_{32}r_{12}$$

Since $r_{12} = p_{21}$,

$$r_{13} = p_{31} + p_{32}p_{21} = \underset{\text{DE}}{.00} + \underset{\text{IE}}{(.50)(.50)} = .25$$

Note that using the appropriate path coefficients r_{13} is reproduced. Note also the separate components of r_{13}. Variable 1 has no direct effect on variable 3. The indirect effect of variable 1 on 3 is .25, which is also the total effect of 1 on 3.

Turning now to r_{23}:

$$r_{23} = \frac{1}{N}\Sigma z_2 z_3 = \frac{1}{N}\Sigma z_2(p_{31}z_1 + p_{32}z_2) = p_{31}r_{12} + p_{32}$$

Since $r_{12} = p_{21}$,

$$r_{23} = p_{31}p_{21} + p_{32} = \underset{\text{S}}{(.00)(.50)} + \underset{\text{DE}}{.50} = .50$$

Again, the correlation between 2 and 3 is reproduced by the use of the path coefficients. Also, the direct effect of 2 on 3 is .50, which is the total effect of 2 on 3. Note that in the present example r_{23} has no spurious component.

The foregoing calculations demonstrate how the correlations among the variables, or more succinctly the correlation matrix **(R)**, may be reproduced by using the path coefficients. As is discussed below, the ability to reproduce **R** by using the path coefficients plays an important role in the assessment of the validity of a given causal model. *It is therefore very important to recognize that in just-identified, or exactly identified, causal models it is possible to reproduce* ***R****, regardless of how questionable, or even bizarre, the causal model may be on substantive or logical grounds*. The topic of identification in causal models is discussed below. At present, it will suffice to point out that a recursive model is just identified when all the variables are interconnected either by curved lines (among the exogenous variables) or by paths (among the exogenous and the endogenous variables, and among the endogenous variables themselves), and the assumptions about the residuals are tenable (see earlier section). Such a model is referred to as fully recursive.

A just-identified model is one in which the number of equations is equal to the number of parameters that are to be estimated, thereby affording a unique solution for each of them. The model of Figure 15.7 is an example of a just-identified model.

The preceding point is now illustrated numerically by changing the causal model among the three variables of Figure 15.7. Assume now that the hypothesized model is as in Figure 15.8. Recall that $r_{12} = .50$; $r_{23} = .50$, and $r_{13} = .25$. Following the procedures used above, calculate the path coefficients for the model of Figure 15.8:

$$p_{13} = \beta_{13} = r_{13} = .25$$

$$p_{23} = \beta_{23.1} = \frac{r_{23} - r_{21}r_{13}}{1 - r^2_{13}} = \frac{(.50) - (.50)(.25)}{1 - .25^2} = \frac{.375}{.9375} = .40$$

$$p_{21} = \beta_{21.3} = \frac{r_{21} - r_{23}r_{13}}{1 - r^2_{13}} = \frac{(.50) - (.50)(.25)}{1 - .25^2} = \frac{.375}{.9375} = .40$$

$$e_1 = \sqrt{1 - r^2_{13}} = \sqrt{1 - .25^2} = .968$$

$$R^2_{2.13} = \frac{r^2_{21} + r^2_{23} - 2r_{21}r_{23}r_{13}}{1 - r^2_{13}} = \frac{(.50)^2 + (.50)^2 - 2(.50)(.50)(.25)}{1 - .25^2} = \frac{.375}{.9375} = .40$$

$$e_2 = \sqrt{1 - R^2_{2.13}} = \sqrt{1 - .40} = .775$$

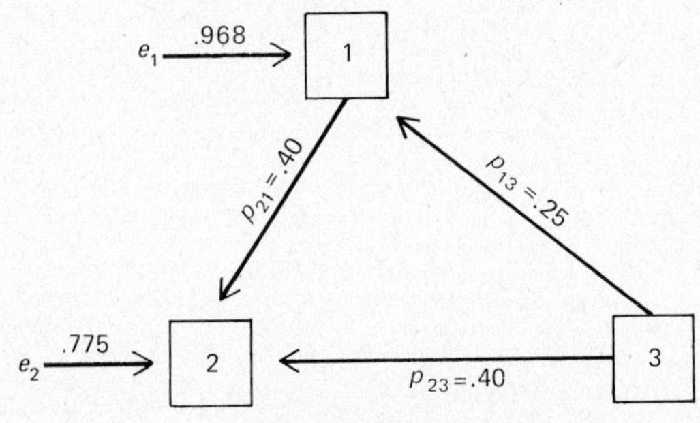

Figure 15.8

The above results are now used to reproduce **R.** The equations for the model of Figure 15.8 are:

$$z_3 = e_3$$

$$z_1 = p_{13}z_3 + e_1$$

$$z_2 = p_{23}z_3 + p_{21}z_1 + e_2$$

$$r_{13} = \frac{1}{N}\Sigma z_3 z_1 = \frac{1}{N}\Sigma z_3(p_{13}z_3) = p_{13} = \underset{\text{DE}}{.25}$$

The direct effect, which is also the total effect, of variable 3 on 1 is .25.

$$r_{23} = \frac{1}{N}\Sigma z_3 z_2 = \frac{1}{N}\Sigma z_3(p_{23}z_3 + p_{21}z_1) = p_{23} + p_{21}r_{13}$$

Since $r_{13} = p_{13}$,

$$r_{23} = p_{23} + p_{21}p_{13} = \underset{\text{DE}}{.40} + \underset{\text{IE}}{(.40)(.25)} = .50$$

The direct effect of 3 on 2 is .4. The indirect effect of 3 on 2 is .1 [(.40)(.25)]. The total effect of 3 on 2 (DE + IE) is .5, which is equal to r_{23}.

$$r_{12} = \frac{1}{N}\Sigma z_1 z_2 = \frac{1}{N}\Sigma z_1(p_{23}z_3 + p_{21}z_1) = p_{23}r_{13} + p_{21}$$

Since $r_{13} = p_{13}$,

$$r_{12} = p_{23}p_{13} + p_{21} = \underset{\text{S}}{(.40)(.25)} + \underset{\text{DE}}{(.40)} = .50$$

Note that the direct effect of 1 on 2 is .40, which is also the total effect of 1 on 2. Further, part of the correlation between 1 and 2 is spurious (.1) because these two variables share a common cause, variable 3.

It has now been demonstrated that using the path coefficients for the model of Figure 15.8 it is possible to reproduce **R.** Clearly, the models of Figures 15.7 and 15.8 are radically different. Yet, the path coefficients obtained in each enable one to reproduce **R.** This is because both models are just identified. Path coefficients for any other just-identified model for the three variables under consideration will be equally effective in reproducing **R.**

In sum, the fact that **R** can be reproduced in just-identified models has no bearing on the assessment of the validity of a specific causal model being considered. It is only in overidentified models, to which we now turn, that one may use the reproduction of **R** for the purpose of assessing the validity of a causal model.

Consider the causal model depicted in Figure 15.9. According to this model, variable 1 affects variable 2, which in turn affects variable 3. Note that the absence of a path from variable 1 to variable 3 indicates that it is hypothesized

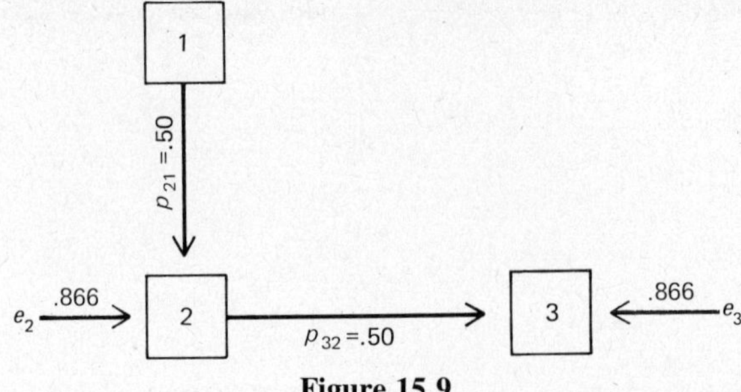

Figure 15.9

that the former has no direct effect on the latter. The model of Figure 15.9 is an example of an overidentified model. Essentially, what this means is that the model contains more information than is necessary to estimate the path coefficients. Specifically, there are three knowns (the correlations among the three variables) and only two unknowns (the two path coefficients). In the present case, one can construct three equations for two unknowns, hence the overidentification.

Assume that the correlations among the variables of model 15.9 are the same as those in the earlier models (i.e., $r_{12} = .50$, $r_{23} = .50$, $r_{13} = .25$). Therefore,

$$p_{21} = \beta_{21} = r_{12} = .50$$

$$p_{32} = \beta_{32} = r_{23} = .50$$

$$e_2 = \sqrt{1 - r_{12}^2} = \sqrt{1 - .50^2} = .866$$

$$e_3 = \sqrt{1 - r_{23}^2} = \sqrt{1 - .50^2} = .866$$

Now, the equations for the model of Figure 15.9 are

$$z_1 = e_1$$

$$z_2 = p_{21}z_1 + e_2$$

$$z_3 = p_{32}z_2 + e_3$$

Using the path coefficients obtained above reproduce the correlation between 1 and 3.

$$r_{13} = \frac{1}{N}\Sigma z_1 z_3 = \frac{1}{N}\Sigma z_1(p_{32}z_2) = p_{32}r_{12}$$

Since $r_{12} = p_{21}$,

$$r_{13} = \underset{\text{IE}}{p_{32}\,p_{21}} = (.50)(.50) = .25$$

The fact that r_{13} could be reproduced on the basis of the calculated path coefficients indicates that the postulated model in Figure 15.9 is consistent with the data. Specifically, this means that postulating a model in which 1 affects 3 only indirectly is consistent with the data.

Two points need to be made in connection with the preceding statement. One, while in this example r_{13} was exactly reproduced, this will generally not happen. But, as discussed below, a close approximation of r_{13} may serve as evidence of the consistency of the model with the data. Two, different overidentified causal models may be equally effective in reproducing **R**. Therefore, as was noted earlier, consistency of a causal model with a set of data does not constitute proof of the validity of the model. This issue is discussed in detail below (see Testing Causal Models). At this stage it will only be demonstrated that path coefficients for a causal model that differs from the one depicted in Figure 15.9 are equally effective in reproducing r_{13}.

Consider the model depicted in Figure 15.10, according to which variable 2 is a common cause of variables 1 and 3. For this model, $p_{12} = r_{12} = .50$, and $p_{32} = r_{23} = .50$. The equations for this model are

$$z_2 = e_2$$

$$z_1 = p_{12}z_2 + e_1$$

$$z_3 = p_{32}z_2 + e_3$$

$$r_{13} = \frac{1}{N}\Sigma z_1 z_3 = \frac{1}{N}\Sigma z_1(p_{32}z_2) = p_{32}r_{12}$$

Since $r_{12} = p_{12}$,

$$r_{13} = p_{32}p_{12} = (.50)(.50) = .25$$

S

Thus, r_{13} was exactly reproduced in the model of Figure 15.10 as well as in that of Figure 15.9. But these two models are radically different from each other. In Figure 15.9 it is postulated the r_{13} is due to the indirect effect of 1 on 3, via 2. In Figure 15.10, on the other hand, it is postulated that r_{13} is spurious. To repeat: from the point of view of reproducing r_{13} both models are consistent with the data.

We turn now to yet another overidentified causal model for the three variables under consideration. This time, it is hypothesized that variable 3 affects

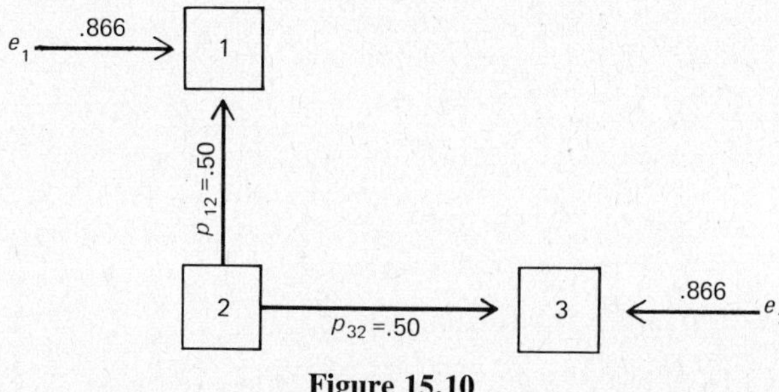

Figure 15.10

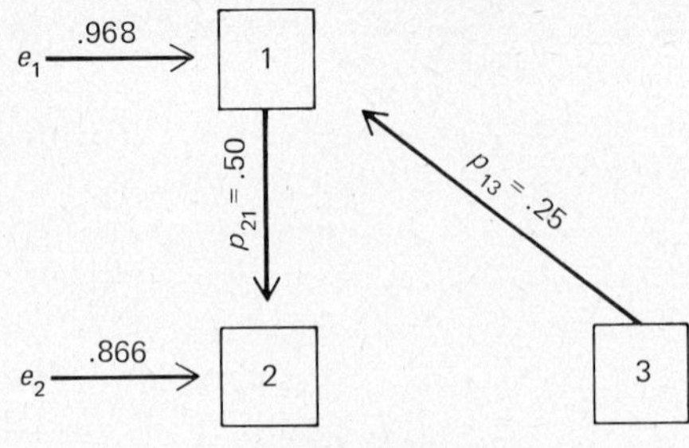

Figure 15.11

variable 1, which in turn affects variable 2. In other words, it is hypothesized that 3 affects 2 indirectly but not directly. This model is depicted in Figure 15.11. The equations for this model are

$$z_3 = e_3$$

$$z_2 = p_{21}z_1 + e_2$$

$$z_1 = p_{13}z_3 + e_1$$

Therefore,

$$p_{13} = r_{13} = .25 \qquad p_{21} = r_{21} = .50$$

Attempting now to reproduce r_{23},

$$r_{23} = \frac{1}{N}\Sigma z_3 z_2 = \frac{1}{N}\Sigma z_3(p_{21}z_1) = p_{21}r_{13}$$

Since $r_{13} = p_{13}$,

$$r_{23} = p_{21}p_{13} = (.50)(.25) = \underset{\text{IE}}{.125}$$

Note that there is a very large discrepancy between the original r_{23} (.50) and the reproduced one (.125), indicating that the model of Figure 15.11 does not fit the data. One possibility is that 3 affects 2 directly as well as indirectly. As was noted earlier, the topic of testing causal models is taken up later in this chapter. At this stage, the sole purpose was to demonstrate that the use of path coefficients to reproduce r_{23} fell far short of the mark.

We turn now to a four-variable model. This time, however, the variables are given substantive meaning in the hope of thereby enhancing the understanding of the use of causal models in behavioral research.

An Example from Educational Research

The causal model of Figure 15.12 was first presented in Chapter 7 (see Figure 7.4) where it was used for the purpose of illustrating incremental partitioning of variance. The illustrative data connected with this model were sub-

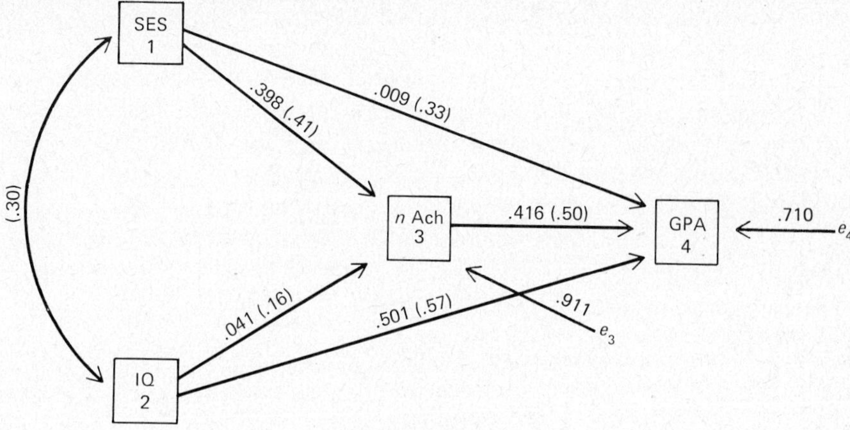

Figure 15.12

sequently used in Chapter 7 for the purpose of illustrating the application of commonality analysis. The same data were used again in Chapter 8 in connection with the study of effects of independent variables on a dependent variable. It was felt that using the same model and the same data here will be instructive in affording comparisons of path analysis with the analytic methods presented earlier. For convenience, the correlations among the variables are repeated in the upper half matrix of Table 15.1.

Assume that the causal model for the variables in this example is the one depicted in Figure 15.12. Note that SES and IQ are treated as exogenous variables; SES and IQ are assumed to affect *n* Ach.; SES, IQ, and *n* Ach are assumed to affect GPA.[6] Since it will be necessary to make frequent reference to these variables in the form of subscripts, it will be more convenient to identify them by the numbers attached to them in Figure 15.12. Accordingly, 1 = SES, 2 = IQ, 3 = *n* Ach, and 4 = GPA.

Table 15.1 Original and Reproduced Correlations for a Four-Variable Model; *N* = 100

	1 *SES*	*2* *IQ*	*3* *n Ach*	*4* *GPA*
1	1.000	.300	.410	.330
2	.300	1.000	.160	.570
3	.410	.123	1.000	.500
4	.323	.555	.482	1.000

NOTE: The original correlations are reported in the upper half of the matrix. The reproduced correlations are reported in the lower half of the matrix. For explanation and discussion, see text below.

In order to calculate the path coefficients for the causal model depicted in Figure 15.12 it is necessary to do two regression analyses. First, variable 3 is regressed on variables 1 and 2 to obtain $\beta_{31.2} = p_{31}$ and $\beta_{32.1} = p_{32}$. Second,

[6]The theoretical considerations that would generate this model are not discussed here, since the sole purpose of the presentation is to illustrate the analysis of such a model.

variable 4 is regressed on variables 1, 2, and 3 to obtain $\beta_{41.23} = p_{41}, \beta_{42.13} = p_{42}$, and $\beta_{43.12} = p_{43}$.

In the interest of space, the calculations of the β's for the present problem and subsequent ones are not shown. Instead, the results are reported and applied in path analysis.[7] Regressing variable 3 on 1 and 2, one obtains $\beta_{31.2} = p_{31} = .398$, and $\beta_{32.1} = p_{32} = .041$. Regressing variable 4 on variables 1, 2, and 3, one obtains $\beta_{41.23} = p_{41} = .009$, $\beta_{42.13} = p_{42} = .501$, and $\beta_{43.12} = p_{43} = .416$. The path from e_3 to variable 3 is $\sqrt{1 - R^2_{3.12}} = \sqrt{1 - .16960} = .911$, and the path from e_4 to variable 4 is $\sqrt{1 - R^2_{4.123}} = \sqrt{1 - .49647} = .710$.

The equations for the endogenous variables of Figure 15.12 are

$$z_3 = p_{31}z_1 + p_{32}z_2 + e_3$$

$$z_4 = p_{41}z_1 + p_{42}z_2 + p_{43}z_3 + e_4$$

The correlations of Table 15.1 will now be decomposed. Recall that correlations among exogenous variables remain unanalyzed. In the present example, r_{12} is unanalyzed. Beginning with r_{13},

$$r_{13} = \frac{1}{N}\Sigma z_1 z_3 = \frac{1}{N}\Sigma z_1(p_{31}z_1 + p_{32}z_2)$$

$$= p_{31} + p_{32}r_{12} = \underset{\text{DE}}{.398} + \underset{\text{U}}{(.041)(.30)} = .41$$

r_{13} is decomposed into two components: the direct effect of SES on *n* Ach (.398) and a component that is left unanalyzed (.012) because SES is correlated with another exogenous variable—namely, IQ.

$$r_{23} = \frac{1}{N}\Sigma z_2 z_3 = \frac{1}{N}\Sigma z_2(p_{31}z_1 + p_{32}z_2)$$

$$= p_{31}r_{12} + p_{32} = \underset{\text{U}}{(.398)(.30)} + \underset{\text{DE}}{(.041)} = .16$$

The direct effect of IQ on *n* Ach is relatively small (.041), while .119 of the correlation between IQ and *n* Ach remains unanalyzed because IQ is correlated with the exogenous variable SES.

$$r_{14} = \frac{1}{N}\Sigma z_1 z_4 = \frac{1}{N}\Sigma z_1(p_{41}z_1 + p_{42}z_2 + p_{43}z_3)$$

$$= p_{41} + p_{42}r_{12} + p_{43}r_{13}$$

Since $r_{13} = p_{31} + p_{32}r_{12}$ (see above),

$$r_{14} = p_{41} + p_{42}r_{12} + p_{43}(p_{31} + p_{32}r_{12})$$

$$= p_{41} + p_{42}r_{12} + p_{43}p_{31} + p_{43}p_{32}r_{12}$$

$$= \underset{\text{DE}}{.009} + \underset{\text{U}}{(.501)(.30)} + \underset{\text{IE}}{(.416)(.398)} + \underset{\text{U}}{(.416)(.041)(.30)} = .33$$

[7]You may wish to perform the calculations as an exercise.

Note that the direct effect of SES on GPA is almost zero (.009). The indirect effect of SES on GPA, via *n* Ach, is .166. Therefore, the total effect of SES on GPA, or the effect coefficient for SES, is .175 (i.e., DE + IE). The remainder of the correlation between SES and GPA (.155) is left unanalyzed because its components include correlated exogenous variables (r_{12}).

$$r_{24} = \frac{1}{N}\Sigma z_2 z_4 = \frac{1}{N}\Sigma z_2(p_{41}z_1 + p_{42}z_2 + p_{43}z_3)$$

$$= p_{41}r_{12} + p_{42} + p_{43}r_{23}$$

Since $r_{23} = p_{31}r_{12} + p_{32}$ (see above),

$$\begin{aligned} r_{24} &= p_{41}r_{12} + p_{42} + p_{43}(p_{31}r_{12} + p_{32}) \\ &= p_{41}r_{12} + p_{42} + p_{43}p_{31}r_{12} + p_{43}p_{32} \\ &= \underset{\text{U}}{(.009)(.30)} + \underset{\text{DE}}{(.501)} + \underset{\text{U}}{(.416)(.398)(.30)} + \underset{\text{IE}}{(.416)(.041)} = .57 \end{aligned}$$

The bulk of the correlation between IQ and GPA is due to the direct effect of the former on the latter (.501). The indirect effect of IQ on GPA, via *n* Ach, is .017. The effect coefficient of IQ on GPA is therefore .518 (DE + IE). The remainder of the correlation between IQ and GPA (.052) is left unanalyzed.

$$r_{34} = \frac{1}{N}\Sigma z_3 z_4 = \frac{1}{N}\Sigma z_3(p_{41}z_1 + p_{42}z_2 + p_{43}z_3)$$

$$= p_{41}r_{13} + p_{42}r_{23} + p_{43}$$

Since $r_{13} = p_{31} + p_{32}r_{12}$, and $r_{23} = p_{31}r_{12} + p_{32}$,

$$\begin{aligned} r_{34} &= p_{41}(p_{31} + p_{32}r_{12}) + p_{42}(p_{31}r_{12} + p_{32}) + p_{43} \\ &= p_{41}p_{31} + p_{41}p_{32}r_{12} + p_{42}p_{31}r_{12} + p_{42}p_{32} + p_{43} \\ &= \underset{\text{S}}{(.009)(.398)} + \underset{\text{S}}{(.009)(.041)(.30)} + \underset{\text{S}}{(.501)(.398)(.30)} + \underset{\text{S}}{(.501)(.041)} + \underset{\text{DE}}{(.416)} = .50 \end{aligned}$$

The direct effect of *n* Ach on GPA is .416. The remainder of the correlation between these variables (.084) is spurious, due to their common causes (SES and IQ).

From the preceding demonstrations it should be clear that path analysis enables one not only to determine the effects of one variable on another but also to identify components of the relations between variables which are spurious because of the effects of common causes, and ambiguous (unanalyzed) because of the operation of correlated causes. When it is desired to determine the expected change in an endogenous variable that is associated with a unit change in one of its causes, it is the effect coefficient (or the total effect) of the cause that should be used for this purpose. It is important to note that using only the direct effect of a variable for such interpretations may be misleading because, being a β, it is calculated while controlling for all the variables that affect a given endogenous variable. That is, the variables that mediate the effect of a causal variable on an endogenous variable are also controlled when the direct effect of the former on the latter is calculated. For example, when the direct effect of SES on GPA is calculated, in the model of Figure 15.12, *n* Ach is also controlled. But when one wishes to consider the effect that SES has on GPA it is necessary to take into account also its indirect effects. In the example under consideration, SES affects GPA indirectly via *n* Ach. Therefore, the total effect of SES on GPA is due to its direct plus its indirect effects, which was also labeled above the effect coefficient.

From the preceding it follows that when it is desired to study the differential effects of several variables on an endogenous variable, it is their effect coefficients that should be compared. Thus, in the example under consideration, the effect coefficients of SES, IQ, and *n* Ach on GPA are .175, .518, and .416, respectively. Accordingly, it may be concluded that IQ has the largest effect on GPA, followed by *n* Ach, and SES. Moreover, the effect of SES on GPA is relatively smaller than the effect of either of the other two variables.[8]

Effect coefficients may be compared with each other only when they impinge on the same endogenous variable (for a detailed discussion, see Schoenberg, 1972). Also, the comparisons made above were possible because all the variables were expressed in standard score form. While this is a decided advantage of using standard scores, there are also serious disadvantages in using such scores (see below, Path Regression Coefficients).

It will be instructive to compare the results of the present analysis with those obtained when other analytic techniques were applied to the same data. In the interest of space, these comparisons will be made only regarding the conclusions reached about the effect of SES on GPA. The model depicted in Figure 15.12 was used in Chapter 7 to illustrate the method of incremental partitioning of variance (see Figure 7.4 and the discussion related to it). Because SES and IQ were treated as exogenous variables, it was argued in Chapter 7 that there was no way of partitioning the variance of GPA that the two of them account for in combination. All one could say is that SES and IQ account for .35268 of the variance in GPA. Recall also that it was reasoned that because incremental partitioning of variance yields asymmetric indices it is inappropriate to compare among them for the purpose of arriving at statements about the relative importance of variables (see Figure 7.3, and the discussion related to it).

The next time the data of Table 15.1 were used in Chapter 7 was to illustrate the application of commonality analysis, where it was found that the uniqueness associated with SES was .00006. Without repeating the detailed discussion of commonality analysis (see Chapter 7), it will only be noted here that if one were to use uniqueness as a criterion for the importance of a variable, it would have to be concluded that SES is not important in explaining GPA.

The data of Table 15.1 were used again in Chapter 8 when the interpretation of β's was discussed. It was found there that when GPA was regressed on SES, IQ, and *n* Ach, the β for SES was .00919. Using this β as an index of the effect, one would have to conclude that SES has practically no effect on SES. Earlier in the present chapter, it was noted that: (1) when one variable is treated as

[8]For a discussion of the usefulness of interpretation of effect coefficients see Lewis-Beck and Mohr (1976).

endogenous and all the others are treated as exogenous (i.e., a single-stage path model), the path coefficients are the same as their respective β's obtained in a multiple regression analysis; and (2) the direct effect of an exogenous variable in a multistage path analysis is the same as the direct effect of the same variable in a single-stage path analysis. In fact, in the analysis related to Figure 15.12 it was found that the direct effect of SES on GPA was .009. Therefore, using only the direct effect as an index of the effect SES on GPA the conclusion will be the same whether one uses multiple regression analysis (as in Chapter 8) or path analysis. But in multiple regression analysis all the independent variables are used as exogenous by default, so to speak. If, on the other hand, one hypothesizes that the causal model is as depicted in Figure 15.12, then it is revealed that although the direct effect of SES on GPA is practically zero, it has an indirect effect on GPA (see above).

The preceding brief discussion should suffice to serve as a contrast between path analysis and the analytic methods presented in Chapters 7 and 8. It is suggested that you reread relevant sections of the aforementioned chapters in order to enhance your understanding of the different analytic methods that were contrasted above.

The model of Figure 15.12 is just identified. It is possible, however, that an overidentified model is consistent with the data of Table 15.1. We turn now to examine one such model.

An Overidentified Model

In the analysis of the causal model depicted in Figure 15.12 it was found that the direct effect of SES on GPA is practically zero (.009). Also, the direct effect of IQ on *n* Ach is small (.041). Suppose that these two paths were to be deleted. In other words, suppose that it is hypothesized that these two paths are equal to zero. This model, which is overidentified, is depicted in Figure 15.13.

The calculation of path coefficients in an overidentified model proceeds in the same manner as in a just-identified model (for a discussion, see Goldberger, 1970). For the model of Figure 15.13, regress variable 3 on variable 1 to obtain

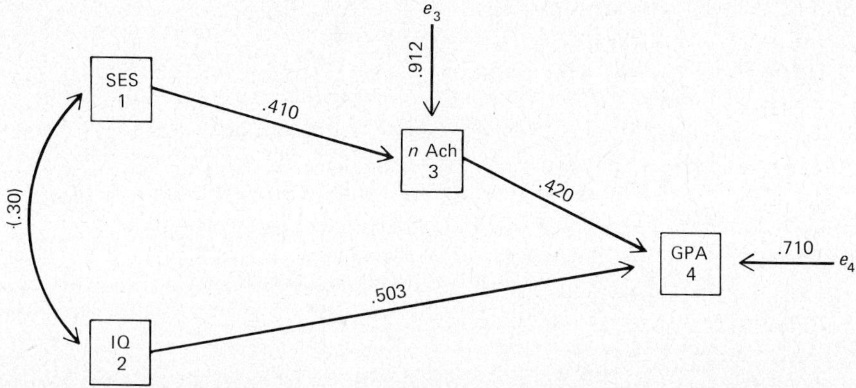

Figure 15.13

$p_{31} = \beta_{31} = r_{13} = .41$. Regress variable 4 on variables 2 and 3 to obtain $p_{42} = \beta_{42.3} = .503$, and $p_{43} = \beta_{43.2} = .420$.

Does this model fit the data? Although it is possible to apply a statistical test in an attempt to answer this question (see below), the approach taken at this stage will be to note whether **R** can be reproduced. The equations for the model of Figure 15.13 are

$$z_3 = p_3 z_1 + e_3$$

$$z_4 = p_{42} z_2 + p_{43} z_3 + e_4$$

Following the procedures outlined earlier, calculate the reproduced correlations, r^*_{ij}:

$$r^*_{13} = p_{31} = .41$$

$$r^*_{23} = \frac{1}{N}\Sigma z_2 z_3 = \frac{1}{N}\Sigma z_2(p_{31} z_1) = p_{31} r_{12} = (.41)(.30) = .123$$

The original r_{23} is .160.

$$r^*_{14} = \frac{1}{N}\Sigma z_1 z_4 = \frac{1}{N}\Sigma z_1(p_{42} z_2 + p_{43} z_3) = p_{42} r_{12} + p_{43} r_{13}$$

Substitute p_{31} for r_{13},

$$r^*_{14} = p_{42} r_{12} + p_{43} p_{31} = (.503)(.30) + (.420)(.410) = .323$$

The original r_{14} is .330.

$$r^*_{24} = \frac{1}{N}\Sigma z_2 z_4 = \frac{1}{N}\Sigma z_2(p_{42} z_2 + p_{43} z_3) = p_{42} + p_{43} r_{23}$$

Substitute $p_{31} r_{12}$ for r_{23},

$$r^*_{24} = p_{42} + p_{43} p_{31} r_{12} = (.503) + (.420)(.410)(.30) = .555$$

The original $r_{24} = .57$.

$$r^*_{34} = \frac{1}{N}\Sigma z_3 z_4 = \frac{1}{N}\Sigma z_3(p_{42} z_2 + p_{43} z_3) = p_{42} r_{23} + p_{43}$$

Substitute $p_{31} r_{12}$ for r_{23},

$$r^*_{34} = p_{42} p_{31} r_{12} + p_{43} = (.503)(.410)(.30) + (.420) = .482.$$

The original $r_{34} = .50$.

The relatively small discrepancies between the original and the reproduced correlations obtained above may plausibly be attributed to sampling errors. Consequently, it may be concluded that the causal model depicted in Figure 15.13 fits the data. (For ease of comparisons between the original and the reproduced correlations, see Table 15.1, where the former are reported in the upper half of the matrix and the latter are reported in the lower half.) Before presenting a method for testing causal models, a general approach for the calculation of effect coefficients is presented.

THE CALCULATION OF EFFECT COEFFICIENTS

The role of effect coefficients in the interpretation of causal models was discussed above, where it was also shown that such coefficients are obtained by adding the Direct Effect (DE) and the Indirect Effects (IE) of a variable on a given endogenous variable. The calculations of DE and IE for the model under consideration were relatively simple. In more complex models, however, the method of calculating IE shown above may become quite cumbersome and, hence, error-prone. Wright (1934) and Li (1975), among others, provide algorithms to calculate IE by tracing the paths in path diagrams. In complex causal models these algorithms, too, become cumbersome and error-prone. A simpler method for the calculation of effect coefficients is therefore presented now.

The method for the calculation of Effect Coefficients (EC) and IE's presented here was developed by Fox (1980); see also Greene (1977). Before presenting this method several things will be noted. (1) The method requires the use of matrix algebra. If necessary, review relevant discussions in Appendix A and in Chapter 4, particularly those of matrix inversion, and multiplication and subtraction of matrices. (2) Of the different methods presented by Fox only one is given here. (3) Fox deals with additional topics (e.g., the reproduction of **R** and nonrecursive models) that deserve careful study. (4) Except for a couple of slight alterations for the purpose of the present discussion, the method presented here follows closely the approach taken by Fox (1980); see, in particular, p. 19. (5) To facilitate the presentation of the method, it will be applied first to the simple models of Figures 15.12 and 15.13. Subsequently, it will be applied to a more complex model. (6) Exogenous variables will be designated by X's, whereas endogenous variables will be designated by Y's. (7) Matrices will be identified by appropriate subscripts. (8) No attempt is made to discuss the derivation of the method, since the sole purpose is to show how its use facilitates the calculation of effect coefficients and indirect effects in complex models. We turn now to the calculation of the matrices of EC and IE's for the model of Figure 15.12.

The matrix of direct effect of exogenous variables on endogenous variables is designated as $\mathbf{D}_{yx}$. The matrix of direct effects of endogenous variables on endogenous variables is designated as $\mathbf{D}_{yy}$. It is, of course, possible to calculate these matrices by using matrix algebra. For the present purposes, however, it is assumed that the direct effects are calculated in the manner shown earlier in the chapter. That is, each endogenous variable is regressed in turn on the variables that affect it, and the β's thus obtained are the indices of the direct effects, or the path coefficients.

For the data of Table 15.1 and the model depicted in Figure 15.12, it was found above:

$$\mathbf{D}_{yx} = \begin{bmatrix} .398 & .041 \\ .009 & .501 \end{bmatrix}$$

Note that in the first row of the matrix .398 is the path coefficient from X_1 (SES) to Y_1 (n Ach), and .041 is the path coefficient from X_2 (IQ) to Y_1. The second row contains the path coefficients from X_1 and X_2, respectively, to Y_2 (GPA).

$$\mathbf{D}_{yy} = \begin{bmatrix} 0 & 0 \\ .416 & 0 \end{bmatrix}$$

In the example under consideration, there is only one direct effect from an endogenous variable to another endogenous variable, namely from Y_1 to Y_2 (.416).

Several matrices are now defined: $\mathbf{I}$ = an identity matrix whose dimensions are the same as $\mathbf{D}_{yy}$. For the present example,

$$\mathbf{I} = \begin{bmatrix} 1 & 0 \\ 0 & 1 \end{bmatrix}$$

$$\mathbf{C} = -\mathbf{D}_{yx} \tag{15.12}$$

For the present example,

$$\mathbf{C} = \begin{bmatrix} -.398 & -.041 \\ -.009 & -.501 \end{bmatrix}$$

$$\mathbf{B} = \mathbf{I} - \mathbf{D}_{yy} \tag{15.13}$$

For the present example,

$$\mathbf{B} = \begin{bmatrix} 1 & 0 \\ 0 & 1 \end{bmatrix} - \begin{bmatrix} 0 & 0 \\ .416 & 0 \end{bmatrix} = \begin{bmatrix} 1 & 0 \\ -.416 & 1 \end{bmatrix}$$

We are ready now to calculate the effect coefficients.

$$\mathbf{E}_{yx} = -\mathbf{B}^{-1}\mathbf{C} \tag{15.14}$$

where $\mathbf{E}_{yx}$ is the matrix of the effect coefficients of the exogenous variables on the endogenous variables, and $\mathbf{B}^{-1}$ is the inverse of $\mathbf{B}$. $\mathbf{C}$ was defined above.

Since $\mathbf{B}$ is a 2×2 matrix, the calculation of its inverse is very simple (see Appendix A and Chapter 4). For the present example,

$$\mathbf{B}^{-1} = \begin{bmatrix} 1 & 0 \\ .416 & 1 \end{bmatrix}$$

and

$$\mathbf{E}_{yx} = -\mathbf{B}^{-1}\mathbf{C} = -\begin{bmatrix} 1 & 0 \\ .416 & 1 \end{bmatrix} \begin{bmatrix} -.398 & -.041 \\ -.009 & -.501 \end{bmatrix}$$

$$= \begin{bmatrix} -1 & 0 \\ -.416 & -1 \end{bmatrix} \begin{bmatrix} -.398 & -.041 \\ -.009 & -.501 \end{bmatrix} = \begin{bmatrix} .398 & .041 \\ .175 & .518 \end{bmatrix}$$

Note that the elements of the first row of the last matrix (.398 and .041) are the EC's of X_1 (SES) and X_2 (IQ) on Y_1 (n Ach). In the present example they are equal to the direct effects of X_1 and X_2 on Y_1 because according to the model there are no variables that mediate the effects of X_1 and X_2 on Y_1. The elements of the second row of the last matrix above are the EC's of X_1 and X_2 on Y_2 (GPA)—that is, .175 is the EC of X_1 (SES) on Y_2 (GPA)—and .518 is the EC of X_2 (IQ) on Y_2. These results are the same as those obtained earlier.

Since an EC is equal to its Direct Effect (DE) plus its Indirect Effect (IE), it follows that having calculated EC one can easily obtain IE by subtracting DE from EC. In matrix notation:

$$\mathbf{I}_{yx} = \mathbf{E}_{yx} - \mathbf{D}_{yx} \tag{15.15}$$

where $\mathbf{I}_{yx}$ is the matrix of indirect effects of the exogenous variables on the endogenous variables. The other two matrices were defined above. For the present example,

$$\mathbf{I}_{yx} = \begin{bmatrix} .398 & .041 \\ .175 & .518 \end{bmatrix} - \begin{bmatrix} .398 & .041 \\ .009 & .501 \end{bmatrix} = \begin{bmatrix} 0 & 0 \\ .166 & .017 \end{bmatrix}$$

According to the model of Figure 15.12, X_1 (SES) and X_2 (IQ) have no indirect effects on Y_1 (n Ach). This is indicated by the row of zeros for Y_1 in the last matrix above. The indirect effect of X_1 on Y_2 (GPA) is .166, and that of X_2 on Y_2 is .017. The same results were obtained in the earlier analysis.

We turn now to the calculation of the matrix of EC's for endogenous variables on endogenous variables:

$$\mathbf{E}_{yy} = \mathbf{B}^{-1} - \mathbf{I} \tag{15.16}$$

where $\mathbf{E}_{yy}$ is the matrix of EC's. The other matrices were defined above. For the present example,

$$\mathbf{E}_{yy} = \begin{bmatrix} 1 & 0 \\ .416 & 1 \end{bmatrix} - \begin{bmatrix} 1 & 0 \\ 0 & 1 \end{bmatrix} = \begin{bmatrix} 0 & 0 \\ .416 & 0 \end{bmatrix}$$

The EC of Y_1 (n Ach) on Y_2 (GPA) is .416. In the present case it is equal to the DE of Y_1 on Y_2 because there are no intervening variables between these two variables.

Although, according to the model depicted in Figure 15.12, Y_1 has no indirect effect on Y_2, it will now be shown how indirect effects of endogenous variables on endogenous variables are calculated.

$$\mathbf{I}_{yy} = \mathbf{E}_{yy} - \mathbf{D}_{yy} \tag{15.17}$$

where $\mathbf{I}_{yy}$ is the matrix of IE's. The other matrices were defined above. For the present example,

$$\mathbf{I}_{yy} = \begin{bmatrix} 0 & 0 \\ .416 & 0 \end{bmatrix} - \begin{bmatrix} 0 & 0 \\ .416 & 0 \end{bmatrix} = \begin{bmatrix} 0 & 0 \\ 0 & 0 \end{bmatrix}$$

As expected, Y_1 has no IE on Y_2, as indicated by the zero element in row 2 and column 1 of the last matrix above.

The procedure outlined above is equally applicable for just-identified and overidentified models. This will now be demonstrated for the overidentified model of Figure 15.13 with minimal comments, since what is being done should be clear from the preceding discussion. Using the values for the direct effects obtained earlier for the model of Figure 15.13,

$$\mathbf{D}_{yx} = \begin{bmatrix} .410 & 0 \\ 0 & .503 \end{bmatrix}$$

Note that the zeros indicate that it was hypothesized that X_2 has no direct effect on Y_1, and that X_1 has no direct effect on Y_2.

$$\mathbf{D}_{yy} = \begin{bmatrix} 0 & 0 \\ .420 & 0 \end{bmatrix}$$

$$\mathbf{I} = \begin{bmatrix} 1 & 0 \\ 0 & 1 \end{bmatrix}$$

$$\mathbf{C} = -\mathbf{D}_{yx} = \begin{bmatrix} -.410 & 0 \\ 0 & -.503 \end{bmatrix}$$

$$\mathbf{B} = \mathbf{I} - \mathbf{D}_{yy} = \begin{bmatrix} 1 & 0 \\ 0 & 1 \end{bmatrix} - \begin{bmatrix} 0 & 0 \\ .420 & 0 \end{bmatrix} = \begin{bmatrix} 1 & 0 \\ -.420 & 1 \end{bmatrix}$$

$$\mathbf{B}^{-1} = \begin{bmatrix} 1 & 0 \\ .420 & 1 \end{bmatrix}$$

$$\mathbf{E}_{yx} = -\mathbf{B}^{-1}\mathbf{C} = \begin{bmatrix} -1 & 0 \\ -.420 & -1 \end{bmatrix} \begin{bmatrix} -.410 & 0 \\ 0 & -.503 \end{bmatrix} = \begin{bmatrix} .410 & 0 \\ .172 & .503 \end{bmatrix}$$

The EC of X_1 on Y_1 is .410, and that of X_2 on Y_1 is zero. The EC of X_1 on Y_2 is .172, and that of X_2 on Y_2 is .503.

$$\mathbf{I}_{yx} = \mathbf{E}_{yx} - \mathbf{D}_{yx} = \begin{bmatrix} .410 & 0 \\ .172 & .503 \end{bmatrix} - \begin{bmatrix} .410 & 0 \\ 0 & .503 \end{bmatrix} = \begin{bmatrix} 0 & 0 \\ .172 & 0 \end{bmatrix}$$

According to the model of Figure 15.13 the only indirect effect is from X_1 (SES) to Y_2 (GPA), via Y_1 (n Ach). This IE is .172, as indicated in the last matrix above. Because X_1 is hypothesized to have no direct effect on Y_2, its EC is equal to its IE.

$$\mathbf{E}_{yy} = \mathbf{B}^{-1} - \mathbf{I} = \begin{bmatrix} 1 & 0 \\ .420 & 1 \end{bmatrix} - \begin{bmatrix} 1 & 0 \\ 0 & 1 \end{bmatrix} = \begin{bmatrix} 0 & 0 \\ .420 & 0 \end{bmatrix}$$

$$\mathbf{I}_{yy} = \mathbf{E}_{yy} - \mathbf{D}_{yy} = \begin{bmatrix} 0 & 0 \\ .420 & 0 \end{bmatrix} - \begin{bmatrix} 0 & 0 \\ .420 & 0 \end{bmatrix} = \begin{bmatrix} 0 & 0 \\ 0 & 0 \end{bmatrix}$$

The preceding illustrations dealt with very simple models and therefore the application of Fox's method probably appeared trivial to you. You may have even wondered whether it is worth the trouble of using it when, as was shown earlier, the same results were obtained fairly easily without the use of matrix algebra. Indeed, if all models were as simple as the ones presented in Figure 15.12 and 15.13, it would not be necessary to resort to Fox's method, whose potency can become evident only when it is applied to a more complex causal model. The reason the method was applied first to the simple models was that it afforded a simple presentation of all the necessary calculations. It should be recognized that when the method is applied to more complex models, it may require matrix inversion and matrix multiplications that may become quite complex, and hence even more error-prone than the method presented earlier when the calculations are done by hand. There is, however, an easy way out of this potential problem by using a computer program for matrix manipulations. One such very useful program is contained in the SAS (Helwig et al., 1979) package.[9] It is this program that will be used to illustrate the application of Fox's method to a more complex causal model.

The causal model and the data to be analyzed were taken from Duncan, Featherman, and Duncan (1972, p. 38, for the 35–44 age group). The correla-

[9]Fox (1980) included an APL program in his paper.

Table 15.2 Correlation Matrix for Non-Negro Men, 35–44 Age Group

	X_1	X_2	X_3	Y_1	Y_2	Y_3
X_1	1.0000	.5300	−.2871	.4048	.3194	.2332
X_2	.5300	1.0000	−.2476	.4341	.3899	.2587
X_3	−.2871	−.2476	1.0000	−.3311	−.2751	−.1752
Y_1	.4048	.4341	−.3311	1.0000	.6426	.3759
Y_2	.3194	.3899	−.2751	.6426	1.0000	.4418
Y_3	.2332	.2587	−.1752	.3759	.4418	1.0000

NOTE: Data taken from O. D. Duncan, D. L. Featherman, and B. Duncan, *Socioeconomic Background and Achievement,* p. 38. Copyright 1972 by Seminar Press. Reprinted by permission. X_1 = father's education; X_2 = father's occupation; X_3 = number of siblings; Y_1 = education; Y_2 = occupation; Y_3 = income.

tion matrix among the variables is reported in Table 15.2, and the causal model is depicted in Figure 15.14, along with the path coefficients.

It will be noted that the path coefficients were obtained by doing three regression analyses: (1) Y_1 on X_1, X_2, and X_3; (2) Y_2 on X_1, X_2, X_3, and Y_1; (3) Y_3 on X_1, X_2, X_3, Y_1, and Y_2. Because the sole purpose here is to illustrate the use of the Matrix program of SAS for obtaining EC's and IE's no comments will be made about the substantive aspects of the causal model, nor about the findings. It is strongly recommended that you read Duncan, Featherman, and Duncan's (1972) penetrating discussions of the causal models they analyze in their book.

One of the reasons the present example was selected is that it was also analyzed by Alwin and Hauser (1975), who have proposed a different method for calculating the EC's and IE's. You will benefit from comparing the method used here and the one used by Alwin and Hauser. It is strongly recommended that you study carefully Alwin and Hauser's discussion and interpretation of the results.

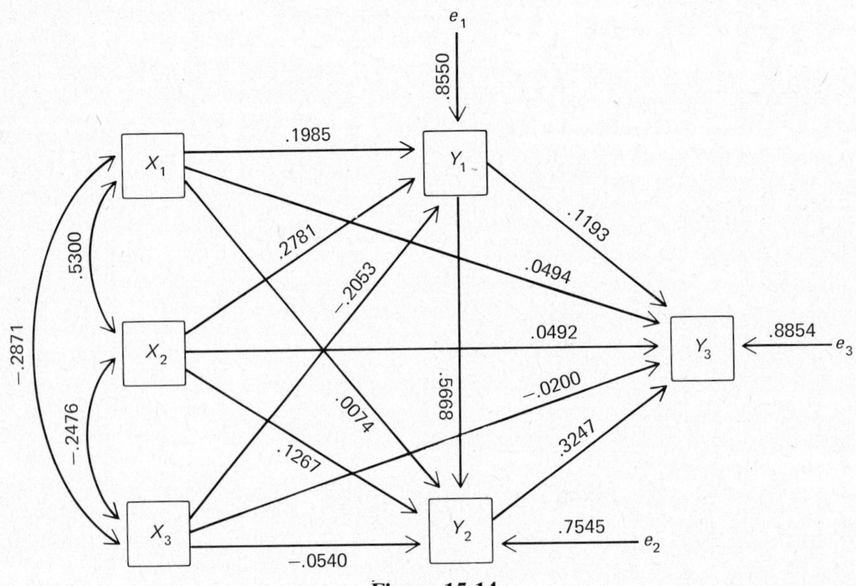

Figure 15.14

Before showing how the Matrix program was used it will be useful to present the $\mathbf{D}_{yx}$ and $\mathbf{D}_{yy}$ for the model of Figure 15.14.

$$\mathbf{D}_{yx} = \begin{bmatrix} .1985 & .2781 & -.2053 \\ .0074 & .1267 & -.0540 \\ .0494 & .0492 & -.0200 \end{bmatrix}$$

$$\mathbf{D}_{yy} = \begin{bmatrix} 0 & 0 & 0 \\ .5668 & 0 & 0 \\ .1193 & .3247 & 0 \end{bmatrix}$$

Control Cards

```
PROC MATRIX PRINT;
DYX = .1985  .2781  -.2053/.0074  .1267  -.0540/.0494  .0492  -.0200;
DYY = 0 0 0 / .5668  0 0 / .1193  .3247  0;
I   = 1 0 0 / 0 1 0 / 0 0 1;
C   = -DYX;
B   = I - DYY;
EYX = -INV(B)*C;
IYX = EYX - DYX;
EYY = INV(B) - I;
IYY = EYY - DYY;
```

Commentary

The above is a listing of the statements used in the MATRIX program of SAS for the calculation of the EC's and IE's for the causal model of Figure 15.14. It will be noted that the results could have been obtained with a more succinct set of matrix statements. For the purpose of consistency with the presentation in the preceding section, it was decided to use the ones listed above. Following are relevant excerpts of the output, along with commentaries.

Output

EYX	COL 1	COL 2	COL 3
ROW 1	.1985	.2781	−.2053
ROW 2	.1199	.2843	−.1704
ROW 3	.1120	.1747	−.0998

Commentary

The above matrix contains the EC's of the X's on the Y's. The values in the first row are the EC's of X_1, X_2, and X_3, respectively on Y_1. The values in the second row are the EC's of the X's on Y_2. The values in row 3 are the EC's of the X's on Y_3. For example, .1120 is the EC of X_1 on Y_3.

Output

IYX	COL 1	COL 2	COL 3
ROW 1	0	0	0
ROW 2	.1125	.1576	−.1164
ROW 3	.0626	.1255	−.0798

Commentary

The above matrix contains the IE's of the X's on the Y's. The first row contains the indirect effects of X_1, X_2, and X_3 on Y_1. Similarly, for row 2, which is associated with Y_2, and row 3, which is associated with Y_3. Thus, for example, −.0798 (row 3, column 3) is the IE of X_3 on Y_3.

Output

EYY	COL 1	COL 2	COL 3
ROW 1	0	0	0
ROW 2	.5668	0	0
ROW 3	.3033	.3247	0

Commentary

The above matrix contains the EC's of Y's on Y's. For example, .3033 is the EC of Y_1 on Y_3.

Output

IYY	COL 1	COL 2	COL 3
ROW 1	0	0	0
ROW 2	0	0	0
ROW 3	.1840	0	0

Commentary

The above matrix contains the IE's of Y's on Y's. In the present example there is only one such IE, namely from Y_1 to Y_3, via Y_2 (.1840).

TESTING CAUSAL MODELS

Path analysis is an important analytic tool for testing causal models. Through its application it is possible to test whether a specific causal model is consistent with the pattern of the intercorrelations among the variables. Before describing approaches to the testing of causal models it is necessary to comment, albeit briefly, on the topic of identification.

Identification

The topic of identification is complex and has received extensive treatments, particularly from econometricians (see, for example, Fisher, 1966; Johnston, 1972, pp. 352–372; Koopmans, 1949; for simpler good discussions in the context of social research see Duncan, 1975, Chapters 6 and 7; Heise, 1975, Chapter 5; Namboodiri, Carter, & Blalock, 1975, Chapters 11 and 12). The present discussion is limited to a brief intuitive overview of the identification problem.

Causal models may be just identified, overidentified, or underidentified. It was already noted in the preceding section that a just-identified model is one in which the number of equations is equal to the number of parameters to be estimated, hence providing a unique solution for each of them. It was also noted earlier that in the context of the recursive models being considered in this chapter a fully recursive model (i.e., one in which all the variables are interconnected) is just identified. Another way of stating this is that the number of β's that can be uniquely estimated is equal to the number of path coefficients that are to be estimated. It is necessary to recognize that the model is just identified as a consequence of assumptions, or restrictions, imposed by the researcher. Thus, for example, one of the restrictions is that the causal flow is unidirectional—that is, path coefficients from a given endogenous variable to its causes are assumed, or constrained, to be equal to zero (see earlier discussion in connection with Equations (15.1)). Another constraint that was necessary to render a fully recursive model just identified concerned the assumptions about the residual terms (see earlier discussion).

An overidentified model, as the name implies, consists of more equations than are necessary for the purpose of parameter estimation. Overidentification is a consequence of restrictions, or constraints, imposed by the researcher on some aspects of the causal model that is being considered. These are referred to as overidentifying restrictions, or constraints. The constraints do not refer to statistical assumptions but to the researcher's hypotheses about the causal model. One of the most commonly used overidentifying restrictions is the postulation that certain path coefficients are equal to zero. In other words, it is hypothesized that a variable has no direct effect on a given endogenous variable, although it may affect it indirectly (see, for example, Figures 15.9 and 15.11).

An underidentified model is one that contains insufficient information for the purpose of obtaining a determinate solution of parameter estimation. Stated differently, this means that an infinite number of solutions may be obtained in an underidentified model. This is why some authors (e.g., Namboodiri, Carter, & Blalock, 1975, p. 503) refer to underidentified models as being "hopeless." As Heise (1975) points out: "Underidentification is a theoretical rather than a statistical problem" (p. 152). The problem cannot be resolved unless the researcher is willing to impose additional restrictions that will render the model just identified or overidentified. Examples of underidentification may be found in factor analytic models, which with added restrictions become identifiable (see, for example, Duncan, 1972; Turner & Stevens, 1959). Finally, it will be noted that it is more useful to consider the question of identification in reference to parameter estimation rather than to the model as a whole. The reason is that in a given model some parameters may be overidentified, whereas others may be underidentified (see Bielby & Hauser, 1977a, p. 149).

As is discussed below, the validity of a causal model is essentially assessed in the light of its efficiency to reproduce, or closely approximate, the correlations among the variables (**R**). In the preceding sections it was shown how path coefficients may be used to reproduce **R.** It was also discussed, and numerically illustrated, that so long as the causal model is just identified, **R** may be reproduced regardless of how untenable and unreasonable the model is on logical and/or theoretical grounds. In other words, a just-identified model may always be shown to fit the data perfectly. Consequently, just-identified models cannot be tested.

There are two broad approaches to the testing of causal models: (1) theory trimming and (2) tests of overidentified models. Following a brief discussion of the former, the latter is discussed in detail.

Theory Trimming

It has been suggested (e.g., Duncan, 1975, p. 49; Heise, 1969) that having calculated the path coefficients for a just-identified model, path coefficients that do not meet criteria of statistical significance and/or meaningfulness be deleted from the model—hence the name theory trimming (Heise, 1969) to characterize this approach. The criteria for deletion of paths will be discussed separately, beginning with statistical significance.

Recall that in the causal models under consideration in this chapter (i.e., recursive models) the path coefficients are β's. Therefore, testing a given β for significance is tantamount to testing the path coefficient that corresponds to it. Earlier in this book (see, for example, Chapter 3) it was shown how each β can be tested for significance, using a t or an F ratio. In the present context, then, following the theory trimming approach one would delete path coefficients whose t ratios are smaller than the tabled t at a prespecified level of significance. But it was also pointed out earlier (see, in particular, Chapter 3) that when more than one β in a given equation is not statistically significant, the deletion of one of them from the equation may lead not only to changes in the magnitudes of the β's that have been retained in the equation but also to changes in the results of their tests of statistical significance (see discussions and illustrations in Chapter 8). Consequently, when it is desired to test whether more than one path coefficient (i.e., β) within a given equation may be deleted, it is more appropriate to test them simultaneously by using the F test that was introduced early in the book and used repeatedly in subsequent chapters.

The discussion thus far was concerned with the deletion of path coefficients (β's) obtained within a single regression equation. But, as was noted above, in a multistage causal model more than one regression equation is calculated. Therefore, testing β's within each equation does not constitute a test of the model. It is possible for tests of given path coefficients within separate equations to indicate that some or all of them are not statistically significant (i.e., that they may be deleted), and yet an overall test of the model may be statistically significant, thereby leading to the conclusion that it does not fit the data. It is therefore more appropriate to use an overall test of the model, as is shown below.[10]

Turning now to the criterion of meaningfulness, it will be recalled that when the sample size is relatively large, even substantively meaningless regression coefficients may be found to be statistically significant. Consequently, many researchers prefer to use a criterion of meaningfulness for the deletion of paths even when their coefficients are statistically significant. As was discussed in earlier chapters, meaningfulness is a judgmental criterion, which depends, among other things, on the specific area being studied, economic considerations, and the consequences of decisions made on the basis of the obtained results. In the absence of guidelines many researchers select a criterion for the deletion of paths arbitrarily—say, all β's $< .05$ are deleted.

The theory trimming approach suffers from the very serious shortcoming of being applied post hoc. It is on these grounds that McPherson (1976) marshals very strong arguments against its use. Without going into the details of his specific points, it will be noted that his major theme is that "The data cannot tell the researcher which hypothesis to test; at best the data may tell when a particular hypothesis is supported or unsupported, when *a priori* grounds exist for testing it" (p. 99), or "The basic criterion for a researcher's deciding wh`ther or not to 'theory trim' is whether he believes that the data can form his hypothesis for him" (p. 102). It is necessary, however, to recognize that at exploratory stages of research one might gain insight by resorting to theory trimming, provided that this is not construed as interchangeable with or a substitute for a priori hypothesis testing. Such hypotheses refer to the postulation of overidentified models, which are tested for significance—a topic to which we now turn.

Testing Overidentified Models

The concept of overidentification was discussed above, where it was noted that when in a just-identified model certain paths are deleted the model becomes overidentified. The deletion of paths reflects hypotheses about certain variables not having direct effects on other variables. Such hypotheses were referred to above as overidentifying restrictions. While overidentifying restrictions other than hypothesizing that certain path coefficients are equal to zero are possible (e.g., that two path coefficients are equal to each other), the present discussion is limited to such restrictions.[11]

As is shown below, an overidentified model can be tested for significance. Rejection of the null hypothesis indicates that the model does not fit the data. It is very important, however, not to equate the failure to reject the null hypothesis with its acceptance. In other words, failure to reject the null hypothesis is logically quite different from accepting it. In a broader context Popper (1959) has argued that the aim of scientific inquiry is falsification. Sci-

[10]For further discussions of this point, as well as issues relating to the α level when multiple tests of significance are performed, see McPherson (1976), McPherson and Haung (1974), and Specht (1975).

[11]For the use of other kinds of restrictions see Chapter 16.

ence cannot prove but only disprove. *"It must be possible for an empirical scientific system to be refuted by experience"* (p. 41). Hypotheses must, in principle, be falsifiable. Rushton (cited in Platt, 1964, p. 349) has expressed this idea most succinctly: "A theory which cannot be mortally endangered cannot be alive."

The methods of testing causal models are eminently suitable for the purpose of testing alternative hypotheses, or engaging in "strong inference" (Platt, 1964). This, of course, should not be construed as an endorsement of the proliferation of overidentified models in search of the one that best fits the data. Researchers can do no better than heed Duncan's (1975) warning on this point:

> It is vital to keep the matter of tests of overidentifying restrictions in perspective. Valuable as such tests may be, they do not really bear upon what may be the most problematic issue in the specification of a recursive model, that is, the causal ordering of variables. *It is the gravest kind of fallacy to suppose that, from a number of competing models involving different causal ordering, one can select the true model by finding the one that comes closest to satisfying a particular set of overidentifying restrictions.* (p. 50; italics added)

Although it is shown below how alternative models are tested, this is done for illustrative purposes only. In other words, the sole purpose is to illustrate the application of the method. Alternative models deserve to be thus labeled only when they are derived from sound theoretical formulations, not because one wonders: "What would happen if I changed the model?"

Generally, tests of overidentified models are performed by using properties of the observed and the reproduced correlation matrices among the variables under consideration. Essentially, determinants of these matrices are used to calculate a χ^2 (chi squared) with degrees of freedom *(df)* equal to the number of overidentifying restrictions (see, for example, Specht, 1975). A significant χ^2 at a prespecified level of α leads to the rejection of the null hypothesis, and it is concluded that the model does not fit the data. The larger the probability associated with the χ^2, the better the fit of the model to the data. When the correlation matrix can be reproduced exactly the χ^2 is zero, indicating a perfect fit. Recall that it was stated above that in fully recursive models the correlation matrix can always be reproduced exactly. Such models have no overidentifying restrictions and therefore cannot be tested.

The foregoing description of tests of overidentified models is admittedly sketchy. The reason is that it was intended only to provide an intuitive understanding that such tests are addressed to the question whether an overidentified model fits the data. Specht (1975) has shown that for recursive models with uncorrelated residuals the χ^2 test discussed above may be obtained directly by using squared residual path coefficients. In other words, the information necessary for the calculation of the χ^2 is available from the estimates of the residual path coefficients. It is this approach that is followed here, using formulas presented by Specht (1975). (For more detailed discussions, see Specht's paper and references cited therein.)

In order to test an overidentified model it is necessary first to calculate R^2_m, which is defined as a generalized squared multiple correlation. R^2_m may be interpreted in a fashion analogous to the ordinary squared multiple correlation, that is, the ratio of explained variance to the variance to be explained. For a single-equation model (i.e., a single-stage path model) R_m^2 is R^2 of the endogenous variable with the exogenous variables. For multistage path models "R_m^2 is the ratio of the generalized variance explained by the causal model to the generalized variance which was to be explained by the model" (Specht, 1975, p. 120; see Specht's paper for a discussion of generalized variance and for the derivation and a more detailed explanation of R_m^2).

Now, Specht shows that for a fully recursive model:

$$R_m^2 = 1 - (1 - R_1^2)(1 - R_2^2) \cdots (1 - R_p^2) \tag{15.18}$$

"where R_i^2 is the ordinary squared multiple correlation coefficient of ith equation in a fully recursive system" (p. 121). Note that in the type of causal models being considered here each term in the parentheses of (15.18) is a squared residual path (see earlier sections in this chapter where it was shown that a residual path is equal to $\sqrt{1 - R_i^2}$). In short, to calculate R_m^2 for a fully recursive model calculate the product of all the squared residual paths and subtract from one.

For an overidentified model one can calculate a statistic analogous to R_m^2:

$$M = 1 - (1 - R_1^2)(1 - R_2^2) \cdots (1 - R_p^2) \tag{15.19}$$

Note that M is calculated in the same manner as is R_m^2, except that some or all of the R^2's of (15.19) are based on a model in which some of the paths have been deleted, whereas the R^2's of (15.18) are based on a fully recursive model. Therefore, M can take values between zero and R_m^2. When the fit of an overidentified model is perfect (i.e., when $\mathbf{R}$ is exactly reproduced), $R_m^2 = M$. The smaller M is in relation to R_m^2 the poorer the fit of the overidentified model. A measure of goodness of fit for an overidentified model is therefore:

$$Q = \frac{1 - R_m^2}{1 - M} \tag{15.20}$$

For large samples, the measure of goodness of fit, Q, can be tested for significance as follows:

$$W = -(N - d)\log_e Q = -(N - d)\log_e\left(\frac{1 - R_m^2}{1 - M}\right) \tag{15.21}$$

where N = sample size; d = number of overidentifying restrictions, that is, the number of path coefficients hypothesized to be equal to zero; $\log_e$ = natural logarithm. W has an approximate χ^2 distribution with $df = d$, the number of overidentifying restrictions.

Note that when $M = R_m^2$, the last term of (15.21) is equal to one. The natural logarithm of one is zero, and therefore χ^2 is equal to zero, indicating a perfect fit. The smaller M is, the smaller is Q $[(1 - R_m^2)/(1 - M)]$, and the larger its natural logarithm, resulting in a larger χ^2.

As with other tests of significance, the χ^2 is affected by the sample size. This can be clearly seen from Formula (15.21), where increasingly larger N's will lead to increasingly larger χ^2's for the same value of Q. Since large samples are mandatory in the type of studies being considered here, there is a high probability that even when a model fits the data well it will be rejected on the grounds of the test of statistical significance. It is therefore suggested that attention be paid to Q, the measure of goodness of fit, which is not a function of sample size. Recall that Q may vary from zero to one. The closer Q is to one, the better the fit of the model to the data. Jöreskog (1974) has suggested that: "The values of χ^2 be interpreted very cautiously" (p. 4). Specifically, he has suggested that a large χ^2 compared to its *df* be taken as an indication that the model does not fit the data. In exploratory studies one would inspect the residuals (in the present context the differences between observed and reproduced correlations) to note how the model may be revised by modifying the overidentifying restrictions. A large drop in χ^2 compared to the difference in *df* between the original and the revised overidentified model is taken as support for the changes in the model (see numerical example below).[12]

It is hoped that the above presentation can best be clarified by illustrating the application of the approach to some numerical examples, to which we now turn.

Numerical Examples

Tests of overidentified models will be applied first to some of the numerical examples used in earlier sections of this chapter. These will be followed by examples of tests of models from a research study from political science. For convenience, figures and results presented in earlier sections will be repeated here, but the calculations will not be repeated. When necessary, refer to earlier sections to see how the results reported here were obtained. To facilitate such references, the numbers of the figures that were presented earlier will be given in parentheses.

Consider the overidentified model depicted in Figure 15.15(a) (presented earlier as Figure 15.11), according to which it is hypothesized that variable 3 has no direct effect on variable 2. A fully recursive model for the three variables

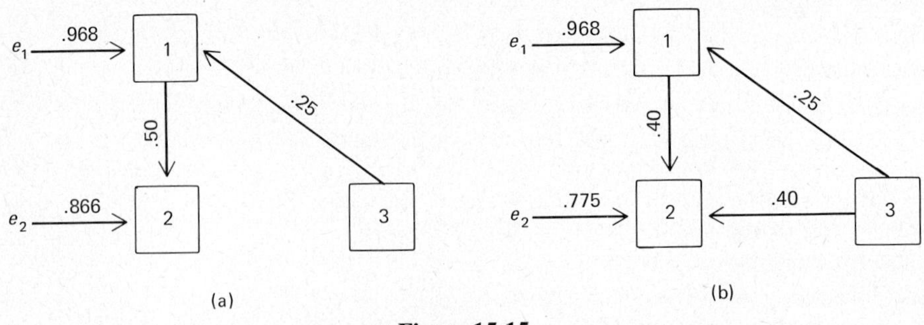

Figure 15.15

[12]For reservations regarding such an approach see Theory Trimming, above.

under consideration is depicted in Figure 15.15(b) (presented earlier as Figure 15.8). The purpose is to test whether the overidentified model (a) fits the data. It should be noted that because we are dealing here with a single path coefficient hypothesized to be equal to zero (i.e., p_{23}) it is not necessary to resort to the method presented in the preceding section. All one needs is test p_{23} of Figure 15.15(b) in the usual manner. If the t ratio for this path coefficient is significant, the null hypothesis that $p_{23} = .00$ is rejected.

But in order to demonstrate the application of the method presented in the preceding section to a very simple example, it will be used instead. For the fully recursive model, Figure 15.5(b), calculate:

$$R_m^2 = 1 - (1 - R_{1.3}^2)(1 - R_{2.13}^2)$$
$$= 1 - (.968)^2(.775)^2 = .437$$

Note that .968 is the residual path for variable 1. It was previously calculated as $\sqrt{1 - R_{1.3}^2} = \sqrt{1 - .25^2} = .968$. Therefore, the first term in the above formula for R_m^2 is the square of this residual path. Similarly, the residual path for variable 2 was obtained earlier by calculating $\sqrt{1 - R_{2.13}^2} = .775$. Therefore, the second term in the above formula for R_m^2 is the square of this residual path.

Turning now to Figure 15.5(a) calculate

$$M = 1 - (1 - R_{1.3}^2)(1 - R_{2.1}^2)$$
$$= 1 - (.968)^2(.866)^2 = .297$$

Calculate now the measure of goodness of fit:

$$Q = \frac{1 - R_m^2}{1 - M} = \frac{1 - .437}{1 - .297} = .8009$$

In order to test Q it will be assumed that the sample size, N, is 100. Applying Formula (15.21),

$$W = -(100 - 1)\log_e .8009 = 21.98$$

with 1 df, $p < .001$. The null hypothesis is rejected, and it is concluded that the model does not fit the data. Earlier, it was shown that while $r_{23} = .50$, the reproduced correlation between these variables on the basis of the estimated path coefficients for the model under consideration is only .125.

We turn now to an illustration of a test of an overidentified model with four variables as depicted in Figure 15.16(a) (presented earlier as Figure 15.13). The fully recursive model for these variables is presented as Figure 15.16(b) (presented earlier as Figure 15.12). The calculations should be clear by now, and will therefore be presented with minimal comments.

Using the residual paths reported in Figure 15.16(b) calculate:

$$R_m^2 = 1 - (.911)^2(.710)^2 = .582$$

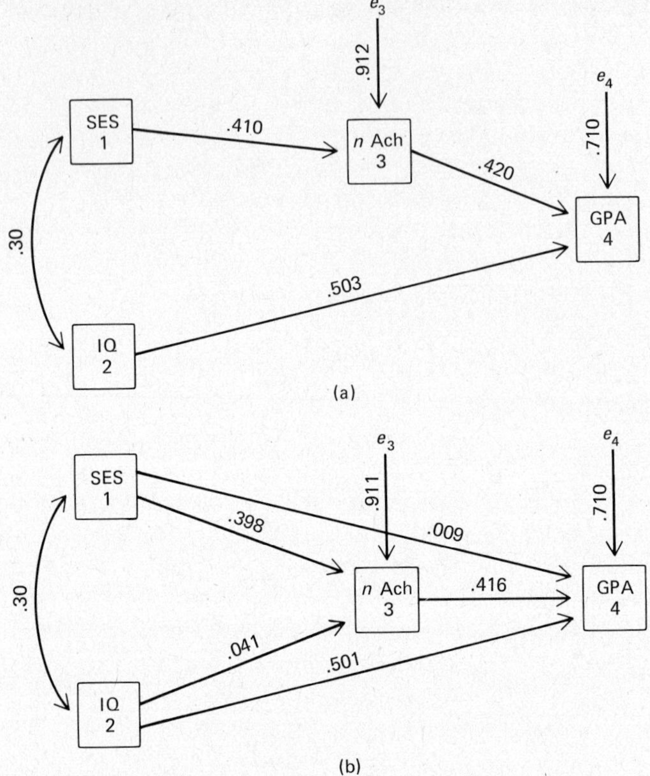

Figure 15.16

Using the residual paths reported in Figure 15.16(a) calculate

$$M = 1 - (.912)^2(.710)^2 = .581$$

$$Q = \frac{1 - .582}{1 - .581} = .9976$$

Assuming $N = 100$,

$$W = -(100 - 2)\log_e .9976 = .235$$

$\chi^2 = .235$ with 2 *df* (two paths were hypothesized to be zero). This χ^2 is between the following two tabled χ^2 values with 2 *df*: .211p = .90, and .446p = .80. It is therefore concluded that the model fits the data.

It is important to reiterate what was said earlier regarding tests of significance. Such tests are addressed to a null hypothesis, which in the present example refers to the hypothesis that two path coefficients (from SES to GPA, and from IQ to *n* Ach) are zero. Failure to reject the null hypothesis should not be construed as its acceptance. Therefore when, on the basis of a test of significance, it is said here, and subsequently, that a model fits the data, this should be understood to mean that the null hypothesis could not be rejected. Recall also that with a sufficiently large sample, the null hypothesis may be rejected even when the model fits the data. Conversely, a small sample size may result in failure to reject the null hypothesis even when the fit of the model to the data is poor.

It was said earlier that the closer Q is to one, the better the fit of the model to the data. In the present example $Q = .9976$, indicating a very good fit of the model to the data. See Table 15.1 for the small discrepancies between the original and the reproduced correlations for this model.

An Example from Political Science Research

In an attempt to explain the roll call behavior of congressmen, Miller and Stokes (1963) studied the pattern of relations among the following variables: attitudes of samples of constituents in each of 116 congressional districts, attitudes of the congressmen representing the districts, congressmen's perceptions of the attitudes held by their constituents, and roll call behavior of the congressmen. In a reanalysis of the Miller and Stokes data, Cnudde and McCrone (1966) formulated three alternative causal models, two of which are presented here as Models I and II in Figure 15.17. Cnudde and McCrone tested their alternative models by employing a technique originally developed by Simon (1954) and elaborated by Blalock (1964, 1968). (See also Namboodiri, Carter, & Blalock, 1975, Chapter 10.) The Simon-Blalock technique is similar in certain respects to path analysis, but is not as powerful.[13]

The presentation here is limited to illustrations of the tests of the three overidentified models given in Figure 15.17. For substantive discussions relevant to this research, see Cnudde and McCrone (1966) and Miller and Stokes (1963). As was discussed earlier (see Theory Trimming), it is inappropriate to engage in tests of different models in search of the *one* that fits the data. As the purpose here is illustrative only, it will be shown that two different models fit the data equally well. To repeat: the model should be derived from theory and not from the data analysis.[14]

One of the areas investigated by Miller and Stokes (1963) was attitudes and roll call behavior pertaining to civil rights. The correlations among the variables in the area of civil rights are reported in the upper half of the matrix in Table 15.3. Each of the three models of Figure 15.17 is dealt with separately. A fully recursive model is also reported in Figure 15.17 not as an alternative model but for the purpose of testing the three overidentified models. It will be noted that for the purpose of testing the three models the fully recursive model need not necessarily be the one presented in Figure 15.17. One could, for example, reverse the direction of the arrow between variables 2 and 3 so that the latter affects the former. While some of the path coefficients will change as a result of this reversal, R^2_m which is used in testing the overidentified models will be the same.

The path coefficients for each model will be given without going through their

[13]See Boudon (1968) and Heise (1969).

[14]For a critique of Cnudde and McCrone's (1966) paper on theoretical grounds see Forbes and Tufte (1968), who also demonstrate that models other than those depicted in Figure 15.17 also fit the data.

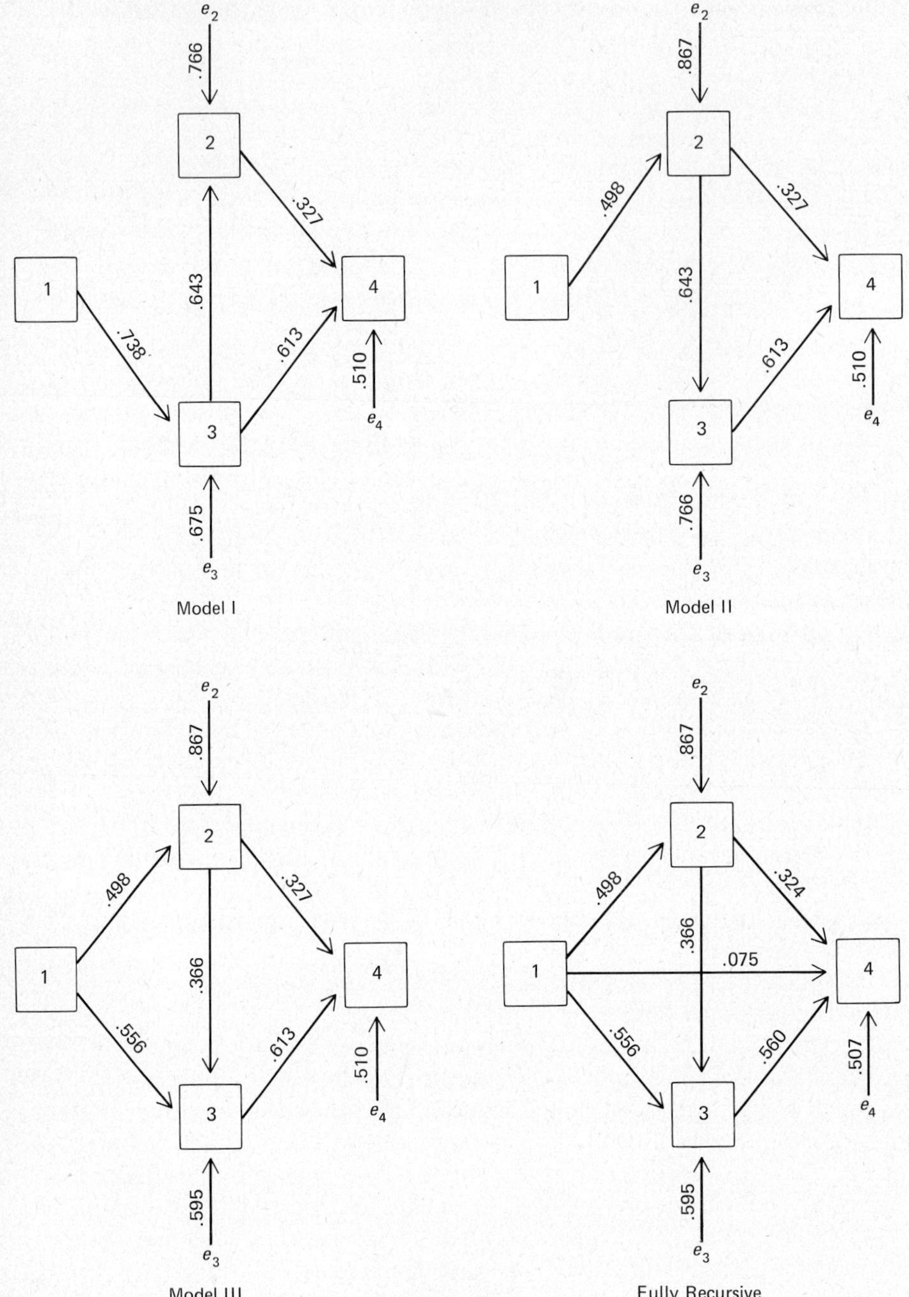

Figure 15.17

calculations. If necessary, refer to earlier sections of this chapter for detailed explanations of the calculations of path coefficients. To facilitate the presentation, the numbers identifying the variables in Figure 15.17 and in Table 15.3 are used. They are: 1 = Constituents' Attitudes, 2 = Congressmen's Attitudes, 3 = Congressmen's Perceptions, and 4 = Roll Call.

Table 15.3 Original and Reproduced Correlations. Attitudes and Roll Call Pertaining to Civil Rights[a]

	1 Constituents' Attitudes	2 Congressmen's Attitudes	3 Congressmen's Perceptions of Constituents' Attitudes	4 Roll Call Behavior
1	1.000	.498	.738	.649
2	.475	1.000	.643	.721
3	.738	.643	1.000	.823
4	.608	.721	.823	1.000

[a]The original correlations, in the upper half of the matrix, are taken from Cnudde and McCrone (1966). In the lower half of the matrix are the correlations as reproduced by the application of Model I. For an explanation and discussion, see text.

Model I. According to this model, Constituents' Attitudes do not affect Congressmen's Attitudes directly, nor do they affect directly Roll Call. Constituents' Attitudes affect Congressmen's Perceptions, which in turn affect Congressmen's Attitudes. Furthermore, Congressmen's Attitudes and Perceptions affect Roll Call.

For this model, $p_{31} = r_{31} = .738$; $e_3 = \sqrt{1 - .738^2} = .675$; $p_{23} = r_{23} = .643$; $e_2 = \sqrt{1 - .643^2} = .766$. Regressing 4 on 2 and 3, obtain $p_{42} = \beta_{42.3} = .327$; $p_{43} = \beta_{43.2} = .613$; $e_4 = \sqrt{1 - R^2_{4.23}} = .510$. The values for the fully recursive model are similarly obtained. They are reported in Figure 15.17.

We turn now to the test of the model. Following the procedures outlined in preceding sections, calculate:

$$R^2_m = 1 - (.867)^2(.595)^2(.507)^2 = .9316$$

Note that the values used for the calculation of R^2_m are the squared residual paths for the fully recursive model in Figure 15.17.

$$M = 1 - (.766)^2(.675)^2(.510)^2 = .9305$$

The values used for the calculation of M are the squared residual paths reported in Model I of Figure 15.17.

$$Q = \frac{1 - R^2_m}{1 - M} = \frac{1 - .9316}{1 - .9305} = .9842$$

It will be recalled that $N = 116$ and that there are two overidentifying restrictions in Model I (i.e., the paths from 1 to 2 and from 1 to 4 are hypothesized to be zero). The test of Q is therefore

$$W = -(N - d)\log_e Q = -(116 - 2) \log_e .9842 = 1.82$$

$\chi^2 = 1.82$ with 2 *df*. From the tabled values of χ^2 it can be seen that $\chi^2 = 2.408$ has a probability of .30. The obtained χ^2 has therefore a probability greater than that. It is concluded that the model fits the data.

Using the path coefficients of Model I and following the method presented in earlier sections, one can reproduce **R,** the correlation matrix among the variables. The reproduced correlations are given in the lower half of the matrix of Table 15.3, although the calculations are not shown here. You may wish to do them as an exercise. Note that the residuals (the discrepancies between the original and the reproduced correlation) are very small, as one would expect when the model fits the data well ($Q = .9842$).

Following methods presented in earlier sections one would also calculate the Effect Coefficients (EC) of the variables in Model I. They are reported here without going through the calculations (again, you may wish to calculate them as an exercise): $EC_{21} = .475$; $EC_{23} = .643$; $EC_{31} = .738$; $EC_{41} = .608$; $EC_{42} = .327$; $EC_{43} = .823$.

Model II. According to this model, which is depicted in Figure 15.17, Constituents' Attitudes do not affect Congressmen's Perception directly, nor do they affect Roll Call directly. Constituents' Attitudes affect Congressmen's Attitudes, which in turn affect Congressmen's Perceptions. Congressmen's Perceptions and Attitudes affect Roll Call.

For this model, $p_{21} = .498$; $e_2 = .867$; $p_{32} = .643$; $e_3 = .766$; $p_{42} = .327$; $p_{43} = .613$; $e_4 = .510$. Using the residual paths, calculate

$$M = 1 - (.867)^2(.766)^2(.510)^2 = .8853$$

$$R^2_m = .9316 \qquad \text{(see calculations above)}$$

$$Q = \frac{1 - .9316}{1 - .8853} = .5963$$

$$W = -(116 - 2)\log_e .5963 = 58.94$$

$\chi^2 = 58.94$ with 2 *df*, $p < .001$. Clearly, Model II does not fit the data. Note the low value of Q. If you use the path coefficients of Model II to reproduce **R,** you will find that $r^*_{13} = .320$, as compared with $r_{13} = .738$—a discrepancy of .418. $r^*_{14} = .359$, whereas $r_{14} = .649$—a discrepancy of .290.

Assuming that Models I and II were derived from two theoretical orientations, one would have to conclude that Model I fits the data and that Model II does not fit the data.

Model III. This model, which is depicted in Figure 15.17, is similar to Model II, except that in the latter it was hypothesized that Constituents' Attitudes do not affect Congressmen's Perception directly, whereas in Model III this path coefficient was not hypothesized to be zero. For this model, $p_{21} = .498$; $e_2 = .867$; $p_{31} = .556$; $p_{32} = .366$; $e_3 = .595$; $p_{42} = .327$; $p_{43} = .613$; $e_4 = .510$.

Using the residual paths, calculate

$$M = 1 - (.867)^2(.595)^2(.510)^2 = .9308$$

$$R^2_m = .9316 \qquad \text{(see calculations above)}$$

$$Q = \frac{1 - .9316}{1 - .9308} = .9884$$

$$W = -(116 - 1)\log_e .9884 = 1.34$$

$\chi^2 = 1.34$ with 1 *df*. The tabled value of $\chi^2 = 1.642$ with 1 *df* has a probability of .20. For the obtained χ^2, therefore, $p > .20$. It is concluded that Model III fits the data.

Several things will be noted. Although both Models I and III fit the data, they reflect different theoretical formulations. In Model I it is hypothesized that variable 3 affects variable 2, whereas in Model III the converse is hypothesized—that is, that variable 2 affects variable 3. In addition, in Model I it is hypothesized that variable 1 does not affect variable 2 directly, whereas in Model III such a direct affect is hypothesized. Note that there are two over-identifying restrictions in Model I, whereas Model III contains only one over-identifying restriction, hence the difference in the *df* for the χ^2's associated with the tests of the two models.

In view of the fact that both models fit the data, which of them is the "correct" or the "true" one? To repeat what was said earlier: different models may fit the same data. It can be shown that various other models also fit the data of Table 15.3. Data analysis should not be used for the purpose of choosing between competing models. It is one's theory that leads to the postulation of causal models. Data analysis can only provide the answer to whether a given model thus derived fits the data. In other words, all one can conclude on the basis of data analysis is whether the model is to be rejected or whether one fails to reject the model.

It was said earlier that in exploratory studies one may revise a model in order to note whether the revision leads to an improvement in the fit to the data. A sharp drop in the χ^2 compared to the difference in the *df*'s associated with the χ^2's for the original and the revised model is taken as an indication of an improvement in the fit. This point is illustrated by contrasting Models II and III. The test of Model II yielded a χ^2 of 58.94 with 2 *df*, whereas the test for Model III yielded a χ^2 of 1.34 with 1 *df*. A drop of 57.6 in the χ^2 is associated with 1 *df*, and it is concluded that the revision of Model II has resulted in a considerable improvement in the fit to the data.

The preceding point can also be demonstrated by showing how the difference between two overidentified models is tested for significance. That is, given that Models II and III are both overidentified, the difference between them can be tested as follows:

$$W = -(N - d)\log_e\left(\frac{1 - M_1}{1 - M_2}\right) \tag{15.22}$$

where N = sample size, and d = the difference between the numbers of over-identifying restrictions of the two models, which in the present case is one. "M_1 is the measure of goodness of fit for the model with the larger number of estimated parameters and M_2 . . . the measure of goodness of fit for the competing model" (Specht, 1975, p. 125). *Note that tests between overidentified models are applicable only when one of the models is nested within the other.* A model is said to be nested within another one if it is obtained by constraining some of the parameters of the latter (see Bentler & Bonett, 1980; and Long, 1976, pp. 169–170, for a discussion of this point). In the present example, Model II of

Figure 15.17 is nested within Model III because the former is obtained from the latter by constraining the path from variable 1 to variable 3 to be equal to zero.

For the present example: $M_1 = .9308$ (obtained above for Model III), and $M_2 = .8853$ (obtained above for Model II). Applying Formula (15.22):

$$W = -(116 - 1)\log_e\left(\frac{1 - .9308}{1 - .8853}\right) = 58.11$$

$\chi^2 = 58.11$ with 1 *df*, $p < .001$. On the basis of this test it is concluded that the deletion of the path from variable 1 to 3 is associated with a significant χ^2, leading to the rejection of Model II in favor of Model III.

PATH REGRESSION COEFFICIENTS

Thus far, the presentation of path analysis was limited to situations in which all the variables have been standardized (i.e., converted to *z* scores). It was shown that when standardized variables are used in recursive models the path coefficients are actually standardized regression coefficients (β's). Accordingly, the advantages and disadvantages of β's, which were discussed in detail earlier in this book (see, in particular, Chapter 8), apply equally to path coefficients. Briefly, it was pointed out that the major advantage of β's is that they are scale-free and can therefore be compared across different variables. But it was also pointed out that the major disadvantage of the β's is that they are population-specific and therefore cannot be used for the purpose of comparisons or generalizations across populations. It is because of this shortcoming that several authors (e.g., Blalock, 1968; Duncan, 1975, Chapter 4; Namboodiri, Carter, & Blalock, 1975, pp. 468–475; Tukey, 1954; Turner & Stevens, 1959) have argued that unstandardized coefficients (b's) be used in the analysis of causal models. Duncan (1975) has perhaps stated this position most forcefully, saying:

> It would probably be salutary if research workers relinquished the habit of expressing variables in standard form. The main reason for this recommendation is that standardization tends to obscure the distinction between the structural coefficients of the model and the several variances and covariances that describe the joint contribution of the variables in a certain population. (p. 51)

In response to the criticisms of the use of path coefficients (β's), Wright (1960a) has maintained that the issue is not one of a choice between two alternative conceptions (i.e., between β's and b's). "It has always seemed to me that these should be looked upon as two aspects of a single theory corresponding to different models of interpretation which, taken together, often give a deeper understanding of a situation than either can give by itself" (p. 189). This is a reasonable position particularly in view of the fact that many, if not most, of the measures used in social science research have no interpretable units. Needless to say, the ultimate solution lies in the development of measures that have meaningful units so that the *b*'s associated with them could be meaningfully interpreted. In the absence of such measures, one may be forced to resort to β's, despite their obvious shortcomings.[15]

Be that as it may, two points will be made. One, both standardized and unstandardized coefficients should be reported so that a reader who wishes to interpret one or the other, or both, will be in a position to do so. At the very least, the standard deviations of all the variables should be reported when only path coefficients (β's) are used, thereby providing the reader with the information necessary to calculate the *b*'s in the event that he or she prefers them over the β's (see below).

Two, while within a given causal model one may use β's to compare the effects of different variables, *b*'s should be used when comparisons of causal models are made across different groups. Very good discussions of comparing causal models across groups, along with numerical examples, may be found in Schoenberg (1972) and Specht and Warren (1976). The remainder of this section will be devoted to a numerical example in which unstandardized coefficients are used.

Numerical Example

In order to distinguish between standardized and unstandardized coefficients, Wright (1960a) has labeled the former *path coefficients* and the latter *path regression coefficients*. Duncan (1975, p. 53) uses the term *structural coefficients* for unstandardized coefficients. The specific label notwithstanding, it was noted above that in recursive models of the type being considered in the present chapter path regression coefficients are partial regression coefficients (*b*'s). Consequently, they are calculated by applying the method of least squares used repeatedly in earlier chapters of this book (see, in particular, Chapter 4).

Beginning with raw data, or with a correlation matrix and standard deviations, one simply regresses each endogenous variable on the exogenous and endogenous variables that are hypothesized to affect it. Alternatively, having calculated path coefficients, one can obtain path regression coefficients by applying a formula presented early in the book—that is, Formula (3.16)—which is repeated here:

$$b_j = \beta_j \frac{s_y}{s_j} \tag{15.23}$$

where b = the unstandardized, or path, regression coefficient for variable j affecting variable y; s_y and s_j = standard deviations of y and j, respectively.

It is the latter approach that will be taken here to illustrate the calculation of path regression coefficients. For this purpose we return to the four-variable causal model presented earlier in Figure 15.12, and which is repeated here as Figure 15.18. The path coefficients for this model were calculated earlier. They

[15]For a detailed discussion of this point see Chapter 8.

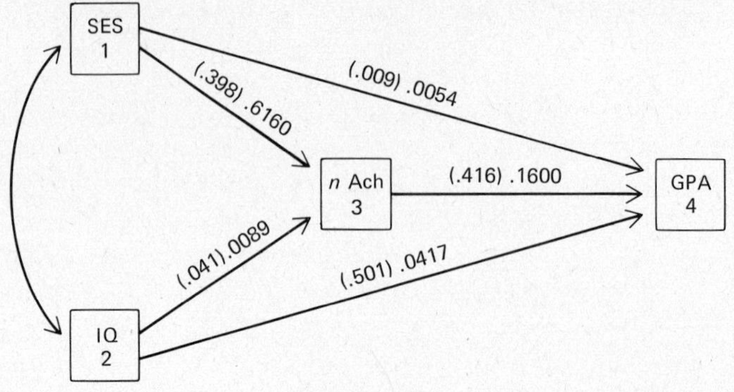

Figure 15.18

are given in parentheses in Figure 15.18. In order to calculate the b's it is necessary to have the standard deviations for the four variables. Assume that these are as follows:

SES = 2.10 IQ = 15.00 n Ach = 3.25 GPA = 1.25

Using these standard deviations and the path coefficients reported in Figure 15.18, apply Formula (15.23) to calculate the path regression coefficients.

$$b_{31.2} = .398 \frac{3.25}{2.10} = .6160$$

$$b_{32.1} = .041 \frac{3.25}{15.00} = .0089$$

$$b_{41.23} = .009 \frac{1.25}{2.10} = .0054$$

$$b_{42.13} = .501 \frac{1.25}{15.00} = .0417$$

$$b_{43.12} = .416 \frac{1.25}{3.25} = .1600$$

A detailed discussion of standardized and unstandardized regression coefficients was given in Chapter 8, and will therefore not be repeated here. It will be noted only that path regression coefficients are interpreted in exactly the same manner as unstandardized regression coefficients. Thus, for example, the path regression coefficient from SES to n Ach (.6160) is interpreted as the expected change in n Ach associated with a unit change in SES, while partialing out the effect of IQ. The remaining path regression coefficients are similarly interpreted. As was noted above, and in Chapter 8, the meaningfulness of such interpretations is predicated on the meaningfulness of the units of the measures of the variables used.

As in the case of path coefficients, path regression coefficients refer to direct effects of one variable on another. In addition, one can calculate indirect effects expressed in path regression coefficients. For example, the direct effect of SES on GPA is .0054. But SES also affects GPA indirectly, via *n* Ach. As in the case of path coefficients, an indirect effect is calculated as the product of two or more path regression coefficients. The path regression coefficient from SES to *n* Ach is .6160, and that from *n* Ach to GPA is .1600. The indirect effect of SES on GPA is therefore (.6160)(.1600) = .0986. Recall that the effect coefficient is equal to the sum of the direct effect and the indirect effect(s). The effect coefficient of SES on GPA is .0054 + .0986 = .1040. Earlier, a matrix approach to the calculation of effect coefficients and indirect effects was introduced in connection with path coefficients. This approach is equally applicable to path regression coefficients, and is now demonstrated for the numerical example under consideration.

Effect Coefficients

Using the matrix approach presented earlier, effect coefficients and indirect effects will be calculated for the present numerical example. Because this approach was discussed in detail earlier, only minimal comments about its application will be given here. If necessary, refer to earlier sections of this chapter.

$$\mathbf{D}_{yx} = \begin{bmatrix} .6160 & .0089 \\ .0054 & .0417 \end{bmatrix}$$

which is the matrix of the direct-effect coefficients of X's (i.e., variables 1 and 2) on the Y's (variables 3 and 4).

$$\mathbf{D}_{yy} = \begin{bmatrix} 0 & 0 \\ .1600 & 0 \end{bmatrix}$$

which is the matrix of direct-effect coefficients of Y (variable 3) on Y (variable 4).

$$\mathbf{I} = \begin{bmatrix} 1 & 0 \\ 0 & 1 \end{bmatrix}$$

$$\mathbf{C} = -\mathbf{D}_{yx} = \begin{bmatrix} -.6160 & -.0089 \\ -.0054 & -.0417 \end{bmatrix}$$

$$\mathbf{B} = \mathbf{I} - \mathbf{D}_{yy} = \begin{bmatrix} 1 & 0 \\ 0 & 1 \end{bmatrix} - \begin{bmatrix} 0 & 0 \\ .1600 & 0 \end{bmatrix} = \begin{bmatrix} 1 & 0 \\ -.1600 & 1 \end{bmatrix}$$

$$\mathbf{E}_{yx} = -\mathbf{B}^{-1}\mathbf{C} = \begin{bmatrix} -1 & 0 \\ -.1600 & -1 \end{bmatrix} \begin{bmatrix} -.6160 & -.0089 \\ -.0054 & -.0417 \end{bmatrix} = \begin{bmatrix} .6160 & .0089 \\ .1040 & .0431 \end{bmatrix}$$

The last matrix consists of the Effect Coefficients (EC) of the X's on the Y's. Specifically, $EC_{31} = .6160$; $EC_{32} = .0089$; $EC_{41} = .1040$; $EC_{42} = .0431$.

$$\mathbf{I}_{yx} = \mathbf{E}_{yx} - \mathbf{D}_{yx} = \begin{bmatrix} .6160 & .0089 \\ .1040 & .0431 \end{bmatrix} - \begin{bmatrix} .6160 & .0089 \\ .0054 & .0417 \end{bmatrix} = \begin{bmatrix} 0 & 0 \\ .0986 & .0014 \end{bmatrix}$$

The last matrix contains the Indirect Effect (IE) of the X's on the Y's: $IE_{41} = .0985$ and $IE_{42} = .0014$.

$$\mathbf{E}_{yy} = \mathbf{B}^{-1} - \mathbf{I} = \begin{bmatrix} 1 & 0 \\ .1600 & 1 \end{bmatrix} - \begin{bmatrix} 1 & 0 \\ 0 & 1 \end{bmatrix} = \begin{bmatrix} 0 & 0 \\ .1600 & 0 \end{bmatrix}$$

The effect coefficient of variable 3 on variable 4 is .1600.

$$\mathbf{I}_{yy} = \mathbf{E}_{yy} - \mathbf{D}_{yy} = \begin{bmatrix} 0 & 0 \\ .1600 & 0 \end{bmatrix} - \begin{bmatrix} 0 & 0 \\ .1600 & 0 \end{bmatrix} = \begin{bmatrix} 0 & 0 \\ 0 & 0 \end{bmatrix}$$

In the present example, the endogenous variable 3 has no indirect effect on variable 4 (see Figure 15.8).

Decomposition of Covariances

It was shown earlier that having calculated path coefficients it is possible to decompose the correlations among the variables in a given causal model. It was also shown how path coefficients obtained in an overidentified model may be used for the purpose of reproducing the correlation matrix. These approaches may be similarly used with path regression coefficients, except that it is the *covariances* among the variables that are being decomposed or reproduced. Detailed descriptions of the application of these procedures in models in which unstandardized variables are used may be found in Duncan (1975, Chapter 4) and in Fox (1980).

CONCLUDING REMARKS

Path analysis was presented as a method for studying patterns of causation among variables. Recognizing that it is a method, it follows that it may be used judiciously or injudiciously. A method is as good or as bad as the use to which it is put by a prudent or imprudent researcher. It was noted in the beginning of the chapter that path analysis is currently in vogue and that it is often misapplied. Misapplications are primarily due to the failure to recognize that the valid use of path analysis is predicated on a theoretical formulation about the pattern of causation among the variables being studied. It is theory that generates the path model; not the other way around.

Even when path analysis is applied according to a theoretical model, it is important to be alert to potential violations of the assumptions on which the method is based. Notable pitfalls are the omission of relevant important variables, the use of measures that are not highly reliable, the possibility that residuals from different equations are intercorrelated. Serious violations of any of the preceding may lead to serious biases in the estimation of path coefficients, hence to erroneous conclusions.

This chapter was limited to recursive models—that is, models in which the causal flow is unidirectional. Needless to say, such models are often unrealistic when they are used to reflect complex phenomena studied by social and behavioral scientists. Although extensions of path analysis are available (see, for example, Turner & Stevens, 1959, and Wright, 1960b, for the analysis of nonrecursive models), these were not presented in this chapter because more powerful approaches to the analysis of complex causal models have been developed in recent years. Chapter 16 is devoted to an introduction to one such approach.

STUDY SUGGESTIONS

1. Distinguish between exogenous and endogenous variables.
2. What is a recursive model? Give examples.
3. Distinguish between exactly identified and overidentified models. What is a serious limitation of an exactly identified model?
4. What is meant by theory trimming? Discuss potential problems in such an approach.
5. Distinguish between path coefficients and path regression coefficients.
6. What is the definition of an effect coefficient?
7. In studies of authoritarianism it has been found that the *F* scale (a measure of authoritarianism) is correlated negatively with mental ability and years of education. Assume that the following causal model is hypothesized:

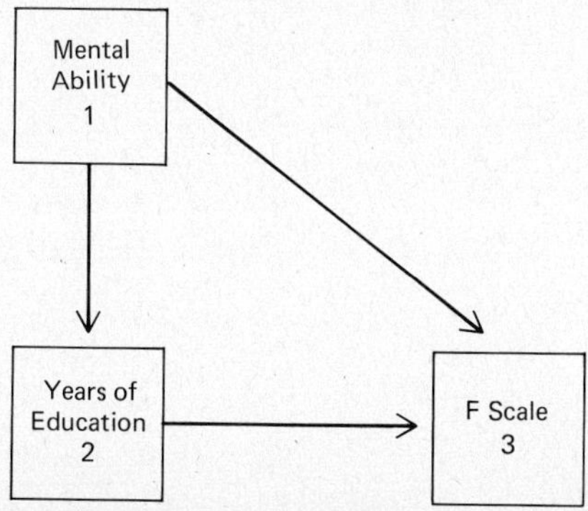

Suppose that the correlations for the above variables are: $r_{12} = .6$; $r_{13} = -.5$; $r_{23} = -.6$. The subscript numbers refer to the variable numbers in the figure. Using the above information, do a path analysis.

(a) What is the direct effect of mental ability on years of education?
(b) What is the direct effect of mental ability on authoritarianism?
(c) What is the direct effect of years of education on authoritarianism?
(d) What is the indirect effect of mental ability on authoritarianism?
(e) Decompose r_{13} and r_{23}.
(f) What are the effect coefficients of mental ability and years of education on authoritarianism?
(g) What are the coefficients for the residual paths to years of education, and to authoritarianism?

8. The following illustrative correlation matrix ($N = 300$) was used earlier in the Study Suggestions for Chapters 6, 7, and 8.

	1 Race	2 IQ	3 School Quality	4 Self-Concept	5 Level of Aspiration	6 Verbal Achievement
1	1.00	.30	.25	.30	.30	.25
2	.30	1.00	.20	.20	.30	.60
3	.25	.20	1.00	.20	.30	.30
4	.30	.20	.20	1.00	.40	.30
5	.30	.30	.30	.40	1.00	.40
6	.25	.60	.30	.30	.40	1.00

The causal model depicted in the following figure is the same as that used in Chapter 7 for the purpose of incremental partitioning of variance.

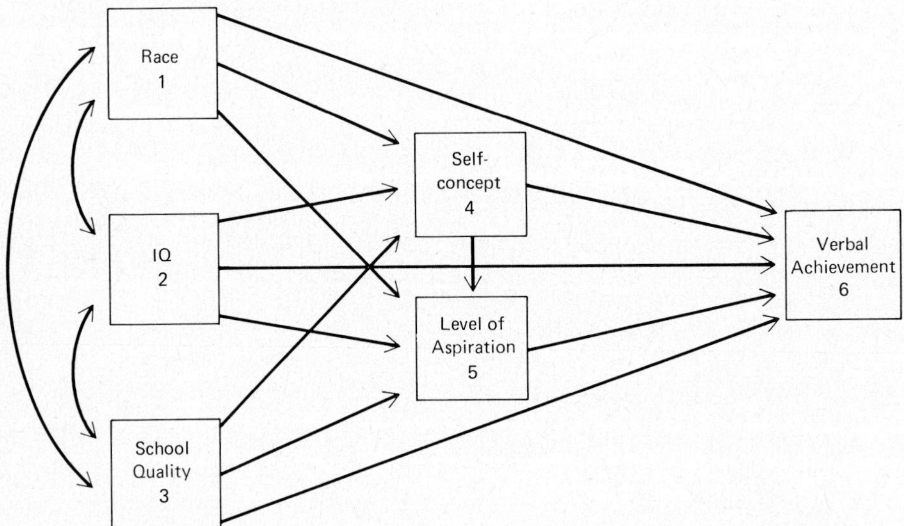

Using the correlation matrix do a path analysis according to the model depicted in the figure.

(a) What are the direct effects of variables 1, 2, and 3 on 4?

(b) What are the direct effects of variables 1, 2, 3, and 4 on 5?

(c) What are the direct effects of variables 1, 2, 3, 4, and 5 on 6?

(d) Using matrix operations, as shown in the chapter, calculate: (1) the effect coefficients of the exogenous variables on the endogenous variables; (2) the indirect effects of the exogenous variables on the endogenous variables; (3) the effect coefficients of endogenous variables on endogenous variables; (4) indirect effects of endogenous variables on endogenous variables.

(e) Calculate the coefficients for the residual paths to variables 4, 5, and 6.

(f) Delete the path from variable 2 to variable 4, and from variable 1 to variable 6, and test the revised model.

(g) What are the path coefficients for the revised model?

Compare the results with those obtained earlier when the same data were subjected to an incremental partitioning of variance (Chapter 7) and to a multiple regression analysis (Chapter 8).

ANSWERS

3. An exactly identified model cannot be tested.
5. Path coefficients are standardized. Path regression coefficients are unstandardized.
6. The effect coefficient is equal to the sum of the direct and indirect effects of a variable on a given endogenous variable.
7. (a) $p_{21} = .6$
   (b) $p_{31} = -.219$
   (c) $p_{32} = -.469$
   (d) IE $= -.281$
   (e) $r_{13} = -.5 = \underbrace{-.219}_{\text{DE}} + \underbrace{(-.281)}_{\text{IE}}$

   $r_{23} = -.6 = \underbrace{-.469}_{\text{DE}} + \underbrace{(-.131)}_{\text{S}}$

   (f) $EC_1 = -.5$; $EC_2 = -.469$
   (g) $p_{2e} = .80$; $p_{3e} = .78$
8. (a) $p_{41} = .239$; $p_{42} = .104$; $p_{43} = .119$
   (b) $p_{51} = .116$; $p_{52} = .171$; $p_{53} = .178$; $p_{54} = .296$
   (c) $p_{61} = -.019$; $p_{62} = .506$; $p_{63} = .130$; $p_{64} = .110$; $p_{65} = .171$
   (d)

   (1) $\mathbf{E}_{yx} = \begin{bmatrix} .239 & .104 & .119 \\ .187 & .202 & .213 \\ .039 & .552 & .180 \end{bmatrix}$

   (2) $\mathbf{I}_{yx} = \begin{bmatrix} 0 & 0 & 0 \\ .071 & .031 & .035 \\ .058 & .046 & .050 \end{bmatrix}$

   (3) $\mathbf{E}_{yy} = \begin{bmatrix} 0 & 0 & 0 \\ .296 & 0 & 0 \\ .161 & .171 & 0 \end{bmatrix}$

   (4) $\mathbf{I}_{yy} = \begin{bmatrix} 0 & 0 & 0 \\ 0 & 0 & 0 \\ .051 & 0 & 0 \end{bmatrix}$

   (e) $p_{4e} = .940$; $p_{5e} = .862$; $p_{6e} = .749$
   (f) $\chi^2 = 3.42$, with 2 *df*.
   (g) $p_{41} = .267$; $p_{42} = 0$; $p_{43} = .133$;
   $p_{51} = .116$; $p_{52} = .171$; $p_{53} = .178$; $p_{54} = .296$;
   $p_{61} = 0$; $p_{62} = .503$; $p_{63} = .128$; $p_{64} = .107$; $p_{65} = .168$

16

INTRODUCTION TO LINEAR STRUCTURAL RELATIONS (LISREL)

In the preceding chapter path analysis was introduced, along with some illustrative applications. It was shown, among other things, how path analysis may be used for the purpose of decomposing relations among variables and for testing causal models. It will be recalled, however, that the validity of the method was predicated on a set of very restrictive assumptions, some of which are that: (1) the variables are measured without error; (2) the residuals are not intercorrelated; and (3) the causal flow is unidirectional (i.e., the causal models are recursive). Needless to say, such assumptions are rarely, if ever, met in applied settings, particularly in nonexperimental research. Following are but a few arguments in support of the preceding statement.

It is a truism that measures are fallible. Many of the measures used in social and behavioral research have at best moderate reliabilities. Moreover, classical approaches to reliability (e.g., Nunnally, 1978) treat errors as being random. Many sources of error are, however, nonrandom or systematic, hence affecting the validity, not the reliability, of measures.

Many of the variables in social and behavioral research are unobservable or latent variables (e.g., motivation, anxiety, intelligence, attitudes). It is unrealistic to expect, as one would have to in path analysis, a single indicator to capture validly and reliably such complex constructs. Instead, multiple indicators are called for.

Often, it is unreasonable to assume, as is done in path analysis, that residuals from different equations are not correlated. Such an assumption is untenable, for example, in longitudinal research when subjects are measured at several points in time on the same variables.

Finally, the formulation of recursive models (i.e., models with unidirectional causation) is unrealistic in many research areas. Moreover, interest in reciprocal causation may be the focus of the research. In studies of academic achievement, for example, one would expect parents' or teachers' expectations to affect students' achievement and in turn to be affected by students' achievement. Similarly, one would expect students' motivation or aspirations to affect students' achievement and to be affected by it.

Path analysis is inapplicable in any of the above noted situations. It was stated in the preceding chapter that extensions of path analysis to accommodate nonrecursive models have been suggested. Other approaches to the analysis of nonrecursive models are available. One such approach—two-stage least squares—is used extensively by econometricians (see, for example, Fox, 1968; Johnston, 1972; Kmenta, 1971; and Rao & Miller, 1971). Methods have also been developed for use with multiple indicator models, notably by Costner (see Costner, 1969; Costner & Schoenberg, 1973; see also Sullivan & Feldman, 1979; and Zeller & Carmines, 1980).

The preceding are but some examples of analytic approaches available for the analysis of causal models that cannot be dealt with in the context of path analysis. More sophisticated and more general approaches to the analysis of causal models have, however, been recently developed. These approaches, generally referred to as structural equation models (see below), "have intertwined the best of psychometric, econometric, and statistical theory" (Bentler, 1978, p. 268). They are not only more powerful than path analysis, but also are based on less restrictive assumptions and subsume path analysis and other approaches as special cases. It is the purpose of this chapter to introduce one such approach. But before doing this, a comment about structural equation models will be made.

Structural Equation Models

The terms *path analysis, causal modeling,* and *structural equation models* have been used by some authors from different disciplines to refer to different and somewhat specialized approaches to the analysis of causal relations among variables. This is particularly true in the use of the term *path analysis* (see Chapter 15). In recent years, however, most authors seem to prefer the use of *structural equation models* as a generic term for the various approaches to the analysis of causality. Excellent reviews of structural equation models will be found in Bentler (1980) and in Bielby and Hauser (1977a). Major recent contributions in this field will be found in Aigner and Goldberger (1977) and in Goldberger and Duncan (1973). One of the approaches that has gained in prominence and is probably the most popular among social scientists was developed by Jöreskog, who labeled it LISREL. It is to this approach that this chapter is exclusively devoted.

LISREL

LISREL is a very versatile approach that may be used for the analysis of causal models with multiple indicators of latent variables, reciprocal causation, measurement errors, correlated errors, and correlated residuals to name but a few. Because of its versatility, LISREL is also very complex. It is therefore important to state the aims of the presentation in this chapter. What follows is meant to serve as an elementary intuitive introduction to LISREL, to the meaning of the elements of the equations used in this approach, and to the application of the computer program LISREL IV (Jöreskog & Sörbom, 1978) to several very simple causal models. Because the models to be analyzed are very simple, they cannot convey the flavor of the complex models that can be handled by LISREL. Nevertheless, it was felt that the use of simple models is best suited to provide a grasp of the basic principles and the basic approach to the application of LISREL. Specifically, the models to be analyzed are (1) recursive models of the type presented in detail in the preceding chapter (i.e., path-analytic models); (2) a model with correlated residuals; (3) a nonrecursive model (i.e., one that includes reciprocal causation between variables); and (4) a model with multiple indicators of unobserved, or latent, variables.

As will become apparent, a good deal of what follows is taken up with detailed descriptions of the use of LISREL IV and comments about its output. This may appear strange, particularly in view of the availability of an extensive manual for this program. Yet, users of LISREL IV encounter difficulties in the formulation of the equations to represent their models and in translating the equations into appropriate computer instructions. Commenting on such difficulties, a colleague said: "My students climb the wall!" It is not at all surprising that Kenny (1979), who provides a very good introduction to LISREL, states: "When I run LISREL I presume I have made an error. I check and recheck my results" (p. 183). While it is worthwhile to follow Kenny's example whenever a complex analytic method is used, it is particularly important to do so when using LISREL.

Before turning to a description of LISREL, some comments about the statistical theory on which it is based are in order. Unlike the methods presented in other chapters of this book, which are based on least-squares statistical theory, LISREL is based on *maximum-likelihood* (ML) statistical theory. It is not possible to discuss ML theory here (for elementary introductions, see Fox, 1968; Hanushek & Jackson, 1977; Mulaik, 1972; Nunnally, 1978; Winer, 1971). It will only be noted that, given specific distributional assumptions, ML estimators are estimators of the parameters most likely to have generated the observed data. Or, as Mulaik puts it:

> The idea of a maximum-likelihood estimator is this: We assume that we know the *general form* of the population distribution from which a sample is drawn. For example, we might assume the population distribution is a multivariate normal distribution. But what we do not know are the population parameters which give this distribution a particular form among all possible multivariate normal distributions. In the absence of such knowledge, however, we can take arbitrary values and treat them *as if* they were the population parameters and ask ourselves what is the *likelihood* . . . of observing certain values for the variables on a single observation drawn from such a population. If we have more than one observation, then we can ask what is the joint likelihood of obtaining such a sample of observation vectors? Finally we can ask: What values for the population parameters make the sample observations have the greatest joint likelihood? When we answer this question, we will take such values to be *maximum-likelihood estimators* of the population parameters. (1972, p. 162)

It will be noted that when the residuals are normally distributed, ML estimators are identical to least-squares estimators. For discussions of advantages and disadvantages of ML estimators, see the references cited above.

Jöreskog has written extensively about ML solutions in general and in connection with their use in LISREL (some of his contributions and those of his associate, Sörbom, have been collected in Jöreskog & Sörbom, 1979). It is suggested, however, that you begin with some simpler introductions before attempting to read Jöreskog's original contributions. Very good introductions to LISREL will be found in Bentler and Woodward (1978, 1979), Burt (1973), Kenny (1979), Long (1976), and Sörbom and Jöreskog (1981). As was noted above, Jöreskog and Sörbom (1978) have also developed an extremely versatile computer program, which is currently in its fourth version, LISREL IV. The manual for LISREL IV contains an excellent introduction to LISREL as well as detailed explanations and examples of its application to different causal models.

LISREL consists of two major subdivisions: (1) the structural equation model and (2) the measurement model. Each of these is now outlined.

The Structural Equation Model

The structural equation model refers to relations among exogenous and endogenous variables. Most often, these variables are constructs and therefore are unobserved. Such variables are also referred to as latent, or true, variables. Latent variables are frequently encountered in the social sciences. In fact, constructs such as intelligence, motivation, attitudes, ambition, anxiety, aspirations, and cognitive styles play a crucial role in the social sciences and in social science research. In LISREL, latent dependent, or endogenous, variables are designated as η (eta), whereas latent independent, or exogenous, variables are designated as ξ (xi). The structural equation model is:

$$\mathbf{B}\boldsymbol{\eta} = \boldsymbol{\Gamma}\boldsymbol{\xi} + \boldsymbol{\zeta} \tag{16.1}$$

where $\boldsymbol{\eta}$ (eta) is an m by 1 vector of latent endogenous variables; $\boldsymbol{\xi}$ (xi) is an n by 1 vector of latent exogenous variables; $\mathbf{B}$ (beta) is an m by m matrix of coefficients of the effects of endogenous on endogenous variables; $\boldsymbol{\Gamma}$ (gamma) is an m by n matrix of coefficients of the effects of exogenous variables (ξ's) on endogenous variables (η's); $\boldsymbol{\zeta}$(zeta) is an m by 1 vector of residuals, or errors in equations. It is assumed that the means of all the variables are equal to zero—that is, that the variables are expressed in deviation scores. Also, it is assumed that ζ and ξ are uncorrelated, and that $\mathbf{B}$ is nonsingular.

The Measurement Model

The measurement model specifies the relations between unobserved and observed, or latent and manifest, variables. Two equations describe this model:

$$\mathbf{y} = \boldsymbol{\Lambda}_y\boldsymbol{\eta} + \boldsymbol{\epsilon} \tag{16.2}$$

where **y** is a p by 1 vector of measures of dependent variables; $\boldsymbol{\Lambda}$ (lambda) is a p by m matrix of coefficients, or loadings, of **y** on the unobserved dependent variables ($\boldsymbol{\eta}$); $\boldsymbol{\epsilon}$ (epsilon) is a p by 1 vector of errors of measurement of **y**.

$$\mathbf{x} = \boldsymbol{\Lambda}_x \boldsymbol{\xi} + \boldsymbol{\delta} \qquad (16.3)$$

where **x** is a q by 1 vector of measures of independent variables; $\boldsymbol{\Lambda}$ (lambda) is a q by n matrix of coefficients, or loadings, of **x** on the unobserved independent variables ($\boldsymbol{\xi}$); and $\boldsymbol{\delta}$ (delta) is a q by 1 vector of errors of measurement of **x**.

In order to clarify the terms introduced in Equations (16.1) through (16.3) a relatively simple causal model will be presented—first graphically and then in matrix form. To highlight the difference between the type of models dealt with here and those presented in Chapter 15, the causal model to be used here for illustrative purposes will parallel one that has been used in Chapter 15. Specifically, the model presented in Figure 16.1 parallels the one presented as Figure 15.13 in Chapter 15. Following Jöreskog, squares are used to represent observed variables, and circles are used to represent unobserved variables. The causal model of Figure 16.1 consists of two latent exogenous variables (ξ_1 and ξ_2) and two latent endogenous variables (η_1 and η_2). Assume that ξ_1 is Socioeconomic Status (SES), and that ξ_2 is Intelligence (IQ). According to the model, SES is measured by three indicators (X_1, X_2, and X_3) and IQ is measured by two indicators (X_4 and X_5). Assume, further, that η_1 is Achievement Motivation (n Ach) and is measured by two indicators (Y_1 and Y_2). η_2 is Achievement (Ach) and is measured by three indicators (Y_3, Y_4, and Y_5).

According to the model depicted in Figure 16.1, SES affects n Ach directly,

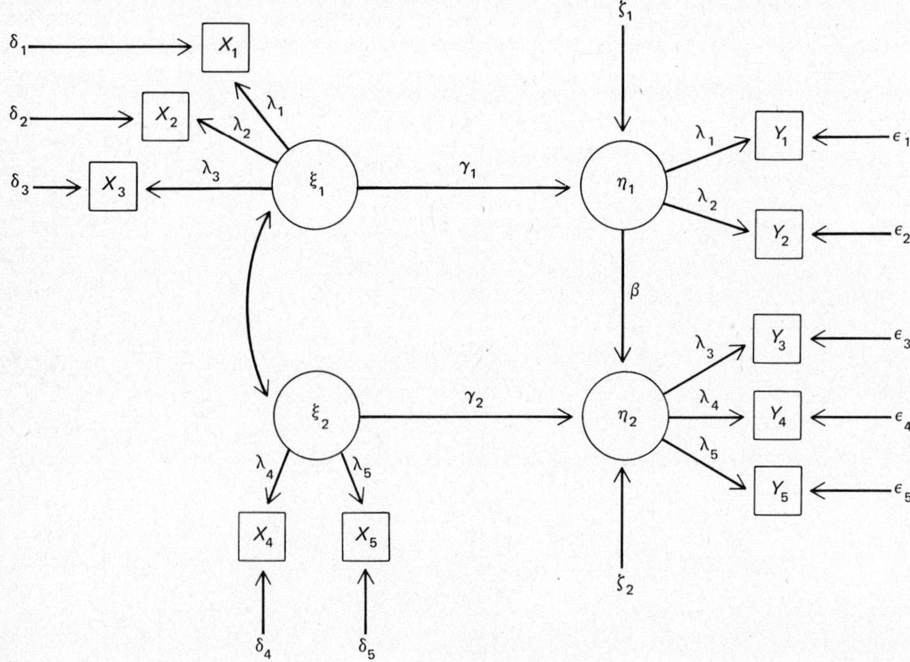

Figure 16.1

and Ach indirectly via *n* Ach. IQ affects Ach directly. This model is the same as that depicted in Figure 15.13, except that in the latter a single measure was used to measure each construct. In other words, in the preceding chapter it was assumed *unrealistically* that the constructs and the scales used to measure them are identities, whereas in the present chapter the constructs are treated as unobserved variables, each of which is measured by two or more fallible measures. Whereas the causal model of Figure 16.1 is recursive, LISREL accommodates also nonrecursive models. For example, in Figure 16.1 it could have been hypothesized that not only does η_1 affect η_2, but also that the latter affects the former. Furthermore, whereas the errors in Figure 16.1 are depicted as being not correlated among themselves, LISREL can accommodate models with correlated errors. The major virtue of LISREL, then, is that it enables one to separate latent variables from errors, thereby affording the study of meaningful relations among the former. This is predicated, among other things, on judicious choices of the indicators, or the manifest variables. "Since the LVs [Latent Variables] are in practice abstractions that presumably underlie MVs [Manifest Variables], a poor choice of MVs will create doubt as to whether a theory's constructs are in fact embedded in a model. Choosing the right number of indicators for each LV is something of an art: in principle, the more the better; in practice, too many indicators make it difficult if not impossible to fit a model to data" (Bentler, 1980, p. 425).

Following is the structural equation model for Figure 16.1.

$$\underset{\mathbf{B}}{\begin{bmatrix} 1 & 0 \\ -\beta & 1 \end{bmatrix}} \underset{\boldsymbol{\eta}}{\begin{bmatrix} \eta_1 \\ \eta_2 \end{bmatrix}} = \underset{\boldsymbol{\Gamma}}{\begin{bmatrix} \gamma_1 & 0 \\ 0 & \gamma_2 \end{bmatrix}} \underset{\boldsymbol{\xi}}{\begin{bmatrix} \xi_1 \\ \xi_2 \end{bmatrix}} + \underset{\boldsymbol{\zeta}}{\begin{bmatrix} \zeta_1 \\ \zeta_2 \end{bmatrix}}$$

Note that the sign of the effect of η_1 on η_2 is negative to compensate for the fact that **B** is placed on the left-hand side of the equal sign. That is, carrying out the matrix operations using the second rows of **B** and **Γ**, one obtains

$$-\beta\eta_1 + \eta_2 = \gamma_2\xi_2 + \zeta_2$$

which may be transformed into

$$\eta_2 = \beta\eta_1 + \gamma_2\xi_2 + \zeta_2$$

The measurement model for Figure 16.1 is as follows:

$$\underset{\mathbf{x}}{\begin{bmatrix} x_1 \\ x_2 \\ x_3 \\ x_4 \\ x_5 \end{bmatrix}} = \underset{\boldsymbol{\Lambda}_x}{\begin{bmatrix} \lambda_1 & 0 \\ \lambda_2 & 0 \\ \lambda_3 & 0 \\ 0 & \lambda_4 \\ 0 & \lambda_5 \end{bmatrix}} \underset{\boldsymbol{\xi}}{\begin{bmatrix} \xi_1 \\ \xi_2 \end{bmatrix}} + \underset{\boldsymbol{\delta}}{\begin{bmatrix} \delta_1 \\ \delta_2 \\ \delta_3 \\ \delta_4 \\ \delta_5 \end{bmatrix}}$$

$$\begin{bmatrix} y_1 \\ y_2 \\ y_3 \\ y_4 \\ y_5 \end{bmatrix} = \begin{bmatrix} \lambda_1 & 0 \\ \lambda_2 & 0 \\ 0 & \lambda_3 \\ 0 & \lambda_4 \\ 0 & \lambda_5 \end{bmatrix} \begin{bmatrix} \eta_1 \\ \\ \eta_2 \end{bmatrix} + \begin{bmatrix} \epsilon_1 \\ \epsilon_2 \\ \epsilon_3 \\ \epsilon_4 \\ \epsilon_5 \end{bmatrix}$$

$$\mathbf{y} = \mathbf{\Lambda}_y \quad \boldsymbol{\eta} + \boldsymbol{\epsilon}$$

Jöreskog (e.g., Jöreskog & Sörbom, 1978, p. 5) shows that on the basis of the assumptions of LISREL the covariance matrix of the observed variables (Σ) is a function of the following eight matrices:

1. $\mathbf{\Lambda}_y$ (lambda) is the matrix of coefficients, or loadings, relating indicators of endogenous variables to latent endogenous variables ($\boldsymbol{\eta}$).
2. $\mathbf{\Lambda}_x$ (lambda) is the matrix of coefficients, or loadings, relating indicators of exogenous variables to latent exogenous variables ($\boldsymbol{\xi}$).
3. **B** (beta) is the matrix of coefficients of the effects of latent endogenous variables on latent endogenous variables.
4. $\mathbf{\Gamma}$ (gamma) is the matrix of coefficients of the effects of latent exogenous variables on latent endogenous variables.
5. $\mathbf{\Phi}$ (phi) is a variance-covariance matrix of the latent exogenous variables ($\boldsymbol{\xi}$).
6. $\boldsymbol{\psi}$ (psi) is a variance-covariance matrix of the residuals (ζ).
7. $\mathbf{\Theta}_\epsilon$ (theta) is a variance-covariance matrix of errors of measurement of y's.
8. $\mathbf{\Theta}_\delta$ (theta) is the variance-covariance matrix of errors of measurement of x's.

Estimation

The elements of the above noted matrices may be of three kinds:

(i) *fixed parameters* that have been assigned given values,
(ii) *constrained parameters* that are unknown but equal to one or more other parameters and
(iii) *free parameters* that are unknown and not constrained to be equal to any other parameter. (Jöreskog & Sörbom, 1978, p. 6)

Using the covariance matrix among the observed variables Jöreskog arrives at estimates of elements in the eight matrices listed above by the method of maximum likelihood. No attempt will be made here to describe the complex estimation process. Instead, the remainder of the chapter will be devoted to some examples of LISREL solutions by using the computer program, LISREL IV, developed by Jöreskog and Sörbom (1978).

LISREL IV

LISREL IV is an extremely versatile, and therefore quite complex, computer program. The manual for LISREL IV contains extensive and detailed descriptions of the models it can handle, as well as detailed instructions and numerical examples. It should be stressed that what follows is *not* meant to supplant the LISREL IV manual. Quite the contrary, it is designed to supplement the manual in the hope of thereby acquainting you with some of the basic features of the program. Therefore it was decided to show first how LISREL IV can be used to solve path-analytic problems of the kind presented and discussed in detail in Chapter 15. This is followed by an example in which residuals are assumed to be correlated, and an example of a nonrecursive model. In all of these examples a single indicator is used for the measurement of each of the variables. The chapter concludes with a simple example in which multiple indicators are used for the measurement of each of the latent variables.

LISREL IV is very flexible in the formats for reading in data, specifying the kinds of parameters in the eight matrices listed above and the assignment of starting values (see below). In the following presentation only one type of format is used for reading in data and for specifying the parameter matrices and starting values. The format to be used is not necessarily the most efficient but is probably the simplest and most straightforward for illustrative purposes. For other formats consult the LISREL IV manual. It is strongly suggested that when you study the examples given below you refer as frequently as is necessary to the LISREL IV manual.

For each example, all the control cards will be listed and commented upon. This will be followed by excerpts of output, along with commentaries. To repeat, very simple examples are purposely used in the hope that this will facilitate your learning how to use LISREL IV. In Study Suggestion 5, references are given to studies in which LISREL IV was used for the analysis of more complex models.

Path Analysis: A Just-Identified Model

In Figure 15.12, a four-variable path model was presented and analyzed in detail. Briefly, Socioeconomic Status (SES) and Intelligence (IQ) were treated as two correlated exogenous variables. It was hypothesized that SES and IQ affect Need Achievement (*n* Ach), and that SES, IQ, and *n* Ach affect achievement as measured by Grade-Point Average (GPA). The causal model for these variables is depicted in Figure 16.2, following the conventions of drawing such models in LISREL (see above). The difference between Figure 16.2 and Figure 15.12 is that in the former a distinction is made between latent variables (enclosed in circles) and manifest variables (enclosed in squares). Note that variable 4 of Figure 15.12 is labeled here Achievement (ACH) to distinguish it from its indicator, GPA. Note that each indicator is treated as being a perfectly reliable and valid measure of the variable that it presumably measures. This is indicated in Figure 16.2 by coefficients that are equal to 1.00 emanating from each latent variable to its indicator and by zero errors associated with the indicators. Needless to say, these assumptions are most unrealistic when one considers the type of variables being studied and the kind of measures generally used to tap them. The virtue of the diagram in Figure 16.2 is that it forcefully brings to light these untenable assumptions. In Figure 15.12,

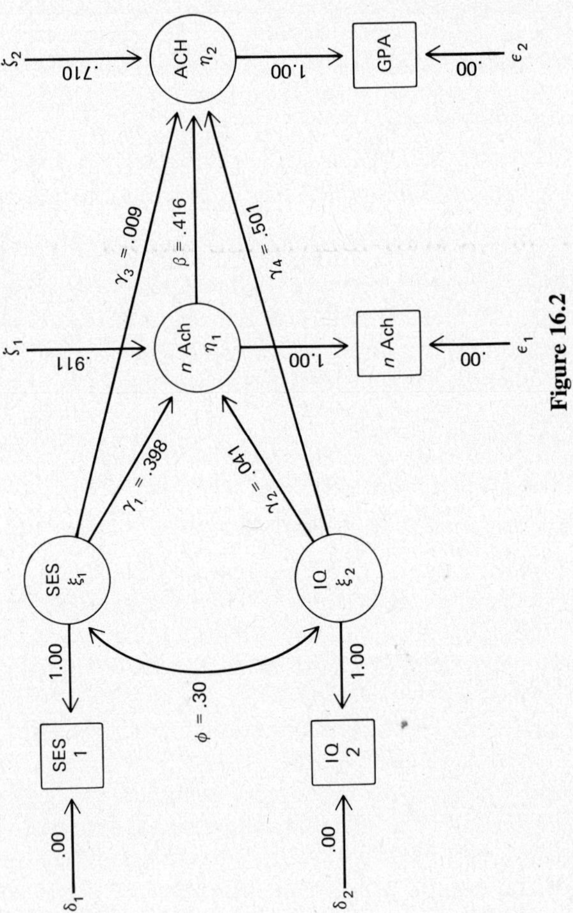
SES
ξ_1
IQ
ξ_2
n Ach
η_1
ACH
η_2
SES
1
IQ
2
n Ach
GPA
δ_1
δ_2
.00
1.00
ϕ = .30
γ_1 = .398
γ_2 = .041
γ_3 = .009
γ_4 = .501
β = .416
ζ_1
.911
ζ_2
.710
ϵ_1
ϵ_2

Figure 16.2

on the other hand, the same assumptions recede into the background, so to speak, and therefore the probability of overlooking them is much greater than when the model is depicted as in Figure 16.2.

Because the illustrative data related to Figure 16.2 were analyzed in detail in Chapter 15, it will be instructive to show how the same data are analyzed using LISREL IV. The correlation matrix among the variables is repeated here in Table 16.1.

Table 16.1 Correlation Matrix for the Four-Variable Model of Figure 16.2; N = 100

	3	*4*	*1*	*2*
	n Ach	*GPA*	*SES*	*IQ*
3	1.00			
4	.50	1.00		
1	.41	.33	1.00	
2	.16	.57	.30	1.00

Control Cards

```
(1) FIGURE 16.2 A JUST-IDENTIFIED MODEL
(2) DA NI=4 MA=KM NO=100
(3) LA
(4) *
(5) 'N ACH' 'GPA' 'SES' 'IQ'
(6) KM
(7) *
(8) 1.0 .5 1.0 .41 .33 1.0 .16 .57 .30 1.0
(9) MO FIXEDX NY=2 NX=2 NE=2 LY=ID PS=FR GA=FR TE=ZE
(10) PA BE
(11) *
(12) 0 0 1 0
(13) MA BE
(14) *
(15) 1 0 −.4 1
(16) MA GA
(17) *
(18) .4 .05 .01 .5
(19) MA PS
(20) *
(21) .8 .5
(22) OU PM MR SE TV
```

Commentary

The cards are numbered here for easy reference. These numbers are *not* punched when LISREL IV is run.

Card 1. A title to be printed on the output.

Card 2. DA refers to DATA. NI is the number of input variables. MA = KM indicates that a correlation matrix is to be analyzed. NO is the number of observations.

Cards 3–5. LA refers to labels. An * (asterisk) in column 1 indicates that what follows is to be read in a free format. Note that this type of format is used throughout in the present example (e.g., cards 11, 14). When * is used, entries are separated by blanks or commas. Note also that each label is placed between apostrophes.

Cards 6–8. KM refers to the correlation matrix. With the type of input format used here (i.e., *) the lower half of the correlation matrix, including the diagonal, is read in a free format row-wise as a single vector. Note that endogenous variables (N ACH and GPA) are read in first, followed by the exogenous variables (SES and IQ). Alternatively, one may use a SELECT statement to reorder the variables so that endogenous variables are taken first (see LISREL IV manual).

Card 9. This card is used to specify the model. FIXEDX means that the exogenous variables (SES and IQ) are treated as being nonrandom. This implies that: (a) $\mathbf{\Lambda}_x = \mathbf{I}$; that is, lambda x is an identity matrix; (b) $\mathbf{\Theta}_\delta = 0$; that is, the x's are measured without error; (c) $\mathbf{\Phi}$, the correlation between the x's is fixed. Taken together, the preceding statements indicate that $\mathbf{x} \equiv \boldsymbol{\xi}$; that is, the latent and manifest exogenous variables are treated as identities.

NE = 2 means there are two latent endogenous variables (η). But specifying that LY = ID ($\Lambda_y = \text{I}$) and that TE = ZE ($\Theta_\epsilon = 0$) means that $\mathbf{y} \equiv \eta$. That is, the latent and manifest endogenous variables are treated as identities.

GA = FR means that all the values of Gamma are free. Consequently, it is not necessary to specify a pattern matrix for Gamma. Similarly, PS = FR means that PSI (ψ) is a diagonal (default) composed of free values, and therefore a pattern matrix for PS is not necessary.

To further clarify the meaning of the model being specified here the matrices will be spelled out.

$$\underset{\mathbf{x}}{\begin{bmatrix} x_1 \\ x_2 \end{bmatrix}} = \underset{\mathbf{\Lambda}_x}{\begin{bmatrix} 1 & 0 \\ 0 & 1 \end{bmatrix}} \underset{\boldsymbol{\xi}}{\begin{bmatrix} \xi_1 \\ \xi_2 \end{bmatrix}} + \underset{\mathbf{\Theta}_\delta}{\begin{bmatrix} 0 & \\ & 0 \end{bmatrix}}$$

The preceding is the measurement model relating latent exogenous variables to their indicators. $\mathbf{\Theta}_\delta$ (THETA DELTA) is a diagonal matrix (default) whose diagonal elements have been fixed to be equal to zero by virtue of specifying FIXEDX on the MODEL card (see card 9)

$$\underset{\mathbf{y}}{\begin{bmatrix} y_1 \\ y_2 \end{bmatrix}} = \underset{\mathbf{\Lambda}_y}{\begin{bmatrix} 1 & 0 \\ 0 & 1 \end{bmatrix}} \underset{\boldsymbol{\eta}}{\begin{bmatrix} \eta_1 \\ \eta_2 \end{bmatrix}} + \underset{\mathbf{\Theta}_\epsilon}{\begin{bmatrix} 0 & \\ & 0 \end{bmatrix}}$$

The preceding is the measurement model relating latent endogenous variables to their indicators. $\mathbf{\Theta}_\epsilon$ (THETA EPSILON) is a diagonal matrix (default) whose diagonal elements have been set equal to zero by specifying TE = ZE on the MODEL card (see card 9, above).

Because of the above specifications, the structural equation model for the present example becomes

$$\mathbf{By} = \mathbf{\Gamma x} + \boldsymbol{\zeta} \qquad (16.4)$$

Compare (16.4) with (16.1) and note that in the former **y** replaces $\boldsymbol{\eta}$ and **x** replaces $\boldsymbol{\xi}$. Spelling out the matrices for the structural equation model:

$$\underset{\mathbf{B}}{\begin{bmatrix} 1 & 0 \\ -\beta & 1 \end{bmatrix}} \underset{\mathbf{y}}{\begin{bmatrix} y_1 \\ y_2 \end{bmatrix}} = \underset{\mathbf{\Gamma}}{\begin{bmatrix} \gamma_1 & \gamma_2 \\ \gamma_3 & \gamma_4 \end{bmatrix}} \underset{\mathbf{x}}{\begin{bmatrix} x_1 \\ x_2 \end{bmatrix}} + \underset{\boldsymbol{\psi}}{\begin{bmatrix} \psi_1 & \\ & \psi_2 \end{bmatrix}}$$

(PSI) is a diagonal matrix (default) of residuals (ζ—ZETAS). Carrying out the matrix operations indicated in the preceding statement:

$$y_1 = \gamma_1 x_1 + \gamma_2 x_2 + \zeta_1$$

$$-\beta y_1 + y_2 = \gamma_3 x_1 + \gamma_4 x_4 + \zeta_2$$

or

$$y_2 = \beta y_1 + \gamma_3 x_1 + \gamma_4 x_2 + \zeta_2$$

Cards 10–12. These specify the pattern matrix for BETA—the coefficients of the effects of endogenous variables on endogenous variables. In card 12 a zero indicates a fixed parameter and a one indicates a free parameter. Accordingly, only one parameter is to be estimated: the effect of y_1 (N ACH) on y_2 (GPA).

Cards 13–15. These refer to the matrix of starting values for **B.** "Starting values for free parameters may be chosen arbitrarily but the closer they are to the final solution the less computer time will be needed to reach the solution" (Jöreskog & Sörbom, 1978, p. 53). Moreover, an injudicious choice of starting values may preclude a solution altogether (see Jöreskog & Sörbom, 1978, p. 53).

Cards 16–18. These specify the starting values for the GAMMA matrix—the coefficients of the effects of exogenous variables on endogenous variables.

Cards 19–21. These specify the starting values for PSI—the variance of the residuals, or errors in the equations.

Card 22. On this card one may specify output to be printed in addition to the standard output. For the various options, see Jöreskog and Sörbom (1978, p. 76).

Output

MATRIX TO BE ANALYZED

	N ACH	GPA	SES	IQ
N ACH	1.000			
GPA	0.500	1.000		
SES	0.410	0.330	1.000	
IQ	0.160	0.570	0.300	1.000

Commentary

This is a listing of the input correlation matrix. When a SELECTION statement is used to reorder variables, or to select a subset of variables, the matrix to be analyzed is reported in the reordered format, and includes only the subset of variables selected (i.e., when not all the input variables are used in the analysis; see LISREL IV manual, pp. 68–69).

Output

PARAMETER SPECIFICATIONS

BETA

	ETA 1	ETA 2
EQ. 1	0	0
EQ. 2	1	0

GAMMA

	KSI 1	KSI 2
EQ. 1	2	3
EQ. 2	4	5

PHI

	KSI 1	KSI 2
KSI 1	0	
KSI 2	0	0

PSI

	EQ. 1	EQ. 2
1	6	7

Commentary

In the preceding matrices the parameters to be estimated are indicated. They are numbered sequentially. Thus, 1 in the BETA matrix indicates that the effect of ETA 1 (N ACH) on ETA 2 (ACH) is to be estimated. In the GAMMA matrix, 2 and 3 indicate that the effects of KSI 1 (SES) and KSI 2 (IQ), respectively, on ETA 1 (N ACH) are to be estimated, and similarly for the other matrices.

Output

STARTING VALUES

BETA

	ETA 1	ETA 2
EQ. 1	1.000	0.0
EQ. 2	−0.400	1.000

GAMMA

	KSI 1	KSI 2
EQ. 1	0.400	0.050
EQ. 2	0.010	0.500

PHI

	KSI 1	KSI 2
KSI 1	1.000	
KSI 2	0.300	1.000

PSI

	EQ. 1	EQ. 2
1	0.800	0.500

Commentary

In the preceding matrices the starting values that have been supplied on the control cards are listed. See Control Cards, above, where the starting values are listed after cards that begin with the letters MA. For example, the starting values for BETA are given after MA BE (card 15). Because in the MODEL statement (card 9) FIXEDX was specified, PHI is fixed and indicates the input correlations between the X's, or the KSI's. In the present example, the correlation between KSI 1 (SES) and KSI 2 (IQ) is .300, and this is listed in the PHI matrix.

Output

LISREL ESTIMATES

BETA

	ETA 1	ETA 2
EQ. 1	1.000	0.0
EQ. 2	−0.416	1.000

GAMMA

	KSI 1	KSI 2
EQ. 1	0.398	0.041
EQ. 2	0.009	0.501

PHI

	KSI 1	KSI 2
KSI 1	1.000	
KSI 2	.300	1.000

PSI

	EQ. 1	EQ. 2
1	0.830	0.504

TEST OF GOODNESS OF FIT
CHI SQUARE WITH 0 DEGREES OF FREEDOM IS 0.0000
PROBABILITY LEVEL = 1.0000

Commentary

In the preceding matrices the estimated parameters are listed. The matrix labeled BETA contains the coefficients of the effects of endogenous variables on endogenous variables. It was noted earlier, however, that the signs of the coefficients have to be reversed to compensate for the fact that **B** is placed on the left-hand side of Equation (16.1). Therefore, the effect of ETA 1 (N ACH) on ETA 2 (ACH) is .416 (i.e., the sign of the β is reversed). In the present example there is only one β. When problems with more than one β are analyzed, the signs of all the β's are reversed.

The GAMMA matrix contains the effects of exogenous variables on endogenous variables. Thus, .398 is the effect of KSI 1 (SES) on ETA 1 (N ACH), and .041 is the effect of KSI 2 (IQ) on ETA 1 (N ACH); .009 is the effect of KSI 1 (SES) on ETA 2 (ACH), and .501 is the effect of KSI 2 (IQ) on ETA 2 (ACH). All of the estimates reported above are identical to those obtained in Chapter 15 when the same data were analyzed by means of multiple regression analysis.

The values listed under PSI are the variances of residuals for each of the ETA's. Because the input in the present example is a correlation matrix, and in view of the assumptions regarding the residuals (see above, and in Chapter 15), the variance of each of the residuals is equal to $1 - R_i^2$, where i is a given ETA. In the present example, .830 is equal to $1 - R^2_{3.12}$, where 3 is N ACH, and 1 and 2 are SES and IQ, respectively. In Chapter 15 it was shown that the path coefficient from the residuals (e) is equal to $\sqrt{1 - R_i^2}$. Therefore, in the present example, the path coefficient from the residual to ETA 1 (N ACH) is equal to $\sqrt{.830} = .911$. The same value was obtained when these data were analyzed in

Chapter 15. The variance of the residual for ETA 2 (ACH) is .504 $(1 - R^2_{4.123})$. The path coefficient from the residual to ETA 2 is $\sqrt{.504} = .710$. Again, the same value was obtained in the analysis of these data in Chapter 15.

In sum, then, when the MODEL is specified as in card 9 (see detailed discussion above of the model specification) the results obtained from LISREL are identical with those obtained when path coefficients are calculated via multiple regression analyses.

Subsequent to the LISREL ESTIMATES the program prints a χ^2 test of goodness of fit of the model to the data. This is the same test that was introduced and discussed in detail in Chapter 15. Because the model being analyzed is just identified, the χ^2 is zero and the *df* are zero. As was noted several times in Chapter 15, a just-identified model cannot be tested for significance.

Output

STANDARD ERRORS

BETA

	ETA 1	ETA 2
EQ. 1	0.0	0.0
EQ. 2	0.078	0.0

GAMMA

	KSI 1	KSI 2
EQ. 1	0.096	0.096
EQ. 2	0.081	0.075

PHI

	KSI 1	KSI 2
KSI 1	0.0	
KSI 2	0.0	0.0

PSI

	EQ. 1	EQ. 2
1	0.118	0.072

Commentary

In the preceding matrices, standard errors for estimated parameters are reported. Note that standard errors for fixed parameters are 0.0. Dividing an estimated parameter by its standard error yields a critical ratio that has an approximate z distribution. LISREL labels the critical ratios as t values.

Output

T-VALUES

BETA

	ETA 1	ETA 2
EQ. 1	0.0	0.0
EQ. 2	−5.317	0.0

GAMMA

	KSI 1	KSI 2
EQ. 1	4.143	0.424
EQ. 2	0.113	6.691

PHI

	KSI 1	KSI 2
KSI 1	0.0	
KSI 2	0.0	0.0

PSI

	EQ. 1	EQ. 2
1	7.036	7.036

Commentary

Small *t* values indicate that the coefficients associated with them may be deleted, thereby arriving at an overidentified model. In the present example, the *t* values associated with the effect of IQ of N ACH (KSI 2 in EQ. 1 above), and with effect of SES on ACH (KSI 1 in EQ. 2 above) are < 1 and are candidates for deletion (see below, An Overidentified Model. For a discussion of the deletion of path coefficients, see Chapter 15, Theory Trimming).

Output

SIGMA, RESIDUALS, ETC.

SIGMA

	N ACH	GPA	SES	IQ
N ACH	1.000			
GPA	0.500	1.000		
SES	0.410	0.330	1.000	
IQ	0.160	0.570	0.300	1.000

RESIDUALS: S − SIGMA

	N ACH	GPA	SES	IQ
N ACH	0.000			
GPA	0.000	0.000		
SES	0.000	0.000	0.000	
IQ	0.000	0.000	0.000	0.000

ESTIMATED REGRESSIONS
ETA ON KSI (= D)

	KSI 1	KSI 2
ETA 1	0.398	0.041
ETA 2	0.175	0.518

Commentary

SIGMA is the reproduced correlation matrix, using the estimated path coefficients and the model equations. Recall that when the model is just identified, the correlation matrix is exactly reproduced (for detailed discussions, see Chapter 15). Since the model being analyzed is just identified, SIGMA is equal to S—the input correlation matrix. Consequently, S − SIGMA (the matrix of residuals) is a null matrix. In an overidentified model, relatively large residuals provide clues about the sources of misspecification of the model.

The ESTIMATED REGRESSIONS are the effect coefficients of exogenous variables on endogenous variables. For example, .175 is the effect coefficient of KSI 1 (SES) on ETA 2 (ACH). See Chapter 15 for a discussion of effect coefficients, and note that the values reported above are the same as those obtained in the analysis of these data in Chapter 15.

A Note on Path Regression Coefficients

In Chapter 15, a distinction has been made between path coefficients (β's) and path regression coefficients (b's). When the input in LISREL is a variance-covariance matrix, or the correlation matrix as well as the standard deviation of all the variables, the estimated coefficients are path regression coefficients. To obtain path regression coefficients for the preceding example it is necessary to (1) read in also a vector of the standard deviations (see LISREL manual pp. 67–68); (2) delete the letters KM on card 2 (the default is CM = covariance matrix); (3) change the starting values, so that the convergence on the solution will be faster.

Path Analysis: An Overidentified Model

In the analysis of the data of Table 16.1 in the preceding section it has been found that KSI 2 (IQ) in EQ. 1 and KSI 1 (SES) in EQ. 2 had coefficients whose associated T−VALUES were < 1. Deleting these two coefficients would result in an overidentified model that can be tested for significance. In order to obtain estimates for such a model, all that is necessary is to make some changes in the specification of the GAMMA matrix. All the other control cards used in the analysis in the preceding section are unaffected. To conserve space, only the necessary changes regarding the GAMMA matrix will be shown here.

In the preceding analysis, GAMMA was specified to be FREE; that is, all the values of GAMMA were to be estimated. In the present analysis, it is desired to fix two of the GAMMA coefficients to be equal to zero. This can be accomplished by adding the following three cards to those used in the preceding analysis:

```
PA GA
*
1 0 0 1
```

PA GA refers to the pattern of the coefficients in the GAMMA matrix, which specifies that the first coefficient in EQ. 1 is free (assigned a 1) and the second coefficient in EQ. 1 is fixed (assigned a 0). Similarly, in EQ. 2 the first coefficient is fixed and the second is free.

In addition to the inclusion of the above three cards the starting values for GAMMA have to be changed. These values, which were given in card 18 in the preceding section, will be changed to:

```
.4 0 0 .5
```

Accordingly, the two fixed parameters, indicated above in PA GA, are set to be equal to zero.

Running LISREL with the above changes will yield the estimates for the overidentified model. The main results of such an analysis are now given.

Output

LISREL ESTIMATES

BETA

	ETA 1	ETA 2
EQ. 1	1.000	0.0
EQ. 2	−0.420	1.000

GAMMA

	KSI 1	KSI 2
EQ. 1	0.410	0.0
EQ. 2	0.0	0.503

PHI

	KSI 1	KSI 2
KSI 1	1.000	
KSI 2	0.300	1.000

```
PSI
              EQ. 1        EQ. 2
            ----------   ----------
1             0.832        0.504
TEST OF GOODNESS OF FIT
CHI SQUARE WITH 2 DEGREES OF FREEDOM IS 0.1921
PROBABILITY LEVEL = 0.9084
```

Commentary

The estimates obtained here are identical to those obtained for the analysis of the same model in Chapter 15 (see Figure 15.13 and the discussion related to it). Therefore, instead of commenting in detail about the solution the coefficients will be identified so as to make sure that you understand which effects they indicate. Beginning with the BETA matrix, it will be recalled that the sign of the coefficient has to be reversed (see discussion above). Therefore, the effect of ETA 1 (N ACH) on ETA 2 (ACH) is .420. In the GAMMA matrix, EQ. 1, .410 refers to the effect of KSI 1 (SES) on ETA 1 (N ACH). Note that the effect of KSI 2 (IQ) on ETA 1 was hypothesized to be zero (see control cards above). In EQ. 2, .503 refers to the effect of KSI 2 (IQ) on ETA 2 (ACH). The effect of KSI 1 (SES) on ETA 2 (ACH) was hypothesized to be zero (see control cards above).

PSI refers to the variance of the residuals. The square root of each PSI is equal to the path coefficient from a residual to a given ETA. Thus $\sqrt{.832} = .912$ is the path from the residual to ETA 1 (N ACH), and $\sqrt{.504} = .710$ is the path from the residual to ETA 2 (ACH). Compare with the results reported in Figure 15.13.

The CHI SQUARE test is the test of the overidentified model. The same test was performed in Chapter 15. Note that the probability of the χ^2 is about .91. Also, the residuals are very small (see below). It is concluded that the model is consistent with the data.

A Note on the χ^2 Test

The χ^2 test for overidentified models was discussed in Chapter 15, where it was noted that it is not addressed to a test of the model but rather to a test of the null hypothesis regarding the overidentifying restrictions in the model. In the present example these restrictions refer to two coefficients (from SES to ACH and from IQ to N ACH) being zero. Recall that the null hypothesis can either be rejected or one may fail to reject it. While failure to reject the null hypothesis may be taken as an indication that the model is consistent with the data, it is important to bear in mind that alternative models may also be consistent with the data. Moreover, because the χ^2 test is affected by the size of the sample, it follows that (1) given a sufficiently large sample an overidentified model may be rejected even when it fits the data well; and (2) when the sample size is small, one may fail to reject the null hypothesis even when the model fits the data poorly. In view of the foregoing, Jöreskog (1974) has suggested that: "The values of χ^2 be interpreted very cautiously" (p. 4).

Therefore, in addition to the test of significance, it is important to inspect the residuals in order to note whether they are relatively small. Jöreskog and Sörbom (1978; see also Sörbom & Jöreskog, 1981) suggest that in exploratory studies the first derivatives of the fixed parameters be inspected in order to note how the model may be revised. A detailed discussion and suggestions about the use of tests of significance in structural equation models will be found in Bentler and Bonett (1980). These authors have also proposed an overall index of fit in such models and approaches to the study of improvement in the fit due to revisions of models.

Output

SIGMA

	N ACH	GPA	SES	IQ
N ACH	1.000			
GPA	0.481	.984		
SES	0.410	0.323	1.000	
IQ	0.123	0.554	0.300	1.000

RESIDUALS: S − SIGMA

	N ACH	GPA	SES	IQ
N ACH	0.000			
GPA	0.019	0.016		
SES	0.000	0.007	0.000	
IQ	0.037	0.016	0.000	0.000

Commentary

SIGMA is the reproduced correlation matrix, using the estimated path coefficients obtained above. The same values were obtained in the analysis of these data in Chapter 15 (see Table 15.1). The RESIDUALS are the differences between the observed and the reproduced correlations. Note that they are very small, indicating a good fit of the model to the data.

A Model with Correlated Residuals

In the models analyzed thus far it was assumed that the residuals are not intercorrelated. We turn now to an analysis of a model in which the residuals are correlated. As in preceding sections, illustrative data are used. Assume that the correlation matrix for five variables is as reported in Table 16.2, and that the causal model is as depicted in Figure 16.3.

It should be noted at the outset that *no claim is being made that the model depicted in Figure 16.3 is theoretically sound.* In fact, it is easy to advance arguments to the contrary. This model and the others used below with the same variables are presented for illustrative purposes only. It would have been safer to refer to the exogenous variables as the *X*'s and to the endogenous variables as the *Y*'s. Nevertheless, it was felt that it would be more instructive to use variables that have substantive meanings. If, however, you feel uncomfortable

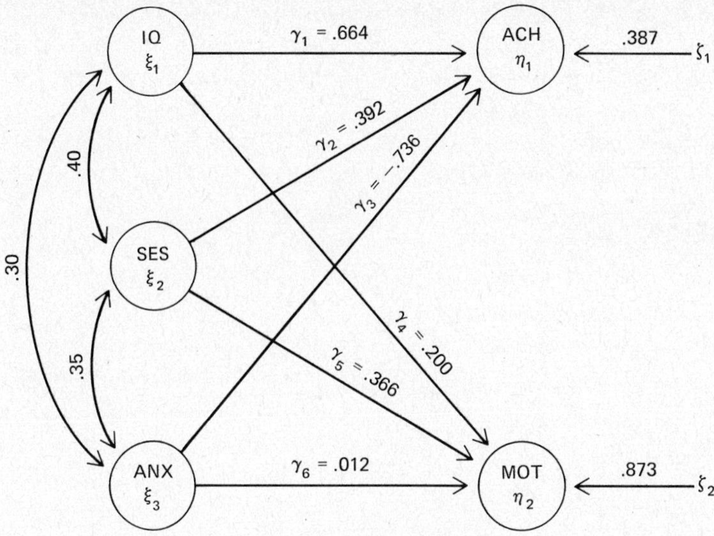

Figure 16.3

with the variables that are being used in connection with the models presented in this section, it is suggested that you substitute for them others with which you may be more comfortable, or that you treat the variables as *X*'s and *Y*'s.

As may be noted from Figure 16.3, Intelligence (IQ), Socioeconomic Status (SES), and Test Anxiety (ANX) are treated as exogenous variables, whereas

Table 16.2 Correlation Matrix for Five Variables, Illustrative Data; $N = 300$

Variables	*ACH*	*MOT*	*IQ*	*SES*	*ANX*
Achievement	1.00				
Motivation	.50	1.00			
Intelligence	.60	.35	1.00		
Socioeconomic Status	.40	.45	.40	1.00	
Test Anxiety	−.40	.20	.30	.35	1.00

Achievement (ACH) and Motivation (MOT) are treated as endogenous variables. Moreover, according to the model the correlation between ACH and MOT is assumed to be spurious. In other words, it assumed to be a consequence of the three common causes of these variables (i.e., IQ, SES, and ANX). Since a single indicator is being used to measure each of the unobserved, or latent, variables, it is necessarily assumed that each indicator is a perfect measure of its corresponding latent variable.[1]

LISREL IV was used to analyze the data of Table 16.2 according to the model depicted in Figure 16.3. Following is the program layout.

Control Cards

```
1) MODEL OF FIGURE 16.3. DATA FROM TABLE 16.2
2) DA  NI=5  MA=KM  NO=300
```

[1]For a discussion of this point, see earlier sections of this chapter.

```
3) LA
4) *
5) 'ACH'  'MOT'  'IQ'  'SES'  'ANX'
6) KM
7) *
8) 1.0  .5  1.0  .6  .35  1.0  .4  .45  .4  1.0  -.4  .2  .3  .35  1.0
9) MO FIXEDX NY=2  NX=3  NE=2  LY=ID  BE=ID  GA=FR
   TE=ZE  PS=FR
10) MA  GA
11) *
12) .6  .4  -.7  .2  .4  .1
13) MA  PS
14) *
15) .2  .7
16) OU  PM  MR  SE  TV
```

Commentary

In view of the detailed comments that were made in connection with the application of LISREL IV to the analysis of the first example (see above), a comment will be made only about one feature of the present layout which differs from that used earlier.

Card 9. Unlike the earlier examples, BE = ID in the present example. This means that BETA is an identity matrix because it is hypothesized that ETA 1 (ACH) does not affect ETA 2 (MOT), nor does the latter affect the former (see Figure 16.3).

Following are excerpts of the output, along with brief commentaries.

Output

PARAMETER SPECIFICATIONS

GAMMA

	KSI 1	KSI 2	KSI 3
EQ. 1	1	2	3
EQ. 2	4	5	6

PHI

	KSI 1	KSI 2	KSI 3
KSI 1	0		
KSI 2	0	0	
KSI 3	0	0	0

PSI

	EQ. 1	EQ. 2
1	7	8

Commentary

The consecutive numbers indicate the free parameters that are to be estimated. The zeros in the PHI matrix indicate that these parameters (in the present case the correlation matrix of the exogenous variables) are fixed.

Output

LISREL ESTIMATES

GAMMA

	KSI 1	KSI 2	KSI 3
EQ. 1	.664	.392	−.736
EQ. 2	.200	.366	.012

PHI

	KSI 1	KSI 2	KSI 3
KSI 1	1.000		
KSI 2	.400	1.000	
KSI 3	.300	.350	1.000

PSI

	EQ. 1	EQ. 2
1	.150	.763

TEST OF GOODNESS OF FIT
CHI SQUARE WITH 1 DEGREE OF FREEDOM IS 205.0325
PROBABILITY LEVEL = .0000

Commentary

The coefficients in the GAMMA matrix indicate the effects of the exogenous variables on the endogenous variables. The coefficients in EQ. 1 are the effects on ETA 1 (ACH), and those in EQ. 2 are the effects on ETA 2 (MOT). The same coefficients would be obtained if one were to do two multiple regression analyses: (1) ACH regressed on IQ, SES, and ANX; and (2) MOT regressed on IQ, SES, and ANX.

PHI is the correlation matrix among the exogenous variables, which has been fixed to be equal to the correlations among the manifest variables. See FIXEDX in the MODEL statement (card 9).

The values reported under PSI are the variances of the residuals. Thus, .150 is the variance of the residuals of ETA 1 (ACH), and .763 is the variance of the residuals of ETA 2 (MOT). Recall that in models of the type analyzed here the variance of the residuals is equal to $1 - R_i^2$, where R_i^2 is the squared multiple correlation of variable i with the variables that affect it.[2] In the present exam-

[2]See Chapter 15 for a detailed discussion of this topic.

ple, R^2 of ACH with IQ, SES, and ANX is .84989. Therefore, the variance of the residuals is 1 − .84989 = .150, as reported above under PSI for EQ. 1. Similarly, R^2 of MOT with IQ, SES, and ANX is .23703. The variance of the residuals of MOT is 1 − .23703 = .763.

The effect of the residuals on variable i is equal to $\sqrt{1 - R_i^2}$. For the present example, the effect of the residuals on ACH is $\sqrt{.150} = .387$, and that on MOT is $\sqrt{.763} = .873$.

The model depicted in Figure 16.3 is overidentified and can therefore be tested for statistical significance.[3] As reported above, $\chi^2\ (1) = 205.03$, $p <$ .00001. Consequently, the model is rejected.

In order to conserve space, SIGMA (the reproduced correlation matrix, in the present case) and the RESIDUALS: S − SIGMA are not reported here. It will be noted, however, that all the residuals are equal to .00, except for the residual corresponding to the correlation between ACH and MOT, which is reported to be .238. Using the estimated coefficients of the model the reproduced correlation coefficient between ACH and MOT is .262. Since the observed correlation between these variables is .50 (see Table 16.2), the residual is .50 − .262 = .238.

It was said earlier that the study of residuals is useful in pinpointing sources of misspecification of a model. In the present example, the relatively large residual indicates that the model is misspecified, at least regarding the relation between ACH and MOT. Needless to say, many alternative models may be formulated in connection with the data of Table 16.2. For example, one may hypothesize that MOT affects ACH. In other words, a path from MOT to ACH would be added in Figure 16.3. Alternatively, one may hypothesize that there is a reciprocal causation between MOT and ACH. In other words, it would be hypothesized that MOT affects ACH, and that ACH affects MOT, thereby positing a nonrecursive model (see below).

The foregoing should not be construed as a sanction for engaging in fishing expeditions of trying out different models, and selecting the one that appears most satisfactory on the basis of statistical tests of significance. Quite the contrary, one could not overemphasize what has been said so many times in this book—namely, that the route is from theory to model testing and not the other way around.[4] To repeat, *the presentation in this section is given for illustrative purposes only*. Before showing the analysis of a nonrecursive model, the model of Figure 16.3 is revised so that it reflects a situation in which the residuals are correlated. This revised model is depicted in Figure 16.4, and the data of Table 16.2 were analyzed by LISREL IV according to this model.

Control Cards

Since the program layout is identical to the one given in the preceding section, except for changes regarding to the residuals, PSI, only the changes will be indicated here.

In the Model statement of the control cards in the preceding section (card 9)

[3]For a detailed discussion of tests of significance of causal models, see Chapter 15.

[4]The intermediate route, so to speak, of Theory Trimming was discussed in Chapter 15.

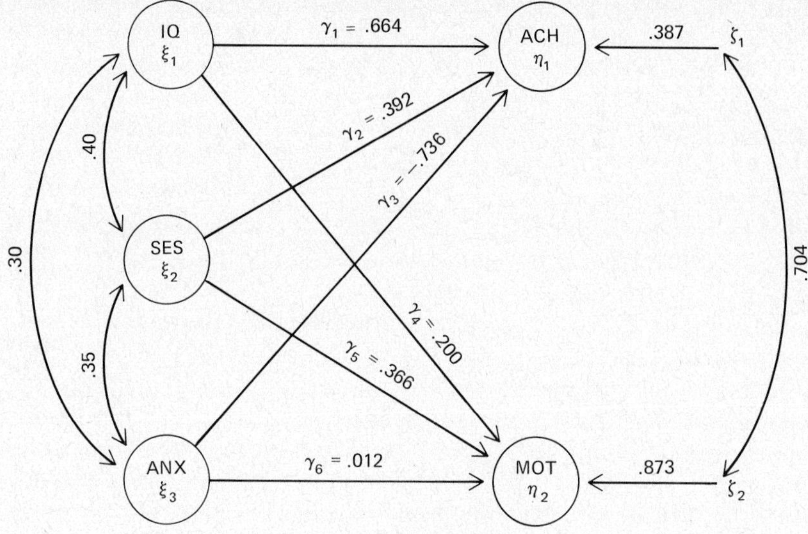

Figure 16.4

it was stated that PS = FR. In the present analysis this is changed to: PS = SY, FR, thereby specifying that PSI is a symmetric matrix whose elements are free. Consequently, the variances of the residuals of ETA 1 (ACH) and ETA 2 (ANX), as well as the covariance of these residuals will be estimated.

Consistent with the change in the specification of PSI, it is necessary to change the matrix of starting values for PS. Accordingly, card 15 is changed to read .2 .3 .7. Recall that: "If the matrix is symmetric the lower half, including the diagonal, should be read as a long vector reading row-wise" (LISREL IV Manual, p. 74).

Because the output for GAMMA and PHI is identical to the one given earlier, it will not be repeated here. Instead, the output for PSI will be given and commented upon. In addition, tests of significance will be reported and commented upon.

Output

PSI

	EQ. 1	EQ. 2
EQ. 1	.150	
EQ. 2	.238	.763

Commentary

The diagonal values of PSI are the variances of the residuals for ETA 1 (ACH) and ETA 2 (MOT). They are identical to those reported and commented upon in the preceding analysis. The covariance between the residuals is .238. Therefore the correlation between the residuals is:

$$\frac{.238}{\sqrt{(.150)(.763)}} = .704$$

It will be noted that the correlation between the residuals is equal to the partial correlation between ACH and MOT, after partialing out the effects of the exogenous variables (IQ, SES, and ANX). In short, $r_{\text{ACH, MOT. IQ, SES, ANX}} =$ .704. It is obvious, then, that the correlation between ACH and MOT is not spurious, at least so far as the causal model depicted in Figure 16.4 is concerned.

Output

TEST OF GOODNESS OF FIT
CHI SQUARE WITH 0 DEGREE OF FREEDOM IS .0000
PROBABILITY LEVEL = 1.0000

Commentary

The model depicted in Figure 16.4 is exactly identified. Hence, it cannot be tested.[5]

Output

T-VALUES
GAMMA

	KSI 1	KSI 2	KSI 3
EQ. 1	26.689	15.475	−30.251
EQ. 2	3.567	6.403	.218

Commentary

It was noted earlier that *t* values are obtained by dividing estimated coefficients by their respective standard errors (in the interest of space, the latter are not reported here). Recall that small *t*'s indicate that the variables with which they are associated are candidates for deletion from the model. In the present example, the *t* for the effect of ANX on MOT is less than 1, and one may therefore consider the deletion of the path from ANX and MOT. In fact, this is what is done in the nonrecursive model, to which we now turn.

[5]See Chapter 15 for a discussion of this topic.

A Nonrecursive Model

Using the variables of Table 16.2, a nonrecursive model is formulated as depicted in Figure 16.5. Note that in this model it is hypothesized that ACH affects MOT, and that MOT affects ACH. Note also that there is no path from ANX to MOT. This is necessary in order to render the model identified. Had there also been a path from ANX to MOT in Figure 16.5 the model would have been underidentified.[6] As the *t* for the path from ANX to MOT is less than 1 (see preceding section), it was decided to delete this path.

LISREL IV was used to analyze the data of Table 16.2 according to the causal model depicted in Figure 16.5. Following is a listing of the program layout.

Control Cards

```
 1) A  NONRECURSIVE  MODEL.  FIGURE  16.5.  DATA  FROM
TABLE 16.2
 2) DA  NI=5  MA=KM  NO=300
 3) LA
 4) *
 5) 'ACH'  'MOT'  'IQ'  'SES'  'ANX'
 6) KM
 7) *
 8) 1.0  .5  1.0  .6  .35  1.0  .4  .45  .4  1.0  -.4  .2  .3  .35  1.0
 9) MO FIXEDX NY=2  NX=3  NE=2  LY=ID  TE=ZE  PS=FR
10) PA  BE
```

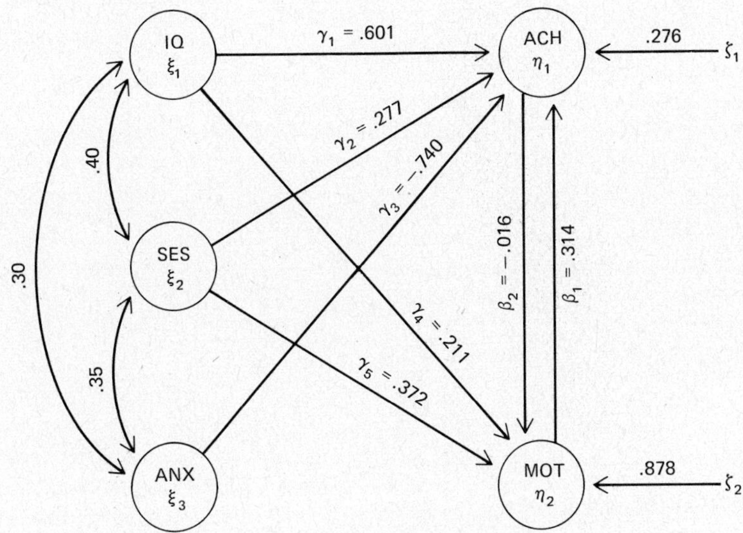

Figure 16.5

[6]See Chapter 15 for a discussion of identification in causal models.

```
11) *
12) 0 1 1 0
13) MA  BE
14) *
15) 1  -.3  .1  1
16) PA  GA
17) *
18) 1  1  1  1  1  0
19) MA  GA
20) *
21) .6  .3  -.7  .2  .4  0
22) MA  PS
23) *
24) .1  .7
25) OU  PM  MR  SE  TV
```

Commentary

Because the control cards of LISREL IV have been discussed in detail earlier, only special features of this problem will be commented upon.

Cards 10–12. These specify the pattern of the BETA matrix. Note that the first and last elements of this matrix are fixed (assigned zero on card 12), whereas the second and the third elements are free (assigned one on card 12). The estimate of the effect of ETA 1 (ACH) on ETA 2 (MOT) will be obtained as the third coefficient, and that of ETA 2 on ETA 1 as the second coefficient (see below).

Cards 13–15. These cards specify the starting values for the BETA matrix. The first and last coefficients in this matrix (i.e., the elements of the principal diagonal) are fixed to be equal to one.

Cards 16–18. These cards specify the pattern of the GAMMA matrix. Note that the last coefficient (i.e., the third coefficient of the second equation) is fixed (assigned a zero). This is the coefficient for the path from ANX to MOT, which is set to be equal to zero on card 21—the card on which the starting values for GAMMA are specified.

Output

PARAMETER SPECIFICATIONS

BETA

	ETA 1	ETA 2
EQ. 1	0	1
EQ. 2	2	0

GAMMA

	KSI 1	KSI 2	KSI 3
EQ. 1	3	4	5
EQ. 2	6	7	0

PHI

	KSI 1	KSI 2	KSI 3
KSI 1	0		
KSI 2	0	0	
KSI 3	0	0	0

PSI

	EQ. 1	EQ. 2
1	8	9

Commentary

The consecutive numbers in the above matrices indicate the parameters to be estimated. Thus, for example, 1 in the BETA matrix refers to the effect of ETA 2 (MOT) on ETA 1 (ACH), whereas 2 refers to the effect of ETA 1 on ETA 2.

Output

LISREL ESTIMATES

BETA

	ETA 1	ETA 2
EQ. 1	1.000	--.314
EQ. 2	.016	1.000

GAMMA

	KSI 1	KSI 2	KSI 3
EQ. 1	.601	.277	−.740
EQ. 2	.211	.372	.000

PHI

	KSI 1	KSI 2	KSI 3
KSI 1	1.000		
KSI 2	.400	1.000	
KSI 3	.300	.350	1.000

PSI

	EQ. 1	EQ. 2
1	.076	.771

TEST OF GOODNESS OF FIT
CHI SQUARE WITH 0 DEGREES OF FREEDOM IS .0000
PROBABILITY LEVEL = 1.0000

Commentary

As was noted several times earlier, the signs of the coefficients in the BETA matrix have to be reversed. Therefore the effect of ETA 2 (MOT) on ETA 1 (ACH) is .314, and the effect of ETA 1 on ETA 2 is −.016.

The coefficients in EQ. 1 of the GAMMA matrix indicate the effects of KSI 1, KSI 2, and KSI 3 (IQ, SES, and ANX), respectively, on ETA 1 (ACH). The coefficients in EQ. 2 indicate the effects of KSI 1, KSI 2, and KSI 3 (IQ, SES, and ANX), respectively, on ETA 2 (MOT). Recall that the effect of KSI 3 on ETA 2 was fixed to be equal to zero. Accordingly, the last coefficient in EQ. 2 of the GAMMA matrix is reported to be 0.0.

PHI is the correlation matrix among the exogenous variables, which has been fixed to be equal to the correlations among the manifest variables. See FIXEDX in the MODEL statement (card 9).

PSI is a diagonal matrix consisting of the variance of the residuals of ETA 1 and ETA 2, respectively.

The model of Figure 16.5 is exactly identified. Consequently, χ^2 and the *df* are equal to zero.

Output

T-VALUES

BETA

	ETA 1	ETA 2
EQ. 1	.0	−15.997
EQ. 2	.217	.0

GAMMA

	KSI 1	KSI 2	KSI 3
EQ. 1	33.232	14.317	−42.836
EQ. 2	3.106	6.505	.0

Commentary

The coefficient for the effect of ETA 1 (ACH) on ETA 2 (MOT) is neither meaningful (−.016) nor statistically significant (t = .217). The remaining coefficients are both meaningful and statistically significant. One may, therefore, revise the model by deleting the path from ACH to MOT, thereby rendering the model recursive. We turn now to the results of the analysis of such a revised model.

The Revised Model

The revised model is depicted in Figure 16.6. The program layout for this model is identical to that for the model depicted in Figure 16.5, except for the

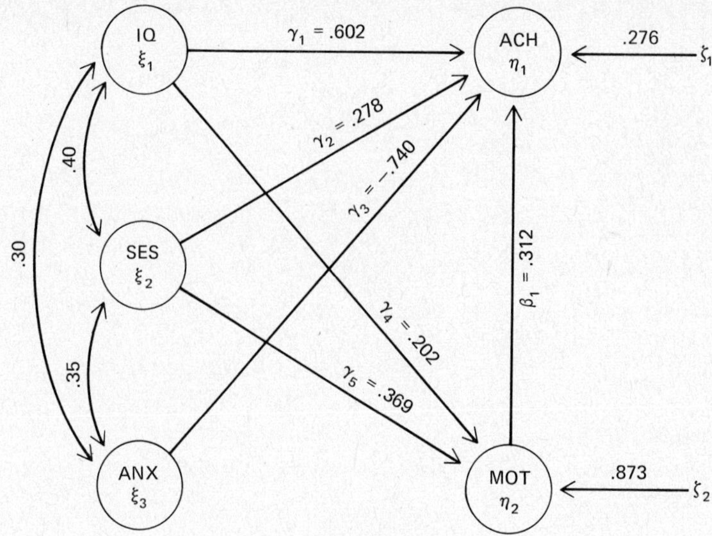

Figure 16.6

BETA matrices. Therefore, only the changes in these matrices will be indicated here. Card numbers are those of the program layout for the model of Figure 16.5.

Card 12. 0 1 0 0
Card 15. 1 −.3 0 1

Commentary

Card 12 refers to the pattern of the BETA matrix. The only free coefficient in this matrix (assigned a one) is for the effect of ETA 2 (MOT) on ETA 1 (ACH). Accordingly, the starting values (card 15) are 1's for the principal diagonal of BETA, −.3 for ETA 2 on ETA 1, and 0 for ETA 1 on ETA 2.

Output

PARAMETER SPECIFICATIONS

BETA

	ETA 1	ETA 2
EQ. 1	0	1
EQ. 2	0	0

GAMMA

	KSI 1	KSI 2	KSI 3
EQ. 1	2	3	4
EQ. 2	5	6	0

PHI

	KSI 1	KSI 2	KSI 3
KSI 1	0		
KSI 2	0	0	
KSI 3	0	0	0

PSI

	EQ. 1	EQ. 2
1	7	8

LISREL ESTIMATES

BETA

	ETA 1	ETA 2
EQ. 1	1.000	−.312
EQ. 2	.000	1.000

GAMMA

	KSI 1	KSI 2	KSI 3
EQ. 1	.602	.278	−.740
EQ. 2	.202	.369	.000

PHI

	KSI 1	KSI 2	KSI 3
KSI 1	1.000		
KSI 2	.400	1.000	
KSI 3	.300	.350	1.000

PSI

	EQ. 1	EQ. 2
1	.076	.763

TEST OF GOODNESS OF FIT
CHI SQUARE WITH 1 DEGREE OF FREEDOM IS .0474
PROBABILITY LEVEL = .8277

Commentary

The results are very much like those obtained when the nonrecursive model was used. Because of the deletion of the path from ACH to MOT the model has become overidentified, and therefore testable. The residuals (see below) are very small, and it is concluded that the model depicted in Figure 16.6 is consistent with the data. Again, you are reminded that different models are used here for illustrative purposes only.

Output

SIGMA, RESIDUALS, ETC.

SIGMA

	ACH	MOT	IQ	SES	ANX
ACH	1.005				
MOT	.507	1.000			
IQ	.600	.350	1.000		
SES	.400	.450	.400	1.000	
ANX	−.403	.190	.300	.350	1.000

RESIDUALS: S − SIGMA

	ACH	MOT	IQ	SES	ANX
ACH	−.005				
MOT	−.007	.000			
IQ	.000	.000	.000		
SES	.000	.000	.000	.000	
ANX	.003	.010	.000	.000	.000

Commentary

SIGMA is the reproduced correlation matrix. The matrix of RESIDUALS is obtained by subtracting SIGMA from the observed correlation matrix. On the basis of the very small residuals it is evident that the model fits the data very well.

No attempt will be made to offer a substantive interpretation of the model because it was not formulated on the basis of theoretical considerations in the first place. As was said earlier, many different models may be shown to fit the data of Table 16.2. The ones used in this section are not necessarily the most plausible from a theoretical frame of reference. They have been presented to illustrate some specific aspects of the analysis of causal models.

It is fitting to conclude this section with a reference to a paper by Nolle (1973), after whose work some of the models analyzed here were, in part, patterned. In an effort to warn researchers against simplistic applications of path analysis, Nolle posited five different causal models about the teacher-student influence process, all of which fit the data perfectly (all were exactly identified models). Nolle (1973) says:

> Although these models do not exhaust the number of possible models, they do reflect four major conceptions of the student-teacher influence process and illustrate the sharp differences and problems which these conceptions can generate with real data. They ultimately become a heuristic device for questioning the simplicity of a literature which gives tacit support to any one model. (p. 417)

A Model with Multiple Indicators

All the models considered thus far consisted of single indicators for each of the latent variables. We turn now to a simple model composed of three latent variables, each of which is measured by two indicators. This model is depicted in Figure 16.7. In order to provide some substantive meaning for the model, assume that the two latent exogenous variables are Intelligence (IQ) and Socioeconomic Status (SES), and that the latent endogenous variable is Achievement (ACH). Each of the latent variables is measured by two indicators. Thus IQ is measured by X_1 and X_2, which may be, for example, the Wechsler and the Stanford-Binet, respectively. SES is measured by X_3 and X_4, which may be, for example, father's education and mother's education, respectively. ACH is measured by Y_1 and Y_2, which may be, for example, a verbal and numeric score, respectively, on a standardized achievement test. You may find it useful to think of other latent variables that are more relevant to a substantive area in which you are interested. For example, ξ_1 (KSI 1) may be Locus of Control, ξ_2 (KSI 2) may be Anxiety, and η (ETA) may be Aggression. Again, each latent variable is measured with two indices, as is indicated in Figure 16.7.

> In order to assess the causal effects it is necessary that the units of measurement in the latent variables be defined in a natural way. This can often be done by specifying the unit of measurement to be the same as one of the observed variables. (Jöreskog, 1979, p. 308; see also LISREL IV manual, and Sörbom, 1975, p. 140)

This is accomplished by setting the coefficient of one indicator for each of the latent variables to be equal to 1.00. These are referred to as reference indicators (Schoenberg, 1972, pp. 15–16). The metric of each of the latent variables becomes that of its reference indicator. Note that in Figure 16.7 the reference indicators are: X_1 for IQ, X_3 for SES, and Y_1 for ACH.

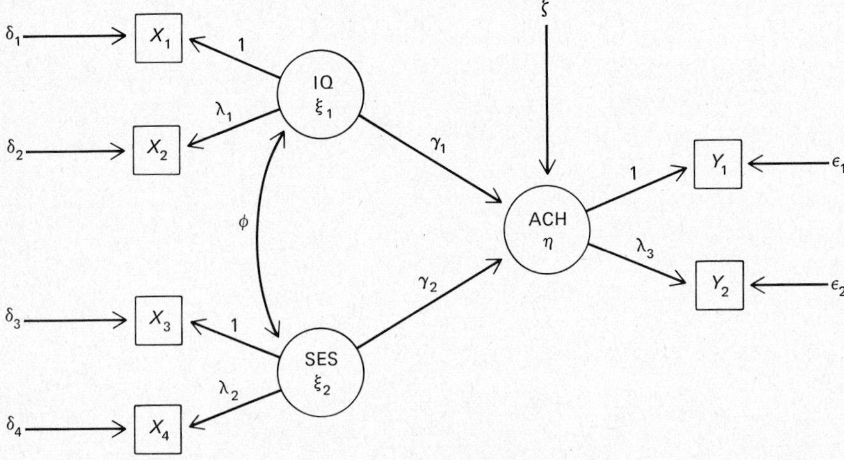

Figure 16.7

The usefulness of reference indicators is predicated on the assumption that the units of such indicators are meaningful. When this is not the case one may use instead a solution in which the latent variables have been standardized. In LISREL IV this solution is obtained by specifying SS on the OU card (see LISREL IV manual, p. 76; also pp. 59–60). It is necessary to recognize, however, that the use of a standardized solution does not solve the problem of establishing a meaningful metric for the latent variables; instead, the problem is evaded.

Before presenting illustrative data and the LISREL IV control cards it will be instructive to spell out the matrices for the measurement and structural models for Figure 16.7.

$$\underset{\mathbf{x}}{\begin{bmatrix} x_1 \\ x_2 \\ x_3 \\ x_4 \end{bmatrix}} = \underset{\boldsymbol{\Lambda}_x}{\begin{bmatrix} 1 & 0 \\ \lambda_1 & 0 \\ 0 & 1 \\ 0 & \lambda_2 \end{bmatrix}} \underset{\boldsymbol{\xi}}{\begin{bmatrix} \xi_1 \\ \xi_2 \end{bmatrix}} + \underset{\boldsymbol{\delta}}{\begin{bmatrix} \delta_1 \\ \delta_2 \\ \delta_3 \\ \delta_4 \end{bmatrix}}$$

The preceding is the measurement model relating the exogenous latent variables (KSI 1 and KSI 2) to the manifest variables (X_1 through X_4). Note that 1's were assigned in $\boldsymbol{\Lambda}$ for the coefficients relating KSI 1 to X_1, and KSI 2 to X_3, thereby designating X_1 and X_3 as reference indicators. $\boldsymbol{\delta}$ (Delta) refers to errors in the manifest variables.

$$\underset{\mathbf{y}}{\begin{bmatrix} y_1 \\ y_2 \end{bmatrix}} = \underset{\boldsymbol{\Lambda}_y}{\begin{bmatrix} 1 \\ \lambda_3 \end{bmatrix}} \eta + \underset{\boldsymbol{\epsilon}}{\begin{bmatrix} \epsilon_1 \\ \epsilon_2 \end{bmatrix}}$$

The preceding is the measurement model relating the latent endogenous variable (ETA) to the manifest variables (Y_1 and Y_2). In the present case, Y_1 is designated as the reference indicator. $\boldsymbol{\epsilon}$ (Epsilon) refers to errors in the manifest variables.

$$\underset{\mathbf{B}}{1} \quad \underset{\boldsymbol{\eta}}{\eta} = \underset{\boldsymbol{\Gamma}}{[\gamma_1 \quad \gamma_2]} \underset{\boldsymbol{\xi}}{\begin{bmatrix} \xi_1 \\ \xi_2 \end{bmatrix}} + \underset{\boldsymbol{\zeta}}{\zeta}$$

The preceding is the structural equation model relating the endogenous variable to the exogenous variables. In the present example there is only one endogenous latent variable, and therefore **B** is equal to 1. ζ (Zeta) refers to the residuals, or the errors in the equation.

A set of illustrative data will be used to illustrate the application of LISREL IV for the estimation of the parameters of the model depicted in Figure 16.7. Table 16.3 gives a correlation matrix for the manifest variables of Figure 16.7, as well as the standard deviations of these variables.

Table 16.3 Correlation Matrix and Standard Deviations for the Manifest Variables of Figure 16.7, Illustrative Data; $N = 200$

	Y_1	Y_2	X_1	X_2	X_3	X_4
Y_1	1.00					
Y_2	.80	1.00				
X_1	.58	.60	1.00			
X_2	.60	.60	.75	1.00		
X_3	.30	.30	.20	.20	1.00	
X_4	.35	.32	.25	.28	.48	1.00
s:	10.00	12.00	15.00	16.00	3.00	4.00

NOTE: s = standard deviation.

Control Cards

```
1) A MODEL WITH MULTIPLE INDICATORS. FIGURE 16.7
2) DA  NI=6  NO=200
3) LA
4) *
5) 'Y1'  'Y2'  'X1'  'X2'  'X3'  'X4'
6) KM
7) *
8) 1.0  .8  1.0  .58  .6  1.0  .6  .6  .75  1.0  .3  .3  .2  .2  1.0  .35
9) .32  .25  .28  .48  1.0
10) SD
11) *
12) 10  12  15  16  3  4
13) MO  NY=2  NX=4  NE=1  NK=2  BE=ID  GA=FR  PH=FR
    PS=FR  TE=FR  TD=FR
14) PA  LY
15) *
16) 0  1
17) MA  LY
18) *
19) 1  1.5
20) PA  LX
21) *
22) 0  0  1  0  0  0  0  1
23) MA  LX
24) *
25) 1  0  1.2  0  0  1  0  1.5
26) MA  GA
27) *
28) .5  1.2
29) MA  PH
30) *
31) 150  10  4
```

```
32) MA  PS
33) *
34) 30
35) MA  TE
36) *
37) 20  30
38) MA  TD
39) *
40) 60  60  5  7
41) OU  PM  MR  SE  TV
```

Commentary

Cards 6–12. These cards are used to read in the correlation matrix (KM) and the standard deviations (SD). Therefore, unlike the preceding examples, the covariance matrix rather than the correlation matrix will be analyzed (see output below).

Card 13. NE refers to the number of ETA variables, which in the present case is one. NK refers to the number of KSI variables, which in the present example is 2. BE = ID indicates that BETA is an identity matrix, which in the present case is a scalar (1). (See above.) All the remaining matrices are specified to be free. PHI is symmetric, whereas PS, TE, and TD are diagonal.

Cards 14–40. These cards specify pattern matrices (PA) for matrices of mixed parameters (i.e., fixed and free) and starting value matrices (MA). Recall that a zero in a PA matrix indicates a fixed parameter, whereas a one indicates a free parameter. For example in the pattern matrix for lambda *Y* (PA LY) the first parameter is fixed and the second is free. In the starting values matrix for lambda *Y* (MA LY) the fixed parameter is set to be equal to 1.00. Note that the matrices that consist of free parameters only (GA, PH, PS, TE, and TD) do not require pattern matrices. Only starting values (MA) have to be provided for such matrices.

Output

MATRIX TO BE ANALYZED

	Y1	Y2	X1	X2	X3	X4
Y1	100.00					
Y2	96.00	144.00				
X1	87.00	108.00	225.00			
X2	96.00	115.20	180.00	256.00		
X3	9.00	10.80	9.00	9.60	9.00	
X4	14.00	15.36	15.00	17.92	5.76	16.00

Commentary

The preceding is the variance-covariance matrix of the manifest variables. The diagonal consists of the variances. For example, 100.00 is the variance of

Y1 (see card 12, where the SD of Y1 is 10). The off-diagonal values are the covariances. The covariance between variables i and j can be expressed as $r_{ij} s_i s_j$, where r_{ij} is the correlation between i and j, and s_i, s_j are the standard deviations of i and j. respectively. For example, the correlation between Y1 and Y2 is .80, and the standard deviations of Y1 and Y2 are 10 and 12, respectively. The covariance between Y1 and Y2 is therefore (.80)(10)(12) = 96, which is the value reported in the above matrix. All the other off-diagonal elements were similarly calculated.

Output

PARAMETER SPECIFICATIONS

LAMBDA Y

	ETA 1
Y1	0
Y2	1

LAMBDA X

	KSI 1	KSI 2
X1	0	0
X2	2	0
X3	0	0
X4	0	3

GAMMA

	KSI 1	KSI 2
EQ. 1	4	5

PHI

	KSI 1	KSI 2
KSI 1	6	
KSI 2	7	8

PSI

	EQ. 1
1	9

THETA EPS

	Y1	Y2
1	10	11

THETA DELTA

	X1	X2	X3	X4
1	12	13	14	15

Commentary

The consecutive numbers in the preceding matrices indicate the parameters that are to be estimated.

Output

```
LISREL ESTIMATES
  LAMBDA Y
            ETA 1
           --------
Y1          1.000
Y2          1.205

  LAMBDA X
            KSI 1     KSI 2
           --------  --------
X1          1.000     0.0
X2          1.086     0.0
X3          0.0       1.000
X4          0.0       1.518

  GAMMA
            KSI 1     KSI 2
           --------  --------
EQ. 1       0.466     1.129

  PHI
            KSI 1     KSI 2
           --------  --------
KSI 1     165.731
KSI 2       9.849     3.796

  PSI
            EQ. 1
           --------
1          28.575

  THETA EPS
            Y1        Y2
           --------  --------
1          20.304    28.362

  THETA DELTA
            X1        X2        X3        X4
           --------  --------  --------  --------
1          59.263    60.516    5.205     7.258

TEST OF GOODNESS OF FIT
CHI SQUARE WITH 6 DEGREES OF FREEDOM IS 2.1403
PROBABILITY LEVEL = 0.9063
```

Commentary

In the preceding matrices the estimated parameters are reported. Note that the effects of IQ (KSI 1) and SES (KSI 2) on ACH (ETA) are .466 and 1.129, respectively (see GAMMA matrix above). Recall that the units of the unobserved variables were fixed to be the same as the units of the measures of X_1, X_3, and Y_1 (see LAMBDA matrices where the coefficients for these variables are equal to 1.00).

The values reported in the PHI matrix refer to the variances of the latent exogenous variables (the diagonal elements) and the covariance between the two latent variables (the off diagonal element). Using these values one may calculate the correlation between the latent variables:

$$r_{\text{IQ.SES}} = \frac{9.849}{\sqrt{(165.731)(3.796)}} = .393$$

This is the value that would be obtained if one were to call for the standardized solution. In this case, the variances of SES and IQ would be reported as equal to 1.00.

The value reported under PSI is the variance of the residuals, or errors in the equation, whereas those reported under THETA EPS and THETA DELTA are the variances of errors in the indicators of the latent endogenous and exogenous variables, respectively.

The χ^2 for the test of the model has a probability of .9063, and the residuals (see below) are small, indicating that the model fits the data.

Output

RESIDUALS: S − SIGMA

	Y1	Y2	X1	X2	X3	X4
Y1	.004					
Y2	.005	.005				
X1	−1.280	1.660	.006			
X2	.124	−.290	.008	.005		
X3	.129	.114	−.849	−1.096	.000	
X4	.537	−.857	.053	1.687	.000	.000

Commentary

Recall that, unlike the previous examples where correlation matrices were analyzed, in the present example a variance-covariance matrix is analyzed. Therefore, the magnitudes of the residuals should be assessed in relation to the variances and the covariances of the observed variables (see MATRIX TO BE ANALYZED, above). In view of the preceding, it can be seen that the residuals are small.

CONCLUDING REMARKS

As was stated in the beginning of the chapter, the aim was to present an elementary introduction to LISREL and to illustrate its application to some very simple models. The virtue of LISREL, however, is that it is well suited for the analysis of complex models that are characteristic of much of social and behavioral research. This can perhaps be recognized by noting that LISREL allows for a more realistic conception of social phenomena—that is, the recognition that, among other things, measures are fallible; errors of manifest variables may be correlated; residuals may be correlated; and causal models may be nonrecursive. Examples of the application of LISREL to complex models will be found in references cited in Study Suggestion 5.

Although the presentation in this chapter was concerned with causal models in nonexperimental research, LISREL is equally applicable to experimental research, particularly when multiple indicators of manipulated variables are taken (see, for example, Alwin & Tessler, 1974; Bagozzi, 1977). Also, the advantages of using LISREL in longitudinal research have been forcefully demonstrated (see, for example, Jöreskog, 1979).

In sum, LISREL has great potential and can be a valuable aid in attempts to unravel complex social and behavioral phenomena.

STUDY SUGGESTIONS

1. Distinguish between the measurement model and the structural equation model in LISREL.
2. In LISREL, what do the following refer to?
   (a) $\boldsymbol{\eta}$
   (b) $\boldsymbol{\xi}$
   (c) $\mathbf{B}$
   (d) $\boldsymbol{\Gamma}$
3. Using LISREL, repeat the analyses done in Study Suggestion 8 of Chapter 15. Compare the results with those given in the answers to Chapter 15.
4. Suppose that a researcher has formulated the following causal model, according to which Socioeconomic Status (SES) affects Locus of Control (LOC) and Aspirations (ASP). In addition, LOC is hypothesized to affect ASP.

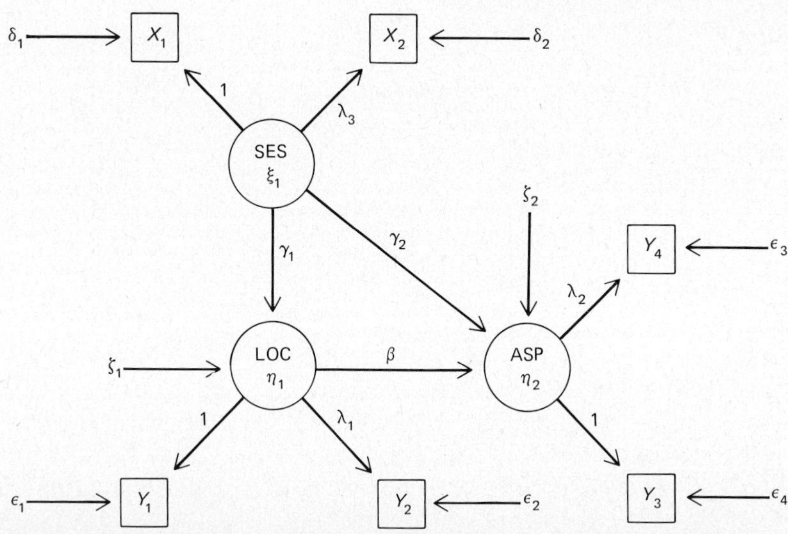

Note that for each latent variable two manifest variables are used. Suppose that the correlation matrix among the manifest variables, and the standard deviation of the manifest variables are as follows ($N = 300$):

	Y_1	Y_2	Y_3	Y_4	X_1	X_2
Y_1	1.00					
Y_2	.70	1.00				
Y_3	.60	.60	1.00			
Y_4	.58	.52	.80	1.00		
X_1	.30	.32	.20	.25	1.00	
X_2	.33	.30	.30	.30	.50	1.00
s:	3.67	2.16	1.32	1.73	2.62	2.13

NOTE: s = standard deviation; Y_1 and Y_2 are the manifest variables for LOC; Y_3 and Y_4 are the manifest variables for ASP; X_1 and X_2 are the manifest variables for SES.

Analyze the data using LISREL.

5. The literature in which LISREL is applied for illustrative purposes or for the solution of substantive problems has been growing recently. Following is a partial listing in which such applications to more complex models than the ones presented in this chapter will be found.

   Various interesting examples of the application of LISREL have been given by Jöreskog and Sörbom. They can be found, among other sources, in the following: the LISREL IV manual, Jöreskog and Sörbom (1979), and Sörbom and Jöreskog (1981). In addition, good examples are given in Alwin and Jackson (1979), Bagozzi and Burnkrant (1979), Bentler and Huba (1979), Bentler and Speckart (1979, 1981), Bentler and Woodward (1978), Bielby and Hauser (1977b), Bielby, Hauser, and Featherman (1977), Burt (1973, 1976), Hauser and Goldberger (1971), Huba, Wingard, and Bentler (1981), Kenny (1979), Maruyama and McGarvey (1980), Maruyama and Miller (1979), Rock, Werts, and Flaugher (1978), Rock, Werts, Linn, and Jöreskog (1977), Saris, de Pijper, and Zegwaart (1978), Werts, Jöreskog, and Linn (1973), Werts, Rock, Linn, and Jöreskog (1976, 1977), and Wheaton, Muthén, Alwin, and Summers (1977).

ANSWERS

2. (a) $\boldsymbol{\eta}$ is a vector of latent endogenous variables.
   (b) $\boldsymbol{\xi}$ is a vector of latent exogenous variables.
   (c) **B** is a matrix of coefficients of the effects of endogenous variables on endogenous variables.
   (d) $\boldsymbol{\Gamma}$ is a matrix of coefficients of the effects of exogenous variables on endogenous variables.
3. Excerpts of LISREL output for Study Suggestion 8 of Chapter 15:

PARAMETER SPECIFICATIONS

BETA

	ETA 1	ETA 2	ETA 3
EQ. 1	0	0	0
EQ. 2	1	0	0
EQ. 3	2	3	0

GAMMA

	KSI 1	KSI 2	KSI 3
EQ. 1	4	5	6
EQ. 2	7	8	9
EQ. 3	10	11	12

PHI

	KSI 1	KSI 2	KSI 3
KSI 1	0		
KSI 2	0	0	
KSI 3	0	0	0

PSI

EQ. 1	EQ. 2	EQ. 3
13	14	15

LISREL ESTIMATES

BETA

	ETA 1	ETA 2	ETA 3
EQ. 1	1.000	0	0
EQ. 2	−.296	1.000	0
EQ. 3	−.110	−.171	1.000

GAMMA

	KSI 1	KSI 2	KSI 3
EQ. 1	.239	.104	.119
EQ. 2	.116	.171	.178
EQ. 3	−.019	.506	.130

PHI

	KSI 1	KSI 2	KSI 3
KSI 1	1.000		
KSI 2	.300	1.000	
KSI 3	.250	.200	1.000

PSI

EQ. 1	EQ. 2	EQ. 3
.884	.743	.561

TEST OF GOODNESS OF FIT
CHI SQUARE WITH 0 DEGREE OF FREEDOM IS .00
PROBABILITY LEVEL = 1.00

Following are excerpts of the LISREL output for the run in which p_{61} and p_{42} were deleted [see (f) of Study Suggestion 8, Chapter 15]

PARAMETER SPECIFICATIONS

GAMMA

	KSI 1	KSI 2	KSI 3
EQ. 1	4	0	5
EQ. 2	6	7	8
EQ. 3	0	9	10

LISREL ESTIMATES

BETA

	ETA 1	ETA 2	ETA 3
EQ. 1	1.000	0	0
EQ. 2	−.296	1.000	0
EQ. 3	−.107	−.168	1.000

GAMMA

	KSI 1	KSI 2	KSI 3
EQ. 1	.267	0	.133
EQ. 2	.116	.171	.178
EQ. 3	0	.503	.128

PSI

EQ. 1	EQ. 2	EQ. 3
.893	.743	.561

TEST OF GOODNESS OF FIT
CHI SQUARE WITH 2 DEGREES OF FREEDOM IS 3.4327
PROBABILITY LEVEL = .1797

4. Following are excerpts from the LISREL output:

MATRIX TO BE ANALYZED

	Y1	Y2	Y3	Y4	X1	X2
Y1	13.469					
Y2	5.549	4.666				
Y3	2.907	1.711	1.742			
Y4	3.682	1.943	1.827	2.993		
X1	2.885	1.811	.692	1.133	6.864	
X2	2.580	1.380	.843	1.105	2.790	4.537

PARAMETER SPECIFICATIONS

LAMBDA Y

	ETA 1	ETA 2
Y1	0	0
Y2	1	0
Y3	0	0
Y4	0	2

LISREL ESTIMATES

LAMBDA Y

	ETA 1	ETA 2
Y1	1.000	0
Y2	.569	0
Y3	0	1.000
Y4	0	1.218

LAMBDA X

	KSI 1
X1	0
X2	3

BETA

	ETA 1	ETA 2
EQ. 1	0	0
EQ. 2	4	0

GAMMA

	KSI 1
EQ. 1	5
EQ. 2	6

PHI

	KSI 1
KSI 1	7

PSI

EQ. 1	EQ. 2
8	9

THETA EPS

Y1	Y2	Y3	Y4
10	11	12	13

THETA DELTA

X1	X2
14	15

LAMBDA X

	KSI 1
X1	1.000
X2	.885

BETA

	ETA 1	ETA 2
EQ. 1	1.000	0
EQ. 2	−.301	1.000

GAMMA

	KSI 1
EQ. 1	.924
EQ. 2	.005

PHI

	KSI 1
KSI 1	3.151

PSI

EQ. 1	EQ. 2
7.057	.612

THETA EPS

Y1	Y2	Y3	Y4
3.724	1.506	.242	.768

THETA DELTA

X1	X2
3.713	2.066

TEST OF GOODNESS OF FIT
CHI SQUARE WITH 6 DEGREES OF FREEDOM IS 13.9757
PROBABILITY LEVEL = .0299

Note, among other things, that the coefficient for the effect of SES on ASP is neither meaningful nor statistically significant (the T–VALUE for this coefficient is .093. The T–VALUES for the other statistics are not reported here).

PART 4

MULTIVARIATE ANALYSIS

17

MULTIPLE REGRESSION, DISCRIMINANT ANALYSIS, AND MULTIVARIATE ANALYSIS OF VARIANCE

In Parts 1 and 2 of this book it was shown how multiple regression analysis may be used for the analysis of data obtained in diverse experimental and nonexperimental designs. While Part 1 was devoted exclusively to designs in which the independent variables are continuous, Part 2 dealt with designs in which the independent variables are categorical only, or combinations of categorical and continuous variables. Despite their diversity, however, all the designs presented in Parts 1 and 2 share a common feature: They are addressed to the analysis of a single dependent variable. In other words, although such designs may consist of multiple independent variables, they can include only one dependent variable.

In behavioral research, as well as in other types of research, one is often interested in using independent variables, or predictors, to explain, or predict, multifaceted phenomena. Consider, for example, the multifaceted phenomenon of academic achievement. While it is true that researchers use students' grade-point average as a dependent variable, this is very often done not because it is believed that this index captures the complex phenomenon of academic achievement, but rather because it is a *single* index that is rather easily obtainable. Needless to say, more insight can be gained by studying the effect of different teaching styles, say, on achievement in reading, spelling, composition, arithmetic, science, to name but a few.

As another example, suppose that an experiment on changing attitudes has been done in which three appeals, A_1, A_2, and A_3, were used with prejudiced individuals.[1] A_1 was a democratic appeal or argument in which prejudice was depicted as being incommensurate with democracy. A_2 was a fair-play appeal:

[1]This idea was taken from an actual experiment by Citron, Chein, and Harding (1950).

The American notion of fair play demands equal treatment for all. A_3 was a religious appeal: Prejudice is a violation of the ethics of the major religions. Now, if it were desired to determine which of the three appeals is most effective in changing prejudicial attitudes toward blacks, say, and if a single measure of such attitudes were used, the analysis would proceed in a manner described in detail in Chapter 9. Suppose, however, that the researcher's conception of prejudice is broader in that it refers to such attitudes toward minority groups, say, blacks, Hispanics, Mexican-Americans. One may attempt to use a single measure of such attitudes, but the validity of doing this is predicated on the assumption that the attitudes toward the three groups are unidimensional; otherwise one may be adding apples and oranges.

The preceding examples referred to experimental research. Similar problems arise very often in nonexperimental research. For example, one may wish to study how males and females differ in their conceptions of sex roles or how members of different ethnic groups differ in their conceptions of human nature. Or one may wish to study differences among preexisting groups in cognitive and affective domains. When the phenomenon that is being studied is multidimensional, one cannot encapsulate it in a single score without thereby distorting it or even entirely stripping it of its meaning.

Thus far, the discussion was limited to situations in which it is desired to study differences among groups on multiple dependent variables. Another common research situation is one in which it is desired to study relations between two *sets* of variables within a single group. For example, one may have five measures of cognitive variables and four measures of affective variables on a sample of schoolchildren and the purpose is to study the relations between these two sets of variables. As is shown in Chapter 18, problems of this kind are handled by canonical analysis.

In the course of reading the foregoing you have probably wondered what would be wrong if one were to analyze each of a set of dependent variables separately, using methods presented in Parts 1 and 2 of this book. Or what would be wrong if one were to calculate zero-order correlations for all possible pairings of variables in situations of the kind described in the last example above. Actually, most researchers do just that. Without going into the details, it will be noted first that the use of multiple univariate tests on the same data affects the level of statistical significance that is preselected by the researcher (see, for example, Bock, 1975, pp. 20–22; Harris, 1975, p. 6). More important, however, is that studying each dependent variable separately, or calculating zero-order correlations only, ignores the very essence and richness of the multifaceted phenomenon being studied. Much of the social world is multivariate in nature, and studying it piecemeal does not hold promise of understanding it. As Harris (1975) so aptly put it:

> If researchers were sufficiently narrowminded, or theories and measurement techniques so well developed or nature so simple as to dictate a single independent variable and a single outcome measure as appropriate in each study, there would be no need for multivariate statistical techniques. (p. 5)

In short, when the phenomenon being studied is multivariate, it is necessary to resort to analytic methods that are commensurate with it. The explication of the complex multivariate methods that have been developed would require a whole volume. Excellent books on this topic are available, among which are Bock (1975), Cooley and Lohnes (1971), Finn (1974), Gnanadesikan (1977), Green (1978), Harris (1975), Maxwell (1977), Overall and Klett (1972), Press (1972), Tatsuoka (1971a), and Timm (1975). It goes without saying that it is not possible to offer an exhaustive treatment of multivariate analysis in a couple of chapters. The presentation here has very limited objectives. In this chapter methods are presented for the analysis of multiple dependent variables for any number of groups or treatments: Discriminant Analysis (DA) and Multivariate Analysis of Variance (MANOVA). In the next chapter Canonical Analysis (CA) is introduced for the purpose of studying relations among sets of variables. It is also shown that CA can be used in lieu of DA and MANOVA. It is hoped that this limited introduction will stimulate you to pursue the study of multivariate analysis and that it will facilitate your efforts in doing so.

Because DA and MANOVA for *two* groups can also be calculated through multiple regression analysis, the chapter begins with a demonstration of how this is done. This is followed by a presentation of DA and MANOVA. Although the equations given for these methods apply to analyses with any number of groups, they are applied in this chapter to two groups only so that the results may be compared with those obtained from the analysis of the same data by multiple regression (the same equations are used in Chapter 18 for the analysis of a numerical example with more than two groups). It is shown that for two groups the three approaches lead to overall identical results, although some intermediate ones differ from one approach to another. Computer programs for multivariate analysis are then discussed, and one of them is used to analyze a numerical example. The chapter concludes with a research example.

MULTIPLE REGRESSION ANALYSIS

Assume that the data reported in Table 17.1 were obtained from two groups in nonexperimental or experimental settings. Thus, for example, A_1 may be males, and A_2 females; or A_1 may be whites and A_2 may be blacks. In short, A_1 and A_2 may represent any two preexisting groups. The dependent variables could be, for example, X_1 = Masculinity, X_2 = Femininity;[2] or X_1 = Locus of

Table 17.1 Illustrative Data on Two Dependent Variables for Two Groups

	A_1		A_2	
	X_1	X_2	X_1	X_2
	8	3	4	2
	7	4	3	1
	5	5	3	2
	3	4	2	2
	3	2	2	5
$\bar{X}$:	5.2	3.6	2.8	2.4

[2]Because the roles of the independent and the dependent variables are reversed for the purpose of the analysis (see below), it was decided to use X's to represent the dependent variables so as to be consistent with the notation used in earlier chapters. Also, this notation is consistent with the one used in discussions of DA in the literature.

Control, X_2 = Anxiety. Alternatively, A_1 and A_2 may be two treatments, or a treatment group and a control group, and the dependent variables may be, for example, X_1 = Reading, X_2 = Arithmetic. It should be noted that while only two dependent variables are used here, this is done for the purpose of minimizing the calculations. The approach presented here applies equally to any number of dependent variables so long as they have been obtained from two groups. The choice of only five subjects per group and single-digit scores was also dictated by considerations of convenience. It was felt that the lack of realism in the numerical example will be more than compensated for by the ease with which all the calculations can be carried out by hand.

The data of Table 17.1 are displayed in Table 17.2 in a format suitable for multiple regression analysis. Also included, at the bottom of the table, are results from intermediate calculations. Note that the two dependent variables, X_1 and X_2, are represented as two column vectors. In addition, a coded vector, Y, is included to represent group membership. Any coding method will do. In the present example, dummy coding is used. Members of group A_1 are assigned 1's, whereas members of group A_2 are assigned 0's. For the purpose of the analysis, the roles of the independent and the dependent variables are reversed. That is, the coded vector representing group membership is treated as the dependent variable, whereas the actual dependent variables are treated as independent variables—but only for analytic purposes.

One could, of course, use a computer program for multiple regression analysis to calculate the regression of Y on X_1 and X_2. But, as was noted above, a small numerical example is used so that all the calculations can be done by hand. Formulas for multiple regression analysis with two independent variables

Table 17.2 Data of Table 17.1, Displayed for Multiple Regression Analysis

	X_1		X_2		Y
	8		3		1
	7		4		1
	5		5		1
A_1	3		4		1
	3		2		1
	4		2		0
	3		1		0
A_2	3		2		0
	2		2		0
	2		5		0
Σ:	40		30		5
M:	4		3		.5
ss:	38		18		2.5
s:	2.0548		1.4142		.5270
Σx_1y =	6	Σx_2y =	3	Σx_1x_2 =	6
r_{x_1y} =	.61559	r_{x_2y} =	.44721	$r_{x_1x_2}$ =	.22942

NOTE: Y = coded vector for group membership; M = mean; ss = deviation sum of squares; s = standard deviation; Σx_1y = sum of cross-product deviations between X_1 and Y, and similarly for the other terms; r_{x_1y} = correlation between X_1 and Y, and similarly for the other terms.

were presented and discussed in detail in Chapter 3. Therefore, although these formulas are used here, they are not commented upon. When necessary, refer to Chapter 3 for explanations. To avoid cumbersome subscripts, X_1 will be referred to as variable 1, and X_2 will be referred to as variable 2. We turn first to the calculation of the squared multiple correlation of Y with X_1 and X_2.

$$R^2_{y\ 12} = \frac{r^2_{y\,1} + r^2_{y\,2} - 2r_{y\,1}r_{y\,2}r_{12}}{1 - r^2_{12}}$$

Using the relevant values from the bottom of Table 17.2:

$$R^2_{y.12} = \frac{(.61559)^2 + (.44721)^2 - 2(.61559)(.44721)(.22942)}{1 - (.22942)^2} = .47778$$

This R^2 can be tested for significance in the usual manner:

$$F = \frac{R^2_{y.12}/k}{(1 - R^2_{y.12})/(N - k - 1)} = \frac{.47778/2}{(1 - .47778)/(10 - 2 - 1)} = 3.20$$

with 2 and 7 *df*, $p > .05$. Assuming that the .05 level of significance was selected, it is concluded that the two groups do not differ significantly on the two dependent variables when they are analyzed simultaneously. Obviously, the failure to reject the null hypothesis is, in part, due to the small number of subjects being used. Since the data are illustrative and since the sole purpose here is to demonstrate the identity of multiple regression analysis, discriminant analysis, and multivariate analysis of variance when applied to data obtained from two groups, we will not be concerned with the failure to reject the null hypothesis.

We now turn to the calculation of the standardized regression coefficients:

$$\beta_1 = \frac{r_{y\,1} - r_{y\,2}r_{12}}{1 - r^2_{12}} = \frac{.61559 - (.44721)(.22942)}{1 - (.22942)^2} = .54149$$

$$\beta_2 = \frac{r_{y2} - r_{y1}r_{12}}{1 - r^2_{12}} = \frac{.44721 - (.61559)(.22942)}{1 - (.22942)^2} = .32298$$

Using these results and the standard deviations reported at the bottom of Table 17.2, calculate the unstandardized regression coefficients:

$$b_1 = \beta_1\left(\frac{s_y}{s_1}\right) = .54149\left(\frac{.5270}{2.0548}\right) = .13888$$

$$b_2 = \beta_2\left(\frac{s_y}{s_2}\right) = .32298\left(\frac{.5270}{1.4142}\right) = .12036$$

The intercept is equal to

$$a = \bar{Y} - b_1\bar{X}_1 - b_2\bar{X}_2$$

$$= .5 - (.13888)(4) - (.12036)(3) = -.41660$$

The regression equation is

$$Y' = -.41660 + .13888X_1 + .12036X_2$$

This equation can be used and interpreted in the usual manner. For example, one may use subjects' scores on the X's to predict Y's, which in the present case indicates group membership. Roughly speaking, if the predicted score is closer to 1, the subject may be classified as "belonging" to group A_1. If, on the other hand, the predicted score is closer to 0, the subject may be classified as "belonging" to group A_2. The b's may be tested for statistical significance in the usual manner. Also, one may use the β's in an attempt to assess the relative importance of the dependent variables. These issues will not be discussed further here because this is done below within the context of Discriminant Analysis (DA). Before presenting DA we turn to a brief discussion of structure coefficients.

Structure Coefficients

It will be recalled that in multiple regression analysis the independent variables, or predictors, are differentially weighted (the weights are the b's or the β's) so that the correlation between the composite scores thus obtained and the dependent variable, or the criterion, is maximized (see Chapter 3 for a detailed discussion). Using the regression equation and scores on the independent variables one can of course calculate each person's score on the composite. These are actually the predicted scores used frequently in earlier chapters. Having calculated composite scores for subjects, it is possible to calculate correlations between each of the original independent variables and the vector of composite scores. Such correlations are referred to as *structure coefficients,* or loadings, since they are interpreted as factor loadings in factor analysis. The square of a structure coefficient indicates the proportion of variance shared by the variable with which it is associated and the vector of composite scores.

The description of how structure coefficients may be calculated was given for explanatory purposes only. There is a much simpler way for calculating them, as is indicated by the following formula:

$$s_i = \frac{r_{yi}}{R_{y.12...k}} \tag{17.1}$$

where s_i = structure coefficient for independent variable X_i; r_{yi} = the correlation between the dependent variable, Y, and X_i; $R_{y.12...k}$ = the multiple correlation of Y with the k independent variables. In short, to obtain structure coefficients, divide the zero-order correlation of each of the independent variables with the dependent variable by the multiple correlation of the dependent variable with the independent variables.

For the numerical example under consideration it was found (see above) that

$$r_{y1} = .61559 \qquad r_{y2} = .44721 \qquad R^2_{y.12} = .47778$$

Therefore,

$$R_{y.12} = \sqrt{.47778} = .69122$$

and

$$s_1 = \frac{.61559}{.69122} = .89058$$

$$s_2 = \frac{.44721}{.69122} = .64699$$

The interpretation of structure coefficients is discussed below and in Chapter 18 in the context of discriminant analysis and canonical analysis. For now, it will only be pointed out that structure coefficients are useful in discriminant analysis, for example, for the purpose of describing or interpreting the dimensions that have been found to discriminate among groups (see below and in Chapter 18). Because the purpose of the preceding section was to show that, with two groups, multiple regression analysis can be used to obtain the same results as those obtained when a discriminant analysis is applied, it was also shown how structure coefficients may be obtained in the context of multiple regression analysis.

It will be noted that some authors (e.g., Thorndike, 1978, pp. 151–156 and 170–172) recommend that structure coefficients also be used for interpretive purposes in general applications of multiple regression analysis. The reason this was not done in this book is that it is believed that such coefficients do not enhance the interpretation of results of multiple regression analysis. This is evident when one considers the manner in which structure coefficients are calculated in the context of multiple regression analysis. From Formula (17.1) it can be seen that such coefficients are simply zero-order correlations of independent variables with the dependent variable divided by a constant, namely, the multiple correlation coefficient. Hence, the zero-order correlations provide the same information.

In addition, it is important to note that because large structure coefficients may be obtained even when the results are meaningless, their use in such instances may lead to misinterpretations. This can best be shown by a numerical example. Assume that the following have been obtained in a study:

$$r_{y1} = .02 \qquad r_{y2} = .01 \qquad r_{12} = .60$$

where Y is the dependent variable, and 1 and 2 are the independent variables. It is clear that the correlations between the independent variables and the dependent variable are not meaningful. Using these data, calculate $R^2_{y.12} = .00041$. Clearly, the squared multiple correlation is not meaningful. But calculate now the structure coefficients:

$$R_{y.12} = \sqrt{.00041} = .02025$$

and applying (17.1),

$$s_1 = \frac{.02}{.02025} = .988$$

$$s_2 = \frac{.01}{.02025} = .494$$

These are impressive coefficients, particularly the first one. True, they are the correlations between the independent variables and the vector of the composite scores obtained by the application of the regression equation. But what is not apparent from inspection of these coefficients is that they have been obtained from meaningless results.

The foregoing should not be taken to mean that the potential problems with the use of structure coefficients are limited to multiple regression analysis. Similar problems occur in discriminant analysis and canonical analysis. But, as is discussed below and in Chapter 18, structure coefficients are calculated only for what are considered meaningful discriminant functions or canonical variates. One can therefore argue that the same be done in the context of multiple regression analysis—that is, that structure coefficients be calculated only after it has been decided that the squared multiple correlation is meaningful. There is, of course, nothing wrong with such an approach, except that, as was pointed out above, essentially the same information is obtained from the zero-order correlations of the independent variables with the dependent variable. We turn now to a presentation of discriminant analysis.

DISCRIMINANT ANALYSIS (DA)

DA was initially developed by Fisher (1936) for the purpose of classifying objects into one of two clearly defined groups. Shortly thereafter, DA was generalized to problems of classification into any number of groups, and has been labeled Multiple Discriminant Analysis (MDA). For some time, DA was used exclusively for taxonomic problems in various disciplines (e.g., botany, biology, geology, clinical psychology, vocational guidance). In recent years, DA has come into use as a method of studying group differences on several variables simultaneously. Because of some common features of DA and Multivariate Analysis Of Variance (MANOVA) some researchers treat the two as interchangeable methods for studying group differences on multiple variables. More often, however, it is suggested that DA be used after a MANOVA for the purpose of identifying the dimensions along which the groups differ.[3] For a comprehensive review of the various uses of DA see Huberty (1975a). Good introductory treatments of DA will be found in Klecka (1980) and Tatsuoka (1970, 1976). More advanced discussions will be found in the books on multivariate analysis cited earlier.

The present chapter is limited to the use of DA for the purpose of studying group differences. Sophisticated classification methods, of which DA is but one, are available and are discussed, among others, by Rulon, Tiedeman, Tatsuoka, and Langmuir (1967), Tatsuoka (1974, 1975), and Van Ryzin (1977). Ad-

[3]See below, and Chapter 18.

ditional discussions will be found in the books on multivariate analysis cited earlier (see, in particular, Overall & Klett, 1972).

Before presenting the formal approach to DA it is necessary to discuss the concept of Sums of Squares and Cross Products (SSCP) matrices.

SSCP

Recall that in the univariate analysis of variance the total sum of squares of the dependent variable is partitioned into two components: (1) pooled within-groups sum of squares and (2) between-groups sum of squares.[4] With multiple dependent variables it is, of course, possible to calculate the within and between sums of squares for each of them. In addition, the total sum of cross products between any two variables can be partitioned into (1) pooled within-groups sum of products and (2) between-groups sum of products. With multiple dependent variables it is convenient to assemble the sums of squares and cross products in the following three matrices: **W** = pooled within-groups SSCP; **B** = between-groups SSCP; **T** = total SSCP. To clarify these notions, assume that there are only two dependent variables. Accordingly, the elements of the above matrices are:

$$\mathbf{W} = \begin{bmatrix} ss_{w_1} & scp_w \\ scp_w & ss_{w_2} \end{bmatrix}$$

where ss_{w_1} = pooled sum of squares within groups for variable 1; ss_{w_2} = pooled sum of squares within groups for variable 2; scp_w = pooled within-groups sum of products of variables 1 and 2.

$$\mathbf{B} = \begin{bmatrix} ss_{b_1} & scp_b \\ scp_b & ss_{b_2} \end{bmatrix}$$

where ss_{b_1} and ss_{b_2} are the between-groups sums of squares for variable 1 and 2, respectively; scp_b is the between-groups sum of cross products of variables 1 and 2.

$$\mathbf{T} = \begin{bmatrix} ss_1 & scp_{12} \\ scp_{12} & ss_2 \end{bmatrix}$$

where ss_1 and ss_2 are the total sums of squares for variables 1 and 2, respectively; scp_{12} is the total sum of cross products of variables 1 and 2. Note that the elements of **T** are calculated as if all the subjects belong to a single group.

[4]See Chapter 9, where it is also shown that when coded vectors are used to represent group membership, the residual sum of squares is equal to the within-groups sum of squares and the regression sum of squares is equal to the between-groups sum of squares.

A Numerical Example

SSCP matrices will now be calculated for the illustrative data presented earlier in Table 17.1, and will be used subsequently for DA. For convenience, these data are repeated in Table 17.3, along with some intermediate results to be used in the calculation of the elements of the SSCP matrices.

Using relevant elements from the bottom of Table 17.3 calculate the elements of the pooled within-groups SSCP matrix (**W**):

$$ss_{w_1} = \left[156 - \frac{(26)^2}{5}\right] + \left[42 - \frac{(14)^2}{5}\right] = 23.6$$

$$ss_{w_2} = \left[70 - \frac{(18)^2}{5}\right] + \left[38 - \frac{(12)^2}{5}\right] = 14.4$$

$$scp_w = \left[95 - \frac{(26)(18)}{5}\right] + \left[31 - \frac{(14)(12)}{5}\right] = -1.2$$

$$\mathbf{W} = \begin{bmatrix} 23.6 & -1.2 \\ -1.2 & 14.4 \end{bmatrix}$$

Now calculate the elements of the between-groups SSCP matrix (**B**):

$$ss_{b_1} = \left[\frac{(26)^2}{5} + \frac{(14)^2}{5}\right] - \frac{(40)^2}{10} = 14.4$$

$$ss_{b_2} = \left[\frac{(18)^2}{5} + \frac{(12)^2}{5}\right] - \frac{(30)^2}{10} = 3.6$$

$$scp_b = \left[\frac{(26)(18)}{5} + \frac{(14)(12)}{5}\right] - \frac{(40)(30)}{10} = 7.2$$

$$\mathbf{B} = \begin{bmatrix} 14.4 & 7.2 \\ 7.2 & 3.6 \end{bmatrix}$$

Table 17.3 Illustrative Data on Two Dependent Variables for Two Groups

	A_1		A_2			
	X_1	X_2	X_1	X_2		
	8	3	4	2		
	7	4	3	1		
	5	5	3	2		
	3	4	2	2		
	3	2	2	5		
ΣX:	26	18	14	12	$\Sigma X_{t_1} = 40$	$\Sigma X_{t_2} = 30$
ΣX^2:	156	70	42	38	$\Sigma X^2_{t_1} = 198$	$\Sigma X_{t_2} = 108$
$\bar{X}$:	5.2	3.6	2.8	2.4		
CP	95		31			$CP_t = 126$

NOTE: The data are repeated from Table 17.1. The sums of squares (ΣX^2) and the sums of cross products (CP) are in raw scores.

Because **T** = **W** + **B**, the elements of the total SSCP matrix (**T**) can be obtained by adding **W** and **B**

$$\mathbf{T} = \underset{\mathbf{W}}{\begin{bmatrix} 23.6 & -1.2 \\ -1.2 & 14.4 \end{bmatrix}} + \underset{\mathbf{B}}{\begin{bmatrix} 14.4 & 7.2 \\ 7.2 & 3.6 \end{bmatrix}} = \begin{bmatrix} 38.0 & 6.0 \\ 6.0 & 18.0 \end{bmatrix}$$

For completeness of presentation, however, the elements of **T** will be calculated directly.

$$ss_{t_1} = 198 - \frac{(40)^2}{10} = 38.0$$

$$ss_{t_2} = 108 - \frac{(30)^2}{10} = 18.0$$

$$scp_t = (95 + 31) - \frac{(40)(30)}{10} = 6.0$$

In conclusion, it will be noted that normally **W**, **B**, and **T** are obtained by using matrix operations on the raw score matrices. This is how computer programs are written. In the present case it was felt that it would be simpler to avoid the matrix operations. Also, as shown above, only two of the three matrices have to be calculated. The third may be obtained by addition or subtraction, whatever the case may be. Thus, **T** was obtained above by adding **W** and **B**. If, instead, **T** and **W** were calculated, then **B** = **T** − **W**—or **W** = **T** − **B**. We are now ready to return to the discussion of DA.

Elements of DA

Although the presentation of DA for two groups may be simplified (see, for example, Green, 1978, Chapter 4; Lindeman, Merenda, & Gold, 1980, Chapter 6), it was felt that it will be more instructive to present the general case—that is, for two groups or more. Therefore, although in the presentation that follows the equations are applied to DA with two groups, *the same equations are applicable to DA with any number of groups* (see Chapter 18). Calculation of DA, particularly the eigenvalues (see below), can become very complicated. Consequently, DA is generally calculated by the use of a computer program (computer programs are discussed later in the chapter). But because the present example is small, it is easy to do all the calculations by hand, thereby providing, it is hoped, a better understanding and familiarity with the elements of DA.

The basic idea of DA is to find a set of weights, **v**, by which to weight the scores of each individual so that the ratio of **B** (between-groups SSCP) to **W** (pooled within-groups SSCP) is maximized, thereby leading to maximum discrimination among the groups. This may be expressed as follows:

$$\lambda = \frac{\mathbf{v}'\mathbf{B}\mathbf{v}}{\mathbf{v}'\mathbf{W}\mathbf{v}} \tag{17.2}$$

where $\mathbf{v}'$ and $\mathbf{v}$ are a row and column vectors of weights, respectively; λ is referred to as the discriminant criterion.

A solution of λ is obtained by solving the following determinantal equation:

$$|\mathbf{W}^{-1}\mathbf{B} - \lambda\mathbf{I}| = 0 \tag{17.3}$$

where $\mathbf{W}^{-1}$ is the inverse of $\mathbf{W}$, and $\mathbf{I}$ is an identity matrix. λ is referred to as the largest eigenvalue, or characteristic root, of the matrix, whose determinant is set equal to zero—that is, Equation (17.3). With two groups, only one eigenvalue may be obtained.[5] Before showing how Equation (17.3) is solved, it is spelled out using the matrices calculated in the preceding section.

$$\left| \underset{\mathbf{W}}{\begin{pmatrix} 23.6 & -1.2 \\ -1.2 & 14.4 \end{pmatrix}^{-1}} \underset{\mathbf{B}}{\begin{pmatrix} 14.4 & 7.2 \\ 7.2 & 3.6 \end{pmatrix}} - \lambda \underset{\mathbf{I}}{\begin{pmatrix} 1 & 0 \\ 0 & 1 \end{pmatrix}} \right| = 0$$

First, the inverse of $\mathbf{W}$ will be calculated. In Chapter 4 and in Appendix A it was shown how the inverse of a 2×2 matrix can be calculated with relative ease. This is done now for the present example without comments. The determinant of $\mathbf{W}$ is:

$$\begin{vmatrix} 23.6 & -1.2 \\ -1.2 & 14.4 \end{vmatrix} = (23.6)(14.4) - (-1.2)(-1.2) = \mathit{338.4}$$

$$\begin{bmatrix} 23.6 & -1.2 \\ -1.2 & 14.4 \end{bmatrix}^{-1} = \begin{bmatrix} \dfrac{14.4}{338.4} & \dfrac{1.2}{338.4} \\ \dfrac{1.2}{338.4} & \dfrac{23.6}{338.4} \end{bmatrix} = \begin{bmatrix} .04255 & .00355 \\ .00355 & .06974 \end{bmatrix}$$

Multiplying $\mathbf{W}^{-1}$ by $\mathbf{B}$,

$$\underset{\mathbf{W}^{-1}}{\begin{bmatrix} .04255 & .00355 \\ .00355 & .06974 \end{bmatrix}} \underset{\mathbf{B}}{\begin{bmatrix} 14.4 & 7.2 \\ 7.2 & 3.6 \end{bmatrix}} = \begin{bmatrix} .63828 & .31914 \\ .55325 & .27662 \end{bmatrix}$$

It is now necessary to solve the following:

$$\begin{vmatrix} .63828 - \lambda & .31914 \\ .55325 & .27662 - \lambda \end{vmatrix} = 0$$

We need to find the value of λ so that the determinant of the matrix will be equal to zero. Therefore,

[5]For solutions with more than two groups, see Chapter 18.

$$(.63828 - \lambda)(.27662 - \lambda) - (.31914)(.55325) = 0$$

$$.17656 - .63828\lambda - .27662\lambda + \lambda^2 - .17656 = 0$$

$$\lambda^2 - .91490\lambda = 0$$

Now, solve the quadratic equation:

$$\lambda = \frac{-b \pm \sqrt{b^2 - 4ac}}{2a}$$

where for the present example,

$$a = 1 \qquad b = -.91490 \qquad c = 0$$

$$\lambda = \frac{.91490 \pm \sqrt{(-.91490)^2 - (4)(1)(0)}}{2} = .91490$$

Having calculated λ the weights, **v**, are calculated by solving the following:

$$(\mathbf{W}^{-1}\mathbf{B} - \lambda\mathbf{I})\mathbf{v} = \mathbf{0} \tag{17.4}$$

The terms in the parentheses are those used in the determinantal equation (17.3). **v** is referred to as the eigenvector, or the characteristic vector. Using the value of λ and the values of the product of $\mathbf{W}^{-1}\mathbf{B}$ obtained above, (17.4) for the present example is:

$$\begin{bmatrix} .63828 - .91490 & .31914 \\ .55325 & .27662 - .91490 \end{bmatrix} \begin{bmatrix} v_1 \\ v_2 \end{bmatrix} = \begin{bmatrix} 0 \\ 0 \end{bmatrix}$$

$$\begin{bmatrix} -.27662 & .31914 \\ .55325 & -.63828 \end{bmatrix} \begin{bmatrix} v_1 \\ v_2 \end{bmatrix} = \begin{bmatrix} 0 \\ 0 \end{bmatrix}$$

This set of homogeneous equations is easily solved by forming the adjoint of the above matrix, which is[6]

$$\begin{bmatrix} -.63828 & -.31914 \\ -.55325 & -.27662 \end{bmatrix}$$

Note that the ratio of the first element to the second element is the first column in the preceding matrix is equal to the ratio of the first element to the second element in the second column. That is,

$$\frac{-.63828}{-.55325} = \frac{-.31914}{-.27662} = 1.15$$

[6]For a discussion of the adjoint of a 2 × 2 matrix, see Appendix A.

The solution of homogeneous equations results in coefficients that have a constant proportionality. One may therefore choose the first or the second column as the values of eigenvector. For that matter, multiplying the adjoint by any constant will result in an equally proportional set of weights. How, then, does one decide which weights to use? Before discussing this issue, the equivalence between the results obtained here and those obtained in the regression analysis of the same data will be shown.

Earlier in this chapter the data analyzed here were subjected to a multiple regression analysis in which the dependent variable was a dummy vector representing group membership. The regression coefficients obtained in that analysis were

$$b_1 = .13888 \qquad b_2 = .12036$$

The ratio of b_1 to b_2 is

$$\frac{.13888}{.12036} = 1.15$$

which is the same as that obtained above. This, then, demonstrates the equivalence of the weights obtained in the two solutions.

Of the various approaches used to resolve the indeterminancy of the weights obtained in DA two will be presented here: (1) raw, or unstandardized, coefficients and (2) standardized coefficients.

Raw Coefficients

The pooled within-groups variance of discriminant scores[7] can be written as follows:

$$\text{Var}(y) = \mathbf{v}'\mathbf{C}\mathbf{v} \tag{17.5}$$

where $\mathbf{v}'$ and $\mathbf{v}$ are row and column eigenvectors, respectively; $\mathbf{C}$ is the pooled within-groups covariance matrix defined as:

$$\mathbf{C} = \frac{\mathbf{W}}{N - g} \tag{17.6}$$

where $\mathbf{W}$ = pooled within-groups SSCP; N = total number of subjects; g = number of groups.

Now, raw coefficients are calculated by setting the constraint that the pooled within-groups variance of the discriminant scores be equal to 1.00. That is, $\mathbf{v}'\mathbf{C}\mathbf{v} = 1.00$. This is accomplished by dividing each element of the eigenvector by $\sqrt{\mathbf{v}'\mathbf{C}\mathbf{v}}$. That is,

[7]Discriminant scores are obtained by applying the discriminant function to subjects' scores. Such scores are calculated below for the subjects in the numerical example under consideration.

$$v_i^* = \frac{v_i}{\sqrt{\mathbf{v'Cv}}} \tag{17.7}$$

where v_i^* = ith raw coefficient; v_i = ith element of the eigenvector; and $\mathbf{v'Cv}$ is as defined for (17.5).

The foregoing formulations will be clarified by applying them to the numerical example under consideration. Earlier **W** was calculated. It is repeated here:

$$\mathbf{W} = \begin{bmatrix} 23.6 & -1.2 \\ -1.2 & 14.4 \end{bmatrix}$$

Applying (17.6), with $N - g = 8$,

$$\mathbf{C} = \frac{1}{8}\begin{bmatrix} 23.6 & -1.2 \\ -1.2 & 14.4 \end{bmatrix} = \begin{bmatrix} 2.95 & -.15 \\ -.15 & 1.8 \end{bmatrix}$$

In order to find $\mathbf{v'Cv}$, one may select as $\mathbf{v}$ either the first or the second column of the adjoint of the matrix obtained above, or one may use instead the b's that were obtained from the multiple regression analysis of the same data. For illustrative purposes, the first column of the adjoint of the matrix obtained above will be used. The elements of this column are $-.63828$ and $-.55325$. As multiplication of these elements by a constant will not affect their proportionality, it will be convenient to multiply them by -1 so as to change their signs. Applying Equation (17.5):

$$\mathbf{v'Cv} = \underset{\mathbf{v'}}{[.63828 \quad .55325]} \underset{\mathbf{C}}{\begin{bmatrix} 2.95 & -.15 \\ -.15 & 1.8 \end{bmatrix}} \underset{\mathbf{v}}{\begin{bmatrix} .63828 \\ .55325 \end{bmatrix}} = 1.64685$$

Equation (17.7) is now used to calculate the raw coefficients:

$$v_1^* = \frac{.63828}{\sqrt{1.64685}} = .49738$$

$$v_2^* = \frac{.55325}{\sqrt{1.64685}} = .43112$$

It can now be seen that $\mathbf{v'^*Cv^*} = 1.00$

$$[.49738 \quad .43112] \begin{bmatrix} 2.95 & -.15 \\ -.15 & 1.8 \end{bmatrix} \begin{bmatrix} .49738 \\ .43112 \end{bmatrix} = 1.00$$

It will be instructive to show that the same raw coefficient can be obtained by using the b's from the multiple regression analysis of the same data. The two

b's are: .13888 and .12036 (see calculations earlier in this chapter). Applying (17.5),

$$\underset{\mathbf{b}'}{[.13888 \quad .12036]} \underset{\mathbf{C}}{\begin{bmatrix} 2.95 & -.15 \\ -.15 & 1.8 \end{bmatrix}} \underset{\mathbf{b}}{\begin{bmatrix} .13888 \\ .12036 \end{bmatrix}} = .07796$$

Calculating the raw coefficients,

$$v_1^* = \frac{.13888}{\sqrt{.07796}} = .49740$$

$$v_2^* = \frac{.12036}{\sqrt{.07796}} = .43107$$

These values are, within rounding errors, the same as those obtained above.

Using the raw coefficients and the means of the dependent variables a constant, c, is obtained:

$$c = -(v_1^*\bar{X}_1 + v_2^*\bar{X}_2 + \cdots + v_k^*\bar{X}_k) \tag{17.8}$$

For the numerical example under consideration, $\bar{X}_1 = 4$ and $\bar{X}_2 = 3$. Using the v^*'s obtained above, c is calculated as follows:

$$c = -[(.49740)(4) + (.43107)(3)] = -3.28281$$

It is now possible to write the discriminant function:

$$Y = -3.28281 + .49740X_1 + .43107X_2$$

As is shown below, this function is used to calculate discriminant scores on the basis of raw scores. At this stage, it will be noted only that the raw coefficients are difficult to interpret, particularly when one wishes to determine the relative importance of the dependent variables. This is because the magnitude of a raw coefficient is dependent, among other things, on the properties and units of the scale that is used to measure the variable with which it is associated. The same problem was encountered earlier in the book when unstandardized coefficients were introduced in the context of multiple regression analysis (see, in particular, Chapter 8). As in multiple regression analysis, researchers using DA often resort to standardized coefficients when they wish to study the relative importance of variables.

Standardized Coefficients

Standardized coefficients in DA are readily obtainable, as is indicated in the following:

$$\beta_i = v_i^*\sqrt{c_{ii}} \tag{17.9}$$

where β_i = standardized coefficient[8] associated with variable i; v_i^* = raw coefficient for variable i; c_{ii} = diagonal element of the pooled within-groups covariance matrix (**C**) associated with variable i. Note that c_{ii} is the pooled within-groups variance of variable i. In short, to convert a raw coefficient to a standardized one, all that is necessary is to multiply the former by the pooled within-groups standard deviation of the variable with which it is associated.

The calculation of standardized coefficients is now demonstrated for the numerical example under consideration. For this example, it was found that v_1^* = .49740 and v_2^* = .43107. Also,

$$\mathbf{C} = \begin{bmatrix} 2.95 & -.15 \\ -.15 & 1.80 \end{bmatrix}$$

Applying (17.9),

$$\beta_1 = (.49740)\sqrt{2.95} = .85431$$

$$\beta_2 = (.43107)\sqrt{1.80} = .57834$$

These coefficients, which are applied to subjects' standard scores (z's), are interpreted in a manner analogous to β's in multiple regression analysis. Accordingly, one may use their relative magnitudes as indices of the relative contribution, or importance, of the dependent variables to the discrimination between the groups. On the basis of this criterion, one would conclude that in the numerical example analyzed above, variable 1 makes a greater contribution than variable 2 to the discrimination between the groups.

It is important, however, to note that the standardized coefficients in DA suffer from the same shortcomings as their counterparts in multiple regression analysis (see Chapter 8 for a detailed discussion of this point). Briefly, the standardized coefficients lack stability since they are affected by the variability of the variables with which they are associated, as can be clearly seen from Formula (17.9), and by the intercorrelations among the variables. Because of the shortcomings of standardized coefficients, various authors (e.g., Cooley & Lohnes, 1971, 1976; Klecka, 1980; Thorndike, 1978) recommend that structure coefficients be used for the interpretation of the discriminant function. We turn now to a brief discussion of this topic.

Structure Coefficients

The notion of structure coefficients was introduced earlier in this chapter in the context of multiple regression analysis. It was said that the structure coefficient is the correlation between an independent variable and the vector of composite scores obtained by applying the regression equation to subjects' scores on the independent variables. As is shown below, the discriminant function may be used for the purpose of calculating a discriminant score for each

[8]There is no consistency in the literature regarding the symbols used for raw and standardized coefficients. Because the standardized coefficients are interpreted in a manner analogous to β's in multiple regression analysis, it was decided to use the same symbol here.

subject. Having done this, one may correlate such scores with each of the original variables. Such correlations, too, are referred to as *structure coefficients* or loadings because, as was noted earlier, they are interpreted as factor loadings in factor analysis. The square of a structure coefficient indicates the proportion of variance of the variable with which it is associated that is accounted for by the given discriminant function. (As is discussed later, with more than two groups, more than one discriminant function may be obtained, and structure coefficients may be calculated for each of the discriminant functions.)

Structure coefficients are primarily useful for the purpose of determining the nature of the function(s) or the dimension(s) on which the groups are discriminated. Some authors also use the relative magnitudes of structure coefficients as an indication of the relative importance of variables on a given function or dimension. These issues will be taken up after it is shown how structure coefficients are calculated in DA.

As in the case of multiple regression analysis, structure coefficients in DA may be obtained without going through the calculations of correlation between the original variables and discriminant scores. The same results may be obtained as follows:

$$\mathbf{s} = \mathbf{R}_t \boldsymbol{\beta}_t \tag{17.10}$$

where $\mathbf{s}$ = vector of structure coefficients on a given discriminant function; $\mathbf{R}_t$ = total correlation matrix (i.e., the correlations are calculated by treating all the subjects as if they belonged to a single group), hence the subscript t to distinguish it from the pooled within-groups correlation matrix; $\boldsymbol{\beta}_t$ = vector of standardized coefficients based on the total number of subjects (see below).

In the preceding section it was shown how raw coefficients, v^*, are calculated subject to the constraint that the pooled within-groups variance of the discriminant scores is equal to 1.00. It was then shown how $\mathbf{v}^*$ is used to obtain standardized discriminant function coefficients (see sections entitled Raw Coefficients and Standardized Coefficients). Exactly the same procedure is followed to obtain $\boldsymbol{\beta}_t$, except that the total covariance matrix, $\mathbf{C}_t$, is used, instead of the pooled within-groups covariance matrix, $\mathbf{C}_w$, which was used in the aforementioned sections.

For the numerical example under consideration, it was found earlier that the total SSCP matrix is:

$$\mathbf{T} = \begin{bmatrix} 38.0 & 6.0 \\ 6.0 & 18.0 \end{bmatrix}$$

The total number of subjects is 10. Therefore, to obtain the total covariance matrix $\mathbf{T}$ is multiplied by the reciprocal of 9 (i.e., $N - 1$).

$$\mathbf{C}_t = \frac{1}{9}\begin{bmatrix} 38.0 & 6.0 \\ 6.0 & 18.0 \end{bmatrix} = \begin{bmatrix} 4.22222 & .66667 \\ .66667 & 2.00000 \end{bmatrix}$$

Analogous to (17.5) above, the coefficients, **v**, obtained earlier from the adjoint of the determinantal matrix are used to calculate **v*** so that the variance of the scores for the total sample is equal to 1.00. For the present example,

$$\underset{\mathbf{v}'}{\mathbf{v}'\mathbf{C}_t\mathbf{v} = [.63828 \quad .55325]} \underset{\mathbf{C}_t}{\begin{bmatrix} 4.22222 & .66667 \\ .66667 & 2.00000 \end{bmatrix}} \underset{\mathbf{v}}{\begin{bmatrix} .63828 \\ .55325 \end{bmatrix}} = \mathit{2.80315}$$

Applying now (17.7),

$$v_1^* = \frac{.63828}{\sqrt{2.80315}} = \mathit{.38123}$$

$$v_2^* = \frac{.55325}{\sqrt{2.80315}} = \mathit{.33044}$$

Note that the ratio of these coefficients is the same as the ratio of the raw coefficients obtained earlier when the pooled within-groups covariance matrix was used (i.e., .38123/.33044 = 1.15).

Now, using v^*, $\boldsymbol{\beta}_t$ is obtained by applying Formula (17.9), except that each v_i^* is multiplied by the square root of the relevant diagonal element from the total covariance matrix instead of elements from the pooled within-groups covariance matrix, which were used when (17.9) was applied earlier. For the present example,

$$\beta_1 = .38123\sqrt{4.22222} = \mathit{.78335}$$

$$\beta_2 = .33044\sqrt{2.00000} = \mathit{.46731}$$

The ratio of the β's based on the total number of subjects is *not* the same as the ratio of the β's obtained earlier when elements from the pooled within-groups covariance matrix were used to calculate the β's. Thus, for the β's calculated here, .78335/.46731 = 1.68, whereas for those calculated earlier, .85431/.57834 = 1.48. Note, however, that the ratio of the β's obtained here is the same as the ratio of the β's obtained in the beginning of this chapter, when the numerical example analyzed here was subjected to a multiple regression analysis with a coded vector as the dependent variable. The β's obtained in that analysis are β_1 = .54149 and β_2 = .32298. Their ratio is: .54149/.32298 = 1.68, which is the same as the ratio of the β's calculated here.

In order to calculate the structure coefficients, **s**, it is necessary to obtain also $\mathbf{R}_t$, the total correlation matrix. In the present case this means that the correlation between X_1 and X_2 has to be calculated. Actually, this has already been reported earlier (see Table 17.2): $r_{x_1x_2}$ = .22942. But for completeness of presentation it is shown how this is done by using $\mathbf{C}_t$, the covariance matrix. In this matrix, 4.22222 is the variance of X_1 and 2.00000 is the variance of X_2 for the total number of subjects. Therefore, $\sqrt{4.22222}$ and $\sqrt{2.00000}$ are the standard deviations of X_1 and X_2, respectively. In $\mathbf{C}_t$ the covariance between X_1 and X_2 is .66667. Dividing a covariance by the product of the standard deviations of the variables yields the correlation coefficient between them; see Formula (2.39). Therefore,

$$\mathbf{R}_t = \begin{bmatrix} \frac{4.22222}{\sqrt{(4.22222)(4.22222)}} & \frac{.66667}{\sqrt{(4.22222)(2.00000)}} \\ \frac{.66667}{\sqrt{(4.22222)(2.00000)}} & \frac{2.00000}{\sqrt{(2.00000)(2.00000)}} \end{bmatrix} = \begin{bmatrix} 1.00000 & .22942 \\ .22942 & 1.00000 \end{bmatrix}$$

It was, of course, not necessary to calculate the diagonal elements of $\mathbf{R}_t$, since they are known to be 1's. Again, for completeness of presentation all the calculations were indicated. The calculation of $\mathbf{R}_t$ could have been presented more succinctly by using matrix notation. The presentation given here was preferred because it was felt that it would be easier to follow.

We are now ready to calculate the structure coefficients, **s**. Using $\boldsymbol{\beta}_t$ and $\mathbf{R}_t$, calculated above, Formula (17.10) is applied:

$$\mathbf{s} = \underset{\mathbf{R}_t}{\begin{bmatrix} 1.0000 & .22942 \\ .22942 & 1.0000 \end{bmatrix}} \underset{\boldsymbol{\beta}_t}{\begin{bmatrix} .78335 \\ .46731 \end{bmatrix}} = \begin{bmatrix} .89056 \\ .64703 \end{bmatrix}$$

It was said earlier that structure coefficients are correlations of original variables with discriminant scores. If you were to calculate the correlation coefficient between the scores on X_1 and the discriminant scores (reported in Table 17.4) *across* the groups you will find it to be .89056. Similarly, the correlation between X_2 and the discriminant scores is .64703. Note that the same coefficients (within rounding errors) were obtained earlier when the data were subjected to a multiple regression analysis.

As a rule of thumb it is suggested that structure coefficients $\geq$ .30 be treated as meaningful. On the basis of this criterion, it is concluded that both variables have meaningful structure coefficients. With two variables only, it is difficult to convey the flavor of the interpretation of structure coefficients. Generally, a large number of variables would be used in DA. Under such circumstances, the meaningful structure coefficients, particularly the high ones, are used in attempts to interpret the discriminant function. Assume, for example, that eight variables are used in a DA and that only three of them have meaningful loadings. One would then examine these variables and attempt to name the function in a manner similar to that done in factor analysis. If, for example, it turns out that the three variables with the meaningful structure coefficients refer to different aspects of socioeconomic status, one would conclude that the function that discriminates between the groups reflects primarily their differences in socioeconomic status. The interpretation is, of course, not always as obvious as in this example. As in factor analysis, one might encounter structures that are difficult to interpret or that elude interpretation altogether. The naming of a function is a creative act—an attempt to capture the flavor of the dimension that underlies a set of variables even when they appear to be diverse.

The square of the first structure coefficient, $.89056^2 = .79310$, indicates that about 79% of the variance of X_1 is accounted for by the discriminant function. The square of the second structure coefficient, $.64703^2 = .41865$, indicates that about 42% of the variance of X_2 is accounted for by the discriminant function. On the basis of the preceding one would conclude that X_1 is more important than X_2. Although the same conclusion has been reached when the β's calculated in the earlier section ($\beta_1 = .85431$ and $\beta_2 = .57834$) were used to determine the relative importance of the variables, this will not always be the case. It is quite possible for the two criteria to lead to radically different conclusions. Which of the two indices (i.e., β's or structure coefficients) is therefore preferable? This depends on the purpose of the interpretation, inasmuch as each of them is addressed to a different question. Tatsuoka (1973) has stated the difference between the two indices succinctly. Reminding the reader that the β's are *partial* coefficients, he says: "This is fine when the purpose is to gauge the contribution of each variable in the company of all others, but it is inappropriate when we wish to give substantive interpretations to the . . . discriminant functions" (p. 280). It is for the latter purpose that structure coefficients are particularly useful. In short: "Both approaches are useful, provided we keep their different objectives clearly in mind" (Tatsuoka, 1973, p. 280).

In conclusion, it should be borne in mind that neither standardized coefficients nor structure coefficients are unambiguous indices of the relative importance of the variables with which they are associated. "As in multiple regression analysis, the notion of variable contribution in discriminant analysis is an evasive one" (Huberty, 1975b, p. 63).

Discriminant Scores and Centroids

The discriminant function may be used for the purpose of calculating discriminant scores for each subject in the groups under study. Earlier, it was said that the topic of classification is not dealt with in this chapter. It will therefore only be noted in passing that discriminant scores may be calculated for subjects who were not members of the groups under study in order to thereby determine which of the existing groups each subject most resembles.[9]

Discriminant scores are now calculated for the subjects in the numerical example analyzed above. The discriminant function that was calculated above is:

$$Y = -3.28281 + .49740X_1 + .43107X_2$$

The scores for the first subject in group A_1 are $X_1 = 8$ and $X_2 = 3$ (see Table 17.3). Accordingly, this subject's discriminant score is:

$$Y = -3.28281 + (.49740)(8) + (.43107)(3) = \mathit{1.9896}$$

Discriminant scores for all subjects were similarly calculated, and are reported in Table 17.4.

[9]References to classification procedures are given earlier in this chapter.

Table 17.4 Discriminant Scores for Data of Table 17.3

	A_1	A_2
	1.9896	−.4311
	1.9233	−1.3595
	1.3595	−.9285
	−.0663	−1.4259
	−.9285	−.1327
Σ:	4.2776	−4.2777
$\bar{Y}$:	.8555	−.8555
ΣY^2:	10.3723	4.9470

At the bottom of the table are reported the mean discriminant scores for groups A_1 and A_2. These means, which are referred to as centroids, are .8555 for group A_1 and −.8555 for group A_2. As the mean of these centroids is zero, it can be readily seen that subjects whose discriminant scores are positive "belong" to group A_1, whereas those whose discriminant scores are negative "belong" to group A_2. On this basis it can be seen in Table 17.4 that the last two subjects in group A_1 resemble more those of group A_2 (they have negative scores, as do all the subjects in group A_2). This kind of misclassification may be used as an indication of the separation of the groups. The stronger the separation, the smaller the number of such misclassifications.

Frequently, one is not interested in the individual discriminant scores. Under such circumstances, the group centroids may be calculated by inserting their means on the dependent variables in the discriminant function. In the present example, the means of the groups are (see Table 17.3):

$$A_1\text{:}\quad \bar{X}_1 = 5.2 \qquad \bar{X}_2 = 3.6$$

$$A_2\text{:}\quad \bar{X}_1 = 2.8 \qquad \bar{X}_2 = 2.4$$

Calculating their centroids:

$$\bar{Y}_{A_1} = -3.28281 + (.49740)(5.2) + (.43107)(3.6) = .8555$$

$$\bar{Y}_{A_2} = -3.28281 + (.49740)(2.8) + (.43107)(2.4) = -.8555$$

One other aspect of the results reported in Table 17.4 is worth noting. At the bottom of the table are reported the sums and the sums of squares of the discriminant scores. Using these values the pooled within-groups deviation sum of squares is calculated:

$$\left[10.3723 - \frac{(4.2776)^2}{5}\right] + \left[4.9470 - \frac{(-4.2777)^2}{5}\right] = 8.00$$

Dividing this pooled sum of squares by its degrees of freedom (i.e., $8 = 10 - 2 = N - g$) yields a pooled within-groups variance equal to 1.00. This confirms what was said earlier—namely, that the raw coefficients are calculated subject to the restriction that the pooled within-groups variance of the discriminant scores be equal to 1.00 (see Equations (17.5)–(17.7) and the discussion related to them).

Measures of Association

As in the case of univariate analysis, it is desirable to have a measure of association between the independent and the dependent variables in multivariate analysis. Of several such measures that have been proposed (see, for example, Huberty, 1972; Shaffer & Gillo, 1974; Smith, 1972; Stevens, 1972a; Tatsuoka, 1970, 1971a) only one will be presented here. The measure to be presented is related to Wilks' Λ (lambda), which is defined as

$$\Lambda = \frac{|\mathbf{W}|}{|\mathbf{T}|} \tag{17.11}$$

where **W** = pooled within-groups SSCP and **T** = total SSCP. Note that Λ is a ratio of the determinants of these two matrices.[10]

Before describing the measure of association that is related to Λ it will be instructive to show how Λ can be expressed for the case of univariate analysis. Recall that in the univariate analysis of variance the total sum of squares (ss_t) is partitioned into between-groups sum of squares (ss_b) and within-groups sum of squares (ss_w). Accordingly, in univariate analysis,

$$\Lambda = \frac{ss_w}{ss_t} \tag{17.12}$$

Since $ss_t = ss_b + ss_w$, Λ can also be written

$$\Lambda = \frac{ss_t - ss_b}{ss_t} = 1 - \frac{ss_b}{ss_t} \tag{17.13}$$

and, from the preceding,

$$\frac{ss_b}{ss_t} = 1 - \Lambda \tag{17.14}$$

As is well known (see Equation (9.5)), the ratio of ss_b to ss_t is defined as η^2—the proportion of variance of the dependent variable accounted for by the independent variable, or group membership. It is clear, then, that (1) Λ indicates the proportion of variance of the dependent variable *not* accounted for by the independent variable, or the proportion of error variance and (2) Λ may vary from zero to one. When $\Lambda = 0$ it means that $ss_b = ss_t$, and that the proportion of error variance is equal to zero. When, on the other hand, $\Lambda = 1$, it means that $ss_b = 0$ ($ss_w = ss_t$) and that the proportion of error variance is equal to one.

[10]Λ plays an important role in multivariate analysis, and is therefore discussed in detail in books on this topic. For a particularly good introduction, see Rulon and Brooks (1968).

In other words, the independent variable does not account for any proportion of the variance of the dependent variable.

It was shown in Chapter 9 that when the dependent variable is regressed on coded vectors that represent a categorical independent variable, the following equivalences hold:

$$ss_w = ss_{\text{res}} \qquad ss_b = ss_{\text{reg}} \qquad \eta^2 = R^2$$

where ss_{res} = residual sum of squares; ss_{reg} = regression sum of squares; R^2 = squared multiple correlation of the dependent variable with the coded vectors. Accordingly, Λ may be expressed as follows:

$$\Lambda = \frac{ss_{\text{res}}}{ss_t} = 1 - \frac{ss_{\text{reg}}}{ss_t} = 1 - R^2 \qquad (17.15)$$

and

$$R^2 = 1 - \Lambda \qquad (17.16)$$

From the foregoing, one may conceive of $1 - \Lambda$ in multivariate analysis as a generalization of η^2 or R^2 of univariate analysis. When in multivariate analysis $\Lambda = 1$ it means that there is no association between the independent and the dependent variables. When, on the other hand, $\Lambda = 0$ it means that there is a perfect association between the independent and the dependent variables.

It will now be shown that for the special case of a DA with two groups, $1 - \Lambda$ is equal to R^2 of a coded vector representing group membership with the dependent variables.

To calculate Λ for the numerical example analyzed above, it is necessary first to calculate the determinants of **W** and **T.** These matrices for the data of Table 17.3 were calculated earlier. They are

$$\mathbf{W} = \begin{bmatrix} 23.6 & -1.2 \\ -1.2 & 14.4 \end{bmatrix}$$

$$\mathbf{T} = \begin{bmatrix} 38.0 & 6.0 \\ 6.0 & 18.0 \end{bmatrix}$$

Calculating the determinants of each of these matrices:

$$|\mathbf{W}| = (23.6)(14.4) - (-1.2)(-1.2) = \mathit{338.4}$$

$$|\mathbf{T}| = (38.0)(18.0) - (6.0)(6.0) = \mathit{648.0}$$

Applying Equation (17.11),

$$\Lambda = \frac{|\mathbf{W}|}{|\mathbf{T}|} = \frac{338.4}{648.0} = \mathit{.52222}$$

and

$$1 - \Lambda = 1 - .52222 = .47778$$

The last value is identical to the R^2 that was obtained in the beginning of this chapter when a coded vector representing membership in groups A_1 and A_2 was regressed on the two dependent variables. Recall that it was said there that for analytic purposes only the roles of the independent and the dependent variables are reversed.

Throughout this section it has been demonstrated that a DA with two groups, regardless of the number of the dependent variables, can be accomplished via a multiple regression analysis in which a coded vector representing group membership is regressed on the dependent variables. As is shown below, the same holds true for multivariate analysis of variance, as well as for tests of significance. Before turning to these topics, it will be useful to show how Λ can be obtained by using other statistics that were calculated in the course of calculating the DA. In Chapter 18 this approach is extended to multiple DA and to multivariate analysis of variance with multiple groups.

In the beginning of this section it was shown how to solve for the eigenvalue, λ, in the following determinantal equation

$$|\mathbf{W}^{-1}\mathbf{B} - \lambda\mathbf{I}| = 0$$

(see Equation (17.3) and the discussion related to it). In the case of two groups,

$$\Lambda = \frac{1}{1 + \lambda} \tag{17.17}$$

For the data of Table 17.3 it was found that $\lambda = .91490$. Therefore

$$\Lambda = \frac{1}{1 + .91490} = .52222$$

which is the same as the value obtained when Equation (17.11) was used. In addition,

$$1 - \frac{1}{1 + \lambda} = R^2 = 1 - .52222 = .47778$$

Another expression using λ is

$$1 - \Lambda = R^2 = \frac{\lambda}{1 + \lambda} \tag{17.18}$$

For the present numerical example,

$$\frac{.91490}{1 + .91490} = .47778 = 1 - \Lambda = R^2$$

A Note on Multiple Discriminant Analysis

Although the equations for DA were applied to the case of two groups, it will be recalled that it was said earlier that the same equations apply to DA with any number of groups. With more than two groups, more than one discriminant function is calculated. The number of discriminant functions that can be calculated is equal to the number of groups minus one, or to the number of dependent variables, whichever is smaller. Thus, with three groups, for example, only two discriminant functions can be calculated, regardless of the number of dependent variables. If, on the other hand, there are six groups but only three dependent variables, the number of discriminant functions that can be calculated is three (the number of the dependent variables). An example of DA for more than two groups is given in Chapter 18.

In the beginning of this chapter it was shown that for the case of two groups, DA can be calculated by multiple regression analysis in which the groups are represented by a coded vector. With more than two groups, it is necessary to use more than one coded vector (see Chapter 9). Under such circumstances, multiple regression analysis cannot be used. As is shown in Chapter 18, canonical analysis with coded vectors may be used to calculate DA for any number of groups.

We turn now to a brief discussion of multivariate analysis of variance.

MULTIVARIATE ANALYSIS OF VARIANCE (MANOVA)

MANOVA is an extension of univariate analysis of variance designed to test simultaneously differences among groups on multiple dependent variables. As is discussed in Chapter 18, several tests have been proposed for this purpose. Probably the most widely used among them is a test of Wilks' Λ. That is, a test of Λ (shown below) serves as an overall test of the null hypothesis of the equality of mean vectors of two or more groups.

In the preceding section, Λ was discussed in detail in the context of DA, though the test of significance for Λ was not shown. A question that naturally arises is: Since Λ may be obtained in both DA and MANOVA, in what way do these approaches differ? Issues of classification to which DA, but not MANOVA, may be applied aside, it was said earlier that some researchers treat MANOVA and DA as interchangeable when the concern is with the study of group differences. But it was also noted that other researchers recommend that MANOVA be applied first in order to determine whether there are overall significant differences among the groups. This is accomplished by testing Λ. If the null hypothesis is rejected, it is recommended that DA be used to identify the variables on which the groups differ mostly, and the nature of the dimensions on which they differ (see discussion of standardized coefficients and structure coefficients in the section on DA).

It was stated above that when more than two groups are being studied, more than one discriminant function is obtained. In such situations, the test of Λ still refers to overall differences among the groups. But if it is found that Λ is statistically significant, it may turn out that only one or two discriminant functions are statistically significant, even though the data afford the calculation of a greater number of such functions (see Chapter 18).

Recall that with two groups, only one discriminant function may be obtained, regardless of the number of dependent variables. Therefore, the test of Λ in such cases provides the same information in both MANOVA and DA. Because the calculation of Λ was shown in detail in the preceding section, it will not be repeated here. Instead, we turn to the topic of tests of significance in MANOVA and DA.

TESTS OF SIGNIFICANCE

The test of Λ for the general case of any number of groups and any number of dependent variables is presented in Chapter 18. In the present section, a special case of this test is presented for the situation in which only two groups are being studied on any number of dependent variables. It is

$$F = \frac{(1 - \Lambda)/t}{\Lambda/(N - t - 1)} \tag{17.19}$$

where t is the number of dependent variables and N is the total number of subjects. The *df* for this F ratio are t and $N - t - 1$. Although different symbols are being used in (17.19) it is identical in form to the test of R^2 used earlier in this chapter when a coded vector representing group membership was regressed on the dependent variables. This can be clearly seen when it is recalled that $1 - \Lambda = R^2$ (see Equation (17.16) and the discussion related to it). Also, because the roles of the independent and the dependent variables are reversed when DA is done via multiple regression analysis, k (used in the formula for testing R^2) is equal to t, which is used in (17.19). t is used here instead of k, so as to be consistent with the symbols used in the general formula for the test of Λ (see Chapter 18).

Earlier, it was found that, for the data of Table 17.3,

$$\Lambda = \frac{|\mathbf{W}|}{|\mathbf{T}|} = .52222$$

Applying Formula (17.19),

$$F = \frac{(1 - .52222)/2}{.52222/(10 - 2 - 1)} = 3.20$$

with 2 and 7 *df*, $p > .05$. Not surprisingly, identical results were obtained when a DA of the same data was done via multiple regression analysis (see Multiple Regression Analysis, above).

It was noted several times earlier that a test of Λ is addressed to differences among groups on all the variables taken simultaneously. When the null hypothesis is rejected, it is of interest to identify specific variables on which the groups differ meaningfully. This brings us back to DA and the study of standardized coefficients and structure coefficients (see section on DA).

It may also be desired to test whether differences on single dependent variables, or on subsets of such variables, are statistically significant. This topic is discussed in Chapter 18 for the case of more than two groups. With two groups only, such tests may be carried out via multiple regression analysis. That is, tests of b's may be used for single variables and tests of differences between two R^2's for subsets of variables. Since the use and interpretation of such tests have been discussed extensively in earlier parts of the book (see, in particular, Chapters 6–8), they are not discussed here.

As in multiple regression analysis, one may use variable-selection procedures in multivariate analysis. For example, it is possible to do a stepwise DA (see research example below). Uses and limitations of variable-selection procedures in multiple regression analysis were discussed in detail in Chapter 6. The points made there regarding the appropriateness of variable-selection procedures in predictive versus explanatory research apply equally to the use of such procedures in multivariate analysis. With two groups, variable-selection procedures may be applied via multiple regression analysis in which the dependent variable is a coded vector representing group membership.

Finally, as with other statistics, the methods presented in this chapter are based on assumptions. These are discussed in detail in books on multivariate analysis cited in the beginning of this chapter. It is suggested that you read such discussions and that you pay special attention to the assumptions that the data follow a multivariate normal distribution, and that the within-groups covariance matrices are homogeneous. The references cited earlier also discuss tests of significance of the latter assumption, as well as the consequences of violating the assumptions.

COMPUTER PROGRAMS

There are a number of excellent computer programs for multivariate analysis. The three packaged programs discussed earlier (i.e., BMDP, SAS, SPSS) include programs for DA, MANOVA, and other multivariate procedures. A highly sophisticated program worthy of special notice is MULTIVARIANCE (Finn, 1977). Because of its great versatility, you may find it not as easy to learn to use as the programs included in the above cited packages. While the manual for MULTIVARIANCE provides detailed explanations and examples, you will benefit from studying Finn's (1974) book, in which several numerical examples analyzed by MULTIVARIANCE are discussed in detail. Examples of applications of MULTIVARIANCE to the analysis of several substantive problems will also be found in Finn and Mattsson (1978). This book is particularly useful because it includes the data, the control cards used, the output, and detailed discussions of the input and the output.

Because of the great popularity of SPSS, it was felt that it will be useful to include here a sample run of the DA program which is part of this package. For comparative purposes, the numerical example analyzed in this chapter will be used. Because this example was discussed in detail earlier, minimal comments will be made about the output.

Control Cards

```
RUN NAME          DISCRIMINANT ANALYSIS TABLE 17.3
SUBFILE LIST      A1(5) A2(5)
VARIABLE LIST     X1, X2
INPUT FORMAT      FIXED (2F2.0)
RUN SUBFILES      (A1, A2)
LIST CASES        CASES = 10/VARIABLES = X1, X2/
DISCRIMINANT      GROUPS = SUBFILES/VARIABLES
                    = X1, X2/ANALYSIS = X1, X2/5, 6
OPTIONS           5, 6
STATISTICS        1, 2, 3
READ INPUT DATA
 8 3
 7 4
 5 5
 3 4
 3 2
 4 2
 3 1
 3 2
 2 2
 2 5
```

Commentary

The DISCRIMINANT program used here is from SPSS Release 8. Although most of the instructions given in the second edition of the SPSS manual (Nie et al., 1975) are the same, some have been changed. It is important therefore that you refer to the SPSS UPDATE (Hull & Nie, 1979) when you use Release 8.

Because the general layout for SPSS was discussed several times earlier (see, for example, Chapter 4) only control cards specific to the DISCRIMINANT program will be commented upon.

SUBFILE LIST. This card describes the groups whose data are to be read, and the number of subjects in each (in parentheses). The data cards have to be sorted so that they are consistent with the subfile list. That is, the cards for the subjects in group A1 come first, followed by the cards for the subjects in group A2. Another method for the identification of group membership is described in the SPSS manual.

RUN SUBFILES. This card indicates which subfiles are to be used in a given analysis. In the present case there are only two subfiles. But when more than two groups are analyzed it is possible to do different DA's by specifying different subfile combinations on this card.

DISCRIMINANT. Calls for the DA procedure. GROUPS = SUBFILES indicates that the groups are sorted by subfiles. Variables = X1, X2 identifies the variables that are to be used in this run, whereas ANALYSIS = X1, X2 specifies the variables to be used in a given DA. In general, then, the total set of variables to be used is specified in the VARIABLES statement. One may then use different ANALYSIS statements to indicate subsets of variables to be used in separate analyses. In the present case, only two variables are read in, and both are to be used in a single analysis. Therefore, VARIABLES and ANALYSIS refer to the same variables.

OPTIONS. Of the various options, two were selected: 5 calls for the printing of a table of classification results, and 6 calls for, among other things, the printing of discriminant scores.

STATISTICS. Selected for this run are the following: 1 = means; 2 = standard deviations; 3 = pooled within-groups covariance matrix.

Following are excerpts of the output, along with brief commentaries.

Output

GROUP MEANS

SUBFILE	X1	X2
1	5.2	3.6
2	2.8	2.4
TOTAL	4.0	3.0

GROUP STANDARD DEVIATIONS

SUBFILE	X1	X2
1	2.28035	1.14018
1	.83666	1.51658
TOTAL	2.05480	1.41421

POOLED WITHIN-GROUPS COVARIANCE MATRIX
8 DEGREES OF FREEDOM

	X1	X2
X1	2.95	
X2	−.15	1.8

POOLED WITHIN-GROUPS CORRELATION MATRIX

	X1	X1
X1	1.00000	
X2	−.06509	1.00000

CANONICAL DISCRIMINANT FUNCTIONS

EIGENVALUE	WILKS' LAMBDA	CHI-SQUARED	D.F.	SIGNIFICANCE
.91489	.52222	4.5476	2	.1029

Commentary

Unlike other programs (e.g., MULTIVARIANCE) this program reports only a χ^2 of Λ. This test is described in Chapter 18.

Output

STANDARDIZED CANONICAL DISCRIMINANT FUNCTION COEFFICIENTS

	FUNC 1
X1	.85430
X2	.57835

UNSTANDARDIZED CANONICAL DISCRIMINANT FUNCTION COEFFICIENTS

	FUNC 1
X1	.49740
X2	.43108
(CONSTANT)	−3.28281

CANONICAL DISCRIMINANT FUNCTIONS EVALUATED AT GROUP MEANS (GROUP CENTROIDS)

	FUNC 1
X1	.85552
X2	−.85552

SUBFILE	CASE SEQNUM	ACTUAL GROUP	DISCRIMINANT SCORES
A1	1	1	1.9896
A1	2	1	1.9233
A1	3	1	1.3595
A1	4	1***	−.0663
A1	5	1***	−.9285
A2	1	2	−.4311
A2	2	2	−1.3595
A2	3	2	−.9285
A2	4	2	−1.4259
A2	5	2	−.1326

CLASSIFICATION RESULTS

ACTUAL GROUP	NO. OF CASES	PREDICTED GROUP MEMBERSHIP 1	2
GROUP 1	5	3	2
SUBFILE A1		60.0%	40.0%
GROUP 2	5	0	5
SUBFILE A2		0.0%	100.0%

PERCENT OF "GROUPED" CASES CORRECTLY CLASSIFIED: 80.00

Commentary

Using the discriminant function, discriminant scores are calculated. The same results were reported in the section on DA (see Table 17.4), where it was noted that the last two cases in group A1 (indicated above by asterisks) are misclassified. The table above summarizes the results of the classification on the basis of the discriminant scores. As is pointed out in the SPSS UPDATE: "The percentage of cases correctly classified will always be optimistic when the same cases are used both to compute the discriminant functions and in classification" (Hull & Nie, 1979, p. 188). For a discussion of this topic see references cited at the beginning of this chapter.

A RESEARCH APPLICATION

In recent years, there has been a proliferation of sex role research in which a variety of scales of dubious validity have been used. Pedhazur and Tetenbaum (1979) offered a detailed critique of one of the most widely used scales, the Bem Sex Role Inventory (BSRI). It is not the purpose here to summarize Pedhazur and Tetenbaum's paper but rather to use one of their analyses as an illustrative application of DA with two groups.

Before doing that the BSRI will be briefly described. It is a scale consisting of 20 "masculine" and 20 "feminine" traits. Respondents are instructed to rate themselves on each trait, using a rating scale ranging from 1 to 7, where 1 indicates "never or almost never true" and 7 indicates "always or almost always true." The ratings on the 20 "masculine" traits are summed to yield what is purported to be a score on Masculinity, and the ratings on the 20 "feminine" traits are summed to yield what is purported to be a score on Femininity. It will be noted in passing that in a series of factor analyses Pedhazur and Tetenbaum have demonstrated that the ratings are factorially complex and have therefore questioned the validity of using them as summated rating scales in the manner indicated above.

Be that as it may, because they are used as summated rating scales, and because researchers often study differences between males and females on Masculinity and Femininity as measured by the BSRI, Pedhazur and Tetenbaum set out to demonstrate that the differences between males and females are primarily due to their self-ratings on two of the 40 traits, namely Masculine and Feminine. This was done by subjecting the self-ratings of 171 males and 400 females on the 40 traits to a DA. Following is a summary of some of the results of this analysis. The standardized coefficients for the traits Feminine and Masculine were $-.70$ and .55, respectively. Of the remaining traits, 32 had coefficients of $< .10$, and six had coefficients between .10 and .15. The structure coefficients for Feminine and Masculine were $-.80$ and .76, respectively. Except for two other traits that had structure coefficients of about .10, the remaining traits had coefficients $< .10$, with most being close to zero. On the basis of these results, it is clear that the discrimination between males and females is primarily due to their self-ratings on the traits Feminine and Masculine.

To further highlight these findings, results of a stepwise DA of the self-ratings on the 40 traits will be briefly summarized. It is important to note first that *no* hierarchy for inclusion of traits in the stepwise analysis has been preestablished. In other words, no traits were forced in, but rather they were entered according to their potency in contributing to the discrimination between the groups.[11] After the traits Masculine and Feminine have been entered, $\Lambda = .241$. Compare this with $\Lambda = .212$ for the entire set of 40 traits. Because only two groups were involved in the analysis, the foregoing can be stated as follows: $R^2 = .759$ when a coded vector representing male-female is regressed on the ratings of Masculine and Feminine only. When the coded vector is regressed on the ratings of all 40 traits, $R^2 = .788$.[12] In other words, the 38 traits add .029 to the proportion of variance accounted for over and above what is accounted for by the traits Masculine and Feminine. It will also be noted that using a function with Masculine and Feminine only, 93.5% of the subjects were correctly classified. Compare this with 97.6% of subjects correctly classified when a function based on the 40 traits were used. Pedhazur and Tetenbaum state:

> In sum, all the indices support the notion that the discrimination between males and females is almost exclusively due to their self-ratings on the two traits Masculine and Feminine. Stated differently, knowledge of the respondents' self-ratings on the remaining 38 traits adds little to the knowledge obtained from their ratings on Masculine and Feminine. Not surprisingly, males rate themselves high on Masculine and low on Feminine. The converse is true for females. (1979, p. 1009)

STUDY SUGGESTIONS

1. In a study with two groups and five dependent variables, how many discriminant functions can be obtained?
2. What is the meaning of a structure coefficient?
3. When Λ (lambda) is calculated for two groups only, what term is it equal to if the data for the two groups are subjected to a multiple regression analysis in which the dependent variable is a coded vector representing group membership?
4. What is the ratio of the determinant of the within-groups SSCP to the determinant of the total SSCP equal to?
5. A researcher studied the differences between males ($N = 180$) and females ($N = 150$) on six dependent variables. Λ was found to be .62342. What is the F ratio for test of Λ?
6. The following is an example of a facet of a study one encounters in research on attribution theory (e.g., Weiner, 1974). Assume that subjects were randomly assigned to perform a task under either a Success or a Failure condition. That is, subjects under the former condition met with success while performing the task, whereas those under the latter condition met with failure. Subsequently, the subjects were asked to rate the degree to which their performance was due to their ability, and to the difficulty of the task they have engaged in. Following are the data (illustrative), where higher ratings indicate greater attributions to ability and to task difficulty.

[11]For discussions of the use of stepwise DA see, for example, Huberty (1975) and Klecka (1980).
[12]See Equation (17.16) and the discussion related to it.

Success		*Failure*	
Ability	*Difficulty*	*Ability*	*Difficulty*
6	5	3	6
7	6	3	6
3	4	2	7
5	5	1	5
6	5	1	7
6	4	5	6
7	6	4	5
7	7	3	6

(a) Do a multiple regression analysis in which the treatments, represented as a dummy vector, are regressed on the two dependent variables.

(b) Do a discriminant analysis of the same data. Compare with the results obtained under (a). Interpret the results.

A miniature example is purposely used so that you may do all the calculations by hand. You may also find it useful to do the analyses by computer and to compare the output with your hand calculations.

ANSWERS

1. Only one function can be obtained, regardless of the number of dependent variables.
2. It is the correlation of an original variable with the discriminant function scores.
3. $1 - R^2$
4. Λ
5. $F = 32.52$, with 6 and 323 *df*.
6. (a) $R^2 = .68762$

   $F = 14.31$, with 2 and 13 *df*.

   $Y' = .64316 + .18069(\text{AB}) - .16398(\text{DIF})$

   $(4.67, p < .001)\ (-1.94, p > .05)$

   The numbers in the parentheses are t ratios associated with each of the b's.

   Structure coefficients: .93173(AB); −.48783(DIF)

   $\beta_{(\text{AB})} = .73081$ $\beta_{(\text{DIF})} = -.30402$

   (b)

$$\mathbf{W} = \begin{bmatrix} 26.375 & 5.250 \\ 5.250 & 11.500 \end{bmatrix}$$

$$\mathbf{B} = \begin{bmatrix} 39.0625 & -9.3750 \\ -9.3750 & 2.2500 \end{bmatrix}$$

$$\mathbf{T} = \begin{bmatrix} 65.4375 & -4.1250 \\ -4.1250 & 13.7500 \end{bmatrix}$$

$\lambda = 2.20127$

$Y = .57789 + .72936(\text{AB}) - .66191(\text{DIF})$

Centroids: Success = 1.38784. Failure = −1.38784.
Standardized coefficients: 1.00109(AB) − .59991(DIF).
Structure coefficients: .93175(AB); −.48778(DIF).
$\Lambda = .31238$. $F = 14.31$, with 2 and 13 *df*.
Ability ratings make a greater contribution to the discrimination between the treatment groups than do ratings of task difficulty. Subjects under the Success condition attribute their performance to a greater extent to their ability than do subjects under the failure condition. The converse is true, though to a much smaller extent, concerning the rating of the difficulty of the task. That is, subjects under the Failure condition perceive the task as being more difficult than do subjects under the Success condition. Following are the means for the two groups:

	Ability	*Difficulty*
Success	5.875	5.250
Failure	2.750	6.000

Note that in the regression analysis of the same data, (a) above, it was found that the regression coefficient for task difficulty is not statistically significant at the .05 level. This is, of course, due in part to the small sample sizes. The mean difference in the ratings of this variable is meaningful when assessed in relation to the pooled within-groups standard deviation.

CANONICAL AND DISCRIMINANT ANALYSIS, AND MULTIVARIATE ANALYSIS OF VARIANCE

Throughout Parts 1 and 2 of this book it has been amply demonstrated that Multiple Regression (MR) is a powerful and versatile analytic method applicable to situations in which the research goal it to explain, or predict, a single dependent variable on the basis of multiple independent variables. It was shown that the independent variables may be continuous, categorical, or a combination of both, but that in all instances the analysis is limited to one dependent variable.

Often, the goal is to study relations between multiple independent and multiple dependent variables or, more generally, between two *sets* of variables. Situations of this kind abound in behavioral and social research, as is evidenced when relations are sought, for example, between (1) mental abilities and academic achievement in several subject areas; (2) attitudes and values; (3) personality characteristics and cognitive styles; (4) a battery of aptitude measures and another battery of such measures; (5) measures of adjustment of husbands and those of their wives; (6) pretests and posttests in achievement, personality, and the like. The list could be extended indefinitely to encompass divers phenomena from various research disciplines and orientations. Examples of potential and actual studies of relations between sets of variables in psychology, education, political science, sociology, communication, marketing will be found, among other sources, in the following: Darlington, Weinberg, and Walberg (1973); Green, Halbert, and Robinson (1966); Levine (1977); Tucker and Chase (1980); and Weiss (1972).

It is for the purpose of studying relations between two sets of variables that Hotelling (1936) has developed the method of Canonical Analysis (CA). It should be noted from the outset that MR can be viewed as a special case of CA—that is, when there is only one dependent variable, or one criterion, CA reduces to MR. Stated differently, CA may be conceived of as an extension of MR or, alternatively, MR may be conceived of as being subsumed under CA.

The generality of CA can be further noted when it is realized that it is not limited, as one might have been led to believe from the examples given above, to continuous variables. Assume, for example, that the interest is in explaining the effects of four treatments on multiple dependent variables, or to study differences among four groups on multiple dependent variables. Using methods described in Chapter 9, one could create three coded vectors to represent the four treatments or the four groups. CA could then be applied, where one set of variables would be the coded vectors and the other set would consist of the dependent variables. Note that the preceding description constitutes an extention of the manner in which MR was applied in Chapter 17, where it was shown that for the case of *two* groups MR can be used to obtain results identical to those obtained through the application of Discriminant Analysis (DA) or Multivariate Analysis of Variance (MANOVA). This, it will be recalled, was accomplished by regressing a coded vector representing group memebership on the dependent variables. With more than two groups, more than one coded vector is necessary to represent group membership. Therefore, MR can no longer be used in lieu of DA or MANOVA. But, as was noted above, CA can be used for such purposes. In sum, CA is a most general analytic approach that subsumes MR, DA, and MANOVA.

This chapter begins with an overview of CA in which it is shown that conceptually the method may be conceived of as a generalization of MR. As will become evident, while the conceptual step from MR to CA is not a large one, the computational one may be very large indeed. Except for the simplest of problems, CA is so complex as to make solutions with only the aid of calculators forbidding. Consequently, intelligent and critical reliance on computer analysis is essential even with moderately complex CA problems. In fact, it was because of the unavailability of computer facilities that CA lay dormant, so to speak, for several decades since its development, except for some relatively simple applications mostly for illustrative purposes. Nowadays, the availability of various computer programs (see below) renders solutions of even extremely complex CA problems easily obtainable. It is safe to say that in view of the great capacity and speed of present-day computers, it is one's theoretical formulations and one's ability to comprehend and interpret the results that set limits on the degree of complexity of CA problems that may be attempted.

Fortunately, as in the case of MR, all the ingredients of the calculations and all aspects of the interpretation of CA can be done with relative ease without a computer when there are only two variables in each set. Gaining an understanding of CA through the use of such simple problems will enable you to then proceed, with the aid of a computer, to more complex ones. Accordingly, after the overview of CA, the calculations and interpretations of the method will be presented via two small numerical examples. The first deals with the general application of CA in studying the relations between two sets of continuous variables. The second example deals with a special application of CA—namely, when one set consists of continuous variables whereas the other set consists of coded vectors representing a categorical variable. By means of this example it will be shown how MANOVA or DA for more than two groups may be done via CA.

In the process of presenting the two examples, all the calculations will be shown. It should be borne in mind that, except for becoming more complex, exactly the same kind of calculations are carried out in CA with more than two variables in each set. But, as was noted above, it is best to do this with the aid of a computer. In order to acquaint you with some of the computer programs for CA, one of the numerical examples presented in this chapter will also be analyzed by computer. At the conclusion of the chapter, two research applications of CA are briefly summarized.

CA: AN OVERVIEW

As noted several times earlier, CA is a method designed to study the relations between two sets of variables, p and q, where $p \geq 2$ could be a set of independent variables, and $q \geq 2$ could be a set of dependent variables. Alternatively, p could be a set of predictors and q a set of criteria. When the preceding designations do not apply (that is, when the aim is to study the relations between two sets of variables without designating one of them as independent or predictors, and the other as dependent or criteria), the p variables are referred to as "the variables on the left," or Set 1, and the q variables are referred to as "the variables on the right," or Set 2. In the sequel, X's will be used to represent variables on the left, and Y's will be used to represent variables on the right.

The basic idea of CA is that of forming two linear combinations, one of the X_p variables and one of the Y_q variables, by differentially weighting them so that the maximum possible correlation between them is obtained. The correlation between the two linear combinations, also referred to as *canonical variates,* is the canonical correlation, R_c. The square of the canonical correlation, R_c^2, is an estimate of the variance shared by the two canonical variates. It is very important to bear in mind that R_c^2 is *not* an estimate of the variance shared between X_p and X_q, *but of the linear combinations of these variables.*[1]

From the foregoing characterization of CA, its analogy with MR should be apparent. When p or q consists of one variable, we are back to MR. Recall that the multiple correlation coefficient is the maximum correlation that can be obtained between the dependent variable, Y, and a linear combination of the independent variables, the X's (see Equation (3.18) and the discussion related to it). Like MR, CA seeks a set of weights that will maximize a correlation coefficient. But unlike MR, in which only the X's can be thus weighted, in CA both the X's and the Y's are differentially weighted. Moreover, after having obtained the maximum R_c in CA, additional R_c's are calculated, subject to the restriction that each succeeding pair of canonical variates of the X's and the Y's not be correlated with all the pairs of canonical variates that precede it. In short, the first pair of linear combinations is the one that yields the highest R_c

[1]See discussion of Redundancy, below.

possible in a given set of data. The second R_c is then based on linear combinations of X_p and Y_q that are not correlated with the first pair and that yield the second largest R_c possible in the given data—and similarly for succeeding R_c's. The maximum number of R_c's that can be extracted is equal to the number of variables in the smaller set, when $p \neq q$. For example, when $p = 5$ and $q = 7$, the maximum number of R_c's is five. This is not to say that all the R_c's that are obtainable are necessarily meaningful or statistically significant. These topics are discussed below. At this stage it will only be noted that CA extracts the R_c's in a descending order of magnitude, subject to the restriction noted above.

Data Matrices for CA

It will be useful to familiarize you with the symbolism of the raw data and correlation matrices that are used in CA. The basic data matrix for CA is depicted in Table 18.1. Note that this is a matrix of N (subjects, cases) by $p + q$ (or $X_p + Y_q$) variables. As usual, the first subscript of each X or Y stands for rows (subjects, cases) and the second subscript for columns (variables, tests, items, and so on). Note the broken vertical line: it partitions the matrix into X_p and Y_q variables, or p variables on the left and q variables on the right. From Table 18.1 it should be clear that MR is a special case of CA. In the former, one variable, Y, is partitioned from the rest, the X's. In the latter, the matrix is partitioned into two sets of variables, X_p and Y_q, where $p \geq 2$ and $q \geq 2$.

Instead of consisting of raw scores, as in Table 18.1, the data matrix may consist of deviation or standard scores. The variables of the data matrix are intercorrelated and a correlation matrix, **R,** is formed. Such a matrix, which is also partitioned, is shown in Table 18.2, where the partitioning is indicated by broken lines. The four partitions of the matrix can be succinctly indicated in this way:

$$\mathbf{R} = \begin{bmatrix} \mathbf{R}_{xx} & \mathbf{R}_{xy} \\ \mathbf{R}_{yx} & \mathbf{R}_{yy} \end{bmatrix}$$

Table 18.1 Basic Data Matrix for CA

Cases	X			Y		
1	X_{11}	$X_{12} \ldots$	X_{1p}	Y_{11}	$Y_{12} \ldots$	Y_{1q}
2	X_{21}	$X_{22} \ldots$	X_{2p}	Y_{21}	$Y_{22} \ldots$	Y_{2q}
.	.	.	.	.	.	.
.	.	. . . .	.	.	. . . .	.
.	.	.	.	.	.	.
N	X_{N1}	$X_{N2} \ldots$	X_{Np}	Y_{N1}	$Y_{N2} \ldots$	Y_{Nq}

NOTE: N = number of cases; p = number of X variables; q = number of Y variables.

Table 18.2 Partitioned Correlation Matrix for CA

		X				*Y*			
		1	2	. . .	*p*	1	2	. . .	*q*
X	1 2 • • • *p*			$\mathbf{R}_{xx}$				$\mathbf{R}_{xy}$	
Y	1 2 • • • *q*			$\mathbf{R}_{yx}$				$\mathbf{R}_{yy}$	

NOTE: p = number of X variables; q = number of Y variables.

where $\mathbf{R}$ = the supermatrix of the intercorrelations among all the variables;[2] $\mathbf{R}_{xx}$ = the correlation matrix of the X_p variables; $\mathbf{R}_{yy}$ = the correlation matrix of the Y_q variables; $\mathbf{R}_{xy}$ = the correlation matrix of the X_p with the Y_q variables; $\mathbf{R}_{yx}$ = the transpose of $\mathbf{R}_{xy}$. It is the preceding four matrices that are used in the solution of the CA problem.

CA WITH CONTINUOUS VARIABLES

In this section, CA is presented for designs in which both sets of variables are continuous. It is for the analysis of data obtained in such designs that CA was initially developed. The adaptation of CA to designs in which one set of variables is continuous and the other set is categorical is dealt with in the next section. The calculations and interpretations of CA when both sets of variables are continuous will be shown by means of a numerical example in which $p = q = 2$, to which we now turn.

Numerical Example

In Table 18.3 a correlation matrix for illustrative data on two X and two Y variables is reported. As noted earlier, the X's may be independent variables and the Y's dependent variables, or the X's may be predictors and the Y's criteria. Most generally, the X's are the variables on the left, or the first set; the Y's are the variables on the right, or the second set. No attempt will be made to attach substantive meanings to the variables under consideration since exam-

[2]For a discussion of supermatrices, see Horst (1963, Chapter 5).

ples of potential applications of CA in various substantive areas were given earlier.

Canonical Correlations

It was said earlier that the number of canonical correlations obtainable in a given set of data is equal to the number of variables in the smaller of the two sets of variables. In the present example, $p = 2$ and $q = 2$. Therefore two canonical correlations may be obtained. The canonical correlations are equal to the square roots of the eigenvalues, λ, or characteristic roots, of the following determinantal equation:

$$\left| \mathbf{R}_{yy}^{-1} \mathbf{R}_{yx} \mathbf{R}_{xx}^{-1} \mathbf{R}_{xy} - \lambda \mathbf{I} \right| = 0 \qquad (18.1)$$

where $\mathbf{R}_{yy}^{-1}$ = inverse of $\mathbf{R}_{yy}$; $\mathbf{R}_{xx}^{-1}$ = inverse of $\mathbf{R}_{xx}$; $\mathbf{I}$ = identity matrix. A problem similar to the one in Equation (18.1) has been solved in Chapter 17 (see Equation (17.3) and the calculations related to it).

First the two inverses will be calculated. Using the data from Table 18.3, the determinant of $\mathbf{R}_{yy}$ is

$$\left| \mathbf{R}_{yy} \right| = \begin{vmatrix} 1.00 & .70 \\ .70 & 1.00 \end{vmatrix} = .51$$

and

$$\mathbf{R}_{yy}^{-1} = \frac{1}{.51} \begin{bmatrix} 1.00 & -.70 \\ -.70 & 1.00 \end{bmatrix} = \begin{bmatrix} 1.96078 & -1.37255 \\ -1.37255 & 1.96078 \end{bmatrix}$$

The determinant of $\mathbf{R}_{xx}$ is:

$$\left| \mathbf{R}_{xx} \right| = \begin{vmatrix} 1.00 & .60 \\ .60 & 1.00 \end{vmatrix} = .64$$

Table 18.3 Correlation Matrix for CA; $N = 300$

		$\mathbf{R}_{xx}$		$\mathbf{R}_{xy}$	
		X_1	X_2	Y_1	Y_2
	X_1	1.00	.60	.45	.48
	X_2	.60	1.00	.40	.38
$\mathbf{R}$ =		$\mathbf{R}_{yx}$		$\mathbf{R}_{yy}$	
	Y_1	.45	.40	1.00	.70
	Y_2	.48	.38	.70	1.00

And,

$$\mathbf{R}_{xx}^{-1} = \frac{1}{.64}\begin{bmatrix} 1.00 & -.60 \\ -.60 & 1.00 \end{bmatrix} = \begin{bmatrix} 1.56250 & -.93750 \\ -.93750 & 1.56250 \end{bmatrix}$$

The matrix operations are now carried in the sequence indicated in (18.1):

$$\mathbf{R}_{yy}^{-1}\mathbf{R}_{yx} = \begin{bmatrix} 1.96078 & -1.37255 \\ -1.37255 & 1.96078 \end{bmatrix}\begin{bmatrix} .45 & .40 \\ .48 & .38 \end{bmatrix} = \begin{bmatrix} .22353 & .26274 \\ .32353 & .19608 \end{bmatrix}$$

$$\mathbf{R}_{yy}^{-1}\mathbf{R}_{yx}\,\mathbf{R}_{xx}^{-1} = \begin{bmatrix} .22353 & .26274 \\ .32353 & .19608 \end{bmatrix}\begin{bmatrix} 1.56250 & -.93750 \\ -.93750 & 1.56250 \end{bmatrix} = \begin{bmatrix} .10295 & .20097 \\ .32169 & .00307 \end{bmatrix}$$

$$\mathbf{R}_{yy}^{-1}\mathbf{R}_{yx}\,\mathbf{R}_{xx}^{-1}\mathbf{R}_{xy} = \begin{bmatrix} .10295 & .20097 \\ .32169 & .00307 \end{bmatrix}\begin{bmatrix} .45 & .48 \\ .40 & .38 \end{bmatrix} = \begin{bmatrix} .12672 & .12578 \\ .14599 & .15558 \end{bmatrix}$$

It is now necessary to solve the following:

$$\begin{vmatrix} .12672 - \lambda & .12578 \\ .14599 & .15558 - \lambda \end{vmatrix} = 0$$

$$(.12672 - \lambda)(.15558 - \lambda) - (.14599)(.12578) = 0$$

$$.01972 - .15558\lambda - .12672\lambda + \lambda^2 - .01836 = 0$$

$$\lambda^2 - .28230\lambda + .00136 = 0$$

Solving the quadratic equation,

$$\lambda = \frac{-b \pm \sqrt{b^2 - 4ac}}{2a}$$

where $a = 1$, $b = -.28230$, and $c = .00136$,

$$\lambda_1 = \frac{.28230 + \sqrt{(-.28230)^2 - (4)(1)(.00136)}}{2} = .27740$$

$$\lambda_2 = \frac{.28230 - \sqrt{(-.28230)^2 - (4)(1)(.00136)}}{2} = .00490$$

It will be noted that the sum of the λ's (.27740 + .00490 = .2823) is equal to the trace (the sum of the elements of the principal diagonal) of the matrix used to solve for λ's. In other words, it is the trace of the matrix whose determinant was set to be equal to zero. Look back at this matrix and note that the two elements in its principal diagonal are .12672 and .15558. Their sum (.2823) is equal to the sum of the λ's, or roots, calculated above. This could serve as a check on the calculations of the λ's.

Taking the positive square roots of the λ's,

$$R_{c1} = \sqrt{\lambda_1} = \sqrt{.27740} = .52669$$

$$R_{c2} = \sqrt{\lambda_2} = \sqrt{.00490} = .07000$$

Recall that R_c^2 indicates the proportion of variance shared by a pair of canonical variates to which it corresponds. Accordingly, the first pair of canonical variates share about 28% of the variance ($R_{c1}^2 = \lambda_1$), and the second pair share about .5% of the variance ($R_{c2}^2 = \lambda_2$). It is shown below how canonical correlations are tested for significance. But, as with other statistics, the criterion of meaningfulness is more important. As a rule of thumb, it is suggested (e.g., Cooley & Lohnes, 1971, p. 176; Thorndike, 1978, p. 183) that $R_c^2 < .10$ (i.e., less than 10% of shared variance) be treated as not meaningful. In any case, the second R_c in the present example is certainly not meaningful. But for completeness of presentation it is retained here.

Canonical Weights

It was said earlier that R_c is a correlation between a linear combination of X's and a linear combination of Y's. It is now shown how the weights used to form such linear combinations—referred to as canonical weights—are calculated. Canonical weights are calculated for each R_c that is retained for purposes of interpretation of the results. Thus, for example, in a given problem seven R_c's may be obtainable, but using a criterion of meaningfulness or statistical significance (see below) it may be decided to retain only the first two. Under such circumstances, the canonical weights associated with the first two R_c's are of interest.

To differentiate between canonical weights to be used with the X's (variables on the left) and the Y's (variables on the right), the letter a will be used for the former and the letter b for the latter. Thus $\mathbf{A}$ is a matrix of canonical weights for the X's and $\mathbf{a}_j$ is the jth column vector of such coefficients associated with the jth R_c. Similarly, $\mathbf{B}$ is a matrix of canonical weights for the Y's and $\mathbf{b}_j$ is the jth column vector of such coefficients.

$\mathbf{B}$ will now be calculated, using relevant results calculated in the preceding section. To obtain $\mathbf{b}_1$ (the canonical weights associated with R_{c1}) it is necessary first to obtain the eigenvector, $\mathbf{v}_1$, or the characteristic vector, associated with λ_1. It was found earlier that $\lambda_1 = .27740$. Following the procedures explained in Chapter 17, the following homogeneous equations are formed:

$$\begin{bmatrix} .12672 - .27740 & .12578 \\ .14599 & .15558 - .27740 \end{bmatrix} \begin{bmatrix} v_1 \\ v_2 \end{bmatrix} = \begin{bmatrix} 0 \\ 0 \end{bmatrix}$$

$$\begin{bmatrix} -.15068 & .12578 \\ .14599 & -.12182 \end{bmatrix} \begin{bmatrix} v_1 \\ v_2 \end{bmatrix} = \begin{bmatrix} 0 \\ 0 \end{bmatrix}$$

A solution for these equations is obtained by forming the adjoint of the preceding matrix:[3]

$$\begin{bmatrix} -.12182 & -.12578 \\ -.14599 & -.15068 \end{bmatrix}$$

Accordingly,

$$\mathbf{v}_1' = [-.12182 \quad -.14599]$$

or, alternatively,

$$\mathbf{v}_1' = [-.12578 \quad -.15068]$$

Recall that there is a constant proportionality between the elements of each column, and that it therefore makes no difference which of the two columns is taken as **v**. Also, it is convenient to change the signs of **v**, since both are negative. Using the values of the first column of the adjoint,

$$\mathbf{v}_1' = [.12182 \quad .14599]$$

Now, β_j is calculated subject to the restriction that the variance of the scores on the jth canonical variate is equal to one. The preceding can be stated as follows:

$$\boldsymbol{\beta}_j'\mathbf{R}_{yy}\,\boldsymbol{\beta}_j = 1.00 \qquad (18.2)$$

To accomplish this, apply

$$\boldsymbol{\beta}_j = \frac{1}{\sqrt{\mathbf{v}_j'\mathbf{R}_{yy}\mathbf{v}_j}}\mathbf{v}_j \qquad (18.3)$$

where $\mathbf{v}_j$ is the jth eigenvector; $\mathbf{v}_j'$ is the transpose of $\mathbf{v}_j$; $\mathbf{R}_{yy}$ is the correlation matrix of the Y's. For the present example,

$$\mathbf{v}_1'\mathbf{R}_{yy}\mathbf{v}_1 = \underset{\mathbf{v}_1'}{[.12182 \quad .14599]} \underset{\mathbf{R}_{yy}}{\begin{bmatrix} 1.00 & .70 \\ .70 & 1.00 \end{bmatrix}} \underset{\mathbf{v}_1}{\begin{bmatrix} .12182 \\ .14599 \end{bmatrix}} = .06105$$

$$\sqrt{\mathbf{v}_1'\mathbf{R}_{yy}\mathbf{v}_1} = \sqrt{.06105} = .24708$$

[3]For a discussion of the adjoint of a 2 × 2 matrix, see Appendix A.

$$\boldsymbol{\beta}_1 = \frac{1}{.24708}\begin{bmatrix} .12182 \\ \\ .14599 \end{bmatrix} = \begin{bmatrix} .49304 \\ \\ .59086 \end{bmatrix}$$

Two canonical weights for Y_1 and Y_2, respectively, are .49304 and .59086. Two things will be noted: (1) These are standardized weights and are therefore applied to standard scores *(z)* on Y_1 and Y_2. (2) These are the weights associated with the first canonical correlation, R_{c1}. Before calculating the weights for the second function, it will be shown that $\boldsymbol{\beta}_1$ satisfies the condition stated in (18.2):

$$\underset{\boldsymbol{\beta}'_1}{[.49304 \quad .59086]} \underset{\mathbf{R}_{yy}}{\begin{bmatrix} 1.00 & .70 \\ \\ .70 & 1.00 \end{bmatrix}} \underset{\boldsymbol{\beta}_1}{\begin{bmatrix} .49304 \\ \\ .59086 \end{bmatrix}} = \mathit{1.00}$$

We turn now to the calculation of $\boldsymbol{\beta}_2$—the canonical weights for Y's associated with the second canonical correlation. The procedure is the same as used for calculating β_1, except that now $\mathbf{v}_2$, the eigenvector associated with λ_2, has to be obtained. Earlier, λ_2 was found to be .00490. Therefore

$$\begin{bmatrix} .12672 - .00490 & .12578 \\ \\ .14599 & .15558 - .00490 \end{bmatrix} \begin{bmatrix} v_1 \\ \\ v_2 \end{bmatrix} = \begin{bmatrix} 0 \\ \\ 0 \end{bmatrix}$$

$$\begin{bmatrix} .12182 & .12578 \\ \\ .14599 & .15068 \end{bmatrix} \begin{bmatrix} v_1 \\ \\ v_2 \end{bmatrix} = \begin{bmatrix} 0 \\ \\ 0 \end{bmatrix}$$

The adjoint of the preceding matrix is

$$\begin{bmatrix} .15068 & -.12578 \\ -.14599 & .12182 \end{bmatrix}$$

and $\mathbf{v}'_2 = [.15068 \quad -.14599]$, or $[-.12578 \quad .12182]$

$$\mathbf{v}'_2\mathbf{R}_{yy}\mathbf{v}_2 = [.15068 \; - .14599] \begin{bmatrix} 1.00 & .70 \\ \\ .70 & 1.00 \end{bmatrix} \begin{bmatrix} .15068 \\ \\ -.14599 \end{bmatrix} = \mathit{.01322}$$

$$\sqrt{\mathbf{v}'\mathbf{R}_{yy}\mathbf{v}} = \sqrt{.01322} = \mathit{.11498}$$

Applying (18.3),

$$\boldsymbol{\beta}_2 = \frac{1}{.11498}\begin{bmatrix} .15068 \\ \\ -.14599 \end{bmatrix} = \begin{bmatrix} 1.31049 \\ \\ -1.26970 \end{bmatrix}$$

The matrix of the canonical weights for the Y's is

$$\mathbf{B} = \begin{bmatrix} .49304 & 1.31049 \\ .59086 & -1.26970 \end{bmatrix}$$

Before dealing with issues concerning the interpretation of these results, the canonical weights for the X's will be calculated. It will be noted first that this could be done by following the same procedure used above to calculate **B**, except that it would begin with the following equation:

$$\left| \mathbf{R}_{xx}^{-1}\mathbf{R}_{xy}\mathbf{R}_{yy}^{-1}\mathbf{R}_{yx} - \lambda\mathbf{I} \right| = 0 \qquad (18.4)$$

Note that the λ's obtained from the solution of (18.4) will be the same as those obtained above from the solution of (18.1). In other words, one may insert in (18.4) the λ's calculated earlier in order to obtain their associated eigenvectors and then calculate **A** in a manner analogous the calculation of **B**. But since **B** is already available, a simpler approach to the calculation of **A** may be taken; that is,

$$\mathbf{A} = \mathbf{R}_{xx}^{-1}\,\mathbf{R}_{xy}\mathbf{B}\mathbf{D}^{-1/2} \qquad (18.5)$$

where $\mathbf{R}_{xx}^{-1}$ = inverse of the correlation matrix of the X's; $\mathbf{R}_{xy}$ = correlation matrix of the X's with the Y's; **B** = canonical weights for the Y's; $\mathbf{D}^{-1/2}$ = diagonal matrix whose elements are the reciprocals of the square roots of the λ's. For the present example, Equation (18.5) translates into

$$\mathbf{A} = \underset{\mathbf{R}_{xx}^{-1}}{\begin{bmatrix} 1.56250 & -.93750 \\ -.93750 & 1.56250 \end{bmatrix}} \underset{\mathbf{R}_{xy}}{\begin{bmatrix} .45 & .48 \\ .40 & .38 \end{bmatrix}} \underset{\mathbf{B}}{\begin{bmatrix} .49304 & 1.31049 \\ .59086 & -1.26970 \end{bmatrix}} \underset{\mathbf{D}^{-1/2}}{\begin{bmatrix} \frac{1}{\sqrt{.27740}} & 0 \\ 0 & \frac{1}{\sqrt{.00490}} \end{bmatrix}}$$

Upon carrying out the matrix operations it is found that

$$\mathbf{A} = \begin{bmatrix} .74889 & -.99914 \\ .35141 & 1.19534 \end{bmatrix}$$

These, then, are the standardized weights for the X's.

Applying the standardized canonical weights to the subjects' standard scores (z) on the X's and the Y's, canonical variate scores are obtained for each subject. These are the linear combinations that were referred to when the concept of the canonical correlation was introduced earlier in the chapter.

In the present example it is, of course, not possible to calculate canonical variate scores because the data were given in the form of a correlation matrix. It will be useful, however, to note that had subjects' scores been available and had canonical variate scores been calculated for them, then the correlation between the canonical variate scores on the first function would have been equal to the value of the first canonical correlation (i.e., $R_{c\,1} = .52669$; see above). Similarly, the correlation between the canonical variate scores on the second function would have been equal to the second canonical correlation (i.e., $R_{c\,2} = .07$; see above).

Standardized canonical weights are interpreted in a manner analogous to the interpretation of standardized regression coefficients (β's) in multiple regression analysis. Accordingly, some researchers use them as indices of the relative importance, or contribution, of the variables with which they are associated. Consider the weights obtained above for the first canonical correlation. They are .49304 and .59086 for Y_1 and Y_2, respectively, and .74889 and .35141 for X_1 and X_2, respectively. On the basis of these results one would probably conclude that Y_1 and Y_2 are about of equal importance, whereas X_1 is more important than X_2. It is, however, important to note that, being standardized coefficients, the canonical weights suffer from the same shortcomings as those of standardized regression coefficients (β's).[4] It is for this reason that some authors (e.g., Cooley & Lohnes, 1971, 1976; Meredith, 1964; Thorndike & Weiss, 1973) prefer the use of structure coefficients for the purpose of interpretation. It is to this topic that we now turn.

Structure Coefficients

Structure coefficients were introduced in connection with discriminant analysis (Chapter 17), where they were defined as the correlations between the original variables and the discriminant function. In canonical analysis, structure coefficients (also referred to by some authors as loadings) are similarly defined: they are the correlations between original variables and the canonical variates. In other words, a structure coefficient is the correlation between a given original variable and the canonical variate scores (see above) on a given function. As in the case of discriminant analysis, it is not necessary to carry out the calculations indicated in the preceding sentence in order to obtain the structure coefficients. Having calculated the standardized canonical weights, structure coefficients are easily obtainable. To calculate the structure coefficients for the X's, apply the following formula:

$$\mathbf{S}_x = \mathbf{R}_{xx}\mathbf{A} \qquad (18.6)$$

where $\mathbf{S}_x$ = matrix of structure coefficients for the X's; $\mathbf{R}_{xx}$ = correlation matrix of the X's; $\mathbf{A}$ = standardized canonical weights for the X's. For the present example,

$$\mathbf{S}_x = \underset{\mathbf{R}_{xx}}{\begin{bmatrix} 1.00 & .60 \\ .60 & 1.00 \end{bmatrix}} \underset{\mathbf{A}}{\begin{bmatrix} .74889 & -.99914 \\ .35141 & 1.19534 \end{bmatrix}} = \begin{bmatrix} .95974 & -.28194 \\ .80074 & .59586 \end{bmatrix}$$

[4]For a detailed discussion of the shortcomings of β's, see Chapter 8.

The correlation between X_1 and the first canonical variate (i.e., the structure coefficient) is .96, and that between X_2 and the first canonical variate is .80. Similarly, the structure coefficients for X_1 and X_2 with the second canonical variate are $-.28$ and .60, respectively. Before dealing with interpretations, the structure coefficients for the Y's will be calculated. The formula for doing this is analogous to (18.6):

$$\mathbf{S}_y = \mathbf{R}_{yy}\mathbf{B} \tag{18.7}$$

where $\mathbf{S}_y$ = matrix of structure coefficients for the Y's; $\mathbf{R}_{yy}$ = correlation matrix of the Y's; $\mathbf{B}$ = standardized canonical weights for the Y's. For the present example,

$$\mathbf{S}_y = \underset{\mathbf{R}_{yy}}{\begin{bmatrix} 1.00 & .70 \\ .70 & 1.00 \end{bmatrix}} \underset{\mathbf{B}}{\begin{bmatrix} .49304 & 1.31049 \\ .59086 & -1.26970 \end{bmatrix}} = \begin{bmatrix} .90664 & .42170 \\ .93600 & -.35236 \end{bmatrix}$$

As a rule of thumb it is suggested that structure coefficients $\geq .30$ be treated as meaningful. Using this criterion, one would conclude that both X_1 and X_2 have meaningful loadings on the first canonical variate, but that only X_2 has a meaningful loading on the second canonical variate. On the other hand, both Y's have meaningful structure coefficients on both canonical variates. *It is important, however, to recall that the second canonical correlation was not meaningful, and that it was decided to retain it here solely for completeness of presentation. Normally, one would not calculate structure coefficients for canonical correlations that are considered not meaningful.*

It is not possible to show here how the structure coefficients are interpreted substantively because no substantive meaning has been given to the variables used in the numerical example. Moreover, the example involves only two variables in each set. Generally, a larger number of variables would be used in canonical analysis. Under such circumstances the variables with the larger structure coefficients on a given canonical variate are used much in the same manner as factor loadings in factor analysis. That is, they provide a means of identifying the dimension on which they load. Assume, for example, that in a given canonical analysis ten X variables have been used, and that only three of them have meaningful loadings on the first canonical variate. One would then examine these variables and attempt to name the first canonical variate in a manner similar to that done in factor analysis. If, for example, it turns out that the three X's with the high structure coefficients deal with different aspects of verbal performance, one might conclude that the first canonical variate is one that primarily reflects verbal ability. Needless to say, the interpretation is not always as obvious as in the example just given. As is the case in factor analysis, it is quite possible to encounter difficulties in the interpretation of a given canonical variate on the basis of the high structure coefficients associated with it. Sometimes the problem may be overcome by rotating the canonical variates, much as one rotates factors in factor analysis. This is a topic that cannot be dealt with here (see, for example, Cliff & Krus, 1976; Hall, 1969; Krus, Reynolds, & Krus, 1976). What was said above about the interpretation of canonical variates with high structure coefficients for the X's applies equally to the interpretation of canonical variates with high structure coefficients for the Y's.

In Chapter 17 it was said that the square of a structure coefficient, or a loading, indicates the proportion of variance of the variable with which it is associated that is accounted for by the discriminant function. Structure coefficients in canonical analysis are similarly interpreted. Accordingly, the first canonical variate accounts for about 92% of the variance of X_1 ($.95974^2 \times 100$), and for about 64% ($.80074^2 \times 100$) of the variance of X_2. Similarly, the first canonical variate accounts for about 82% and 88% of the variance of Y_1 and Y_2, respectively.

The sum of the squared structure coefficients of a set of variables (i.e., the X's or the Y's) on a given canonical variate indicates the amount of variance of the set that is accounted for, or extracted, by the canonical variate. Dividing the amount of variance extracted, by the number of variables in the set (i.e., p for the X's and q for the Y's) yields the proportion of its total variance that is extracted by the canonical variate.

Recalling that premultiplying a column vector by its transpose is the same as squaring and summing its elements (see Appendix A), the foregoing can be stated as follows:

$$PV_{x_j} = \frac{\mathbf{s}'_{x_j}\mathbf{s}_{x_j}}{p} \tag{18.8}$$

where PV_{x_j} is the proportion of the total variance of the X's extracted by canonical variate j; $\mathbf{s}_{x_j}$ and $\mathbf{s}'_{x_j}$, respectively, are a column vector of structure coefficients of the X's on canonical variate j, and its transpose; p is the number of X variables. Similarly,

$$PV_{y_j} = \frac{\mathbf{s}'_{y_j}\mathbf{s}_{y_j}}{q} \tag{18.9}$$

where PV_{y_j} is the proportion of the total variance of the Y's that is extracted by canonical variate j; $\mathbf{s}_{y_j}$ and $\mathbf{s}'_{y_j}$, respectively, are a column vector of structure coefficients of the Y's on canonical variate j and its transpose; q is the number of Y variables.

For the numerical example analyzed above, the matrix of structure coefficients for the X's (**A**) was found to be:

$$\mathbf{A} = \begin{bmatrix} .95974 & -.28194 \\ .80074 & .59586 \end{bmatrix}$$

Applying, successively, (18.8) to each of the columns of **A**:

$$PV_{x_1} = \frac{1}{2}[.95974 \quad .80074]\begin{bmatrix} .95974 \\ .80074 \end{bmatrix} = .78114$$

Thus, about 78% of the total variance of the X's is extracted by the first canonical variate.

$$PV_{x_2} = \frac{1}{2}\,[-.28194 \quad .59586] \begin{bmatrix} -.28194 \\ .59586 \end{bmatrix} = .21727$$

About 22% of the total variance of the X's is extracted by the second canonical variate.

The matrix of structure coefficients for the Y's (**B**) was found above to be:

$$\mathbf{B} = \begin{bmatrix} .90664 & .42170 \\ .93600 & -.35236 \end{bmatrix}$$

Applying, successively, (18.9) to each of the columns of **B:**

$$PV_{y_1} = \frac{1}{2}\,[.90664 \quad .93600] \begin{bmatrix} .90664 \\ .93600 \end{bmatrix} = .84905$$

About 85% of the total variance of the Y's is extracted by the first canonical variate.

$$PV_{y_2} = \frac{1}{2}\,[.42170 \quad -.35236] \begin{bmatrix} .42170 \\ -.35236 \end{bmatrix} = .15099$$

About 15% of the total variance of the Y's is extracted by the second canonical variate.

Note that the sum of the proportions of variance of the X's extracted by the two canonical variates is .78114 + .21727 = *1.00*. The sum of the proportions of variance of the Y's extracted by the two canonical variates is .84905 + .15099 = *1.00*. In general, the sum of the proportions of variance of the set with the smaller number of variables that is extracted by all the canonical variates is 1.00 (or 100%). In the present example, both sets consist of the same number of variables, namely two. Therefore, the sum of the proportions of variance extracted by the two canonical variates in each set is 1.00.

Recalling that when the two sets consist of different numbers of variables, the maximum number of canonical variates obtainable is equal to the number of variables in the smaller set, it follows that under such circumstances the maximum number of canonical variates cannot extract all of the variance of the variables in the larger set. Depending on the number of variables in each set, and on the patterns of relations among them, it is possible that while 100% of the variance of the variables of the smaller set is extracted, only a small fraction of the percent of the variance of the variables in the larger set is extracted.

As is shown in the next section, the PV's play an important role in an index of redundancy. Before turning to this topic it is important to underscore that canonical weights and structure coefficients should be interpreted with caution, particularly when they have not been cross-validated. As in multiple regression analysis,[5] cross-validation is of utmost importance in canonical analysis. A very good discussion of cross-validation in canonical analysis will be found in Thorndike (1978), who says: "It might be argued that cross-validation is more important for canonical analysis because there are two sets of weights, each of which will make maximum use of sample-specific covariation, rather than just one" (p. 180).

Redundancy

Using the concepts of proportion of variance extracted by a canonical variate, Stewart and Love (1968) and Miller (1969) have, independently, proposed a redundancy index, which for the X variables is defined as follows:

$$Rd_{x_j} = PV_{x_j}R^2_{c_j} \tag{18.10}$$

where Rd_{x_j} is the redundancy of the X's given the jth canonical variate of Y; PV_{x_j} is the proportion of the total variance of the X's extracted by the jth canonical variate of the X's (see (18.8)); $R^2_{c_j}$ is the square of the jth canonical correlation. Basically the redundancy of X_j is the product of the proportion of the variance of the X's the jth canonical variate of X extracts (PV_{x_j}) by the variance that the jth canonical variate of X's shares with the jth canonical variate of Y's ($R^2_{c_j}$). This could perhaps be clarified when it is recalled that a canonical variate is a linear combination of variables, and that R^2_c is the squared correlation between two linear combinations: one for the X's and one for the Y's. Now, the redundancy X_j is the proportion of the variance of the X's that is redundant with (or predicted from, or explained by) the jth linear combination of the Y's.

The foregoing will be further clarified, it is hoped, by illustrating its calculation. In the example analyzed above it was found that $PV_{x_1} = .78114$ and $PV_{x_2} = .21727$. Also, $R^2_{c_1} = .27740$ and $R^2_{c_2} = .00490$. Applying (18.10),

$$Rd_{x_1} = (.78114)(.27740) = .21669$$

This means that about 22% of the total variance of the X's is predictable from the first canonical variate (linear combination) of the Y's. Also,

$$Rd_{x_2} = (.21727)(.00490) = .00106$$

This means that about .1% of the total variance of the X's is predictable from the second canonical variate (linear combination) of the Y's.

The total redundancy of X, given all the linear combinations of the Y's is simply the sum of the separate redundancies; that is,

$$\overline{Rd_x} = \Sigma Rd_{x_j} \tag{18.11}$$

[5]For a discussion of cross-validation in multiple regression analysis, see Chapter 6.

where $\overline{Rd_x}$ is the total redundancy and ΣRd_{x_j} is the sum of the separate redundancies. For the present example,

$$\overline{Rd_x} = .21669 + .00106 = .21775$$

Before showing how the redundancies of Y are calculated, and before further elaborating on the meaning of these indices, it is believed that it will be useful to examine the concept of redundancy from yet another perspective—namely, multiple regression analysis. For this purpose, zero-order correlations between the X's and the Y's reported in Table 18.3 are repeated here:

$$r_{x_1y_1} = .45 \qquad r_{x_1y_2} = .48 \qquad r_{x_2y_1} = .40 \qquad r_{x_2y_2} = .38 \qquad r_{y_1y_2} = .70$$

Using these correlations two R^2's will now be calculated: $R^2_{x_1 . y_1y_2}$ and $R^2_{x_2 . y_1y_2}$.

$$R^2_{x_1 . y_1y_2} = \frac{(.45)^2 + (.48)^2 - 2(.45)(.48)(.70)}{1 - (.70)^2} = .25588$$

The proportion of variance of X_1 that is predictable from all the variables in the other set (in the present case, Y_1 and Y_2) is .25588.

$$R^2_{x_2 . y_1y_2} = \frac{(.40)^2 + (.38)^2 - 2(.40)(.38)(.70)}{1 - (.70)^2} = .17961$$

The proportion of variance of X_2 that is predictable from all the variables in the other set (the Y's) is .17961.

Now, calculate the average of the R^2's obtained above:

$$\frac{.25588 + .17961}{2} = .21775$$

This is the same as $\overline{Rd_x}$ obtained above. The total redundancy of X given Y, then, is equal to the average of the squared multiple correlations of each of the X's with all of the Y's. In other words, redundancy "is synonymous with average predictability" (Cramer & Nicewander, 1979, p. 43).

We turn now to a definition and calculation of redundancies of Y given the X's. Analogously to Rd_{x_j},

$$Rd_{y_j} = PV_{y_j} R^2_{c_j} \tag{18.12}$$

where Rd_{y_j} is the redundancy of the Y's given the jth canonical variate of X; PV_{y_j} is the proportion of the total variance of the Y's extracted by the jth canonical variate of the Y's (see (18.9)); $R^2_{c_j}$ is the square of the jth canonical correlation.

Using the following values that were calculated earlier, the redundancies of Y will be calculated.

$$PV_{y_1} = .84905 \qquad PV_{y_2} = .15099 \qquad R^2_{c_1} = .27740 \qquad R^2_{c_2} = .00490$$

Applying (18.12),

$$Rd_{y_1} = (.84905)(.27740) = .23553$$

That is, about 24% of the total variance of the Y's is redundant with (or predictable from) the first linear combination (canonical variate) of the X's. Also,

$$Rd_{y_2} = (.15099)(.00490) = .00074$$

That is, about .07% of the total variance of the Y's is redundant with the second canonical variate of the X's. Now,

$$\overline{Rd_y} = \Sigma Rd_{y_j} \qquad (18.13)$$

where $\overline{Rd_y}$ is the total redundancy of Y and ΣRd_{y_j} is the sum of the separate redundancies. For the present example,

$$\overline{Rd_y} = (.23553) + (.00074) = .23627$$

The total redundancy of Y given the X's is about 24%. In a manner analogous to that shown above for the total redundancy of X, it can be shown that the total redundancy of Y is equal to the average of the squared multiple correlations of each of the Y's with all the variables in the other set (the two X's, in the present example).

It is important to note that redundancy is an asymmetric index; that is, $Rd_{y_j} \neq Rd_{x_j}$ or $\overline{Rd_{y_j}} \neq \overline{Rd_{x_j}}$. That this is so can be seen by inspecting the formulas for the calculation of Rd_{x_j} and Rd_{y_j}—Equations (18.10) and (18.12), respectively. Both equations contain a common term (i.e., $R^2_{c_j}$). But each uses the proportion of variance extracted (PV) by its canonical variate. These PV's are not necessarily equal to each other. Their magnitudes depend, of course, on a specific set of data. It is safe to say, however, that the probability of the two PV's being equal to each other is very small.

Speaking of the total redundancy, Stewart and Love (1968) point out that it should be viewed "as a summary index. In general it is not to be viewed as an analytic tool" (p. 162). This does not diminish its great utility, which, among other things, is in serving as a guard against wandering into a world of fantasy. An elaboration of the preceding statement will serve to explain the substantive meaning of redundancy, as well as to shed further light on R^2_c.

When R^2_c was introduced, it was underscored that it is an estimate of the shared variance of two linear combinations of variables; *not* of the variance of the variables themselves. From the discussion of redundancy it should be clear that even when R^2_c is high, the redundancy of Y, X, or both may be very low. This may best be clarified by a numerical example. Assume that the first canonical correlation between two sets of variables, X and Y, is relatively high, say .80. Therefore the shared variance of the first pair of linear combinations of the X's and the Y's is .64. So far as proportions of variance shared or accounted for, this is a value that in most circumstances would be considered meaningful, and even very impressive in many research areas.

Assume now that PV_{y_1} (proportion of variance extracted by the first linear combination of the Y's) is .10, and that $PV_{x_1} = .07$. Accordingly, $Rd_{y_1} = .064$ ($.64 \times .10$), and $Rd_{x_1} = .045$ ($.64 \times .07$). The predictable variance of the Y's from the linear combination of the X's is only about 6%, and the predictable variance of the X's from the linear combinations of the Y's is only about 4%. Although it is not possible to discuss such results in the absence of a substantive example, it is nevertheless safe to say that in many, perhaps most, areas of social research they will be considered not impressive, and even not meaningful. Be that as it may, the main point being made here is that the sole reliance on R_c^2 poses a real threat of wandering into a world of fantasy in which impressive figures that may have little to do with the variability of the variables themselves are cherished and heralded as meaningful scientific findings.[6]

Several concluding remarks will now be made about the uses of the redundancy index. One, when only the meaningful or statistically significant canonical correlations are retained in a given analysis, redundancy indices would generally be calculated only for the canonical variates that have been retained.

Two, although the redundancies of X and Y were quite similar to each other in the numerical example analyzed above, this is not necessarily the case. It is possible for the redundancies of the two sets to be radically different from each other.

Three, depending on the research design, redundancies may be meaningfully calculated for only one of the two sets of variables. For example, when in a given study the X's are treated as predictors and the Y's are treated as criteria, it is meaningful to calculate redundancies only for the Y's because the interest is in determining the proportion of variance of the criteria that is predictable from the predictors—not vice versa. In experimental research, one would, similarly, calculate redundancies only for the dependent variables.

Four, in the discussions of the interpretation of the redundancy index terms such as variance redundant with, or predictable from, or explained by, have been used interchangeably. Needless to say, these are not equivalent terms. Because no substantive examples have been used, it was not possible to select the most appropriate term. In actual applications the choice should generally be clear. Thus, for example, the term "variance predictable from" is appropriate in predictive research, whereas the stronger term "variance explained by" is more appropriate in explanatory research.[7]

Finally, as pointed out by Cramer and Nicewander (1979), the redundancy index is not a measure of multivariate association. After discussing several such measures, Cramer and Nicewander raise the question of whether a single measure can provide satisfactory information about the relation between two sets of variables, and conclude: "In our view the answer to this question generally is, 'No.' " (p. 53).[8]

[6]Good discussions and numerical examples of the use of the redundancy index will be found in Cooley and Lohnes (1971, 1976), and in Love and Stewart (1968).

[7]See earlier chapters (particularly Chapters 6–8) for discussions of differences between predictive and explanatory research.

[8]For a discussion of measures of association in the context of canonical analysis, see Darlington et al. (1973).

Tests of Significance

As is discussed later in this chapter, several different approaches have been proposed regarding statistical tests of significance in multivariate analysis. At this stage, it will only be noted that the most widely used test of significance in canonical analysis is Bartlett's (1947) test of Wilks' Λ (lambda). It is this test that is presented here.

In Chapter 17, Wilks' Λ was presented as a ratio of the determinants of two matrices (the Within-Groups SSCP to the Total SSCP; see Equation (17.11) and the discussion related to it). An analogous expression of Λ that can be made in the context of canonical analysis is not shown here (see Tatsuoka, 1971, p. 188). Instead, it will be shown how Λ is calculated using R_c^2.

$$\Lambda = (1 - R_{c_1}^2)(1 - R_{c_2}^2) \cdots (1 - R_{c_j}^2) \tag{18.14}$$

where Λ = Wilks' lambda; $R_{c_1}^2$ = the square of the first canonical correlation, $R_{c_2}^2$ = the square of the second canonical correlation, and so on up to the square of the jth canonical correlation.

In the numerical example analyzed earlier it was found that $R_{c_1}^2 = .27740$ and $R_{c_2}^2 = .00490$. Applying (18.14),

$$\Lambda = (1 - .27740)(1 - .00490) = \mathit{.71906}$$

Bartlett (1947) proposed the following test of significance of Λ:

$$\chi^2 = -[N - 1 - .5(p + q + 1)]\log_e \Lambda \tag{18.15}$$

where N = number of subjects; p = number of variables on the left; q = number of variables on the right; $\log_e$ = natural logarithm. The degrees of freedom associated with this χ^2 are pq. For the present example, $\log_e .71906 = -.32981$; $p = q = 2$; $N = 300$ (see Table 18.3). Applying (18.15),

$$\chi^2 = -[300 - 1 - .5(2 + 2 + 1)](-.32981)$$
$$= -(299 - 2.5)(-.32981) = (-296.5)(-.32981) = \mathit{97.79}$$

with $pq = 4$ degrees of freedom, $p < .001$.

The test just performed refers to all the R_c^2's; that is, it is an overall test of the null hypothesis that all the R_c^2 are equal to zero. In the present example it refers to the two R_c^2's. It is, however, desirable to determine which of the R_c^2's obtainable from a given set of data are statistically significant. This is accomplished by applying (18.15) sequentially as follows.

First, the overall Λ is tested (as above). If the null hypothesis is rejected, it is concluded that at least the first R_c^2 is statistically significant, and a Λ' based on the remaining R_c^2's is tested for significance, using (18.15). The Λ' is calculated as was Λ—that is, using (18.14)—except that $R_{c_1}^2$ is removed from the equation. If Λ' is statistically significant, it is concluded that the first two R_c^2's are statistically significant. Equation (18.14) is then applied to calculate Λ'' on the basis of the remaining R_c^2's. Λ'' is then tested for significance, using (18.15).

The procedure is continued until a given Λ is found to be not statistically significant at a prespecified α, at which point it is concluded that the R_c^2's preceding this step are statistically significant, whereas the remaining ones are not. The *df* for the χ^2 test of Λ' (i.e., after removing the first R_c^2) are $(p - 1)(q - 1)$; for the χ^2 test of Λ'' (after the first two R_c^2's have been removed) are $(p - 2)(q - 2)$, and so on.[9]

This procedure is now applied to the numerical example under consideration. It was found above that Λ is statistically significant. $R_{c_1}^2$ is therefore removed, and (18.14) is applied to calculate Λ'. Recalling that $R_{c_2}^2 = .00490$,

$$\Lambda' = (1 - .00490) = .9951$$

$$\log_e .9951 = -.00491$$

Applying now (18.15),

$$\chi^2 = -[300 - 1 - .5(2 + 2 + 1)](-.00491)$$

$$= (-296.5)(-.00491) = 1.46$$

with 1, $(p - 1)(q - 1)$, *df*, $p > .05$.

It is concluded that $R_{c_2}^2$ is not statistically significant. In the present example, there are only two R_c^2's. Had there been more than two, and had Λ' been found not statistically significant, it would have been concluded that all but the first R_c^2 are not statistically significant.

Having retained the significant R_c^2's, one would proceed and interpret only the statistics (e.g., canonical weights, structure coefficients) that are associated with them. For illustrative purposes, canonical weights and structure coefficients were calculated earlier for both functions, even though it was clear that the second one was not meaningful. It will be recalled that it was suggested earlier that the main criterion used for retaining a R_c^2 be whether it is meaningful. It was noted that some authors have suggested that $R_c^2 < .10$ be treated as not meaningful.

Finally, it is convenient to provide a summary of the results in tabular form. An example of such a summary for the numerical example analyzed in this section is given in Table 18.4. Again, for completeness of presentation, the results associated with both R_c^2's are given, even though the second one is not meaningful.

Computer Analysis

BMDP, SAS, and SPSS each contain a program for canonical analysis. Of the three, the one contained in the BMDP package is the most versatile in input as well as output options. The output of the SPSS program is meager. Among other things, it does not even report the structure coefficients. If you have access to SPSS only you will have to calculate structure coefficients by hand,

[9]Harris (1975, p. 144; 1976) questioned the validity of the testing sequence outlined above. The issues raised by Harris cannot be dealt with here.

Table 18.4 Summary of Canonical Analysis for Data of Table 18.3

	Root 1		Root 2			Root 1		Root 2	
Variables	β	s	β	s	*Variables*	β	s	β	s
X_1	.75	.96	−1.00	−.28	Y_1	.49	.91	1.31	.42
X_2	.35	.80	1.20	.60	Y_2	.59	.94	−1.27	−.35
PV:		.78		.22			.85		.15
Rd:		.22		.00			.24		.00
$\overline{Rd}$:			.22					.24	
$R^2_{c_1} = .2774$	$R^2_{c_2} = .0049$								

NOTE: β = standardized coefficients; s = structure coefficient; PV = proportion of variance extracted; Rd = redundancy; $\overline{Rd}$ = total redundancy.

using the standardized canonical weights, that SPSS does report, and the zero-order correlation matrices (see Equations (18.6) and (18.7) and the calculations related to them). It will be noted that the CDC version of SPSS has a very versatile subprogram (MANOVA) whose output is very detailed. MANOVA can be used, among other things, for canonical analysis. The same holds true for the MULTIVARIANCE program which was described in Chapter 17.

For illustrative and comparative purposes, the control cards and excerpts of output from BMDP6M are given for the numerical example analyzed in this chapter. In view of the fact that the results were commented upon in detail, only brief comments will be made here. When necessary, refer to earlier discussions.

Control Cards

```
/ PROBLEM TITLE IS 'CHAPTER 18, TABLE 18.3'.
/ INPUT VARIABLES ARE 4. TYPE = CORR. SHAPE = LOWER.
        FORMAT IS '(4F4.2)'. CASES ARE 300.
/ VARIABLE NAMES ARE X1, X2, Y1, Y2.
/ CANONICAL FIRST ARE X1, X2. SECOND ARE Y1, Y2.
/ PRINT MATRICES ARE COEF, LOAD.
/ END
 100
  60 100
  45  40 100
  48  38  70 100
```

Commentary

In the INPUT paragraph, TYPE = CORR. indicates that a correlation matrix is to be read as input. SHAPE = LOWER. means that the matrix is lower triangular. Note that each row is punched on a separate card. The first row consists of one element (the diagonal, which is equal to 1.00). The second row consists of two elements, and so forth. The variable format statement refers to the longest row, which in the present case consists of four elements.

In the CANONICAL paragraph, FIRST refers to the first set of variables, or the variables on the left. SECOND refers to the second set of variables, or the variables on the right.

The PRINT paragraph calls for additional output. Specifying COEF and LOAD will result in printing the canonical variates and the loadings.

Output

EIGENVALUE	CANONICAL CORRELATION	NUMBER OF EIGENVALUES	BARTLETT'S TEST FOR REMAINING EIGENVALUES CHI-SQUARE	D.F.	SIGNIFICANC
0.27742	0.52671	0	97.79	4	0.00000
0.00487	0.06979	1	1.45	1	0.22892

BARTLETT'S TEST ABOVE INDICATES THE NUMBER OF CANONICAL VARIABLES NECESSARY TO EXPRESS THE DEPENDENCY BETWEEN THE TWO SETS OF VARIABLES. THE NECESSARY NUMBER OF CANONICAL VARIABLES IS THE SMALLEST NUMBER OF EIGENVALUES SUCH THAT THE TEST OF THE REMAINING EIGENVALUES IS NONSIGNIFICANT. FOR EXAMPLE, IF A TEST AT THE .01 LEVEL WERE DESIRED, THEN 1 VARIABLE WOULD BE CONSIDERED NECESSARY. HOWEVER, THE NUMBE OF CANONICAL VARIABLES OF PRACTICAL VALUE IS LIKELY TO BE SMALLER.

STANDARDIZED COEFFICIENTS FOR CANONICAL VARIABLES FOR FIRST SET OF VARIABLES (THESE ARE THE COEFFICIENTS FOR THE STANDARDIZED VARIABLES -- MEAN ZERO, STANDARD DEVIATION ONE.)

	CNVRF1	CNVRF2
	1	2
X1 1	0.749	−1.001
X2 2	0.351	1.200

STANDARDIZED COEFFICIENTS FOR CANONICAL VARIABLES FOR THE SECOND SET OF VARIABLES (THESE ARE THE COEFFICIENTS FOR THE STANDARDIZED VARIABLES -- MEAN ZERO, STANDARD DEVIATION ONE.)

	CNVRS1	CNVRS2
	1	2
Y1 1	0.493	1.311
Y2 2	0.591	−1.270

Commentary

The printout also includes raw coefficients, which in the present case are the same as the standardized ones because a correlation matrix has been read as input.

Output

CANONICAL VARIABLE LOADINGS (CORRELATIONS OF CANONICAL VARIABLES WITH ORIGINAL VARIABLES)

	CNVRF1	CNVRF2
	1	2
X1 1	0.960	−0.281
X2 2	0.801	0.599
	CNVRS1	CNVRS2
	1	2
Y1 1	0.907	0.422
Y2 2	0.936	−0.352

Commentary

The preceding are the matrices of the structure coefficients. The first matrix refers to the variables on the left and has been labeled in the chapter as **A.** The second matrix is what has been labeled in the chapter as **B.**

CA, MANOVA, AND DA

Thus far, the presentation dealt with CA in which both sets of variables are continuous. We turn now to designs in which one set of variables is continuous, whereas the other set consists of coded vectors representing a categorical variable. Such designs are used in experimental as well as nonexperimental research. In the former, the categorical variable consists of more than two treatments (e.g., teaching methods, modes of communication, drugs), whereas in the latter it represents more than two preexisting groups (e.g., national, racial, religious, political).[10]

As in univariate analysis, multivariate analysis proceeds in the same manner, regardless of whether the data were obtained in experimental or nonexperimental research. Needless to say, however, interpretations of results are greatly determined by the type of research setting in which they were obtained.[11]

Conventionally, the type of designs described above are analyzed by either one-way MANOVA or DA. Some researchers begin with MANOVA and apply DA only when the results of the former are found to be statistically significant.

In this section it is shown that designs in which the dependent variables, or criteria, are continuous, and the independent variable, or predictor, is categorical may be conceived of as a special case of CA. A numerical example, consisting of two dependent variables and a categorical variable consisting of three categories, is used first to show how CA is carried out and interpreted. It is

[10]When there are only two treatments, or two groups, the analysis proceeds as shown in Chapter 17.

[11]The detailed discussions of this issue given in earlier chapters are equally applicable here, and are therefore not repeated.

then shown how the same results are obtained when the data are analyzed via MANOVA and DA.

Numerical Example

Assume that a researcher wishes to study how Conservatives (A_1), Republicans (A_2), and Democrats (A_3) differ in their expectations regarding government spending on social welfare programs (Y_1) and on defense (Y_2). Illustrative data for such a design are given in Table 18.5.

Table 18.5 Illustrative Data for Three Groups and Two Dependent Variables

	A_1		A_2		A_3	
	Y_1	Y_2	Y_1	Y_2	Y_1	Y_2
	3	7	4	5	5	5
	4	7	4	6	6	5
	5	8	5	7	6	6
	5	9	6	7	7	7
	6	10	6	8	7	8
Σ:	23	41	25	33	31	31
$\bar{Y}$:	4.6	8.2	5.0	6.6	6.2	6.2

Before proceeding with the analysis, several points will be made about this example. One, it is admittedly contrived, and is being offered solely to provide an opportunity to illustrate the interpretation of results obtained in the kinds of analyses presented in this section. Two, in order to encourage you to think of other variables from areas of your interest, the terms groups (A_1, A_2, and A_3) and variables (Y_1 and Y_2) will be used throughout the analyses. References to the variables noted above will be made only when results are interpreted. In general, you may think of A_1, A_2, and A_3 as representing any three preexisting groups, or any three treatments, of your choice. Similarly, Y_1 and Y_2 may be viewed as any two criterion, or dependent, variables. Three, only two dependent variables and a very small number of subjects are used so that all the calculations may be done easily by hand. But in doing this one necessarily pays the price of not being able to show the full potential of multivariate analyses when they are applied to relatively large numbers of variables. It is hoped that the research examples given at the end of the chapter will make up for these deficiencies.

With the foregoing in mind, we turn to a CA of the data of Table 18.5. Following the procedure used in designs consisting of one dependent variable and one independent categorical variable (see Chapter 9), the measures of the two dependent variables for all the subjects are placed in two vectors, Y_1 and Y_2. The categorical variable is coded in the usual manner. That is, two coded vectors are used to represent the three groups, or treatments. In the present example, dummy coding is used. The data of Table 18.5 are displayed in this fashion in Table 18.6.

It should be clear that exactly the same procedure will be followed, regardless of the number of the dependent variables, or categories of the independent variable. For example, if the design consisted of eight dependent variables, Y, and five treatments, X, then one would generate eight Y vectors of dependent variable measures for all the subjects and four coded vectors to represent the five categories of the independent variable.

Having generated the vectors as in Table 18.6, one proceeds and applies CA in exactly the same manner as was done earlier in the chapter when the design consisted of two sets of continuous variables. Therefore, while the calculations will be shown, comments about them will be brief. When necessary, refer to earlier sections for more detailed explanations.

Canonical Correlations

First, the zero-order correlations among the four vectors of Table 18.6 are calculated. These are reported in the following supermatrix:

$$\mathbf{R} = \left[\begin{array}{cc:cc} \multicolumn{2}{c}{\mathbf{R}_{xx}} & \multicolumn{2}{c}{\mathbf{R}_{xy}} \\ 1.00000 & -.50000 & -.41959 & .60000 \\ -.50000 & 1.00000 & -.16784 & -.20000 \\ \hdashline \multicolumn{2}{c}{\mathbf{R}_{yx}} & \multicolumn{2}{c}{\mathbf{R}_{yy}} \\ -.41959 & -.16784 & 1.00000 & .25175 \\ .60000 & -.20000 & .25175 & 1.00000 \end{array}\right]$$

Table 18.6 Data from Table 18.5 Displayed for Canonical Analysis

	X_1	X_2	Y_1	Y_2
	1	0	3	7
	1	0	4	7
A_1	1	0	5	8
	1	0	5	9
	1	0	6	10
	0	1	4	5
	0	1	4	6
A_2	0	1	5	7
	0	1	6	7
	0	1	6	8
	0	0	5	5
	0	0	6	5
A_3	0	0	6	6
	0	0	7	7
	0	0	7	8
s:	.48795	.48795	1.16292	1.46385

NOTE: s = standard deviation; X_1 and X_2 = dummy coding for groups; Y_1 and Y_2 = dependent variables.

Second, calculate $\mathbf{R}_{yy}^{-1}\mathbf{R}_{yx}\mathbf{R}_{xx}^{-1}\mathbf{R}_{xy}$. For the present data,

$$\underset{\mathbf{R}_{yy}^{-1}}{\begin{bmatrix} 1.06766 & -.26879 \\ -.26879 & 1.06766 \end{bmatrix}} \quad \underset{\mathbf{R}_{yx}}{\begin{bmatrix} -.41959 & -.16784 \\ .60000 & -.20000 \end{bmatrix}} \quad \underset{\mathbf{R}_{xx}^{-1}}{\begin{bmatrix} 1.33333 & .66667 \\ .66667 & 1.33333 \end{bmatrix}} \quad \underset{\mathbf{R}_{xy}}{\begin{bmatrix} -.41959 & .60000 \\ -.16784 & -.20000 \end{bmatrix}}$$

$$\mathbf{R}_{yy}^{-1}\mathbf{R}_{yx} = \begin{bmatrix} 1.06766 & -.26879 \\ -.26879 & 1.06766 \end{bmatrix} \begin{bmatrix} -.41959 & -.16784 \\ .60000 & -.20000 \end{bmatrix} = \begin{bmatrix} -.60925 & -.12544 \\ .75338 & -.16842 \end{bmatrix}$$

$$\mathbf{R}_{yy}^{-1}\,\mathbf{R}_{yx}\,\mathbf{R}_{xx}^{-1} = \begin{bmatrix} -.60925 & -.12544 \\ .75338 & -.16842 \end{bmatrix} \begin{bmatrix} 1.33333 & .66667 \\ .66667 & 1.33333 \end{bmatrix} = \begin{bmatrix} -.89596 & -.57342 \\ .89222 & .27770 \end{bmatrix}$$

$$\mathbf{R}_{yy}^{-1}\,\mathbf{R}_{yx}\,\mathbf{R}_{xx}^{-1}\,\mathbf{R}_{xy} = \begin{bmatrix} -.89596 & -.57342 \\ .89222 & .27770 \end{bmatrix} \begin{bmatrix} -.41959 & .60000 \\ -.16784 & -.20000 \end{bmatrix} = \begin{bmatrix} .47218 & -.42289 \\ -.42098 & .47979 \end{bmatrix}$$

Third, calculate the eigenvalues (λ), or characteristic roots, by solving the following determinantal equation (see (18.1) and the discussion related to it):

$$\left|\mathbf{R}_{yy}^{-1}\mathbf{R}_{yx}\mathbf{R}_{xx}^{-1}\mathbf{R}_{xy} - \lambda\mathbf{I}\right| = 0$$

For the present data,

$$\begin{vmatrix} .47218 - \lambda & -.42289 \\ -.42098 & .47979 - \lambda \end{vmatrix} = 0$$

$$(.47218 - \lambda)(.47979 - \lambda) - (-.42098)(-.42289) = 0$$

$$.22655 - .47218\lambda - .47979\lambda + \lambda^2 - .17803 = 0$$

$$\lambda^2 - .95197\lambda + .04852 = 0$$

$$\lambda_1 = \frac{.95197 + \sqrt{(-.95197)^2 - (4)(1)(.04852)}}{2} = .89793$$

$$\lambda_2 = \frac{.95197 - \sqrt{(-.91597)^2 - (4)(1)(.04852)}}{2} = .05404$$

$$R_{c_1}^2 = \lambda_1 = .89793$$

$$R_{c_2}^2 = \lambda_2 = .05404$$

Tests of Significance

Using the R_c^2's, apply (18.14) to obtain Wilks' Λ:

$$\Lambda = (1 - R_{c_1}^2)(1 - R_{c_2}^2) = (1 - .89793)(1 - .05404) = .09655$$

To apply Bartlett's χ^2 test of Λ it is necessary to take the natural logarithm of Λ: $\log_e .09655 = -2.33769$. Recalling that $N = 15$, and $p = q = 2$, Bartlett's χ^2 test (see Formula (18.15)) is

$$\chi^2 = -[15 - 1 - .5\,(2 + 2 + 1)]\,(-2.33769)$$
$$= (-11.5)(-2.33769) = \mathit{26.88}$$

with 4 (pq) degrees of freedom, $p < .001$.

It is concluded that the first R_c^2 is statistically significant. To test whether the second R_c^2 is also statistically significant, calculate first Λ', that is, after the first R_c^2 has been removed.

$$\Lambda' = (1 - R_{c2}^2) = (1 - .05404) = \mathit{.94596}$$

$$\log_e .94596 = -.05556$$

$$\chi^2 = -[15 - 1 - .5(2 + 2 + 1)](-.05556)$$
$$= (-11.5)(-.05556) = \mathit{.64}$$

with $1[(p - 1)(q - 1)]df$, $p > .05$. It is concluded the $R_{c_2}^2$ is not statistically significant. Recalling the suggestion that $R_c^2 < .10$ be treated as not meaningful, it is evident the $R_{c_2}^2$ is not meaningful either. Therefore only the first R_c^2 is retained.

Canonical Weights

Because the primary interest in the present example is in the statistics associated with the dependent variables, Y's, in order to conserve space, only these will be calculated. Using $\lambda_1 = .89793$ and the values of the matrix whose determinant was set to be equal to zero (see above):

$$\begin{bmatrix} .47218 - .89793 & -.42289 \\ -.42098 & .47979 - .89793 \end{bmatrix} \begin{bmatrix} v_1 \\ v_2 \end{bmatrix} = \begin{bmatrix} 0 \\ 0 \end{bmatrix}$$

$$\begin{bmatrix} -.42575 & -.42289 \\ -.42098 & -.41814 \end{bmatrix} \begin{bmatrix} v_1 \\ v_2 \end{bmatrix} = \begin{bmatrix} 0 \\ 0 \end{bmatrix}$$

Forming the adjoint of the preceding matrix:

$$\begin{bmatrix} -.41814 & .42289 \\ .42098 & -.42575 \end{bmatrix}$$

$$\mathbf{v}_1' = [-.41814 \quad .42098] \quad \text{or} \quad [.42289 \quad -.42575]$$

In order to obtain the standardized coefficients, calculate first:

$$\underset{\mathbf{v}_1'}{\mathbf{v}_1'\mathbf{R}_{yy}\,\mathbf{v}_1 = [-.41814 \quad .42098]} \underset{\mathbf{R}_{yy}}{\begin{bmatrix} 1.00000 & .25175 \\ .25175 & 1.00000 \end{bmatrix}} \underset{\mathbf{v}_1}{\begin{bmatrix} -.41814 \\ .42098 \end{bmatrix}} = .26343$$

Apply now (18.3):

$$\boldsymbol{\beta}_1 = \frac{1}{\sqrt{\mathbf{v}_1'\mathbf{R}_{yy}\,\mathbf{v}_1}}\,\mathbf{v}_1 = \frac{1}{\sqrt{.26343}}\begin{bmatrix} -.41814 \\ .42098 \end{bmatrix} = \begin{bmatrix} -.81468 \\ .82022 \end{bmatrix}$$

On the basis of the standardized weights, it appears that both variables contribute equally to the separation among the three groups. The signs of these weights indicate that in forming the linear combination of the two variables, Y_1 is weighted negatively and Y_2 is weighted positively. Or, referring to the example given in the beginning of this section, expectations regarding government spending on social welfare programs are weighted negatively, whereas expectations regarding defense spending are weighted positively.

When it is desired to obtain raw canonical weights, $\mathbf{v}_j^*$, these can be easily calculated using the following formula:

$$v_j^* = \frac{\beta_j}{s_j} \qquad (18.16)$$

where v_j^* is the raw coefficient for variable j; β_j is the standardized coefficient for variable j; s_j is the standard deviation of variable j. For the present example, $s_{y_1} = 1.16292$ and $s_{y_2} = 1.46385$ (see Table 18.6). Applying (18.16),

$$v_1^* = \frac{-.81468}{1.16292} = -.70055$$

$$v_2^* = \frac{.82022}{1.46385} = .56032$$

Structure Coefficients

The structure coefficients for the Y's on the first canonical variate are now calculated, using Formula (18.7).

$$\mathbf{s}_y = \mathbf{R}_{yy}\,\boldsymbol{\beta} = \begin{bmatrix} 1.00000 & .25175 \\ .25175 & 1.00000 \end{bmatrix} \begin{bmatrix} -.81468 \\ .82022 \end{bmatrix} = \begin{bmatrix} -.60819 \\ .61512 \end{bmatrix}$$

Thus, the correlation between Y_1 and the scores on the first canonical variate is $-.61$, and that of Y_2 with the scores on the first canonical variate is .62. On the basis of the criterion that a structure coefficient of .3 or greater be considered meaningful, it is concluded that both Y_1 and Y_2 have equally meaningful loading on the first canonical variate.

It was said earlier that structure coefficients are interpreted as loadings in factor analysis. When, in factor analysis, some variables have high positive loadings on a factor, and other variables have high negative loadings on the same factor, it is referred to as being bipolar. In the present example, the first canonical variate is bipolar. Referring to the example presented in the beginning of this section, where Y_1 was said to be expectations regarding government spending on social welfare programs, and Y_2 was said to be expectations regarding defense spending, it is clear that the three groups are separated on a single dimension that may be named social welfare versus defense. Groups that have high expectations regarding defense spending tend to have lower expectations regarding spending on social welfare programs, and vice versa.

Generally, more than two dependent variables are used. Under such circumstances, the variables with the high structure coefficients on a given canonical variate serve to identify it. Thus, when more than one canonical correlation is meaningful, it is possible to study the number and the nature of the dimensions that separate the groups.

Redundancy

In order to calculate the redundancy of Y given X, the proportion of the total variance of the Y's that is extracted by the first canonical variate is calculated, using (18.9). That is,

$$PV_{y_j} = \frac{\mathbf{s}'_{y_j}\mathbf{s}_{y_j}}{q} = \frac{1}{2}\,[-.60819 \quad .61512]\begin{bmatrix}-.60819\\ .61512\end{bmatrix} = .37413$$

The first canonical variable extracts about 37% of the total variance of the Y's.

Now the redundancy of Y given X, see (18.12), is

$$Rd_{y_j} = PV_{y_j}R^2_{c_j} = (.37413)(.89793) = .33594$$

This means that about 34% of the total variance of the Y's is explained by the first linear combination of the X's. Recalling that in the present example the Y's are the dependent variables and the X's represent three groups (A_1, A_2, and A_3), or three treatments, it is concluded that the differences among the groups explain about 34% of the total variance of the dependent variables. Referring to the example given earlier, this means that about 34% of the variability in expectations regarding government spending is due to the differences among Conservatives, Republicans, and Democrats.

The foregoing was based on the first canonical variate. Because the second canonical correlation was neither meaningful nor statistically significant, the proportion of variance of the Y's accounted for by the second X canonical variate is not calculated. In any case, if you were to calculate it as an exercise you would find that it is very small (about 4%).

MULTIVARIATE ANALYSIS OF VARIANCE

The data given in Table 18.5 and analyzed in the preceding section via CA will now be analyzed via MANOVA. For convenience, these data are repeated in Table 18.7. Also included, at the bottom of the table, are the following Sums of Squares and Cross Products matrices: **B** (between groups); **W** (pooled within groups); **T** (total). In the interest of space, the calculations of these matrices are not shown here. If necessary, refer to Chapter 17 (section entitled SSCP) for detailed explanations of the calculations of SSCP matrices.

It has already been shown in Chapter 17 that one can obtain Wilks' Λ (lambda) by using the following:

$$\Lambda = \frac{|\mathbf{W}|}{|\mathbf{T}|} \tag{18.17}$$

where $|\mathbf{W}|$ = determinant of the pooled within groups SSCP; $|\mathbf{T}|$ = determinant of the total SSCP.

Taking these matrices from Table 18.7, their determinants are calculated:

$$|\mathbf{W}| = \begin{vmatrix} 12.00 & 13.20 \\ 13.20 & 18.80 \end{vmatrix} = (12.00)(18.80) - (13.20)^2 = \mathit{51.36}$$

$$|\mathbf{T}| = \begin{vmatrix} 18.93333 & 6.00000 \\ 6.00000 & 30.00000 \end{vmatrix} = (18.93333)(30.00000) - (6.00000)^2 = \mathit{531.9999}$$

Applying now (18.17),

$$\Lambda = \frac{51.36}{531.9999} = \mathit{.09654}$$

Table 18.7 Illustrative Data for Three Groups and Two Dependent Variables

	A_1		A_2		A_3	
	Y_1	Y_2	Y_1	Y_2	Y_1	Y_2
	3	7	4	5	5	5
	4	7	4	6	6	5
	5	8	5	7	6	6
	5	9	6	7	7	7
	6	10	6	8	7	8
Σ:	23	41	25	33	31	31
$\bar{Y}$:	4.6	8.2	5.0	6.6	6.2	6.2

$$\underset{\mathbf{B}}{\begin{bmatrix} 6.93333 & -7.20000 \\ -7.20000 & 11.20000 \end{bmatrix}} \quad \underset{\mathbf{W}}{\begin{bmatrix} 12.00 & 13.20 \\ 13.20 & 18.80 \end{bmatrix}} \quad \underset{\mathbf{T}}{\begin{bmatrix} 18.93333 & 6.00000 \\ 6.00000 & 30.00000 \end{bmatrix}}$$

NOTE: The same data were analyzed in the preceding section via CA. **B** = between-groups SSCP; **W** = within-groups SSCP; **T** = total SSCP.

This is the same as the value of Λ that was obtained when these data were analyzed via CA in the preceding section.

Tests of Significance

One could, of course, now use Bartlett's χ^2 test of Λ. But this was already done in the preceding section ($\chi^2 = 26.88$, with 4 *df*). Instead, another approach to the testing of Λ, proposed by Rao (1952), will be given here:

$$F = \frac{1 - \Lambda^{1/s}}{\Lambda^{1/s}} \left[\frac{ms - v}{t(k - 1)} \right] \tag{18.18}$$

where t = number of dependent variables; k = number of treatments, or groups.

$$m = \frac{2N - t - k - 2}{2}$$

$$s = \sqrt{\frac{t^2 (k - 1)^2 - 4}{t^2 + (k - 1)^2 - 5}}$$

$$v = \frac{t(k - 1) - 2}{2}$$

N in the above definition of m is the total number of subjects.

The F ratio has $t(k - 1)$ and $ms - v$ degrees of freedom for the numerator and the denominator, respectively.

For the present example, $N = 15$, $t = 2$, and $k = 3$. Calculate m, s, and v:

$$m = \frac{(2)(15) - 2 - 3 - 2}{2} = 11.5$$

$$s = \sqrt{\frac{(2)^2(3 - 1)^2 - 4}{(2)^2 + (3 - 1)^2 - 5}} = \sqrt{\frac{12}{3}} = 2$$

$$v = \frac{(2)(3 - 1) - 2}{2} = 1$$

Now apply (18.18):

$$F = \frac{1 - .09654^{1/2}}{.09654^{1/2}} \left[\frac{(11.5)(2) - 1}{2(3 - 1)} \right] = \frac{1 - \sqrt{.09654}}{\sqrt{.09654}} (5.50) = 12.20$$

with 4 $[t(k - 1)]$ and 22 $(ms - v)$ degrees of freedom, $p < .001$. It is concluded that there are significant differences among the three groups on the two dependent variables, when these are analyzed simultaneously (see below for different conclusions when these data are subjected to univariate analyses). For the sub-

Table 18.8 Exact F Tests of Λ for Special Cases

k (Groups)	t (Variables)	F	Degrees of Freedom (v_1, v_2)
Any number	2	$\frac{1-\sqrt{\Lambda}}{\sqrt{\Lambda}}\left[\frac{N-k-1}{k-1}\right]$	$2(k-1), 2(N-k-1)$
2	Any number	$\frac{1-\Lambda}{\Lambda}\left[\frac{N-t-1}{t}\right]$	$t, N-t-1$
3	Any number	$\frac{1-\sqrt{\Lambda}}{\sqrt{\Lambda}}\left[\frac{N-t-2}{t}\right]$	$2t, 2(N-t-2)$

NOTE: v_1 = degrees of freedom for numerator; v_2 = degrees of freedom for denominator.

stantive example presented earlier, this means that Conservatives, Republicans, and Democrats differ significantly in their expectations regarding government spending. If A_1, A_2, and A_3 were treatments it would have been concluded that they have differential effects on the dependent variables.

Generally, the F of Formula (18.18) is approximately distributed, except for some special cases when it is exact. These are given in Table 18.8. Note that in these special cases the formula is greatly simplified. Note also that the numerical example under consideration is one of the special cases of the category listed last in Table 18.8. For a very good discussion of Formula (18.18), see Rulon and Brooks (1968, pp. 72–76).

Other Test Criteria

Unlike univariate analysis of variance, more than one criterion is currently used by researchers for the purpose of performing tests of significance in multivariate analysis. While the various criteria generally yield similar tests of significance results, it is possible for the different test criteria not to agree. It is not the purpose of this section to review the merits and demerits of available criteria for tests of significance in multivariate analysis, but rather to introduce, in addition to Λ, two criteria that are obtainable from the canonical analysis without further calculations.[12]

The first criterion was developed by Roy (1957), and is referred to as Roy's largest root criterion because it uses the largest root, λ, obtained in the CA, or the largest R_c^2. When the numerical example analyzed here was analyzed earlier via CA, it was found that the largest $\lambda = R_c^2 = .89793$. It is this root that is tested for significance. Heck (1960) has provided charts for the significance of the largest characteristic root. Pillai (1960) has provided tables for the significance of the largest root. The tables and/or the charts are reproduced in various books on multivariate analysis (e.g., Morrison, 1976; Press, 1972; Timm, 1975). The charts as well as the tables are entered with three values: s, m, and n. For CA, s = number of nonzero roots; $m = .5\,(q - p - 1)$, where $q \geq p$; $n = .5\,(N - p - q - 2)$.

[12]For a review and a discussion of different test criteria in multivariate analysis, see Olson (1976).

For the numerical example that was analyzed in the preceding section via CA,

$$s = 2$$

$$m = .5(2 - 2 - 1) = -.5$$

$$n = .5(15 - 2 - 2 - 2) = 4.5$$

It is with these values that one enters Heck's charts, for example. If the value of the largest root exceeds the value found in the chart, the result is significant at the level indicated in that chart.

A second criterion for the multivariate analysis is the sum of the roots. The sum of the roots is equal to the trace (the sum of the elements in the principal diagonal) of the matrix used to solve for λ's in the CA. In other words, it is the trace of the matrix whose determinant was set equal to zero. Look back at this matrix in the section on CA and note that the two elements in its principal diagonal are .47218 and .47979. Their sum (.95197) is equal to the sum of the roots extracted: .89793 + .05404 = .95197. Pillai (1960) has provided tables for testing the sum of the roots. The tables are entered with values of s, m, and n, where these are as defined above.

Finally, it will be noted that some computer programs (e.g., SPSS MANOVA, available only on the CDC version) report approximate F ratios for Wilks' Λ, Roy's largest root, and Pillai's trace criteria.

Multiple Comparisons among Groups and Variable Contributions

An overall test of significance in MANOVA leads to the rejection of the null hypothesis that the mean vectors of the groups are equal. When more than two groups are involved, it is necessary to determine which pairs, or combinations, of groups differ significantly from each other. It has been shown earlier (see Chapter 9) that in univariate analysis this is accomplished by performing multiple comparisons among the means. It was also shown that, depending on one's hypotheses, such comparisons may be a priori (orthogonal and nonorthogonal) or post hoc. In MANOVA, too, methods of multiple comparisons among groups are available. Detailed discussions of this topic will be found in texts on multivariate analysis (see, in particular, Bock, 1975; Finn, 1974; Kramer, 1972; Morrison, 1976; Stevens, 1972b; Timm, 1975).

In univariate analysis, a statistically significant comparison indicates that the groups being compared differ significantly on the dependent variable under investigation. But when a significant comparison is obtained in MANOVA it is not clear which of the multiple dependent variables contribute mostly to the difference between the groups that are being compared. Among various approaches that have been recommended for the study of the contribution of specific variables to the separation between groups are discriminant analysis (see below) and simultaneous confidence intervals. These and other methods are discussed in the references cited above. Wilkinson (1975), who provides a good discussion and a numerical example of different approaches to multiple comparisons in MANOVA, concludes: "Except in the rarest cases of known independent or known equicorrelated responses, no one of these measures sufficiently describes the relation between treatment and response" (p. 412). In short, the relatively neat situation of multiple comparisons in univariate analysis occurs rarely in MANOVA.

Univariate *F* Ratios

Some authors (e.g., Hummel & Sligo, 1971) have suggested that an overall statistically significant result in MANOVA be followed by the calculation of univariate F ratios for each of the dependent variables. This suggestion is ill advised because it ignores the intercorrelations among the dependent variables and thereby subverts the very purpose of doing MANOVA in the first place. It is possible that no significant differences will be detected when each dependent variable is analyzed separately, but that a MANOVA of the same data will indicate significant differences.[13] In fact, the numerical example analyzed here was expressly constructed to show this possibility. This will now be demonstrated by the calculation of separate F ratios for each of the two dependent variables of the numerical example analyzed above.

The statistics necessary for the calculation of the two univariate F ratios are available in the principal diagonals of the **B** (between-groups or between-treatments SSCP) and **W** (within-groups or within-treatments SSCP) given in Table 18.7. Specifically, the between-groups sums of squares for Y_1 and Y_2, respectively, are 6.93333 and 11.20000. The within-groups sums of squares for Y_1 and Y_2, respectively, are 12.00 and 18.80. Recall that mean squares between groups and within groups are obtained by dividing sums of squares by their degrees of freedom and that the F ratio is a ratio of the mean square between groups to the mean square within groups. In the present example, the number of groups is three, and therefore the degrees of freedom for the mean square between them are two. The degrees of freedom for the mean square within groups are 12 $[g(n_j - 1)]$, where g = number of groups, or treatments and n_j = number of subjects in group j.

Turning first to the test of the differences among the three groups on Y_1,

$$F = \frac{6.93333/2}{12.00/12} = 3.47$$

with 2 and 12 *df*, $p > .05$. It is concluded that the three groups do not differ significantly, at the .05 level of significance.

Calculate now the F ratio for Y_2:

$$F = \frac{11.20/2}{18.80/12} = 3.57$$

with 2 and 12 *df*, $p > .05$. It is concluded that the three groups do not differ significantly at the .05 level of significance. Thus the results of the univariate F

[13]For clear discussions and demonstrations of this point, see Li (1964, pp. 405–410), and Tatsuoka (1971b, pp. 22–24).

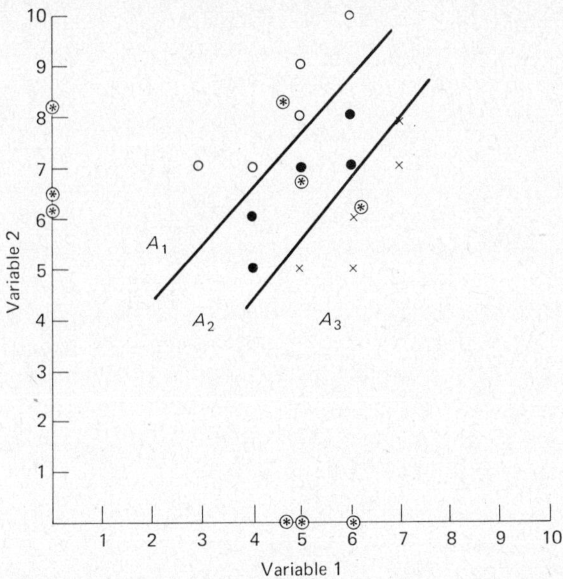

Figure 18.1

tests contradict the results obtained earlier where it was concluded on the basis of CA and MANOVA of the same data that there are significant differences among the three groups. How can such a result happen? Following Li (1964, Chapter 30), this is now demonstrated graphically.

In Figure 18.1, the paired scores of the dependent variables, Y_1 and Y_2, are plotted. The plotted pairs of A_1 are shown with open circles, those of A_2 with black circles, and those of A_3 with crosses. The means of the three groups have also been plotted—indicated by circled asterisks. Notice that the plotted points overlap a good deal if viewed horizontally or vertically. If we visualize the projections of all the plotted points on the 1-axis first, we see the substantial overlap. In addition, the three means of the 1 groups have been projected on the 1-axis (circled asterisks): 4.6, 5.0, 6.2. Now visualize the projections on the 2-axis of all the points. Again, there is considerable overlap. The plotted means' projections on the 2-axis have been indicated: 8.2, 6.6, 6.2. Note when considering variable 1 alone, that there is little difference between the means of A_1, the lowest mean, and A_2, but both are different from A_3, the highest mean. When considering variable 2 alone, on the other hand, the mean of A_1, now the highest mean, is quite different from the means of A_2 and A_3—and the latter is now the lowest mean.

If, instead of regarding the plotted points one-dimensionally, we regard them two-dimensionally in the 1-2 plane, the picture changes radically. There are clear separations between the plotted points and the plotted means of A_1, A_2, and A_3. In fact, it is possible to draw straight lines to separate the clusters of plotted points. Considering the two dependent variables together, then, the groups are separated in the two-dimensional space. And the multivariate analysis faithfully reflects the separation.

Although, as was noted above, the present example was contrived to demonstrate that MANOVA and univariate analyses of the same data may lead to contradictory conclusions, it should be realized that this is not necessarily a rare occurrence in actual research. This is particularly so when more than two dependent variables and more independent variables are used. Under such circumstances the possibilities and complexities increase enormously, and it is only by resorting to multivariate analyses that one may hope to begin to unravel them. The promise held by the application of multivariate analysis to the study of complex phenomena should, it is hoped, be evident even on the basis of the almost trivial example given here.

It was said several times earlier that various authors (e.g., Borgen & Seling, 1978; Tatsuoka, 1971a) have suggested that an overall significant finding in MANOVA be followed by a DA for the purpose of shedding light on the nature of the dimensions on which the groups differ. It was also said earlier that the overall results and tests of significance in CA, MANOVA, and DA are identical. These points are now elaborated by applying a DA to the same numerical example that was analyzed above by CA and MANOVA.

DISCRIMINANT ANALYSIS

The topic of DA was discussed in detail in Chapter 17. Although the analysis in that chapter was limited to the case of two groups, the same approach is taken with more than two groups, except that, unlike the case of two groups, more than one discriminant function is calculated. In general, the number of discriminant functions obtainable in a set of data is equal to the number of groups minus one, or the number of dependent variables, whichever is smaller. Thus, with three groups, for example, only two discriminant functions may be derived, regardless of the number of dependent variables. On the other hand, given ten groups and four dependent variables, for example, only four discriminant functions may be derived. (This is not to say that all the obtainable discriminant functions are meaningful and/or statistically significant.) The numerical example analyzed in the preceding sections consisted of three groups and two dependent variables. Therefore, a maximum of two discriminant functions may be derived.

Because the general approach in DA is the same as that presented in Chapter 17, comments about the calculations will be kept to a minimum. In the process of doing the calculations, references will be made to equations introduced in Chapter 17 in order to facilitate your consulting, whenever necessary, the detailed discussions of them.

It was shown in Chapter 17 (see Equation (17.3)) that DA begins with the solution of the roots, λ, of the following determinantal equation:

$$\left|\mathbf{W}^{-1}\mathbf{B} - \lambda\mathbf{I}\right| = 0 \tag{18.19}$$

where $\mathbf{W}^{-1}$ is the inverse of the pooled within-groups SSCP; $\mathbf{B}$ is the between-groups SSCP; λ are the eigenvalues, or characteristic roots; $\mathbf{I}$ is an identity matrix. For the numerical example analyzed previously via CA and MANOVA, $\mathbf{W}$ and $\mathbf{B}$ are (see Table 18.7):

$$\mathbf{W} = \begin{bmatrix} 12.00 & 13.20 \\ 13.20 & 18.80 \end{bmatrix}$$

$$\mathbf{B} = \begin{bmatrix} 6.93333 & -7.20000 \\ -7.20000 & 11.20000 \end{bmatrix}$$

The determinant of **W** is:

$$|\mathbf{W}| = (12.00)(18.80) - (13.20)^2 = \mathit{51.36}$$

The inverse of **W** is:

$$\mathbf{W}^{-1} = \frac{1}{51.36}\begin{bmatrix} 18.80 & -13.20 \\ -13.20 & 12.00 \end{bmatrix} = \begin{bmatrix} .36604 & -.25701 \\ -.25701 & .23364 \end{bmatrix}$$

$$\mathbf{W}^{-1}\mathbf{B} = \begin{bmatrix} .36604 & -.25701 \\ -.25701 & .23364 \end{bmatrix}\begin{bmatrix} 6.93333 & -7.20000 \\ -7.20000 & 11.20000 \end{bmatrix} = \begin{bmatrix} 4.38835 & -5.51400 \\ -3.46414 & 4.46724 \end{bmatrix}$$

$$\begin{vmatrix} 4.38835 - \lambda & -5.51400 \\ -3.46414 & 4.46724 - \lambda \end{vmatrix} = 0$$

Thus

$$(4.38835 - \lambda)(4.46724 - \lambda) - (-5.51400)(-3.46414) = 0$$

$$19.60381 - 4.46724\lambda - 4.38835\lambda + \lambda^2 - 19.10127 = 0$$

$$\lambda^2 - 8.85559\lambda + .50254 = 0$$

from which

$$\lambda_1 = \frac{8.85559 + \sqrt{(-8.85559)^2 - (4)(1)(.50254)}}{2} = \mathit{8.79847}$$

$$\lambda_2 = \frac{8.85559 - \sqrt{(-8.85559)^2 - (4)(1)(.50254)}}{2} = \mathit{.05712}$$

Index of Discriminatory Power

Having calculated the two roots it is possible to calculate the proportion of discriminatory power of each of the discriminant functions that are associated with these roots. In general,

$$P_j = \frac{\lambda_j}{\Sigma\lambda} \tag{18.20}$$

where P_j = the proportion of discriminatory power of the discriminant function that is associated with the jth root; $\Sigma\lambda$ = sum of the roots.

For the present example,

$$P_1 = \frac{8.79847}{8.79847 + .05712} = .99355$$

$$P_2 = \frac{.05712}{8.79847 + .05712} = .00645$$

Thus, 99.35% of the discriminatory power is due to the first discriminant function, whereas that associated with the second function is only about .65%. It is important to note that P_j indicates the discriminatory power of the jth function in relation to the other functions—*not* the proportion of variance of the dependent variables accounted by the jth function. Stated differently, P_j is an index of the proportion of the discriminatory power of the jth function of whatever the total amount of discriminatory power all the functions may possess. Therefore a large P_j does not necessarily mean that the discriminant function associated with it leads to a meaningful discrimination among the groups. Nevertheless, P_j is a useful descriptive index in that it provides, at a glance, an indication of the relative power of each of the discriminant functions. As demonstrated in the present numerical example, P_2 is so small as to lead to the conclusion that, the total discriminatory power of both functions notwithstanding, the second function is useless.

Tests of Significance

Using the roots of the determinantal equation (18.19), Wilks' Λ is calculated as follows:

$$\Lambda = \frac{1}{(1 + \lambda_1)(1 + \lambda_2) \cdots (1 + \lambda_j)} \tag{18.21}$$

For the present example,

$$\Lambda = \frac{1}{(1 + 8.79847)(1 + .05712)} = .09654$$

This is, within rounding error, the same value as the one obtained in the analysis of these data via CA. As in CA, one may remove the first root to obtain Λ':

$$\Lambda' = \frac{1}{1 + .05712} = .94597$$

Again, the same value of Λ' was obtained when the data were analyzed via CA. Therefore, Bartlett's χ^2 could be applied to test the discriminatory power of all the functions as well as to determine the number of functions that are statistically significant.

Alternatively, instead of calculating Λ, Bartlett's χ^2 may be applied to the roots obtained in DA. It takes the following form:

$$\chi^2 = [N - 1 - .5(p + k)]\Sigma \log_e (1 + \lambda_j) \tag{18.22}$$

where N = total number of subject; p = number of dependent variables; k = number of treatments, or groups; $\log_e$ = natural logarithm. The degrees of freedom associated with the χ^2 are $p\ (k - 1)$.

For the present example,

$$\chi^2 = [15 - 1 - .5(2 + 3)]\ [\log_e 9.79847 + \log_e 1.05712]$$

$$= (11.5)(2.28223 + .05555) = \mathit{26.88}$$

with 4 df, $p < .001$. This is the same as the result obtained in the analysis of these data via CA.

Removing the first root amounts to removing its logarithm (i.e., 2.28223) from the last expression above. Therefore, for the remaining root,

$$\chi^2 = (11.5)(.05555) = \mathit{.64}$$

with 1 $[(p - 1)(k - 2)]$ df, $p > .05$. Again, exactly the same result was obtained earlier when the data were subjected to CA.

Before turning to the calculation of the discriminant functions, it should be evident from the foregoing presentation that the other test criteria discussed in the section entitled MANOVA are easily obtainable from DA. Thus, Roy's largest root, or $R^2_{c_1}$, is:

$$\frac{\lambda_1}{1 + \lambda_1} = \frac{8.79847}{9.79847} = \mathit{.89794}$$

Pillia's trace is similarly obtained:

$$\frac{\lambda_1}{1 + \lambda_1} + \frac{\lambda_2}{1 + \lambda_2} = \frac{8.79847}{9.79847} + \frac{.05712}{1.05712} = \mathit{.95198}$$

Compare these results with those obtained in the sections on CA and MANOVA of the same data.

Discriminant Functions

The first discriminant function will now be calculated. Again, because the procedure of doing this was discussed in detail in Chapter 17, comments on the calculations will be kept to a minimum. For easy reference, formulas introduced in Chapter 17 will be repeated with their original numbers. It is felt that application of the formulas to the numerical example would suffice to indicate the meaning of their terms. When in doubt, consult Chapter 17 for detailed explanations.

Subtract the first root, 8.79847, from the elements of the principal diagonal of $\mathbf{W}^{-1}\mathbf{B}$, calculated above, and form the following:

$$\begin{bmatrix} 4.38835 - 8.79847 & -5.51400 \\ -3.46414 & 4.46724 - 8.79847 \end{bmatrix} \begin{bmatrix} v_1 \\ v_2 \end{bmatrix} = \begin{bmatrix} 0 \\ 0 \end{bmatrix}$$

$$\begin{bmatrix} -4.41012 & -5.51400 \\ -3.46414 & -4.33123 \end{bmatrix} \begin{bmatrix} v_1 \\ v_2 \end{bmatrix} = \begin{bmatrix} 0 \\ 0 \end{bmatrix}$$

Form the adjoint of the preceding matrix:

$$\begin{bmatrix} -4.33123 & 5.51400 \\ 3.46414 & -4.41012 \end{bmatrix}$$

$$\mathbf{v}' = [-4.33123 \quad 3.46414] \quad \text{or} \quad [5.51400 \quad -4.41012]$$

Now, calculate $\mathbf{C}_w$—the pooled within-groups covariance matrix:

$$\mathbf{C}_w = \frac{1}{12}\begin{bmatrix} 12.0 & 13.2 \\ 13.2 & 18.8 \end{bmatrix} = \begin{bmatrix} 1.00000 & 1.10000 \\ 1.10000 & 1.56667 \end{bmatrix}$$

Equation (17.5) is now applied:

$$\mathbf{v}'\mathbf{C}\mathbf{v} = \underset{\mathbf{v}'}{[-4.33123 \quad 3.46414]} \underset{\mathbf{C}}{\begin{bmatrix} 1.00000 & 1.10000 \\ 1.10000 & 1.56667 \end{bmatrix}} \underset{\mathbf{v}}{\begin{bmatrix} -4.33123 \\ 3.46414 \end{bmatrix}} = 4.55124$$

The raw coefficients are now calculated by using Formula (17.7):

$$v_i^* = \frac{\mathrm{v}_i}{\sqrt{\mathbf{v}'\mathbf{C}\mathbf{v}}}$$

Hence

$$v_1^* = \frac{-4.33123}{\sqrt{4.55124}} = -2.03024$$

$$v_2^* = \frac{3.46414}{\sqrt{4.55124}} = 1.62379$$

When the data were analyzed earlier in this chapter via CA, it was found that the raw coefficients on the first canonical variate are −.70055 and .56032 for Y_1 and Y_2, respectively. It will be noted that the ratio of these coefficients is the same as the ratio of the ones obtained here. That is,

$$\frac{-.70055}{.56032} = \frac{-2.03024}{1.62379} = -1.25$$

Using the treatment means, grand means for Y_1 and Y_2 are calculated. From Table 18.7,

	A_1	A_2	A_3
$\overline{Y}_1$:	4.6	5.0	6.2
$\overline{Y}_2$:	8.2	6.6	6.2

$$\overline{Y}_1 = \frac{4.6 + 5.0 + 6.2}{3} = 5.26667$$

$$\overline{Y}_2 = \frac{8.2 + 6.6 + 6.2}{3} = 7.00000$$

Formula (17.8) is now used to obtain the constant, c, for the first discriminant function.

$$c = -(v_1^*\overline{Y}_1 + v_2^*\overline{Y}_2)$$

$$= -[(-2.03024)(5.26667) + (1.62379)(7.00000)] = -.67393$$

The first discriminant function is

$$X_1 = -.67393 - 2.03024Y_1 + 1.62379Y_2$$

Inspection of the coefficients of this function indicates that subjects who have relatively high scores on Y_2 and relatively low scores on Y_1 will have relatively high positive discriminant scores. Conversely, subjects whose scores are relatively high on Y_1 and relatively low on Y_2 will have relatively high negative discriminant scores (see discussion of Group Centroids, below).

Recall that some researchers use standardized coefficients for the purpose of determining the relative importance of variables in a given function, whereas others use structure coefficients instead.[14] The standardized coefficients for the first function are calculated by applying (17.9): $\beta_i = v_i^* \sqrt{c_{ij}}$. Hence

$$\beta_1 = -2.03024\sqrt{1.00000} = -2.03024$$

$$\beta_2 = 1.62379\sqrt{1.56667} = 2.03244$$

Using the magnitude of the β as a criterion of the relative importance of the variable with which it is associated, one would conclude that in the present example Y_1 and Y_2 are virtually of equal importance.[15]

Following the procedures used above, the second function may be calculated. For completeness of presentation, the second function will be reported. But in the interest of space, its calculation is not shown (you may wish to do this as an exercise).

[14]This point was discussed in detail in Chapter 17.
[15]Structure coefficients are calculated below.

The second function is

$$X_2 = -5.60054 + .52025Y_1 + .40865Y_2$$

The standardized coefficients for the second function are

$$\beta_1 = .52025 \qquad \beta_2 = .51149$$

Recall that the second function was found to be neither meaningful (see section entitled Index of Discriminatory Power) nor statistically significant. It is therefore not interpreted. As was noted above, it was given here for completeness of presentation.

Group Centroids

Using the group means and the discriminant functions, given above, group centroids are calculated. For the first function,

$$X_{1(A_1)} = -.67393 - 2.03024(4.6) + 1.62379(8.2) = 3.30$$

$$X_{1(A_2)} = -.67393 - 2.03024(5.0) + 1.62379(6.6) = -.11$$

$$X_{1(A_3)} = -.67393 - 2.03024(6.2) + 1.62379(6.2) = -3.19$$

The three groups are almost equally spaced on the first discriminant variate, with A_1 and A_3 at the two extremes, and A_2 occupying the intermediate position. Referring to the substantive example given when these data were introduced, one would conclude that Conservatives, Republicans, and Democrats are about equally separated in their expectations of government spending on the dimension of defense versus social welfare programs. Specifically, the Conservatives' relatively high centroid indicates that their expectations regarding defense spending are relatively high, whereas their expectations regarding spending on social welfare are relatively low. The converse is true about the Democrats, whereas the Republicans occupy an intermediate position on the dimension under consideration.

As an aid in the interpretation of results from DA it is very useful to plot the group centroids. Before doing this, the group centroids on the second discriminant variate are calculated. Using the second function and the group means, given above, the centroids are

$$X_{2(A_1)} = -5.60054 + .52025(4.6) + .40865(8.2) = .14$$

$$X_{2(A_2)} = -5.60054 + .52025(5.0) + .40865(6.6) = -.30$$

$$X_{2(A_3)} = -5.60054 + .52025(6.2) + .40865(6.2) = .16$$

A plot of the centroids is given in Figure 18.2, where the abscissa represents the first discriminant variate, and the ordinate represents the second. Note how clearly the three groups are separated by the first function, whereas the second function hardly separates them. That is, the centroids are almost on a straight

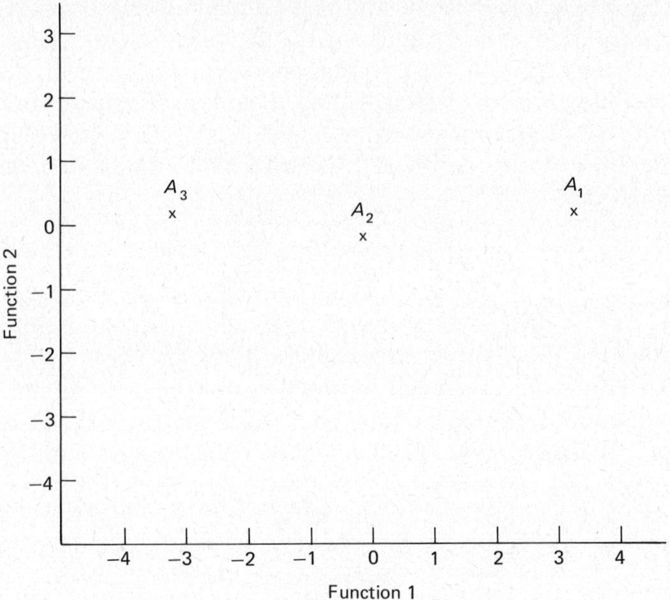

Figure 18.2

line. This, of course, is not surprising in view of what we know about the second discriminant function.

For illustrative purposes, another plot on two discriminant variates for three groups is given in Figure 18.3. Note carefully that this plot *does not* refer to the numerical example analyzed above. Suppose that such a plot were obtained in a study with three preexisting groups, or with three treatments. It can be seen at a glance that the first function discriminates between A_1 and A_2, on the one

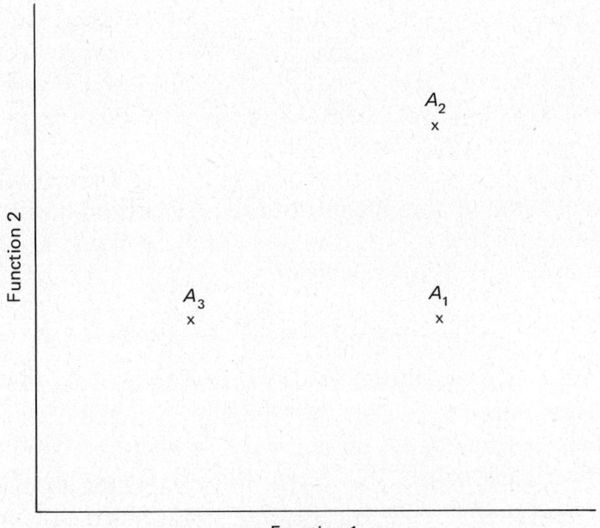

Figure. 18.3

hand, and A_3, on the other hand. The second function discriminates between A_2, on the one hand and A_1 and A_3, on the other hand. Using structure coefficients associated with the two functions one would be in a position to determine the dimension on which A_1 and A_2 are discriminated from A_3, and that on which A_2 is discriminated from A_1 and A_3. It will be noted that computer programs for DA (e.g., SPSS, DISCRIMINANT; BMDP7M) include various plotting options.

Structure Coefficient

Following the procedures discussed in detail in Chapter 17, structure coefficients will now be calculated for the first discriminant variate. It will be recalled that for this purpose the total covariance matrix, C_t, is used. Taking the total SSCP matrix from Table 18.7, and recalling that $N = 15$, C_t is:

$$\mathbf{C}_t = \frac{1}{14}\begin{bmatrix} 18.93333 & 6.00000 \\ 6.00000 & 30.00000 \end{bmatrix} = \begin{bmatrix} 1.35238 & .42857 \\ .42857 & 2.14286 \end{bmatrix}$$

Earlier, the first eigenvector, $\mathbf{v}'$, was found to be: $[-4.33123 \quad 3.46414]$
Calculate now:

$$\mathbf{v}'\mathbf{C}_t\mathbf{v} = \underset{\mathbf{v}'}{[-4.33123 \quad 3.46414]}\underset{\mathbf{C}_t}{\begin{bmatrix} 1.35238 & .42857 \\ .42857 & 2.14286 \end{bmatrix}}\underset{\mathbf{v}}{\begin{bmatrix} -4.33123 \\ 3.46414 \end{bmatrix}} = \mathit{38.22442}$$

Applying now (17.7), or $v_i^* = v_i/\sqrt{\mathbf{v}'\mathbf{C}\mathbf{v}}$, calculate

$$v_1^* = \frac{-4.33123}{\sqrt{38.22442}} = -.70055$$

$$v_2^* = \frac{3.46414}{\sqrt{38.22442}} = .56031$$

These raw coefficients, $\mathbf{v}^*$, are identical to those obtained earlier when these data were analyzed via CA.

Using (17.8), or $\beta_i = v_i^* \sqrt{c_{ii}}$, calculate

$$\beta_1 = -.70055\sqrt{1.35238} = -.81468$$

$$\beta_2 = .56031\sqrt{2.14286} = .82021$$

As was explained in Chapter 17, these β's are standardized coefficients based on the total covariance matrix, $\mathbf{C}_t$; hence it is the diagonal elements of this matrix that are used in their calculation. Again, exactly the same values for the β's were obtained earlier in the CA of these data.

Finally, to obtain the structure coefficients, **s**, it is necessary to apply (17.10): $\mathbf{s} = \mathbf{R}_t\,\beta_t$. First, calculate the total correlation matrix, $\mathbf{R}_t$, using $\mathbf{C}_t$:

$$\mathbf{R}_t = \begin{bmatrix} \dfrac{1.35238}{\sqrt{(1.35238)(1.35238)}} & \dfrac{.42857}{\sqrt{(1.35238)(2.14286)}} \\ \dfrac{.42857}{\sqrt{(1.35238)(2.14286)}} & \dfrac{2.14286}{\sqrt{(2.14286)(2.14286)}} \end{bmatrix} = \begin{bmatrix} 1.00000 & .25175 \\ .25175 & 1.00000 \end{bmatrix}$$

$$\mathbf{s} = \begin{bmatrix} 1.00000 & .25175 \\ .25175 & 1.00000 \end{bmatrix} \begin{bmatrix} -.81468 \\ .82021 \end{bmatrix} = \begin{bmatrix} -.60819 \\ .61511 \end{bmatrix}$$

These values are the same as those obtained for the structure coefficients when CA was applied to these data. Because their interpretation was discussed in the CA section, they are not discussed here, except to note that had one done only a DA on the numerical example under consideration, these coefficients would have been used for the purpose of interpreting the dimension on which the groups are separated in the same manner as was done earlier.

The calculations of the structure coefficients associated with the second function are not shown here (you may wish to do this as an exercise). They are $s_1 = .79$ and $s_2 = .79$.

The DA is summarized in Table 18.9.

Table 18.9 Summary of DA for Data of Table 18.7

Function	*Variables*	*Raw*	β	s	*Group*	*Centroids*
1	Y_1	−2.03	−2.03	−.61	A_1	3.30
	Y_2	1.62	2.03	.62	A_2	−.11
					A_3	−3.19
2	Y_1	.52	.52	.79	A_1	.14
	Y_2	.41	.51	.79	A_2	−.30
					A_3	.16
$\lambda_1 = 8.80$	$P_1 = .99$					
$\lambda_2 = .06$	$P_2 = .01$					

NOTE: Raw = raw coefficient; β = standardized coefficient; s = structure coefficient; λ = eigenvalue; P = proportion of discriminatory power.

RECAPITULATION AND EXTENSIONS

When a design consists of multiple dependent variables, or criteria, and a categorical independent variable representing treatments, or preexisting groups, the data may be analyzed by CA, MANOVA, or DA. It was shown in this section that the three approaches lead to identical results. The three approaches are briefly summarized.

Using CA, create Y vectors of the dependent variables for all the subjects treated as a single group. Using one of the coding methods presented in Chapter 9, code the categorical variable as the X's. Do a CA using the Y's as one set and the X's as the other set. Calculate the squared canonical correlations, R_c^2's, and test them for significance. Retain the R_c^2's that meet the criteria of meaningfulness and statistical significance. Calculate canonical weights, structure coefficients, and redundancy indices. Interpret the results.

Using MANOVA, calculate Λ and test for statistical significance. If Λ is statistically significant, do multiple comparisons between groups and determine the variables that primarily contribute to the differences between the groups. It will be recalled that these procedures were not shown. Instead, it was shown how MANOVA is followed up by a DA.

Using DA, determine the number of meaningful and statistically significant discriminant functions. Using these functions, calculate group centroids and plot them. Calculate structure coefficients. Interpret the results.

The presentation in this section was limited to a single categorical independent variable. As in the case of univariate analysis, the approaches presented here can be extended to designs with more than one categorical variable, or factorial designs. These are discussed in books on multivariate analysis cited several times earlier (see also Pruzek, 1971).

RESEARCH APPLICATIONS

Two research studies will be used to illustrate applications of analytic methods presented in this chapter. Because of space considerations, it is not possible to deal here with either theoretical or research design aspects of these studies. If you are interested in issues other than the strict illustrative applications given here, it is suggested that you read the original studies.[16]

Sex-Typed Traits

In Chapter 17, one aspect of a study by Pedhazur and Tetenbaum (1979) was briefly described. We return to this study to describe another of its aspects. It will be recalled that Pedhazur and Tetenbaum questioned the validity of a scale constructed by Bem (1974) to measure sex roles. The Bem Sex Role Inventory (BSRI) consists of 60 traits, 20 of which are presumably "masculine," 20 "feminine," and 20 "neutral." The concern here is solely with some aspects of the method of trait selection and their classification into the aforementioned categories. More specifically, it will be noted that two of the 60 traits of the BSRI are Masculine and Feminine. It is with the role played by these two traits, as contrasted with the remaining 58, that this presentation is concerned.

Following is a brief description of the approach taken by Bem in the selection and the classification of traits into the three categories. A group of college students was asked to rate the desirability of each of about 400 traits for a woman in American society. Another group of college students was asked to rate the desirability of the same traits for a man in American society. Tests of significance (t ratios) were performed on the difference between the mean ratings of each of the traits. Traits whose mean desirability ratings were statistically significantly higher for a man than for a women were designated as masculine.

[16]For other research applications, see Cooley and Lohnes (1971, 1976) and Love and Stewart (1968).

Conversely, traits whose mean ratings of desirability were statistically significantly higher for a woman than for a man were designated as feminine. Traits whose mean ratings for a man or a woman did not differ significantly were designated as neutral.

For reasons that will not be gone into here, Pedhazur and Tetenbaum (1979) added another condition; that is, they sought ratings of desirability of traits also for an adult in American society. Using Bem's instructions three groups of students were asked to rate the desirability of the 60 BSRI traits as follows: for a man ($N = 493$), for a woman ($N = 426$), and for an adult ($N = 545$). Pedhazur and Tetenbaum, unlike Bem, used multivariate analyses to analyze the ratings. Results of canonical analysis (CA) and discriminant analysis (DA) are now summarized.

Turning first to CA, it will be noted that this is an example in which one set of variables is continuous, whereas the other set consists of coded vectors that represent a categorical variable. Specifically, one set consists of the ratings of desirability of the 60 traits, and the other set consists of two coded vectors to represent the three conditions under which the traits were rated (i.e., for man, for woman, and for adult). Recall that under such circumstances, the maximum number of canonical correlations is two (the number of variables—coded vectors in the present case—in the smaller set).

The first squared canonical correlation ($R^2_{c_1}$) was .817, and $R^2_{c_2} = .348$. Using these R^2_c's, Wilks' Λ can be calculated and tested for significance (see (18.14) and (18.15)):

$$\Lambda = (1 - .817)(1 - .348) = \mathit{.119}$$

It will be noted that both R^2_c's are meaningful and statistically significant. We focus here on the structure coefficients of the traits for the first canonical variate. Specifically, the structure coefficient for Feminine was $-.64$, and that for Masculine was .73. Except for nine other traits whose structure coefficients were about .30, all the remaining traits had very low structure coefficients. It appears, then, that the first canonical variate is primarily a bipolar gender factor, with Feminine on one side and Masculine on the other side. To underscore the role played by these two traits, another CA was done. This time only the traits Masculine and Feminine were used as one set, and the coded vectors as the other set. In this analysis, $R^2_{c_1} = .803$ and $R^2_{c_2} = .164$. Therefore, $\Lambda = (1 - .803)(1 - .164) = .165$. Note the very strong similarity of the results of the two analyses. Clearly, the separation among the three conditions on the first canonical variate is primarily due to the ratings of Masculine and Feminine. To further shed light on these results, we turn to DA of the same data.

Two DA's were done: (1) forcing in all 60 traits and (2) a stepwise DA. Following is a brief summary of the results. When all 60 traits were forced into the analysis, it was found that the discriminatory power (see Index of Discriminatory Power, earlier in this chapter) of the first function was about 89% and that of the second function about 11%. The standardized coefficients for Masculine and Feminine on the first function were $-.60$ and .73, respectively. The absolute values of the coefficients associated with 44 other traits were less than .05, the remaining 14 traits having coefficients whose absolute values ranged from

.05 to .12. Consistent with the results reported above, then, it is clear that the ratings of Masculine and Feminine are primarily responsible for the discrimination among the three conditions.

Using the first function for the 60 traits, the centroids for the three conditions were as follows: man = 2.34; adult = .22; woman = −2.99. For comparative purposes, the centroids on the second function are: man = .63; adult = −.94; and woman = .48. Two things will be noted: (1) the separation among the groups is much more pronounced on the first discriminant variate than on the second (see also discriminatory power above); (2) on the first discriminant variate, the centroids for three conditions are about equally spaced, with the one for the "adult" condition occupying the intermediate position. On the second discriminant variate, on the other hand, the conditions "man" and "woman" are contrasted with the "adult" condition.

Turning now to the stepwise DA, it will be noted first that no hierarchy for inclusion of traits in the analysis was preestablished. In other words, it was left for each trait to be entered according to its contribution to the separation among the three conditions. The first trait to enter in this analysis was Masculine. This was followed by the trait Feminine. After this step, the remaining 58 traits added very little to the discrimination among the three conditions. Specifically, with these two traits only, $R^2_{c_1} = .803$, and $R^2_{c_2} = .164$. Therefore, $\Lambda = (1 - .803)(1 - .164) = .165$. Compare these results with the ones obtained with all 60 traits and it will become evident that it is the ratings of Masculine and Feminine that carry the main burden of the separation among the three conditions. For example, Λ for 60 traits is .119, whereas for the two traits only it is .165.

For comparison purposes the centroids for the three conditions on the first function when Masculine and Feminine only were used are as follows: man = 2.27; adult = .16; woman = −2.83. Note the striking resemblance between these centroids and the ones given above for the function based on the 60 traits.

Finally, about 89% of the subjects were correctly classified on the basis of the two functions in which the 60 traits were used. Compare this with 87% of the subjects correctly classified by the functions in with the traits Masculine and Feminine only were used.

In sum, the analyses summarized above demonstrate the utility of multivariate analyses in determining the relative contribution of variables in the discrimination among groups, as well as in identifying the nature of the dimensions on which the groups differ.

Personality Structure and Drug Use

Wingard, Huba, and Bentler (1979) studied the relations among 26 personality variables (e.g., agility, ambition, extraversion, law abidance, liberalism) and the use of 13 different substances and drugs (e.g., cigarettes, beer, liquor, cocaine, marijuana). The subjects were 1634 adolescents from the Los Angeles metropolitan area. An interesting feature of this study is that the authors split the sample randomly into two subsamples for the purpose of cross-validation.

From the foregoing brief description it should come as no surprise that the major analytic approach used by the authors was CA. Having subjected the data of each subsample separately to a CA, it was found that the first two canonical variates were statistically significant (.05 level) in Sample 1, and that the first three canonical variates were statistically significant in Sample 2. But because the third canonical correlation in Sample 2 was relatively low (.282), and for comparative purposes, only the first two canonical variates were retained in both samples.

Following is a brief summary of the findings. The first two canonical correlations in Sample 1 were .597 and .310. In Sample 2, the first two canonical correlations were .582 and .311. Among substances with high structure coefficients on the first dimension in Sample 1 were: Cigarettes (.843), Beer (.757), Liquor (.787), Marijuana (.691). Among personality variables with relatively high structure coefficients on the first dimension in Sample 1 were : Law-Abidance (−.824), Extraversion (.553), Liberalism (.398), Leadership (.368). It appears, then, that the first dimension for the substance use reflects experimentation with substances that are presumably less harmful, more readily available, and that involve less severe legal penalties for possession and use. The personality dimension reflects primarily nonabidance with the law and extraversion. It is interesting to note that there is a larger number of meaningful, and higher, loadings for the substances as compared to those for the personality variables. In other words, the first canonical variates extracts a larger proportion of the variance of substance use as compared with the proportion of variance of the personality variables extracted by the first dimension (see (18.8) and (18.9) and the discussion related to them).

The patterns of the loadings on the first dimension in Sample 2 was very similar to those of Sample 1. This, however, was not the case for the patterns of the loadings in the two samples on the second dimension, which were quite different from each other. In an effort to achieve greater congruence between the two solutions, the authors rotated the loadings. But the rotated solutions were less satisfactory than the unrotated ones. On the basis of these and other considerations the authors concluded that, though statistically significant, the second canonical variate reflects "trivial, sample-specific sources of covariation between the drug use and personality domains" (p. 139). Here, then, is a good example of the utility of cross-validation.

Finally, the authors calculated the redundancy of drug use, given the personality variables, and found it to be about 10.3% in Sample 1, and about 9.4% in Sample 2.

In sum, CA enabled the authors to identify a single dimension of substance use that is related to some aspects of personality. But as the authors themselves conclude, on the basis of the redundancy indices, "the ability of personality to account for variations in adolescent substance use was relatively low" (p. 131).

STUDY SUGGESTIONS

1. It is desired to study the relations between a set of personality measures and a set of achievement measures. If six personality measures and four achievement measures are obtained from a group of subjects, how many canonical correlations may be calculated?
2. In a canonical analysis with three variables in Set 1 and four variables in Set

2, the following results were obtained: $R^2_{c_1} = .432$, $R^2_{c_2} = .213$, $R^2_{c_3} = .145$. The structure coefficients for the two sets were:

Set 1			*Set 2*		
.876	.521	.237	.220	.839	.430
.072	.972	.473	.836	.127	.376
−.736	.163	.406	.511	.647	.483
			.764	.256	.331

The number of subjects was 350.

(a) Calculate the overall Λ.

(b) What is the χ^2 associated with Λ?

(c) What is the total redundancy: (1) of Set 1 given Set 2; (2) of Set 2 given Set 1?

3. A researcher wishes to study the differences among five groups on ten dependent variables. Assuming that the data are to be subjected to a canonical analysis:

   (a) How many coded vectors are required?

   (b) How many canonical correlations may be obtained in such an analysis?

   (c) Would the overall results obtained in such an analysis differ from those that would be obtained if the data were analyzed via MANOVA?

4. A researcher was interested in studying differences among lower-class, middle-class, and upper-class adolescents in perceptions of their control of their destiny and in their career aspirations. A measure of locus of control and a measure of career aspirations were administered to samples from the three populations. Following are the data (illustrative), where higher scores indicate greater feelings of control and higher career aspirations.

   (a) Do a canonical analysis in which one set of variables consists of the measures of locus of control and career aspirations, and the other set consists of coded vectors representing group membership.

   (b) Do a discriminant analysis of the above data. Plot the centroids and interpret the results. Compare with the results obtained under (a), above.

Lower Class		*Middle Class*		*Upper Class*	
Locus of Control	*Career Aspirations*	*Locus of Control*	*Career Aspirations*	*Locus of Control*	*Career Aspirations*
2	2	3	5	3	6
3	4	5	5	4	6
4	5	5	4	5	6
4	3	6	6	5	6
3	5	5	6	5	5
5	4	4	7	6	7
4	4	7	7	5	6
5	5	6	6	5	7

ANSWERS

1. 4
2. (a) $\Lambda = .382$

   (b) $\chi^2 = 332.01$, with 12 *df*.

   (c) $\overline{Rd}_1 = .299$; $\overline{Rd}_2 = .260$

3. (a) 4
   (b) 4
   (c) No
4. (a) $R^2_{c_1} = .53109$ $R^2_{c_2} = .06593$
   $\Lambda = .43799$ $\chi^2 = 16.92$, with 4 *df*.
   χ^2 for $R^2_{c_2} = 1.40$, with 1 *df*.
   The second canonical correlation is neither statistically significant nor meaningful. Results reported below are associated with $R^2_{c_1}$ only. Canonical weights and structure coefficients are reported for the dependent variables only. LOC = locus of control; ASP = career aspirations. Standardized weights: LOC = .09379; ASP = .94332. Raw weights: LOC = .07957; ASP = .72481. Structure coefficients: LOC = .63405; ASP = .99704. $Rd_1 = .37073$.
   (b) $\lambda_1 = 1.13261$ $\lambda_2 = .07059$
   Tests of significance are the same as under (a), above. $P_1 = .94132$ $(\lambda_1/\Sigma\lambda)$
   Only the first discriminant function is retained.
   $Y = -5.85629 + .11103(\text{LOC}) + 1.01141(\text{ASP})$
   Centroids: Lower = −1.3943. Middle = .52833. Upper = .86597.
   Standardized coefficients: .11838(LOC) + .94609(ASP).
   Note that: (1) ASP makes a greater contribution to the discrimination among the groups than does LOC. (2) From the centroids it is evident that the discrimination is primarily between lower class, on the one hand, and middle and upper class, on the other hand.

APPENDIX A

MATRIX ALGEBRA: AN INTRODUCTION

Matrix algebra is one of the most useful and powerful branches of mathematics for conceptualizing and analyzing psychological, sociological, and educational research data. As research becomes more and more multivariate, the need for a compact method of expressing data becomes greater. Certain problems require that sets of equations and subscripted variables be written. In many cases the use of matrix algebra simplifies and, when familiar, clarifies the mathematics and statistics. In addition, matrix algebra notation and thinking fit in nicely with the conceptualization of computer programming and use.

This chapter provides a brief introduction to matrix algebra. The emphasis is on those aspects that are related to subject matter covered in this book. Thus many matrix algebra techniques, important and useful in other contexts, are omitted. In addition, certain important derivations and proofs are neglected. Although the material presented here should suffice to enable you to follow the applications of matrix algebra in this book, it is strongly suggested that you expand your knowledge of this topic by studying one or more of the following texts: Dorf (1969), Green (1976), Hohn (1964), Horst (1963), and Searle (1966). In addition, you will find good introductions to matrix algebra in the books on multivariate analysis that were cited in Chapter 17.

BASIC DEFINITIONS

A *matrix* is an n-by-k rectangle of numbers or symbols that stand for numbers. The order of the matrix is n by k. It is customary to designate the rows first and the columns second. That is, n is the number of rows of the matrix and k the number of columns. A 2-by-3 matrix called **A** might be

$$\begin{array}{cc} & \begin{array}{ccc} 1 & 2 & 3 \end{array} \\ \mathbf{A} = \begin{array}{c} 1 \\ 2 \end{array} & \begin{bmatrix} 4 & 7 & 5 \\ 6 & 6 & 3 \end{bmatrix} \end{array}$$

Elements of a matrix are identified by reference to the row and column that they occupy. Thus, a_{11} refers to the element of the first row and first column of **A,** which in the above example is 4. Similarly, a_{23} is the element of the second row and third column of **A,** which in the above example is 3. In general, then a_{ij} refers to the element in row i and column j.

The *transpose* of a matrix is obtained simply by exchanging rows and columns. In the present case, the transpose of **A,** written **A**$'$, is

$$\mathbf{A}' = \begin{bmatrix} 4 & 6 \\ 7 & 6 \\ 5 & 3 \end{bmatrix}$$

If $n = k$, the matrix is square. A square matrix can be symmetric or asymmetric. A *symmetric* matrix has the same elements above the principal diagonal as below the diagonal except that they are transposed. The principal diagonal is the set of elements from the upper left corner to the lower right corner. Symmetric matrices are frequently encountered in multiple regression analysis and in multivariate analysis. The following is an example of a correlation matrix, which is symmetric:

$$\mathbf{R} = \begin{bmatrix} 1.00 & .70 & .30 \\ .70 & 1.00 & .40 \\ .30 & .40 & 1.00 \end{bmatrix}$$

Diagonal elements refer to correlations of variables with themselves, hence the 1's. Each off-diagonal element refers to a correlation between two variables and is identified by row and column numbers. Thus, $r_{12} = r_{21} = .70$; $r_{23} = r_{32} = .40$. And similarly for other elements.

A *column vector* is an n-by-1 array of numbers. For example:

$$\mathbf{b} = \begin{bmatrix} 8.0 \\ 1.3 \\ -2.0 \end{bmatrix}$$

A *row vector* is a 1-by-n array of numbers:

$$\mathbf{b}' = [8.0 \quad 1.3 \quad -.20]$$

$\mathbf{b}'$ is the *transpose* of **b.** Note that vectors are designated by lowercase boldface letters, and that a prime is used to indicate a row vector.

A *diagonal* matrix is frequently encountered in statistical work. It is simply a matrix in which some values other than zero are in the principal diagonal of the matrix, and all the off-diagonal elements are zeros. Here is a diagonal matrix:

$$\begin{bmatrix} 2.759 & 0 & 0 \\ 0 & 1.643 & 0 \\ 0 & 0 & .879 \end{bmatrix}$$

A particularly important form of a diagonal matrix is an *identity* matrix, **I,** which has 1's in the principal diagonal:

$$\mathbf{I} = \begin{bmatrix} 1 & 0 & 0 \\ 0 & 1 & 0 \\ 0 & 0 & 1 \end{bmatrix}$$

MATRIX OPERATIONS

The power of matrix algebra becomes apparent when we explore the operations that are possible. The major operations are addition, subtraction, multiplication, and inversion. A large number of statistical operations can be done by knowing the basic rules of matrix algebra. Some matrix operations are now defined and illustrated.

Addition and Subtraction

Two or more vectors can be added or subtracted provided they are of the same dimensionality. That is, they have the same number of elements. The following two vectors are added:

$$\underset{\mathbf{a}}{\begin{bmatrix} 4 \\ 3 \\ 5 \end{bmatrix}} + \underset{\mathbf{b}}{\begin{bmatrix} 7 \\ 7 \\ 4 \end{bmatrix}} = \underset{\mathbf{c}}{\begin{bmatrix} 11 \\ 10 \\ 9 \end{bmatrix}}$$

Similarly, matrices of the same dimensionality may be added or subtracted. The following two 3-by-2 matrices are added:

$$\underset{\mathbf{A}}{\begin{bmatrix} 6 & 4 \\ 5 & 6 \\ 9 & 5 \end{bmatrix}} + \underset{\mathbf{B}}{\begin{bmatrix} 7 & 4 \\ 7 & 4 \\ 1 & 3 \end{bmatrix}} = \underset{\mathbf{C}}{\begin{bmatrix} 13 & 8 \\ 12 & 10 \\ 10 & 8 \end{bmatrix}}$$

Now, **B** is subtracted from **A:**

$$\underset{\mathbf{A}}{\begin{bmatrix} 6 & 4 \\ 5 & 6 \\ 9 & 5 \end{bmatrix}} - \underset{\mathbf{B}}{\begin{bmatrix} 7 & 4 \\ 7 & 4 \\ 1 & 3 \end{bmatrix}} = \underset{\mathbf{C}}{\begin{bmatrix} -1 & 0 \\ -2 & 2 \\ 8 & 2 \end{bmatrix}}$$

Multiplication

To obtain the product of a row vector by a column vector, corresponding elements of each are multiplied and then added. For example, the multiplication of **a**′ by **b,** each consisting of three elements, is:

$$\underset{\mathbf{a}'}{[a_1 \quad a_2 \quad a_3]} \underset{\mathbf{b}}{\begin{bmatrix} b_1 \\ b_2 \\ b_3 \end{bmatrix}} = a_1b_1 + a_2b_2 + a_3b_3$$

Note that the product of a row by a column is a single number called a *scalar*. This is why the product of a row by a column is referred to as the scalar product of vectors.

Here is a numerical example:

$$[4 \quad 1 \quad 3]\begin{bmatrix}1\\2\\5\end{bmatrix} = (4)(1) + (1)(2) + (3)(5) = 21$$

Scalar products of vectors are very frequently used in statistical analysis. For example, to obtain the sum of the elements of a column vector it is premultiplied by a unit row vector of the same dimensionality. Thus,

$$\Sigma X: \qquad [1 \quad 1 \quad 1 \quad 1 \quad 1]\begin{bmatrix}1\\4\\1\\3\\7\end{bmatrix} = 16$$

The sum of the squares of a column vector is obtained by premultiplying the vector by its transpose.

$$\Sigma X^2: \qquad [1 \quad 4 \quad 1 \quad 3 \quad 7]\begin{bmatrix}1\\4\\1\\3\\7\end{bmatrix} = 76$$

Similarly, the sum of the products of X and Y is obtained by multiplying the row of X by the column of Y, or the row of Y by the column of X.

$$\Sigma XY: \qquad [1 \quad 4 \quad 1 \quad 3 \quad 7]\begin{bmatrix}3\\-5\\7\\2\\-1\end{bmatrix} = -11$$

Scalar products of vectors are used frequently in this book, particularly in Chapters 17 and 18.

Instead of multiplying a row vector by a column vector, one may multiply a column vector by a row vector. The two operations are entirely different from each other. It was shown above that the former results in a scalar. The latter operation, on the other hand, results in a matrix. This is why it is referred to as the matrix product of vectors. For example,

$$\begin{bmatrix}3\\-5\\7\\2\\-1\end{bmatrix}[1 \quad 4 \quad 1 \quad 3 \quad 7] = \begin{bmatrix}3 & 12 & 3 & 9 & 21\\-5 & -20 & -5 & -15 & -35\\7 & 28 & 7 & 21 & 49\\2 & 8 & 2 & 6 & 14\\-1 & -4 & -1 & -3 & -7\end{bmatrix}$$

Note that each element of the column is multiplied, in turn, by each element of the row to obtain one element of the matrix. The products of the first element of the column by the row elements become the first row of the matrix. Those of the second element of the column by the row become the second row of the matrix, and so forth. Thus, the matrix product of a column vector of k elements and a row vector of k elements is a $k \times k$ matrix.

Matrix multiplication is done by multiplying rows by columns. An illustration is easier than verbal explanation. Suppose we want to multiply two matrices, **A** and **B,** to produce the product matrix, **C:**

$$\underset{\mathbf{A}}{\begin{bmatrix} 3 & 1 \\ 5 & 1 \\ 2 & 4 \end{bmatrix}} \times \underset{\mathbf{B}}{\begin{bmatrix} 4 & 1 & 4 \\ 5 & 6 & 2 \end{bmatrix}} = \underset{\mathbf{C}}{\begin{bmatrix} 17 & 9 & 14 \\ 25 & 11 & 22 \\ 28 & 26 & 16 \end{bmatrix}}$$

Following the rule of scalar product of vectors, we multiply and add as follows (follow the arrows):

$$\begin{array}{lll} (3)(4) + (1)(5) = 17 & (3)(1) + (1)(6) = 9 & (3)(4) + (1)(2) = 14 \\ (5)(4) + (1)(5) = 25 & (5)(1) + (1)(6) = 11 & (5)(4) + (1)(2) = 22 \\ (2)(4) + (4)(5) = 28 & (2)(1) + (4)(6) = 26 & (2)(4) + (4)(2) = 16 \end{array}$$

From the foregoing illustration it may be discerned that in order to multiply two matrices it is necessary that the number of columns of the first matrix be equal to the number of rows of the second matrix. This is referred to as the *conformability* condition. Thus, for example, an n-by-k matrix can be multiplied by a k-by-m matrix because the number of columns of the first (k) is equal to the number of rows of the second (k). In this context, the k's are referred to as the "interior" dimensions; n and m are referred to as the "exterior" dimensions.

Two matrices are conformable when they have the same "interior" dimensions. There are no restrictions on the "exterior" dimensions when two matrices are multiplied. It is useful to note that the "exterior" dimensions of two matrices being multiplied become the dimensions of the product matrix. For example, when a 3-by-2 matrix is multiplied by a 2-by-5 matrix, a 3-by-5 matrix is obtained:

$$(3\text{-by-}2) \times (2\text{-by-}5) = (3\text{-by-}5)$$

In general,

$$(n\text{-by-}k) \times (k\text{-by-}m) = (n\text{-by-}m)$$

A special case of matrix multiplication often encountered in statistical work is the multiplication of a matrix by its transpose to obtain a matrix of raw score, or deviation, Sums of Squares and Cross Products (SSCP). Assume that there are n subjects for whom measures on k variables are available. In other words, assume that the data matrix, **X**, is an n-by-k. To obtain the raw score SSCP calculate **X′X**. Here is a numerical example:

$$\underset{\mathbf{X}'}{k\overset{n}{\begin{bmatrix} 1 & 4 & 1 & 3 & 7 \\ 2 & 3 & 3 & 4 & 6 \\ 2 & 5 & 1 & 3 & 5 \end{bmatrix}}} \; \underset{\mathbf{X}}{n\overset{k}{\begin{bmatrix} 1 & 2 & 2 \\ 4 & 3 & 5 \\ 1 & 3 & 1 \\ 3 & 4 & 3 \\ 7 & 6 & 5 \end{bmatrix}}} = \underset{\mathbf{X}'\mathbf{X}}{\begin{bmatrix} 76 & 71 & 67 \\ 71 & 74 & 64 \\ 67 & 64 & 64 \end{bmatrix}}$$

In statistical symbols, **X′X** is

$$\Sigma X_i X_j = \begin{bmatrix} \Sigma X_1^2 & \Sigma X_1 X_2 & \Sigma X_1 X_3 \\ \Sigma X_2 X_1 & \Sigma X_2^2 & \Sigma X_2 X_3 \\ \Sigma X_3 X_1 & \Sigma X_3 X_2 & \Sigma X_3^2 \end{bmatrix}$$

Using similar operations one may obtain deviation SSCP matrices. Such matrices are used frequently in this book (see, in particular, Chapters 4, 17, and 18).

A matrix can be multipled by a scalar: each element of the matrix is multiplied by the scalar. Suppose, for example, we want to calculate the mean of each of the elements of a matrix of sums of scores. Let $N = 10$. The operation is

$$\frac{1}{10}\begin{bmatrix} 20 & 48 \\ 30 & 40 \\ 35 & 39 \end{bmatrix} = \begin{bmatrix} 2.0 & 4.8 \\ 3.0 & 4.0 \\ 3.5 & 3.9 \end{bmatrix}$$

Each element of the matrix is multiplied by the scalar $^1/_{10}$.

A matrix can be multiplied by a vector. The first example given below is premultiplication by a vector, the second is postmultiplication:

$$[6 \quad 5 \quad 2]\begin{bmatrix} 7 & 3 \\ 7 & 2 \\ 4 & 1 \end{bmatrix} = [85 \quad 30]$$

$$\begin{bmatrix} 7 & 7 & 4 \\ 3 & 2 & 1 \end{bmatrix}\begin{bmatrix} 6 \\ 5 \\ 2 \end{bmatrix} = \begin{bmatrix} 85 \\ 30 \end{bmatrix}$$

Note that in the latter example, (2-by-3) × (3-by-1) becomes (2-by-1). This sort of multiplication of a matrix by a vector is done frequently in multiple regression analysis (see, for example, Chapter 4).

Thus far, nothing has been said about the operation of division in matrix algebra. In order to show how this is done it is necessary first to discuss some other concepts, to which we now turn.

DETERMINANTS

A *determinant* is a certain numerical value associated with a square matrix. The determinant of a matrix is indicated by vertical lines instead of brackets. For example, the determinant of a matrix **B** is written

$$\det \mathbf{B} = |\mathbf{B}| = \underset{\mathbf{B}}{\begin{vmatrix} 4 & 2 \\ 1 & 5 \end{vmatrix}}$$

The calculation of the determinant of a 2 × 2 matrix is very simple: it is the product of the elements of the principal diagonal minus the product of the remaining two elements. For the above matrix,

$$|\mathbf{B}| = \begin{vmatrix} 4 & 2 \\ 1 & 5 \end{vmatrix} = (4)(5) - (1)(2) = 20 - 2 = \mathit{18}$$

or, symbolically,

$$|\mathbf{B}| = \begin{vmatrix} b_{11} & b_{12} \\ b_{21} & b_{22} \end{vmatrix} = b_{11}b_{22} - b_{12}b_{21}$$

The calculation of determinants for larger matrices is quite tedious, and will not be shown here (see references cited in the beginning of the chapter). In any event, matrix operations are most often done with the aid of a computer. The purpose here is solely to indicate the role played by determinants in some applications of statistical analysis.

Applications of Determinants

To give the flavor of the place and usefulness of determinants in statistical analysis, we turn first to two simple correlation examples. Suppose we have two correlation coefficients, r_{y1} and r_{y2}, calculated between a dependent variable, Y, and two variables, 1 and 2. The correlations are $r_{y1} = .80$ and $r_{y2} = .20$. We set up two matrices that express the two relations, but this is done immediately in the form of determinants, whose numerical values are calculated:

$$\begin{array}{cc} 1 & y \end{array}$$
$$\begin{vmatrix} 1.00 & .80 \\ .80 & 1.00 \end{vmatrix} = (1.00)(1.00) - (.80)(.80) = \mathit{.36}$$

and

$$\begin{array}{cc} 2 & y \\ \end{array}$$
$$\begin{vmatrix} 1.00 & .20 \\ .20 & 1.00 \end{vmatrix} = (1.00)(1.00) - (.20)(.20) = .96$$

The two determinants are .36 and .96.

Now, to determine the percentage of variance shared by y and 1 and by y and 2, square the r's:

$$r^2_{y1} = (.80)^2 = .64$$

$$r^2_{y2} = (.20)^2 = .04$$

Subtract each of these from 1.00: 1.00 − .64 = *.36*, and 1.00 − .04 = *.96*. These are the determinants just calculated. They are $1 - r^2$, or the proportions of the variance not accounted for.

As an extension of the foregoing demonstration, it may be shown how the squared multiple correlation, R^2, can be calculated with determinants:

$$R^2_{y.12...k} = 1 - \frac{|\mathbf{R}|}{|\mathbf{R}_x|}$$

where $|\mathbf{R}|$ is the determinant of the correlation matrix of al the variables, that is, the independent variables as well as the dependent variable; $|\mathbf{R}_x|$ is the determinant of the correlation matrix of the independent variables. From the foregoing it can be seen that the ratio of the two determinants indicates the proportion of variance of the dependent variable, Y, *not* accounted by the independent variables, X's. (See Study Suggestions 6 and 7 at the end of this Appendix.)

The ratio of two determinants is also frequently used in multivariate analyses (see the sections of Chapters 17 and 18 dealing with Wilks' Λ).

Another important use of determinants is related to the concept of linear dependencies, to which we now turn.

Linear Dependence

Linear dependence means that one or more vectors of a matrix, rows or columns, are a linear combination of other vectors of the matrix. The vectors $\mathbf{a}' = [3 \quad 1 \quad 4]$ and $\mathbf{b}' = [6 \quad 2 \quad 8]$ are dependent since $2\mathbf{a}' = \mathbf{b}'$. If one vector is a function of another in this manner, the coefficient of correlation between them is 1.00. Dependence in a matrix can be defined by reference to its determinant. If the determinant of the matrix is zero it means that the matrix contains at least one linear dependency. Such a matrix is referred to as being *singular*. For example, calculate the determinant of the following matrix:

$$\begin{vmatrix} 3 & 1 \\ 6 & 2 \end{vmatrix} = (3)(2) - (1)(6) = 0$$

The matrix is singular, that is, it contains a linear dependency. Note that the values of the second row are twice the values of the first row.

A matrix whose determinant is not equal to zero is referred to as being *nonsingular*. The notions of singularity and nonsingularity of matrices play very important roles in statistical analysis. For example, in Chapter 8 issues regarding multicollinearity are discussed in reference to the determinant of the correlation matrix of the independent variables. As is shown below, a singular matrix has no inverse.

We turn now to the operation of division in matrix algebra, which is presented in the context of the discussion of matrix inversion.

MATRIX INVERSE

Recall that the division of one number into another number amounts to multiplying the dividend by the reciprocal of the divisor:

$$\frac{a}{b} = \frac{1}{b} a$$

For example, 12/4 = 12(1/4) = (12)(.25) = 3. Analogously, in matrix algebra, instead of dividing a matrix **A** by another matrix **B** to obtain matrix **C,** we multiply **A** by the *inverse* of **B** to obtain **C.** The inverse of **B** is written $\mathbf{B}^{-1}$. Suppose, in ordinary algebra, we had $ab = c$, and we wanted to find b. We would write

$$b = \frac{c}{a}$$

In matrix algebra, we write

$$\mathbf{B} = \mathbf{A}^{-1}\mathbf{C}$$

(Note that **C** is premultiplied by $\mathbf{A}^{-1}$ and not postmultiplied. In general, $\mathbf{A}^{-1}\mathbf{C} \neq \mathbf{C}\mathbf{A}^{-1}$.)

The formal definition of the inverse of a square matrix is: Given **A** and **B,** two square matrices, if $\mathbf{AB} = \mathbf{I}$, then **A** is the inverse of **B.**

Generally, the calculation of the inverse of a matrix is very laborious and, therefore, error prone. This is why it is best to use a computer program for such purposes (see below). Fortunately, however, the calculation of the inverse of a 2 × 2 matrix is very simple, and is shown here because: (1) it affords an illustration of the basic approach to the calculation of the inverse; (2) it affords the opportunity of showing the role played by the determinant in the calculation of the inverse; (3) inverses of 2 × 2 matrices are frequently calculated in some chapters of this book (see, in particular, Chapters 4, 17, and 18).

In order to show how the inverse of a 2 × 2 matrix is calculated it is necessary first to discuss briefly the *adjoint* of a such a matrix. This is shown in reference to the following matrix:

$$\mathbf{A} = \begin{bmatrix} a & b \\ c & d \end{bmatrix}$$

The adjoint of **A** is:

$$\text{adj } \mathbf{A} = \begin{bmatrix} d & -b \\ -c & a \end{bmatrix}$$

Thus, to obtain the adjoint of a 2 × 2 matrix interchange the elements of its principal diagonal (a and d in the above example), and change the signs of the other two elements (b and c in the above example).[1]

Now the inverse of a matrix **A** is:

$$\mathbf{A}^{-1} = \frac{\text{adj } \mathbf{A}}{|\mathbf{A}|} = \frac{1}{|\mathbf{A}|} \text{adj } \mathbf{A}$$

where $|\mathbf{A}|$ is the determinant of **A.**

The inverse of the following matrix, **A,** is now calculated.

$$\mathbf{A} = \begin{bmatrix} 6 & 2 \\ 8 & 4 \end{bmatrix}$$

First, calculate the determinant of **A:**

$$|\mathbf{A}| = \begin{vmatrix} 6 & 2 \\ 8 & 4 \end{vmatrix} = (6)(4) - (2)(8) = 8$$

Second, form the adjoint of **A:**

$$\text{adj } \mathbf{A} = \begin{bmatrix} 4 & -2 \\ -8 & 6 \end{bmatrix}$$

Third, multiply the adj **A** by the reciprocal of $|\mathbf{A}|$ to obtain the inverse of **A:**

$$\mathbf{A}^{-1} = \frac{1}{|\mathbf{A}|} \text{adj } \mathbf{A} = \frac{1}{8} \begin{bmatrix} 4 & -2 \\ -8 & 6 \end{bmatrix} = \begin{bmatrix} .50 & -.25 \\ -1.00 & .75 \end{bmatrix}$$

[1]For a general definition of the adjoint of a matrix, see references cited in the beginning of this chapter. Adjoints of 2 × 2 matrices are used frequently in Chapters 17 and 18.

It was said above that $\mathbf{A}^{-1}\mathbf{A} = \mathbf{I}$. For the present example,

$$\mathbf{A}^{-1}\mathbf{A} = \underset{\mathbf{A}^{-1}}{\begin{bmatrix} .50 & -.25 \\ -1.00 & .75 \end{bmatrix}} \underset{\mathbf{A}}{\begin{bmatrix} 6 & 2 \\ 8 & 4 \end{bmatrix}} = \underset{\mathbf{I}}{\begin{bmatrix} 1.00 & 0 \\ 0 & 1.00 \end{bmatrix}}$$

It was said above that a matrix whose determinant is zero is singular. From the foregoing demonstration of the calculation of the inverse it should be clear that a singular matrix has no inverse. Although one does not generally encounter singular matrices in social science research, an unwary researcher may introduce singularity in the treatment of the data. For example, suppose that a test battery consisting of five subtests is used to predict a given criterion. If, under such circumstances, the researcher uses not only the scores on the five subtests but also a total score, obtained as the sum of the five subscores, he or she has introduced a linear dependency (see above), thereby rendering the matrix singular. Similarly, when one uses scores on two scales as well as the differences between them in the same matrix. Other situations when one should be on guard not to introduce linear dependencies in a matrix occur when coded vectors are used to represent categorical variables (see Chapter 9).

CONCLUSION

It is realized that this brief introduction to matrix algebra cannot serve to demonstrate its great power and elegance. To do this, it would be necessary to use matrices whose dimensions are larger than the ones used here for simplicity of presentation. To begin to appreciate the power of matrix algebra it is suggested that you think of the large data matrices frequently encountered in behavioral research. Using matrix algebra one can manipulate and operate upon large matrices with relative ease, when ordinary algebra will simply not do. For example, when in multiple regression analysis only two independent variables are used, it is relatively easy to do the calculations by ordinary algebra (see Chapter 3). But with increasing numbers of independent variables, the use of matrix algebra for the calculation of multiple regression analysis becomes a must. And, as is amply demonstrated in Parts 3 and 4 of this book, matrix algebra is the language of linear structural equation models and multivariate analysis. In short, to understand and be able to intelligently apply these methods it is essential that you develop a working knowledge of matrix algebra. It is therefore strongly suggested that you do some or all the calculations of the matrix operations presented in the various chapters, particularly those in Chapter 4, and in Parts 3 and 4 of the book. Furthermore, it is suggested that you learn to use computer programs when you have to manipulate relatively large matrices. Of the various computer programs for matrix manipulations, one of the best and most versatile is the MATRIX program of the SAS package. Examples of applications of this program are given in Chapters 8 and 15.

STUDY SUGGESTIONS

1. You will find it useful to work through some of the rules of matrix algebra. Use of the rules occurs again and again in multiple regression, factor analysis, discriminant analysis, canonical correlation, and multivariate analysis of variance. The most important of the rules are as follows:

(1) $\mathbf{ABC} = (\mathbf{AB})\mathbf{C} = \mathbf{A}(\mathbf{BC})$

This is the *associative rule* of matrix multiplication. It simply indicates that the multiplication of three (or more) matrices can be done by pairing and multiplying the first two matrices and then multiplying the product by the remaining matrix, or by pairing and multiplying the second two and then multiplying the product by the first matrix. Or we can regard the rule in the following way:

$$\mathbf{AB} = \mathbf{D}, \text{ then } \mathbf{DC}$$
$$\mathbf{BC} = \mathbf{E}, \text{ then } \mathbf{AE}$$

(2) $\mathbf{A} + \mathbf{B} = \mathbf{B} + \mathbf{A}$

That is, the order of addition makes no difference. And the associative rule applies:

$$\mathbf{A} + \mathbf{B} + \mathbf{C} = (\mathbf{A} + \mathbf{B}) + \mathbf{C} = \mathbf{A} + (\mathbf{B} + \mathbf{C})$$

(3) $\mathbf{A}(\mathbf{B} + \mathbf{C}) = \mathbf{AB} + \mathbf{AC}$

This is the *distributive rule* of ordinary algebra.

(4) $(\mathbf{AB})' = \mathbf{B}'\mathbf{A}'$

The transpose of the product of two matrices is equal to the transpose of their product in reverse order.

(5) $(\mathbf{AB})^{-1} = \mathbf{B}^{-1}\mathbf{A}^{-1}$

This rule is the same as that in (4), above, except that it is applied to matrix inverses.

(6) $\mathbf{AA}^{-1} = \mathbf{A}^{-1}\mathbf{A} = \mathbf{I}$

This rule can be used as a proof that the calculation of the inverse of a matrix is correct.

(7) $\mathbf{AB} \neq \mathbf{BA}$

This is actually not a rule. It is included to emphasize that the order of the multiplication of matrices is important.

Here are three matrices, **A, B,** and **C.**

$$\underset{\mathbf{A}}{\begin{pmatrix} 2 & 3 \\ 1 & 2 \end{pmatrix}} \quad \underset{\mathbf{B}}{\begin{pmatrix} 3 & 4 \\ 0 & 1 \end{pmatrix}} \quad \underset{\mathbf{C}}{\begin{pmatrix} 0 & 2 \\ 5 & 3 \end{pmatrix}}$$

(a) Demonstrate the associative rule by multiplying:

$$\mathbf{A} \times \mathbf{B}; \text{ then } \mathbf{AB} \times \mathbf{C}$$
$$\mathbf{B} \times \mathbf{C}; \text{ then } \mathbf{A} \times \mathbf{BC}$$

(b) Demonstrate the distributive rule using **A, B,** and **C** of (a), above.

(c) Using **B** and **C**, above, show that $\mathbf{BC} \neq \mathbf{CB}$.

2. What are the dimensions of the matrix that will result from multiplying a 3-by-6 matrix **A** by a 6-by-2 matrix **B?**
3. Given:

$$\mathbf{A} = \begin{bmatrix} 1.26 & -.73 \\ 2.12 & 1.34 \\ 4.61 & -.31 \end{bmatrix} \quad \mathbf{B} = \begin{bmatrix} 4.11 & 1.12 \\ \\ -2.30 & -.36 \end{bmatrix}$$

What is **AB?**

4. When it is said that a matrix is singular, what does it imply about its determinant?
5. Calculate the inverse of the following matrix:

$$\begin{bmatrix} 15 & -3 \\ 6 & 12 \end{bmatrix}$$

6. In a study of Holtzman and Brown (1968), the correlations among measures of study habits and attitudes, scholastic aptitude, and grade-point averages were reported as follows:

	SHA	SA	GPA
SHA	1.00	.32	.55
SA	.32	1.00	.61
GPA	.55	.61	1.00

The determinant of this matrix is .4377. Calculate R^2 for GPA with SHA and SA. (*Hint:* You need to calculate the determinant of the matrix of the independent variables, and then use the two determinants for the calculation of R^2.)

7. Liddle (1958) reported the following correlations among intellectual ability, leadership ability, and withdrawn maladjustment:

	IA	LA	WM
IA	1.00	.37	−.28
LA	.37	1.00	−.61
WM	−.28	−.61	1.00

The determinant of this matrix is .5390. Calculate:

(a) the proportion of variance of WM *not* accounted for by IA and LA.

(b) R^2 of WM with IA and LA.

(c) using matrix algebra, the regression equation of WM on IA and LA. (See Chapter 4 for matrix equation.)

8. It is strongly suggested that you study one or more of the references cited in the beginning of this Appendix.

ANSWERS

1. (a)

$$\mathbf{ABC} = \begin{bmatrix} 55 & 45 \\ 30 & 24 \end{bmatrix}$$

(b)

$$\mathbf{A(B + C)} = \begin{bmatrix} 21 & 24 \\ 13 & 14 \end{bmatrix}$$

(c)

$$\mathbf{BC} = \begin{bmatrix} 20 & 18 \\ 5 & 3 \end{bmatrix} \qquad \mathbf{CB} = \begin{bmatrix} 0 & 2 \\ 15 & 23 \end{bmatrix}$$

2. 3-by-2

3.

$$\mathbf{AB} = \begin{bmatrix} 6.8576 & 1.6740 \\ 5.6312 & 1.8920 \\ 19.6601 & 5.2748 \end{bmatrix}$$

4. The determinant is zero.

5.

$$\begin{bmatrix} .06061 & .01515 \\ -.03030 & .07576 \end{bmatrix}$$

6. The determinant of the matrix of the independent variables is .8976.

$$R^2 = 1 - \frac{.4377}{.8976} = .5124$$

7. (a) .62449
   (b) .37551
   (c)

$$\boldsymbol{\beta} = \mathbf{R}^{-1}\mathbf{r} = \begin{bmatrix} -.06291 \\ \\ -.58672 \end{bmatrix}$$

APPENDIX B

TABLES OF F, CHI SQUARED DISTRIBUTIONS, AND ORTHOGONAL POLYNOMIALS

The 5 (Roman Type) and 1 (Boldface Type) Percent Points for the Distribution of F*

n_2	n_1 degrees of freedom (for greater mean square)																					
	1	2	3	4	5	6	7	8	9	10	11	12	14	16	20	24	30	40	50	75	100	200	500	∞
1	161	200	216	225	230	234	237	239	241	242	243	244	245	246	248	249	250	251	252	253	253	254	254	254
	4,052	**4,999**	**5,403**	**5,625**	**5,764**	**5,859**	**5,928**	**5,981**	**6,022**	**6,056**	**6,082**	**6,106**	**6,142**	**6,169**	**6,208**	**6,234**	**6,258**	**6,286**	**6,302**	**6,323**	**6,334**	**6,352**	**6,361**	**6,366**
2	18.51	19.00	19.16	19.25	19.30	19.33	19.36	19.37	19.38	19.39	19.40	19.41	19.42	19.43	19.44	19.45	19.46	19.47	19.47	19.48	19.49	19.49	19.50	19.50
	98.49	**99.00**	**99.17**	**99.25**	**99.30**	**99.33**	**99.34**	**99.36**	**99.38**	**99.40**	**99.41**	**99.42**	**99.43**	**99.44**	**99.45**	**99.46**	**99.47**	**99.48**	**99.48**	**99.49**	**99.49**	**99.49**	**99.50**	**99.50**
3	10.13	9.55	9.28	9.12	9.01	8.94	8.88	8.84	8.81	8.78	8.76	8.74	8.71	8.69	8.66	8.64	8.62	8.60	8.58	8.57	8.56	8.54	8.54	8.53
	34.12	**30.82**	**29.46**	**28.71**	**28.24**	**27.91**	**27.67**	**27.49**	**27.34**	**27.23**	**27.13**	**27.05**	**26.92**	**26.83**	**26.69**	**26.60**	**26.50**	**26.41**	**26.35**	**26.27**	**26.23**	**26.18**	**26.14**	**26.12**
4	7.71	6.94	6.59	6.39	6.26	6.16	6.09	6.04	6.00	5.96	5.93	5.91	5.87	5.84	5.80	5.77	5.74	5.71	5.70	5.68	5.66	5.65	5.64	5.63
	21.20	**18.00**	**16.69**	**15.98**	**15.52**	**15.21**	**14.98**	**14.80**	**14.66**	**14.54**	**14.45**	**14.37**	**14.24**	**14.15**	**14.02**	**13.93**	**13.83**	**13.74**	**13.69**	**13.61**	**13.57**	**13.52**	**13.48**	**13.46**
5	6.61	5.79	5.41	5.19	5.05	4.95	4.88	4.82	4.78	4.74	4.70	4.68	4.64	4.60	4.56	4.53	4.50	4.46	4.44	4.42	4.40	4.38	4.37	4.36
	16.26	**13.27**	**12.06**	**11.39**	**10.97**	**10.67**	**10.45**	**10.27**	**10.15**	**10.05**	**9.96**	**9.89**	**9.77**	**9.68**	**9.55**	**9.47**	**9.38**	**9.29**	**9.24**	**9.17**	**9.13**	**9.07**	**9.04**	**9.02**
6	5.99	5.14	4.76	4.53	4.39	4.28	4.21	4.15	4.10	4.06	4.03	4.00	3.96	3.92	3.87	3.84	3.81	3.77	3.75	3.72	3.71	3.69	3.68	3.67
	13.74	**10.92**	**9.78**	**9.15**	**8.75**	**8.47**	**8.26**	**8.10**	**7.98**	**7.87**	**7.79**	**7.72**	**7.60**	**7.52**	**7.39**	**7.31**	**7.23**	**7.14**	**7.09**	**7.02**	**6.99**	**6.94**	**6.90**	**6.88**
7	5.59	4.74	4.35	4.12	3.97	3.87	3.79	3.73	3.68	3.63	3.60	3.57	3.52	3.49	3.44	3.41	3.38	3.34	3.32	3.29	3.28	3.25	3.24	3.23
	12.25	**9.55**	**8.45**	**7.85**	**7.46**	**7.19**	**7.00**	**6.84**	**6.71**	**6.62**	**6.54**	**6.47**	**6.35**	**6.27**	**6.15**	**6.07**	**5.98**	**5.90**	**5.85**	**5.78**	**5.75**	**5.70**	**5.67**	**5.65**
8	5.32	4.46	4.07	3.84	3.69	3.58	3.50	3.44	3.39	3.34	3.31	3.28	3.23	3.20	3.15	3.12	3.08	3.05	3.03	3.00	2.98	2.96	2.94	2.93
	11.26	**8.65**	**7.59**	**7.01**	**6.63**	**6.37**	**6.19**	**6.03**	**5.91**	**5.82**	**5.74**	**5.67**	**5.56**	**5.48**	**5.36**	**5.28**	**5.20**	**5.11**	**5.06**	**5.00**	**4.96**	**4.91**	**4.88**	**4.86**
9	5.12	4.26	3.86	3.63	5.48	3.37	3.29	3.23	3.18	3.13	3.10	3.07	3.02	2.98	2.93	2.90	2.86	2.82	2.80	2.77	2.76	2.73	2.72	2.71
	10.56	**8.02**	**6.99**	**6.42**	**6.06**	**5.80**	**5.62**	**5.47**	**5.35**	**5.26**	**5.18**	**5.11**	**5.00**	**4.92**	**4.80**	**4.73**	**4.64**	**4.56**	**4.51**	**4.45**	**4.41**	**4.36**	**4.33**	**4.31**
10	4.96	4.10	3.71	3.48	3.33	3.22	3.14	3.07	3.02	2.97	2.94	2.91	2.86	2.82	2.77	2.74	2.70	2.67	2.64	2.61	2.59	2.56	2.55	2.54
	10.04	**7.56**	**6.55**	**5.99**	**5.64**	**5.39**	**5.21**	**5.06**	**4.95**	**4.85**	**4.78**	**4.71**	**4.60**	**4.52**	**4.41**	**4.33**	**4.25**	**4.17**	**4.12**	**4.05**	**4.01**	**3.96**	**3.93**	**3.91**
11	4.84	3.98	3.59	3.36	3.20	3.09	3.01	2.95	2.90	2.86	2.82	2.79	2.74	2.70	2.65	2.61	2.57	2.53	2.50	2.47	2.45	2.42	2.41	2.40
	9.65	**7.20**	**6.22**	**5.67**	**5.32**	**5.07**	**4.88**	**4.74**	**4.63**	**4.54**	**4.46**	**4.40**	**4.29**	**4.21**	**4.10**	**4.02**	**3.94**	**3.86**	**3.80**	**3.74**	**3.70**	**3.66**	**3.62**	**3.60**
12	4.75	3.88	3.49	3.26	3.11	3.00	2.92	2.85	2.80	2.76	2.72	2.69	2.64	2.60	2.54	2.50	2.46	2.42	2.40	2.36	2.35	2.32	2.31	2.30
	9.33	**6.93**	**5.95**	**5.41**	**5.06**	**4.82**	**4.65**	**4.50**	**4.39**	**4.30**	**4.22**	**4.16**	**4.05**	**3.98**	**3.86**	**3.78**	**3.70**	**3.61**	**3.56**	**3.49**	**3.46**	**3.41**	**3.38**	**3.36**
13	4.67	3.80	3.41	3.18	3.02	2.92	2.84	2.77	2.72	2.67	2.63	2.60	2.55	2.51	2.46	2.42	2.38	2.34	2.32	2.28	2.26	2.24	2.22	2.21
	9.07	**6.70**	**5.74**	**5.20**	**4.86**	**4.62**	**4.44**	**4.30**	**4.19**	**4.10**	**4.02**	**3.96**	**3.85**	**3.78**	**3.67**	**3.59**	**3.51**	**3.42**	**3.37**	**3.30**	**3.27**	**3.21**	**3.18**	**3.16**

*Reproduced from Snedecor *Statistical Methods*, Iowa State College Press, Ames, Iowa, by permission of the author and publisher.

The 5 (Roman Type) and 1 (Boldface Type) Percent Points for the Distribution of F*—Continued

n_2	n_1 degrees of freedom (for greater mean square)																							
	1	2	3	4	5	6	7	8	9	10	11	12	14	16	20	24	30	40	50	75	100	200	500	∞
14	4.60	3.74	3.34	3.11	2.96	2.85	2.77	2.70	2.65	2.60	2.56	2.53	2.48	2.44	2.39	2.35	2.31	2.27	2.24	2.21	2.19	2.16	2.14	2.13
	8.86	**6.51**	**5.56**	**5.03**	**4.69**	**4.46**	**4.28**	**4.14**	**4.03**	**3.94**	**3.86**	**3.80**	**3.70**	**3.62**	**3.51**	**3.43**	**3.34**	**3.26**	**3.21**	**3.14**	**3.11**	**3.06**	**3.02**	**3.00**
15	4.54	3.68	3.29	3.06	2.90	2.79	2.70	2.64	2.59	2.55	2.51	2.48	2.43	2.39	2.33	2.29	2.25	2.21	2.18	2.15	2.12	2.10	2.08	2.07
	8.68	**6.36**	**5.42**	**4.89**	**4.56**	**4.32**	**4.14**	**4.00**	**3.89**	**3.80**	**3.73**	**3.67**	**3.56**	**3.48**	**3.36**	**3.29**	**3.20**	**3.12**	**3.07**	**3.00**	**2.97**	**2.92**	**2.89**	**2.87**
16	4.49	3.63	3.24	3.01	2.85	2.74	2.66	2.59	2.54	2.49	2.45	2.42	2.37	2.33	2.28	2.24	2.20	2.16	2.13	2.09	2.07	2.04	2.02	2.01
	8.53	**6.23**	**5.29**	**4.77**	**4.44**	**4.20**	**4.03**	**3.89**	**3.78**	**3.69**	**3.61**	**3.55**	**3.45**	**3.37**	**3.25**	**3.18**	**3.10**	**3.01**	**2.96**	**2.89**	**2.86**	**2.80**	**2.77**	**2.75**
17	4.45	3.59	3.20	2.96	2.81	2.70	2.62	2.55	2.50	2.45	2.41	2.38	2.33	2.29	2.23	2.19	2.15	2.11	2.08	2.04	2.02	1.99	1.97	1.96
	8.40	**6.11**	**5.18**	**4.67**	**4.34**	**4.10**	**3.93**	**3.79**	**3.68**	**3.59**	**3.52**	**3.45**	**3.35**	**3.27**	**3.16**	**3.08**	**3.00**	**2.92**	**2.86**	**2.79**	**2.76**	**2.70**	**2.67**	**2.65**
18	4.41	3.55	3.16	2.93	2.77	2.66	2.58	2.51	2.46	2.41	2.37	2.34	2.29	2.25	2.19	2.15	2.11	2.07	2.04	2.00	1.98	1.95	1.93	1.92
	8.28	**6.01**	**5.09**	**4.58**	**4.25**	**4.01**	**3.85**	**3.71**	**3.60**	**3.51**	**3.44**	**3.37**	**3.27**	**3.19**	**3.07**	**3.00**	**2.91**	**2.83**	**2.78**	**2.71**	**2.68**	**2.62**	**2.59**	**2.57**
19	4.38	3.52	3.13	2.90	2.74	2.63	2.55	2.48	2.43	2.38	2.34	2.31	2.26	2.21	2.15	2.11	2.07	2.02	2.00	1.96	1.94	1.91	1.90	1.88
	8.18	**5.93**	**5.01**	**4.50**	**4.17**	**3.94**	**3.77**	**3.63**	**3.52**	**3.43**	**3.36**	**3.30**	**3.19**	**3.12**	**3.00**	**2.92**	**2.84**	**2.76**	**2.70**	**2.63**	**2.60**	**2.54**	**2.51**	**2.49**
20	4.35	3.49	3.10	2.87	2.71	2.60	2.52	2.45	2.40	2.35	2.31	2.28	2.23	2.18	2.12	2.08	2.04	1.99	1.96	1.92	1.90	1.87	1.85	1.84
	8.10	**5.85**	**4.94**	**4.43**	**4.10**	**3.87**	**3.71**	**3.56**	**3.45**	**3.37**	**3.30**	**3.23**	**3.13**	**3.05**	**2.94**	**2.86**	**2.77**	**2.69**	**2.63**	**2.56**	**2.53**	**2.47**	**2.44**	**2.42**
21	4.32	3.47	3.07	2.84	2.68	2.57	2.49	2.42	2.37	2.32	2.28	2.25	2.20	2.15	2.09	2.05	2.00	1.96	1.93	1.89	1.87	1.84	1.82	1.81
	8.02	**5.78**	**4.87**	**4.37**	**4.04**	**3.81**	**3.65**	**3.51**	**3.40**	**3.31**	**3.24**	**3.17**	**3.07**	**2.99**	**2.88**	**2.80**	**2.72**	**2.63**	**2.58**	**2.51**	**2.47**	**2.42**	**2.38**	**2.36**
22	4.30	3.44	3.05	2.82	2.66	2.55	2.47	2.40	2.35	2.30	2.26	2.23	2.18	2.13	2.07	2.03	1.98	1.93	1.91	1.87	1.84	1.81	1.80	1.78
	7.94	**5.72**	**4.82**	**4.31**	**3.99**	**3.76**	**3.59**	**3.45**	**3.35**	**3.26**	**3.18**	**3.12**	**3.02**	**2.94**	**2.83**	**2.75**	**2.67**	**2.58**	**2.53**	**2.46**	**2.42**	**2.37**	**2.33**	**2.31**
23	4.28	3.42	3.03	2.80	2.64	2.53	2.45	2.38	2.32	2.28	2.24	2.20	2.14	2.10	2.04	2.00	1.96	1.91	1.88	1.84	1.82	1.79	1.77	1.76
	7.88	**5.66**	**4.76**	**4.26**	**3.94**	**3.71**	**3.54**	**3.41**	**3.30**	**3.21**	**3.14**	**3.07**	**2.97**	**2.89**	**2.78**	**2.70**	**2.62**	**2.53**	**2.48**	**2.41**	**2.37**	**2.32**	**2.28**	**2.26**
24	4.26	3.40	3.01	2.78	2.62	2.51	2.43	2.36	2.30	2.26	2.22	2.18	2.13	2.09	2.02	1.98	1.94	1.89	1.86	1.82	1.80	1.76	1.74	1.73
	7.82	**5.61**	**4.72**	**4.22**	**3.90**	**3.67**	**3.50**	**3.36**	**3.25**	**3.17**	**3.09**	**3.03**	**2.93**	**2.85**	**2.74**	**2.66**	**2.58**	**2.49**	**2.44**	**2.36**	**2.33**	**2.27**	**2.23**	**2.21**
25	4.24	3.38	2.99	2.76	2.60	2.49	2.41	2.34	2.28	2.24	2.20	2.16	2.11	2.06	2.00	1.96	1.92	1.87	1.84	1.80	1.77	1.74	1.72	1.71
	7.77	**5.57**	**4.68**	**4.18**	**3.86**	**3.63**	**3.46**	**3.32**	**3.21**	**3.13**	**3.05**	**2.99**	**2.89**	**2.81**	**2.70**	**2.62**	**2.54**	**2.45**	**2.40**	**2.32**	**2.29**	**2.23**	**2.19**	**2.17**
26	4.22	3.37	2.98	2.74	2.59	2.47	2.39	2.32	2.27	2.22	2.18	2.15	2.10	2.05	1.99	1.95	1.90	1.85	1.82	1.78	1.76	1.72	1.70	1.69
	7.72	**5.53**	**4.64**	**4.14**	**3.82**	**3.59**	**3.42**	**3.29**	**3.17**	**3.09**	**3.02**	**2.96**	**2.86**	**2.77**	**2.66**	**2.58**	**2.50**	**2.41**	**2.36**	**2.28**	**2.25**	**2.19**	**2.15**	**2.13**

*Reproduced from Snedecor: *Statistical Methods*, Iowa State College Press, Ames, Iowa, by permission of the author and publisher.

The 5 (Roman Type) and 1 (Boldface Type) Percent Points for the Distribution of F*—Continued

n_2	n_1 degrees of freedom (for greater mean square): 1	2	3	4	5	6	7	8	9	10	11	12	14	16	20	24	30	40	50	75	100	200	500	∞
27	4.21	3.35	2.96	2.73	2.57	2.46	2.37	2.30	2.25	2.20	2.16	2.13	2.08	2.03	1.97	1.93	1.88	1.84	1.80	1.76	1.74	1.71	1.68	1.67
	7.68	**5.49**	**4.60**	**4.11**	**3.79**	**3.56**	**3.39**	**3.26**	**3.14**	**3.06**	**2.98**	**2.93**	**2.83**	**2.74**	**2.63**	**2.55**	**2.47**	**2.38**	**2.33**	**2.25**	**2.21**	**2.16**	**2.12**	**2.10**
28	4.20	3.34	2.95	2.71	2.56	2.44	2.36	2.29	2.24	2.19	2.15	2.12	2.06	2.02	1.96	1.91	1.87	1.81	1.78	1.75	1.72	1.69	1.67	1.65
	7.64	**5.45**	**4.57**	**4.07**	**3.76**	**3.53**	**3.36**	**3.23**	**3.11**	**3.03**	**2.95**	**2.90**	**2.80**	**2.71**	**2.60**	**2.52**	**2.44**	**2.35**	**2.30**	**2.22**	**2.18**	**2.13**	**2.09**	**2.06**
29	4.18	3.33	2.93	2.70	2.54	2.43	2.35	2.28	2.22	2.18	2.14	2.10	2.05	2.00	1.94	1.90	1.85	1.80	1.77	1.73	1.71	1.68	1.65	1.64
	7.60	**5.42**	**4.54**	**4.04**	**3.73**	**3.50**	**3.33**	**3.20**	**3.08**	**3.00**	**2.92**	**2.87**	**2.77**	**2.68**	**2.57**	**2.49**	**2.41**	**2.32**	**2.27**	**2.19**	**2.15**	**2.10**	**2.06**	**2.03**
30	4.17	3.32	2.92	2.69	2.53	2.42	2.34	2.27	2.21	2.16	2.12	2.09	2.04	1.99	1.93	1.89	1.84	1.79	1.76	1.72	1.69	1.66	1.64	1.62
	7.56	**5.39**	**4.51**	**4.02**	**3.70**	**3.47**	**3.30**	**3.17**	**3.06**	**2.98**	**2.90**	**2.84**	**2.74**	**2.66**	**2.55**	**2.47**	**2.38**	**2.29**	**2.24**	**2.16**	**2.13**	**2.07**	**2.03**	**2.01**
32	4.15	3.30	2.90	2.67	2.51	2.40	2.32	2.25	2.19	2.14	2.10	2.07	2.02	1.97	1.91	1.86	1.82	1.76	1.74	1.69	1.67	1.64	1.61	1.59
	7.50	**5.34**	**4.46**	**3.97**	**3.66**	**3.42**	**3.25**	**3.12**	**3.01**	**2.94**	**2.86**	**2.80**	**2.70**	**2.62**	**2.51**	**2.42**	**2.34**	**2.25**	**2.20**	**2.12**	**2.08**	**2.02**	**1.98**	**1.96**
34	4.13	3.28	2.88	2.65	2.49	2.38	2.30	2.23	2.17	2.12	2.08	2.05	2.00	1.95	1.89	1.84	1.80	1.74	1.71	1.67	1.64	1.61	1.59	1.57
	7.44	**5.29**	**4.42**	**3.93**	**3.61**	**3.38**	**3.21**	**3.08**	**2.97**	**2.89**	**2.82**	**2.76**	**2.66**	**2.58**	**2.47**	**2.38**	**2.30**	**2.21**	**2.15**	**2.08**	**2.04**	**1.98**	**1.94**	**1.91**
36	4.11	3.26	2.86	2.63	2.48	2.36	2.28	2.21	2.15	2.10	2.06	2.03	1.98	1.93	1.87	1.82	1.78	1.72	1.69	1.65	1.62	1.59	1.56	1.55
	7.39	**5.25**	**4.38**	**3.89**	**3.58**	**3.35**	**3.18**	**3.04**	**2.94**	**2.86**	**2.78**	**2.72**	**2.62**	**2.54**	**2.43**	**2.35**	**2.26**	**2.17**	**2.12**	**2.04**	**2.00**	**1.94**	**1.90**	**1.87**
38	4.10	3.25	2.85	2.62	2.46	2.35	2.26	2.19	2.14	2.09	2.05	2.02	1.96	1.92	1.85	1.80	1.76	1.71	1.67	1.63	1.60	1.57	1.54	1.53
	7.35	**5.21**	**4.34**	**3.86**	**3.54**	**3.32**	**3.15**	**3.02**	**2.91**	**2.82**	**2.75**	**2.69**	**2.59**	**2.51**	**2.40**	**2.32**	**2.22**	**2.14**	**2.08**	**2.00**	**1.97**	**1.90**	**1.86**	**1.84**
40	4.08	3.23	2.84	2.61	2.45	2.34	2.25	2.18	2.12	2.07	2.04	2.00	1.95	1.90	1.84	1.79	1.74	1.69	1.66	1.61	1.59	1.55	1.53	1.51
	7.31	**5.18**	**4.31**	**3.83**	**3.51**	**3.29**	**3.12**	**2.99**	**2.88**	**2.80**	**2.73**	**2.66**	**2.56**	**2.49**	**2.37**	**2.29**	**2.20**	**2.11**	**2.05**	**1.97**	**1.94**	**1.88**	**1.84**	**1.81**
42	4.07	3.22	2.83	2.59	2.44	2.32	2.24	2.17	2.11	2.06	2.02	1.99	1.94	1.89	1.82	1.78	1.73	1.68	1.64	1.60	1.57	1.54	1.51	1.49
	7.27	**5.15**	**4.29**	**3.80**	**3.49**	**3.26**	**3.10**	**2.96**	**2.86**	**2.77**	**2.70**	**2.64**	**2.54**	**2.46**	**2.35**	**2.26**	**2.17**	**2.08**	**2.02**	**1.94**	**1.91**	**1.85**	**1.80**	**1.78**
44	4.06	3.21	2.82	2.58	2.43	2.31	2.23	2.16	2.10	2.05	2.01	1.98	1.92	1.88	1.81	1.76	1.72	1.66	1.63	1.58	1.56	1.52	1.50	1.48
	7.24	**5.12**	**4.26**	**3.78**	**3.46**	**3.24**	**3.07**	**2.94**	**2.84**	**2.75**	**2.68**	**2.62**	**2.52**	**2.44**	**2.32**	**2.24**	**2.15**	**2.06**	**2.00**	**1.92**	**1.88**	**1.82**	**1.78**	**1.75**
46	4.05	3.20	2.81	2.57	2.42	2.30	2.22	2.14	2.09	2.04	2.00	1.97	1.91	1.87	1.80	1.75	1.71	1.65	1.62	1.57	1.54	1.51	1.48	1.46
	7.21	**5.10**	**4.24**	**3.76**	**3.44**	**3.22**	**3.05**	**2.92**	**2.82**	**2.73**	**2.66**	**2.60**	**2.50**	**2.42**	**2.30**	**2.22**	**2.13**	**2.04**	**1.98**	**1.90**	**1.86**	**1.80**	**1.76**	**1.72**
48	4.04	3.19	2.80	2.56	2.41	2.30	2.21	2.14	2.08	2.03	1.99	1.96	1.90	1.86	1.79	1.74	1.70	1.64	1.61	1.56	1.53	1.50	1.47	1.45
	7.19	**5.08**	**4.22**	**3.74**	**3.42**	**3.20**	**3.04**	**2.90**	**2.80**	**2.71**	**2.64**	**2.58**	**2.48**	**2.40**	**2.28**	**2.20**	**2.11**	**2.02**	**1.96**	**1.88**	**1.84**	**1.78**	**1.73**	**1.70**

*Reproduced from Snedecor: *Statistical Methods*, Iowa State College Press, Ames, Iowa, by permission of the author and publisher.

The 5 (Roman Type) and 1 (Boldface Type) Percent Points for the Distribution of F*—Concluded

n_2	n_1 degrees of freedom (for greater mean square)																							
	1	2	3	4	5	6	7	8	9	10	11	12	14	16	20	24	30	40	50	75	100	200	500	∞
50	4.03	3.18	2.79	2.56	2.40	2.29	2.20	2.13	2.07	2.02	1.98	1.95	1.90	1.85	1.78	1.74	1.69	1.63	1.60	1.55	1.52	1.48	1.46	1.44
	7.17	**5.06**	**4.20**	**3.72**	**3.41**	**3.18**	**3.02**	**2.88**	**2.78**	**2.70**	**2.62**	**2.56**	**2.46**	**2.39**	**2.26**	**2.18**	**2.10**	**2.00**	**1.94**	**1.86**	**1.82**	**1.76**	**1.71**	**1.68**
55	4.02	3.17	2.78	2.54	2.38	2.27	2.18	2.11	2.05	2.00	1.97	1.93	1.88	1.83	1.76	1.72	1.67	1.61	1.58	1.52	1.50	1.46	1.43	1.41
	7.12	**5.01**	**4.16**	**3.68**	**3.37**	**3.15**	**2.98**	**2.85**	**2.75**	**2.66**	**2.59**	**2.53**	**2.43**	**2.35**	**2.23**	**2.15**	**2.06**	**1.96**	**1.90**	**1.82**	**1.78**	**1.71**	**1.66**	**1.64**
60	4.00	3.15	2.76	2.52	2.37	2.25	2.17	2.10	2.04	1.99	1.95	1.92	1.86	1.81	1.75	1.70	1.65	1.59	1.56	1.50	1.48	1.44	1.41	1.39
	7.08	**4.98**	**4.13**	**3.65**	**3.34**	**3.12**	**2.95**	**2.82**	**2.72**	**2.63**	**2.56**	**2.50**	**2.40**	**2.32**	**2.20**	**2.12**	**2.03**	**1.93**	**1.87**	**1.79**	**1.74**	**1.68**	**1.63**	**1.60**
65	3.99	3.14	2.75	2.51	2.36	2.24	2.15	2.08	2.02	1.98	1.94	1.90	1.85	1.80	1.73	1.68	1.63	1.57	1.54	1.49	1.46	1.42	1.39	1.37
	7.04	**4.95**	**4.10**	**3.62**	**3.31**	**3.09**	**2.93**	**2.79**	**2.70**	**2.61**	**2.54**	**2.47**	**2.37**	**2.30**	**2.18**	**2.09**	**2.00**	**1.90**	**1.84**	**1.76**	**1.71**	**1.64**	**1.60**	**1.56**
70	3.98	3.13	2.74	2.50	2.35	2.23	2.14	2.07	2.01	1.97	1.93	1.89	1.84	1.79	1.72	1.67	1.62	1.56	1.53	1.47	1.45	1.40	1.37	1.35
	7.01	**4.92**	**4.08**	**3.60**	**3.29**	**3.07**	**2.91**	**2.77**	**2.67**	**2.59**	**2.51**	**2.45**	**2.35**	**2.28**	**2.15**	**2.07**	**1.98**	**1.88**	**1.82**	**1.74**	**1.69**	**1.62**	**1.56**	**1.53**
80	3.96	3.11	2.72	2.48	2.33	2.21	2.12	2.05	1.99	1.95	1.91	1.88	1.82	1.77	1.70	1.65	1.60	1.54	1.51	1.45	1.42	1.38	1.35	1.32
	6.96	**4.88**	**4.04**	**3.56**	**3.25**	**3.04**	**2.87**	**2.74**	**2.64**	**2.55**	**2.48**	**2.41**	**2.32**	**2.24**	**2.11**	**2.03**	**1.94**	**1.84**	**1.78**	**1.70**	**1.65**	**1.57**	**1.52**	**1.49**
100	3.94	3.09	2.70	2.46	2.30	2.19	2.10	2.03	1.97	1.92	1.88	1.85	1.79	1.75	1.68	1.63	1.57	1.51	1.48	1.42	1.39	1.34	1.30	1.28
	6.90	**4.82**	**3.98**	**3.51**	**3.20**	**2.99**	**2.82**	**2.69**	**2.59**	**2.51**	**2.43**	**2.36**	**2.26**	**2.19**	**2.06**	**1.98**	**1.89**	**1.79**	**1.73**	**1.64**	**1.59**	**1.51**	**1.46**	**1.43**
125	3.92	3.07	2.68	2.44	2.29	2.17	2.08	2.01	1.95	1.90	1.86	1.83	1.77	1.72	1.65	1.60	1.55	1.49	1.45	1.39	1.36	1.31	1.27	1.25
	6.84	**4.78**	**3.94**	**3.47**	**3.17**	**2.95**	**2.79**	**2.65**	**2.56**	**2.47**	**2.40**	**2.33**	**2.23**	**2.15**	**2.03**	**1.94**	**1.85**	**1.75**	**1.68**	**1.59**	**1.54**	**1.46**	**1.40**	**1.37**
150	3.91	3.06	2.67	2.43	2.27	2.16	2.07	2.00	1.94	1.89	1.85	1.82	1.76	1.71	1.64	1.59	1.54	1.47	1.44	1.37	1.34	1.29	1.25	1.22
	6.81	**4.75**	**3.91**	**3.44**	**3.14**	**2.92**	**2.76**	**2.62**	**2.53**	**2.44**	**2.37**	**2.30**	**2.20**	**2.12**	**2.00**	**1.91**	**1.83**	**1.72**	**1.66**	**1.56**	**1.51**	**1.43**	**1.37**	**1.33**
200	3.89	3.04	2.65	2.41	2.26	2.14	2.05	1.98	1.92	1.87	1.83	1.80	1.74	1.69	1.62	1.57	1.52	1.45	1.42	1.35	1.32	1.26	1.22	1.19
	6.76	**4.71**	**3.88**	**3.41**	**3.11**	**2.90**	**2.73**	**2.60**	**2.50**	**2.41**	**2.34**	**2.28**	**2.17**	**2.09**	**1.97**	**1.88**	**1.79**	**1.69**	**1.62**	**1.53**	**1.48**	**1.39**	**1.33**	**1.28**
400	3.86	3.02	2.62	2.39	2.23	2.12	2.03	1.96	1.90	1.85	1.81	1.78	1.72	1.67	1.60	1.54	1.49	1.42	1.38	1.32	1.28	1.22	1.16	1.13
	6.70	**4.66**	**3.83**	**3.36**	**3.06**	**2.85**	**2.69**	**2.55**	**2.46**	**2.37**	**2.29**	**2.23**	**2.12**	**2.04**	**1.92**	**1.84**	**1.74**	**1.64**	**1.57**	**1.47**	**1.42**	**1.32**	**1.24**	**1.19**
1000	3.85	3.00	2.61	2.38	2.22	2.10	2.02	1.95	1.89	1.84	1.80	1.76	1.70	1.65	1.58	1.53	1.47	1.41	1.36	1.30	1.26	1.19	1.13	1.08
	6.66	**4.62**	**3.80**	**3.34**	**3.04**	**2.82**	**2.66**	**2.53**	**2.43**	**2.34**	**2.26**	**2.20**	**2.09**	**2.01**	**1.89**	**1.81**	**1.71**	**1.61**	**1.54**	**1.44**	**1.38**	**1.28**	**1.19**	**1.11**
∞	3.84	2.99	2.60	2.37	2.21	2.09	2.01	1.94	1.88	1.83	1.79	1.75	1.69	1.64	1.57	1.52	1.46	1.40	1.35	1.28	1.24	1.17	1.11	1.00
	6.64	**4.60**	**3.78**	**3.32**	**3.02**	**2.80**	**2.64**	**2.51**	**2.41**	**2.32**	**2.24**	**2.18**	**2.07**	**1.99**	**1.87**	**1.79**	**1.69**	**1.59**	**1.52**	**1.41**	**1.36**	**1.25**	**1.15**	**1.00**

*Reproduced from Snedecor: *Statistical Methods*, Iowa State College Press, Ames, Iowa, by permission of the author and publisher.

Table of χ^{2}*

Degrees of Freedom *df*	P = .99	.98	.95	.90	.80	.70	.50	.30	.20	.10	.05	.02	.01
1	.000157	.000628	.00393	.0158	.0642	.148	.455	1.074	1.642	2.706	3.841	5.412	6.635
2	.0201	.0404	.103	.211	.446	.713	1.386	2.408	3.219	4.605	5.991	7.824	9.210
3	.115	.185	.352	.584	1.005	1.424	2.366	3.665	4.642	6.251	7.815	9.837	11.341
4	.297	.429	.711	1.064	1.649	2.195	3.357	4.878	5.989	7.779	9.488	11.668	13.277
5	.554	.752	1.145	1.610	2.343	3.000	4.351	6.064	7.289	9.236	11.070	13.388	15.086
6	.872	1.134	1.635	2.204	3.070	3.828	5.348	7.231	8.558	10.645	12.592	15.033	16.812
7	1.239	1.564	2.167	2.833	3.822	4.671	6.346	8.383	9.803	12.017	14.067	16.622	18.475
8	1.646	2.032	2.733	3.490	4.594	5.527	7.344	9.524	11.030	13.362	15.507	18.168	20.090
9	2.088	2.532	3.325	4.168	5.380	6.393	8.343	10.656	12.242	14.684	16.919	19.679	21.666
10	2.558	3.059	3.940	4.865	6.179	7.267	9.342	11.781	13.442	15.987	18.307	21.161	23.209
11	3.053	3.609	4.575	5.578	6.989	8.148	10.341	12.899	14.631	17.275	19.675	22.618	24.725
12	3.571	4.178	5.226	6.304	7.807	9.034	11.340	14.011	15.812	18.549	21.026	24.054	26.217
13	4.107	4.765	5.892	7.042	8.634	9.926	12.340	15.119	16.985	19.812	22.362	25.472	27.688
14	4.660	5.368	6.571	7.790	9.467	10.821	13.339	16.222	18.151	21.064	23.685	26.873	29.141
15	5.229	5.985	7.261	8.547	10.307	11.721	14.339	17.322	19.311	22.307	24.996	28.259	30.578
16	5.812	6.614	7.962	9.312	11.152	12.624	15.338	18.418	20.465	23.542	26.296	29.633	32.000
17	6.408	7.255	8.672	10.085	12.002	13.531	16.338	19.511	21.615	24.769	27.587	30.995	33.409
18	7.015	7.906	9.390	10.865	12.857	14.440	17.338	20.601	22.760	25.989	28.869	32.346	34.805
19	7.633	8.567	10.117	11.651	13.716	15.352	18.338	21.689	23.900	27.204	30.144	33.687	36.191
20	8.260	9.237	10.851	12.443	14.578	16.266	19.337	22.775	25.038	28.412	31.410	35.020	37.566
21	8.897	9.915	11.591	13.240	15.445	17.182	20.337	23.858	26.171	29.615	32.671	36.343	38.932
22	9.542	10.600	12.338	14.041	16.314	18.101	21.337	24.939	27.301	30.813	33.924	37.659	40.289
23	10.196	11.293	13.091	14.848	17.187	19.021	22.337	26.018	28.429	32.007	35.172	38.968	41.638
24	10.856	11.992	13.848	15.659	18.062	19.943	23.337	27.096	29.553	33.196	36.415	40.270	42.980
25	11.524	12.697	14.611	16.473	18.940	20.867	24.337	28.172	30.675	34.382	37.652	41.566	44.314
26	12.198	13.409	15.379	17.292	19.820	21.792	25.336	29.246	31.795	35.563	38.885	42.856	45.642
27	12.879	14.125	16.151	18.114	20.703	22.719	26.336	30.319	32.912	36.741	40.113	44.140	46.963
28	13.565	14.847	16.928	18.939	21.588	23.647	27.336	31.391	34.027	37.916	41.337	45.419	48.278
29	14.256	15.574	17.708	19.768	22.475	24.577	28.336	32.461	35.139	39.087	42.557	46.693	49.588
30	14.953	16.306	18.493	20.599	23.364	25.508	29.336	33.530	36.250	40.256	43.773	47.962	50.892

*Reprinted from Table III of Fisher: *Statistical Methods for Research Workers,* Oliver & Boyd Ltd., Edinburgh, by permission of the author and publishers.

For larger values of *df*, the expression $\sqrt{2\chi^2} - \sqrt{2(df) - 1}$ may be used as a normal deviate with unit standard error.

Coefficients of Orthogonal Polynomials

Polynomial	X = 1	2	3	4	5	6	7	8	9	10
Linear	−1	0	1							
Quadratic	1	−2	1							
Linear	−3	−1	1	3						
Quadratic	1	−1	−1	1						
Cubic	−1	3	−3	1						
Linear	−2	−1	0	1	2					
Quadratic	2	−1	−2	−1	2					
Cubic	−1	2	0	−2	1					
Quartic	1	−4	6	−4	1					
Linear	−5	−3	−1	1	3	5				
Quadratic	5	−1	−4	−4	−1	5				
Cubic	−5	7	4	−4	−7	5				
Quartic	1	−3	2	2	−3	1				
Linear	−3	−2	−1	0	1	2	3			
Quadratic	5	0	−3	−4	−3	0	5			
Cubic	−1	1	1	0	−1	−1	1			
Quartic	3	−7	1	6	1	−7	3			
Linear	−7	−5	−3	−1	1	3	5	7		
Quadratic	7	1	−3	−5	−5	−3	1	7		
Cubic	−7	5	7	3	−3	−7	−5	7		
Quartic	7	−13	−3	9	9	−3	−13	7		
Quintic	−7	23	−17	−15	15	17	−23	7		
Linear	−4	−3	−2	−1	0	1	2	3	4	
Quadratic	28	7	−8	−17	−20	−17	−8	7	28	
Cubic	−14	7	13	9	0	−9	−13	−7	14	
Quartic	14	−21	−11	9	18	9	−11	−21	14	
Quintic	−4	11	−4	−9	0	9	4	−11	4	
Linear	−9	−7	−5	−3	−1	1	3	5	7	9
Quadratic	6	2	−1	−3	−4	−4	−3	−1	2	6
Cubic	−42	14	35	31	12	−12	−31	−35	−14	42
Quartic	18	−22	−17	3	18	18	3	−17	−22	18
Quintic	−6	14	−1	−11	−6	6	11	1	−14	6

This table is adapted with permission from B. J. Winer, *Statistical Principles in Experimental Design* (New York: McGraw Hill, 1962).

REFERENCES

Abelson, R. P. A note on the Neyman-Johnson technique. *Psychometrika,* 1953, *18,* 213–218.

Ahlgren, A., & Walberg, H. J. Generalized regression analysis. In D. J. Amick & H. J. Walberg (Eds.), *Introductory multivariate analysis.* Berkeley, Calif.: McCutchan, 1975.

Aigner, D. J., & Godlberger, A. S. (Eds.). *Latent variables in socioeconomic models.* Amsterdam: North-Holland, 1977.

Aitkin, M. A. Fixed-width confidence intervals in linear regression with applications to the Johnson-Neyman technique. *British Journal of Mathematical and Statistical Psychology,* 1973, *26,* 261–269.

Alexander, C. N., & Campbell, E. Q. Peer influences on adolescent educational aspirations and attainments. *American Sociological Review,* 1964, *29,* 568–575.

Alexander, K., & Eckland, B. K. Contextual effects in the high school attainment process. *American Sociological Review,* 1975, *40,* 402–416.

Alexander, K. L., & Griffin, L. J. School district effects on academic achievement: A reconsideration. *American Sociological Review,* 1976, *41,* 144–152.

Alker, H. R. Causal inference and political analysis. In J. Brend (Ed.), *Mathematical applications in political science,* II. Dallas: Southern Methodist University Press, 1966.

Alker, H. R. A typology of ecological fallacies. In M. Dogan & S. Rokkan (Eds.), *Quantitative ecological analysis in the social sciences.* Cambridge, Mass.: M.I.T. Press, 1969.

Allison, P. D. Testing for interaction in multiple regression. *American Journal of Sociology,* 1977, *83,* 144–153.

Althauser, R. P. Multicollinearity and non-additive regression models. In H. M. Blalock (Ed.), *Causal models in the social sciences.* Chicago: Aldine, 1971.

Alwin, D. F. Assessing school effects: Some identities. *Sociology of Education,* 1976, *49,* 294–303.

Alwin, D. F., & Hauser, R. M. The decomposition of effects in path analysis. *American Sociological Review,* 1975, *40,* 37–47.

Alwin, D. F., & Jackson, D. J. Measurement models for response errors in surveys: Issues and applications. In K. F. Schuessler (Ed.), *Sociological methodology 1980.* San Francisco: Jossey-Bass, 1979.

Alwin, D. F., & Otto, L. B. High school context effects on aspirations. *Sociology of Education,* 1977, *50,* 259–273.

Alwin, D. F., & Tessler, R. C. Causal models, unobserved variables, and experimental data. *American Journal of Sociology,* 1974, *80,* 58–86.

Anderson, G. L. *A comparison of the outcomes of instruction under two theories of learning.* Unpublished doctoral dissertation, University of Minnesota, 1941.

Anderson, N. H. Comparison of different populations: Resistance to extinction and transfer. *Psychological Review,* 1963, *70,* 162–179.

Anscombe, F. J. Rejection of outliers. *Technometrics,* 1960, *2,* 123–147.

Anscombe, F. J. Graphs in statistical analysis. *American Statistician,* 1973, *27,* 17–21.

Anscombe, F. J., & Tukey, J. W. The examination and analysis of residuals. *Technometrics,* 1963, *5,* 141–160.

Applebaum, M. I., & Cramer, E. M. Some problems in the nonorthogonal analysis of variance. *Psychological Bulletin,* 1974, *81,* 335–343.

Armor, D. J. School and family effects on black and white achievement: A reexamination of the USOE data. In F. Mosteller & D. P. Moynihan (Eds.), *On equality of educational opportunity.* New York: Vintage Books, 1972.

Astin, A. W. Undergraduate achievement and institutional excellence. *Science,* 1968, *161,* 661–668.

Astin, A. W. The methodology of research on college impact, part one. *Sociology of Education,* 1970, *43,* 223–254.

Astin, A. W., & Panos, R. J. *The educational and vocational development of college students.* Washington, D.C.: American Council on Education, 1969.

Bagozzi, R. P. Structural equation models in experimental research. *Journal of Marketing Research,* 1977, *14,* 209–226.

Bagozzi, R. P., & Burnkrant, R. E. Attitude organization and the attitude–behavior relationship. *Journal of Personality and Social Psychology,* 1979, *37,* 913–929.

Bartlett, M. S. Multivariate analysis. *Journal of the Royal Statistical Society,* Series B, 1947, *9,* 176–197.

Bayley, N. On the growth of intelligence. *American Psychologist,* 1955, *10,* 805–818.

Beaton, A. E. Scaling criterion of questionnaire items. *Socio-Economic Planning Sciences,* 1969, *2,* 355–362. (a)

Beaton, A. E. Some mathematical and empirical properties of criterion scaled variables. In G. W. Mayeske et al., *A study of our nation's schools.* Washington, D.C.: U.S. Office of Education, 1969. (b)

Beaton, A. E. *Commonality.* Unpublished manuscript, 1973.

Bem, S. L. The measurement of psychological androgyny. *Journal of Consulting and Clinical Psychology,* 1974, *42,* 155–162.

Bentler, P. M. The interdependence of theory, methodology, and empirical data: Causal modeling as an approach to construct validation. In D. B. Kandel (Ed.), *Longitudinal research on drug use.* New York: Wiley, 1978.

Bentler, P. M. Multivariate analysis with latent variables: Causal modeling. *Annual Review of Psychology,* 1980, *31,* 419–456.

Bentler, P. M., & Bonett, D. G. Significance tests and goodness of fit in the analysis of covariance structures. *Psychological Bulletin,* 1980, *88,* 588–606.

Bentler, P. M., & Huba, G. J. Simple minitheories of love. *Journal of Personality and Social Psychology,* 1979, *37,* 124–130.

Bentler, P. M., & Speckart, G. Models of attitude-behavior relations. *Psychological Review,* 1979, *86,* 452–464.

Bentler, P. M., & Speckart, G. Attitudes "cause" behaviors: A structural equation analysis. *Journal of Personality and Social Psychology,* 1981, *40,* 226–238.

Bentler, P. M., & Woodward, J. A. A head start reevaluation: Positive effects are not yet demonstrable. *Evaluation Quarterly,* 1978, *2,* 493–510.

Bentler, P. M., & Woodward, J. A. Nonexperimental evaluation research: Contributions of causal modeling. In L. Datta & R. Perloff (Eds.), *Improving evaluations.* Beverly Hills, Calif.: Sage, 1979.

Berliner, D. C., & Cahen, L. S. Trait-treatment interaction and learning. In F. N. Kerlinger (Ed.), *Review of research in education 1.* Itasca, Ill.: F. E. Peacock, 1973.

Bibby, J. The general linear model—a cautionary tale. In C. A. O'Muircheartaigh & C. Payne (Eds.), *The analysis of survey data* (Vol. 2). New York: Wiley, 1977.

Bidwell, C. E., & Kasarda, J. D. School district organization and student achievement. *American Sociological Review,* 1975, *40,* 55–70.

Bidwell, C. E., & Kasarda, J. D. Reply to Hannan, Freeman and Meyer, and Alexander and Griffin. *American Sociological Review,* 1976, *41,* 152–160.

Bielby, W. T., & Hauser, R. M. Structural equation models. *Annual Review of Sociology,* 1977, *3,* 137–161. (a)

Bielby, W. T., & Hauser, R. M. Response error in earnings functions for nonblack males. *Sociological Methods and Research,* 1977, *6,* 241–280. (b)

Bielby, W. T., Hauser, R. M., & Featherman, D. L. Response errors of black and nonblack males in models of intergenerational transmission of socioeconomic status. *American Journal of Sociology,* 1977, *82,* 1242–1288.

Bielby, W. T., & Klugel, J. R. Statistical inference and statistical power in applications of the general linear model. In D. R. Heise (Ed.), *Sociological methodology 1977.* San Francisco: Jossey-Bass, 1977.

Binder, A. Considerations of the place of assumptions in correlational analysis. *American Psychologist,* 1959, *14,* 504–510.

Blalock, H. M. *Causal inferences in nonexperimental research.* Chapel Hill: University of North Carolina Press, 1964.

Blalock, H. M. Theory building and causal inferences. In H. M. Blalock and A. B. Blalock (Eds.), *Methodology in social research.* New York: McGraw-Hill, 1968.

Blalock, H. M. (Ed.). *Causal models in the social sciences.* Chicago: Aldine, 1971.

Blalock, H. M. *Social statistics* (2nd ed.). New York: McGraw-Hill, 1972.

Blalock, H. M., Wells, C. S., & Carter, L. F. Statistical estimation with random measurement error. In E. F. Borgatta & G. W. Bohrnstedt (Eds.), *Sociological Methodology 1970.* San Francisco: Jossey-Bass, 1970.

Blau, P. Structural effects. *American Sociological Review,* 1960, *25,* 178–193.

Bock, R. D. *Multivariate statistical methods in behavioral research.* New York: McGraw-Hill, 1975.

Bohrnstedt, G. W. Observations on the measurement of change. In E. F. Borgatta & G. W. Bohrnstedt (Eds.), *Sociological methodology 1969.* San Francisco: Jossey-Bass, 1969.

Bohrnstedt, G. W., & Carter, T. M. Robustness in regression analysis. In H. L. Costner (Ed.), *Sociological methodology 1971.* San Francisco: Jossey-Bass, 1971.

Borgatta, E. F., & Jackson, D. J. (Eds.). *Aggregate data: Analysis and interpretation.* Beverly Hills, Calif.: Sage, 1980.

Borgen, F. H., & Seling, M. J. Use of discriminant analysis following MANOVA: Multivariate statistics for multivariate purposes. *Journal of Applied Psychology,* 1978, *63,* 689–697.

Borich, G. D., Godbout, R. C., & Wunderlich, K. W. *The analysis of aptitude-treatment interactions: Computer programs and calculations.* Chicago: International Educational Services, 1976.

Boudon, R. A new look at correlation analysis. In H. M. Blalock & A. B. Blalock (Eds.), *Methodology in social research.* New York: McGraw-Hill, 1968.

Bowers, W. J. Normative constraints on deviant behavior in the college context. *Sociometry,* 1968, *31,* 370–385.

Bowles, S., & Levin, H. M. The determinants of scholastic achievement: An appraisal of some recent evidence. *Journal of Human Resources,* 1968, *3,* 3–24. (a)

Bowles, S., & Levin, H. M. More on multicollinearity and the effectiveness of schools. *Journal of Human Resources,* 1968, *3,* 393–400. (b)

Box, G. E. P. The exploration and exploitation of response surfaces: Some general considerations and examples. *Biometrics,* 1954, *10,* 16–60.

Box, G. E. P. Use and abuse of regression. *Technometrics,* 1966, *8,* 625–629.

Box, G. E. P. Response surfaces. In D. L. Sills (Ed.), *International encyclopedia of the social sciences* (Vol. 5, pp. 254–259). New York: Macmillan, 1968.

Bracht, G. H. Experimental factors related to aptitude-treatment interactions. *Review of Educational Research,* 1970, *40,* 627–645.

Bradley, R. A., & Srivastava, S. S. Correlation in polynomial regression. *American Statistician,* 1979, *33,* 11–14.

Braithwaite, R. B. *Scientific explanation.* Cambridge: Cambridge University Press, 1953.

Brewer, M. B., Crano, W. D., & Campbell, D. T. Testing a single-factor model as an alternative to the misuse of partial correlations in hypothesis-testing research. *Sociometry,* 1970, *33,* 1–11.

Brodbeck, M. Logic and scientific method in research on teaching. In N. L. Gage (Ed.), *Handbook of research on teaching.* Skokie, Ill.: Rand McNally, 1963.

Brodbeck, M. (Ed.). *Readings in the philosophy of the social sciences.* New York: Macmillan, 1968.

Bryk, A. S., & Weisberg, H. I. Value-added analysis: A dynamic approach to the estimation of treatment effects. *Journal of Educational Statistics,* 1976, *1,* 127–155.

Bryk, A. S., & Weisberg, H. I. Use of the nonequivalent control group design when subjects are growing. *Psychological Bulletin,* 1977, *84,* 950–962.

Burks, B. S. On the inadequacy of the partial and multiple correlation technique. *Journal of Educational Psychology,* 1926, *17,* 532–540. (a)

Burks, B. S. On the inadequacy of the partial and multiple correlation technique. *Journal of Educational Psychology,* 1926, *17,* 625–630. (b)

Burks, B. S. Statistical hazards in nature–nurture investigations. In M. Whipple (Ed.), *National society for the study of education: 27th yearbook* (Part 1). Bloomington, Ill.: Public School Publishing Company, 1928.

Burstein, L. The choice of unit of analysis in the investigation of school effects: IEA in New Zealand. *New Zealand Journal of Educational Studies,* 1976, *11,* 11–24.

Burstein, L. Assessing differences between grouped and individual-level regression coefficients. *Sociological Methods and Research,* 1978, *7,* 5–28.

Burstein, L. The role of levels of analysis in the specification of education effects. In R. Dreeben & J. A. Thomas (Eds.), *The analysis of educational productivity. Vol. I: Issues in microanalysis.* Cambridge, Mass.: Ballinger, 1980. (a)

Burstein, L. The analysis of multilevel data in educational research and evaluation. In D. C. Berliner (Ed.), *Review of research in education 8.* Washington, D.C.: American Educational Research Association, 1980. (b)

Burstein, L., Linn, R. L., & Capell, F. J. Analyzing multilevel data in the presence of heterogeneous within-class regressions. *Journal of Educational Statistics,* 1978, *3,* 347–383.

Burt, C. *Mental and scholastic tests.* London: P. S. King and Son, 1921.

Burt, C. *The young delinquent.* New York: D. Appleton, 1925.

Burt, C. *Mental and scholastic tests* (4th ed.). London: Staples Press, 1962.

Burt, R. S. Confirmatory factor-analytic structures and the theory construction process. *Sociological Methods and Research,* 1973, *2,* 131–190.

Burt, R. S. Interpretational confounding of unobserved variables in structural equation models. *Sociological Methods and Research,* 1976, *5,* 3–52.

Cain, G. G. Regression and selection models to improve nonexperimental comparisons. In C. A. Bennett & A. A. Lumsdaine (Eds.), *Evaluation and experiment: Some critical issues in assessing social programs.* New York: Academic Press, 1975.

Cain, G. G., & Watts, H. W. The controversy about the Coleman Report: Comment. *Journal of Human Resources,* 1968, *3,* 389–392.

Cain, G. G., & Watts, H. W. Problems in making policy inferences from the Coleman Report. *American Sociological Review,* 1970, *35,* 228–242.

Campbell, D. T., & Boruch, R. F. Making the case for randomized assignment to treatments by considering the alternatives: Six ways in which quasi-experimental evaluations in compensatory education tend to underestimate effects. In C. A. Bennett & A. A. Lumsdaine (Eds.), *Evaluation and experiment: Some critical issues in assessing social programs.* New York: Academic Press, 1975.

Campbell, D. T., & Erlebacher, A. E. How regression artifacts in quasi-experimental evaluations can mistakenly make compensatory education look harmful. In J. Hellmuth (Ed.), *Compensatory education: A national debate* (Vol. 3): *Disadvantaged child.* New York: Brunner/Mazel, 1970.

Campbell, D. T., & Stanley, J. C. Experimental and quasi-experimental designs for research on teaching. In N. L. Gage (Ed.), *Handbook of research on teaching.* Skokie, Ill.: Rand McNally, 1963.

Carlson, J. E., & Timm, N. H. Analysis of nonorthogonal fixed-effects designs. *Psychological Bulletin,* 1974, *81,* 563–570.

Carroll, J. B. *The teaching of French as a foreign language in eight countries.* New York: Wiley, 1975.

Carter, D. S. Comparison of different shrinkage formulas in estimating population multiple correlation coefficients. *Educational and Psychological Measurement,* 1979, *39,* 261–266.

Carver, R. P. The case against statistical significance testing. *Harvard Educational Review,* 1978, *48,* 378–399.

Cattell, R. B., & Butcher, H. J. *The prediction of achievement and creativity.* Indianapolis: Bobbs-Merrill, 1968.

Chatterjee, S., & Price, B. *Regression analysis by example.* New York: Wiley, 1977.

Citron, A., Chein, I., & Harding, J. Anti-minority remarks: A problem for action research. *Journal of Abnormal and Social Psychology,* 1950, *45,* 99–126.

Cleary, T. A. Test bias: Prediction of grades of Negro and white students in integrated colleges. *Journal of Educational Measurement,* 1968, *5,* 115–124.

Clemans, W. V. An analytical and empirical examination of some properties of ipsative measures. *Psychometrika, Monograph Supplement* (No. 14), 1965.

Cliff, N., & Krus, D. J. Interpretation of canonical analysis: Rotated vs. unrotated solutions. *Psychometrika,* 1976, *41,* 35–42.

Cnudde, C. F., & McCrone, D. J. The linkage between constituency attitudes and congressional voting behavior: A causal model. *American Political Science Review,* 1966, *60,* 66–72.

Cochran, W. G. Analysis of covariance: Its nature and uses. *Biometrics,* 1957, *13,* 261–281.

Cochran, W. G. Errors of measurement in statistics. *Technometrics,* 1968, *10,* 637–666.

Cochran, W. G. Some effects of errors of measurement on multiple correlation. *Journal of the American Statistical Association,* 1970, *65,* 22–34.

Cochran, W. G., & Cox, G. M. *Experimental designs.* New York: Wiley, 1950.

Cochran, W. G., & Rubin, D. B. Controlling bias in observational studies: A review. *Sankhyā, The Indian Journal of Statistics,* Series A, 1973, *35,* 417–446.

Cohen, J. Multiple regression as a general data-analytic system. *Psychological Bulletin,* 1968, *70,* 426–443.

Cohen, J. *Statistical power analysis for the behavioral sciences* (Rev. ed.). New York: Academic Press, 1977.

Cohen, J. Partialed products *are* interactions; partialed vectors *are* curve components. *Psychological Bulletin,* 1978, *85,* 858–866.

Cohen, J., & Cohen, P. *Applied multiple regression/correlation analysis for the behavioral sciences.* Hillsdale, N.J.: Lawrence Erlbaum, 1975.

Cole, N. S. Bias in selection. *Journal of Educational Measurement,* 1973, *10,* 237–255.

Coleman, J. S. Equality of educational opportunity: Reply to Bowles and Levin. *Journal of Human Resources,* 1968, *3,* 237–246.

Coleman, J. S. Reply to Cain and Watts. *American Sociological Review,* 1970, *35,* 242–249.

Coleman, J. S. The evaluation of equality of educational opportunity. In F. Mosteller & D. P. Moynihan (Eds.), *On equality of educational opportunity.* New York: Vintage Books, 1972.

Coleman, J. S. Methods and results in the IEA studies of effects of school on learning. *Review of Educational Research,* 1975, *45,* 335–386. (a)

Coleman, J. S. Social research advocacy: A response to Young and Bress. *Phi Delta Kappan,* 1975, *55,* 166–169. (b)

Coleman, J. S. Regression analysis for the comparison of school and home effects. *Social Science Research,* 1976, *5,* 1–20.

Coleman, J. S., Campbell, E. Q., Hobson, C. J., McPartland, J., Mood, A. M., Weinfeld, F. D., & York, R. L. *Equality of educational opportunity*. Washington, D.C.: U.S. Government Printing Office, 1966.

Coleman, J. S., & Karweit, N. L. *Information systems and performance measures in schools*. Englewood Cliffs, N.J.: Educational Technology Publications, 1972.

Comber, L. C., & Keeves, J. P. *Science education in nineteen countries*. New York: Wiley, 1973.

Conger, A. J. A revised definition for suppressor variables: A guide to their identification and interpretation. *Educational and Psychological Measurement,* 1974, *34,* 35–46.

Conger, A. J., & Jackson, D. N. Suppressor variables, prediction, and the interpretation of psychological relationships. *Educational and Psychological Measurement,* 1972, *32,* 579–599.

Conrad, H. Information which should be provided by test publishers and testing agencies on the validity and use of their tests. *Proceedings, 1949 Invitational Conference on Testing Problems*. Princeton, N.J.: Educational Testing Service, 1950, 63–68.

Converse, P. E. Survey research and the decoding of patterns in ecological data. In M. Dogan & S. Rokkan (Eds.), *Quantitative ecological analysis in the social sciences*. Cambridge, Mass.: M.I.T. Press, 1969.

Cook, T. D., & Campbell, D. T. *Quasi-experimentation: Design and analysis issues for field settings*. Skokie, Ill.: Rand McNally, 1979.

Cooley, W. W., & Lohnes, P. R. *Multivariate data analysis*. New York: Wiley, 1971.

Cooley, W. W., & Lohnes, P. R. *Evaluation research in education*. New York: Wiley, 1976.

Coser, L. A. Presidential address: Two methods in search of a substance. *American Sociological Review,* 1975, *40,* 691–700.

Costner, H. L. Theory, deduction, and rules of correspondence. *American Journal of Sociology,* 1969, *75,* 245–263.

Costner, H. L., & Schoenberg, R. Diagnosing indicator ills in multiple indicator models. In A. S. Goldberger & O. D. Duncan (Eds.), *Structural equation models in the social sciences*. New York: Seminar Press, 1973.

Cox, D. R. *Planning of experiments*. New York: Wiley, 1958.

Cramer, E. M. Significance tests and tests of models in multiple regression. *American Statistician,* 1972, *26,* 26–30.

Cramer, E. M., & Appelbaum, M. I. Nonorthogonal analysis of variance—once again. *Psychological Bulletin,* 1980, *87,* 51–57.

Cramer, E. M., & Nicewander, W. A. Some symmetric, invariant measures of multivariate association. *Psychometrika,* 1979, *44,* 43–54.

Creager, J. A. Orthogonal and nonorthogonal methods of partitioning regression variance. *American Educational Research Journal,* 1971, *8,* 671–676.

Cronbach, L. J. Intelligence? Creativity? A parsimonious reinterpretation of the Wallach-Kogan data. *American Educational Research Journal,* 1968, *5,* 491–511.

Cronbach, L. J. Test validation. In R. L. Thorndike (Ed.), *Educational measurement* (2nd ed.). Washington, D.C.: American Council on Education, 1971.

Cronbach, L. J. *Research on classrooms and schools: Formulation of questions, design and analysis*. Occasional paper of the Stanford Evaluation Consortium, Stanford University, Stanford, Calif., 1976.

Cronbach, L. J., & Furby, L. How should we measure "change"—or should we? *Psychological Bulletin,* 1970, *74,* 68–80.

Cronbach, L. J., & Gleser, G. C. *Psychological tests and personnel decisions* (2nd ed.). Urbana: University of Illinois Press, 1965.

Cronbach, L. J., Rogosa, D., Floden, R. E., & Price, G. G. *Analysis of covariance in nonrandomized experiments: Parameters affecting bias*. Occasional paper of the Stanford Evaluation Consortium, Stanford University, Stanford, Calif., 1977.

Cronbach, L. J., & Snow, R. E. *Aptitudes and instructional methods*. New York: Irvington, 1977.

Cronbach, L. J., & Webb, N. Between-class and within-class effects in a reported aptitude × treatment interaction: Reanalysis of a study by G. L. Anderson. *Journal of Educational Psychology,* 1975, *67,* 717–724.

Cureton, E. E. Validity. In E. F. Lindquist (Ed.), *Educational measurement*. Washington, D.C.: American Council on Education, 1951.

Daniel, C., & Wood, F. S. *Fitting equations to data* (2nd ed.). New York: Wiley, 1980.

Darlington, R. B. Multiple regression in psychological research and practice. *Psychological Bulletin,* 1968, *69,* 161–182.

Darlington, R. B., & Rom, J. F. Assessing the importance of independent variables in nonlinear causal laws. *American Educational Research Journal,* 1972, *9,* 449–462.

Darlington, R. B., Weinberg, S. L., & Walberg, H. J. Canonical variate analysis and related techniques. *Review of Educational Research,* 1973, *43,* 433–454.

Davidson, M. L. Univariate versus multivariate tests in repeated-measures experiments. *Psychological Bulletin,* 1972, *77,* 446–452.

Davis, D. J. Flexibility and power in comparisons among means. *Psychological Bulletin,* 1969, *71,* 441–444.

Davis, J. A. The campus as a frog pond: An application of the theory of relative deprivation to career decisions of college men. *American Journal of Sociology,* 1966, *72,* 17–31.

Deegan, J. Specification error in causal models. *Social Science Research,* 1974, *3,* 235–259.

De Groot, A. D. *Methodology.* The Hague: Mouton, 1969.

Dixon, W. J., & Brown, M. B. (Eds.). *BMDP–79.* Los Angeles: University of California Press, 1979.

Doby, J. T. Explanation and prediction. In J. T. Doby (Ed.), *An introduction to social research* (2nd ed.). New York: Appleton-Century-Crofts, 1967.

Dogan, M., & Rokkan, S. (Eds.). *Quantitative ecological analysis in the social sciences.* Cambridge, Mass.: M.I.T. Press, 1969.

Dorf, R. C. *Matrix algebra.* New York: Wiley, 1969.

Dowaliby, F. J., & Schumer, H. Teacher-centered versus student-centered mode of college classroom instruction as related to manifest anxiety. *Journal of Educational Psychology,* 1973, *64,* 125–132.

Draper, N., & Smith, H. *Applied regression analysis* (2nd ed.). New York: Wiley, 1981.

DuBois, P. H. *Multivariate correlational analysis.* New York: Harper & Row, 1957.

Duncan, O. D. Inheritance of poverty or inheritance of race? In D. P. Moynihan (Ed.), *On understanding poverty: Perspectives from the social sciences.* New York: Basic Books, 1969.

Duncan, O. D. Partials, partitions, and paths. In E. F. Borgatta & G. W. Bohrnstedt (Eds.), *Sociological Methodology 1970.* San Francisco: Jossey-Bass, 1970.

Duncan, O. D. Unmeasured variables in linear models for panel analysis. In H. L. Costner (Ed.), *Sociological methodology 1972.* San Francisco: Jossey-Bass, 1972.

Duncan, O. D. *Introduction to structural equation models.* New York: Academic Press, 1975.

Duncan, O. D., Cuzzort, R. P., & Duncan, B. *Statistical geography.* New York: Free Press, 1961.

Duncan, O. D., Featherman, D. L., & Duncan, B. *Socioeconomic background and achievement.* New York: Seminar Press, 1972.

Dunn, O. J. Multiple comparisons among means. *Journal of the American Statistical Association,* 1961, *56,* 52–64.

Dunnett, C. W. A multiple comparison procedure for comparing several treatments with a control. *Journal of the American Statistical Association,* 1955, *50,* 1096–1121.

Edwards, A. L. *Expected values of discrete random variables and elementary statistics.* New York: Wiley, 1964.

Edwards, A. L. *Experimental design in psychological research* (4th ed.). New York: Holt, Rinehart and Winston, 1972.

Edwards, A. L. *Multiple regression and the analysis of variance and covariance.* San Francisco: W. H. Freeman, 1979.

Elashoff, J. D. Analysis of covariance: A delicate instrument. *American Educational Research Journal,* 1969, *6,* 383–401.

Eysenck, H. J. *Fact and fiction in psychology.* New York: Penguin, 1965.

Ezekiel, M., & Fox, K. A. *Methods of correlation and regression analysis* (3rd ed.). New York: Wiley, 1959.

Farkas, G. Specification, residuals and contextual effects. *Sociological Methods and Research,* 1974, *2,* 333–363.

Farrar, D. E., & Glauber, R. R. Multicollinearity in regression analysis: The problem revisited. *Review of Economics and Statistics,* 1967, *49,* 92–107.

Federal Register, August 25, 1978, Part IV.

Feigl, H., & Brodbeck, M. (Eds.). *Readings in the philosophy of science.* New York: Appleton-Century-Crofts, 1953.

Feldt, L. S. A comparison of the precision of three experimental designs employing a concomitant variable. *Psychometrika,* 1958, *23,* 335–354.

Finn, J. D. Multivariate analysis of repeated measures data. *Multivariate Behavioral Research,* 1969, *4,* 391–413.

Finn, J. D. *A general model for multivariate analysis.* New York: Holt, Rinehart and Winston, 1974.

Finn, J. D. *MULTIVARIANCE VI.* Chicago: National Educational Resources, 1977.

Finn, J. D., & Mattsson, I. *Multivariate analysis in educational research: Applications of the MULTIVARIANCE program.* Chicago: National Educational Resources, 1978.

Finney, D. J. Standard errors of yields adjusted for regression on an independent measurement. *Biometrics Bulletin,* 1946, *2,* 53–55.
Finney, J. M. Indirect effects in path analysis. *Sociological Methods and Research,* 1972, *1,* 175–186.
Firebaugh, G. A rule for inferring individual-level relationships from aggregate data. *American Sociological Review,* 1978, *43,* 557–572.
Firebaugh, G. Assessing group effects: A comparison of two methods. *Sociological Methods and Research,* 1979, *7,* 384–395.
Fisher, F. M. *The identification problem in econometrics.* New York: McGraw-Hill, 1966.
Fisher, R. A. The use of multiple measurements in taxonomic problems. *Annals of Eugenics,* 1936, *7,* 179–188.
Fisher, R. A. *Statistical methods for research workers* (13th ed.). New York: Hafner, 1958.
Fisher, R. A., & Yates, F. *Statistical tables for biological, agricultural and medical research* (6th ed.). New York: Hafner, 1963.
Forbes, H. D., & Tufte, E. R. A note of caution in causal modelling. *American Political Science Review,* 1968, *62,* 1258–1264.
Fox, J. Effect analysis in structural equation models. *Sociological Methods and Research,* 1980, *9,* 3–28.
Fox, K. A. *Intermediate economic statistics.* New York: Wiley, 1968.
Freedman, J. L. Involvement, discrepancy, and change. *Journal of Abnormal and Social Psychology,* 1964, *69,* 290–295.

Gaito, J. Repeated measurements designs and counterbalancing. *Psychological Bulletin,* 1961, *58,* 46–54.
Games, P. A. Multiple comparisons of means. *American Educational Research Journal,* 1971, *8,* 531–565.
Games, P. A. Limitations of analysis of covariance on intact group quasi-experimental designs. *Journal of Experimental Education,* 1976, *44,* 51–54.
Gnanadesikan, R. *Methods for statistical data analysis of multivariate observations.* New York: Wiley, 1977.
Gocka, E. F. Stepwise regression for mixed mode predictor variables. *Educational and Psychological Measurement,* 1973, *33,* 319–325.
Goldberger, A. S. *Econometric theory.* New York: Wiley, 1964.
Goldberger, A. S. On Boudon's method of linear causal analysis. *American Sociological Review,* 1970, *35,* 97–101.
Goldberger, A. S., & Duncan, O. D. (Eds.). *Structural equation models in the social sciences.* New York: Seminar Press, 1973.
Gordon, R. A. Issues in multiple regression. *American Journal of Sociology,* 1968, *73,* 592–616.
Gorsuch, R. L. *Factor analysis.* Philadelphia: W. B. Saunders, 1974.
Grant, G. Shaping social policy: The politics of the Coleman Report. *Teachers College Record,* 1973, *75,* 17–54.
Graybill, F. A. *An introduction to linear statistical models* (Vol. 1). New York: McGraw-Hill, 1961.
Green, H. A. J. *Aggregation in economic analysis: An introductory survey.* Princeton, N.J.: Princeton University Press, 1964.
Green, P. E. *Mathematical tools for applied multivariate analysis.* New York: Academic Press, 1976.
Green, P. E. *Analyzing multivariate data.* Hinsdale, Ill.: Dryden Press, 1978.
Green, P. E., Halbert, M. H., & Robinson, P. J. Canonical analysis: An exposition and illustrative application. *Journal of Marketing Research,* 1966, *3,* 32–39.
Greene, V. L. An algorithm for total and indirect causal effects. *Political Methodology,* 1977, *4,* 369–381.
Greenhouse, S. W., & Geisser, S. On methods in the analysis of profile data. *Psychometrika,* 1959, *24,* 95–112.
Greenwald, A. G. Within-subjects designs: To use or not to use? *Psychological Bulletin,* 1976, *83,* 314–320.
Guilford, J. P. *Psychometric methods* (2nd ed.). New York: McGraw-Hill, 1954.
Guilford, J. P. *The nature of human intelligence.* New York: McGraw-Hill, 1967.
Guilford, J. P., & Fruchter, B. *Fundamental statistics in psychology and education* (5th ed.). New York: McGraw-Hill, 1978.
Gunst, R. F., & Mason, R. L. Advantages of examining multicollinearities in regression analysis. *Biometrics,* 1977, *33,* 249–260.
Gupta, K. L. *Aggregation in economics: A theoretical and empirical study.* Rotterdam: Rotterdam University Press, 1969.

Haitovsky, Y. Multicollinearity in regression analysis: A comment. *Review of Economics and Statistics*, 1969, *51*, 486–489.

Hall, C. E. Rotation of canonical variates in multivariate analysis of variance. *Journal of Experimental Education*, 1969, *38*, 31–38.

Hammond, J. L. Two sources of error in ecological correlations. *American Sociological Review*, 1973, *38*, 764–777.

Hannan, M. T. *Aggregation and disaggregation in sociology*. Lexington, Mass.: Heath, 1971.

Hannan, M. T., & Burstein, L. Estimation from grouped observations. *American Sociological Review*, 1974, *39*, 374–392.

Hannan, M. T., Freeman, J. H., & Meyer, J. W. Specification of models for organizational effectiveness. *American Sociological Review*, 1976, *41*, 136–143.

Hannan, M. T., & Young, A. A. *Small sample results on estimation from grouped observations*. Milwaukee, Wis.: Vasques Associates, 1976, Technical Report No. 24, Consortium on Methodology for Aggregating Data in Educational Research.

Hanson, N. R. *Patterns of discovery*. Cambridge: Cambridge University Press, 1958.

Hanson, N. R. *Observation and explanation: A guide to the philosophy of science*. New York: Harper & Row, 1971.

Hanushek, E. A., & Jackson, J. E. *Statistical methods for social scientists*. New York: Academic Press, 1977.

Hanushek, E. A., Jackson, J. E., & Kain, J. F. Model specification, use of aggregate data, and the ecological correlation fallacy. *Political Methodology*, 1974, *1*, 89–107.

Hanushek, E. A., & Kain, J. F. On the value of *Equality of educational opportunity* as a guide to public policy. In F. Mosteller & D. P. Moynihan (Eds.), *On equality of educational opportunity*. New York: Vintage Books, 1972.

Hargens, L. L. A note on standardized coefficients as structural parameters. *Sociological Methods and Research*, 1976, *5*, 247–256.

Harman, H. H. *Modern factor analysis* (3rd ed.). Chicago: University of Chicago Press, 1976.

Härnqvist, K. The international study of educational achievement. In F. N. Kerlinger (Ed.), *Review of research in education 3*. Itasca, Ill.: F. E. Peacock, 1975.

Harris, C. W. (Ed.). *Problems in measuring change*. Madison: University of Wisconsin Press, 1963.

Harris, R. J. *A primer of multivariate statistics*. New York: Academic Press, 1975.

Harris, R. J. The invalidity of partitioned-U tests in canonical correlation and multivariate analysis of variance. *Multivariate Behavioral Research*, 1976, *11*, 353–366.

Harvard Educational Review. *Environment, heredity, and intelligence*. Reprint series No. 2. Cambridge, Mass., 1969.

Hauser, R. M. Context and Consex: A cautionary tale. *American Journal of Sociology*, 1970, *75*, 645–664.

Hauser, R. M. *Socioeconomic background and educational performance*. Rose Monograph Series. Washington, D.C.: American Sociological Association, 1971.

Hauser, R. M. Contextual analysis revisited. *Sociological Methods and Research*, 1974, *2*, 365–375.

Hauser, R. M., & Goldberger, A. S. The treatment of unobservable variables in path analysis. In H. L. Costner (Ed.), *Sociological methodology 1971*. San Francisco: Jossey-Bass, 1971.

Hays, W. L. *Statistics* (3rd ed.). New York: Holt, Rinehart and Winston, 1981.

Heck, D. L. Charts of some upper percentage points of the distribution of the largest characteristic root. *Annals of Mathematical Statistics*, 1960, *31*, 625–642.

Heim, J., & Perl, L. *The educational production function: Implications for educational manpower policy*. Ithaca, N.Y.: New York State School of Industrial and Labor Relations, Cornell University, 1974.

Heise, D. R. Problems in path analysis and causal inference. In E. F. Borgatta & G. W. Bohrnstedt (Eds.), *Sociological methodology 1969*. San Francisco: Jossey-Bass, 1969.

Heise, D. R. *Causal analysis*. New York: Wiley, 1975.

Helwig, J. T., & Council, K. A. (Eds.). *SAS user's guide* (1979 edition). Cary, N.C.: SAS Institute, 1979.

Hempel, C. G. *Fundamentals of concept formation in empirical science*. Chicago: University of Chicago Press, 1952.

Hempel, C. G. *Aspects of scientific explanation*. New York: Free Press, 1965.

Herzberg, P. A. The parameters of cross-validation. *Psychometrika, Monograph Supplement* (No. 16), 1969.

Himmelfarb, S. What do you do when the control group doesn't fit into the factorial design? *Psychological Bulletin*, 1975, *82*, 363–368.

Hoaglin, D. C., & Welsch, R. E. The hat matrix in regression and ANOVA. *American Statistician*, 1978, *32*, 17–22.

Hocking, R. R. Misspecification in regression. *American Statistician,* 1974, *28,* 39–40.
Hocking, R. R. The analysis and selection of variables in linear regression. *Biometrics,* 1976, *32,* 1–49.
Hodges, S. D., & Moore, P. G. Data uncertainties and least squares regression. *Applied Statistics,* 1972, *21,* 185–195.
Hohn, F. E. *Elementary matrix algebra* (2nd ed.). New York: Macmillan, 1964.
Hoffman, S. Long road to theory. In S. Hoffman (Ed.), *Contemporary theory in international relations.* Englewood Cliffs, N.J.: Prentice-Hall, 1960.
Holtzman, W. H., & Brown, W. F. Evaluating study habits and attitudes of high school students. *Journal of Educational Psychology,* 1968, *59,* 404–409.
Holzinger, K. J., & Freeman, F. N. The interpretation of Burt's regression equation. *Journal of Educational Psychology,* 1925, *16,* 577–582.
Horel, A. E., & Kennard, R. W. Ridge regression: Biased estimation for nonorthogonal problems. *Technometrics,* 1970, *12,* 55–67. (a)
Horel, A. E., & Kennard, R. W. Ridge regression: Applications to nonorthogonal problems. *Technometrics,* 1970, *12,* 69–82. (b)
Hornbeck, F. W. Factorial analyses of variance with appended control groups. *Behavioral Science,* 1973, *18,* 213–220.
Horst, P. *Matrix algebra for social scientists.* New York: Holt, Rinehart and Winston, 1963.
Horst, P. *Psychological measurement and prediction.* Belmont, Calif.: Wadsworth, 1966.
Hottelling, H. Relations between two sets of variates. *Biometrika,* 1936, *28,* 321–377.
Howe, H. Education research—The promise and the problem. *Educational Researcher,* 1976, *5*(6), 2–7.
Huba, G. J., Wingard, J. A., & Bentler, P. M. A comparison of two latent variable causal models for adolescent drug use. *Journal of Personality and Social Psychology,* 1981, *40,* 180–193.
Huberty, C. J. Multivariate indices of strength of association. *Multivariate Behavioral Research,* 1972, *7,* 523–526.
Huberty, C. J. Discriminant analysis. *Review of Educational Research,* 1975, *45,* 543–598. (a)
Huberty, C. J. The stability of three indices of relative variable contribution in discriminant analysis. *Journal of Experimental Education,* 1975, *44,* 59–64. (b)
Huitema, B. E. *The analysis of covariance and alternatives.* New York: Wiley, 1980.
Hull, C. H., & Nie, N. H. *SPSS update.* New York: McGraw-Hill, 1979.
Hummel, T. J., & Sligo, J. R. Empirical comparison of univariate and multivariate analysis of variance procedures. *Psychological Bulletin,* 1971, *76,* 49–57.
Humphreys, L. G. Doing research the hard way: Substituting analysis of variance for a problem in correlational analysis. *Journal of Educational Psychology,* 1978, *70,* 873–876.
Humphreys, L. G., & Fleishman, A. Pseudo-orthogonal and other analysis of variance designs involving individual-differences variables. *Journal of Educational Psychology,* 1974, *66,* 464–472.
Hunter, J. E., & Schmidt, F. L. Critical analysis of the statistical and ethical implications of various definitions of *Test bias. Psychological Bulletin,* 1976, *83,* 1053–1071.
Huynh, H., & Feldt, L. S. Conditions under which mean square ratios in repeated measurements designs have exact *F*-distributions. *Journal of the American Statistical Association,* 1970, *65,* 1582–1589.
Huynh, H., & Feldt, L. S. Estimation of the Box correction for degrees of freedom from sample data in randomized blocks and split-plot designs. *Journal of Educational Statistics,* 1976, *1,* 69–82.

Igra, A. On forming variable set composites to summarize a block recursive model. *Social Science Research,* 1979, *8,* 253–264.
Inkeles, A. The international evaluation of educational achievement. *Proceedings of the National Academy of Education,* 1977, *4,* 139–200.
Irwin, L., & Lichtman, A. J. Across the great divide: Inferring individual level behavior from aggregate data. *Political Methodology,* 1976, *3,* 411–439.

Jencks, C. S. The Coleman Report and the conventional wisdom. In F. Mosteller & D. P. Moynihan (Eds.), *On equality of educational opportunity.* New York: Vintage Books, 1972.
Jencks, C., et al. *Inequality.* New York: Basic Books, 1972.
Jencks, C., et al. *Who gets ahead?.* New York: Basic Books, 1979.
Jensen, A. How much can we boost IQ and scholastic achievement? *Harvard Educational Review,* 1969, *39,* 1–123.
Johnson, P. O., & Fay, L. C. The Johnson-Neyman technique, its theory and application. *Psychometrika,* 1950, *15,* 349–367.

Johnson, P. O., & Jackson, R. W. B. *Modern statistical methods: Descriptive and inductive.* Skokie, Ill.: Rand McNally, 1959.

Johnson, P. O., & Neyman, J. Tests of certain linear hypotheses and their applications to some educational problems. *Statistical Research Memoirs,* 1936, *1,* 57–93.

Johnston, J. *Econometric methods* (2nd ed.). New York: McGraw-Hill, 1972.

Jöreskog, K. G. Analyzing psychological data by structural analysis of covariance matrices. In D. H. Krantz, R. C. Atkinson, D. Luce, & P. Suppes (Eds.), *Contemporary developments in mathematical psychology* (Vol. 2). San Francisco: Freeman, 1974.

Jöreskog, K. G. Statistical estimation of structural models in longitudinal-developmental investigations. In J. R. Nesselroade & P. B. Baltes (Eds.), *Longitudinal research in the study of behavior and development.* New York: Academic Press, 1979.

Jöreskog, K. G., & Sörbom, D. *LISREL IV.* Chicago: National Educational Resources, 1978.

Jöreskog, K. G., & Sörbom, D. *Advances in factor analysis and structural equation models.* Cambridge, Mass.: Abt Books, 1979.

Kahneman, D. Control of spurious association and the reliability of the controlled variable. *Psychological Bulletin,* 1965, *64,* 326–329.

Kaplan, A. *The conduct of inquiry.* San Francisco: Chandler, 1964.

Karweit, N., Fennessey, J., & Daiger, D. C. *Examining the credibility of offsetting contextual effects.* Report No. 250. Center for Social Organization of Schools. The Johns Hopkins University, Baltimore, 1978.

Kean, M. H., Summers, A. A., Raivetz, M. J., & Farber, I. J. *What works in reading?* Philadelphia: Office of Research and Evaluation, The School District of Philadelphia, 1979.

Keesling, J. W. *Some explorations in multilevel analysis.* Paper presented at the annual meeting of the American Educational Research Association, Toronto, March 1978.

Keesling, J. W., & Wiley, D. *Regression models for hierarchical data.* Paper presented at the annual meeting of the Psychometric Society, Stanford University, Stanford, Calif., 1974.

Kemeny, J. G., Snell, J. L., & Thompson, G. L. *Introduction to finite mathematics* (2nd ed.). Englewood Cliffs, N.J.: Prentice-Hall, 1966.

Kendall, M. G. Regression, structure and functional relationship. *Biometrika,* 1951, *38,* 11–25.

Kendall, P. L., & Lazarsfeld, P. F. The relation between individual and group characteristics in "The American soldier." In P. F. Lazarsfeld & M. Rosenberg (Eds.), *The language of social research.* New York: Free Press, 1955.

Kenny, D. A. A quasi-experimental approach to assessing treatment effects in the nonequivalent control group design. *Psychological Bulletin,* 1975, *82,* 345–362.

Kenny, D. A. *Correlation and causality.* New York: Wiley, 1979.

Kerlinger, F. N. Research in education. In R. L. Ebel, V. H. Noll, & R. M. Bauer (Eds.), *Encyclopedia of educational research* (4th ed.). New York: Macmillan, 1969.

Kerlinger, F. N. *Foundations of behavioral research* (2nd ed.). New York: Holt, Rinehart and Winston, 1973.

Kim, J. O., & Mueller, C. W. Standardized and unstandardized coefficients in causal analysis. *Sociological Methods and Research,* 1976, *4,* 423–438.

Kirk, R. E. *Experimental design: Procedures for the behavioral sciences.* Belmont, Calif.: Brooks/Cole, 1968.

Kish, L. Selection of the sample. In L. Festinger & D. Katz (Eds.), *Research methods in the behavioral sciences.* New York: Dryden, 1953.

Kish, L. *Survey Sampling.* New York: Wiley, 1965.

Kish, L. Representation, randomization, and control. In H. M. Blalock, A. Aganbegian, F. M. Borodkin, R. Boudon, & V. Capecchi (Eds.), *Quantitative sociology.* New York: Academic Press, 1975.

Klecka, W. R. *Discriminant analysis.* Beverly Hills, Calif: Sage, 1980.

Kmenta, J. *Elements of econometrics.* New York: Macmillan, 1971.

Knapp, T. R. The unit-of-analysis problem in applications of simple correlation analysis to educational research. *Journal of Educational Statistics,* 1977, *2,* 171–186.

Koopmans, T. C. Identification problems in economic model construction. *Econometrica,* 1949, *17,* 125–143.

Kramer, C. Y. *A first course in methods of multivariate analysis.* Ann Arbor, Mich.: Edwards Brothers, 1972.

Krus, D. J., Reynolds, T. J., & Krus, P. H. Rotation in canonical variate analysis. *Educational and Psychological Measurement,* 1976, *36,* 725–730.

Kumer, T. K., Multicollinearity in regression analysis. *Review of Economics and Statistics,* 1975, *57,* 365–366.

Lana, R. E., & Lubin, A. The effect of correlation on the repeated measures design. *Educational and Psychological Measurement,* 1963, *23,* 729–739.

Langbein, L. I. Schools or students: Aggregation problems in the study of student achievement. In M. Guttentag (Ed.), *Evaluation studies: Review annual 2*. Beverly Hills, Calif.: Sage, 1977.
Langbein, L. I., & Lichtman, A. J. *Ecological inference*. Beverly Hills, Calif.: Sage, 1978.
Larsen, W. A., & McCleary, S. J. The use of partial residual plots in regression analysis. *Technometrics,* 1972, *14,* 781–790.
Lazarsfeld, P. F., & Menzel, H. On the relation between individual and collective properties. In A. Etzioni (Ed.), *Complex organizations*. New York: Holt, Rinehart and Winston, 1961.
Lemieux, P. H. A note on the detection of multicollinearity. *American Journal of Political Science,* 1978, *22,* 183–186.
Lerner, D. (Ed.). *Cause and effect*. New York: Free Press, 1965.
Levine, M. S. *Canonical analysis and factor comparison*. Beverly Hills, Calif.: Sage, 1977.
Lewis-Beck, M. S. Stepwise regression: A caution. *Political Methodology,* 1978, *5,* 213–240.
Lewis-Beck, M. S., & Mohr, L. B. Evaluating effects of independent variables. *Political Methodology,* 1976, *3,* 27–47.
Li, C. C. *Introduction to experimental statistics*. New York: McGraw-Hill, 1964.
Li, C. C. *Path analysis: A primer*. Pacific Grove, Calif.: Boxwood Press, 1975.
Li, J. C. R. *Statistical Inference*. Ann Arbor, Mich.: Edwards Brothers, 1964.
Liddle, G. Overlap among desirable and undesirable characteristics in gifted children. *Journal of Educational Psychology,* 1958, *49,* 219–223.
Lindeman, R. H., Merenda, P. F., & Gold, R. Z. *Introduction to bivariate and multivariate analysis*. Glenview, Ill.: Scott, Foresman, 1980.
Lindquist, E. F. *Statistical analysis in educational research*. Boston: Houghton Mifflin, 1940.
Lindquist, E. F. *Design and analysis of experiments in psychology and education*. Boston: Houghton Mifflin, 1953.
Linn, R. L. Fair test use in selection. *Review of Educational Research,* 1973, *43,* 139–161.
Linn, R. L., & Werts, C. E. Assumptions in making causal inferences from part correlations, partial correlations, and partial regression coefficients. *Psychological Bulletin,* 1969, *72,* 307–310.
Linn, R. L., & Werts, C. E. Errors of inference due to errors of measurement. *Educational and Psychological Measurement,* 1973, *33,* 531–543.
Linn, R. L., Werts, C. E., & Tucker, L. R. The interpretation of regression coefficients in a school effects model. *Educational and Psychological Measurement,* 1971, *31,* 85–93.
Lohnes, P. R., & Cooley, W. W. *Regarding criticisms of commonality analysis*. Paper presented at the annual meeting of the American Educational Research Association, Toronto, Canada, March 1978.
Long, J. S. Estimation and hypothesis testing in linear models containing measurement error. *Sociological Methods and Research,* 1976, *5,* 157–206.
Longley, J. W. An appraisal of least squares programs for the electronic computer from the point of view of the user. *American Statistical Association Journal,* 1967, *62,* 819–841.
Lord, F. M. Elementary models for measuring change. In C. W. Harris (Ed.), *Problems in measuring change*. Madison: University of Wisconsin Press, 1963.
Lord, F. M. A paradox in the interpretation of group comparisons. *Psychological Bulletin,* 1967, *68,* 304–305.
Lord, F. M. Statistical adjustments when comparing preexisting groups. *Psychological Bulletin,* 1969, *72,* 336–337.
Lord, F. M. Significance test for a partial correlation corrected for attenuation. *Educational and Psychological Measurement,* 1974, *34,* 211–220.
Lord, F. M., & Novick, M. R. *Statistical theories of mental test scores*. Reading, Mass.: Addison-Wesley, 1968.
Love, W. A., & Stewart, D. K. *Interpreting canonical correlations: Theory and practice*. Pittsburgh: American Institute for Research and University of Pittsburgh, 1968.
Lubin, A. The interpretation of significant interaction. *Educational and Psychological Measurement,* 1961, *21,* 807–817.

McCall, R. B., & Appelbaum, M. I. Bias in analysis of repeated-measures designs: Some alternative approaches. *Child Development,* 1973, *44,* 401–415.
McClelland, D. C., Atkinson, J. W., Clark, R. A., & Lowell, E. L. *The achievement motive*. New York: Appleton-Century-Crofts, 1953.
McDill, E. L., Rigsby, L. C., & Meyers, E. D. Educational climates of high schools: Their effects and sources. *American Journal of Sociology,* 1969, *74,* 567–586.
MacDonald, K. I. Path analysis. In C. A. O'Muircheartaigh & C. Payne (Eds.), *The analysis of survey data* (Vol. 2). New York: Wiley, 1977.
MacDonald, K. I. Interpretation of residual paths and decomposition of variance. *Sociological Methods and Research,* 1979, *7,* 289–304.

McNemar, Q. *Psychological Statistics* (3rd ed.). New York: Wiley, 1962.
McNemar, Q. *Psychological Statistics* (4th ed.). New York: Wiley, 1969.
McPherson, J. M. Theory triming. *Social Science Research,* 1976, *5,* 95–105.
McPherson, J. M., & Haung, C. J. Hypothesis testing in path models. *Social Science Research,* 1974, *3,* 127–139.
Madaus, G. F., Kellaghan, T., Rakow, E. A., & King. D. J. The sensitivity of measures of school effectiveness. *Harvard Educational Review,* 1979, *49,* 207–230.
Marquardt, D. W., & Snee, R. D. Ridge regression in practice. *American Statistician,* 1975, *29,* 3–20.
Maruyama, G., & McGarvey, B. Evaluating causal models: An application of maximum-likelihood analysis of structural equations. *Psychological Bulletin,* 1980, *87,* 502–512.
Maruyama, G., & Miller, N. Reexamination of normative influence processes in desegregated classrooms. *American Educational Research Journal,* 1979, *16,* 273–283.
Mason, R., & Brown, W. G. Multicollinearity problems and ridge regression in sociological models. *Social Science Research,* 1975, *4,* 135–149.
Maxwell, A. E. Limitations on the use of the multiple linear regression model. *British Journal of Mathematical and Statistical Psychology,* 1975, *28,* 51–62.
Maxwell, A. E. *Multivariate analysis in behavioral research.* New York: Wiley, 1977.
Mayeske, G. W. Teacher attributes and school achievement. In *Do teachers make a difference?* Washington, D.C.: U.S. Office of Education, 1970.
Mayeske, G. W., & Beaton, A. E. *Special studies of our nation's students.* Washington, D.C.: U.S. Government Printing Office, 1975.
Mayeske, G. W., Cohen, W. M., Wisler, C. E., Okada, T., Beaton, A. E., Proshek, J. M., Weinfeld, F. D., & Tabler, K. A. *A study of our nation's schools.* Washington, D.C.: U.S. Government Printing Office, 1972.
Mayeske, G. W., Okada, T., & Beaton, A. E. *A study of the attitude toward life of our nation's students.* Washington, D.C.: U.S. Government Printing Office, 1973. (a)
Mayeske, G. W., Okada, T., Beaton, A. E., Cohen, W. M., & Wisler, C. E. *A study of the achievement of our nation's students.* Washington, D.C.: U.S. Government Printing Office, 1973. (b)
Mayeske, G. W., Wisler, C. E., Beaton, A. E., Weinfeld, F. D., Cohen, W. M., Okada, T., Proshek, J. M., & Tabler, K. A. *A study of our nation's schools.* Washington, D.C.: U.S. Dept. of Health, Education, and Welfare, Office of Education, 1969.
Meehl, P. E. Wanted—a good cookbook. *American Psychologist,* 1956, *11,* 263–272.
Meehl, P. E. Nuisance variables and the ex post facto design. In M. Radner & S. Winokur (Eds.), *Minnesota studies in the philosophy of science* (Vol 4). Minneapolis: University of Minnesota Press, 1970.
Menzel, H. Comment on Robinson's "Ecological correlations and the behavior of individuals." *American Sociological Review,* 1950, *15,* 674.
Meredith, W. Canonical correlation with fallible data. *Psychometrika,* 1964, *29,* 55–65.
Merritt, R. L., & Rokkan, S. (Eds.). *Comparing nations.* New Haven: Yale University Press, 1966.
Meyer, D. L. Response surface methodology in education and psychology. *Journal of Experimental Education,* 1963, *31,* 329–336.
Meyer, J. W. High school effects on college intentions. *American Journal of Sociology,* 1970, *76,* 59–70.
Michelson, S. The association of teacher resourceness with children's characteristics. In *Do teachers make a difference?* Washington, D.C.: U.S. Office of Education, 1970.
Milgram, S., Bickman, L., & Berkowitz, L. Note on the drawing power of crowds of different size. *Journal of Personality and Social Psychology,* 1969, *13,* 79–82.
Miller, J. *The development and application of bi-multivariate correlation.* Unpublished doctoral dissertation, State University of New York at Buffalo, 1969.
Miller, M. K., & Stokes, C. S. Path analysis in sociological research. *Rural Sociology,* 1975, *40,* 193–201.
Miller, R. G. *Simultaneous statistical inference.* New York: McGraw-Hill, 1966.
Miller, W. E., & Stokes, D. E. Constituency influence in congress. *American Political Science Review,* 1963, *57,* 45–56.
Mood, A. M. Macro-analysis of the American educational system. *Operations Research,* 1969, *17,* 770–784.
Mood, A. M. Do teachers make a difference? In *Do teachers make a difference?* Washington, D.C.: U.S. Office of Education, 1970.
Mood, A. M. Partitioning variance in multiple regression analyses as a tool for developing learning models. *American Educational Research Journal,* 1971, *8,* 191–202.
Mood, A. M. Foreward to G. W. Mayeske et al., *A study of the attitude toward life of our nation's students.* Washington, D.C.: U.S. Government Printing Office, 1973. (a)

Moore, M. Aggression themes in a binocular rivalry situation. *Journal of Personality and Social Psychology,* 1966, *3,* 685–688.

Morrison, D. E., & Henkel, R. E. (Eds.). *The significance test controversy: A reader.* Chicago: Aldine, 1970.

Morrison, D. F. *Multivariate statistical methods* (2nd ed.). New York: McGraw-Hill, 1976.

Mosier, C. I. Problems and designs of cross-validation. *Educational and Psychological Measurement,* 1951, *11,* 5–11.

Mosteller, F., & Moynihan, D. P. (Eds.). *On equality of educational opportunity.* New York: Vintage Books, 1972. (a)

Mosteller, F., & Moynihan, D. P. A pathbreaking report. In F. Mosteller & D. P. Moynihan (Eds.), *On equality of educational opportunity.* New York: Vintage Books, 1972. (b)

Mulaik, S. A. *The foundations of factor analysis.* New York: McGraw-Hill, 1972.

Myers, J. L. *Fundamentals of experimental design* (3rd ed.). Boston: Allyn and Bacon, 1979.

Nagel, E. Types of causal explanation in science. In D. Lerner (Ed.), *Cause and effect.* New York: Free Press, 1965.

Namboodiri, N. K. Experimental designs in which each subject is used repeatedly. *Psychological Bulletin,* 1972, *77,* 54–64.

Namboodiri, N. K. (Ed.). *Survey sampling and measurement.* New York: Academic Press, 1978.

Namboodiri, N. K., Carter, L. F., & Blalock, H. M. *Applied multivariate analysis and experimental designs.* New York: McGraw-Hill, 1975.

Nelson, J. I. High school context and college plans: The impact of social structure on aspirations. *American Sociological Review,* 1972, *37,* 143–148.

Newton, R. G., & Spurrell, D. J. A development of multiple regression for the analysis of routine data. *Applied Statistics,* 1967, *16,* 51–64. (a)

Newton, R. G., & Spurrell, D. J. Examples of the use of elements for clarifying regression analyses, *Applied Statistics,* 1967, *16,* 165–172. (b)

Nie, N. H., Hull, C. H., Jenkins, J. G., Steinbrenner, K., & Bent, D. H. *SPSS* (2nd ed.). New York: McGraw-Hill, 1975.

Nolle, D. B. Alternative path analytic models of student-teacher influence: The implications of different strokes for different folks. *Sociology of Education,* 1973, *46,* 417–426.

Nunnally, J. The place of statistics in psychology. *Educational and Psychological Measurement,* 1960, *20,* 641–650.

Nunnally, J. C. *Psychometric theory* (2nd ed.). New York: McGraw-Hill, 1978.

Olson, C. L. On choosing a test statistic in multivariate analysis of variance. *Psychological Bulletin,* 1976, *83,* 579–586.

Overall, J. E., & Klett, C. J. *Applied multivariate analysis.* New York: McGraw-Hill, 1972.

Overall, J. E., Spiegel, D. K., & Cohen, J. Equivalence of orthogonal and nonorthogonal analysis of variance. *Psychological Bulletin,* 1975, *82,* 182–186.

Overall, J. E., & Woodward, J. A. Common misconceptions concerning the analysis of covariance. *Multivariate Behavioral Research,* 1977, *12,* 171–186. (a)

Overall, J. E., & Woodward, J. A. Nonrandom assignment and the analysis of covariance. *Psychological Bulletin,* 1977, *84,* 588–594. (b)

Peaker, G. F. *An empirical study of education in twenty-one countries: A technical report.* New York: Wiley, 1975.

Pedhazur, E. J. Analytic methods in studies of educational effects. In F. N. Kerlinger (Ed.), *Review of research in education 3.* Itasca, Ill.: Peacock, 1975.

Pedhazur, E. J. Coding subjects in repeated measures designs. *Psychological Bulletin,* 1977, *84,* 298–305.

Pedhazur, E. J., & Tetenbaum, T. J. Bem sex role inventory: A theoretical and methodological critique. *Journal of Personality and Social Psychology,* 1979, *37,* 996–1016.

Perlmutter, J., & Myers, J. L. A comparison of two procedures for testing multiple contrasts. *Psychological Bulletin,* 1973, *79,* 181–184.

Pillai, K. C. S. *Statistical tables for tests of multivariate hypotheses.* Manila, Philippines: University of the Philippines, 1960.

Platt, J. R. Strong inference. *Science,* 1964, *146.* 347–353.

Poor, D. D. S. Analysis of variance for repeated measures designs: Two approaches. *Psychological Bulletin,* 1973, *80,* 204–209.

Popper, K. R. *The logic of scientific discovery.* New York: Basic Books, 1959.

Porter, A. C., & Chibucos, T. R. Selecting analysis strategies. In G. D. Borich (Ed.), *Evaluating educational programs and products.* Englewood Cliffs, N.J.: Educational Technology Publications, 1974.

Potthoff, R. F. On the Johnson-Neyman technique and some extensions thereof. *Psychometrika,* 1964, *29,* 241–256.
Press, S. J. *Applied multivariate analysis.* New York: Holt, Rinehart and Winston, 1972.
Price, B. Ridge regression: Application to nonexperimental data. *Psychological Bulletin,* 1977, *84,* 759–766.
Pruzek, R. M. Methods and problems in the analysis of multivariate data. *Review of Educational Research,* 1971, *41,* 163–190.
Prysby, C. L. Community partisanship and individual voting behavior: Methodological problems of contextual analysis. *Political Methodology,* 1976, *3,* 183–198.
Przeworski, A. Contextual models for political behavior. *Political Methodology,* 1974, *1,* 27–60.
Purves, A. C. *Literature education in ten countries.* New York: Wiley, 1973.
Purves, A. C., & Levine, D. U. (Eds.). *Educational policy and international assessment.* Berkeley, Calif.: McCutchan, 1975.

Rao, C. R. Advanced statistical methods in biometric research. New York: Wiley, 1952.
Rao, P., & Miller, R. L. *Applied econometrics.* Belmont, Calif.: Wadsworth, 1971.
Reichardt, C. S. The statistical analysis of data from nonequivalent group designs. In T. D. Cook & D. T. Campbell, *Quasi-experimentation.* Skokie, Ill.: Rand McNally, 1979.
Roberts, K. H., & Burstein. L. (Eds.). *Issues in aggregation.* San Francisco: Jossey-Bass, 1980.
Robinson, J. E., & Gray, J. L. Cognitive style as a variable in school learning. *Journal of Educational Psychology,* 1974, *66,* 793–799.
Robinson, W. S. Ecological correlations and the behavior of individuals. *American Sociological Review,* 1950, *15,* 351–357.
Rock, D. A., Werts, C. E., & Flaugher, R. L. The use of analysis of covariance structures for comparing the psychometric properties of multiple variables across populations. *Multivariate Behavioral Research,* 1978, *13,* 403–418.
Rock, D. A., Werts, C. E., Linn, R. L., & Jöreskog, K. G. A maximum likelihood solution to the errors in variables and errors in equations model. *Multivariate Behavioral Research,* 1977, *12,* 187–198.
Rockwell, R. C. Assessment of multicollinearity. *Sociological Methods and Research,* 1975, *3,* 308–320.
Rogosa, D. Comparing nonparallel regression lines. *Psychological Bulletin,* 1980, *88,* 307–321.
Rogosa, D. On the relationship between the Johnson-Neyman region of significance and statistical tests of parallel within-group regressions. *Educational and Psychological Measurement,* 1981, *41,* 73–84.
Rosenberg, M. *The logic of survey analysis.* New York: Basic Books, 1968.
Rouanet, H., & Lépine, D. Comparison between treatments in a repeated-measures design: ANOVA and multivariate methods. *British Journal of Mathematical and Statistical Psychology,* 1970, *23,* 147–163.
Roy, S. N. *Some aspects of multivariate analysis.* New York: Wiley, 1957.
Rozeboom, W. W. The fallacy of the null-hypothesis significance test. *Psychological Bulletin,* 1960, *57,* 416–428.
Rozeboom, W. W. Ridge regression: Bonanza or beguilement? *Psychological Bulletin,* 1979, *86,* 242–249.
Rubin, D. B. Estimating causal effects of treatments in randomized and nonrandomized studies. *Journal of Educational Psychology,* 1974, *66,* 688–701.
Rubin, D. B. Assignment to treatment group on the basis of a covariate. *Journal of Educational Statistics,* 1977, *2,* 1–26.
Rulon, P. J., & Brooks, W. D. On statistical tests of group differences. In D. K. Whitla (Ed.), *Handbook of measurement and assessment in behavioral sciences.* Reading, Mass.: Addison-Wesley, 1968.
Rulon, P. J., Tiedeman, D. V., Tatsuoka, M. M., & Langmuir, C. R. *Multivariate statistics for personnel classification.* New York: Wiley, 1967.
Russett, B. M., Alker, H. R., Deutsch, K. W., & Lasswell, H. D. (Eds.). *World handbook of political and social indicators.* New Haven: Yale University Press, 1964.
Ryan, T. A. Multiple comparisons in psychological research. *Psychological Bulletin,* 1959, *56,* 26–47. (a)
Ryan, T. A. Comments on orthogonal components. *Psychological Bulletin,* 1959, *56,* 394–396. (b)

Saris, W. E., de Pijper, W. M., & Zegwaart, P. Detection of specification errors in linear structural equation models. In K. F. Schuessler (Ed.), *Sociological methodology 1979.* San Francisco: Jossey-Bass, 1978.
Scheffé, H. *The analysis of variance.* New York: Wiley, 1959.
Scheffler, I. Explanation, prediction, and abstraction. *British Journal for the Philosophy of Science,* 1957, *7,* 293–309.

Scheuch, E. K. Cross-national comparisons using aggregate data: Some substantive and methodological problems. In R. L. Merritt & S. Rokkan (Eds.), *Comparing nations*. New Haven: Yale University Press, 1966.
Scheuch, E. K. Social context and individual behavior. In M. Dogan & S. Rokkan (Eds.), *Quantitative ecological analysis in the social sciences*. Cambridge, Mass.: M.I.T. Press, 1969.
Schmidt, P., & Muller, E. N. The problem of multicollinearity in a multistage causal alienation model: A comparison of ordinary least squares, maximum-likelihood and ridge estimators. *Quality and Quantity*, 1978, *12*, 267–297.
Schoenberg, R. Strategies for meaningful comparison. In H. L. Costner (Ed.), *Sociological methodology 1972*. San Francisco: Jossey-Bass, 1972.
Schoenberger, R. A., & Segal, D. R. The ecology of dissent: The southern Wallace vote in 1968. *Midwest Journal of Political Science*, 1971, *15*, 583–586.
Schuessler, K. *Analyzing social data*. Boston: Houghton Mifflin, 1971.
Schwille, J. R. Predictors of between-student differences in civic education cognitive achievement. In J. V. Torney, A. N. Oppenheim, & R. F. Farnen, *Civic education in ten countries*. New York: Wiley, 1975.
Scriven, M. Explanation and prediction in evolutionary theory. *Science*, 1959, *130*, 477–482.
Scriven, M. The logic of cause. *Theory and Decision*, 1971, *2*, 49–66.
Scriven, M. Causation as explanation. *Noûs*, 1975, *9*, 3–16.
Searle, S. R. *Matrix algebra for the biological sciences*. New York: Wiley, 1966.
Searle, S. R. *Linear models*. New York: Wiley, 1971.
Sechrest, L. Incremental validity: A recommendation. *Educational and Psychological Measurement*, 1963, *23*, 153–158.
Serlin, R. C., & Levin, J. R. Identifying regions of significance in aptitude-by-treatment-interaction research. *American Educational Research Journal*, 1980, *17*, 389–399.
Sewell, W. H., & Armer, J. M. Neighborhood context and college plans. *American Sociological Review*, 1966, *31*, 159–168.
Shaffer, J. P., & Gillo, M. W. A multivariate extension of the correlation ratio. *Educational and Psychological Measurement*, 1974, *34*, 521–524.
Shaw, B. *Complete plays with prefaces* (Vol. 1). New York: Dodd, Mead, 1963.
Sherif, M. Social psychology: Problems and trends in interdisciplinary relationships. In S. Koch (Ed.), *Psychology: A study of a science* (Vol. 6). New York: McGraw-Hill, 1963.
Simon, H. A. Spurious correlation: A causal interpretation. *Journal of the American Statistical Association*, 1954, *49*, 467–479.
Simon, H. A. *Models of man*. New York: Wiley, 1957.
Simon, H. A. Causation. In D. L. Sills (Ed.), *International encyclopedia of the social sciences*. New York: Macmillan, 1968.
Sjoberg, G., & Nett, R. *A methodology for social research*. New York: Harper & Row, 1968.
Smith, H. F. Interpretation of adjusted treatment means and regressions in analysis of covariance. *Biometrics*, 1957, *13*, 282–308.
Smith, I. L. The eta coefficient in MANOVA. *Multivariate Behavioral Research*, 1972, *7*, 361–372.
Smith, K. W. Another look at the clustering perspective on aggregation problems. *Sociological Methods and Research*, 1977, *5*, 289–316.
Smith, K. W., & Sasaki, M. S. Decreasing multicollinearity. *Sociological Methods and Research*, 1979, *8*, 35–56.
Smith, M. S. Equality of educational opportunity: Comments on Bowles and Levin. *Journal of Human Resources*, 1968, *3*, 384–387.
Smith, M. S. *Equality of educational opportunity:* The basic findings reconsidered. In F. Mosteller & D. P. Moynihan (Eds.), *On equality of educational opportunity*. New York: Vintage Books, 1972.
Snedecor, G. W., & Cochran, W. G. *Statistical methods* (6th ed.). Ames: Iowa State University Press, 1967.
Snow, R. E. Research on aptitude for learning: A progress report. In L. S. Shulman (Ed.), *Review of research in education 4*. Itasca, Ill.: Peacock, 1977.
Sockloff, A. L. Behavior of the product-moment correlation coefficient when two heterogeneous subgroups are pooled. *Educational and Psychological Measurement*, 1975, *35*, 267–276.
Sörbom, D. Detection of correlated errors in longitudinal data. *British Jounal of Mathematical and Statistical Psychology*, 1975, *28*, 138–151.
Sörbom, D., & Jöreskog, K. G. The use of LISREL in sociological model building. In D. J. Jackson & E. F. Borgatta (Eds.), *Factor analysis and measurement in sociological research*. Beverly Hills, Calif.: Sage, 1981.
Southwood, K. E. Substantive theory and statistical interaction: Five models. *American Journal of Sociology*, 1978, *83*, 1154–1203.

Specht, D. A. On the evaluation of causal models. *Social Science Research,* 1975, *4,* 113–133.

Specht, D. A., & Warren, R. D. Comparing causal models. In D. R. Heise (Ed.), *Sociological methodology 1976.* San Francisco: Jossey-Bass, 1975.

Sprague, J. Estimating a Boudon-type contextual model: Some practical and theoretical problems of measurement. *Political Methodology,* 1976, *3,* 333–353.

Stevens, J. P. Global measures of association in multivariate analysis of variance. *Multivariate Behavioral Research,* 1972, *7,* 373–378. (a)

Stevens, J. P. Four methods of analyzing between variation for the k-group MANOVA problem. *Multivariate Behavioral Research,* 1972, *7,* 499–522. (b)

Stewart, D., & Love, W. A general canonical correlation index. *Psychological Bulletin,* 1968, *70,* 160–163.

Stimson, J. A., Carmines, E. G., & Zeller, R. A. Interpreting polynomial regression. *Sociological Methods and Research,* 1978, *6,* 515–524.

Stolzenberg, R. M. Estimating an equation with multiplicative and additive terms, with an application to analysis of wage differentials between men and women in 1960. *Sociological Methods and Research,* 1974, *2,* 313–331.

Stolzenberg, R. M. The measurement and decomposition of causal effects in nonlinear and nonadditive models. In K. F. Schuessler (Ed.), *Sociological methodology 1980.* San Francisco: Jossey-Bass, 1979.

Sudman, S. *Applied sampling.* New York: Academic Press, 1976.

Sullivan, J. L., & Feldman, S. *Multiple indicators: An introduction.* Beverly Hills, Calif.: Sage, 1979.

Summers, A. A., & Wolfe, B. L. *Equality of educational opportunity quantified: A production function approach.* Paper presented at the meeting of the Econometric Society, December 1974.

Summers, A. A., & Wolfe, B. L. Which school resources help learning? Efficiency and equity in Philadelphia public schools. *Federal Reserve Bank of Philadelphia Business Review,* February 1975.

Summers, A. A., & Wolfe, B. L. Do schools make a difference? *American Economic Review,* 1977, *67,* 639–652.

Tannenbaum, A. S., & Bachman, J. G. Structural versus individual effects. *American Journal of Sociology,* 1964, *69,* 585–595.

Tatsuoka, M. M. *Discriminant analysis.* Champaign, Ill.: Institute for Personality and Ability Testing, 1970.

Tatsuoka, M. M. *Multivariate analysis: Techniques for educational and psychological research.* New York: Wiley, 1971. (a)

Tatsuoka, M. M. *Significance tests: Univariate and multivariate.* Champaign, Ill.: Institute for Personality and Ability Testing, 1971. (b)

Tatsuoka, M. M. Multivariate analysis in educational research. In F. N. Kerlinger (Ed.), *Review of research in education 1.* Itasca, Ill.: Peacock, 1973.

Tatsuoka, M. M. *Classification procedures: Profile similarity.* Champaign, Ill.: Institute for Personality and Ability Testing, 1974.

Tatsuoka, M. M. Classification procedures. In D. J. Amick & H. J. Walberg (Eds.), *Introductory multivariate analysis.* Berkeley, Calif.: McCutchan, 1975.

Tatsuoka, M. M. Discriminant analysis. In P. M. Bentler, D. J. Lettieri, & G. A. Austin (Eds.), *Data analysis strategies and designs for substance abuse research.* Washington, D.C.: U.S. Government Printing Office, 1976.

Taylor, C. L. (Ed.). *Aggregate data analysis.* Paris: Mouton, 1968.

Terman, L. M. (Ed.). *Genetic studies of genius* (Vol. 1, 2nd ed.). Stanford: Stanford University Press, 1926.

Theil, H. *Linear aggregation of economic relations.* Amsterdam: North-Holland, 1954.

Theil, H. *Statistical decomposition analysis.* Amsterdam: North-Holland, 1972.

Thorndike, E. L. On the fallacy of imputing the correlations found for groups to the individuals or smaller groups composing them. *American Journal of Psychology,* 1939, *52,* 122–124.

Thorndike, R. L. *Personnel selection.* New York: Wiley, 1949.

Thorndike, R. L. *Reading comprehension education in fifteen countries.* New York: Wiley, 1973.

Thorndike, R. L., & Hagen, E. P. *Measurement and evaluation in psychology and education* (4th ed.). New York: Wiley, 1977.

Thorndike, R. M. *Correlational procedures for research.* New York: Gardner Press, 1978.

Thorndike, R. M., & Weiss, D. J. A study of the stability of canonical correlations and canonical components. *Educational and Psychological Measurement,* 1973, *33,* 123–134.

Timm, N. H. *Multivariate analysis with applications in education and psychology.* Monterey, Calif.: Brooks/Cole, 1975.

Torney, J. V., Oppenheim, A. N., & Farnen, R. F. *Civic education in ten countries*. New York: Wiley, 1975.
Tucker, R. K., & Chase, L. J. Canonical correlation. In P. R. Monge & J. N. Cappella (Eds.), *Multivariate techniques in human communication research*. New York: Academic Press, 1980.
Tukey, J. W. Causation, regression and path analysis. In O. Kempthorne, T. A. Bancroft, J. W. Gowen, & J. D. Lush (Eds.), *Statistics and mathematics in biology*. Ames: Iowa State College Press, 1954.
Tukey, J. W. Analyzing data: Sanctification or detective work? *American Psychologist*, 1969, *24*, 83–91.
Turner, M E., & Stevens, C. D. The regression analysis of causal paths. *Biometrics*, 1959, *15*, 236–258.
Tzelgov, J., & Stern, I. Relationships between variables in three variable linear regression and the concept of suppressor. *Educational and Psychological Measurement*, 1978, *38*, 325–335.

Ulam, S. M. *Adventures of a mathematician*. New York: Scribner's, 1976.

Valkonen, T. Individual and structural effects in ecological research. In M. Dogan & S. Rokkan (Eds.), *Quantitative ecological analysis in the social sciences*. Cambridge, Mass.: M.I.T. Press, 1969.
Van Ryzin, J. (Ed.). *Classification and clustering*. New York: Academic Press, 1977.
Velicer, W. F. Suppressor variables and the semipartial correlation coefficient. *Educational and Psychological Measurement*, 1978, *38*, 953–958.

Walker, H. M., & Lev, J. *Statistical inference*. New York: Holt, Rinehart and Winston, 1953.
Ward, J. H. Partitioning variance and contribution or importance of a variable: A visit to a graduate seminar. *American Educational Research Journal*, 1969, *6*, 467–474.
Warren, W. G. Correlation or regression: Bias or precision. *Applied Statistics*, 1971, *20*, 148–164.
Weiner, B. (Ed.). *Achievement motivation and attribution theory*. Morristown, N.J.: General Learning Press, 1974.
Weiss, D. J. Canonical correlation analysis in counseling psychology research. *Journal of Counseling Psychology*, 1972, *19*, 241–252.
Weisberg, H. I. Statistical adjustments and uncontrolled studies. *Psychological Bulletin*, 1979, *86*, 1149–1164.
Werts, C. E., Jöreskog, K. G., & Linn, R. L. Identification and estimation in path analysis with unmeasured variables. *American Journal of Sociology*, 1973, *78*, 1469–1484.
Werts, C. E., & Linn, R. L. Analyzing school effects: How to use the same data to support different hypotheses. *American Educational Research Journal*, 1969, *6*, 439–447.
Werts, C. E., & Linn, R. L. Considerations when making inferences within the analysis of covariance model. *Educational and Psychological Measurement*, 1971, *31*, 407–416.
Werts, C. E., Rock, D. A., Linn, R. L., & Jöreskog, K. G. Comparison of correlations, variances, covariances, and regression weights with or without measurement error. *Psychological Bulletin*, 1976, *83*, 1007–1013.
Werts, C. E., Rock, D. A., Linn, R. L., & Jöreskog, K. G. Validating psychometric assumptions within and between several populations. *Educational and Psychological Measurement*, 1977, *37*, 863–872.
Werts, C. E., & Watley, D. J. Analyzing college effects: Correlation vs. regression. *American Educational Research Journal*, 1968, *5*, 585–598.
Wheaton, B., Muthén, B., Alwin, D. F., & Summers, G. F. Assessing reliability and stability in panel models. In D. R. Heise (Ed.), *Sociological methodology 1977*. San Francisco: Jossey-Bass, 1977.
Wiggins, J. S. *Personality and prediction: Principles of personality assessment*. Reading, Mass.: Addison-Wesley, 1973.
Wilkinson, L. Response variable hypotheses in the multivariate analysis of variance. *Psychological Bulletin*, 1975, *82*, 408–412.
Williams, E. J. *Regression analysis*. New York: Wiley, 1959.
Winer, B. J. *Statistical principles in experimental design* (2nd ed.). New York: McGraw-Hill, 1971.
Wingard, J. A., Huba, G. J., & Bentler, P. M. The relationship of personality structure to patterns of adolescent substance use. *Multivariate Behavioral Research*, 1979, *14*, 131–143.
Wisler, C. E. Partitioning the explained variation in a regression analysis. In G. W. Mayeske et al., *A study of our nation's schools*. Washington, D. C.: U.S. Dept. of Health, Education, and Welfare, Office of Education, 1969.
Wold, H. Causal inference from observational data: A review of ends and means. *Journal of the Royal Statistical Society* (Series A), 1956, *119*, 28–61.
Wold, H., & Juréen, L. *Demand analysis*. New York: Wiley, 1953.

Wonnacott, R. J., & Wonnacott, T. H. *Econometrics*. New York: Wiley, 1970.

Wood, C. G., & Hokanson, J. E. Effects of induced muscular tension on performance and the inverted U function. *Journal of Personality and Social Psychology,* 1965, *1,* 506–510.

Wright, G. C. Linear models for evaluating conditional relationships. *American Journal of Political Science,* 1976, *20,* 349–373.

Wright, S. Correlation and causation. *Journal of Agricultural Research,* 1921, *20,* 557–585.

Wright, S. The method of path coefficients. *Annals of Mathematical Statistics,* 1934, *5,* 161–215.

Wright, S. The interpretation of multivariate systems. In O. Kempthorne, T. A. Bancroft, J. W. Gowen, & J. D. Lush (Eds.), *Statistics and mathematics in biology*. Ames: Iowa State College Press, 1954.

Wright, S. Path coefficients and path regressions: Alternative or complementary concepts? *Biometrics,* 1960, *16,* 189–202. (a)

Wright, S. The treatment of reciprocal interaction, with and without lag, in path analysis. *Biometrics,* 1960, *16,* 423–445. (b)

Wright, S. *Genetic and biometric foundations* (Vol. 1). Chicago: University of Chicago Press, 1968.

Young, B. W., & Bress, G. B. Coleman's retreat and the politics of good intentions. *Phi Delta Kappan,* 1975, *55,* 159–166.

Zeller, R. A., & Carmines, E. G. *Measurement in the social sciences.* New York: Cambridge University Press, 1980.

INDEX OF NAMES

INDEX OF SUBJECTS